Entrepreneurship in Developing Countries

The International Library of Entrepreneurship

Series Editor: David B. Audretsch
*Max Planck Institute of Economics, Jena, Germany
and Ameritech Chair of Economic Development
Indiana University, USA*

1. Corporate Entrepreneurship and Growth
    Shaker A. Zahra

2. Women and Entrepreneurship: Contemporary Classics
    Candida G. Brush, Nancy M. Carter, Elizabeth J. Gatewood, Patricia G. Greene and Myra M. Hart

3. The Economics of Entrepreneurship
    Simon C. Parker

4. Entrepreneurship and Technology Policy
    Albert N. Link

5. Technological Entrepreneurship
    Donald S. Siegel

6. Entrepreneurship and Economic Growth
    Martin Carree and A. Roy Thurik

7. New Firm Startups
    Per Davidsson

8. International Entrepreneurship
    Benjamin M. Oviatt and Patricia Phillips McDougall

9. Entrepreneurship Education
    Patricia G. Greene and Mark P. Rice

10. Entrepreneurship and Global Capitalism (Volumes I and II)
    Geoffrey G. Jones and R. Daniel Wadhwani

11. The Political Economy of Entrepreneurship
    Magnus Henrekson and Robin Douhan

12. Financing Entrepreneurship
    Philip Auerswald and Ant Bozkaya

13. Entrepreneurial Teams and New Business Creation
    Mike Wright and Iris Vanaelst

14. Innovation and Entrepreneurship
    David B. Audretsch, Oliver Falck and Stephan Heblich

15. Entrepreneurship in Developing Countries
    Thorsten Beck

Future titles will include:

The Knowledge Spillover Theory of Entrepreneurship
Zoltan Acs

Strategies for New Venture Development
Ari Ginsberg

Entrepreneurship and Public Policy
David Smallbone

Wherever possible, the articles in these volumes have been reproduced as originally published using facsimile reproduction, inclusive of footnotes and pagination to facilitate ease of reference.

For a list of all Edward Elgar published titles visit our site on the World Wide Web at
www.e-elgar.com

Entrepreneurship in Developing Countries

Edited by

Thorsten Beck

Professor of Economics and Chairman
European Banking Center
Tilburg University, The Netherlands
and Research Fellow, CEPR, London, UK

THE INTERNATIONAL LIBRARY OF ENTREPRENEURSHIP

An Elgar Reference Collection
Cheltenham, UK • Northampton, MA, USA

Published by
Edward Elgar Publishing Limited
The Lypiatts
15 Lansdown Road
Cheltenham
Glos GL50 2JA
UK

Edward Elgar Publishing, Inc.
William Pratt House
9 Dewey Court
Northampton
Massachusetts 01060
USA

A catalogue record for this book is available from the British Library

Library of Congress Control Number: 2009930879

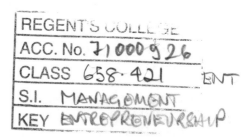

Mixed Sources
Product group from well-managed
forests and other controlled sources
www.fsc.org Cert no. SA-COC-1565
© 1996 Forest Stewardship Council
FSC

ISBN 978 1 84844 434 8

Printed and bound by MPG Books Group, UK

Contents

Acknowledgements

The editor and publishers wish to thank the authors and the following publishers who have kindly given permission for the use of copyright material.

American Economic Association for articles: Raymond Fisman (2001), 'Estimating the Value of Political Connections', *American Economic Review*, **91** (4), September, 1095–102; John McMillan and Christopher Woodruff (2002), 'The Central Role of Entrepreneurs in Transition Economies', *Journal of Economic Perspectives*, **16** (3), Summer, 153–70; Simon Johnson, John McMillan and Christopher Woodruff (2002), 'Property Rights and Finance', *American Economic Review*, **92** (5) 1335–56; Mara Faccio (2006), 'Politically Connected Firms', *American Economic Review*, **96**, March, 369–86.

Berkeley Economic Press for article: Raymond J. Fisman (2003), 'Ethnic Ties and the Provision of Credit: Relationship-Level Evidence from African Firms', *Advances in Economic Analysis and Policy*, **3** (1), Article 4, i–iii, 1–18.

Blackwell Publishing for articles: Philippe Aghion and Patrick Bolton (1997), 'A Theory of Trickle-Down Growth and Development', *Review of Economic Studies*, **64** (2), April, 151–72; Huw Lloyd-Ellis and Dan Bernhardt (2000), 'Enterprise, Inequality and Economic Development', *Review of Economic Studies*, **67** (1), January, 147–68; Mike Burkart, Fausto Panunzi and Andrei Shleifer (2003), 'Family Firms', *Journal of Finance*, **LVIII** (5), October, 2167–201; Thorsten Beck, Asli Demirgüç-Kunt and Vojislav Maksimovic (2005), 'Financial and Legal Constraints to Growth: Does Firm Size Matter?', *Journal of Finance*, **LX** (1), February, 137–77.

Elsevier for articles: Leo Sleuwaegen and Micheline Goedhuys (2002), 'Growth of Firms in Developing Countries, Evidence from Côte d'Ivoire', *Journal of Development Economics*, **68**, 117–35; Anna L. Paulson and Robert Townsend (2004), 'Entrepreneurship and Financial Constraints in Thailand', *Journal of Corporate Finance*, **10**, 229–62; Robert Cull and Lixin Colin Xu (2005), 'Institutions, Ownership, and Finance: The Determinants of Profit Reinvestment Among Chinese Firms', *Journal of Financial Economics*, **77**, 117–46; Daniel Berkowitz and John E. Jackson (2006), 'Entrepreneurship and the Evolution of Income Distributions in Poland and Russia', *Journal of Comparative Economics*, **34**, 338–56; Leora Klapper, Luc Laeven and Raghuram Rajan (2006), 'Entry Regulation as a Barrier to Entrepreneurship', *Journal of Financial Economics*, **82**, 591–629; Christopher Woodruff and Rene Zenteno (2007), 'Migration Networks and Microenterprises in Mexico', *Journal of Development Economics*, **82**, 509–28; Christian Ahlin and Neville Jiang (2008), 'Can Micro-Credit Bring Development?', *Journal of Development Economics*, **86**, 1–21; Marianne Bertrand, Simon Johnson, Krislert Samphantharak and Antoinette Schoar (2008), 'Mixing Family with

Business: A Study of Thai Business Groups and the Families Behind Them', *Journal of Financial Economics*, **88**, 466–98; Stijn Claessens, Erik Feijen and Luc Laeven (2008), 'Political Connections and Preferential Access to Finance: The Role of Campaign Contributions', *Journal of Financial Economics*, **88**, 554–80.

MIT Press Journals for articles: Kevin M. Murphy, Andrei Shleifer and Robert W. Vishny (1991), 'The Allocation of Talent: Implications for Growth', *Quarterly Journal of Economics*, **106** (2), May, 503–30; Simeon Djankov, Rafael La Porta, Florencio Lopez-de-Silanes and Andrei Shleifer (2002), 'The Regulation of Entry', *Quarterly Journal of Economics*, **CXVII** (1), February, 1–37; Signe-Mary McKernan (2002), 'The Impact of Microcredit Programs on Self-Employment Profits: Do Noncredit Program Aspects Matter?', *Review of Economics and Statistics*, **84** (1), February, 93–115; Simeon Djankov, Yingyi Qian, Gérard Roland and Ekaterina Zhuravskaya (2006), 'Entrepreneurship in China and Russia Compared', *Journal of the European Economic Association*, **4** (2–3), April–May, 352–65; Luc Laeven and Christopher Woodruff (2007), 'The Quality of the Legal System, Firm Ownership, and Firm Size', *Review of Economics and Statistics*, **89** (4), November, 601–14; Suresh de Mel, David McKenzie and Christopher Woodruff (2008), 'Returns to Capital in Microenterprises: Evidence from a Field Experiment', *Quarterly Journal of Economics*, **CXXIII** (4), November, 1329–72.

Small Science and Business Media for article: Murat F. Iyigun and Ann L. Owen (1999), 'Entrepreneurs, Professionals, and Growth', *Journal of Economic Growth*, **4**, June, 213–32.

University of Chicago Press via Rightslink for articles: David S. Evans and Boyan Jovanovic (1989), 'An Estimated Model of Entrepreneurial Choice under Liquidity Constraints', *Journal of Political Economy*, **97** (4), August, 808–27; William J. Baumol (1990), 'Entrepreneurship: Productive, Unproductive, and Destructive', *Journal of Political Economy*, **98** (5), Part 1, October, 893–921; Abhijit V. Banerjee and Andrew F. Newman (1993), 'Occupational Choice and the Process of Development', *Journal of Political Economy*, **101** (2), April, 274–98; Anna L. Paulson, Robert M. Townsend and Alexander Karaivanov (2006), 'Distinguishing Limited Liability from Moral Hazard in a Model of Entrepreneurship', *Journal of Political Economy*, **114** (1),100–144.

Every effort has been made to trace all the copyright holders but if any have been inadvertently overlooked the publishers will be pleased to make the necessary arrangement at the first opportunity.

In addition the publishers wish to thank the Library of Indiana University at Bloomington, USA, for their assistance in obtaining these articles.

Introduction

Thorsten Beck

1 Introduction

Entrepreneurship is a critical phenomenon to understand the process of economic development and to understand the cross-country variation in economic growth. Early on, economists emphasized the important role of entrepreneurs (Knight, 1921 and Schumpeter, 1934), with innovations being their crucial contribution. Specifically, Schumpeter mentions the role of entrepreneurs in discovering or introducing new products, new methods, new markets, new sources of supply or new forms of organization.

As economic theory moved away from the idea of complete markets and started modeling different market frictions, the individual choice to become an entrepreneur and the impact of financing and other institutional constraints on this decision became a central element in development theory. Empirical work over the past 20 years has used an array of data sources, on the aggregate, firm- and household-level, to better understand the causes and consequences of entrepreneurship. While better data availability and quality in industrialized countries have led to most of entrepreneurship research being conducted in these countries, the focus is increasingly shifting towards developing countries. This has to be seen in the context of policy makers and donors alike stressing private sector development as a critical tool to promote economic growth and reduce poverty. New data collection efforts on the firm- and household-level as well as on the institutional constraints faced by entrepreneurs have enabled an array of new research projects.

This volume contains a number of articles written over the past decades that help us understand the role of entrepreneurs in the development process, both theoretically and empirically. While some of these contributions focus specifically on developing countries, others employ large cross-country samples. The papers span a wide methodological range, from theoretical models, over cross-country studies, to firm- and household-level studies, utilizing both regression analysis and simulation techniques. The list of papers is by no means exhaustive; rather, the editor has chosen the – in his opinion – most significant contributions to give the reader an introduction into this area of economic research. The papers in this volume also show the gaps in our knowledge that still exist; recent working papers and research projects are aimed at filling some of these gaps.

This introductory chapter provides a short survey of the articles contained in this book, but also points to ongoing research and gaps in our knowledge. The remainder of this chapter is structured according to the parts of the book. Section 2 presents an overview of theoretical papers that help us better understand the role of entrepreneurship in the development process. Section 3 discusses the role of financing constraints for entrepreneurship and the role of microfinance institutions in alleviating these constraints. Section 4 surveys the role of institutional barriers to entrepreneurship, while section 5 discusses the characteristics of entrepreneurs in developing economies, especially the role of family enterprises. Section 6 presents work on the relationship between entrepreneurs and politicians and the resultant rent-seeking activities. Section 7 concludes and provides directions for future research.

2   The Theory of Entrepreneurship

Modeling an economy with complete markets and perfect information does not require explicitly introducing a role for entrepreneurs. Anyone can become an entrepreneur and there is no differential impact of one more entrepreneur on innovation, productivity or economic growth. Modeling the role of entrepreneurs thus requires introducing market frictions. Most theoretical models have put capital market imperfections and the resulting lack of access to external funding at the center of the relationship between entrepreneurship and economic development. As entrepreneurs' wealth is not necessarily sufficient to realize their investment projects, they depend on external funding. Aghion and Bolton (1997, Chapter 1), model an economy with wealth inequality and endogenous financial intermediation where the effort employed by the entrepreneur cannot be observed without cost by the lender. This agency problem and the resulting moral hazard risk prevent poorer agents from accessing external funding and from realizing their entrepreneurial project. Capital market frictions are thus the critical mechanism through which initial wealth inequality persists and dampens economic growth.

Endogenous labor market decisions and capital market imperfections are also the central elements of Banerjee and Newman (1993, Chapter 2), who model an economy where agents decide between self-employment, wage employment or entrepreneurship. Because of capital market imperfections – modeled as the possibility for borrowers of reneging on their repayment commitment – poor agents without sufficient wealth that can be used as collateral choose wage employment and wealthy agents choose entrepreneurship, which implies hiring salaried workers. Again, income distribution plays a critical role by determining whether an economy relies in the long-run mostly on self-employment or on entrepreneurship with repercussions for economic development. Evans and Jovanovic (1989, Chapter 3), also point to the critical role of financing constraints resulting in a positive correlation between initial wealth and the likelihood of becoming an entrepreneur. The critical mechanism in their model is the limited liability of entrepreneurs, which imposes a limit on their borrowing capacity up to a certain multiple of their initial wealth. Unlike the previous articles, they also test their theoretical predictions, with survey data from the USA; nevertheless, their results have repercussions for the developing world. In addition to capital market frictions, as in Banerjee and Newman, Lloyd-Ellis and Bernhardt (2000, Chapter 4), also introduce a variation in entrepreneurial skills, with a lack of such skills dampening long-run economic development. The relative scarcity of entrepreneurial talent, in conjunction with limited access to credit, is thus the critical element in their model that determines whether an economy enters the traditional long-term development process or enters in long-term distributional cycles with conflict between wage earners and entrepreneurs.

Using longitudinal household data for several regions of Thailand – a country that has not only grown rapidly, but also undergone significant institutional changes over the past decades, including in the financial sector – Robert Townsend has, together with several co-authors, simulated theoretical models and assessed their capability to mimic real world trends. Two of these papers are included here. Paulson and Townsend (2004, Chapter 6), confirm the results by Evans and Jovanovic that wealthier households are more likely to start businesses. Financing constraints place greater restrictions on entrepreneurial activities in poorer regions of Thailand. Further, the largest lenders seem to have a bigger impact on entrepreneurship through selection of borrowers rather than through lending itself. Paulson, Townsend and Karaivanov (2006, Chapter 5), explore which of the different market frictions – limited liability as modeled by Evans and Jovanovic or moral hazard as modeled by Aghion and Bolton – is more relevant in a developing economy like Thailand. The critical difference between the two models is that the limited liability model predicts a positive relationship between wealth and the amount borrowed, while the moral hazard model predicts a negative relationship. Paulson *et al.* find relatively more evidence for the moral hazard mechanism of financing constraints, especially in wealthier parts of Thailand. Limited liability alone can thus not explain financing constraints and restrictions on entrepreneurial activities in a developing economy, such as Thailand.

The payoff of entrepreneurial activities might very well vary across countries at different levels of income and therefore the share of population that decides to invest in entrepreneurial human capital. Iyigun and Owen (1999, Chapter 7), analyze the incentives for agents to invest in either entrepreneurial or professional human capital and show that entrepreneurial human capital plays a more important role in middle-income countries while professional human capital plays a more important role in high-income countries. As economies grow richer the payoff to professional human capital increases and agents are less willing to take the risk of investing in entrepreneurial human capital. While not formally testing their model, Iyigun and Owen show that cross-country correlations are in line with their theory.

The chapters in Part I underline the importance of financial market imperfections in preventing potential entrepreneurs from realizing their investment projects and in perpetuating income inequalities and economic underdevelopment. While most theoretical models take these imperfections as given, financial economists have recently focused on policies that can help alleviate these market imperfections and thus foster entrepreneurship without the need for redistribution (see Demirgüç-Kunt and Levine, 2008, for a more detailed discussion). Theoretical work that directly links reductions in financial market frictions with more equality in economic opportunities and entrepreneurship would certainly be welcome.

3   Entrepreneurs, Financing Constraints, and Microfinance

Since financing constraints are often the critical market friction that prevents potential entrepreneurs from realizing their projects and thus condemns them to either self- or wage employment, microcredit has gained an important role in helping overcome the financing constraints of poor potential entrepreneurs. Nobel Prize winner and Grameen Bank founder Muhamed Yusuf claims that access to credit is the primary obstacle to productive self-employment for the poor.[2] And recent research shows that financing constraints might be indeed the most binding constraint on firms of all sizes (Ayyagari, Demirgüç-Kunt and Maksimovic, 2008), more so than other elements of the business environment such as macroeconomic instability or infrastructure.

To what extent can microfinance help the poor overcome restrictions on entrepreneurial activities? Can microfinance foster economic development by alleviating financing constraints of poor entrepreneurs? In an important theoretical contribution, Ahlin and Jiang (2008, Chapter 8), show that microcredit can either foster or dampen economic development, i.e. there is no unambiguous relationship between microcredit and economic development. Critically, only if microfinance institutions allow graduation of self-employed borrowers into entrepreneurs will microfinance unambiguously raise income per capita. Important in this context is the role of microsavings, in addition to microcredit; only if microfinance institutions offer the poor savings products, are they able to accumulate sufficient capital to eventually graduate to the formal banking sector.[3]

One important constraint for microentrepreneurs might be the non-linearity of investment. In the presence of large scale economies, poor microentrepreneurs might be simply stuck in poverty gaps and even relatively large capital grants or loans might not be able to help them. De Mel, McKenzie and Woodruff (2008, Chapter 9), use a randomized experiment in Sri Lanka to measure returns on capital and assess this constraint. Specifically, they compare a treatment group of microentrepreneurs that receive grants in cash or in-kind with a control group of microentrepreneurs without such grants. They find very high returns to capital – over 50 percent per annum and thus significantly higher than market interest rates – and thus evidence that access to finance can help the poor overcome restrictions on entrepreneurial activities.[4]

McKernan (2002, Chapter 10), assesses another important aspect of microfinance – non-credit services, such as technical advice, vocational training, health information etc. – that complements lending and is often provided by the same microcredit institution. She finds a large significant effect of both the credit and the non-credit components of microfinance for several Bangladeshi microfinance programs, including Grameen Bank and Bangladesh Rehabilitations Assistance Committee (BRAC), on self-employment profits. This effect is strongest for the poorest participants in the microcredit programs.[5]

A very different way of alleviating financing constraints of entrepreneurs in developing countries is through remittance flows from migrants to developed economies to their families in their home countries. Remittance flows constitute by now the second largest source of capital inflows for developing countries, although their size is still underestimated as a large share of remittances flows through unofficial channels and is thus not captured in official statistics. Woodruff and Zenteno (2007, Chapter 11), show that entrepreneurs from Mexican regions with traditionally stronger migration flows towards the USA have higher investment and profit levels. This is especially true for capital-intensive sectors that depend most on capital inflows to alleviate capital constraints. It still remains to be assessed whether direct remittances or remittances channeled through banks are more efficient in terms of improving capital allocation, questions that are the subject of ongoing research projects.

Given the importance of financing constraints, significant research resources have been recently channeled into better understanding of how to overcome these constraints. Randomized experiments, similar to de Mel *et al.*, help assess the success of specific microcredit programs and mechanisms, such as group-lending (Giné and Karlan, 2006). However, recent research also confirms the theoretical predictions by Ahlin and Jiang that credit is only one financial service needed by microentrepreneurs and financial products such as savings, payment and remittance and insurance play an increasingly important role.

4   Institutional Barriers to Entrepreneurship

While financing constraints are important in restricting entrepreneurial activity, there are other market frictions and government failures that prevent large segments of the population in many developing countries from taking up formal entrepreneurial activity and limit their activities to the shadow or informal economy.[6] Consequently, a large share of economic activity in many countries is still undertaken in the informal sector, with estimates of the size of this sector ranging from less than 10 percent in Austria and Switzerland to 70 percent in the Philippines and Thailand. What prevents enterprises from becoming formal? Recent data collection efforts at the World Bank under the catchy name of *Doing Business* have shed significant light on institutional barriers for new enterprises to enter the formal economy. These barriers include firm registration costs, costs of property registration and transfer, contract enforcement and labor legislation. Other institutional arrangements, such as credit registries or bankruptcy regimes, have an important effect on enterprises, as they impact the degree and cost of access to external finance. While facing certain limitations, such as capturing only the official rules and costs and other measurement problems, these indicators are an important step towards measuring the institutional framework in which entrepreneurs work and advances on other dimensions, such as properly capturing the degree of entrepreneurship in society (discussed below in section 5) will allow more rigorous exploration of the causes of entrepreneurship.

Registration processes are one important entry hurdle. As documented by Djankov *et al.* (2002, Chapter 12), the number of steps, the time and the costs of registering a company vary enormously across countries. Take the example of official costs of registration, which range from less than 0.5 percent of GDP per capita in the USA to over 4.6 times GDP per capita in the Dominican Republic. Although high barriers are sometimes justified with the need to protect consumers and workers, Djankov *et al.* (2002, Chapter 12), show that countries with higher entry barriers have higher levels of corruption and larger informal economies, but no better quality in private or public good provision. High entry barriers have a negative impact on entrepreneurial activity, as shown by Klapper, Laeven and Rajan (2006, Chapter 13), for a sample of Western and Eastern European countries. They show that costly registration procedures dampen the registration of new enterprises, especially in industries that are naturally high-entry sectors. They also force new enterprises to start with a larger size, while dampening subsequent growth. It is important to stress that these restrictions are in addition to financing constraints; entrepreneurial activity is larger in countries that have better systems in place to share information about borrowers.

Institutional constraints do not only affect entry of new enterprises, but also their subsequent growth, as shown by Beck, Demirgüç-Kunt and Maksimovic (2005, Chapter 14). Using firm-level surveys, they show that smaller firms do not only feel more constrained by deficiencies in the financial and legal system, but these constraints also translate into slower growth. Financing and institutional constraints thus create an uneven playing field between small and large enterprises, a gap that is larger in countries with deficient financial and legal systems. The uneven playing field can also explain the divergent growth patterns of firms of different sizes, as shown by Sleuwaegen and Goedhuys (2002, Chapter 15), for Côte d'Ivoire and Germany. While in Germany, small manufacturing firms grow typically faster than large firms, this relationship is reversed in Côte d'Ivoire. The authors explain this with stronger growth obstacles, especially for medium-sized enterprises, related to infrastructure and access to finance. These growth constraints can also explain the phenomenon of the missing middle in the size distribution of firms in Africa and other parts of the developing world.

Institutional constraints do not only prevent firms – especially small firms – from growing, but also from reaching their optimal size, and influence their corporate structure. This is shown by Laeven and Woodruff (2007, Chapter 16), using data across Mexican states. They find that firms in states with weaker legal systems are smaller than in states with strong legal systems. The effect of legal system quality is stronger for proprietorships than for incorporated enterprises. This is consistent with theory predicting that proprietors are relatively more reluctant to invest in their companies than incorporated firms in weak legal environment, given the absence of risk diversification possibilities of such an enterprise.

Not surprisingly, the effect of higher entry barriers into the formal sector has also negative repercussions for economic development. Barseghyan (2008) shows for a cross-section of 61 industrial and developing countries that higher entry barriers, as measured by the Djankov *et al.* data, is associated with lower income per capita and lower levels of total factor productivity, a relationship that is robust to controlling for reverse causation and simultaneity bias by instrumenting for the entry costs with historic and geographic variables.

Transition economies are an especially rich laboratory for research on entrepreneurship given that market economies were built up from ground after the start of transition. The socialist economies were dominated by large enterprises and the initial focus of the reform process was privatizing them rather than enabling the set-up of new private enterprises. As McMillan and Woodruff (2002, Chapter 17), argue, new entrepreneurs reacted to the incentives given by the reform process, which varied significantly across transition economies. Entrepreneurs in Russia, for example, are much more afraid of corruption and less inclined to invest than entrepreneurs in Poland. The lack of privatization of state-owned enterprises was also a deterrent to new entrepreneurship as the state-owned enterprises tend to stifle new entrants through regulatory capture or preventing them from accessing credit. For example, Berkowitz and Jackson (2006, Chapter 18), compare the experience in Poland and Russia and find that the lower entry barriers in Poland did not only lead to a higher share of small enterprises after the start of transition than in Russia but also a significantly smaller increase in income inequality.

Only a few papers so far have tried to explore which dimension of the business environment is the decisive constraint for entrepreneurs. Johnson, McMillan and Woodruff (2002, Chapter 19), use survey data for five transition economies to test the binding constraint on reinvestment by small new firms. They find that weak property rights – as proxied by survey responses about the payments of bribes – are more binding for reinvestment than access to bank loans, proxied by the availability of physical collateral. Cull and Xu (2005, Chapter 20), on the other hand, find that Chinese entrepreneurs are more likely to reinvest their profits if they are more confident in the system of property rights protection and have easier access to credit, with this effect being stronger for small firms. While the work for the Eastern and Central European countries shows the dominance of legal system constraints, access to finance is at least as important a constraint for Chinese entrepreneurs. Disentangling the effect of different dimensions of the business environment is an important area of further research, but will be difficult to undertake, as many of these dimensions are highly correlated. Time-varying policy implementation across different subnational units can provide natural experiments that can be utilized for research, as Bruhn (2008) shows for the business registration reform in Mexico.

5 Who are the Entrepreneurs?

Measuring the degree of entrepreneurship in a society is difficult for several reasons. On the one hand, the Global Entrepreneurship Monitor (Reynolds *et al.*, 2005) relies on survey information about new enterprises and intentions to form an enterprise. Further, it measures the share of population involved in managing their own company. Measurement is consistent across countries, but coverage is limited to 41 countries and does not measure formal enterprise formation, as new entrepreneurial activity could be undertaken in the informal economy. On the other hand, a recent data collection effort by the World Bank (Klapper *et al.*, 2007) focuses on legal entities registered with a public registry and data collection relies on official sources whose quality might vary across countries. However, the sample comprises over 100 countries with data up to eight years. Neither of the two data sources captures properly the degree to which entrepreneurial activity is innovative. Further, both sources provide indications of entry into entrepreneurship, but not exit, so that turnover or levels of entrepreneurship are hard to assess. Both databases, however, are valuable sources of information and offer promising venues of research towards exploring the causes and consequences of entrepreneurship across countries.

Who are the entrepreneurs? Recent surveys of both entrepreneurs and non-entrepreneurs have tried to shed light on this question. Djankov *et al.* (2006, Chapter 21), compare survey results from China and Russia. These surveys carefully match a sample of several hundred entrepreneurs to a similar-sized sample of non-entrepreneurs with similar individual characteristics such as age, gender, educational attainment etc. In both countries, entrepreneurs have more entrepreneurs among friends and families than non-entrepreneurs, value work relatively more than leisure and have higher wealth ambitions. The study found that in Russia entrepreneurs have relatively better educational backgrounds but also parents that were more likely to have been part of the Communist elite than non-entrepreneurs, while in China, entrepreneurs are relatively more risk-taking and more motivated by greed. The authors have undertaken similar studies for Brazil, Nigeria and India.

In the absence of formal market institutions in many developing countries, personal relationships between entrepreneurs are important. For the case of Africa, several studies have found that entrepreneurs of European and Asian descent have closer ties within their own ethnic community, which facilitates access to trade credit as well as input and output markets. Fisman (2003, Chapter 22), uses data on specific supplier relationships between African firms and shows that firms are twice as likely to obtain credit from suppliers within the ethnic group as from outsiders. However, these close ethnic community ties account only for 15 percent of the preferential access to credit that entrepreneurs of non-African descent enjoy in Sub-Saharan Africa. While personal relationships are thus important, their significance should not be overestimated for success of enterprises.

Many enterprises, especially new and small ones and especially in developing countries, are family enterprises, with no significant outside shareholding or management influence. One important issue for family entrepreneurs is the question of succession. Specifically, Burkart, Panunzi and Shleifer (2003, Chapter 23), model an enterprise where the founder has to decide between outsourcing management to a professional or leaving it to her heir. Assuming that the professional would be the better manager, they show that the decision is shaped by the legal framework. In economies with strong minority shareholder rights, founding entrepreneurs are more likely to pass the enterprise on to professional management and float part of their equity on the stock exchange. In weak legal environments, the founder passes the firm on his heir, while in intermediate regimes, the founder hires an external manager, but does not sell part of the equity. The model and its predictions match well cross-country variation in the share of family enterprises and the reluctance of firms to open to outside management and investment.

Bertrand *et al.* (2008, Chapter 24), confirm some of Burkart *et al.*'s predictions in a study of 93 of the largest Thai business families and their enterprises. They find that larger families are more likely to be involved with management of the family business. The founder's sons play an important role in both board membership and management, with negative repercussions for firm-level performance. They interpret their findings with the hypothesis that the dilution of ownership and control over many sons results in a race to the bottom in tunneling resources out of the family's firms.

6   Entrepreneurs, Politicians and Rent-Seeking

As pointed out by Baumol (1990, Chapter 25), and already discussed above, not all entrepreneurial activity focuses on innovation. The incentives and pay-offs offered by society determine the relative share of entrepreneurs focused either on productive or unproductive activities, and therefore the productive contribution of these entrepreneurs to society varies significantly across countries. Baumol offers several historical examples, such as Rome or ancient China, where innovative entrepreneurship was frowned upon and rent-seeking activities had a very high and culturally accepted return. In today's world, rent-seeking is a prominent entrepreneurial activity in developed and developing countries alike. Such rent-seeking is often based on connections between entrepreneurs and politicians.

Murphy, Shleifer and Vishny (1991, Chapter 26) formalize Baumol's hypothesis in a theoretical model and show how the choice between becoming an innovative entrepreneur or an unproductive rent-seeker depends on the return to either activity. In economies where rent-seeking is more rewarding the most talented will go forgo entrepreneurial activity and rather seek rents, with negative repercussions for growth. Simple cross-country growth regressions confirm the predictions of this model: a higher share of engineering college graduates is associated with higher GDP per capita growth, while a higher share of law graduates with lower growth.

Measuring political connections is difficult as is measuring their benefits. Faccio (2006, Chapter 27), assembles data on over 20000 publicly traded firms across 47 countries and on their political connections. A firm is defined as politically connected if one of their large shareholders or senior managers is a member of parliament, a minister or is closely related to a top politician. She finds such political connections in 35 of the 47 countries and the incidence of political connections increases with firm size, the level of corruption and with restrictions on foreign investment. Using the event study approach around political announcements affecting the respective firm, she finds a significant increase in the share price when either a large shareholder or senior manager enters politics or a politician joins the Board.

Fisman (2001, Chapter 28), estimates the value of political connections for the case of Indonesia. Focusing on a single country helps alleviate measurement problems, as the

Indonesian political system of that time was completely organized around strongman Suharto. Using the last years of Suharto's government and a string of adverse rumors about the health of Suharto, Fisman looks at the relative excess returns of firms closely connected to Suharto's family over the Jakarta Stock Exchange Index. He finds that firms connected to the Suharto family experienced a significantly larger drop in their share prices following adverse rumors about the president's health.

Relationships between politicians and entrepreneurs can also be formed using campaign contributions that translate into benefits for the contributors after successful elections. Using data on campaign contributions around the 1998 and 2002 federal elections in Brazil, Claessens, Feijen and Laeven (2008, Chapter 29), find that firms that provided contributions to elected federal congressmen experienced higher stock returns than firms that did not. One of the channels through which these firms reaped the return on their 'investment' into relationships was through improved access to credit after the elections. Given that 40 percent of the Brazilian banking system is still dominated by two large banks owned by the federal government and long-term financing is concentrated in a government-owned development bank, such findings are not surprising.

7 Conclusions

The papers in this volume have provided students of entrepreneurship in developing countries with important insights. Theoretical models have shown the importance of entrepreneurs for economic development, but have also pointed to the important role of financing constraints that restrict entrepreneurial activity. Governments in many developing countries impose high entry barriers into the formal economy with negative repercussions for entrepreneurship. Personal relationships and ethnic ties as well as political connections replace formal market institutions in many developing countries. The lack of market-conducive institutions also has negative repercussions for the growth of such firms and for their corporate form, preventing many from accessing external equity.

While the papers in this volume show the enormous progress achieved over the past decades in our understanding of entrepreneurship in developing countries, they also point to important gaps. Among these gaps are understanding the channels through which entrepreneurship can contribute to economic growth – capital accumulation, innovation, competition etc. – and policies that can help foster entrepreneurship. What is the role of entrepreneurs and enterprises in innovation and productivity growth? Is there a gender dimension to entrepreneurship; is there a stronger effect of the institutional barriers discussed above on women? A combination of different data sources, including household surveys and data bases of institutional features across countries, along the lines of *Doing Business*, will help us answer these and related questions in the future.

Several recent data collections and new research approaches seem interesting and important. First, better data on the importance of entrepreneurship across countries are necessary. While the Global Entrepreneurship Monitor (GEM), data have provided important insights into the potential for entrepreneurial activity, they do not measure actual entrepreneurial activity. Recent data collection efforts at the World Bank are helpful in this context (Klapper *et al.*, 2007). Such data might help assess more rigorously the impact of entrepreneurship on economic development, but also the relative importance of different market frictions and government failures in subduing entrepreneurial activity.

Household data and randomized experiments can provide similarly fruitful insights into impediments to entrepreneurship. By 'treating' a randomly chosen sample of microentrepreneurs to certain interventions – be it capital grants, such as in de Mel *et al.* (Chapter 9), technical assistance, financial literacy programs or help with registration – and comparing them afterward to a non-treated control group, one can assess the effect of such interventions. Household surveys such as employed by Djankov *et al.* can also give greater insights into the personal characteristics of entrepreneurs.

A critical area of future research, however, should be the evaluation of different government programs and policies to foster entrepreneurship. There is a wide array of policies and programs employed by national and sub-national governments around the world. These include reforms of business registration, partial credit guarantee programs, venture capital funds, business development agencies and others. Many of these support mechanisms are supported by the donor community. However, little research has been undertaken to rigorously assess the success of such schemes and their cost–benefit ratio compared to other policies.

Many of the gaps are currently addressed with new and ongoing research.[7] The importance of private sector development and the critical role that entrepreneurs have in the development of the private sector make these times exciting and important ones for more research in entrepreneurship in developing countries.

Notes

1. Helpful comments and suggestions from Leora Klapper and David McKenzie are gratefully acknowledged, without implicating them.
2. For an excellent introduction into microfinance, see Amendariz de Aghion and Morduch (2005).
3. The ambiguous theoretical prediction about the effect of microcredit programs is matched by ambiguous empirical results, as summarized in World Bank (2008).
4. McKenzie and Woodruff (2008) find very similar results for a randomized experiment in Mexico.
5. A recent working paper by Karlan and Valdivia (2006) finds similar positive results of entrepreneurship training for microfinance clients in Peru. Like de Mel *et al.*, they utilize a randomized experiment, comparing microcredit borrowers with and without such extension services.
6. See Schneider and Ernste (2000) for an overview of the measurement, causes and consequence of informal economic activities.
7. See for example, this recent NBER conference, the proceedings of which will be published shortly: http://www.nber.org/~confer/2008/IDE/program.html

References

Armendariz de Aghion, Beatriz, and Jonathan Morduch (2005), *The Economics of Mirofinance*, Cambridge, MA: MIT Press.
Ayyagari, Meghana, Asli Demirgüç-Kunt and Vojislav Maksimovic (2008), 'How important are financing constraints? The role of finance in the business environment', *World Bank Economic Review*, **22** (3), 483–516.
Barseghyan, Levon (2008), 'Entry costs and cross-country differences in productivity and output'.

Bruhn, Miriam (2008), 'License to Sell: The Effect of Business Registration Reform on Entrepreneurial Activity in Mexico', Washington, D.C.: World Bank Policy Research Working Paper 4538.

Demirgüç-Kunt, Asli and Ross Levine (2008), 'Finance and Economic Opportunity', Washington, D.C.: World Bank Policy Research Working Paper 4468.

Giné, Xavi and Dean Karlan (2006), 'Group vs. Individual Liability: A Field Experiment in the Philippines', Washington, D.C.: World Bank Policy Research Working Paper 4008.

Karlan, Dean and Martin Valdivia (2006), 'Teaching Entrepreneurship: Impact of Entrepreneurship Training on Microfinance Clients and Institutions', New Haven, CT: Yale University mimeo.

Klapper, Leora, Raphael Amit, Mauro Guillen and Juan Manuel Quesada (2007), 'Entrepreneurship and Firm Formation Across Countries', Washington, D.C.: World Bank Policy Research Working Paper 4313.

Knight, Frank (1921), *Risk, Uncertainty and Profit*. New York: Houghton Mifflin.

McKenzie, David and Christopher Woodruff (2008), 'Experimental evidence on returns to capital and access to finance in Mexico', *World Bank Economic Review*, **22** (3), 457–482.

Reynolds, Paul, Niels Bosma, Erkko Autio, Steve Hunt, Natalie de Bono, Isabel Servais, Paloma Lopez-Garcia and Nancy Chin (2005), 'Global entrepreneurship monitor: Data collection, design and implementation: 1998–2003', *Small Business Economics*, **24** (3), 205–31.

Schneider, Friedrich and Dominik Ernste (2000), 'Shadow economies: Size, causes and consequences', *Journal of Economic Literature*, **38** (1), 77–114.

Schumpeter, Joseph (1934), *The Theory of Economic Development*. Cambridge, MA: Harvard University Press.

World Bank (2008), 'Finance for All? Policies and Pitfalls in Expanding Access', Washington, D.C.: World Bank Policy Research Report.

Part I
The Theory of Entrepreneurship

[1]

Review of Economic Studies (1997) **64**, 151–172
0034-6527/97/00080151$02.00
© 1997 The Review of Economic Studies Limited

A Theory of Trickle-Down Growth and Development

PHILIPPE AGHION

University College London and European Bank for Reconstruction and Development

and

PATRICK BOLTON

ECARE, Université Libre de Bruxelles and CENTER, Tilburg University

First version received October 1993; *final version accepted September* 1996 *(Eds.)*

This paper develops a model of growth and income inequalities in the presence of imperfect capital markets, and it analyses the trickle-down effect of capital accumulation. Moral hazard with limited wealth constraints on the part of the borrowers is the source of both capital market imperfections and the emergence of persistent income inequalities. Three main conclusions are obtained from this model.

First, when the rate of capital accumulation is sufficiently high, the economy converges to a unique invariant wealth distribution. Second, even though the trickle-down mechanism can lead to a unique steady-state distribution under laissez-faire, there is room for government intervention: in particular, redistribution of wealth from rich lenders to poor and middle-class borrowers improves the production efficiency of the economy both because it brings about greater equality of opportunity and also because it accelerates the trickle-down process. Third, the process of capital accumulation initially has the effect of widening inequalities but in later stages it reduces them: in other words, this model can generate a Kuznets curve.

1. INTRODUCTION

It is widely believed that the accumulation of wealth by the rich is good for the poor since some of the increased wealth of the rich trickles down to the poor. This paper formalizes an important mechanism through which wealth may trickle down from the rich to the poor.

The mechanism we focus on is borrowing and lending in the capital market: as more capital is accumulated in the economy more funds may be available to the poor for investment purposes. This in turn enables them to grow richer.[1] In our model, persistent wealth inequalities arise because investment projects generate random returns and entrepreneurs do not insure themselves perfectly against this income risk.[2] While in the existing literature on endogenous income distribution the supply side of the credit market is not explicitly modelled and the interest rate is given exogenously, in our model the equilibrium

---

1. What we call a "loan contract" can also be reinterpretated as an "employment contract" and our capital market could be reinterpreted as a labour market. It is important to highlight this reinterpretation of our model since empirically trickle-down may be as (or even more) important in the labour market. In a stripped-down model like ours it is not surprising that we cannot give a satisfactory answer to the question of what distinguishes a credit relationship from an employment relationship, besides the difference in the timing of monetary transfers.

2. We thus follow a distinguished transition in modelling inequalities initiated by Champernowne (1953) and successively refined by Loury (1981) and Banerjee and Newman (1991), among others. See Cowell (1977), Aghion and Bolton (1992) for brief overviews of this literature.

interest rate schedule is determined endogenously by the interplay between the supply and demand for investment funds. Endogeneizing the interest rate schedule is a necessary modelling step in order to fully address the question of the effects of capital accumulation on the income distribution.

When the interest rate schedule is determined endogenously it is no longer possible to simply trace the wealth of a single individual in isolation from the rest of the economy, since the stochastic evolution of her wealth depends on the evolution of the state of the economy through the equilibrium interest rate schedule. As a result, the dynamics of an individual's wealth are now nonlinear. It turns out that there are no general mathematical methods for dealing with nonlinear Markov processes. However, we show that with sufficiently fast capital accumulation the equilibrium interest rate schedule converges to a fixed schedule. Once this schedule is attained standard linear methods again apply to the stochastic evolution of an individual's wealth. We are thus able to derive sufficient conditions for the convergence of our complicated Markov process to a unique invariant distribution. This proposition is by no means obvious or general. Indeed, in related work Banerjee and Newman (1993) and Piketty (1993) provide examples of nonlinear Markov processes which have multiple invariant distributions.[3]

The main economic insight which comes out of our analysis in this paper is that, even though wealth does trickle-down from the rich to the poor and leads to a unique steady-state distribution of wealth under sufficiently high rates of capital accumulation, there is still room for wealth redistribution policies to improve the long-run efficiency of the economy. In other words, the trickle down mechanism is not sufficient to eventually reach an efficient distribution of resources, even in the best possible scenario. The reason why redistribution improves production efficiency is that with redistribution the poor need to borrow less to invest and therefore their incentives to maximize profits are distorted less. Thus, redistribution improves the efficiency of the economy because it brings about greater equality of opportunity and because it accelerates the trickle-down process.

However, one-shot redistributions in our model only have temporary effects. In order to improve the efficiency of the economy permanently, permanent redistribution policies must be set up. This observation is a direct consequence of our convergence result to a unique invariant distribution. In contrast, one-shot redistribution policies may have permanent effects in the models considered in Banerjee and Newman (1993) and Piketty (1993).

It is worth pointing out that the need for redistribution arises from the existence of an incentive problem. In the absence of incentive considerations there is no need for redistribution in our model. Our justification should be contrasted with most other motivations for redistribution in the literature which emphasize insurance or fairness considerations that must be weighed against incentive efficiency considerations (see e.g. Mirrless (1971)).

The paper is organized as follows: Section 2 outlines the model; Section 3 characterizes the equilibrium in the capital market. Section 4 analyses the interaction between growth and redistribution. Section 5 establishes the convergence to a unique invariant

---

3. The set up considered by Piketty is most similar to ours, with the interest rate also being endogenously determined by the supply and demand for investment funds. However, the focus of Piketty's analysis is on situations where the rate of capital accumulation is not sufficiently high for the economy to converge to a unique wealth distribution. Rather, there exist multiple invariant distributions. When there are multiple steady-state distributions, a one-shot redistribution of wealth may push the economy from one steady-state to another and therefore have long-run effects. However, since little is known about the *dynamics* of wealth distribution in these models, it is not always clear *a priori* what the long-run effects of a one-shot redistribution might be.

distribution. Finally, Section 6 discusses redistribution and explains why the positive incentive effects of redistribution for the borrowers outweigh the negative incentive effects for the wealthy entrepreneurs, who may see some of their accumulated wealth taxed away.

2. THE MODEL

We consider a closed economy with a continuum of identical agents of total mass 1. Each agent lives for one period during which he or she works and invests. The resulting income is divided between consumption and bequests. Each agent has one offspring and generations succeed other each *ad infinitum*.

The only source of heterogeneity among individuals is assumed to be their initial wealth endowments. We denote by $G_t(w)$ the distribution of wealth endowments at the beginning of period t which results from the previous generation's bequests (where $w \geq 0$). All the agents in the economy are endowed with one unit of labour which they supply (inelastically) at no disutility cost.

Our detailed description of this economy begins with the technological assumptions. At the beginning of each period t an agent has the following options:

(a) she can use her unit of labour to work on a "backyard" (or "routine") activity which requires no capital investment. The return to this activity is assumed to be deterministic and small, equal to $n > 0$.

(b) alternatively, she may choose to be self-employed and invest her unit of labour in a high yield "entrepreneurial" activity which requires a fixed initial capital outlay of $\hat{k} = 1$. The uncertain revenue from investment in this high yield project is given by[4]

$$F(k, l) = \begin{cases} r \text{ with probability } p \\ 0 \text{ with probability } 1-p \end{cases} \quad \text{if } k \geq \hat{k} = 1 \text{ and } l \geq 1; \quad (2.1)$$

$$F(k, l) = 0 \text{ otherwise};$$

The probability of success p can be influenced by the individual's effect. We denote by $C(p)$ the effort cost of reaching probability p, and for computational simplicity we only

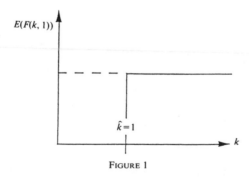

FIGURE 1

4. The high-yield technology defined by (2.1) corresponds to an extreme form of U-shaped average cost curve with respect to capital outlays. What is important for the analysis that follows is that the cost function is U-shaped; and especially that the production technology exhibit diminishing returns. The specific form chosen in the text is otherwise not important.

consider the quadratic cost function

$$C(p) = \frac{rp^2}{2a}, \qquad \text{where } a \in (0, 1].$$ (2.2)

(c) the agent's initial endowment of capital w_t can be used in the entrepreneurial activity or it can be invested in an economy-wide mutual fund. The equilibrium unit (gross) return of this mutual fund, A_t, is determined endogenously by equating aggregate savings with aggregate investment. As in Diamond (1984) or Green (1987) we suppose that there is free-entry into the mutual fund market so that all extra-normal profits from the intermediation activity are competed away and borrowers obtain funding in exchange for an expected unit repayment on the loan of A_t.

To complete our description of the model, we must specify individual preferences and the chronology of the main events of an agent's life. We assume that agents are risk-neutral and their utility depends only on consumption and bequests. We assume that parents have "warm-glow" preferences over bequests (see Andreoni (1989)). That is, parents derive utility by giving to their children, independently of the extent to which their children actually benefit from the bequest.

The chronology of an agent's main events and decisions in her life is as shown in Figure 2.

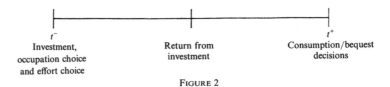

t^-	Return from	t^+
Investment,	investment	Consumption/bequest
occupation choice		decisions
and effort choice		

FIGURE 2

At the beginning of each period each individual decides to invest her unit of labour and her inherited wealth w_t in one (or two) of the above activities. At the end of her lifetime, the individual allocates her net final wealth between consumption and bequests. Agents are assumed to have Leontieff preferences over consumption and bequests,[5] so that optimal bequests are a linear function of end of period wealth. Let $w(t^+)$ denote wealth at the end of period t, then $b_{t+1} = w_{t+1} = (1 - \delta) w(t^+)$.

3. STATIC EQUILIBRIUM IN THE CAPITAL MARKET

We shall assume that, initially at least, the aggregate wealth in the economy is not high enough for all individuals to be able to invest in their high yield entrepreneurial projects.

Assumption 1

$$\int_{w \geq 0} w \, dG_0(w) = W_0 < 1.$$

The economy should comprise three classes of agents, at least in the early periods[6]:

5. Ex-ante, preferences have the form $U = \min \{(1 - \delta) c; \delta b\} - C(p)$, where $c, b, C(p)$ denote respectively the agent's consumption, bequests and effort cost; ($C(p) = 0$ whenever the individual does not engage in entrepreneurial activities).

6. This heuristic claim will be formally established in the remaining part of the section.

AGHION & BOLTON   TRICKLE-DOWN GROWTH   155

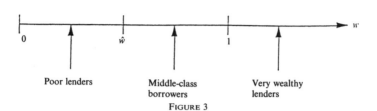

FIGURE 3

the very wealthy (with initial wealth $w_i > 1$) who have enough funds to invest both in their high-yield project and in the projects of other agents via the capital market; the middle-class composed of agents investing only in their own high-yield project but who need to complement their initial wealth $w_i < 1$ with a loan of $(1 - w_i)$ to cover the set up cost $\hat{k} = 1$; finally the poor who do not invest in their own project. This is illustrated in Figure 3.

The equilibrium terms at which the middle-class will borrow are determined by equalizing the aggregate demand for funds (emanating from this class) with aggregate supply (from the very wealthy and the poor).

Second, we assume that the (effort-driven) probability of success p is not observable, and that

Assumption 2

A borrower's repayment to her lenders cannot exceed her end of period wealth.

Thus, the incentive problem here is a moral hazard problem with limited wealth constraints, as in Sappington (1983).

3.1. *The optimal lending contract*

An optimal investment contract between a borrower with initial wealth $w < 1$ and his lender(s) will then specify a repayment schedule $R(w)$ such that:

$$R(w) = \begin{cases} (1-w)\rho(w) & \text{if the project succeeds;} \\ 0 & \text{if the project fails,} \end{cases}$$

where $(1 - w)$ is the amount borrowed and $\rho(w)$ is the unit repayment rate.

Given this contract, a borrower chooses p to maximize her expected revenue net of both repayment and effort costs

$$\max_{p} \{ pr - p(1 - w)\rho(w) - C(p) \}. \tag{3.1}$$

The solution is given by

$$p(w) = a \left(1 - (1 - w) \frac{\rho(w)}{r} \right). \tag{3.2}$$

We see from equation (3.2) that when $\rho(w)$ is fixed and independent of w the lower the borrower's initial wealth the less effort she devotes to increasing the probability of success of her project. The more individuals need to borrow in order to invest, the less incentives they have to supply effort since they must share a larger fraction of the marginal returns from effort with lenders.

The very wealthy, who do not need to borrow in order to invest in their own project, supply the first-best level of effort since they remain residual claimants on all returns from such effort

$$w \geq 1 \Rightarrow p(w) = \arg \max \ (pr - C(p)) = p^{fb}(w),$$

$$= a. \tag{3.3}$$

This implies that only those individuals who need to borrow funds to invest in their project actually choose to do so; the very wealthy prefer not to borrow in order to achieve first-best efficiency.[7]

So far we have treated the repayment schedule ρ as independent of the initial wealth w. However, since the risk of default on a loan may vary with the size of the loan, the unit repayment rate ρ must vary with w to reflect the change in default risk.

In equilibrium, all loans must yield the same expected return, so that the following condition must hold[8]

$$p(w)\rho(w) = A_t, \tag{3.4}$$

where A_t is the equilibrium unit rate of return of the mutual fund. We assume that A_t is a certain return.[9] Combining (3.2) and (3.4), the required repayment rate $\rho(w)$ must satisfy

$$a\rho(w)\left[1 - (1-w)\frac{\rho(w)}{r}\right] = A_t. \tag{3.5}$$

From equations (3.2), (3.4) and (3.5) one derives the important proposition, that even when $\rho(w)$ varies with w, effort supply is increasing in w.

Proposition 0. *In equilibrium effort supply is increasing in w: $p'(w) > 0$.*

Proof. From equation (3.4) we know that $p(w) = A_t/\rho(w)$. Thus the sign of $p'(w)$ is given by the sign of $\{-\rho'(w)\}$. Define the function

$$f(\rho, w) = a\left[\rho - \rho^2\frac{1-w}{r}\right].$$

The left-hand intersection point of $f(p, w)$ with the horizontal line A_t defines the solution $\rho(w)$ to equation (3.5), see figure 4.

This solution is given by

$$\rho(w) = \left[1 - \sqrt{1 - \frac{4A_t(1-w)}{ar}}\right]\frac{r}{2(1-w)}.$$

It is easy to see that $\rho'(w) < 0$. ‖

7. The existence of a fixed-cost indivisibility in the entrepreneurial technology might create incentives for our risk-neutral individuals to buy *lotteries*. For example, an agent with initial wealth $w < k$ would take the lottery: (invest 0 with probability $1 - w/k$; invest k with probability w/k). For the sake of expositional clarity we shall rule out lotteries in the analysis below.

8. Because they are all risk-neutral, lenders will never invest in a high-yield project whose expected repayment revenue is strictly less than the market rate of return A_t.

9. Since a continuum (number) of i.i.d. projects are being financed by the mutual fund, one can appeal to the law of large numbers and assume without loss of generality that the expected rate of return A_t accruing to investors in the mutual fund is a safe rate of return. Introducing even a little amount of risk-aversion into individual preferences would suffice to rule out random rates of return in equilibrium.

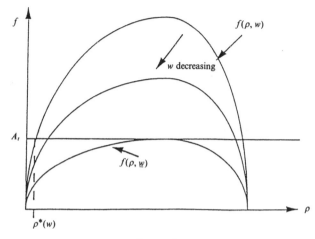

FIGURE 4

Because effort supply is decreasing when the agent borrows more, the unit repayment $\rho(w)$ must be commensurately increased to ensure that the lender obtains the same expected repayment. In other words, the poorer the borrower, the higher is her unit repayment—$\rho(w)$—to compensate for a lower probability of repayment, $p(w)$.

When

$$w < \underline{w}(A_t) \equiv 1 - \frac{ar}{4A_t},$$

there is no solution to equation (3.5). This means that the maximum expected return on a loan $1 - w$, with $w < \underline{w}$, is strictly less than A_t. Thus all agents with wealth $w \in [0, \underline{w}(A_t)]$ won't be able to borrow, even if they want to borrow.

Definition. We say that there may be *credit rationing* in the capital market when $\underline{w}(A_t) > 0$. All agents with wealth $w \in [0, \underline{w}(A_t)]$ are said to be *credit rationed* if they would like to borrow but cannot since they cannot guarantee a return of A_t.

As will become clear in section 5, Proposition 0 is of fundamental importance for the wealth dynamics. Indeed, a consequence of this proposition is that an individual's bequest is stochastically increasing with her inherited wealth, so that the iterated map representing the dynamics of a lineage's wealth distribution is monotonic in the lineage's initial wealth.

3.2. *Equilibrium credit rationing*

When $\underline{w}(A_t) > 0$ it does not follow that all agents with wealth $w \in [0, w(A_t)]$ are credit rationed, since all these agents may actually prefer not to undertake the high-yield project and borrow. The higher the cost of capital, A_t, the less attractive it is to borrow and the more attractive it is to lend. Thus, we should expect that no credit-rationing takes place in equilibrium when A_t is high.

More formally, let $\tilde{w} = \tilde{w}(A_t)$ denote the initial wealth endowment of an individual of generation t who is *indifferent between borrowing and lending*. We have

$$p(\tilde{w})r - A_t(1-\tilde{w}) - C(p(\tilde{w})) - 1 = A_t\tilde{w} + n. \tag{3.6}$$

The L.H.S. of (3.6) is the expected utility from being a borrower {using the fact that $p(\tilde{w})p(\tilde{w}) = A_t$}, the R.H.S. of (3.6) is the expected utility from being a lender.

We can rewrite the above indifference condition as

$$p(\tilde{w})r - C(p(\tilde{w})) - 1 = A_t + n. \tag{3.7}$$

Lemma 1. *All individuals with initial wealth $w < \tilde{w}$ strictly prefer to be lenders; all individuals with initial wealth $w \in (\tilde{w}, 1)$ strictly prefer to be borrowers. Moreover, $\tilde{w} = \tilde{w}(A)$ is increasing with the market rate of return A.*

Proof. Let $\theta(p) = pr - C(p) - 1$. By assumption $\theta(p)$ is concave, which implies that θ is increasing on $[0, a]$ since $a = p^{fb} = \arg \max \theta(p)$. The lemma then follows from the fact that $p(w) < p^{fb} = a$ for all $w < 1$ and that $p(w)$ is increasing in w on that same wealth interval. ‖

Now we can both determine the equilibrium rate of return A_t on the capital market and characterize the situations in which credit-rationing occurs in equilibrium. The net suppliers of funds are first the wealthy, with initial wealth $w > 1$; they put $(w-1)$ in the mutual fund; second, the poor who either are denied access to borrowing $(w < \underline{w}(A_t) = 1 - ar/4A_t)$ or prefer to lend rather than borrow on the capital market $(w < \tilde{w}(A_t))$; they put w in the mutual fund. The aggregate supply of funds on the capital market, for given A_t, is then equal to

$$S(A_t) = \int_0^{\hat{w}(A_t)} w \, dG_t(w) + \int_1^{\infty} (w-1) \, dG_t(w). \tag{3.8}$$

where $\hat{w}(A_t) = \max (\underline{w}(A_t), \tilde{w}(A_t))$ is increasing in A_t.

By complementarity, the aggregate demand for funds at the same market rate of return A_t is equal to

$$D(A_t) = \int_{\hat{w}(A_t)}^1 (1-w) \, dG_t(w). \tag{3.9}$$

Clearly, $S(A_t)$ is increasing in A_t and $D(A_t)$ is decreasing in A_t. Thus, an equilibrium rate of return corresponding to the wealth distribution $G_t(w)$, whenever it exists, is uniquely defined by

$$S(A_t) = D(A_t). \tag{3.10}$$

The description of the capital-market equilibrium at each period t is now completed. Credit-rationing occurs in equilibrium whenever the set of poor individuals who would prefer to borrow but are denied access to credit is non-empty, i.e. whenever

$$\underline{w}(A_t) > \max \{0, \tilde{w}(A_t)\}. \tag{3.11}$$

Then all individuals with wealth

$$w \in [\max \{0, \tilde{w}(A_t)\}, \underline{w}(A_t)],$$

are credit-rationed.

The following proposition characterizes the situations in which condition (3.11) is satisfied.

Proposition 1.   *There is credit-rationing in equilibrium whenever*

$$\frac{ar}{4} < A_t < \frac{3}{8}\,ar - n - 1.$$

Proof.   See Appendix.   ‖

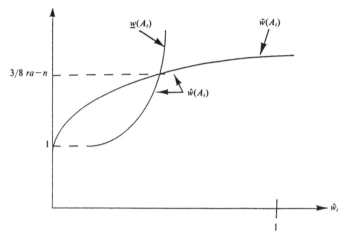

FIGURE 5

This result, depicted in Figure 5, may appear somehow surprising, especially in light of the existing literature on credit-rationing (see Stiglitz and Weiss (1981) and Bernanke and Gertler (1989)).

Indeed, this literature predicts that credit-rationing is more likely when the cost of capital is high while here we predict the opposite. The main reason why our prediction differs from the existing literature is that the identity of lenders and borrowers is fixed exogenously in all existing models of credit-rationing, while in our model agents can choose to be borrowers or lenders. Their choice depends on the size of inherited wealth and the rate of return on the capital market.[10] When the cost of capital (or market return), A_t, is high, poor agents prefer to lend at rate A_t; this rate is highly favourable to lenders and highly unfavorable to borrowers, especially those who need to borrow large amounts.

Conversely, when the cost of capital A_t is low (that is sufficiently close to 1) and the lending terms are shifted in favour of the borrowers, the same poor agents prefer to borrow at such a low rate but may be denied access to credit. This explains why credit-rationing is more likely to occur when the cost of capital is low. Finally, when $A_t \leq ar/4$, the cost of capital is sufficiently low that it is worth lending to all borrowers with wealth $w \geq 0$.

---

10. We obtain the same conclusion as Stiglitz–Weiss and Bernanke–Gertler if, as they implicitly do, we assume $\tilde{w}(A_t) = 0$.

4. THE EVOLUTION OF EQUILIBRIUM INTEREST RATES

Once the equilibrium unit cost of borrowing in period t, A_t, has been determined one can specify the stochastic process of lineage wealth as follows.

Let $\hat{w}_t$ denote the cut-off wealth level below which individuals are either unwilling or unable to invest in the risky project (that is, $\hat{w}_t = \min(\tilde{w}(A_t), \underline{w}(A_t))$). Then

$$\text{For } w_t \in [0, \hat{w}_t], \quad w_{t+1} = (1-\delta)(A_t w_t + n) \text{ with probability one;}$$
$$\text{For } w_t \in [\hat{w}_t, \infty], \quad w_{t+1} = f_t(w_t, \theta_t),$$
(4.1)

where

(a) $\theta_t \in \{0, 1\}$ is an i.i.d. variable that refers to the high yield project being successful ($\theta_t = 1$) or unsuccessful ($\theta_t = 0$). Recall from Section 3 that the probability distribution for θ_t when $w_t = w$ is given by

$$\text{prob } (\theta_t = 1/w) = h(1, w) \begin{cases} = a \text{ for } w \geq 1; \\ = p(w) \text{ for } w < 1, \end{cases}$$

and

$$\text{prob } (\theta_t = 0/w) = h(0, w) = 1 - h(1, w).$$

(b)

$$f_t(w, 1) = (1-\delta)(r - (1-w)A_t) \qquad \text{for } w \geq 1;$$
$$f_t(w, 1) = (1-\delta)(r - (1-w)p(w)) \quad \text{for } w < 1,$$

and

$$f_t(w, 0) = \max \{0, (1-\delta)(w-1)A_t\}.$$

Given that the economy comprises a continuum of agents and that the random returns on each risky project (with equity participation by the entrepreneur of w) are independently identically distributed, the aggregate wealth level and its distribution function can be interpreted as deterministic variables, by the law of large numbers. The wealth distribution G_{t+1} in period $t+1$ is then obtained from the distribution in period t as follows.

Consider an individual with an inherited wealth of w_{t+1}. This wealth can come from a parent who successfully invested in the risky project, in which case the parent's initial wealth was

$$w_t = \psi_t(w_{t+1}, 1) \quad \text{where } \psi_t(\cdot, 1) = f_t^{-1}(\cdot, 1).$$

Or it can come from a parent who invested unsuccessfully in the risky project, in which case the parent's initial wealth was

$$w_t = \psi_t(w_{t+1}, 0) \quad \text{where } \psi_t(\cdot, 1) = f_t^{-1}(\cdot, 0).$$

Finally, it can come from a parent who did not invest in the risky project, who had initial wealth

$$w_t = \frac{1}{A_t} \left(\frac{w_{t+1}}{1-\delta} - n \right).$$

This latter possibility only arises if $w_t < \hat{w}_t$.

Then the wealth distribution in period $(t+1)$ is simply obtained by adding up the total mass of lineages who end up with wealth less than w_{t+1}. In the special case where $\hat{w}_t = 0$[11] one obtains

$$G_{t+1}(w) = \int_0^{\psi_t(w,1)} h(x, 1)dG_t(x) + \int_0^{\psi_t(w,0)} h(x, 0)dG_t(x), \qquad (4.2)$$

where the fraction of successful and unsuccessful parents, respectively $h(x, 1)$ and $h(x, 0)$, have been specified above.

The dynamics of the wealth distribution, together with the determination of the equilibrium cost of capital A_t, fully describe the evolution of the capital market and the evolution of lineage wealth over time.

We shall mostly be interested in the evolution of this economy under conditions of rapid capital accumulation. Namely, we shall assume that the returns on individual projects (r) and the saving propensity of individuals $(1-\delta)$ are both sufficiently large that

Assumption 3

$$\tfrac{3}{8}ar(1-\delta) > 1 + n.$$

Now, it is easy to see that, in the absence of credit-rationing, the economy will grow until *all* investment opportunities have been exploited. Indeed, take any period in which some investment projects have not been undertaken. This cannot be a long-run equilibrium: first, since $p(0)r(1-\delta) > (ar/2)(1-\delta) > 1$, by Assumption 3 all individuals who are undertaking a risky project will, as a group, leave more wealth than they started out with to their offspring. There will thus be more funds available to finance risky projects at the end of the period and thus, whenever the equilibrium cost of capital A_t is strictly greater than 1, A_{t+1} will necessarily be strictly lower than A_t and more risky projects will be financed in period $t+1$. If the cost of capital, A_t is equal to 1, Assumption 3 implies that all individuals choose to invest in the risky projects rather than in the safe activity[12]. Therefore, all the investment opportunities will end up being exploited. Once all investment opportunities have been exploited growth tapers off and the cost of capital stays at the lower bound $A = 1$.

There is an important proviso to this convergence argument: even if there is no credit-rationing with $A = 1$, there may be credit-rationing along the development path where $A_t > 1$. The persistence of credit-rationing along the development path may prevent further risky investments from being undertaken even when more funds become available for such investments. This, in turn, creates problems with our convergence argument and with the existence of a unique steady-state. We shall briefly return at the end of this section to these problems. The next assumption, which is again satisfied under joint conditions of high productivity and high saving propensity, that is under fast capital accumulation,

---

11. When aggregate wealth accumulation is sufficiently rapid, the economy ends up with $\hat{w}_t \leq 0$ after a finite number of periods. See Proposition 2 below.

12. More precisely, the poorest individual will strictly prefer to invest in the risky project if and only if:

$$p(0)r - C(p(0)) - 1 > n.$$

But the L.H.S. of the above inequality is greater than:

$$\frac{a}{2}r - \frac{a}{8}r - 1 = \frac{3}{8}ar - 1$$

since $p(0) > a/2$. That $\tfrac{3}{8}ar - 1 > n$ is in turn clearly implied by Assumption 3.

removes the difficulties that might result from credit-rationing[13] and thus guarantees convergence of the economy to a no-growth/low interest rate steady-state equilibrium. In making such an assumption, we are de facto focusing our attention on the most favourable case for trickle-down.[14] Nevertheless, as we shall argue in Section 6 below, even in that case, laissez-faire trickle-down does not work optimally and therefore it leaves room for efficiency improving redistribution policies. So, let us assume

Assumption 4

$$\frac{ar}{4}(1-\delta) > 1$$

One can then establish

Proposition 2.   *Given Assumptions 3 and 4 the cost of capital A_t converges to 1 in finite time.*

Proof.   See Appendix.   ‖

In words, as more capital is accumulated (and is accumulated quickly enough) there are more and more funds available in the economy to finance a smaller and smaller pool of borrowers. Thus the equilibrium lending terms are progressively shifted in favour of borrowers.

This effect of capital accumulation on the evolution of A_t can give rise to a Kuznets curve[15] type relation between growth and wealth inequality: indeed, to the extent that in the early phases of development the lending terms are favourable to the lenders (A_t is initially high if aggregate wealth is small) the wealth of rich lenders (with $w > 1$) grows relatively faster.[16] In later stages of development we know from Proposition 2 that lending terms become more favourable to borrowers so that the wealth of the middle-class tends to catch up with that of the rich whilst an increasing fraction of the poor can borrow and thus invest in their own individual projects.[17] In other words, initial phases of growth tend to increase inequalities while later stages tend to reduce them. This Kuznets effect is reinforced by the existence of capital market imperfections, since the higher the cost of capital, A_t, the more rapidly the (second-best) probability of success $p(w)$ increases with the initial wealth of borrowers w. Whereas the first-best probability of success is the same for all investors and equal to a (see Aghion and Bolton (1993)).

---

13. This assumption does not rule out credit rationing everywhere along the adjustment path, but it rules out credit rationing for low enough interest rates: that is, assumption A4 implies that $\underline{w}(A_t) \leqq 0$ for A_t sufficiently close to 1.

14. Indeed, in less favourable cases where there is a multiplicity of steady-state equilibria, some of these steady-states are necessarily inefficient (from the point of view of surplus maximization) and therefore reflect immediately a failure of the trickle-down mechanism.

15. See Glomm–Ravikumar (1994) for a good survey of recent theories of the Kuznets curve.

16. This is all the more true since the less favourable lending terms for the middle-class borrowers has a negative effect on their effort supply relative to the first best effort.

17. The emergence of a Kuznets curve in our model depends on the entrepreneurial technology having *decreasing* returns for high values of k. The introduction of increasing returns or of technological progress opening new investment opportunities to the rich, tend to counter the Kuznets effect obtained in this model.

AGHION & BOLTON   TRICKLE-DOWN GROWTH   163

5. THE LIMIT WEALTH DISTRIBUTION

In this section we determine the long run behaviour of the wealth distribution in the general case where $0 < a < 1$, under Assumptions 1 and 3. We know from Proposition 2 that when these assumptions hold, $A_t \to 1$ in finite time. Accordingly, our analysis here starts at the earliest date for which $A_t = 1$. We denote that date T. We begin by considering the long run evolution of lineage wealth for a single lineage in this economy. We show that the probability distribution of lineage wealth converges to a unique stationary distribution. This stationary distribution can be interpreted as the long run wealth distribution for the economy since all lineage wealth processes are identically and independently distributed, and since there is a continuum of lineages. To establish the convergence of the probability distribution of lineage wealth to a unique stationary distribution we appeal to recent results of convergence for monotonic Markov processes in Hopenhayn and Prescott (1992). The evolution of lineage wealth when $A_t = 1$ is entirely described by

$$w_{t+1} = f(w_t, \theta_t), \tag{5.1}$$

where

$$f(w, 1) \begin{cases} = (1-\delta)(r - (1-w)) \text{ for } w \geq 1; \\ = (1-\delta)(r - (1-w)\rho(w)) = (1-\delta)(r - (1-w)/p(w)) \quad \text{for } w < 1; \end{cases}$$

$$f(w, 0) = \max\{0, (1-\delta)(w-1)\}.$$

[Recall that $\theta_t \in \{0, 1\}$ is an i.i.d. random variable that refers to the high yield project being successful ($\theta_t = 1$) or unsuccessful ($\theta_t = 0$); and that prob $(\theta_t = 1/w) = p(w) = 1 - \text{prob } (\theta_t = 0/w)$ for all w.]

Let $\bar{w}$ denote the highest sustainable wealth level, defined by: $f(\bar{w}, 1) = \bar{w}$, i.e. $\bar{w} = (r-1)(1-\delta)/\delta^{-1}$ (see Figure 6 below); let $W = [0, \bar{w}]$ and let Ω denote the set of Borel subsets of W.

Given that the random variable θ_t is i.i.d., the stochastic process of lineage wealth described by (5.1) is a stationary linear Markov process. The corresponding transition function: $P: W \times \Omega \to [0, 1]$ is simply defined by

$$P(w, A) = \text{prob } \{f(w, \theta) \in A\}, \text{ for all Borel subsets } A \in \Omega. \tag{5.2}$$

We shall describe the long run dynamic behaviour implied by $P(\cdot, \cdot)$ by determining the existence of a unique invariant distribution G.

Notation. For any wealth distribution $G(\cdot)$, let $T^*G(\cdot)$ be the Markov transformation of G defined by

$$T^*G(A) = \int P(w, A) dG(w), \tag{5.3}$$

for all Borel subsets $A \subset W$.

Definition. A wealth distribution G on W is invariant for P if for all Borel subsets $A \subset W$, one has the equality

$$T^*G(A) = G(A).$$

To see intuitively why an invariant distribution $G(\cdot)$ exists for our Markov process of lineage wealth it is helpful to look at Figure 6.

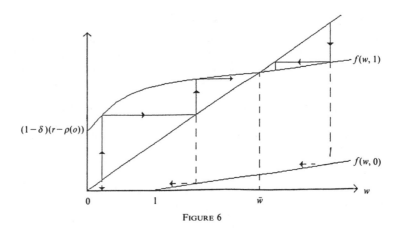

FIGURE 6

As can be seen from Figure 6, if lineage wealth at some date t is such that $w_t > \bar{w}$, then in finite time it can only shrink to a level less than or equal to $\bar{w}$, the highest sustainable wealth level. This wealth level can only be maintained if the high-yield project's returns are the highest possible. Once lineage wealth is less than or equal to $\bar{w}$ it can never exceed $\bar{w}$ but the Figure 6 suggests that it may take any value in the interval $[0, \bar{w}]$ with positive probability. Thus, any (measurable) subset of $[0, \bar{w}]$ may be visited an infinite number of times on average by the lineage wealth w_t. In the theory of Markov chains with a finite number of states existence of a unique invariant distribution is obtained only if the state variable can move from any recurrent state to any other with positive probability (see for example Cinlar (1975)). The above figure suggests that wealth lineages may move from any (measurable) subset $[0, \bar{w}]$ to any other (measurable) subset of $[0, \bar{w}]$ and thus one might expect this Markov process to have a unique invariant distribution.

As it turns out, one can indeed establish the following result.

Proposition 3. *There exists a unique invariant distribution G for the Markov process corresponding to $P(w, A)$. Moreover, for any initial wealth distribution G_0, the sequence $(T^*)^n(G_0)$ converges "weakly"[18] to G.*

Proof. See Appendix. ‖

The proof is a straightforward application of Hopenhayn and Prescott's (1992) analysis of existence, uniqueness and convergence properties of monotonic stochastic processes. Indeed, an immediate consequence of Proposition 0 (that is, of the fact that effort supply is increasing in wealth) is that the transition function $P(w, A)$ is increasing in w in terms of first-order stochastic dominance.

The unique invariant distribution G derived in Proposition 3 satisfies the following equation

$$T^*G = G, \tag{5.4}$$

18. The term "weakly" refers to the weak-* topology on the set of wealth distributions over the interval $[0, \bar{w}]$.

where:

$$T^*G(w) = \int_0^{\psi(w,1)} p(x)dG(x) + \int_0^{\psi(w,0)} (1-p(x))dG(x),$$

and

$$\psi(\cdot, 1) = f^{-1}(\cdot, 1), \qquad \psi(\cdot, 0) = f^{-1}(\cdot, 0).$$

In particular, when $0 < a < 1$, the unique stationary distribution G has full support on $[0, \bar{w}]$, so that some wealth inequality remains in the long run. Therefore, despite the trickle-down nature of growth in this model, wealth inequalities cannot be completely eliminated in the long run. One might be tempted to argue, however, that the long run wealth inequalities are unimportant since the Markov-operator T associated with the transition probability P is ergodic, which means that in the long run all lineages fare equally well on average. It is therefore unnecessary or even counter-productive, one would argue, to redistribute wealth in the long run. If all lineages are equally well off on average in the long run then on the basis of distributive justice alone there seems to be little reason to redistribute wealth. Moreover, a one-time distribution can only have temporary effects as the distribution of wealth tends to move back towards the stationary distribution.

However, we shall argue in the next section that permanent redistribution policies can improve the productive efficiency of the economy. By redistributing wealth the government can equalize opportunities of investment and thus improve productive efficiency. To illustrate this point we shall compare the stationary distribution obtained in our economy with the stationary distribution obtained in a first-best-economy.

6. THE CASE FOR A PERMANENT REDISTRIBUTION OF WEALTH

In a first-best world, a borrower can commit to choosing effort level $p = a$.[19] Thus, wealth accumulates faster over time than in a second-best economy where $p(w) < a$ for all $w < 1$. Moreover, it is straightforward to establish a stronger result than Proposition 2 for the first-best economy; that is, under weaker assumptions than 3 and 4, there exists $T < \infty$ such that $\int_0^\infty w dG_t(w) > 1$ and $A_t = 1$ for all $t \geq T$. As in the second-best economy, one can show that the stationary Markov process of lineage wealth for the first-best economy has a unique invariant probability measure. Thus, we can define the stationary wealth distribution for the first-best economy, as follows

$$T^*_{FB}G(w) = \int_0^{\psi(w,1)} a dG(x) + \int_0^{\psi(w,0)} (1-a)dG(x). \qquad (6.1)$$

We are now in a position to compare the stationary wealth distributions in the first-best and second-best economies, G_{FB} and G_{SB}, where G_{FB} is given by $T^*_{FB}G = G$ and G_{SB} is defined by $T^*G = G$.

---

19. How can a borrower commit to choosing $p = a$? In practice this is often impossible but one can imagine a world in which the borrower's choice of effort can be easily monitored at low cost; then, for example, the loan contract can specify that the borrower may not obtain the payoffs (net of repayments) from his/her investment if he/she is seen not to choose $p = a$. The threat of such a punishment is clearly more effective when the agent borrows less since then his/her payoffs (net of repayments) are higher. Thus, as long as monitoring of effort involves costs an agent wishing to borrow less is going to be served before an agent wishing to borrow more since the lender must incur smaller costs of monitoring for the agent borrowing less.

Proposition 4.   *The second-best stationary distribution is dominated by the first-best stationary distribution*:

$$G_{SB}(w) \geq G_{FB}(w) \quad \text{for all } w,$$

the inequality being strict for all $w < r(1-\delta)$.

Proof.   See Appendix. ‖

In steady-state equilibrium the second-best economy has both a lower output per capita and a wealth distribution which puts more weight on poorer individuals than the first-best economy (the latter observation follows from the fact that in steady state both wealth distributions have the same support). The source of the problem is, of course, moral hazard with limited wealth. Because borrowers cannot appropriate the full marginal return of their effort-investment, they tend to underinvest in effort and therefore they tend to get lower expected returns than wealthier agents who do not need to borrow to invest. There is a natural policy response available to correct this productive inefficiency: redistribute wealth permanently from the rich lenders to the poor and the middle-class who need to borrow funds to invest. The positive effect of such redistribution is to equalize opportunities by letting all agents have access to profitable activities on similar terms. Note that redistribution is desirable here not because it is an ex-post Pareto-improvement, but because it increases productive efficiency[20].

One might argue that redistribution is undesirable, because of the disincentive effect it might have on effort supply of the rich and because redistribution could be undone by a corresponding change in individuals' bequest decisions.

Concerning first the issue of effort supply, one can easily design a redistribution policy that increases the output and effort of the subsidized borrowers by more than it decreases the output and effort of the taxed rich, thereby increasing aggregate productive efficiency of the overall economy. For example, suppose that, starting from the second-best invariant distribution G_{SB}, the government imposes a profit tax on the returns r earned by a unit mass of rich individuals and uses the proceeds of this tax in order to increase the initial wealth of a unit mass of borrowers from w to say $w + \varepsilon$. Since only a fraction a of rich investors do generate positive returns r on their risky investments, each successful investor must pay a profit tax at least equal to ε/a if the government's budget balance is to be preserved. Let p_R and p'_R denote the effort of a rich individual respectively before and after the above redistribution policy has been introduced. Similarly, let p_P and p'_P denote the effort supplied by a borrower with initial wealth w respectively before and after the subsidy. We have[21] $C'(p_R) = r$ and $C'(p'_R) = r - \varepsilon/a$ hence

$$p_R - p'_R = \frac{r}{a} \frac{\varepsilon}{a}, \tag{6.2}$$

---

20. Pareto-improvements can always be achieved through private contracting. No state intervention is necessary for redistribution unless some agents are made worse off (ex-post) by the redistribution policy. This is typically what happens in this model. Note also that state invervention may be justified even when it does not achieve a Pareto-improvement. A good example of such state invervention is enforcement of property rights. Any tightening of enforcement of property rights benefits the owners but hurts the thieves. Thus, such a tightening is not Pareto-improving.

21. Note that future expected subsidies in the event that an agent does badly do not affect effort supply. The reason is once again that we do not assume a Ricardian model of bequests. We have assumed a "warm-glow" motive for bequests, so that an increase in future subsidies of poor children does not reduce the parents incentive to accumulate wealth.

and $C'(p_P) = r - p(w)(1-w)$, $C'(p'_P) = r - p(w+\varepsilon)(1-w+\varepsilon)$, hence

$$p'_P - p_P = \frac{r}{a}[h(w+\varepsilon) - h(w)]$$

$$\approx \frac{r}{a}h'(w)\varepsilon \text{ for } \varepsilon \text{ sufficiently small,} \qquad (6.3)$$

where

$$h(w) = \rho(w)(1-w) = \left[\sqrt{1 - \frac{4(1-w)}{ar}}\right]\frac{r}{2}.$$

That $p'_P - p_P > p_R - p'_R$ simply follows from the fact that $h'(w) = (2/ra)(1/h(w)) > 2/a$, so that

$$p'_P - p_P > 2(p_R - p'_R). \qquad (6.4)$$

We thus obtain a net gain in aggregate productive efficiency from a policy that would permanently implement the redistribution suggested in this example.[22] In addition, since individual preferences over bequests are assumed to be "warm-glow", a [proportional] tax on beginning of period wealth of rich individuals would reduce the disincentive effects of taxation on the rich relative to those given in the example.

This brings us to the second potential objection to redistribution, that subsidies and bequests may be perfect substitutes. However, when parents have "warm-glow" preferences for bequests, we know from Andreoni (1989) that bequests and subsidies are imperfect substitutes. Therefore the disincentive effect of subsidies on bequests will not be complete.[23] It is worth noting here that empirically the "warm-glow" model of bequests tends to perform better than the Ricardian model. For example one prediction of the Ricardian model is that in a growing economy (with technical progress) bequests should be negative on average. Similarly, parents should leave more to the worst-off children. None of these predictions are empirically verified. Note that the "warm-glow" model would predict positive bequests even in a growing economy and equal division among children even when the latter are not equally well off.

An important consequence of Proposition 3 is that one shot redistributions cannot have long-lasting effects in the sense that they do not affect the unique invariant distribution G_{SB}. This in turn follows from the convergence result. Permanent redistribution policies must be set up in order to durably improve the efficiency of the economy in steady state[24]. Temporary redistribution policies may, however, help the economy achieve its long-run steady-state faster; in other words, the government can improve productive efficiency along the growth-adjustment path.

---

22. This example may seem to rely heavily on the cost function $C(p)$ being quadratic. However its conclusion can easily be generalized to the case where C is sufficiently convex.

23. Even if agents had Ricardian preferences, subsidies and bequests are not necessarily perfect substitutes because parents may be wealth constrained and thus unable to borrow to bequeath to their children. In that case they won't cut back their bequests when their children receive a greater subsidy.

24. The idea that redistribution policies may have positive incentive effects has already been suggested by Bernanke and Gertler (1990), among others. However their discussion does not take into account the lending side of the capital market. In particular, it ignores the potential disincentive effects that redistribution might have on the lenders. Moreover, their analysis remains purely static and does not distinguish between a one-shot and a permanent redistribution policy.

To see this, let M_t be the aggregate wealth in period t. Then M_{t+1} in the second-best economy is given by

$$\frac{M_{t+1}}{(1-\delta)} = n\int_0^{\hat{w}_t} dG_t + r\left[\int_{\hat{w}_t}^1 p(w)dG_t + \int_1^\infty a\,dG_t\right] + A_t\left[M_t - \int_{\hat{w}_t}^\infty dG_t\right]. \tag{6.5}$$

It is clear from this expression that the growth rate $[M_{t+1} - M_t/M_t]$ depends not only on the stock of wealth in period t but also on its distribution. Thus, the process of capital accumulation affects and is affected by the distribution of wealth. In the first-best economy, on the other hand, the growth rate is not affected by the distribution of wealth.[25] To see this, formally replace $\hat{w}_t$ by $v_t \leq \hat{w}_t$, $p(w)$ by $a \geq p(w)$ and A_t by $((ra/2)-n) \geq A_t$ in (6.5), to obtain

$$\frac{M_{t+1}^{FB}}{1-\delta} = ar M_t + \frac{r}{1-M_t}. \tag{6.6}$$

Comparing (6.5) and (6.6) one observes that growth in the second-best economy is always slower than in the first-best economy. However, through (costless) redistribution of wealth one can always achieve the first-best growth rate in the second-best economy. If *per capita* wealth $M_t < 1$, the first-best growth rate is achieved by letting a mass M_t of agents start out with $w = 1$ and the other agents have $w = 0$. This form of redistribution may actually increase inequalities.[26] If $M_t > 1$, the first-best is achieved by letting all agents have $w = M_t$. That is, the first-best is achieved by implementing perfect equality.

APPENDIX

Proof of Proposition 1

Let

$$V(p) = pr - \frac{rp^2}{2a} - 1.$$

Using the formula for $\rho^*(w)$, we have for all A

$$\rho^*(\underline{w}(A)) = \rho^*\left(1 - \frac{ar}{4a}\right) = \frac{2A}{a}.$$

Hence

$$p(\underline{w}(A)) = \frac{A}{\rho^*(\underline{w}(A))} = \frac{a}{2},$$

which in turn implies that

$$V(p(\underline{w}(A))) = \tfrac{3}{8}ar - 1.$$

25. That the distribution of wealth does not affect the aggregate wealth M_{t+1} in the first-best is not surprising since all individual investors supply the same effort $p = a$ and achieve the same random return (r with probability a, 0 with probability $1 - a$) independently of their initial wealth. This is no longer true in the second-best world where a borrower's probability of success $p(w)$ is strictly increasing with her wealth w.

26. The need for such (inequality increasing) redistribution within the wealth interval [0, 1] disappears if one allows for lotteries: in that case the unique invariant distribution should have mass points at 0 and 1, but the negative incentive effects of borrowing for those agents with wealth $w = 0$ would still call for redistribution of wealth away from rich lenders (with $w > 1$).

AGHION & BOLTON   TRICKLE-DOWN GROWTH   169

Now we know from Lemma 1 that the wealth level $\tilde{w}(A)$ at which individuals are indifferent between borrowing and lending, satisfies equation (3.7), or equivalently

$$V(p(\tilde{w})A)) = A_t + n.$$

The proof of Proposition 1 is now straightforward: first, the two wealth schedules $\underline{w}(A)$ and $\tilde{w}(A)$ intersect at a market rate A^* such that

$$V(p(\underline{w}(A^*))) = V(p(\tilde{w}(A^*))).$$

Using equations (A1) and (A2), we obtain the unique solution

$$A^* = \tfrac{3}{8} ar - n - 1.$$

Using equations (A1) and (A2), again, we have, for all $A_t > A^*$

$$V(p(\tilde{w}(A_t))) > V(p(\underline{w}(A_t))),$$

or: $\tilde{w}(A_t) > \underline{w}(A_t)$ since both V and p are increasing over the relevant range of variables. Similarly, whenever $A_t < A^*$ we must have $\tilde{w}(A_t) < \underline{w}(A_t)$ by the same reasoning. Finally, $A_t \leq ar/4 \Rightarrow \underline{w}(A_t) \leq 0$. This completes the proof of Proposition 1. ‖

Proof of Proposition 2

The proof proceeds in three steps.
   Step 1.   *The cost of capital A_t cannot remain above $1/(1-\delta)$ for more than a finite number of periods.*

Suppose indeed that $A_t > 1/(1-\delta)$ for infinitely many t.
   Then all investors in risky projects would see their expected lineage wealth increase over time, by an amount uniformly bounded away from zero.
   More formally, if w_t denotes the initial wealth of an investor $(w_t \geq \hat{w}_t)$, we have, when $A_t > 1/(1-\delta)$:

$$E(w_{t+1}|w_t) - w_t = [p(w_t)r - A_t(1-w_t)](1-\delta) - w_t$$

$$\geq p(0)r(1-\delta) - A_t(1-\delta)$$

$$\geq 2A_t(1-\delta) - A_t(1-\delta)$$

$$= A_t(1-\delta) > 1 > 0.$$

The last inequality follows from the fact that $p(0) = A/\rho(0) \geq 2A/r$.
   Also, whenever $A_t > 1/(1-\delta)$, the fraction of the population with wealth $w_t > \hat{w}_t$ is uniformly bounded away from zero. To see this, suppose instead that the fraction of investors was not bounded away from zero. One could then exhibit a subsequence (t_k) from the infinite set $\{t/A_t > 1/(1-\delta)\}$, such that the total mass of investors $\int_{\hat{w}_{t_k}}^{\infty} dG_{t_k} \to 0$ as $t_k \to \infty$. But then, as $t_k \to \infty$, there would eventually be an excess supply of funds unless $A_{t_k} \to 1$. However, having $A_{t_k} \to 1$ contradicts the fact that $A_{t_k} > 1/(1-\delta)$ for all t_k.
   It follows from the above two remarks that whenever $A_t > 1/(1-\delta)$, the total wealth of investors will increase by an amount which is uniformly bounded away from zero. In all other periods where $A_t \leq 1/(1-\delta)$ investors (i.e. with initial wealth $w_t > \hat{w}_t$) will still get richer on average, although by a smaller amount: $E(w_{t+1}|w_t > \hat{w}_t) - w_t \geq A_t(1-\delta) \geq 1 - \delta > 0$, since A_t is bounded below by 1.
   Thus if $A_t > 1/(1-\delta)$ for infinitely many t, the total wealth of investors would go to $(+\infty)$ over time, so for t sufficiently large there would necessarily be excess supply of funds in the economy; this in turn implies that A_t cannot remain indefinitely above $1/(1-\delta)$. ‖

   Step 2.   *Under assumption A4, there cannot be credit-rationing when $A_t \in [1, 1/(1-\delta)]$*

Indeed, credit rationing can only occur at wealth levels less than $\underline{w}(A_t)$. But since the $\underline{w}(\cdot)$ function is increasing in A, we have $\underline{w}(A_t) \leq \underline{w}(1/(1-\delta))$ for $A_t \leq 1/(1-\delta)$. Finally, by Assumption 4, $\underline{w}(1/(1-\delta)) < 0$. This establishes Step 2.[27] ‖

   Step 3. $A_t = 1$ *for t sufficiently large.*

27. A weaker condition for avoiding credit-rationing is, from Proposition 1:

$$A4 \text{ or } \frac{1}{1-\delta} > \frac{3}{8} ar - n.$$

This step follows immediately from: (a) Assumption 3 which implies that, abstracting from credit-rationing considerations, the cost of capital A_t shall converge to 1 in finite time; (b) Assumption 4, which rules out the possibility of credit-rationing for $A_t \leq 1/(1-\delta)$; (c) Step 1, which guarantees that A_t falls below $1/(1-\delta)$ in finite time. This establishes Proposition 2. ‖

Proof of Proposition 3

   Lemma 1. (*Monotonicity of P*)   The transition function $P(w, A)$ is increasing in its first argument w in the following (*first-order stochastic dominance*) sense: For all $(w, w') \in W^2$, $w \leq w' \Rightarrow \forall x \in W$, $P(w', [0, x]) \leq P(w, [0, x])$.

   Proof of Lemma 1.   This follows immediately from Proposition 0. More specifically, we have for all $(x, w) \in W^2$

$$P(w, [0, x]) = p(w)1_{f(w,1)<x} + (1-p(w))1_{f(w,0)<x},$$

where

$$1_{f(w,\theta)<x} \begin{cases} =1 & \text{if } f(w, \theta) < x \\ =0 & \text{otherwise.} \end{cases}$$

Thus, for all $(w, w') \in W^2$ such that $w' \geq w$, we get

$$P(w', [0, x]) - P(w, [0, x]) = (p(w') - p(w))(1_{f(w,1)<x} - 1_{f(w,0)<x}) + p(w')[1_{f(w',1)<x} - 1_{f(w,1)<x}]$$
$$+ (1-p(w'))[1_{f(w',0)<x} - 1_{f(w,0)<x}].$$

The first term is negative since $p(w') \geq p(w)$ [Proposition 0] and $f(w, 1) > f(w, 0)$ (success is better than failure). The second and third terms are also negative since $f(w', \theta) \geq f(w, \theta)$ for $w' \geq w$.
   This establishes Lemma 1. ‖

   Lemma 2. (*Monotone Mixing Condition*)   The monotonic transition function P satisfies the following property:
   For any $w^* \in (0, \bar{w})$ there exists an integer m such that:

$$P^m(0, [w^*, \bar{w}]) > 0 \quad \text{and} \quad P^m(\bar{w}, [0, w^*]) > 0^{28}.$$

In words, even the poorest individual will have his lineage wealth end up above w^* after m consequent successes; similarly, even the richest individual will have his lineage wealth end up below w^* after m consequent failures.

   Proof of Lemma 2.   Take any $w^* \in (0, \bar{w})$. Then, since $(f(w, 1) - w)$ is always strictly positive and continuous on $[0, w^*]$, it remains uniformly bounded below by some positive number α. Thus, there exists an integer n_1 such that: $n \geq n_1 \Leftrightarrow f^{(n)}(0, 1) > w^*$, where $f^{(n)}(\cdot, 1)$ denotes the n-th iterate of $f(\cdot, 1)$.[29]
   Similarly, since $[w - f(w, 0)]$ is strictly positive and continuous on $[w^*, \bar{w}]$, it remains uniformly bounded below by some positive number β. Thus, there exists an integer n_0 such that: $n \geq n_0 \Leftrightarrow f^{(n)}(\bar{w}, 0) < w^*$, where $f^{(n)}(\cdot, 0)$ denotes the n-th iterate of $f(\cdot, 0)$.
   Let $m = \max(n_0, n_1)$. We have

$$P^m(0, [w^*, \bar{w}]) \geq p(0)^m > 0,$$

and

$$P^m(\bar{w}, [0, w^*]) \geq (1 - p(\bar{w}))^m > 0.$$

This establishes Lemma 2. ‖

   From here on, the proof of Proposition 3 proceeds in two immediate steps.

   28. where $P^m(w, A)$ denotes the probability of reaching A from w after m generations (i.e. after m iterations of the Markov Process defined by P).
   29. n_1 is less than or equal to the smallest integer n such that $n \cdot \alpha > w^*$. Similarly n_0 is at most equal to the smaller integer n such that $\bar{w} - n\beta < w^*$.

Step 1. *Existence*

The existence of an invariant distribution G for the Markov process defined by $P(w, A)$ follows immediately from the monotonicity of P established in Lemma 1 and from Hopenhayn–Prescott's Corollary 4. ‖

Step 2. *Uniqueness and Convergence*

This step follows from the monotonicity of P (Lemma 1), its monotone mixing property (Lemma 2), and Hopenhayn–Prescott's theorem 2 and Corollary 2.

Proposition 3 is now fully established. ‖

Proof of Proposition 4   From (5.4) and (6.1) we have

$$T^*G_{SB}(w) - T^*_{FB}G_{SB}(w) = \int_{\psi(w,1)}^{\psi(w,0)} (a - p(x))dG_{SB}(w).$$

Since $\psi(w, 1) < \psi(w, 0)^{30}$ and $p(x) \leqq a$, we have

$$T^*G_{SB}(w) = G_{SB}(w) \geqq T^*_{FB}G_{SB}(w),$$

with a strict inequality if $\psi(w, 1) < 1$ or equivalently if $w < r(1 - \delta)$.

Since T^*_{FB} is increasing we also have

$$T^*_{FB}G_{SB}(w) \geqq T^*_{FB}(T^*_{FB}G_{SB}(w)),$$

and more generally

$$T^*_{FB}G_{SB}(w) \geqq T^{*n}_{FB}G_{SB}(w), \text{ for all } n > 1.$$

(T^{*n} denotes the n-th iterate of T^*).

Since $T^{*n}_{FB}G_{SB}$ converges weakly to G_{FB} when $n \to +\infty$ (as in Proposition 3), we know that eventually $G_{SB}(w) \geqq G_{FB}(w)$ for all w, with a strict inequality for $w < r(1 - \delta)$. This establishes Proposition 4. ‖

Acknowledgements. We are grateful to Steve Alpern, Abhijit Banerjee, Roland Benabou, Francois Bourguignon, Pierre-Andre Chiappori, Mathias Dewatripont, Leonard Mirman, Andrew Newman, Khalid Sekkat, three referees and Ian Jewitt for their suggestions, and to seminar participants at Nuffield College, the London School of Economics, Bristol, MIT, Paris, Stanford and Tilburg, for their comments. We are especially grateful to Tony Atkinson and Hugo Hopenhayn for detailed and insightful comments.

REFERENCES

AGHION, P. and BOLTON, P. (1992), "Distribution and Growth in Models of Imperfect Capital Markets," *European Economic Review*, **36**, 603–611.

AGHION, P. and BOLTON, P. (1993), "A Theory of Trickle-Down Growth and Development" (mimeo, Nuffield College, Oxford).

ANDREONI, J. (1989), "Giving with Impure Altruism: Applications to Charity and Ricardian Equivalence", *Journal of Political Economy*, **97**, 1447–1458.

BANERJEE, A. V. and NEWMAN, A. F. (1991), "Risk-Bearing and the Theory of Income Distribution", *Review of Economic Studies*, **58**, 211–255.

BANERJEE, A. and NEWMAN, A. (1993), "Occupational Choice and the Process of Development", *Journal of Political Economy*, **101**, 274–298.

BERNANKE, B. and GERTLER, M. (1990), "Financial Fragility and Economic Performance", *Quarterly Journal of Economics*, **105**, 87–114.

BERNANKE, B. and GERTLER, M. (1989), "Agency Costs, Collateral, and Business Fluctuations", *American Economic Review*, **79**, 14–31.

CHAMPERNOWNE, D. (1953), "A Model of Income Distribution", *Economic Journal*, **63**, 318–351.

CINLAR, E. (1975), *Introduction to Stochastic Processes* (Englewood Cliffs, New Jersey: Prentice Hall).

30. Indeed, we have

$$\psi(w, 1) = z \Leftrightarrow w = f(z, 1) \text{ and}$$

$$\psi(w, 0) = y \Leftrightarrow w = f(y, 0).$$

Thus $z < w < y$ be definition of $f(\cdot, 1)$ and $f(\cdot, 0)$.

172 **REVIEW OF ECONOMIC STUDIES**

COWELL, F. A. (1977), *Measuring Inequality*, (Oxford: Philip Allen).

DIAMOND, D. W. (1984), "Financial Intermediation and Delegated Monitoring, *Review of Economic Studies*, **51**, 393–414.

FIELDS, G. (1980), *Poverty, Inequality and Development* (Cambridge: Cambridge University Press).

GALOR, O. and ZEIRA, J. (1993), "Income Distribution and Macroeconomics", *Review of Economics Studies*, **60**, 35–52.

GLOMM, G. and RAVIKUMAR, B. (1994), "Equilibrium Theories of the Kuznets Curve" (University of Virginia).

GREEN, E. J. (1987), "Lending and the Smoothing of Uninsurable Income", in Prescott, E. and Wallace, N. (eds.), *Contractual Arrangements for Intertemporal Trade*, (Minnesota: University of Minnesota Press).

HOPENHAYN, H. and PRESCOTT, E. (1992), "Stochastic Monotonicity and Stationary Distributions for Dynamic Economies", *Econometrica*, **60**, 6.

LOURY, G. (1981), "Intergenerational Transfers and the Distribution of Earnings", *Econometrica*, **49**, 843–867.

MIRRLEES, J. (1971), "An Exploration in the Theory of Optimum Income Taxation", *Review of Economic Studies*, **38**, 175–208.

PIKETTY, T. (1993), "Imperfect Capital Markets and Persistence of Initial Wealth Inequalities", *Working Paper STICERD-LSE*, No. TE92255.

SAPPINGTON, D. (1983), "Limited Liability Contracts between Principal and Agent", *Journal of Economic Theory*, **29**, 1–21.

STIGLITZ, J. E. and WEISS, A. (1981), "Credit Rationing in Markets with Imperfect Information", *American Economic Review*, **71**, 393–410.

[2]

Occupational Choice and the Process of Development

Abhijit V. Banerjee

Harvard University

Andrew F. Newman

Northwestern University

This paper models economic development as a process of institutional transformation by focusing on the interplay between agents' occupational decisions and the distribution of wealth. Because of capital market imperfections, poor agents choose working for a wage over self-employment, and wealthy agents become entrepreneurs who monitor workers. Only with sufficient inequality, however, will there be employment contracts; otherwise, there is either subsistence or self-employment. Thus, in static equilibrium, the occupational structure depends on distribution. Since the latter is itself endogenous, we demonstrate the robustness of this result by extending the model dynamically and studying examples in which initial wealth distributions have long-run effects. In one case the economy develops either widespread cottage industry (self-employment) or factory production (employment contracts), depending on the initial distribution; in the other example, it develops into prosperity or stagnation.

I. Introduction

Why does one country remain populated by small proprietors, artisans, and peasants while another becomes a nation of entrepreneurs employing industrial workers in large factories? Why should two

We are grateful to Tim Besley, Allan Drazen, Drew Fudenberg, Maitreesh Ghatak, Rodi Manuelli, Kiminori Matsuyama, Joel Mokyr, Andrei Shleifer, Nancy Stokey, Aldo Rustichini, Peter Streufert, Chris Udry, an anonymous referee, and the editors of this *Journal* for helpful discussion and comments.

[*Journal of Political Economy*, 1993, vol. 101, no. 2]

seemingly identical countries follow radically different development paths, one leading to prosperity, the other to stagnation? Questions like these are of central concern to both development economists and economic historians, who have been interested in the study of the evolution of institutional forms, particularly those under which production and exchange are organized. Yet most of these institutional questions have resisted formal treatment except in a static context (see Stiglitz [1988] for a review), whereas the dynamic issues that are peculiarly developmental have for the most part been restricted to the narrower questions of output growth or technical change. This paper takes a first step in the direction of providing a dynamic account of institutional change by focusing on the evolution of occupational patterns, the contractual forms through which people exchange labor services.[1]

There are several ways in which the dynamics of occupational choice influence the process of development. Most obvious among them is the effect on the distribution of income and wealth. Insofar as distribution can affect saving, investment, risk bearing, fertility, and the composition of demand and production, there is a clear link with the economy's rate of growth and hence with development in its narrowest sense.

Just as important is the connection that arises when one considers development to mean institutional transformation as well as economic growth (Stiglitz 1988; Townsend 1988; Khan 1989). One of the most significant elements of the institutional structure of any economy is the dominant form of organization of production: it has "external" consequences considerably beyond the efficiency of current production. Some of these effects may be politico-economic, but there are also some that are purely economic. It has been argued, for example, that the introduction of the factory system in the early years of the Industrial Revolution left the technology unaffected and generated little efficiency gain initially. But it seems very likely that in the long run this new form of production organization helped to make possible the major innovations of the Industrial Revolution (see, e.g., Cohen 1981; Millward 1981; North 1981).

Conversely, the process of development also affects the structure of occupations. It alters the demand for and supply of different types of labor and, hence, the returns to and allocations of occupations. It transforms the nature of risks and the possibilities for innovations. And, of course, it changes the distribution of wealth. Since one's wealth typically affects one's incentives to enter different occupations,

[1] We use the term "occupation" to mean a contractual arrangement rather than a productive activity. A bricklayer and an accountant are in the same occupation if each is an independent contractor or if each works for a wage.

the effect on the wealth distribution generates a parallel effect on the occupational structure.

Our aim here is to build a model that focuses directly on this interplay between the pattern of occupational choice and the process of development. The basic structure of interaction is very simple. Because of capital market imperfections, people can borrow only limited amounts. As a result, occupations that require high levels of investment are beyond the reach of poor people, who choose instead to work for other, wealthier, employers; thus wage contracts are viewed primarily as substitutes for financial contracts. The wage rate and the pattern of occupational choice are then determined by the condition that the labor market must clear.[2] Depending on labor market conditions and on their wealth, other agents become self-employed in low-scale production or remain idle.

The pattern of occupational choice is therefore determined by the initial distribution of wealth, but the structure of occupational choice in turn determines how much people save and what risks they bear. These factors then give rise to the new distribution of wealth. We shall be concerned with the long-run behavior of this dynamic process.

Despite its simplicity, our model's structure is somewhat nonstandard. As a rule, the dynamics are nonlinear and the state space—the set of all wealth distributions—is very large, so that reasonably complicated behavior may be expected. While a complete mathematical analysis of the model is beyond the scope of this paper, we confine our attention to two special cases that admit considerable dimensional reduction. These examples afford complete study: they are simple enough to allow diagrammatic exposition in which we trace out entire paths of development, including institutional evolution, and with them we generate robust and natural instances of hysteresis or long-run dependence on initial conditions.

In one of our examples (Sec. IV*D*), the ultimate fate of the economy—prosperity or stagnation—depends in a crucial way on the initial distribution of wealth. If the economy initially has a high ratio of very poor people to very rich people, then the process of development runs out of steam and ends up in a situation of low employment and low wages (this may happen even when the initial per capita income is quite high, as long as the distribution is sufficiently skewed). By contrast, if the economy initially has few very poor people (the per capita income can still be quite low), it will "take off" and converge to a high-wage, high-employment steady state.

[2] This static model of occupational choice is a simplified version of the one in Newman (1991), which also discusses the advantages of the capital market imperfections approach over preference-based approaches such as that of Kihlstrom and Laffont (1979). See also the related work of Eswaran and Kotwal (1989).

That an economy's long-term prosperity may depend on initial conditions is a familiar idea in the development literature, and some recent papers capture different aspects of this phenomenon in a formal model (e.g., Romer 1986; Lucas 1988; Murphy, Shleifer, and Vishny 1989*a*, 1989*b*; Matsuyama 1991; Galor and Zeira, in press). Our paper differs from these in several respects. First, most of the papers study technological increasing returns, originating either in the production technology itself or in various kinds of productivity spillovers. We consider instead a kind of "pecuniary" increasing returns stemming from an imperfect capital market (Galor and Zeira also follow this tack). Second, distribution tends not to play a causal role in this literature. A notable exception is Murphy et al. (1989*a*), but there the mechanism is the structure of demand for produced commodities rather than the occupational choice mediated by the capital market: moreover, their model is static and therefore does not endogenize the distribution.

Third, and most important, none of these papers emphasizes the endogeneity of economic institutions as part of the process of development. This distinction is highlighted by the example we examine in Section IV*C*, in which there appears a different kind of dependence on initial conditions. We show that the economy might converge to a steady state in which there is (almost) only self-employment in small-scale production; alternatively, it may end up in a situation in which an active labor market and both large- and small-scale production prevail. Which of the two types of production organization eventually predominates once again depends on the initial distribution of wealth. Specifically, an economy that starts with a large number of relatively poor people is more likely to develop wage employment and large-scale production than an economy with few very poor people. This result provides a formalization of the classical view that despite the fact that capitalism is the more dynamic economic system, its initial emergence does depend on the existence of a population of dispossessed whose best choice is to work for a wage.

In Section II we set up the basic model. Section III examines single-period equilibrium. The main results on the dynamics of occupational choice and the process of development are in Section IV. We conclude in Section V with a brief discussion of some qualitative properties of this class of models.

II. The Model

A. *Environment*

There is a large population (a continuum) of agents with identical preferences; the population at time t is described by a distribution function $G_t(w)$, which gives the measure of the population with wealth less than w.

At the beginning of life, agents receive their initial wealth in the form of a bequest from their parents. They also have an endowment of one unit of labor; the effort they actually exert, however, is not observable except under costly monitoring by another agent.

When agents become economically active, they may apply for a loan. Enforcement of loan contracts is imperfect, and agents immediately have an opportunity to renege; lenders will limit borrowing and require collateral in order to ensure that agents do not. The agents choose an occupation, which determines how they invest their labor and capital. They then learn investment outcomes and settle outside claims. Finally, they bequeath to their children, consume what remains, and pass from the scene.

Although the model is naturally recursive, we prefer to study dynamics in continuous time and to impose an overlapping demographic structure. These modifications permit us to avoid unrealistic jumps and overshooting, which can arise as artifacts of discrete time and simultaneous demographics. We therefore shall assume that all the economic activity other than inheritance—borrowing, investment, work, and bequests—takes place at the instant the agents reach maturity. The age of maturity in turn is distributed exponentially with parameter λ across the population and independently from wealth.[3] The total population is stationary and is normalized to unity; that is, a cohort of size λ is active at each instant.

These assumptions, though artificial, greatly simplify the analysis. For instance, they imply that in an interval of time dt, a measure $\lambda G_t(w)\,dt$ of agents with wealth below w are active: the measure of active agents in a wealth interval is always proportional to the measure of the entire (immature) population in that interval. Thus differential changes in the wealth distribution at each instant will depend only on the current distribution. Moreover, the differential dynamics will be related to the recursive dynamics in a transparent manner so that it will be easy to switch attention from the (recursive) dynamics of a lineage to the (continuous) dynamics of the economy.

Agents are risk-neutral: preferences over commodities are represented by $c^\gamma b^{1-\gamma} - z$, where c is an agent's consumption of the sole physical good in the economy, b is the amount of this good left as a bequest to his offspring (the "warm glow" [Andreoni 1989] is much more tractable than other bequest motives), and z is the amount of

---

[3] That is, an agent born at s is "immature" with probability $e^{\lambda(s-t)}$ at time $t > s$ ($1/\lambda$ is the average age of maturity of the population). These demographics resemble those in Blanchard (1985), although he does not assume instantaneous economic activity.

labor he supplies. Denote the income realization by y; utility then takes the form $\delta y - z$, where $\delta \equiv \gamma^\gamma (1 - \gamma)^{1-\gamma}$.

B. Production Technology and Occupations

The economy's single good may be used for consumption or as capital. There are three ways to invest. First, there is a divisible, safe asset that requires no labor and yields a fixed gross return $\hat{r} < 1/(1 - \gamma)$.[4] One may think of it as financial claims mediated by foreign banks that borrow and lend at the fixed international interest rate $\hat{r} - 1$.[5] Agents may invest in this asset regardless of how they use their labor. Anyone who invests only in the safe asset is said to be idle or to be subsisting.

Second, there is a risky, indivisible investment project such as a farm or machine that requires no special skill to operate. To succeed, it must have an initial investment of I units of capital and one unit of labor; with any lower level of either input, it will not generate any returns. If the project succeeds, it generates a random return rI, where r is r_0 or r_1 with probabilities $1 - q$ and q, respectively ($0 < r_0 < r_1$), and has mean $\bar{r}$. Such a project may be operated efficiently by a self-employed agent insofar as it produces enough output to cover its labor cost: $I(\bar{r} - \hat{r}) - (1/\delta) \geq \max\{0, I(r_0 - \hat{r})\}$.

Finally, there is a monitoring technology that permits aggregated production. By putting in an effort of one, one entrepreneur can perfectly monitor the actions of $\mu > 1$ individuals; less effort yields no information. This activity is indivisible, and it is impossible to monitor another monitor.

Using this technology, an entrepreneur can hire μ workers, each at a competitive wage v. Workers undertake projects that require I' units of capital and one unit of labor and generate random returns $r'I'$; r' takes on the values r_0' and r_1' (also with $0 < r_0' < r_1'$) with probabilities $1 - q'$ and q'. It is natural to imagine that the projects individual workers are running are similar to the projects being run by the self-employed. To facilitate this interpretation, we assume that $I' = I$ and that r' and r have the same mean (note that $q' \neq q$, however). The returns on each of the projects belonging to a single entrepreneur are perfectly correlated. Entrepreneurial production is feasible in the sense that at the lowest possible wage rate (which is $1/\delta$, since at a lower wage the worker is better off idle) it is more

---

[4] The restriction on the safe return ensures that the long-run dynamics are reasonable in the sense that people's wealth levels do not grow without bound.

[5] Of course, $\hat{r}$ might instead represent the return to some physical subsistence activity that requires wealth but no effort; arbitrage considerations then dictate that this also be the return on loans.

profitable than self-employment: $\mu[I(\bar{r} - \hat{r}) - (1/\delta)] - (1/\delta) \geq \max\{I(\bar{r} - \hat{r}) - (1/\delta), \mu[I(r'_0 - \hat{r}) - (1/\delta)]\}$.

The main difference between the two types of production lies not so much in the technology but rather in the contracts under which output is distributed. In one, the worker runs a project for himself: he is the claimant on output and therefore needs no monitoring. In the other, the worker runs it for someone else, which entails the monitoring function of the entrepreneur.

To summarize, there are four occupational options: (1) subsistence, (2) working, (3) self-employment, and (4) entrepreneurship. There may be a question of how we rule out other possibilities. Entrepreneurs cannot control more than μ projects because one cannot monitor a monitor. Being a part-time entrepreneur (sharing with someone else) is ruled out by the indivisible monitoring technology and in any case would not be attractive because of risk neutrality. Raising capital through partnership is precluded by the same contract enforcement problems that exist between the bank and borrowers: one partner could as easily default on another partner as default on the bank (thus without loss of generality we need consider only debt and can ignore equity). The same arguments rule out combining self-employment with any other activity.

C. Markets

In the market for labor, demand comes from entrepreneurial production and supply from individuals' occupational choices. This market is competitive, with the wage moving to equate supply and demand. The goods market is competitive as well, but it is otherwise pretty trivial.

It remains to discuss the market for loans. We assume that lenders can enter freely; what distinguishes this market is the possibility that a borrower might renege on a debt. The story we have in mind is similar to that proposed by Kehoe and Levine (in press). To abstract from bankruptcy issues, assume that project returns are always high enough to ensure that borrowers can afford repayment. Suppose that an agent puts up all his wealth w (the maximum he can provide) as collateral and borrows an amount L. He may now attempt to avoid his obligations by fleeing from his village, albeit at the cost of lost collateral $w\hat{r}$; flight makes any income accruing to the borrower inaccessible to lenders. Fleeing does not diminish investment opportunities, however, and having L in hand permits the agent to achieve $V(L)$ in expected gross income net of effort (under our assumptions, his ensuing decisions and therefore $V(L)$ are independent of his choice whether to renege). At the end of the production period, he will have succeeded in escaping the lender's attempts to find him with a large probability $1 - \pi$, in which case he avoids paying $L\hat{r}$. Should he be caught, though, he will have had ample time to dispose of his income, and therefore he can be subjected to only a nonmonetary punishment F (such as flogging or imprisonment), which enters additively into his utility. Reneging therefore yields a payoff of $V(L) - \pi F$, and repaying yields $V(L) + w\hat{r} - L\hat{r}$; the borrower will renege whenever $w\hat{r} + \pi F < L\hat{r}$. Knowing this, lenders will make only loans that satisfy $L \leq w + (\pi F/\hat{r})$. All loans made in equilibrium will satisfy this constraint, and the borrower will never renege.[6]

The only reason to borrow in this model is to finance self-employment or entrepreneurship. The target levels of capital are therefore I and μI (we assume that wages are paid at the end of the period so there is no need to finance them). Someone with a wealth level $w < I$ who wants to become self-employed therefore uses w as collateral and needs to borrow I.[7] He will be able to borrow this amount if and only if $I \leq w + (\pi F/\hat{r})$. Thus the minimum wealth level w^* necessary to qualify for a loan large enough to finance self-employment is equal to $I - (\pi F/\hat{r})$ (the escape probability $1 - \pi$ is large enough that $w^* > 0$). The smallest wealth needed to borrow enough to be an entrepreneur, denoted w^{**}, is derived by a parallel argument and is equal to $\mu I - (\pi F/\hat{r})$. Since μ exceeds unity, w^{**} is greater than w^*; moreover, neither of these values depends on the wage.

The model of the capital market we have chosen here yields a rather extreme version of increasing returns to wealth. In effect, it is not terribly different from the models of Sappington (1983) and Bernanke and Gertler (1989, 1990) or the numerous discussions of credit markets in the development literature (see Bell [1988] for a survey). Using such models would not alter the dependence of borrowing costs on wealth or of occupational structure on distribution. But as we shall see, the present model is simple enough in some cases to allow reduction to a dynamical system on the two-dimensional simplex, a procedure that would be impossible with a more elaborate specification.

III. Static Equilibrium

Recall that the distribution of wealth at time t is denoted by $G_t(w)$ and that because the age to maturity is exponentially distributed and

---

[6] An alternative interpretation is that πF is equal to a moving cost incurred by the borrower when he flees, with no chance for the lender to catch him.

[7] By using all his wealth as collateral, the borrower maximizes the size of the loan he can obtain.

independent of wealth, $\lambda G_t(w)$ represents the distribution of wealth for the cohort active at t. The (expected) returns to self-employment and subsistence are given exogenously by the model's parameters; the wage v determines the returns to the other two occupations. The returns and the borrowing constraints determine the occupational choice made at each level of wealth. Integrating these choices with respect to $\lambda G_t(w)$ gives us the demand for and the supply of labor. To find the instantaneous equilibrium, we need only find the wage that clears the labor market (we can assume that the goods market clears; as for the capital market, the interest rate has already been fixed at $\hat{r}$).

All agents who do not choose subsistence will have the incentive to expend full effort. Therefore, the payoffs to each occupation (for someone who can choose any of them) are subsistence, $\delta w\hat{r}$; worker, $\delta(w\hat{r} + v) - 1$; self-employed, $\delta[w\bar{r} + I(\bar{r} - \hat{r})] - 1$; and entrepreneur, $\delta[w\hat{r} + \mu I(\bar{r} - \hat{r}) - \mu v] - 1$. Since only entrepreneurs demand labor, these expressions imply that demand will be positive only if the wage does not exceed $\bar{v} \equiv [(\mu - 1)/\mu]I(\bar{r} - \hat{r})$. Moreover, since only agents with $w \geq w^{**}$ will be entrepreneurs, the labor demand correspondence is

$$
\begin{array}{ll}
0 & \text{if } v > \bar{v}, \\
[0, \mu\lambda[1 - G_t(w^{**})]] & \text{if } v = \bar{v}, \\
\mu\lambda[1 - G_t(w^{**})] & \text{if } v < \bar{v}.
\end{array}
$$

Similar reasoning tells us that the supply of labor is (denote the minimum wage $1/\delta$ by $\underline{v}$)

$$
\begin{array}{ll}
0 & \text{if } v < \underline{v}, \\
[0, \lambda G_t(w^*)] & \text{if } v = \underline{v}, \\
\lambda G_t(w^*) & \text{if } \underline{v} < v < I(\bar{r} - \hat{r}), \\
[\lambda G_t(w^*), \lambda] & \text{if } v = I(\bar{r} - \hat{r}), \\
\lambda & \text{if } v > I(\bar{r} - \hat{r}).
\end{array}
$$

The equilibrium wage will be $\underline{v}$ if $G_t(w^*) > \mu[1 - G_t(w^{**})]$ and $\bar{v}$ if $G_t(w^*) < \mu[1 - G_t(w^{**})]$. The singular case in which $G_t(w^*) = \mu[1 - G_t(w^{**})]$ gives rise to an indeterminate wage in $[\underline{v}, \bar{v}]$. The facts that the wage generically assumes one of only two values, that it depends on no more information about the distribution $G_t(\cdot)$ than its value at w^* and w^{**}, and that w^* and w^{**} do not depend on any endogenous variables of the model are the keys to the dimensional reduction that so simplifies our analysis below.

   To summarize, the pattern of occupational choice that is generated
in equilibrium is as follows: (1) Anyone with initial wealth less than
$w*$ will be a worker unless wages are exactly $\underline{v}$, in which case the labor
market clears by having some of the potential workers remain idle.
(2) Agents with initial wealth between $w*$ and $w**$ will become self-
employed; although they could choose working, they would do so
only if $v \geq I(\bar{r} - \hat{r})$, which cannot occur in equilibrium. (3) Anybody
who starts with wealth at or above $w**$ will be an entrepreneur as
long as $v < \bar{v}$. If $v = \bar{v}$, all the potential entrepreneurs are equally
happy with self-employment, so $1 - [G_t(w*)/\mu] - G_t(w**)$ of them
opt for the latter, and the labor market clears.
   Thus despite the fact that everybody has the same abilities and
the same preferences, different people choose different occupations.
What is more, the occupational choices made by individuals depend
on the distribution of wealth. For example, if everyone is above $w*$,
everyone will be self-employed. Employment contracts emerge only
if some people are below $w*$ and others are above $w**$. With everyone
below $w*$, subsistence becomes the only option. Thus, as in Newman
(1991), the institutional structure of the economy, represented by the
pattern of occupations, depends on the distribution of wealth.[8] The
question, of course, is whether this dependence of institutional structure on distribution that obtains in the short run also obtains in the
long run, when the distribution itself is endogenous.

IV. Dynamics

We have described how the equilibrium wage and occupational
choices at time t are determined, given an initial wealth distribution.
Knowledge of the realization of project returns then gives us each
person's income and bequests, from which we can calculate the rate
of change of this distribution.

A. *Individual Dynamics*

A person active at t leaves $1 - \gamma$ of his realized income as a bequest
b_t. The intergenerational evolution of wealth is then represented as
follows: (1) subsistence: $b_t = (1 - \gamma)w_t\hat{r}$; (2) working: $b_t = (1 - \gamma)(w_t\hat{r} + v)$; (3) self-employment: $b_t = (1 - \gamma)[w_t\hat{r} + I(r - \hat{r})]$, which is

---

   [8] So does static efficiency. In this model, a first-best Pareto optimum is achieved only
when everyone is self-employed. Even though the employment contract is optimal
from the point of view of the parties involved, an equilibrium with employment contracts cannot be first-best efficient (some resources are being spent on monitoring
instead of direct production).

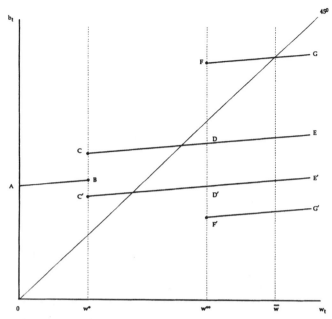

FIG. 1.—Individual recursion diagram for $v = \bar{v}$

random; and (4) entrepreneurship: $b_t = (1 - \gamma)\{w_t \hat{r} + \mu[I(r' - \hat{r}) - v]\}$, also random.

The transition diagram in figure 1 represents the dynamics of lineage wealth for the case $v = \bar{v}$. Everybody with wealth between zero and w^* will choose working, and their offspring's wealth as a function of their own wealth is given by the line segment AB. Agents between w^* and w^{**} will be self-employed, and their wealth dynamics are given by the two parallel lines CD and $C'D'$, each indicating one realization of the random variable r. Since the wage is $\bar{v}$, everyone above w^{**} will either be an entrepreneur or be self-employed; the two parallel lines DE and $D'E'$ represent the dynamics for a self-employed person and FG and $F'G'$ represent those for an entrepreneur.

A similar diagram can be constructed for the case in which $v = \underline{v}$. The specific positions of the different lines in these diagrams depend, of course, on the parameters of the model.

B. The Dynamics of Distribution and Occupational Choice

From the point of view of an individual lineage, wealth follows a Markov process. If this process were stationary, we could go ahead and use the standard techniques (see, e.g., Stokey and Lucas 1989) to establish existence and global stability of an ergodic measure on the wealth space and, since we are assuming a continuum of agents, reinterpret this to be the limiting wealth distribution for the economy. Under the stationarity assumption, one can study Markov processes by considering (deterministic) maps from the space of distributions to itself; such maps are well known to be linear.

In our model, however, the stationarity assumption is not justified. At the time a lineage is active, its transition rule depends on the prevailing wage. The wage in turn depends on the current distribution of wealth across all active agents in the economy (which, as we have said, is the same as that for the entire population); as the distribution changes over time, so does the wage, thereby destroying the stationarity of the process.

In short, the state space for our model is not simply the wealth interval, but the set of distributions on that interval: this is the smallest set that provides us with all the information we need to fully describe the economy and predict its path through time. We have already shown that given the current distribution of wealth, we can determine the equilibrium level of wages and the pattern of occupational choices. Then, using the transition equations, the current distribution of wealth $G_t(\cdot)$, and the fact that we have a large number of agents receiving independent project returns, we can in principle derive the (deterministic) change in the distribution of wealth at time t. We therefore have a well-defined, deterministic, dynamical system on the space of wealth distributions.

Ordinarily, the dynamical system so derived may be quite complex, and unlike a system induced by the familiar stationary Markov process, which is defined on the same space, it is nonlinear. The nonlinearity already tells us that uniqueness, global stability, and other nice, easy-to-verify properties of linear systems are unlikely to obtain. But we want to say more about our economy than to simply state abstractly that it might display hysteresis, nonuniqueness, cycles, or other nonlinear behavior.[9]

Fortunately, if we restrict attention to certain sets of parameter values, we can achieve a rather precise characterization of the economy's behavior using methods that are elementary. In the rest of this section we shall look at two examples that obtain when the individual transition diagrams like figure 1 have certain configurations; these

---

[9] As this article was going to press, we became aware of the work of Conlisk (1976) on interactive Markov chains, to which our model is closely related. His results do not apply to our case, however.

cases are illustrative of interesting historical patterns of development and occupational structure.

C. The Cottage versus the Factory

Consider the case in which the transition diagrams for $v = \underline{v}$ and $v = \bar{v}$ are given by figure 2a and b. The configuration represented in these diagrams will obtain when $\bar{v}$ is relatively high, $1 - \gamma$ is relatively low, and the riskiness of production (given by $r_1 - r_0$ and $r_1' - r_0'$) is quite large.

Look now at figure 2a. Define $\bar{w}$ to be the fixed point of the intergenerational wealth transition map $b(w_t) = (1 - \gamma)\{w_t \hat{r} + \mu[I(r_1' - \hat{r}) - \underline{v}]\}$, and observe that this is the highest possible wealth level that can be sustained in the long run (any lineage with wealth greater than this value is sure to fall below it eventually). Without loss of generality then, we restrict all our attention to wealth distributions on the interval $[0, \bar{w}]$.

Observe now that in figure 2a, a lineage currently with wealth in $[0, w^*)$ remains in that range in the next period. Any lineage initially in $[w^*, w^{**})$ either goes to $[w^{**}, \bar{w}]$ (if the project return is high) or remains in $[w^*, w^{**})$ (if the project return is low). Finally, the offspring of an agent who is in $[w^{**}, \bar{w}]$ either remains there (if lucky) or goes to $[w^*, w^{**})$ (if unlucky). The important point is that these transitions depend only on what interval one is in and not on the precise wealth level within that interval. Similarly, inspection of figure 2b shows that when the prevailing wage is $\bar{v}$, the transitions between the same three intervals also depend only on those intervals and not on the wealth levels within them.

As we showed in Section III, the equilibrium wage and the occupational structure depend only on the ratio of the number of people in $[0, w^*)$ and the number of people in $[w^{**}, \bar{w}]$, and not on any other properties of the distribution. Identify the three intervals $[0, w^*)$, $[w^*, w^{**})$, and $[w^{**}, \bar{w}]$ with three "classes" L, M, and U (for lower, middle, and upper); wealth distributions (fractions of the population in the three classes) are then given by probability vectors $\mathbf{p} = (p_L, p_M, p_U)$, that is, points in Δ^2, the two-dimensional unit simplex. The state space for our economy is then just this simplex: for our purposes, it contains all the information we need.[10]

---

[10] Thus if $G(\cdot)$ is the current wealth distribution, then $p_L = G(w^*)$, $p_M = G(w^{**}) - G(w^*)$, and $p_U = 1 - G(w^{**})$. Of course, some information is lost by our dimensional reduction: if $H(\cdot)$ is another distribution with $H(w^*) = G(w^*)$ and $H(w^{**}) = G(w^{**})$, then it will be indistinguishable from $G(\cdot)$, even if the two distributions have different means. The limits to which they converge will generally differ as well but will be equal at w^* and w^{**}.

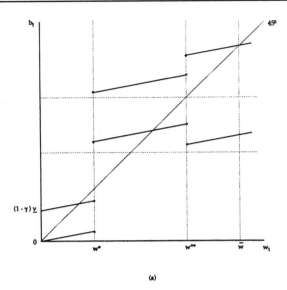

(a)

(b)

Fig. 2.—*a*, $v = \underline{v}$. *b*, $v = \bar{v}$

Now suppose that at some instant t, $\lambda p_L > \mu \lambda p_U$ so that there is excess supply in the labor market and $v = \underline{v}$. In an interval of time dt a measure $\lambda p_U dt$ of the current upper class is active. The people in this class are replaced by their children, of whom a fraction q' will have parents who are lucky with their investment and therefore remain in the upper class. Among the children in the currently active middle class, q have lucky parents and ascend into the upper class. The change in the upper-class population in this interval is therefore

$$dp_U = \lambda(qp_M dt + q'p_U dt - p_U dt).$$

The evolution of the entire wealth distribution can be represented by a dynamical system on Δ^2, which may be written

$$\frac{d\mathbf{p}}{dt} = \mathbf{A}(\mathbf{p}(t))\mathbf{p}(t), \tag{1}$$

where $\mathbf{A}(\mathbf{p}(t))$ is a 3×3 matrix that depends on the current distribution $\mathbf{p}(t)$ in the sense that it takes two different forms depending on whether p_L is greater or less than μp_U. If $\lambda p_L > \mu \lambda p_U$, so that $v = \underline{v}$, then we have (for brevity, we set $\lambda = 1$ for the remainder of the paper)

$$\mathbf{A}(\mathbf{p}) = \begin{bmatrix} 0 & 0 & 0 \\ 0 & -q & 1-q' \\ 0 & q & q'-1 \end{bmatrix}, \quad p_L > \mu p_U. \tag{2}$$

For the case $v = \bar{v}$, the situation is slightly more complicated since the individual transition probabilities for members of the class U depend on their occupation:

$$\mathbf{A}(\mathbf{p}) = \begin{bmatrix} -1 & 0 & (1-q')p_L/\mu p_U \\ 1 & -q & (1-q)[1-(p_L/\mu p_U)] \\ 0 & q & q+(q'-q)(p_L/\mu p_U)-1 \end{bmatrix}, \quad p_L < \mu p_U. \tag{3}$$

The third column of this matrix is derived by noting that $p_L/\mu p_U$ of the agents with wealth greater than w^{**} become entrepreneurs; of these, q' get the high return and remain above w^{**}, and $1 - q'$ fall below w^*; the remaining agents in U become self-employed and enter L and U in the proportions $1 - q$ and q.

Now it will be convenient to study the dynamics of our economy by using a phase diagram; to do so we restrict our attention to the two variables p_L and p_U, since knowledge of them gives us p_M. This

PROCESS OF DEVELOPMENT   289

procedure gives us a piecewise-linear system of differential equations:

$$\dot{p}_L = \begin{cases} 0, & p_L > \mu p_U \\ \left(\dfrac{1 - q'}{\mu} - 1\right) p_L, & p_L < \mu p_U \end{cases} \tag{4}$$

and

$$\dot{p}_U = \begin{cases} q - q p_L + (q' - q - 1) p_U, & p_L > \mu p_U \\ q - \left(q + \dfrac{q}{\mu} - \dfrac{q'}{\mu}\right) p_L - p_U, & p_L < \mu p_U. \end{cases} \tag{5}$$

The phase diagram for this set of differential equations is given in figure 3a. The upper triangle represents distributions for which $v = \bar{v}$, and the lower triangle represents those for which $v = \underline{v}$. The heavy line is the "boundary" $p_L = \mu p_U$ between the two linear systems.[11]

In the upper triangle the point C represents a stationary distribution that is locally stable. In the lower triangle there is a continuum of stationary distributions since the $\dot{p}_L = 0$ locus includes the whole lower triangle. This is a consequence of the fact that there is no way in or out of state L. Hysteresis of a degenerate sort is therefore built into this model.

Since our interest lies in hysteresis generated by the workings of the labor market, we feel that it is best to eliminate the degeneracy. This is legitimate since all we need to do to get rid of it is to perturb the dynamics slightly by allowing individuals very small probabilities of moving from state L to the other two states and from the other two states to L.[12] The phase diagram for one such perturbation is given in figure 3b. As expected, the $\dot{p}_U = 0$ loci in both triangles have moved only very slightly, as has the $\dot{p}_L = 0$ locus in the upper triangle. The most significant change is that now we have a $\dot{p}_L = 0$ locus in the lower triangle that intersects the $\dot{p}_U = 0$ locus in that triangle at the point F'.

Both F' and C' represent stationary distributions, and both are locally stable. But they represent very different social situations. Point F' is an economy in which there are three distinct classes with very little social mobility between the top two and the bottom one (all mobility in and out of L is due to the small random perturbations we used to eliminate the degeneracy). The principal reason behind the

[11] We have assumed that on the boundary the high-wage dynamics apply. The behavior at the boundary is, of course, affected by which wage prevails there. Making alternative assumptions will not significantly change our results.

[12] Think of these small probabilities as corresponding to winning the lottery and having a thunderbolt hit your house and factory.

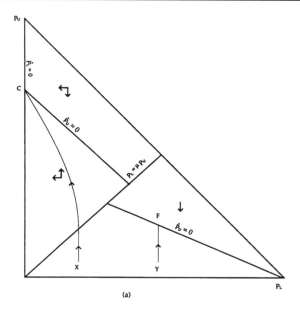

(a)

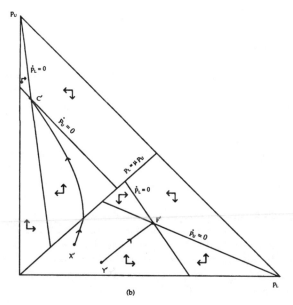

(b)

FIG. 3.—The cottage and the factory: *a*, original dynamics; *b*, perturbed dynamics

PROCESS OF DEVELOPMENT   291

limited mobility is that the ratio of workers to entrepreneurs is high; the consequent low wage rate makes it virtually impossible, given the propensity to bequest, for workers to accumulate enough wealth to enter state M. At the same time, the wage rate is low enough and the project returns (in particular the low ones) are high enough to ensure the self-employed and entrepreneurs against going to L.

By contrast, C' is a situation in which there is really only one occupation in the economy: the overwhelming majority of the population (in the unperturbed version of the model, *everyone*) is self-employed. While there are a substantial number of people in class U who therefore are wealthy enough to be entrepreneurs, most of them are self-employed because they cannot find any workers. Since the low outcome for the self-employed is still high enough to keep the next generation in state M, the supply of people in state L remains small and the original configuration is able to reproduce itself.

The economy always converges to one of these stationary states. Which of the two will result depends on the initial conditions. With the aid of the phase diagram we see what types of economies converge to C' rather than to F'. Roughly speaking, economies with a small fraction of poor relative to middle- and upper-class people tend to converge to C'.

By looking at some trajectories, we can be more precise and better understand the dynamics. The points X' and Y' are two points close to each other in the lower triangle that both have a small upper class but have slightly different mixes of the classes. Consider the trajectory starting at X', which has the relatively smaller lower class. Since the middle class is large and the upper class small, those moving up from M to U outnumber those who are moving the other way. The upper class grows. Because the size of the lower class changes very slowly, the ratio of the upper class to the lower class increases over time until μp_U becomes greater than p_L. At this point the wage increases to $\bar{v}$ and the dynamics change. The workers start rising into the middle class, reducing the fraction of potential entrepreneurs who can find workers. The rest of the upper class now adopts self-employment and the transitions into the lower class decline (the self-employed remain in the middle class even when they are unlucky). The fraction of the lower class in the population thus continues to decline, and the economy converges to a distribution like C'.

The trajectory that starts at Y' also moves in the same direction at first, but since the initial fraction of the middle class was smaller, the rate of increase in the upper class will be smaller. For this reason, and also because the initial fraction of the lower class was larger, p_L remains larger than μp_U, wages do not rise, and employing people remains profitable. Instead of converging to C', the economy ends up at F', which is a situation with both self-employment and entrepreneurial production.

If we identify self-employment with self-sufficient peasants and cottage industries and entrepreneurial production with large-scale capitalist agriculture and factory production, the dynamic patterns we describe above have historical parallels. The most famous of these might be the instance of England and France, which in terms of the level of development and technology were roughly comparable at the middle of the eighteenth century (O'Brien and Keyder 1978; Crafts 1985; Crouzet 1990) and yet went through radically different paths of development. England went on to develop and benefit hugely from the factory system and large-scale production, whereas France remained a nation of small farms and cottage industries for the next hundred years. In terms of our model, one possible explanation would be that England started at a point like Y' and France started at a point like X'.[13]

D. Prosperity and Stagnation

A somewhat different set of development paths can be generated with an alternative configuration of parameter values. Consider the case in which the transition map is as in figure 4a and b (corresponding once again to the cases $v = \underline{v}$ and $v = \bar{v}$). As before, the aggregate dynamic behavior can be reduced to a two-dimensional dynamical system in the simplex. Using the same definitions for the states as above, we follow a similar procedure to derive the dynamics of the wealth distribution. This process is described by the following system of piecewise-linear differential equations:

$$\dot{p}_L = \begin{cases} 1 - q - (1 - q)p_L + (q - q')p_U, & p_L > \mu p_U \\ 1 - q - \left(2 - q + \dfrac{q'}{\mu} - \dfrac{q}{\mu}\right)p_L, & p_L < \mu p_U \end{cases} \tag{6}$$

and

$$\dot{p}_U = \begin{cases} q - qp_L + (q' - q - 1)p_U, & p_L > \mu p_U \\ q - \left(q + \dfrac{q}{\mu} - \dfrac{q'}{\mu}\right)p_L - p_U, & p_L < \mu p_U. \end{cases} \tag{7}$$

[13] A full study of the relevant data would be the subject of another paper, but there seems to be abundant evidence both for the poor performance of credit markets, at least in England (Deane 1965; Shapiro 1967; Ashton 1968), and for a more equal land distribution in France (especially after the Revolution) than in England (where the enclosure movement had generated a large population of landless poor). See Clapham (1936), Grantham (1975), and Soltow (1980).

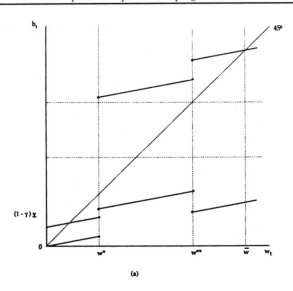

(a)

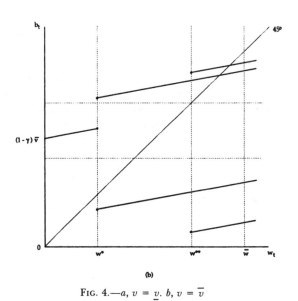

(b)

FIG. 4.—a, $v = \underline{v}$. b, $v = \bar{v}$

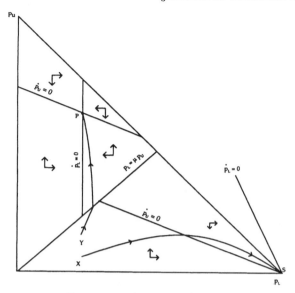

FIG. 5.—Prosperity and stagnation

The corresponding phase diagram appears in figure 5. There are two stationary distributions, labeled S and P, and both are locally stable, with large basins of attraction.[14] Again, these stationary distributions are very different from each other. The distribution S is a state of economic collapse or stagnation: $p_L = 1$, so all agents have low wealth, which entails that they all remain in the subsistence sector. By contrast, P is a prosperous economy with both self-employment and an active labor market in which workers receive high wages; since the transition probabilities between the states are relatively high, there is also considerable social mobility. This contrasts with the case of factory production discussed above (point F' in fig. 3b) in which there is little mobility between L and the other two states.

As before, the long-run behavior of this economy depends on the initial conditions: economies in which the initial ratio of workers to entrepreneurs is low are more likely to be above the boundary line, where they will be subject to the high-wage dynamics, and are therefore more likely to converge to P. Where the initial ratio of poor to

[14] Figure 5 is not the only possible phase diagram that can correspond to the configurations in fig. 4a and b. If q, q', and μ satisfy $\mu q(1 - q) < 1 + q' + q(q - q')$, the stationary point of the high-wage dynamics will actually lie *below* the $p_L = \mu p_U$ boundary. Then there is a unique steady state since in converging to the high-wage stationary point, the economy crosses the boundary and the low-wage dynamics take over: the economy inevitably stagnates.

wealthy is high, the economy will be subject instead to the low-wage dynamics.

Of course, by examining figure 5, we can see that even if an economy initially has a high ratio of poor to wealthy, it is not necessarily doomed to stagnate, particularly if the middle class is sufficiently large (distributions with a large middle class are located near the origin). Consider the path starting at the point Y. Here most agents in the economy are self-employed, and the few workers that there are receive low wages because there are so few entrepreneurs demanding their labor (recall that some agents in state L must be idle). Over time, some of the self-employed become entrepreneurs and the rest fall into the lower wealth class. Along this particular path, the number of agents in U grows sufficiently fast that all agents in L are eventually hired as workers, and the economy is brought to the boundary. Now there is excess demand for labor and the high-wage dynamics take over, with the number of wealthy agents growing rapidly (the number of workers declines slightly along this part of the development path, from which we infer that the ranks of the self-employed must be growing). Thus even though this economy begins with a high ratio of poor to wealthy, it eventually achieves prosperity.

Notice, however, that if we start at the nearby point X instead of Y, the upper class grows slightly faster than the lower class, with both growing at the expense of the middle class of self-employed. The wage remains low, however, and eventually the lower class begins to dominate until the economy collapses to the stationary point S.

We can also check whether an economy might adhere to standard accounts of development such as the Kuznets hypothesis. The present example shows that the path to prosperity need not follow this pattern. Along the path emanating from Y, equality, measured by the relative size of the middle class, declines all the way to the prosperous steady state P. We can, however, easily generate versions of figure 5 in which some paths to prosperity are indeed of the Kuznets type. An example is shown in figure 6, which is obtained when the probability q' of high returns for entrepreneurs is fairly large. Beginning at Y, the middle class declines until point Z, after which it grows as the economy converges to P. Thus, as Kuznets suggested, while mean wealth rises along the entire development path, inequality first increases and then decreases.

V. Conclusion

In dynamic studies of income and wealth distribution, economists have tended to rely on what we have referred to as linear models, in which individual transitions are independent of aggregate variables

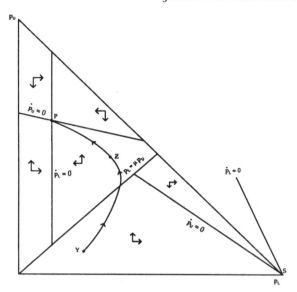

FIG. 6.—A development path that follows a Kuznets curve

(see Banerjee and Newman [1991] and the references therein). Our model of a developing economy, by contrast, is nonlinear because it violates this property of individual dynamics (see also Aghion and Bolton 1991). While it seems unlikely that other nonlinear models will admit the kind of dimensional reduction we have exploited, our examples do illustrate some of the fundamental differences between the two types of model.

For one thing, they may have distinct policy implications. Under the guidance of the linear model, which usually displays global stability, one is led to conclude that continual redistributive taxation, with the distortion it often entails, is required for achieving equity. The nonlinear model, by contrast, raises the possibility that one-time redistributions may have permanent effects, thereby alleviating the need for distortionary policy.

The nonlinear model also provides a way to capture the empirically appealing notion that the same individual characteristics (e.g., wealth levels) can be observed under different stationary distributions. For all practical purposes, the very richest people in India are as wealthy as the very richest in the United States, and the very poorest Americans are no wealthier than their Indian counterparts. Yet standard Markov process models (including deterministic representative agent models) that give rise to multiple steady states or hysteresis preclude this possibility: any state observed under one stationary distribution cannot be observed under another, so that if India and the United States correspond to different equilibria of the same standard model, then no Indian can enjoy the same wealth as any American.

Our examples (particularly C' and F' in fig. 3b) underscore a related point. Individual lineages can travel all over the wealth space under two very different stationary distributions.[15] Moreover, random perturbations to the individual-level dynamics will not significantly affect these distributions and cannot destroy the dependence of aggregate behavior on initial conditions. Contrary to the lessons of linear models, there need be no contradiction between individual mobility and aggregate hysteresis.

References

Aghion, Philippe, and Bolton, Patrick. "A Trickle-down Theory of Growth and Development with Debt Overhang." Manuscript. Paris: DELTA, 1991.

Andreoni, James. "Giving with Impure Altruism: Applications to Charity and Ricardian Equivalence." *J.P.E.* 97 (December 1989): 1447–58.

Ashton, Thomas S. *The Industrial Revolution, 1760–1830.* London: Oxford Univ. Press, 1968.

Banerjee, Abhijit V., and Newman, Andrew F. "Risk-bearing and the Theory of Income Distribution." *Rev. Econ. Studies* 58 (April 1991): 211–35.

Bell, Clive. "Credit Markets, Contracts and Interlinked Transactions." In *Handbook of Development Economics,* edited by Hollis Chenery and T. N. Srinivasan. New York: North-Holland, 1988.

Bernanke, Ben, and Gertler, Mark. "Agency Costs, Net Worth, and Business Fluctuations." *A.E.R.* 79 (March 1989): 14–31.

———. "Financial Fragility and Economic Performance." *Q.J.E.* 105 (February 1990): 87–114.

Blanchard, Olivier J. "Debt, Deficits, and Finite Horizons." *J.P.E.* 93 (April 1985): 223–47.

Clapham, John H. *Economic Development of France and Germany, 1815–1914.* 4th ed. Cambridge: Cambridge Univ. Press, 1936.

Cohen, Jon S. "Managers and Machinery: An Analysis of the Rise of Factory Production." *Australian Econ. Papers* 20 (June 1981): 24–41.

Conlisk, John. "Interactive Markov Chains." *J. Math. Sociology* 4 (July 1976): 157–85.

Crafts, N. F. R. "Industrial Revolution in England and France: Some Thoughts on the Question, 'Why Was England First?' " In *The Economics of the Industrial Revolution,* edited by Joel Mokyr. Totowa, N.J.: Rowman & Allanheld, 1985.

Crouzet, François. *Britain Ascendant: Comparative Studies in Franco-British Economic History.* Cambridge: Cambridge Univ. Press, 1990.

Deane, Phyllis. *The First Industrial Revolution.* Cambridge: Cambridge Univ. Press, 1965.

---

[15] The idea that a stationary economy is one in which aggregate characteristics are fixed, but in which individuals may occupy different states over time, is already common in economics (examples are Loury [1981], Banerjee and Newman [1991], and Hopenhayn [1992]); it is one motivation for seeking ergodic distributions. What is new here is the presence of multiple ergodic distributions with common support.

Eswaran, Mukesh, and Kotwal, Ashok. "Why Are Capitalists the Bosses?" *Econ. J.* 99 (March 1989): 162–76.

Galor, Oded, and Zeira, Joseph. "Income Distribution and Macroeconomics." *Rev. Econ. Studies* (in press).

Grantham, George W. "Scale and Organization in French Farming, 1840–1880." In *European Peasants and Their Markets: Essays in Agrarian Economic History,* edited by William N. Parker and Eric L. Jones. Princeton, N.J.: Princeton Univ. Press, 1975.

Hopenhayn, Hugo Andreas. "Entry, Exit, and Firm Dynamics in Long Run Equilibrium." *Econometrica* 60 (September 1992): 1127–50.

Kehoe, Timothy J., and Levine, David K. "Debt-constrained Asset Markets." *Rev. Econ. Studies* (in press).

Khan, M. Ali. "In Praise of Development Economics." Manuscript. Baltimore: Johns Hopkins Univ., 1989.

Kihlstrom, Richard E., and Laffont, Jean-Jacques. "A General Equilibrium Entrepreneurial Theory of Firm Formation Based on Risk Aversion." *J.P.E.* 87 (August 1979): 719–48.

Loury, Glenn C. "Intergenerational Transfers and the Distribution of Earnings." *Econometrica* 49 (July 1981): 843–67.

Lucas, Robert E., Jr. "On the Mechanics of Economic Development." *J. Monetary Econ.* 22 (July 1988): 3–42.

Matsuyama, Kiminori. "Increasing Returns, Industrialization, and Indeterminacy of Equilibrium." *Q.J.E.* 106 (May 1991): 617–50.

Millward, R. "The Emergence of Wage Labor in Early Modern England." *Explorations Econ. Hist.* 18 (January 1981): 21–39.

Murphy, Kevin M.; Shleifer, Andrei; and Vishny, Robert W. "Income Distribution, Market Size, and Industrialization." *Q.J.E.* 104 (August 1989): 537–64. (*a*)

———. "Industrialization and the Big Push." *J.P.E.* 97 (October 1989): 1003–26. (*b*)

Newman, Andrew F. "The Capital Market, Inequality, and the Employment Relation." Manuscript. Evanston, Ill.: Northwestern Univ., 1991.

North, Douglass C. *Structure and Change in Economic History.* New York: Norton, 1981.

O'Brien, Patrick K., and Keyder, Caglar. *Economic Growth in Britain and France, 1780–1914: Two Paths to the Twentieth Century.* London: Allen & Unwin, 1978.

Romer, Paul M. "Increasing Returns and Long-Run Growth." *J.P.E.* 94 (October 1986): 1002–37.

Sappington, David. "Limited Liability Contracts between Principal and Agent." *J. Econ. Theory* 29 (February 1983): 1–21.

Shapiro, Seymour. *Capital and the Cotton Industry in the Industrial Revolution.* Ithaca, N.Y.: Cornell Univ. Press, 1967.

Soltow, Lee. "Long-Run Changes in British Income Inequality." In *Wealth, Income, and Inequality,* 2d ed., edited by Anthony B. Atkinson. Oxford: Oxford Univ. Press, 1980.

Stiglitz, Joseph E. "Economic Organization, Information, and Development." In *Handbook of Development Economics,* edited by Hollis Chenery and T. N. Srinivasan. New York: North-Holland, 1988.

Stokey, Nancy L., and Lucas, Robert E., Jr. *Recursive Methods in Economic Dynamics.* Cambridge, Mass.: Harvard Univ. Press, 1989.

Townsend, Robert M. "Models as Economies." *Econ. J.* 98 (suppl., 1988): 1–24.

[3]

An Estimated Model of Entrepreneurial Choice under Liquidity Constraints

David S. Evans

National Economic Research Associates

Boyan Jovanovic

New York University

Is the capitalist function distinct from the entrepreneurial function in modern economies? Or does a person have to be wealthy before he or she can start a business? Knight and Schumpeter held different views on the answer to this question. Our empirical findings side with Knight: Liquidity constraints bind, and a would-be entrepreneur must bear most of the risk inherent in his venture. The reasoning is roughly this: The data show that wealthier people are more inclined to become entrepreneurs. In principle, this could be so because the wealthy tend to make better entrepreneurs, but the data reject this explanation. Instead, the data point to liquidity constraints: capital is essential for starting a business, and liquidity constraints tend to exclude those with insufficient funds at their disposal.

I. Introduction

Do liquidity constraints hinder people from starting businesses? The answer to this question is important for several reasons. First, liquidity

We thank seminar participants at Columbia University, at the University of Florida at Gainesville, and at the National Bureau of Economic Research at Cambridge for helpful comments; the C. V. Starr Center for Applied Economics at New York University for technical assistance; and Francesco Goletti and Zheng Gu for excellent research assistance. We are greatly indebted to Linda Leighton for developing the data set used in this paper and to the referee for many valuable comments and suggestions. This work was done while Evans was a visitor at the C. V. Starr Center.

[*Journal of Political Economy*, 1989, vol. 97, no. 4]

constraints may explain the finding by Evans and Leighton (1989) that the hazard into self-employment is constant in age.[1] This finding is not consistent with the occupational choice stories told by Johnson (1978), Jovanovic (1979), and Miller (1984), which imply that individuals will try riskier occupations such as entrepreneurship when they are younger. But entrepreneurship may in fact not be an option for younger workers because they will have had less time to build up the capital needed to start a business and, with liquidity constraints, will have difficulty borrowing enough start-up funds.

Second, the belief that capital markets do not provide adequate funds for new businesses is one of the rationales for government assistance programs to small business.[2] The U.S. Small Business Administration provides subsidized loans and loan guarantees to small businesses for start-up and expansion. Great Britain, France, Belgium, and the Netherlands have recently adopted financial assistance programs for unemployed workers who start businesses (see Bendick and Egan 1987). The U.S. Department of Labor plans to conduct an experiment in which a sample of unemployment insurance recipients will be given the option of receiving business start-up funds instead of unemployment benefits (see U.S. Department of Labor 1988).

Third, the liquidity constraint is central to the dispute between Frank Knight and Joseph Schumpeter over the nature of entrepreneurship. Knight (1921) argues that bearing risk is one of the essential characteristics of entrepreneurship.[3] He apparently recognizes that capital markets provide too little capital to entrepreneurs because of moral hazard and adverse selection problems (see LeRoy and Singell 1987). Consequently, entrepreneurs must finance themselves and bear the risk of failure. Schumpeter (1934, 1950), on the other hand, argues that the functions of the entrepreneur and the capitalist are quite separate:[4] The role of the entrepreneur is to identify arbitrage opportunities in the economy, while modern capital markets generally enable him to find a capitalist to bear the risks for him.[5]

---

[1] Data from the National Longitudinal Survey of Young Men indicate that the probability of entering self-employment is independent of both age and labor market experience for men who are under 40. Data from a much larger sample of individuals from the *Current Population Survey* indicate that the probability of entering self-employment is independent of age for those under 50.

[2] This is not to say that these programs are cost effective. As far as we know, there is no evidence on whether the Small Business Administration loan programs are efficient. Bendick and Egan (1987) suggest that the unemployment programs may not be efficient.

[3] See Kanbur (1979) and Kihlstrom and Laffont (1979) for models based on Knight.

[4] This view continues among the Austrians (see Kirzner 1973).

[5] For example, Schumpeter (1934, p. 77) says that "most economists up to the time of the younger Mill failed to keep capitalist and entrepreneur distinct because the manufacturer of a hundred years ago was both; and certainly the course of events since then

This paper examines the importance of liquidity constraints by estimating a model of entrepreneurial choice in which the tightness of the liquidity constraint is a parameter. People have endowments of entrepreneurial ability and assets that may be correlated. The financial capital that they can devote to a business is a multiple of these assets. This multiple is a measure of the degree of liquidity constraints. In Section II we present the model and discuss evidence for our assumption that individuals face an L-shaped liquidity constraint.

The model is estimated with data on roughly 1,500 white males who were wage workers in 1976 and either wage workers or self-employed workers in 1978. The data were drawn from the National Longitudinal Survey of Young Men. After discussing the data, in Section III we report reduced-form results and other evidence consistent with the model.

We present maximum likelihood estimates of the structural parameters of the model in Section IV. The key parameters are the degree of the liquidity constraint, the returns to capital in entrepreneurship, the mean and variance of the distribution of entrepreneurial ability in the population, and the correlation between entrepreneurial ability and assets. It is important to note that we find that a person cannot use more than 1.5 times his or her initial assets for starting a new venture. Thus we reject Schumpeter in favor of Knight: Most individuals who enter self-employment face a binding liquidity constraint and as a result use a suboptimal amount of capital to start up their businesses. Further work is needed to find out if these structural estimates are robust to alternative specifications and samples. Moreover, our findings have no normative implications without added assumptions on why liquidity constraints are there in the first place.

In Section V we summarize the results and present suggestions for further research. While we focus on liquidity constraints, we make several contributions of more general interest. First, we estimate the parameters of the entrepreneurial ability distribution, which we find to be nondegenerate. Thus we confirm Knight's conjecture (1921)— recently elaborated on by Lucas (1978) and Jovanovic (1982)—that one of the key determinants of entrepreneurship is the distribution of "business acumen" in the population. To our knowledge, this paper reports the first structural estimates of the distribution of this key parameter.

Second, the selection problem analyzed in this paper is not stan-

---

has facilitated the making of this distinction." He notes that the entrepreneur and the capitalist are sometimes one and the same. But in his extensive discussions of the relationship between the entrepreneur and the capitalist, he shows no awareness that market forces might require the entrepreneur to be his own capitalist.

dard and may have applications in other areas. The interaction of selection on ability and liquidity constraints gives rise to a complicated set of selection conditions for which we derive the likelihood function. A similar problem would arise in, for example, the demand for durables with heterogeneous consumers subject to liquidity constraints.

II. The Model

The model is static. At the start of the period, the individual must decide whether to work for himself (i.e. become an entrepreneur) or continue to work for someone else (i.e. remain a wage worker). At the end of the period, self-employment opportunity will yield him a gross payoff equal to y, while wage work will yield him a wage of w. We assume away unemployment or withdrawal from the labor force.

A person takes up self-employment if his expected net income is higher there. Otherwise he chooses wage work. The wage equation is

$$w = \mu x_1^{\gamma_1} x_2^{\gamma_2} \xi. \tag{1}$$

Here x_1 is the person's previous experience as a wage worker, x_2 is his education, μ is a constant, and ξ is a disturbance whose logarithm has variance σ_ξ^2, independent across workers. Entrepreneurial earnings are[6]

$$y = \theta k^\alpha \epsilon. \tag{2}$$

Here θ is "entrepreneurial ability," k is the amount of capital invested in the business, ϵ is a lognormal disturbance whose logarithm has variance σ_ϵ^2, independent across entrepreneurs, and $\alpha \in (0, 1)$.[7] An abler entrepreneur has a higher total product and a higher marginal product of capital at all levels of capital. This restriction on the relationship between average and marginal products over entrepreneurs can be found in Lucas (1978) and Jovanovic (1982). It is consistent with the empirical finding that *total profits* increase with firm size when the latter is measured by assets.[8]

---

[6] Two exogenous observables were included in the wage equation but not in the entrepreneurial earnings equation; see the last paragraph of app. C (available from the authors).

[7] We assume that $E(\epsilon) = 1$ so that $E[\log(\epsilon)] = -\sigma_\epsilon^2/2$. The disturbance term ϵ reflects an independent and identically distributed productivity shock.

[8] Most studies of the relationship between firm size and the rate of return find that the rate of return either increases with firm size or is constant in firm size. See Scherer (1980) for a review of studies. Therefore, total profits must increase with firm size. A potentially important assumption here is that θ and μ are uncorrelated. We tried to model the case in which they are correlated but found that the resulting model was analytically intractable. A correlated θ and μ should not affect the theoretical implications of the model, although it would affect the characteristics of the constrained entrepreneurs and the likelihood estimates. If θ and μ were positively (negatively) correlated, we would expect that liquidity constraints would be less (more) empirically

Now a word about ϵ. This is the unforeseen component of his income from choosing to become an entrepreneur. Its time-series properties are, strictly speaking, of no import for the analysis. It could, for instance, be a permanent component that affects the entrepreneur's productivity for as long as he is self-employed, or it could represent an independent and identically distributed disturbance to his productivity over time. If ϵ did have a permanent component, revealed only ex post, then we would have a theory of exit as in Jovanovic (1982). The present paper will not explore this intuition any farther because of the great complexity that it would impose on the empirical analysis.

An entrepreneur's net income is

$$y + r(z - k). \tag{3}$$

Here r is *one plus* the rate of interest, and z is the entrepreneur's beginning-of-period wealth. If $z < k$, the entrepreneur is a net borrower, and $r(z - k)$ is the amount he repays at the end of the period. He cannot default, no matter how his business turns out. The latter assumption is not too implausible if people can borrow only a limited amount or have to put up collateral (as indeed appears to be the case as discussed below).[9] We shall assume that each person can borrow up to an amount that is proportional to his wealth; the factor of proportionality is denoted by $\lambda - 1$. Since the amount borrowed cannot exceed $(\lambda - 1)z$, the most that a person can invest in the business is $z + (\lambda - 1)z = \lambda z$.[10] The entrepreneur therefore faces the constraint

$$0 \le k \le \lambda z, \tag{4}$$

---

important. Entrepreneurs will tend to be high- (low-) wage people who are more (less) likely to have accumulated sufficient start-up funds. The results below provide some evidence that entrepreneurs may be relatively poor wage workers. The argument is that individuals who have accumulated a lot of assets will tend to be relatively good wage workers. Therefore, assets can be viewed as a proxy for wage ability. We find that entrepreneurial ability and assets are negatively correlated, which suggests that entrepreneurial and wage ability may be negatively correlated.

[9] The default rate among business exits appears to be fairly small. In 1976 the fraction of all concerns that defaulted was one-third of 1 percent. While comparable estimates on exits are not available, Evans (1987b) found that about 21 percent of manufacturing firms exited between 1976 and 1981, for an annual exit rate of about 4 percent per year. His sample was weighted toward larger manufacturing firms. The exit rate of all firms is likely to be higher.

[10] In a more realistic model, λ would depend not only on z but also on observed characteristics, x, since the latter affect y and, hence, the probability of repayment. Ando (1985) finds, e.g., that, for established businesses, the probability of having a loan application accepted increases with the amount of business experience of the applicant, the size of the firm, and the past credit record of the firm. These factors are probably less important for the new businesses considered here since most people starting a business have no previous business experience or credit history. Nevertheless, in future work it would be useful to explore whether the liquidity constraint and the interest rate depend on demographic characteristics.

ENTREPRENEURIAL CHOICE   813

where the parameter λ satisfies

$$\lambda \geq 1, \tag{5}$$

and it is equal for everyone. The constraint tells us the maximum amount of capital that the entrepreneur can control. The interest factor, r, is also equal for everyone. Moreover, for simplicity we assume that the lending rate equals the borrowing rate.[11]

This form for the liquidity constraint is analytically convenient. Moreover, evidence indicates that the liquidity constraint facing businesses is similar to the L-shaped constraint (4). Ando (1985, p. C.5) finds that most new businesses are likely to face even more severe constraints:[12] "Several conclusions emerge from these studies. One is the critical role of personal savings and loans from friends and relatives, particularly in business formation. It is by far the largest source of capital in new firms and in firms beginning to grow. Once the firm is established, the role of personal savings diminishes as institutional investors perceive less risk and become more willing to provide capital." A study by Scott and Dunkelberg (cited by Ando) for the National Federation of Independent Businessmen found that firms that had been in existence for less than 4 years reported that, on average, only 50 percent of their initial loan request was met. These findings suggest that new businesses are liquidity constrained and that the amount of capital available to them is limited by their personal assets.[13]

---

[11] The assumption of a constant interest rate is at least a crude approximation to reality. A significant portion of loan applications are rejected, and many new businesses claim difficulty in obtaining financing (see below). This suggests that the supply curve of capital is not upward sloping over a wide range. Banks do not appear to fine-tune risk premia to individual borrowers. For a theoretical discussion of credit raticning, see Stiglitz and Weiss (1981). For a recent study of consumer credit rationing, see Mariger (1987), who finds that almost 20 percent of his sample of families were liquidity constrained. Loans from friends and relatives may be one means to evade the liquidity constraint. There is some evidence, e.g., that the entrepreneurial success of some immigrant groups is due to their access to capital from family and communal networks. Koreans, e.g., participate in rotating credit associations for business start-ups. See Light (1972) for a discussion. Among the established male business owners surveyed by Ando (1985), loans from friends and relatives constituted about 10 percent of the start-up capital, while bank loans constituted about 41 percent.

[12] She reports that, of loans taken in the previous three years, 40 percent required personal collateral and 39.5 percent required business collateral. Although there is some ambiguity, if loans required either personal or business collateral, then 80 percent of the loans would have required some collateral. Of loans that had been rejected, 70.8 percent required personal collateral and 64.5 percent business collateral.

[13] Ham and Melnik (1987) find evidence of liquidity constraints even for firms much larger than those considered here. They report that most credit agreements place an upper limit on borrowing and that about 20 percent of the firms in their sample reached the maximum amount of their commitment size. See their discussion for an alternative interpretation, however.

The Entrepreneur's Investment Decision

At the time that the investment decision is made, the entrepreneur cannot foretell the realization of ϵ, although he does know θ. Under the assumption that he is risk neutral, his investment decision, k, solves

$$\max_{k \in [0, \lambda z]} \ [\theta k^\alpha + r(z - k)]. \tag{6}$$

At an interior maximum, the first-order condition is

$$\theta \alpha k^{\alpha - 1} - r = 0, \tag{7}$$

which leads to the solution

$$k = \left(\frac{\theta \alpha}{r} \right)^{1/(1 - \alpha)}, \tag{8}$$

which is valid as long as the right-hand side is no greater than λz. When the latter is true, we say that the entrepreneur is not constrained with respect to how much he can borrow, or is simply "unconstrained." For the entrepreneur to be unconstrained, his θ must satisfy

$$\theta \leq (\lambda z)^{1 - \alpha} \frac{r}{\alpha}. \tag{9}$$

Otherwise he is constrained.

Since our data do not contain precise enough information on how much is invested, we shall substitute out from the entrepreneurial earnings equation (2) the optimal capital invested (as given by [8] for the unconstrained and by λz for the constrained). This leads to the following expression for entrepreneurial income:

$$y = \begin{cases} \theta^{1/(1 - \alpha)} \left(\dfrac{\alpha}{r} \right)^{\alpha/(1 - \alpha)} \epsilon & \text{if } \theta \text{ satisfies (9)} \\[2ex] \theta (\lambda z)^\alpha \epsilon & \text{otherwise.} \end{cases} \tag{10}$$

Clearly, if θ satisfies (9), y does not depend on z. If, on the other hand, θ does not satisfy (9), then $\partial y / \partial z = \alpha y / z$ and $\partial y / \partial \theta = y/\theta$, so that the slope of the indifference curves in figure 1 is $d\theta/dz|_{y \, \text{const}} = -\alpha\theta/z$.

Selection into Entrepreneurship

The would-be entrepreneur, we assume, knows θ *before* he commits himself on whether to start a business. In this we deviate from Jovanovic (1982) and instead follow Lucas (1978). Since the individual knows his θ, he will choose to start a business if and only if his ex-

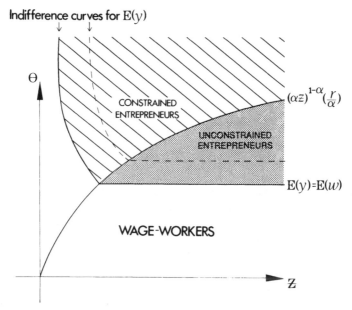

FIG. 1.—Nature of the selection into entrepreneurship

pected net income from doing so exceeds that from wage work:

$$\max[\theta k^{\alpha} + r(z - k)] \geq \mu x_1^{\gamma_1} x_2^{\gamma_2} + rz. \qquad (11)$$

Since the left-hand side of (11) increases with θ while the right-hand side does not, we have the following proposition.

PROPOSITION 1: A person with characteristics (θ, z, x) chooses entrepreneurship if $\theta \in (f(z, x), \infty)$, where $f(z, x)$ is the value of θ that solves (11) as an exact equality.

That higher-θ people select into entrepreneurship and that the preferred region in θ-space is a half-open interval is a property that does not depend on the nature of the production function. All that matters is that output is increasing in θ at all levels of the capital stock. On the other hand, the shape of the three regions in figure 1 depends on our assumption that an increase in θ raises the marginal product of capital everywhere. That is, k and θ are gross complements.

Canceling the term rz from both sides of (11) and substituting the optimal k (from [8] for the unconstrained and from λz for the constrained) leaves us with the following *selection conditions*: (1) Equation (9) holds and

$$\theta^{1/(1-\alpha)}\left(\frac{\alpha}{r}\right)^{\alpha/(1-\alpha)} - r\left(\frac{\alpha}{r}\right)^{1/(1-\alpha)}\theta^{1/(1-\alpha)} \geq \mu x_1^{\gamma_1} x_2^{\gamma_2},$$

or (2) equation (9) does not hold and $\theta(\lambda z)^{\alpha} - r\lambda z > \mu^{\gamma}$. Appendix B (available from the authors on request, together with apps. A and C) shows that selection conditions 1 and 2 are equivalent to the following selection conditions:

$$\mu^{1-\alpha}\left(\frac{r}{\alpha}\right)^{\alpha}(1 - \alpha)^{\alpha - 1}x_1^{\gamma_1(1-\alpha)}x_2^{\gamma_2(1-\alpha)} \leq \theta \leq (\lambda z)^{1-\alpha}\left(\frac{r}{\alpha}\right) \quad (1')$$

or

$$\theta > \max\left[(\lambda z)^{1-\alpha}\left(\frac{r}{\alpha}\right), \mu x_1^{\gamma_1}x_2^{\gamma_2}(\lambda z)^{-\alpha} + r(\lambda z)^{1-\alpha}\right]. \quad (2')$$

If θ satisfies either constraint, the individual chooses self-employment. The complicated nature of these constraints stems from the wealth constraint on investment. The special case of *no* wealth constraints obtains when $\lambda = \infty$. Then the right-hand side of condition $2'$ is ∞ as is the right-hand side of condition $1'$, so that the selection rule takes on a simple one-sided form. Figure 1 shows the nature of the selection.

The Joint Distribution of θ and z

Since θ and z may be correlated in the population, we take the following steps to control for this. The parameter θ is assumed to be independent of everything except possibly z. We write

$$\ln \theta = \delta_0 + \delta_1 \ln z + \eta, \quad (12)$$

where $\eta \sim N(0, \sigma_\eta^2)$, so that $\ln \theta \sim N(\delta_0 + \sigma_1 \ln z, \sigma_\eta^2)$.

We shall not dwell too long on δ_1—the parameter determining the population correlation between θ and z. It may reflect greater past savings by those high-θ people who, knowing their θ, expected to become entrepreneurs one day. Or, if we stretch the interpretation a bit, it may reflect lower absolute risk aversion of wealthy people, making them more inclined to become entrepreneurs (as in Kihlstrom and Laffont [1979]).[14] Whatever the source of the correlation between θ and z, the parameter δ_1 will not, in general, be invariant to changes in other parameters of the model. We include it so as to avoid interpreting the apparent correlation between z on the one hand and entrepreneurial choice and success on the other as being caused entirely by the presence of liquidity constraints: A positive δ_1 would imply that, even in the absence of liquidity constraints (i.e., $\lambda = \infty$), wealthier people would be more likely to become entrepreneurs sim-

---

[14] We thank Larry Samuelson for this interpretation.

ply because of a "spurious" correlation between z and the unobservable θ. As it turns out, we find no evidence that δ_1 is positive.[15]

III. The Data and Reduced-Form Results

We use data from the National Longitudinal Survey of Young Men (NLS) to estimate the structural parameters of the model. This survey consists of a sample of 5,225 men who were between the ages of 14 and 24 in 1966 and who were queried periodically between 1966 and 1981. Individuals reported net family assets, the key variable for our purposes, in 1971, 1976, and 1981. We look at a subsample of 1,949 white males who were wage workers in 1976, who either were wage workers or were self-employed in 1978, and who were not unemployed, out of the labor force, in the military, or in school full-time in either 1976 or 1978.[16] Of these individuals, 89 (4.5 percent) entered self-employment. Unfortunately, we lost a number of other individuals who failed to report information we needed. Asset and income variables were often missing. For the maximum likelihood analysis we also had to delete some individuals who reported negative net worth or negative self-employment income (since we take the logs of these variables), leaving us with 1,443 white men for the actual estimation. Given that this subsample consists of less than half of the 3,918 white males who started in the survey in 1966, our results may not be representative of the population at large. For the reduced-form results reported below, we include all individuals for whom the relevant information is available. Table 1 reports variable definitions, summary statistics, and sample selection. Further details are discussed in Evans and Leighton (1987).

The men in our sample were between the ages of 24 and 34 in 1976. This age range covers a portion of the life cycle during which a large proportion of the men who will eventually become self-employed make the transition. According to *Current Population Survey* data, approximately 2.5 percent of 21–25-year-old males were self-

---

[15] In fact, δ_1 is negative and statistically significant. This result suggests that high-asset people tend to be relatively poor entrepreneurs. But it is also possible that this is a sign that the model is misspecified. Some of the results for the model with δ_1 negative are implausible, as we discuss below.

[16] Note that we have eliminated workers who were unemployed in 1976. Ongoing work by Evans and Leighton finds that unemployed workers are about twice as likely to switch into self-employment than other workers. A few of the individuals in our sample, however, did experience spells of unemployment between the 1976 and 1978 survey weeks and were not eliminated. Of the entrants, six (10 percent of the 59) experienced some unemployment, and of the nonentrants, 97 (7 percent of the 1,384 nonentrants) experienced some unemployment. In the reduced-form results reported below, we included a dummy variable for workers who experienced some unemployment between survey weeks but found that it had no substantive effect on the results.

TABLE 1

DEFINITION OF VARIABLES

Name	Mean (Standard Deviation)	Definition
Enter	.0409 (.2022)	Equals 0 if wage worker in 1976 and 1978 survey weeks and 1 if wage worker in 1976 survey week and self-employed in 1978 survey week; defined only for individuals who were employed in both survey weeks and who were not full-time students
Assets	20.0092 (50.0533)	Net family assets in 1976 survey week (in thousands of dollars)
Income	17.6553 (19.1731)	Individual wage earnings in 1978 for wage workers and individual self-employment earnings in 1978 for self-employed workers (in thousands of dollars)*
Work experience	11.9959 (12.5343)	Years of wage experience as of 1978 survey week[†]
Education	13.9390 (14.1546)	Years of education as of 1978 survey week

NOTE.—Data drawn from the National Longitudinal Survey of Young Men, 1966–81. The initial sample size consisted of 3,918 white young men aged 14–24 in 1966. Data were available for 2,536 in both 1976 and 1978. Of these men, 1,986 were employed in both survey weeks and were not enrolled in school full-time. The resulting sample consisted of 126 entrants and 1,860 nonentrants on the basis of the self-employment indicator variable available from the NLS. Of the 126 entrants, 37 were deleted because in 1978 they reported having been self-employed more than 2 years. Most of the deletions were incorporated self-employed who apparently reported themselves as wage workers in 1976 even though they were running their own businesses. Approximately 110 individuals had missing asset data, and 60 individuals had missing income data. The maximum likelihood estimation also deleted individuals who reported nonpositive assets or self-employment earnings.

* Two adjustments were made to self-employment income: (1) Some individuals who run incorporated businesses report self-employment income as wage and salary income. If an individual was incorporated, reported no self-employment income, and reported wage and salary income, we used his wage and salary income in place of self-employment income. (2) For individuals who had operated their businesses for less than a year (as measured by tenure as of the 1978 survey week), we prorated self-employment income by the length of time in business to obtain an estimate of annual self-employment earnings.

† Wage experience accumulated from 1966. An estimate of pre-1966 job experience was used for workers who had jobs prior to the start of the survey. See app. A to Evans and Leighton (1987) for details.

employed, 5.7 percent of 26–30-year-old males, 9.0 percent of 31–35-year-old males, and 11.2 percent of 36–40-year-old males. The population fraction of self-employment remains fairly constant between age 40 and retirement age.[17]

In 1978 the average self-employed man in our sample earned $15,746 compared with $16,760 for wage earners. The average increase in earnings was smaller for those who switched into self-employment than for those who remained wage workers.[18] Of the 89

[17] These results are based on averages for 1976–86. See Evans and Leighton (1987) for details on the data and Evans and Leighton (1989) for a discussion of the dynamics of changes in the stock of self-employed workers over the life cycle.

[18] A possible reason for the discrepancy is that self-employment income gets more favorable tax treatment.

TABLE 2

ESTIMATED PROBABILITY OF ENTERING SELF-EMPLOYMENT:
REDUCED-FORM RESULTS, 1976–78

VARIABLE	PROBIT ESTIMATES*	
	(1)	(2)
Assets	.0053	.0075
	(.0282)	(.0032)
Assets^2/100	−.0010	−.0015
	(.0008)	(.0011)
Wage experience	.0248	.0320
	(.0144)	(.0148)
Education	−.0128	−.0038
	(.0163)	(.0174)
Married	−.4799	−.4491
	(.1162)	(.1183)
Urban	−.1511	−.0879
	(.1124)	(.1166)
Handicapped	−.1376	−1730
	(.2131)	(.2152)
Wage income in 1976/1,000	. . .	−.0222
		(.0104)
Constant	−1.3915	−1.3991
	(.3057)	(.3143)
Log likelihood	−330.0562	−327.4762
Observations	1,839	1,835

NOTE.—Standard errors are in parentheses.
* The F-statistic for assets and assets^2 was 2.24 (p-value of .0107) for the regression in the first column and 3.64 (p-value of .0264) in the second column.

individuals who switched into self-employment, 20 percent formed incorporated businesses.

Before we estimate the structural parameters of the model, it is useful to consider some simple tests of the model. If one assumes a zero correlation between assets and entrepreneurial ability, our model has two implications. First, there is a positive correlation between the probability of starting a business and assets *if and only if* there are liquidity constraints: Such constraints mean that a wealthier person can start a business with a more efficient capital level and thereby realize a greater return than a poorer one. Table 2 reports probit estimates of the relationship between the probability of entering self-employment and initial assets. The estimates in the first column control for education, experience, and several demographic characteristics. The effect of assets on the probability of starting a business is positive (at the sample mean) and is statistically significant at the 10 percent level. The estimates in the second column also condition on wage earnings in the previous period. The effect of

JOURNAL OF POLITICAL ECONOMY

TABLE 3

ESTIMATED EFFECT OF LOG ASSETS ON LOG SELF-EMPLOYMENT EARNINGS:
REDUCED-FORM RESULTS

	REGRESSION ESTIMATES	
VARIABLE	1978	1981
Log assets	.1424	−.0683
	(.0538)	(.1239)
Log experience	.2290	1.0010
	(.3534)	(1.0273)
Log education	−.3344	.4627
	(.5589)	(1.1865)
Married	−.1422	.1532
	(.2694)	(.5536)
Urban	−.0054	.2044
	(.2059)	(.4828)
Handicapped	.9884	−.9083
	(.5423)	(1.0332)
Constant	8.8066	1.2021
	(3.1708)	(8.6413)
R^2	.2267	.0806
F-statistic	2.54	.45
Observations	59	37

NOTE.—Dependent variable is log self-employment earnings. Semilog regressions yielded qualitatively similar results. Standard errors are in parentheses.

assets on the probability of starting a business is positive (at the sample mean) and is statistically significant at the 2 percent level.[19]

The second implication is that the correlation between entrepreneurial earnings and initial assets is positive since wealthier people will have started businesses with more efficient capital levels. Table 3 reports regression estimates that show a statistically significant positive correlation between log self-employment earnings and log assets after controlling for education, experience, and several demographic characteristics.[20]

A third implication is that people with smaller assets will be forced to devote a larger proportion of their assets to their businesses. Ando (1985) estimates that a 10 percent increase in assets leads to a 4 percent increase in the amount of personal savings devoted to a business. Thus poorer individuals do devote a larger proportion of their wealth to their businesses, just as our model implies.

Although the model is static, it suggests several dynamic implications. Constrained firms will start with a suboptimal amount of capital and therefore will be smaller than unconstrained firms. As a result,

[19] Evans and Leighton (1989) report similar results for 1980–81.
[20] We obtain similar results using a semilog regression and using only levels.

constrained businesses will have a greater tendency to reinvest earnings back into the business than unconstrained firms since the return on capital invested in the business is higher for the constrained firms. Therefore, smaller firms will grow faster than larger firms that entered at the same time. Evans (1987a, 1987b) and Dunne, Roberts, and Samuelson (1987) confirm that smaller firms do indeed grow faster than larger firms when business age and other characteristics are held constant.[21]

As firms grow over time, the importance of the initial liquidity constraint will diminish. We have checked this implication by comparing the effect of initial (1976) assets on entrepreneurial earnings in 1978 and 1981. The results reported in table 3 are consistent with the diminishing importance of assets over time.[22] The elasticity of earnings with respect to initial assets is positive and statistically significant for 1978 and negative and highly insignificant for 1981. This suggests that assets are not acting as a proxy for entrepreneurial ability, whose effect should persist over time.[23]

Recent attempts to subsidize small business start-ups by unemployed workers also provide some weak evidence for our model. Relaxing binding liquidity constraints by providing unemployment benefits in a lump sum or otherwise providing start-up assistance should increase business formations. Bendick and Egan (1987) report that the British Enterprise Allowance Program roughly doubled the formation of businesses among unemployed workers.[24]

IV. Maximum Likelihood Estimates

The likelihood function is derived in the appendix (available from the authors). The regressions reported above indicate that work experi-

[21] Another related implication of the model is that firms that face a tighter liquidity constraint will grow more rapidly. We tested this implication by regressing the growth of income between 1978 and 1981 for entrants who were self-employed in both years against the log of assets (35 observations were available). The relationship was negative, as predicted, but statistically insignificant.

[22] We might also expect that failures will experience smaller growth in assets than successes. The average change in nominal assets between 1976 and 1981 was 250 percent for successes and 111 percent for failures. The price level increased 159.7 percent between these years. Therefore, failures had negative asset growth and successes had positive asset growth.

[23] We also estimated the 1978 earnings equation using the 1981 sample to determine whether the change in the sign of the asset variable is due to self-selection. The estimated coefficient on assets was smaller for the restricted sample (about .6) but remained statistically significant at the 5 percent level.

[24] The Enterprise Allowance Program gave workers an operating subsidy for up to 1 year instead of unemployment benefits. Workers had to have $1,500 of their own to invest in the business before they could be eligible. Bendick and Egan note that workers received more from participating in the program than if they had remained unemployed.

ence and education were not substantively or statistically significant determinants of entrepreneurial earnings. Therefore, entrepreneurial earnings are assumed to depend only on assets. Wage earnings are assumed to depend on education and experience.[25]

Table 4 reports the maximum likelihood estimates. The estimated correlation between entrepreneurial ability and assets is negative and statistically significant. Thus we can reject the hypothesis that assets are a positive proxy for entrepreneurial ability. The key finding is that there are binding capital constraints. In the second column, which constrains δ_1 to be zero, the point estimate of λ is 1.44 with a 99 percent (plus or minus three standard deviations) confidence interval of (1.31, 1.59). Our results support Knight ($\lambda = 1$) over Schumpeter ($\lambda = \infty$).

The estimate of α in the second column means that a 10 percent increase in the capital devoted to a business leads to a 2.2 percent increase in earnings. This coefficient is highly significant.[26] The estimate of σ_θ is almost the same as the estimate of σ_ϵ. This means that entrepreneurs face considerable risk, not just as perceived by outsiders (who can see neither ϵ nor θ), but also as perceived by themselves since they cannot see ϵ until after they have committed their investment. Surprisingly, the distribution of unanticipated earnings shocks seems to be more variable for wage workers than for entrepreneurs.

---

[25] As mentioned in the appendix, α is constrained to lie in the unit interval (i.e., marginal product of capital is positive and diminishing) and λ is constrained to be positive. Our rough expectation is that α would be about a third—the share of capital in income (see n. 26 for more on this point). The assumption that $0 < \alpha < 1$ implies that there are diminishing returns to capital and that capital and ability are complements. The assumption that $\lambda > 0$ precludes the implausible implication that liquidity decreases with assets. Both assumptions are necessary because $\log(\alpha)$, $\log(1 - \alpha)$, and $\log(\lambda)$ appear in the likelihood function. It was not possible to keep all the parameter estimates within the permissible range during the likelihood estimation without these constraints. In order to ensure that the estimates reported are for a global maximum of the likelihood function, we perturbed the values of the key parameters and checked to see that the likelihood function was indeed lower and that the parameters moved toward the estimates at the maximum. We tried several high and low combinations of α and λ in this process. We also tried several alternative functional forms for the capital constraint (e.g., including higher-order terms in assets and allowing the capital constraint to depend on some of the exogenous variables) but had difficulty obtaining convergence.

[26] The estimates of α of .39 and .22 are not too far from those obtained elsewhere using the Cobb-Douglas production function. In models without liquidity constraints, α should equal capital's share in income, which is about one-third. In our model, however, α is the share of capital in the income of *unconstrained* entrepreneurs only. As for a constrained entrepreneur, he spends $r\lambda z$ on capital and expects $\theta(\lambda z)^\alpha$ in income. This yields a capital share of $r(\lambda z)^{1-\alpha}/\theta$. But since a constrained entrepreneur's θ violates (9), this means that $1/\theta < [(\lambda z)^{1-\alpha} r/\alpha]^{-1}$, which means that the empirical share of capital *exceeds* α for the constrained. Therefore, our estimate of α should be *less* than one-third, and on these grounds, again, the estimates in the second column of table 4 are more plausible than those in the first column.

TABLE 4

Maximum Likelihood Estimates of Entrepreneurial Selection under Liquidity Constraints for 1976–78

COEFFICIENT	NAME	ESTIMATE	
		(1)	(2)
Capital returns	α	.3862	.2186
		(.0822)	(.0200)
Capital constraint	λ	1.7263	1.4401
		(.0782)	(.0429)
Log entrepreneurial ability—constant	δ_0	2.3388	2.2732
		(.0498)	(.0404)
Log entrepreneurial ability—assets	δ_1	−.1160	...
		(.0343)	
Wage constant	μ	.2098	.1947
		(.2168)	(.2115)
Experience returns	γ_1	.3225	.3281
		(.0390)	(.0386)
Education returns	γ_2	.7200	.7207
Standard deviations for:			
Entrepreneurial ability	σ_θ	.2682	.2849
		(.0139)	(.0118)
Entrepreneurial earnings	σ_ϵ	.2666	.2797
		(.0222)	(.0163)
Wage earnings	σ_ξ	.4114	.4114
		(.0043)	(.0043)
Log likelihood		−954.0183	−959.8647
Observations		1,443	1,443

Note.—Estimation performed with the MAXLIK procedure in Gauss. Asymptotic standard errors are in parentheses.

Given the stringent functional form assumptions and the extensive attrition from our sample, the reader should regard the estimated structural parameters merely as suggestive of what more refined research will reveal. Nonetheless, let us take the estimates seriously and use them to evaluate the impact of liquidity constraints on business start-ups. We shall use the estimates from column 2 of table 4 for these calculations.[27]

The optimal amount of start-up capital for a white person with average education and experience is estimated to be $16,739 for someone with log entrepreneurial ability three standard deviations above the mean, $8,603 for two standard deviations above the mean, and $4,421 for one standard deviation above the mean. The geometric mean assets in our sample were $7,433. Someone with these assets could control business capital of $10,704. Thus only the

---

[27] Most of the results were similar if col. 1 is used instead, with the exception of the effect of removing the constraint. The correlated case predicts that removing the constraints leads to roughly a sixfold increase in the rate of entry, an implausible inference. Complete results are available from the authors on request.

ablest would not be able to obtain sufficient capital if they decided to start a business.[28] Most people are not constrained in the sense that, if they did decide to start a business, they would have sufficient capital according to our estimates.

Only high-ability/low-asset people are affected by the wealth constraint. But it is precisely these people who are most likely to want to switch to self-employment. Those with high ability can earn more in self-employment than in wage work, especially if they have poor wage earnings. But those with poor wage earnings are also likely to have accumulated relatively few assets. Indeed, compared with nonentrants, entrants had lower average wage earnings ($12,339 for entrants vs. $13,592 for nonentrants in 1976) and lower geometric mean assets ($5,927 for entrants and $7,504 for nonentrants in 1976).

Using the estimated structural parameters, we can calculate the fraction of the population that has values of θ (and of the other characteristics) satisfying constraints 1′ and 2′.[29] The average probability of being a constrained entrepreneur (i.e., satisfying 1′) is 3.75 percent, and the average probability of being an unconstrained entrepreneur (i.e., satisfying 2′) is 0.06 percent. Thus the liquidity constraint is binding for virtually all the individuals who are likely to start a business.

The liquidity constraint reduces the amount of capital flowing to entrepreneurship in two ways.[30] First, it will prevent some people from trying entrepreneurship. If the liquidity constraint were removed, the estimates indicate that the average probability of becoming an entrepreneur over the period would increase to 5.11 percent from 3.81 percent. Thus we estimate that the liquidity constraint deters 1.3 percent of the population from trying entrepreneurship.[31] Second, individuals who do try entrepreneurship use less capital because of the constraint. For example, an individual with $5,927 of assets (the geometric mean for entrants) and with log entrepreneurial ability two standard deviations above the mean uses $68 too little capital ($8,603 − 1.44 × $5,927). The difference between optimal and actual capital is lower for people with lower ability—an individual

---

[28] In fact, for individuals with average characteristics and assets, only those with log entrepreneurial ability 2.33 standard deviations above the mean would be constrained.

[29] These figures are obtained by taking the logarithmic values of the elements of the constraints and using the assumption that ln θ is normally distributed to calculate the probability that an individual with observed characteristics will satisfy the constraint. The sample mean of these individual probabilities is then taken.

[30] The figures reported below are in 1976 dollars. Prices have roughly doubled since 1976.

[31] This, of course, is a partial equilibrium result. Increasing the supply of entrepreneurs would decrease entrepreneurial rewards and thereby reduce the number of individuals who would like to switch.

with $5,927 of assets and log entrepreneurial ability three standard deviations above the mean would use the optimal amount of capital—and higher for people with less assets—an individual with $3,717 of assets and log entrepreneurial ability two standard deviations above the mean uses $3,250 too little capital.

The structural parameters also give a rough idea of the aggregate self-employment investment that might not be made because of the liquidity constraint. There were 50.3 million white male members of the labor force in 1976. The average annual entry rate into self-employment for the NLS sample between 1976 and 1978 was 2.25 percent. Therefore, 1.26 million whites are estimated to have entered self-employment annually. If we assume that each of these people used $68 too little capital (as would be the case for an individual whose log entrepreneurial ability is two standard deviations above the mean and who has assets of $5,917—the geometric mean for entrants), the total lost investment because of suboptimal investment by initial entrants is $86 million a year. Additionally, 1.30 percent of our sample were deterred from entering self-employment for a 2-year period (0.65 percent annually) or 0.3 million people annually. If we assume that these individuals would have invested the optimal start-up capital of $8,603 (the amount for a person with log entrepreneurial ability two standard deviations above the mean), the total lost investment because of deterred entry is $2,580 million. We thus obtain a total "lost" investment of $2.7 billion in 1976 dollars. By way of comparison, gross private domestic investment in 1976 was $174 billion. Again, it is important to emphasize that (1) these calculations are meant to be illustrative[32] and (2) without a better understanding of the nature of the liquidity constraints, the welfare implications of these calculations are unclear.

V. Conclusions

This paper develops and estimates a behavioral model of entrepreneurial choice under liquidity constraints. Several interesting results emerge. One can reject Schumpeter's view that capital markets allow a separation of the entrepreneurial and capitalist functions: Liquidity constraints bind. It is estimated that entrepreneurs are limited to a capital stock that is no more than about one and one-half times their wealth. As a result, almost all the entrepreneurs in our sample are estimated to devote less capital to their businesses than they would like to. Our findings are consistent with those of Fazzari, Hubbard,

---

[32] More accurate calculations would require integrating over the joint distribution of ability, assets, education, and experience.

826   JOURNAL OF POLITICAL ECONOMY

and Petersen (1987), who find evidence of significant capital market imperfections even for publicly traded manufacturing corporations.

We conclude with several words of caution and some suggestions for further research. Our results are based on a simple static model of entrepreneurship. Further work on entrepreneurial selection and asset accumulation over the life cycle would be useful. The estimates rely on a sample that is subject to several potential selection biases whose correction could alter our conclusions. Because of sample attrition and missing values, only about half of the initial sample was used in the estimation. An interesting extension would have only a fraction q of 1976 wage workers observing a self-employment opportunity, and then q could be estimated; currently q is assumed to be one. The model also relies on a simple formulation of the liquidity constraints. Estimating more general liquidity constraints in which income and demographic characteristics play a role would enrich our understanding of the role that liquidity constraints play in entrepreneurial choice.

References

Ando, Faith. *Access to Capital by Subcategories of Small Business.* Report prepared for the U.S. Small Business Administration. Fort Washington, Pa.: JACA Corp., December 1985.

Bendick, Marc, Jr., and Egan, Mary Lou. "Transfer Payment Diversion for Small Business Development: British and French Experience." *Indus. and Labor Relations Rev.* 40 (July 1987): 528–42.

Dunne, Timothy; Roberts, Mark; and Samuelson, Laurence. "Plant Failure and Employment Growth in the U.S. Manufacturing Sector." Manuscript. University Park: Pennsylvania State Univ., Dept. Econ., January 1987.

Evans, David S. "The Relationship between Firm Growth, Size, and Age: Estimates for 100 Manufacturing Industries." *J. Indus. Econ.* 35 (June 1987): 567–81. (*a*)

———. "Tests of Alternative Theories of Firm Growth." *J.P.E.* 95 (August 1987): 657–74. (*b*)

Evans, David S., and Leighton, Linda S. *Self-Employment Selection and Earnings over the Life Cycle.* Washington: Small Bus. Admin., December 1987.

———. "Some Empirical Aspects of Entrepreneurship." *A.E.R.* 79 (June 1989).

Fazzari, Steven; Hubbard, R. Glenn; and Petersen, Bruce C. "Financing Constraints and Corporate Investment." Working Paper no. 2387. Cambridge, Mass.: NBER, September 1987.

Ham, John C., and Melnik, Arie. "Loan Demand: An Empirical Analysis Using Micro Data." *Rev. Econ. and Statis.* 69 (November 1987): 704–9.

Johnson, William R. "A Theory of Job Shopping." *Q.J.E.* 92 (May 1978): 261–78.

Jovanovic, Boyan. "Job Matching and the Theory of Turnover." *J.P.E.* 87, no. 5, pt. 1 (October 1979): 972–90.

ENTREPRENEURIAL CHOICE 827

―――. "Selection and the Evolution of Industry." *Econometrica* 50 (May 1982): 649–70.

Kanbur, Steven M. "Of Risk Taking and the Personal Distribution of Income." *J.P.E.* 87 (August 1979): 769–97.

Kihlstrom, Richard E., and Laffont, Jean-Jacques. "A General Equilibrium Entrepreneurial Theory of Firm Formation Based on Risk Aversion." *J.P.E.* 87 (August 1979): 719–48.

Kirzner, Israel M. *Competition and Entrepreneurship.* Chicago: Univ. Chicago Press, 1973.

Knight, Frank H. *Risk, Uncertainty and Profit.* New York: Houghton Mifflin, 1921.

LeRoy, Stephen F., and Singell, Larry D., Jr. "Knight on Risk and Uncertainty." *J.P.E.* 95 (April 1987): 394–406.

Light, Ivan H. *Ethnic Enterprise in America: Business and Welfare among Chinese, Japanese, and Blacks.* Berkeley: Univ. California Press, 1972.

Lucas, Robert E., Jr. "On the Size Distribution of Business Firms." *Bell J. Econ.* 9 (Autumn 1978): 508–23.

Mariger, Randall P. "A Life-Cycle Consumption Model with Liquidity Constraints: Theory and Empirical Results." *Econometrica* 55 (May 1987): 533–57.

Miller, Robert A. "Job Matching and Occupational Choice." *J.P.E.* 92 (December 1984): 1086–1120.

Scherer, Frederic M. *Industrial Market Structure and Economic Performance.* 2d ed. Boston: Houghton Mifflin, 1980.

Schumpeter, Joseph A. *The Theory of Economic Development.* Cambridge, Mass.: Harvard Univ. Press, 1934.

―――. *Capitalism, Socialism, and Democracy.* 3d ed. New York: Harper and Row, 1950.

Stiglitz, Joseph E., and Weiss, Andrew. "Credit Rationing in Markets with Imperfect Information." *A.E.R.* 71 (June 1981): 393–410.

U.S. Department of Labor. *Self Employment Demonstration Project Request for Proposal RFP-DAA-88-23.* Washington: Employment and Training Admin., U.S. Dept. Labor, January 15, 1988.

[4]

Review of Economic Studies (2000) **67**, 147–168
© 2000 The Review of Economic Studies Limited

0034-6527/00/00080147$02.00

Enterprise, Inequality and Economic Development

HUW LLOYD-ELLIS
University of Toronto

and

DAN BERNHARDT
University of Illinois Urbana–Champaign

First version received November 1995; final version accepted February 1999 (Eds.)

We characterize an equilibrium development process driven by the interaction of the distribution of wealth with credit constraints and the distribution of entrepreneurial skills. When efficient entrepreneurs are relatively abundant, a "traditional" development process emerges in which the evolution of macroeconomic variables accord with empirical regularities and income inequality traces out a Kuznets curve. If, instead, efficient entrepreneurs are relatively scarce, the model generates long-run "distributional cycles" driven by the endogenous interaction between credit constraints, entrepreneurial efficiency and equilibrium wages.

1. INTRODUCTION

Research in developing economies typically identifies two key obstacles to the creation and expansion of small and medium sized enterprises: a lack of access to credit, especially to finance working capital, and a relative scarcity of entrepreneurial skills.[1] This paper characterizes an equilibrium development process driven by the interaction of the distribution of wealth with credit constraints and the distribution of entrepreneurial efficiency. When efficient entrepreneurs are relatively abundant, a "traditional" development process emerges (*e.g.* Lewis (1954) and Fei and Ranis (1966)), in which the evolution of macroeconomic variables accord with key empirical regularities and income inequality traces out a Kuznets curve. If, instead, efficient entrepreneurs are relatively scarce, our model generates long-run "distributional cycles" driven by the endogenous interaction between credit constraints, entrepreneurial efficiency and equilibrium wages.

Our model features single-period lived agents who value both consumption and bequests to their children. Individuals, who differ in both entrepreneurial efficiency and inherited wealth, choose whether to work as entrepreneurs, as wage labourers in industry or in subsistence agriculture. An entrepreneur uses his inherited wealth as collateral in return for a loan to pay for start-up costs and working capital. Potential moral hazard in debt repayment limits borrowing. He hires labour at the prevailing equilibrium wage, which he pays out of earned revenues, receiving the balance as profit.

Initially, few agents are efficient enough to become entrepreneurs and those who do operate on a small scale. With little competition for labour, the equilibrium wage is just sufficient to entice workers away from the rural sector. Over time, the distribution of

---

1. See Levy (1993) and Fidler and Webster (1996).

wealth grows in the *first-order stochastic sense*, permitting the extent and scale of entrepreneurial activity to expand, so that profits rise and income inequality worsens. When wages are low, even relatively inefficient projects are worth undertaking if sufficient capital can be employed—wealth rather than entrepreneurial efficiency is the primary determinant of economic activity. Consequently, even though entrepreneurial efficiency is uncorrelated across generations, wealth inequality persists.

Eventually, competition amongst entrepreneurs for workers bids up the equilibrium wage, so that profits eventually fall, and income and wealth inequality start to decline. At this point, the skewness of the efficiency distribution is crucial in determining whether growth continues unabated, or whether cycles appear as the economy matures. With decreasing returns to scale, past wage increases effectively transfer wealth from the rich with low marginal products to the poor with high marginal products, (the "productivity effect"). However, if entrepreneurial efficiency is skewed so that low cost entrepreneurs are scarce, then this transfer reduces the supply of entrepreneurs coming from the rich by more than it increases that coming from the poor (the "enterprise effect").

If the productivity effect dominates, the supply of entrepreneurs and their demand for labour still rise. Wages are bid up further, output expands and the distributions of wealth and income grow in the *second-order sense*. As wages rise, less efficient agents prefer to enter the labour force (though they could profitably become entrepreneurs) and production becomes increasingly efficient. Gradually, entrepreneurial efficiency replaces wealth as the primary determinant of occupational choice, so that wealth becomes less persistent along family lineages. This benchmark process matches several empirical regularities associated with development:

- Market-clearing wages remain low initially, but then rise monotonically;
- There is continuous rural–urban migration and increasing participation in manufacturing;[2]
- The labour share of GNP and of value-added in manufacturing rises with *per capita* GNP;[3]
- The capital–output ratio initially rises, but levels off and may decline as wages rise;[4]
- Average firm size grows and then declines. The dispersion in firm sizes also grows and then falls;
- Equilibrium growth rates are high in early stages, decline as workers leave the rural sector, then increase after all workers leave subsistence, before declining again as the economy matures;
- Income inequality rises in the Lorentz dominance sense during the early phases of development, then gradually falls as the economy matures.[5]

If, instead, the enterprise effect dominates, then the redistribution of inheritances caused by past wage increases actually causes the supply of entrepreneurs and their

2. Young (1993) finds that the recent rapid growth of East Asian NICs was largely due to the accumulation of capital and increased participation in the manufacturing sector rather than total factor productivity growth.

3. The prediction holds for a cross-section of countries (Lloyd-Ellis and Bernhardt (1998)) and for the industrial revolution in Europe (Mathias and Postan (1978)). Labour share of GNP also rose in the U.S. but labour share of manufacturing value-added has been constant for the last 100 years.

4. See Maddison (1989) and Kim and Lau (1994) for related evidence.

5. This Kuznets relationship holds for a cross-section of market economies (Paukert (1973), Ahluwalia (1976), Lydall (1979), Summers, Kravis and Heston (1984)). Although inequality declined in most developed countries during the twentieth century (Fields and Jakubsen (1994)), studies of the U.K. and U.S. that include nineteenth century data find support for Kuznets' hypothesis (*e.g.* Lindert and Williamson (1980)).

LLOYD-ELLIS & BERNHARDT   ENTERPRISE AND INEQUALITY 149

demand for labour to *decline*. Wages fall and aggregate output contracts. The resulting redistribution towards the rich increases the supply of entrepreneurs and their demand for labour, so that the economy's decline is reversed. The process continues in this fashion, generating endogenous "distributional cycles" in economic activity which persist into the long run. Wages evolve procyclically so that income inequality worsens during recessions and improves during economic booms.

Our model is most closely related to those of Banerjee and Newman (1993), and Aghion and Bolton (1997).[6] Both models feature one-period lived, risk-neutral agents who *ex ante* differ *only* in their inheritances but not their efficiency, and whose entrepreneurs face *ex post* production risk. Banerjee and Newman have the same moral hazard problem in credit markets as we do, and consider an environment in which entrepreneurs employ workers and capital in one of two exogenously-specified combinations. Their analysis focuses on how the long-run distribution of wealth is related to technology parameters: they find that because of the non-convexities in the feasible technology choices of entrepreneurs, the long-run distributions of wealth may depend on initial conditions. In Aghion and Bolton, agents either invest in a fixed-size, risky project, lending any remaining wealth or borrowing if necessary; or they earn a safe, low income and lend. Limited liability and the dependence of the success probability on non-contractable effort induces credit-rationing based on inherited wealth. Equilibrium between borrowers and lenders determines a market interest rate which, in contrast to ours, varies with the distribution of wealth. As wealth accumulates, demand for credit declines and supply rises, so that interest rates fall and, although it may initially rise, wealth inequality eventually falls. Neither model features a fully-specified labour market, *ex ante* differences in entrepreneurial efficiency or working capital, so they are silent with respect to the evolution of key macroeconomic aggregates.

A crucial distinction between our model and theirs is the timing of the revelation of information regarding entrepreneurial efficiency. In our economy, agents learn their potential efficiency *before* choosing occupations, and we abstract from *ex post* production risk.[7] This timing captures, to some extent, the feature that if there were multiple production periods within a lifetime, agents would condition actions on their revealed efficiency. As a result of this timing, both potential efficiency and inherited wealth affect agent decision-making—occupational choice, capital employed and labour hired—and consequently the paths of macroeconomic aggregates. The impacts of inherited wealth and efficiency are distinct and vary as the economy develops. While in initial stages, wealth is the primary determinant of occupation because wealthy agents can invest in capital and profitably exploit cheap labour on a grander scale; in later stages, entrepreneurial efficiency matters more both because fewer agents are wealth constrained and because higher wages reduce the profitability of large scale production. The consequence for the dynamics of income and wealth inequality is that they first rise and persist along family lineages, and then fall and are less persistent along lineages. If the efficiency distribution is skewed, the importance of entrepreneurial efficiency relative to wealth is cyclical; rising during booms and falling during recessions.

Section 2 of our paper lays out the economic environment and characterizes the periodic equilibrium of the economy. Section 3 details the mechanisms driving the economy through each phase of the development cycle and characterizes the movements of

---

6. Other related contributions to the literature include Greenwood and Jovanovic (1990), Galor and Zeira (1993) and Piketty (1997).

7. Production risk would play no real role if, as in Banerjee and Newman, it is bounded in such a way that default never occurs (see Lloyd-Ellis and Bernhardt (1998)). In contrast, production risk plays a central role in Aghion and Bolton because of the possibility of default.

key macroeconomic variables and the evolution of inequality over this cycle. Section 4 shows how a highly skewed distribution of entrepreneurial efficiency can lead to endogenous cycles. All proofs are in the Appendix.

2. THE MODEL

There are countably many times periods, $t = 0, 1, 2, \ldots$. The economy is populated by a continuum of family lineages of measure one. Each agent is active for one period, then reproduces one agent. An agent's endowment consists of a bequest inherited from his parent. Agents have identical preferences over consumption, C_t, and bequests to their children, B_{t+1}, represented by

$$u(C_t, B_{t+1}). \tag{1}$$

The utility function is homogeneous of degree one, strictly increasing in both arguments and strictly quasi-concave. The assumption that the preference is for the bequest itself, not for the offspring's utility, simplifies the analysis and captures the idea of a tradition for bequest-giving (see Andreoni (1989)). Homegeneity can be relaxed considerably without changing the results.

At time $t = 0$ a new production technology comes into existence. Entrepreneurs who pay the necessary start-up costs (discussed below), combine labour, l_t, and capital, k_t, to produce a single consumption good according to the common production function,

$$f(k_t, l_t). \tag{2}$$

The production function is strictly increasing in both arguments, strictly concave and quasi-homothetic. Capital and labour are complements and third-order derivatives are negligible, so the product function is well approximated by a second-order Taylor series expansion.

Agents are distinguished by two characteristics: their initial wealth inheritances, b, and their personal costs of undertaking a project, x. Project start-up costs are drawn from a time-invariant distribution, $H(x)$, with support $[0, 1]$ and a linear density

$$h(x) = mx + 1 - \frac{m}{2}, \tag{3}$$

where $m \in [-2, 2]$. Start-up costs reflects innate entrepreneurial efficiency and are uncorrelated with inherited wealth. Linearity can be relaxed considerably without changing our results.

Entrepreneurs can borrow to finance their investments. However, the capital market is limited by a moral hazard problem as in Sappington (1983) and Banerjee and Newman (1993). Specifically, there exists an alternative activity which yields a safe gross return of $r \geq 1$. Competition amongst lenders then drives the interest on loans down to r. Entrepreneurs can borrow L, but they must put up their inheritance b as collateral. After production they can abscond, losing rb, but escaping the repayment obligation, rL. If absconders are apprehended, which they are with probability p, they can hide their income from the authorities, but they receive a punishment which imposes on them an additive disutility of d. With homogeneous preferences, borrowers would renege if $\beta rb + pd < \beta rL$, where β is a positive preference parameter. Recognizing this, lenders only make loans that satisfy $L \leq b + \Delta$, where $\Delta = pd/\beta r$. The scale of the project is therefore limited by an agent's inheritance, start-up cost and the degree of market completeness summarized by Δ.

LLOYD-ELLIS & BERNHARDT   ENTERPRISE AND INEQUALITY 151

Given his type (b, x), each agent chooses his occupation taking the equilibrium wage and his own potential profits as given. If his inheritance is large enough, he can become an entrepreneur in the manufacturing sector. Both project set-up costs and productive capital employed must be financed out of bank loans. Alternatively, agents can work in the manufacturing sector at the prevailing equilibrium wage rate, w_t, and invest their inheritance in the alternative activity, earning rb. Finally, agents may prefer to remain in rural areas and receive the subsistence income, γ. The manufacturing sector is located in urban areas, where agents incur a cost of living equal to $v \geq 0$. With homogeneous preferences, one can interpret this cost as a disutility of labour incurred by entrepreneurs and workers, but not by subsisters.

The occupational choice of an agent of type (b, x) determines his lifetime income given the equilibrium obtaining that period, $y(b, x, w_t)$. His total lifetime wealth equals

$$W_t = W(b, x, \iota_t, w_t) = y(b, x, w_t) - \iota_t v + rb, \tag{4}$$

where $\iota_t = 1$ if the agent lives in an urban area and $\iota_t = 0$ otherwise.

2.1. *Optimal behaviour*

An agent with wealth W_t maximizes $u(C_t, B_{t+1})$ subject to $C_t + B_{t+1} = W_t$, yielding optimal linear consumption and bequest policies, $C(W_t)$ and $B(W_t)$. We assume that the pre-industrial economy has reached a steady state with constant bequests defined by $b^0 = B(\gamma + rb^0)$.

Agents who are efficient enough become entrepreneurs. Wages are paid out of end-of-period revenues. After paying the start-up cost, x, an entrepreneur chooses capital to maximize profits subject to the constraint that capital must be financed out of the remainder of his loan, $b + \Delta - x$. Thus, the net profits earned by a type (b, x) entrepreneur equal

$$\pi(b, x, w_t) = \max_{k_t, l_t} \{ f(k_t, l_t) - w_t l_t - r(k_t + x) \text{ s.t. } 0 \leq k_t \leq b + \Delta - x \}. \tag{5}$$

Profit maximization yields capital and labour demand functions, $k(b, x, w_t) \leq k^u(w_t)$ and $l(b, x, w_t) \leq l^u(w_t)$, where u denotes unconstrained levels.[8] We assume that most agents are initially borrowing constrained, *i.e.* $\Delta < k^u(\underline{w}) + x^* - b^0$, where x^* is sufficiently small, and $\underline{W} = \gamma + v$ is the reservation wage below which potential workers prefer to remain in subsistence.

For an agent with inherited wealth b to undertake a project, he must draw a start-up cost that is less than $b + \Delta$. Even if such an agent can afford to become an entrepreneur there may still exist a marginal set-up cost level, $x^m(b, w_t)$, defined implicitly by $\pi(b, x^m, w_t) = w_t$, at which the agent would be indifferent between working and becoming an entrepreneur. We assume that $\pi(b^0, \underline{x}, \underline{w}) > \underline{w}$ so that some projects are always undertaken.[9] The start-up cost of an agent with inherited wealth b who is just willing and able to undertake a project at time t is given by

$$z(b, w_t) = \min [b + \Delta, x^m(b, w_t)]. \tag{6}$$

Lemma 1. $z(b, w)$ *is increasing and also concave in b, decreasing in w and* $\lim_{b \to \infty} z_b(b, w) = 0$.

---

8. The assumption of quasi-homotheticity implies that the demand for labour by a constrained entrepreneur increases linearly with firm size.

9. This condition is sufficient for the limiting distribution to be ergodic.

2.2. *Macroeconomic equilibrium*

Let $G_t(\cdot)$ denote the time t distribution of inheritances. Then, integrating the optimal decisions of agents over their types, (b, x), yields the following aggregates:

Enterprise: $\quad E_t(w_t) \quad = \int H(z(b, w_t))G_t(db);$ (7)

Start-up costs: $\quad X_t(w_t) \quad = \int \int_0^{z(b,w_t)} x H(dx)G_t(db);$ (8)

Labour force: $\quad L_t(w_t) \quad = \int \int_0^{z(b,w_t)} l(b, x, w_t)H(dx)G_t(db);$ (9)

Capital invested: $\quad K_t(w_t) = \int \int_0^{z(b,w_t)} k(b, x, w_t)H(dx)G_t(db);$ (10)

Output: $\quad Q_t(w_t) \quad = \int \int_0^{z(b,w_t)} f(k(b, x, w_t), l(b, x, w_t))H(dx)G_t(db);$ (11)

Net income: $\quad Y_t(w_t) \quad = \int \left(\int_0^{z(b,w_t)} \pi(b, x, w_t)H(dx) \right) G_t(db) + w_t L_t(w_t).$ (12)

Aggregate subsistence is given by $S_t(w_t) = 1 - E_t(w_t) - L_t(w_t)$. These aggregates are time-varying functions of the wage because they also depend on the distribution of inherited wealth.

A *competitive equilibrium* for an economy with inheritance distribution $G_t(\cdot)$ is a tuple $\{w_t^e, E_t^e, L_t^e, S_t^e\}$ such that:

- Given the wage w_t^e, an agent of type (b, x) selects his occupation to maximize utility;
- Type (b, x) entrepreneurs choose capital and labour to maximize profits subject to $k \leq b + \Delta - x$;
- Markets clear: $E_t^e(w_t^e) + L_t^e(w_t^e) + S_t^e(w_t^e) = 1$, where $S_t^e(w_t^e) = 0$ if $w_t^e > \underline{w}$.

Two kinds of equilibria can arise. In a *dual economy* equilibrium, the supply of entrepreneurs and their labour is insufficient to draw all agents out of subsistence and the wage settles at its reservation level, $\underline{w}$. In an *advanced economy* equilibrium the supply of entrepreneurs and their labour demand are high enough that the surplus labour is exhausted and the wage is bid up above $\underline{w}$. The following lemma is useful for understanding how the economy evolves in such an equilibrium:

Lemma 2. *Aggregate income, Y_t, is equal to the area below the upper envelope generated by the supply and demand curves for labour.*

At time t, a fraction $S_t^e/G_t(b^0)$ of agents that inherit b^0 remain in subsistence. A proportion $z(b, w_t)$ of agents with inheritance b realize a low enough start-up cost, $x < z(b, w_t)$, to undertake their projects. Let $\bar{x}(y^*, b, w_t)$ be the value of x such that $\pi(b, x, w_t) = y^*$. Then the distribution of income conditional on inherited wealth and the

LLOYD-ELLIS & BERNHARDT   ENTERPRISE AND INEQUALITY 153

equilibrium obtaining at time t can be represented by the cumulative distribution function

$$\Phi(y|b, w_t) = \begin{cases} 0, & \text{if } y < \gamma \text{ or } y < w_t, b > b^0, \\ S_t/G_t(b^0), & \text{if } \gamma \leq y < w_t, b = b^0, \\ 1 - H(z(b, w_t)), & \text{if } w_t \leq y < \underline{\pi}(b, w_t), \\ 1 - H(\tilde{x}(y, b, w_t)), & \text{if } \underline{\pi}(b, w_t) \leq y \leq \bar{\pi}(b, w_t), \\ 1, & \text{otherwise.} \end{cases} \tag{13}$$

Here $\underline{\pi}(b, w_t) = \max[w_t, \pi(b, b + \Delta, w_t)]$ is the lower support on profits and $\bar{\pi}(b, w_t) = \pi(b, \underline{x}, w_t)$ is the upper support. The unconditional distribution of incomes is therefore $\Phi_t(y) = \int \Phi(y|b, w_t)G_t(db)$.

An agent's final wealth is simply the sum of the return on his inheritance and his lifetime income, net of any urban living costs. An agent of type (b_t, x_t) bequests $b_{t+1} = B(y(b_t, x_t, w_t) - \iota_t v + rb_t)$. Note that an agent's inheritance depends not only on his parent's inheritance and cost realization, but also on the past distribution of wealth via its effect on the equilibrium wage. The distribution of wealth evolves according to an endogenous non-stationary probability transition function, so the unconditional distribution of bequests is

$$G_{t+1}(b') = \int P(b'|b, w_t)G_t(db), \tag{14}$$

where $P(b'|b, w_t) = \Phi(B^{-1}(b') + \iota_t v - rb|b, w_t)$.

A firm's "size" corresponds to the amount of capital it employs. The distribution of firm size conditional on inherited wealth b is

$$J(k|b, w_t) = \begin{cases} 0, & \text{if } b > \hat{b}(w_t), k < k^u(w_t), \\ \dfrac{H(z(b, w_t)) - H(b + \Delta - k)}{H(z(b, w_t))}, & \text{if } b < \hat{b}(w_t), k < k^u(w_t), \\ 1, & \text{otherwise,} \end{cases} \tag{15}$$

where $\hat{b}(w_t)$ is the inheritance level such that all wealthier entrepreneurs are unconstrained. Thus, the time t distribution of firm sizes is $J_t(k) = \int J(k|b, w_t)G_t(db)$.

3. A LEWIS–KUZNETS DEVELOPMENT PROCESS

In this section we detail the dynamic evolution of the economy when entrepreneurial ability is uniformly distributed ($m = 0$). The results hold more generally as long as the distribution is not too skewed towards high start-up costs (*i.e.* m is not too large). The implications of more skewed distributions for the development process are discussed in Section 4.

3.1. *The phases of economic development*

Proposition 1. *Following the time $t = 0$ introduction of a new production technology to the long-run pre-industrial economy, the economy passes through four distinct phases of development:*

Phase 1 (*The Dual Economy*, $0 \le t < \tau_1$): *Wages remain at $\underline{w}$. Incomes and wealths grow in the first-order stochastic sense.*

Phase 2 (*The Transition*, $\tau_1 \le t < \tau_2$): *Wages begin to rise, but incomes and wealths continue to grow in the first-order stochastic sense.*

Phase 3 (*Advanced Economic Development*, $t > \tau_2$): *Wages rise, and incomes and wealths grow in the second-order stochastic sense.*

Phase 4 (*Long Run*): *Wages converge and the distributions of incomes and wealths converge to unique limiting distributions, $\Phi^*(\cdot)$ and $G^*(\cdot)$, which are independent of the initial distribution.*

At $t = 0$, agents with sufficiently low start-up costs migrate to urban areas to become entrepreneurs. They employ additional agents at the prevailing wage. If b^0 is sufficiently low, a dual economy equilibrium obtains: Surplus labour remains in the rural sector earning the subsistence income, γ, and the equilibrium wage settles at $\underline{w}$. At the end of their lives, workers and farmers bequeath b^0. However, entrepreneurs bequeath more than b^0, so that the distribution of inheritances at $t = 1$, $G_1(\cdot)$, dominates $G_0(\cdot)$ in the first-order stochastic sense.

The stochastic increase in wealth encourages more generation $t = 1$ agents to engage in entrepreneurial activities and on a greater scale. The associated increase in labour demand draws migrants from the rural sector, output rises and the distribution of income at $t = 1$, dominates that at $t = 0$ in the first-order stochastic sense. Although most agents still receive $\underline{w}$ or less, entrepreneurial profits increase in the first-order stochastic sense. The development process continues in this fashion as long as there is surplus labour in the economy and the wage remains at $\underline{w}$.

Eventually, the supply of subsistence labour is exhausted. At some date τ_1, an advanced economy equilibrium obtains: increased competition for workers by entrepreneurs bids the wage rate above $\underline{w}$.[10] Although wages rise, profits may still rise due to the relaxation of financing constraints. So long as the bequests of the richest lineages do not decline, the distribution of inheritances continues to grow in the first-order stochastic sense for several periods after τ_1. During this transitional phase, labour demand rises and supply declines, so that both wage and aggregate income rise. However, with strict concavity in production, the largest entrepreneurs eventually achieve the optimal scale so their incomes start to decline. Eventually, this declining income offsets the rising lineage wealth, so that at some time $\tau^2 \ge \tau^1$, $\bar{b}_{\tau^2+1} > \bar{b}_{\tau^2}$, and the next phase of development begins.

To understand how the economy evolves in the advanced phase, suppose the distribution of inheritances at date $t \ge \tau^2$, $G_t(\cdot)$, dominates $G_{t-1}(\cdot)$ in the second-order stochastic sense. Since the production function is strictly concave and quasi-homothetic, a unit transfer of wealth from rich to poor entrepreneurs raises labour demand. Although some high cost projects become undesirable, the uniform distribution of entrepreneurial efficiencies ensures that the redistribution of wealth does not reduce the supply of entrepreneurs. Hence, the equilibrium wage and aggregate incomes rise.

The children of entrepreneurs are more likely to be entrepreneurs themselves, but receive lower profits than their parents. Conversely, the children of workers are predominantly workers and experience an increase in income. As a result, the distribution of income evolves in the manner illustrated in Figure 1. Formally, there exists a y^* such that

---

10. A sufficient condition for $\tau_1 < \infty$, is given in the Appendix in Lemma A4.

LLOYD-ELLIS & BERNHARDT   ENTERPRISE AND INEQUALITY 155

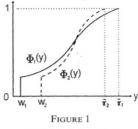

FIGURE 1

Declining *X*-dispersion

$0 < \Phi_t(y^*) < 1$ and $0 < \Phi_{t-1}(y^*) < 1$ and

$$\Phi_t(y) \geq \Phi_{t-1}(y) \quad \forall y < y^*,$$
$$\Phi_t(y) \leq \Phi_{t-1}(y) \quad \forall y \geq y^*,$$ (16)

where the inequality is strict on an interval of positive measure. We say that distribution $\Phi_t(\cdot)$ is more *X-Dispersed* than distribution $\Phi_{t-1}(\cdot)$.

Since average income also increases, the distribution of income must grow in the second-order stochastic sense. Similar results hold for wealth so that the distribution of inheritances, $G_{t+1}(\cdot)$, dominates $G_t(\cdot)$ in the second-order stochastic dominance, the result follows by induction from period $t = \tau^2$.

The economy cannot grow without bound. In particular, there exists an efficient state in which all agents who wish to become entrepreneurs can do so at the unconstrained optimum scale given the equilibrium wage rate. The associated market clearing condition, $[1 + l''(\bar{w})]x'''(\bar{w}) = 1$, implicitly defines an upper bound for the equilibrium wage, $\bar{w}$. Since the wage increases monotonically with time and is bounded, it must converge to some long-run value $w^* \in [\underline{w}, \bar{w}]$. It follows that the transitional dynamics governing the distribution of wealth converge to a stationary Markov process, $P(\cdot | b, w^*)$. This process satisfies the Monotone Mixing Condition (Hopenhayn and Prescott (1992)), so that the distributions of wealth and income converge to unique limiting distributions.

The limiting distributions are non-degenerate: wealth disparities continue to exist, *but do not persist forever between lineages.* Since the limiting distributions are independent of the initial distribution of inheritances, $G_0(\cdot)$, economies that start out with more unequal distributions, while they may not follow the same cycle of development, will end up with the same long-run distribution.

If the share of wealth bequeathed is sufficiently high, then the efficient state is eventually reached. In this case, the conditional distribution of income is independent of inherited wealth: $\Phi(y | b, \bar{w}) = \Phi(y | \bar{w})$, $\forall b$, and inequality is low because the wage is at its highest possible level, $\bar{w}$. If the share of wealth bequeathed is very low, the economy never achieves enough momentum to leave the dual economy phase (*i.e.* $\tau^1 = \infty$). Consequently, the wage remains at $\underline{w}$, production is inefficient because most entrepreneurs are constrained, wealth and income inequality remain very high and even though the economy satisfies the mixing condition, wealth is very persistent along lineages.

3.2. *The macrodynamics of development*

We now detail the evolution of key macroeconomic variables over the economy's development cycle. We illustrate the results using the following specifications for preferences and technology

$$u(C_t, B_{t+1}) = C_t^{1-\omega} B_{t+1}^{\omega}, \tag{17}$$

$$f(k_t, l_t) = \alpha k_t - \beta k_t^2 + \xi l_t - \rho l_t^2 + \sigma l_t k_t. \tag{18}$$

To emphasize the robustness of the results, we allow for some skewness in the distribution of start-up costs (*i.e.* $m > 0$). Figure 2 illustrates the time paths for key aggregate variables.[11]

Growth rates of wages and aggregate income are non-monotonic. After leaving the dual economy phase, wage growth first accelerates because, with decreasing returns to scale, the demand for labour from low wealth entrepreneurs expands more rapidly than the reduction in demand from high wealth entrepreneurs. In general, the growth rate in aggregate income first rises then declines gradually in the dual phase, rises again when the wage starts to increase, and then declines as the economy develops further. The first growth spurt occurs because as some lineages become wealthy, the supply of entrepreneurs increases rapidly, offsetting the decline in the marginal return to wealth. The growth rate then declines as agents become less constrained and the marginal return to their wealth falls. Output growth rises again when wages rise due to the effective redistribution of wealth towards poorer agents who are more productive on the margin. As the economy develops further, because there is no engine for long-run growth, wage increases decline and growth rates fall.

Proposition 2 (Occupations). *During the dual phase the rate of enterprise, $E_t(\underline{w})$ and labour force participation, $L_t(\underline{w})$, grow over time. There exists a $\theta > |f_{kl}^2/f_{kk}|$ such that if the slope of the marginal product curve for labour is sufficiently small, $|f_{ll}| < \theta$, then during later phases the rate of enterprise, $E_t(w_t)$, still increases but wage labouring, $L_t(w_t)$, declines.*

We have already described the mechanism driving the increase in enterprise and labour force participation in the early phases of the cycle. In the advanced phase, second-order stochastic growth is sufficient to cause labour supply to fall and labour demand to rise. In general, whether the equilibrium number of labourers rises or falls depends on the wage elasticities of supply and demand. If the wage elasticity of demand is sufficiently high ($|f_{ll}|$ sufficiently small), then the number of entrepreneurs increases over time.[12]

Proposition 3 (Factor Shares). *There exists a $\delta > 0$ and a $\theta > |f_{kl}^2/f_{kk}|$ such that if the optimal firm-level demand for labour is sufficiently great, $l(\underline{w}) > \delta$, and the slope of the marginal product of labour curve is sufficiently small, $|f_{ll}| < \theta$, then the labour share of value-added in manufacturing rises monotonically throughout the development cycle.*

During the dual phase, the manufacturing labour force expands and the wage is constant. If the wage elasticities of supply and demand are high enough (*e.g.* when the sufficient conditions on primitives in Proposition 3 hold), then the labour share of value-added rises as the manufacturing sector expands. In the advanced phase, when the equilibrium labour force may decline, continued growth in the labour share requires that the equilibrium wage, w_t, rises sufficiently rapidly relative to aggregate income, Y_t. Again, if

11. Parameter values are $m = 0.5, \omega = 0.2, \gamma = 0.12, v = 0.08, \alpha = 1.1, \beta = 50, \xi = 3.2, \rho = 0.5, \sigma = 4, r = 1, b^0 = 0.03, \Delta = 0.01$. The numerical example tracks the entire distribution of wealth on a discretized support. The associated code is available from the authors.

12. The qualitative implications for the wage rate, aggregate income and inequality do not depend on this elasticity.

LLOYD-ELLIS & BERNHARDT   ENTERPRISE AND INEQUALITY 157

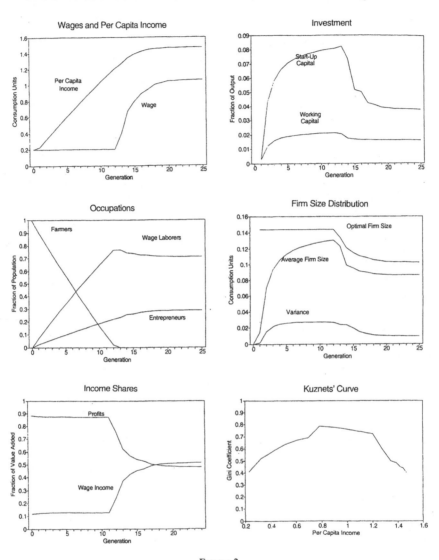

FIGURE 2

The macrodynamics of development

the wage elasticities of labour demand and supply are sufficiently high, the increments to aggregate profits are always proportionately less than the increments in the aggregate wage bill.

Proposition 4 (Investment). *During the early phases both aggregate working capital, K_t, and aggregate start-up capital, X_t, grow monotonically. However, during the advanced phase these variables may evolve non-monotonically.*

In the dual phase, first-order stochastic growth in wealth causes both aggregate working capital, $K_t(w_t)$, and aggregate start-up costs, $X_t(w_t)$, to grow. Later in the development cycle, the time paths of these aggregates depend on the net effect of two opposing forces: the second-order stochastic increase in inheritances causes the demand for start-up and working capital to rise for a given wage, however, the rising wage induces less efficient agents to become workers, causing the equilibrium level of capital to fall. If the wage elasticity of demand for capital is high enough,[13] then the aggregate working capital stock falls (see Figure 2). Similarly, aggregate start-up costs, $X_t(\cdot)$, decline as long as the wage elasticity of the supply of entrepreneurs is sufficiently high.

Proposition 5. *The distribution of firm sizes, $J_t(\cdot)$, becomes increasingly X-Dispersed during phases 1 and 2, before becoming gradually less X-Dispersed in the advanced phase.*

During the dual phase, the wealth of agents drawing a particular cost level, stochastically increases with each generation. Hence, the level of capital employed by them (firm size) also stochastically increases. Although during later phases, the rising wage implies that average firm size eventually falls, the dispersion of firm sizes evolves in a way similar to that of incomes and wealths. Figure 2 depicts the time paths of the average and variance of firm sizes for the parameterized economy. Recall that the rate of enterprise, E_t, increases throughout the process, but that the aggregate capital stock first falls and then rises during the advanced stages. The evolution of the average firm size reflects this. The variance rises, reaching a peak during the dual stage and then declining throughout the advanced stage. If maximum efficiency is attained, the variance falls to zero because all entrepreneurs produce at the optimal scale, $k''(\bar{w})$. Otherwise, the limiting distribution of firm sizes is non-degenerate and the variance converges to a positive value.

Proposition 6 (The Lorentz Curve).

(a) *There exists a time period $t^* < \tau^1$, such that for all $t < t^*$, income inequality increases in the Lorentz dominance sense.*

(b) *There exists a $\delta > 0$ and a $\theta > |f_{kl}^2/f_{kk}|$ such that if the optimal firm level demand for labour is sufficiently great, $l''(\bar{w}) > \delta$ and the slope of the marginal product of labour curve is sufficiently small, $|f_{ll}| < \theta$, then for all $t > \tau^2$, income inequality declines in the Lorentz dominance sense.*

The first panel of Figure 3 depicts a typical Lorentz curve, $Z_t(p)$, during the dual stage of development.[14] The linear segment OA corresponds to the traditional sector, the linear segment AB corresponds to wage labourers and the convex segment BC corresponds to entrepreneurs. Inequality increases in the *Lorentz dominance* sense if the entire Lorentz curve shifts to the right (*i.e.* the curve shifts from $OABC$ to $OA'B'C$). Sufficient conditions are that (1) the growth rate in *per capita* income exceeds the growth rate in the income of migrating agents; and, (2) the largest entrepreneur's profit, $\pi_t(\bar{b}_t, \underline{x}, \underline{w})$, increases faster than mean income, Y_t. Both conditions are trivially true in the first period and hold subsequently as long as the marginal product of capital is sufficiently high and $\underline{w}$ is sufficiently low.

---

13. That is, if labour and capital are sufficiently strong complements, the supply of entrepreneurs is sufficiently wage elastic and the fraction of constrained entrepreneurs is small enough.

14. The Lorentz curve is $Z_t(p) = 1/Y_t \int_0^{\hat{y}_t(p)} y\Phi(dy)$, where $\Phi_t(\hat{y}_t) = p$. Our analysis here is influenced by Bourguignon (1990).

LLOYD-ELLIS & BERNHARDT   ENTERPRISE AND INEQUALITY 159

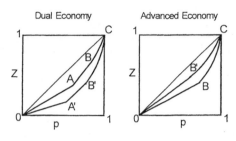

FIGURE 3

Evolution of Lorenz curves

During the advanced stages of economic development, the Lorentz curve no longer includes the segment corresponding to the traditional sector. The maximum income in the economy falls and the mean rises, so the slope at C declines. For inequality to decline unambiguously, the wage must grow more quickly than *per capita* income. This will be the case if the elasticities of the demand for, and supply of, labour are sufficiently large (*i.e.* the sufficient conditions in Proposition 6(b) apply), because this ensures that a wage increase has a large negative impact on aggregate profits. Figure 3 illustrates the implied relationship betwen the Gini coefficient[15] and *per capita* income.

A key factor driving these development dynamics is that an agent's ability to borrow is limited by his inherited wealth. As the value of Δ is increased (see Figure 4), the development cycle occurs more rapidly, but its nature remains much the same. Income inequality rises to a high value much more rapidly before declining. As the borrowing constraint is relaxed further the economy reaches the efficient state. For $\Delta \geq k''(w) + \bar{x} - b^0$, the economy jumps immediately to the efficient state and the degree of income inequality reflects only variations in entrepreneurial efficiency.

4. ECONOMIC DEVELOPMENT WHEN EFFICIENT ENTREPRENEURS ARE SCARCE

A key problem facing developing economies is the relative scarcity of high skilled entrepreneurs. As Fidler and Webster (p. 25, 1996) point out "Poorly developed business skills

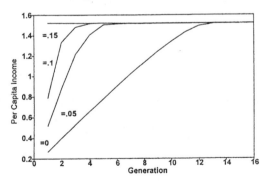

FIGURE 4

Relaxing the collateral requirement

15. Twice the area between the Lorenz curve and the 45° line.

are a binding constraint to enterprise growth, even more than lack of access to credit in many cases. Entrepreneurs' complaints about lack of access to credit often mask technical and managerial inadequacies ...". This section considers the implications for the development process when we incorporate the feature that efficient entrepreneurs are a relatively scarce resource—*i.e.* the distribution of entrepreneurial efficiency is skewed towards high cost entrepreneurs: $m > 0$.

During the dual-economy phase, the qualitative nature of our results are independent of the shape of the distribution of entrepreneurial efficiency. However, in later phases, when the wage rate is endogenous, the nature of the development path is sensitive to the skewness of this distribution:

If the distribution of entrepreneurial efficiency is sufficiently skewed towards high cost projects, then the economy exhibits endogenous long-run cycles in production. Wages evolve pro-cyclically so that income inequality falls during booms and rises during recessions.

To understand the mechanism driving this result, consider the special case where no working capital is used in production and the skill density is highly skewed ($m = 2$). Then the relationship between the rate of enterprise and wealth for any given wage w is

$$\psi(b, w) = H(z(b, w)) = \min [b^2, x_m^2(w)]. \tag{19}$$

Consider two wealth levels b^l and b^h and the agents who inherit them (see Figure 5). If $b^l < x_m(w) < b^h$, then a unit transfer of wealth from the rich agents to the poor agents unambiguously increases the supply of entrepreneurs. If, however, $b^l < b^h < x_m(w)$ (*i.e.* both wealth levels lie on the convex segment) then such a transfer decreases the supply of entrepreneurs from the high wealth group by more than it increases the supply from the low wealth group.

Past wage increases result in many such transfers from rich to poor agents. If the support of the distribution of inheritances is such that the measure of agents with wealth greater than $x_m(w)$ is small and if the increase in mean inheritance is sufficiently small, then a second-order stochastic increase in the distribution of inherited wealth, can cause the aggregate supply of entrepreneurs at the wage w, to *decline*. If this is the case at each and every wage, the supply curve for labour must shift inward.

With no capital in production and $m = 2$, the demand for labour from entrepreneurs with wealth b is proportional to the supply of entrepreneurs:

$$\lambda(b, w) = l(w) \min [b^2, x_m^2(w)]. \tag{20}$$

Hence, a second-order stochastic increase in the distribution of wealth reduces the aggregate demand for labour at each wage. From Lemma 2, both the wage and aggregate income must decline in equilibrium as a consequence of this "enterprise effect".

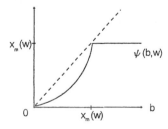

FIGURE 5

Occupational choice with a skewed distribution of skills

LLOYD-ELLIS & BERNHARDT   ENTERPRISE AND INEQUALITY   161

As the wage falls, wealth starts to be redistributed away from poorer lineages and back towards richer lineages. By a converse argument to that given above, this causes an increase in the supply of entrepreneurs and an increase in their demand for labour, even if the inheritances fall slightly. By Lemma 2, the equilibrium wage and aggregate income rise and the economy's decline is reversed. As wages rise, wealth is redistributed towards the centre and the process begins all over again.

When the production function exhibits decreasing returns to working capital, the wealth transfer due to rising wages in the past represents a transfer from agents with low marginal products to those with high marginal products. This "productivity effect" tends to increase the supply of entrepreneurs and the demand for labour. However, so long as the enterprise effect dominates, which it will if m is large enough, the redistribution of wealth resulting from past wage increases can still cause a decline in the equilibrium wage and reduce aggregate income. The economy continues to evolve in this fashion so that the long run path exhibits recurrent "distributional cycles" in economic activity.

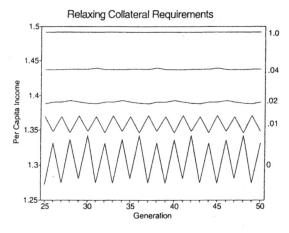

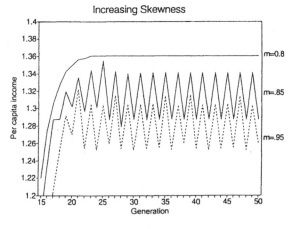

FIGURE 6

Endogenous cycles

These cycles are intimately related to the interaction between capital market imperfections, the skewness of the distribution of entrepreneurial efficiency and the labour market equilibrium. As m is increased, so that relatively efficient entrepreneurs become increasingly scarce, the economy moves from no cycles, to cycles of gradually increasing amplitude relative to the mean. Eventually, efficient entrepreneurs become so scarce that the economy cannot escape from the first development phase. Relaxing the borrowing constraints (*i.e.* raising Δ, holding m constant) causes the cycles to decline and eventually disappear.

Thus, both the severity of capital market imperfections and the skewness of entrepreneurial efficiency offer a potential explanation for differences in the amplitude and persistence of long-run cycles across economies. Moreover, these factors may help us to understand differences in the long run variability of factor shares and income inequality across economies. For example, as Blanchard (1997) documents, factor shares have been more variable in European than in Anglo-Saxon economies (the U.S., the U.K. and Canada); one potential explanation is that credit-market imperfections are more severe in Europe. Cross-country evidence on cyclical movements in income inequality is mixed (Deninger and Squire (1996)). However, Beach (1976) finds that U.S. Income inequality tends to fall during booms and rise during recessions.

5. CONCLUDING REMARKS

In the model described here, the distribution of entrepreneurial efficiency is time invariant so the only source of economic growth comes from the reduced importance of borrowing constraints as agents accumulate wealth. If the distribution of start-up costs were to improve over time, this would reinforce the results of Section 3. As Figure 6 suggests, in the long-run cyclical economy, an improving distribution of skills would eventually eliminate the cycles.

Our analysis could be extended in several directions. The impacts of the shocks of the mid-1970s varied considerably across economies according to their stage of development. Some economies have yet to recover to their 1973 levels of *per capita* income and many have experienced large increases in inequality. When such shocks are incorporated into our model, the time taken to recover depends crucially on the interaction between the distribution of entrepreneurial efficiency and the extent of credit market imperfections. Relatedly, the recent financial crisis in Asia can be represented by an increase in potential entrepreneurial moral hazard leading to a decline in the ratio of lending to wealth. Our model can be used to trace out the consequences. Models such as that described here can also be used to study and evaluate the impacts of macroeconomic policy. Townsend (1997) argues that such models are crucial to the systematic formation of development policies.

APPENDIX

Lemma A1. *For constrained firms:* $k_b(b, x, w) = -k_x(b, x, w) = 1$, $l_h(b, x, w) = -l_x(b, x, w) = -(f_{kl}/f_{ll})$, $k_w(b, x, w) = 0$, $l_w(b, x, w) = 1/f_{ll}$. *For unconstrained firms* $k_b(b, x, w) = k_x(b, x, w) = l_b(b, x, w) = l_x(b, x, w) = 0$, $k_w(b, x, w) = -f_{kl}/(f_{kk}f_{ll} - f_{kl}^2) < 0$, $l_w(b, x, w) = f_{kk}/(f_{kk}f_{ll} - f_{kl}^2) < 0$.

Lemma A2. $\pi_b(\cdot) = f_k - r \geqq 0$; $\pi_x(\cdot) = -f_k \lessgtr -r$; $\pi_w(\cdot) = -l(b, x, w) < 0$.

Lemma A3. *Let $\tilde{x}$ be implicitly defined by $\pi(b, \tilde{x}, w) = y$. Total differentiation reveals that $\tilde{x}_y < 0$, $\tilde{x}_b \geqq 0$, $\tilde{x}_w < 0$. Also $\tilde{x}_{yy} = \tilde{x}_{bb} = \tilde{x}_{yb} < 0$, $\tilde{x}_{bw} = \tilde{x}_{yw} < 0$ and $\tilde{x}_{ybb} > 0$.*

LLOYD-ELLIS & BERNHARDT   ENTERPRISE AND INEQUALITY 163

Proof of Lemma 1. Let $\bar{b}(w_t)$ denote the inheritance below which the marginal entrepreneur is constrained on the extensive margin, so that $x'''(\bar{b}, w_t) = \bar{b} + \Delta$. Let $\hat{b}(w_t)$ denote the inheritance level above which marginal entrepreneurs are unconstrained, so that $x'''(\hat{b}, w_t) = \hat{x}'''(w_t)$. Then if

$$b \in [0, \bar{b}(w_t)]: z_w(b, w_t) = 0, \qquad z_b(b, w_t) = 1, \qquad z_{bb} = 0;$$

$$b \in [\bar{b}(w_t), \hat{b}(w_t)]: z_w(b, w_t) = -\frac{1 + l(b, z(b, w_t), w_t)}{f_k} < 0, \quad z_b(b, w_t) = \frac{f_k - r}{f_k} > 0, \quad z_{bb} = \frac{f_{kk}f_{ll} - f_{kl}^2}{f_{ll}f_k^3} < 0;$$

$$b \in [\hat{b}(w_t), \infty): z_w(b, w_t) = -(1 + l''(w_t)), \qquad z_b(b, w_t) = z_{bb} = 0.$$

Since $z_b(b, w) = 0$ for all $\underline{b} > \hat{b}(w)$, it follows that $\lim_{b \to \infty} z_b(b, w) = 0$. ||

Proof of Lemma 2. Aggregate income is given in (12). This can be written as

$$Y_t(w_t) = \int_b \int_{w_t}^{\infty} \left[-\int_0^{z(b,w)} \pi_w(b, x, w)H(dx) - wh(z)z_w(b, w) \right] dwG_t(db) + w_t L_t(w_t). \tag{A1}$$

From Lemma A2, $\pi_w(b, x, w) = -l(b, x, w)$, so that this can be reduced to

$$Y_t(w_t) = \int_b \int_{w_t}^{\infty} \left[\int_0^{z(b,w)} l(b, x, w)H(dx) - wh(z)z_w(b, w) \right] dwG_t(db) + w_t L_t(w_t). \tag{A2}$$

But $(d/dw)[wH(z(b, w))] = wh(z)z_w(b, w) + Hz(b, w))$, and so

$$Y_t(w_t) = \int_b \int_{w_t}^{\infty} \left(\int_0^{z(b,w)} [1 + l(b, x, w)]H(dx) \right.$$

$$\left. - \frac{d}{dw}[wH(z(b, w))] \right) dwG_t(db) + w_t L_t(w_t). \tag{A3}$$

However,

$$-\int_{w_t}^{\infty} \frac{d[wH(z(b, w))]}{dw} dw = w_t H(z(b, w_t)),$$

and so

$$Y_t(w_t) = \int_b \int_{w_t}^{\infty} \int_0^{z(b,w)} [1 + l(b, x, w)]H(dx)dwG_t(db) + w_t E_t(w_t) + w_t L_t(w_t), \tag{A4}$$

which is the area under the upper envelope created by the supply and demand curves. ||

Theorem 1 (Hadar and Russell (1971)). *Let* $M_t = \int \mu(b)G_t(db)$, *where* $\mu_b(b) \geq 0, \forall b$; $\mu_b(b) > 0$ *on an interval. If* $G_t(b)$ *FSD (first-order stochastically dominates)* $G_{t-1}(b)$ *then* $M_t > M_{t-1}$.

Theorem 2 (Hadar and Russell (1971)). *Let* $M_t = \int \mu(b)G_t(db)$, *where* $\mu_{bb}(b) \leq 0$, $\mu_{bb}(b) < 0$ *for some b and* $\lim_{b \to \infty} \mu_b(b) = 0$. *If* $G_t(\cdot)$ *SSD (second-order stochastically dominates)* $G_{t-1}(\cdot)$ *then* $M_t > M_{t-1}$.

Lemma A4. *Suppose that the increase in the urban population between time* $t = 0$ *and* $t = 1$ *is sufficient to absorb all immigrant entrepreneurs,*

$$E_1(\underline{w}) + L_1(\underline{w}) - E_0(\underline{w}) - L_0(\underline{w}) > E_0(\underline{w})(1 - E_0(\underline{w})). \tag{A5}$$

Then if the distribution of wealth grows in the first-order stochastic sense, migration occurs in the rural-to-urban direction only.

Proof. See Lloyd-Ellis and Bernhardt (1998). ||

Proof of Proposition 1.

Phase 1 (The Dual Economy). Suppose that for some $t, G_t(\cdot)$ FSD $G_{t-1}(\cdot)$ and $w_t = \underline{w}$. The resulting change in the distribution of income for any y equals

$$\Phi_t(y) - \Phi_{t-1}(y) = \int \Phi_b(y|b, \underline{w})[G_{t-1}(b) - G_t(b)]db. \tag{A6}$$

But $\Phi_b(y|b, \underline{w}) = -\tilde{x}_b \leq 0$, from Lemma A3. Hence, from Theorem 1, $\Phi_t(b)$ FSD $\Phi_{t-1}(b)$. Analogous results hold for the distribution of final wealth and, hence, bequests: $G_{t+1}(\cdot)$ FSD $G_t(\cdot)$. Since $G_1(\cdot)$ FSD $G_0(\cdot)$, the first part of Proposition 1 follows by induction.

Phase 2 (The Transition). Suppose that for some period t, $w_t > w_{t-1}$, $\bar{b}_{t+1} > \bar{b}_t$ and $G_t(\cdot)$ FSD $G_{t-1}(\cdot)$. Since $\Phi_t(y) = 0$ and $\Phi_{t-1}(y) \geq 0$, $\forall y < w_t$ it must be that $\Phi_t(y) \leq \Phi_{t-1}(y)$ $\forall y < w_{st}$. For incomes $y > w_t$, decompose the change in the distribution of income as follows:

$$\Phi_t(y) - \Phi_{t-1}(y) = \int_b \Phi(y|b, w_t)G_t(db) - \int_b \Phi(y|b, w_{t-1})G_{t-1}(db)$$

$$= \int_b \Phi(y|b, w_t)G_t(db) - \int_b \Phi(y|b, w_t)G_{t-1}(db)$$

$$+ \int_b \Phi(y|b, w_t)G_{t-1}(db) - \int_b \Phi(y|b, w_{t-1})G_{t-1}(db)$$

$$= \int_b [G_{t-1}(b) - G_t(b)]\Phi_b(y|b, w_t)db + \int_b \int_{w_{t-1}}^{w_t} \Phi_w(y|b, w)dwG_{t-1}(db). \tag{A7}$$

Since $\Phi_b(y|b, \underline{w}) = \tilde{x}_b \leq 0$ and $G_t(\cdot)$ FSD $G_{t-1}(\cdot)$, the first term must be negative. Since $w_t > w_{t-1}$ and $\Phi_w(y|b, w) = -\tilde{x}_w > 0$, from Lemma A3, the second term is positive. Hence, the sign of the expression is, in general, ambiguous. However, differentiating with respect to y, for $y \in (w_t, \bar{\pi}_t]$ the change in the slope of the distribution function is

$$\phi_t(y) - \phi_{t-1}(y) = \int [G_{t-1}(b) - G_t(b)]\Phi_{yb}(y|b, w_t)db + \int_{w_{t-1}}^{w_t} \Phi_{yw}(y|b, w)dwG_{t-1}(db). \tag{A8}$$

From Lemma A3, $\Phi_{yb}(y|b, w_t) = -\tilde{x}_{yb} > 0$ and $\Phi_{yw}(y|b, w) = -\tilde{x}_{yw} > 0$. Hence, using Theorem 1, $\Phi_t(y) - \Phi_{t-1}(y)$ must increase with y on $(w_t, \bar{\pi}_t]$. If $\bar{\pi}_t > \bar{\pi}_{t-1}$, this implies that the cumulative distribution functions do not intersect. It follows that $\Phi_t(\cdot)$ FSD $\Phi_{t-1}(\cdot)$. A similar decomposition can be carried out for the distribution of inheritances:

$$G_{t+1}(b') - G_t(b') = \int [G_{t-1}(b) - G_t(b)]P_b(b'|b, w_t)db + \int \int_{w_{t-1}}^{w_t} P_w(b'|b, w)dwG_{t-1}(db). \tag{A9}$$

Since $P_{bb'} > 0$ and $P_{wb'} > 0$ it follows that $G_{t+1}(b') - G_t(b')$ increases with b'. Hence, $\bar{b}_{t+1} > \bar{b}_t$ implies $G_{t+1}(b')$ FSD $G_t(b')$. Since $G_{t^1}(\cdot)$ FSD $G_{t^1-1}(\cdot)$, the proposition follows by induction.

Phase 3 (Advanced Economic Development). Suppose that for some t, $G_t(\cdot)$ SSD $G_{t-1}(\cdot)$. Since, from Lemma A4, $\lim_{b \to \infty} z_b(b, w) = 0$, the change in the supply of entrepreneurs equals

$$E_t(w) - E_{t-1}(w) = \int z_{bb}(b, w) \int_0^b [G_t(\hat{b}) - G_{t-1}(\hat{b})]d\hat{b}db. \tag{A10}$$

Since $z_{bb}(b, w) \leq 0$, where the inequality is strict on a set of positive measure, Theorem 2 implies that the supply of entrepreneurs increases for a given wage. In turn, the increase in the supply of entrepreneurs implies that the supply of labour must fall. Since $\lim_{b \to \infty} z_b(b, w) = 0$, the shift in the demand schedule for labour equals

$$L_t(w) - L_{t-1}(w) = \int \frac{d^2}{db^2} \left(\int_0^{z(b,w)} l(b, x, w)dx \right) \int_0^b [G_t(\hat{b}) - G_{t-1}(\hat{b})]d\hat{b}db, \tag{A11}$$

where $(d^2/db^2) (\int_0^{z(b,w)} l(b, x, w)dx) = -(1 - z_b(b, w))^2 l_k(w) + z_{bb}(b, w)l(b, z(b, w), w) \leq 0$. By Theorem 2, the demand for labour rises, so that $w_t > w_{t-1}$ and $Y_t > Y_{t-1}$ (Lemma 2). The change in the slope of the income distribution function is given by (A8). Since $w_t > w_{t-1}$, the second term is positive. Since $G_t(\cdot)$ SSD $G_{t-1}(\cdot)$ and, from Lemma A3, $\Phi_{ybb} = -\tilde{x}_{ybb} < 0$, Theorem 2 implies that the first term is also positive. Hence, $\Phi_t(y) - \Phi_{t-1}(y)$ increases with $y \in (w_t, \bar{\pi}_t]$. Hence, $\bar{\pi}_t < \bar{\pi}_{t-1}$ implies the c.d.f.'s intersect only once:

$$\Phi_t(y) \leq \Phi_{t-1}(y) \quad \text{if } y < y_t^*,$$
$$\Phi_t(y) \geq \Phi_{t-1}(y) \quad \text{if } y \geq y_t^*. \tag{A12}$$

Since $Y_t > Y_{t-1}$, it follows that $\Phi_t(\cdot)$ SSD $\Phi_{t-1}(\cdot)$. An analogous argument establishes that $G_{t+1}(\cdot)$ SSD $G_t(\cdot)$. Since $G_{t^2}(\cdot)$ SSD $G_{t^2-1}(\cdot)$, the proposition follows by induction.

LLOYD-ELLIS & BERNHARDT   ENTERPRISE AND INEQUALITY 165

Phase 4 (*The Long Run*).   The wage increases monotonically and is bounded above by $\bar{w}$. Hence, it must converge to some $w^* \in [\underline{w}, \bar{w}]$. In particular, for all $\varepsilon > 0$ there must exist a T such that

$$w^* - w_T < \frac{\varepsilon}{l''(w_T)}. \tag{A13}$$

Since the L.H.S. decreases over time and the R.H.S. increases, if this inequality holds for $t = T$ it must hold for all $t > T$. Using the differentiability of $\Phi(y|b, w)$ in w, we have

$$\Phi(y|b, w^*) - \Phi(y|b, w_t) = \int_{w_t}^{w^*} \Phi_w(y|b, w)dw, \quad \forall y, b. \tag{A14}$$

Using Lemma A4 this can be expressed as

$$\Phi(y|b, w^*) - \Phi(y|b, w_t) = \int_{w_t}^{w^*} \frac{l(b, \tilde{x}(y, b, w), w)}{f_k(b, \tilde{x}(y, b, w), w)}dw. \tag{A15}$$

But $l(b, \tilde{x}(y, b, w), w) \le l''(w_t), \forall w > w_t$ and $f_k(b, \tilde{x}(y, b, w), w) \ge 1$, and so

$$\Phi(y|b, w^*) - \Phi(y|b, w_t) \le (w^* - w_t)l''(w_t). \tag{A16}$$

Hence, for all $t \ge T$, $\Phi(y|b, w^*) - \Phi(y|b, w_t) < \varepsilon, \forall y, b$. The same analysis holds for the distribution of inherited wealth, so that the evolution of the distribution of inheritances converges to a stationary, monotone Markov process, $P(\cdot|b, w^*)$. Hopenhayn and Prescott (1992) detail conditions for this class of Markov processes that ensure the limiting distribution is unique and invariant. Thus, given any initial distribution at time $t \ge T$, $G_t(\cdot)$, the associated sequence converges:

$$\lim_{n \to \infty} G_{t+n}(\cdot) = \int \lim_{n \to \infty} P^n(\cdot|b)G_t(db) = P^*(\cdot). \quad \| \tag{A17}$$

Proof of Proposition 2. $E_t(\underline{w})$ and $L_t(w)$ are both expected values of increasing functions of b and, hence, by Theorem 1, grow monotonically during the dual economy phase. In the later phases, when the wage rises, decompose the equilibrium change in the labour force into

$$L_t(w_t) - L_{t-1}(w_{t-1}) = \int \frac{d}{db}\left(\int_0^{z(b, w_t)} l(b, x, w_t)dx\right)[G_{t-1}(b) - G_t(b)]db$$

$$+ \int \int_{w_{t-1}}^{w_t} \left(\int_0^{z(b, w)} l_w(b, x, w)dx + l(b, z(b, w), w)z_w(b, w)\right)dw G_{t-1}(db). \tag{A18}$$

The slope of the individual firm's labour demand curve, l_w, increases with $|f_{ll}|$ (see Lemma A1). A value of f_{ll} that is sufficiently close to f_{kl}^2 / f_{kk}, (thus preserving the concavity of the production function) ensures that $L_t < L_{t-1}$. $\|$

Proof of Proposition 3.   The slope of labour supply is equal to minus the slope of entrepreneurial supply: $-E_w = -\int_b z_w(b, w)G_t(db)$. Using Lemma A2, the greater is $l''(w)$, the greater is the slope of the labour supply curve. From Lemma A1, as $(f_{ll} \to (f_{kl}^2 / f_{kk}), l_w \to -\infty$. *Ceteris paribus*, if these slopes are sufficiently large, then the increment in the equilibrium wage proportionately exceeds the increment in *per capita* income. $\|$

Proof of Proposition 4. $X_t(\underline{w})$, $K_t(\underline{w})$ and $Q_t(\underline{w})$ are all expected values of increasing functions of b and, hence, by Theorem 1, must grow monotonically during the dual economy phase. $\|$

Proof of Proposition 5.   During the dual phase, the change in the distribution of firm sizes is

$$J_t(k) - J_{t-1}(k) = \int_b J_b(k|b)[G_{t-1}(b) - G_t(b)]db, \tag{A19}$$

where

$$J_b(k|b, w_t) = \frac{b + \Delta - k}{z(b, w_t)}\left[\frac{z_b(b, w_t)}{z(b, w_t)} - \frac{1}{b + \Delta - k}\right]. \tag{A20}$$

Since $z_b(b, w) \le 1$ and $z(b, w) > b + \Delta - k, \forall k < k''(w_t)$, this expression is negative. Thus, by Theorem 1, $G_t(\cdot)$ FSD $G_{t-1}(\cdot)$ implies that $J_t(\cdot)$ FSD $J_{t-1}(\cdot)$. Since the lower support on firm sizes is fixed at $\underline{k}(b^0, \underline{w}) = b^0 + \Delta - z(b^0, \underline{w})$

and a strictly positive measure of firms are of this size, the distribution of firm sizes must exhibit increasing X-Dispersion throughout this phase.

During the later phases, the upper support on firm size is $k''(w_t)$. Since the wage increases over time, the upper support on firm size falls. The lower support on firm size is $\underline{k}_t = \underline{b}_t + \Delta - z(\underline{b}_t, w_t)$. Both $\underline{b}_t$, and w_t rise, so $\underline{k}_t$ must also rise over time. The c.d.f. for the distribution of firm sizes for $k \in [\underline{k}_t, k''(w_t)]$ is given by

$$J_t(k) = \int_{\underline{b}} \left[1 - \frac{b + \Delta - k}{z(b, w_t)} \right] G_t(db), \tag{A21}$$

which is linear in k. Hence, the distributions $j_t(\cdot)$ and $J_{t-1}(\cdot)$ intersect only once on $[\underline{k}_t, k''(w_t)]$. ||

Proof of Proposition 6(a).   Since migration is strictly positive and Y_t increases, A' lies above and to the left of A. The horizontal component of $A'B'$ exceeds that of AB because L_t increases and its slope is lower since Y_t rises. The slope of $A'A$ exceeds the slope of $A'B'$ if

$$\frac{Y_t - Y_{t-1}}{Y_{t-1}} > \frac{v}{\gamma} \left(\frac{S_{t-1} - S_t}{S_{t-1}} \right). \tag{A22}$$

Since E_t increases, the horizontal component of $B'C$ exceeds that of BC. Hence, if (A22) holds, the fact that AB is steeper than $A'B'$ implies that B' must lie below and to the left of B.

Now consider the change in the convexity of the Lorentz curve segment BC

$$Z_t''(p) - Z_{t-1}''(p) = \frac{\hat{y}_t'(p)}{Y_t} - \frac{\hat{y}_{t-1}'(p)}{Y_{t-1}} = \frac{1}{\phi_t(\hat{y}_t(p)) Y_t} - \frac{1}{\phi_{t-1}(\hat{y}_{t-1}(p)) Y_{t-1}}. \tag{A23}$$

During the dual economy stage of development, if $\Phi_t(\cdot)$ FSD $\Phi_{t-1}(\cdot)$ then $\hat{y}_t(p) \geq \hat{y}_{t-1}(p)$. Now

$$\phi_t(\hat{y}_t) - \phi_{t-1}(\hat{y}_{t-1}) = \int \phi(\hat{y}_t | b, \underline{w}) G_t(db) - \int \phi(\hat{y}_{t-1} | b, \underline{w}) G_{t-1}(db)$$

$$= \int \phi_b(\hat{y}_t | b, \underline{w}) [G_{t-1}(b) - G_t(b)] db + \int [\phi(\hat{y}_t | b, \underline{w}) - \phi(\hat{y}_{t-1} | b, \underline{w})] G_{t-1}(db). \tag{A24}$$

Now $\phi_b(y | b) = -\tilde{x}_{yb}(y, b, \underline{w}) \geq 0$ and so, since $G_t(\cdot)$ FSD $G_{t-1}(\cdot)$, the first term is positive. Also, since $\hat{y}_t(p) > \hat{y}_{t-1}(p)$ and $\tilde{x}_{yy} < 0$,

$$\phi(\hat{y}_t | b) - \phi(\hat{y}_{t-1} | b) = \tilde{x}_y(\hat{y}_{t-1}, b, \underline{w}) - \tilde{x}_y(\hat{y}_t, b, \underline{w}) \geq 0. \tag{A25}$$

Hence, the second term is positive, so that $\phi_t(\hat{y}_t) > \phi_{t-1}(\hat{y}_t)$. Since $Y_t > Y_{t-1}$,

$$Z_t''(p) < Z_{t-1}''(p), \qquad \forall p \geq 1 - E_{t-1}. \tag{A26}$$

It follows that if the slope at C is increasing, the Lorentz curves cannot intersect on this segment. This is the case if

$$\frac{\pi(\bar{b}_t, \underline{x}, \underline{w})}{Y_t} \geq \frac{\pi(\bar{b}_{t-1}, \underline{x}, \underline{w})}{Y_{t-1}}. \tag{A27}$$

If this holds throughout the dual phase, then t^* is the period in which the profit of the richest entrepreneur ceases to grow faster than mean income. Hence, for all $t > t^*$, the slope of the Lorentz curve at C must decline. ||

Proof of Proposition 6(b).   Consider the percentile–income combination (p^*, y^*) at which $\Phi_t(\cdot)$ and $\Phi_{t-1}(\cdot)$ intersect: $p^* = \Phi_t(y^*) = \Phi_{t-1}(y^*)$. Since $\Phi_t(y) > \Phi_{t-1}(y)$ for all $y > y^*$, it must be true that for any $p > p^*$, $\hat{y}_t(p) < \hat{y}_{t-1}(p)$. Given that $Y_t(w_t) > Y_{t-1}(w_{t-1})$, this implies that

$$\frac{\hat{y}_t(p)}{Y_t} < \frac{\hat{y}_{t-1}(p)}{Y_{t-1}}, \qquad \forall p > p^*. \tag{A28}$$

But this says that the slope of the Lorentz curve must be less at time t than at time $t - 1$ for all $p > p^*$. Since the Lorentz curves meet at $p = 1$, it follows that

$$Z_t(p) > Z_{t-1}(p), \qquad \forall p > p^*. \tag{A29}$$

LLOYD-ELLIS & BERNHARDT   ENTERPRISE AND INEQUALITY 167

For $p < p^*$ we know that $\hat{y}_t(p) > \hat{y}_{t-1}(p)$, so the above argument cannot hold. Consider, now, the change in the density function for any $p < p^*$. This can be decomposed into

$$\phi_t(\hat{y}_t) - \phi_{t-1}(\hat{y}_{t-1}) = \int \phi_b(\hat{y}_t(p)|b, w_t)[G_{t-1}(b) - G_t(b)]db$$

$$+ \int \int_{w_{t-1}}^{w_t} \phi_w(\hat{y}_t(p)|b, w)dwG_{t-1}(db) + \int [\phi(\hat{y}_t|b, w_t) - \phi(\hat{y}_{t-1}|b, w_t)]G_{t-1}(db). \quad (A30)$$

As in Lemma A3, the first two terms must be positive and, as in Proposition 6(a), the third term must also be positive. Hence, the Lorentz curve at t must be less convex than at $t - 1$

$$Z_t''(p) < Z_{t-1}''(p), \qquad \forall p \in [1 - E_{t-1}, p^*]. \quad (A31)$$

Thus, the Lorentz curves intersect at most once. If the supply and demand curves for labour are so wage elastic that $(w_t/Y_t) > (w_{t-1}/Y_{t-1})$, then the Lorentz curves cannot intersect at all. ‖

Acknowledgements. This paper has benefitted from the comments of David Andolfatto, Charles Beach, Jim Bergin, V. V. Chari, Mick Devereux, Burton Hollifield, Arthur Hosios, Tom McCurdy, Aloysius Siow, Robert Townsend, Dan Usher, and seminar participants at Brock, Cornell, Minnesota, Northwestern, Pennsylvania, Queen's, Rutgers, Toronto, UBC, and Waterloo. All remaining errors and omissions are our own. Funding from the Social Sciences and Humanities Research Council of Canada is gratefully acknowledged.

REFERENCES

ADREONI, J. (1989), "Giving with Impure Altruism: Applications to Charity and Ricardian Equivalence", *Journal of Political Economy*, **97**, 1447–1458.
AGHION, P. and BOLTON, P. (1997), "A Theory of Trickle-Down Growth and Development", *Review of Economic Studies*, **64**, 151–172.
AHLUWALIA, M. S. (1974), "Income Distribution and Development: Some Stylized Facts", *American Economic Review*, **66**, 128–135.
BANERJEE, A. V. and NEWMAN, A. F. (1993), "Occupational Choice and the Process of Development", *Journal of Political Economy*, **101**, 274–298.
BEACH, C. M. (1976), "Cyclical Impacts on the Personal Distribution of Income", *Annals of Economic and Social Measurement*, **5**, 29–52.
BLANCHARD, O., (1997) "The Medium Run", *Brookings Papers on Economic Activity* (Macroeconomics), **??**, ???–???.
BOURGIGNON, F. (1990), "Growth and Inequality in the Dual Model of Development: The Role of Demand Factors", *Review of Economic Studies*, **57**, 215–228.
FEI, J. C. H. and RANIS, G. (1966), "Agrarianism, Dualism and Economic Development", in I. Adelman and E. Thorbecke (eds.), *The Theory and Design of Economic Development* (Baltimore: Johns Hopkins Press), 3–44.
FIDLER, L. and WEBSTER, R. P. (eds.) *The Informal Sector and Microfinance Institutions in West Africa*, World Bank Regional and Sectoral Studies, 1996.
FIELDS, G. and JAKUBSEN, G. H. (1994), "New Evidence on the Kuznets Curve" (Mimeo, Cornell University).
GALOR, O. and ZEIRA, J. (1993), "Income Distribution and Macroeconomics", *Review of Economic Studies*, **60**, 35–52.
GREENWOOD, J. and JOVANOVIC, B. (1990), "Financial Development, Growth and the Distribution of Income", *Journal of Political Economy*, **5**, 1076–1107.
HADAR, J. and RUSSELL, W. (1971), "Stochastic Dominance and Diversification", *Journal of Economic Theory*, **3**, 288–305.
HOPENHAYN, H. and PRESCOTT, E. C. (1992), "Stochastic Monotonicity for Dynamic Economies", *Econometrica*, **60**, 1387–1406.
KIM, J.-I. and LAU, L. J. (1994), "The Sources of Economic Growth of the East Asian Newly Industrialized Countries", *Journal of the Japanese and International Economies*, **8**, 235–271.
KUZNETS, S. (1955), "Economic Growth and Income Inequality", *American Economic Review*, **45**, 1–28.
LLOYD-ELLIS, H. and BERNHARDT, D. (1998), "Enterprise, Inequality and Economic Development" (Mimeo, University of Toronto).
LEVY, B. (1993), "Obstacles to Developing Indigenous Small and Medium Enterprises: An Empirical Assessment", *The World Bank Economic Review*, 7, 65–83.
LEWIS, A. W. (1954), "Economic Development with Unlimited Supplies of Labour", *Manchester School of Economics and Social Studies*, **22**, 139–151.
LINDERT, P. H. and WILLIAMSON, J. G. (1985), "Growth, Equality and History", *Explorations in Economic History*, **22**, 341–377.

LYDALL, H. (1979) *A Theory of Income Distribution* (Oxford: Clarendon Press).

MADDISON, A. (1989) *The World Economy in the 20th Century* (Paris: Development Centre of the Organization for Economic Co-operation and Development).

PAUKERT, F. (1973), "Income Distribution at Different Levels of Development: A Survey of Evidence", *International Labor Review*, **108**, ???–???.

PIKETTY, T. (1997), "The Dynamics of the Wealth Distribution and the Interest Rate with Credit Rationing", *Review of Economic Studies*, **64**, 173–191.

RODRIK, D. (1994), "Getting Interventions Right: How South Korea and Taiwan Grew Rich" (NBER Working Paper No. 4964).

SAPPINGTON, D. (1983), "Limited Liability Contracts between Principal and Agent", *Journal of Economic Theory*, **29**, 1–21.

SCHUMPETER, J. A. (1934) *The Theory of Economic Development* (Cambridge: Harvard University Press).

SUMMERS, R., KRAVIS, I. B. and HESTON, A. (1984), "Changes in the World Income Distribution", *Journal of Policy Modeling*, **6**, 237–269.

TODARO, M. P. (1994), *Economic Development in the Third World* New York: Longman.

TOWNSEND, R. M. (1997), "Microenterprise and Macropolicy", in D. M. Kreps and K. F. Wallis (eds.), *Advances in Economics and Econometrics: Theory and Applications*, **2** (Cambridge: Cambridge University Press).

WILLIAMSON, J. G. (1985) *Did British Capitalism Breed Inequality?* (Boston: Allen & Unwin).

YOUNG, A. (1993), "Lessons from the East Asian NICs: A Contrarian View" (NBER Working Paper No. 4482).

[5]

Distinguishing Limited Liability from Moral Hazard in a Model of Entrepreneurship

Anna L. Paulson

Federal Reserve Bank of Chicago

Robert M. Townsend

University of Chicago and Federal Reserve Bank of Chicago

Alexander Karaivanov

Simon Fraser University

We present and estimate a model in which the choice between entrepreneurship and wage work may be influenced by financial market imperfections. The model allows for limited liability, moral hazard, and a combination of both constraints. The paper uses structural techniques to estimate the model and identify the source of financial market imperfections using data from rural and semiurban households in Thailand. Structural, nonparametric, and reduced-form estimates provide independent evidence that the dominant source of credit market imperfections is moral hazard. We reject the hypothesis that limited liability alone can explain the data.

A previous version of this paper has been circulated under the title "Distinguishing Limited Commitment from Moral Hazard in Models of Growth with Inequality." Comments from Daron Acemoglu, Patrick Bolton, Lars Hansen, Boyan Jovanovic, Andreas Lehnert, Bernard Salanié, Chris Udry, two anonymous referees, the editor of this *Journal*, and conference and seminar participants at the Federal Reserve Bank of Chicago, DELTA, Indiana University–Purdue University at Indianapolis, Massachusetts Institute of Technology, University of California at Los Angeles, University of Toulouse, Stanford, and Yale are gratefully acknowledged. We also thank Francisco Buera, Xavier Giné, and Yukio Koriyama for excellent research assistance as well as the National Institutes of Health and the National Science Foundation for funding. We are much indebted to Sombat Sakuntasathien for collaboration and for making the data collection possible. The views expressed in this paper are those of the authors and do not necessarily represent those of the Federal Reserve Bank of Chicago or the Federal Reserve System. The usual disclaimer applies.

[*Journal of Political Economy*, 2006, vol. 114, no. 1]

I. Introduction

Financial market imperfections shape economic outcomes in many areas. In studying these outcomes, many papers posit a particular financial market imperfection and exclude the possibility of alternative sources of imperfections. The goal of this paper is to identify the source of financial constraints that limit entry into entrepreneurship. We use structural, nonparametric, and reduced-form techniques to distinguish the source of financial market imperfections using microeconomic data from Thailand.

Earlier work demonstrates that financial constraints have an important effect on who starts businesses and on how existing businesses are run in Thailand (see Paulson and Townsend 2004). A symptom of financial constraints is that wealth will be positively correlated with the probability of starting a business, with the characteristics of potential entrepreneurs held constant. A strong positive correlation between becoming an entrepreneur and beginning-of-period wealth can be seen in the nonparametric regression displayed in figure 1.[1] However, a positive correlation between wealth and entrepreneurship only demonstrates that financial constraints are likely to be important but does not illuminate the source of the constraint.[2]

The literature identifies two main sources of financial constraints that influence the decision to become an entrepreneur. In Evans and Jovanovic (1989), the financial constraint is due to limited liability. Agents can supplement their personal stake in entrepreneurial activities by borrowing. Wealth plays the role of collateral and limits default. In this environment low-wealth households may be prevented from borrowing enough to become entrepreneurs, and others that are able to start businesses may be constrained in investment. Limited liability is also featured in a variety of empirical studies of occupational choice. Evans and Jovanovic (1989) and Magnac and Robin (1996) provide structural estimates of this model for the United States and for France, respectively. In a limited-liability environment, constrained entrepreneurs borrow more when wealth increases. With limited liability, borrowing does not automatically imply being constrained. Some entrepreneurs may be able to borrow enough to invest the optimal amount of capital, as though there were no constraints.

---

[1] For each observation in fig. 1, a weighted regression is performed using 80 percent (bandwidth = 0.8) of the data around that point. The data are weighted using a tricube weighting procedure that puts more weight on the points closest to the observation in question. The weighted regression results are used to produce a predicted value for each observation. Because the graphs can be fairly sensitive to outliers, we have dropped the wealthiest 1 percent of the sample.

[2] In a dynamic setting with borrowing constraints, as in Buera (2005), the predicted probability of entrepreneurship can decrease at higher levels of wealth.

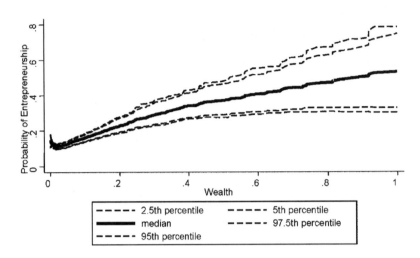

FIG. 1.—Lowess estimates of the probability of being an entrepreneur and wealth. Five hundred bootstrap estimates of the relationship between being an entrepreneur and wealth were created using a bandwidth of 0.8. The 2.5th percentile (dashed line), fifth percentile (dashed line), median (solid line), ninety-fifth percentile (dashed line), and 97.5th percentile (dashed line) estimates are shown in the figure.

Financial constraints that arise from moral hazard are the focus of the model of occupational choice featured in Aghion and Bolton (1997). Since entrepreneurial effort is unobserved and repayment is feasible only if a project is successful, poor borrowers have little incentive to be diligent, increasing the likelihood of project failure and default. In order to break even, lenders charge higher interest rates to low-wealth borrowers. Some low-wealth potential entrepreneurs will be unable, or unwilling at such high interest rates, to start businesses at any scale. Low-wealth entrepreneurs who do succeed in getting loans will be subject to a binding incentive compatibility constraint that ensures that they exert the appropriate level of effort. In contrast to the limited-liability case, when there is moral hazard and wealth increases, constrained entrepreneurs will increasingly self-finance and borrowing diminishes. In a moral hazard environment, all entrepreneurs who borrow will be constrained.[3]

The model that we estimate takes into account entrepreneurial talent and allows investment to be divisible and agents to be risk averse. Because the scale of the business can vary, the relationship between wealth and borrowing is not driven by indivisibilities. In addition, the model allows entrepreneurial talent to depend on wealth and formal education.

[3] This is true if the moral hazard environment does not produce the same solution as the first-best, which is generally the case.

Regardless of the assumptions regarding financial constraints, the model implies that entrepreneurship will be positively related to preexisting wealth. Of course the specific functional relationship between entrepreneurship and wealth will depend on the financial constraint. In addition, as discussed above, the relationship between being a borrower and being constrained and the response of constrained entrepreneurs to an increase in wealth depend on the financial market imperfection. In particular, if limited liability constrains financial markets, increases in wealth will allow constrained entrepreneurs to borrow more. However, not all borrowers need be constrained when there is limited liability. If moral hazard is the source of constraints, increases in wealth will be associated with less borrowing, and all borrowers will be constrained.

A central goal of this paper is to see whether limited liability can be distinguished from moral hazard in structural estimates using cross-sectional data from a sample of households from Thailand. We also consider the possibility that both are important.[4] The estimated models share a common technology, as well as common preferences and assumptions about the distribution of talent. They differ only in the assumed financial constraint. The appropriate Vuong (1989) test is used to compare the structural estimates and to determine which single financial constraint is most consistent with the data on entrepreneurial status, initial wealth, and education or if both are important. The Vuong test is also featured in Fafchamps (1993) and Wolak (1994). The structural model comparison tests are augmented with nonparametric and reduced-form estimates that capitalize on the richness of the data, which include information on household characteristics, borrowing, and collateral.

This paper is related to other work that tries to identify the underlying source of market imperfections. For example, Abbring et al. (2003) use dynamic data to distinguish moral hazard from adverse selection in the insurance context. Their work takes the insurance contract as given, on the basis of the regulatory environment. Our treatment of the limited-liability constraint is conceptually similar. We assume a standard debt contract and estimate the parameter that determines how much a potential entrepreneur can borrow as a function of wealth and entrepreneurial talent. The estimation is more innovative when the financial environment is affected by moral hazard. The estimated financial contract is the endogenous solution to the mechanism design problem that satisfies the incentive compatibility constraint. To our knowledge, this

---

[4] We have also considered the possibility that occupation choices are first-best and that there is *neither* limited liability nor moral hazard. Structural, reduced-form, and nonparametric findings reject this possibility.

is the first paper to provide structural estimates of a moral hazard model of occupational choice based on a mechanism design approach.

The Thai data come from a socioeconomic survey that was fielded in March–May of 1997 to 2,880 households, approximately 21 percent of which run their own businesses.[5] The sample focuses on households living in two distinct regions of the country: rural and semiurban households living in the central region, close to Bangkok, and more obviously rural households living in the semiarid and much poorer northeastern region.[6] The data include current and retrospective information on wealth (household, agricultural, business, and financial), occupational history (transitions to and from farm work, wage work, and entrepreneurship), and access to and use of a wide variety of formal and informal financial institutions (commercial banks, agricultural banks, village lending institutions, and money lenders as well as friends, family, and business associates). The data also provide detailed information on household demographics, education, and entrepreneurial activities.

The results indicate that progress can be made in identifying the nature of financial constraints. The dominant source of constraints is moral hazard. We reject the hypothesis that limited liability alone can explain the data. The evidence in favor of moral hazard is particularly strong for the wealthier central region. For the poorer northeastern region, we cannot rule out that limited liability may have a role to play, but only in combination with moral hazard.

These conclusions are based both on the formal financial regime comparison tests from the structural estimation, which use data on wealth, education, and entrepreneurial status, and on reduced-form and nonparametric estimates, which use data on wealth, entrepreneurial status, net savings, and other important household characteristics. The formal financial regime comparison tests are necessarily informative only about the relative success of a given financial regime for the particular set of assumptions regarding preferences, technology, and so forth that are imposed by the model. In contrast, the reduced-form and nonparametric estimates examine implications that are likely to distinguish moral hazard from limited liability for a large class of potential assumptions.

The rest of the paper is organized as follows. In Section II, the model and the financial constraints are presented. Section III describes the computational algorithm for the structural maximum likelihood estimation. Section IV describes the data. Section V reports on the structural maximum likelihood parameter estimates. In Section VI, we determine

---

[5] For estimation purposes, the data are restricted to households that have nonzero wealth and either currently own a business that was founded in the five years prior to the survey (14 percent) or have no business at the time of the survey (86 percent).

[6] See Binford, Lee, and Townsend (2001) for more details on the sampling methodology.

which financial regime best fits the data using structural, reduced-form, and nonparametric techniques. Section VII presents conclusions and suggests directions for future research.

II. Model and Implications

In this section, we describe the model of occupational choice and provide intuition for the solutions and the relationships among key variables. Since structural estimation lends itself to characterizing the model in a different, but equivalent, way, this section also describes the general linear programming problem that forms the basis of the structural estimation. The basic structure of the model—preferences, endowments, and technology—is the same regardless of the financial environment. The financial environment depends on which constraints are assumed to bind: limited liability, moral hazard, or both.

A. *Economic Environment*

Households are assumed to derive utility, U, from their own consumption, c, and disutility from effort, z:

$$U(c, z) = \frac{c^{1-\gamma_1}}{1 - \gamma_1} - \kappa \frac{z^{\gamma_2}}{\gamma_2}. \tag{1}$$

We assume that utility displays constant relative risk aversion in consumption. The parameter $\gamma_1 \geq 0$ determines the degree of risk aversion. The parameters $\kappa > 0$ and $\gamma_2 \geq 1$ determine the loss in utility from expending effort. Consumption, c, and effort, z, must be nonnegative.

In discussing the implications of the model, we begin by assuming that agents are risk neutral, in other words, that $\gamma_1 = 0$. We reintroduce risk aversion in the presentation of the linear programming problem that forms the basis for the structural estimation.

There are three sources of household heterogeneity in the model: initial wealth, A, entrepreneurial talent, θ, and years of education, S. All these variables are determined ex ante and can be observed by all the agents in the model.[7] Wealth is normalized to lie in the interval $(0, 1]$. We assume that talent is lognormally distributed. Specifically,

$$\ln \theta = \delta_0 + \delta_1 \ln (A) + \delta_2 \ln (1 + S) + \eta, \tag{2}$$

where η is normally distributed with mean zero and variance $\sigma_\eta^2 = 1$. In order to avoid the spurious inference that wealth rather than talent is the source of constraints, an individual's expected talent can be cor-

---

[7] The complications in estimation that arise from the fact that the econometrician cannot observe θ are addressed in Sec. III.

related with wealth through δ_1. Talent may also be correlated with formal education via δ_2.

Entrepreneurs produce output q from their own effort z and from capital k. Output q can take on two values, namely, $q = \theta$, which corresponds to success and occurs with positive probability, and $q = 0$, which is equivalent to bankruptcy and occurs with the remaining probability. Note that output is increasing in entrepreneurial talent, θ. The technology is stochastic and is written $P(q = \theta|z, k > 0)$, the probability of achieving output q given effort z and capital k. Specifically,[8]

$$P(q = \theta|z, k > 0) = \frac{k^\alpha z^{1-\alpha}}{1 + k^\alpha z^{1-\alpha}}. \tag{3}$$

Output can be costlessly observed by everyone.

When $k = 0$, the firm is not capitalized. This means that the household works in the wage sector. Earnings, w, in the wage sector are also stochastic and depend on effort. They are equal to one with probability $z/(1 + z)$ and equal to zero with the residual probability.[9]

All households are price takers and take as given the gross cost of borrowing, $r(A, \theta)$, which may vary with wealth and entrepreneurial talent. Entrepreneurs who do not borrow (who have $k < A$) and wage workers earn the given, riskless gross interest rate, r, on their net savings.

Occupational assignments are determined by a social planner who maximizes agents' utility subject to constraints that describe the financial intermediary and any financial market imperfections. This approach is equivalent to a situation in which a large number of financial institutions compete to attract clients so that in the end it is as though the agents in the economy maximize their utility subject to the financial institution earning zero profits, and subject, of course, to constraints having to do with financial market imperfections.

In sum, when agents are risk neutral, the planner makes an effort recommendation, z, and a capital recommendation, k to solve

$$\max_{z,k} \left\{ w\frac{z}{1 + z} - \kappa\frac{z^{\gamma_2}}{\gamma_2} + rA \right\} \quad \text{if } k = 0,$$

$$\max_{z,k} \left\{ \theta\frac{k^\alpha z^{1-\alpha}}{1 + k^\alpha z^{1-\alpha}} - \kappa\frac{z^{\gamma_2}}{\gamma_2} + r(A - k) \right\} \quad \text{if } k > 0, \ k \le A,$$

$$\max_{z,k} \left\{ \theta\frac{k^\alpha z^{1-\alpha}}{1 + k^\alpha z^{1-\alpha}} - \kappa\frac{z^{\gamma_2}}{\gamma_2} + r(A, \theta)(A - k)\frac{k^\alpha z^{1-\alpha}}{1 + k^\alpha z^{1-\alpha}} \right\} \quad \text{if } k > A. \tag{4}$$

---

[8] The probability of entrepreneurial success is scaled by $1 + k^\alpha z^{1-\alpha}$ to guarantee that it will lie between zero and one.

[9] Again, this formulation guarantees that the probability of success in the wage sector will lie between zero and one.

As one can see above, agents have three possibilities: (1) working for wages, which corresponds to $k = 0$; (2) becoming an entrepreneur but not borrowing, which happens when capital is positive and less than or equal to wealth, $k > 0$ and $k \leq A$; or (3) becoming an entrepreneur and borrowing, which happens when capital is positive and exceeds wealth, $k > 0$, $k > A$.

The first term in the maximand is the expected utility of a risk-neutral wage worker: expected wages minus the cost of effort, plus a riskless return on wealth. The second term is the expected utility of a risk-neutral entrepreneur who does not need to borrow to carry out the recommended k: expected output minus the cost of effort, plus a riskless return on any wealth not invested in the project. The final term is the expected utility of an entrepreneur who must borrow to carry out the assigned k: expected output minus the cost of effort, minus the expected cost of repaying the loan. Note that the loan is repaid only when the project is successful. The planner's problem is subject to a constraint that guarantees that the expected rate of repayment on such loans covers the cost of outside funds, so that lenders break even:

$$r(A, \theta)\frac{k^{\alpha}z^{1-\alpha}}{1 + k^{\alpha}z^{1-\alpha}} = r \quad \text{for } k > A, \forall\theta, \forall A. \tag{5}$$

B. Financial Environment

We introduce variations in the financial environment through additional constraints on the planner's problem. When financial markets are "first-best" and are subject to neither limited liability nor moral hazard, no further constraints are imposed.

Limited liability.—To model limited liability, we assume, as in Evans and Jovanovic (1989), that households can borrow up to some fixed multiple of their total wealth, but no more. The maximum amount that can be invested in a firm is equal to λA, and the maximum amount that a household can borrow is given by $(\lambda - 1)A$. When limited liability is a concern, the planner's maximization problem will be subject to

$$k \leq \lambda A \tag{6}$$

in addition to equation (5).

Moral hazard.—When there is moral hazard, entrepreneurial effort is unobservable and the financial contract cannot specify an agent's effort. In terms of the planner's problem, this translates into a requirement that the capital assignment and the interest rate schedule are compatible with the effort choice that a borrowing entrepreneur would have made on his or her own. In other words, the capital assignment and the interest rate schedule must not violate the first-order condition with respect to effort of the entrepreneur's own maximization problem. In this case, in addition to equation (5), the planner's maximization problem will be subject to

$$[\theta - r(A, \theta)(k - A)]\left[\frac{(1 - \alpha)k^{\alpha}z^{-\alpha}}{(1 + k^{\alpha}z^{1-\alpha})^{2}}\right] - \kappa z^{\gamma_2 - 1} = 0, \tag{7}$$

which is an entrepreneurial household's first-order condition for effort, z, for a given interest rate schedule and capital, k.[10] Equation (7) requires that the planner's effort recommendation equate the marginal benefit of effort with the marginal cost of effort plus a term that represents the marginal impact of effort on loan repayment, through the effect of effort on the probability that an entrepreneurial project will be successful: $k^{\alpha}z^{1-\alpha}/(1 + k^{\alpha}z^{1-\alpha})$.

Note that when agents are risk neutral, moral hazard is an issue only for entrepreneurs who borrow. The lack of observability of effort is not an issue for wage workers and entrepreneurs who self-finance. The planner can assign effort to them without having to satisfy the incentive compatibility constraint, equation (7), because there is no moral hazard problem when the optimal capital investment does not require borrowing.

Moral hazard and limited liability.—We also consider the possibility that credit markets are characterized by both moral hazard and limited liability. This is modeled by assuming that the entrepreneurial choice problem is subject to both equation (6) and equation (7) in addition to equation (5).

C. Characterization of Solutions

Risk-neutral case.—Figure 2 describes the optimal assignment of effort and capital for a risk-neutral entrepreneurial household for each of the three potential financial regimes and compares them to the first-best solution in which there are no financial constraints. We assume that the household has wealth, A, equal to 0.1 and talent, θ, equal to 2.56.[11] The first-best capital, effort, and welfare levels are, as one might imagine, highest. The ellipses that radiate out from the first-best solution are the agent's indifference curves in effort and capital. Utility is decreasing as one moves away from the first-best solution.

---

[10] See Karaivanov (2005) for a proof that this approach is valid here.

[11] A wealth level of 0.1 corresponds to the eighty-ninth percentile of wealth in the data. Figure 2 shows the optimal assignment of effort and capital for an entrepreneurial household assuming that $\alpha = 0.78$, $\kappa = 0.08$, $\gamma_2 = 1$, and $\lambda = 2.50$. These parameter values are within the range of the values produced by the structural estimation.

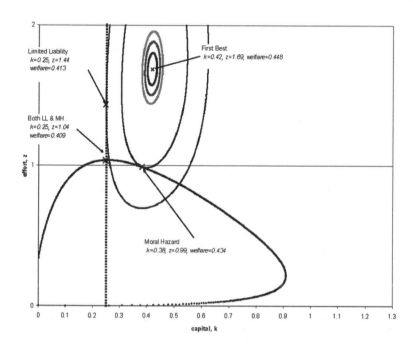

Fig. 2.—Assignments of capital (k) and effort (z) for the entrepreneurs in the risk-neutral model: moral hazard, limited liability, and both moral hazard and limited liability assumptions: $\theta = 2.56$, $A = 0.10$, $\alpha = 0.78$, $\kappa = 0.08$, $\gamma_2 = 1.00$, $r = 1.10$, and $\lambda = 2.50$.

The vertical dotted line to the left of the first-best solution represents the set of potential allocations of capital and effort when there is a *binding* limited-liability constraint and investment can be at most λA, or 0.25 in this example. As seen in the graph, imposing the limited-liability constraint results in lower capital and effort and, naturally, lower welfare.

The set of possible allocations of capital and labor in the moral hazard case are described by the ear-shaped curve that begins in the lower left-hand corner of the graph. When there is moral hazard, utility is maximized at the point at which the allocation possibilities are tangent to the entrepreneur's indifference curve. In this example, this occurs where investment is equal to 0.38 (of which 0.1 comes from the agent's own wealth and the remaining 0.28 must be borrowed) and effort is equal to 0.99. When there is moral hazard and binding limited liability, both constraints must be satisfied, and the solution is found where the moral hazard allocation curve intersects the vertical line that describes the limited-liability constraint, where investment is equal to 0.25 and effort is equal to 1.04. Note that for these parameter values, welfare is lowest when both limited liability and moral hazard are an issue and that moral hazard alone delivers higher welfare than limited liability alone.

Regardless of the financial constraint, when wealth increases, capital and effort both increase toward the first-best solution, although the path will of course depend on the financial environment. If there are no constraints and the solution is first-best, the solution is unchanged when wealth increases.

Special cases.—The risk-neutral model described above includes special cases that have been studied in the literature. For example, the model of Evans and Jovanovic (1989) can be derived by first eliminating the role for entrepreneurial effort by setting z to one and setting the disutility of effort, κ, to zero. Next, assume that output is a deterministic function of capital, k, so that $q = \theta k^\alpha$ and loans must be fully repaid in the amount rk, no matter what. The maximum loan size is determined by the limited-liability constraint, equation (6), which requires $k \leq \lambda A$. Apart from the normalized probabilities, these assumptions deliver the limited-liability model of Evans and Jovanovic. The likelihood of becoming an entrepreneur is increasing in wealth and entrepreneurial talent. With wealth held fixed, more talented entrepreneurs are more likely to be constrained. Entrepreneurial households that face a binding limited-liability constraint will borrow and invest *more* when wealth increases.[12]

We can also use our framework to generate the model of Aghion and Bolton (1997). Assume that capital can be either zero or one. In other words, firms must be capitalized at $k = 1$. Eliminate any role for entrepreneurial talent by setting θ equal to one, and assume that the income of wage workers is unaffected by effort or, equivalently, assume that $z = 1$ for wage workers. Finally, assume that $\gamma_2 = 2$ so that the disutility of effort is quadratic. Apart from the normalized probabilities, these assumptions deliver the model of Aghion and Bolton. As they stress, effort, z, which must be incentive compatible, will be a monotonically increasing function of wealth. As wealth increases, the probability of entrepreneurial success increases, which means that wealthier households will face lower interest rates. Low-wealth households face such high interest rates that they may choose not to borrow and become wage workers rather than entrepreneurs. Entrepreneurial households with wealth less than one must borrow an amount equal to $1 - A$ to finance their firm, which, again, must be capitalized at one. These households are subject to a binding incentive compatibility constraint. In

---

[12] A version of the model in which there is no credit, as in Lloyd-Ellis and Bernhardt (2000), can be derived by assuming that $\lambda = 1$, so that no borrowing is possible. Giné and Townsend (2004) extend that model and use it to assess the aggregate growth effects and the distributional consequences of financial liberalization in Thailand from 1976 to 1996.

contrast to the limited-liability model of Evans and Jovanovic (1989), when wealth increases for these constrained households, they will borrow *less* and continue to invest the same amount in their firms.

D.   The Linear Programming Problem

In this subsection, we restate the occupational choice problem faced by an agent with wealth A, schooling S, and entrepreneurial talent θ as a principal-agent problem between the agent and a competitive financial intermediary. The optimal contract between the two parties consists of prescribed investment, k, recommended effort, z, and consumption, c. Consumption can be contingent on the output realization, q. Agents assigned zero investment are referred to as "workers," and agents assigned a positive level of investment are called "entrepreneurs." Agents may now be risk averse, with risk neutrality embedded as a special case.

Nonconvexities arising from the incentive constraints, from the indivisibility of the choice between wage work and entrepreneurship, and from potential indivisibilities in k mean that, in general, standard numerical solution techniques that rely on first-order conditions will fail. By writing the principal-agent problem as a linear programming problem with respect to lotteries over consumption, output, effort, and investment, we can restore convexity and compute solutions.

Let the probability that a particular allocation (c, q, z, k) occurs in the optimal contract for agent (θ, A, S) be denoted by $\pi(c, q, z, k|\theta, A, S)$. The choice object, $\pi(c, q, z, k|\theta, A, S)$, enters linearly into the objective function as well as in every constraint. See Prescott and Townsend (1984) and Phelan and Townsend (1991) for a detailed description of this methodology. The linear programming approach allows us to use a set of well-known maximization routines in the structural estimation.

In particular, we solve the following linear programming problem:

$$\max_{\pi(c,q,z,k|\theta,A,S)\geq 0} \sum_{c,q,z,k} \pi(c, q, z, k|\theta, A, S)U(c, z) \tag{LP}$$

subject to

$$\sum_c \pi(c, q, z, k|\theta, A, S) = \tilde{p}(q|z, k, \theta) \sum_{c,q} \pi(c, q, z, k|\theta, A, S)$$

$$\text{for all } q, z, k, \tag{8}$$

$$\sum_{c,q,z,k} \pi(c, q, z, k|\theta, A, S)(c - q) = r \sum_{c,q,z,k} \pi(c, q, z, k|\theta, A, S)(A - k), \tag{9}$$

$$\sum_{c,q} \pi(c, q, z, k|\theta, A, S)U(c, z) \gtreqless$$

$$\sum_{c,q} \pi(c, q, z, k|\theta, A, S)\frac{\tilde{p}(q|z', k, \theta)}{\tilde{p}(q|z, k, \theta)} U(c, z')$$

$$\text{for all } k > 0, \; z, \; z' \neq z, \tag{10}$$

and

$$\sum_{c,q,z,k} \pi(c, q, z, k|\theta, A, S) = 1. \tag{11}$$

The function $\tilde{p}(q|z, k, \theta)$ defines the probability of output q, given effort, capital, and entrepreneurial talent. It is analogous to the original $P(q = \theta|z, k > 0)$ (see eq. [3]), but here it is conditioned on θ as well as on z and k, and it is also relevant for wage workers, who have $k = 0$.

The first constraint, equation (8), is a Bayesian consistency constraint, ensuring that the conditional probabilities, $\tilde{p}(q|z, k, \theta)$, are consistent with the production function. The second constraint, equation (9), is a break-even condition, which ensures that the financial intermediary earns zero profits. Intuitively, financial intermediary payments, $c - q$, must equal interest earnings, $r(A - k)$. The third constraint, equation (10), is the incentive compatibility constraint, which ensures that the recommended effort, z, will be undertaken rather than any alternative effort, z'. Because agents may be risk averse and value insurance that is provided by the financial intermediary, the incentive compatibility constraint may bind for all firms, not just firms that require outside capital. The final constraint, equation (11), ensures that the probabilities sum to one.

We consider three alternative specifications of the above linear programming problem, which correspond to different assumptions about the informational and financial constraints faced by agents in the model. In the first specification, moral hazard, we assume that effort is unobservable and that the incentive compatibility constraint, equation (10), must be satisfied. In this specification, the feasible investment levels are independent of A; that is, each agent can invest any feasible amount no matter what her wealth is.

In the second specification, limited liability, we assume that effort is observable and that the incentive compatibility constraint does not have to be satisfied. In the case of limited liability, the investment levels that an agent with wealth A can undertake are constrained to lie in the interval $[0, \lambda A]$, with $\lambda > 0$ as in Evans and Jovanovic (1989). In the final specification, both limited liability and moral hazard, we assume that effort is unobservable and that investment must be less than λA.

The contract elements c, q, z, and k are assumed to belong to the finite discrete sets C, Q, Z, and K, respectively. These sets, which are represented for computational purposes by grids of real numbers, are defined in more detail below.

III.   Computational Algorithm for Structural Estimation

The algorithm for computing and estimating the occupational choice problem uses a structural maximum likelihood approach and consists of the following main stages.

- Stage 1: Solve for the optimal contract between the financial intermediary and an agent with given ability, θ, education, S, and initial wealth, A. As discussed above, three alternative specifications of the constraints on the optimal contract are considered: moral hazard, limited liability, and both moral hazard and limited liability.
- Stage 2: Construct the likelihood function from the solutions of the stage 1 problems for the occupational choices, wealth, and education observed in the data.
- Stage 3: Maximize the likelihood function to obtain estimates for the structural parameters of the model and standard errors.

The general idea of the algorithm is to obtain the probability of being an entrepreneur for given model parameters and input data, θ, S, and A in stage 1, and then integrate over entrepreneurial ability θ, which is not observed by the econometrician, to obtain the expected probability that an agent with wealth A and education S would be in business for all wealth and education levels in the data. The expected probabilities generated from the model are then used to construct and maximize the appropriate likelihood function. The rest of this section details the procedures followed in each of the above stages.

A.   Solve the Linear Programming Problem

The numerical procedure for solving the linear programming problem (LP) takes the following steps:

1. Create grids for c, q, z, and k: We use 10 linearly spaced grid points for c on $[0, 10]$ and 10 linearly spaced grid points for z on $[0.0001, 5]$. For capital we use 16 log-spaced grid points for k on $[0, 5]$, when limited liability is not a concern. This range for capital was chosen to ensure that it did not place restrictions on capital choices in a "first-best" environment. When limited liability constrains financial contracts, the investment grid, K, consists of 16 points on $[0, \lambda A]$ for each given A at which the linear program is computed. As explained in the model description, output, q, can take three possible values: zero (entrepreneurial failure), θ (entrepreneurial success), and one (success in wage work).[13]

2. Use Matlab to construct the matrices of coefficients corresponding to the constraints and the objective of the linear program (LP). We use the single-crossing property to eliminate some of the incentive constraints since they do not bind at the solution.

3. Solve for the optimal contract, $\pi^*(c, q, z, k|\theta, A, S)$, using a call to the linear programming commercial library CPLEX[14] and obtain the probability of being an entrepreneur:

$$\pi^E(\theta, A, S) \equiv \sum_{c,q,z,k} \pi^*(c, q, z, k|\theta, A, S, k > 0).$$

The probability of being a worker is simply $1 - \pi^E(\theta, A, S)$.

Stage 1 is the building block of each of the following stages. Since it is moderately time-consuming, it is crucial to minimize the number of linear programs computed in the estimation procedure.

B.   *Construct the Likelihood Function*

In stage 2, we construct the log likelihood function that is used to estimate the structural models. For estimation purposes, observed wealth in Thai baht is rescaled on $(0, 1]$, where 1 corresponds to the wealth of the wealthiest household in the data. Recall that entrepreneurial

---

[13] The dimension of the grids was influenced by computational time considerations. Notice that even with these grid dimensions, we still have to solve a constrained optimization problem with 2,400 variables (the π's) and, potentially, 802 constraints for each (θ, A, S) we consider. When limited liability is the only constraint, the 320 incentive compatibility constraints are eliminated. We can handle a much larger number of variables, but then computational time increases exponentially in the estimation stage of the algorithm.

[14] Using CPLEX instead of Matlab's internal linear programming routine (*linprog*) improves computational time by a factor of 10–15.

ability is given by

$$\ln \theta = \delta_0 + \delta_1 \ln A + \delta_2 \ln (S + 1) + \eta, \tag{12}$$

where η is distributed $N(0, 1)$. For a given wealth level, A, and education level, S, we compute the *expected* probability that an agent (A, S) will be an entrepreneur by numerically integrating over the ability distribution. In other words, we numerically approximate the following expression:[15]

$$\bar{\pi}^E(A, S) = \int_{-\infty}^{\infty} \pi^E(\theta, A, S) d\phi(\eta). \tag{13}$$

Since the linear programming stage 1 is costly in terms of computation time,[16] we cannot afford to compute $\bar{\pi}^E(A, S)$ at all possible combinations of A and S (more than 2,000) because it would take at least 1.5 hours for *each* likelihood function evaluation. We overcome this problem by constructing a 20-point log-spaced grid for wealth, A.[17] The function $\bar{\pi}^E(A, S)$ is computed only at these 20 grid points.

In order to be able to compute the probability for all data points, which is necessary to evaluate the likelihood, we use a cubic spline interpolation of $\bar{\pi}^E(A, S)$ over the wealth points in the data, which generates the expected probability of being an entrepreneur, predicted by the model, for an agent with wealth A_i in the data. We denote this by $H(A_i|\psi)$,[18] where $\psi \equiv (\gamma_1, \gamma_2, \kappa, \alpha, \delta_0, \delta_1, \delta_2, \lambda)$ is the vector of model parameters. This procedure reduces the computational time to 30–50 seconds per likelihood evaluation, depending on the regime. The log likelihood function is given by

$$L(\psi) = \frac{1}{n} \sum_{i=1}^{n} E_i \ln H(A_i|\psi) + (1 - E_i) \ln [1 - H(A_i|\psi)]. \tag{14}$$

In equation (14), n is the number of observations, E_i is a binary

[15] The numerical integration method used is Gauss-Legendre quadrature with five nodes for η on $[-3, 3]$ (see Judd 1998). This method was chosen because it minimizes the number of linear program computations (we solve only five linear programs for a given A, S pair) and because it has desirable asymptotic properties.

[16] Three seconds for each A, S pair. All calculations were performed on a 3 GHz Pentium 4 machine with 1 GB RAM running Windows XP with hyperthreading.

[17] The log-spaced grid takes into account that the actual wealth data are heavily skewed toward the low end of the wealth distribution. In order to compute $\bar{\pi}^E(A, S)$, we also need values for education, S, that correspond to the grid points for wealth, A. We obtain these by running a nonparametric lowess regression of education on wealth using all the data. The resulting nonlinear function that relates education to wealth is then evaluated at the 20 wealth grid points to obtain the corresponding 20 values for S. This method is preferable to simply picking an education value corresponding to the data point closest to a particular wealth grid point since more information is used in the nonparametric regression to compute the education values corresponding to the wealth grid points.

[18] Notice that H is implicitly a function of agents' education levels.

variable that takes the value of one if agent i is an entrepreneur in the data and zero otherwise, and A_i is the wealth level of agent i (again from the data).

C. Solve for Optimal Parameter Values

In stage 3, we solve for the parameter values that maximize the likelihood of model occupational assignments that correspond to the occupational assignments in the data. In other words, we maximize the likelihood function, equation (14), over the choice of parameter values—the vector $\psi \equiv (\gamma_1, \gamma_2, \kappa, \alpha, \delta_0, \delta_1, \delta_2, \lambda)$, given the data.[19]

The riskless interest rate is assumed to be 10 percent, that is, $r = 1.1$ in the model. In comparison, the net annual interest rate on collateralized loans to individuals from the Bank for Agriculture and Agricultural Cooperatives (BAAC) is roughly 13 percent in the data, and interest rates on loans from commercial banks, the vast majority of which are collateralized, average 22 percent. In addition, there are many informal loans, often between relatives, in which the reported interest rate is zero (see Giné [2005] for further details). The relevant interest rate for the model is a riskless one, with default not an option. Clearly default is a possibility for the loans and interest rates observed in the data, so we assume that the riskless gross interest rate is lower than those observed in the data.

The actual maximization of the log likelihood function $L(\psi)$ is performed in the following way. First, in order to ensure that a global maximum is reached, we do an extensive deterministic grid search over the parameters and pick the parameter configuration that maximizes L.[20] The best parameter configuration from the grid search is then taken as the initial parameter guess for a second-stage likelihood optimization procedure.[21]

Finally, we compute the standard errors for the estimated parameters using standard bootstrapping methods drawing with replacement from the original sample.[22]

---

[19] In some specifications only a subset of these parameters is estimated. Section V reports on the parameter estimates for each specification.

[20] The grid search is computationally time-intensive and can take up to two to three days depending on the number of estimated parameters.

[21] This latter procedure solves the nonlinear optimization problem of maximizing L by using the Matlab routine *fminsearch*, which is a generalization of the polytope method using the Nelder-Mead simplex algorithm. We chose this method because of its high reliability, relative insensitivity to initial values, and good performance with low-curvature objective functions. Typically the optimization takes 300–400 iterations, which amounts to two and a half to seven hours of computer time depending on the regime.

[22] Even with a fairly small number of bootstrap draws (10), this is the most time-intensive part of the algorithm and can take up to three to four days for each estimated parameter configuration.

IV. Data and Background Information

This section briefly describes some of the salient features of the data and reviews the evidence that financial constraints seem to play an important role in determining who becomes an entrepreneur and how existing businesses are run. The reader who is interested in more details is referred to Paulson and Townsend (2004).

The data we analyze cover four provinces in Thailand. Two of the provinces are in the central region and are relatively close to Bangkok. The other two provinces are much further from Bangkok and are located in the relatively poor northeastern region. The contrast between the survey areas is deliberate and has obvious advantages. Within each province a stratified random sample of 12 geographic areas (*tambons*, typically 10–12 villages) was selected. The stratification ensured that the sample was ecologically diverse. In each tambon, four villages were selected at random. In each village, a random sample of 15 households were interviewed.

The businesses we study are quite varied and include shops and restaurants, trading activities, shrimp or livestock raising, and the provision of construction or transportation services.[23] While there are many different types of businesses, shrimp or fish raising, shops, and trade account for 70 percent of the businesses in the whole sample and make up a similar percentage of the businesses in each region. Median initial investment in the household businesses varies substantially with business type.

Despite this variation, the median initial investment appears to be relatively similar across regions for the same type of business, particularly for the most common business types. For example, the median investment in a shop is 16,000 baht in both the northeastern and the central regions. In the Northeast, the median initial investment in trade is 21,000 baht compared to 23,000 baht in the central region.[24] For future reference, note that average annual household income in Thailand at the time of the survey is 105,125 baht, or roughly $4,200.

Most business households run a single business and rely heavily on

---

[23] We are aware that some farms are run like businesses and that the dividing line between businesses and farms is not always clear. However, farming, particularly of rice and other crops, can be thought of as a "default" career choice. An active decision to do something else has been made by the households that we define to be business households. We experimented with alternative categorizations and found that the one we use has content in the sense that the performance of the structural estimation deteriorates when entrepreneurial status is randomly assigned compared to when entrepreneurial status is determined by the data.

[24] Median investment in shrimp or fish does differ depending on the region: in the Northeast it is 9,000 baht compared to 51,000 baht in the central region. The reason is that shrimp farming, which requires substantial initial investment, is concentrated in the central region, whereas fish farms are more important in the Northeast.

family workers. Only 10 percent of the businesses paid anyone for work during the year prior to the survey.[25] More than 60 percent of the businesses were established in the past five years. In the empirical work we restrict our attention to these businesses.[26] Savings (either in the form of cash or through asset sales) is the most important source of initial business investment. Approximately 60 percent of initial investment in household businesses comes from savings. Loans from commercial banks account for about 9 percent of initial business investment, and the BAAC accounts for another 7 percent. In the Northeast, the BAAC plays a larger role than commercial banks, and in the central region the opposite is true.

Entrepreneurial households are a bit younger and more educated than nonbusiness households. The current median income of business households is about twice that of nonbusiness households. This difference is used to calibrate the talent parameter, δ_0, in the baseline structural estimates. Business households are wealthier both at the time of the survey and prior to starting a business, compared to their nonbusiness counterparts. In addition, business households are more likely to be customers of commercial banks and the BAAC and to participate in village financial institutions.

Table 1 summarizes the data for business and nonbusiness households that are used in the structural maximum likelihood estimates and the business household information that is used in the reduced-form and nonparametric analysis. The wealth variable measures the value of real, nonfinancial wealth that the household owned six years prior to the survey. It is equal to the total value of the household, agricultural, and land assets that the household owned then. This corresponds to beginning-of-period wealth, that is, wealth prior to choosing an occupation. The value of any business assets that the household may have owned six years ago is excluded.[27]

---

[25] This means that the set of entrepreneurial firms is unlikely to be very affected by the case in which wealthy, but untalented, households hire poor, but talented, managers to run their firms.

[26] Although these results are not presented in the paper, we have also looked at businesses that were established in the past 10 years. This group includes 83 percent of the businesses in the sample. None of the results are sensitive to which group of businesses we examine. The decision to focus on businesses that were started in the past five years was the result of weighing the benefit of having more accurate measures of beginning-of-period wealth against the cost of eliminating the 224 households that started businesses more than five years ago.

[27] The past value of real assets is found by depreciating the purchase price of the asset (in 1997 baht) from the time of purchase to what it would have been worth six years prior to the survey. We assume that the depreciation rate for all household and agricultural assets is 10 percent per year. If the household purchased a tractor 10 years before the survey for 100,000 baht, we would first convert the purchase price to 1997 baht (using the Thai consumer price index) and then multiply this figure by $(0.90)^4$ to account for four years of depreciation between the purchase date and six years prior to the survey.

TABLE 1
SUMMARY STATISTICS

	Whole Sample	Northeast	Central Region
	A. Variables Used in Structural and Reduced Form/Nonparametric Estimation (All Households)		
Number of households	2,313	1,209	1,104
Business households	14%	9%	19%
Years of schooling:			
All households	4.03	3.97	4.09
	(2.56)	(2.45)	(2.67)
Business households	4.70	5.00	4.50
	(2.90)	(3.00)	(2.80)
Wealth six years prior to survey:			
All households	1,007,166	355,996	1,712,046
	(3,929,520)	(648,590)	(5,545,901)
Business households	2,532,464	428,490	3,614,755
	(7,603,877)	(558,630)	(9,168,505)
Constrained business households*	1,199,500	313,093	1,655,471
	(5,770,877)	(546,497)	(7,051,744)
Unconstrained business households	1,562,854	137,406	2,296,109
	(5,550,756)	(343,281)	(6,713,852)
	B. Variables Used in Reduced Form/Nonparametric Estimation (Business Households Only)		
Number of households	361	122	239
Initial business investment	148,734	81,311	179,349
	(339,562)	(176,918)	(388,312)
Net savings	4,562	−13,680	13,946
	(714,701)	(410,166)	(829,564)
% that are net borrowers	55%	61%	51%
% that report they are constrained*	56%	68%	50%
Age of head	49.5	48.4	50.1
	(13.9)	(13.6)	(14.1)
Adult women in the household	1.6	1.6	1.7
	(.9)	(.8)	(.9)
Adult men in the household	1.6	1.5	1.7
	(.9)	(.9)	(.9)
Children (< 18 years) in the household	1.5	1.5	1.6
	(1.2)	(1.1)	(1.3)
	C. Business Households That Were Member/Customer of Organization/Institution Six Years Ago		
Formal financial institution	23%	16%	27%
Village institution/organization	11%	10%	12%
Agricultural lender	33%	33%	33%
BAAC group	22%	29%	18%
Money lender	4%	5%	4%

NOTE.—Standard deviations are in parentheses. Wealth is in Thai baht. The exchange rate at the time of the survey is 25 baht to $1.00.

* Households that reported that their businesses would be more profitable if it were expanded are labeled "constrained"; households that report that their business would *not* be more profitable if it were expanded are labeled "unconstrained."

In addition to using data on past wealth, entrepreneurial status, and years of education, the reduced-form and nonparametric analyses make use of additional data on the demographic characteristics of the head of the business household (age and age squared) and on characteristics of the household (the number of adult men, adult women, and children in the household). All these variables are measured at the time of the survey. We also use data on net financial savings at the time of the survey, which is equal to the financial savings of the household plus the value of loans that are owed to them minus current debt. In some estimates, we control for the impact of credit market availability by including measures of whether or not the household was a member or a customer of various financial institutions in the past.

Household business reports of whether or not they are "constrained" are a key variable in the reduced-form and nonparametric analysis. Household businesses are considered constrained if they answer yes to the question "Would your business be more profitable if it were expanded?" Fifty-six percent of business households answer yes to this question. Further information from the survey suggests that household responses to this question may reasonably approximate the theoretical notion of being constrained or being subject to a binding limited-liability or incentive compatibility constraint. For example, of the businesses that reported that they were constrained, 37 percent said that they had not expanded their business because they lacked sufficient funds to do so. Another 30 percent said that they did not have enough land to expand. An additional 13 percent reported that they lacked time or labor for expansion.[28]

V.   Structural Maximum Likelihood Estimates

In this section the structure of the model is taken literally to determine how well it fits the observed pattern of who becomes an entrepreneur as a function of wealth, the imputed distribution of entrepreneurial talent in the Thai data, and various assumptions about the financial regime. We consider three financial regimes: moral hazard, limited liability, and both moral hazard and limited liability.

Each structural maximum likelihood estimate produces a measure of

---

This procedure would give us the value of the tractor six years prior to the survey. Past values of land are treated differently. Households were asked to report the current value of each plot that they own. In calculating past land values, we assume that there have been no real changes in land prices. So if the household has had one plot for 10 years and the current value of that plot is 100,000 baht, then six years ago the value of that plot would also be 100,000 baht (in 1997 baht). In addition, information on land purchases and sales is used to measure the value of land that a household owned in the past.

[28] See Townsend et al. (1997) for further details on the survey design and implementation.

the likelihood that a given set of assumptions about the financial environment could have generated the patterns of wealth, education, and entrepreneurial status observed in the Thai data. In addition, the estimation delivers the maximized values of the model parameters, the probability that each agent will become an entrepreneur, and assignments of capital, effort, and consumption for each agent.

Most of the structural estimates are produced assuming that the talent parameters δ_0, δ_1, and δ_2 are fixed. This is done to ensure that a given agent has the same expected talent regardless of the financial environment. The talent parameter δ_1 is set equal to 0.06, which means that a 10 percent increase in wealth raises entrepreneurial talent by 0.6 percent. The parameter δ_2 is set equal to 0.125, which means that a 10 percent increase in years of schooling increases entrepreneurial talent by 1.25 percent. Throughout the estimation, we also assume that the standard deviation of shocks to entrepreneurial talent, σ_η, is one. The values of δ_1, δ_2, and σ_η were chosen to be consistent with structural estimates of a version of the model of Evans and Jovanovic (1989) using the Thai data.[29] Because these estimates also use income data, they bring additional information to bear on the relationship between entrepreneurial talent, wealth, and education. Computational constraints prevent us from using income data in the structural estimates discussed below.

We consider two methods of fixing the talent parameter, δ_0. In the first method, which is referred to as "income" in the tables, δ_0 is assigned on the basis of the observed income of entrepreneurs relative to non-entrepreneurs. When the scaling required to ensure that probabilities lie between zero and one is ignored, the model implies that the output of a successful entrepreneur is equal to θ and the output of a successful wage worker is equal to one. The data reveal that the median entrepreneur has income that is 2.56 times higher than that of the median wage worker. When we map from the data back into the model, this implies that the median entrepreneur has a θ of 2.56. From equation (2), which maps wealth and schooling into log talent, as well as the assumptions about δ_1 and δ_2 discussed above, this implies that δ_0 must be equal to 0.922.

In the second method, which we refer to as the "% entrepreneur" case, δ_0 is chosen so that the predicted percentage of entrepreneurs from the structural estimation of the model matches the percentage of

---

[29] These estimates were produced using the methods described in Evans and Jovanovic (1989). Their methodology cannot be used to estimate the model discussed in this paper.

entrepreneurs observed in the data, namely 14 percent. In this case, δ_0 is set equal to 1.295.[30]

We also estimate δ_0, δ_1, and δ_2 for each of the financial regimes. These estimates are labeled "estimated delta" in the tables. Both the model and common sense suggest that entrepreneurial talent plays an important role in occupational choice and, potentially, in determining the availability and cost of credit. However, success in this area is necessarily incomplete since direct data on the distribution, let alone the level, of entrepreneurial talent are not available.[31] Therefore, we allow estimated talent parameters to vary freely with the financial regimes and compare these estimates with estimates in which the talent parameters are fixed a priori, as described above.

Table 2 reports on the structural estimates for the whole sample for the three financial market possibilities: moral hazard, limited liability, and both. Each column of information in the table corresponds to a financial market regime. There are four sets of estimates for each financial market regime. The first set assumes that average entrepreneurial talent is set according to the "income" method described above and that agents may be risk averse. We treat these estimates as the "benchmark" case and use the others to make sure that our conclusions are robust. The second set makes the same assumptions about entrepreneurial talent but assumes that agents are risk neutral. The third set of estimates returns to the assumption that agents may be risk averse and uses the % entrepreneur method to set the average talent parameter. In the final set of estimates, talent parameters are estimated as discussed above and agents are assumed to be risk averse. The predicted relationships between capital, effort, consumption, and wealth for entrepreneurs in the benchmark case are described in figure 3.

A. Parameter Estimates

Across the financial regimes, in the benchmark case (panel A of table 2), the production parameter, α, is estimated to range from 0.69 to 0.78. This means that, all else equal, a 10 percent increase in business investment would lead to a 4.2–5.1 percent increase in the probability of entrepreneurial success. The parameter estimates for α can be used together with predicted values for effort and investment to calculate the implied probability that the average business will be successful. In the

---

[30] We assumed that financial markets were characterized by moral hazard and used the whole sample to calibrate δ_0 so as to deliver the percentage of entrepreneurs observed in the data.

[31] Other researchers have used information from the distribution of test scores to pin down the talent distribution (see, e.g., Cunha, Heckman, and Navarro 2004). Equivalent information for the individuals in the Thai data is not available.

TABLE 2
PARAMETER VALUES FROM STRUCTURAL ESTIMATION: WHOLE SAMPLE

	Moral Hazard	Limited Liability	Both
	A. Risk Aversion, Talent (Income)		
γ_1	.0985	.0982	.1025
	(.0125)	(.0003)	(.0046)
γ_2	2.1007	1.1713	2.4753
	(.3216)	(.0037)	(.1797)
κ	.1257	.1079	.1190
	(.0227)	(.0003)	(.0062)
α	.7775	.6937	.7208
	(.0325)	(.0165)	(.0108)
λ	. . .	22.9885	20.8082
		(.0727)	(1.4882)
	B. Risk Neutrality, Talent (Income)		
γ_2	1.5801	1.3475	1.5511
	(.0243)	(.0167)	(.0171)
κ	.0530	.0675	.0789
	(.0009)	(.0009)	(.0008)
α	.7700	.6800	.6902
	(.0099)	(.0273)	(.0043)
λ	. . .	24.5000	28.3848
		(.3307)	(.3095)
	C. Risk Aversion, Talent (% Entrepreneur)		
γ_1	1.0737	.0668	.7781
	(.0123)	(.0004)	(.0035)
γ_2	1.0000	1.0000	1.0000
	(.0192)	(.0141)	(.0105)
κ	.0904	.0722	.1219
	(.0001)	(.0001)	(.0016)
α	.9780	.9702	.5062
	(.0032)	(.0003)	(.0066)
λ	. . .	10.7281	1.9014
		(.0305)	(.0042)
	D. Risk Aversion, Estimated Talent		
γ_1	.5753	.0957	.1002
	(.0175)	(.0002)	(.0005)
γ_2	1.0494	1.2314	1.0939
	(.0171)	(.0120)	(.0061)
κ	1.2312	.9889	1.0022
	(.0649)	(.0049)	(.0065)
α	.7931	.2283	.7985
	(.0148)	(.0030)	(.0188)
δ_0	1.0175	.8853	.1002
	(.0464)	(.0108)	(.0007)
δ_1	.0604	.0285	.0503
	(.0218)	(.0002)	(.0004)
δ_2	.0516	$-.2226$	.3005
	(.0053)	(.0046)	(.0018)
λ	. . .	21.0118	5.0088
		(.2223)	(.0970)

NOTE.—Bootstrap standard errors are in parentheses.

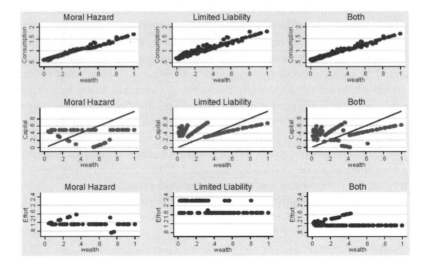

FIG. 3.—Expected assigned consumption, capital, and effort relative to wealth for entrepreneurs from benchmark structural estimates of moral hazard, limited liability, and both moral hazard and limited-liability financial regimes. The 45-degree line is included in capital figures

baseline case, an entrepreneur who invests the average amount of capital and exerts the average amount of effort has a 32 percent chance of success in the moral hazard case, 41 percent in the limited-liability case, and 33 percent when both moral hazard and limited liability are a concern. These figures are relatively low partly because of the normalization that ensures that the probability of success will always lie between zero and one (see eq. [3]). When we ignore the normalization, the probability of success is 47 percent in the moral hazard case, 71 percent in the case of limited liability, and 49 percent when both limited liability and moral hazard are important. By comparison, survey data from Thailand suggest that 67 percent of businesses started in 1998 were still in operation in 2001.

Estimates of α are very similar when the income method is used to determine talent and risk neutrality is assumed (panel B of table 2). When the benchmark income method (panel A) is compared with the estimates in which talent parameters are estimated (panel D), α stays roughly the same for the moral hazard and both cases and falls from 0.69 to 0.23 in the case of limited liability. When the % entrepreneur method is used to pin down talent (panel C), the estimates produce values of α that are close to one for the moral hazard and limited-liability cases. With these assumptions, the predicted probability of entrepreneurial success is 46 percent for moral hazard, 42 percent for limited liability, and 36 percent when financial markets are characterized by both moral hazard and limited liability.

The degree of risk aversion is estimated to be fairly consistent both across financial regimes and across assumptions about the talent parameters. The estimates for γ_1 are generally close to 0.1, which implies that households are not particularly risk averse. There are three exceptions to this general finding. Estimated risk aversion is considerably higher when the % entrepreneur method is used to calibrate talent and there is moral hazard (see panel C). In the case of moral hazard alone, $\gamma_1 = 1.07$, and when there is moral hazard together with limited liability, γ_1 is estimated to be 0.78. Moral hazard alone generates a γ_1 of 0.58 when talent parameters are estimated (panel D).

There are two parameters that determine the disutility of effort, κ and γ_2 (see eq. [1]). Estimates of κ, a scale parameter measuring the distastefulness of effort, are very consistent across the three financial regimes, ranging from 0.11 to 0.13 in the benchmark case, 0.05 to 0.08 when we assume risk neutrality, and 0.09 to 0.12 when the % entrepreneur method is used to calibrate talent. However, when talent parameters are estimated, κ is much higher, ranging from 0.99 to 1.23.

There is some variation in the parameter γ_2 across financial regimes. This parameter, which is similar to a risk aversion parameter, measures the extent to which agents dislike variability in effort. For example, in the benchmark case, this parameter is lowest in the limited-liability case at 1.2, goes up to 2.1 in the case of moral hazard, and reaches 2.5 when both moral hazard and limited liability are a concern. This reveals some interesting interaction between the financial regime and the parameters. In the limited-liability case, the estimates want to assign relatively low disutility of effort compared to the moral hazard and "both" cases when effort assignments must satisfy an incentive compatibility constraint. This is also consistent with information on how effort assignments are made across the financial regimes (see fig. 3). Entrepreneurs are assigned higher levels of effort in the limited-liability financial regime than in the regime in which moral hazard is also a concern. There is some tendency for the structural estimation to produce parameters that make higher effort less costly to agents when there is limited liability and no moral hazard.

Estimates of the parameter λ, which determines how much agents can borrow in the limited-liability and both cases, seem too high. In the benchmark estimates, λ is estimated to be between 21 and 23. This means that agents can borrow between 20 and 22 times their wealth.

The limited liability parameter, λ, is very sensitive to assumptions about average talent, δ_0. When average talent is calibrated to fit the observed percentage of entrepreneurs in the data (see panel C of table 2), estimates of λ decline markedly, ranging from 1.9 when both moral hazard and limited liability are a concern to 10.7 when the financial environment is characterized by limited liability alone.

To further explore this issue, we have estimated the limited-liability model fixing the value of λ at two (i.e., households can borrow an amount equal to their own wealth). In these estimates, the other parameter values are similar to the values that are obtained when λ is also estimated, although the overall fit of the model, as measured by the log likelihood, declines compared to the case in which λ is estimated. (These estimates are available from the authors.)

An examination of the data reveals that, in practice, loan to collateral values are typically quite low, and very often the value of the loan is significantly less than the value of the collateral used to secure it, consistent with a λ of less than one.[32] On the other hand, there are also many unsecured loans in the data. That is, there are many loans in which λ would appear to be infinite.

As discussed above, in the first three sets of estimates, the parameters that describe the relationship between entrepreneurial talent and wealth and schooling are held fixed at $\delta_1 = 0.06$ and $\delta_2 = 0.125$. These two parameters remain the same, and δ_0 is set equal to 0.922 for the benchmark income case and is higher, at $\delta_0 = 1.295$, in the % entrepreneur case. In the final set of results (panel D of table 2), these parameters are estimated for each of the financial regimes. Estimates of δ_0 range from a low of 0.1 in the case of both limited liability and moral hazard to a high of 1.0175 when moral hazard alone is assumed to govern financial constraints. Estimates of δ_1, which measures the relationship between wealth and entrepreneurial talent, are all positive and range from 0.03 in the limited-liability case to 0.06 in the moral hazard case. This range includes the assigned value for δ_1, 0.06, that is assumed in the other sets of estimates.

Estimates of the parameter δ_2, which captures the relationship between entrepreneurial talent and formal schooling, display the most variation across the financial regimes. In the case of limited liability and no moral hazard, estimates of δ_2 suggest that entrepreneurial talent decreases with formal schooling, with each additional year of schooling decreasing entrepreneurial talent by 4 percent. When moral hazard is a concern, either on its own or together with limited liability, additional schooling is associated with higher entrepreneurial talent, with an additional year of schooling increasing entrepreneurial talent by 0.9 percent in the case of moral hazard alone and by 8 percent in the case of moral hazard and limited liability.

---

[32] Land is the most common source of collateral, and indivisibilities in land may account for some of the very low loan/collateral ratios that we see. For example, if a household wishes to borrow 10,000 baht and has a plot of land worth 100,000 baht that it uses as collateral, the loan/collateral ratio will be 0.1.

Despite the variation in talent parameters across the financial regimes, especially in δ_2, average entrepreneurial talent is estimated to be relatively similar across the regimes: 2.8 in the case of moral hazard, 2.1 in the case of limited liability, and 2.0 when both moral hazard and limited liability are an issue. By comparison, average entrepreneurial talent is estimated to be about 3.0 for all the financial regimes in the benchmark income case and about 3.9 in the % entrepreneur case.

B.   Benchmark Assignments of Capital, Effort, and Consumption

Figure 3 uses simulated data from each of the three model regimes evaluated at their respective structural maximum likelihood parameter estimates to describe how expected assigned entrepreneurial capital, effort, and consumption vary with wealth for the whole-sample, benchmark case with risk aversion. To illustrate more clearly the distinctions between the regimes and the intuition behind the solutions to the corresponding linear programs from Section II, the simulations were performed at all actual wealth and schooling levels from the data; that is, no splines were used, in contrast to the actual estimation. Each graph shows the expected assignment of consumption, capital, and effort as a function of wealth for agents that the structural estimates assign to have $k > 0$, in other words, entrepreneurs. The discreteness of the grids we use for computational reasons and the heterogeneity in average entrepreneurial talent, which fluctuates with schooling through δ_2 and thus plays an important role in determining capital, effort, and consumption, account for the variability and "clustering" displayed in the figures.

In the case of consumption, the figure shows that consumption increases more or less linearly with wealth, regardless of what is assumed about financial market imperfections. This is what we would expect for unconstrained entrepreneurs, regardless of what is assumed about financial market imperfections. In the limited-liability case, most entrepreneurs turn out to be unconstrained. However, in the moral hazard case, all risk-averse entrepreneurs are subject to a binding incentive compatibility constraint. For these households the roughly linear relationship between consumption and wealth is a result of the large fraction of capital assignments that are the same regardless of wealth. With recommended investment often invariant to wealth, additional wealth is invested at the gross interest rate, r, and augments consumption by the gross interest rate multiplied by any additional net savings.

Looking at the relationship between capital and wealth reveals differences in what is expected across the models. The straight line in the capital figures is the 45-degree line. Capital assignments above the 45-degree line correspond to borrowing, and capital assignments below the line involve no borrowing. When financial markets are characterized by moral hazard alone, there appear to be two groups of entrepreneurs. The largest group has investment that is largely unchanged with wealth. For this group, borrowing decreases unambiguously with wealth, which we would expect as constrained entrepreneurs relax the incentive compatibility constraint by relying less on outside funding when wealth goes up. This group has higher average talent and wealth. The second group, with lower talent and lower wealth, has investment that first declines with wealth and then increases with wealth. The range in which investment decreases when wealth increases is also a range in which borrowing is decreasing, which has the effect of relaxing the incentive compatibility constraint. The range in which investment increases with wealth is a range in which the entrepreneurs are net savers and do not rely on outside funding for their businesses.

Entrepreneurial investment and, hence, borrowing increase sharply with wealth along several distinct lines when limited liability is a concern. This effect is driven by λ. Constrained entrepreneurs increase investment and borrowing since increasing wealth relaxes the limited-liability constraint. Note that the rate of increase in investment is higher for low-wealth entrepreneurs that borrow (their capital assignments are above the 45-degree line) than it is for higher-wealth households that are net savers. When both moral hazard and limited liability are a concern, the relationship between investment and wealth is a combination of what was observed for the cases in which there was only moral hazard or only limited liability, with the exception that there is no group of entrepreneurs for whom investment appears to be the same regardless of wealth.

Effort tends to be higher when there is limited liability and no moral hazard, as one might expect. In this case, the structural estimates predict essentially two levels of effort, high and low, that do not vary with wealth. There is some tendency for the low-wealth entrepreneurs to have higher effort and wealthier entrepreneurs to have lower effort.[33] In addition, although this cannot be seen in the figure, the low-wealth, high-effort group tends to have greater entrepreneurial talent, on average, than the high-wealth, low-effort group.

When moral hazard constrains financial contracts, there is also a large group of entrepreneurs who have the same, relatively low, effort regardless of wealth. This group accounts for 78 percent of the businesses produced by the moral hazard estimation. However, there is another, much smaller, group of entrepreneurs with low to medium wealth who

---

[33] Notice that there are relatively more points on the upper effort level "line" in the "effort" panel of the limited-liability part of fig. 3 for low wealth levels and relatively more points on the low-level "line" for higher wealth levels.

exert more effort as wealth increases. This group has lower average entrepreneurial talent than the group whose effort does not vary with wealth. When both moral hazard and limited liability are a concern, the data produced by the structural estimation more closely mimic the situation in which there is only moral hazard.

VI.   Comparison of the Financial Regimes

In this section the financial regimes are compared using two complementary techniques. First, we distinguish between the financial regimes using formal tests based on the structural estimates discussed above. Next, nonparametric and reduced-form techniques are used to provide additional, independent evidence about the source of financial market imperfections in the Thai data.

While the structural estimates impose a number of restrictions on the data, they rely on a very limited subset of the available data: past wealth, the entrepreneurial status of the household, and the years of schooling of the household head. In contrast, the nonparametric estimates impose almost no structure on relationships between the key variables of interest and explore relationships between variables that are not used in the structural estimation. The reduced-form estimates draw on the richness of the available survey data, while imposing a particular functional form on the relationship between the dependent and independent variables. Both the nonparametric and the reduced-form findings offer completely independent evidence of the nature of financial constraints and enhance the overall interpretation of what we see in the data.

A.   *Structural Evidence*

In this subsection, we provide formal tests of which of the candidate financial regimes best fit the whole sample and the various subsamples of the data that were described earlier. The financial regimes are compared using the Vuong likelihood ratio test (see Vuong 1989). One attractive feature of the Vuong test is that it does not require either model to be correctly specified. This feature is appealing given the necessity of studying models that are much simpler than reality. The null hypothesis is that the two models are equally near the actual data-generating process. The Vuong test delivers an asymptotic test statistic that measures the weight of the evidence in favor of one model or the other.[34]

---

[34] One could use the same procedure in which the null hypothesis was that one model was closer to the actual data-generating process. The test statistic would remain the same; however, the critical values for rejecting the null would of course change.

We use the Vuong test for strictly nonnested models. For the purposes of this test, model A nests model B if, for any possible allocation that can arise in model B, there exist parameter values such that this is the allocation in model A. In the current context, the case with both limited liability and moral hazard nests the case in which financial markets are characterized by only moral hazard. The reason is that for a sufficiently large λ, the "both" case will reproduce the exact same assignment of households to occupations as the moral hazard alone case. On the other hand, the "both" case does not nest the limited-liability case, because there is no parameter that can make effort observable, "turn off" the moral hazard constraint, and deliver the same assignment of entrepreneurial status as in the limited liability alone case. In any case, the likelihood ratio test statistic that Vuong proposes is appropriate regardless of whether the three financial regimes are completely nonnested, overlapping, or nested. However, the asymptotic distribution of the test statistic depends on the relationship between the models.[35] Using the distribution that is appropriate for nonnested models is the conservative choice, in the sense that is makes it more difficult to statistically distinguish the financial regimes.

1. Whole Sample Findings

Table 3 reports the log likelihoods for each of the three possible financial regimes (moral hazard, limited liability, and both) and the four sets of assumptions we make in estimation (income with risk aversion and with risk neutrality, % entrepreneur with risk aversion, and the case in which the talent parameters are estimated). The likelihoods are reported for the whole sample (panel A), the Northeast (panel B), and the central region (panel C). The results of the comparison tests for the three possible financial regimes—moral hazard, limited liability, and both—are provided in panels A–C of table 4 for the whole sample, Northeast, and central region, respectively.

For the whole sample, the case in which moral hazard alone describes financial markets significantly outperforms the limited-liability case and the case in which financial markets are characterized by both moral hazard and limited liability.[36] This finding is robust to alternative assumptions about risk aversion and to alternative methods of calibrating average entrepreneurial talent. Because the moral hazard case performs best even when talent is calibrated to match the observed percentage

---

[35] In the case of strictly nested models, the test statistic has a χ^2 distribution. In the case of nonnested models, the test statistic is normally distributed.

[36] Using different methods and data, Ligon (1998) finds that a model with moral hazard better explains the degree of consumption smoothing in Indian villages relative to either a model with full risk sharing or a model in which only self-insurance is possible.

TABLE 3
LOG LIKELIHOODS FROM STRUCTURAL ESTIMATION

	Moral Hazard	Limited Liability	Both
		A. Whole Sample	
Risk aversion, talent (income)	−.4038	−.4706	−.4683
Risk neutrality, talent (income)	−.4104	−.4608	−.4372
Risk aversion, talent (% entrepreneur)	−.4590	−.7514	−.6064
Risk aversion, estimated talent	−.3996	−.4134	−.4035
		B. Northeast	
Risk aversion, talent (income)	−.3044	−.3474	−.3258
Risk neutrality, talent (income)	−.3046	−.3474	−.3474
Risk aversion, talent (% entrepreneur)	−.3408	−.4588	−.4250
Risk aversion, estimated talent	−.3040	−.3045	−.3029
		C. Central	
Risk aversion, talent (income)	−.5014	−.5966	−.5668
Risk neutral, talent (income)	−.5190	−.5966	−.5553
Risk aversion, talent (% entrepreneur)	−.6104	−.8658	−.7902
Risk aversion, estimated talent	−.4991	−.5355	−.5185

of entrepreneurs in the data, we gain confidence that the results are not in some way driven by the relatively low number of entrepreneurs produced by the estimates that use the relative income of entrepreneurs and nonentrepreneurs to fix the mean of the talent distribution.[37]

When the estimation also produces estimates of the talent parameters (the fourth row), the distinction between the moral hazard and the both cases decreases somewhat. While these estimates strongly reject the possibility that financial markets are characterized by limited liability alone, they do allow for the possibility that limited liability in concert with moral hazard might be as good a candidate for explaining the data as moral hazard alone.

2. Regional Findings

We next consider the possibility that the financial regime varies by region. There are a number of reasons to consider this possibility, the

---

[37] The benchmark income results imply that 3 percent of the sample will become entrepreneurs when there is moral hazard, 6 percent when there is limited liability, and 5 percent when there is limited liability and moral hazard. In the data, 14 percent of households have a business. By design, the % entrepreneur estimates imply that 14 percent of households will have a business when there is moral hazard. When there is limited liability or limited liability and moral hazard, 26 percent of households are predicted to have a business in the % entrepreneur case.

TABLE 4

COMPARISON OF FINANCIAL REGIMES, VUONG TEST RESULTS

	MH vs. LL	MH vs. Both	LL vs. Both	Best Overall Fit
	A. Whole Sample			
Risk aversion, talent (income)	MH*** (.0000)	MH*** (.0001)	Both (.8866)	MH
Risk neutrality, talent (income)	MH*** (.0010)	MH** (.0252)	Both*** (.0033)	MH
Risk aversion, talent (% entrepreneur)	MH*** (.0000)	MH*** (.0000)	Both*** (.0000)	MH
Risk aversion, estimated talent	MH*** (.0046)	MH (.3402)	Both*** (.0046)	MH or both
	B. Northeast			
Risk aversion, talent (income)	MH*** (.0071)	MH* (.0519)	Both*** (.0081)	MH
Risk neutrality, talent (income)	MH*** (.0073)	MH*** (.0073)	Tie (.1018)	MH
Risk aversion, talent (% entrepreneur)	MH*** (.0000)	MH*** (.0012)	Both*** (.0000)	MH
Risk aversion, estimated talent	MH (.4213)	Both (.3718)	Both (.1846)	MH, LL or both
	C. Central			
Risk aversion, talent (income)	MH*** (.0003)	MH*** (.0008)	Both (.1897)	MH
Risk neutrality, talent (income)	MH*** (.0007)	MH** (.0263)	Both** (.0133)	MH
Risk aversion, talent (high)	MH*** (.0000)	MH*** (.0000)	Both*** (.0027)	MH
Risk aversion, estimated talent	MH*** (.0004)	MH** (.0426)	Both (.1342)	MH

NOTE.—MH = moral hazard, LL = limited liability, both = moral hazard and limited liability. The abbreviation for the model that best fits the data in the pairwise comparison is reported. The *p*-values for the Vuong tests are in parentheses.

* Significant at at least the 10 percent level.
** Significant at at least the 5 percent level.
*** Significant at at least the 1 percent level.

first being the large differences in wealth between the more developed central region and the less developed northeastern region. In addition to this difference, the dominant financial institution is different in the two regions, and one prominent lender, the BAAC, appears to operate differently in the two regions.

In the Northeast the percentage of total funds lent is very concentrated compared to the central region. The BAAC accounts for 39 percent of all funds lent. Other formal lenders account for only 11 percent of lending. In the central region, lending is much more dispersed. The BAAC accounts for 24 percent of lending. Commercial banks and relatives account for another 21 percent and 17 percent of lending, respectively.

Despite these regional differences, the comparisons of the financial regimes for the northeastern and the central regions in panels B and C of table 4 reinforce the findings for the whole sample. Hidden information, specifically hidden action, drives the key financial constraint in Thailand. For the central region, the findings are even stronger than for the whole sample. Regardless of assumptions about risk aversion and talent, these estimates favor moral hazard alone as an explanation for the patterns of entrepreneurship in the central region. In the Northeast, the same pattern emerges, with one exception. When the estimation allows talent parameters to vary with the financial regime, the three financial regimes cannot be statistically distinguished from one another.

3. Robustness Checks

Grid sizes and bounds.—In producing the structural estimates, we have experimented with different grid sizes for investment and effort, as well as with different upper bounds on the potential range for investment and effort.[38] The superior fit of the moral hazard financial regime is not affected by alternative assumptions about the number of grids or the range of potential investment and effort levels.

Sensitivity of results to outliers.—In order to ensure that the findings are not driven by outliers in the data, we have estimated the model, under the benchmark assumptions, for each of the financial regimes, dropping observations that fall into the top 5 percent or the bottom 5 percent of the wealth distribution. When the influence of potential outliers is eliminated, the moral hazard regime continues to significantly outperform the limited-liability regime as well as the regime in which both moral hazard and limited liability are a concern.

Identification of business households.—We return now to the issue of whether the assignment of entrepreneurial and nonentrepreneurial status to the sample households has content. This is evaluated using simulations of the Evans and Jovanovic (1989) limited-liability model, because this model is relatively speedy to estimate numerically. We construct 100 samples of the Thai data in which entrepreneurial status is randomly assigned, ignoring the actual occupation of the household. The overall fraction of randomly assigned entrepreneurs is fixed at the proportion of business households actually observed in the original data. The overall fit of the limited-liability model deteriorates substantially when it is estimated using the simulated data.

---

[38] Specifically, we computed versions of the model with five grid points for effort, versions with 10 grid points for investment, and versions with higher upper bounds on the grids for effort and investment (10 instead of five).

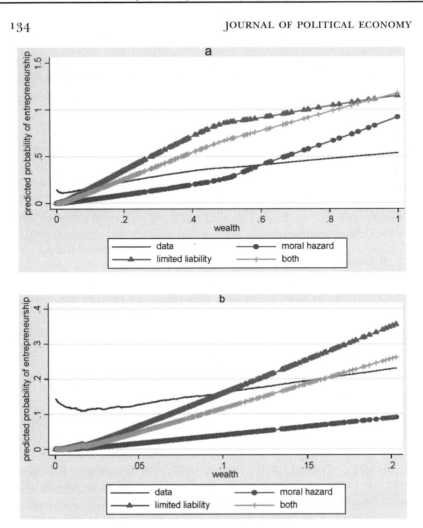

FIG. 4.—Predicted probability of entrepreneurship and wealth. *a*, Entire wealth domain. *b*, Fifth to ninety-fifth percentiles of wealth. Lowess estimates of the relationship between entrepreneurial status and wealth from survey data and entrepreneurial status assigned in benchmark structural estimates (moral hazard, limited liability, and both moral hazard and limited liability). Bandwidth = 0.8.

4.   Summary of Structural Evidence

Taking together all the evidence from the formal comparison of the three financial regimes, we conclude that moral hazard is the key financial market imperfection that affects who becomes an entrepreneur in Thailand. We reject the possibility that limited liability alone could explain the data.

Figure 4 compares the predicted likelihood of starting a business as a function of wealth at the maximized parameter values produced by each financial regime for the benchmark whole-sample results. The figure also includes nonparametric estimates of the probability of starting a business as a function of wealth from the survey data. In the case of the structural estimates, the graphs represent the nonparametric relationship between entrepreneurship and wealth implied by the assignments of capital and effort produced by the structural estimates. For each wealth and talent value, the structural estimates generate the probability that a household with that wealth and talent will become an entrepreneur. The curve labeled "data" in both panels of figure 4 is the nonparametric estimate of the relationship between the survey reports of entrepreneurial status and wealth. For each structural estimate and the data, nonparametric estimates of the relationship between entrepreneurship and wealth were produced using the same techniques as in figure 1 (see n. 1 for details).

Figure 4a shows what happens to the likelihood of starting a business over the entire domain of wealth, and figure 4b restricts the wealth domain to the fifth through the ninety-fifth percentiles. It is important to keep in mind that the probability of starting a business as a function of wealth produced by the structural estimates also includes the impact of integrating out over the talent distribution. Similarly, the estimates produced from the survey data make no attempt to control for entrepreneurial talent or schooling.

From figure 4a, it appears that the predicted probability of being an entrepreneur generated by the moral hazard regime is closest to the Thai data. Further, from figure 4b, one can see that while the moral hazard estimate underpredicts the percentage of entrepreneurs relative to most of the data, this estimate does a good job of matching the slope observed in the data. In other words, the moral hazard regime closely mimics the relatively constant observed rate of increase of entrepreneurship with wealth in the data.

In contrast, the limited-liability and the "both" estimates overestimate the rate of increase in entrepreneurship with wealth for the majority of households. Specifically, both of these regimes suggest that the rate of increase in entrepreneurship with wealth is highest among low-wealth households, and this slows down only when wealth reaches approximately 0.55, or nearly the ninety-ninth percentile of the wealth distribution (see fig. 4a). In comparison, the moral hazard estimate implies that entrepreneurship increases more modestly with wealth for almost all the wealth distribution and then increases sharply with wealth at the highest wealth levels. Some intuition is provided by an examination of figure 2, the risk-neutral case, and figure 3. Under limited liability, increases in wealth for constrained entrepreneurs sharply increase the level of capital with only a small variation in effort. In contrast, under moral hazard, capital is, on average, not moving much with wealth whereas effort increases, starting from a lower value. Evidently the moral hazard constraint is more damaging at low levels of wealth than limited liability is.

B.   Nonparametric and Reduced-Form Evidence

In addition to comparing the financial regimes on the basis of the structural evidence about who will start a business as a function of wealth and talent, we can also use nonparametric and reduced-form techniques and additional variables to try to distinguish financial regimes. While none of the findings presented here is definitive on its own, taken together they reinforce the findings from the structural model comparisons: the financial market constraint is dominant because of moral hazard.

Limited liability and moral hazard have different implications for how borrowing will change with wealth, particularly for constrained business owners. Recall that constrained business households are those that report that their business would be more profitable if it were expanded and that 56 percent of the business households are "constrained" according to this definition. In the limited-liability case, constrained business owners have borrowed up to the maximum multiple of wealth allowed, so increases in wealth will necessarily lead to increased borrowing for these businesses. In the moral hazard case, the opposite is true: borrowing will decrease with wealth for constrained business owners. Business owners can relax the incentive compatibility constraint by borrowing less. We investigate these implications by examining the relationship between the likelihood of being a borrower and wealth and the level of net savings and wealth for constrained business households.

1.   Nonparametric Evidence

Figure 5a summarizes the nonparametric relationship between the probability of being a borrower and wealth for constrained business households. Figure 5b reports on the predicted relationship between net savings and wealth for constrained business households. Both figures were produced using the same nonparametric techniques that were used to create figure 1. The domain of wealth is restricted to the fifth to the ninety-fifth percentiles. The dashed lines in the figures represent the twenty-fifth percentile and the seventy-fifth percentile bootstrap estimates of the relationship between borrowing and wealth and between net savings and wealth.

Turning first to figure 5a, we see that the probability of being a borrower decreases as wealth goes from zero to about 0.02. Approximately

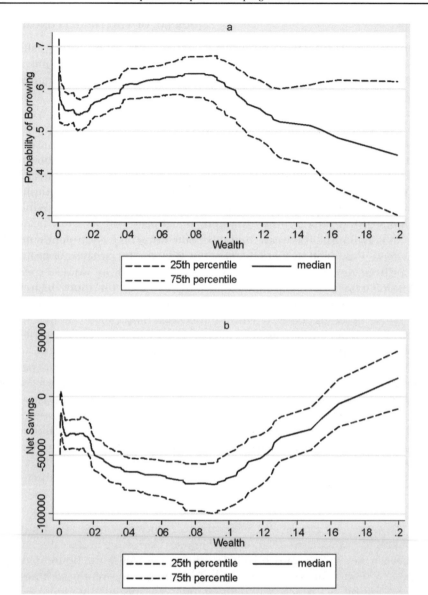

FIG. 5.—*a*, Lowess estimate of the probability of being a borrower for constrained business households. *b*, Lowess estimate of net savings and wealth for constrained business households. Five hundred bootstrap estimates of the relationship between being a borrower and wealth (*a*) and between net savings and wealth (*b*) were created using a bandwidth of 0.8. The twenty-fifth percentile (dashed line), median (solid line), and seventy-fifth percentile estimates (dashed line) are shown in the figure. Note that the figure shows the relationship for the fifth to the ninety-fifth percentiles of wealth.

60 percent of the survey households have wealth in this range. This relationship is consistent with moral hazard. As wealth goes from 0.02 to about 0.05, the likelihood of borrowing increases with wealth, as we would expect if limited liability constrained financial markets. This range corresponds to about 17 percent of the survey households. When wealth is greater than 0.08, the probability of borrowing again decreases with wealth, which would be expected if moral hazard were responsible for restrictions on financial contracts. This range accounts for about 9 percent of households. Thus for the majority of households in the Thai data, the relationship between borrowing and wealth is consistent with moral hazard, although we cannot rule out the possibility that limited liability also plays a role in shaping financial markets.

The relationship between the *level* of borrowing and, equivalently, net savings is examined in figure 5*b*. Here we see a similar pattern. As wealth goes from zero to 0.005, net savings increases, which we would expect if moral hazard were important. This range accounts for approximately one-third of households. As wealth goes from 0.005 to 0.09, net savings decrease or, equivalently, borrowing increases. This range is consistent with limited liability and corresponds to about 55 percent of households in the sample. When wealth is greater than 0.09, net savings again increases with wealth, and this range accounts for the remaining 12 percent of households. These estimates suggest that both moral hazard and limited liability may be important for explaining the data, with about half of the observations being consistent with each financial constraint. However, limited liability alone cannot account for the relationship between the likelihood of borrowing and borrowing levels and wealth described in figure 5.[39]

2. Reduced-Form Evidence

Whole-sample findings.—We now turn to reduced-form parametric estimates to examine the relationship between borrowing and wealth and between net savings and wealth for constrained business households. Table 5 reports on probit estimates of whether entrepreneurial households borrow as a function of demographic controls, past use of various financial institutions, past wealth, and whether or not the household reports that its business is constrained. For the whole sample, these results suggest that constrained business households are 8.5 percentage points more likely to borrow than their unconstrained counterparts.

This finding is more consistent with moral hazard than with limited liability. When financial markets are characterized by moral hazard and incentive constraints bind, everyone who borrows will be constrained.

---

[39] Small sample sizes preclude us from creating regional versions of these estimates.

DISTINGUISHING LIMITED LIABILITY   139

TABLE 5
PROBIT ESTIMATES OF BEING A NET BORROWER (Net Savings < 0), BUSINESS
HOUSEHOLDS

	WHOLE SAMPLE		NORTHEAST		CENTRAL REGION	
	*dF/dx**	*Z*-Statistic	*dF/dx**	*Z*-Statistic	*dF/dx**	*Z*-Statistic
Constrained (= 1 if constrained, 0 otherwise)*	.0849	1.55	−.0491	−.48	.1321	1.97
Wealth six years ago†	−.0013	−.24	.1880	1.75	.0007	.12
Age of head	−.0115	−.82	−.0149	−.58	−.0116	−.67
Age of head squared	.0001	.65	.0001	.47	.0001	.49
Years of schooling— head	.0049	.47	−.0027	−.16	.0010	.07
Adult women in household	.0494	1.37	.1320	1.81	.0268	.62
Adult men in household	−.0701	−2.05	−.1838	−2.64	−.0334	−.82
Children (< 18 years) in household	.0344	1.47	.1338	2.63	.0059	.21
Observed frequency	.5457		.6066		.5146	
Predicted frequency at mean of X	.5483		.6367		.5153	
Log likelihood	−237.02		−70.50		−158.47	
Pseudo *R²*	4.70%		13.79%		4.28%	
Observations	361		122		239	

NOTE.—Net savings is defined to be financial assets plus loans owed to household minus debt. Numbers in the table are the estimated coefficient multiplied by 1 million. The sample excludes the top 1 percent of households by wealth. The estimates also include controls for past membership/patronage of various financial institutions and organizations.
  * Dummy variables.
  † Wealth six years ago is made up of the value of household assets, agricultural assets, and land.

In the limited-liability case, the relationship between borrowing and being constrained is much weaker. Some households that borrow will be able to invest the optimal amount of capital and will not be constrained, and others will not be able to borrow enough to invest the optimal amount and will be constrained.

Table 6 reports on the relationship between the extent of borrowing, or, equivalently, net savings, and wealth for constrained and unconstrained business households. This table includes regression estimates of net savings for business households as a function of various demographic controls and wealth for business households. The effect of wealth is allowed to differ depending on whether the business is constrained or not. For the whole sample, net savings is positively correlated (or, equivalently, borrowing is negatively correlated) with wealth for constrained businesses. A 1,000,000-baht increase in wealth for a constrained business would increase net savings (decrease borrowing) by 48,000 baht.

TABLE 6
Regression Estimates of Net Savings, Business Households

	Whole Sample		Northeast		Central Region	
	Coefficient	t-Statistic	Coefficient	t-Statistic	Coefficient	t-Statistic
Wealth six years ago:*						
Constrained business†	.048	4.32	-.004	.05	.048	3.63
Unconstrained business†	.012	1.42	.383	3.31	.012	1.19
Age of head	9,592.724	.52	5,639.596	.29	15,814.300	.60
Age of head squared	-93.922	-.56	-71.272	-.41	-161.393	-.68
Years of schooling (head)	-23,179.890	-1.67	-12,283.410	-.96	-28,433.790	-1.35
Adult women in household	-105,875.200	-2.18	-133,223.000	-2.59	-104,812.200	-1.56
Adult men in household	108,636.700	2.37	60,962.520	1.22	140,117.500	2.22
Children (<18 years) in household	377,10.180	1.21	-60,660.900	-1.68	64,761.760	1.54
Constant	-234,535.400	-.48	121,595.300	.25	-461,081.300	-.65
Adjusted R^2	7.86%		9.94%		8.71%	
Observations	361		122		239	

Note.—Net savings is defined to be financial assets plus loans owed to household minus debt. Numbers in the table are estimated coefficients multiplied by 1 million. The sample excludes the top 1 percent of households by wealth.
* Wealth six years ago is made up of the value of household assets, agricultural assets, and land.
† Dummy variable.

The same increase in wealth for an unconstrained business is predicted to increase net savings by 12,000 baht, and the coefficient on wealth for unconstrained businesses is not statistically different from zero. This is the relationship we would expect to see between net savings and wealth among constrained businesses if financial markets are characterized by moral hazard and households are risk neutral. By decreasing borrowing when wealth goes up, constrained businesses can relax the incentive compatibility constraint associated with moral hazard. If financial markets were characterized by limited liability, we would expect net savings to go down (borrowing to increase) with wealth for constrained businesses.

Regional findings.—The results for the central region favor moral hazard and are very similar to the results for the whole sample. The likelihood of being a borrower is predicted to be 13 percentage points higher among constrained business households in the central region (see table 5). Table 6 shows that a 1,000,000-baht increase in wealth is predicted to increase net savings by 48,000 baht in the central region, which we would expect if moral hazard were a concern.

According to the estimates reported in table 5, being constrained has no statistically significant effect on the likelihood of borrowing for businesses in the Northeast. When financial markets are characterized by limited liability, the probability of borrowing should not be related to wealth, which is consistent with the findings in table 5 for the Northeast. A much stronger case would exist if the point estimate for the effect of being constrained on the probability of borrowing were close to zero and precisely estimated. As it is, the precision of the estimate is consistent with the impact of being constrained having either a negative or a positive impact on the likelihood of borrowing in the Northeast.

We also find that the level of net savings is imprecisely related to wealth among constrained businesses in the Northeast (see table 6). We cannot rule out the possibility that an increase in wealth would be associated with a decrease in net savings (increase in borrowing), which we would expect if limited liability constrains financial markets. On the other hand, the results do not allow us to rule out the opposite either.

3.   Summary of Nonparametric and Reduced-Form Evidence

Taken together, the nonparametric and reduced-form evidence indicates that limited liability alone cannot explain the observed relationship between borrowing and wealth and net savings and wealth. Figure 5 suggests that both moral hazard and limited liability have a role to play in explaining patterns of entrepreneurship in Thailand. The strength of the evidence in favor of moral hazard for the central region and the lack of evidence to distinguish moral hazard from limited liability in the Northeast provide independent confirmation of the patterns observed in the formal model comparison tests for the two regions.

VII.   Conclusions and Discussion

Identifying the source of financial constraints that limit entry into entrepreneurship was a key objective of the paper. Nonparametric, reduced-form, and structural evidence all indicate that moral hazard is the key financial constraint that restricts entrepreneurship in Thailand. To the extent that limited liability plays a role in constraining entrepreneurs and potential entrepreneurs, it does so in conjunction with moral hazard.

The paper emphasizes different potential assumptions regarding the constraints on financial contracting. The model has common assumptions about utility, production, the distribution of talent, and error terms, regardless of financial constraints. Therefore, these aspects of the model do not account for the success of the moral hazard model in the structural estimates. In addition, nonparametric and reduced-form evidence, which is independent of assumptions regarding utility functions, production, talent, and errors, also points to moral hazard as the dominant financial market imperfection.

The issues raised in the paper contribute to the discussion of the desirability of policy interventions that are intended to alleviate financial constraints. In particular, the paper highlights the fact that the presence of financial constraints does not establish grounds for a policy intervention. Given the financial market imperfections, the existing set of contracts may be the optimal ones. Nonetheless, the findings suggest useful directions for policy discussions.

Currently the BAAC emphasizes joint liability lending groups for poor farmers. Our findings suggest that these groups, which may use superior information that villagers have about one another to mitigate moral hazard problems, could be usefully extended to more households. Indeed, we find some evidence that wealthier households that participate in BAAC borrowing groups may be less constrained in the central region (see Paulson and Townsend 2004), as though the BAAC were using these groups as a screening mechanism and channeling larger loans to individuals who are deemed acceptable group members by their peers. In contrast, a program to establish secure property rights in land (so that it could serve as collateral and overcome limited-liability constraints) might be a lower priority for much of Thailand. The main point is that a successful policy intervention must address the underlying financial market imperfection rather than its symptoms.

Our work suggests a number of fruitful avenues for future research. Clearly more work on the role of entrepreneurial talent is a priority.

Success in this area is likely to require additional data to help pin down both the distribution of talent and its role in production. In addition, it would be valuable, from both a theoretical and an empirical perspective, to extend the cross-sectional framework and findings reported on here to a dynamic setting. Finally, it would be interesting to explore the extent to which the findings for Thailand generalize to other developing and developed countries.

References

Abbring, Jaap H., Pierre-André Chiappori, James J. Heckman, and Jean Pinquet. 2003. "Adverse Selection and Moral Hazard in Insurance: Can Dynamic Data Help to Distinguish?" *J. European Econ. Assoc.* 1 (April/May): 512–21.

Aghion, Phillippe, and Patrick Bolton. 1997. "A Theory of Trickle-Down Growth and Development." *Rev. Econ. Studies* 64 (April): 151–72.

Binford, Michael, Tae Jeong Lee, and Robert M. Townsend. 2001. "Sampling Design for an Integrated Socioeconomic and Ecologic Survey Using Satellite Remote Sensing and Ordination." Manuscript, Univ. Chicago.

Buera, Francisco. 2005. "A Dynamic Model of Entrepreneurial Choice with Borrowing Constraints." Manuscript, Northwestern Univ.

Cunha, Flavio, James J. Heckman, and Salvador Navarro. 2004. "Separating Uncertainty from Heterogeneity in Life Cycle Earnings." IZA Discussion Paper no. 1437, Inst. Study Labor, Bonn.

Evans, David S., and Boyan Jovanovic. 1989. "An Estimated Model of Entrepreneurial Choice under Liquidity Constraints." *J.P.E.* 97 (August): 808–27.

Fafchamps, Marcel. 1993. "Sequential Labor Decisions under Uncertainty: An Estimable Household Model of West-African Farmers." *Econometrica* 61 (September): 1173–97.

Giné, Xavier. 2005. "Access to Capital in Rural Thailand: An Estimated Model of Formal versus Informal Credit." Policy Research Working Paper no. 3502, World Bank, Washington, DC.

Giné, Xavier, and Robert M. Townsend. 2004. "Evaluation of Financial Liberalization: A General Equilibrium Model with Constrained Occupation Choice." *J. Development Econ.* 74 (August): 269–307.

Judd, Kenneth L. 1998. *Numerical Methods in Economics.* Cambridge, MA: MIT Press.

Karaivanov, Alexander. 2005. "Incomplete Financial Markets and Occupational Choice: Evidence from Thai Villages." Manuscript, Simon Fraser Univ.

Ligon, Ethan. 1998. "Risk Sharing and Information in Village Economies." *Rev. Econ. Studies* 65 (October): 847–64.

Lloyd-Ellis, Huw, and Dan Bernhardt. 2000. "Enterprise, Inequality and Economic Development." *Rev. Econ. Studies* 67 (January): 147–68.

Magnac, Thierry, and Jean-Marc Robin. 1996. "Occupational Choice and Liquidity Constraints." *Ricerche Economiche* 50 (June): 105–33.

Paulson, Anna L., and Robert M. Townsend. 2004. "Entrepreneurship and Financial Constraints in Thailand." *J. Corporate Finance* 10 (March): 229–62.

Phelan, Christopher, and Robert M. Townsend. 1991. "Computing Multi-period, Information-Constrained Optima." *Rev. Econ. Studies* 58 (October): 853–81.

Prescott, Edward C., and Robert M. Townsend. 1984. "Pareto Optima and Competitive Equilibria with Adverse Selection and Moral Hazard." *Econometrica* 52 (January): 21–45.

Townsend, Robert M. [principal investigator], with Anna L. Paulson, Sombat Sakuntasathien, Tae Jeong Lee, and Michael Binford. 1997. "Questionnaire Design and Data Collection for NICHD Grant 'Risk, Insurance and the Family' and NSF Grants." Manuscript, Univ. Chicago.

Vuong, Quang H. 1989. "Likelihood Ratio Tests for Model Selection and Non-nested Hypotheses." *Econometrica* 57 (March): 307–33.

Wolak, Frank A. 1994. "An Econometric Analysis of the Asymmetric Information, Regulator-Utility Interaction." *Annales d'Economie et de Statistique*, no. 34 (April–June): 13–69.

[6]

ELSEVIER

Available online at www.sciencedirect.com

SCIENCE @ DIRECT®

Journal of Corporate Finance 10 (2004) 229–262

Journal of
CORPORATE
FINANCE

www.elsevier.com/locate/econbase

Entrepreneurship and financial constraints in Thailand

Anna L. Paulson[a,*], Robert Townsend[a,b]

[a] *Federal Reserve Bank of Chicago, 230 S. LaSalle Street, Chicago, IL 60604, USA*
[b] *University of Chicago, Chicago, USA*

Abstract

We use new data from rural and semi-urban Thailand to examine how financial constraints affect entrepreneurial activity. The analysis uses nonparametric and reduced form techniques. The results indicate that financial constraints play an important role in shaping the patterns of entrepreneurship in Thailand. In particular, wealthier households are more likely to start businesses. Wealthier households are also more likely to invest more in their businesses and face fewer constraints. We also provide evidence that financial constraints place greater restrictions on entrepreneurial activity in the poor Northeast compared to the more developed Central region.
© 2003 Elsevier B.V. All rights reserved.

JEL classification: M13; O16; O321
Keywords: Entrepreneurship; Financial constraints; Thailand

1. Introduction

It is difficult to overstate the importance of entrepreneurial activity for both developed and developing economies. Small, entrepreneurial firms are an important source of innovation, jobs and economic growth. There are striking similarities between small entrepreneurial firms in the US and Thailand, despite the obvious differences between the two countries. In Thailand, small firms employ 60% of the workforce and account for approximately 50% of GDP. In the US, roughly 50% of the workforce is employed in a small firm and small firms account for 38% of GDP. In addition, the typical small firm is very small. In both Thailand and the US, the vast majority of small firms have just one or two employees. Savings and funds from friends and family provide the bulk of start-up

---

* Corresponding author. Tel.: +1-312-322-2169; fax: +1-312-913-2626.
E-mail address: anna.paulson@chi.frb.org (A.L. Paulson).

0929-1199/$ - see front matter © 2003 Elsevier B.V. All rights reserved.
doi:10.1016/S0929-1199(03)00056-7

230   *A.L. Paulson, R. Townsend / Journal of Corporate Finance 10 (2004) 229–262*

financing for small firms. In both US and Thailand, two-thirds of the initial investment in small firms comes from these sources. The goal of this paper is to use new data to systematically investigate the role of financial constraints in determining who becomes an entrepreneur in Thailand and to examine how financial constraints affect the way entrepreneurial activities are conducted. While some of the insights provided by this exercise will be specific to Thailand, others will have implications for small firms generally.

The average annual income of business owners in rural and semi-urban Thailand is double that of nonbusiness owners. One-third of households report that they would like to change occupations. Of the households who would like to change occupations, most would like to open a business. Many of these households report that they do not start businesses because they do not have the necessary funds. Among entrepreneurial households, 54% report that their business would be more profitable if they could expand it. When asked why they do not undertake this profitable opportunity, 56% of households report that they do not have enough money to do so. Both the formation of new businesses and the way that existing businesses are run appears to be affected by financial constraints.

If financial constraints are important, then we expect that business start-ups will be sensitive to the wealth of potential entrepreneurs. If financial constraints were not important, then potential entrepreneurs will make the decision to start a business based solely on the expected profitability of the planned endeavour. If necessary, they will be able to get outside financing to start the project, and their own wealth not be a factor in whether or not the business is started. When financial constraints are important, however, outside financing may be unavailable or insufficient—creating a link between the wealth of the potential entrepreneur and the decision to start a business. Wealthier households will be more likely to start a business. Holtz-Eakin et al. (1994) and Evans and Jovanovic (1989) use US data to investigate the impact of wealth on entrepreneurship in the US and conclude that financial constraints are important.

The operation of existing businesses will also be affected by the entrepreneur's wealth when financial constraints are present. In particular, financial constraints may prevent entrepreneurs from investing the optimal amount in their businesses. If financial constraints did not exist, then entrepreneurs would be able to make up the shortfall between their own funds and the profit maximizing level of investment by borrowing. In this situation, entrepreneurial investment and entrepreneurial wealth will be independent of one another. However, financial constraints may mean that entrepreneurs are unable to borrow, or may only be able to borrow a limited amount. In this case, wealthier entrepreneurs will be able to invest more in their businesses because they are less dependent on the availability of outside funding. Fazzari et al. (1988) explore this implication of financial constraints for a sample of publicly traded manufacturing firms in the US and show that, for some firms, investment is sensitive to cash flows.

Despite the general presence of financial constraints in the economy, entrepreneurial households who are sufficiently wealthy will not be constrained in how they operate their businesses because they do not need to rely on outside financing. As entrepreneurial wealth increases, we would expect household reports of being constrained and other measures of constraints, like returns to investment, to go down.

More generally, financial constraints will cause the supply and the demand for credit to be related to the characteristics of the borrower and the business, to the characteristics of

A.L. Paulson, R. Townsend / Journal of Corporate Finance 10 (2004) 229–262   231

the lender as well as to the characteristics of the market where the borrower resides and the lender operates. For example, the borrower's creditworthiness, the monitoring capabilities of the lender, the competitiveness of the lending market and the size of the market for the borrower's products are all likely to affect how much the business owner would like to borrow and how much, or whether, a potential lender is willing to lend. Measuring the impact and separating out cause from effect for many of these factors is complicated. The point is that these are important factors to control for in investigating the clear predicted relationships between entrepreneurship, wealth and entrepreneurial talent in the presence of financial constraints.

The implications of financial constraints that we investigate can come out of a wide variety of assumptions about how financial markets operate. They do not depend on a particular type of financial market imperfection. For example, all of these implications are shared by a model where there is no credit (see Lloyd-Ellis and Bernhardt, 2000); a model where credit is exogenously limited to be a fixed multiple of household wealth (see Evans and Jovanovic, 1989) and a model where credit is allocated as the optimal solution to an information constrained moral hazard problem (see Aghion and Bolton, 1996).[1] They are also consistent with the asymmetric information framework emphasized by Fazzari et al. (1988, 2000). The analysis of the implications that are presented below corresponds to a general evaluation of the impact of financial constraints rather than to an evaluation of a particular model.[2]

The data that we analyze come from our own socioeconomic survey that was fielded in March–May of 1997 to 2880 households, approximately 21% of whom run their own businesses. The sample focuses on households living in two distinct regions of Thailand: rural and semi-urban households living in the Central region which is close to Bangkok and more obviously rural households living in the semi arid and much poorer Northeastern region. The Central region is wealthier and more developed than the Northeast. The data include current and retrospective information on wealth (household, agricultural, business and financial), occupational history (transitions to and from farm work, wage work and entrepreneurship), access and use of a wide variety of formal and informal financial institutions (commercial banks, agricultural banks, village lending institutions, money-lenders, as well as friends, family and business associates). The data also provide detailed information on household demographics, entrepreneurial activities and education. The retrospective data on wealth and interactions with financial institutions helps our efforts to disentangle the effects of running a business from the forces which make it possible to start a business in the first place.

Because these data provide rich and detailed information about both the firm and the entrepreneurial household as well as information on financial intermediaries, they are

---

[1] Whether investment and the likelihood of being constrained increase or decrease with entrepreneurial talent clearly depends on a model's assumption about whether talent and capital are complements or substitutes. Lloyd-Ellis and Bernhardt (2000) assume that talent and capital are substitutes. That model implies that investment and constraints will decrease when entrepreneurial talent increases. In contrast, Evans and Jovanovic (1989) assume that talent and capital are complements. That model implies that investment and constraints will increase when talent increases.

[2] In related work, Paulson and Townsend (2002), we formally evaluate two alternative models of financial market imperfections and discuss which model best fits the Thai data.

232   *A.L. Paulson, R. Townsend / Journal of Corporate Finance 10 (2004) 229–262*

particularly well designed for studying the relationship between entrepreneurship and the financial system. Economic theory emphasizes that both firm and household characteristics are important in determining the supply and the demand for credit. In many studies the available data force a focus on either the firm or the household as potential entrepreneur, but do not allow for both to be treated with equal thoroughness. For example, Evans and Jovanovic (1989) use data from the National Longitudinal Study of Young Men, which has detailed information on the self-employed, but very sparse information about the businesses they run. In their studies of banking relationships and access to credit in small businesses, Petersen and Rajan (1994, 1995) analyze data collected by the Small Business Administration (SBA). The SBA data provide a wealth of detail about the firm, but very little information about the entrepreneur. Holtz-Eakin et al. (1994) use data from US individual tax returns. These data provide detailed information about inheritances and some information about both the entrepreneur and the firm; however, they do not include important firm and household variables, like the nature of the business and the education of the entrepreneur, for example.

Our results indicate that financial constraints play an important role in shaping the patterns of entrepreneurship in Thailand. In particular, wealthier households are more likely to start businesses. In the Central region, wealthier households are also more likely to invest more in their businesses and face fewer constraints. We also provide evidence that financial constraints place greater restrictions on entrepreneurial activity in the Northeast compared to the Central region. In addition, there is some intriguing evidence that the largest lender in rural and semi-urban areas has a greater impact on entrepreneurial activity through selection rather than through lending.

The rest of the paper is organized as follows. In the next section, we describe the household and small business data that are used in the analysis. In Section 3, we use nonparametric and reduced form techniques to evaluate how financial constraints effect which businesses are started and how existing businesses are run. We stratify the data by wealth and education and compare and contrast salient patterns of the data with the implications financial constraints using nonparametric methods. Next we introduce statistical controls and estimate reduced-form OLS and probit equations. The reduced form estimates allow us to control for the key variables that are suggested by the presence of financial constraints as well as for other variables which may be important sources of variation in the data. Section 4 concludes and discusses the policy implications of the findings.

2. Project background and the survey data

The data that we analyze in this paper are the product of a large on-going socioeconomic and institutional study in Thailand that is funded by the U.S. National Institute of Health and the National Science Foundation (see Townsend et al., 1997). The initial survey of households, village financial institutions and village key informants was completed in May of 1997 and covers regions both on the doorstep of Bangkok as well as in the relatively poor Northeast. The data provide a wealth of pre-financial crisis socioeconomic and financial data on 2880 households, 606 small businesses, 192 villages, 161 local financial institutions, 262 borrowing groups of the Bank for Agriculture and

A.L. Paulson, R. Townsend / Journal of Corporate Finance 10 (2004) 229–262 233

Agricultural Cooperatives (BAAC) and soil samples from 1880 agricultural plots. We focus on the household survey data in this paper.

The data that we analyze cover four provinces in Thailand. Two of the provinces, Lopburi and Chachoengsao are in the Central region and are relatively close to Bangkok. Chachoengsao borders the Bangkok Metropolitan Area and forms part of the industrial corridor that extends to Thailand's eastern seaboard. The other two provinces, Buriram and Sisaket are much further from Bangkok and are located in the relatively poor northeastern region. Sisaket is one of the poorest provinces in the country. The contrast between the survey areas is deliberate and has obvious advantages.

2.1. The financial environment

The financial environment that is prevalent in each survey region also differs substantially. There are two main formal sector lenders: the BAAC and commercial banks. Of these two institutions, the BAAC is much more active in rural areas. Ninety-five percent of northeastern Thai villages and 89% of Central Thai villages had at least one BAAC borrower in 1994 (Thai Community Development Department data). The BAAC offers two types of loans. One is a standard collateralized loan and the other requires no formal collateral and is secured instead through a joint liability agreement with a group of farmers who all belong to a BAAC group.

While the bulk of the BAAC's loans are uncollateralized, these loans tend to be small and the majority of funds are lent through collateralized loans. Commercial banks are active lenders in 41% of Thai villages. However, commercial bank borrowers tend to be concentrated in the relatively prosperous Central region, where 50% of villages have at least one commercial bank borrower. In contrast, only 31% of northeastern villages have a commercial bank borrower. Commercial bank loans are almost always secured with a land title. In addition to these formal sector lenders, there are a number of quasi-formal institutions that offer savings and lending services to villagers: village savings and lending institutions and rice banks. It is also common for households to borrow from relatives and neighbors and moneylenders. Often households will borrow from several sources to finance one investment project (see Kaboski and Townsend, 2000 for more details).

2.2. Sample and survey instruments

In each of the four provinces, a stratified random sample of 12 tambons (subset of an amphoe or county) was chosen. The stratification ensured an ecologically balanced sample that included two "forested" tambons. Within each sample tambon, four villages were selec-ted at random. Fifteen households were randomly selected from each of the sample villages. Soil samples were collected from randomly chosen plots belonging to the first 10 of these households. In each village, a key informant was interviewed, usually the village headman or woman. In addition, interviews were conducted with the committee members of each village financial institution. If the sample village included BAAC borrowing groups, they were also interviewed. The sampling strategy is described in more detail in Binford et al. (2001).

234   *A.L. Paulson, R. Townsend / Journal of Corporate Finance 10 (2004) 229–262*

Table 1A
Number and percentage of different types of businesses by region

Business type	Whole sample		Northeast	Central
	Number	Percentage (%)	Percentage (%)	Percentage (%)
Shrimp and/or fish	157	26	13	32
Shop	154	25	41	18
Trade	115	19	12	22
Restaurant/noodle shop	31	5	6	5
Transport and construction	31	5	3	6
Sewing/silk/embroidery	26	4	6	3
Mechanic/repair shop etc.	20	3	4	3
Rice threshing	19	3	9	0
Services (haircut, laundry, etc.)	14	2	1	3
Other	39	6	6	7
Total	606	100	100	100
Total from shrimp/fish, shops and trade	426	70	66	72

The survey instruments were designed to incorporate the latest advances in economic theory. The theories that guided the design of the questionnaires include models of financial constraints in occupation choice and in input financing; models of growth with costly financial expansion; and models which take into consideration private information and incentives.[3] We proceeded by extrapolating from the theory what the true story underlying Thailand's growth and the accompanying increase in inequality and rapid expansion of the financial sector might have been, or, more formally, by writing down and simulating a variety of economic models.[4] This process generated a list of variables that were crucial to assessing the validity of a particular story or economic model. This list of variables formed the basis for designing the questionnaires and the field research.

2.3. Business and household characteristics

In this section, we highlight some of the key features of the data that are important for this study. The businesses we study are quite varied and include shops and restaurants, trading activities, raising shrimp or livestock and the provision of construction or transportation services (see Table 1A).[5] While there are many different types of businesses, shrimp and/or fish raising, shops and trade account for 70% of the businesses in the whole sample and make up a similar percentage of the businesses in each region. Median initial investment in the households business varies substantially with business type (see Table

---

[3] Examples are the models mentioned above, all of which can generate the implications that we evaluate: Lloyd-Ellis and Bernhardt (2000), Evans and Jovanovic (1989) and Aghion and Bolton (1996).

[4] From the beginning of the 1980s until the middle of the 1990s, the Thai economy grew very rapidly. Over this period, real per capita GDP grew 8% per year. During this period of rapid growth the financial sector grew even more rapidly. The period of rapid growth was also accompanied by substantial increases in inequality. From 1981 to 1992, the Thai gini coefficient increased by 21%.

[5] We rely on household reports on whether or not they ran a business except in the case of shrimp and fish farming. All of these activities are treated as businesses. It is quite common for households to run a business in addition to farming, usually rice, and working for wages.

A.L. Paulson, R. Townsend / Journal of Corporate Finance 10 (2004) 229–262   235

Table 1B
Median initial investment by region and business type, 1000s of 1997 baht

Business type	Whole sample	Northeast	Central
Shrimp/shrimp and fish/fish	50	9	51
Shop	16	16	16
Trade	21	21	23
Restaurant/noodle shop	7	32	6
Transport and construction	278	855	181
Sewing/silk/embroidery	10	5	17
Mechanic/repair shop etc.	31	23	84
Rice threshing	47	59	12
Services (haircut, laundry, etc.)	20	25	14
Other	45	34	68
Total	32	19	38

1B). Despite this variation, the median initial investment appears to be relatively similar across regions for the same type of business, particularly for the most common business types. For example, the median investment in a shop is 16,000 baht in both the Northeast and the central region. In the Northeast, the median initial investment in trade is 21,000 baht compared to 23,000 baht in the central region.[6] For future reference, note that the average annual income in Thailand in 1996 is 105,125 baht, or roughly US$4200.

Most business households run only a single business (see Table 1C) and rely very heavily on family workers. Only 10% of the businesses paid anyone for work during the year prior to the survey.[7] More than 60% of the businesses were established in the past 5 years. In the empirical work, we restrict our attention to these businesses. Although these results are not presented in the paper, we have also looked at businesses that were established in the past 10 years. This group includes 83% of the businesses in the sample. None of the results are sensitive to which group of businesses we examine. The decision to focus on businesses that were started in the past 5 years was the result of weighing the benefit of having more accurate measures of beginning of period wealth against the cost of eliminating the 224 households that start businesses more than 5 years ago.

Households rely heavily on savings (either in the form of cash or through asset sales) to fund initial investment in their businesses. Approximately 60% of the total initial investment in household businesses comes from savings. Loans from commercial banks account for about 9% of total business investment and the Bank for Agriculture and Agricultural Cooperatives (BAAC) accounts for another 7%. In the Northeast, the BAAC plays a larger role compared to commercial banks, and in the central region the opposite is true.

Each respondent with a household business was asked, "If you could increase the size of your business, do you think it would be more profitable?". We call the households who

---

[6] Median investment in shrimp and/or fish does differ depending on the region: in the Northeast it is 9000 baht compared to 51,000 baht in the central region. This is because shrimp farming, which requires substantial initial investment, is concentrated in the central region, while fish farms are more important in the Northeast.

[7] This means that the set of entrepreneurial firms is unlikely to be very affected by the case where wealthy, but untalented, households hire poor, but talented, managers to run their firms.

Table 1C
Business characteristics

	Whole sample	Northeast	Central
Number of businesses per household—%			
One	82	89	79
More than one	18	11	21
Year established—%			
1–5 years ago	63	68	60
6–10 years ago	20	21	21
11+ years ago	17	11	19
Businesses completely owned by hh—%	97	96	98
Number of workers—%			
1–2 people	71	77	68
3–5 people	23	18	26
>5 people	6	5	6
Percentage who are family workers	94	96	93
Percentage who paid for work during past year	10	6	11
Sources of initial funding—percentage of total from each source			
Savings	39	31	40
Selling land/other assets	24	31	23
Store credit	2	2	2
Commercial bank	9	4	9
BAAC	7	10	6
Agricultural cooperative	2	3	2
Production credit group	0	0	0
Other organization	0	0	0
Relatives	0	0	0
Non-relatives	0	0	0
Moneylender	2	9	1
Gift	6	0	7
Employer	0	0	0
Other	9	9	9
Percentage of total funds from cash/savings	63	62	63
Percentage of total funds from loans	22	28	20
Percentage of businesses that are constrained*	54	64	50
Reason for constraint—%			
Not enough money to expand	56	72	47
Not enough land to expand	9	3	13
Not enough labor	12	6	15

*Households who reported that their businesses would be more profitable if it were expanded are labeled "constrained".

answered yes to this question "constrained". The respondents appear to consider the availability of capital an important factor in whether their business is operating at an optimal scale. Sixty-four percent of the household businesses in the Northeast and 50% of the households in the Central region answered yes to this question (see the bottom of Table 1C). Those who answered yes were asked to name the main barriers to expanding the business. The most common answer, especially in the Northeast, was "not enough money to expand". Seventy-two percent of the constrained businesses in the Northeast gave this answer, compared with 47% in the Central region. Scarce land and labor were also

A.L. Paulson, R. Townsend / Journal of Corporate Finance 10 (2004) 229–262 237

important reasons for not expanding, particularly in the Central region. Thirteen percent of constrained businesses in the Central region reported that they did not have enough land to expand and 15% reported that they did not have enough labor.

Table 1D provides a summary of household characteristics by region and whether or not the household has a business. Twenty-one percent of the sample households have a business, and these businesses are concentrated in the relatively prosperous Central region where 28% of the households have a business. In the Northeast, only 13% of households have a business. Business owners tend to be a bit younger and substantially more educated than their nonentrepreneurial counterparts. This is especially true in the Northeast, where 31% of the heads of business owning households have more than 4 years of schooling compared with only 14% of nonbusiness owning heads. In the Central region the difference is less dramatic: 21% of the heads of business owning households have more than 4 years of schooling compared with 15% of the heads of nonbusiness households. The percentage of business owning households who have less than 4 years of schooling is consistently lower than for nonbusiness households. In the empirical work that follows, we will use years of schooling as a proxy for entrepreneurial talent. In related work, we provide evidence that formal education and entrepreneurial talent are closely related in Thailand (Paulson and Townsend, 2002).

In both the Northeast and the Central region, the median annual income of business households is more than twice that of nonbusiness households. In addition to having higher incomes, business households are also wealthier—both at the time of the survey and prior to starting a business. In the Northeast, the average wealth of business owners is 38% higher

Table 1D
Household characteristics and current and past wealth by region and business ownership

	Whole sample		Northeast		Central	
	No business	Business	No business	Business	No business	Business
Observations	2,282	593	1,253	185	1,029	408
Percentage of sample (%)	79	21	87	13	72	28
Median household size	4	4	5	4	4	4
Median age of head	51	47	50	46	54	48
Years of schooling: head						
0–3 years (%)	21	11	20	9	21	12
4 years (%)	65	65	66	60	63	67
5–16 years (%)	14	24	14	31	15	21
Median annual income*	40,000	102,450	27,420	55,680	64,800	130,450
	Current wealth from land and agricultural and household assets 1000s of baht					
Mean	876	3,241	405	559	1,450	4,456
Standard deviation	3,046	9,295	661	641	4,411	11,000
Median	238	603	212	336	306	884
	Wealth from land and agricultural and household assets 6 years ago 1000s of baht					
Mean	699	2,211	329	405	1,150	3,030
Standard deviation	2,759	6,444	645	553	4,002	7,622
Median	130	225	125	180	140	304

* Median annual income includes income from wages and salaries and net income from farming, livestock and business activities. Income is measured in current (1997) baht. At the time of the survey, US$1 was equal to approximately 25 baht.

than that of nonbusiness owners, and median wealth is 58% higher. The difference between business and nonbusiness households is even larger in the Central region. Average wealth is 207% higher and median wealth is 188% higher.

Because households were asked to report when they acquired household and agricultural assets and land, the data provide an indication of past wealth as well as current wealth. In the empirical work, we examine the relationship between past wealth (i.e. prior to starting a business) and entrepreneurship. This allows us to avoid some problems of endogeneity that are likely to plague current wealth measures. The past value of real assets is found by depreciating the purchase price of the asset (in 1997 baht) from the time of purchase to what it would have been worth 6 years ago. We assume that the depreciation rate for all household and agricultural assets is 10% per year. If the household purchased a tractor 10 years before the survey for 100,000 baht, we would first convert the purchase price to 1997 baht (using the Thai consumer price index) and then multiply this figure by $(0.90)^4$ to account for 4 years of depreciation between the purchase data and 6 years prior to the survey. This procedure would give us the value of the tractor 6 years prior to the survey.

Past values of land are treated differently. Households were asked to report the current value of each plot that they own. In calculating past land values, we assume that there have been no real changes in land prices. So if the household has had one plot for 10 years and the current value of that plot is 100,000 baht, then 6 years ago the value of that plot will also be 100,000 baht (in 1997 baht). We also incorporate land purchase and sale information to measure the value of land that a household owned in the past. Summary statistics for past wealth are reported in Table 1D.

The indicators of past wealth that we compute are incomplete in (at least) two respects. The first issue is that we only have information on household and agricultural assets that the household still owns. If the household purchased a car 10 years ago and sold it 3 years ago, the value of the car will not be included in past wealth.[8] If the household still owns the car, then it will be included in the measure of past wealth. Since we have information about land transactions, this issue is not a concern for the past value of land. The bulk of household wealth is held in the form of land, so distortions induced by the lack of transactions data for household and agricultural assets are likely to be small. The second concern is that we do not have any information on past financial assets and liabilities. Since financial assets and liabilities tend to make up a small fraction of current household wealth, leaving them out of our measures of past wealth is probably not too big of a problem.

The measures of past wealth indicate that current business households were wealthier than nonbusiness households, regardless of whether they had a business in the past, in the past as well as at the time of the survey, especially in the Central region. Six years ago, business households in the Northeast were 23% wealthier than nonbusiness households, on average. In the Central region, business households were 163% wealthier on average.

Table 1E examines the magnitudes and the sources of real and financial wealth for business and nonbusiness households in each region. Sources of wealth differ across business and nonbusiness households. One thing that stands out is the difference in the

---

[8] Except to the extent that the proceeds from selling the car are used to buy assets that the household owns at the time of the survey.

A.L. Paulson, R. Townsend / Journal of Corporate Finance 10 (2004) 229–262 239

Table 1E

Composition of wealth and participation in financial markets by region and business ownership

	Whole sample		Northeast		Central	
	No Business	Business	No Business	Business	No Business	Business
Composition of wealth—median (1000s of baht)						
House	130	300	100	150	200	400
Household assets	17	58	9	45	32	68
Total value of land	200	515	190	244	250	893
Land that can be collateral	30	300	40	100	15	632
Agricultural assets	7	24	17	23	0	25
Business assets	0	16	0	9	0	22
Savings in goods	0	0	5	6	0	0
Financial assets	0.5	5	0.4	2.9	1.0	7.7
Financial liabilities	6.0	23	10	23	0	22
Participation in financial markets—percentage who have						
Debts to commercial banks	3	9	2	8	3	9
Debts to BAAC and agricultural cooperative	34	40	40	54	28	34
Debts to others	32	30	36	37	27	27
Savings in gold	70	85	57	69	86	92
Loans owed to hh	10	16	11	20	8	14
Percentage who are currently members/customers of institutions/organizations						
Formal financial institution	40	67	34	55	48	73
Village institution/organization	35	40	41	51	29	36
Agricultural organization	50	56	56	74	43	48
Moneylender	15	14	16	14	14	14
ROSCA	3	9	0	0	6	13
Percentage who were members/customers of institutions/organizations 6 years ago						
Formal financial institution	15	29	11	18	19	34
Village institution/organization	12	13	14	14	10	13
Agricultural organization	26	32	26	36	26	30
Moneylender	4	4	4	4	4	4
ROSCA	0	2	0	0	1	3

Wealth is measured in current (1997) baht. At the time of the survey, US$1 was equal to approximately 25 baht.

percentage of households who own titled land, which can be used as collateral.[9] In the Northeast, the median value of land that can be used as collateral is 100,000 baht for business owners and only 40,000 baht for nonbusiness owners. In the Central region, the difference is even more dramatic. The median value of land that can be used as collateral is 632,000 baht for business owners and 15,000 baht for nonbusiness owners.

---

[9] Keep in mind that cause and effect are not distinguished here and business households may have used their profits to invest in land. In many areas in Thailand, people farm land which they do not have full title to. Some people have "land-use" certificates which do not confer the same legal rights as full title. Land held by certificate cannot be used as collateral in the formal lending market, nor can it be officially sold. According to Feder et al. (1988) approximately 50% of privately held land cannot be used as collateral and can be transferred only through limited means, like inheritance. The vast majority of formal sector loans require land title as collateral. There are some smaller loan programs and lenders that allow borrowers to use savings or to pledge crops as collateral.

240   *A.L. Paulson, R. Townsend / Journal of Corporate Finance 10 (2004) 229–262*

Table 1E also compares current and past participation in formal and informal financial market by business and nonbusiness households. We group formal and informal financial institutions into five categories. The first, formal financial institutions, includes commercial banks, finance companies, insurance companies as well as national employee credit unions like the Teachers Credit Union. The second, village institutions and organizations, is made up of PCGs, rice and buffalo banks as well as village poor and elderly funds. The BAAC, the Agricultural Cooperative and local farmer's groups are included in the third group, agricultural organizations.[10] Moneylenders and Rotating Savings and Credit Associations (ROSCAs) make up the fourth and fifth groups, respectively.

The most prominent type of institution varies across the two regions. In the Northeast, agricultural organizations have the highest participation rate among both business and nonbusiness households. Formal financial institutions have the highest participation rate in the Central region. Participation includes saving as well as borrowing. In both the Northeast and the Central region, business owners are more likely to be current customers of formal financial institutions, village institutions, and agricultural organizations. Interestingly, about 14% of all households are currently customers of a moneylender and there is essentially no difference in this fraction across regions and across business and nonbusiness households. No households in the Northeast are members of a ROSCA, but ROSCAs do seem to be important in the Central region. Thirteen percent of business households in the Central region are current members of a ROSCA compared with 6% of nonbusiness households.

Households were asked to report when they became a customer or member of each organization, so we are also able to look at past participation in these same organizations. We examine the impact of these variables on the decision to start a business and the likelihood of being constrained in the analysis that follows. Six years ago, participation in all types of organizations appears to have been much lower and formal financial institutions were less prominent. Agricultural organizations had the highest participation rate for all groups, except business owners in the Central region, who were a bit more likely, even then, to be customers of a formal financial institution. Although past participation rates are lower in general, participation among eventual business owners was still higher than that of nonbusiness owners. For example, 11% of nonbusiness owners in the Northeast report being a customer of a formal financial institution 6 years ago, compared with 18% of business households. In the Central region, the same figures are 19% and 34%. The fact that households who eventually opened a business have higher levels of participation in financial markets, even prior to starting a business, suggests that access to capital may be a important component of the transition to entrepreneurship.

3. Nonparametric and reduced form evaluation of implications of financial constraints

In this section, we use the Thai data to examine how entrepreneurship is affected by financial constraints. In particular, we consider to what extent the likelihood of starting a

---

[10] In the analysis that follows, we distinguish between customers of the BAAC who have collateralized loans and customers whose loans are secured through joint liability arrangements.

A.L. Paulson, R. Townsend / Journal of Corporate Finance 10 (2004) 229–262 241

business is related to household wealth; whether evidence of financial constraints tends to decline with wealth; and how business investment is affected by household wealth. We present two types of evidence to evaluate the implications of financial constraints. We first construct tables and graphs that describe how the percentage of entrepreneurs and of constrained and unconstrained business owners varies with wealth. We also construct tables and graphs that describe how investment varies with wealth. These methods have the advantage of requiring very little structure or statistical assumptions. On the other hand, they do not control for important variation in the data that is not captured by the bivariate relationships that they focus on. In order to address these concerns, we also examine reduced form ordinary least squares and maximum likelihood probit counterparts to the implications of financial constraints.

We need to come up with appropriate measures of entrepreneurial talent and wealth in order to evaluate the implications of financial constraints. The proxy we use for entrepreneurial talent is education. While education is certainly not a perfect indicator of entrepreneurial talent, it is likely to be positively correlated with business skill.[11] As we mentioned earlier, in Paulson and Townsend (2002) we show that, at least for Thailand, formal education seems to be strongly associated with entrepreneurial talent. The appropriate wealth variable is beginning of period wealth, that is, wealth at the time the decision to start a business is made. As an empirical counterpart to this variable, we use wealth 6 years prior to the survey, and exclude households already in business at that time from the analysis. The items that are included in this measure are: the value of household and agricultural assets and titled and untitled land. We do not include the value of business assets that the household may have owned 6 years ago. By using past, rather than current wealth, and by excluding business assets acquired before the business was started, we hope to avoid issues of endogeneity: wealthier people are more likely to start businesses and business owners have higher earnings than wage-workers, which allows business owners to become still richer. In this scenario, current wealth captures both the cause and the effect of having been able to start a business in the past. Since 60% of businesses were founded in the past 5 years, our measure of past wealth captures conditions prior to opening the business for most households.[12]

It may be the case that households that eventually start businesses have higher past wealth because they have been saving at a higher rate in anticipation of starting a business in the future. This is in fact turns out to be true in the data.[13] Given this pattern, if we find that wealth is an important predictor of who starts a business, then it is particularly strong evidence that financial constraints are important since households have to wait to start a

---

[11] We have also experimented with including a variable that captures the likelihood that the head of the household would have migrated to Bangkok 5 years ago. We hypothesize that people with a high propensity to migrate may also have more entrepreneurial talent. Adding this variable does not substantively change the results.

[12] We eliminate households who started businesses more than 5 years ago so that we are comparing business and nonbusiness households. In addition, we have also experimented with examining households who started businesses in the past 10 years as a function of wealth 11 years ago. The results are the same regardless of whether we look at businesses started in the past 5 years or businesses started in the past 10 years.

[13] Eleven years prior to the survey, the median wealth of households that started a business in the 5 years prior to the survey was only 58% of that of households who never started a business. However, 6 years prior to the survey, the median wealth of business households was 152% times the median wealth of nonbusiness households.

242   *A.L. Paulson, R. Townsend / Journal of Corporate Finance 10 (2004) 229–262*

Table 2A
Entrepreneurship and constraints by wealth and education

Schooling	Wealth			
	Lowest quartile	Second quartile	Third quartile	Fourth quartile
Whole sample				
0–3 years #	*150*	*149*	*127*	*108*
No business—%	91	87	89	85
Business—%	9	13	11	15
Constrained—%	36	74$^{\#\#}$	57	44
Unconstrained—%	64	26	43	56
4 years #	429	479	483	480
No business—%	83	83	84	68
Business—%	17^{++}	17	16	32***,+++,###
Constrained—%	61^{+}	55	61	45**,##
Unconstrained—%	39	45	39	55
5–16 years #	127	84	95	111
No business—%	72	69	72	59
Business—%	28$^{ooo,+++}$	31$^{ooo,+++}$	28$^{ooo,+++}$	41**,ooo,+,#
Constrained—%	50	62	52	63^{++}
Unconstrained—%	50	38	48	37
Central region				
0–3 years #	*76*	*78*	*67*	*46*
No business—%	86	81	82	80
Business—%	14	19	18	20
Constrained—%	27	67$^{\#\#}$	50	56
Unconstrained—%	73	33	50	44
4 years #	218	225	228	257
No business—%	74	77	75	57
Business—%	26^{++}	23	25	43***,+++,##
Constrained—%	55$^{\#}$	46	45	44
Unconstrained—%	45	54	55	56
5–16 years #	61	53	60	49
No business—%	67	68	70	45
Business—%	33^{oo}	32°	30	55**,ooo,###
Constrained—%	55	65	56	59
Unconstrained—%	45	35	44	41
Northeast				
0–3 years #	*73*	*74*	*63*	*57*
No business—%	96	92	95	93
Business—%	4	8	5	7
Constrained—%	67	67	67	50
Unconstrained—%	33	33	33	50
4 years #	212	249	242	240
No business—%	92	89	89	84
Business—%	8	11	11	16***,+
Constrained—%	82	64	63	72
Unconstrained—%	18	36	37	28

A.L. Paulson, R. Townsend / Journal of Corporate Finance 10 (2004) 229–262 243

Table 2A (*continued*)

Schooling	Wealth			
	Lowest quartile	Second quartile	Third quartile	Fourth quartile
Northeast				
5–16 years #	67	33	44	50
No business—%	76	70	77	66
Business—%	$24^{\text{ooo},+++}$	$30^{\text{ooo},+++}$	$23^{\text{ooo},++}$	$34^{\text{ooo},+++}$
Constrained—%	44^{++}	50	60	65
Unconstrained—%	56	50	40	35

*, **, *** indicate the significance of the change in proportion of businesses, constrained businesses or unconstrained businesses when the lowest wealth quartile is compared to the highest wealth quartile at the 10%, 5% and 1% levels, respectively. ^{o}, ^{oo}, ^{ooo} indicate the significance of the change in the proportion of businesses, constrained businesses or unconstrained businesses when the lowest education category is compared to the highest education category at the 10%, 5% and 1% levels, respectively. $^{\#}$, $^{\#\#}$, $^{\#\#\#}$ indicate the significance of the change in the proportion of businesses, constrained businesses or unconstrained businesses when the wealth quartile indicated in the column heading is compared to the next lowest wealth quartile at the 10%, 5% and 1% levels, respectively. $^{+}$, $^{++}$, $^{+++}$ indicate the significance of the change in the proportion of businesses, constrained businesses or unconstrained businesses when the education category indicated in the row heading is compared to the next lowest education category at the 10%, 5% and 1% levels, respectively.

business until they have accumulated enough wealth to finance it. This suggests that they are unable to borrow to start the business.

We also need to be able to tell whether or not businesses are constrained. We consider households who answered yes to the question "If you could increase the size of your business, do you think it would be more profitable?" to be constrained. There are several issues surrounding the use of this measure. First, the question refers to current, not past conditions. Second, it is unclear to what extent the respondents' interpretations of the question match the definition of constrained suggested by economic theory. However, as was discussed above, the responses to follow-up questions about why the household did not expand the business suggest that there is at least a rough correspondence between the theoretical and the practical definitions of being constrained. In addition to this measure of being constrained, we also examine how returns to business investment vary with wealth and education. Constrained households are likely to operate on a portion of the production function where the returns to investment are greater than the optimal level.

In the discussion that follows, we consider each of the implications of financial constraints. For each implication, we consider the evidence that is found in [Tables 2A, Table 2B or Table 2C, followed by a discussion of the nonparametric estimates which are presented in Figs. 1–3. Finally, we discuss the relevant reduced form estimates which are found in Tables 3A–5.

3.1. Implications of financial constraints

3.1.1. Implication #1: holding entrepreneurial talent fixed and increasing wealth, the percentage of businesses will increase

Table 2A summarizes the percentage of nonbusiness owners, the percentage of constrained business owners and the percentage of unconstrained business owners by the education of the head of household and wealth. We split years of schooling into three

244   A.L. Paulson, R. Townsend / Journal of Corporate Finance 10 (2004) 229–262

Table 2B
Median returns to business investment in business by wealth

	Wealth			
	Lowest quartile	Second quartile	Third quartile	Fourth quartile
Whole sample				
Business	56.7%	38.4%	20.7%	16.2%**
Constrained	96.9%	67.2%	13.8%	16.4%***
Unconstrained	10.5%++	31.2%	32.3%	16.1%
Central				
Business	80.8%	48.8%	39.1%	16.0%***
Constrained	98.2%	79.3%	28.2%	14.4%***
Unconstrained	48.0%	34.8%	56.6%	21.0%
Northeast				
Business	21.2%	12.7%	6.6%	10.0%
Constrained	57.9%	35.7%	23.2%	17.1%
Unconstrained	4.0%+	8.9%	3.2%+	0.0%

	Education		
	0–3 years	4 years	5–16 years
Whole sample			
Business	5.80%	28.54%	22.77%
Constrained	32.59%	30.44%	25.63%
Unconstrained	2.90%	28.46%	19.37%
Central			
Business	6.42%	38.99%	25.63%
Constrained	21.84%	37.84%	25.63%
Unconstrained	6.42%	43.89%	24.98%
Northeast			
Business	4.10%	12.71%	21.40%
Constrained	35.59%	18.69%	26.52%
Unconstrained	− 5.43%++	4.32%+	4.53%

*, **, *** indicate the significance of the difference in median returns to investment for businesses, constrained businesses or unconstrained businesses when the lowest wealth quartile is compared to the highest wealth quartile at the 10%, 5% and 1% levels, respectively. °, °°, °°° indicate the significance of the difference in median returns to investment for businesses, constrained businesses or unconstrained businesses when the lowest education category is compared to the highest education category at the 10%, 5% and 1% levels, respectively. #, ##, ### indicate the significance of the difference in median returns to investment for businesses, constrained businesses or unconstrained businesses when the wealth quartile indicated in the column heading is compared to the next lowest wealth quartile at the 10%, 5% and 1% levels, respectively. +, ++, +++ indicate the significance of the difference in median returns to investment within the category indicated by the column heading, for constrained businesses and unconstrained businesses at the 10%, 5% and 1% levels, respectively.

groups: 0–3, 4 and 5–16 years. About 60% of the heads of household in the survey have 4 years of schooling, which was the statutory minimum when most of them attended school. Wealth is divided into quartiles. The division depends on the sample under consideration. So, for example, only northeastern households were taken into account in determining the quartiles for the Northeast. The figures in this table summarize the key features of the data

A.L. Paulson, R. Townsend / Journal of Corporate Finance 10 (2004) 229–262 245

Table 2C
Median initial investment in business by wealth and education

	Wealth			
	Lowest quartile	Second quartile	Third quartile	Fourth quartile
Whole sample				
Business	17,053	12,317	16,917	30,583
Constrained	13,494	12,317	25,664	30,905
Unconstrained	20,257	12,536	11,658	29,639
Central				
Business	22,562	14,147	15,727	32,478
Constrained	13,603	18,191	19,130	43,000*
Unconstrained	38,504	10,926	13,970	28,695^{+}
Northeast				
Business	12,732	12,131	5205	21,705
Constrained	12,732	7617	4856	15,720
Unconstrained	11,614	21,202	5877	33,343

	Education		
	0–3 years	4 years	5–16 years
Whole sample			
Business	15,420	18,401	18,674
Constrained	9920	25,664	14,211
Unconstrained	36,263	14,147^{+}	23,467
Central			
Business	15,727	30,905	18,218
Constrained	7710	32,478$^{\#\#}$	10,419$^{\#}$
Unconstrained	44,398	15,942^{++}	33,478
Northeast			
Business	15,329	10,063	26,677
Constrained	12,131	11,600	30,844
Unconstrained	15,420	5615	16,917$^{\#}$

*, **, *** indicate the significance of the difference in median initial investment for businesses, constrained businesses or unconstrained businesses when the lowest wealth quartile is compared to the highest wealth quartile at the 10%, 5% and 1% levels, respectively. °, °°, °°° indicate the significance of the difference in median initial investment for businesses, constrained businesses or unconstrained businesses when the lowest education category is compared to the highest education category at the 10%, 5% and 1% levels, respectively. #, ##, ### indicate the significance of the difference in median initial investment for businesses, constrained businesses or unconstrained businesses when the wealth quartile, or the education category, indicated in the column heading is compared to the next lowest wealth quartile, or the next lowest education category, at the 10%, 5% and 1% levels, respectively. +, ++, +++ indicate the significance of the difference in median returns to investment, within the category indicated by the column heading, for constrained businesses and unconstrained businesses at the 10%, 5% and 1% levels, respectively.

along the lines suggested by the presence of financial constraints without making a commitment to a particular statistical model.

Financial constraints imply that, holding business skill fixed, as wealth increases the percentage of business owners will increase. This prediction appears to be borne out in the

246 *A.L. Paulson, R. Townsend / Journal of Corporate Finance 10 (2004) 229–262*

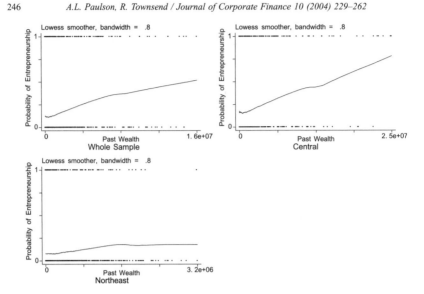

Fig. 1. Probability of entrepreneurship and past wealth. These figures represent nonparametric estimates of the relationship between having started a business in the 5 years prior to the survey and wealth 6 years prior to the survey. The dots represent the actual data points and the lines depict the estimated relationship between the likelihood of starting a business and past wealth. For each observation, a weighted regression is performed using 80% (bandwidth = 0.8) of the data around that point. The data are weighted using a tri-cube weighting procedure that puts more weight on the points closest to the observation in question. The weighted regression results are used to produce a predicted value for each observation. Because the graphs can be fairly sensitive to outliers, the wealthiest 1% of the sample is dropped.

data. Comparing the percentage of business owners in the lowest wealth category to the percentage of business owners in the highest wealth category, we find that the percentage of business owners increases substantially for each region and for all education groups. The percentage of business owners increases from 14% to 20% in the Central region and from 4% to 7% in the Northeast for the lowest education group. For people with 4 years of schooling, the percentage of business owners goes from 26% to 43% (significant at the 1% level) in the Central region and from 8% to 16% in the Northeast (significant at the 5% level). For the group with 5–16 years of schooling, the percentage goes from 33% to 55% in the Central region (significant at the 5% level) and increases from 24% to 34% in the Northeast.

The increasing likelihood of becoming an entrepreneur as wealth grows can also be seen very dramatically in Fig. 1. These graphs (as well as Figs. 2 and 3) are nonparametric estimates of the relationship between entrepreneurship and wealth. For each observation, a weighted regression is performed using 80% (bandwidth = 0.8) of the data around that point. The data are weighted using a tri-cube weighting procedure that puts more weight on the points closest to the observation in question. The weighted regression results are used to produce a predicted value for each observation. Because the graphs can be fairly sensitive to outliers, we have dropped the wealthiest 1% of the sample. The graphs indicate

A.L. Paulson, R. Townsend / Journal of Corporate Finance 10 (2004) 229–262　　　　247

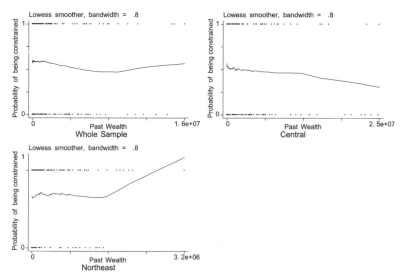

Fig. 2. Probability of being a constrained business and past wealth. These figures represent nonparametric estimates of the relationship between a businesses report of being constrained at the time of the survey and wealth 6 years prior to the survey. The sample consists of businesses that were started in the 5 years prior to the survey. The dots represent the actual data and the lines depict the estimated relationship between being constrained and past wealth. For each observation, a weighted regression is performed using 80% (bandwidth = 0.8) of the data around that point. The data are weighted using a tri-cube weighting procedure that puts more weight on the points closest to the observation in question. The weighted regression results are used to produce a predicted value for each observation. Because the graphs can be fairly sensitive to outliers, the wealthiest 1% of the sample is dropped.

that the likelihood of becoming an entrepreneur increases dramatically with wealth, particularly in the Central region.

So far we have examined the implications of financial constraints for who will become an entrepreneur without making any statistical assumptions and without controlling for other characteristics of the households. In the next set of tables, Tables 3A and 3B, we estimate probit models of who becomes an entrepreneur. The dependent variable is equal to one if the household currently runs a business that was founded in the last 5 years. The explanatory variables include characteristics of the household head that may be indicators of business talent: age, age squared, and years of schooling.[14] There are also variables that control for the amount of household labor that is available: the number of adult males, the

---

[14] In addition to including a variable that captures the likelihood of migrating to Bangkok, as discussed above, we have experimented with including parent's characteristics, in case entrepreneurial talent is inherited. Having parents in the top half of the wealth distribution, having parents who held a village position and having parents who had an occupation other than rice farmer have no impact on the results presented here. However, parents education does effect the likelihood of starting a business. For the whole sample, households whose parents had no education were 3 percentage points less likely to start a business and households who had a parent with more than 4 years of schooling were 10 percentage points more likely to start a business. The impact of the other independent variables is unchanged when the parental characteristics were included.

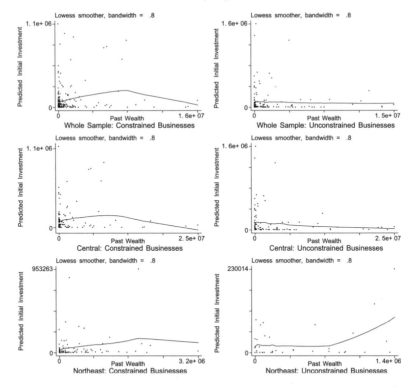

Fig. 3. Initial investment and past wealth. These figures represent nonparametric estimates of the relationship between initial business investment and wealth 6 years prior to the survey. The sample consists of businesses that were started in the 5 years prior to the survey. The dots represent the actual data and the lines depict the estimated relationship between initial business investment and past wealth. For each observation, a weighted regression is performed using 80% (bandwidth = 0.8) of the data around that point. The data are weighted using a tri-cube weighting procedure that puts more weight on the points closest to the observation in question. The weighted regression results are used to produce a predicted value for each observation. Because the graphs can be fairly sensitive to outliers, the wealthiest 1% of the sample is dropped.

number of adult females and the number of children living in the household. The figures reported in the tables indicate the marginal effect of an infinitesimal change in each continuous variable on the probability of starting a business. For dummy variables, the impact of changing the variable in question from zero to one is reported.

We also include measures of household wealth, being careful to take issues of endogeneity into consideration. The wealth variables are: the value 6 years ago of household, agricultural and land assets that the household owned then. We also include the past wealth squared. If the likelihood of starting a business increases with wealth at a decreasing rate, the coefficient on this variable should be negative.

We control for credit market availability by including measures of whether or not the household was a member or a customer of various financial institutions in the past. Like

A.L. Paulson, R. Townsend / Journal of Corporate Finance 10 (2004) 229–262   249

Table 3A
Probit estimates of having started business in last 5 years

	Whole sample		Northeast		Central region	
	dF/dx*	Z-statistic	dF/dx*	Z-statistic	dF/dx*	Z-statistic
Age of head	− 0.0105	− 3.18	− 0.0106	− 3.01	− 0.0111	− 1.84
Age of head squared	0.0001	2.52	0.0001	2.68	0.0001	1.21
Years of schooling—head	0.0080	3.01	0.0102	3.74	0.0034	0.67
Number of adult females in household	0.0013	0.15	0.0089	0.96	− 0.0131	− 0.85
Number of adult males in household	0.0158	2.03	0.0013	0.16	0.0345	2.41
Number of children (< 18 years) in household	− 0.0045	− 0.79	− 0.0115	− 1.80	0.0103	0.99
Wealth 6 years ago[†]	0.0276	3.25	0.0861	2.15	0.0246	2.82
Wealth squared[†]	0.0000	− 1.78	0.0000	− 1.20	0.0000	− 0.79
Member/customer in organization/institution 6 years ago						
Formal financial institution*	0.0199	1.10	0.0040	0.19	0.0314	1.03
Village institution/organization*	− 0.0224	− 1.05	− 0.0400	− 1.96	0.0239	0.55
Agricultural lender*	0.0278	1.39	0.0145	0.67	0.0511	1.40
BAAC group*	0.0397	1.72	0.0519	2.06	0.0084	0.20
Moneylender*	0.0014	0.04	0.0130	0.36	− 0.0176	− 0.31
Observed frequency	0.1407		0.0915		0.2070	
Predicted frequency at mean of X	0.1105		0.0699		0.1720	
Log likelihood	− 860.30		− 363.62		− 488.65	
χ^2 for significance of fixed effects	152.96		28.83		85.69	
Prob>χ^2	0.00		0.19		0.00	
Pseudo R-squared (%)	14.14		10.87		15.59	
Number of observations	2467		1333		1135	

The sample excludes the top 1% of households by wealth.

* dF/dx is equal to the infinitesimal change in each continuous independent variable. For dummy variables, it is equal to the discrete change in probability when the dummy variable changes from 0 to 1. Dummy variables are marked by an asterisk.

[†] Wealth 6 years ago is made up of the value of household assets, agricultural assets and land. Number in table is estimated coefficient multiplied by 1,000,000.

the labor supply variables, we include these variables so that we can appropriately interpret the talent and wealth variables as evidence either in favor of, or against, the presence of financial constraints.

In order to separate the impact of the availability of a particular credit institution in the local area from the impact of being a client of the institution, the estimates also include controls for each of the tambons that were sampled.[15] The tambon controls are meant to

---

[15] There are two tambons in the Central region where no households have started businesses in the past 5 years. The 117 households in these tambons are dropped from the analysis of which households start businesses because there is no variation in the dependent variable within these tambons. We also experimented with using village fixed-effects. Using village fixed-effects requires dropping about 30 villages (542 households) because no households in the villages have started businesses in the past 5 years or because all of the households in the village have started businesses in the past 5 years. We prefer the estimates with tambon fixed-effects because fewer observations are dropped. In any case, the village fixed-effects and the tambon fixed-effects results are very similar. Any substantive differences in the two estimates are discussed in the text below.

Table 3B
Probit estimates of having started business in last 5 years

	Whole sample		Northeast		Central region	
	dF/dx*	Z-statistic	dF/dx*	Z-statistic	dF/dx*	Z-statistic
Age of head	− 0.0106	− 3.20	− 0.0107	− 3.03	− 0.0112	− 1.85
Age of head squared	0.0001	2.56	0.0001	2.71	0.0001	1.25
Years of schooling—head	0.0080	3.00	0.0101	3.68	0.0035	0.68
Number of adult females in household	0.0009	0.11	0.0088	0.95	− 0.0145	− 0.93
Number of adult males in household	0.0154	1.96	0.0017	0.20	0.0336	2.30
Number of children (< 18 years) in household	− 0.0035	− 0.61	− 0.0114	− 1.79	0.0121	1.15
Wealth 6 years ago[‡]	0.0279	3.00	0.0856	2.03	0.0220	2.17
Wealth squared[‡]	0.0000	− 1.74	0.0000	− 0.98	0.0000	− 0.63
(Wealth + inheritance) × member/customer in organization/institution 6 years ago						
Formal financial institution[‡]	− 0.0126	− 1.76	− 0.0275	− 0.66	− 0.0098	− 1.26
Village institution/organization[‡]	0.0055	0.48	0.0287	0.53	− 0.0020	− 0.12
Agricultural lender[‡]	0.0085	1.07	− 0.0292	− 0.71	0.0082	1.00
BAAC group[‡]	0.0068	0.70	0.0207	0.49	0.0204	1.49
Moneylender[‡]	− 0.0235	− 1.09	− 0.0041	− 0.06	− 0.0282	− 0.93
Member/customer in organization/institution 6 years ago						
Formal financial institution*	0.0394	1.85	0.0198	0.65	0.0553	1.56
Village institution/organization*	− 0.0270	− 1.18	− 0.0477	− 1.76	0.0186	0.39
Agricultural lender*	0.0161	0.72	0.0304	0.99	0.0350	0.83
BAAC group*	0.0320	1.24	0.0387	1.17	− 0.0269	− 0.56
Moneylender*	0.0210	0.56	0.0156	0.32	0.0145	0.22
Observed frequency	0.1407		0.0915		0.2070	
Predicted frequency at mean of X	0.1105		0.0695		0.1729	
Log likelihood	− 856.43		− 363.01		− 484.71	
χ^2 for significance of fixed effects	154.69		28.79		87.93	
Prob>χ^2	0.00		0.19		0.00	
Pseudo R-squared (%)	14.53		11.02		16.27	
Number of observations	2467		1333		1135	

The sample excludes the top 1% of households by wealth.

　* dF/dx is equal to the infinitesimal change in each continuous independent variable. For dummy variables, it is equal to the discrete change in probability when the dummy variable changes from 0 to 1. Dummy variables are marked by an asterisk.

　[‡] Number in table is estimated coefficient multiplied by 1,000,000.

capture geographic variations in the supply of credit along with other important character-istics, infrastructure and the size of the market, for example, that are likely to vary depending on the tambon. The inclusion of the tambon controls means that the credit market variables provide an indication of the average probability that patrons of the various institutions will start businesses, relative to the probability that households in a particular tambon will start a business.

In Table 3B, we augment the set of explanatory variables so that they correspond roughly to an environment where credit is allocated as a function of wealth. We do this by adding interactions of wealth with the measures of past use of financial institutions in order to capture the effect of wealth on credit constraints. If wealthier households are more likely

A.L. Paulson, R. Townsend / Journal of Corporate Finance 10 (2004) 229–262   251

Table 4A

Probit estimates that business would be more profitable if expanded, business started in last 5 years

	Whole sample		Northeast		Central region	
	dF/dx*	Z-statistic	dF/dx*	Z-statistic	dF/dx*	Z-statistic
Age of head	− 0.0012	− 0.07	0.0760	2.18	− 0.0248	− 1.26
Age of head squared	0.0000	− 0.23	− 0.0007	− 2.25	0.0002	0.95
Years of schooling—head	0.0091	0.73	− 0.0036	− 0.16	0.0153	0.96
Number of adult females in household	0.0740	1.72	0.0055	0.06	0.0948	1.96
Number of adult males in household	− 0.0151	− 0.38	− 0.0840	− 0.99	0.0296	0.65
Number of children (< 18 years) in household	0.0153	0.53	− 0.0272	− 0.39	0.0095	0.30
Wealth 6 years ago[†]	− 0.0160	− 0.49	− 0.3140	− 0.74	− 0.0010	− 0.05
Wealth squared[‡]	0.0000	0.90	0.0000	0.80	0.0000	− 0.14
Member/customer in organization/institution 6 years ago						
Formal financial institution*	− 0.0843	− 1.07	− 0.1586	− 1.01	− 0.0546	− 0.60
Village institution/organization*	0.0118	0.10	0.3368	1.56	− 0.0340	− 0.26
Agricultural lender*	0.1430	1.44	− 0.0998	− 0.53	0.1941	1.74
BAAC group*	− 0.0824	− 0.78	0.0734	0.37	− 0.0842	− 0.69
Moneylender*	0.2264	1.37	0.0833	0.26	0.1798	0.84
Observed frequency	0.5131		0.5870		0.4732	
Predicted frequency at mean of X	0.5136		0.6056		0.4703	
Log likelihood	− 188.05		− 53.59		− 135.00	
χ^2 for significance of fixed effects	33.56		9.00		26.89	
Prob>χ^2	0.63		0.91		0.14	
Pseudo R-squared (%)	11.30		14.09		12.87	
Number of observations	306		92		224	

The sample excludes the top 1% of households by wealth.

* dF/dx is equal to the infinitesimal change in each continuous independent variable. For dummy variables, it is equal to the discrete change in probability when the dummy variable changes from 0 to 1. Dummy variables are marked by an asterisk.

[†] Wealth 6 years ago is made up of the value of household assets, agricultural assets and land. Number in table is estimated coefficient multiplied by 1,000,000.

[‡] Number in table is estimated coefficient multiplied by 1,000,000.

to get credit from particular institutions and use these funds to start businesses, then these variables will increase the likelihood of opening a business.

Again because we are concerned with the impact of outliers, we exclude the wealthiest 1% of households in both Tables 3A and 3B. We also exclude households who have businesses that were established more than 5 years ago so that we compare households who have started businesses in the past 5 years to nonbusiness.

We find that the likelihood of starting a business increases significantly with wealth in all of the estimates presented in Tables 3A and 3B. For example, in Table 3A for the whole sample, we find that a 1,000,000 baht increase in wealth would increase the likelihood of starting a business by about 3 percentage points.[16] This is an increase of 21% above the

---

[16] A 1,000,000 baht increase in wealth corresponds to doubling the current wealth of the median business owner and tripling the wealth of the median nonbusiness owner. By comparison, the standard deviation of current wealth is 8,850,000 baht for business owners and 4,079,000 baht for nonbusiness owners.

Table 4B
Probit estimates that business would be more profitable if expanded, business started in last 5 years

	Whole sample		Northeast		Central region	
	dF/dx*	Z-statistic	dF/dx*	Z-statistic	dF/dx*	Z-statistic
Age of head	− 0.0035	− 0.21	0.0854	2.45	− 0.0272	− 1.37
Age of head squared	0.0000	− 0.11	− 0.0008	− 2.62	0.0002	1.05
Years of schooling—head	0.0099	0.78	− 0.0117	− 0.47	0.0165	1.03
Number of adult females in household	0.0766	1.77	− 0.0058	− 0.06	0.1038	2.07
Number of adult males in household	− 0.0216	− 0.53	− 0.1040	− 1.17	0.0257	0.55
Number of children (< 18 years) in household	0.0157	0.53	− 0.0087	− 0.12	0.0201	0.60
Wealth 6 years ago‡	− 0.0027	− 0.08	− 0.0829	− 0.18	0.0056	0.23
Wealth squared‡	0.0000	0.49	0.0000	0.38	0.0000	− 0.34
(Wealth + inheritance) × member/customer in organization/institution 6 years ago						
Formal financial institution‡	− 0.0316	− 1.07	0.7040	1.87	− 0.0186	− 1.08
Village institution/organization‡	0.0393	0.84	0.2510	0.43	0.0382	1.63
Agricultural lender‡	0.0188	0.56	− 0.4900	− 1.20	− 0.0099	− 0.54
BAAC group‡	− 0.0212	− 0.61	− 0.0729	− 0.18	0.0068	0.32
Moneylender‡	− 0.4040	− 1.37			− 0.3350	− 1.15
Member/customer in organization/institution 6 years ago						
Formal financial institution*	− 0.0435	− 0.48	− 0.4472	− 1.93	0.0038	0.04
Village institution/organization*	− 0.0467	− 0.35	0.2861	0.80	− 0.1745	− 1.20
Agricultural lender*	0.1353	1.15	0.0600	0.22	0.2696	1.99
BAAC group*	− 0.0454	− 0.37	0.1485	0.52	− 0.1470	− 1.03
Moneylender*	0.4438	2.00			0.4191	1.51
Observed frequency	0.5131		0.5870		0.4732	
Predicted frequency at mean of X	0.5131		0.6091		0.4661	
Log likelihood	− 185.18		− 51.17		− 131.38	
χ^2 for significance of fixed effects	32.00		9.26		26.11	
Prob>χ^2	0.70		0.90		0.16	
Pseudo R-squared (%)	12.65		17.95		15.21	
Number of observations	306		92		224	

The sample excludes the top 1% of households by wealth.

* dF/dx is equal to the infinitesimal change in each continuous independent variable. For dummy variables, it is equal to the discrete change in probability when the dummy variable changes from 0 to 1. Dummy variables are marked by an asterisk.

‡ Number in table is estimated coefficient multiplied by 1,000,000.

observed percentage of households who have started a business in the past 5 years. The impact of the same increase in wealth in the Northeast is much larger. The likelihood of starting a business goes up by 8.6 percentage points, a 93% increase. The magnitude of the effect for the Central region is similar to the results for the whole sample. Table 3A suggests that the impact of wealth decreases as households get wealthier. The coefficient on wealth squared is significant and negative, although very small, for the whole sample. For the Northeast and the Central region, the sign on wealth squared is also negative but the effect is not significant.

The coefficients on the wealth variable in the regressions presented in Table 3B are very similar to the results for Table 3A. Increases in wealth appear to significantly increase the

A.L. Paulson, R. Townsend / Journal of Corporate Finance 10 (2004) 229–262   253

Table 5
Regression estimates of initial investment in business, business started in last 5 years

	Whole sample		Northeast		Central region	
	Coefficient	T-statistic	Coefficient	T-statistic	Coefficient	T-statistic
Age of head	− 0.0132	− 0.23	− 0.0261	− 0.27	− 0.0577	− 0.83
Age of head squared	− 0.0001	− 0.15	0.0000	0.01	0.0003	0.54
Years of schooling—head	0.1208	3.13	0.1376	2.36	0.1321	2.67
Number of adult females in household	0.1250	0.89	0.2621	1.06	0.0810	0.52
Number of adult males in household	0.2007	1.55	0.3608	1.48	0.1212	0.81
Number of children (< 18 years) in household	− 0.0318	− 0.34	− 0.0497	− 0.26	− 0.0144	− 0.14
Wealth 6 years ago[†]	0.3390	3.13	− 0.3100	− 0.31	0.1230	1.68
Wealth squared[‡]	0.0000	− 2.51	0.0000	1.24	0.0000	− 1.82
Constant	10.2197	6.71	9.6242	3.87	11.8264	6.31
Adjusted R-squared (%)	8.52		11.77		5.38	
Number of observations	252		83		177	

The sample excludes the top 1% of households by wealth and initial investment.

[†] Wealth 6 years ago is made up of the value of household assets, agricultural assets and land. Number in table is estimated coefficient multiplied by 1,000,000.

[‡] Number in table is estimated coefficient multiplied by 1,000,000.

likelihood of starting a business. Most of the variables which capture the interaction between past wealth and past patronage of various financial institutions are insignificant. However, for the whole sample, the likelihood of starting a business appears to be decreasing in the interaction between wealth and being a customer of a formal financial institution in the past. This finding is consistent with other evidence that households use commercial banks primarily to save rather than to borrow. There is some tentative evidence that agricultural organizations (primarily the BAAC through both collateralized and joint liability loans) facilitate business start-ups for wealthy households in the Central region.

In addition, the likelihood of starting a business is affected directly by household patronage of various financial institutions prior to starting a business. In the whole sample, households who were customers of commercial banks 6 years ago are 4 percentage points more likely to start a business, a 28% increase in the overall likelihood of business start-ups. There is a similar effect for the Central region. However, in the Northeast, past patronage of commercial banks has no significant effect on the likelihood of starting a business. In the Northeast, households who used to belong to village institutions/organizations are 5 percentage points less likely to start businesses. Many village institutions in the Northeast, rice banks, for example, cater to relatively poor households. The fact that households who relied on this type of assistance in the past may be correlated with other unmeasured household characteristics that are negatively associated with entrepreneurship.[17]

---

[17] On-going work suggests that the negative impact of village banks may be largely due to selection. Kaboski and Townsend (2000) show that villages with particular institutions (Production Credit Groups) and particular policies (making loans) have positive effects on business start-ups, once selection effects have been controlled for.

254   *A.L. Paulson, R. Townsend / Journal of Corporate Finance 10 (2004) 229–262*

The fact that entrepreneurship is also significantly affected by the age of the household head (Northeast and Central regions), the number of adult males in the household (Central region) and the number of children in the household (Northeast) can also be interpreted as evidence of financial constraints. For example, in the Central region, the presence of one additional male in the household increases the likelihood of starting a business by 3.5 percentage points. In the absence of financial constraints, we would expect households to be able to get the necessary funding to hire additional non-household labor. Similarly, each additional child under 18 reduces the likelihood of starting a business in the Northeast by 1 percentage point. In the absence of financial constraints, the household should be able to use additional funds to hire additional laborers, either to do childcare or to work in the household firm. This would eliminate the link between the number of children in the household and the likelihood of starting a business.[18]

Taking the evidence presented in Table 2A, Fig. 1 and Tables 3A and 3B together, there is overwhelming evidence that financial constraints play an important role in determining who will start a business and that wealthier households are much more likely to start businesses. There is also some tentative evidence that financial constraints may operate through existing financial institutions, particularly BAAC borrowing groups in the Central region. In addition, the correlation of demographic characteristics with the probability of starting a business points to the importance of financial constraints.

3.1.2. Implication #2: holding entrepreneurial talent fixed and increasing wealth, the percentage of constrained businesses will decrease

In addition to predicting that business ownership will increase with wealth, the presence of financial constraints also implies that, holding entrepreneurial skill constant, the percentage of constrained business owners should fall as wealth increases. We can examine this implication by comparing the percentage of business owners who are constrained in the lowest wealth category to the percentage who are constrained in the highest wealth category (see Table 2A). Here the results are mixed. In the Central region, the percentage of business owners who report that they are constrained increases from 27% to 56% from the lowest to the highest wealth quartile for heads with 0–3 years of schooling. For heads with 4 years of schooling, the percentage of constrained business owners decreases from 55% to 44%. For the most educated group, the percentage of constrained business owners increases slightly from 55% to 59%. In the Northeast, for heads with 0–3 years of schooling, the percentage of constrained business owners decreases from 67% to 50% from the lowest to the highest wealth quartile. For those with 4 years of schooling the percentage goes from 82% to 72%. For the most educated group, the percentage of constrained business owners increases from 44% to 65%.

The only significant difference in the proportion of businesses who report that they are constrained is consistent with financial constraints. In the whole sample, among households whose heads have 4 years of schooling, the percentage of constrained businesses

---

[18] Other interpretations of the impact of these variables lead to similar conclusions about the presence of financial constraints. For example, the negative coefficient on children may reflect the need to divert resources away from the household business in order to pay for educational expenses. Again, if financial constraints were not an issue, the household would be able to borrow to start a business or to finance educational expenses.

A.L. Paulson, R. Townsend / Journal of Corporate Finance 10 (2004) 229–262 255

decreases from 61% to 45% from the lowest to the highest wealth quartile. This decrease is significant at a 5% level.

Turning our attention to Fig. 2 which contains graphical representations of the nonparametric relationship between the likelihood of being constrained and wealth, we see that for the Central region, financial constraints appear to be important for existing businesses. The likelihood of being constrained seems to decrease substantially with wealth. For the Northeast, the relationship is perverse and is driven perhaps by an outlier. For most households in this region, there does not appear to be much relationship between being constrained and wealth. For the whole sample, the graphs indicate that the likelihood of being constrained is decreasing in wealth for most of the sample.

Tables 4A and 4B use the same sets of variables as the estimates presented in Tables 3A and 3B to predict who will be a constrained business owner, among households who started a business in the past 5 years. These tables suggest that being constrained at the time of the survey is unrelated to past wealth. While the coefficients on past wealth are negative, as financial constraints would imply, none of the coefficients are significant. Increases in wealth may also reduce the likelihood of being constrained by freeing up borrowing constraints.

This effect is included in the estimates in Table 4B via the variables that interact wealth with membership in various financial institutions. There is some evidence that the joint effect of past wealth and past membership in a village organization can actually increase the likelihood of being constrained at the time of the survey. For households in the Central region, holding other things fixed, a 1,000,000 baht increase in wealth will increase the likelihood of being constrained by 4 percentage points through this effect. As indicated above, this suggests that selection in the credit market may be important. Village institutions often cater to the poor, so a relatively wealthy household that patronizes a village financial institution may indicate that the household has particularly poor prospects despite its wealth.

Curiously, customers of formal financial institutions in the Northeast are more likely to be constrained through the wealth effect. This effect disappears if village rather than tambon fixed-effects are included and the direct effect of being a customer of a formal financial institution in the Northeast is to reduce the likelihood of being constrained by almost 45 percentage points. There is some weak evidence that the interaction of wealth with being the customer of a moneylender reduces the probability of being constrained for the whole sample. Note, however, that the direct effect of being a customer of a moneylender significantly increases the probability of being constrained. In the Central region, being the customer of an agricultural lender (usually borrowing from the BAAC with collateral) is associated with a 27 percentage point increase in the probability that the business is constrained. This finding hints at a potential source of financial constraints. In an environment with moral hazard, optimal credit allocations will be subject to a binding incentive compatibility constraint, which means that borrowing will be associated with being constrained.[19]

---

[19] In Paulson and Townsend (2002), we use structural econometric techniques to examine whether the data can best be explained by a model with this type of financial constraint or by financial constraints that arise when credit is limited in a mechanical way by wealth.

256   *A.L. Paulson, R. Townsend / Journal of Corporate Finance 10 (2004) 229–262*

Taking the evidence presented in Table 2A, Fig. 2 and Tables 4A and 4B together, there is little evidence of a systematic relationship between past wealth and household reports of being constrained. However, there is intriguing evidence that household reports of being constrained are related to the interaction of household wealth and participation in various financial institutions and that they are directly affected by household participation in both formal and informal financial institutions.

When we move away from household reports of constraints and consider other indications of constraints, there is clear evidence that constraints decline with wealth. The top panel of Table 2B reports on how returns to business investment vary with wealth. If financial constraints are important, then returns will be high for low wealth households and lower when wealth increases. For the whole sample, median returns decrease from 57% for business households in the lowest wealth quartile to 16% for households in the highest wealth quartile (significant at a 5% level). The same pattern is observed in the Central region (significant at a 1% level) and in the Northeast (not significant). The evidence that is presented in this table also bolsters the view that household reports of being constrained correspond to theoretical definitions of constraints. With two exceptions (out of 12 comparisons), the median return to business investment is higher for households who report that they are constrained, compared to households who do not complain of constraints. This difference is sometimes significant, particularly in the Northeast.

3.1.3. Implication #3: initial investment increases with wealth

If financial constraints are important, then entrepreneurial households may invest less than the optimal amount in existing businesses. If wealth were to increase, investment could go up as well. Table 2C examines how median initial investment in the business varies by past wealth and education. The patterns in the data are consistent with financial constraints. In every case, median investment is higher for previously wealthier households compared to poorer households. Median business investment for firms in the lowest wealth quartile is 22,562 baht in the Central region, compared to 32,478 baht for firms in the highest wealth quartile. In the Northeast, median investment increases from 12,732 to 21,705 baht. For the whole sample, median investment increases from 17,053 to 30,583 baht. Although the table suggests that investment increases with wealth, these differences in investment are not significant, except for constrained businesses in the Northeast.

Fig. 3 presents graphs of the nonparametric relationship between household wealth and business investment for constrained and unconstrained businesses separately. For constrained businesses in the whole sample, the bulk of the data is consistent with the presence of financial constraints: initial investment increases with wealth. For unconstrained businesses, there is very little relationship between wealth and initial investment. We would expect this to be the case if these households are in fact unconstrained and are able to invest the optimal amount of capital in their businesses regardless of their personal wealth. The graphs for the Central region are very similar to the graphs for the whole sample. Initial investment increases with wealth for most constrained businesses and there is little relationship between wealth and investment for unconstrained businesses. In the Northeast, initial investment increases with wealth for both constrained and unconstrained businesses.

A.L. Paulson, R. Townsend / Journal of Corporate Finance 10 (2004) 229–262 257

We can also evaluate investment's relationship with other important variables using reduced-form techniques. Table 5 presents regression estimates of the log of initial business investment as a function of some of the same variables we have discussed earlier: age and education, the number of adult males, females and children in the household and past wealth.[20] While we are examining the relationship between initial investment in the business and wealth, our approach is similar to that taken by Fazzari et al. (1988). They show that firm investment is sensitive to proxies for the availability of internal funds for a sample of publicly traded US manufacturing firms. When financial constraints are important, then the availability of internal funds (i.e. wealth) will have a significant positive effect on initial investment as well. Wealth is an important predictor of initial investment in the whole sample as well as in the Central region. If past wealth were to increase by 1,000,000 baht, for the whole sample, business investment would increase by 40%. The same increase in wealth would lead to an increase in investment of 13% in the Central region. Wealth appears to affect investment at a decreasing rate. The sign on the wealth-squared term is negative and significant for both the whole sample and the Central region. Wealth does not appear to play a significant role in determining initial investment in the Northeast.

The nonparametric estimates suggest that there is a strong relationship between wealth and investment in the Northeast. However, we do not find evidence of this relationship when we impose the assumptions of the linear regression model. For the Central region and the whole sample the message of the various statistical techniques reinforce one another: investment increases significantly with wealth.

3.1.4. Implication #4: investment and constraints increase with entrepreneurial talent (if talent and investment are complements) or decrease with talent (if they are substitutes)

If entrepreneurial talent and investment are substitutes, then initial investment in the business will be decreasing with entrepreneurial talent. Less talented individuals will need to invest more than their more talented counterparts who start businesses. More talented entrepreneurs should also report fewer constraints. In contrast, if talent and investment are complements, potential entrepreneurs who are highly skilled would like to invest more, although they are more likely to be constrained. On average, however, this implies that investment will increase with talent. We can examine these implications by looking at how initial business investment and constraints vary with education. This information is summarized in Table 2A (constraints) and in the bottom panel of Table 2C (investment). The pattern of initial investment and education does not favor the possibility that talent and investment are substitutes. Instead of finding that initial investment decreases with education, we tend to find the opposite. In the Central region, median investment increases by 16% from the lowest education category to the highest. In the Northeast, the increase is even more dramatic: investment goes up by 74%. This finding offers evidence that capital and entrepreneurial talent are complements. It is important to note, however, that the differences in investment between the education groups are not always monotone or statistically significant.

---

[20] We look at initial investment in the business because the level of this variable is the counterpart to the decision about whether or not to start a business.

When we examine how household reports of constraints vary with education (Table 2A), the pattern seems to depend on the region. In the Central region, the pattern is consistent with investment and talent being complements: more households tend to report constraints when we compare households with 0–3 years of schooling with households with more than 4 years of schooling within a particular wealth quartile. In the Northeast, the percentage of constrained businesses tends to decline slightly with education, which is more consistent with investment and talent being substitutes. None of these comparisons are significant however.

If we look at how an alternative measure of constraints, returns to business investment, varies with education the evidence from both the Central region and the Northeast favors the view that investment and entrepreneurial talent are complements rather than substitutes. The bottom panel of Table 2B reports median returns to business investment for businesses whose heads have 0–3 years of schooling, 4 years of schooling and more than 4 years of schooling. In all cases, median returns to investment increase when the lowest education group is compared to the medium or highest education group. Again, these comparisons, while suggestive, are not statistically significant or monotone.

We can also examine this implication by looking at the effect of education on initial investment in the regressions presented in Table 5. In addition to the years of schooling of the head of the household, the regressions include the age and age squared of the head of the household, the number of adult males, adult females, and children in the household, as well as the wealth of the household 6 years prior to the survey. In the whole sample, the Northeast and the Central region business investment increases significantly with schooling. In the whole sample, the results suggest that a household head with 8 years of schooling would invest 67% more than an otherwise similar household whose head had gone to school for 4 years. The weight of the evidence presented in Tables 2A–2C and Table 5 clearly favors the assumption that capital and entrepreneurial talent are complements, rather than substitutes.

3.2. Regional differences and financial institutions

In addition to documenting the overall importance of financial constraints, the contrast between the Northeast and the Central region allows us to explore how the effect of financial constraints may differ with economic and financial development. This comparison draws largely on the reduced form results. If median past wealth were to increase by 100%, the percentage of business households would increase by approximately 1 percentage point in the Northeast and by 0.5 percentage points in the Central region. This corresponds to a 9% increase in the percentage of business households in the Northeast and a 1.5% increase in the percentage of business households in the Central region. The process of starting a business is more sensitive to wealth in the Northeast compared to the Central region. This finding makes sense since the Central region is wealthier and has a relatively sophisticated financial system. Financial constraints are important in both regions; however, they restrict business start-ups more in the Northeast.

However, investment increases significantly with wealth in the Central region. In the Northeast, there is no statistically significant relationship between investment and wealth. At first glance, it seems puzzling that investment would be independent of wealth in the relatively poor and financially backward Northeast. However, we argue that it is precisely those characteristics of the Northeast that leads to these findings. Because financial constraints are so severe in the Northeast, only very selected businesses are founded. Conditional on being able to start a business, northeastern households are able to break the link between investment and wealth. In order to start a business in the Northeast, households must accumulate enough wealth to fund the business at close to the optimal level because future outside financing is unlikely to materialize. In addition to reconciling the relationship between business start-ups and wealth and investment and wealth in the Northeast and the Central region, this analysis also explains why an equivalent increase in wealth has a larger impact on business start-ups in the Northeast.

The data also allow us to examine the role of particular financial institutions in overcoming financial constraints. Here we focus on the role of the BAAC. Membership in a BAAC group (prior to starting a business) interacted with wealth facilitates business start-ups in the Central region (see Table 3B). In the Northeast, the direct effect of membership in a BAAC group is positively associated with starting a business (see Table 3A). The loans that are available through membership in a BAAC group are quite small, so it seems unlikely that BAAC group loans are playing the key role in promoting business start-ups. However, BAAC membership may reveal important characteristics about the potential entrepreneur. BAAC groups are self-selected—potential members must be accepted by the rest of the group. Therefore, membership in a BAAC group may indicate that the potential entrepreneur is very talented, a better credit risk, has access to particularly good projects and so on. The role of selection appears to be related to wealth in the Central region. To the extent that being a member of a BAAC group reveals something about entrepreneurial talent, this finding provides alternative support for the hypothesis that entrepreneurial talent and wealth are complementary.

While BAAC group membership is associated with a higher likelihood of starting a business for wealthy households in the Central region, having a collateralized loan from the BAAC (again prior to starting a business) increases the chance that a business in the Central region is currently constrained (see Table 4B).[21] Collateralized loans from the BAAC can be of considerable size, so it seems puzzling that these loans do not reduce the probability that the business is constrained. However, as we suggest above, the finding that BAAC loans are associated with constraints may be due to the nature of the financial constraint. The regional differences in the impact of the BAAC echo Ahlin and Townsend (2000), who show that BAAC joint liability borrowing groups operate differently, depending on the region.

4. Conclusions and discussion

Overall, we find substantial evidence that financial constraints play an important role in determining which households will start businesses in rural and semi-urban Thailand. In

---

[21] This variable is not significant in the estimates for the Northeast. However, there is some tentative evidence that the interaction of having a collateralized loan from the BAAC and wealth reduces constraints in the Northeast (see Table 4B).

particular, nonparametric as well as reduced form evidence demonstrates that wealthier households are more likely to start businesses. The importance of financial constraints is reinforced by the fact that household demographic characteristics are also key determinants of who becomes an entrepreneur. The evidence that households who eventually start businesses have been accumulating wealth more quickly than households who do not start businesses prior to starting a business—as though they were saving in an effort to overcome an inability to borrow to finance business start-up costs—also underscores the importance of financial constraints.

Financial constraints also significantly affect the way existing household businesses in Thailand are run. The nonparametric and reduced form evidence shows that returns to business investment tend to decrease with wealth and investment increases with wealth as well as with entrepreneurial talent. We have also provided evidence that entrepreneurial talent and investment are complements, rather than substitutes. This implies that the burden of being constrained falls disproportionately on more capable entrepreneurs.

In addition, the special features of the Thai data allow us to conclude that financial constraints impose a greater restrictions on entrepreneurial activity in the less developed Northeast compared to the wealthier Central region. The BAAC appears to play a key role in promoting entrepreneurial activity in both the Northeast and the Central region. However, the evidence suggests that BAAC group membership signals important characteristics of the potential entrepreneur. Loans provided by this institution do not predict business start-ups and tend to increase the likelihood that businesses are constrained. This would happen if talented entrepreneurs were more likely to join BAAC groups, and talent and investment were complements, as the results suggest.

These conclusions are strengthened by the use of a variety of statistical approaches that allow us to make sure findings are robust to alternative functional forms and the inclusion of further control variables. The nonparametric estimates rely only on limited data—examining bilateral relationships between variables of interest. Although the nonparametric estimates, which are summarized in Figs. 1–3, often reveal largely linear relationships between key variables, there are some important nonlinearities in the relationship between investment and wealth for constrained businesses.

While we are concerned with the impact of financial constraints on small, entrepreneurial firms in a developing country, these issues are also important for large firms, who in principle have access to sophisticated financial markets. For example, Fazzari et al. (2000) survey the literature that shows that firm investment is sensitive to proxies for the availability of internal funds across many different samples.

The type of evidence for financial constraints that we have presented is often used to justify policy interventions that are aimed at relieving constraints, often through subsidized credit.[22] Despite the overwhelming evidence that financial constraints have an important impact on entrepreneurial activity, it would be inappropriate to extrapolate from this evidence what would happen if wealth were reallocated or credit were subsidized. For one

---

[22] The Small Business Innovation Research program in the US is one example. This program provides subsidized credit for research and development for small firms. From 1983 to 1997, this program allocated approximately US$7 billion to small high-technology firms (Lerner, 1999).

thing, while we have been careful to deal with some sources of endogeneity in wealth by looking at the relationship between wealth prior to starting a business and the decision to start a business, there are other potential sources of endogeneity. For example, if individuals with high levels of entrepreneurial ability accumulate wealth more quickly, so that they can start a business sooner and capitalize on their ability, then the coefficient on past wealth in the probit models for starting a business will capture the impact of wealth and of ability.

Even if one had fully accounted for all the potential sources of endogeneity in wealth, the impact of a policy intervention will still depend on the financial market imperfection that is responsible for financial constraints. For example, in Thailand a program to increase property rights in land would be particularly effective if limited commitment meant that collateral played a key role in borrowing arrangements. However, if credit were constrained because of informational constraints, as in Aghion and Bolton (1996), this program would be unlikely to ease financial constraints.

Acknowledgements

Comments from Daron Acemoglu, Patrick Bolton, David Denis, Lars Hansen, Boyan Jovanovic, Andreas Lehnert, Bernard Salanié, Chris Udry and from conference and seminar participants at the Federal Reserve Bank of Chicago, DELTA, IUPUI, MIT, UCLA, the University of Toulouse, Stanford and Yale are gratefully acknowledged. We also thank Francisco Buera, Xavier Giné and Alexander Karaivanov for their excellent research assistance as well as the National Institute of Health and the National Science Foundation for funding. We are much indebted to Sombat Sakuntasathien for collaboration and for making the data collection possible. The first draft of this paper was completed while Paulson was a National Fellow at the Hoover Institution and a second was completed while Townsend was visiting MIT and we thank them both for their hospitality. The views expressed in this paper are those of the authors and do not necessarily represent those of the Federal Reserve Bank of Chicago or the Federal Reserve System.

References

Aghion, P., Bolton, P., 1996. A trickle-down theory of growth and development with debt overhang. Review of Economic Studies 64, 151–172.

Ahlin, C., Townsend, R., 2000. Using Repayment Data to test Across Models of Joint Liability Lending, Manuscript. University of Chicago, Chicago.

Binford, M., Lee, T.J., Townsend, R., 2001. Sampling Design for an Integrated Socioeconomic and Ecologic Survey Using Satellite Remote Sensing and Ordination, Manuscript. University of Chicago, Chicago.

Evans, D.S., Jovanovic, B., 1989. An estimated model of entrepreneurial choice under liquidity constraints. Journal of Political Economy 97, 808–827.

Fazzari, S., Hubbard, R.G., Petersen, B., 1988. Financing constraints and corporate investment. Brookings Papers on Economic Activity 1, 141–195.

Fazzari, S., Hubbard, R.G., Petersen, B., 2000. Investment-cash flow sensitivities are useful: a comment on Kaplan and Zingales. Quarterly Journal of Economics 115, 695–705.

Feder, G., et al., 1988. Land Policies and Farm Productivity in Thailand. Johns Hopkins Univ. Press, Baltimore.

Holtz-Eakin, D., Joulfian, D., Rosen, H.S., 1994. Sticking it out: entrepreneurial survival and liquidity constraints. Journal of Political Economy 102, 53–75.

Kaboski, J., Townsend, R., 2000. Borrowing and Lending in Semi-Urban and Rural Thailand, Manuscript. University of Chicago, Chicago.

Lerner, J., 1999. The government as venture capitalist. Journal of Business 72, 285–318.

Lloyd-Ellis, H., Bernhardt, D., 2000. Enterprise, inequality and economic development. Review of Economic Studies 67, 147–168.

Paulson, A.L., Townsend, R., 2002. The Nature of Financial Constraints: Distinguishing the Micro Underpinnings of Macro Models, Manuscript. University of Chicago, Chicago.

Petersen, M.A., Rajan, R.G., 1994. The benefits of lender relationships: evidence from small business data. Journal of Finance 49, 3–37.

Petersen, M.A., Rajan, R.G., 1995. The effect of credit market competition on lending relationships. Quarterly Journal of Economics 110, 407–444.

Townsend, R., principal investigator with Paulson, A., Sakuntasathien, S., Lee, T.J., Binford, M., 1997. Questionnaire design and data collection for NICHD grant. 'Risk, Insurance and the Family' and NSF grants.

[7]

Journal of Economic Growth, 4: 213–232 (June 1999)
© 1999 Kluwer Academic Publishers, Boston.

Entrepreneurs, Professionals, and Growth

MURAT F. IYIGUN

Board of Governors of the Federal Reserve System

ANN L. OWEN

Hamilton College

We examine the implications for growth and development of the existence of two types of human capital: entrepreneurial and professional. Entrepreneurs accumulate human capital through a work-experience intensive process, whereas professionals' human capital accumulation is education-intensive. Moreover, the return to entrepreneurship is uncertain. We show how skill-biased technological progress leads to changes in the composition of aggregate human capital; as technology improves, individuals devote less time to the accumulation of human capital through work experience and more to the accumulation of human capital through professional training. Thus, our model explains why entrepreneurs play a relatively more important role in intermediate-income countries and professionals are relatively more abundant in richer economies. It also shows that those countries that initially have too little of either entrepreneurial or professional human capital may end up in a development trap.

Keywords: education, work experience, self-employment, growth

JEL classification: J24, O11, O40

1. Introduction

Both entrepreneurial and professional skills are important components of an economy's human capital stock, but they influence the level of technology and aggregate production in potentially different ways. Entrepreneurial skills generate new ideas, innovations, and products, while professional skills help to facilitate economic transactions. Both skills are important for the process of development. Yet while professional and entrepreneurial skills can complement each other in aggregate production, they can compete for an individual's time in their accumulation. This article explores the implications for growth of the existence of more than one type of human capital, showing how the choice between entrepreneurship and professional employment evolves as an economy develops and examining how individuals' decisions to accumulate different types of human capital affect the economy's long-run potential.

There are two main results. First, entrepreneurial human capital plays a relatively more important role in intermediate income countries, whereas professional human capital is relatively more important in richer economies. We demonstrate that as an economy develops, individuals choose to invest more time accumulating professional skills through schooling than accumulating entrepreneurial human capital. The resulting change in the relative stocks of entrepreneurial and professional human capital is a direct consequence of our assumption that providing professional services is a relatively safe activity and providing entrepreneurial skills is risky. As per capita income grows and the payoff to being a professional increases, individuals are less willing to gamble on entrepreneurial ventures. This phenomenon occurs even though the expected value of entrepreneurship rises with per capita income. While entrepreneurs in a more developed economy face a clearly better lottery than entrepreneurs in a less developed economy, the price of the lottery ticket— foregone professional earnings—is higher in the developed economy, making individuals less willing to take the bet. Second, we find that, in an economy where both entrepreneurial and professional human capital affect the future level of technology, the initial stocks of both types of human capital are important for the process of development.

Our approach is related to that of Banerjee and Newman (1993), who show how the distribution of wealth and credit market imperfections influence occupational choice. In their model, there is a fixed cost to becoming an entrepreneur and the distribution of wealth determines the percent of the population that undertakes such a venture.[1] We take a slightly different view on the defining characteristic of entrepreneurship, choosing to focus on the element of risk inherent in the concept rather than the financial requirements. Thus, while both models generate the result that high-income economies will have more employer-employee relationships, our model focuses particularly on how the incentives to accumulate professional and entrepreneurial human capital change as an economy grows. Specifically, while Banerjee and Newman (1993) demonstrate that economic development may foster entrepreneurial investment, our model shows that, as economies develop, the increasing relative return to professional employment has an offsetting negative effect on resources devoted to entrepreneurship relative to that devoted to professional activities. Our use of more than one type of human capital also ties into recent work such as Galor and Tsiddon (1997), who study the interaction between technological progress and the return to different dimensions of skills (i.e., specific human capital and ability).

Another idea that has been discussed in recent literature that is relevant to our article is that the risk associated with economic activity evolves with development. Acemoglu and Zilibotti (1997) show that when there are indivisible investment projects, in the early stages of development, diversification is not possible. As wealth accumulates, however, diversification becomes possible, and investment risk is reduced. In the same vein, Levine and Zervos (1998) show that stock market liquidity and banking development are associated with higher growth rates, suggesting that the more developed financial markets associated with higher levels of income reduce the disincentive for investment by reducing liquidity risk. We also examine investment risk in our model. However, there is an important distinction: we look at the risk of human capital investment and not physical capital investment. In our model, as per capita income increases, the variability of payoffs to the uncertain activity (entrepreneurship) increases, raising the risk of some kinds of human capital investment. In response to the increased variability of payoffs to entrepreneurial skills and the increase in the certain payoff to professionalism, individuals in the more developed economies reallocate their time toward the safer activity. Thus, although development is associated with increased risk for some types of human capital investment, it also provides individuals with better opportunities to reduce their investment in risky activities.

In what follows, we present a two-period overlapping-generations model in which aggregate human capital is the sum of both professional and entrepreneurial human capital. Individuals of differing abilities choose to accumulate human capital when their wages as human capital providers would be greater than their wages as laborers. They accumulate professional human capital by investing time in schooling and entrepreneurial human capital by investing time working as an entrepreneur. A key difference between the two types of human capital is that the reward paid to professional human capital is certain but the payoff to entrepreneurial human capital is not.

The level of technology employed by any one generation of workers is determined by the level of professional and entrepreneurial human capital of the previous generation. Thus, in an environment where technological change is skill-biased, the compensation to professional human capital and the expected compensation to entrepreneurial human capital increase as the stock of professional and entrepreneurial skills grow. For fixed factor prices, this raises the incentive to become a human capital provider, lowers the threshold level of ability above which individuals accumulate skills, and increases the number of individuals who invest in human capital. However, when individuals are compensated for their manual labor as well as their aggregate human capital input, skill-biased technological change induces more variability in the entrepreneurial payoff. Thus, as the return to the safe activity increases and the payoffs to the risky activity become more variable, human capital accumulators devote more time to schooling and less time to gaining entrepreneurial experience. In essence, individuals in high-income economies with higher wages to professionals have more to lose by gambling on an entrepreneurial venture. In contrast, individuals in low-income countries face less variable payoffs to entrepreneurship and a lower return to their investment in professional skills and are therefore more willing to invest in entrepreneurial skills.

In our model, entrepreneurial activities are more risky than professional activities. Entrepreneurial skills are accumulated through a more work-experience-intensive process and, as a result, are distinct from those accumulated through an education-intensive process. These unique skills contribute to the development or adoption of the economywide technology in a way that is potentially different from skills accumulated through education. While some entrepreneurial skills may be employed in the R&D sector, it is not necessary for all of them to be for the average level of entrepreneurial skills to influence the level of technology. Entrepreneurs may also indirectly influence the level of technology by starting new businesses that put competitive pressures on existing businesses to innovate. Thus, even if an entrepreneurial venture serves only to increase the variety of goods produced and does not directly enhance current technology, its existence spurs others to invent. At the same time, professionals are also capable of creating improvements in the level of technology. Some professionals may be directly employed with the invention of new technology (such as an engineer who works for a large company) or may aid with the administration of that new technology (such as a corporate lawyer who helps a company obtain patents for its inventions). In either case, we assume that because professional skills are accumulated in a different way than entrepreneurial skills, the skills of the professional and the skills of the entrepreneur are different and may contribute in a different way to the level of technology.

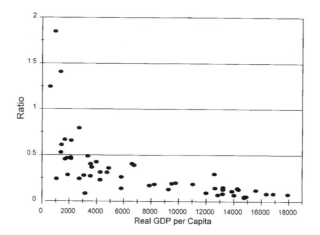

Figure 1. Real GDP per capita and the employers and self-employed to employees ratio (excluding agricultural workers). Data source: Summers and Heston (1991); *Mark 5.6*; International Labour Office (1993). Note: One observation per country is reported within the period 1986 to 1992.

If the way professional and entrepreneurial human capital are combined in output production is different from the way the two types of human capital are combined to determine the level of technology, then time devoted to schooling will be inefficient. In other words, if developing the technology utilizes the two types of human capital in a different way than implementing the technology, individuals, whose compensation is based on their contribution to output production, will not choose the socially optimal combination of schooling and entrepreneurial investment. In particular, if entrepreneurial ventures are more important in determining the level of technology and less important in its utilization, then the steady-state level of education will be too high, and per capita income would be higher with more entrepreneurial skills and fewer professional skills.[2]

These results are developed in the following: Section 2 presents some supporting empirical evidence, Section 3 describes the basic model, Section 4 discusses its dynamic behavior, and Section 5 concludes.

2. Empirical Evidence

This article is motivated, in part, by a stylized fact: in economies with higher per capita income, fewer individuals are employers compared to the number of individuals who work for others (see Figure 1).[3] Moreover, the fraction of workers classified in managerial and professional occupations increases with per capita income (see Figure 2).[4] This pattern of occupational change is also evident when examining individual countries over time; Bregger (1996) shows that the percentage of self-employed workers in nonagricultural industries steadily decreased in the United States from 12 percent in 1948 to 7.5 percent in 1994.

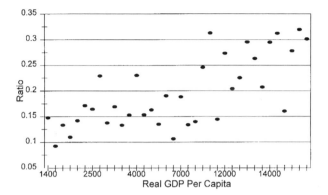

Figure 2. Real GDP per capita and managers and professionals as a share of nonagricultural workers. Data source: Summers and Heston (1991); *Mark 5.6*; International Labour Office (1993). Note: One observation per country is reported for either 1989 or 1990.

Table 1. Average age, education, and experience of self-employed and salaried workers.

	Respondent's Occupational Choice	
	Self-Employed	Salaried
Age	47.5	40.8
Education	13.8	13.5
Job tenure	13.2	8.2

Data source: Federal Reserve (1995).
Note: All variables measured in years. Individuals not working at the time of the survey are excluded from the sample.

Other empirical regularities also shed light on how occupational choice and the process of human capital accumulation might be related. First, the channels of human capital accumulation for entrepreneurs are more work-experience intensive than for wage and salary workers. Summary statistics from the *1995 Survey of Consumer Finances* show that self-employed workers are on average older and have longer job tenures than those who work for others, suggesting that experience gained with age may be an important component of entrepreneurial human capital (see Table 1).[5] These results are supported by Evans and Leighton (1989) and Evans and Jovanovich (1989), who show that the probability of being self-employed increases with labor-market experience but not with education.[6]

The second empirical observation that bears on our analysis is that both entrepreneurs and professionals contribute to the process of technological change. They contribute directly by being the inventors of new technology: the U.S. patent office reports that 22 percent of the patents for inventions granted over the period 1963 to 1984 were awarded to independent inventors and 75 percent were awarded to organizations.[7] In addition, people in both types of occupations contribute indirectly to the development of new technology. Entrepreneurs start new businesses that help to increase competitive pressures on existing businesses to innovate, and professionals help to administer an economic system that fosters invention.

Finally, education and work experience do not seem to be perfect substitutes in the accumulation of human capital. Evans and Leighton (1989) show that the probability of being an entrepreneur depends positively on previous business experience but not on education, suggesting that work experience may be an avenue of human capital accumulation particularly suited for the self-employed. Anecdotal evidence of entrepreneurs who did not receive degrees from traditional four-year college help this claim ring true.[8]

3. The Model

3.1. Production

Consider a small open company that operates in a perfectly competitive world in which economic activity extends over an infinite discrete time. The output of the economy Y_t is a single homogeneous good that can be produced by two technologies—one that uses physical capital K_t and efficiency units of skilled labor (or human capital) H_t and another that uses an unskilled labor aggregate L_t only. The output produced at time t in the skilled sector Y_t^h and the unskilled sector Y_t^l are given by

$$Y_t^h = F(K_t, \lambda_t H_t), \quad \text{and} \quad Y_t^l = \phi L_t, \quad \phi > 0; \qquad Y_t = Y_t^h + Y_t^l, \tag{1}$$

where F is a concave production function with constant returns to scale (CRS), and the endogenously determined technology level, denoted by λ_t, complements human capital H_t. The latter indicates that technological change in this economy is skill-biased.[9]

We assume that markets are competitive, which implies that factor inputs earn their marginal products:

$$r_t = F_K(K_t, \lambda_t H_t), \quad w_t^h = \lambda_t F_{\lambda H}(K_t, \lambda_t H_t), \quad \text{and} \quad w^l = \phi, \tag{2}$$

where r_t is the rental rate of physical capital, and w_t^h, w^l, respectively, denote the returns to human capital and unskilled labor.

Suppose that the world interest rate is constant at $\bar{r}$. Since the small open economy permits unrestricted physical capital mobility, its interest rate is constant at $\bar{r}$ as well. Given that F exhibits CRS, this implies that the ratio $K_t/\lambda_t H_t$ as well as $F_{\lambda H}(K_t, \lambda_t H_t)$ are also constant. Thus, with $F_{\lambda H}(K_t, \lambda_t H_t)$ normalized to one, factor payments are given by the following:

$$r_t = \bar{r} = F_K(K_t, \lambda_t H_t) \quad \Rightarrow \quad F_{\lambda H}(K_t, \lambda_t H_t) = \bar{w} \equiv 1 \quad \Rightarrow \quad w_t^h = \lambda_t. \tag{3}$$

ENTREPRENEURS, PROFESSIONALS, AND GROWTH   219

3.2. Individuals

Individuals, who live for two periods in overlapping generations, are endowed with one unit of time in every period. At birth, they are also endowed with an innate mental ability level a_i, which we assume to be drawn from a uniform distribution. That is,

$$\int_{\underline{a}}^{\bar{a}} \frac{1}{\bar{a} - \underline{a}} da = 1, \tag{4}$$

where $\bar{a}$, $\underline{a}$ respectively denote the upper and lower bounds of the support of the ability distribution. Individuals' innate mental ability levels a_i augment their human capital and labor input.

In the first period, individuals decide whether they will be labor or human capital suppliers during their lifetime. If they choose to become labor providers, they devote all of their time endowment in the first and second periods to work, saving their first-period income in the world capital market. If they choose to become human capital suppliers, they also decide what fraction of their time in the first period to devote to accumulating professional human capital through education and to acquiring entrepreneurial human capital by working in a business venture. In the second period, individuals supply their total human capital and labor endowment and they consume. The size of the population is normalized to one, and there is no population growth.

Regardless of individuals' choice of occupation, we assume that their innate abilities are unobservable without any schooling or work experience. More specifically, because employers cannot observe the ability of young workers, they pay these workers an unskilled wage that is proportional to the expected innate ability level of unskilled labor in that period. In contrast, employers pay old unskilled workers a wage that is dependent on their specific innate ability, as old workers' experience in the previous period reveals their type.[10] Therefore, individual i's income from being a lifetime labor provider in both periods is given by

$$(I^i)^u = \begin{cases} w^l \alpha_t & \text{when young,} \\ w^l a_i & \text{when old,} \end{cases} \tag{5}$$

where α_t denotes the expected ability of unskilled workers in period t. Note that when all individuals choose to become labor providers in any given period t, the expected ability of unskilled workers α_t will equal $\frac{\bar{a}+\underline{a}}{2} \equiv 1$.

For those individuals who choose to become human capital providers, skills require time to develop, and thus, these individuals earn no income when they are young. We assume that the time devoted to education in the first period s_t^i increases an individual's stock of professional capital in the second period p_{t+1}^i, whereas time devoted to work x_t^i increases his entrepreneurial capital e_{t+1}^i:

$$e_{t+1}^i = a_i f(x_t^i), \tag{6}$$

and

$$p_{t+1}^i = a_i f(s_t^i), \tag{7}$$

where $x_t^i + s_t^i \leq 1$, the standard Inada conditions hold, and $\forall\, x_t^i,\, s_t^i \geq 0,\, f' > 0,\, f'' < 0$. One can think of the initial time devoted to augment entrepreneurial human capital as a startup cost for entrepreneurial ventures.

As the above specification implies, we have chosen to allow a single individual to supply both entrepreneurial and professional human capital even though individuals tend to be classified empirically as either entrepreneurs or professionals. We believe this formulation to be quite plausible to the extent that performing any job requires some combination of each type of human capital and markets reward each of those potentially differently. That noted, one can reconcile the results of our model with the empirical classification of occupations by interpreting the percentage of time human capital providers allocate to each activity as the percent of the skilled labor force involved in each occupation. More realistically, if we incorporated another dimension of ability into our model so that some individuals had a comparative advantage in supplying entrepreneurial human capital while others had a comparative advantage in supplying professional human capital, we could classify individuals as either entrepreneurs or professionals based on how they accumulated the majority of their human capital.

We assume that there is uncertainty in the return to entrepreneurial ventures but that the return to education (which generates professional human capital in the following period) is not subject to any uncertainty. Specifically, individual i's income from becoming an entrepreneur, $(I_{t+1}^i)^e$, is

$$(I_{t+1}^i)^e = \begin{cases} w_{t+1}^h e_{t+1}^i = \lambda_{t+1} e_{t+1}^i & \text{with probability } q \\ 0 & \text{with probability } 1 - q, \end{cases} \tag{8}$$

and his income from professional activities $(I_{t+1}^i)^p$ is

$$(I_{t+1}^i)^p = w_{t+1}^h p_{t+1}^i = \lambda_{t+1} p_{t+1}^i, \tag{9}$$

where $0 < q \leq 1$. In equation (8), the probabilities q and $1 - q$ are the odds of success and failure faced by each entrepreneur. In aggregate, given a sufficiently large number of entrepreneurs, q percent will succeed and $1 - q$ percent will fail.

Finally, we assume that the level of technology in period $t + 1$, λ_{t+1}, is determined by the average levels of the entrepreneurial and professional human capital in the previous period.[11] Specifically,

$$\lambda_{t+1} = \lambda(e_t, p_t), \tag{10}$$

where $\frac{\partial \lambda_{t+1}}{\partial e_t}, \frac{\partial \lambda_{t+1}}{\partial p_t} > 0,\ \frac{\partial^2 \lambda_{t+1}}{\partial e_t^2}, \frac{\partial^2 \lambda_{t+1}}{\partial p_t^2} < 0$ and $\frac{\partial^2 \lambda_{t+1}}{\partial e_t \partial p_t}, \frac{\partial^2 \lambda_{t+1}}{\partial p_t \partial e_t} > 0$.

Individuals maximize expected utility from consumption in the second period and their rate of time preference is zero. The expected utility of individual i of generation t takes the following specific form:

$$E\left[u(c_{t+1}^i) \mid t\right] = q \ln(c_{t+1,q}^i) + (1 - q) \ln(c_{t+1,1-q}^i), \tag{11}$$

where $c_{t+1,q}^i$ and $c_{t+1,1-q}^i$, respectively, denote the consumption of individual i in the good and bad states.[12]

ENTREPRENEURS, PROFESSIONALS, AND GROWTH   221

In addition to $s_t^i + x_t^i \leq 1$, individual i is subject to the budget constraint below:

$$I_{t+1}^i = \begin{cases} [(1+\bar{r})\alpha_t + a_i]\phi & \text{if } i \text{ is a labor provider} \\ \phi a_i + (I_{t+1}^i)^e + (I_{t+1}^i)^p & \text{if } i \text{ is a human capital provider,} \end{cases} \tag{12}$$

where $(I_{t+1}^i)^e$ and $(I_{t+1}^i)^p$ are given by equations (8) and (9).[13]

Given the problem specified above, there exists a threshold innate ability level for every period t — that, henceforth we will denote by $\tilde{a}_t$ — below which individual i will choose to be a labor supplier. Combining equations (6) to (9), (11), and (12), we can show that $\tilde{a}_t$ satisfies the following equality:

$$q \ln\left\{\phi\tilde{a}_t + \lambda_{t+1}\tilde{a}_t[f(s_t^i) + f(1 - s_t^i)]\right\} + \{(1-q)\ln\{\phi\tilde{a}_t + \lambda_{t+1}\tilde{a}_t f(s_t^i)]\}$$

$$= \ln\{[(1+\bar{r})\alpha_t + \tilde{a}_t]\phi\}. \tag{13}$$

If individual i's innate mental ability level is such that $a_i > \tilde{a}_t$, individual i — while young — chooses to accumulate human capital instead of supplying labor. In that case, the optimal amount of time allocated to education by the individual s_t^i satisfies

$$\frac{q}{1-q} = -\frac{\phi + \lambda_{t+1}[f(s_t^i) + f(1 - s_t^i)]}{\phi + \lambda_{t+1}f(s_t^i)} \frac{f'(s_t^i)}{f'(s_t^i) - f'(1 - s_t^i)}. \tag{14}$$

Note that the first-order condition above implies that the amount of time individual i devotes to schooling is independent of his innate ability level a_i. Put differently, $s_t^i = s_t \,\forall\, i$ such that $a_i > \tilde{a}_t$.

Equations (13) and (14) lead to the propositions below:

Proposition 1: $\forall\, t \geq 0$ *such that* $\tilde{a}_t < \bar{a}$, *the threshold innate ability level in period* t, $\tilde{a}_t$, *is a decreasing function of average levels of entrepreneurial and professional human capital in the same period,* e_t *and* p_t. *Namely,*

$$\frac{\partial \tilde{a}_t}{\partial e_t}, \quad \frac{\partial \tilde{a}_t}{\partial p_t} \quad < 0. \tag{15}$$

Proof: Using equation (13) and the implicit function theorem, it is straightforward to show

$$\frac{\partial \tilde{a}_t}{\partial e_t} = -\frac{\tilde{a}_t(3\tilde{a}_t + \underline{a})}{\underline{a}}\left[\frac{q[f(s_t) + f(1 - s_t)]}{\phi + \lambda_{t+1}[f(s_t) + f(1 - s_t)]} + \frac{(1-q)f(s_t)}{\phi + \lambda_{t+1}f(s_t)}\right]\frac{\partial \lambda_{t+1}}{\partial e_t}$$

$$< 0, \tag{16}$$

and

$$\frac{\partial \tilde{a}_t}{\partial p_t} = -\frac{\tilde{a}_t(3\tilde{a}_t + \underline{a})}{\underline{a}}\left[\frac{q[f(s_t) + f(1 - s_t)]}{\phi + \lambda_{t+1}[f(s_t) + f(1 - s_t)]} + \frac{(1-q)f(s_t)}{\phi + \lambda_{t+1}f(s_t)}\right]\frac{\partial \lambda_{t+1}}{\partial p_t}$$

$$< 0. \tag{17}$$

∎

The above proposition shows that, in the early stages of development when the returns to both types of human capital input are relatively small, only those with the highest ability levels choose to supply human capital, whereas a majority of the population chooses to supply labor. As improvements in technology raise the relative return to human capital, however, a larger fraction of the population chooses to accumulate human capital while young by allocating time to education and working as entrepreneurs.[14]

Proposition 2: *(i)* $\forall q, 0 < q \leq 1$, *and* $\forall t \geq 0$ *such that* $\tilde{a}_t < \bar{a}$, *the optimal amount of time individual i chooses to devote to education* s_t *is such that* $s_t \geq \frac{1}{2}$. *(ii)* $\forall q, 0 < q < 1$, *and* $\forall t \geq 0$ *such that* $\tilde{a}_t < \bar{a}$, *the amount of time individual i chooses to devote to education in period t*, s_t, *is an increasing function of average levels of entrepreneurial and professional human capital in the same period*, e_t *and* p_t. *Namely,*

$$\frac{\partial s_t}{\partial e_t}, \quad \frac{\partial s_t}{\partial p_t} \quad > 0. \tag{18}$$

Proof: (i) Given that the lhs and the first term on the rhs of equation (14) are positive, we establish that the term $\frac{f'(s_t)}{f'(s_t)-f'(1-s_t)}$ on the rhs needs to be nonpositive. Thus, $f'(s_t) - f'(1 - s_t) \leq 0 \Leftrightarrow s_t \geq \frac{1}{2} \forall i$ such that $a_i > \tilde{a}_t$.

(ii) Using the first-order condition given by (14) and invoking — once again — the implicit function theorem, we get

$$\frac{\partial s_t}{\partial e_t} = -\frac{1}{\eta} \frac{\phi f(1 - s_t) f'(s_t)}{\phi + \lambda_{t+1} f(s_t)} \frac{\partial \lambda_{t+1}}{\partial e_t} > 0, \tag{19}$$

where

$$\eta = \begin{cases} -\dfrac{\phi \lambda_{t+1} f'(s_t) f'(1-s_t) + \lambda_{t+1}^2 f(s_t) f'(1-s_t) + \lambda_{t+1}^2 f(1-s_t) f'(s_t)}{\phi + \lambda_{t+1} f(s_t)} \\ -\{\phi + \lambda_{t+1}[f(s_t) + f(1 - s_t)]\} \dfrac{f''(s_t) f'(1-s_t) + f''(1-s_t) f'(s_t)}{f'(s_t) - f'(1-s_t)} \end{cases} < 0.$$

$\frac{\partial s_t}{\partial p_t}$ is equal to an expression almost identical to (19), where $\frac{\partial \lambda_{t+1}}{\partial e_t}$ is replaced by $\frac{\partial \lambda_{t+1}}{\partial p_t}$. ∎

Proposition 2 shows how increases in the human capital stock, which raise the level of technology and per capita income, affect the accumulation of the two different types of human capital. Specifically, it demonstrates that technological change, by inducing human capital suppliers to devote more time to schooling, leads to a shift away from entrepreneurial human capital accumulation.[15] The reason is that technological change not only raises the relative return to human capital, but it also increases the *risk* of time invested in entrepreneurial human capital accumulation in the sense that the discrepancy between the payoffs in the good and bad states increases as the economy develops.[16] As a result, those individuals who find it optimal to become human capital suppliers choose to stay in school longer and develop a higher ratio of professional to entrepreneurial skills. As will be seen in the next section, the change in the ratio of professional to entrepreneurial skills does not necessarily imply a reduction in aggregate entrepreneurial skills because the aggregate value is also affected by decreases in $\tilde{a}_t$ which cause more individuals to become human capital providers.

One can see from equation (14) that, besides the inherent risk in the payoff to entrepreneurial skills, there are two key elements in generating the dynamics discussed above. First, individuals get paid for their raw labor ($\phi \neq 0$) even when they are human capital providers. Second, technological progress is skill-biased. The implications of both of these assumptions, taken together, is that the variability of payoffs in the good and bad states increases with development. If either human capital providers were not compensated for their raw labor ($\phi = 0$) or if the payment to raw labor increased proportionally with λ_{t+1} (for example, the return to raw labor was equal to $\phi\lambda_{t+1}$), then λ_{t+1} would drop out of the first-order condition and individuals would not reallocate their time away from investing in entrepreneurial skills. When all individuals get paid for their raw labor ($\phi \neq 0$), however, skill-biased technological change induces higher variability in the payoffs in the good and bad states. Thus, as an optimal response to this increased variability of payoffs, individuals increase their level of schooling s_t.

4. The Evolution of the Economy

Given (13) and the specification of the technology parameter λ_{t+1} in (10), we identify that there exists a minimum level of technology below which all individuals choose to work as labor and no one allocates time to activities that foster human capital accumulation. Let

$$
\mu = \left\{ (e_t, p_t) \,\middle|\, \begin{array}{l} q \ln\{\phi\bar{a} + \lambda_{t+1}\bar{a}[f(s_t) + f(1 - s_t)]\} \\ + (1 - q) \ln\{\phi\bar{a} + \lambda_{t+1}\bar{a}f(s_t)]\} \end{array} \leq \ln((1 - \bar{r} + \bar{a})\phi) \right\}. \quad (20)
$$

Thus, when $(e_t, p_t) \in \mu, \bar{a} \leq \tilde{a}_t$, not even the highest-ability individuals choose to devote time to education or work experience and $e_{t+1} = p_{t+1} = 0$.

In contrast, for all pairs of entrepreneurial and professional human capital in any given period t, $(e_t, p_t) \notin \mu$, the dynamical system is characterized by the two equations that govern the evolution of entrepreneurial and professional human capital stocks. Namely,

$$
e_{t+1} = \begin{cases} \int_{\tilde{a}_t}^{\bar{a}} \frac{1}{\bar{a}-\underline{a}} f(x_t^i)da_i = \frac{\bar{a}-\tilde{a}_t}{\bar{a}-\underline{a}} f(x_t) = \frac{\bar{a}-\tilde{a}_t}{\bar{a}-\underline{a}} f(1 - s_t) & \text{when } \bar{a} > \tilde{a}_t > \underline{a} \\ f(1 - s_t) & \text{when } \tilde{a}_t \leq \underline{a} \end{cases}
$$

$$
p_{t+1} = \begin{cases} \int_{\tilde{a}_t}^{\bar{a}} \frac{1}{\bar{a}-\underline{a}} f(s_t^i)da_i = \frac{\bar{a}-\tilde{a}_t}{\bar{a}-\underline{a}} f(s_t) & \text{when } \bar{a} > \tilde{a}_t > \underline{a} \\ f(s_t) & \text{when } \tilde{a}_t \leq \underline{a}. \end{cases} \quad (21)
$$

Given that both $\tilde{a}_t$ and s_t are functions of the technology level in period $t + 1$, λ_{t+1}, which in turn is a function of the entrepreneurial and professional human capital in the previous period, e_t and p_t,

$$
e_{t+1} = \Gamma(e_t, p_t) \quad \text{and} \quad p_{t+1} = \psi(e_t, p_t). \quad (22)
$$

In this economy, a steady-state is characterized by $(\bar{e}, \bar{p})$ such that, $\forall t \geq T, \bar{e} = \Gamma(\bar{e}, \bar{p})$ and $\bar{p} = \Psi(\bar{e}, \bar{p})$.

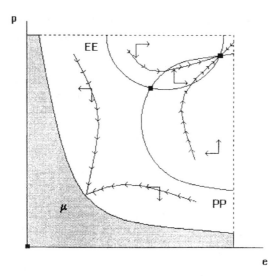

Figure 3. Entrepreneurial and professional human capital accumulation dynamics.

Proposition 3: $\forall q, \tilde{q} \leq q \leq 1$ and $(e_0, p_0) \notin \mu$, $\exists$ *a nontrivial, stable, steady-state equilibrium for the dynamical system specified in (22) if*

(i) the technology of human capital production f is sufficiently productive,

(ii) ϕ is sufficiently small.

Proof: See Appendix for the derivation of the dynamical system.

   The reason for the first condition in Proposition 3 is intuitive: the technology of human capital production must be effective enough to induce individuals to accumulate entrepreneurial and professional skills. The reason for the second condition is intuitive as well: because ϕ is the opportunity cost of providing human capital, when it is too large, individuals will not invest in either professional or entrepreneurial skills, and a nontrivial steady state will not exist.
   Figure 3 presents the phase diagram of the dynamical system. As shown, only when the initial stocks of entrepreneurial *and* professional human capital, $(e_0, p_0) \notin \mu$, are sufficiently large, does the system converge to a nontrivial, stable steady-state, $(\bar{e}, \bar{p}) \gg 0$. In that case, the production technology used in the skilled sector continually improves along with increases in fraction of individuals who become human capital providers. Until the system reaches its steady-state, such individuals allocate an increasing share of their time to formal education in order to accumulate relatively more professional human capital. However, when $(e_0, p_0) \ll (\bar{e}, \bar{p})$, the stock of entrepreneurial human capital may still increase during some part of the transition to the steady-state despite the fact that human

capital providers allocate a decreasing fraction of their time to entrepreneurial activities during the transition. The reason is that, throughout the transition, more individuals are choosing to become human capital providers instead of remaining unskilled. Otherwise, if the initial stocks of entrepreneurial *and* professional human capital, (e_0, p_0), are not sufficiently large, then the initial level of technology is not sophisticated enough to guarantee that an increasing fraction of individuals become human capital providers. As a result, fewer and fewer individuals allocate their time to augmenting their human capital, and the system converges to a steady-state in which production is carried out solely in the unskilled sector.

There are several important implications of the dynamics of our model. First, entrepreneurial human capital plays a relatively (but not absolutely) more important role in intermediate income countries, whereas professional human capital is relatively (and absolutely) more abundant in richer economies. For those countries that start off with a sufficiently high combination of entrepreneurs and professionals, an increasing fraction of the population chooses to invest in both skills during the transition to the steady state. Moreover, those who choose to do so devote an increasing amount of time to the accumulation of professional human capital and a decreasing amount of time to entrepreneurial human capital. The reason, as we have stated earlier, is that as per capita income grows and the payoff to being a professional increases, individuals are less willing to gamble on enterpreneurial ventures. Of course, higher probabilities of entrepreneurial success (higher values of q) generate higher stocks of entrepreneurial skills.

The key mechanism that generates the decline in the relative importance of entrepreneurial skills as an economy grows is that the opportunity cost of being self-employed increases faster than its expected return. While the major conclusions of our model would hold if either the probability of a successful venture or the payoff to a failed entrepreneur increased as an economy develops, these increases must not be too large. If they are too large, then the expected benefit of self-employment would increase more than its opportunity cost, and individuals would allocate more time to it as per capita income grows.

A second important implication of the dynamics of our model is that the initial stock of *both* entrepreneurial and professional human capital are important for the process of development. Notably, those countries that start off with too little entrepreneurial or professional human capital end up in a development trap in which production is carried out in the unskilled sector only and there is no human capital investment of any type. This result obtains because both entrepreneurial and professional human capital play a role in the determination of the level of technology. Therefore, when either type of human capital is relatively small initially, the level of technology and the return to human capital investment relative to the labor input are also small. As a result, an increasing fraction of individuals choose to become labor suppliers instead of becoming human capital providers.[17]

A relevant example of the importance of this second point may be found in the former east-bloc countries. As some have pointed out (e.g., Overland and Spagat, 1996), these economies have a highly educated labor force and may be primed for an economic takeoff. However, our model highlights the possibility that these economies, if short on entrepreneurs, may be further away from the high-income steady state than education levels alone would indicate. In fact, some of them may even be unable to reach it.

A third implication of our model is that because the social marginal returns to work and education may differ from the private marginal returns, it is likely that even the steady state with positive human capital investment is inefficient. However, because in our model the alternative to education is also a productive activity, the source of the inefficiency is not standard: there may be too much investment in education in the steady state. Specifically, when entrepreneurs are more important in determining the level of technology than professionals, the high-income steady state may be characterized by overinvestment in education. Similarly, when professional human capital has greater influence on the technology in use, the high-income steady state has too little education. The key feature of the model that produces these unique inefficiencies is that entrepreneurial and professional human capital may be combined in different ways in production and in the formation of the technology of production. Therefore, it is important to note that inefficiencies may result not from too much human capital but from a misallocation of the existing human capital stock between professional and entrepreneurial skills. In fact, a more socially efficient ratio of professionals to entrepreneurs will raise the steady-state level of technology and increase the wages paid to human capital providers and the economy's human capital stock.

5. Conclusion

The model we present above demonstrates why both entrepreneurial and professional skills are important for development. It shows that the private incentives to accumulate entrepreneurial relative to professional skills are greater in intermediate income countries and that—due to the inherent riskiness of entrepreneurial ventures—those incentives decline relative to the incentives to become a professional as countries grow richer. Nonetheless, the initial stock of *both* types of human capital matter because together they determine the return to human capital relative to raw labor. Thus, the initial conditions are important in determining whether countries converge to an equilibrium in which, for a larger fraction of the population, investing time in human capital accumulation will be more profitable relative to labor provision.

Our model also demonstrates that when more than one type of human capital exists, individuals may not allocate their time in a socially efficient way to the accumulation of these different skills. More generally, our results indicate that a thorough macroeconomic investigation of all channels of human capital accumulation is necessary to formulate the appropriate tests of the role of human capital in development and to effectively design and implement the most successful policies. This is a fruitful area for further research.

Appendix

Proof of Proposition 3:   We prove this proposition in three steps:

- *Step 1:* We assume that the *EE* and *PP* loci do not lie within μ (i.e., $\tilde{a}_t < \bar{a} \,\forall\, t$ and equation (20) holds) and demonstrate that they have the form shown in Figure 3.

- *Step 2:* We then show that when $q = 1$, the *EE* and *PP* loci intersect when $f(\frac{1}{2})$ is large enough. We relax the assumption that the entire *EE* and *PP* loci derived in step 1 lie outside of μ, but show that the intersection of the two loci is still outside of μ.

- *Step 3:* Finally, we show that decreases in q shift the *EE* and *PP* loci continuously, guaranteeing that the *EE* and *PP* loci intersect for $\forall q, \tilde{q} \leq q \leq 1$.

Step 1   Let

$$EE = \{(e_t, p_t) \mid e_{t+1} - e_t = \Delta e = 0\} \tag{23}$$

and

$$PP = \{(e_t, p_t) \mid p_{t+1} - p_t = \Delta p = 0\}. \tag{24}$$

Assume that $\tilde{a}_t < \bar{a} \ \forall \ t$. Then, using the implicit function theorem, we are able to show that

$$\left.\frac{\partial p_t}{\partial e_t}\right|_{EE} = -\frac{\Gamma_e - 1}{\Gamma_p} = -\frac{\left(\frac{\bar{a}-\tilde{a}_t}{\bar{a}-\underline{a}}\right) f'(1-s_t)\frac{\partial s_t}{\partial e_t} + \left(\frac{1}{\bar{a}-\underline{a}}\right) f(1-s_t)\frac{\partial \tilde{a}_t}{\partial e_t} + 1}{\left(\frac{1}{\bar{a}-\underline{a}}\right) f(1-s_t)\frac{\partial \tilde{a}_t}{\partial p_t} + \left(\frac{\bar{a}-\tilde{a}_t}{\bar{a}-\underline{a}}\right) f'(1-s_t)\frac{\partial s_t}{\partial p_t}}, \tag{25}$$

where Γ_e and Γ_p respectively denote $\frac{\partial \Gamma}{\partial e_t}$ and $\frac{\partial \Gamma}{\partial p_t}$. Similarly,

$$\left.\frac{\partial p_t}{\partial e_t}\right|_{PP} = -\frac{\psi_e}{\psi_p - 1} = -\frac{\left(\frac{\bar{a}-\tilde{a}_t}{\bar{a}-\underline{a}}\right) f'(s_t)\frac{\partial s_t}{\partial e_t} - \left(\frac{1}{\bar{a}-\underline{a}}\right) f(s_t)\frac{\partial \tilde{a}_t}{\partial e_t}}{\left(\frac{\bar{a}-\tilde{a}_t}{\bar{a}-\underline{a}}\right) f'(s_t)\frac{\partial s_t}{\partial p_t} - \left(\frac{1}{\bar{a}-\underline{a}}\right) f(s_t)\frac{\partial \tilde{a}_t}{\partial p_t} - 1} \tag{26}$$

where ψ_e and ψ_p respectively denote $\frac{\partial \psi}{\partial e_t}$ and $\frac{\partial \psi}{\partial p_t}$. By combining (16) and (19) with (25), we find that if ϕ is relatively small then $\frac{\partial s_t}{\partial e_t}$ and $\frac{\partial s_t}{\partial p_t}$ are also small and Γ_e, $\Gamma_p \geq 0 \ \forall \ (e_t, p_t) \notin \mu$. Thus,

$$\left.\frac{\partial p_t}{\partial e_t}\right|_{EE} \begin{cases} \leq 0 & \text{when} \quad \Gamma_e \geq 1 \\ > 0 & \text{when} \quad \Gamma_e < 1, \end{cases} \tag{27}$$

and, since Ψ_e, $\Psi_p \geq 0 \ \forall \ (e_t, p_t) \notin \mu$, for all parameter specifications,

$$\left.\frac{\partial p_t}{\partial e_t}\right|_{PP} \begin{cases} \leq 0 & \text{when} \quad \Psi_p \geq 1 \\ > 0 & \text{when} \quad \Psi_p < 1. \end{cases} \tag{28}$$

Let e^* and p^*, respectively, denote (for given values of p_t and e_t) the values of e_t and p_t that set $q \ln\{\lambda_{t+1}\bar{a}[f(s_t) + f(1-s_t)]\} + (1-q)\ln\{\bar{a}[\phi + \lambda_{t+1}f(s_t)]\} = \ln[(1+\bar{r}+\bar{a})\phi]$. Given that $\tilde{a}_t < \bar{a}$, $\frac{\partial^2 \tilde{a}_t}{\partial e_t^2}$, $\frac{\partial^2 \tilde{a}_t}{\partial p_t^2}$ are positive, and $\frac{\partial^2 s_t}{\partial e_t^2}$, $\frac{\partial^2 s_t}{\partial p_t^2}$ are negative—as can be verified from (16) (17), and (19)—we determine that

$$\lim_{e_t \to e^*} \left(\left.\frac{\partial p_t}{\partial e_t}\right|_{EE}\right) < 0 \quad \text{and} \quad \lim_{e_t \to \infty} \left(\left.\frac{\partial p_t}{\partial e_t}\right|_{EE}\right) > 0 \tag{29}$$

and that

$$\lim_{p_t \to p^*} \left(\frac{\partial p_t}{\partial e_t} \bigg|_{PP} \right) < 0 \quad \text{and} \quad \lim_{p_t \to \infty} \left(\frac{\partial p_t}{\partial e_t} \bigg|_{PP} \right) > 0. \tag{30}$$

Moreover, given that s_t and $\tilde{a}_t$ are continuous in e_t and p_t—as implied by Propositions 1 and 2—along the *EE* locus $\exists$ $(e', p') \notin \mu$ such that

$$\frac{\partial p_t}{\partial e_t} \bigg|_{EE} = 0 \tag{31}$$

and that, along the *PP* locus $\exists$ $(e'', p'') \notin \mu$ such that

$$\frac{\partial p_t}{\partial e_t} \bigg|_{PP} = 0. \tag{32}$$

Thus, we establish the general forms of the *EE* and *PP* loci on the (e, p) map as shown in Figure 3.

Step 2 Next, we need to demonstrate that, for a nontrivial, stable steady-state to exist, $\exists$ $(\bar{e}, \bar{p}) \notin \mu$.

First consider the case in which $q = 1$. When $q = 1$, $s_t = \frac{1}{2}$ and $f(s_t) = f(1 - s_t) = f(\frac{1}{2}) \equiv \tilde{f}$ $\forall$ t. Moreover, $\frac{\partial s_t}{\partial e_t} = \frac{\partial s_t}{\partial p_t} = 0$. Thus, (21) simplifies to

$$e_{t+1} = p_{t+1} = \begin{cases} \tilde{f} \int_{\tilde{a}_t}^{\bar{a}} \frac{1}{\bar{a} - \underline{a}} da_i = \frac{\bar{a} - \tilde{a}_t}{\bar{a} - \underline{a}} \tilde{f} & \text{when } \tilde{a}_t > \underline{a} \\ \tilde{f} & \text{when } \tilde{a}_t \leq \underline{a}. \end{cases} \tag{33}$$

Under this case, if a nontrivial steady state equilibrium $(\bar{e}, \bar{p}) \notin \mu$ exists, it satisfies $\bar{e} = \bar{p}$. It also follows directly from (33) that if $\exists$ $(\hat{e}, \hat{p}) \in EE$ such that $\hat{e} = \hat{p}$ and $\exists$ $(\tilde{e}, \tilde{p}) \in PP$ such that $\tilde{e} = \tilde{p}$, then $\hat{e} = \tilde{e} = \bar{e}$ and $\hat{p} = \tilde{p} = \bar{p}$ (that is, if the *EE* and *PP* loci cross the 45 degree line, they must cross at the same place).

Suppose that, there does not exist $(\bar{e}, \bar{p}) \notin \mu$. This implies that $\forall$ $e_t = p_t$, $(e_t, p_t) \notin \mu$, Δp and Δe are both negative. However, (33) indicates that, for a large enough value of $\tilde{f}$, $\exists$ $(e_t, p_t) \notin \mu$ s.t. $e_t = p_t$ and Δp and Δe are both positive. Thus, we can ensure that $\exists$ $(e_t, p_t) \notin \mu$ s.t. $e_t = p_t$ and $\Delta p = \Delta e = 0$.

Step 3 We now show that as q is reduced, $\exists$ $(\bar{e}, \bar{p}) \notin \mu$. First note that, when $q = 1$,

$$\frac{\partial p_t}{\partial e_t} \bigg|_{EE} \neq \frac{\partial p_t}{\partial e_t} \bigg|_{PP}, \tag{34}$$

when evaluated at $(\bar{e}, \bar{p})$. Thus, we can rule out a tangency at $(\bar{e}, \bar{p})$ when $q = 1$.

Using (21), (23), and (24) and the fact that s_t and $\tilde{a}_t$ are continuous in q, we can also establish that the *EE* and the *PP* locus shift continuously in response to changes in q. Taken together with the fact that EE and PP are not tangent at $(\bar{e}, \bar{p})$ when $q = 1$, we conclude that $\exists\, q, \tilde{q} \leq q < 1$, such that $(\bar{e}, \bar{p}) \notin \mu$ (with $\bar{e} < \bar{p}$) exists.

Remark. Note that increases in the effectiveness of education and experience in human capital accumulation — as given by the function f — shift EE and PP in the opposite direction as decreases in q. Thus, the more effective f is in converting education and experience into human capital, the lower is $\tilde{q}$. ∎

Acknowledgments

John M. Heitkemper provided valuable research assistance. We are grateful to Gerhard Glomm, Lant Pritchett, two anonymous referees, and the editor, Oded Galor, for useful comments and suggestions. All remaining errors are, of course, our own. This article represents the views of the authors and should not be interpreted as reflecting those of the Board of Governors of the Federal Reserve System or other members of its staff.

Notes

1. Evans and Jovanovich (1989) and Holtz-Eakin, Joulfaian, and Rosen (1994) provide some empirical support for the role that credit constraints play in shaping occupational choice by showing that wealthier people are more likely to become entrepreneurs and Holtz-Eakin, Joulfaian, and Rosen (1994) find that individuals who receive inheritances are more likely to remain entrepreneurs. Holtz-Eakin and Dunn (1995), however, show that financial assets influence the probability of being self-employed only modestly among a sample of young men and not at all in sample of young women, placing some doubt on the importance of credit market imperfections.

2. In fact, Murphy, Shleifer, and Vishny (1991) find some evidence that individuals may not choose to accumulate their human capital in a socially optimal way: countries with more students concentrating in legal studies grow slower. McGoldrick and Robst (1996) also report some evidence on this point by noting that a significant fraction of the U.S. labor force may be overeducated. They compare estimates of required schooling for each occupation as reported in the *Dictionary of Occupational Titles* to actual levels of schooling reported by the respondents to the *1985 Panel Study of Income Dynamics* and find that over half of the sample is overeducated. When they compare actual levels of education to individuals' own estimates of the educational requirements of their jobs, that fraction falls but remains substantial.

3. Following Evans and Jovanovich (1989), Evans and Leighton (1989), and Holtz-Eakin, Joulfaian, and Rosen (1994), we empirically associate entrepreneurship with self-employment and use the terms *entrepreneur* and *self-employed* interchangeably in this section. Clearly, not all self-employed individuals are entrepreneurs, particularly if we define entrepreneurs to be only those engaged in R&D (see Knight, 1921; Schumpeter, 1950, or even Baumel, 1990, for competing views on the definition of entrepreneurship). However, the self-employed do share an important characteristic with entrepreneurs: they face more uncertain returns to their labor than wage and salary workers. It is this common characteristic that we choose to highlight in our model.

   In addition, we should point out that, although individuals tend to be classified empirically as either entrepreneurs or professionals, our model takes a broader view of the process of human capital accumulation and allows a single individual to accumulate both entrepreneurial and professional skills.

4. Obviously, being self-employed and being a professional are not mutually exclusive activities. However, taken together, Figures 1 and 2 illustrate our major point: more developed economies have more people working for others and more people engaged in professional and managerial activities.

5. Even though both groups of workers have about the same level of education, self-employed workers' higher levels of job tenure and age suggest that these workers have accumulated their human capital through a more experience-intensive process.

6. More support for the idea that the human capital of the self-employed is more experience intensive can be found in Bregger (1996), who uses data from the Current Population Survey to show that workers are more likely to become self-employed as they become older. In addition, Fujii and Hawley (1991) show that self-employed workers have more work experience and a higher return to experience than wage and salary workers. Finally, LaFerrere and McEntee (1995), using French data, show that individuals are less likely to be self-employed if they have a third-level education.

7. The remaining patents were awarded to the U.S. and foreign governments.

8. Michael Dell, CEO of Dell Computers and Inc. Magazine's 1989 entrepreneur of the year, attended University of Texas at Austin but never finished. Bill Gates, cofounder of Microsoft, dropped out of Harvard in his junior year, and Ross Perot, founder of the multimillion-dollar corporation, Electronic Data Systems (EDS), attended Texarkana Junior College.

9. Skill-biased technological change is not essential for our results. Rather, what is crucial for the dynamics we describe below is a positive link between educated labor and skill-biased technological change. Put differently, the basic model we lay out below could easily accommodate directed technological change along the lines proposed by Acemoglu (1998). In his model, increases in the number of skilled workers generate economywide incentives for investment in skill-biased technological change. Extending that reasoning to cover our model, coefficients on human capital and raw labor in equation (1) could be modified so that they respectively depend positively and negatively on the ratio of skilled to unskilled labor. The thrust of our qualitative conclusions would not change under such a modification.

10. The results we present below are not dependent on this specification either. Under a technically more complicated alternative, for example, labor income could be fixed and independent of innate ability throughout the lifetime.

11. As will become clear in what follows, the dynamics of the model depend on the lag with which the existing stock of human capital affects the *level* of technology. Alternatively, we could have chosen to follow Romer (1990) and adopt what is by now a more conventional approach where the *rate* of technological progress or adoption depends on the existing stock of human capital. Our main arguments would go through unaffected under such a modification as well.

    Note also that this general form does not require us to make the assumption that both entrepreneurs and professionals are required—only that entrepreneurs and professionals are both capable of contributing to the level of technology or to its adoption. As we state in the introduction, both independent inventors and corporations are responsible for a significant portion of patent applications in the United States, suggesting that both entrepreneurs and professionals play a role in fostering innovation. We are, of course, implicitly assuming that the marginal contribution of each new entrepreneur to the level of technology is the same regardless of whether or not this entrepreneur works in the R&D sector. This would occur if we assume that the fraction of entrepreneurs in the R&D sector remains constant over time or if entrepreneurial skills applied in the non-R&D sector are just as effective in improving the technology.

12. We have chosen logarithmic preferences to demonstrate that increasing relative risk aversion is not necessary to generate the declining willingness to gamble on entrepreneurship as per capita income grows. Clearly, this result could be generated with any utility function that features increasing relative risk aversion, and some, but not all, utility functions that feature decreasing relative risk aversion.

13. In our setup, individuals are compensated for each of the three types of labor they provide. This is similar to the specification used in Galor and Weil (1996) in which individuals are compensated for both their physical and mental abilities. See the discussion at the end of this section for the implications of alternative schemes in which human capital providers are not compensated for their physical abilities (that is, $\phi = 0$ for human capital providers).

14. In our model, individuals must pass the innate-ability threshold in order to become human capital providers. As mentioned in the introduction, there may also be a threshold level of wealth required of entrepreneurs in the absence of perfect capital markets. One could adapt our model to other rationing rules such as one that takes into account both parental wealth and ability (similar to that found in Owen and Weil, 1998) without altering its major conclusions.

15. Our formulation abstracts from how the magnitude of improvements in the level of technology—due to higher human capital—might affect relative returns to different components of the human capital stock. For a relevant discussion on this issue, see Galor and Tsiddon (1997).

16. It is relatively straightforward to demonstrate that the risk of an entrepreneurial venture increases with technological change. In addition, if abilities were perfectly observable and we were to allow competitive insurance companies to provide coverage, the insurance premium an entrepreneur would pay to insure against potential loss π_t^i would equal

$$\pi_t^i = (1 - q)\lambda_{t+1}a_t^i f(1 - s_t^i).$$

For a fixed level of schooling, a higher level of technology λ implies that this premium is greater. In the absence of insurance against entrepreneurial loss, it is clear that raising the time devoted to schooling s_t^i is an optimal response to improvements in technology.

17. Obviously, the existence of a development trap in this model is not a consequence of having two types of human capital but is rather related to whether human capital accumulation has an opportunity cost (that is, labor wage income). That noted, however, the model presented above demonstrates that when a development trap exists, the initial stocks of both types of human capital need to be taken into account in assessing the potential evolution of the economy.

References

Acemoglu, D. (1998). "Why Do New Technologies Complement Skills? Directed Technical Change and Wage Inequality," *Quarterly Journal of Economics* 113, 1055–89.

Acemoglu, D., and F. Zilibotti. (1997). "Was Prometheus Unbound by Chance? Risk, Diversification and Growth," *Journal of Political Economy* 105, 709–751.

Azariadis, C., and A. Drazen. (1990). "Threshold Externalities in Economic Development," *Quarterly Journal of Economics* 105, 501–526.

Banerjee, A., and A. Newman. (1993). "Occupational Choice and the Process of Economic Development," *Journal of Political Economy* 101, 274–298.

Baumol, W. J. (1990). "Entrepreneurship: Productive, Unproductive, and Destructive," *Journal of Political Economy* 98, 893–921.

Becker, G. S. (1993). *Human Capital: A Theoretical and Empirical Analysis, with Special Reference to Education.* Chicago: University of Chicago Press.

Bregger, J. E. (1996). "Measuring Self-Employment in the United States," *Monthly Labor Review* 119, 3–9.

Evans, D. S., and B. Jovanovic. (1989). "An Estimated Model of Entrepreneurial Choice Under Liquidity Constraints." *Journal of Political Economy* 97, 808–827.

Evans, D. S., and L. S. Leighton. (1989). "Some Empirical Aspects of Entrepreneurship." *American Economic Review* 79, 519–535.

Federal Reserve Board of Governors. (1995). *1995 Survey of Consumer Finances.* http://www.federalreserve.gov/pubs/oss.

Fujii, E. T., and C. B. Hawley. (1991). "Empirical Aspects of Self-Employment." *Economics Letters* 36, 323–329.

Galor, O., and D. Tsiddon. (1997). "Technological Progress, Mobility and Economic Growth." *American Economic Review* 87, 363–382.

Galor, O., and D. N. Weil. (1996). "The Gender Gap, Fertility and Growth." *American Economic Review* 86, 374–387.

Holtz-Eakin, D., and T. Dunn. (1995). "Capital Market Constraints, Parental Wealth and Transition to Self-Employment Among Men and Women." Bureau of Labor Statistics, NLS Discussion Paper, 96-29.

Holtz-Eakin, D., D. Joulfaian, and H. S. Rosen. (1994). "Sticking It Out: Entrepreneurial Survival and Liquidity Constraints." *Journal of Political Economy* 102, 53–75.

International Labour Office. (1993). *1993 Year Book of Labour Statistics.* Geneva: International Labour Office.

Knight, F. (1921). *Risk, Uncertainty, and Profit.* New York: Houghton Mifflin.

LaFerrerre, A., and P. McEntee. (1995). "Self-Employment and Intergenerational Transfers of Physical and Human Capital: An Empirical Analysis of French Data." *Economic and Social Review* 27, 43–54.

Levine, R., and S. Zervos. (1998). "Stock Markets, Banks and Economic Growth." *American Economic Review* 88, 537–558.

Lucas, R. E. (1988). "On the Mechanics of Economic Development." *Journal of Monetary Economics* 22, 3–42.

Lucas, R. E. (1993). "Making a Miracle." *Econometrica* 61, 251–272.

McGoldrick, K. M., and J. Robst. (1996). "Gender Differences in Overeducation: A Test of the Theory of Differential Overqualification." *American Economic Review, Papers and Proceedings* 86, 280–284.

Mincer, J. (1993). *Studies in Human Capital: Collected Essays of Jacob Mincer* (vol. 1). Brookfield, VT: Edward Elgar.

Mincer, J. (1996). "Economic Development, Growth of Human Capital and the Dynamics of the Wage Structure." *Journal of Economic Growth* 1, 29–48.

Murphy, K. M., A. Shleifer, and R. Vishny. (1991). "The Allocation of Talent: Implications for Growth." *Quarterly Journal of Economics* 106, 503–530.

Overland, J., and M. Spagat. (1996). "Human Capital and Russia's Economic Transformation." *Transition* 2, 12–15.

Owen, A. L., and D. N. Weil. (1998). "Intergenerational Earnings Mobility, Inequality and Growth." *Journal of Monetary Economics* 41, 71–104.

Romer, P. M. (1990). "Endogenous Technological Change." *Journal of Political Economy* 98, 571–602.

Schumpeter, J. (1950). *Capitalism, Socialism, and Democracy* (3rd ed.) New York: Harper & Row.

Stokey, N. L. (1988). "Learning by Doing and the Introduction of New Goods." *Journal of Political Economy* 96, 701–717.

Summers, Robert, and Alan Heston. (1991). "The Penn World Table: An Expanded Set of International Comparisons, 1950–1988." *Quarterly Journal of Economics* 106, 327–443 Mark 5.6.

U.S. Patent Office. (19). *Historic Data: All Technologies Report*. Washington, DC: U.S. Government Printing Office. http://www.uspto.gov/web/offices/ac/ido/ocip/taf.

Part II
Entrepreneurs, Financing Constraints, and Microfinance

[8]

ELSEVIER

Journal of Development Economics 86 (2008) 1–21

JOURNAL OF
Development
ECONOMICS

www.elsevier.com/locate/econbase

Can micro-credit bring development? [☆]

Christian Ahlin [a,*], Neville Jiang [b]

[a] *Department of Economics, Michigan State University, United States*
[b] *Department of Economics, University of Massachusetts Lowell, United States*

Received 15 July 2005; received in revised form 12 July 2007; accepted 14 August 2007

Abstract

We examine the long-run effects of micro-credit on development in an occupational choice model similar to Banerjee and Newman (JPE, 1993). Micro-credit is modeled as a pure improvement in the credit market that opens up self-employment options to some agents who otherwise could only work for wages or subsist. Micro-credit can either raise or lower long-run GDP, since it can lower use of both subsistence and full-scale industrial technologies. It typically lowers long-run inequality and poverty, by making subsistence payoffs less widespread. Thus, an equity-efficiency tradeoff may be involved in the promotion of micro-credit. However, in a worst case scenario, micro-credit has purely negative long-run effects. The key to micro-credit's long-run effects is found to be the "graduation rate", defined as the rate at which the self-employed build up enough wealth to start full-scale firms. We distinguish between two avenues for graduation: "winner" graduation (of those who earn above-average returns in self-employment) and "saver" graduation (due to gradual accumulation of average returns in self-employment). Long-run development is not attainable via micro-credit if "winner" graduation is the sole avenue for graduation. In contrast, if the saving rate and self-employment returns of the *average* micro-borrower are jointly high enough, then micro-credit can bring an economy from stagnation to full development through "saver" graduation. Thus the lasting effects of micro-credit may partially depend on simultaneous facilitation of micro-saving. Eventual graduation of the average borrower, rather than indefinite retention, should be the goal of micro-banks if micro-credit is to be a stepping stone to broad-based development rather than at best an anti-poverty tool.
© 2007 Elsevier B.V. All rights reserved.

JEL classification: D31; D82; O11
Keywords: Micro-credit; Occupational choice; Long-run development; Poverty; Inequality

1. Introduction

[☆] We are grateful for the encouragement and helpful comments of Dilip Mookherjee (the editor), two anonymous referees, Francesco Caselli, James Foster, Mercedes Garcia-Escribano, Maitreesh Ghatak, Xavier Gine, Hyeok Jeong, Andrew Newman, Kenichi Ueda, Clara Vega, Bruce Wydick, and seminar participants at Vanderbilt and NEUDC 2006. All errors are our own.

* Corresponding author.
E-mail addresses: ahlinc@msu.edu (C. Ahlin),
nienhuei_jiang@uml.edu (N. Jiang).

Micro-credit has been called "one of the most significant innovations in development policy of the past twenty-five years."[1] This movement aims to extend small amounts of capital to poor borrowers throughout the world, typically to facilitate income-generating self-employment activities. In the process it has popularized creative, perhaps

[1] Timothy Besley, quoted introducing Armendariz de Aghion and Morduch (2005). This book, Ghatak and Guinnane (1999), and Morduch (1999) provide broad introductions to the topic.

2   *C. Ahlin, N. Jiang / Journal of Development Economics 86 (2008) 1–21*

ingenious, lending techniques. For example, group lending employed by the Grameen Bank in Bangladesh and the Bank for Agriculture (BAAC) in Thailand, among others, has been shown theoretically to offer efficiency gains in contracting.[2] Other aspects of micro-lending practice have also received attention, including its use of sequential loans and local information flows.[3] Empirically, there is evidence that some of the mechanisms highlighted in theory are at work in practice.[4] There is also some evidence for positive effects on household consumption and other outcomes from these programs.[5]

Virtually all of the research thus far focuses on partial effects of micro-credit, often in a static context. The literature seems relatively quiet about the longer-run issues involved in micro-lending. On the empirical side, this may be explained by the relative youthfulness of the research agenda and the programs themselves. However, it does not seem too early to examine theoretically the potential long-run effects of micro-credit. Taking a step in this direction is the goal of the current paper.

Specifically, we study the long-run effects of micro-credit on development, measured by income per capita, inequality, and poverty. We use the occupational choice setting of Banerjee and Newman (1993). One advantage of this model for our purposes is its distinction between self-employment and entrepreneurship. Entrepreneurial activities are assumed to require a relatively large scale of capital and employment of wage laborers, while engaging in self-employment requires capital and only one's own labor. The latter provides a fitting description of many activities funded by micro-credit.[6]

We modify the model in two significant ways. First, we assume entrepreneurship is more efficient than self-employment. This creates a hierarchy of three technologies ranked by productivity and scale; in ascending order, they are subsistence, self-employment, and entrepreneurship. Second, we model micro-credit as the use of group lending to harness social pressure. This follows Besley and Coate (1995), and results in the borrower facing a higher cost of default. Assuming that micro-credit tends to

target low-wealth borrowers, it increases access to self-employment but not entrepreneurship.

Thus micro-credit is modeled as a pure but limited improvement in the credit market. It opens up self-employment options to some agents who otherwise could only work for wages or subsist; but it does not directly affect access to full-scale entrepreneurship.

In the cases we analyze, micro-credit nearly always lowers poverty, defined as the number of people earning subsistence-level income. It does so by directly removing financial barriers and lifting some subsisters into self-employment. It can also do so more broadly by affecting the wage. Specifically, if enough households' occupational choices are expanded to include self-employment, entrepreneurs must attract workers by paying a higher market wage, equal to the self-employment certainty-equivalent payoff. This allows all subsisters – even those without access to micro-credit – to escape from poverty.

Micro-credit also tends to lower inequality, by raising incomes of erstwhile poor subsisters and (potentially) lowering incomes at the top of the distribution by raising the wage paid by entrepreneurs.

Yet, though micro-credit is modeled as a pure credit market improvement, we find that it can raise *or lower* long-run output per capita. On the positive side, it lessens or eliminates use of the least-productive subsistence technology by removing financial barriers to self-employment. On the negative side, it can diminish use of the most productive entrepreneurial technology. Necessary for this to occur is that micro-credit raises the wage, which lowers entrepreneurial profits and can increase attrition of unsuccessful entrepreneurs from the entrepreneurial class — the set of households with sufficient wealth, given credit market imperfections, to run a full-scale firm. Since micro-credit can lower total income, it may therefore involve a long-run equity-efficiency tradeoff rather than being a "win–win" proposition.

Further, we find an exception even to the general rule that micro-credit lowers poverty in the long-run. In this perverse scenario, even though micro-credit initially raises income and reduces the number of subsisters, in the long run there are more subsisters, fewer entrepreneurs, lower aggregate income, and greater poverty. Key conditions for this scenario are that a) the rate of entrepreneurial attrition increases with the initial rise in the wage, and b) the odds of accumulating enough wealth from self-employment to start a full-scale firm are low relative to the odds of failing in both self-employment and entrepreneurship, where failing implies not having enough wealth to continue the venture (attrition). If these conditions hold, micro-credit can raise the wage only temporarily, since a critical mass of entrepreneurs (and hence labor demand) cannot be

---

[2] See Stiglitz (1990), Banerjee et al. (1994), Besley and Coate (1995), and Ghatak (1999, 2000), among others.

[3] For example, see Armendariz de Aghion and Morduch (2000) and Rai and Sjöström (2004).

[4] See Wydick (1999), Karlan (2007), and Ahlin and Townsend (2007a,b), among others.

[5] Armendariz de Aghion and Morduch (2005) provide a review of impact studies. In part, they argue that current knowledge of impacts could be significantly improved.

[6] For example, Grameen Bank founder Muhammad Yunus was reported to advocate frequently, as paraphrased by Bornstein (1997, p. 331), that "self-employment should be preferred over wage-employment as a faster and more humane way to combat poverty".

C. Ahlin, N. Jiang / Journal of Development Economics 86 (2008) 1–21

maintained. Meanwhile, the depletion of the entrepreneurial class may be so significant that the economy ends up with fewer entrepreneurs and more subsisters in the long-run.

The main question considered in this paper is whether micro-credit can bring an underdeveloped economy to full development, defined (in this model) as the steady state with high wages and only the most efficient technology in use. The critical condition for full development is that there be a sufficiently large entrepreneurial class, that is, wealthy households who therefore have access to the most efficient technology and provide strong labor demand. Since micro-credit cannot directly enable full-scale entrepreneurship (by assumption), its long-run effects turn on the possibilities for "graduation" into the entrepreneurial class by households using the self-employment technology funded by micro-credit. Here "graduation" refers to sufficient accumulation of wealth by the self-employed (or those working for comparable wages) to enable entrepreneurship, operation of a full-scale firm.

The answer to our main question requires distinguishing between two potential avenues for graduation from self-employment to entrepreneurship. Households may eventually save enough wealth to graduate to entrepreneurship via sustained earning of normal (average) self-employment returns. This possibility we refer to as "saver graduation". If saver graduation is possible, graduation is non-exceptional, though it may require saving over a significant period of time. On the other hand, if the savings rate and average returns in self-employment are jointly low, it may be impossible to accumulate enough wealth to graduate earning only normal self-employment returns. Graduation may still be possible, however, for those who earn supernormal (above-average) returns in self-employment — their high income can translate into sufficient wealth to start a full-scale firm. In this case, micro-credit can be viewed as opening self-employment opportunities to many individuals and allowing the market to select the particularly skilled or lucky ones for entrepreneurship. This type of graduation is referred to as "winner graduation", since micro-credit essentially picks winners for graduation. In summary, winner graduation is open to those who earn relatively high returns in self-employment, while saver graduation comes from gradual accumulation of average self-employment returns.

If the self-employment technology funded by micro-credit allows *winner graduation* but not saver graduation, then micro-credit cannot bring development. That is, regardless of the frequency of supernormal returns in self-employment (holding the mean fixed), the entrepreneurial class cannot be sufficiently built. The reason is that, as the entrepreneurial class grows toward the key

critical size, labor demand grows; consequently, a growing number of the agents who could be self-employed choose wage labor instead and earn a fixed wage equal to the average self-employment payoff. But wage labor does not involve the risk, upside or downside, that self-employment does. Thus, a declining segment of the middle class has the chance to earn supernormal returns on this road to development. As a result, growth in the entrepreneurial class stalls short of the critical mass. However, though a high winner graduation rate does not allow micro-credit to bring full development, it does result in higher long-run output. In fact, any mean-preserving spread that increases the frequency of both supernormal and subnormal returns in self-employment unambiguously raises long-run output.

On the other hand, if the self-employment technology funded by micro-credit allows for saver graduation, then sufficiently widespread micro-credit can bring development. Ultimately, it can move an economy from low output and subsistence wages to efficient technology and scale and to high wages, vanishing as an institution in the long-run. Necessary for this is that the rate at which households graduate via accumulation of normal self-employment returns be high enough relative to the rate of attrition out of the entrepreneurial class due to bad luck; if this condition holds, the entrepreneurial class grows until it reaches its critical value for development. In this scenario, micro-credit essentially breaks a subsistence-level poverty trap by offering access to more efficient capital intensity and technology; but breaking through the potential barriers to entrepreneurship must rely on jointly high savings rates and average self-employment incomes.

Together, the results imply that if micro-credit raises incomes but leaves the average borrower trapped at a new, intermediate income level (non-poor but non-developed), then it cannot by itself be a stepping stone to full development; it is at best an anti-poverty tool.

Our paper has similarities with others in the literature. It borrows the basic framework from Banerjee and Newman (1993). Our focus on the effect of credit market improvements is different from theirs. Our results also differ due to a different technology assumption, which is discussed in the next section. We discuss briefly in Section 4.1 what effect the introduction of micro-credit (as modeled here) would have in their framework.

Matsuyama addresses similar issues in different models. Matsuyama (2007) shows that credit market improvements that increase access to non-frontier technologies may lower long-run efficiency, a phenomenon seen here. Matsuyama (2006) examines how the introduction of a moderately productive self-employment technology affects the set of potential steady states. He concludes

4   *C. Ahlin, N. Jiang / Journal of Development Economics 86 (2008) 1–21*

that self-employment may raise or lower long-run income levels, similar to what we find here. These models differ from ours in significant ways. For example, they abstract from technological uncertainty, while uncertainty parameters figure prominently into the key conditions behind our analysis and results.

The policy conclusions we draw support a focus on "micro-finance" rather than on "micro-credit" exclusively. That is, the model identifies a novel complementarity between enabling saving and micro-lending: micro-lending can break a poverty trap, but it needs help from micro-saving to break any existing middle-income traps. Of course, the average level of technology made available by micro-lending is also critical; if low, graduation may be impossible even with high savings rates.[7]

The model also suggests that micro-credit institutions ought to be oriented toward graduating their borrowers toward larger undertakings,[8] and even to different credit institutions; the common focus on borrower *retention* may actually be a pitfall. A focus on graduation may make it hard to structure incentives for employees – to work themselves out of a job – and for borrowers – to repay loans when they are on the verge of graduating. Both of these incentive problems might be mitigated by information sharing among credit institutions, or by micro-credit institutions aspiring not to remain exclusively *micro*-credit institutions forever. These incentive problems seem worthy of greater exploration.

Section 2 introduces the basic static elements of the model, with Section 2.1 detailing the credit market and micro-credit. Section 3 introduces the dynamics. Section 4 presents the central examples and results: no graduation (Section 4.1), only winner graduation (Section 4.2), and only saver graduation (Section 4.3). Section 5 briefly discusses alternative approaches to this paper's question, and Section 6 discusses policy implications and concludes.

2. Model

The model borrows significantly from Banerjee and Newman (1993, hereafter BN); major departures will be noted. At any date t there is a unit continuum of agents differing in wealth w. Let $G_t(w)$ be the fraction of agents with wealth less than w at time t. Agents come to maturity at a random time distributed exponentially

according to λ, independent of wealth. At the instant of maturity they engage in all economic activity. Each mature agent is then replaced by, and leaves a bequest to, an offspring. The offspring is dormant until his random instant of maturity is realized. This process gives rise to a stationary population, with identical wealth distributions for the active population and the entire population.[9] We set $\lambda \equiv 1$.

Agents have identical preferences over own consumption C and bequest B: $B^s C^{1-s}$. These preferences imply a fixed fraction of income s being used as a bequest. They also imply that indirect utility is linear in income, and thus agents are risk-neutral.[10]

We assume a small open economy facing world (gross) interest rate ρ. To restrict attention to finite wealth accumulation, we assume $s\rho < 1$.[11]

All agents are endowed with one unit of labor and choose the occupation in which to spend it. There are three production technologies available to produce the only final good: (1) a subsistence technology which requires no capital and one unit of labor; (2) a self-employment technology which requires K^S units of the final good as an initial investment and one unit of labor; and (3) an entrepreneurial technology which requires a larger investment K^E ($> K^S$) and $n \geq 1$ units of labor in addition to the entrepreneur's.

These technologies result in four occupations from which to choose: subsistence, self-employment, entrepreneurship, and wage labor (for an entrepreneur). The subsistence technology produces $\underline{v}$ units of output. Thus an agent with endowment w who subsists ends life with a net worth of $\underline{v} + \rho w$. Similarly, choosing to be a wage worker results in earned income of v_t, the market wage, and ending net worth of $v_t + \rho w$.

The remaining two occupations involve uncertainty. Self-employment produces a random rate of return $\tilde{R}^S$, where this and other rates of return are taken net of the opportunity cost of capital ρ. For simplicity, $\tilde{R}^S$ can take one of three values, high/supernormal (R_h^S), medium/normal (R_m^S), and low/subnormal (R_l^S), with probabilities π_i^S, $i = h, m, l$, respectively. We assume that the expected

---

[7] Relatedly, Kaboski and Townsend (2005) find that village-level institutions that promote savings and that offer training and advice register the greatest positive impacts. Karlan and Valdivia (2006) also find positive impacts from a training program attached to micro-lending.
[8] This seems to support one of the well-known Grameen Bank 'Sixteen Decisions': "For higher income we shall collectively undertake bigger investments." See Bornstein (1997, p. 97).

[9] See BN (p. 278). As with them, our choice of overlapping generations in continuous time is to avoid jumps and overshooting.
[10] See BN. Unlike them, we assume labor is supplied inelastically, which is inconsequential to the results.
[11] If $s\rho > 1$, any positive amount of wealth grows without bound. This eventually makes the credit market restrictions discussed below irrelevant (with fixed technology levels), and any economy will converge to full development regardless of initial wealth levels and distribution. In a version of the model with exogenously growing technology and capital requirements, the economy's development path would depend on relative paces of growth of technology, capital requirements, and wealth, if $s\rho > 1$.

C. Ahlin, N. Jiang / Journal of Development Economics 86 (2008) 1–21 5

net return, $\bar{R}^S$, equals the normal return, R_m^S. A self-employed agent with wealth w ends with net worth of $\bar{R}^S K^S + \rho w$.

Entrepreneurship generates a random (net) rate of return $\tilde{R}^E$. $\tilde{R}^E$ can take two values, high (R_h^E) and low (R_l^E), with probabilities π_i^E, $i = h, l$, respectively. Let $\bar{R}^E$ denote the expected return. An entrepreneur with wealth w ends with net worth of $\tilde{R}^E K^E - n v_t + \rho w$, after paying the wages of n workers.

Let $\hat{v} \equiv \bar{R}^S K^S$ and $\bar{v} \equiv \bar{R}^E K^E / (n+1)$ be the expected output per unit of labor of the self-employment and entrepreneurial technologies, respectively. We assume that

$$\underline{v} < \hat{v} < \bar{v}. \tag{A1}$$

This assumption creates a hierarchy of three technologies, with entrepreneurial production most efficient, subsistence least efficient, and self-employment in the middle. Assumption (A1) is critical to our results and is our key departure from BN. (However, it is quite similar to the technology structure in Matsuyama, 2006, where self-employment is assumed less productive than entrepreneurship.) There are essentially two production technologies in BN;[12] three technologies are necessary here given our construction of micro-credit as a credit market improvement that increases access to better, but not best, technology and capital intensity (see next section).

This three-technology hierarchy can be justified on several grounds. One rationale for this hierarchy is that capital intensity is a key to productivity. It has been assumed that $K^S < K^E$; if further $K^S < K^E / (n+1)$,[13] then per-person capital requirements across occupations vary monotonically with efficiency. A second, complementary rationale for entrepreneurship's greater efficiency is that production organized within a firm is often more efficient than production organized across autonomous individuals. This can be due to scale economies and/or greater scope for specialization within firms.

---

[12] Entrepreneurship is not a separate production technology in BN, but a separate *institution*: one agent monitoring n other agents who each use the self-employment technology. In fact, in BN entrepreneurship is less productive than self-employment, since it uses up the entrepreneur's unit of labor in non-productive monitoring; however, they do not stress the efficiency differences between these occupations. It seems to us that their technology assumptions are not meant to take a stand on the relative efficiencies of self-employment and entrepreneurship, but are made as streamlined as possible while still allowing their points about institutions and history dependence to be made.

[13] This can be assumed without affecting any results, but is not needed for any of them given Assumption (A1).

Assumption (A1) seems to accord broadly with several empirical facts. First, the large share of production accounted for by wage labor and the capital of relatively large firms in developed countries makes it empirically plausible that entrepreneurship is in general more productive than self-employment (defining both occupations as we do here). Scale economies and/or easier within-firm specialization seem to constitute an empirical regularity in the many sectors in which large firms dominate. Second, while micro-credit improves micro-borrowers' access to capital and technology, it does not seem in general to allow them to reach optimal capital scale and technology levels. Most micro-loans are fractions of domestic GDP/capita, and micro-lenders often appear to ration funds, perhaps aiming for broader outreach or to provide repayment incentives via promises of larger future loans. It seems clear that most micro-credit funded enterprises work with less capital and less advanced technology than the average developed country worker. In this context, micro-credit may be useful to a stagnant economy as a stepping stone to fully efficient production, but it does not represent the ideal long-run solution. The three-technology hierarchy will allow us to define micro-credit in a way that matches this stylized fact; micro-credit will open access to self-employment, thereby increasing capital intensity and technology levels, but not to fully developed levels.

The first-best of this economy is achieved when exclusively entrepreneurial technology is used, that is, when there are $1/(n+1)$ entrepreneurs and $n/(n+1)$ workers. A perfect credit market would give this outcome, but we assume there are imperfections.

2.1. Credit market and micro-credit

The credit market is competitive, leading to a (gross) interest rate of $r = \rho$ charged on all loans that involve no default risk. Following BN, we assume a borrower always can repay but may choose not to after production. Specifically, an agent who borrows K can refuse to repay at the cost of facing a (non-monetary) punishment F with probability q and losing whatever collateral was pledged, C. Borrowers then face the choice of whether to default, saving principal and interest rK but losing collateral rC and facing expected penalty qF. If $rK > rC + qF$, i.e. $C < K - qF/r$, an agent will choose to default.

In equilibrium, lenders will demand sufficient collateral so that no default occurs. Thus $r = \rho$, and collateral $C \geq w^* \equiv K^S - qF/\rho$ is required from any agent seeking to become self-employed and $C \geq w^{**} \equiv K^E - qF/\rho$ from any agent seeking to become an entrepreneur.[14] We assume the credit market imperfection is severe enough (qF small enough) so that $w^* > 0$.

The credit market imperfection divides the population into three classes that differ in occupational possibilities. The wealthiest class, those with $w \geq w^{**}$, can choose any occupation. We call them the "entrepreneurial class", or for convenience, the "upper class" and let $P_t^U \equiv 1 - G_t(w^{**})$ denote their measure at date t. Similarly, the "lower class" with wealth $w < w^*$ can only subsist or work for wages; its measure is $P_t^L \equiv G_t(w^*)$. Finally, the residual "middle class" can choose any occupation but entrepreneurship; its measure is $P_t^M \equiv G_t(w^{**}) - G_t(w^*)$.

In this context, micro-credit will be defined as a pure credit market improvement that improves low-wealth borrowers' access to credit. To do so, we follow the literature that views micro-credit as innovative use of joint liability contracts to enable more efficient lending; specifically, as in Besley and Coate (1995, hereafter BC), micro-credit makes default less attractive by harnessing social penalties.

Assume the lender pairs borrowers together in groups of two and makes each one responsible for the other's repayment. Specifically, if borrowers i and j are paired together and j defaults, i faces penalty F' with probability q'; and vice versa. This penalty is additional to any potential penalty incurred for his own default (F).

The key assumption, adapted from BC, is that an informal, social penalty is imposed on a borrower who defaults, since default led to his partner facing additional penalty $q'F'$. The social penalty could involve ostracism, withholding of informal aid or insurance, and/or the breaking of productive relationships. Let ϕ be the magnitude of the social penalty imposed on a borrower who defaults.

Repayment calculus changes with micro-credit. If a borrower chooses to default rather than repay, he saves principal and interest ρK, loses collateral ρC and faces expected penalty qF, as before; in addition, there is the social penalty for defaulting, ϕ. (He may also be penalized $q'F'$ by the lender for his partner's default, but this is independent of his own repayment decision.) Thus if $\rho K > \rho C + qF + \phi$, i.e. $C < K - (qF + \phi)/\rho$, default will occur. To acquire a loan K, collateral at least $K - (qF + \phi)/\rho$ is required; this collateral requirement is directly lowered by the social penalty, ϕ, which

augments the official penalty qF. Group lending therefore represents a pure credit market improvement here.

Micro-credit with group lending and social penalties could in principle lower both wealth cutoffs, w^* and w^{**} (defined above), in the amount ϕ/ρ. Empirically, however, micro-credit tends to be targeted to low-wealth borrowers rather than borrowers of all wealth levels. Further, the types of projects undertaken by micro-borrowers are commonly small-scale micro-enterprises rather than full-scale firms. In order to match the empirical reality of micro-credit, we assume that only the wealth cutoff for self-employment, w^*, is lowered, and that access to entrepreneurship, w^{**}, is not affected. This assumption is critical to results, but it will be straightforward to see how results change without it.

There are several potential micro-foundations for this assumption. First, it is plausible that dependence on informal insurance networks, which can be the basis for informal penalties (as in Paal and Wiseman, 2005), declines with wealth. Group lending would then offer little or no enforcement enhancement among richer borrowers, who are less vulnerable to informal penalties. Second, one could assume the social penalty is occupation-specific, positive for self-employment and zero for entrepreneurship. This would be justified if the entrepreneurial technology had to be employed in an anonymous or high-mobility urban context, while the self-employment technology could be operated in a village, with tight social networks. Banerjee and Newman (1998) tell a related story. Third, other factors could cause the attractiveness of group loans to decline with wealth. Madajewicz (2005) shows in a hidden action environment how joint liability loans may not be optimal for higher-wealth borrowers since the increased risk from liability for partners' loans dominates the benefit of increased monitoring incentives. Incorporating one or more of these mechanisms is beyond the scope of this paper, and we directly assume that the social penalties harnessed by group lending affect w^* but not w^{**}.

In summary, micro-credit is modeled as a pure but limited improvement in the credit market. It has the immediate effect of growing the middle class P_t^M at the expense of the lower-class P_t^L, without changing the upper-class P_t^U.

2.2. Labor market equilibrium

Occupational choices depend on the equilibrium wage. The wage in turn depends on the wealth distribution as summarized through P_t^U, P_t^M, and P_t^L,

---

[14] In this model, an agent partially or fully self-financing is equivalent to an agent financing the full amount externally, since wealth is equally effective as collateral or productive capital. We can thus think of all agents as financing externally.

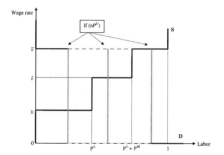

Fig. 1. Labor market equilibrium.

since these determine labor supply and demand; these are graphed in Fig. 1.

Labor demand can only arise from the upper class, who are able to become entrepreneurs. Given Assumption (A1), it is straightforward to show that entrepreneurship gives the best payoff as long as $v_t < \bar{v}$. This critical wage $\bar{v}$ equates the wage labor payoff, v_t, with the expected entrepreneurial payoff, $\bar{R}^E K^E - nv_t$. If $v_t > \bar{v}$, wage labor gives the highest payoff. Thus, since each entrepreneur hires n workers, total demand will be nP_t^U if $v_t < \bar{v}$; 0 if $v_t > \bar{v}$; and any amount in $[0, nP_t^U]$ if $v_t = \bar{v}$, since the upper class are then indifferent between wage labor and entrepreneurship.

Turning to labor supply, note that there are three levels for the wage that put wage labor on par with the three respective occupations: $\underline{v}$ for subsistence, $\bar{v}$ for entrepreneurship, and $\hat{v}$ for self-employment. Given the occupational restrictions placed by the credit market, labor supply is then zero when $v_t < \underline{v}$; P_t^L when $\underline{v} < v_t < \hat{v}$; $P_t^L + P_t^M$ when $\hat{v} < v_t < \bar{v}$; and 1 when $\bar{v} < v_t$. If v_t equals $\underline{v}$, $\hat{v}$, or $\bar{v}$, a mass of agents is indifferent between labor and some other occupation, and labor supply can take any value between its limits from below and above.

Combining supply and demand leads to one of the following three equilibrium wages.[15]

- If $nP_t^U < P_t^L$, the equilibrium wage rate is $v_t = \underline{v}$.
- If $P_t^L < nP_t^U < P_t^L + P_t^M$, the equilibrium wage rate is $v_t = \hat{v}$.
- If $P_t^L + P_t^M < nP_t^U$, that is, $P_t^U > 1/(1+n)$, the equilibrium wage rate is $v_t = \bar{v}$.

In the first case, the pool of potential entrepreneurs is too small relative to the population whose only options

are wage labor or subsistence. The wage is bid down to subsistence level. All upper-class agents take advantage of the low wages to become entrepreneurs; all middle-class agents choose self-employment; and some of the lower-class work in firms (nP_t^U) while the rest subsist $(P_t^L - nP_t^U)$.

In the second case, there are enough potential entrepreneurs to need some middle-class workers, so they pay $\hat{v}$. All upper-class agents become entrepreneurs, all lower-class and some middle-class agents become workers, and the rest of the middle-class $(1 - (n+1) P_t^U)$ become self-employed.

In the third case, the potential entrepreneurial pool is so large that it needs to attract some of its own members to work. The equilibrium wage makes working in a firm as attractive as running one. All lower- and middle-class agents, and some upper-class agents, become workers and receive the same labor income[16] as entrepreneurs (in expected value). Since everyone in this economy is working in a firm with the entrepreneurial technology, the highest aggregate output is achieved; and the high wages guarantee perfect equality in (expected) income.

The wealth distribution thus determines the current wage rate, which determines occupations, incomes, and the future wealth distribution.[17] These dynamics are analyzed next.

3. Dynamics

In Section 3.1, we present the family wealth dynamics under each of the three potential equilibrium wages discussed above. Section 3.2 considers aggregate wealth dynamics.

3.1. Family dynamics

An agent passes a fraction s of his ending net worth to his offspring. Let $V(v_t, w)$ be the occupation-specific income earned by an agent of wealth w who comes to maturity when the wage is v_t; these values are readily calculated from the discussion of the three cases in Section 2.2. The bequest his offspring receives, i.e. his offspring's wealth, is then $w' = s[V(v_t, w) + \rho w]$.

Recall from Section 2.2 that P_t^U and P_t^L are the only features of the wealth distribution needed to calculate the wage v_t at any time t. However, generally the entire

---

[15] In contrast, there are *two* potential equilibrium wages in BN, due to their assumption that self-employment is more productive than entrepreneurship.

[16] "Labor income" and "income" are used synonymously with the occupation-specific component of income. They exclude interest income ρw.

[17] The cases where nP_t^U exactly equals either P_t^L or $P_t^L + P_t^M$ can see any of a range of wages. We assume for simplicity that the highest possible wage prevails in these cases.

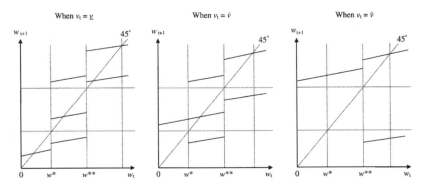

Fig. 2. Family wealth transition.

wealth distribution is needed in order to track the evolution of P_t^U and P_t^L over time. For tractability, we follow BN and restrict analysis to cases exhibiting the following Markov property: the wealth *class* and occupational choice of any agent, together with the market wage, fully determine probabilities of transition to future wealth classes. This "BN Markov assumption" dramatically reduces the state-space, to the two-dimensional simplex (P_t^L, P_t^U).

One set of parameter values that allows for this dimensional reduction is displayed in Fig. 2. There are three panels, one for each possible market wage. The first panel corresponds to $v_t = \underline{v}$. At this wage the lower-class work or subsist to earn $\underline{v}$. The graph depicts them as stuck in the lower class: given the saving and interest rates, they can never accumulate enough to finance self-employment.[18] The middle class are all self-employed. The graph depicts them remaining in the middle class if they earn normal returns, graduating to the upper class if they receive supernormal returns (i.e. "win"), and falling into the lower class if they receive subnormal returns. Finally, the upper class work as entrepreneurs. The graph depicts them always earning enough to stay in the upper class: even if unlucky, the wage bill is low enough to keep them wealthy.

The second panel applies to $v = \hat{v}$ and differs from the first in two regards. First, the lower class now earn wages equal to the expected payoff from self-employment; we assume this is sufficient to transit to the middle class. Second, entrepreneurs face a high enough wage

bill that bad luck causes them to drop to the middle class. This increased downward mobility for the entrepreneurial class resulting from the higher wages will be the key to the equity-efficiency tradeoff potentially inherent in micro-credit; but it does not drive the key results on whether micro-credit can bring development (Propositions 1 and 2 below). The middle-class payoffs are unchanged since they continue to choose self-employment, or else work for similar wages.

The third panel applies to $v = \bar{v}$. There, wages are so high that both low- and middle-class families transit to the upper class. The down side is that unlucky entrepreneurs now transit to the lower class after paying the high-wage bill. Results would not change if unlucky entrepreneurs transited to the middle class — everyone earns the same high (expected) income regardless, and the dynamics will guarantee that the wage remains high if it ever gets high (since $\pi_t^E < n$).

In summary, the main restriction in Fig. 2 is the BN Markov assumption discussed above. Beyond this, a few additional restrictions are imposed. Regarding the *lowest class*, the main restriction is that the subsistence wage is too low to provide poor households any upward mobility. This low-wage induced poverty trap seems empirically plausible, and such traps are not uncommon in models like this (including BN). Regarding the *middle class*, the main assumption is that only "winners" can graduate from the middle class, while the mean self-employment outcome leaves a household in the middle class. This creates a second, middle-income trap for the average self-employed household, which is the one assumption critical to Proposition 1 below. This middle-income trap is removed in the discussion of "saver graduation" in Section 4.3 (Fig. 6). The middle class are otherwise modeled flexibly: mobility from self-employment to any

---

[18] The condition for this is $s(\underline{v} + \rho w^*) < w^*$, that is, $s\underline{v}/(1 - s\rho) < w^*$. This is satisfied when the savings rate, return to savings, and subsistence wages are jointly low enough compared with the wealth cutoff for operating a micro-enterprise, which reflects the degree of imperfection in the credit market.

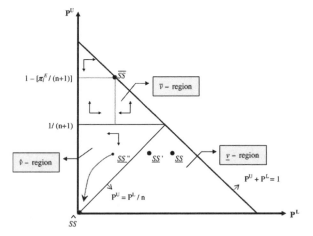

Fig. 3. Aggregate wealth dynamics (when π_l^S, $\pi_h^S = 0$).

class is allowed, and we will address the entire parameter space governing these transition probabilities. Finally, assumptions on the *upper class* guarantee that successful entrepreneurs remain in the upper class regardless of the wage — this is necessary for the possibility of a fully developed steady state. The most substantive assumptions address what happens to unsuccessful entrepreneurs: namely, they remain wealthy if wages are low, drop to the middle class if wages are moderate, and drop to the lowest class when wages are high. As noted, these assumptions do not drive either of the propositions below. However, while the specifics are not important, the idea that higher wages lead to greater downward mobility of unsuccessful entrepreneurs is critical to the existence of an equity-efficiency tradeoff involved in micro-credit.

3.2. Aggregate dynamics

Given the family wealth evolution described in the previous section and Fig. 2, we can accomplish our ultimate objective: tracing the economy-wide wealth and income distributions. Each of the panels in Fig. 2 leads to a pair of first-order differential equations in P_t^L and P_t^U. For example, when $v_t = \underline{v}$

$$\dot{P}_t^U = \pi_h^S(1 - P_t^L - P_t^U)$$
$$\dot{P}_t^L = \pi_l^S(1 - P_t^L - P_t^U). \tag{1}$$

These equations reflect the fact that when $v_t = \underline{v}$ the only class mobility comes from the middle class, all $(1 - P_t^L - P_t^U)$ of whom are self-employed. A fraction

π_h^S of the middle class who are active at date t are winners and graduate to the upper class, causing P_t^U to grow. Similarly, a fraction π_l^S are unlucky and drop to the lower class, causing P_t^L to grow.

When $v_t = \hat{v}$,

$$\dot{P}_t^U = \pi_h^S[1 - (n+1)P_t^U] - \pi_l^E P_t^U$$
$$\dot{P}_t^L = \pi_l^S[1 - (n+1)P_t^U] - P_t^L. \tag{2}$$

Again, the middle class provides mobility, but only those who are self-employed. Recall that the middle class divides itself between wage labor and self-employment when $v_t = \hat{v}$. In fact, the entire population is running a firm or working in one, except the self-employed middle class. Since there are P_t^U firms, the measure of self-employed must be $1 - (n+1)P_t^U$. Mobility also comes from active lower-class agents; at this wage they immediately move up to the middle class (hence the $-P_t^L$ term in $\dot{P}_t^L$). Active upper-class agents whose firms perform poorly now drop out of the upper class (hence the $-\pi_l^E P_t^U$ term in $\dot{P}_t^U$).

When $v_t = \bar{v}$,

$$\dot{P}_t^U = (1 - P_t^U) - \frac{\pi_l^E}{n+1}$$
$$\dot{P}_t^L = -P_t^L + \frac{\pi_l^E}{n+1}. \tag{3}$$

The first term in $\dot{P}_t^U$ is because everyone not in the upper class $(1 - P_t^U)$ transits there, due to the high wages. The second term reflects the fraction of unlucky entrepreneurs who drop to the lower class. The maximum number of entrepreneurs in the economy is $1/(n+1)$; this is also the actual number whenever the wage is this high. The first term in $\dot{P}_t^L$ is because lower-class agents transit upward; the second term captures the unlucky entrepreneurs.

The economy can be described at any time t by a point on the two-dimensional simplex (P_t^L, P_t^U); see Fig. 3. This triangle is subdivided into three "regions" corresponding to the three equilibrium wages (see Section 2.2). Points in the upper triangle where $P_t^U > 1/(n+1)$ involve the high-wage $v_t = \overline{v}$. Points in the lower right triangle where $P_t^U < P_t^L/n$ involve the low-wage $v_t = \underline{v}$. The remaining triangle involves the medium wage, $v_t = \hat{v}$. The economy's initial location thus determines which of the dynamics (Eqs. (1)–(3)) apply at the outset and whether the economy may ultimately progress to higher wages and greater efficiency.

4. Micro-credit and long-run development

We illustrate the possibilities opened up by micro-credit through several examples. Our strategy is to compare the long-run outcomes of two initially identical economies, only one of which experiences the introduction of micro-credit.

4.1. Dynamics with no graduation

Consider the simple case in which uncertainty in self-employment returns is eliminated: $\pi_h^S = \pi_l^S = 0$. This implies that the self-employed middle class cannot graduate upward.

Fig. 3 shows the evolution of the wealth distribution. We see from Eq. (1) that $\dot{P}_t^U = \dot{P}_t^L = 0$ in the $\underline{v}$-region. Each class is absorbing, so that a wealth distribution in this region stagnates at the same location forever; see point $\underline{SS}$ in Fig. 3. A wealth distribution in the $\hat{v}$-region, however, converges to the origin (point $\widehat{SS}$), since both $\dot{P}_t^U$ and $\dot{P}_t^L$ are negative (Eq. (2)).[19] The $\hat{v}$-region thus involves shrinking upper and lower classes (both due to higher wages) and an absorbing middle class; in the end, all are self-employed. In the $\overline{v}$-region, any distribution converges to point $\overline{SS}$ defined as $\left(P_{\overline{SS}}^L, P_{\overline{SS}}^U\right) = \left(\frac{n}{n+1}, 1 - \frac{n}{n+1}\right)$. All agents are employing the most efficient technology and have the same expected income. Here, each region of the simplex is self-contained, that is, there are no paths from one v-region to another.

We can compare the (labor) income distributions of these possible long-run economies in terms of both average

level, inequality, and poverty. To facilitate discussion about poverty, we assume the poverty line p satisfies

$$\underline{v} < p < \hat{v}. \tag{A2}$$

As mentioned, economy $\overline{SS}$ involves use of only the most efficient technology; further, everyone earns the high-wage $\overline{v}$ (in expected value), so there is no poverty or inequality. This ideal outcome is referred to as "development". Economy $\widehat{SS}$ also has perfect equality and no poverty since everyone is self-employed. Average income is of course lower, equal to $\hat{v}$. Finally, economy $\underline{SS}$ clearly has higher poverty and inequality than the others, as the lower class earn $\underline{v}$, the middle class earn $\hat{v}$, and the upper class earn $\overline{R}^E K^E - n\underline{v}$. Average income is a weighted average of the three technologies' productivities. It is thus clearly lower than at $\overline{SS}$, but can be higher than at $\widehat{SS}$, since it involves both more entrepreneurship and more subsistence. In particular, there is a critical line from the origin, with slope less than $1/n$ and therefore lying in the $\underline{v}$-region. If P_0^U/P_0^L is high enough so that $\underline{SS}$ lies above this line, then $\underline{SS}$ has higher income than $\widehat{SS}$; and vice versa.[20]

Now imagine two economies at $\underline{SS}$ and the introduction of micro-credit in one. Can this financial development bring the economy to development? Recall from Section 2.1 that the introduction of micro-credit is equivalent to a decline in P_t^L mirrored by a rise in P_t^M, with P_t^U unchanged. In Fig. 3 this would be represented by a leftward shift from point $\underline{SS}$. There are two qualitative cases to consider. First, micro-credit may impact few enough people that the treated economy remains in the $\underline{v}$-region (pictured as the shift to $\underline{SS}'$). The only change in this economy is that the agents impacted by micro-credit move from subsistence or wage labor to self-employment. Clearly, micro-credit leads to higher average income and lower poverty. The treated and untreated economies' Lorenz curves cross, though, so inequality is less clear; but the treated economy's *generalized* Lorenz curve dominates the untreated economy's.[21] Second, micro-credit may impact enough people, that is, improve enough agents' productive options, to raise the wage to $\hat{v}$ (pictured as the shift to $\underline{SS}''$). As analyzed above, the treated economy will converge to steady state $\widehat{SS}$, getting

---

[19] One can show that the trajectory stays within the $\hat{v}$-region.

[20] Income at $\underline{SS}$ can be written as $(n+1)P_0^U \times \overline{v} + P_0^M \times \hat{v} + (P_0^L - nP_0^U) \times \underline{v}$. The critical line in the $\underline{v}$-region, along which average income is $\hat{v}$, is then $p^U = p^L/\left[n\left(1 + \frac{\overline{v} - \hat{v}}{\hat{v} - \underline{v}} \frac{n+1}{n}\right)\right]$.

[21] The generalized Lorenz curve is the Lorenz curve multiplied by the mean income. Generalized Lorenz dominance is the extension of Lorenz dominance to generalized Lorenz curves.

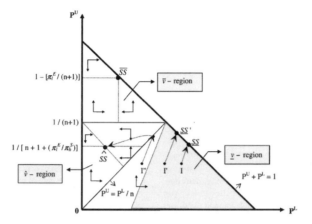

Fig. 4. Aggregate wealth dynamics (when π_l^S, $\pi_h^S \neq 0$ and $a > 1/n$).

rid of inequality and poverty, but potentially lowering total output if the initial point *SS* was high enough.[22]

In summary, the introduction of micro-credit lowers poverty and inequality (though if it fails to raise the wage, there are exceptions under Lorenz dominance but not generalized Lorenz dominance). Micro-credit may or may not raise total income, however, since it can reduce the use of the most productive, entrepreneurial technology; if sufficiently widespread, it raises the wage and lowers entrepreneurial profits, causing attrition from the entrepreneurial class. Thus micro-credit may involve an equity-efficiency tradeoff. In any case, micro-credit cannot bring full development when $\pi_l^S = \pi_h^S = 0$.[23]

---

[22] Even if $\pi_l^E = 0$, or for some other reason the higher wages do not cause any entrepreneurs to face downward mobility, development cannot be reached. In this case, the steady state is horizontally to the left at (0, P_0^U). However, output will be higher and inequality and poverty lower than before micro-credit; thus, there is no equity-efficiency tradeoff if the higher wages do not dampen entrepreneurial prospects over time.

[23] The assumption that entrepreneurial technology is the most productive is critical to these results. If instead self-employment is most productive, as in BN, then micro-credit immediately promotes the best technology and can bring full development if sufficiently widespread. This can be seen by a leftward shift (as described above) in Fig. 3 of BN. The impact of our assumption that micro-credit lowers w^* but does not affect w^{**} is also clear. If instead micro-credit also lowered w^{**}, an economy would move leftward *and* upward after the introduction of micro-credit, since the entrepreneurial class would grow. Micro-credit could then bring development if the immediate growth it brought in the upper class was sufficient to raise the wage to $\bar{v}$ (i.e. if micro-credit immediately lifted P_0^U above $1 / (n + 1)$). This highlights the interpretation of our results: they hold when micro-credit is an institution that promotes access to more productive, but not the most productive, technology and scale.

4.2. Dynamics with winner graduation

The development prospects of micro-credit may be enhanced if it provides a substantial possibility of graduating from self-employment to entrepreneurship. Assume now that with probability $\pi_h^S > 0$ an agent experiences supernormal returns allowing his offspring to graduate to entrepreneurship, while with probability $\pi_l^S > 0$ an agent experiences subnormal returns and puts his offspring in the lower class.

Fig. 4 shows the evolution of the wealth distribution. The $\bar{v}$-region sees the same dynamics (convergence to $\overline{SS}$) as in Section 4.1, since π_h^S and π_l^S do not figure into Eq. (3). Dynamics in the $\underline{v}$-region now reflect a shrinking middle class: there remains no mobility out of the upper and lower classes, but a constant flow into each from the middle class. The economy moves upward and to the right along a linear trajectory whose steepness depends on the relative rates of graduating upward out of self-employment (π_h^S) and dropping into poverty out of self-employment (π_l^S). Specifically, Eq. (1) gives its slope $\dot{P}_t^U / \dot{P}_t^L$ as

$$a \equiv \pi_h^S / \pi_l^S.$$

4.2.1. Dynamics with a large

We consider first the most promising case, where *a* is large. Specifically, assume $a > 1/n$. This implies that the trajectory within the $\underline{v}$-region is steeper than the region's upper boundary, $P_t^U = P_t^L / n$. Some initial distributions will therefore hit and cross the upper boundary into the $\hat{v}$-region as the growth of the upper class raises wages.

12   *C. Ahlin, N. Jiang / Journal of Development Economics 86 (2008) 1–21*

These starting points have relatively high P_0^U compared to P_0^L; they correspond to the non-shaded area of the v-region in Fig. 4. The remaining initial distributions, in the shaded area, will converge to points on the upper right leg of the v-region where $P_t^U + P_t^L = 1$; one example is denoted by $\underline{SS}$.

It can be verified that all distributions in the $\hat{v}$-region will converge to

$$\left(P_{\widehat{SS}}^L, P_{\widehat{SS}}^U \right) = \left(\frac{\pi_l^E / a}{n + 1 + \frac{\pi_l^E}{\pi_h^S}}, \frac{1}{n + 1 + \frac{\pi_l^E}{\pi_h^S}} \right). \tag{4}$$

Fig. 4 depicts the phase diagram and steady state denoted by $\widehat{SS}$.

Can micro-credit bring an underdeveloped (low- or mid-wage) economy to full development? No. Fig. 4 makes clear that a leftward shift of any economy may eventually bring the economy to the mid-wage steady state $\widehat{SS}$, but it cannot bring it to the high-wage steady state $\overline{SS}$. This is also clear from Eq. (4): $P_{\widehat{SS}}^U$ is less than the critical value of $1/(n+1)$ no matter what the value of π_h^S.[24] These arguments rely on the specific class transitions of Fig. 2. However, this result holds for any class transitions that satisfy the BN Markov assumption, Assumption (A1), and the assumption that only winners graduate, that is, that average returns in self-employment ($\hat{v}$) are not sufficient to allow graduation to the upper class:

$$s(\hat{v} + \rho w^{**}) < w^{**}; \quad \text{i.e.} \quad \frac{s\hat{v}}{1 - s\rho} < w^{**}. \tag{A3}$$

Proposition 1. *Under the BN Markov assumption and Assumptions (A1) and (A3), micro-credit cannot bring an underdeveloped (low- or mid-wage) economy to full development.*

Proof. See Appendix.

This result is somewhat surprising; one might think that a sufficient proportion of self-employed winners graduating could more than compensate for attrition of entrepreneurs and raise the number of entrepreneurs P_t^U to its critical value $1/(n+1)$. But the intuition is as follows. Micro-credit can raise the wage to $\hat{v}$ but not to $\bar{v}$. In the $\hat{v}$-region, if the number of entrepreneurs P_t^U were to increase toward the critical value $1/(n+1)$, labor demand would grow; as a

result, more of the middle class would engage in wage labor rather than self-employment (two occupations between which they are indifferent). In the limit, if P_t^U were to approach $1/(n+1)$, the number of self-employed would approach zero as all the middle class worked for wages instead. But, upward mobility into entrepreneurship comes only from the self-employed; workers earn the mean self-employment payoff with certainty, which by assumption does not allow graduation. Thus, mobility into entrepreneurship vanishes as the number of entrepreneurs approaches the critical value.

This result is robust to any assumptions about uncertainty in the three occupations (including $\pi_l^E = 0$ and/or π_h^S near 1). The critical assumption is the mid-wage trap, i.e. the inability of households earning *average* returns in self-employment ever to graduate to the entrepreneurial class. The model implies, then, that if micro-credit promotes technologies that cannot raise the wealth level of the *average* borrowing household enough to fund larger endeavors – via accumulating saved earnings, over a period of time that admittedly may be a generation or more – then micro-credit is at best an anti-poverty tool rather than a stepping stone to broader development.

While not a panacea in this case, micro-credit can have positive long-run effects. Economies starting in the shaded area of the v-region in Fig. 4 will have their long-run outcomes altered. (All other economies have the same long-run destiny with or without micro-credit.) As in Section 4.1, there are two qualitative cases to consider. First, micro-credit may impact few enough people that the treated economy remains in the shaded area of the v-region (pictured as the shift from I to I'). Some of the agents lifted to self-employment eventually graduate to become entrepreneurs, leaving the long-run treated economy with more entrepreneurs and fewer subsisters ($\underline{SS'}$ instead of $\underline{SS}$). Clearly, average income is higher and poverty is lower due to micro-credit. The Lorenz curves of the treated and untreated economies cross, but the treated economy's generalized Lorenz curve dominates the untreated economy's.

Second, micro-credit may impact enough people to move the treated economy out of the shaded area (the shift from I to I'') and thus ultimately to $\widehat{SS}$. Micro-credit would then clearly have lowered poverty, since everyone earns at least $\hat{v}$ in the treated economy ($\widehat{SS}$) while some agents earn v (as workers or subsisters) in the untreated economy ($\underline{SS}$).

In this case, the effect on long-run average income can be positive or negative. Average income in the untreated economy, y_{SS}, is a convex combination of the entrepreneurial and subsistence productivities, while average income in the treated economy, $y_{\widehat{SS}}$, is a convex

---

[24] Even if $\pi_l^E = 0$ contrary to our assumption, so that $P_{\widehat{SS}}^U = 1/(n+1)$, the economy will not reach $\widehat{SS}$; P_t^U will get arbitrarily close to $1/(n+1)$ but can be shown always to be smaller at any finite t.

C. Ahlin, N. Jiang / Journal of Development Economics 86 (2008) 1–21 13

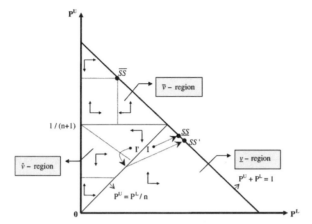

Fig. 5. Aggregate wealth dynamics (when π_l^S, $\pi_h^S \neq 0$ and $a < \pi_l^F / n$).

combination of the entrepreneurial and self-employment productivities:

$$y_{\widehat{SS}} = \bar{v} \cdot P_{\widehat{SS}}^U(n+1) + \hat{v} \cdot \left[1 - P_{\widehat{SS}}^U(n+1)\right]$$

$$y_{\underline{SS}} = \bar{v} \cdot P_{\underline{SS}}^U(n+1) + \underline{v} \cdot \left[1 - P_{\underline{SS}}^U(n+1)\right]. \tag{5}$$

Both equations reflect the fact that the total population working in firms is $P_t^U(n+1)$. While $y_{\widehat{SS}}$ is fixed strictly below $\bar{v}$ since $P_{\widehat{SS}}^U$ is strictly less than $1/(n+1)$ (see Eq. (4)), $y_{\underline{SS}}$ can be arbitrarily close to $\bar{v}$, since $P_{\underline{SS}}^U$ can be arbitrarily close to $1/(n+1)$, depending on initial conditions. Thus there is a range of steady states $\underline{SS}$ in the $\underline{v}$-region that involve higher average income than $\widehat{SS}$.[25] That is, micro-credit can lower average income even as it lowers poverty. The intuition is the same as in Section 4.1. On the positive side, micro-credit reduces use of subsistence technology in favor of self-employment technology; on the negative side, it raises the wage and the amount of attrition out of entrepreneurship, potentially lowering use of the entrepreneurial technology in the long-run.

Both steady states involve inequality, and inequality comparisons can be ambiguous. What is clear is that when $\widehat{SS}$ has higher income than $\underline{SS}$, $\widehat{SS}$ also *generalized* Lorenz dominates $\underline{SS}$ (though it may be Lorenz dominated). When $\widehat{SS}$ has lower income than $\underline{SS}$, the generalized Lorenz curves cross; but $\widehat{SS}$ Lorenz dominates $\underline{SS}$ if

$$\frac{\hat{v}}{\bar{v}} \left(1 + \frac{\hat{v} - \underline{v}}{\bar{v} - \hat{v}}\right) \geq \frac{n+1}{n}. \tag{A4}$$

Thus,[26] either $\widehat{SS}$ achieves higher income without sacrificing equality, or it achieves lower income but a more equal distribution (under condition (A4)).

We finally note that risk-taking in self-employment gives long-run benefits to economies transiting toward $\widehat{SS}$. Consider a mean-preserving spread in returns that raises π_h^S and π_l^S while holding fixed their ratio a as well as R_h^S, R_m^S, and R_l^S. This raises $P_{\widehat{SS}}^U$ (see Eq. (4)), which unambiguously raises output (see Eq. (5)). The resulting income distribution generalized Lorenz dominates the original. This result suggests that encouraging risk-taking in self-employment activities rather than failsafe approaches (which deliver high repayment rates) may improve long-run outcomes.[27]

Micro-credit cannot bring full development if it relies only on winner graduation for mobility into the entrepreneurial class; but it can lower poverty and inequality and, under some conditions, raise total income. We next show that micro-credit can have a purely negative long-run impact when a is small.

---

[25] Specifically, $y_{\underline{SS}} > y_{\widehat{SS}}$ iff $P_{\underline{SS}}^U > Q$, where $Q = \frac{1}{n+1} \left[\frac{P_{\widehat{SS}}^U(n+1) + \frac{\hat{v} - \underline{v}}{\bar{v} - \underline{v}}}{1 + \frac{\hat{v} - \underline{v}}{\bar{v} - \underline{v}}}\right] < \frac{1}{n+1}$.

[26] Even without condition A4, $\widehat{SS}$ is never Lorenz dominated by $\underline{SS}$ when $y_{\underline{SS}} > y_{\widehat{SS}}$; but there may be low-wage steady states (with high enough $P_{\underline{SS}}^U$) whose Lorenz curves cross that of $\widehat{SS}$.

[27] This holds when graduation is limited to winner graduation; the presence of saver graduation (analyzed in Section 4.3) could eliminate the economy-wide gains from risk-taking. Also, including risk aversion in the model might alter this conclusion; the net effect on long-run welfare from the increase in both risk-taking and income might be ambiguous. If the lender absorbed a sufficient amount of project risk, however, the welfare effect would be positive. We discuss risk aversion in more detail in Section 5.

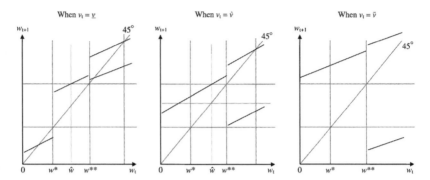

Fig. 6. Family wealth transition with saver graduation.

4.2.2. Dynamics with a small

Assume that winner graduation is relatively rare, specifically $a < \pi_l^E/n$.[28] In this case, there is no steady state in the $\hat{v}$-region; all economies there eventually drop into the $\underline{v}$-region, as is evident from Fig. 5. In much of the $\hat{v}$-region, the middle class is growing at the expense of both the lower and upper classes. But, under the assumed parameter values, the upper class continues to decline even as the lower class begins to rebound. This lower-class resurgence occurs after the middle class has gotten so big that downward mobility out of it dominates upward mobility into it from the lower class. The continuing decline of the upper class even when the middle class is big is because the rate of graduation from middle to upper class, π_h^S, is so low relative to the rate of falling out of the upper class, π_l^E. Eventually, the upper class decline and lower-class resurgence is sufficient to lower the wage to $\underline{v}$. At this point, $\underline{v}$-region dynamics take over and the steady state is on the upper right leg of the $\underline{v}$-region.

Under these parameters, micro-credit can make an economy unambiguously worse off in the long-run. It can do so, paradoxically, only if it is widespread enough to effect a transition to the mid-wage $\hat{v}$. It provides the economy a temporary spell of higher wages ($v=\hat{v}$), depleting both upper and lower classes; but if the decline in the upper class is sufficiently dominant, the mix of upper

and lower-class agents when the wage drops back to $\underline{v}$ can lead to a worse steady state. Fig. 5 depicts such a case. The untreated economy beginning at I reaches steady state $\underline{SS}$, while the treated economy beginning at I reaches steady state $\underline{SS}'$. Economy $\underline{SS}$ has higher output and lower poverty than $\underline{SS}'$ and generalized Lorenz dominates $\underline{SS}'$.

Without a careful calibration of the model, it is hard to gauge how likely such a scenario is. But, the model does shed light on necessary conditions. This scenario requires $a < \pi_l^E/n$, or equivalently,

$$\pi_h^S < \frac{\pi_l^E \pi_l^S}{n}.$$

In words, if self-employment returns that are high enough to allow graduation to full-scale entrepreneurship are encountered sufficiently rarely, compared to the frequency of bad outcomes in self-employment and entrepreneurship,[29] then micro-credit can make an economy strictly worse off in the long-run.

4.3. Dynamics with saver graduation

Another kind of graduation into the entrepreneurial class may come from saving normal returns rather than achieving supernormal returns. Such "saver" graduation is explicitly ruled out by Assumption (A3). In this section, we assume the reverse of (A3), which guarantees that the savings rate and normal returns in self-employment are jointly high enough to allow for eventual graduation into the upper class. Our goal is

---

[28] The case where $\pi_l^E/n < a < 1/n$ is very similar to the case where $a > 1/n$. One difference is that trajectories in the $\underline{v}$-region have slopes less than $1/n$ and thus never exit the region. This implies there is no possibility to raise the wage from $\underline{v}$ to $\hat{v}$ without micro-credit. Graphically, the whole $\underline{v}$-region would be shaded in Fig. 4. A second difference is that it is possible to exit the $\hat{v}$-region (from its lower left quadrant only) into the $\underline{v}$-region. Apart from these differences, previous results apply.

[29] At the same time, the mean self-employment return must allow continuation in self-employment.

C. Ahlin, N. Jiang / Journal of Development Economics 86 (2008) 1–21 15

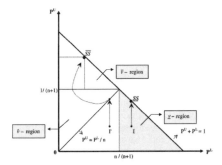

Fig. 7. Aggregate wealth dynamics with saver graduation.

more modest than the generality of Proposition 1; it is to show that there exist sufficient conditions under which micro-credit can catalyze full development.

Generational class transitions are now pictured in Fig. 6, which is the same as Fig. 2 except that the average return, middle class bequest line crosses the w^{**} line. We also return to the uncertainty structure of Section 4.1, assuming π_h^S, $\pi_l^S = 0$. This eliminates uncertainty from self-employment, and with it the possibility for winner graduation. It is done for simplicity and to allow an exclusive focus on saver graduation.[30]

The middle class now divides into two subclasses, depending on whether or not one's wealth level is high enough to raise one's descendant to the upper class. We denote the new, intermediate cutoff wealth level $\hat{w}$,[31] where by assumption $\hat{w} \in (w^*, w^{**})$, and the subclasses as the lower middle (P_t^{LM}) and upper middle (P_t^{UM}). For purposes of aggregate dynamics, the wealth distribution becomes a point in the three-dimensional simplex.

Two of the differential equations describing aggregate dynamics, 1 and 2, need to be modified. Eq. (3) is unmodified since the new assumption does not affect the dynamics when $v_t = \bar{v}$. When $v_t = \underline{v}$, the lower class sees no mobility in or out; thus $\dot{P}_t^L = 0$ and $P_t^L = P_0^L$. Further,

$$\dot{P}_t^U = P_t^{UM}$$
$$\dot{P}_t^{UM} = \left(1 - P_t^U - P_t^L - P_t^{UM}\right) - P_t^{UM}. \qquad (6)$$

The upper-class P_t^U grows due to the bequests of the upper middle class, P_t^{UM}. The upper middle-class P_t^{UM}

grows due to the bequests of the lower middle class (the term in parentheses) and declines due to its own members graduating to the upper class.

Fig. 7 displays the economy's dynamics. It is clear that the trajectory of an economy in the $\underline{v}$-region is straight upward. The lower class is not changing, while the middle class is gradually moving up to the upper class. The economy ends up on the upper right leg of the $\underline{v}$-region (iff it begins in the shaded area of Fig. 7) or it transits to the $\hat{v}$-region.

When $v_t = \hat{v}$, all active lower-class agents exit the lower class. Thus $\dot{P}_t^L = -P_t^L$, which gives $P_t^L = P_0^L e^{-t}$. Further,

$$\dot{P}_t^U = P_t^{UM} - \pi_l^E P_t^U$$
$$\dot{P}_t^{UM} = \left(1 - P_t^U - \gamma P_t^L - P_t^{UM}\right) - P_t^{UM}. \qquad (7)$$

There are two differences between Eqs. (6) and (7). First, there is exit out of the upper class by unlucky entrepreneurs, due to the higher wages. Second, it is not only the lower middle class who move up to the upper middle class, but also some of the lower class; see Fig. 6. We let this fraction be $(1-\gamma)P_t^L$, so that γP_t^L reach the lower middle, but not upper middle, class.[32]

Achieving development from the $\hat{v}$-region is now possible. The lower class vanishes with time. The middle class progresses inevitably upward to the upper class. The only drawback is the unlucky entrepreneurs who are dropping into the (lower) middle class.

Now consider the effect of micro-credit. Its main effect will be to move economies that are otherwise destined to remain in the $\underline{v}$-region, into the $\hat{v}$-region. If the $\hat{v}$-region is a transitory step en route to development, then micro-credit can be the economy's stepping stone to full development.

Proposition 2. *Under Assumption (A1) and family dynamics as displayed in Fig. 6, if $\pi_l^E < n/2$, micro-credit can bring an underdeveloped (low-wage) economy to full development.*

Proof. See Appendix.

Fig. 7 displays an economy in the shaded area, I, along with its destination without micro-credit $\underline{SS}$ and its path to development with micro-credit. Note that micro-credit exists temporarily en route to full-scale, entrepreneurial development. Its ultimate effect is to raise income and lower poverty and inequality.

---

[30] If winner graduation and saver graduation are simultaneously possible, it appears necessary to track a minimum of five classes, and the system of differential equations becomes non-linear. However, it seems clear that allowing some uncertainty in self-employment will not change the result (below) that micro-credit can bring development, though sufficient uncertainty skewed in a negative direction could alter this conclusion.

[31] This cutoff $\hat{w}$ satisfies $s(\hat{v} + \rho \hat{w}) = w^{**}$.

[32] Define two lower classes, lower lower and upper lower, based on whether agents transit to the lower middle or upper middle class, respectively. Then $\dot{P}_t^{LL} = -P_t^{LL}$ and thus $P_t^{LL} = P_0^{LL} e^{-t}$; and similarly for P_t^{UL}. Since $P_t^L = P_0^L e^{-t}$, it is clear that $\gamma = P_0^{LL}/P_0^L$, a constant, during any spell in the $\hat{v}$-region.

This result requires that the leakage out of the upper class, π_I^E, be not too large.[33] The intuition comes from the steady state distribution under $\hat{v}$-dynamics. If in steady state the entrepreneurial class is of measure X, then $\pi_{II}^E X$ will be in the lower middle class and $\pi_{If}^E X$ will be in the upper middle class. Thus the entrepreneurial class measures $1/(2\pi_I^E + 1)$. The condition for this to be greater than the critical value $1/(n+1)$ is that $\pi_I^E < n/2$. More generally, if an unlucky entrepreneur spends k periods outside of the upper class before regaining enough assets to graduate, the required condition appears to be $\pi_I^E < n/k$.

The key condition in this example is that there must not be an income trap at the level of the average endeavor that micro-credit enables. Absent such a trap – that is, if the road to (eventual) wealth accumulation and raised incomes via larger endeavors is open for the *average* micro-borrower – then micro-credit can be the tool that breaks the initial poverty trap and sets households and the economy on the path to prosperity.

5. Extensions and alternative approaches

Of course, the model cannot pretend to give a final answer to the main question of this paper. It does not deal with some significant issues that bear upon the question. Here we discuss several of these issues.

5.1. Risk aversion

Both this model and the original BN model abstract from risk aversion. If there were positive risk aversion here, market wages would be lowered, since they are the certainty-equivalent values of the occupational payoffs. For example, the middle wage would no longer equal the mean return from self-employment $\hat{v}$, but something less. Risk aversion would therefore lower the wealth transition paths of wage earners. As a result, the economy might in general have a harder time reaching higher wages and incomes. There may also be no steady states in the $\hat{v}$- and/or $\bar{v}$-regions.

Micro-credit would have a harder time bringing full development. As shown above, a necessary condition for it to spur full development is that the *average return* in self-employment allows eventual graduation to the upper class. In a model with risk aversion, the condition would

instead be on the *certainty equivalent* of the self-employment payoff. The intuition, again, is that as the economy approaches the critical labor demand value, most of the middle class is working for wages rather than engaging in self-employment; and if the wage, which equals the certainty equivalent of the self-employment payoff, does not allow graduation, the entrepreneurial class stalls short of its threshold value for development. This makes clear that sufficient risk aversion will make micro-credit unable to catalyze full development even in cases where it could have under risk neutrality.[34]

Risk aversion would also open the possibility of additional scenarios in which micro-credit lowers income and raises poverty. By lowering the self-employment certainty-equivalent wage, risk aversion could make exit of the poverty trap hard or impossible for low-wealth households. If so, there may be no steady state in the $\hat{v}$-region, and an economy that moves there due to micro-credit would return to the v-region, potentially with a mix of upper and lower-class agents that leads to lower income and higher poverty in the long-run.

The negative effect of risk aversion could be mitigated, however, to the extent that lenders shoulder the risk of self-employment projects — this would raise the certainty equivalent of the self-employment payoff. It seems quite plausible that lenders are often better positioned than borrowers to bear risk, especially when they have many borrowers and are geographically diversified.[35]

5.2. Foreign entry

Entry of foreign entrepreneurs can be examined in this model. The main effect would be a rise in labor demand, which could raise the wage. If foreign entry was sufficient to raise the wage to $\bar{v}$, the economy would reach maximal income (GNP) with no ill effects; even though there could be fewer domestic entrepreneurs, everyone earns the mean return from entrepreneurship. If it raised the wage to $\hat{v}$, then poverty would certainly decline but the same long-run equity-efficiency tradeoffs that are potentially involved in micro-credit could surface. Again, the intuition is that the higher wage can diminish the domestic entrepreneurial class in the long-run.

Assume the foreign entrants are permanent upper-class fixtures, rather than facing the downward mobility

---

[33] If instead $\pi_{II}^E > n/2$, the $\hat{v}$-region contains an interior steady-state. Computation shows that the economy converges to this steady state without exiting the $\hat{v}$-region from nearly all starting points within this region. Thus, assessing the effect of micro-credit would involve comparing an economy in the $\hat{v}$-region with one in the v-region, with the potential equity-efficiency tradeoff of previous sections.

[34] This assumes there is some risk in self-employment and that the lowest potential outcome in self-employment does not allow eventual graduation to the upper class.

[35] Townsend and Yaron (2001) discuss practices used by the Bank for Agriculture in Thailand (BAAC) to absorb some of its borrowers' risk.

C. Ahlin, N. Jiang / Journal of Development Economics 86 (2008) 1–21 17

possibilities that domestic entrepreneurs face. In this case, foreign entry can lower income and crowd out domestic entrepreneurship even if it does not affect the wage. It does this (in the $\hat{v}$-region) by causing more middle-class agents to work rather than engage in self-employment. Hence fewer people take risk, so fewer graduate into the higher incomes of the entrepreneurial class; fewer drop to the lower class, but income does not drop with this downward transition when the wage is $\hat{v}$.

In summary, sufficient foreign entry of entrepreneurs can bring full development by raising labor demand and wages. If the magnitude of entry is smaller, it can raise the wage moderately and bring the same equity-efficiency tradeoff that micro-credit does. Even if it does not affect the wage, it can lower domestic income and crowd out domestic entrepreneurship.

5.3. "Macro"-credit

By assumption, the introduction of micro-credit lowers w^* but not w^{**}, that is, it raises access to better technology but not the best. If instead the credit market improvement raises access to the best technology, entrepreneurship, it can bring full development directly (see footnote 23). But there are also cases in which it can harm an economy, if the increased access to credit is limited.[36] For one, it can give rise to the same kind of perverse scenario that micro-credit can when $a < \pi_l^E/n$ (see Section 4.2.2): raising wages temporarily to $\hat{v}$, but eventually leaving the economy with a less advantageous mix of upper and lower-class agents, lower income and higher poverty.

As another example, assume that entrepreneurship is so risky that entrepreneurs fall to the lowest class when the wage is $\hat{v}$ and they do not succeed. (This would require modification of the second panel of Fig. 2.) Imagine the economy to be in a mid-wage steady state when a credit market improvement broadens access to the entrepreneurial technology. If the entrepreneurial failure rate is high enough,[37] the increase in number of entrepreneurs could eventually cause the lower class to grow enough to lower the wage to subsistence level, $\underline{v}$. The steady state would then likely be in the $\underline{v}$-region, with higher poverty and potentially lower aggregate income.[38]

In short, "macro"-credit can directly bring development if sufficiently widespread, but if not, can in some instances leave an economy worse off.

5.4. Dynamic incentives

This paper abstracts from the decline in repayment incentives that may occur as borrowers build up their own wealth and lower their need for external finance. However, this issue could be important in answering this paper's question, since micro-credit would have a difficult time promoting development if it relies on poverty to give incentives for repayment.

The sovereign debt literature has addressed this issue in the context of inter-country debt. The standard assumption is that no direct sanctions for default are available, only the denial of future loans. Making this assumption, Eaton et al. (1986, p. 491) argue and Rosenthal (1991) shows formally that lending for the purpose of capital accumulation (as opposed to consumption smoothing, say) is not possible. The basic intuition is that since transfers to the borrower are concentrated in the early stages of any such relationship, transfers away from the borrower must predominate in later stages — guaranteeing that at some point the borrower will want to default. Anticipating this, the lender will not lend.

This logic suggests that micro-credit cannot facilitate wealth accumulation if repayment is supported only by the threat of future credit denial; it is instead limited to more modest goals, such as aiding consumption smoothing. In contrast, our focus is not on self-enforcing debt contracts but on labor market equilibrium effects of micro-credit. In particular, we follow BN in assuming lenders do have access to direct sanctions (F), rather than being limited only to withdrawing future credit access; and micro-credit is modeled as a credit market improvement that increases direct sanctions by harnessing social pressure.

5.5. Human capital

The model focuses on physical capital/wealth constraints and ignores human capital. Human capital is clearly a key concern, however. Can poor borrowers graduate to better technologies and greater capital intensity without increases in human capital? Might the increase in wages from micro-credit spur greater human capital investment and catalyze development in this alternative way?

The model can offer some insight into these issues because of the similarities between physical and human capital. For example, in the model micro-credit can raise the wage and allow parents to endow their offspring with

---

[36] We thank a referee for pointing this out, in particular, the scenario of the next paragraph.
[37] Specifically, if $\pi_h^S = \pi_l^S = 0$, the condition needed is $\pi_l^E \geq n/(n+1)$.
[38] It would surely be in the $\underline{v}$-region if the first panel of Fig. 2 applies and either $\pi_h^S = \pi_l^S = 0$ or $a < 1/n$. If failed entrepreneurs transit to a lower class in the $\underline{v}$-region and $\pi_h^S = \pi_l^S = 0$, aggregate income would certainly be lower.

greater physical capital, potentially opening up higher income opportunities; it would presumably have a similar effect in a human capital model. In a simple modification of the model that incorporates both physical and human capital,[39] we find no qualitative change in the necessary conditions for micro-credit to bring development: average returns in the technology that micro-credit facilitates must be high enough to enable eventual graduation into entrepreneurship through accumulation of physical and human capital. Without this, micro-credit can break the poverty trap but not the mid-wage income trap (for enough people), as in Section 4.2.

That said, there may be differences between human and physical capital that matter for answering this paper's question. Technological non-convexities and income traps may exist at different levels for the two capitals. In particular, there may be no middle-income trap associated with human capital. Further, the rate of return to human capital could depend in interesting ways on the human capital distribution. Human capital may also interact with technological change. While a fuller analysis of human capital accumulation is beyond the scope of this paper, we believe that some of the insights from our physical capital model would likely carry over.

6. Policy implications and conclusions

Micro-credit in this model reduces poverty in most of the cases we examine. Thus it can indeed bring development, if development is defined as positive impact on the lives of the poorest half of the population (as Muhammad Yunus has advocated).

Can micro-credit bring about the more ambitious goal of high wages and widespread use of efficient technology and capital intensity? This model marks as critical the possibility for saver graduation. That is, graduation must be possible as a rule rather than as an exception – it must be possible to accumulate normal self-employment returns to reach efficient firm scale – if micro-credit is to serve as a stepping stone to long-run development. This possibility depends on two separate quantities, which jointly must be sufficiently high: a) the average return to self-employment activities and b) the savings rate.

Focusing on quantity a) suggests that the productive efficiency of the self-employment undertakings funded by micro-credit institutions is important. This is hardly surprising. It suggests that information sharing, technology transfer, and training programs can provide significant value-added in the long-run.

Micro-credit institutions are also uniquely positioned to affect quantity b). Financial access of all kinds is costly in many contexts in which they operate, due to geographical distances and due to the small amounts in question. In essence, these difficulties can act as a tax on savings. One can show that the savings rate in the presence of a flat-rate tax on savings τ would be $s' = s/(1-\tau)$. A micro-credit institution can make use of its employee network, village organizational structures (e.g. groups), and geographical extension to offer savings vehicles cost-effectively. This would lower the 'tax' and raise the effective savings rate s', potentially enabling saver graduation.

Thus the model uncovers a novel *complementarity* between micro-lending and facilitating micro-saving. Not only does savings mobilization raise funds that can be lent (not modeled here), it also enhances the household wealth accumulation process that this model suggests is critical to the long-run success of micro-lending. Here, micro-lending can break the poverty trap, but it must rely on micro-saving for help in breaking the mid-wage income trap. A combination of micro-lending and micro-saving facilitation allows for sufficient graduation into entrepreneurship and eventual raising of the wage.[40]

The model also supports a focus on graduation as a matter of course, which ought to be incorporated into incentives and evaluation of micro-credit programs. Loan officers should be rewarded not only for number of clients and client retention, but also for clients who leave the program for formal financial institutions. On the institutional level, programs might be judged in part on the number of their customers that have moved upward from the micro-credit sector. Information sharing between micro-credit and formal credit institutions would be crucial, enabling graduation to be tracked as well as allowing for mitigation of the default incentives (and adverse selection issues) involved with borrowers on the verge of graduation.

As an alternative to graduation between credit institutions, micro-credit institutions may commit to

---

[39] Specifically, we assume that there are three discrete human capital endowments, $1 < \sigma < \eta$, and that each agent receives as part of his bequest the human capital endowment commensurate with his wealth class, lower, middle, or upper. An agent with human capital endowment x can supply x units of labor. The only change in the simplex partition (e.g. Fig. 4) is that the boundary dividing the $\hat{v}$- and $\bar{v}$-regions intersects the $P_t^L = 0$ line at $\sigma/(n+\sigma)$ rather than $1/(n+1)$. All the potential scenarios of the model without human capital are present in this model as well.

[40] Technically, the model has no room for mobilizing saving since all economic activity takes place in an instant. A richer model would allow for saving from the time entrepreneurial returns are realized until bequest takes place, or from the time returns are realized until a new investment opportunity is learned of.

their members indefinitely, providing larger and larger loans and shifting contract terms as needed. It would then be the underlying technological graduation that would be desirable to track and reward. Serving such an array of customers, however, may take most micro-credit institutions beyond their core competencies.

However, the model suggests that graduation is not optional, not simply an added benefit of micro-credit. It is precisely when the rate of graduation is minimal that micro-credit may lower total income and even raise poverty in the long-run. More research on the incentives involved in promoting graduation seems critical.

The model we analyze provides rich ground for examining various micro-credit scenarios that differ in initial conditions, amount of micro-credit, and so on. As with the original BN model, its potential drawbacks include the simplifying assumptions and focus on special, analytically tractable cases. Though we believe there was and is insight to be gained from these cases, the policy implications should be put in that context. Future policy extensions involving computational analysis may be helpful. Endogenizing the capital and/or labor choices of the self-employed and entrepreneurs, and carrying out simulation with (even roughly) calibrated technology, preference, and uncertainty parameters,[41] appear to be fruitful avenues of research.

Appendix A. Proofs of Propositions

Proof of Proposition 1. Relying on the BN Markov assumption, let $\pi_{jk}^{o,v}$ be the probability that an agent of class j transitions to class k when the wage is $v \in \{\underline{v}, \hat{v}, \bar{v}\}$ and the agent chooses occupation $o \in \{SU, L, SE, E\}$, where "SU" indexes subsistence, "L" (wage) labor, "SE" self-employment, and "E" entrepreneurship. Assumption (A3) is reflected as $\pi_{MH}^{L,\hat{v}}=0$. This of course implies that $\pi_{LH}^{L,\hat{v}}=0$ and $\pi_{LH}^{L,\underline{v}}=0$, the latter because $\underline{v}<\hat{v}$ by Assumption (A1).

An underdeveloped economy by definition begins with $P_0^U<1/(n+1)$, and given that micro-credit does not affect P_0^U, an underdeveloped economy affected by micro-credit is either in the $\hat{v}$-region or the $\underline{v}$-region. The differential equation describing upper-class evolution in the $\hat{v}$-region is

$$\dot{P}_t^U = \pi_{MH}^{SE,\hat{v}}\left[1-(n+1)P_t^U\right]-\left(1-\pi_{HH}^{E,\hat{v}}\right)P_t^U. \quad (8)$$

The first term captures mobility into the upper class, which comes only from the lucky self-employed, whose number includes everyone not working in a firm or running one;

[41] Caucutt and Kumar (2004) carry out a calibration exercise with the original BN model.

wage-earners have no upward mobility by Assumption A3 ($\pi_{LH}^{L,\hat{v}}, \pi_{MH}^{L,\hat{v}}=0$). The second term captures mobility out of the upper class. Solving Eq. (8) gives

$$P_t^U = P_{\widehat{SS}}^{U'}\left(1-e^{-\left[\pi_{MH}^{SE,\hat{v}}(n+1)+1-\pi_{HH}^{E,\hat{v}}\right]t}\right)$$

$$+ P_0^U e^{-\left[\pi_{MH}^{SE,\hat{v}}(n+1)+1-\pi_{HH}^{E,\hat{v}}\right]t},$$

where $P_{\widehat{SS}}^{U'}$ is equal to $P_{\widehat{SS}}^{U}$ defined in Eq. (4), except that $\pi_{MH}^{SE,\hat{v}}$ is substituted for π_h^S and $(1-\pi_{HH}^{E,\hat{v}})$ is substituted for π_l^E. This expression makes clear that (i) if $P_0^U=P_{\widehat{SS}}^{U'}$, then $P_t^U=P_0^U$ for all $t\in(0,\infty)$ and (ii) if $P_0^U\neq P_{\widehat{SS}}^{U'}$, then $P_t^U<\max\{P_{\widehat{SS}}^{U'}, P_0^U\}$ for all $t\in(0,\infty)$. Since $P_{\widehat{SS}}^U<1/(n+1)$ and $P_{\widehat{SS}}^{U'}\leq 1/(n+1)$ (with equality only when $\pi_{HH}^{E,\hat{v}}=1$), we can conclude that $P_t^U<1/(n+1)$ for all $t<\infty$, i.e. that an economy cannot achieve development from the $\hat{v}$-region.

Turning to the $\underline{v}$-region, upper-class evolution is described by

$$\dot{P}_t^U = \pi_{LH}^{SU,\underline{v}}\left(P_t^L-nP_t^U\right)$$

$$+\pi_{MH}^{SE,\underline{v}}\left(1-P_t^U-P_t^L\right)-\left(1-\pi_{HH}^{E,\underline{v}}\right)P_t^U. \quad (9)$$

The first term captures mobility into the upper class from the subsisting lower class, whose number includes all the lower class not employed in firms; the wage-earning lower class has no upward mobility by Assumptions (A1) and (A3) ($\pi_{LH}^{L,\underline{v}}=0$). The second term captures upward mobility from the middle class, all of whom are self-employed and only the "winners" among whom graduate. The final term captures mobility out of the upper class.

Define ϵ_t as the shortfall of the upper class from its critical value for development:

$$\epsilon_t \equiv \frac{1}{n+1}-P_t^U.$$

By hypothesis, $\epsilon_0>0$. Also, $\dot{\epsilon}_t=-\dot{P}_t^U$, so Eq. (9) can be rewritten

$$\dot{\epsilon}_t = -\pi_{LH}^{SU,\underline{v}}\left(P_t^L-nP_t^U\right)$$

$$-\pi_{MH}^{SE,\underline{v}}\left(1-P_t^U-P_t^L\right)$$

$$+\left(1-\pi_{HH}^{E,\underline{v}}\right)\left(\frac{1}{n+1}-\epsilon_t\right). \quad (10)$$

20   *C. Ahlin, N. Jiang / Journal of Development Economics 86 (2008) 1–21*

Note that the numbers of subsisters $(P_t^L - nP_t^U)$ and self-employed $(1 - P_t^U - P_t^L)$ are nonnegative and together sum to $1 - (n+1)P_t^U$, which is equivalent to $(n+1)\epsilon_t$. Given this fact, take two cases. First, consider $\pi_{HH}^{E,y} < 1$. Inspection of Eq. (10) shows that $\dot{\epsilon}_t > 0$ when ϵ_t is close enough to zero. Thus ϵ_t is bounded away from zero. Second, consider $\pi_{HH}^{E,y} = 1$ and define $\bar{\pi}$ as the maximum of $\{\pi_{LH}^{SU,y}, \pi_{MH}^{SE,y}\}$. Then

$$\dot{\epsilon}_t \geq -\bar{\pi}\left(P_t^L - nP_t^U\right) - \bar{\pi}\left(1 - P_t^U - P_t^L\right)$$

$$= -\bar{\pi}(n+1)\epsilon_t,$$

from which it follows that

$$\epsilon_t \geq \epsilon_0 e^{-\bar{\pi}(n+1)t}.$$

Thus, ϵ_t is bounded away from zero for any finite t. This establishes that development is not attainable from the $\underline{v}$-region. $\square$

Proof of Proposition 2. Sufficient micro-credit guarantees a wage of $\hat{v}$, since it can lift enough of the lower class to guarantee that $P_0^L \leq nP_0^U$. Assumption (A1) and the family dynamics of Fig. 6 give rise to the system of equations described by $P_t^L = P_0^L e^{-t}$ and differential Eq. (7), when $v_t = \hat{v}$. Solving gives[42]

$$P_t^U = P_{SS}^U$$

$$- e^{-(1+\pi_I^E/2)t}\left[\delta^U \cos(\beta t) + \frac{\delta^{UM} + (1 - \pi_I^E/2)\delta^U}{\beta}\sin(\beta t)\right]$$

$$- \frac{\gamma P_0^L e^{-t}}{\pi_I^E}\left[1 - e^{-\pi_I^E t/2}\left(\cos(\beta t) + \frac{\pi_I^E}{2\beta}\sin(\beta t)\right)\right],$$

$$(11)$$

where $P_{SS}^{UM} = \pi_I^E/(2\pi_I^E + 1)$, $P_{SS}^U = 1/(2\pi_I^E + 1)$, $\delta^U = P_{SS}^U - P_0^U$, $\delta^{UM} = P_{SS}^{UM} - P_0^{UM}$, and $\beta = \sqrt{\pi_I^E(4 - \pi_I^E)/2}$. It is clear from Eq. (11) that P_t^U approaches P_{SS}^U as t gets large. Manipulation of the P_{SS}^U expression gives that $P_{SS}^U > 1/(n+1)$ if $\pi_I^E < n/2$. This condition then guarantees that under $\hat{v}$-dynamics, P_t^U will reach the critical value $1/(n+1)$ in finite time and $\bar{v}$-dynamics will take over. Eq. (3) guarantees that when $v_t = \bar{v}$, P_t^U will monotonically increase toward its steady state value of $(n+1-\pi_I^E)/(n+1)$.

It remains to show that the trajectory through the $\hat{v}$-region never crosses into the $\underline{v}$-region; if it did, the dynamics would change and the above analysis would no

longer apply. Trajectories in the $\hat{v}$-region satisfy $\dot{P}_t^L = -P_t^L$. If $P_t^L = 0$, it is impossible to enter the $\underline{v}$-region, that is, to satisfy $P_t^L > nP_t^U$; assume $P_t^L > 0$. Since P_t^L is declining, to exit the $\hat{v}$-region requires that $\dot{P}_t^U < 0$ and that $\left|\frac{\dot{P}_t^L}{\dot{P}_t^U}\right| > 1/n$. Note from Eq. (7) that $\dot{P}_t^U \geq -\pi_I^E P_t^U$. Combining this with $\dot{P}_t^L = -P_t^L$ gives that $\left|\frac{\dot{P}_t^L}{\dot{P}_t^U}\right| \leq \pi_I^E \frac{P_t^U}{P_t^L}$ (when $\dot{P}_t^U < 0$). Now consider a point in the interior of the $\hat{v}$-region near the boundary with the $\underline{v}$-region, the line $P_t^L = nP_t^U$. This point can be expressed as $(P_t^L, P_t^U) = (nk, \lambda k)$, where $k \in [0, \frac{1}{n+1})$ and $\lambda \in \left(1, \frac{1}{k(n+1)}\right)$. We know that here $\left|\frac{\dot{P}_t^L}{\dot{P}_t^U}\right| \leq \pi_I^E \frac{\lambda}{n}$ (if $\dot{P}_t^U < 0$), which is less than $1/n$ for λ satisfying $1 < \lambda < 1/\pi_I^E$. This establishes that economies close to the boundary (λ near 1) are not following trajectories that allow for exit from the $\hat{v}$-region into the $\underline{v}$-region; that is, exit downward is impossible. $\square$

References

Ahlin, Christian, Townsend, Robert M., 2007a. Selection into and across contracts: theory and field research. Journal of Econometrics 136 (2), 665–698 (February).

Ahlin, Christian, Townsend, Robert M., 2007b. Using repayment data to test across theories of joint liability lending. Economic Journal 117 (517), F11–F51 (February).

Armendariz de Aghion, Beatriz, Morduch, Jonathan, 2000. Microfinance beyond group lending. Economics of Transition 8 (2), 401–420.

Armendariz de Aghion, Beatriz, Morduch, Jonathan, 2005. The Economics of Microfinance. MIT Press, Cambridge MA.

Banerjee, Abhijit V., Newman, Andrew F., 1993. Occupational choice and the process of development. Journal of Political Economy 101 (2), 274–298 (April).

Banerjee, Abhijit V., Newman, Andrew F., 1998. Information, the dual economy, and development. Review of Economic Studies 65 (4), 631–653 (October).

Banerjee, Abhijit V., Besley, Timothy, Guinnane, Timothy W., 1994. Thy neighbor's keeper: the design of a credit cooperative with theory and a test. Quarterly Journal of Economics 109 (2), 491–515 (May).

Besley, Timothy, Coate, Stephen, 1995. Group lending, repayment incentives and social collateral. Journal of Development Economics 46 (1), 1–18 (February).

Bornstein, David, 1997. The Price of a Dream: The Story of the Grameen Bank. University of Chicago Press, Chicago.

Caucutt, Elizabeth M., Kumar, Krishna B., 2004. Evaluating explanations for stagnation. Working Paper. December.

Eaton, Jonathan, Gersovitz, Mark, Stiglitz, Joseph E., 1986. The pure theory of country risk. European Economic Review 30 (3), 481–513 (June).

Ghatak, Maitreesh, 1999. Group lending, local information and peer selection. Journal of Development Economics 60 (1), 27–50 (October).

Ghatak, Maitreesh, 2000. Screening by the company you keep: joint liability lending and the peer selection effect. Economic Journal 110 (465), 601–631 (July).

Ghatak, Maitreesh, Guinnane, Timothy W., 1999. The economics of lending with joint liability: theory and practice. Journal of Development Economics 60 (1), 195–228 (October).

Kaboski, Joseph P., Townsend, Robert M., 2005. Policies and impact: an analysis of village-level microfinance institutions. Journal of the European Economic Association 3 (1), 1–50 (March).

---

[42] For completeness: $P_t^{UM} = P_{SS}^{UM} - e^{-(1+\pi_I^E/2)t}\left[\delta^{UM}\cos(\beta t) - \frac{(1-\pi_I^E/2)\delta^{UM} + \delta^U}{\beta}\sin(\beta t)\right] + \frac{(1-\pi_I^E/2)\gamma P_0^L e^{-t}}{\pi_I^E}\left[1 - e^{-\pi_I^E t/2}\left(\cos(\beta t) + \frac{\pi_I^E(3-\pi_I^E)}{2\beta(1-\pi_I^E)}\sin(\beta t)\right)\right].$

Karlan, Dean S., 2007. Social connections and group banking. Economic Journal 117 (517), F52–F84 (February).

Karlan, Dean, Valdivia, Martin, 2006. Teaching entrepreneurship: impact of business training on microfinance clients and institutions. Working Paper. November.

Madajewicz, Malgosia, 2005. Joint liability versus individual liability in credit contracts. Working Paper. June.

Matsuyama, Kiminori, 2006. The 2005 Lawrence R. Klein Lecture: emergent class structure. International Economic Review 47 (2), 327–360 (May).

Matsuyama, Kiminori, 2007. Credit traps and credit cycles. American Economic Review 97 (1), 503–516 (March).

Morduch, Jonathan, 1999. The microfinance promise. Journal of Economic Literature 37 (4), 1569–1614 (December).

Paal, Beatrix, Wiseman, Thomas, 2005. Group lending with endogenous social collateral. Working Paper.

Rai, Ashok S., Sjöström, Tomas, 2004. Is Grameen lending efficient? Repayment incentives and insurance in village economies. Review of Economic Studies 71 (1), 217–234 (January).

Rosenthal, Robert W., 1991. On the incentives associated with sovereign debt. Journal of International Economics 30 (1–2), 167–176 (February).

Stiglitz, Joseph E., 1990. Peer monitoring and credit markets. World Bank Economic Review 4 (3), 351–366 (September).

Townsend, Robert M., Yaron, Jacob, 2001. The credit risk-contingency system of an Asian development bank. Federal Reserve Bank of Chicago Economic Perspectives 25 (3), 31–48.

Wydick, Bruce, 1999. Can social cohesion be harnessed to repair market failures? Evidence from group lending in Guatemala. Economic Journal 109 (457), 463–475 (July).

[9]

THE
QUARTERLY JOURNAL
OF ECONOMICS

Vol. CXXIII   November 2008   Issue 4

RETURNS TO CAPITAL IN MICROENTERPRISES:
EVIDENCE FROM A FIELD EXPERIMENT*

SURESH DE MEL
DAVID MCKENZIE
CHRISTOPHER WOODRUFF

We use randomized grants to generate shocks to capital stock for a set of Sri Lankan microenterprises. We find the average real return to capital in these enterprises is 4.6%–5.3% per year), substantially higher than market interest rates. We then examine the heterogeneity of treatment effects. Returns are found to vary with entrepreneurial ability and with household wealth, but not to vary with measures of risk aversion or uncertainty. Treatment impacts are also significantly larger for enterprises owned by males; indeed, we find no positive return in enterprises owned by females.

I. INTRODUCTION

Small and informal firms are the source of employment for half or more of the labor force in most developing countries. A central question for policymakers is whether these firms hold the potential for income growth for their owners, or whether they merely represent a source of subsistence income for low-productivity individuals unable to find alternative work. The rapid increase in development funding being channeled to microfinance organizations is based on the belief that these firms

*The authors thank David I. Levine for early discussions on this project, and Shawn Cole, Xavier Gine, Gordon Hanson, Larry Katz, Craig McIntosh, Jonathan Morduch, Edward Vytlacil, Bilal Zia, three anonymous referees, and participants at various seminars for comments. Susantha Kumara, Jose Martinez, and Jayantha Wickramasiri provided outstanding research assistance. AC Nielsen Lanka administered the surveys on which the data are based. Financial support from National Science Foundation Grant SES-0523167 and the World Bank is gratefully acknowledged. This paper was drafted in part while Woodruff was visiting LSE, whose support is also gratefully acknowledged.

The Quarterly Journal of Economics, November 2008

can earn high returns to capital if given the opportunity. Evidence that *some* firms have high marginal returns is suggested by the very high interest rates paid to moneylenders, and by literature that identifies the effect of credit shocks on those who apply for credit (see Banerjee and Duflo [2005] for an excellent recent summary). However, the sample of firms who apply for credit or who belong to microfinance organizations does not represent the full universe of firms for a number of reasons.[1] We lack a credible estimate of returns among firms not borrowing from formal sources.

In this paper we use a randomized experiment to identify the effect of incremental cash investments on the profitability of all enterprises, irrespective of whether they choose to apply for credit at market interest rates. We then examine the heterogeneity of returns in order to test which theories can explain why firms may have marginal returns well above the market interest rate. We accomplish this by surveying microenterprises in Sri Lanka and providing small grants to a randomly selected subset of the sampled firms. We purposely restricted our survey to firms with less than 100,000 Sri Lankan rupees (LKR, about US$1,000) in capital other than land and buildings. The grants were either 10,000 LKR (about US$100), or 20,000 LKR (about US$200). The larger grants were equal to more than 100% of the 18,000 LKR baseline median level of invested capital.

An accurate measurement of returns to capital is critical to understanding the potential of microfinance. With more than 70 million clients worldwide, microfinance nongovernmental organizations (NGOs) are now the most common source of credit for household enterprises and one of the largest channels for development aid. But available evidence on take-up rates suggests that only a small percentage of those informed about microfinance programs desire loans. Is the return to capital lower than interest rates for nonborrowers? Or do other factors—risk aversion or low levels of financial literacy, for example—prevent potentially beneficial loans from being requested? Despite the rapid spread of microfinance in recent years, there is surprisingly little evidence

---

1. These reasons include both selection among entrepreneurs as to whether or not to apply for credit, determined by factors such as their attitudes to risk, access to alternative sources of finance, perceptions of the returns on investment, and expectations of getting a loan; as well as selection on the part of the lender as to which firms to accept as clients. Microfinance lending methodologies like group lending may also cause some potential borrowers to forgo loans (Gine and Karlan 2007).

of its effectiveness in raising incomes of borrowers. Reviewing the literature, Armendáriz de Aghion and Morduch (2005, p. 199) conclude: "The number of careful impact studies is small but growing, and their conclusions, so far, are [measured]." The small number of studies is due in part to the difficulty of identifying a comparison sample (Karlan 2001; Morduch 1999). We generate an identical comparison among firms in our sample through randomization.

Measuring returns at low levels of capital stock also provides important feedback to theory. The theoretical literature on occupational choice has posited a minimum scale below which returns to capital are very low or even zero.[2] Low returns at low levels of capital stock would suggest that individuals without access to a sufficient amount of capital would face a permanent disadvantage. That is, they would fall into a poverty trap. If, on the other hand, returns are high at low levels of capital stock, then entrepreneurs entering with suboptimal capital stocks would be able to grow by reinvesting profits. In this case, entrepreneurs might remain inefficiently small for some period of time, but would not be permanently disadvantaged. In the absence of minimum scale, we might expect returns to be high. Because small-scale entrepreneurs lack access to credit at market interest rates, risk-adjusted returns may well be higher than market interest rates.

There is an increasing number of estimates of returns to capital in small-scale productive activities in developing countries (see Banerjee and Duflo [2005]). Some of the estimates come from broad cross sections of producers, and others from the subset of firms exposed to some shock. Among the former, McKenzie and Woodruff (2006) estimate returns to capital among the smallest urban microenterprises in Mexico, those with less than US$200 invested, of around 15% per month, or an uncompounded rate of 180% per year. Returns in the Mexican data fall to around 40%–60% per year above US$500 of capital stock. McKenzie and Woodruff (forthcoming, 2008) undertake an experiment similar to that reported here among a small sample of enterprises in Mexico with less than US$900 of capital stock. They find returns in the range of 250%–360% per year, higher than the cross-sectional estimates in their earlier work. Udry and Anagol (2006) estimate

---

2. Banerjee and Newman (1993) and Aghion and Bolton (1997) are seminal papers in this literature. Because we study a sample of enterprises that existed at the time of the baseline survey, we can only provide evidence on the importance of nonconvexities conditional on entry. The loss of income resulting from starting an unsuccessful business might be an additional barrier to entry for low-wealth households.

1332   *QUARTERLY JOURNAL OF ECONOMICS*

returns in a sample of small-scale agricultural producers in Ghana to be 50% per year among those producing traditional crops on a median-sized plot and 250% per year among those producing nontraditional crops on median-sized plots. Banerjee and Duflo (2004) take advantage of changes in the criteria identifying firms eligible for earmarked credit from Indian banks. The changes in the laws result in credit supply shocks to identifiable sets of firms, allowing for the identification of the impact of changes in access to finance among this subset of firms. Banerjee and Duflo derive estimates of returns for this set of firms of between 74% and 100% per year.

The central challenge in estimating returns to capital is that the optimal level of capital stock is likely to depend on attributes of entrepreneurial ability, which are difficult to measure. Banerjee and Duflo point to one way around this problem—exploiting an exogenous shock that is uncorrelated with entrepreneurial ability. But this approach has a downside in that the sample is limited to firms or entrepreneurs exposed to the shock. In the case of Banerjee and Duflo's estimates, the estimates apply only to those firms applying for credit. This resolves one problem at the cost of creating another: while estimated returns are less subject to ability bias, self-selection of the subsample suggests that the returns likely overstate those for the full spectrum of firms. However, low returns to capital are only one of several possible reasons entrepreneurs may fail to apply for loans. Firms may lack information about lenders or overestimate the probability that they will be denied a loan. Estimating returns of firms not applying for formal credit is a first step to developing policies to address the constraints faced by small firms.

The difficulty of obtaining an unbiased estimate of returns to capital for all microenterprises, regardless of whether they are active borrowers, is the motivation for the field experiment on which the data used in this paper are based. We use random grants of either cash or equipment to generate changes in capital against which changes in profits can be measured. Randomized experiments have quickly become an important part of the toolkit of development economics (Duflo, Glennerster, and Kremer 2006), although this is the first experiment of which we are aware involving payments to firms, rather than to households or schools. The random allocation of the grants ensures that the changes in capital stock are uncorrelated with entrepreneurial ability, demand shocks, and other factors associated with the differences in the profitability of investments across firms.

We first use the data to measure the effect of assignment to each of four treatments on capital stock, profits, and hours worked by the owner. After establishing that the treatments did have the expected positive effect on capital stock and profits, we examine the reasonableness of pooling both the four treatments and the data from the various waves of the survey. We then describe the conditions under which we can use the random treatments as instruments for capital stock, and estimate the real marginal return on capital using IV regressions.

We find that both the treatment effects and, for reasonable values of the owner's labor time, the returns to capital range from 4.6% to 5.3% per month, on the order of 60% per year. We find that there is considerable heterogeneity of the returns along measurable dimensions. We set out a model consistent with our data that can be used to investigate the importance of imperfect credit markets and imperfect insurance markets. The model predicts that with imperfect finance and insurance markets, returns to the shocks to capital stock should be higher for more constrained entrepreneurs and those who are more risk averse and face greater uncertainties in sales and profits. Examination of the heterogeneity of treatment effects shows that returns to capital are generally higher for entrepreneurs who are more severely capital constrained—those with higher ability and with fewer other wage workers in the household who can provide liquidity. One important exception to this is that while the conventional wisdom holds that women are more severely credit constrained, we find that the returns are much higher in enterprises owned by males than in enterprises owned by females. We do not find that the treatment effects vary significantly with measures of risk aversion or uncertainty. Taken at face value, the heterogeneity of returns suggests that the high returns are more closely associated with missing credit markets than missing insurance markets.

We show that the results are robust to accounting for spillovers on firms located near the treated firms, to attrition from the sample, and to measurement issues. Finally, we use both the baseline data and the untreated panel to compare returns generated by OLS, random-, and fixed-effects regressions with those generated by the experiment. We find that the experimental returns are more than twice as large as the nonexperimental returns. Attenuation bias arising from the imprecise measurement of capital stock appears to be the most plausible reason for the underestimate of the nonexperimental returns.

II. Description of Experiment

II.A. The Sample

We carried out a baseline survey of microenterprises in April 2005 as the first wave of the Sri Lanka Microenterprise Survey (SLMS).[3] Eight additional waves of the panel survey were then conducted at quarterly intervals, through April 2007. The survey took place in three southern and southwestern districts of Sri Lanka: Kalutara, Galle, and Matara. The survey is designed to also study the process of recovery of microenterprises from the December 26, 2004, Indian Ocean tsunami, and so these districts were selected as ones where coastal areas had received tsunami damage. The sample was drawn equally from areas along the coast where firms suffered direct damage from the tsunami; areas slightly inland where firms did not suffer direct damage, but where demand may have been affected; and inland areas where neither assets nor demand are likely to have been affected by the tsunami. We refer to these areas as directly affected, indirectly affected, and unaffected zones. We set out to draw a sample of firms with invested capital of 100,000 LKR (about US$1,000) or less, excluding investments in land and buildings. This size cutoff was chosen so that our treatments (described below) would be a large shock to business capital.

We began by using the 2001 Sri Lankan Census to select 25 Grama Niladhari (GN) divisions in these three districts. A GN is an administrative unit containing on average around 400 households. We used the Census to select GNs with a high percentage of own-account workers and modest education levels, because these were most likely to yield enterprises with invested capital below the threshold we had set.[4] The GNs were stratified according to whether the area was directly affected, indirectly affected, or unaffected by the tsunami. A door-to-door screening survey was then carried out among households in each of the selected GNs. This survey was given to 3,361 households, with fewer than 1% of households refusing to be listed. The screening survey identified self-employed workers outside of agriculture, transportation,

---

3. Fieldwork was carried out by ACNielsen Lanka (Pvt) Ltd.
4. Although we avoided GNs with high average education levels, the median education level in our sample (10 years) is the same as the median level in the Sri Lankan labor force survey for all adults ages 20–65 years. The mean level of education is only slightly lower (8.9 vs. 9.4 years). We believe the resulting sample is representative of a substantial majority of the own-account workers in Sri Lanka.

fishing, and professional services who were between the ages of 20 and 65 and had no paid employees.

The full survey was given to 659 enterprises meeting these criteria. After reviewing the baseline survey data, we eliminated 41 enterprises either because they exceeded the 100,000 LKR maximum size or because a follow-up visit could not verify the existence of an enterprise. The remaining 618 firms constitute the baseline sample. We present results later in the paper indicating that returns to capital were higher among firms directly affected by the tsunami, but we exclude these firms for most of the analysis because the tsunami recovery process might affect returns to capital. We leave the full analysis of the impact of the capital shocks on enterprise recovery to another paper. Excluding the directly affected firms leaves us with a baseline sample of 408 enterprises.

The 408 firms are almost evenly split across two broad industry categories, with 203 firms in retail sales and 205 in manufacturing/services. Firms in retail sales are typically small grocery stores. The manufacturing/services firms cover a range of common occupations of microenterprises in Sri Lanka, including sewing clothing, making lace products, making bamboo products, repairing bicycles, and making food products such as hoppers and string hoppers.

II.B. The Experiment

The aim of our experiment was to provide randomly selected firms with a positive shock to their capital stock and to measure the impact of the additional capital on business profits. Firms were told before the initial survey that we would survey them quarterly for five periods, and that after the first wave of the survey, we would conduct a random prize drawing, with prizes of equipment for the business or cash. The random drawing was framed as compensation for participating in the survey. We indicated to the owners that they would receive at most one grant. For logistical reasons, we distributed just over half the prizes awarded after the first wave of the survey, and the remaining prizes after the third wave; enterprises not given a prize after the first wave were not told whether or not they had won one of the prizes to be awarded in the second distribution until after the third wave. The prize consisted of one of four grants: 10,000 LKR (~US$100) of equipment or inventories for their business, 20,000 LKR in equipment/inventories, 10,000 LKR in cash, or 20,000 LKR in cash.

In the case of the in-kind grants, the equipment was selected by the enterprise owner and purchased by our research assistants.[5] Subsequently, we received funding to extend the panel to nine waves. Because this represented an extension of the survey relative to what firms were told before the baseline survey, we granted each of the untreated firms 2,500 LKR (~US$25) after the fifth wave.

The randomization was stratified within district (Kalutara, Galle, and Matara) and zone (unaffected and indirectly affected by the tsunami). Allocation to treatment was done *ex ante* among the 408 firms kept in the sample after the baseline survey.[6] A total of 124 firms received a treatment after wave 1, with 84 receiving a 10,000-LKR treatment and 40 receiving a 20,000-LKR treatment. Another 104 firms were selected at random to receive a treatment after the third survey wave: 62 receiving the 10,000-LKR treatment and 42 the 20,000-LKR treatment. In each case, half the firms receiving a treatment amount received cash, and the other half equipment.

The 10,000-LKR treatment is equivalent to about three months of median profits reported by the firms in the baseline survey, and the larger treatment is equivalent to six months of median profits. The median initial level of invested capital, excluding land and buildings, was about 18,000 LKR, implying that the small and large treatments correspond to approximately 55% and 110% of the median initial invested capital. By either measure, the treatment amounts were large relative to the size of the firms.

Although the amount offered for the in-kind treatment was either 10,000 or 20,000 LKR, in practice the amount spent on inventories and equipment sometimes differed from this amount. Only 4 of the 116 firms receiving in-kind grants spent as much as 50 LKR (US$0.50) less than the amount we offered. More commonly, the entrepreneurs contributed funds of their own to purchase a larger item. This occurred in 65 of the 116 in-kind

5. To purchase the equipment for these entrepreneurs receiving equipment treatments, research assistants visited several firms in the evening to inform them that they had won an equipment prize. The winning entrepreneurs were asked what they wanted to buy with the money, and where they would purchase it. The research assistants then arranged to meet them at the market where the goods were to be purchased at a specified time the next day. Thus, the goods purchased and the place/market where they were purchased were chosen by the entrepreneurs with no input from the research assistants.

6. The authors carried out the randomization privately by computer. The *ex ante* treatment allocation was kept private from both the survey firm and the firms participating in the survey, with firms only learning they had received a treatment at the time it was given out. Seven firms assigned to receive a treatment after wave 3 attrited between the second and third waves.

treatments. However, in 44 of the 65 cases, the owners contributed less than 500 LKR, or US$5. The entrepreneurs contributed 2,000 LKR or more in only 13% of the cases. We use the amount offered rather than the amount spent in our analysis of the effects of treatment. We have both receipts and pictures of the goods purchased with the in-kind grants. Approximately 57% of the purchases were inventories or raw materials, 39% machinery or equipment, and 4% construction materials for buildings.

Cash treatments were given without restrictions. Those receiving cash were told that they could purchase anything they wanted, whether for their business or for other purposes. In reality, the grant was destined to be unrestricted because we lacked the ability to monitor what recipients did with the funds, and because cash is fungible. Being explicit about this was intended to produce more honest reporting regarding use of the funds. In the survey subsequent to the treatment, we asked how they had used the treatment.[7] On average, 58% of the cash treatments was invested in the business between the time of the treatment and the subsequent survey. An additional 12% was saved, 6% was used to repay loans, 5% was spent on household consumption, 4% was spent on repairs to the house, 3% was spent on equipment or inventories for another business, and the remaining 12% was spent on "other items." Of the amount invested in the enterprise, about two-thirds was invested in inventories and the rest in equipment.

Both the cash and in-kind treatments invested in the firm were almost exclusively spent on expanding the existing line of business, purchasing similar types of inventories and equipment as firms would do with reinvestments of retained earnings. Only three of the treated firms reported changing their line of business after treatment, and these were changes to different products within retail sales. Treated firms were also not more likely to introduce new products: 18.9% of treated firms introduced a new product during the year following the baseline survey, compared to 15.6% of never-treated firms ($p = .40$). Thus, it was not the case that the treatments were being used to fund particularly risky new endeavors.[8]

---

7. Our question noted that some entrepreneurs had told us they had spent the money on furniture or other items for the household, some had spent it on food and clothing, and some had invested in their business. In fact, they had told us this during piloting of the wave 2 survey.

8. Furthermore, we find no relationship between the share of the cash treatment invested in the business and the risk aversion of the owner, which is consistent with the view that the treatments were not being used for particularly risky investments.

III. Data and Measurement of Main Variables

The baseline survey gathered detailed information on the firm and the characteristics of the firm owner. The main outcome variable of interest in this paper is the profits of the firm. Firm profits were elicited directly from the firm by asking,

> What was the total income the business earned during March after paying all expenses including wages of employees, but not including any income you paid yourself. That is, what were the profits of your business during March?

The reported mean and median profits in the baseline are 3,850 and 3,000 LKR, respectively. The survey also asked detailed questions about revenues and expenses. Profits calculated as reported revenues minus reported expenses are lower, awave 2,500 LKR at the mean and 1,350 LKR at the median. Profits calculated in this manner are positively correlated with reported profits, with a correlation coefficient of 0.32. This is about the same level as one finds in other microenterprise surveys. In de Mel, McKenzie, and Woodruff (2008a), we analyze the measurement of profits in detail, reporting on experiments conducted with different questions, bookkeeping, and monitoring of sales. The biggest reason that reported and calculated profits differ is a mismatch of the timing of purchases and the sales associated with those purchases. Some of the expenses in one month are associated with sales the following month. Correcting for this mistiming increases the correlation with reported profits to awave 0.70. We conclude from the more detailed analysis of measurement issues that the reported profit is the best measure of the firm's profitability, and we use those data for the remainder of this paper. In the Online Appendix, we show that the effects we find are robust to other outcome measures.

The baseline survey also gathered detailed information on the replacement cost of assets used in the enterprise, and whether they were owned or rented. Almost all (99%) assets excluding land and buildings are owned by the enterprises. The majority of assets owned by the enterprises are land and buildings. In the baseline sample, these average 121,000 LKR (US$1,200), though about a sixth (15%) of firms report they own no assets in this category. The firms also reported an average of 14,400 LKR (US$145) worth of machinery and equipment and 13,000 LKR (US$130) in inventories.

In each subsequent wave of the survey, we asked firms to report on the purchase of new assets, the disposition of assets by sale or damage, and the repair and return to service of any previously damaged assets. Changes in the market value of fixed assets are calculated from the responses to these questions. Combined with the data from each previous quarter, these data allow us to estimate equipment investment levels for each quarter of the survey.[9] The survey also asks the current value of inventories of raw material, work in progress, and final goods each quarter. The specific questions related to the measurement of capital stock are described in the Online Appendix.

Of the 408 firms in the baseline survey, 369 completed the ninth wave, an attrition rate of only 9.6%. However, only 391 of the 408 firms completed the survey questions on profits in the first wave, 368 in the fifth, and 343 in the ninth. We concentrate our analysis on the unbalanced panel of 385 firms reporting at least three waves of profit data. We show that our results are robust to corrections for attrition.

Table I summarizes the characteristics of the enterprise owners and their firms, and compares the baseline characteristics of firms ever assigned to treatment with those firms always in the control group. The median owner in our sample is 41 years old, has 10 years of education, and has been running his or her firm for 5 years. The sample is almost equally divided between male and female owners. The household asset index is the first principal component of a set of indicators of ownership of durable assets, measured in the baseline survey.[10] The Digit Span Recall Test is a measure of numeracy and short-term cognitive processing ability. Respondents were first shown a three-digit number. The number was then taken away, and the respondents were asked to repeat it from memory after a delay of ten seconds. Those successfully repeating the three-digit number were shown a four-digit number, and so on up to eleven digits. The coefficient of relative risk aversion (CRRA) comes from a lottery game played in wave 2 of the survey, described in more detail in the Online Appendix. Respondents were asked whether they would choose a certain payoff of 40 LKR—about two hours of mean reported earnings—or a gamble with payoffs of 10 or 100 LKR. We varied the percentage

---

9. We expect that the owners do not make adjustments for depreciation of machinery and equipment. We show in the Online Appendix that the results are unchanged when we adjust the value of machinery and equipment owned at the beginning of each quarter for depreciation of 2.5% per quarter. This depreciation rate is in the middle of the range of 8%–14% estimated by Schündeln (2007) for small and medium sized enterprises in Indonesia.

10. We use the following seventeen asset indicators to construct this principal component: cell phone; landline phone; household furniture; clocks and watches; kerosene, gas, or electric cooker; iron and heaters; refrigerator or freezer; fans; sewing machines; radios; television sets; bicycles; motorcycles; cars and vans; cameras; pressure lamps; and gold jewelry.

TABLE I
DESCRIPTIVE STATISTICS AND VERIFICATION OF RANDOMIZATION

Baseline characteristic	Total number of observations in R1	Full sample		Means by treatment		t-test p-value
		Mean	SD	Assigned to any treatment	Assigned to control	
Profits March 2005	391	3,851	3,289	3,919	3,757	.63
Revenues March 2005	408	12,193	14,933	11,796	12,739	.53
Total invested capital March 2005	408	146,441	224,512	155,626	133,837	.33
Total invested capital excluding land and buildings March 2005	408	26,530	25,259	25,633	27,761	.40
Own hours worked March 2005	408	52.6	22.3	51.8	53.7	.39
Hours worked, unpaid family, March 2005	405	18.1	28.8	18.2	15.4	.31
Age of entrepreneur	408	41.8	11.4	41.8	41.9	.92
Age of firm in years	403	10.3	10.5	10.8	9.7	.34
Proportion female	387	0.491	0.5	0.459	0.533	.15
Years of schooling of entrepreneur	408	9.0	3.1	8.9	9.2	.40
Proportion whose father was an entrepreneur	408	0.385	0.49	0.373	0.401	.56
Proportion of firms that are registered	408	0.235	0.45	0.254	0.209	.32
Number of household members working in wage jobs	408	0.7	0.83	0.7	0.7	.73
Household asset index	408	0.276	1.610	0.118	0.494	.02
Number of digits recalled in Digit Span Recall Test	370	5.9	1.23	5.9	5.9	.96
Implied coefficient of relative risk aversion from lottery game	403	0.143	1.57	0.206	0.053	.33

Note: All data based on baseline survey. Profits, revenue, and capital stock data in Sri Lankan rupees. The last column reports the p-value for the t-test of the equivalence of means in the samples assigned to control on the one hand and any of the four treatments on the other. The household asset index is the first principal component of variables representing ownership of seventeen household durables, listed in the Online Appendix; Digit Span Recall is the number of digits the owner was able to repeat from memory ten seconds after viewing a card showing the numbers (ranging from 3 to 11); risk aversion is the CRRA calculated from a lottery exercise described in the text and Online Appendix.

chance of winning the higher payoff from 10% to 100%. The CRRA is calculated from the switchover point from the certain payoff to the gamble.

Randomization was done by computer, and so any differences between the treatment and control groups are purely due to chance. In general the randomization appears to have created groups that are comparable in terms of baseline characteristics, with the only significant difference in means occurring for a household durable asset index, with firm owners in the control group having slightly higher mean baseline assets. Our main specifications will include enterprise fixed effects to improve precision and account for such chance differences between treatment groups.

IV. ESTIMATION OF BASIC EXPERIMENTAL TREATMENT EFFECTS

We begin by examining the impact of treatment on the outcomes of interest. The first marker is capital stock, where the treatments were designed to have a direct effect. We are also interested in the effect of the treatments on enterprise profits and the number of hours worked by the owner. We estimate regressions of the following form:

$$(1) \qquad Y_{it} = \alpha + \sum_{g=1}^{4} \beta_g \text{Treatment}_{git} + \sum_{t=2}^{9} \delta_t + \lambda_i + \varepsilon_{it},$$

where Y represents the outcome of interest; $g = 1$ to 4, the four treatment types granted to enterprise i any time before wave t; δ_t are wave fixed effects and λ_i are enterprise fixed effects. We cluster all standard errors at the enterprise level. We estimate (1) in both levels and logs, though as we will discuss, the interpretation of the treatment effect measured in logs is less straightforward. We begin by pooling all waves of the survey. We also remove outliers at the top of the sample, trimming the top 0.5% of both the absolute and percentage changes in profits measured from one period to the next. We discuss both of these issues in the next section. The results are reported in Table II.

The first column of the table verifies that the treatment did increase capital stock as intended. All four treatments are significantly associated with higher levels of capital stock. The measured impact of the cash treatments is somewhat higher than the impact of the in-kind treatments, though the large standard errors on the individual treatments mean that the differences

TABLE II
EFFECT OF TREATMENTS ON OUTCOMES

Impact of treatment amount on:	Capital stock (1)	Log capital stock (2)	Real profits (3)	Log real profits (4)	Owner hours worked (5)
10,000 LKR in-kind	4,793*	0.40***	186	0.10	6.06**
	(2,714)	(0.077)	(387)	(0.089)	(2.86)
20,000 LKR in-kind	13,167***	0.71***	1,022*	0.21*	−0.57
	(3,773)	(0.169)	(592)	(0.115)	(3.41)
10,000 LKR cash	10,781**	0.23**	1,421***	0.15*	4.52*
	(5,139)	(0.103)	(493)	(0.080)	(2.54)
20,000 LKR cash	23,431***	0.53***	775*	0.21*	2.37
	(6,686)	(0.111)	(643)	(0.109)	(3.26)
Number of enterprises	385	385	385	385	385
Number of observations	3,155	3,155	3,248	3,248	3,378

Notes: Data from quarterly surveys conducted by the authors reflecting nine survey waves of data from March 2005 through March 2007. Capital stock and profits are measured in Sri Lankan rupees, deflated by the Sri Lankan CPI to reflect March 2005 price levels. Columns (2) and (4) use the log of capital stock and profits, respectively. Profits are measured monthly and hours worked are measured weekly. All regressions include enterprise and period (wave) fixed effects. Standard errors, clustered at the enterprise level, are shown in parentheses. Sample is trimmed for top 0.5% of changes in profits.
*** $p < .01$, ** $p < .05$, * $p < .1$.

between cash and in-kind treatments are not significant. Trimming the top and bottom 1% of capital stock reduces these differences.[11] Column (2) shows the treatment effects measured in logs rather than levels. Logs have the advantage of dampening the effect of outliers. The coefficient measures the percentage change in capital stock for each treatment. Because enterprises had different levels of pretreatment capital stock, a treatment represents a different percentage increase of each firm's capital stock. Nevertheless, all four treatments have the expected positive effects on capital stock using logs, and the effects are roughly proportional to the size of the treatment. At the mean baseline capital stock, the effect of the in-kind treatments on capital stock (120%–130% of the treatment amount) is larger than that measured with levels, whereas the effect of the cash treatments (70%–90% of the treatment amounts) is somewhat smaller.

11. The treatment effects after trimming capital stock are 5,780 (6,227) for the 10,000 LKR in-kind (cash) treatment and 13,443 (17,325) for the 20,000 LKR in-kind (cash) treatment.

Though capital stock represents the most direct measure of impact, we are most interested in the impact of the treatment on the profits generated by the business. This is shown in column (3) in levels and column (4) in logs. Profits are measured monthly and deflated by the Sri Lanka Consumers' Price Index to reflect April 2005 price levels.[12] In either case, three of the four treatments have significant, positive effects on profit levels. The smaller in-kind treatment has measured positive but insignificant effects, while the smaller cash treatment has surprising large measured impacts. Only the difference between the 10,000 LKR cash and 10,000 LKR in-kind treatments is significant at the .05 level. The four coefficients in column (3) indicate increases in monthly profits ranging from 2% to 14% of the treatment amount, and the coefficients in column (4) indicate returns of 4%–6% per month at the mean of baseline profits. The last column of Table II shows the impact of the treatment on hours worked. Both 10,000 LKR treatments are associated with a higher number of hours worked. Those receiving the smaller treatments work 4–6 hours per week longer than the untreated owners, against a baseline of just over 50 hours per week. The treatments might also affect the use of the labor of family members or hired workers in the enterprises as well. In results reported in the Online Appendix, we find no effects of the treatment on nonowner labor hours.

IV.A. *Trimming Outliers*

We next examine the impact of trimming the sample for outliers and confirm that it is reasonable to pool treatments across time, by level, and by treatment type. We focus on the effect of treatments on profit levels. We begin by assuming each enterprise is characterized by a linear production function and that the treatments have homogeneous effects on the enterprises. We later relax both of these assumptions.

The data we obtained from the survey firm contained several observations with large positive or negative changes in profit levels reported by the same firm across time. These outliers were rechecked for coding errors, and a handful of errors were found and corrected. Among the remaining outliers, the survey firm was

12. Data are from Sri Lanka Department of Census and Statistics, http://www.statistics.gov.lk/price/slcpi/slcpi_monthly.htm (accessed February 17, 2007). Capital stock data are not deflated because they are based on market values reported as of March 2005. These market values are not adjusted for inflation or depreciation, a point we discuss further in the next section.

able to confirm that several of the large drops in profits resulted from a temporary suspension of the firm's activities, sometimes because of illness of the owner and sometimes from a lack of demand. Because these types of events represent risks of running a business, it is important that they not be trimmed from the data. In other cases, the survey firm was not able to confirm the reason for the large changes in either direction. Some of these are likely due to errors made by the survey enumerators in recording the responses in the field. We believe it is reasonable to trim the sample for large changes in profits when these are unlikely to be caused by events such as owner illness, to prevent them from having undue influence on the results. The first column of Table III shows the mean treatment effect in the untrimmed sample, with the treatment variable collapsed into a single measure taking the value of 100 for a cash or in-kind treatment of 10,000 LKR and 200 for a cash or in-kind treatment of 20,000 LKR.[13] Measuring the treatment in units of 100 LKR allows us to interpret the coefficients directly as a percentage of the treatment amount. The second column trims out the top 0.5% of the percentage and level increases in profits. This trims observations in which an enterprise reported an increase in profits of more than 948%, or more than 20,350 LKR from one wave to the next, six and four standard deviations from the mean change, respectively. A comparison of coefficients in columns (1) and (2) of Table III shows that trimming has the effect of slightly decreasing both the estimated impact of the treatment and the standard error.[14]

IV.B. Pooling of Treatment Effects

The remaining columns of Table III report results from splitting the treatment in various dimensions. In column (3), we test

13. The 2,500 LKR payment made to untreated enterprises after wave 5 is coded as 25.

14. In many contexts, quantile (median) regressions provide an alternative to trimming. Quantile regressions of real profits on the treatment amount and wave dummies using the untrimmed data give a coefficient of 500 at the 25th quantile and 75th quantiles and 464 at the median—similar in size to the trimmed-fixed-effects mean treatment effect of 541. However, these quantile regression coefficients tell us, for example, the change in median profits from the treatment, which is not the same as the median change in profits arising from our treatment (Abadie, Angrist, and Imbens 2002). The median treatment effect cannot be identified without imposing strong assumptions. Furthermore, quantile regressions are not estimable with fixed effects, and more restrictive approaches to estimating quantile regression models with panel data are still in their infancy, with many theoretical issues still to be resolved (Koenker 2004). Given that trimming appears to have only modest effects on the estimated mean effects, and that we believe most of the trimmed observations reflect measurement errors, we use trimming rather than quantile regression for the remainder of the paper.

TABLE III
POOLING OF TREATMENT EFFECTS (DEPENDENT VARIABLE: REAL PROFITS)

	(1) FE	(2) FE	(3) FE	(4) FE	(5) FE	(6) FE
Treatment amount	5.68*** (2.18)	5.41*** (2.09)				
Treatment amount × being 1–4 quarters posttreatment			5.47** (2.08)			
Treatment amount × being 5–8 quarters posttreatment			4.88* (2.85)			
In-kind treatment amount				4.17 (2.58)		
Cash treatment amount				6.70** (2.81)		
Treated amount 10,000 LKR					7.65** (3.31)	
Treated amount 20,000 LKR					8.95* (4.53)	
Treatment amount × coastal zone (tsunami affected)						9.08** (4.36)
Treatment amount × near-coastal zone						5.10** (2.38)
Treatment amount × inland zone						5.34 (3.33)

TABLE III
(CONTINUED)

	(1) FE	(2) FE	(3) FE	(4) FE	(5) FE	(6) FE
Constant	3,841***	3,824***	3,824***	3,823***	3,823***	3,665***
	(185)	(174)	(174)	(174)	(174)	(152)
Trimming top 0.5% of changes in profits	No	Yes	Yes	Yes	Yes	Yes
F-test of equality of treatment effects p-value			0.76	0.45	0.80	0.44
F-test p-value: $2 \times 10{,}000$ treatment $= 20{,}000$ treatment					0.39	
Firm-period observations	3,274	3,248	3,248	3,248	3,248	4,913
Number of enterprises	385	385	385	385	385	585

Notes: Data from quarterly surveys conducted by the authors reflecting nine waves of data from March 2005 through March 2007. Capital stock and profits are measured in Sri Lankan rupees, deflated by the Sri Lankan CPI to reflect March 2005 price levels. To make interpretation easier, the coefficients in columns (1)–(4) and (6) show the effect of a 100-rupee treatment on profits; the coefficients in column (5) show the effect of a 100- and 200-rupee treatment. Profits are measured monthly and hours worked are measured weekly. All regressions include enterprise and period (wave) fixed effects. The sample in column (6) includes enterprises directly affected by the tsunami, which are excluded from other regressions reported in the paper. Standard errors, clustered at the enterprise level, are shown in parentheses.
*** $p < .01$, ** $p < .05$, * $p < .1$.

whether pooling all of the posttreatment waves of the sample is reasonable. We compare the returns in the four quarters following treatment with the returns five to eight quarters after treatment. We find that a 10,000 LKR treatment increases profits by 547 LKR (5.5% of the treatment amount) in the first four quarters after treatment and 488 LKR (4.9%) in the subsequent four quarters, an insignificant difference ($p = 0.76$). Next, we allow the effect of the in-kind treatment to differ from the effect of the cash treatment. In column (4), we find that the measured effect of the cash treatment is larger than the effect of the in-kind treatment (a 6.7% vs. 4.2% monthly return), but the difference is not significant at conventional levels ($p = .45$). Column (5) shows that we cannot rule out linearity of the returns measured by the two treatment levels. Profits increase by 760 LKR per month with the smaller treatment, 7.6% of the treatment amount, whereas they increase by 900 LKR per month, or 4.5% of the larger treatment. The difference in returns is not significant. Finally, column (6) adds the sample of firms in the coastal area that were directly affected by the tsunami and allows returns to differ in each of the three zones. The data indicate that the effect of the treatment is identical in the inland and near-coastal areas, making the combination of these reasonable. Among enterprises directly affected by the tsunami, the impact is larger and less precisely measured. Though the difference between the coastal area and the other two zones is not statistically significant ($p = .44$ for the combined inland and near-coastal areas), we believe the nature of the recovery process justifies separation of the coastal area from the other two zones. We examine the recovery issues in more detail in de Mel, McKenzie, and Woodruff (2008b).[15]

V. Estimating the Return to Capital

The results to this point show the impact of the experiment on profit levels of firms, without saying anything about the channel through which the treatment effect operates. This may be the

---

15. While the aggregate returns are larger but not statistically different, we show in de Mel, McKenzie, and Woodruff (2008b) that the returns among tsunami-affected firms are very high in the retail sector, and zero in the manufacturing/services sector. There is no difference in the return across sector in the other two areas. We also show that, compared to the inland firms, revenues of firms in the near coastal zone were reduced for only two quarters following the tsunami, whereas revenues remained lower even after nine waves for the directly affected firms.

most relevant analysis for lenders, who are likely to be interested in whether the additional profits are sufficient to allow repayment of loans, or to NGOs, governments, or others providing cash to microenterprise owners. But we are also interested in isolating the returns to the additional capital stock generated by the treatments. Doing this requires some additional assumptions. We must estimate

$$(2) \qquad \text{profits}_{i,t} = \alpha + \beta_i K_{i,t} + \sum_{t=2}^{9} \delta_t + \lambda_i + \varepsilon_{i,t}$$

using the treatments as an instrument for capital stock, $K_{i,t}$. Profits and capital may be measured in either levels or logs, reflecting a linear or constant elasticity of substitution (CES) production function, respectively. In the Online Appendix we present additional analysis showing that we cannot reject that the level of profits is linear in capital.

For the random treatments to be valid instruments for changes in capital stock, they must affect capital stock alone, and not be associated with changes in either the levels or the marginal products of other factors affecting production. Table II shows that although the treatments do indeed increase capital stock, they also affect the number of hours worked by the owner in the enterprise, violating this condition. In addition, treatment could also increase the quality of labor supplied by the owner. While the treatment might lead to an initial burst in energy from the owner, our assumption is that this is mainly manifested through hours of work supplied, and any further effects are not prolonged. We have no instrument that varies across time for changes in the owner's labor effort or the effect of effort on output by the firm (i.e., the cross partial of capital and labor). Instead, we proceed by adjusting profits to reflect the value of the owner's time in the production of profits. We discuss this adjustment in more detail below.

If the marginal return to capital is the same for all firms, $\beta_i = \beta$, then after the adjustment for own labor hours, the IV estimator will provide a consistent estimate of the marginal return to capital, β. However, if there are heterogeneous returns to capital, stronger assumptions are needed in order for the IV estimator to consistently estimate the average marginal return to capital. Adapting the discussion in Card (2001, p. 1142) on identifying returns to education,[16] the IV estimator will consistently identify the average marginal return to capital if the treatment induces an equal change in capital stock for all firms receiving the 10,000 LKR treatment, and twice this change in capital stock for all firms receiving the 20,000 LKR treatment, or if, more generally, the change in capital stock induced by the treatment is independent of the marginal return to capital, β_i. If these conditions do not hold, and we assume that the change in capital stock induced by the treatment is nonnegative for all firms, then the IV estimator provides a local average treatment effect (LATE), which is a weighted average of the marginal returns to capital, with the marginal return to each firm weighted by how much that firm's capital stock responds to the treatment.

The change in capital stock induced by the treatment is unlikely to be identical across firms because firms were free to choose how much of the cash treatment to invest in their business and how much of the in-kind treatments to decapitalize. If individuals with higher marginal returns to capital invest more of the treatment in their business, then the LATE estimated by instrumental variables will exceed the average marginal return to capital. However, as we show below with our theoretical model, enterprise owners with high marginal returns to capital in the business also have high returns to further cash in their household (otherwise they would reallocate cash from household uses to business uses). As such, the pretreatment marginal return to capital in the business will be equated to the opportunity cost of capital in the household for each firm owner, leaving him or her indifferent between investing a marginal unit in the firm or in the household. Then high-marginal-return firm owners will invest more of the treatment in their firm only if the household return to capital falls at a faster rate than the return to capital in the firm.

We can test whether the percentage of treatment invested in the enterprise is associated with characteristics potentially correlated with the return to capital, such as the measured levels of ability, risk aversion, and pretreatment measures of the success of the enterprise. In results reported in the Online Appendix, we find no relationship between the percentage invested and baseline household assets, years of schooling, Digit Span scores, the baseline profit/sales and profit/capital stock ratios, or the CRRA

16. We thank a referee for drawing this issue to our attention.

estimated from the lottery exercise.[17] These are reassuring results and suggest that it may be reasonable to interpret the IV
estimator as indeed providing the average marginal return to capital. Nevertheless, we are unable to rule out possible correlations
between the response of capital stock to the treatment and unobserved characteristics such as unmeasured ability or demand
shocks.

With these caveats in mind, Table IV reports the results of IV
regressions measuring returns to capital. The first two columns
use real profits and log real profits as dependent variables. In
levels, we find that the shock is associated with a rate of return of
5.85% per month. The treatment amount is highly significant in
the first stage, and has a coefficient of 0.91. The log specification
also shows a highly significant instrumented return to capital. At
the mean baseline capital stock (26,500 LKR) and mean baseline
profit levels (3,850), this implies a return of 5.51% per month,
almost identical to the return calculated in levels. At the median
baseline profit/capital stock ratio (0.17), the return is 6.46% per
month. Thus, the log specification appears to produce estimates
very similar to the linear specification.

Column (3) of Table IV uses the four individual treatments
as instruments for changes in capital stock, rather than the single measure of the treatment amount. The individual treatments
result in a slightly lower estimated return to capital, 5.16% per
month. Following Kling, Liebman, and Katz (2007, p. 95), one
can visually display the variation underlying this IV estimate by
means of a scatterplot of the 41 adjusted profit and capital stock
means for each of the treatment groups in each time period, normalized so that each time period has mean zero (Figure I). The
figure shows that there is a consistent pattern across time periods
and groups in which higher capital stock is associated with higher
levels of adjusted profits. The slope of the fitted line is the 2SLS
estimator.

None of these first three specifications makes any attempt to
adjust for the changes in the owner's hours worked. Recall that
business profits include the earnings of the firm owner. Hence the
increase in real profits from the treatment reflects both the return
to the additional capital and the return to the additional hours

17. The interaction with the profit/capital ratio comes closest to being significant ($p = .11$), but is negative, indicating that less profitable firms invested more
of the grant.

TABLE IV

INSTRUMENTAL VARIABLE REGRESSIONS MEASURING RETURN TO CAPITAL FROM EXPERIMENT

	Real profits IV-FE (1)	Log real profits IV-FE (2)	Real profits 4 instruments (3)	Real profits adjusted (1) IV-FE (4)	Real profits adjusted (2) IV-FE (5)
Capital stock/log capital stock (excluding land & buildings)	5.85** (2.34)	0.379*** (0.121)	5.16** (2.26)	5.29** (2.28)	4.59** (2.29)
First-stage					
Coefficient on treatment amount	0.91***	0.33***		0.91***	0.91***
F statistic	27.81	49.26	6.79	27.81	27.81
Observations	3,101	3,101	3,101	3,101	3,101
Number of enterprises	384	384	384	384	384

Notes: Data from quarterly surveys conducted by the authors reflecting nine waves of data from March 2005 through March 2007. Capital stock and profits are measured in Sri Lankan rupees, deflated by the Sri Lankan CPI to reflect March 2005 price levels. Profits are measured monthly. The estimated value of the owner's labor is subtracted from profits in columns (4) and (5), as described in the text. In column (4), the owner's time is valued by regression coefficients from a production function using baseline data; in column (5), we use the median hourly earnings in the baseline sample for each of six gender/education groups. A single variable measuring the rupee amount of the treatment is used as the instrument in columns (1) and (2) and (4) and (5). In column (3), we use four separate variables indicating receipt of each treatment type. Except in column (2), the coefficients show the effect of a 100-rupee increase in the capital stock. All regressions include enterprise and period (wave) fixed effects. Standard errors, clustered at the enterprise level, are shown in parentheses. The F statistic is the partial F statistic in the first-stage regression on the excluded instruments.
*** $p < .01$, ** $p < .05$, * $p < .1$.

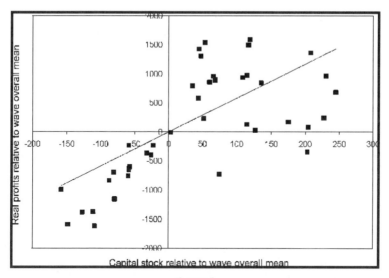

FIGURE I
Partial Regression Leverage Plot

Notes: The unit of observation is the wave*treatment group, for four treatments and nine waves. The line passes through the origin with a slope of 5.85 representing the IV-FE estimation of column (1), Table IV, of real profits on capital stock and wave indicators, using treatment group by wave interactions as instrumental variables.

worked by the owner. As we noted, we have no instrument for the changes in hours worked. An alternative approach is to create a measure of profits stripped of the value of the owner's labor hours. To do this, we need an estimate of the additional profit generated when the owner increases the number of hours (s)he works in the enterprise. We derive two estimates of the value of the owner's time, which can be thought of as lower and upper bounds. First, we estimate the marginal return to owner labor by using the baseline data to regress profits on capital stock (exclusive of land and buildings), age of the owner, six education/gender dummy variables, and the interaction of these six variables with the owner's monthly labor hours. The education/gender categories allow the return to labor to vary with the characteristics of the owner. Given the cross-sectional nature of the regression, there are endogeneity issues with both capital stock and hours. Nevertheless, the coefficients on owner's labor hours, which range from 0 to 9 LKR per hour, provide some indication of the value of an additional hour worked by the owner. We multiply the appropriate coefficient by

the reported hours worked in each wave of the survey, and sub-
tract that from the reported profits. Doing so results in negative
real profits for approximately 10% of the firm-period observations.
The negative profits make estimation of the CES production function problematic. So, we estimate the adjusted profit regressions
using only a linear specification. Column (4) of Table IV shows
that returns to capital thus measured are 5.29% per month.

As an alternative estimate of the value of hours worked, we
take the median hourly earnings reported in the baseline survey,
again using the six education/gender categories. Dividing profits
by hours worked reported in the baseline survey produces median
values ranging from 7.9 LKR per hour for females with fewer
than 8 years of schooling to 17.3 LKR per hour for males with
8 to 10 years of schooling. These estimates assume that there is
zero *average* return to capital in the median firm in each of these
six categories, and are thus likely an overestimate of the value
of the owner's time. Indeed one-third of the firm-period observations have negative profits using this measure. Nevertheless, the
returns to capital fall only to 4.59% per month when owner's labor
is valued in this manner. Given that the changes in hours worked
by the owner are modest, a fairly wide range of estimated values of the owner's time has only a modest effect on the estimated
returns to capital in the enterprises.

VI. HETEROGENEITY OF TREATMENT EFFECTS

We find that the treatment increased real monthly business
profits by between 5% and 6%. Even if all these additional profits
are consumed by the household and not compounded by reinvestment in the business, this would still give a real annual return in
excess of 60%. This greatly exceeds the market interest rate on
loans being charged by banks and microfinance institutions. Typical *nominal* market interest rates are 16%–24% per annum for
two-year loans. Assuming a 4% inflation rate, this equates to an
effective annualized real rate of 12%–20% per annum. The presence of marginal returns well in excess of the market interest rate
therefore raises the question of why firms are not taking advantage of these high returns, an issue we address in this section.

VI.A. A Model of Heterogeneous Returns

In the baseline survey, 78% of firm owners reported that their
business was smaller than the size they would like. When asked

what they view as constraints to the growth of their business, the most prevalent constraint reported is lack of finance, which 93% of firms say is a constraint. The second most prevalent constraint, lack of inputs, which 53% of firms list as a constraint, is also likely to reflect in part liquidity constraints, as firms said that they couldn't afford to buy all the inputs they would need. The perception of financial constraints is supported by the relatively rare use by firms of formal finance. Only 3.1% of our firms have a bank account for business use, and 89% of firms got *no* start-up financing from a bank or microfinance organization. Formal credit is scarcely used at all for financing additional equipment purchases. Instead the major source of funds is personal savings of the entrepreneur and loans from family. On average, 69% of start-up funds came from this source, and 71% of firms relied entirely on own savings and family for start-up funds.

After finance, the second most common set of constraints to growth according to the firms themselves can be broadly interpreted as reflecting uncertainty among firms about realizing the gains from investment. The possibility of lack of demand for products (which 34% of firms say is a constraint), lack of market information (16% say is a constraint), and economic policy uncertainty (15% say is a constraint) all suggest that the riskiness of returns could be important.

These perceptions suggest that missing markets for credit or for insurance against risk could be important factors in explaining the high marginal returns to capital.[18] We provide a simple model of microenterprise production to illustrate how these missing markets can give rise to marginal returns in excess of the market interest rate, and to suggest dimensions along which to examine the heterogeneity of returns.

Consider a one-period model in which the enterprise owner supplies labor inelastically to the business.[19] The household has an endowment of assets A and allocates the number of other working-age adults in the household, n, to the labor market, where they are paid a fixed wage w. The household can finance capital

18. These are two of the most common explanations considered in the literature. See Banerjee and Duflo (2005) for an excellent recent review of different explanations. Missing credit and insurance markets appear the most important for our setting among the different theories they summarize.

19. This simple model is an adaptation of the agricultural household model set out in Bardhan and Udry (1999). We show in the Online Appendix the consequences of relaxing the inelastic labor supply assumption on the model's main results.

stock (K) through the formal credit market by borrowing (B), and through its internal household capital market, by allocating A_K of household assets and I_K of household labor income to financing capital stock.

The household's problem is then to choose the amount of capital stock, K, to invest in the business, subject to its budget and borrowing constraints:

$$\text{Max} \quad \text{EU(c)}$$
$$\{K, B, A_K, I_K\}$$

subject to:

(3) $c = \varepsilon f(K, \theta) - rK + r(A - A_K) + (nw - I_K),$

(4) $K \le A_K + I_K + B,$

(5) $B \le \overline{B},$

(6) $A_K \le A,$

(7) $I_K \le nw,$

where ε is a random variable with positive support and mean 1, reflecting the fact that production is risky, and r is the market interest rate. The production function of the firm, $f(.)$ depends on the level of capital stock, and on θ, the ability of the entrepreneur.

With well-functioning credit and insurance markets, households will choose K to maximize expected profits and as a result, households choose K such that

(8) $f'(K, \theta) = r.$

That is, households will choose capital stock so that the marginal return to capital equals the market interest rate. In this case, the marginal return to capital will be the same for all firms, and will not depend on the characteristics of the owner or household.

The more general solution to the household's first-order condition for K is

(9) $f'(K, \theta) = \dfrac{1}{1 + \frac{\text{Cov}(U'(c), \varepsilon)}{EU'(c)}} \left[r + \dfrac{\lambda}{EU'(c)} \right],$

where λ is the Lagrange multiplier on condition (4), and is a measure of how tightly overall credit constraints bind. We can consider two subcases.

Perfect Insurance Markets, Missing Credit Market. With perfect insurance, risk and uncertainty do not matter, and (9) reduces to $f'(K, \theta) = r + \lambda$. That is, the marginal return will exceed the market interest rate by the shadow cost of capital. Solving the first-order conditions for the optimal choices of B, I_K, and A_K yields

(10) $$\lambda = \mu_B = \mu_A + r = \mu_I + 1,$$

where μ_B, μ_A, and μ_I are the Lagrange multipliers on constraints (5), (6), and (7), respectively. Credit constraints will therefore be binding if and only if both the external (formal) and internal (household) credit markets are binding. Given the lack of access to bank finance by our firms, it therefore appears that the critical determinant of whether or not credit constraints bind will be the shadow cost of capital within the household.

In our model, λ will then depend on the amount of internal capital available, which is increasing in household assets A and in the number of workers n. However, it will also depend on what the firms' unconstrained level of capital will be. If ability θ and capital are complements, then higher ability individuals will desire more capital, and so will be more likely to be constrained for a given level of assets and workers. As a result, if credit constraints are the reason for high returns, we predict that the marginal return to capital will be higher for firms with greater ability, lower for households with more workers, and lower for households with more liquid household assets. We will test for this by examining whether the effect of our treatments varies with these factors.

Perfect Credit Markets, Missing Insurance Market. An alternative explanation for the high marginal returns could be that credit markets function well, but that households are risk averse and insurance markets are missing. In this case equation (9) simplifies to

(11) $$f'(K, \theta)\text{Cov}(U'(c), \varepsilon) = [r - f'(K, \theta)]EU'(c).$$

Because consumption increases with ε, $\text{Cov}(U'(c), \varepsilon) < 0$. Because $U'(c) < 0$ this implies that $r < f'(K, \theta)$. The size of the gap between the market interest rate and the marginal return to capital will be increasing in the level of risk in business profits, and in the level of risk aversion displayed by the household. We test this by interacting the treatment effect with measures of the risk aversion of the entrepreneurs and the perceived uncertainty they have in their profits.

VI.B. *Estimation of Heterogeneous Treatment Effects and Measurement of Factors Determining Heterogeneity*

The above theory shows that the pattern of heterogeneity of treatment effects can inform us about the reasons why returns are so high and exceed market interest rates. We allow for heterogeneity in treatment effects through estimation of variants of the following fixed-effects regression:

$$\text{profits}_{i,t} = \beta \text{Amount}_{i,t} + \sum_{s=1}^{S} \gamma_s \text{Amount}_i * X_{s,i}$$

$$(12) \qquad + \sum_{t=2}^{9} \phi_t \delta_t + \sum_{s=1}^{S} \left(\sum_{t=2}^{9} \phi_{s,t} \delta_t * X_{s,i} \right) + \alpha_i + \varepsilon_{i,t}.$$

The parameter γ_s then shows how the effect of the treatment amount varies with characteristic s.[20] Because the evolution of profits over time may vary with $X_{s,i,t}$ even in the absence of treatment, we allow the wave effects δ_t to also differ with individual characteristics. The theoretical model suggests that the heterogeneity of returns could vary with the number of workers in the household, household wealth, entrepreneurial ability, risk aversion, and uncertainty. The Online Appendix discusses how each of these characteristics is measured. We also directly test whether returns differ by gender, because women are argued to be poorer than men on average (e.g., Burjorjee, Deshpande, and Weidemann [2002]; FINCA [2007]), to have less collateral, and hence to be more credit constrained (e.g., Khandker [1998]; SEAGA [2002]).

VI.C. *Results on Treatment Effect Heterogeneity*

Table V presents the results from estimating equation (12) allowing for different forms of heterogeneity in the treatment effects. We focus on the treatment effects, not attempting to isolate

---

20. The upper limit of 100,000 LKR of capital stock may result in an interaction between ability and some of the characteristics we are interacting with the treatment. For example, an entrepreneur of a given ability level may stay within the sample criteria if there are no additional workers in the household but grow beyond that limit if there are additional workers. The presence of additional workers would then be negatively correlated with entrepreneurial ability in the sample. This should be kept in mind when interpreting the coefficients on the interaction effects.

1358 *QUARTERLY JOURNAL OF ECONOMICS*

TABLE V
TREATMENT EFFECT HETEROGENEITY (DEPENDENT VARIABLE: REAL PROFITS)

					Females	Males
	(1)	(2)	(3)	(4)	(5)	(6)
	FE	FE	FE	FE	FE	FE
Treatment amount	5.41***	7.35**	5.29***	4.96**	2.83	6.74**
	(2.09)	(2.86)	(2.15)	(2.19)	(2.39)	(3.09)
Interaction of treatment amount with:						
Female owner		−7.51*				
		(4.02)				
Number of wage workers			−3.69			
			(2.38)			
Household asset index			−2.43**		−2.88**	−3.05
			(1.14)		(1.35)	(2.06)
Years of education			1.56***		0.24	2.03**
			(0.59)		(0.78)	(0.82)
Digit Span Recall			3.80**		7.34***	1.84
			(1.88)		(2.32)	(2.80)
Risk aversion				0.54		
				(1.25)		
Uncertainty				−7.82		
				(7.31)		
Constant	3,824***	3,777***	3,823***	3,840***	2,860***	4,700
	(174)	(179)	(175)	(174)	(211)	(283)
Firm-period observations	3,248	3,084	3,149	3,218	1,484	1,510
Number of enterprises	385	365	369	381	174	176

Notes: Data from quarterly surveys conducted by the authors reflecting 9 waves of data from March 2005 through March 2007. Capital stock and profits are measured in Sri Lankan rupees, deflated by the Sri Lankan CPI to reflect March 2005 price levels. Profits are measured monthly. The sample in column (2) excludes 20 enterprises that are either jointly owned or in which the identity of the owner changes in at least one wave of the survey. The household asset index is the first principal component of variables representing ownership of 17 household durables; digit span recall is the number of digits the owner was able to repeat from memory, ten seconds after viewing a card showing the numbers (ranging from 3 to 11); risk aversion is the CRRA calculated from a lottery exercise described in the text; and uncertainty is the coefficient of variation of expected sales three months from the date of survey. All of the interaction terms are calculated as deviations from the sample mean. The coefficients show the effect of a 100 rupee increase in the capital stock. All regressions include enterprise and period (wave) fixed effects, as well as the interaction of period effects and each included measure of heterogeneity. Standard errors, clustered at the enterprise level, are shown in parentheses.
*** $p < .01$, ** $p < .05$, * $p < .1$.

the portion of the impact operating through increased capital stock. All of the reported regressions are based on a linear production function. Column (1) presents the overall treatment effect, repeating column (2) of Table III. Column (2) separates the treatment effect by gender. We limit the sample to those enterprises in which either a male or a female reports being the owner in each of the nine waves of the survey. There are twenty enterprises in the sample where the gender of the person responding as the owner changes, or where the respondents report that the enterprise is jointly owned by the male and female. Surprisingly, we find a very large positive effect of the treatment for males and no significant effect for females. This runs counter to the idea that women are more constrained than men, though there are other explanations beside capital constraints. Our ongoing research examines this result and the potential explanations in more detail, with preliminary results discussed in de Mel, McKenzie, and Woodruff (2007).

In column (3), we allow the return to vary with two measures of household wealth and liquidity and two measures of the owner's ability. About half of the households report having at least one paid wage worker. We expect the shadow value of capital to be lower in households with wage workers, as the wages generate a source of funds for investing in the enterprise. Similarly, we expect the shadow value of capital to be lower in wealthier households, which we measure with the first principal component of a vector of household durable assets. We find (column (3)) that both of these variables have the expected sign. When they are included together, the household asset measure is significant at the .05 level, and the wage worker variable just misses the .10 cutoff. Either is significant when included without the other.

The two ability measures are highly significant. Both indicate that more able owners experienced larger impacts from the treatment. An additional year of schooling (one-third of a standard error) increases profits from the 10,000 LKR treatment by 156 LKR, and an additional digit recited (0.8 of a standard error) increases profits from the same treatment by 380 LKR. These results imply that treatment has a larger effect on more able entrepreneurs. This is again consistent with credit constraints, because it implies that the return deviates further from market interest rates for more able entrepreneurs.

Column (4) shows no significant interaction of the treatment amount with risk aversion or uncertainty.[21] Risk aversion is assessed through lottery experiments played with real money with each firm owner, while uncertainty is measured by the coefficient of variation in the subjective distribution of profits elicited from

---

21. These results are robust to using a subjective measure of willingness to take risk based on questions modeled on the German Socioeconomic Panel Survey. Recall as well that we find no relationship between risk aversion and the proportion of the grant invested in the enterprise.

each firm owner.[22] The coefficient of uncertainty on firm profits is negative, which would suggest that firm owners facing more uncertainty have lower returns. These results are inconsistent with risk-averse entrepreneurs facing missing insurance markets causing high marginal returns, as this would lead us to expect that both coefficients would be significantly positive.

The results are very similar if we include the wealth, ability, risk, and uncertainty measures together, although the uncertainty measure becomes larger and significantly negative at the .05 level. Columns (4) and (5) of Table V break the sample into enterprises owned by males and by females. While the returns are clearly higher for males at the sample means of all of the variables, there is significant heterogeneity in both the male and the female samples. We use the coefficients on the treatment amount and the treatment interaction terms to derive a predicted return for each individual in the survey. The data show that about 60% of female owners and just over 20% of male owners have predicted returns below the market interest rate.

Taken together, the heterogeneity of returns supports the view that the high marginal returns from treatment reflect credit constraints rather than missing insurance markets. Credit constraints bind more tightly, and thus marginal returns are higher, for more able entrepreneurs and for entrepreneurs with a high shadow cost of capital within the household, measured by the presence of fewer paid wage workers. The large variance of the returns may explain why lenders are hesitant to lend to the enterprises.

VII. ROBUSTNESS TO SPILLOVERS, HAWTHORNE EFFECTS, AND ATTRITION

VII.A. Controlling for Potential Treatment Spillovers

A key condition for randomization to provide valid estimates of the treatment effect is the stable unit treatment value assumption. This requires that the potential outcomes for each firm are independent of its treatment status and of the treatment status of any other firm (Angrist, Imbens, and Rubin 1996). As Miguel and Kremer (2004) and Duflo, Glennerster, and Kremer (2006)

---

22. This was obtained in wave 3 of the survey rather than the baseline. Thus, the measure may be affected by the treatment.

note, the presence of spillovers can cause this assumption to be violated, leading to biased estimates of the treatment effect. It is therefore important to test for spillover effects arising from our grants to firms.

We collected the GPS coordinates of each firm in our survey, taking advantage of improvements in precision and technology which allow location to be measured accurately to within 15 meters, 95% of the time (Gibson and McKenzie 2007). This allows us to construct a measure of the number of treated firms in the same industry at any given point in time within a given radius of each firm. In our baseline survey, the median firm reported that 80% of its revenue came from customers within one kilometer of the business. With this in mind, we examine the effects of treatments provided to firms in a radius of either 500 meters or 1 kilometer from each firm. After the second set of treatments, the median firm in our sample has one firm in its industry treated within 500 meters, and also one firm treated within 1 kilometer. The means are 1.6 firms within 500 meters and 2.8 firms within 1 kilometer.

We then estimate the treatment effect regression as

$$\text{profits}_{i,t} = \alpha + \beta \text{Amount}_{i,t} + \gamma N_{i,t}^d$$

$$(13) \qquad\qquad + \sum_{t=2}^{5} \delta_t + \lambda_i + \varepsilon_{i,t},$$

where $N_{i,t}^d$ is the number of treated firms in the same industry within radius d of firm i at time t. The average overall treatment effect on profits for treated firms is then $\beta + \gamma \bar{N}^d$, where $\bar{N}^d$ is the average number of treated firms in the neighborhood of distance d of a treated firm. We likewise augment the returns to capital regression in equation (2) to include this spillover effect. The estimated returns to capital will be just the coefficient β on capital, which gives the marginal impact on profits of a change in capital, controlling for any firms getting treated nearby. Importantly, the mean number of treated firms within 500 meters is identical in the sample of treated and untreated firms (1.82 for treated firms vs. 1.77 for untreated firms). Thus, each treatment negatively affects other treated and control firms in an identical manner, implying that β remains the estimated average impact of the treatment on the treated firm.

Table VI reports the results of estimating (13). Columns (1) and (3) show a negative and significant spillover effect when

TABLE VI
TESTING FOR TREATMENT SPILLOVERS (DEPENDENT VARIABLE: REAL PROFITS)

	(1) FE	(2) FE	(3) IV-FE	(4) IV-FE	(5) FE
Treatment amount	5.50***	5.51***			7.50***
	(2.09)	(2.10)			(2.82)
Capital stock			5.39**	5.41**	
(excluding land & buildings)			(2.28)	(2.28)	
Number of firms in industry treated					
Within 500 m	−1.41**		−1.23*		−2.66***
	(0.61)		(0.62)		(0.85)
Within 1 km		−0.53		−0.49	
		(0.45)		(0.45)	
Amount * female owner					−7.77*
					(3.98)
Within 500m * female owner					3.52***
					(1.17)
Constant	3,829***	3,827***	1,697***	1,619***	3,775***
	(172)	(173)	(520)	(529)	(177)
Observations	3,248	3,248	3,101	3,101	3,084
Number of enterprises	385	385	385	385	365

Notes: Data from quarterly surveys conducted by the authors reflecting nine waves of data from March 2005 through March 2007. Capital stock and profits are measured in Sri Lankan rupees, deflated by the Sri Lankan CPI to reflect March 2005 price levels. Profits are measured monthly. The number of treated firms surwaveing each individual firm is calculated from GPS coordinates and the *circnum* command in STATA. Columns (3) and (4) use a single instrument measuring the rupee value of the treatment. The coefficients show the effect of a 100-LKR increase in the capital stock. All regressions include enterprise and period (wave) fixed effects. Standard errors, clustered at the enterprise level, are shown in parentheses.
*** $p < .01$, ** $p < .05$, * $p < .1$.

estimating the treatment effect and return to capital, respectively. Each treated firm within 500 meters lowers real profits by 141 LKR, and real profits adjusted for the value of the owner's hours (calculated from the regression coefficients discussed above) by 123 LKR. However, even after controlling for the number of firms treated within the neighborhood of a firm, the estimated return to capital for a treated firm is awave 5.4% per month, very close to that estimated in Table IV. The spillover effects are insignificant when we consider a neighborhood of radius 1 kilometer awave the firm, although they are similar in size when taken at the mean.

Exploring the data further allows us to say something about the nature of the spillovers. The distribution of the number of firms within a neighborhood of a treated firm is highly skewed. When we examine this by industry, we find that the bamboo industry is an outlier. All of our 29 bamboo product firms are located in two adjacent GNs, and the median (mean) bamboo firm had 12 (10) treated bamboo firms within 500 meters by wave 5 of our survey. In contrast, all other industries have mean and median numbers of treated firms of three or fewer in wave 4. In results shown in the Online Appendix, we find that excluding the firms in the bamboo sector causes the spillover effect to shrink by half and to lose statistical significance.[23] Column (5) of Table VI shows that the gender differences remain after we control for spillovers. The other results reflecting heterogeneity of treatment impacts are also unaffected when we control for spillovers.

The significant spillovers therefore seem confined to the bamboo industry. The relevant spillovers among bamboo firms appear to be on the supply side. There are restrictions imposed by the government on the harvesting of bamboo, limiting the supply of raw materials. Treated firms apparently purchased all of the supplies available, crowding out the supplies of other firms in the same industry. The fact that spillovers lose significance when the bamboo sector is removed suggests that demand-side spillovers may be less important. However, we should keep in mind that we measure the impact of spillovers only on those enterprises included in the sample. The measure does not reflect spillovers—positive or negative—on enterprises not included in the sample. Therefore, controlling for spillovers as we have does not allow us to make any statement about the impact of the treatments on overall economic activity or income.

VII.B. Robustness to Reporting Effects

Our main outcome of interest is the profits reported by the firm. Given the self-reported nature of the profit data, we should be concerned with both general misreporting and changes in reporting behavior caused by the treatment themselves. We address both of these here. We note that the small enterprises in our sample often keep no written records and generally purchase goods for resale at shops where they receive no receipts.

Owners tell us that "firms like theirs" generally underreport both revenues and profits, most commonly over concern that the

---

23. A spillover radius of 100 meters produces results that are similar in all respects to the radius of 500 meters. Spillovers are significant for the full sample, but insignificant once the bamboo sector is excluded. The coefficient is larger, reflecting the fact that many fewer firms have a treated enterprise within 100 meters. Spillovers at any radius are not significant when measured using a broader industry category. These results are also included in the Online Appendix.

data may be reported to tax authorities. For the linear regressions, underreporting by all firms would lead to an underestimate of returns. Firms may also misreport unintentionally, because they fail to remember operating data accurately. We provided half of the firms, randomly selected, with simple account ledgers at the time we administered the second through the fifth waves of the survey. We asked firms to record revenues, expenses, and goods and cash taken from the business for household purposes on a daily or weekly basis. We find that neither assignment to the books treatment nor the interaction of this assignment and the treatment amount are significant when included in the profits regression. (See the Online Appendix for details.) We interpret this as an indication that noise from recall does not have a significant effect on the estimated treatment effect.

A second concern is that owners change their reporting of profits as a result of the treatment. Deliberate overreporting of profits in response to treatment is likely to be a concern in evaluation of business loans or business training programs, where firms who wish to receive more help from the program in the future wish to show that they are benefiting from the treatment they have received. We believe this is not driving the treatment impacts we describe for several reasons. First, the treatment was presented to the firm as a "prize" received as compensation for participating in a survey, awarded randomly. As such, owners had no reason to think future prizes would be forthcoming on the basis of how they used the prize. Second, the pattern of results suggests that if the treatment affected reporting, it did so only for some types of owners. We find large treatment effects among males, but not among females. In the tsunami-affected area, we find large significant effects among retailers, but not among manufacturers. We find large effects among those with higher ability measures, but not among those with lower ability measures. These within-sample differences in returns are more difficult to justify on the basis of reporting bias, unless we believe profits actually fall after treatment for certain groups of firms. Third, we would expect the Hawthorne-type effects to dissipate over time. Yet, on Table III we showed that there is only a small difference between the treatment impact 5–8 quarters after treatment and the impact 1–4 quarters after treatment. Moreover, we also find significant and large treatment effects that remain over time when we regress expenses or inventory levels against the treatment amount. We find no effect of the treatment on the profit-to-sales ratio, or on the reported markup of sales price over marginal cost.

Finally, if firms were deliberately overreporting, we would expect those receiving cash grants to overreport the share of the cash that they had invested in their business. However, on average, firms report they invested 58% of the cash treatment in the business and saved an additional 12%. When we estimate the effect of treatment on capital stock for the two waves immediately following treatment, the coefficient on the cash amount is 0.74, very close to the amount reported as being spent on the business or saved. The fact that owners are responding honestly to the question of how they invest the cash makes it less likely they are deliberately overreporting profits.

VII.C. Attrition

The attrition rate in the SLMS was remarkably low for a quarterly firm panel survey: 369 of the original 408 firms were still in the ninth wave of the survey. Nevertheless, not all firms report profits in every wave, and the combination of attrition, missing profit data, and trimming firms with large changes in profits reduces our sample for the main treatment effects specification (column (2), Table III) to 3,248 firm-period observations compared to the maximum possible of $408 * 9 = 3{,}672$ observations. The attrition rate is thus 11.5% firm-period observations. Comparing firms assigned to treatment and to control, the attrition rate is 14.3% for the control group and 9.6% for the group assigned to treatment.

To examine the robustness of our results to this differential attrition, we use the bounding approach of Lee (2005) to construct upper and lower bounds for the treatment effect. The key identifying assumption required for implementing the Lee (2005) bounds is a monotonicity assumption that treatment assignment affects sample selection only in one direction. In our context, this requires assuming that there are some firms who would have attrited if they had not been assigned to treatment, but that no firm attrits as a result of being assigned to treatment. This seems plausible in our context.

To construct the Lee (2005) bounds we trim the distribution of profits for the group assigned to treatment by the difference in attrition rates between the two groups as a proportion of the retention rate of the group assigned to treatment. In our application, this requires trimming the upper or lower 5.2% of the real profits distribution for the group assigned to treatment. Doing this then gives a lower bound for the treatment effect of 404 LKR and an upper bound of 754 LKR, compared to the treatment effect of 541 in column (2), Table III. Similarly, the bounds for the return to capital of 5.3% estimated in column (4), Table IV, are 2.6% and 6.7%. The lower bounds occur only if it is the most profitable control firms that attrit. However, a panel regression predicting attrition as a function of the previous period's profit finds no significant effect of having high profits on attrition, and that having the previous period's profit in the bottom 10% lowers the probability of staying in the sample by five percentage points ($p = .054$). Attrition of the least profitable firms from the control sample would lead us to understate the returns, making the upper bounds more relevant. Thus our estimated treatment effects and return to capital appear robust to attrition.

VIII. EXPERIMENTAL VS. NONEXPERIMENTAL RETURNS

We believe this project and a related one undertaken by two of the authors in Mexico (McKenzie and Woodruff forthcoming, 2008) provide the first experimental evidence on the returns to capital in small-scale enterprises. Estimates of rates of return currently in the literature come from cross-sectional or quasi-experimental data. The random capital shocks generated by our grants generate exogenous shocks to capital stock. The assumptions required to obtain unbiased estimates of returns to capital are much less stringent than is typically the case in cross-sectional or panel data. The experiment also allows us to say something about the nature of bias in cross-sectional estimates of returns to capital (McKenzie and Woodruff 2006; Udry and Anagol 2006). Estimating the direction and magnitude of the bias in cross-sectional data is important because nonexperimental estimates are less expensive to generate, and hence are more prevalent.

The direction of bias in returns estimated from cross-sectional bias is theoretically ambiguous. Most commonly, bias is thought to be related to the inability to fully measure the ability of the enterprise owner. The unmeasured component of ability may be complementary to capital—that is, unmeasured ability and capital stock may be positively correlated. Alternatively, if only the most able entrepreneurs are able to survive when operating at very low levels of capital stock (as, for example, Lloyd-Ellis and Bernhardt [2000]), then unmeasured ability and capital stock may

TABLE VII

COMPARING EXPERIMENTAL TO NONEXPERIMENTAL ESTIMATES (DEPENDENT
VARIABLE: REAL PROFITS ADJUSTED FOR VALUE OF OWNER'S HOURS WORKED)

	Nonexperimental results			Experimental results
	(1) OLS	(2) Random effects	(3) Firm FE	(4) Firm FE
Invested capital	2.58***	1.71*	0.07	5.29**
(excluding land	(0.70)	(1.02)	(1.07)	(2.28)
and buildings)				
Age of owner	−45.7***	−38.3*		
	(15.5)	(20.3)		
Education of owner	−215.3***	−105.8		
	(59.7)	(72.9)		
Owner is female	−1,359***	−2,430***		
	(339)	(491)		
Constant	6,485***	5,800***	2,299***	1,487***
	(985)	(1,163)	(300)	(498)
Observations	349	698	698	3,101
Number of enterprises	349	151	151	384

Notes: The sample for the regression in column (1) includes all firms but uses only the baseline (pretreatment) data. The second and third columns use only untreated firms and the first five waves of data. The final column repeats the regression shown in Table IV, column (4). The coefficients show the effect of a 100-LKR increase in the capital stock. The second through fourth regressions include period (wave) fixed effects, and the third and fourth include period and enterprise fixed effects. Standard errors, clustered at the enterprise level, are shown in parentheses.
*** $p < .01$, ** $p < .05$, * $p < .1$.

be negatively correlated. Finally, as we have discussed, microenterprise data are also inherently noisy. If capital stock is subject to significant measurement error, then cross-sectional estimates of return may be reduced by attenuation bias.[24]

Table VII estimates returns using the baseline (pretreatment) data and OLS regressions, and using the panel of untreated firms with random- and fixed-effects regressions. We present a basic specification, but we find that the coefficient on capital stock is not much affected by inclusion of other variables. We also use a linear production function and trim the sample for the top 0.5% of changes in profits. The dependent variable is real profits adjusted for the value of the owner's labor using the regression coefficients, as described above. The pattern of results is not affected by any of these decisions, with the exception that using logs results in a

---

24. See Card (2001) for related discussion of the bias in returns to education from unobserved ability and measurement error.

different ordering in the nonexperimental returns. The OLS regression on the baseline (pretreatment) sample implies a profit rate of 2.6% (profit increases by between 2.58 LKR per month for each additional 100 LKR invested). The estimated profit is only 1.7% when we use random effects on the first five waves of the panel of untreated firms,[25] and very nearly zero when we run enterprise-level fixed effects on the untreated panel. These compare to experimental returns of 5.3% per month, meaning that the experimental returns are at least twice any of the nonexperimental estimates. Estimated in logs using real profits, the results are qualitatively similar, though somewhat less extreme. The OLS, RE, and enterprise FE coefficients on log capital stock are 0.22, 0.26, and 0.12, respectively. The coefficient from the experiment (Table IV, column (2)) is 0.38, again, at least half as large. These results are included in the Online Appendix.

The nonexperimental estimates may differ from the experimental estimates because of unobserved ability or measurement error biasing the nonexperimental estimates. Alternatively, the experiment may produce a weighted average treatment effect that differs from the treatment effect being estimated nonexperimentally. We have shown that the response of capital stock to the treatment does not vary with owner characteristics thought to influence the marginal return to capital, suggesting we are indeed capturing the average treatment effect. The difference between estimates is of similar magnitude when we add controls for several measures of ability—years of schooling, Digit Span Recall, and the time to solve a maze—leading us to believe that attenuation bias due to measurement error is the most plausible explanation for the lower returns generated from the nonexperimental regressions.[26] Compared with the measure of capital stock in the cross section, our capital shocks are very precisely measured.

As a check on the generalizability of the finding of higher returns with the experimentally generated data, we ran a smaller version of the project in Mexico. These data are described in McKenzie and Woodruff (forthcoming, 2008). We find the same pattern: experimental returns are awave twice the level of

---

25. We limit the sample to the first five waves because of the 2,500-LKR payment made to the untreated firms after wave 5. The results are nearly identical if we use all nine waves.

26. The very low nonexperimental estimates using fixed effects also suggest measurement error is causing attenuation bias.

returns estimated parametrically or semi-parametrically with cross-sectional data. This suggests that the increasing number of studies using cross-sectional data are likely to represent a lower bound on the return to capital, at least at low levels of capital stock. Given the wide range of countries and settings from which these estimates come, our experimental results provide important support for the generalizability of findings in the literature.

IX. Conclusions

We find that random cash or in-kind grants increase profits of microenterprises by over 5% per month, or at least 60% per year. These treatment impacts appear to be flat or decreasing—we do not find evidence of increasing returns over our sample range. Marginal returns are highest for entrepreneurs with more ability and with fewer other workers in the household. In contrast, returns do not differ with risk aversion of the entrepreneur, or with the perceived uncertainty about future profits. We also find that impacts are higher in male-owned enterprises. Indeed, we find that the average impact of the treatment among female-owned enterprises is not different from zero. We also find evidence of negative spillovers on firms in the neighborhood of the treated firms. The impacts at the firm level are unchanged when we control for an account for these spillovers. But an inability to measure any spillovers affecting enterprises not included in our sample makes assessment of the economywide impact of the treatments impossible.

The variance in the impact of the treatments appears to be very large. About half of the female owners have characteristics suggesting negative returns, and almost 60% have returns lower than market interest rates of 12%–18% per year. Even among male-owned enterprises, where the average return is very high, just over 20% of the enterprises have predicted returns that are lower than market interest rates. The high variance in returns may explain why so few of the enterprises in our sample borrow from formal lenders. The strong negative correlation between treatment impact and measures of household liquidity, and the strong positive correlation between treatment impact and ability suggest that these measures may be useful screening devices to identify microenterprises where investments are likely to be most profitable.

1370   *QUARTERLY JOURNAL OF ECONOMICS*

The grants are associated with both an increase in capital stock and an increase in the hours the owner works in the enterprise. Arguably, this total treatment impact is of most interest to lenders, who are concerned that the additional resources generate enough profit to repay loans. But the returns to the additional capital, isolated from other impact channels, is also of interest to discussions in the economics literature. With some additional assumptions, we are able to use the random treatments to estimate marginal returns to capital in the enterprises. Using different estimates of the marginal productivity of the owner's additional work effort, we find returns of 4.6%–5.3% per month, 55%–63% per year. These high returns at very low levels of capital stock imply that nonconvex production sets are unlikely to lead to permanent poverty traps. One caveat to this optimistic conclusion is that our sample includes only individuals who ran an enterprise at the time of the baseline sample. Entry may be prevented not by a requirement to invest a large amount of capital, but by the possibility of an initial period of very low profitability. Our data do not allow us to examine this possibility.

Although the variance in returns may limit the willingness of banks to lend to these firms, we still view the high level of returns as something of a puzzle. The majority of the treatments were invested in working capital. If returns to these investments are so high, what prevents firms from growing incrementally by reinvesting profits? Is it a lack of savings institutions—or a lack of knowledge about how the savings institutions operate—recurrent shocks to households, or time-inconsistent preferences? Because working capital investments are unlikely to involve indivisibilities, a lack of savings institutions by itself is unlikely to provide a full answer to this puzzle. What the results point to is the need for a better understanding of how these microentrepreneurs make investment decisions. We see this as a fertile area for future research.

UNIVERSITY OF PERADENIYA
WORLD BANK
UNIVERSITY OF CALIFORNIA, SAN DIEGO

REFERENCES

Abadie, Alberto, Joshua Angrist, and Guido Imbens, "Instrumental Variables Estimates of the Effect of Subsidized Training on the Quantiles of Trainee Earnings," *Econometrica*, 70 (2002), 91–117.

RETURNS TO CAPITAL IN MICROENTERPRISES   1371

Aghion, Philippe, and Patrick Bolton, "A Theory of Trickle-Down Growth and Development," *Review of Economic Studies*, 64 (1997), 151–172.

Angrist, Joshua, Guido Imbens, and Donald Rubin, "Identification of Causal Effects Using Instrumental Variables," *Journal of the American Statistical Association*, 91 (1996), 444–455.

Armendáriz de Aghion, Beatriz, and Jonathan Morduch, *The Economics of Microfinance* (Cambridge, MA: MIT Press, 2005).

Banerjee, Abhijit, and Esther Duflo, "Do Firms Want to Borrow More? Testing Credit Constraints Using a Directed Lending Program," Working Paper, MIT, 2004.

——,"Growth Theory through the Lens of Development Economics," in *Handbook of Economic Growth*, Philippe Aghion and Steven Durlauf, eds. (Amsterdam: Elsevier Press, 2005).

Banerjee, Abhijit V., and Andrew F. Newman, "Occupational Choice and the Process of Development," *Journal of Political Economy*, 101 (1993), 274–298.

Bardhan, Pranab, and Christopher Udry, *Development Microeconomics* (Oxford, UK: Oxford University Press, 1999).

Burjorjee, Deena M., Rani Deshpande, and C. Jean Weidemann, "Supporting Women's Livelihoods: Microfinance that Works for the Majority—A Guide to Best Practices," United Nations Capital Development Fund, Special Unit for Microfinance, 2002. Available at http://www.uncdf.org/english/microfinance/pubs/thematic_papers/gender/supporting/part_1.php.

Card, David, "Estimating the Return to Schooling: Progress on Some Persistent Econometric Problems," *Econometrica*, 69 (2001), 1127–1160.

de Mel, Suresh, David McKenzie, and Christopher Woodruff, "Who Does Microfinance Fail to Reach? Experimental Evidence on Gender and Microenterprise Returns," BREAD Working Paper No. 157, 2007.

——, "Measuring Microenterprise Profits: Must We Ask How the Sausage is Made?" *Journal of Development Economics*, forthcoming, 2008a.

——, "Enterprise Recovery following Natural Disasters," Working Paper, UCSD, 2008b.

Duflo, Esther, Rachel Glennerster, and Michael Kremer, "Using Randomization in Development Economics: A Toolkit," BREAD Working Paper No. 136, 2006.

FINCA, "Frequently Asked Questions," 2007, Available at http://www.villagebanking.org/site/c.erKPI2PCIoE/b.2394157/k.8161/Frequently_Asked_Questions.htm [accessed August 15, 2007].

Gibson, John, and David McKenzie, "Using the Global Positioning System (GPS) in Household Surveys for Better Economics and Better Policy," *World Bank Research Observer*, 22 (2007), 217–241.

Gine, Xavier, and Dean Karlan, "Group vs. Individual Liability: A Field Experiment in the Philippines," Working Paper, Yale University, 2007.

Khandker, Shahidur R. "Using Microcredit to Advance Women," World Bank Premnote (November) No. 8, 1998. Available at http://www1.worldbank.org/prem/PREMNotes/premnote8.pdf [accessed August 15, 2007].

Karlan, Dean, "Microfinance Impact Assessments: The Perils of Using New Members as a Control Group," *Journal of Microfinance*, 3 (2001), 76–85.

Kling, Jeffrey R., Jeffrey B. Liebman, and Lawrence F. Katz, "Experimental Analysis of Neighborhood Effects," *Econometrica*, 75 (2007), 83–119.

Koenker, Roger, "Quantile Regression for Longitudinal Data," *Journal of Multivariate Analysis*, 91 (2004), 74–89

Lee, David, "Training, Wages, and Sample Selection: Estimating Sharp Bounds on Treatment Effects," NBER Working Paper No. 11721, 2005.

Lloyd-Ellis, Huw, and Dan Bernhardt, "Enterprise, Inequality and Economic Development," *Review of Economic Studies*, 67 (2000), 147–168.

McKenzie, David, and Christopher Woodruff, "Do Entry Costs Provide an Empirical Basis for Poverty Traps? Evidence from Mexican Microenterprises," *Economic Development and Cultural Change*, 55 (2006), 3–42.

——, "Experimental Evidence on Returns to Capital and Access to Finance in Mexico," *World Bank Economic Review* (forthcoming, 2008).

Miguel, Edward, and Michael Kremer, "Worms: Identifying Impacts on Education and Health in the Presence of Treatment Externalities," *Econometrica*, 72 (2004), 159–217.

Morduch, Jonathan, "The Microfinance Promise," *Journal of Economic Literature*, 37 (1999), 1569–1614.

SEAGA (Socio-economic and Gender Analysis Programme), "A Guide to Gender Sensitive Microfinance," FAO, 2002. Available at http://www.fao.org/sd/seaga/downloads/En/Microfinanceen.pdf [accessed August 15, 2007].

Schündeln, Matthias, "Appreciating Depreciation: A Note on Physical Capital Depreciation in a Developing Country," Working Paper, Harvard University, 2007.

Udry, Christopher, and Santosh Anagol, "The Return to Capital in Ghana," *American Economic Review*, 96 (2006), 388–393.

[10]

THE IMPACT OF MICROCREDIT PROGRAMS ON SELF-EMPLOYMENT PROFITS: DO NONCREDIT PROGRAM ASPECTS MATTER?

Signe-Mary McKernan*

Abstract—Microcredit programs provide a two-tiered approach to poverty alleviation: credit for the purchase of capital inputs in order to promote self-employment and noncredit services and incentives. These noncredit aspects may be an important component of the success of microcredit programs. However, because they are costly to deliver and their contribution to the success of the programs is difficult to measure, they may not be properly valued. —This paper uses primary data on household participants and nonparticipants in Grameen Bank and two similar microcredit programs to measure the total and noncredit effects of microcredit program participation on productivity. The total effect is measured by estimating a profit equation and the noncredit effect by estimating the profit equation conditional on productive capital. Productive capital and program participation are treated as endogenous variables in the analysis. I find large positive effects of participation and the noncredit aspects of participation on self-employment profits.

I. Introduction

Microcredit programs, most notably the Grameen Bank of Bangladesh, have recently been in the spotlight as a means of poverty alleviation. The Grameen Bank was founded in 1976 by Muhammad Yunus, an economics professor, with the idea that lack of capital was the primary obstacle to productive self-employment among the poor. Today, the Grameen Bank has more than two million members, better than 90% loan recovery rates, and has been replicated in more than forty developing and developed countries (including the United States) worldwide.

Microcredit programs, such as the Grameen Bank, provide a two-tiered approach to poverty alleviation. They provide credit to the poor for the purchase of capital inputs in order to promote productive self-employment. They also provide noncredit services (often referred to as social development programs) such vocational training, information in areas of health, civil responsibilities and rights, and information sharing and monitoring among members. These noncredit services, which serve to differentiate group-lending programs from banks or individual-lending institutions, may be an important component of the success of microcredit programs and thus a critical element to maintain when expanding and replicating programs. As Rahman (1993) warns in his article "The General Replicability of the Grameen Bank Model," "one should never compromise with the social development program which [. . .] appears to

be the glue that cements the very base of the program" (p. 218). However, because these noncredit services can be costly to deliver[1] and their contribution to the success of the programs difficult to measure, they may not be properly valued.

The substantial resources, more than $200 million, being invested in expanding and replicating microcredit programs are testimony to their perceived potential for worldwide poverty alleviation. As such, it is crucial to know the answer to two key questions. First, do microcredit programs increase self-employment productivity? And second, do the noncredit aspects of microcredit programs have a positive effect on self-employment productivity above and beyond the provision of credit? This paper investigates these two questions. It presents measures of the total and noncredit effects of microcredit programs on productivity. The total effect is measured by estimating a profit equation and the noncredit effect by estimating the profit equation conditional on productive capital. Because credit from microcredit programs is used to purchase capital, estimating the effect of program participation while controlling for the level of productive capital provides an estimate of the programs' noncredit effect. In doing so, this paper provides the first measure of the noncredit effects of microcredit programs and the first known study of the impact of microcredit programs on self-employment productivity.

The paper is divided into six major sections. The remainder of this section provides background information on the functions of microcredit programs. Section II presents a theoretical model that highlights the issues involved in determining self-employment profits and provides empirical implications for the effect of microcredit programs on self-employment profits. Section III outlines the estimation strategies used to measure the total and noncredit effects of participation in each of three microcredit programs in Bangladesh: Grameen Bank (GB), Bangladesh Rural Advancement Committee (BRAC), and Bangladesh Rural Development Board's (BRDB) Rural Development RD-12 program. Section IV describes the household survey data from Bangladesh. Section V presents the results, and section VI concludes.

Received for publication September 21, 1998. Revision accepted for publication September 1, 2000.

* The Urban Institute

I gratefully acknowledge financial support from a Watson Institute Dissertation Fellowship, a National Institute of Child Health and Human Development (NICHD) Demography Traineeship, and a Mellon Foundation travel grant. I thank Mark M. Pitt, Rachel M. Friedberg, Robert A. Moffitt, Deon Filmer, Shahidur Khandker, Martin Ravallion, and a referee for valuable comments, and the staffs of Grameen Bank and BRAC in Bangladesh for their help and hospitality. All remaining errors are my own. The views expressed are those of the author and should not be attributed to the Urban Institute.

A. The Role of Microcredit Programs

Traditionally, the poor have had little access to credit. The high transaction costs associated with small loans and a lack of collateral make the poor an unattractive group for formal banks. Money lenders may step in to fill the credit void, but,

[1] Training accounted for 29% of Grameen Bank total administrative and personnel costs in 1989 (Yaron (1994, p. 63)).

at the high interest rates charged (up to 150% a year (Varian, 1990)), the poor are neither able to obtain the resources necessary to substantially increase productivity nor reap the benefits of any additional income generated. Hoff and Stiglitz (1990) explain that the collateral and high interest rates that serve to deny the poor affordable credit are most likely the market's response to the costly problems of screening, monitoring, and enforcement.[2]

Group-based microcredit programs, such as the Grameen Bank, provide an innovative and promising mechanism for delivering credit to the poor. These programs design incentive schemes that induce group members to undertake the burden of screening, monitoring, and enforcement that would otherwise fall on the lender (Hoff & Stiglitz, 1990; Ghatak & Guinnane, 1999). Interested members form self-selected small groups of approximately five people. Although loans are given to individual group members, the whole group becomes ineligible for further loans or is financially liable if any member of their group defaults. This system of joint liability induces group members to screen and monitor one another to ensure that loans are repaid. Group-based programs thus use joint liability to exploit the local knowledge of group members. By replacing collateral with joint liability and working with groups rather than individuals to lower transactions costs, these programs have made formal credit available to the poorest of the poor.

The Grameen Bank and other microcredit programs do not provide credit alone; they bundle noncredit services along with credit. These noncredit services provide program members with vocational training, organizational help, and social development inputs aimed at improving health, literacy, leadership skills, and social empowerment. In BRAC,[3] BRDB,[4] and GB,[5] the noncredit programs are primarily composed of social development and specialized skill training workshops, and a set of pledges (the Seventeen Promises in BRAC, the Sixteen Decisions in Grameen Bank, and the Bittaheen Cooperative Members' Oaths in BRDB) that serve as a social constitution for the programs. The social development workshops and pledges are used to disseminate practical information to tackle some of the health and social problems associated with poverty. They emphasize issues such as the importance of educating children, not giving or receiving dowry, working hard, planting trees and vegetable gardens, drinking tubewell or boiled water, and storing savings in the bank rather than at home. The spe-

cialized skill training workshops provide technical instruction (such as how to produce silk or maintain rice husking machinery) and an opportunity for members to share their expertise with each other.

Group-based credit programs, which have been so successful in developing countries, may also be a viable strategy for poverty alleviation in developed countries. Organizations replicating or planning to replicate the Grameen Bank model can be found in the United States, France, Italy, and Canada (Rahman, 1993).[6] In the inner cities and poorer rural areas of the United States, group-based lending programs offer a creative way to deliver credit to the "microentrepreneurs," those who have businesses with virtually no access to bank credit and that are too small to qualify for Small Business Administration loan guarantees. Mary Houghton, president of Shorebank Corporation and one of the founders of Women's Self-Employment Project of Chicago — an urban adaptation of the Grameen Bank model, felt that, in inner cities, the Grameen Bank approach "reduced the transaction cost of lending by providing loans in a group setting to several borrowers at once; peer pressure could substitute for collateral; and peer groups could provide encouragement, emotional support, indigenous informal technical assistance, and a mechanism for screening out unpromising business ideas" (Balkin, 1993, p. 237). The Good Faith Fund of Arkansas is another example of a Grameen Bank replication in the United States; its stated objectives are to enhance "the 'income, assets, employment and self-esteem of significant numbers of the poorest economically active' entrepreneurs or potential entrepreneurs" (Mondal & Tune, 1993, p. 223).

II. Theory

In this section of the paper, I present a simple theoretical model designed to derive the determinants of profits and describe the mechanisms by which microcredit programs may affect profits. To derive the determinants of self-employment profits when markets are absent or imperfect, as in Bangladesh, consider the restricted profit function when production decisions are separable and nonseparable from household utility considerations.[7] Subsection IIA models the profit function under separability, subsection IIB describes the absent or imperfect markets in rural Bang-

---

[2] The screening or adverse selection problem: "borrowers differ in the likelihood that they will default, and it is costly to determine the extent of that risk to each borrower." The monitoring or moral hazard problem: "it is costly to ensure that borrowers take those actions which make repayment most likely." The enforcement problem: "it is difficult to compel repayment."

[3] For a description of the BRAC credit and social development program, see Lovell (1992) and Khandker and Khalily (1996).

[4] For a description of BRDB's program, see Khandker, Khan, and Khalily (1995).

[5] For a description of Grameen Bank's program, see Hossain (1988), Fuglesang and Chandler (1993), and Khandker, Khalily, and Khan (1993).

[6] Examples of organizations in developed countries replicating the Grameen Bank include Micro-Business International (Washington), The Good Faith Fund (Arkansas), Lakota Friend (South Dakota), Katalysis, and Micro-Enterprise Capital Corporation (Washington), Cherokee Community Loan Fund and Trickleup Program (New York), ADIE Credit Project for Self-Employment (France), Micro Credit Rainbow (Italy), The First People's Fund, Calmedow Foundation (Canada).

[7] The term *restricted profit function* is used here to refer to production behavior under circumstances in which some inputs are variable and other inputs are fixed over the period of production. Samuelson (1953–1954) is an early pioneer of the concept of restricted profit functions. For a characterization of the restricted profit function, see Lau (1976) and, for the methodological framework, Lau and Yotopoulos (1979) and Lau, Lin, and Yotopoulos (1979).

ladesh that violate assumptions needed for separability, and subsection IIC models the profit function under nonseparability. Subsection IID then models the household's decision to undertake a self-employment enterprise, subsection IIE describes the mechanisms by which microcredit programs may affect profits, and subsection IIF presents empirical implications based on the theory.

A. Restricted Profit Function Under Separability

Households consisting of two working-age adults, a female and a male, produce a good Y for market sale. Production of output Y is given by the production function

$$Y = \Gamma(L_{fY}, L_{mY}, A; K, H, N, \epsilon), \tag{1}$$

where hired or household female and male labor, L_{fY} and L_{mY}, and a vector of inputs, A, are variable inputs in the production of Y; capital assets K, human capital H, and quantity of land N are fixed inputs in the production of Y;[8] and ϵ is the realization of a mean zero stochastic shock to production (such as weather). H represents the stock of entrepreneurial and cognitive ability in the household.[9] H may directly affect productivity or may affect the productivity of other inputs to Y $\left(\text{for example, } \frac{\partial^2 Y}{\partial KH} > 0\right)$. However, due to the manual nature of rural wage labor market opportunities, there is no return to H in the wage labor market.[10]

Profit, π, is defined as

$$\pi = p_Y Y - w_f L_{fY} - w_m L_{mY} - p_A A \tag{2}$$

where p_Y, w_f, w_m, and p_A are prices of the output and variable inputs to production.

Given the assumptions of profit-maximizing and price-taking behavior on the part of the households, the local strong concavity of the production function in the variable inputs, and the short-run fixity of the quantities of the fixed inputs, the household's decision variables are the quantity of output and the quantities of the variable inputs. The restricted profit function defined as the maximized value of profit given the production technology, the prices of the variable commodities, and the quantity of the fixed commodities is given by

$$\pi = \pi(p_Y, w_f, w_m, p_A, K, H, N, \epsilon) \tag{3}$$

where all variable are as defined previously.

The restricted profit function given by equation (3) is a function only of the exogenous prices of the output and variable inputs and the fixed factors. It does not contain other household characteristics or the prices of consumption goods because, by assuming separability, household production decisions can be made independently of consumption and labor supply (or leisure) decisions. However, if household labor and hired labor are imperfect substitutes or if the household is not a price-taker in any of the markets for the inputs or output, then production decisions are no longer separable from household utility considerations and the restricted profit function given in equation (3) is inappropriate.[11]

B. Absent or Imperfect Markets in Rural Bangladesh

The rural credit market literature exhaustively describes imperfections in these markets. Bell (1988) describes the incomplete or imperfect market structures that result in information and enforcement problems: creditors cannot be sure that debtors will settle their accounts when they are due. These problems generate considerations that involve important departures from the standard competitive framework in which agents might as well be anonymous because prices then convey all relevant information costlessly to buyers and sellers alike.

Besley (1994) explains that—although collateral security, underdevelopment in complementary institutions, and covariant risks characterize all credit markets to some extent—these problems are particularly acute in rural credit markets. Collateral, which may serve as a solution to the enforcement problem, is hard to come by in rural areas in which poor households lack assets that could be collateralized. Also, the property rights necessary to appropriate collateral may be poorly developed. Rural areas also lack the literate and numerate populations and well-developed information systems that often are taken for granted in wealthier urban areas. Finally, covariant risks among farmers and segmented markets mean that a lender's portfolio of loans is concentrated on a group of individuals facing common shocks to their incomes in one particular geographic area. As a result of these rural credit market problems and the high transaction costs associated with the small loans required by the poor, poor households in rural areas do not have access to formal credit.

Labor markets are also imperfect in rural Bangladesh. Very few women in rural Bangladesh work in the wage

---

[8] Capital assets K will be treated as statistically endogenous in the empirical section of the paper.

[9] For simplicity, I do not differentiate H by sex; doing so will not change the results of the model. Some attributes of H, such as entrepreneurial ability, are unmeasured in the data. Econometric methods used to control for such unobserved heterogeneity are described in the estimation section.

[10] The assumption that there are returns to human capital in self-employment that involve managing a business, but not to wage labor in rural areas is consistent with empirical findings for rural labor markets. For example, using microdata from rural India, Rosenzweig (1980) finds evidence consistent with the hypothesis that schooling enhances agricultural production efficiency, but no correlation between human capital characteristics and the wage received.

[11] For a summary of the theoretical and empirical issues involved in estimating agricultural household models, see Singh, Squire, and Strauss (1986). For empirical tests of household labor supply in the context of rural labor markets, see Rosenzweig (1980), and, for empirical tests of the separability of household labor supply and production decisions, see Pitt and Rosenzweig (1986) and Benjamin (1992).

labor market. The interpretation of the Muslim practice of purdah in rural Bangladesh dictates that women should not be seen by men outside the family (Fuglesang & Chandler, 1993). As a result, women do work that can be done within the bounds of the homestead. With an absent market for female labor, female labor supplied to the production of the self-employment activity, L_{fY}, is restricted to household labor. Thus, production decisions cannot be made independently of labor supply decisions, and the shadow or virtual wage w_f^*, which is endogenous to the household, will be a determinant of profit.

C. Profits Under Nonseparability

To illustrate how the determinants of household utility become determinants of the household profit function in the presence of absent or imperfect markets, consider the households' maximization problem when there is no female wage labor market.

For any production cycle, a well-behaved (quasi-concave with positive partial derivatives) household utility function is assumed to exist. Let this function be given by

$$U = U(X, l_f, l_m),$$ (4)

where X is a market purchased good, and l_f and l_m denote leisure or household time of the female and the male.

The time constraints of the female and male are given by

$$L_f = L_{fY} + l_f$$ (5)
$$L_m = L_{mY} + L_{mw} + l_m.$$

The female's time is allocated to the production of Y, L_{fY}, and to leisure, l_f.[12] The male's time is spent in the production of Y, L_{mY}, wage labor, L_{mw}, and in leisure, l_m.

The household's budget constraint given in equation (6) sets expenditures equal to full income:

$$p_X X + l_m w_m = \pi + L_m w_m.$$ (6)

Households maximize utility subject to the time constraint, the budget constraint, and the production technology given in equation (1). The solution to the households' maximization problem will be characterized by these three constraints and by an additional condition: equality of household demand and household supply (Strauss, 1986) for female labor. This additional constraint can be seen in the first-order condition (assuming interior solutions):[13]

$$\frac{\partial U}{\partial L_{fY}} = -\lambda \left(p_Y \frac{\partial Y}{\partial L_{fY}} \right),$$

[12] Distinguishing between leisure and other types of household time such as child rearing or the production of household goods could be added to the model but would not clarify the basic point to be made.
[13] I later allow for a corner solution: the activity not to operate.

where λ is the marginal utility of income. Rather than equating the supply of female labor and the demand for female labor to the exogenous female wage, the household directly equates the supply and demand for labor. As a result, the shadow wage, w_f^*, which implicitly induces the household to equate supply and demand, is a function of all market prices (both consumption and production), the time endowments, and fixed inputs:[14]

$$w_f^* = w_f^*(p_X, p_Y, w_m, p_A, L_f, L_m, K, H, N).$$ (7)

Substituting w_f^* for w_f in the profit function under separability given by equation (3) we arrive at the determinants of the profit function when there is no female labor market and household consumption and production decisions are nonseparable:

$$\pi^n = \pi^n(p_X, p_Y, w_m, p_A, L_f, L_m, K, H, N, \epsilon).$$ (8)

Profits are now a function of the exogenous prices of the output and variable inputs, the quantity of the fixed factors, and all exogenous prices in the household's utility function. Unlike a profit function under separability, there is no one-to-one correspondence between the profit function and the production function. The marginal effects of productive inputs on profits are unsigned because they now represent optimal levels given technology and preferences.

D. The Decision to Undertake a SE Enterprise

With the determinants of household profits in hand, I turn to the household's decision to undertake a self-employment (SE) activity. For simplicity, the model described abstracts from dynamic considerations of the household. However, it is clear that, at some point in time prior to the optimization over the variable inputs above, households decide whether to undertake a self-employment enterprise and choose the levels of capital to be used in the enterprise.[15]

At any point in time, we observe profits only for a select group of households that have chosen to undertake an enterprise. In the prior period, before capital and human capital levels are set and before ϵ and prices are realized and profits and household utility are known with certainty, households make the decision of whether or not to undertake an SE enterprise. In this initial period, households calculate expected profits conditional on optimally choosing inputs (which now include capital) given their fixed quantity of land. Households then compare indirect utility of expected profits from undertaking the activity, V_1, defined by

$$V_1 = V_1(p_X, p_Y, w_m, p_A, p_K, L, H, N),$$ (9)

[14] The shadow wage will also be a function of fixed household characteristics if they are introduced into the model.
[15] The level of capital is thus endogenous to the household. As previously mentioned, this endogeneity is accounted for in the estimation section.

with indirect expected utility when not undertaking the activity, where V_0 equals

$$V_0 = V_0(p_X, w_m), \tag{10}$$

where p_K is the price of capital, and all other variables are as defined previously. If V_1 is greater than V_0, households undertake the SE enterprise.

E. The Effect of Microcredit on SE Profits

Microcredit programs may affect profits by increasing access to capital and by increasing the stock of human capital.

The Effect of Microcredit on Profits via Physical Capital:
As described previously, rural credit market imperfections, high transaction costs associated with the small loans required by the poor, and a lack of collateral serve to exclude the poor from formal banks. With little or no access to credit[16] and with minimal savings,[17] production may never be undertaken or may be held at suboptimal levels. By targeting the poor, working with groups rather than individuals, and substituting joint liability for collateral, microcredit programs are able to overcome some of the market imperfections and provide formal credit to the poor at an affordable interest rate of 15% to 20% per year. Thus, microcredit programs may affect profits by providing additional capital assets, thereby raising the level of capital and enabling households to initiate or expand an SE enterprise.

To see the possible effects of a microcredit program, consider the village credit market and self-employment decisions before and after a microcredit program intervention. Prior to the program intervention, assume households are in equilibrium with respect to their self-employment decisions. Given credit market and other constraints, some households operate self-employment activities and others do not. Then a microcredit program comes to the village and relaxes the credit market constraint. The intervention lowers the price of credit and increases the amount of capital available to households. Given the lower cost of credit, some households that were not previously operating a self-employment enterprise now find it optimal to do so. Other households that were operating an enterprise find it optimal to expand the enterprise.

Microcredit programs should have an especially large effect on productivity where labor markets are absent, as in rural Bangladesh. Capital inputs may be needed to use labor productivity at home. Thus, by eliminating credit market failures and providing capital, microcredit programs may have the additional effect of making labor more productive.

---

[16] The poor can borrow from local money lenders, but the interest rate charged may be up to 150% per year.
[17] Gersovitz (1983) shows that, at low levels of income and consumption, reducing consumption to accumulate assets may not be optimal because it may seriously threaten health, production efficiency, and life expectancy.

The Effect of Microcredit on Profits via Human Capital:
Microcredit programs may increase the stock of human capital directly through their social development programs, or indirectly through incentive schemes used to encourage peer monitoring. Because their ultimate objective is poverty alleviation, not banking, microcredit programs typically bundle social development programs with the provision of credit. These social development programs provide human capital in areas such as literacy, bank rules, investment strategies, health, civil responsibilities, the empowerment of women, and vocational training.

Group-based microcredit programs such as BRAC, BRDB, and Grameen Bank encourage group members to help one another. For instance, as part of Grameen Bank's social development program, all members are required to memorize, chant, and follow the Sixteen Decisions, one of which states "We shall always be ready to help each other. If anyone is in difficulty, we shall all help him" (Fuglesang & Chandler, 1993). In all three programs, individuals are encouraged to turn to their group members when in need of advice or help rather than seeking help from bank staff.

Beyond encouragement, group-based microcredit programs also provide incentives for members to share human capital. Group-lending programs use incentive schemes that induce group members to monitor one another. Examples of such incentive schemes include loss of access to future credit for all group members if any member defaults (Grameen Bank) and group liability for loans if any member defaults (BRAC). Because the optimal incentive scheme to encourage peer monitoring typically involves making the payments to one agent (group member) depend on the outputs of other agents (Varian, 1990; Holmstrom, 1979), group-lending programs also create incentives for group members to share information, provide advice, and help each other. Varian (1990) provides a model that illustrates that two-period incentive schemes may affect the principal's profits by providing incentives for high-productivity agents to share information with low-productivity agents, thereby increasing the number of agents with high productivity.

By increasing the stock of human capital, microcredit programs may directly affect profits by providing additional inputs to produce the self-employment output or indirectly by increasing the productivity of other inputs. Households with high levels of human capital may be more likely to undertake a self-employment activity because there are returns to human capital only if households are engaged in a self-employment enterprise.

F. Empirical Implications of the Theory

The theory presented has several interesting empirical implications. If microcredit programs increase access to physical and human capital, they will enable households to undertake or expand self-employment enterprises. If these programs are bundling social development and training with credit and if they induce members to share information as in

Varian's incentive scheme, we should see an increase in profits above and beyond the effect of capital on profits. These empirical implications can be summarized in three hypotheses regarding the effect of microcredit programs of self-employment profits:

- Microcredit programs enable households to undertake self-employment activities.
- Microcredit programs increase the level of self-employment profits for households already engaged in a self-employment activity.
- Bundling training with credit increases self-employment profits.

Testing these three hypotheses requires an estimation strategy that enables me to evaluate the effects of participation in microcredit programs on profit. Section III outlines the issues involved in evaluating programs such as microcredit programs and develops an estimation strategy that enables me to test the hypotheses.

III. Estimation

A. Program Evaluation Issues

Choice-based sampling, self-selection into programs, and nonrandom program placement can contribute to biased estimates of the effects of credit programs. The data available for analyzing the impact of a credit program (or a training program) on an outcome are often nonrandom samples. Frequently, they consist of pooled data from two sources: a sample of program participants from program records, and a sample of nonparticipants from some national sample. Typically such pooled samples over-represent program participants relative to their proportion in the population, thus creating the problem of choice-based sampling. That is, if the data from the two sources are combined and the sample proportion of program participants does not converge to the population proportion of program participants, the combined sample is a choice-based sample (Heckman & Robb, 1985a). If the probability that a program participant appears in the sample and the probability that a program participant appears in the population are known, it is possible to reweight the data back to a sample with proportions of program participants that would be produced by a random sample to obtain consistent estimates of the program's effect. Choice-based sampling, if not corrected for, can lead to inconsistent estimates of a program's effect.

The classic program evaluation problem of selection bias must also be addressed when employing nonexperimental data to evaluate the effect of microcredit programs on an outcome such as profit.[18] To understand how selection issues may bias the measure of a program's effect, consider

a comparison of profits for households that have participated in a credit program and for households who have not participated. If participation is determined by a randomized controlled trial in which individuals are randomly assigned to treatment status (participant) or control status (nonparticipant), as in experimental data, then the difference between profits for participants and nonparticipants is a valid estimate of the program effect (Moffitt, 1991).

However, if participants are "selected" or "self-selected" into treatment status, then the population of nonparticipants constitutes a nonequivalent comparison group, and the difference between profits of participants and nonparticipants may not be a valid measure of the program effect. For example, if households that join microcredit programs are better entrepreneurs or have a greater taste for work before joining the program than those who do not join, then a comparison of profits between participating and nonparticipating households would wrongly ascribe to the credit program that part of the profits due to the better entrepreneurship or harder work of households that self-select themselves into the program.

Nonrandom placement of credit programs may also bias estimates of the program effect. It is unlikely that poverty alleviation programs such as microcredit programs are randomly allocated across geographic areas. Treating the timing and placement of programs as random can lead to serious mismeasurement of program effectiveness (Pitt, Rosenzweig, & Gibbons, 1993). For example, if microcredit programs are placed in remote villages where households are poorer and have less access to markets to purchase inputs for production and to sell outputs, then a comparison of household profits in program and nonprogram villages would lead to a downward bias in the estimated program effect.

B. Participation in a Microcredit Program

What determines whether an individual participates in BRAC, BRDB, or Grameen Bank? First, participation is determined by whether there is a credit program in the village where the household resides. As the three credit programs target the rural poor, programs are located in rural villages. Program officials note that they are more likely to start a microcredit program in poorer areas, as well as in areas in which villagers have requested program services.

Second, participation is determined by whether or not the household is considered poor enough for eligibility. All three credit programs target the poor. Thus, the primary criteria for program eligibility is that the household is functionally landless. In all three programs, only one member of a household that owns less than half an acre of cultivable land is eligible to join.

Given that households have a program available to them and are eligible to join, considerations such as access to alternative sources of capital, level of human capital, value of time, and taste parameters (such as taste for self-

---

[18] See Moffitt (1991) and Heckman and Robb (1985a, 1985b) for a formal statement of the selection bias problem and discussion of possible econometric solutions.

enrichment or distaste for attending program meetings, managing finances, and violating social norms set by purdah) affect whether an individual joins a credit program.

A brief description of the participation process in Grameen Bank as described by Hossain (1988) will help further illuminate what it means to participate in one of the group-based microcredit programs:

> Interested persons are asked to form groups of five like-minded people of similar economic standing [. . .]. Only one person from a household can be a member, and relatives must not be in the same group. Male and female members form separate groups. [. . .]
>
> Loans are given to individuals (for a maximum of 5,000 taka) without any collateral. A borrower may use the credit in any productive activity, but the loan has to be used immediately and the principal repaid in 50 weekly installments.
>
> Disbursement of loans is not a simple matter. When a group is formed, it is kept under close observation for a month by the bank worker to see if members are conforming to the discipline of the Grameen Bank. The prospective borrowers are obliged to participate in a group training program for a minimum of seven days of continuous instruction by the bank worker. The training is intended to make the members thoroughly conversant with the rules and regulations of the bank. This includes understanding the purpose of the various bank procedures . . . health, children's education, and other social development programs . . . . The group is accorded formal recognition when all members are found to be well versed in the rules and procedures. Two members of the group then receive loans and their loan-repayment behavior is observed for a month or two. If they pay the weekly installments on a regular basis, the next two members become eligible for loans. . . . A repeat loan is not approved for any member until the accounts of all members of the group are settled (pp. 25–26).

C. Estimation Strategy

In this paper, I have proposed that household participation in a group-based credit program may affect household profits in several ways: by providing credit for productive capital and by providing or creating incentives for additional human capital that may affect profits directly or indirectly via its effect on other inputs to production such as capital. These effects can be generalized into two effects on profits: the so-called "credit effect" and "noncredit effect." In model 1, I outline a strategy for estimating the total effect of microcredit programs on profit. In model 2, I describe the estimation of that part of the total effect due to the noncredit aspects of the programs.

D. Model 1: The Total Effect of Participation on Profits

To measure the total effect of participation in a microcredit program on profit, I estimate a restricted profit equation that conditions profit on the household's participation in a microcredit program. As emphasized in the discussion of program evaluation, participation in a program cannot be treated as exogenous because individuals who participate in microcredit programs may systematically differ from those who do not participate. Thus, the model for the effect of program participation on profit (model 1) models both the decision to participate in a credit program and profit conditional on participation.

For a household i in village j, the reduced-form equation for credit program participation C_{ij} is

$$C_{ij} = X_{ij}\beta^c + Z_{ij}\delta^c + V_j\gamma^c + \epsilon_{ij}^c, \tag{11}$$

and the equation for profits π_{ij} is

$$\pi_{ij}^* = C_{ijk}\alpha + X_{ij}\beta^\pi + Z_{ij}\delta^\pi + V_j\gamma^\pi + \epsilon_{ij}^\pi$$

$$\pi_{ij} = \begin{cases} \pi_{ij}^* \text{ if } \pi_{ij}^* > \pi_0 \\ 0 \text{ if } \pi_{ij}^* \le \pi_0 \end{cases}, \tag{12}$$

where credit program participation C_{ijk} is a dummy for participation such that $C_{ijk} = 1$ if an individual in the household participates in program k and $C_{ijk} = 0$ otherwise,

k = BRAC, BRDB, and Grameen Bank,[19]
restricted profit π_{ij} equals current revenue less current variable costs,
X_{ij} is a vector of household characteristics (such as sex, land holdings, and measures of human capital–age and education),
Z_{ij} is a vector of household characteristics distinct from the X_{ij}'s,
V_j is a vector of village characteristics (such as prices, wages, and community infrastructure),
π_{ij}^* is latent profit, π_{ij} is observed profit,
π_0 is an unknown threshold but the same for all households, and
β, δ, and γ are unknown parameters to be estimated.

The error terms of the participation and profit equations, ϵ_{ij}^c and ϵ_{ij}^π, are composed of three parts

$$\epsilon_{ij}^c = \eta_{ij}^c + \mu_j^c + e_{ij}^c$$

$$\epsilon_{ij}^\pi = [\rho_v^{c\pi}\mu_j^{c\pi} + \mu_j^\pi] + [\rho_h^{c\pi}\eta_{ij}^{c\pi} + \eta_{ij}^\pi] + e_{ij}^\pi, \tag{13}$$

where μ_j^c, $\mu_j^{c\pi}$, and μ_j^π are unobserved village-specific effects in the participation equation, common to the participation and profit equations, and specific to the profit

---

[19] As each village had only one type of credit program available in the early 1990s, there is no need to model which of the programs an individual from a household joins.

equation, respectively. Similarly, η_{ij}^c, $\eta_{ij}^{c\pi}$, and η_{ij}^π are unobserved household-specific effects. Examples of unobserved village- and household-specific effects that may be common to both the participation and profit equations include the proximity of a village to market and entrepreneurial ability of household members. The remaining parts of the error terms, $\{e_{ij}^c$ and $e_{ij}^\pi\}$, are i.i.d. drawings from a bivariate normal distribution with zero mean, variance σ_c^2, σ_π^2, and covariance $\sigma_{c\pi}$. The parameter $\rho_v^{c\pi}$ corresponds to the correlation of village-specific unobservables common to both the participation and profit equations. The parameter $\rho_h^{c\pi}$ corresponds to the correlation coefficient for household-specific unobservables common to both the participation and profit equations. If the correlation coefficients (ρ's) are not both equal to zero, the errors ϵ_{ij}^c and ϵ_{ij}^π are correlated. Estimation that does not take this correlation into account will yield biased estimates of the parameters of the profit equation due to the endogeneity of credit program participation C_{ijk}.

I model self-employment profits as a limited dependent variable rather than continuous because we do not observe profits for households that are not engaged in a self-employment activity. The Tobit model specification for the profit equation thus addresses selection into a self-employment activity and captures the effect of participation in a microcredit program on profits through both the effect on the probability of undertaking a self-employment activity and the effect on profits conditional on already doing a self-employment activity. The standard Tobit model outlined in equation (12) imperfectly captures the household decision to undertake a self-employment activity as described in subsection IID. The model captures the decision to the extent that, in deciding whether to undertake a self-employment activity, households calculate what profits would be if they undertook the self-employment activity and compare these expected profits, π_{ij}^*, to some (unobserved) reservation level of profits, π_0.[20] But, because the Tobit model assumes that the unobserved reservation level of profits is the same for all households, it imperfectly captures the household's decision. A more complete specification would allow for the censoring threshold to be both unobserved and stochastic, as in the modified Tobit model of Nelson (1977). However, because I lack the identification necessary for the Nelson model, I do not use it. Identification in the case of such a censored regression model with a stochastic and unobserved threshold requires one of two conditions: an exogenous variable that affects the reservation level of profit but not expected profit, or the covariance of expected and reservation profit equal to zero (Maddala, 1983). But, as seen in subsection IID, no such exogenous variable exists: all the determinants of the reservation level of profit V_0 are also determinants of expected profits, and it

is not plausible to assume the covariance of expected and reservation profits is zero.

Identification in Model 1: To identify α, the effect of participation on profit, in the presence of nonrandom program placement and self-selection, I must control for the common individual- and village-specific unobservables $\eta_{ij}^{c\pi}$ and $\mu_j^{c\pi}$ and have exogenous variation in my participation variable. The techniques I use to solve this identification problem are adapted from Pitt and Khandker (1998) and are outlined below.

To control for the common household-specific unobservables (self-selection) $\eta_{ij}^{c\pi}$, I use limited information maximum likelihood (LIML) with endogenous and exogenous switching.[21] LIML enables me to jointly estimate the participation and profit equations, thereby allowing the errors ϵ_{ij}^c and ϵ_{ij}^π to be correlated. To understand what is meant by endogenous and exogenous switching, think of households as in two different regimes: participants and nonparticipants in one of the microcredit programs. Those who could choose to participate are endogenously in their regime, whereas those who could not choose to participate are exogenously in their regime.

Households that are eligible to join one of the programs (own less than half an acre of cultivable land) and that live in a village with a program available can choose whether to participate in the microcredit program available to them. The decision to participate (and thus the switch between the two regimes) is endogenous to the household. These households with choice do not provide the necessary identification of the program effect because, as previously discussed, unobservables (such as taste for work) that affect their decision to participate may also affect their profits. Measuring the program effect via a comparison of the profits (conditional on observed attributes) from households who choose to participate with those who choose not to participate may confound the participation effect with these unobservables.

Households who are exogenously excluded from participating provide the necessary identification. If credit programs are randomly placed across villages, then households living in nonprogram villages serve as an exogenous control group with which to compare the profits of program participants. However, if program placement is not random, then these households cannot serve as an exogenous control group, and estimation must control for the village-specific unobservables.

To control for village-specific unobservables, I use a village-level fixed-effects (FE) technique that treats the village-specific errors μ_j as parameters to be estimated and thus controls for village-specific unobservables.[22] Two dis-

---

[20] As profits are continuous around $\pi_{ij} = 0$, the data support using a standard Tobit model that treats profits as the latent equation behind the decision to undertake a self-employment activity (Moffitt, 1982).

[21] The likelihood function for model 1 is presented in the appendix.
[22] Fixed-effects estimation with limited dependent variables raises the issue of consistency. Without a large number of observations per fixed-effects unit, parameter estimates in limited dependent variable models

tinct sets of village-level dummy variables are estimated in the model: one set of 72 dummy variables for target households living in program villages (households with choice) in the credit program participation equation, and a second set of 87 dummy variables for all households included in the profit equation. Thus, the model explicitly allows program placement to be responsive only to target households by modeling unobservables in the participation equation as specific to target households within villages and not just those that affect all villages equally.

In estimates that use the FE technique to control for nonrandom program placement, households that are excluded from participating in the credit programs by an exogenous rule are used to identify the program effect. This exogenous rule is the restriction that households owning more than half an acre of cultivable land are precluded from joining any of the three credit programs. The half-an-acre land rule acts to exogenously separate households into quasi-experimental treatment and control groups. Thus, households that own more than half an acre of cultivable land act as the control group and provide the exogenous variation (switch) necessary to identify the participation effect.[23] A comparison of profits between households with program choice and households without program choice, conditioning on all village effects and observed household and individual attributes, is an estimate of the program's effect on profits. To ensure that these "landed" (no choice) households can be pooled in the estimation with the "landless" households that are eligible to participate, I limit the set of landed households to those that own less than five acres of land.

Identification on the basis of land ownership requires that land ownership be exogenous to the population studied, in this case, households in rural Bangladesh. Market sales of land in South Asia are well documented to be low.[24] As a result, land ownership is treated as an exogenous regressor in most empirical work on household behavior in South Asia. (See, for example, Rosenzweig (1980).)[25]

---

may be inconsistent. Heckman (1981) provides Monte Carlo evidence that, with eight or more observations per fixed-effects unit, the inconsistency problem becomes relatively inconsequential. The average number of households per village in this study is twenty.

[23] Using land ownership for identification precludes a fully nonparametric estimation strategy. If the linear relationship between land holdings and profits in my model is replaced with a nonparametric relationship, the exogenous variation necessary to identify the program effect α would be lost. To ensure that the program effect measured is not driven by this linear relationship, I estimate the model while allowing for land to enter as a successively higher-level polynomial (log (land), [log (land)]², and [log (land)]³). The program effect results, presented in appendix table A5, were not qualitatively altered by these changes.

[24] For example, using a sample consisting of Indian rural farm households, Rosenzweig and Wolpin (1985) find a very low incidence of land sales: less than 1.75% of land-holding households that sold land in the sample year.

[25] Theories to explain the scarcity of land sales include the absence of an active land market; positive spatial correlation of incomes, underdeveloped national credit markets, the collateral value of land, and limited nonagricultural investment opportunities (Binswanger & Rosenzweig,

Parameters of Interest in Model 1: In model 1, α is the primary parameter of interest. It is the parameter on the credit program participation dummy (C_{ijk}) and measures the effect of participation on profits through both the credit and noncredit mechanisms of microcredit programs. The correlation coefficient $corr(\epsilon_{ij}^c, \epsilon_{ij}^\pi)$ provides evidence of screening into the programs. The correlation coefficient tells us whether, conditional on the regressors, households that join group lending programs are likely to have higher or lower profits.

E. Model 2: The Noncredit Effect of Participation on Profits

Besides the provision of credit for productive capital, is there any additional effect from the noncredit services that microcredit programs bundle with credit? The impact of the noncredit aspects—such as vocational training, the provision of health and other information, and information sharing and monitoring among members—is difficult to measure. Yet they are what serve to differentiate group-lending programs from banks or individual-lending institutions. To measure the impact of these noncredit aspects of program participation on profits, I condition the profit function not only on program participation, as in model 1, but also on productive capital. By holding constant productive capital while measuring the effect of program participation, I am able to provide a measure of the noncredit services provided by microcredit programs.

I condition on capital instead of credit in the profit function because this allows me to include households that have purchased their capital from savings or other sources. The noncredit aspects of microcredit programs may affect the productivity of all capital, not just capital purchased with microcredit. For example, vocational training provided by a microcredit program, such as how to use a sewing machine, will affect the productivity of all sewing machines owned, not just those purchased with credit from a microcredit program. In this respect, the noncredit effect of participation may be proportional to the total level of productive capital owned by the household.

In model 2, both credit program participation and productive capital must be treated as endogenous variables. As explained previously, credit program participation is endogenous because unobservables that affect the decision to participate may also affect profits. Similarly, unobservables that affect the amount of capital chosen may also affect profits. For example, astute business people may be able to acquire more capital, or poor business people may overinvest in capital.

To model the noncredit effect of participation of profits, consider the reduced-form equation for credit program participation C_{ij} of household i in village j

---

1986); and plot-specific skills associated with cultivation (Rosenzweig & Wolpin, 1985).

$$C_{ij} = X_{ij}\beta^c + Z_{ij}\delta^c + V_j\gamma^c + \epsilon_{ij}^c \tag{14}$$

and the jointly determined equations for capital K_{ij} and profits π_{ij}

$$K_{ij}^* = X_{ij}\beta^k + Z_{ij}\delta^k + V_j\gamma^k + \epsilon_{ij}^k$$

$$K_{ij} = \begin{cases} K_{ij}^* & \text{if } \pi_{ij}^* > \pi_0 \\ 0 & \text{if } \pi_{ij}^* \le \pi_0 \end{cases} \tag{15}$$

$$\pi_{ij}^* = C_{ijk}\alpha_1 + (C_{ijk} * K_{ij})\alpha_2 + K_{ij}\psi + X_{ij}\beta^\pi$$
$$+ V_j\gamma^\pi + \epsilon_{ij}^\pi$$

$$\pi_{ij} = \begin{cases} \pi_{ij}^* & \text{if } \pi_{ij}^* > \pi_0 \\ 0 & \text{if } \pi_{ij}^* \le \pi_0 \end{cases}, \tag{16}$$

where all variables are defined the same way as in model 1 except for the error term of the profit equation, ϵ_{ij}^π, which now also includes the village- and household-specific unobservables common to the capital and profit equations.

The error terms for the three equations are now given by

$$\epsilon_{ij}^c = \eta_{ij}^c + \mu_j^c + e_{ij}^c$$

$$\epsilon_{ij}^k = \eta_{ij}^k + \mu_j^k + e_{ij}^k \tag{17}$$

$$\epsilon_{ij}^\pi = [\rho_h^{c\pi}\eta_{ij}^{c\pi} + \rho_h^{k\pi}\eta_{ij}^{k\pi} + \eta_{ij}^\pi] + [\rho_v^{c\pi}\mu_j^{c\pi} + \rho_v^{k\pi}\mu_j^{k\pi}$$
$$+ \mu_j^\pi] + e_{ij}^\pi.$$

The parameters $\rho_v^{c\pi}$ and $\rho_h^{c\pi}$ correspond to correlation coefficients for the village- and household-specific unobservables common to the participation and profit equations. The parameters $\rho_v^{k\pi}$ and $\rho_h^{k\pi}$ correspond to correlation coefficients for the village- and household-specific unobservables common to the capital and profit equations. As in model 1, if any of the correlation coefficients are not equal to zero, then the error term of the profit equation ϵ_{ij}^π is correlated with the regressor(s). Estimation that does not take this correlation into account will yield biased estimates of the parameters of the profit equation.

Identification in Model 2: To identify the noncredit effects of program participation, α_1 and α_2, I need to control for the endogeneity of program participation and capital. I control for village-specific unobservables by using distinct village-level fixed effects in all three equations: a total of 246 village-level dummy variables. To control for the household-specific heterogeneity, I use limited information maximum likelihood (LIML) to jointly estimate the participation equation, the capital equation, and the profit equation conditional on participation.[26] As in model 1, households that cannot choose to participate in a credit program are used to identify the participation equation. The exogenous variables, Z_{ij}, that affect capital and participation but not profits conditional on capital and participation, identify

[26] The likelihood function for model 2 is presented in the appendix.

the capital equation. These identifying instruments measure access to, and indirectly the price of, interhousehold transfers. These 28 variables indicate the number of landed and living relatives by relationship to the head and spouse of the household (for example, the number of head's parents (brothers, sisters, uncles, aunts, sons, daughters) who own land).

For the potential transferees, Z_{ij}, to be identifying instruments for the capital equation, potential transferees cannot affect profits except through capital or participation in a microcredit program. One possible objection to using potential transferees as an instrument arises from the nonseparability of the household's utility and profit functions. If households are risk averse and trade mean profits for lower variance and if potential transferees act as insurance and decrease the variance of consumption, then households may undertake higher mean and variance profits than they would without potential transferees. In this case, potential transferees would affect profits other than through capital or group lending, and my instruments would not be valid.

Parameters of Interest in Model 2: In model 2, α_1 measures the direct noncredit effect on the level of profits, and α_2 measures the difference between how participating households and nonparticipating households use capital to affect profits (the indirect noncredit effect). As in model 1, the correlation coefficient $corr(\epsilon_{ij}^c, \epsilon_{ij}^\pi)$ may provide evidence of screening. Conditional on assets and other regressors, are households that join group-lending programs likely to have higher or lower profits?

IV. Data

I estimate models 1 and 2 using primary data drawn from a survey of 1,798 households conducted in 87 villages in rural Bangladesh during 1991–1992. The survey was designed for use in evaluating the three microcredit programs of interest: BRAC, BRDB's RD-12 program, and Grameen Bank. As such, it was designed quasi-experimentally to include both target (qualify to participate) and nontarget (do not qualify to participate) households from both program and nonprogram villages.

As described previously, households owning more than half an acre of cultivable land do not qualify for participation in any of the three credit programs. These nontarget households are used to identify the program effect in models that control for village-level fixed effects and treat participation as endogenously determined. I limit the set of nontarget households to those that own fewer than five acres of land in most specifications to ensure that nontarget households are comparable to target households.

Morduch (1998) raises the issue of mistargeting in these data. Indeed, I find that 17% of participating households owned more than half an acre of cultivable land prior to joining BRAC, BRDB, or Grameen Bank. Pitt (1999) finds evidence that what looks like mistargeting is really the credit programs making adjustments for land quality in judging the eligibility of a household: the participating households owning more than half an acre of total land at the time of the survey have dramatically lower land values. Even so, a targeting issue remains. Land quality is unobserved, and so we cannot be certain whether nonparticipating households with more than half an acre of land do not participate because they are ineligible or because they choose not to participate. As a result, some target households may be inappropriately classified as nontarget households. In the results presented here, I use the definitions of target and nontarget households-based on the half-an-acre land rule—as classified by the survey team. However, I also include additional specifications to ascertain the sensitivity of my estimates to this targeting issue. I find that the results regarding the effects of participation in BRAC and BRDB are not sensitive, but that those for Grameen Bank are somewhat sensitive.

The survey sample design is choice based: program participants and target nonparticipants are oversampled. Appropriate weights are used throughout the analysis to weight the choice-based sample back to random sample proportions. A description of the survey design is provided in the Appendix.

The household survey covers a wide variety of household characteristics and includes detailed information on self-employment enterprises. A village-level survey was also conducted in all 87 villages and provides complementary information on prices and infrastructure.

A. Self-Employment Profits

Restricted profit, the dependent variable used in the analysis, is defined as total household monthly gross revenue from self-employment, plus the value of household consumption from production less monthly operating expenses (primarily raw materials and hired labor). Profit is defined gross of the cost of capital and of the opportunity costs of household labor. The cost of capital, measured here as the price of the loan, is not deducted from profit so as to ensure that differences in profits do not arise from less expensive credit from microcredit programs. The opportunity cost of household labor is not deducted from profit because, given labor market imperfections, the village wage is a poor measure of the opportunity cost of household labor.[27] However, village-level price, wage, and infrastructure control variables are included in models that do not use village-level fixed effects. I choose not to control for household labor by including it as a regressor in the profit equation for two reasons. First, controlling for labor in the profit equation is not appropriate given the nonseparability

of production and household utility considerations due to the absent female labor market in Bangladesh. As a consequence of this nonseparability, credit program participation has an effect on the value of labor; it prices female labor, thereby moving its return from zero to positive. As a result, credit program participation may have a large impact on household labor-leisure decisions, and, under nonseparability, these decisions affect profit. Part of the participation effect, then, is this labor effect. Second, even if it were appropriate to control for household labor, household labor is an endogenous variable to the profit equation and is correlated with program participation. Thus, including labor as an independent variable in the profit equation may bias the estimate of the impact of microcredit program participation on profit.[28] My estimates of the effect of participation on profits will include the impacts via program-induced changes in physical capital, human capital, and labor.

Profit is the sum of profits from all self-employment activities undertaken by the household. Of the 1,757 households included in the analysis,[29] 60% are self-employed in agriculture, 39% in livestock activities, 39% in nonfarm enterprises (such as trading, rickshaw transport, or managing a shop or business), 1% in processing, and 15% are not self-employed.[30] As described in the estimation strategy, I control for selection into self-employment by using a Tobit model for the profit equation.

Table 1 presents the percentage of households that are self-employed and the average profit for households managing an enterprise for program participants, and target and nontarget nonparticipants in villages with and without programs available. The percentage of households undertaking a self-employment enterprise is eight to twenty percentage points higher for households participating in a program than for target nonparticipants. This suggests that the credit programs may play an important role in the household's decision to undertake an SE enterprise.

For the subsample of households for which profits are observed (those self-employed), table 1 also indicates that participants have higher mean profits than do target nonparticipants and slightly lower mean profits than do nontarget nonparticipants. A test that mean profits are equal for all participating and nonparticipating households cannot be rejected ($t = 0.714$).

---

[27] The female wage labor market is largely absent (as discussed previously), and so no female wage is available in many villages. Although there is a male wage labor market in Bangladesh, male hired and household labor may be imperfect substitutes because of extra monitoring or transactions costs associated with hired labor.

[28] The direction of the bias is not clear. Theory predicts that microcredit program participation (which increases physical and human capital) and labor will have a positive impact on profits. Thus, the sign of the bias depends on the unsigned covariance between participation and labor supply in my mixed sample of households with male or female program participants. Pitt and Khandker (1998) find a negative effect of participation on male labor supply and a positive effect of participation on female labor supply.

[29] To ensure that nontarget households (those who own more than half an acre of land) can be pooled in the estimation with target households, I limit the set of nontarget households to those that own fewer than five acres of land. As a result, 41 of the 1,798 households in the sample are excluded from the analysis.

[30] Percentages do not sum to 100 because households often undertake more than one self-employment activity.

TABLE 1.—Weighted[a] Percentage of HHS Self-Employed and Weighted Mean and Standard Error of Profit for those Self-Employed

	# Obs	Self-Employed	Mean Profit	Standard Error
BRAC program participants	285	82%	1875.45	260.45
BRDB program participants	308	91%	1928.78	228.06
GB program participants	312	94%	1721.60	201.09
Target in program village	378	75%	1515.76	218.18
Target in nonprogram village	255	74%	1039.91	176.66
Nontarget in program village	179	99%	2768.16	259.63
Nontarget in nonprogram village	40	98%	2099.14	427.56
All households (HH)	1757	85%	1937.32	109.62

[a] Weights are used to adjust choice-based sample to random sample proportions.

Finally, table 1 provides some evidence that village differences may be important: mean profits are higher for target and nontarget nonparticipants in villages with a program available than in villages without. However, a hypothesis test that these mean differences are equal cannot be rejected at the 0.05 significance level ($t = 1.695$ and $t = 1.337$, for target and nontarget households, respectively).

A description of the independent variable definitions can be found in the appendix. Table A1, also in the appendix, presents the weighted mean and standard deviations of all variables used in the regressions. Because the samples drawn are not representative of the village population,[31] the means of the variables are adjusted using weights based on the population and sample distribution of households covered in the study villages.

V. Empirical Results

In this section, I present and interpret results from estimating the impact of participation in a credit program on profit. The results from estimating model 1 provide mea-

[31] See Survey Design in the appendix.

sures of the total effect of participation on profits, whereas the model 2 estimates measure the noncredit effect (effect after conditioning on capital) of participation on profits.

All results reported use weighted exogenous sampling maximum likelihood (WESML) methods to correct for the choice-based nature of the sample. Results denoted with LIML use limited information maximum likelihood to control for self-selection into the microcredit programs, and results denoted with FE use village-level fixed effects to control for nonrandom program placement.

A. Model 1 Results

Table 2 and 3 report the participation coefficients for model 1's profit equation.[32] All three sets of estimates show a positive and significant effect of credit program participation on the natural logarithm of profit.[33]

Nonrandom Program Placement: A comparison of the WESML and WESML-FE results provides evidence of whether BRAC, BRDB, and Grameen Bank are randomly placed with respect to self-employment profits. The WESML estimates treat program participation and placement as exogenous, whereas the WESML-FE results treat participation as exogenous, but include village-level fixed

[32] The full set of coefficients for the WESML-LIML-FE model are presented in appendix table A2. As described later, the three credit programs, which provide access to capital and human capital, have a positive effect on profits. Additional human capital as measured by age and education does not significantly affect profits. This may in part be due to the low levels of education in the sample: average of 1.6 years for the most-educated female in the household and 2.5 years for the most-educated male in the household. Land holdings have a positive and significant effect on profits.

[33] To use the logarithmic functional form, 198 households (11% of sample) with negative profits were excluded from the profit equation. Dropping low-profit households raises the issue of selection bias. To test for this, I ran alternative specifications of the dependent variable, which allowed me to include low-profit households. These specifications, presented in appendix table A6, were (i) add a constant to profit before taking logs and (ii) assume zero log (profit) for households with negative profit. My results were robust to all three specifications of the dependent variable.

TABLE 2.—Model 1 Results
Estimates of the Total Effect of Participation on Log (Monthly Profit)

Explanatory Variables	WESML Tobit (1)	WESML-FE Tobit (2)	WESML-LIML-FE (3)	WESML-LIML-FE (4)
BRAC participant	0.883	1.025	1.223[a]	0.969
	(2.87)	(2.90)	(3.27)	(2.73)
BRDB participant	1.526	1.138	1.371[a]	1.093
	(5.79)	(3.90)	(2.75)	(3.72)
GB participant	1.977	1.955	1.414[a]	1.296[a]
	(7.61)	(6.48)	(3.38)	(3.18)
ρ BRAC			−0.069	
			(−1.31)	
ρ BRDB			−0.068	
			(−0.57)	
ρ GB			0.186	0.207
			(1.91)	(2.16)
Number observations	1558	1558	1703	1703

[a] Participation treated as an endogenous variable. Asymptotic *t*-ratios in parentheses. Presents only selected regressors. See appendix table A2 for full WESML-LIML-FE set.

THE IMPACT OF MICROCREDIT PROGRAMS ON SELF-EMPLOYMENT PROFITS   105

TABLE 3.—MODEL 1 RESULTS
SENSITIVITY ESTIMATES OF THE TOTAL EFFECT OF PARTICIPATION ON LOG (MONTHLY PROFIT)

Explanatory Variables	Land Rule for Participation Eligibility						
	0.5 acre (1)	Strict 0.5 acre (2)	1.0 acre (3)	1.5 acre (4)	2.0 acre (5)	2.0 acre (6)	2.0 acre (7)
BRAC participant	0.969	0.811	0.825	0.756	0.696	0.778	1.410
	(2.73)	(2.10)	(2.37)	(2.19)	(2.08)	(2.34)	(2.78)
BRDB participant	1.093	1.209	0.936	0.849	0.894	0.955	2.596
	(3.72)	(3.81)	(3.26)	(3.00)	(3.26)	(3.50)	(5.93)
GB participant	1.296[a]	1.155[a]	0.496[a]	0.151[a]	0.169[a]	1.542	1.561[a]
	(3.18)	(2.58)	(0.86)	(0.23)	(0.26)	(5.77)	(2.61)
BRAC * log (land)							−0.304
							(−2.25)
BRDB * log (land)							−0.687
							(−6.28)
GB * log (land)							−0.651
							(−5.33)
ρ GB	0.207	0.258	0.318	0.370	0.358		0.477
	(2.16)	(2.71)	(2.52)	(2.58)	(2.45)		(4.25)
Number observations	1703	1546	1712	1714	1754	1596	1754

Selected coefficients with asymptotic *t*-ratios in parentheses.
[a] GB participation treated as an endogenous variable; specifications estimated using WESML-LIML-FE. Results presented in column 6 treat participation as exogenous variables and are estimated using WESML-FE.

effects to control for nonrandom placement of programs. If the credit programs are randomly placed with respect to profits, then the WESML estimates are consistent and efficient, and the WESML-FE estimates are consistent but inefficient. If program placement is nonrandom, the WESML estimates are inconsistent (Pitt & Khandker, 1998). To provide a measure of whether the fixed-effects estimates differ significantly from the nonfixed estimates, a Hausman-like test for fixed effects (Greene, 1990) was attempted. The test statistic calculated is $(\hat{\beta}_{FE} - \hat{\beta})'(\hat{\Sigma}_{FE} - \hat{\Sigma})^{-1}(\hat{\beta}_{FE} - \hat{\beta})$, but the covariance matrix of the difference of the covariance matrices of the parameter estimates, $(\hat{\Sigma}_{FE} - \hat{\Sigma})^{-1}$, was not positive definite; the differences between the diagonal elements of the WESML-FE covariance matrix and the WESML covariance matrix were very close to zero and sometimes negative. This provides evidence that the WESML-FE estimates are as efficient as the WESML estimates, that the test statistic is essentially infinitely large, and that the null hypothesis of equal fixed effects and nonfixed parameters should be rejected. Based on this evidence and on evidence of nonrandom program placement from previous work,[34] I will focus on models that control for village level heterogeneity.

Village Externalities and the Interpretation of Program Effects: If microcredit programs affect the self-employment profits of households that do not participate in the programs as well as those who do (for example through demonstration effects), then the full effect of the program on profits should include any such village "externalities" and

[34] Using the same source data to study the effect of participation in BRAC, BRDB, and Grameen Bank on reproductive behavior, Pitt et al. (1999) find evidence that the programs are not randomly placed with respect to reproductive behavior and that fixed-effects estimates differ substantially from nonfixed effects estimates.

not just the direct effect of the program on participants.

The discussion of village heterogeneity thus far has been concerned with heterogeneity due to nonrandom program placement. But consider the limiting case in which program placement is in fact random, but the programs successfully increase the taste for work or entrepreneurship of nonparticipants in the program village. In this case, village unobservables would be correlated with program placement, but the causation would go from program placement to village unobserved effects, not from village unobserved effects to program placement. Unfortunately, the only way these external effects can be measured is to have data on villages before and after program introduction.

The presence of village externalities affects the interpretation, but not the consistency of the program participation coefficients (denoted by α in equation (12) and (19)). The program coefficients capture all program effects only if there are no external effects, that is, if none of the village-specific heterogeneity is caused by programs. If village externalities do exist, the WESML-LIML-FE estimate of the program impact captures only the effect above and beyond its effect on nonparticipants in the village.

Selection into the Microcredit Programs: The WESML-LIML-FE estimates presented in column 3 of table 2 control for the possible endogeneity of the participation variables and for nonrandom program placement. The GB correlation coefficient (ρ) indicates a positive correlation between unobservables (such as entrepreneurial ability) that affect both profits and participation; households that are likely to have higher profits are also more likely to join GB than are nonparticipating households. This positive correlation provides evidence that GB may successfully screen bad credit risks—either because low-profit households are turned away or because high-profit households choose to join—and is consistent with recent theoretical work that suggests that joint liability can alleviate adverse selection problems (Ghatak & Guinnane, 1999).

A comparison of the GB participant coefficient in the WESML-LIML-FE results (which control for selection into GB) and the WESML-FE results (which do not control for selection) underscores the importance of controlling for selection bias when evaluating the impact of GB. The WESML-LIML-FE coefficient of 1.41 estimates that participation in GB increases profits by 263%, whereas the WESML-FE coefficient of 1.96 indicates a 518% increase in profits.[35] By confounding the selection and program effect, the WESML-FE result overestimates the effect of GB by more than 200 percentage points. The correlation coefficients for BRAC and BRDB are not statistically different from zero, so the exogeneity of participation in BRAC and BRDB cannot be rejected. The WESML-LIML-FE specification in column 4 of table 2 thus treats participation in GB as endogenous, but participation in BRAC and BRDB as exogenous. This is the specification that I will focus on in the next section, which interprets the results for model 1.

The Total Effect of Participation on Profits: The WESML-LIML-FE results, shown in column 4 of table 2, demonstrate a positive and significant effect of participation in all three microcredit programs on profit. The Tobit coefficients presented measure the effect of the participation dummy variable on the latent or underlying equation for log profit, in this case the profit households would expect to earn if they undertook an SE enterprise. To interpret these Tobit coefficients in terms of the effect of the regressor (participation) on realized profits, I use the following formula derived in the appendix.

The effect of participation on observed (realized) profits is given by $(e^\alpha - 1) F(z)$, where α denotes the Tobit coefficient on the dummy variable indicating participation, $z = X_{ij}\beta/\sigma$, and $F(z)$ is the cumulative normal distribution function evaluated at the means of the regressors (X_{ij}). $F(z)$ gives the probability of being above the limit (undertaking an SE enterprise) and is approximated by the fraction of the sample self-employed: 0.85. Thus, participation in BRAC, BRDB, and Grameen Bank increases profit by 139%, 169%, and 226%, respectively. These individual effects of the three programs are not substantially different; the hypothesis that the three parameters are equal cannot be rejected at the 0.05 level of significance ($\chi^2(2) = 0.48$, $p = 0.79$). For a household earning the sample average of 1,654 taka ($45) from SE profit, the combined credit and noncredit inputs from participation result in an average 2,944 taka ($80) increase in monthly profit.[36]

---

[35] The method used to interpret the coefficients is explained in the next section and in the appendix.

[36] 1991 Exchange rate $1 US = 37 taka. Source: The Europa World Yearbook (1995).

Sensitivity of Results to Identification Assumptions: As discussed previously, a targeting issue arises because some participating households owned more than half an acre of cultivable land prior to joining the credit programs. Whether due to mistargeting or adjustments for land quality, this targeting issue raises the possibility that the half-an-acre eligibility land rule used for identification is inappropriate. Some nonparticipating households with slightly more than half an acre of land may be inappropriately classified as nontarget and treated as exogenously excluded from participating, when they may have been eligible and thus should have been classified as target and treated as endogenously choosing not to participate.

To measure the sensitivity of the results to the half-acre-land rule used for identification, table 3 presents estimates of the total effect of participation on profits (model 1) based on specifications that vary the land rule used for identification. For comparison purposes, column 1 of table 3 repeats the final model 1 results—estimated using the half-acre land rule—presented in column 4 of table 2. Column 2 of table 3 strictly imposes the half-acre rule, as recommended by Morduch (1998), by excluding participating households who owned more than half an acre of cultivable land prior to joining the programs. A comparison of columns 1 and 2 shows no qualitative or statistically significant difference in the results: participation in all three programs continues to have a large, positive effect on self-employment profits.

Next, columns 3, 4, and 5 of table 3 present results from model 1 specifications that use a progressively higher land cutoff for program eligibility, as recommended by Pitt (1999). These specifications take nonparticipating households with somewhat more than half an acre of cultivable land and treats them as if they have the choice to participate, that is treats them endogenously.[37] A comparison of column 1 with columns 3, 4, and 5 shows no significant change in the BRAC and BRDB participation coefficients, but the GB coefficient becomes smaller and statistically insignificant.

There are two explanations as to why the effect of participation in Grameen Bank becomes smaller as the land rule for participation eligibility increases. First, because higher-profit households were more likely to participate in Grameen Bank ($\rho GB > 0$), enforcing the half-acre land rule for nonparticipants but not participants, as I do in column 1, may mean that some low-profit households are in the nontarget control group, rather than in the target treatment group. Consequently, the column 1 results may overestimate the Grameen Bank program effect. The second explanation is that, by increasing the land eligibility rule used in estimation, I reduce the size of the control group of nontarget households and the power of my identification

---

[37] The specifications shown in table 3 treat participation in Grameen Bank endogenously and participation in BRAC and BRDB exogenously. I also estimated specifications (not shown) that treat participation in all three programs endogenously. In all of these specifications, I could not reject the exogeneity of participation in BRAC and BRDB (ρ BRAC and ρ BRDB are zero).

Entrepreneurship in Developing Countries

TABLE 4.—MODEL 2 RESULTS
ESTIMATES OF THE NONCREDIT EFFECT OF PARTICIPATION ON LOG (MONTHLY PROFIT)

Explanatory Variables	WESML Tobit (1)	WESML-FE Tobit (2)	WESML-LIML-FE (3)	WESML-LIML-FE (4)
BRAC participant	0.804	0.915	0.965[a]	0.858
	(2.54)	(2.55)	(2.44)	(2.39)
BRDB participant	1.387	0.997	0.934[a]	0.955
	(5.15)	(3.41)	(1.41)	(3.27)
GB participant	1.876	1.879	1.134[a]	1.110[a]
	(7.05)	(6.26)	(2.61)	(2.73)
Log (K)	2.260[a]	2.038[a]	1.940[a]	1.945[a]
	(2.79)	(3.26)	(3.18)	(3.23)
ρ BRAC			−0.031	
			(−0.56)	
ρ BRDB			0.007	
			(0.04)	
ρ GB			0.242	0.246
			(2.45)	(2.59)
Number observations	1756	1756	1757	1757

Presents only selected regressors. See table A3 for full WESML-LIML-FE set.
[a] Treated as an endogenous variable. Asymptotic *t*-ratios in parentheses.

diminishes. There are fewer and fewer nontarget households identifying the program effect, thereby resulting in a smaller participation coefficient and larger standard error.[38]

Column 6 of table 3 illustrates that what looks to be a smaller or insignificant effect for Grameen Bank when the two-acre land eligibility rule is used is not a fundamental difference between Grameen Bank and the other two programs, but results only because participation in Grameen Bank is treated as an endogenous variable in the analysis and participation in BRAC and BRDB as exogenous variables.[39] The specification in column (6) treats participation in all three programs exogenously. In this case, none of the results are sensitive to changes in the land eligibility rule: participation in all three programs continues to have a large, positive effect on self-employment profits.

Column 7 of table 3 indicates that, even when the two-acre land rule is used and participation in Grameen Bank is treated as an endogenous variable, participation in all three credit programs has a large effect for landless households.[40] The returns to participating in the microcredit programs decreases as the land holdings of the participating household increases. In summary, table 3 illustrates that the effect of two out of the three microcredit programs is robust to all sensitivity tests and that all three programs have a large, positive total effect of participation on self-employment profits for the landless poor.

[38] Nontarget households living in program villages represent 10% of the sample using the half-acre land eligibility rule and 5% of the sample using the two-acre land eligibility rule.
[39] Had I proceeded in a more restrictive fashion, restricting the correlation of unobservables to be the same across the three programs as Pitt and Khandker (1998) did, I would have found the combined correlation coefficient was zero and found no sensitivity in my results to changing the land eligibility rule. In other words, where I do find some sensitivity, another sensible approach would find no sensitivity.
[40] Many participating household are landless: 13%, 21%, and 41% of participating households have log (land) holdings of less than or equal to 0, 1, and 2, respectively.

B. Model 2 Results

The model 2 results provide measures of the noncredit effect of participation in BRAC, BRDB, and Grameen Bank on the natural logarithm of monthly profit. Table 4 presents selected coefficients from alternative estimates of model 2 that control for differing levels of individual- and village-level heterogeneity.[41] Table 5 provides coefficients of interest from alternative specifications of model 2 WESML-LIML-FE estimates. Results indicate that the identifying instruments used in the first-stage capital equation are important determinants of capital ($\chi^2(28) = 48.11, p = 0.01$).[42] All results in table 4 and table 5 are consistent with a positive noncredit effect of BRAC, BRDB, and Grameen Bank on profit. A discussion of the results follows.

Selection into the Microcredit Programs: The WESML-LIML-FE results in column 3 of table 4 control for the possible endogeneity of all three participation variables and for nonrandom program placement. The correlation coefficients (ρ's) indicate whether, conditional on capital and all other regressors, households that join one of the microcredit programs are likely to have higher or lower profits. Once again, there is a positive correlation between unobservables that affect both participation in GB and profits. Households that are more likely to join GB are likely to have higher profits than those that do not join. A comparison of the

[41] The full set of coefficients for the WESML-LIML-FE model are presented in appendix table A3. As described later, the three credit programs, which provide access to capital and human capital, have a positive effect on profits even after controlling for capital owned by the household. As in model 1, additional human capital as measured by age and education does not significantly affect profits. This may in part be due to the low levels of education in the sample. Land holdings no longer have a significant effect on profits.
[42] Results from the reduced-form capital and participation equations are presented in appendix table A4.

TABLE 5.—MODEL 2 RESULTS
ALTERNATIVE SPECIFICATIONS OF THE NONCREDIT EFFECT OF PARTICIPATION ON LOG (MONTHLY PROFIT)

Explanatory Variables	WESML-LIML-FE (1)	WESML-LIML-FE (2)	WESML-LIML-FE (3)
BRAC participant	0.858		3.698
	(2.39)		(1.42)
BRDB participant	0.955		5.083
	(3.27)		(2.75)
GB participant	1.110[a]		6.300[a]
	(2.73)		(2.67)
BRAC participant * log (K)		0.114	−0.419
		(2.17)	(−1.11)
BRDB participant * log (K)		0.115	−0.576
		(2.90)	(−2.35)
GB participant * log (K)		0.122[a]	−0.737[a]
		(2.20)	(−2.40)
Log (K)	1.945[a]	1.904[a]	1.980[a]
	(3.23)	(3.14)	(3.32)
ρ GB	0.246	0.296	0.223
	(2.59)	(3.30)	(2.15)
Number observations	1757	1757	1757

Presents only selected regressors. See table A3 for full set. Asymptotic *t*-ratios in parentheses.
[a] Participation treated as an endogenous variable. Log (K) treated as an endogenous variable in all three specifications.

WESML-FE and WESML-LIML-FE GB participant coefficient indicates that not controlling for this selection overestimates the GB noncredit program effect by nearly 300 percentage points.

As in model 1, the BRAC and BRDB correlation coefficients are not significant. Thus, a test of the hypothesis that participation in these two programs is uncorrelated with profits cannot be rejected, and I will turn to the WESML-LIML-FE results that treat participation in GB as endogenous, and participation in BRAC and BRDB as exogenous. These results are presented in column 4 of table 4 and, for comparison purposes, once again in column 1 of table 5, along with two other specifications of the model.

The Noncredit Effect of Participation of Profits: Table 5 presents alternative specifications of the WESML-LIML-FE model 2 coefficients of interest. Specification 1 measures the noncredit effect as a change in the level of profit. Specification 2, which interacts participation and capital, treats the noncredit effect of participation in the credit programs on profit as proportionate to the amount of productive capital the household owns. And specification 3, which includes both intercept and interaction effects of participation, allows for the noncredit effect to be measured both as a difference in the level of profit and in the use of productive capital. All three specifications show a positive effect of participation in BRAC, BRDB, and Grameen Bank after conditioning on capital. These results indicate that the three microcredit programs increase profits above and beyond the provision of capital and are consistent with a positive noncredit effect on profits.[43]

The three different specifications provide similar measures of the noncredit effect. To interpret the Tobit coefficients on the participation dummy variable, I use the following formula derived in the appendix. Percentage change in observed profit equals $(e^{\alpha_1}e^{\alpha_2 \log(K)} - 1) F(Z)$, where α_1 and α_2 denote the coefficients on the dummy variable for participation, and the interaction of the dummy variable for participation and log (K), respectively. The program effects are evaluated at the mean of predicted log (capital) in the sample, 7.18 taka, for specifications 2 and 3. The average effect of BRAC ranges from an 84% increase in profit in specification 3 to a 115% increase in specification 1. The effect of BRDB ranges from a 109% increase in specification 2 to a 135% increase in specifications 1 and 3. And the average effect of Grameen Bank ranges from a 119% increase in profit in specification 2 to a 173% increase in specification 1. Although these noncredit effects of participation are large, it is important to remember that they include the programs' impact on profits via increases in human capital, and changes in the supply and value of household labor.[44]

The noncredit effects by program are also strikingly similar; the hypothesis that the BRAC, BRDB, and GB coefficients are equal cannot be rejected in any of the specifications ($p = 0.87$, $p = 0.99$, and $p = 0.85$). Across the three specifications, the noncredit effect is approximately 125%. For the average household in the sample earning 1,654 taka, a 125% increase means an additional 2,068 taka or $56 a month in self-employment profits. However, as seen in specification 3, the impact of the program depends on the amount of capital owned by the household.

Specification 3, which includes both intercepts for participation and interactions for participation and the amount of capital owned by the household, indicates that the returns

[43] Additional specifications estimated to ascertain the sensitivity of the model 2 estimates to the land eligibility rule used for identification are consistent with the model 1 sensitivity estimates discussed previously.

[44] Pitt and Khandker (1998) also find a large positive effect of participation on female labor supply.

to participating in the microcredit programs are decreasing in capital. The average effect of participation for households at the mean of the first quartile of the predicted log (capital) distribution is 494%, whereas it is only 18% for households at the mean of the fourth quartile. These results suggest that the microcredit programs have the greatest impact on households that need the credit the most: those with the least capital.

VI. Conclusion

Microcredit programs, most notably the Grameen Bank of Bangladesh, have recently drawn much attention as a means of alleviating poverty. By using joint liability to help overcome the costly problems of screening, incentive, and enforcement, these programs provide credit for the purchase of capital inputs and complementary noncredit services (including vocational training) in order to promote productive self-employment among the poor. Given their potential for poverty alleviation and the large amounts of resources being spent on expanding and replicating them, two important research questions are whether microcredit programs increase self-employment productivity and whether the noncredit aspects of the program have an important effect above and beyond the provision of credit.

This paper models the role of microcredit programs in determining the restricted self-employment profits of rural households. Using data from a special survey carried out in 87 rural Bangladeshi villages during 1991–1992, this study then estimates the impact of participation in three microcredit programs (BRAC, BRDB's RD-12 program, and Grameen Bank) on self-employment profits. Making use of the fact that credit from microcredit programs is used to purchase capital, this paper also provides a measure of the noncredit effect of the programs by estimating the effect of program participation while controlling for the level of productive capital.

Productive capital is treated as an endogenous variable in the profit equation and is identified by instrumental variables that measure access to, and indirectly the price of, intrahousehold transfers. The program evaluation issue of selection bias is addressed by jointly estimating the program participation and self-employment profit equations thereby controlling for any correlation between the error terms of the two equations. Village-level fixed-effects methods are used to control for bias arising from nonrandom program placement. The effect of participation on profits is identified by exploiting a quasi-experimental component of the programs.

The empirical results presented suggest a positive selection effect between participation in Grameen Bank and profits; conditional on their village of residence and observed characteristics, high-profit households are more likely to participate in Grameen Bank. A comparison of results from models that do and do not control for this selection indicate that the bias may overestimate the effect

of participation on profits by more than 200 percentage points. This positive selection finding provides empirical evidence that joint liability, as used in Grameen Bank, may successfully screen out bad credit risks and is consistent with recent theoretical work that suggests that joint liability can alleviate adverse selection (or screening) problems (Ghatak & Guinnane, 1999).

Results on the impact of the three programs illustrate a large positive and significant (approximately 175% or $80 increase) total effect of participation on monthly self-employment profits and a large positive and significant (125% or $55 increase) noncredit effect of participation after conditioning on capital. In two of the three programs, these positive results are robust to all sensitivity tests, and in all three programs the results are robust for the landless poor. The effect of participation is decreasing in the amount of assets held by the household; households with the fewest assets benefit most from participating in a program. To provide a context for the magnitude of these effects, consider that 1991 annual GNP per capita for Bangladesh was $220;[45] thus, the average monthly income for a household of four in Bangladesh at the time of the survey was $73.

These findings have several important implications. First, the large positive impact these programs have on productivity suggests that microcredit programs may be a viable strategy for the alleviation of poverty among the landless poor. Second, the large noncredit effects of the programs provide evidence that group lending programs do more than just overcome credit market imperfections to increase access to credit for the poor. The group cohesion, joint liability, incentives to share information, and social development programs that serve to differentiate group-lending programs from banks or individual-lending institutions are an important part of microcredit programs' success. The noncredit program aspects do matter.

REFERENCES

Balkin, Steven, "A Grameen Bank Replication: The Full Circle Fund of the Women's Self-Employment Project of Chicago" chapter 14 in Abu N. M. Wahid (Ed.), *The Grameen Bank: Poverty Relief in Bangladesh* (Boulder, CO: Westview Press, 1993), 235–266.

Bell, Clive, "Credit Markets and Interlinked Transactions" (pp. 763–830), in H. Chenery and T. N. Srinivasan (Eds.), *Handbook of Development Economics,* vol. I (Amsterdam: North-Holland, 1988).

Benjamin, Dwayne, "Household Composition, Labor Markets, and Labor Demand: Testing for Separation in Agricultural Household Models," *Econometrica* 60:2 (March 1992), 287–322.

Besley, Timothy, "How Do Market Failures Justify Interventions in Rural Credit Markets?" *The World Bank Research Observer* 9:1 (January 1994), 27–47.

Binswanger, Hans P., and Mark R. Rosenzweig, "Behavioural and Material Determinants of Production Relations in Agriculture," *The Journal of Development Studies* 32 (1986), 503–539.

Europa Publications Limited, *The Europa World Yearbook 1995 Volume II* (London: Europa Publications, 1995), p. 492.

Fuglesang, Andreas, and Dale Chandler, *Participation as Process—Process as Growth* (Dhaka: Grameen Trust, 1993).

---

[45] Source: World Bank (1993).

110 THE REVIEW OF ECONOMICS AND STATISTICS

Gersovitz, Mark, "Savings and Nutrition at Low Incomes," *Journal of Political Economy* 91:5 (1983), 841–855.

Ghatak, Maitreesh, and Timothy W. Guinnane, "The Economics of Lending with Joint Liability: Theory and Practice," *Journal of Development Economics* 60 (1999), 195–228.

Greene, William H., *Econometric Analysis* (New York: Macmillan Publishing Company, 1990).

Heckman, James J., "The Incidental Parameters Problem and the Problem of Initial Conditions in Estimating a Discrete Time-Discrete Data Stochastic Process" (pp. 178–195), in C. F. Manski and D. McFadden (Eds.), *Structural Analysis of Discrete Data with Econometric Applications* (Cambridge, MA: The MIT Press, 1981).

Heckman, James J., and Richard Robb, Jr., "Alternative Methods for Evaluating the Impact of Interventions: An Overview," *Journal of Econometrics* 30 (1985a), 239–267.

Heckman, James J., and Richard Robb, Jr., "Alternative Methods for Evaluating the Impact of Interventions," (pp. 156–246), in J. Heckman and B. Singer (Eds.), *Longitudinal Analysis of Labor Market Data* (Cambridge, MA: Cambridge University Press, 1985b).

Hoff, Karla, and Joseph E. Stiglitz, "Introduction: Imperfect Information and Rural Credit Markets—Puzzles and Policy Perspectives," *The World Bank Economic Review* 4:3 (1990), 235–250.

Holmstrom, B., "Moral Hazard and Observability," *Bell Journal of Economics* 10 (1979), 74–91.

Hossain, Mahabub, *Credit for Alleviation of Rural Poverty: The Grameen Bank in Bangladesh*, International Food Policy Research Institute Research report no. 65 (Washington DC: Bangladesh Institute of Development Studies, 1988).

Khandker, Shahidur R., and Baqui Khalily, "The Bangladesh Rural Advancement Committee's Credit Programs: Performance and Sustainability," World Bank discussion paper no. 324 (1996).

Khandker, Shahidur R., Baqui Khalily, and Zahed Khan, "Grameen Bank: Performance and Sustainability," World Bank discussion paper no. 306 (October 1993).

Khandker, Shahidur R., Zahed Khan, and Baqui Khalily, "Sustainability of a Government Targeted Credit Program: Evidence from Bangladesh," World Bank discussion paper no. 316 (1995).

Lau, Lawrence J., "A Characterization of the Normalized Restricted Profit Function," *Journal of Economic Theory* 12 (1976), 131–163.

Lau, Lawrence J., and Pan A. Yotopoulos, "The Methodological Framework," *Food Research Institute Studies* 27: (1979), 11–22.

Lau, Lawrence J., Wuu-Long Lin, and Pan A. Yotopoulos, "Efficiency and Technological Change in Taiwan's Agriculture," *Food Research Institute Studies* 27:1 (1979), 23–50.

Lovell, Catherine H., *Breaking the Cycle of Poverty: The BRAC Strategy* (West Hartford, CN: Kumarian Press Inc., 1992).

Maddala, G. S., *Limited-Dependent and Qualitative Variable in Econometrics* (Cambridge, MA: Cambridge University Press, 1983).

McDonald, John F., and Robert A. Moffitt, "The Uses of Tobit Analysis," this REVIEW 62:2 (May 1980), 318–321.

Moffitt, Robert, "The Tobit Model, Hours of Work and Institutional Constraints," this REVIEW 64:3 (August 1982), 510–515.

——, "Program Evaluation with Nonexperimental Data," *Evaluation Review* 15:3 (June 1991), 291–314.

Mondal, Wali I., and Ruth Anne Tune, "Replicating the Grameen Bank in North America: The Good Faith Fund Experience" (pp. 223–234), in Abu N. M. Wahid (Ed.), *The Grameen Bank: Poverty Relief in Bangladesh* (Boulder, CO: Westview Press, 1993).

Morduch, Jonathan, "Does Microfinance Really Help the Poor? New Evidence from Flagship Programs in Bangladesh," Harvard University and Stanford University manuscript (June 26, 1998).

Nelson, Forrest, "Censored Regression Models with Unobserved, Stochastic Censoring Thresholds," *Journal of Econometrics* 6 (November 1977), 309–327.

Pitt, Mark M., "Reply to Jonathan Morduch's 'Does Microfinance Really Help the Poor? New Evidence from Flagship Programs in Bangladesh'," Brown University manuscript (October 14, 1999).

Pitt, Mark M., and Shahidur R. Khandker, "Household and Intrahousehold Impacts of the Grameen Bank and Similar Targeted Credit Programs in Bangladesh," Brown University manuscript (March 1995).

——, "The Impact of Group-Based Credit Programs on Poor Households in Bangladesh: Does the Gender of Participants Matter?" *Journal of Political Economy* 106:5 (1998), 958–996.

——, Signe-Mary McKernan, and M. Abdul Latif, "Credit Programs for the Poor and Reproductive Behavior in Low Income Countries: Are the Reported Causal Relationships the Result of Heterogeneity Bias?" *Demography* 36:1 (February 1999), 1–21.

Pitt, Mark M., and Mark R. Rosenzweig, "Agricultural Prices, Food Consumption, and the Health and Productivity of Indonesian Farmers" (pp. 153–182), in Singh, Squire, and Strauss (Eds.) *Agricultural Household Models* (Baltimore, MD: Johns Hopkins Press, 1986).

Pitt, M., M. R. Rosenzweig, and D. M. Gibbons, "The Determinants and Consequences of the Placement of Government Programs in Indonesia," *World Bank Economic Review* (September 1993), 319–348.

Rahman, Atiur, "The General Replicability of the Grameen Bank Model," chapter 12 in Abu N. M. Wahid (Ed.), *The Grameen Bank: Poverty Relief in Bangladesh* (Boulder, CO: Westview Press, 1993), 209–222.

Rosenzweig, Mark R., "Neoclassical Theory and the Optimizing Peasant: An Econometric Analysis of Market Family Labor Supply in a Developing Country," *The Quarterly Journal of Economics* 94 (1980), 31–55.

Rosenzweig, Mark R., and Kenneth I. Wolpin, "Specific Experience, Household Structure, and Intergenerational Transfers: Farm Family Land and Labor Arrangements in Developing Countries," *The Quarterly Journal of Economics* 100 (supplement) (1985), 961–987.

Samuelson, P. A., "Prices of Factors and Goods in General Equilibrium," *Review of Economics Studies* 21 (1953–1954), 1–20.

Singh, Inderjit, Lyn Squire, and John Strauss, "The Basic Model: Theory, Empirical Results, and Policy Conclusions" (pp. 17–70), in I. Singh, L. Squire, and J. Strauss (Eds.), *Agricultural Household Models: Extensions, Applications and Policy* (Baltimore, MD: Johns Hopkins Press, 1986).

Strauss, John, "The Theory and Comparative Statics of Agricultural Household Models: A General Approach" (pp. 71–91), in *Agricultural Household Models: Extensions, Applications and Policy* (Baltimore, MD: Johns Hopkins Press, 1986).

Varian, Hal R., "Monitoring Agents With Other Agents," *Journal of Institutional and Theoretical Economics* 146 (1990), 153–174.

World Bank, *World Development Report 1993: Investing in Health* (Oxford University Press, Inc, 1993).

Yaron, Jacob, "What Makes Rural Finance Institutions Successful?" *The World Bank Research Observer* 9:1 (January 1994), 49–70.

APPENDIX

Survey Design

A multipurpose quasi-experimental survey of 1,798 households was conducted in 87 villages in rural Bangladesh. The 87 villages in the sample are located in 29 thanas (subdistricts). These 29 thanas were randomly drawn from 391 thanas in Bangladesh. Of the 29 thanas sampled, 24 had at least one of the three microcredit programs in operation, whereas five had none of them. Three villages in each of the program thana were then randomly selected from a list, supplied by the program's local office, of villages in which the program had been in operation at least three years. Three villages in each nonprogram thana were randomly drawn from the village census of the Government of Bangladesh.

A village census was conducted in each of the 87 villages in the sample to classify households as target (those who qualify to join a program) or nontarget households and to identify program participating and nonparticipating households among the target households. A stratified random sampling technique was used to oversample households participating in one of the credit programs and target nonparticipating households. Of the 1,798 households surveyed, 1,538 are target households and 260 nontarget (Pitt & Khandker, 1995, 1998).

Variable Definitions

Capital is defined as the current value (at time of survey) of productive capital used in all four types of self-employment activities. These include transport assets (bike, motorcycle, boat, rickshaw, handcart, bullock, horsecart); agricultural assets (ploughs, other agricultural equipment, dairy cattle, calves, goats, sheep, poultry, and other animals); tools (hammer, spade); processing equipment (looms, dekhi); and inventory used for nonfarm enterprises.

Human capital is measured by the education (highest grade completed) of the head and of an adult female in the household and by the age of the household head. Fixed quantity of land is measured in decimals by total household land ownership.

The exogenous variables denoted by Z in the estimation section are a set of 28 variables indicating the existence of nonresident relations of various types who are living and who are landowners. These nonresident relations are potential sources of transfers that may substitute for credit or provide access to capital.

The dummy variables "no adult female in HH" and "no spouse in HH" (household) are included as regressors to control for variables such as "Highest grade completed by adult female in HH" and "# [relative] of HH head's spouse . . ." which are undefined but coded as zero if no female or spouse resides in the HH. These dummy variables thus measure the difference between having zero as the highest grade completed or number of relatives and not having a female or spouse in the household.

In specifications that do not include village-level fixed effects, the male wage, female wage, and a dummy controlling for the absence of a wage, six goods prices, and five measures of village infrastructure are included.

Likelihood Functions

Model 1

Model 1 is described by the reduced-form equation for credit program participation C_{ij}

$$C_{ij} = X_{ij}\beta^c + Z_{ij}\delta^c + V_j\gamma^c + \epsilon_{ij}^c \tag{18}$$

and the equation for profits π_{ij}

$$\pi_{ij}^* = C_{ijk}\alpha + X_{ij}\beta^\pi + Z_{ij}\delta^\pi + V_j\gamma^\pi + \epsilon_{ij}^\pi$$
$$\pi_{ij} = \begin{cases} \pi_{ij}^* \text{ if } \pi_{ij}^* > \pi_0 \\ 0 \text{ if } \pi_{ij}^* \leq \pi_0 \end{cases} \tag{19}$$

where i denotes household and j denotes village.

For notational convenience in writing out the likelihood function, I will drop subscripts and denote all credit and profit equation regressors by X^c and X^π and coefficients by β^c and β^π, respectively. Using village-level fixed effects to control for village level heterogeneity, equation (18) and (19) can be rewritten as

$$C = X^c\beta^c + e^c \tag{20}$$

and

$$\pi^* = X^\pi\beta^\pi + e^\pi$$
$$\pi = \begin{cases} \pi^* \text{ if } \pi^* > \pi_0 \\ 0 \text{ if } \pi^* \leq \pi_0 \end{cases}, \tag{21}$$

where $\{e^c$ and $e^\pi\}$ are i.i.d. drawings from a bivariate normal distribution with covariance matrix

$$\Sigma = \begin{bmatrix} \Sigma_{11} & \Sigma_{12} \\ \Sigma_{21} & \Sigma_{22} \end{bmatrix} = \begin{bmatrix} \sigma_c^2 & \sigma_{c\pi} \\ \sigma_{c\pi} & \sigma_\pi^2 \end{bmatrix} = \begin{bmatrix} \sigma_c^2 & \rho^{c\pi}\sigma_c\sigma_\pi \\ \rho^{c\pi}\sigma_c\sigma_\pi & \sigma_\pi^2 \end{bmatrix}.$$

$\rho^{c\pi}$ is the correlation between C and $\pi \left(\rho^{c\pi} = \dfrac{\sigma_{c\pi}}{\sigma_c\sigma_\pi} \right)$ and is specific to each of the three credit programs. If the household lives in a BRAC village, $\rho^{c\pi} = \rho_{BRAC}$; in a BRDB village, $\rho^{c\pi} = \rho_{BRDB}$; and, in a GB village, $\rho^{c\pi} = \rho_{GB}$. The variance of the binomial credit participation equation, σ_c^2, is normalized to 1.

Defining $C = 1$ as program participant and $C = -1$ as nonprogram participant, the likelihood for model 1 can be described by

$$\log L = \Sigma_{noSE}^{choice} w \log \Pr(C = 1, \pi = 0) + \Sigma_{noSE}^{choice} w \log \Pr(C = -1, \pi$$
$$- 1, \pi = 0) + \Sigma_{SE}^{choice} w \log \Pr(C = 1, \pi) + \Sigma_{SE}^{choice} w \log \Pr(C$$
$$= -1, \pi) + \Sigma_{noSE}^{nochoice} w \log \Pr(\pi = 0) + \Sigma_{SE}^{nochoice} w \log \Pr(\pi),$$

where *choice* refers to households that can choose to join a credit program because they are landless and live in a village that has a credit program available,

nochoice refers to households that cannot choose to join a credit program because they are landed or do not live in a village where a credit program is available,

SE corresponds to households that undertake a self-employment activity, and *noSE* to those who do not,

w denotes the weight used to adjust for the choice-based sample and is equal to the inverse probability that we observe a household due to our sampling strategy. (That is, $w = (\%$ type A households in population)$/(\%$ type A households in sample), where A = target nonparticipating, target participating, and nontarget households.)

Noting that the joint density is equivalent to the product of a conditional density and a marginal density (that is, $f(C, \pi) = f(C|\pi)f(\pi)$), and that the conditional distribution of C given π is $C|\pi \sim N(X^c\beta^c + \Sigma_{12}\Sigma_{22}^{-1}(\pi - X^\pi\beta^\pi), \Sigma_{11} - \Sigma_{12}\Sigma_{22}^{-1}\Sigma_{21})$ (Greene, 1990, p. 78), the model 1 likelihood can be written as

$$\log L = \Sigma_{noSE}^{choice} w \log \Phi_2\left[\frac{-X^\pi\beta^\pi}{\sigma_\pi}, \frac{X^c\beta^c}{\sigma_c} C, \rho^{c\pi}(-C)\right]$$
$$+ \Sigma_{SE}^{choice} w \log \left\{\frac{1}{\sigma_\pi}\phi\left[\frac{\pi - X^\pi\beta^\pi}{\sigma_\pi}\right]\right.$$
$$\Phi\left[\frac{X^c\beta^c + \Sigma_{12}\Sigma_{22}^{-1}(\pi - X^\pi\beta^\pi)}{(\Sigma_{11} - \Sigma_{12}\Sigma_{22}^{-1}\Sigma_{21})^{1/2}} (C)\right]\right\}$$
$$+ \Sigma_{noSE}^{nochoice} w \log \Phi\left[\frac{-X^\pi\beta^\pi}{\sigma_\pi}\right]$$
$$+ \Sigma_{SE}^{nochoice} w \log \frac{1}{\sigma_\pi}\phi\left[\frac{\pi - X^\pi\beta^\pi}{\sigma_\pi}\right]$$

where Φ_2, Φ, and ϕ are the bivariate standard normal distribution, univariate standard normal distribution, and standard normal density, respectively. I used Fortran to program the model 1 likelihood function and Fortran's gqopt library to maximize the likelihood function.

Model 2

Model 2 is described by the reduced-form equation for credit program participation C_{ij}

$$C_{ij} = X_{ij}\beta^c + Z_{ij}\delta^c + V_j\gamma^c + \epsilon_{ij}^c \tag{22}$$

and the jointly determined equations for capital K_{ij} and profits π_{ij}

$$K_{ij}^* = X_{ij}\beta^k + Z_{ij}\delta^k + V_j\gamma^k + \epsilon_{ij}^k$$
$$K_{ij} = \begin{cases} K_{ij}^* \text{ if } \pi_{ij}^* > \pi_0 \\ 0 \text{ if } \pi_{ij}^* \leq \pi_0 \end{cases} \tag{23}$$

$$\pi_{ij}^* = C_{ijk}\alpha_1 + (C_{ijk} * K_{ij})\alpha_2 + K_{ij}\psi + X_{ij}\beta^\pi + V_j\gamma^\pi + \epsilon_{ij}^\pi$$
$$\pi_{ij} = \begin{cases} \pi_{ij}^* \text{ if } \pi_{ij}^* > \pi_0 \\ 0 \text{ if } \pi_{ij}^* \leq \pi_0 \end{cases} \tag{24}$$

The three equations are estimated jointly using limited information maximum likelihood.

Once again, I simplify notation by dropping subscripts and denoting all credit, capital, and profit equation regressors by X^c, X^k, and X^π, and coefficients by β^c, β^k, and β^π, respectively. Using village-level fixed effects to control for village-level heterogeneity, equation (22), (23), and (24) can be rewritten as

$C = X^c\beta^c + e^c$

$K^* = X^k\beta^k + e^k$

$K = \begin{cases} K^* & \text{if } \pi^* > \pi_0 \\ 0 & \text{if } \pi^* \le \pi_0 \end{cases}$

and

$\pi^* = X^\pi\beta^\pi + e^\pi$

$\pi = \begin{cases} \pi^* & \text{if } \pi^* > \pi_0 \\ 0 & \text{if } \pi^* \le \pi_0 \end{cases}.$

Redefining $C = 1$ as program participant and $C = -1$ as nonprogram participant, the likelihood for model 2 can be written as

$$\log L = \Sigma_{noSE}^{choice} w \log \Phi_2\left[\frac{-X^\pi\beta^\pi}{\sigma_\pi}, \frac{X^c\beta^c}{\sigma_c} C, \rho^{c\pi}(-C)\right]$$

$$+ \Sigma_{SE}^{choice} w \log \left\{ \frac{1}{\sigma_\pi} \phi\left[\frac{\pi - X^\pi\beta^\pi}{\sigma_\pi}\right] \frac{1}{\sigma_k} \phi\left[\frac{K - X^k\beta^k}{\sigma_k}\right] \right.$$

$$\Phi\left[\frac{X^c\beta^c + \Sigma_{12}\Sigma_{22}^{-1}(\pi - X^\pi\beta^\pi)}{(\Sigma_{11} - \Sigma_{12}\Sigma_{22}^{-1}\Sigma_{21})^{1/2}}(C)\right] \right\}$$

$$+ \Sigma_{noSE}^{nochoice} w \log \Phi\left[\frac{-X^\pi\beta^\pi}{\sigma_\pi}\right]$$

$$+ \Sigma_{SE}^{nochoice} w \log \left\{ \frac{1}{\sigma_\pi} \phi\left[\frac{\pi - X^\pi\beta^\pi}{\sigma_\pi}\right] \frac{1}{\sigma_k} \phi\left[\frac{K - X^k\beta^k}{\sigma_k}\right] \right\},$$

where Φ_2, Φ, ϕ, Σ_{11}, Σ_{12}, Σ_{21}, and Σ_{22} are as defined for model 1. I used Fortran to program the model 2 likelihood function and Fortran's gqopt library to maximize the likelihood function.

Interpretation of Coefficients

To interpret my estimates of the effect of credit program participation on self-employment profits, consider the Tobit profit equation

$\log \pi_{ij}^* = C_{ijk}\alpha_1 + (C_{ijk} * \log K_{ij})\alpha_2 + \log K_{ij}\psi + X_{ij}\beta^\pi + V_j\gamma^\pi + \epsilon_{ij}^\pi$

$\log \pi_{ij} = \begin{cases} \log \pi_{ij}^* & \text{if } \log \pi_{ij}^* > \pi_0 \\ 0 & \text{if } \log \pi_{ij}^* \le \pi_0 \end{cases}$ (25)

where π_{ij} is observed profit,
π_{ij}^* is latent profit,
π_0 is an unknown threshold but the same for all households,
C_{ijk} is a dummy for participation such that $C_{ijk} = 1$ if an individual in the household participates in program k and $C_{ijk} = 0$ otherwise,
$k =$ BRAC, BRDB, and Grameen Bank,
K_{ij} denotes capital,
X_{ij} is a vector of household characteristics,
V_j is either a vector of village characteristics or village-fixed-effect dummies,

ϵ_{ij} is the error term,
α_1 and α_2, are the parameters of interest, and
log denotes natural logarithm.

In the more standard case, when the variable of interest is not a dummy variable, the marginal effect of a regressor (participation) on a latent dependent variable (profit) is given by

$$\frac{\partial E[\pi^*]}{\partial C} = \alpha_1 + \alpha_2 \log K,$$

and the marginal effect for observed profit, given the censoring, is given by

$$\frac{\partial E[\pi]}{\partial C} = [\alpha_1 + \alpha_2 \log K]F(Z)$$

where $z = X_{ij}\beta/\sigma$, and $F(z)$ is the cumulative normal distribution function evaluated at the means of the regressors (X_{ij}). However, when the variable of interest is a dummy variable, we are not interested in marginal changes in the regressor, but a change from zero to one. Another method of interpretation is necessary (although this standard method can work as a close approximation when the coefficient is small).

The method I use involves looking at the impact of a 0-to-1 change in the binary regressor on the dependent variable and is outlined below. Calculating the difference between log profits for participants

$\log \pi_{participants}^* = \alpha_1 + \alpha_2 \log K_{ij} + \log K_{ij}\psi + X_{ij}\beta^\pi + V_j\gamma^\pi + \epsilon_{ij}^\pi$ (26)

and nonparticipants

$\log \pi_{nonparticipants}^* = \log K_{ij}\psi + X_{ij}\beta^\pi + V_j\gamma^\pi + \epsilon_{ij}^\pi$ (27)

I find

$\log \pi_{participants}^* - \log \pi_{nonparticipants}^* = \alpha_1 + \alpha_2 \log K_{ij}$ (28)

which is equivalent to

$\log \left(\dfrac{\pi_{participants}^*}{\pi_{nonparticipants}^*}\right) = \alpha_1 + \alpha_2 \log K_{ij}.$ (29)

Taking the antilog and subtracting 1 to express the change in latent profits in percentage terms yields

$\dfrac{\pi_{participants}^* - \pi_{nonparticipants}^*}{\pi_{nonparticipants}^*} = e^{\alpha_1}e^{\alpha_2 \log K_{ij}} - 1.$ (30)

The impact of participation on observed profits is then given by

$\dfrac{\pi_{participants} - \pi_{nonparticipants}}{\pi_{nonparticipants}} = (e^{\alpha_1}e^{\alpha_2 \log K_{ij}} - 1)F(Z),$ (31)

where $F(z)$ gives the probability of being above the limit (undertaking an SE enterprise) and is approximated by the fraction of the sample self-employed: 0.85.

THE IMPACT OF MICROCREDIT PROGRAMS ON SELF-EMPLOYMENT PROFITS   113

TABLE A1.—WEIGHTED MEANS AND STANDARD DEVIATIONS OF VARIABLES
HOUSEHOLD ATTRIBUTES

	# Obs	Mean	Standard Deviation
Monthly self-employment profits	1756	1653.96	3192.10
Dummy BRAC participant	1757	0.12	0.32
Dummy BRDB participant	1757	0.07	0.25
Dummy GB participant	1757	0.09	0.28
Log (capital)	1756	7.18	1.33
Highest grade completed by household (HH) head	1757	2.48	3.50
Highest grade completed by adult female in HH	1757	1.60	2.85
Age of HH head (years)	1757	40.80	12.79
Dummy HH head male	1757	0.95	0.22
Dummy no adult female in HH	1757	0.02	0.13
Dummy no adult male in HH	1757	0.04	0.19
Household land (decimals)	1757	75.49	106.06
# Parents of HH head who own land	1757	0.25	0.56
# Brothers of HH head who own land	1757	0.80	1.30
# Sisters of HH head who own land	1757	0.74	1.20
# Uncles of HH head who own land	1757	0.93	1.55
# Aunts of HH head who own land	1757	0.65	1.33
# Sons of HH head who own land	1757	0.34	1.00
# Daughters of HH head who own land	1757	0.34	0.93
# Parents of HH head's spouse who own land	1757	0.52	0.78
# Brothers of HH head's spouse who own land	1757	0.91	1.42
# Sisters of HH head's spouse who own land	1757	0.74	1.20
# Uncles of HH head's spouse who own land	1757	1.13	1.92
# Aunts of HH head's spouse who own land	1757	0.75	1.54
# Sons of HH head's spouse who own land	1757	0.30	0.90
# Daughters of HH head's spouse who own land	1757	0.31	0.88
# Parents of HH head who are living	1757	0.73	0.74
# Brothers of HH head who are living	1757	2.03	1.62
# Sisters of HH head who are living	1757	1.84	1.53
# Uncles of HH head who are living	1757	1.66	1.91
# Aunts of HH head who are living	1757	1.45	1.90
# Sons of HH head who are living	1757	1.70	1.58
# Daughters of HH head who own land	1757	1.62	1.52
# Parents of HH head's spouse who are living	1757	1.03	0.83
# Brothers of HH head's spouse who are living	1757	1.98	1.64
# Sisters of HH head's spouse who are living	1757	1.92	1.67
# Uncles of HH head's spouse who are living	1757	2.02	2.27
# Aunts of HH head's spouse who are living	1757	1.56	1.95
# Sons of HH head's spouse who are living	1757	1.49	1.48
# Daughters of HH head's spouse who are living	1757	1.46	1.47
Dummy no spouse in HH	1757	0.13	0.33
Average male daily wage	1757	37.89	9.40
Average female daily wage	1757	16.13	9.61
Dummy no female wage	1757	0.19	0.40
Dummy primary school in village	1757	0.69	0.46
Dummy rural health center in village	1757	0.30	0.46
Dummy family planning center in village	1757	0.10	0.30
Dummy dai/midwife available in village	1757	0.67	0.47
Distance to bank (km)	1757	3.48	2.85
Price of rice	1757	11.15	0.85
Price of wheat flour	1757	9.59	1.00
Price of mustard oil	1757	52.65	5.97
Price of hen egg	1757	2.46	1.81
Price of milk	1757	12.55	3.04
Price of potato	1757	3.74	1.49

TABLE A2.—MODEL 1 RESULTS
WESML-LIML-FE ESTIMATES OF THE TOTAL EFFECT OF PARTICIPATION ON
LOG (MONTHLY PROFIT)

Explanatory Variables	Coefficient	Asymptotic t-Ratio
BRAC participant	0.969	2.73
BRDB participant	1.093	3.72
GB participant	1.296[a]	3.18
Highest grade completed by household (HH) head	−0.001	−0.04
Highest grade completed by adult female in HH	−0.035	−0.90
Age of HH head (years)	−0.011	−0.98
Dummy HH head male	1.046	1.48
Dummy no adult female in HH	−1.879	−2.05
Dummy no adult male in HH	0.149	0.18
Log (household land in decimals)	0.584	8.38
# Parents of HH head who own land	0.376	1.96
# Brothers of HH head who own land	0.123	1.37
# Sisters of HH head who own land	−0.021	−0.23
# Uncles of HH head who own land	0.043	0.45
# Aunts of HH head who own land	0.035	0.35
# Sons of HH head who own land	0.371	1.80
# Daughters of HH head who own land	−0.224	−0.94
# Parents of HH head's spouse who own land	0.194	1.25
# Brothers of HH head's spouse who own land	−0.011	−0.14
# Sisters of HH head's spouse who own land	0.211	2.43
# Uncles of HH head's spouse who own land	0.046	0.55
# Aunts of HH head's spouse who own land	−0.115	−1.30
# Sons of HH head's spouse who own land	−0.478	−2.17
# Daughters of HH head's spouse who own land	0.291	1.21
# Parents of HH head who are living	−0.037	−0.22
# Brothers of HH head who are living	0.061	0.79
# Sisters of HH head who are living	0.020	0.28
# Uncles of HH head who are living	0.132	1.64
# Aunts of HH head who are living	−0.099	−1.19
# Sons of HH head who are living	−0.300	−2.16
# Daughters of HH head who own land	0.288	1.65
# Parents of HH head's spouse who are living	−0.153	−0.91
# Brothers of HH head's spouse who are living	0.150	2.21
# Sisters of HH head's spouse who are living	−0.801	−1.16
# Uncles of HH head's spouse who are living	−0.143	−1.90
# Aunts of HH head's spouse who are living	0.072	0.90
# Sons of HH head's spouse who are living	0.440	3.18
# Daughters of HH head's spouse who are living	−0.344	−1.96
Dummy no spouse in HH	−0.609	−1.34
ρ GB	0.207	2.16
σ	2.721	34.97
Number observations		1703

[a] Treated as an endogenous variable.

TABLE A3.—MODEL 2 RESULTS
WESML-LIML-FE SPEC. 1 ESTIMATES OF THE NONCREDIT EFFECT OF
PARTICIPATION ON LOG (MONTHLY PROFIT)

Explanatory Variables	Coefficient	Asymptotic t-Ratio
BRAC participant	0.858	2.39
BRDB participant	0.955	3.27
GB participant	1.110[a]	2.73
Log (capital)	1.945[a]	3.23
Highest grade completed by household (HH) head	0.030	0.65
Highest grade completed by adult female in HH	−0.063	−1.08
Age of HH head (years)	−0.019	−1.45
Dummy HH head male	−0.496	−0.45
Dummy no adult female in HH	2.272	1.14
Dummy no adult male in HH	0.394	0.35
Log (household land in decimals)	−0.071	−0.26
ρ GB	0.246	2.59
σ	2.748	34.38
Number observations	1757	

[a] Treated as an endogenous variable.

TABLE A4.—REDUCED-FORM EQUATIONS

	Dependent Variable			
	Program Participant		Log (Capital[a])	
	WESML-FE Probit		WESML-FE	
Explanatory Variables	Coefficient	Asymptotic t-Ratio	Coefficient	Asymptotic t-Ratio
Highest grade completed by household (HH) head	0.027	1.60	−0.016	−0.82
Highest grade completed by adult female in HH	−0.030	−1.42	0.016	0.71
Age of HH head (years)	−0.004	−0.59	−0.001	−0.08
Dummy HH head male	−0.831	−1.76	0.824	2.19
Dummy no adult female in HH	−0.667	−1.99	−2.200	−4.24
Dummy no adult male in HH	−0.284	−0.70	−0.146	−0.32
Log (household land in decimals)	0.022	0.85	0.343	8.64
# Parents of HH head who own land	0.034	0.37	0.176	2.22
# Brothers of HH head who own land	0.031	0.64	0.015	0.41
# Sisters of HH head who own land	−0.036	−0.72	−0.027	−0.69
# Uncles of HH head who own land	−0.168	−3.88	−0.017	−0.41
# Aunts of HH head who own land	0.184	3.77	0.076	1.60
# Sons of HH head who own land	0.253	1.50	0.114	1.38
# Daughters of HH head who own land	0.025	0.17	0.030	0.28
# Parents of HH head's spouse who own land	−0.019	−0.25	0.050	0.76
# Brothers of HH head's spouse who own land	−0.052	−1.22	−0.024	−0.72
# Sisters of HH head's spouse who own land	0.057	1.15	0.105	2.51
# Uncles of HH head's spouse who own land	0.043	1.15	0.054	1.41
# Aunts of HH head's spouse who own land	−0.058	−1.25	−0.042	−1.22
# Sons of HH head's spouse who own land	0.149	0.79	−0.026	−0.25
# Daughters of HH head's spouse who own land	0.125	0.78	−0.010	−0.09
# Parents of HH head who are living	0.053	0.66	−0.011	−0.19
# Brothers of HH head who are living	−0.054	−1.83	0.047	1.42
# Sisters of HH head who are living	0.086	2.58	−0.004	−0.13
# Uncles of HH head who are living	0.096	2.72	0.053	1.68
# Aunts of HH head who are living	−0.074	−2.09	−0.047	−1.41
# Sons of HH head who are living	0.041	0.71	−0.093	−1.74
# Daughters of HH head who are living	0.005	0.05	0.076	1.12
# Parents of HH head's spouse who are living	−0.054	−0.68	−0.013	−0.19
# Brothers of HH head's spouse who are living	0.048	1.47	0.085	2.83
# Sisters of HH head's spouse who are living	−0.014	−0.47	−0.055	−1.73
# Uncles of HH head's spouse who are living	−0.050	−1.67	−0.065	−2.08
# Aunts of HH head's spouse who are living	0.033	0.95	0.350	1.15
# Sons of HH head's spouse who are living	0.042	0.67	0.193	3.18
# Daughters of HH head's spouse who are living	−0.001	−0.02	−0.046	−0.62
Dummy no spouse in HH	−0.361	−1.53	−0.044	−0.23
Dummy nontarget HH			0.422	3.83
Number observations	1283		1486	

[a] Capital is the taka value of productive capital used in self-employment (such as tools, rickshaw, and livestock). The 28 variables indicating the number of living and landed nonresident relations represent potential sources of transfers to the household and are used as instruments for the log (capital) equation. A joint test for significance indicates that they are important determinants of capital ($\chi^2(28) = 48.11$, $p = 0.01$).

THE IMPACT OF MICROCREDIT PROGRAMS ON SELF-EMPLOYMENT PROFITS 115

TABLE A5.—MODEL 2 RESULTS
WESML-LIML-FE ESTIMATES OF THE NONCREDIT EFFECT OF PARTICIPATION ON LOG (MONTHLY PROFIT): LAND HOLDINGS ENTER AS POLYNOMIAL

Explanatory Variables	WESML-LIML-FE Spec. 1	WESML-LIML-FE Spec. 2	WESML-LIML-FE Spec. 3
BRAC participant	0.965[a]	0.918[a]	0.848[a]
	(2.44)	(2.42)	(2.24)
BRDB participant	0.934[a]	1.069[a]	0.944[a]
	(1.41)	(2.08)	(1.93)
GB participant	1.134[a]	1.160[a]	1.072[a]
	(2.61)	(2.93)	(2.72)
Log (capital)	1.940[a]	1.662[a]	1.701[a]
	(3.18)	(2.81)	(3.03)
Highest grade completed by household (HH) head	0.030	0.027	0.027
	(0.65)	(0.64)	(0.64)
Highest grade completed by adult female in HH	−0.062	−0.073	−0.068
	(−1.09)	(−1.35)	(−1.26)
Age of HH head (years)	−0.019	−0.020	−0.019
	(−1.45)	(−1.61)	(−1.57)
Dummy HH head male	−0.048	−0.246	−0.252
	(−0.44)	(−0.24)	(−0.26)
Dummy no adult female in HH	2.263	.607	.658
	(1.11)	(0.83)	(0.88)
Dummy no adult male in HH	0.400	0.259	0.423
	(0.35)	(0.26)	(0.42)
Log (household land in decimals)	−0.068	−0.264	−0.286
	(−0.025)	(−1.01)	(−1.14)
(Log (household land in decimals))^2		0.065	0.194
		(3.11)	(3.84)
(Log (household land in decimals))^3			−0.022
			(−3.04)
ρ BRAC	−0.031	−0.041	−0.038
	(−0.56)	(−0.73)	(−0.68)
ρ BRDB	0.007	−0.045	−0.023
	(0.04)	(−0.36)	(−0.19)
ρ GB	0.242	0.220	0.235
	(2.45)	(2.32)	(2.46)
σ	2.748	.737	2.729
	(34.29)	(34.53)	(34.39)
Number observations	1757	1757	1757

Asymptotic *t*-ratios in parentheses.
[a] Treated as an endogenous variable.

TABLE A6.—MODEL 1 RESULTS
WESML-LIML-FE ESTIMATES OF THE TOTAL EFFECT OF PARTICIPATION ALTERNATE SPECIFICATIONS OF DEPENDENT VARIABLE

Explanatory Variable	Dependent Variable		
	Spec. 1 Log (Profit) Drop if Profit < 0	Spec. 2 Log (Profit + c)	Spec. 3 Log (Profit) = 0 if Profit < 0
BRAC participant	0.969	0.989	1.014
	(2.73)	(2.48)	(2.77)
BRDB participant	1.093	0.859	0.718
	(3.72)	(2.68)	(2.30)
GB participant	1.296[a]	1.124[a]	0.959[a]
	(3.18)	(2.72)	(2.03)
ρ GB	0.207	0.121	0.210
	(2.16)	(1.57)	(2.29)
Number observations	1703	1703	1703

Asymptotic *t*-ratios in parentheses.
[a] Treated as an endogenous variable. Presents only selected regressors.

[11]

ELSEVIER

Journal of Development Economics 82 (2007) 509–528

JOURNAL OF
Development
ECONOMICS

www.elsevier.com/locate/econbase

Migration networks and microenterprises in Mexico

Christopher Woodruff [a],[*], Rene Zenteno [b]

[a] *Graduate School of International Relations and Pacific Studies, UCSD, La Jolla, CA 92093, United States*
[b] *Monterrey Institute of Technology and Graduate Studies, Mexico*

Received 18 June 2004; received in revised form 6 March 2006; accepted 9 March 2006

Abstract

Are migration networks associated with lower capital costs, or the alleviation of capital constraints? We examine these questions with data measuring access to remittance flows among small-scale entrepreneurs in Mexico. Using a survey of more than 6000 self-employed workers and small firm owners located in 44 urban areas of Mexico, we estimate the impact of attachment to migration networks on the level of capital investment, the capital–output ratio, sales, and profits of microenterprises. The impact is identified from the geographic pattern of migration from Mexico driven by the completion of rail lines in the early 1900s. For the full sample of firms, we find that migration is associated with higher investment levels and higher profits, but not higher sales. The strongest effects on investment are in the categories of automobiles, tools and inventories. When the sample is limited to firms in high-capital sectors, investment, sales, and profits all increase with attachment to the migration networks, suggesting that attachment to the migration network alleviates capital constraints in those sectors.
© 2006 Elsevier B.V. All rights reserved.

JEL classification: O16; J23; F22
Keywords: Microenterprises; Remittances; Migration; Capital networks

1. Introduction

There is growing empirical evidence of the role networks play in shaping economic activity. Networks allow for trade over long distances (Greif, 1993) and in locations where formal legal enforcement is not available (McMillan and Woodruff, 1999). Where capital markets are imperfect, networks may play a role in allocating capital among uses and users (Banerjee and Munshi, 2004). In countries with high rates of international emigration, migration networks may

* Corresponding author.
  E-mail address: cwoodruff@ucsd.edu (C. Woodruff).

0304-3878/$ - see front matter © 2006 Elsevier B.V. All rights reserved.
doi:10.1016/j.jdeveco.2006.03.006

510   *C. Woodruff, R. Zenteno / Journal of Development Economics 82 (2007) 509–528*

play an particularly important role in determining economic outcomes. Munshi (2003) provides evidence that networks are an important feature of Mexico–U.S. migration. In this paper, we examine the impact of the migration networks in Mexico on the development of microenterprises in the country.

Migration to the United States has long been an important feature of Mexican life. In 2000, more than 9 million Mexican-born individuals were resident in the United States, about 9% of the population born in Mexico. Early migration of workers from Mexico to the United States came in two waves associated with guest worker, or *Bracero*, programs. The first of these was during the 1910s, at the start of World War I. The second began in 1942 during World War II. The distribution within Mexico of the points of origin of early migrants to the United States was closely associated with the location of rail lines which went northward to the Texas border. Though railroads are no longer the most important means of transport for U.S. bound migrants, the rail lines remain closely associated with migration. The early migrants formed the foundation for migration networks that persist to the present day.

We examine the impact of migration networks on microenterprises using data from a very detailed survey of more than 6000 microenterprises located in 44 urban areas of Mexico, representing 92% of Mexico's urban population. We show that migration is associated with a significantly higher rate of investment and a significantly higher capital/output ratio. The effects are large. A one standard deviation increase in the migration rate in an entrepreneur's state of birth is associated with a 35%–40% increase in the level of capital invested in the enterprise. Examining the level of investment by type of asset, we find that investments in tools, inventories and vehicles are all associated with stronger links to migration networks. Migration is correlated with higher capital–output ratios as well. In the full sample, we find no robust relationship between migration and the level of output of an enterprise. The results from the full sample are strikingly similar to those described by Banerjee and Munshi (2004) for a sample of firms in the Indian knitted shirt industry. However, for Mexico we do find that the increased investment is associated with higher profit levels. Moreover, when we isolate firms operating in high-capital sectors, we find a positive relationship between migration on the one hand and all four of the outcome measures—including sales—on the other. In the low capital sector, we find a much weaker connection between migration and investment, and a strong relationship only for the capital–output ratio. These results suggest that migration networks may play a role in alleviating capital constraints in high capital sectors.

Our identification strategy exploits variation in the degree to which individuals in Mexico are connected to historical migration networks. We measure connection to the migration network with a group level variable, the rate of migration in an individual's state of birth. We then instrument for this with the distance from the capital of the state in which an individual was born to the nearest station on the north/south rail lines as they existed in the early 1900s. Of course, rail lines may affect local economic activity in many ways, potentially invalidating the instrument. Partly for this reason, we limit our focus to the approximately 28% of individuals who currently reside in a state in Mexico which is different from their state of birth. Note that these individuals may differ in important (and unmeasured) ways from those who reside in their state of birth, so the implication of our results should be viewed as being limited to the sub-group of internal migrants.

The paper relates to two literatures. The first is the growing literature on the impact of migration on sending country development. There is an extensive and established literature on the relationship between migration and economic development of sending regions. Much of the literature, however, focuses on rural–urban migration within countries (Stark, 1978, 1980; Rozelle et al., 1999). Earlier studies focusing on international migrants generally examined the

C. Woodruff, R. Zenteno / Journal of Development Economics 82 (2007) 509–528 511

impact in rural areas within the countries from which migrants emigrate. Examples of this include Lucas (1987) and Lucas and Stark (1985), who analyze the impact on earnings returned by migrant workers in South African mines. Taylor (1992) and Taylor and Wyatt (1996) examine agricultural asset accumulation in a sample of rural households receiving remittances in Mexico.

There is smaller, but growing literature examining the impact of migration on non-agricultural activities. Dustmann and Kirkchamp (2002) provide evidence that savings of returning migrants may be an important source of startup capital for microenterprises. They find that 50% of a sample of Turkish emigrants returning from Germany started a microenterprise within 4 years of resettling in Turkey, using money saved while working abroad. Mesnard (2004) and Mesnard and Ravallion (2005) also find a connection between return migration to Tunisia and entry into self-employment, and Ilahi (1999) finds similar evidence in Pakistan. Early evidence of a correlation between migration, remittances and entry into self-employment in Nicaragua is provided by Funkhouser (1992). With respect to Mexico, Massey and Parrado (1998) examine enterprise formation in a sample of 30 communities in central-west Mexico, including five neighborhoods in large cities. They conclude that earnings from work in the United States provided an important source of startup capital in 21% of the new business formations. Escobar Latapi and Martinez Castellanos (1991) report that earnings from U.S. migration were an important source of startup capital in 7 of 19 manufacturing firms they surveyed in Guadalajara.

The second literature which relates to the issues addressed in the paper is the literature on capital constraints, and particularly the importance of networks in the provision of finance. In this regard, recent papers by Banerjee and Munshi (2004) on the Indian knitted shirt industry and Banerjee and Duflo (2003) on changes in the lending laws in India are particularly relevant. Banerjee and Munshi study production in a single industry where members of a relatively capital rich community (Gounders) face lower costs of capital than do members of a capital poor community (Outsiders). Banerjee and Munshi show that entrepreneurs in the capital rich community (or network) have higher capital-investment levels and higher capital–output ratios. Capital-rich (Gounder) firms also have higher sales levels when very young, but grow more slowly than the capital-constrained Outsiders. Banerjee and Munshi conclude that imperfections in capital markets prevent the capital costs from equating across communities. Banerjee and Duflo (2003) show that increases in access to capital may also alleviate capital constraints.[1] The variation in the Banerjee–Duflo data comes not from networks but from changes in Indian laws dictating set-aside lending for firms with certain characteristics. They find that increased access to capital is associated with higher sales and higher profits, suggesting that firms use the increased access to make fresh investments rather than using the bank loans to pay off non-bank loans bearing higher interest rates. When we use our full sample, our results are quite similar to those of Banerjee–Munshi. Like them, we find that attachment to liquidity is associated with higher investment and capital–output ratios, but not to higher sales. When the sample is limited to firms in high capital sectors, our results are close to Banerjee–Duflo. For this subsample, we do find evidence that sales are higher among firms with stronger attachment to the network.

The main challenge in both of these literatures is to cleanly identify impacts of migration or credit constraints. For migration, the cleanest identification strategies in the existing literature derive from short-terms shocks.[2] Munshi (2003) uses changes in rainfall (e.g., droughts) to

---

[1] Using a sample of much larger, publicly traded firms in the Unite States, Lamont (1997) shows that liquidity shocks increase investment in units of firms, even where those units themselves experienced no shock, and hence, no change in the marginal productivity of capital.

[2] Mesnard and Ravallion (2005) use a change in policies by destination countries of Tunisian migrants as a source of exogenous variation.

512   C. Woodruff, R. Zenteno / Journal of Development Economics 82 (2007) 509–528

identify the strength of migration networks among a set of communities in high migration states in Mexico. Yang (2004) uses the Asian currency crisis as a source of changes in the value of remittances received by Filipino families with migrants overseas. He takes advantage of the fact Filipino migrants work in many different countries. We use cross-sectional data and are not aware of any identifiable exogenous shock to exploit in our data. Given our identification strategy, our results should be interpreted as representing the longer-term effect of migration on microenterprises in Mexico. These may differ from the response to transient shocks identified by Yang.

Because the use of distance from rail lines as an instrument is so critical to the interpretation of our results, we begin by examining the validity of this instrument, and discussing other issues related to identification, in Sections 2 and 3. The data are described in Section 4 and the regression results presented in Section 5. Section 6 offers some conclusions.

2. Migration patterns

Mexican workers were recruited to work in the United States in large numbers during the first two decades of the 20th century. The largest source of demand came from the railroads and farms in the southwestern United States. After the start of World War I, the United States established a guest worker, or *Bracero* program, in part to offset the decline in immigration from Europe during the war. Encouraged by this and by the chaos surrounding the Mexican revolution, the flow of workers from Mexico to the United States increased markedly during the 1910s and 1920s.

Three rail lines built between 1884 and 1900 were the major means of transporting labor recruiters south into Mexico and transporting workers north to the United States.[3] The first, the Central Mexican Railroad went south from what is now Ciudad Juarez to Irapuato in the state of Guanajuato, where it branched east to Mexico City and west through Guadalajara to Colima near the Pacific Coast. In the north, the Central Mexican Railway connected to the Southern Pacific and Texas Pacific Railroads in Texas. A second line, the Mexican International railroad, ran a shorter distance Durango through Chihuahua to Piedras Negras, where it connected with the Southern Pacific in Eagle Pass Texas. Finally, the Mexican National Railroad traveled north from Mexico City through San Luis Potosi and Monterrey, reaching the border at Nuevo Laredo and Brownsville in eastern Texas. This third line was less well connected to rail lines in the United States.

Foerster (1925) provides data on the state of origin of migrants registering in Texas, California, Arizona and New Mexico during the year 1924. (In 1920, these states represented more than 90% of the Mexican-born population in the United States, see Borjas and Katz, 2005.) We calculated the distance from the capital city of each state to a stop on any of the main north/south rail lines as they existed in the early 1900s (see Mexican Central Railway, 1900). Where the line passed through the state, as is the case in 16 states, we assigned a distance of zero. For border states not served by the rail line and for Baja California Sur, we used the distance from the capital city to the border. The link between distance to the rail line and migration measured in 1924 is very strong. The correlation between these distances and percentage of the population of each of Mexico's 32 federal entities migrating in 1924 is 0.72.

These same rail lines remained linked to migration during the second *Bracero* program, which began in 1942. The state-level correlation between distance to the rail lines and migration between

---

[3] Railroads were the only practical means for traveling long distances over land in Mexico in the early 1900s. According to Coatsworth (1972, Chapter 3), stage coach travel was five times more costly and one-fifth as fast in 1910.

1955 and 1959, the peak years of the Bracero Program, is 0.75. The correlation between migration rates in the 1920s and 1950s is 0.78. We use the distance to these rail lines as an instrument for current migration patterns. The rail lines were directly related to migration in the early 1900s. This early migration led to the establishment of migration networks, which persisted even after other rail lines were constructed and other means of transportation became more commonly used. There are several potential concerns with the use of rail lines as an instrument, which we address in the next section.

3. A framework and identification issues

To clarify the issues related to identification of network effects, consider a simple Lucas-style span of control model (Lucas, 1978). Potential entrepreneurs weigh their earnings from wage work against the earnings from self-employment. The latter are a function of the individual's entrepreneurial ability and market conditions. For example, suppose an entrepreneur faces a simple production function of the sort $Y=\theta DK^{\alpha}L^{1-\alpha}$, where K and L are capital and labor, θ_i represents entrepreneurial ability, and D represents (perhaps temporary) shocks to demand in the industry in which the firm operates. Demand for capital of entrepreneur i will then be a function of the interest rate (r), the wage rate (w), θ_i, and D:[4]

$$K_{id} = f(r, w, \theta_i, D) \tag{1}$$

where the subscript i indexes the individual and the subscript d indicates demand for capital. The wage rate affects investment through the decision to enter self-employment.[5]

The relevant interest rate is the rate of interest earned on savings up to the level of an individual's wealth and the rate of interest paid on loans after that point. We refer to this interest rate schedule as the supply of capital. Capital may come from the entrepreneur's personal wealth, or from loans from either formal sources (e.g., banks) or informal sources (e.g., family members or friends). In reality, formal bank lending to firms of the size in our sample is very rare in Mexico. Less than 3% of enterprises in our sample report receiving loans from banks.[6] Personal wealth and loans from family members and friends are the most common sources of capital. The supply of capital is a function of:

$$K_{is} = g(W, B, I, T) \tag{2}$$

where the subscript i indexes the individual, s indicates supply of capital, and W is the entrepreneur's wealth or savings,[7] B represents access to bank loans, I access to informal loans

---

[4] Demand for investment capital may also depend on factors such as the security of property rights (Besley, 1995; Johnson et al., 2002). Empirically, we find no evidence of this among our sample of firms, perhaps because their small size leaves them outside the formal institutional structures in Mexico, and below the radar screen of regulators.

[5] Lucas (1978) develops a model to show that under similar assumptions, those with entrepreneurial ability above some endogenously determined threshold will become entrepreneurs, while remaining agents will become wage workers. An increase in per capita income is associated with an increase in wage rates, leading the lowest ability entrepreneurs to abandon self-employment in favor of wage work.

[6] By comparison, 51% of firms in a sample drawn using the same size criteria in the United States report having a loan from a formal financial institution. The U.S. data are drawn from the Federal Reserve's *National Survey of Small Business Finances, 1994.*

[7] Wealth or savings may include profits from the business which are reinvested in the enterprise. In the Fazzari et al. (1988) framework, reinvestment of cash flow allows a credit-constrained firm to adjust towards its optimal capital stock over time. This suggests that the age of the firm will affect the level of investment. The business cycle might affect investment levels as well, through its impact on cash flows. We control for both of these in the regressions.

514   C. Woodruff, R. Zenteno / Journal of Development Economics 82 (2007) 509–528

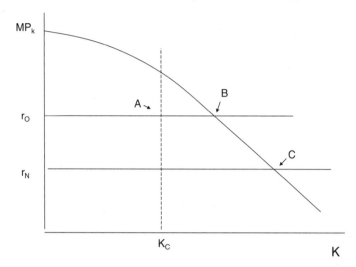

Fig. 1. The effect of constriants and capital networks on the level of invested capital.

and T access to trade credit. The level of capital invested in the firm then depends on both the demand for capital and its supply.

If the migration network has more liquidity, then those in the network will face a lower cost of capital than those outside the network. The network might also serve to alleviate capital constraints faced by microentrepreneurs. These two possibilities are illustrated in Fig. 1, which shows the marginal product of capital at any level of capital stock. The figure is drawn for the case of diminishing marginal product of capital. The cost of capital for those outside networks, denoted r_O, is higher than the cost of capital within migration networks, r_N. A constrained firm outside the network finds itself at a point like that labeled A, associated with capital level K_c where the marginal product of capital exceeds the market cost of capital. An unconstrained firm outside the network will be at the point labeled B, and an unconstrained firm in the migration network at point C. In either case, the implication is that networked firms will use capital. For many production functions (for example, Cobb–Douglass), networked firms will also have higher capital–output ratios. If the network alleviates capital constraints (i.e., a movement from A to C), then firms will certainly have higher sales and higher profits as well. If the network only reduces the cost of capital (i.e., a movement from point B to point C), then whether sales increase depends on the elasticity of demand. For small niche markets with inelastic demand, sales of unconstrained firms may not increase.[8]

Our data do not allow us to differentiate directly between the case of lower capital costs and the case of constraint alleviation with lower capital costs. But the effect of the network on output provides a weak test of this. If we find no effect on output, we would conclude that the networks

---

[8] Profits will increase mechanically with the fall in interest rates from the market to the migration network level. However, it is less clear that this increase will be reflected in our data. A very small percentage of firms report having formal bank loans. Most invested capital is from the owner's personal resources or informal loans from family members. The informal loans often have no explicit interest rate, and hence the reduction in the cost of external credit may not be reflected in the firms' reported expenses and profits.

C. Woodruff, R. Zenteno / Journal of Development Economics 82 (2007) 509–528   515

serve only to lower the cost of capital. If sales increase as well, increased capital may be alleviating capital constraints as well.

3.1. Issues with identification

Our intent is to isolate the effect of migration networks operating through the supply or cost of capital. In order to do that, we must be able separate that effect from the other effects of migration. One obvious issue is that individuals who migrate, or family members of those who migrate, might be expected to have unmeasured characteristics which differ from individuals who do not migrate. The migrants, on average, might be expected to be more entrepreneurial than non-migrants. We address this concern by using a group level measure of migration: the overall migration rate in an individual's state of birth. The question of identification then becomes a question of the independence of the overall migration rate from the overall average unmeasured characteristics. That is, the identification question is one of correlation between state-level migration rates and the distribution of entrepreneurial ability at the state level.

At the group level, there are at least two broad concerns with identification of the effects of migration on the supply of capital. The first is that the strength of migration networks may be correlated with the overall distribution of entrepreneurial ability, θ_i, in the population. The second is that migration may be correlated with other factors affecting the demand for capital of microenterprises. In either case, the effect of migration on the level of capital employed could be causal–for example, remittances flowing from migration may increase the demand for goods and services produced by microenterprises–or spurious. We discuss each of these issues, and how we address them, in turn.

With respect to the distribution of entrepreneurial ability, one concern is that high migration regions may have been selected by U.S. labor recruiters early on because people inhabiting those regions are particularly entrepreneurial. The fact that major north/south rail lines connected Mexico's largest cities–Mexico City and Guadalajara–with important border cities, combined with the fact that migration followed those rail lines alleviates to some extent a causal story linking entrepreneurial ability with migration. But there could still be a spurious connection between the rail lines and entrepreneurial ability. A second concern related to the distribution of entrepreneurial ability is the selection of who migrates. Almost 10% of the population born in Mexico resides in the United States—and the percentage is much higher in some states. Given that our data are limited to individuals resident in Mexico in 1998, the distribution of θ_i among the population in our sample will be affected by the selection of who migrates. We argue in this section that the available evidence suggests that the rail lines were not significantly correlated with the distribution of entrepreneurial ability at the time of early migration.

With regard to the connection between early migration and the entrepreneurial ability of the region, we note that the northern terminus of all three rail lines was determined by their U.S. owners (Coatsworth, 1972; Kuntz Ficker, 2000). In the case of the Mexican Central Railway, the crossing point of El Paso was selected to link with the existing network of the company's parent, the Atchison, Topeka and Santa Fe. The Mexican National Railroad was linked to the railway system controlled by its major investor, Jay Gould. The southern terminus of both lines in Mexico City was determined by the centrality of that city to the life of the country. While the specific route of the rail line might have been affected by the lobbying ability of individual municipalities, at the level of the state, the route was largely determined by geography given the two end points. There might be slightly more concern about politics playing a large role in these two parts of the lines: the western spur of the Central Railway to Guadalajara, which was completed in 1889, and the

516   C. Woodruff, R. Zenteno / Journal of Development Economics 82 (2007) 509–528

line to Colima near the Pacific coast, completed in 1907. Perhaps these lines resulted from particularly adept lobbying on the part of the states of Jalisco and Colima. As we note below, the main results are robust to excluding individuals born in these two states.

Even if there were no causal link between regional entrepreneurial ability and access to the rail line, there may have been a spurious correlation. We have literacy data from the population census of 1910, and somewhat more detailed education and occupation data from the census of 1940. The earlier period predates the first wave of migration during the 1910s and 1920s, when the percentage of Mexican-born population living abroad was very low. The second precedes the larger wave of migration associated with the second Bracero program in effect from 1942 to 1965. Moreover, the percentage of Mexican-born individuals residing in the United States decreased during the 1930s due to a large return migration during the Depression. The population missing from Mexico's 1940 census due to migration abroad was reduced as a result.

Data from the population census of 1910 suggest there is no significant correlation between literacy rates in that year and subsequent migration rates when the latter are measured either using the data for 1924 (Foerster, 1925) or data from the peak migration years of the second Bracero program, 1955–1959.[9] There is a small positive correlation (0.08) between literacy in 1910 and 1924 migration rates, and a small negative correlation (−0.03) between literacy in 1910 and 1955–1959 migration rates. Data from the 1940 census on the level of self-employment (self-employed as a percent of all employed) indicate that self-employment rates are insignificantly correlated with subsequent migration rates. We find similarly small and insignificant correlations between migration rates during the peak of the *Bracero* program, 1955–1959, and occupation structure in 1940.[10] There is some negative correlation between levels of education in 1940 and subsequent migration rates. Migration rates are higher in states with a larger percentage of residents with less than 6 years of schooling (0.31) and smaller in state with more population having 68 years of schooling (−0.31) or 9–11 years of schooling (−0.19), though the latter correlation is not significant at the 0.10 level. To the extent that educational attainment is correlated with entrepreneurial ability (a standard assumption in the literature), the education data suggest that there may be some negative correlation between migration rates and entrepreneurial ability. If so, this will bias our results downward.

We also have some concern that the railroads may have had a direct effect on the profitability of microenterprise investments, perhaps because they increased the economic growth in the areas where they passed. While limited data from the first half of the century make it difficult to fully address this concern, we note that by mid-century, the railroad network extended to every state in Mexico. The growth-inducing effects of railroads thus had a half-century to take hold even in those places which were far from rails when the migration networks were first formed. Of course, it might be the case that regions with earlier access to railroads gained advantages over those obtaining rail lines at a later time, and that time has not dissipated this advantage.

A separate concern related to the endogeneity of the distribution of θ_i is that of selection. Almost 10% of the individuals born in Mexico currently reside in the United States. These individuals are clearly not randomly selected from the population born in Mexico. Hence, even if

---

[9] The *Bracero* migration rate data come from González Navarro (1974).

[10] The measured correlation between self-employment in 1940 and *Bracero* (1955–1959) migration is low and negative (−0.05), while the correlations between the 1940 self-employment rate and current (1995–2000) migration rates is low and positive (0.07). The correlation between Bracero migration rates and the percentage of employment in agriculture (0.07), trade (−0.10), manufacturing (−0.07) and professional services (−0.03) are all low and highly insignificant.

C. Woodruff, R. Zenteno / Journal of Development Economics 82 (2007) 509–528   517

Table 1
Regression results: labor force participation and self-employment status

	Males				Females			
	(1)	(2)	(3)	(4)	(5)	(6)	(7)	(8)
	LFP	LPF	SE status	SE status	LFP	LFP	SE status	SE status
	OLS	IV	OLS	IV	OLS	IV	OLS	IV
Migration rate,	−0.125	−0.10	−0.38	−0.21	−0.29	−0.397	0.145	0.002
state of birth	(1.21)	(0.36)	(1.85)	(0.83)	(2.37)	(1.45)	(0.59)	(0.01)
State fixed effects	Yes	Yes	Yes	Yes	Yes	Yes	Yes	Yes
Industry fixed effects	No	No	Yes	Yes	No	No	Yes	Yes
Number of	28123	28123	20707	20707	31120	31120	8342	8342
observations								
R^2	0.07	0.09	0.17	0.18	0.03	0.03	0.30	0.27

t-values in parentheses. Standard errors are corrected for clustering at the state of birth level. Data are from the 1998 National Employment Survey. The sample is limited to individuals 18–65 years of age residing in urban areas. Labor force participation is defined as working 35 h or more per week. For the self-employment regressions, those working in agriculture are excluded.

the distribution of entrepreneurial talent were identical in high and low migration states prior to migration, that distribution might differ in important ways after migration.

We can provide little direct evidence on the characteristics of migrants residing outside of Mexico. The data to examine even measured characteristics of Mexican migrants are less than perfect. As a result, there is little consensus on the measured characteristics of those missing from Mexico.[11] We can, however, look at the data on outcomes related to self-employment. We do this first by running regressions on labor force participation and entry into self-employment, reported in Table 1. We find no robust relationship between links to migration networks and either labor force participation or entry into self-employment. We define labor force participation as working full time, 35 h/week or more. All of the results are very similar if we instead use a threshold of 20 h/week. All of the regressions control for the age and estimated work experience of the individual, the squares of both of these, and for GDP per capita in the individual's state of birth. The regressions on self-employment status include controls for seven broad industry categories, though again, the results are not sensitive to this.

The regressions in Columns 1 and 2 report the labor force participation results for males, and those in Columns 5 and 6 report the similar results for females. For males, we find no relationship between connection to the migration networks and participation in the labor force. For females, we find a significant negative relationship between work force participation and migration in the OLS regression, but again this is not robust to instrumenting for migration using distance from the capital of the individual's state of birth and the north/south rail lines. Columns 3–4 and 7–8 report the results of regressions on self-employment, conditional on labor force participation, for males

---

[11] See Chiquiar and Hanson (2005), who examine the patterns of migration from Mexico based on information provided by migrants in 1990 U.S. population census. They construct counterfactual wage distributions in including U.S. migrants in the Mexican labor market. Their findings suggest that migrants would have wages slightly higher than the median in Mexico, centered in the 5th and 6th deciles (see Figs. 6 and 7). Ibarraran and Lubotsky (2005), on the other hand use data from the Mexican population census to show that migrants are negatively selected. The U.S. census is more likely to undercount young single migrants who are less well established in the U.S., while the Mexican census undercounts migrants who move as a household, who are more likely to be urban and have higher levels of education than other migrants.

518   *C. Woodruff, R. Zenteno / Journal of Development Economics 82 (2007) 509–528*

and females, respectively. For males, we find a negative relationship between the probability of being self-employed and migration networks in the OLS regression, significant at the 0.10 level. This result, however, is not significant when migration is instrumented. For females, we find no significant relationship in either the OLS or the IV regressions. We conclude that there is no robust relationship between migration and labor force participation or occupational choice.

What do these results suggest about selection of who migrates? In a world without capital constraints, the lack of a robust connection between migration and self-employment would suggest that migrants are selected equally from all parts of the distribution of θ_i. But other researchers have found evidence that migration helps overcome capital constraints, suggesting that the unconstrained capital case is the relevant case.[12] One scenario consistent with both capital constraints and the results in Table 1 is that selection of who migrates offsets the positive effect of migration on entry into self-employment in Mexico. That is, if those with higher entrepreneurial ability are disproportionately likely to migrate, then migration will be negatively correlated with entrepreneurial ability in the sample of individuals remaining behind in Mexico. We caution that this does not necessarily imply that our estimates of the effect of migration on the performance of microenterprises will be biased in a downward direction. None of the results in Table 1 provides information on whether the migrants come disproportionately from the highest end of the range of θ_i, from the range just above the θ_i associated with entry into self employment, or equally from all parts of the range above $\theta_{\min}$. Having reached the limits of what these data allow us to say about any selection bias, we leave the issue of selection as a caveat to the interpretation of our findings.

3.2. Migration and product demand

Aside from the distribution of entrepreneurial talent, migration networks may also affect the demand by microentrepreneurs for capital through an increase in the demand for the goods and services they produce, or through an increase in the wage rates in the regions where they work. Massey and Parrado (1994) use the term "migradollars" for the first possibility. Even absent direct causation, the regions with high migration may differ in ways that affect demand for the output of microenterprises. Large firms may not find markets there attractive, for example, leaving larger market shares for microenterprises. A final related concern is that the rail lines themselves might have affected the industrial structure of the region.

We address this issue by focusing our attention on individuals who currently reside in a state other than their state of birth. About 28% of those in the sample live in a state other than their state of birth. Among this group, the correlation between the migration rate in the state of birth and state of residence is positive but low, 0.16. The birth state provides us with a measure of the individual's connection to migration networks, while the internal migration separates that network connection from the other effects of migration on the local economy. To take an example, we can compare a sample of individuals who currently live in Mexico City, some of whom were born in high migration regions and some in low migration regions. Given the size of firms in our

---

[12] Mesnard (2004) and Mesnard and Ravallion (2005) find that migrants returning to Tunisia with larger savings are more likely to enter self-employment. Dustmann and Kirkchamp (2002) and Ilahi (1999) reach similar conclusions looking a sample of migrants returning to Turkey and Pakistan, respectively. Indeed, at first glance our results appear to be at odds with these other findings. It is important, and relevant, to point out that they are not entirely comparable in this regard. The other authors use samples of returning migrants, while we use a sample of those remaining in the country of origin (which may include some returned migrants). Hence, our sample is affected by selection in very different way from theirs.

C. Woodruff, R. Zenteno / Journal of Development Economics 82 (2007) 509–528 519

Table 2
Receipt of remittances

	Males	Females
	(1)	(2)
	Internal migrants only	Internal migrants only
Migration rate in state of residence	4.49 (3.32)	12.82 (5.79)
Migration rate in state of birth	3.27 (3.96)	5.68 (7.28)
Number of observations	278,778	312,079
% of sample receiving remittances	0.69%	1.51%
Pseudo R^2	0.035	0.027

t-values in parentheses. Standard errors for the migration rate in state of residence are adjusted for clustering at the level of state of residence, and standard errors for the migration rate in the state of birth are adjusted for clustering at the level of the state of birth.

sample, their markets are primarily local.[13] Hence, individuals born in different states will have different levels of connection to migration networks, but face similar market characteristics.

Do international migration networks survive internal migration? We verify that they do using data from Mexico's 2000 census of population. The census includes information on whether individuals receive remittances from anyone currently residing outside of Mexico. When we examine the probability an individual household receives remittances, we find that the receipt of remittances is increase both in the migration rate of the household head's state of residence and state of birth. That is, after controlling for the migration rate in the state of residence, the migration rate in the state of birth is positively associated with the receipt of remittances. Regressions demonstrating this are shown in Table 2. The sample is divided between males and females, and limited to individuals residing in a state other than their state of birth. For both males and females, the overall migration rate in the state of residence has a larger measured effect, but for both, the probability of receiving remittances is increasing in the migration rate of their state of birth as well.

In sum, we address identification issues in the following way: In all of the regressions we report, we use distance to the railroads as an instrument for migration. We also measure the link to the migration network through migration rates in an individual's state of birth, and focus on individuals currently residing in a state other than their state of birth. Even so, we want to stress two caveats. First, by using historical migration, we are identifying the long run effects of migration on microenterprises. Second, the results are based on a sample of individuals who have migrated internally within Mexico since their birth. These individuals may differ in unmeasured ways from those who remain in their state of birth. Hence, the results may not generalize to the overall population.

4. Microenterprise data

We use enterprise investment data from Mexico's 1998 National Survey of Microenterprises (ENAMIN for its Spanish initials). The sample for the ENAMIN is drawn from the self-employed workers surveyed in the National Urban Employment Survey (ENEU for its Spanish initials) in

---

[13] All of the firms in the data have fewer than five employees, with the exception of those in the manufacturing sector, where the upper limit is 15. We verify that the main results are robust to excluding manufacturers from the sample, and excluding the handful of firms (seven) engaged in wholesale trade.

520   C. Woodruff, R. Zenteno / Journal of Development Economics 82 (2007) 509–528

the fourth calendar quarter of 1998. The ENEU is a household-based survey. Hence, the ENAMIN sample includes both registered and unregistered firms. The ENAMIN survey is restricted to firms with fewer than 15 workers (including the owner) in manufacturing and fewer than 5 workers in other sectors. The survey asks enterprise owners about their sales, investments, and employees. The survey also includes some information on the founding of the enterprise, the sources of capital, and the owner's work history. The questions related to investments in the enterprise are quite detailed. Owners are asked about up capital investments in seven categories (tools, vehicles, buildings, and so on), and also about inventories of finished goods and inputs.

The 1998 ENAMIN contains data for 12,005 microenterprises owned by 11,823 individuals in 44 urban areas in Mexico. Each of Mexico's 32 federal entities (31 states and the Federal District) is represented. Where a single individual owns two enterprises, we combine the data on those enterprises. Many of the enterprises are operated to supplement income earned in wage work. In about one-third of the cases, the owners report working less than 35 h/week in the enterprise. In regressions on the size of the enterprise, we focus on enterprises in which the owner works full time, at least 35 h/week. We also limit the sample to firms whose owners are between 18 and 65 years of age. Using these criteria, the sample consists of 7588 firms.[14] Missing data reduce the sample size to 6044 enterprises. Most of this reduction (1482 of 1544 cases) is due to missing data on capital stock. While this is of some concern, we note there is no correlation between missing information on capital stock and the independent variables of interest. We focus on a the sample of individuals who currently reside in a state other than their state of birth. A total of 1675 individuals fit these criteria, 1269 males and 406 females. These internal migrants represent 28% of the sample of enterprises meeting the other criteria. Compared with the full sample, internal migrants have slightly lower levels of schooling (about 1/3rd of a year less) and are a year older. On average, their enterprises have the same amount of invested capital and have been operating for the same number of years. In measured characteristics, then, the subsample of internal migrants is similar to full sample.

The majority (58%) of owners in the sample are self-employed workers hiring no employees. Only 20% of the firms employ at least one paid worker, and 22% of the firms employ family members working without pay. Just over 3% of the firms are partnerships. The reported owner of the majority (76%) of the enterprises is a male, and we use the gender of the owner to differentiate enterprises. The most common activity of the firms is commerce (35%), almost all of which is retail trade. Repair services (16%) and manufacturing (12%) are next most common activities. The remaining firms operate restaurants (11%), in construction (8%), miscellaneous personal services (including cleaning services, 7%), professional services (5%) and transportation services (6%).

Enterprise owners are asked the replacement cost of the capital equipment used in the business (tools, equipment, vehicles, real estate, and so on), and the value of inventories of finished and unfinished goods. We sum these data to obtain an estimate of the capital invested in the firm. For each asset identified in the survey, owners are also asked if they own, rent, or have borrowed the asset. We exclude assets that are rented or borrowed, since these do not represent investments by the owner. The median firm reports a replacement cost of owned assets of $752. The range is quite large, with 25% of the firms investing less than $125, and 10% investing more than $9500. Only a small part of the invested capital–6% for males and 15% for females–is in inventories.

---

[14] The age restriction has no effect on either the significance or magnitude of the results we report below. Including enterprises whose owners work part time does not affect the statistical significance of the results, but does decrease the magnitude of the measured effects by about 20% for males and 30% for females.

C. Woodruff, R. Zenteno / Journal of Development Economics 82 (2007) 509–528 521

The level of capital investment varies considerably with the sector in which the firm operates. At one end, those in transportation and professional services have the highest investment levels, with the median firm reporting a replacement cost of about $6100 and $2800, respectively. At the other extreme, firms in the construction industry have median investment level of only $97, and firms in miscellaneous personal services $184. The most common activity, commerce, has a median replacement cost of invested capital of $1330.

Entrepreneurs finance their investment almost entirely through personal savings and loans from family members and friends. The survey includes questions on sources of startup finance and also on loans and trade credit currently received by the enterprise. About 24% of the firms reported having received loans to start their business. Four-fifths of the firms receiving loans report that the source of the loan was a family member or friend. Only 2.5% of the firms received bank credit at startup. About 8% of firms report that they currently have a loan, with just over one-quarter of those loans coming from banks or other formal credit institutions.

The upper limits on firm size in the ENAMIN sampling criteria produce a potentially biased sample. If remittances relieve capital constraints enough that firms grow beyond the upper limits for sampling, then they will be excluded from the survey. This does not appear to be cause for major concern. Only 1% of the sample outside of manufacturing has 5 employees, and only two manufacturing firms have more than 11 employees. Moreover, the ENAMIN data from which the sample is drawn indicate that only a small percentage of firms exceed these size criteria (3% for manufacturing, 4% for other firms). Hence, we expect that any bias resulting from the selection of the ENAMIN sample criteria is likely to be small.

5. Regression results

The framework developed in Section 3 suggests that we investigate the effect of migration networks on a series of outcomes. First, we expect networked firms to have higher investment levels and higher capital output ratios. If non-networked firms are capital constrained (and even if they are not under some circumstances), we also expect to find higher output and higher profits. We examine each of these four outcomes in this section. We begin by estimating a reduced form regression for capital investment, derived from Eqs. (1) and (2). Denoting the level of migration in an individual's state of residence as M_k and the migration rate in an individual's state of birth as M_j, we can write:

$$K_{ijkl} = c + \varphi w_{kl} + \beta \Gamma_i + \delta \Phi_k + \gamma \Omega_j + \eta_1 M_j + \eta_2 M_k + I_l + \varepsilon_{ijkl} \tag{3}$$

The level of capital invested by entrepreneur i from state of origin j and state of residence k, operating in industry l, is a constant c, an industry fixed effect I_l, a vector of entrepreneur and firm level characteristics Γ_i (e.g., education, age, and age of firm), a vector of state of residence characteristics Φ_k (e.g., GDP per capita, bank credit per capita), a vector of characteristics of the state of birth Ω_j (e.g., per capita income), the wage rate in the state and industry in which the firm operates w_{kl}, the migration rates in the state of birth and residence, and an error term. Given the underlying equations, we interpret the coefficient on M_k as the combined impact of demand for capital and supply of capital, and M_j as indicating a capital supply effect.

The basic regressions include several variables measuring the economic conditions in the state in which the firm is located (the vector Φ). If important state level controls correlated with migration rates are missing, however, our estimate of the impact of remittances may be biased. We therefore focus most of our attention on regressions which control for state fixed effects, of the form:

$$K_{ijkl} = c + \beta\boldsymbol{\Gamma}_i + \gamma\boldsymbol{\Omega}_j + S_k + \eta_1 M_j + I_l + \varepsilon_{ijkl} \tag{4}$$

where S_k is a state fixed effect for the state of residence. The state fixed effects subsume the variation in migration rates in the individual's state of residence. The state and industry variables account for nearly all of the variation in state/industry wage rates, so we drop that from the specification as well.

5.1. Enterprise investment and capital–output ratios

Table 3 reports the results of a regressions on the log of invested capital. We combine the data for males and females because the female sample is small and because separate regressions indicated that the effects we are most interested in are of similar magnitude across genders. (These results are available from the authors.) In the first column, an individual's connection to the migration network is measured by the rate of migration in the state of residence and the rate in the state of birth. The sample is limited to internal migrants, so these variables always take different values. The controls include the level of education, estimated work experience (age minus education minus 6), age of the firm, the square of each of these, the log of per capita income in the individual's state of birth, and industry fixed effects. The standard errors in this and all reported regressions are adjusted for clustering at the state-of-birth level. The rate of migration in the state

Table 3

	(1)	(2)	(3)	(4)	(5)
	OLS	IV	IV	IV	IV
	Internal migrants only	Internal migrants only	With state FE	Without manufacturing, wholesale	All individuals, state FE
(A) Regression results: log of replacement cost of invested capital					
Migration rate, state of residence	−1.53 (0.62)				
Migration rate, state of birth	7.87 (5.79)	7.18 (4.22)	9.10 (3.65)	8.00 (2.94)	9.35 (3.52)
State fixed effects	No	No	Yes	Yes	Yes
Industry controls	Yes	Yes	Yes	Yes	Yes
Number of Observations	1675	1675	1675	1475	6044
R^2	0.29	0.29	0.32	0.33	0.29
(B) First stage for IV regressions: migration rate in the entrepreneur's state of birth					
Distance to north/south rail lines		−0.010 (5.38)	−0.009 (5.29)	−0.009 (5.19)	−0.007 (4.61)
State fixed effects		No	Yes	Yes	Yes
Industry controls		Yes	Yes	Yes	Yes
Number of Observations		1675	1675	1475	6044
Partial R^2 of instrument		0.55	0.45	0.45	0.24

t-values in parentheses. Standard errors are corrected for clustering at the state of birth level. Sample limited to owners 18–65 years of age working at least 35 h/week.

In addition to the variables shown, all regressions include 7 variables indicating the sector of activity. Other controls included in the regression are years of schooling of the owner, the estimated labor market experience (age minus years of schooling minus 6), the age of the firm in years, the square of each of these variables, a dummy indicating the owner reports data for two enterprises and the income per capita in the owner's state of birth.

of birth is positively related to the level of investment, while the rate of migration in the state of residence is not.

The remaining regressions in Table 3 focus on the rate of migration in the individual's state of birth. In Column 2, we instrument for the migration rate using the distance to the railway lines. The measured effect of migration falls slightly for males and increases slightly for females, and both remain statistically significant. The bottom panel of Table 3 shows the first stage regression. As with the main regressions, the standard errors in the first stage are adjusted for clustering at the state-of-birth level. The first stage regression indicates that the location of rail lines explains a large portion (55%) of the variance in current migration rates. Column 3 adds state fixed effects to the regressions. The measured impact of attachment to the migration network increases, though not significantly so, when the state fixed effects are added. The measure of attachment to migration networks is significant not only statistically, but economically as well. A one standard deviation change in the migration rate (0.039) is associated with a 0.35 log point change in the investment level, indicating a very large impact.

Next, we check to see if the results are robust to dropping manufacturing firms and wholesalers from the sample. Migration measured by the individual's state of birth may have an effect on the demand for goods and services sold by the enterprise if the firm's market is not limited to local areas. Because all of the firms outside manufacturing have fewer than five workers–about 80% have no paid workers–it is reasonable to assume that these firms generally face local markets. Both the nature of the goods produced and the size limits mean that manufacturers may face geographically dispersed markets. Remittances flowing into their birth states may result in higher demand for their products. The same is true for firms engaged in wholesale trade, though there are only seven of these in the sample. The regression in Column 4 shows that eliminating these firms has no significant effect on the results. Finally, Column 5 reports the results when we expand the sample to include individuals living in their state of birth. We find results quite close to those reported in Column 3 for the sample of internal migrants.

The results in Table 3 take the capital stock as a whole. The ENAMIN data report investments in several different categories. To see which types of investments are associated with migration networks, Table 4 reports regressions on the level of investment in each of

Table 4
Log of replacement cost of invested capital by type of investment

	(1)	(2)	(3)	(4)	(5)
	IV	IV	IV	IV	IV
	Real estate	Tools and equipment	Vehicles	Inventories	Other investments
Migration rate, state of birth	3.04 (0.85)	4.70 (1.69)	9.35 (2.38)	6.38 (2.00)	3.44 (1.01)
State fixed effects	Yes	Yes	Yes	Yes	Yes
Industry controls	Yes	Yes	Yes	Yes	Yes
Number of observations	1675	1675	1675	1675	1675
R^2	0.13	0.42	0.34	0.41	0.34

t-values in parentheses. Standard errors are corrected for clustering at the state of birth level. Sample limited to owners 18–65 years of age working at least 35 h/week. The migration rate is instrumented with the distance from the north/south railway lines, as described in the text. In addition to the variables shown, all regressions include 7 variables indicating the sector of activity. Other controls included in the regression are years of schooling of the owner, the estimated labor market experience (age minus years of schooling minus 6), the age of the firm in years, the square of each of these variables, a dummy indicating the owner reports data for two enterprises and the income per capita in the owner's state of birth.

five categories: real estate, tools and equipment, vehicles, inventories, and other investments. Some firms report no investment in a given category. Table 4 uses the log of the investment level plus $1, so that the zero investment level is defined. We discuss below the differences in results when we look at the log investment level conditional on having positive investment.

Across the full sample, about a third of the investment firms make is in real estate and almost a third is in vehicles. Of the remainder, 16% is in tools, 8% in inventories, and 12% in other investments. Using the same specification as in Column 3 of Table 3, we find that attachment to the migration network is associated with increases in investment in tools and equipment, vehicles, and inventories. The latter two are significant at the 0.05 level; the first at the 0.10 level. The largest increase is in vehicles. We also ran regressions on the investment level conditional on reporting some investment in the category (results available from the authors). These produce several differences in the pattern of significance: migration networks are associated with higher levels of investment in real estate ($\beta=9.07$, $t=4.14$) and the category of other investments ($\beta=6.21$, $t=2.93$); and tools and equipment are no longer significant.

We next turn to the capital–output ratio, total output, and profits. Table 5 reports the results of regressions where the dependent variable is the capital–output ratio, defined at the total capital invested in the firm divided by gross sales in the month before the survey. The specification is the same as that shown in Eq. (4). We find a very strong relationship between attachment to the migration network and the capital–output ratio. The results with the IV are slightly larger than the OLS results. A one standard deviation increase in the migration rate of an individual's state of birth is associated with a one-fifth of a standard deviation increase in the log capital–output ratio.

Table 5
Capital/output, sales, and profits

	(1)	(2)	(3)	(4)	(5)	(6)
	OLS	IV	OLS	IV	IV	IV
	Log capital/output	Log capital/output	Log sales	Log sales	Log of profits	Log of profits
Migration rate, state of birth	3.18 (4.09)	4.78 (4.17)	2.09 (1.88)	0.73 (0.54)	1496 (2.17)	401 (0.52)
Capital stock						0.046 (4.56)
Capital^2						− 6.91E−07 (3.46)
Capital^3						3.54E−12 (2.90)
Capital^4						− 5.34E−18 (2.58)
State fixed effects	Yes	Yes	Yes	Yes	Yes	Yes
Industry controls	Yes	Yes	Yes	Yes	Yes	Yes
Number of observations	1623	1225	1623	1623	1626	1626
R^2	0.22	0.21	0.32	0.32	0.15	0.22

t-values in parentheses. Standard errors are corrected for clustering at the state of birth level. Sample limited to owners 18–65 years of age working at least 35 h/week.

The migration rate is instrumented with the distance from the north/south railway lines, as described in the text. In addition to the variables shown, all regressions include 7 variables indicating the sector of activity. Other controls included in the regression are years of schooling of the owner, the estimated labor market experience (age minus years of schooling minus 6), the age of the firm in years, the square of each of these variables, a dummy indicating the owner reports data for two enterprises and the income per capita in the owner's state of birth.

C. Woodruff, R. Zenteno / Journal of Development Economics 82 (2007) 509–528 525

5.2. Sales and profits

We next turn to sales and profits. If networks are alleviating capital constraints, we should certainly expect sales and profits to increase. If they are only lowering the cost of capital for networked firms, then sales and profits will not necessarily increase. For sales (Columns 3 and 4 of Table 5), there is a significant increase in sales in the OLS regressions (0.10 level). But the measured effect is much smaller in the IV regressions, and the coefficient is insignificant.

Does the increased investment result in higher profits for the microentrepreneurs? The answer appears to be yes. Columns 5 and 6 show the results of regressions with the total profit, measured in dollars, as the dependent variable. The regression in Column 5 does not control for the firm's capital stock. Without controlling for capital stock, attachment to the migration network is associated with higher profit levels. A one standard deviation increase in the migration rate is associated with almost US$60 per month in increased profits, about 15% of the mean profit reported by firms in the sample. Once we control for capital stock (Column 6), the direct effect of the migration network becomes insignificant. This suggests that migration affects profits only through the returns earned on the increased investments associated with migration.

5.3. Discussion of results

Collectively, we find that migration is associated with higher investment levels, higher capital–output ratios, and higher profits. There is no robust finding on sales. These results suggest that the migration networks provide access to capital, which leads to higher investment levels and profits. But, like the networks described by Banerjee and Munshi (2004), the lack of any increase in the sales level casts some doubt on whether the liquidity from migration networks is relieving capital constraints.

We can think of several alternative explanations for the initial pattern of results, but they find little support in the data. We explored the possibility that micro entrepreneurs connected to the migration network may substitute capital for labor, but found no evidence in the data that they were doing so. Neither their own hours worked, nor the likelihood of hiring paid or unpaid workers are significantly associated with migration networks. We also explored the possibility that they were purchasing equipment they would otherwise rent. Again, we find no evidence that amount of rented equipment is negatively associated with migration.

We can make a bit more progress if we divide the sample into high capital and low capital sectors. Table 6 shows the mean and median capital by sector, ranked by median capital.

Table 6
Mean and median invested capital by sector

	Mean invested capital	Median invested capital
Construction	$686	$97
Miscellaneous services	$3399	$184
Repair services	$2461	$369
Restaurants	$2183	$337
Manufacturing	$5210	$1566
Trade	$4229	$1330
Professional services	$9725	$2811
Transportation	$13,219	$6054

Data in US dollars, translated using the exchange rate in the fourth calendar quarter of 1998.

Table 7
High and low capital sectors

	High capital sectors				Low capital sectors			
	(1)	(2)	(3)	(4)	(5)	(6)	(7)	(8)
	IV	IV	IV	IV	IV	IV	IV	IV
	Log capital	Log of sales	Log capital/ output	Profits	Log capital	Log of sales	Log capital/ output	Profits
Migration rate,	13.73	3.92	5.85	1272	4.93	−2.01	3.49	148
state of birth	(3.74)	(1.85)	(3.07)	(1.03)	(1.70)	(0.96)	(3.08)	(0.20)
Invested capital				0.045				0.035
				(5.32)				(4.75)
State fixed effects	Yes	Yes	Yes	Yes	Yes	Yes	Yes	Yes
Industry controls	Yes	Yes	Yes	Yes	Yes	Yes	Yes	Yes
Number of	967	927	927	937	708	696	696	689
Observations								
R^2	0.27	0.26	0.21	0.25	0.31	0.39	0.20	0.26

t-values in parentheses. Standard errors are corrected for clustering at the state of birth level. Sample limited to owners 18–65 years of age working at least 35 h/week.
The migration rate is instrumented with the distance from the north/south railway lines, as described in the text. In addition to the variables shown, all regressions include 7 variables indicating the sector of activity. Other controls included in the regression are years of schooling of the owner, the estimated labor market experience (age minus years of schooling minus 6), the age of the firm in years, the square of each of these variables, a dummy indicating the owner reports data for two enterprises and the income per capita in the owner's state of birth.

Construction, miscellaneous services, repair services and restaurants have less than the overall median level of invested capital, and we label these low capital sectors. The remaining sectors are labeled high capital. Table 7 reports the four sets of regressions—invested capital, log sales, capital output, and profits—with the sample broken into high and low capital intensity. In the high capital sectors, closer attachment to the migration network is associated with higher investment, higher sales, higher capital output ratios, and higher profits. The latter are caused only by the higher investment level.[15]

The results for the low capital sectors are much different. Here, the measured effect on the level of invested capital is about a third what it is in the high capital sector, a statistically significant difference. Migration has a negative but insignificant effect on sales, and a positive and significant effect on the capital–output ratio. Profits are increasing in the level of capital stock, with no direct impact of attachment to the migration network on profits. With the sample broken into high and low capital sectors, the results suggest that the increased availability of capital is not relieving constraints in low-capital sectors, but is relieving capital constraints in high-capital sectors.

6. Concluding remarks

We find evidence that migration is associated with larger investments and higher capital–output ratios among microenterprises in Mexico. There is also evidence that the higher investments are associated with higher levels of profits and, at least in more capital intensive sectors, with higher sales levels as well.

---

[15] Regressions available from the authors indicate that connection to the migration network is not associated with the choice of entry in to high or low capital sectors.

C. Woodruff, R. Zenteno / Journal of Development Economics 82 (2007) 509–528 527

The results are consistent with the sort of community effects found by Banerjee and Munshi among tee shirt manufacturers in India. Membership in a more liquid community leads to higher investment which is consistent with individuals in that community facing lower costs of capital. For entrepreneurs operating in more capital-intensive sectors, the results are perhaps closer to those found by Banerjee and Duflo among Indian firms gaining and losing access to bank finance. Our results suggest that in these sectors, migration networks may help overcome capital constraints in Mexico. Though we focus on capital stock and not entry, these latter results complement recent research from countries other than Mexico which suggests that migration relieves credit constraints and allows increased entry into self employment (Mesnard and Ravallion, 2005; Ilahi, 1999; Dustmann and Kirkchamp, 2002).

One final qualification of the results is worth reiterating. Identification issues led us to focus on the sample of individuals residing in a state in Mexico other than their state of birth. These individuals represent 28% of the full sample. They may differ in unmeasured ways from individuals residing in their birth state. Hence, the results may not extend to the larger population.

Acknowledgements

We thank Gordon Hanson, Simon Johnson, Peter Murrell, Jim Rauch, Raymond Robertson and participants in numerous seminars for comments. Daniel Chiquiar and Susana Ferreira provided exceptional research assistance. Financial support from UC MEXUS-CONACYT is also acknowledged.

References

Banerjee, Abhijit, Duflo, Esther, 2003. Do Firms want to Borrow More? Testing Credit Constraints Using a Directed Lending Program. working paper MIT.

Banerjee, Abhijit, Munshi, Kaivan, 2004. How efficiently is capital allocated. Evidence from the knitted garment industry in Tirupur. Review of Economic Studies 71 (1), 19–42.

Besley, Timothy, 1995. Property rights and investment incentives: theory and evidence from Ghana. Journal of Political Economy 103, 903–937.

Borjas, George, Katz, Lawrence, 2005. The evolution of the Mexican-Born workforce in the United States. NBER working paper 11281.

Chiquiar, Daniel, Hanson, Gordon, 2005. International migration, self-selection and the distribution of wages: evidence from mexico and the United States. NBER working paper No. 9242.

Coatsworth, John, 1972. The Impact of Railroads on the Economic Development of Mexico, 1877–1910, PhD Dissertation, University of Wisconsin.

Dustmann, Christian, Kirkchamp, Oliver, 2002. The optimal migration duration and activity choice after re-migration. Journal of Development Economics 67 (2), 351–372.

Escobar Latapi, Agustin, Martinez Castellanos, Maria de la O., 1991. Small-scale industry and international migration in Guadalajara, Mexico. In: Diaz-Briquets, Weintraub (Eds.), Migration, Remittances, and Small Business Development. Westview Press, Boulder.

Fazzari, Steven, Hubbard, R. Glenn, Petersen, Bruce C., 1988. Financing constraints and corporate investment. Brookings Papers on Economic Activity 1, 141–195.

Foerster, Robert F., 1925. The Racial Problems Involved in Immigration from Latin America and the West Indies to the United States. United States Department of Labor.

Funkhouser, Edward, 1992. Migration from Nicaragua: some recent evidence. World Development 20 (8), 1209–1218.

González Navarro, Moisés, 1974. Poblacíon y Sociedad en México (1900–1970). Univeridad Autónoma de México Press, Mexico City.

Greif, Avner, 1993. Contract enforceability and economic institutions in early trade: the Maghribi traders' coalition. American Economic Review 83 (3), 525–548 (June).

Ibarraran, Pablo, Lubotsky, Darren, 2005. Mexican Immigration and Self Selection: New Evidence from the 2000 Mexican Census. Working paper UI, Urbana-Champaign.

Ilahi, Nadeem, 1999. Return migration and occupational change. Review of Development Economics 3 (2), 170–186.

Johnson, Simon, McMillan, John, Woodruff, Christopher, 2002. Property rights and finance. American Economic Review 92 (5), 1335–1356.

Kuntz Ficker, Sandra, 2000. Economic backwardness and firm strategy: an American railroad corporation in nineteenth century Mexico. Hispanic American Historical Review 80 (2), 267–298.

Lamont, Owen, 1997. Cash flows and investment: evidence from internal capital markets. Journal of Finance 51 (2), 83–109.

Lucas Jr., Robert E., 1978. On the size distribution of firms. Bell Journal of Economics 9, 508–523.

Lucas, Robert E.B., 1987. Emigration to South Africa's mines. American Economic Review 77:3, 313–330 (June).

Lucas, Robert E.B., Stark, Oded, 1985. Motivations to remit: evidence from Botswana. Journal of Political Economy 93, 901–918 (October).

Massey, Douglas S., Parrado, Emilio A., 1994. Migradollars: the remittances and savings of Mexican migrants to the USA. Population Research and Policy Review 13, 3–30.

Massey, Douglas S., Parrado, Emilio A., 1998. International migration and business formation in Mexico. Social Science Quarterly 79 (1), 1–20.

McMillan, John, Woodruff, Christopher, 1999. Interfirm relationships and informal credit in Vietnam. Quarterly Journal of Economics 114 (4), 1285–1320.

Mesnard, Alice, 2004. Temporary migration and capital market imperfections. Oxford Economic Papers 56, 242–262.

Mesnard, Alice, Ravallion, Martin, 2005. The Wealth Effect on New Business Startups in a Developing Country. Working paper, World Bank.

Mexican Central Railway Company, 1900. Facts and Figures about Mexico and her Great Railroad The Mexican Central. The Mexican Central Railway Company, Mexico City.

Munshi, Kaivan, 2003. Networks in the modern economy: Mexican migrants in the US labor market. Quarterly Journal of Economics 118 (2), 549–599.

Rozelle, Scott, Taylor, J. Edward, DeBrauw, 1999. Migration, remittances, and agricultural productivity in China. American Economic Review 89 (2), 287–291.

Stark, Oded, 1978. Economic–Demographic Interaction in Agricultural Development: The Case of Rural-to-Urban Migration. UN Food and Agriculture Organization, Rome.

Stark, Oded, 1980. On the role of urban-to-rural remittances in rural development. Journal of Development Studies 16.

Taylor, J. Edward, 1992. Remittances and inequality reconsidered: direct, indirect, and intertemporal effects. Journal of Policy Modeling 14 (2), 187–208.

Taylor, J. Edward, Wyatt, T.J., 1996. The shadow value of migrant remittances, income and inequality in a household-farm economy. Journal of Development Studies 32 (6), 899–912.

Yang, Dean, 2004. International Migration, Human Capital, and Entrepreneurship: Evidence from Philippine Migrants' Exchange Rate Shocks, working paper, University of Michigan.

Part III
Institutional Barriers to Entrepreneurship

[12]

THE

QUARTERLY JOURNAL
OF ECONOMICS

Vol. CXVII   February 2002   Issue 1

THE REGULATION OF ENTRY*

SIMEON DJANKOV
RAFAEL LA PORTA
FLORENCIO LOPEZ-DE-SILANES
ANDREI SHLEIFER

We present new data on the regulation of entry of start-up firms in 85 countries. The data cover the number of procedures, official time, and official cost that a start-up must bear before it can operate legally. The official costs of entry are extremely high in most countries. Countries with heavier regulation of entry have higher corruption and larger unofficial economies, but not better quality of public or private goods. Countries with more democratic and limited governments have lighter regulation of entry. The evidence is inconsistent with public interest theories of regulation, but supports the public choice view that entry regulation benefits politicians and bureaucrats.

I. INTRODUCTION

Countries differ significantly in the way in which they regulate the entry of new businesses. To meet government requirements for starting to operate a business in Mozambique, an entrepreneur must complete 19 procedures taking at least 149 business days and pay US$256 in fees. To do the same, an entrepreneur in Italy needs to follow 16 different procedures, pay US$3946 in fees, and wait at least 62 business days to acquire the

* We thank Tatiana Nenova, Ekaterina Trizlova, and Lihong Wang for able research assistance, and three anonymous referees, Abhijit Banerjee, Richard Caves, Edward Glaeser, Roumeen Islam, Simon Johnson, Lawrence Katz, David Laibson, Guy Pfeffermann, and seminar participants at George Mason University and the University of Maryland at College Park for helpful comments. The collection of data for this paper was financed by the World Bank's Research Advisory Group and the World Development Report 2002: Building Institutions for Markets. An appendix describing country data is available from the authors on request.

The Quarterly Journal of Economics, February 2002

1

2   *QUARTERLY JOURNAL OF ECONOMICS*

necessary permits. In contrast, an entrepreneur in Canada can finish the process in two days by paying US$280 in fees and completing only two procedures.

In this paper we describe the required procedures governing entry regulation, as well as the time and the cost of following these procedures, in 85 countries. We focus on legal requirements that need to be met before a business can officially open its doors, the official cost of meeting these requirements, and the minimum time it takes to meet them if the government does not delay the process. We then use these data to evaluate economic theories of regulation. Our work owes a great deal to De Soto's [1990] path-breaking study of entry regulation in Peru. Unlike De Soto, we look at the official requirements, official cost, and official time—and do not measure corruption and bureaucratic delays that further raise the cost of entry.

Pigou's [1938] public interest theory of regulation holds that unregulated markets exhibit frequent failures, ranging from monopoly power to externalities. A government that pursues social efficiency counters these failures and protects the public through regulation. As applied to entry, this view holds that the government screens new entrants to make sure that consumers buy high quality products from "desirable" sellers. Such regulation reduces market failures such as low quality products from fly-by-night operators and externalities such as pollution. It is "done to ensure that new companies meet minimum standards to provide a good or service. By being registered, new companies acquire a type of official approval, which makes them reputable enough to engage in transactions with the general public and other businesses" [SRI 1999, p. 14]. The public interest theory predicts that stricter regulation of entry, as measured by a higher number of procedures in particular, should be associated with socially superior outcomes.

The public choice theory [Tullock 1967; Stigler 1971; Peltzman 1976] sees the government as less benign and regulation as socially inefficient. It comes in two flavors. In Stigler's [1971] theory of regulatory capture, "regulation is acquired by the industry and is designed and operated primarily for its benefit." Industry incumbents are able to acquire regulations that create rents for themselves, since they typically face lower information and organization costs than do the dispersed consumers. In this theory the regulation of entry keeps out the competitors and raises incumbents' profits. Because stricter regulation raises barriers to entry, it should lead to greater market power and profits rather than benefits to consumers.

A second strand of the public choice theory, which we call the *tollbooth* view, holds that regulation is pursued for the benefit of politicians and bureaucrats [McChesney 1987; De Soto 1990; Shleifer and Vishny 1998]. Politicians use regulation both to create rents and to extract them through campaign contributions, votes, and bribes. "An important reason why many of these permits and regulations exist is probably to give officials the power to deny them and to collect bribes in return for providing the permits" [Shleifer and Vishny 1993, p. 601]. The capture and tollbooth theories are closely related, in that they both address rent creation and extraction through the political process. The capture theory emphasizes the benefits to the industry, while the tollbooth theory stresses those to the politicians even when the industry is left worse off by regulation.

In principle, the collection of bribes in exchange for release from regulation can be efficient. In effect, the government can become an equity holder in a regulated firm. In practice, however, the creation of rents for the bureaucrats and politicians through regulation is often inefficient, in part because the regulators are disorganized, and in part because the policies they pursue to increase the rents from corruption are distortionary. The analogy to tollbooths on a highway is useful. Efficient regulation may call for one toll for the use of a road, or even no tolls if the operation of the road is most efficiently financed through general tax revenues. In a political equilibrium, however, each town through which the road passes might be able to erect its own tollbooth. Toll collectors may also block alternative routes so as to force the traffic onto the toll road. For both of these reasons, political toll collection is inefficient.

In the tollbooth theory the regulation of entry enables the regulators to collect bribes from the potential entrants and serves no social purpose. "When someone has finally made the decision to invest, he then is subjected to some of the worst treatment imaginable. . . In a few cases this treatment consists of outright extortion: presenting the investor with insurmountable delays or repeated obstacles unless he makes a large payoff . . ." [World Bank 1999, p. 10]. More extensive regulation should be associated with socially inferior outcomes, particularly corruption.

We assess the regulation of entry around the world from the perspective of these theories by addressing two broad sets of

4   *QUARTERLY JOURNAL OF ECONOMICS*

questions. First, what are the consequences of the regulation of entry, and in particular, who gets the rents? If the regulation of entry serves the public interest, it should be associated with higher quality of goods, fewer damaging externalities, and greater competition. Public choice theory, in contrast, predicts that stricter regulation is most clearly associated with less competition and higher corruption.

A second question we examine to distinguish the alternative theories of regulation is which governments regulate entry? The public interest model predicts that governments whose interests are more closely aligned with those of the consumers, which we think of as the more representative and more limited governments, should ceteris paribus regulate entry more strictly. In contrast, the public choice model predicts that the governments least subject to popular oversight should pursue the strictest regulations, to benefit themselves and possibly the incumbent firms. Knowing who regulates thus helps to discriminate among the theories.

Our analysis of exhaustive data on entry regulation in 85 countries leads to the following conclusions. The number of procedures required to start up a firm varies from the low of 2 in Canada to the high of 21 in the Dominican Republic, with the world average of around 10. The minimum official time for such a start-up varies from the low of 2 business days in Australia and Canada to the high of 152 in Madagascar, assuming that there are no delays by either the applicant or the regulators, with the world average of 47 business days. The official cost of following these procedures for a simple firm ranges from under 0.5 percent of per capita GDP in the United States to over 4.6 times per capita GDP in the Dominican Republic, with the worldwide average of 47 percent of annual per capita income. For an entrepreneur, legal entry is extremely cumbersome, time-consuming, and expensive in most countries in the world.

In a cross section of countries, we do not find that stricter regulation of entry is associated with higher quality products, better pollution records or health outcomes, or keener competition. But stricter regulation of entry *is* associated with sharply higher levels of corruption, and a greater relative size of the unofficial economy. This evidence favors public choice over the public interest theories of regulation.

In response, a public interest theorist could perhaps argue that heavy regulation in some countries is a reflection of both significant market failures and the unavailability of alternative mechanisms of addressing them, such as good courts or free press. In addition, corruption and a large unofficial economy may be inadvertent consequences of benevolent regulation, and hence cannot be used as evidence against the public interest view. Such inadvertent consequences might obtain as a side effect of screening out bad entrants [Banerjee 1997; Acemoglu and Verdier 2000], or simply as a result of a well-intended but misguided transplant of rich-country regulations into poor countries. Because of this logic, the question of which countries regulate entry more heavily may be better suited conceptually to distinguish the alternative theories.

We find that the countries with more open access to political power, greater constraints on the executive, and greater political rights have less burdensome regulation of entry—even controlling for per capita income—than do the countries with less representative, less limited, and less free governments. The per capita income control is crucial for this analysis because it could be argued that richer countries have both better governments and a lower need for the regulation of entry, perhaps because they have fewer market failures or better alternative ways of dealing with them. The fact that better governments regulate entry less, along with the straightforward interpretation of the evidence on corruption and the unofficial economy, point to the tollbooth theory: entry is regulated because doing so benefits the regulators.

The next section describes the sample. Section III presents our basic results on the extent of entry regulation around the world. Section IV asks who gets the rents from regulation. Section V presents the main results on which governments regulate. Section VI concludes.

II. DATA

A. Construction of the Database

This paper is based on a new data set, which describes the regulation of entry by start-up companies in 85 countries in 1999. We are interested in all the procedures that an entrepreneur needs to carry out to begin legally operating a firm involved in industrial or commercial activity. Specifically, we record all procedures that are officially required of an entrepreneur in order to

6   *QUARTERLY JOURNAL OF ECONOMICS*

obtain all necessary permits and to notify and file with all requisite authorities. We also calculate the official costs and time necessary for the completion of each procedure under normal circumstances. The study assumes that the information is readily available and that all governmental bodies function efficiently and without corruption.

We collect data on entry regulation using all available written information on start-up procedures from government publications, reports of development agencies such as the World Bank and USAID, and government web pages on the Internet. We then contact the relevant government agencies to check the accuracy of the data. Finally, for each country we commission at least one independent report on entry regulation from a local law firm, and work with that firm and government officials to eliminate disagreements among them.

We use official sources for the number of procedures, time, and cost. If official sources are conflicting or the laws are ambiguous, we follow the most authoritative source. In the absence of express legal definitions, we take the government official's report as the source. If several official sources have different estimates of time and cost, we take the median. Absent official estimates of time and cost, we take the estimates of local incorporation lawyers. If several unofficial (e.g., a private lawyer) sources have different estimates, we again take the median.

Our countries span a wide range of income levels and political systems. The sample includes fourteen African countries, nine East Asian countries including China and Vietnam, three South Asian countries (India, Pakistan, and Sri Lanka), all Central and Eastern European countries except for Albania and some of the former Yugoslav republics, eight former Soviet Union republics and Mongolia, ten Latin American countries, two Caribbean countries (Dominican Republic and Jamaica), six Middle Eastern countries (Egypt, Israel, Jordan, Lebanon, Morocco, and Tunisia), and all major developed countries.

We record the procedures related to obtaining all the necessary permits and licenses, and completing all the required inscriptions, verifications, and notifications for the company to be legally in operation. When there are multiple ways to begin operating legally, we choose the fastest in terms of time. In some countries, entrepreneurs may not bother to follow official procedures or bypass them by paying bribes or hiring the services of "facilitators." An entrepreneur in Georgia can start up a company after going through 13 procedures in 69 business days and paying $375 in fees. Alternatively, he may hire a legal advisory firm that completes the start-up process for $610 in three business days. In the analysis, we use the first set of numbers. We do so because we are primarily interested in understanding the structure of official regulation.

Regulations of start-up companies vary across regions within a country, across industries, and across firm sizes. For concreteness, we focus on a "standardized" firm, which has the following characteristics: it performs general industrial or commercial activities, it operates in the largest city[1] (by population), it is exempt from industry-specific requirements (including environmental ones), it does not participate in foreign trade and does not trade in goods that are subject to excise taxes (e.g., liquor, tobacco, gas), it is a domestically owned limited liability company,[2] its capital is subscribed in cash (not in-kind contributions) and is the higher of (i) 10 times GDP per capita in 1999 or (ii) the minimum capital requirement for the particular type of business entity, it rents (i.e., does not own) land and business premises, it has between 5 and 50 employees one month after the commencement of operations all of whom are nationals, it has turnover of up to 10 times its start-up capital, and it does not qualify for investment incentives. Although different legal forms are used in different countries to set up the simplest firm, to make comparisons we need to look at the same form.

Our data almost surely underestimate the cost and complexity of entry.[3] Start-up procedures in the provinces are often slower than in the capital. Industry-specific requirements add procedures. Foreign ownership frequently involves additional verifications and procedures. Contributions in kind often require assessment of value, a complex procedure that depends on the quality of property registries. Finally, purchasing land can be quite difficult and even impossible in some of the countries of the sample (for example, in the Kyrgyz Republic).

1. In practice, the largest city coincides with the capital city except in Australia (Melbourne), Brazil (Sao Paulo), Canada (Toronto), Germany (Frankfurt), Kazakhstan (Almaty), the Netherlands (Amsterdam), South Africa (Johannesburg), Turkey (Istanbul), and the United States (New York).
2. If the Company Law allows for more than one privately owned business form with limited liability, we choose the more popular business form among small companies in the country.
3. The World Economic Forum [2001] surveys business people on how important administrative regulations are as an obstacle to new business. Our three measures are strongly positively correlated with these subjective assessments.

8   *QUARTERLY JOURNAL OF ECONOMICS*

B. Definitions of Variables

We use three measures of entry regulation: the number of procedures that firms must go through, the official time required to complete the process, and its official cost. In the public interest theory, a more thorough screening process requires more procedures and demands more time. In the public choice theory, more procedures and longer delays facilitate bribe extraction (tollbooth view) or make entry less attractive to potential competitors (capture view).

Theoretical predictions regarding our measure of cost are ambiguous. A benevolent social planner who wants to spend significant resources on screening new entrants may choose to finance such activity with broad taxes rather than with the direct fees that we measure, leading to low costs as we measure them. A corrupt regulator may also want to set fees low in order to raise his own bribe income if, for example, fees are verifiable and cannot be expropriated by the regulator.[4] In contrast, higher fees are unambiguously desirable as a tool to deter entry under the *capture theory*. Because of these ambiguities, we present statistics on cost mainly to describe an important attribute of regulation and not to discriminate among theories.

We keep track of all the procedures required by law to start a business. A separate activity in the start-up process is a "procedure" only if it requires the entrepreneur to interact with outside entities: state and local government offices, lawyers, auditors, company seal manufacturers, notaries, etc. For example, all limited liability companies need to hold an inaugural meeting of shareholders to formally adopt the Company Articles and Bylaws. Since this activity involves only the entrepreneurs, we do not count it as a procedure. Similarly, most companies hire a lawyer to draft their Articles of Association. However, we do not count that as a procedure unless the law requires that a lawyer be involved. In the same vein, we ignore procedures that the entrepreneur can avoid altogether (e.g., reserving exclusive rights over a proposed company name until registration is completed) or that can be performed after business commences.[5] Finally, when ob-

---

4. Shleifer and Vishny [1993] distinguish corruption with theft from corruption without theft. In the latter case, the regulator must remit the official fee to the Treasury, and therefore has no interest in that fee being high.

5. In several countries, our consultants advised us that certain procedures, while not required, are highly recommended, because failure to follow them may result in significant delays and additional costs. We collected data on these

taining a document requires several separate procedures involving different officials, we count each as a procedure. For example, a Bulgarian entrepreneur receives her registration certificate from the Company Registry in Sofia, and then has to pay the associated fee at an officially designated bank. Even though both activities are related to "obtaining the registration certificate," they count as two separate procedures in the data.

To measure time, we collect information on the sequence in which procedures are to be completed and rely on official figures as to how many business days it takes to complete each procedure. We ignore the time spent to gather information, and assume that all procedures are known from the very beginning. We also assume that procedures are taken simultaneously whenever possible, for maximum efficiency. Since entrepreneurs may have trouble visiting several different institutions within the same day (especially if they come from out-of-town), we set the minimum time required to visit an institution to be one day.[6] Another justification for this approach is that the relevant offices sometimes open for business only briefly: both the Ministry of Economy and the Ministry of Justice in Cairo open for business only between 11 a.m. and 2 p.m.

We estimate the cost of entry regulation based on all identifiable official expenses: fees, costs of procedures and forms, photocopies, fiscal stamps, legal and notary charges, etc. All cost figures are official and do not include bribes, which De Soto [1990] has shown to be significant for registration. Setup fees often vary with the level of start-up capital. As indicated, we report the costs associated with starting to operate legally a firm with capital equivalent to the larger of (i) ten times per capita GDP in 1999 or (ii) the minimum capital requirement stipulated in the law. We have experimented with other capital levels and found our results to be robust.

Theoretical predictions for the cost of entry regulation are ambiguous. As an alternative measure, we consider only the

---

procedures, but did not include them in the variables presented here because we wanted to stick to the mandatory criterion. We have rerun the regressions discussed below including these highly recommended procedures. The inclusion does not have a material impact on the results.

6. In the calculation of time, when two procedures can be completed on the same day in the same building, we count that as one day rather than two (following the urgings of officials in several countries, where several offices are located in the same building). Our results are not affected by this particular way of computing time.

component of the cost that goes to the government, which in the sample averages about half the total cost. The results for this cost variable are generally weaker than for the total out-of-pocket cost, but go in the same direction. Our basic cost estimates also ignore the opportunity cost of the entrepreneur's time and the forgone profits associated with bureaucratic delay. To address this concern, we calculate a "full cost" measure, which adds up the official expenses and an estimate of the value of the entrepreneur's time, valuing his time at the country's per capita income per working day. We report this number below, and have replicated the analysis using it as a measure of cost. The results obtained using this cost measure are very similar to those using the raw data on time and cost, and hence are not presented.

Table I lists typical procedures associated with setting up a firm in our sample. The procedures are further divided by their function: screening (a residual category, which generally aims to keep out "unattractive" projects or entrepreneurs), health and safety, labor, taxes, and environment. The basic procedure in starting up a business, present everywhere, is registering with the Companies' Registry. This can take more than one procedure; sometimes there is a "preliminary license" and a "final" license. Combined with that procedure, or as a separate procedure, is the check for uniqueness of the proposed company name. Add-on procedures comprise the requirements to notarize the Company Deeds, to open a bank account and deposit of start-up capital, and to publish a notification of the company's establishment in an official or business paper. Additional screening procedures that include obtaining different certificates and filing with agencies other than the Registry may add up to 97 days in delays, as is the case in Madagascar. Another set of basic screening procedures, present in almost every country in the data set, covers certain mandatory municipal procedures, registrations with statistical offices and with Chambers of Commerce and Industry (or respective Ministries). In the Dominican Republic these procedures take seven procedures and fourteen days. There is large cross-country variation in terms of the number, time, and cost of screening procedures as the Company Registry performs many of these tasks automatically in the most efficient countries but the entrepreneur does much of the legwork in the less efficient ones.

Additional procedures appear in four areas. The first covers tax-related procedures, which require seven procedures and twenty days in Madagascar. The second is labor regulations,

THE REGULATION OF ENTRY 11

TABLE I

LIST OF PROCEDURES FOR STARTING UP A COMPANY

This table provides a list of common procedures required to start up a company in the 85 countries of the sample.

1. Screening procedures
- Certify business competence
- Certify a clean criminal record
- Certify marital status
- Check the name for uniqueness
- Notarize company deeds
- Notarize registration certificate
- File with the Statistical Bureau
- File with the Ministry of Industry and Trade, Ministry of the Economy, or the respective ministries by line of business
- Notify municipality of start-up date
- Obtain certificate of compliance with the company law
- Obtain business license (operations permit)
- Obtain permit to play music to the public (irrespective of line of business)
- Open a bank account and deposit start-up capital
- Perform an official audit at start-up
- Publish notice of company foundation
- Register at the Companies Registry
- Sign up for membership in the Chamber of Commerce or Industry or the Regional Trade Association

2. Tax-related requirements
- Arrange automatic withdrawal of the employees' income tax from the company payroll funds
- Designate a bondsman for tax purposes
- File with the Ministry of Finance
- Issue notice of start of activity to the Tax Authorities
- Register for corporate income tax
- Register for VAT
- Register for state taxes
- Register the company bylaws with the Tax Authorities
- Seal, validate, rubricate accounting books

3. Labor/social security-related requirements
- File with the Ministry of Labor
- Issue employment declarations for all employees
- Notarize the labor contract
- Pass inspections by social security officials
- Register for accident and labor risk insurance
- Register for health and medical insurance
- Register with pension funds
- Register for Social Security
- Register for unemployment insurance
- Register with the housing fund

4. Safety and health requirements
- Notify the health and safety authorities and obtain authorization to operate from the Health Ministry
- Pass inspections and obtain certificates related to work safety, building, fire, sanitation, and hygiene

5. Environment-related requirements
- Issue environmental declaration
- Obtain environment certificate
- Obtain sewer approval
- Obtain zoning approval
- Pass inspections from environmental officials
- Register with the water management and water discharge authorities

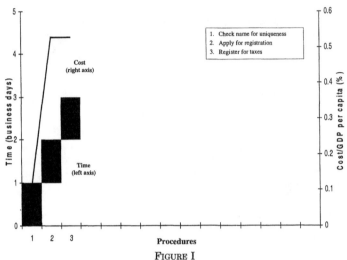

FIGURE I

Start-up Procedures in New Zealand

Procedures are lined up sequentially on the horizontal axis and described in the text box. The time required to complete each procedure is described by the height of the bar and measured against the left scale. Cumulative costs (as a percentage of per capita (GDP) are plotted using a line and measured against the right scale.

which require seven procedures and 21 days in Bolivia. The third area is health and safety regulations, which demand five procedures and 21 business days in Malawi. The final area covers compliance with environmental regulations, which take two procedures and ten days in Malawi if all goes well.

Figures I and II describe the number, time, and cost of the procedures needed to begin operating legally in New Zealand and France, respectively. New Zealand's streamlined start-up process takes only three procedures and three days. The entrepreneur must first obtain approval for the company name from the website of the Registrar of Companies, and then apply online for registration with both the Registrar of Companies and the tax authorities.

In contrast, the process in France takes 15 procedures and 53 days. To begin, the founder needs to check the chosen company name for uniqueness at the Institut National de la Propriété Industrielle (INPI). He then needs the mayor's permit to use his home as an office. (If the office is to be rented, the founder must secure a notarized lease agreement.) The following documents must then be obtained, each from a different authority: proof of a

THE REGULATION OF ENTRY   13

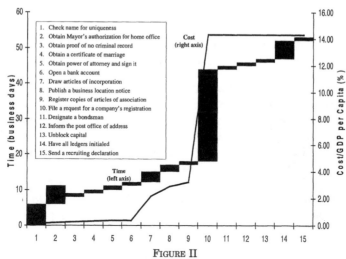

FIGURE II
Start-up Procedures in France
Procedures are lined up sequentially on the horizontal axis and described in the
text box. The time required to complete each procedure is described by the height
of the bar and measured against the left scale. Cumulative costs (as a percentage
of per capita GDP) are plotted using a line and measured against the right scale.

clean criminal record, an original extract of the entrepreneur's
certificate of marital status from the City Hall, and a power of
attorney. The start-up capital is then deposited with a notary
bank or Caisse des Dépôts, and is blocked there until proof of
registration is provided. Notarization of the Articles of Association follows. A notice stating the location of the headquarters
office is published in a journal approved for legal announcements,
and evidence of the publication is obtained. Next, the founder
registers four copies of the articles of association at the local tax
collection office. He then files a request for registration with the
Centre de Formalités des Entreprises (CFE) which handles declarations of existence and other registration-related formalities.
The CFE must process the documents or return them in case the
request is incomplete. The CFE automatically enters the company information in the Registre Nationale des Entreprises
(RNE) and obtains from the RNE identification numbers: numero
SIRENE (Système Informatique pour le Répertoire des Entreprises), numero SIRET (Système Informatique pour le Répertoire
des Etablissements), and numero NAF (Nomenclature des Activi-
tées Francaises). The SIRET is used by, among others, the tax

14   *QUARTERLY JOURNAL OF ECONOMICS*

authorities. The RNE also publishes a notice of the company formation in the official bulletin of civil and commercial announcements. The firm then obtains a proof of registration form "K-bis," which is effectively its identity card. To start legal operations, the entrepreneur completes five additional procedures: inform the post office of the new enterprise, designate a bondsman or guarantee payment of taxes with a cash deposit, unblock the company's capital by filing with the bank a proof of registration (K-bis), have the firm's ledgers and registers initialed, and file for social security. The magazine L'Entreprise comments: "To be sure that the file for the Company Registry is complete, many promoters check it with a counselor's service, which costs FF200 in Paris (about US$30). But there's always something missing, and most entrepreneurs end up using a lawyer to complete the procedure."

III. BASIC RESULTS

Table II describes all the variables used in this study. Table III presents the basic information from our sample. Countries are ranked in ascending order first by the total number of entry procedures, then by the time it takes to complete them, and finally by the cost of entry. We classify each procedure as one of five types: safety and health, environmental, tax, labor, and a residual category which we label "screening," whose purpose under the public interest theory is to weed out the undesirable entrepreneurs. We then compute and report the total number of procedures and their breakdown into our five categories for each country. We also report the minimum number of business days that are officially required to comply with entry regulations, the costs arising from the official fees, and the total costs which impute the entrepreneur's time (as a fraction of GDP per capita). Finally, we take averages by income level and report *t*-tests comparing the regulation of entry across income groups.

The data show enormous variation in entry regulation across countries. The total number of procedures ranges from 2 in Canada to 21 in the Dominican Republic and averages 10.48 for the whole sample. Very few entry regulations cover tax and labor issues. The worldwide average number of labor and tax procedures are 1.94 and 2.02, respectively. Procedures involving environmental issues and safety and health matters are even rarer (0.14 and 0.34 procedures on average, respectively). Instead, much of what governments do to regulate entry falls into the category of screening procedures. The worldwide average number of such procedures facing a new entrant is 6.04.

The number of procedures is highly correlated with both the time and cost variables (see Table VI). The correlation of the (log) number of procedures with (log) time is 0.83 and with (log) cost is 0.64. Translated into economic terms, this means that entrepreneurs pay a steep price in terms of fees and delays in countries that make intense use of ex ante screening. For example, completing 19 procedures demands 149 business days and 111.5 percent of GDP per capita in Mozambique. In Italy the completion of 16 procedures takes up 62 business days and 20 percent of GDP per capita. The Dominican Republic is in a class of its own: completing its 21 procedures requires 80 business days and fees of at least 4.63 times per capita GDP. These figures are admittedly extreme within the sample, yet meeting the official entry requirements in the average sample country requires roughly 47 days and fees of 47 percent of GDP per capita.

When we aggregate time and out-of-pocket costs into an aggregate cost measure, the results for some countries become even more extreme. The world average full cost measure rises to 66 percent of per capita GDP, but varies from 1.7 percent of per capita GDP for New Zealand to 4.95 times per capita GDP in the Dominican Republic.

Panel B of Table III reports averages of the total number of procedures and its components, time and cost by quartiles of per capita GDP in 1999. Two patterns emerge. First, the cost-to-per-capita-GDP ratio decreases uniformly with GDP per capita. The average cost-to-per-capita-GDP ratio for countries in the top quartile of per capita GDP ("rich countries") is 10 percent and rises to 108 percent in countries in the bottom quartile of per capita GDP. This pattern merely reflects the fact that the income elasticity of fees (in log levels) is about 0.2. Second, countries in the top quartile of per capita GDP require fewer procedures and their entrepreneurs face shorter delays in starting a legal business than those in the remaining countries.[7] The total number of procedures in an average rich country is 6.8 which is significantly lower than the rest-of-sample average of 11.8 (*t*-statistics are

---

7. One objection to this finding is that entrepreneurs in rich countries might face more postentry regulations than they do in poor countries. We have data on one aspect of postentry regulation, namely the regulation of labor markets (see Djankov et al. [2001a]). The numbers of entry and of labor market regulations are positively correlated across countries, contrary to this objection.

TABLE II
THE VARIABLES

This table describes the variables collected for the 85 countries included in our study. The first column gives the name of the variable. The second column describes the variable and provides the sources from which it was collected.

Variable	Description
Number of procedures	The number of different procedures that a start-up has to comply with in order to obtain a legal status, i.e., to start operating as a legal entity. Source: *Authors' own calculations.*
Safety & Health	The number of different safety and health procedures that a start-up has to comply with to start operating as a legal entity. Source: *Authors' own calculations.*
Environment	The number of different environmental procedures that a start-up has to comply with to start operating as a legal entity. Source: *Authors' own calculations.*
Taxes	The number of different tax procedures that a start-up has to comply with to start operating as a legal entity. Source: *Authors' own calculations.*
Labor	The number of different labor procedures that a start-up has to comply with to start operating as a legal entity. Source: *Authors' own calculations.*
Screening	The number of different steps that a start-up has to comply with in order to obtain a registration certificate that are not associated with safety and health issues, the environment, taxes, or labor. Source: *Authors' own calculations.*
Time	The time it takes to obtain legal status to operate a firm, in business days. A week has five business days and a month has twenty-two. Source: *Authors' own calculations.*
Cost	The cost of obtaining legal status to operate a firm as a share of per capita GDP in 1999. It includes all identifiable official expenses (fees, costs of procedures and forms, photocopies, fiscal stamps, legal and notary charges, etc.). The company is assumed to have a start-up capital of ten times per capita GDP in 1999. Source: *Authors' own calculations.*
Cost + time	The cost of obtaining legal status to operate a firm as a share of per capita GDP in 1999. It includes all identifiable official expenses (fees, costs of procedures and forms, photocopies, fiscal stamps, legal and notary charges, etc.) as well as the monetized value of the entrepreneur's time. The time of the entrepreneur is valued as the product of time and per capita GDP in 1999 expressed in per business day terms. The company is assumed to have a start-up capital of ten times the GDP per capita level in 1999. Source: *Authors' own calculations.*
GDP/POP$_{1999}$	Gross domestic product per capita in current U. S. dollars in 1999. Source: *World Bank [2001].*
Quality standards	Number of ISO 9000 certifications per thousand inhabitants issued by the International Organization for Standardization as of 1999 to each country in the sample. "ISO standards represent an international consensus on the state of the art in the technology concerned. . . . ISO 9000 is primarily concerned with quality management. . . . ISO develops voluntary technical standards that contribute to making the development, manufacturing and supply of products and services more efficient, safer and cleaner. . . . ISO standards also serve to safeguard consumers. . . . When an organization has a management system certified to an ISO 9000. . . , this means that the process influencing quality (ISO 9000). . . conforms to the relevant standard's requirements." Source: *International Organization for Standardization (www.iso.ch).*
Water pollution	Emissions of organic water pollutants (kilograms per day per worker) for 1998. Measured in terms of biochemical oxygen demand, which refers to the amount of oxygen that bacteria in water will consume in breaking down waste. Emissions per worker are total emissions divided by the number of industrial workers. Source: *World Bank [2001].*

Deaths from accidental poisoning	Log of the number of deaths caused by accidental poisonings (including by drugs, medications, bio-products, solid and liquid substances, gases and vapors) per million inhabitants. Average of the years 1981 through 1994 (the most recent available figure). Source: The number of accidental deaths from poisoning is taken from *World Health Organization [1998]*. Population figures are taken from *World Bank [2001]*.
Deaths from intestinal infections	Log of the number of deaths caused by intestinal infections (including digestive disorders) per million inhabitants. Average of the years 1981 through 1994 (the most recent available figure). Source: The number of deaths from intestinal infections is taken from *World Health Organization [1998]*. Population figures are taken from *World Bank [2001]*.
Size of the unofficial economy	Size of the shadow economy as a percentage of GDP (varying time periods). Source: *Authors' own computations based on averaging over all estimates reported in Schneider and Enste [2000] for any given country as well as Sananikone [1996] for Burkina Faso, Chidzero [1996] for Senegal, Turnham and Schwartz [1990] for Indonesia and Pakistan, and Kasnakoglu and Yayla [2000] for Turkey.*
Employment in the unofficial economy	Share of the labor force employed in the unofficial economy in the capital city of each country as a percent of the official labor. Figures are based on surveys and, for some countries, on econometric estimates. Source: *Schneider [2000] and the Global Urban Indicators Database [2000] (www.urbanobservatory.org/indicators/database).*
Product market competition	Survey measure of the extent to which respondents agree with the following statement: "Competition in the local market is intense and market shares fluctuate constantly." Scale from 1 (strongly disagree) through 7 (strongly agree). Source: *IMD [2001]*.
Corruption	Corruption perception index for 1999. Corruption is defined broadly as "the misuse of public power for private benefits, e.g., bribing of public officials, kickbacks in public procurement, or embezzlement of public funds." The index averages the corruption scores given by the following sources: (1) Freedom House Nations in Transit (FH); (2) Gallup International (GI); (3) The Economist Intelligence Unit (EIU); (4) the Institute for Management Development, Lausanne (IMD); (5) the International Crime Victim Survey (ICVS); (6) the Political and Economic Risk Consultancy, Hong Kong (PERC); (7) The Wall Street Journal, Central European Economic Review (CEER); (8) the World Bank and University of Basel (WB/UB), (9) the World Economic Forum (WEF). Descending score from 1 (most corrupt) to 10 (least corrupt). Source: *Transparency International (www.transparency.de/).*
Executive de facto independence	Index of "operation (de facto) independence of chief executive." Descending scale from 1 to 7 (1 = pure individual; 2 = intermediate category; 3 = slight to moderate limitations; 4 = intermediate category; 5 = substantial limitations; 6 = intermediate category; 7 = executive parity or subordination). Average of the years 1945 through 1998. Source: *Jaggers and Marshall [2000]*.
Constraints on executive power	Index of constraints on the executive power based on the number of effective veto points in a country. Veto points include (1) an effective legislature (represents two veto points in the case of bicameral systems); (2) an independent judiciary; and (3) a strong federal system. Average of the years 1945 through 1998. Source: *Henisz [2001]*.
Effectiveness of legislature	Index of the effectiveness of the legislature. Ascending scale from 1 to 4 (1 = no legislature; 2 = largely ineffective; 3 = partly effective; 4 = effective). Average of the years 1945 through 1998. Source: *The Cross-National Time-Series Data Archive (www.databanks.sitehosting.net/www/main.htm).*
Competition in the legislature's nominating process	Index of the competitiveness of the nominating process for seats in the legislature. Ascending scale from 1 to 4 (1 = no legislature; 2 = noncompetitive; 3 = partly competitive; 4 = competitive). Average of the years 1945 through 1998. Source: *The Cross-National Time-Series Data Archive (www.databanks.sitehosting.net/www/main.htm).*
Autocracy	Indicates the "general closedness of political institutions." Scale from 0 to 10 with 0 being low in autocracy and 10 being high in autocracy. Average of the years 1945 through 1998. Source: *Jaggers and Marshall [2000]*.
Political rights	Indicates the "general closedness of political rights. Higher ratings indicate countries that come closer to the ideals suggested by the checklist questions of (1) free and fair elections; (2) those elected rule; (3) there are competitive parties or other competitive political groupings; (4) the opposition has an important role and power; and (5) the entities have self-determination or an extremely high degree of autonomy. Average of the years 1972 through 1998. Source: *Freedom House [2001]*.
Legal origin	Identifies the legal origin of each Company Law or Commercial Code of each country. There are five possible origins: (1) English Common Law; (2) French Commercial Code; (3) German Commercial Code; (4) Scandinavian Commercial Code; and (5) Socialist/Communist laws. Source: *La Porta et al. [1998]; Reynolds and Flores [1989]; CIA World Factbook [2001].*

TABLE III
The Data

Panel A reports the total number of procedures and their breakup in the following five categories: (1) safety and health; (2) environment; (3) taxes; (4) labor; and (5) screening. The table also reports the time, direct cost (as a fraction of GDP per capita in 1999) associated with meeting government requirements, and direct cost plus the monetized value of the entrepreneur's time (as a fraction of GDP per capita in 1999) as well as the level of GDP per capita in dollars in 1999. Countries are sorted in ascending order on the basis of (1) the total number of procedures; (2) time; and (3) cost. Panel B presents means of the variables by quartiles of GDP per capita in 1999. Panel C presents *t*-statistics for differences in means across quartiles of per capita GDP in 1999. Table II describes the variables in detail.

	Number of procedures	Safety & Health	Environment	Taxes	Labor	Screening	Time	Cost	Cost + time	GDP/ POP$_{1999}$
				Panel A: Data						
Canada	2	0	0	1	0	1	2	0.0145	0.0225	19,320
Australia	2	0	0	1	0	1	2	0.0225	0.0305	20,050
New Zealand	3	0	0	1	0	2	3	0.0053	0.0173	13,780
Denmark	3	0	0	1	0	2	3	0.1000	0.1120	32,030
Ireland	3	0	0	1	0	2	16	0.1157	0.1797	19,160
United States	4	0	0	1	1	2	4	0.0049	0.0169	30,600
Norway	4	0	0	1	1	2	18	0.0472	0.1192	32,880
United Kingdom	5	0	0	1	1	3	4	0.0143	0.0303	22,640
Hong Kong	5	0	0	0	1	4	15	0.0333	0.0933	23,520
Mongolia	5	0	0	1	0	4	22	0.0331	0.1211	350
Finland	5	0	0	1	3	1	24	0.0116	0.1076	23,780
Israel	5	0	0	2	1	2	32	0.2132	0.3412	15,860
Zimbabwe	5	0	0	2	1	2	47	0.1289	0.3169	520
Sweden	6	0	0	1	1	4	13	0.0256	0.0776	25,040
Jamaica	6	0	0	2	1	3	24	0.1879	0.2839	2,330
Zambia	6	0	0	2	1	3	29	0.6049	0.7209	320
Panama	7	0	0	1	1	5	15	0.3074	0.3674	3,070
Switzerland	7	0	0	2	1	4	16	0.1724	0.2364	38,350
Singapore	7	0	0	1	2	4	22	0.1191	0.2071	29,610
Latvia	7	0	0	2	1	4	23	0.4234	0.5154	2,470
Malaysia	7	0	0	1	1	5	42	0.2645	0.4325	3,400

THE REGULATION OF ENTRY   19

Country										
Sri Lanka	8	0	0	1	1	6	23	0.1972	0.2892	820
Netherlands	8	0	1	0	2	5	31	0.1841	0.3081	24,320
Belgium	8	0	0	2	1	5	33	0.0998	0.2318	24,510
Taiwan, China	8	0	0	2	1	5	37	0.0660	0.2140	13,248
Hungary	8	0	0	1	1	6	39	0.8587	1.0147	4,650
Pakistan	8	0	0	1	2	5	50	0.3496	0.5496	470
Peru	9	0	0	2	2	4	83	0.1986	0.5306	2,390
South Africa	9	0	0	2	2	5	26	0.0844	0.1884	3,160
Kyrgyz Republic	9	0	0	1	1	7	32	0.2532	0.3812	300
Thailand	9	0	1	2	3	4	35	0.0639	0.2039	1,960
Nigeria	9	0	0	1	2	5	36	2.5700	2.7140	310
Austria	9	0	0	1	2	6	37	0.2728	0.4208	25,970
Tunisia	9	0	0	2	0	7	41	0.1722	0.3362	2,100
Slovenia	9	0	0	1	0	8	47	0.2103	0.3983	9,890
Lebanon	10	0	0	1	1	7	63	1.5672	1.8192	3,700
Uruguay	10	0	0	4	1	5	23	0.4949	0.5869	5,900
Bulgaria	10	0	0	0	2	8	27	0.1441	0.2521	1,380
Chile	10	0	0	2	3	5	28	0.1308	0.2428	4,740
Germany	10	0	1	2	1	7	42	0.1569	0.3249	25,350
Ghana	10	0	0	4	1	4	45	0.2175	0.3975	390
Lithuania	10	2	0	1	2	5	46	0.0546	0.2386	2,620
Czech Republic	10	0	0	2	1	7	65	0.0822	0.3422	5,060
India	11	0	0	3	3	4	77	0.5776	0.8856	450
Japan	11	0	0	2	2	7	26	0.1161	0.2201	32,230
Uganda	11	2	0	1	2	6	29	0.3040	0.4200	320
Egypt, Arab Rep.	11	0	0	1	2	8	51	0.9659	1.1699	1,400
Kenya	11	0	0	3	2	6	54	0.5070	0.7230	360
Armenia	11	0	0	1	1	9	55	0.1267	0.3467	490
Poland	11	2	0	3	3	5	58	0.2546	0.4866	3,960
Spain	11	0	0	4	4	5	82	0.1730	0.5010	14,000
Indonesia	12	0	0	2	2	8	128	0.5379	1.0499	580
Croatia	12	1	0	1	2	6	38	0.4503	0.6023	4,580
Kazakhstan	12	0	0	3	1	8	42	0.4747	0.6427	1,230
Portugal	12	0	0	1	2	8	76	0.1844	0.4884	10,600
Slovak Republic	12	0	0	2	2	7	89	0.1452	0.5012	3,590
China	12	0	0	2	5	5	92	0.1417	0.5097	780

(continued overleaf)

Entrepreneurship in Developing Countries

TABLE III
(CONTINUED)

	Number of procedures	Safety & Health	Environment	Taxes	Labor	Screening	Time	Cost	Cost + time	GDP/ POP$_{1999}$
Korea, Rep.	13	0	0	2	4	7	27	0.1627	0.2707	8,490
Tanzania	13	1	0	5	2	5	29	3.3520	3.4680	240
Ukraine	13	0	0	2	3	8	30	0.2569	0.3769	750
Turkey	13	0	0	2	2	9	44	0.1932	0.3692	2,900
Malawi	13	5	2	1	1	4	52	0.1886	0.3966	190
Morocco	13	1	0	3	3	6	57	0.2126	0.4406	1,200
Georgia	13	2	0	1	1	9	69	0.6048	0.8808	620
Burkina Faso	14	0	0	3	2	9	33	3.1883	3.3203	240
Philippines	14	0	0	5	1	8	46	0.1897	0.3737	1,020
Argentina	14	0	0	4	5	5	48	0.1019	0.2939	7,600
Jordan	14	1	0	2	1	10	64	0.5369	0.7929	1,500
Venezuela	14	1	1	3	3	6	104	0.1060	0.5220	3,670
Greece	15	0	0	4	2	9	36	0.5860	0.7300	11,770
France	15	0	0	3	1	11	53	0.1430	0.3550	23,480
Brazil	15	0	0	7	5	3	63	0.2014	0.4534	4,420
Mexico	15	1	2	2	3	7	67	0.5664	0.8344	4,400
Mali	16	1	0	3	2	10	59			240
Italy	16	0	0	5	3	8	62	0.2002	0.4482	19,710
Senegal	16	0	0	3	2	11	69	1.2331	1.5091	510
Ecuador	16	2	0	2	4	8	72	0.6223	0.9103	1,310
Romania	16	1	2	1	3	9	97	0.1531	0.5411	1,520
Vietnam	16	0	1	1	5	9	112	1.3377	1.7857	370
Madagascar	17	0	0	7	3	7	152	0.4263	1.0343	250
Colombia	18	2	0	4	5	7	48	0.1480	0.3400	2,250
Mozambique	19	4	0	1	3	11	149	1.1146	1.7106	230
Russian Federation	20	0	0	2	5	13	57	0.1979	0.4259	2,270
Bolivia	20	0	1	2	7	10	88	2.6558	3.0078	1,010
Dominican Republic	21	0	0	2	3	16	80	4.6309	4.9509	191
Sample average	10.48	0.34	0.14	2.04	1.94	6.04	47.40	0.4708	0.6598	8,226

Panel B: Means by Quartiles of GDP per capita in 1999

1st Quartile	6.77	0.00	0.05	1.59	1.14	4.00	24.50	0.10	0.20	24,372
2nd Quartile	11.10	0.24	0.14	2.14	2.38	6.19	49.29	0.33	0.53	5,847
3rd Quartile	12.33	0.52	0.14	2.19	2.33	7.14	53.10	0.41	0.62	1,568
4th Quartile	11.90	0.62	0.24	2.24	1.95	6.90	63.76	1.08	1.34	349

Panel C: Test of means (t-statistics)

1st vs. 2nd Quartile	−4.20[a]	−2.07[b]	−0.87	−1.35	−3.64[a]	−3.34[a]	−3.71[a]	−3.03[a]	−3.97[a]	12.03[a]
1st vs. 3rd Quartile	−4.58[a]	−3.02[a]	−0.87	−1.64[b]	−2.82[a]	−4.07[a]	−4.21[a]	−2.54[b]	−3.19[a]	16.35[a]
1st vs. 4th Quartile	−4.04[a]	−2.08[a]	−1.55	−1.61	−2.43[b]	−3.18[a]	−4.09[a]	−3.53[a]	−4.06[a]	17.31[a]
2nd vs. 3rd Quartile	−1.17	−1.34	0.00	−0.11	0.10	−1.51	−0.54	−0.52	−0.59	6.14[a]
2nd vs. 4th Quartile	−0.72	−1.17	−0.61	−0.21	1.10	−0.89	−1.46	−2.54[b]	−2.73[a]	8.05[a]
3rd vs. 4th Quartile	0.33	−0.27	−0.61	−0.11	0.82	0.26	−1.06	−2.17[b]	−2.27[b]	8.53[a]

a. Significant at 1 percent; b. significant at 5 percent; c. significant at 10 percent.

reported in Panel C). Rich countries also have fewer safety and health, tax, and labor start-up procedures than the rest of the sample. Similarly, meeting government requirements takes approximately 24.5 business days in rich countries, statistically significantly lower than the rest-of-sample mean of 55.4 days. In contrast, countries in the other three quartiles of per capita income are not statistically different from each other in the number of procedures and the time it takes to complete them.

To summarize, the regulation of entry varies enormously across countries. It often takes the form of screening procedures. Rich countries (i.e., those in the top quartile of per capita GDP) regulate entry relatively less than do all the other countries. In principle, these findings are consistent with both the public choice and public interest theories. Market failures might be more pervasive in countries with incomes just below the first quartile of GDP per capita, generating a greater demand for benign regulation in these countries. Alternatively, income levels may proxy for characteristics of political systems that allow politicians or incumbent firms to capture the regulatory process for their own benefit. In the next two sections we relate these patterns in the data to the theories of regulation.

IV. WHO GETS THE RENTS FROM REGULATION?

Theories of regulation differ in their predictions as to who gets its benefits. The public interest theory predicts that stricter entry regulation is associated with higher measured consumer welfare. In contrast, the public choice theory sees regulation as a tool to create rents for bureaucrats or incumbent firms. Stricter regulation should then be associated with higher corruption and less competition.

Measuring rents is inherently extremely difficult, especially across countries. In this section, we present some measures that we have been able to find that bear—albeit quite imperfectly—on the relevant theories. To begin, consider some variables bearing on the public interest theory. These variables reflect the activities of all firms in the country, and not just the entrants. The first is a measure of a country's compliance with international quality standards. It is a natural variable to focus on if the goal of regulation is to screen out entrants who might sell output of inferior quality. Second, we consider the level of water pollution, which should fall if entry regulation aims to control externalities and does so successfully.[8] Third, we consider two measures of health outcomes that publicly interested entry regulation would guard against: the number of deaths from accidental poisoning and from intestinal infections.[9] In addition, we include two measures of the size of the unofficial economy based on estimates of unofficial output and employment, respectively. Since firms operating unofficially avoid nearly all regulations, a large size of the unofficial economy in countries with more regulations undermines the prediction of the public interest theory that regulation effectively protects consumers.[10] Finally, we use a survey measure of "product market competition." Stiffer entry regulation should be associated with greater competition in the public interest theory, and lacking competition in the public choice theory, especially in its regulatory capture version.

Table IV presents the results on these seven measures of consequences of regulation using the number of procedures as dependent variables. For two reasons, we run each regression with and without the log of per capita GDP. First, the number of procedures is correlated with income per capita, and we want to make sure that we are not picking up the general effects of good governance associated with higher income. Second, we use GDP per capita as a rough proxy of the prevalence of market failures in a country. Including per capita income as a control is a crude way to keep the need for socially desirable regulation constant, which allows us to focus on the consequences (and later causes) of regulation separately from the need.

The results in Table IV show that compliance with international quality standards declines as the number of procedures rises. Pollution levels do not fall with regulation levels. The two measures of accidental poisoning are not lower in countries with more regulations (if anything, the opposite seems to be true even controlling for per capita income). More regulation is associated with a larger unofficial economy, and statistically significantly so if we use the unofficial employment variable. Competition in countries with more regulation is perceived to be less intense,

8. We have tried measures of air pollution and obtained similar results.
9. Due to reporting practices in poor countries, the second variable might better capture deaths from accidental poisoning in the poor countries, according to the World Health Organization [1998].
10. There is a large literature detailing how regulation can drive firms into the unofficial economy, where they can avoid some or all of these regulations. See, for example, Johnson, Kaufmann, and Shleifer [1997] and Friedman, Johnson, Kaufmann, and Zoido-Lobaton [2000].

TABLE IV

EVIDENCE ON REGULATION AND SOCIAL OUTCOMES

The table presents the results of OLS regressions using the following seven dependent variables: (1) Quality standards as proxied by the number of ISO 9000 certifications; (2) Water pollution; (3) Deaths from accidental poisoning; (4) Deaths from intestinal infection; (5) Size of the unofficial economy as a fraction of GDP; (6) Employment in the unofficial economy; and (7) Product market competition. The independent variables are the log of the number of procedures and the log of per capita GDP in dollars in 1999. Table II describes all variables in detail. Robust standard errors are shown below the coefficients.

Dependent variable	Number of procedures	Ln GDP/POP$_{1999}$	Constant	R^2 N
Quality standards (ISO Certifications)	-0.2781^a		0.7649^a	0.3311
	(0.0496)		(0.1268)	85
	-0.1595^a	0.0771^a	-0.1140	0.5384
	(0.0443)	(0.0131)	(0.1484)	85
Water pollution	0.0127^b		0.1557^a	0.0247
	(0.0084)		(0.0174)	76
	-0.0037	-0.0131^a	0.2984^a	0.2310
	(0.0076)	(0.0027)	(0.0314)	76
Deaths from accidental poisoning	0.6588^a		1.6357^a	0.1179
	(0.2057)		(0.4381)	57
	0.0637	-0.4525^a	6.8347^a	0.4109
	(0.1958)	(0.0933)	(1.0929)	57
Deaths from intestinal infection	2.3049^a		-2.2697^a	0.3451
	(0.3081)		(0.6778)	61
	1.0501^a	-0.8717^a	7.8494^a	0.6259
	(0.2971)	(0.1012)	(1.3048)	61
Size of the unofficial economy^d	14.7553^a		-3.7982	0.2482
	(2.5698)		(5.2139)	73
	6.4849^b	-6.1908^a	67.1030^a	0.5187
	(2.5385)	(1.0834)	(13.7059)	73
Employment in the unofficial economy	19.4438^a		-4.1103	0.3132
	(2.5756)		(5.9160)	46
	13.8512^a	-4.4585^a	41.5133^b	0.4477
	-3.6056	(1.3918)	(17.6836)	46
Product market competition	-0.4012^a		5.7571^a	0.1405
	(0.1213)		(0.2511)	54
	-0.1418	0.2108^a	3.3579^a	0.3087
	(0.1202)	(0.0680)	(0.7749)	54

a. Significant at 1 percent; b. significant at 5 percent; c. significant at 10 percent.

d. The regression on the size of the unofficial economy controls for the log of GDP per capita plus unofficial economy income (i.e., GDP per capita* (1 + unofficial economy)) and not just by GDP per capita as all other regressions on the table do.

although this result is only statistically significant without the income control. We have also run all regressions using cost and time as independent variables, and obtained qualitatively similar results. While the data are noisy, none of the results support the predictions of the public interest theory.[11]

The negative results in Table IV should be interpreted with caution. First, some of our measures of public goods, such as deaths from accidental poisoning, are probably more relevant for poor countries, and in particular are unlikely to be influenced by entry regulation for rich countries. Accordingly, it might be more appropriate to perform the analysis separately for countries at different income levels. To this end, we divide the sample at the median per capita income and rerun the regressions in Table IV for each subsample. The data do not support the proposition that, in the subsample of poorer countries, heavier regulation of entry is associated with better social outcomes or more competition.

Second, an even deeper concern with the results in Table IV is that, despite our control for per capita income, there is important unobserved heterogeneity among countries correlated with regulation, which accounts for the results. For example, suppose that some countries have particularly egregious market failures, but also especially poor alternative mechanisms for dealing with them, such as the press and the courts. Regulation, for example, might be less infected by corruption than either the press or the judiciary. A publicly interested regulator in such countries would choose to use more regulatory procedures because the alternative methods of dealing with market failure are even worse, but still end up with inferior outcomes.

We cannot dismiss this concern with the results of Table IV, although our later findings cast doubt on its validity. We run the regressions in Table IV using information on the freedom of the press from Djankov, McLiesh, Nenova, and Shleifer [2001], and find that, holding constant various measures of freedom of the press and per capita income, the number of procedures is still not associated with superior social outcomes. We also run the regressions in Table IV using a number of measures of citizen access to

---

11. Using data for publicly traded firms, we have found no evidence that countries with heavier entry regulation have more profitable firms, as measured by the return on assets. These profitability numbers, however, are very crude. We also measured profitability using the return on World-Bank-financed projects from the World Bank Operations Evaluation Department. These data also yield no evidence that more regulations are associated with greater returns.

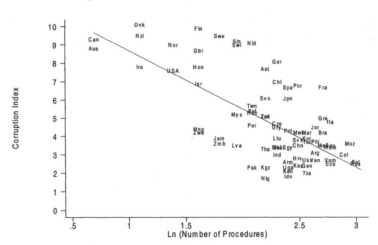

FIGURE III
Corruption and Number of Procedures
The scatter plot shows the values of the corruption index against the (log)
number of procedures for the 78 countries in our sample with nonmissing data on
corruption.

justice and of efficiency of the judiciary from Djankov et al.
[2001b]. Again, we find that, holding constant these measures
and per capita income, the number of procedures is associated, if
anything, with inferior social outcomes.

A direct implication of the *tollbooth* hypothesis is that corruption levels and the intensity of entry regulation are positively
correlated. In fact, since in many countries in our sample politicians run businesses, the regulation of entry produces the double
benefit of corruption revenues and reduced competition for the
incumbent businesses already affiliated with the politicians. Figure III presents the relationship between corruption and the
number of procedures without controlling for per capita GDP.[12]
Panel A of Table V shows statistically that, consistent with the
tollbooth theory, more regulation is associated with worse corruption scores. The coefficients are statistically significant (with and
without controlling for income) and large in economic terms. The
estimated coefficients imply that, controlling for per capita GDP,
reducing the number of procedures by ten is associated with a

12. We have tried a number of measures of corruption, all yielding similar
results. We have made sure that our results do not depend on "red tape" being part
of the measure of corruption.

TABLE V

EVIDENCE ON THE TOLLBOOTH THEORY

The table presents the results of OLS regressions using corruption as the dependent variable. The independent variables are (1) the log of the number of procedures; (2) the log of time; (3) the log of cost; and the log of per capita GDP in dollars in 1999. Panel A presents results for the 78 observations with available corruption data. Panel B reports results separately for the subsample of countries with GDP per capita in 1999 above and below the sample median. Table II describes all variables in detail. Robust standard errors are shown in parentheses below the coefficients.

Panel A: Results for the whole sample						
Independent variable	(1)	(2)	(3)	(4)	(5)	(6)
Number of procedures	−3.1811[a] (0.2986)	−1.8654[a] (0.2131)				
Time			−1.7566[a] (0.1488)	−0.8854[a] (0.1377)		
Cost					−1.2129[a] (0.1206)	−0.4978[a] (0.1285)
Ln GDP/POP$_{1999}$		0.9966[a] (0.0864)		0.9765[a] (0.1014)		0.9960[a] (0.1118)
Constant	11.8741[a] (0.7380)	1.1345 (0.9299)	11.0694[a] (0.5932)	0.0677 (1.1176)	2.7520[a] (0.2414)	−4.0893[a] (0.7867)
R^2	0.4656	0.8125	0.4387	0.7662	0.4256	0.7306
N	78	78	78	78	78	78

	Panel B: Results for countries above and below the world median GDP per capita					
	Countries above median GDP/POP$_{1999}$			Countries below median GDP/POP$_{1999}$		
Independent variable	(1)	(2)	(3)	(4)	(5)	(6)
Number of procedures	−1.8729[a] (0.2971)			−0.7841[b] (0.3304)		
Time		−0.8135[a] (0.1762)			−0.0923 (0.2850)	
Cost			−0.5327[a] (0.1894)			−0.3408[a] (0.1021)
Ln GDP/POP$_{1999}$	1.4811[a] (0.2265)	1.5871[a] (0.2789)	1.7621[a] (0.2913)	0.3993[b] (0.1735)	0.3680[c] (0.1802)	0.2117 (0.1718)
Constant	−3.6970 (2.4628)	−5.9027[c] (2.9942)	−11.3736[a] (2.5773)	2.3246[c] (1.2849)	1.0098 (1.8813)	1.3125 (1.1136)
R^2	0.7820	0.7155	0.6728	0.2362	0.1324	0.2830
N	40	40	40	38	38	38

a. Significant at 1 percent; b. significant at 5 percent; c. significant at 10 percent.

reduction in corruption of .8 of a standard deviation, roughly the difference between France and Italy. The results using the cost and the time of meeting the entry regulations as independent

28   *QUARTERLY JOURNAL OF ECONOMICS*

variables are also statistically significant, pointing further to the robustness of this evidence in favor of the tollbooth theory.

One way to reconcile the findings in Table V with the public interest theory is to argue that regulation has unintended consequences. Thus, benign politicians in emerging markets imitate the regulations of rich countries with best intentions in mind, but are stymied by corruption and other enforcement failures. This theory is not entirely consistent with our earlier finding that poorer countries in fact have more entry regulations than rich countries do. A further implication of this theory is that regulations should have a bigger impact on corruption in poorer countries. Panel B of Table V addresses this hypothesis by examining separately the relationship between entry regulations and corruption in countries with above and below world median income. The results show that regulations actually have a stronger effect on corruption in the subsample of richer countries.

On the second version of the unintended consequences argument, it may be impossible for a benevolent government to screen bad entrants without facilitating corruption [Banerjee 1997; Acemoglu and Verdier 2000]. In countries whose markets are fraught with failures, it might be better to have corrupt regulators than none at all. Corruption may be the price to pay for addressing market failures. We turn next to the evidence regarding the political attributes of countries that regulate entry to disentangle the competing theories of regulation.

V. WHO REGULATES ENTRY?

In this section we focus on the political attributes of countries that regulate entry. These attributes are intimately related to the competing hypotheses about regulation. In the public interest theory, regulation remedies market failures. The implication is that countries whose political systems are characterized by higher congruence between policy outcomes and social preferences should regulate entry more strictly. In the empirical analysis that follows, we identify such countries with more representative and limited governments.

In the public choice theory, despotic regimes are more likely to be captured by incumbents and to have regulatory systems aimed at maximizing the bribes and profits of a few cronies rather than address market failures [Olson 1991; De Long and Shleifer 1993]. Such dictators need the political support of various interest groups, and use distortionary policies to favor their friends and to abuse their opponents. The dictator's choice of distortionary policies is not mitigated by public pressure, since he faces no elections. When the public is less able to assert its preferences, then, we expect more distortionary policy choices. Specifically, we expect more representative and limited government to be associated with lighter regulation of entry.

One might argue, in contrast, that dictators should pursue efficient economic policies, including light regulation of entry, if they are politically secure and can "tax" the fruits of entry and growth. One response, discussed by Olson [1991] and De Long and Shleifer [1993], is that while a few dictators are politically secure and pursue enlightened policies, most are not. Insecure dictators extract what they can from the economy as fast as they can both to prolong their tenure, and to enrich themselves and their supporters while still in power. Democracy might not lengthen the horizons of politicians, but it does limit their opportunities.

We collect data on a variety of characteristics of political systems, partly because we want to be flexible regarding the meaning of "good government." Where possible, we use variables from different sources to check the robustness of our results. Our political variables fall into four broad groups. The first includes the de facto independence of the executive and an index of constraints on the executive. The second group includes an index of the effectiveness of the legislature and a measure of competition in the legislature's nominating process. The third group includes a measure of autocracy and one of political rights.

An additional variable that we focus on, used in the earlier work by La Porta et al. [1998, 1999] is legal origin. We classify countries based on the origin of their commercial laws into five broad groups: English, French, German, Scandinavian, and Socialist. Legal origin has been viewed as a proxy for the government's proclivity to intervene in the economy and the stance of the law toward the security of property rights in a country [La Porta et al. 1999].

Correlations among the political variables are presented in Table VI. Political variables tend to be strongly correlated within blocks. For example, the measure of constraints on the executive power is highly correlated with de facto independence of the executive (0.9761) and with the effectiveness of the legislature (0.9078). Yet, we report results on all three variables as each

30   *QUARTERLY JOURNAL OF ECONOMICS*

TABLE VI

CORRELATION TABLE FOR POLITICAL ATTRIBUTES

The table reports correlations among measures of regulation and the variables used in Table VII. All variables are defined in Table II. Significance levels are Bonferroni-adjusted.

	Exec de facto independence	Constraints on executive power	Effectiveness legislature	Competition nominating	Autocracy	Political rights	French LO
Exec de facto independence	1.0000						
Constraints on exec. power	0.9761[a]	1.0000					
Effectiveness legislature	0.9210[a]	0.9078[a]	1.0000				
Competition nominating	0.8243[a]	0.8069[a]	0.8484[a]	1.0000			
Autocracy	−0.9085[a]	−0.8844[a]	−0.8514[a]	−0.7819[a]	1.0000		
Political rights	0.8440[a]	0.8448[a]	0.8485[a]	0.7191[a]	−0.8564[a]	1.0000	
French legal origin	−0.1814	−0.1814	−0.1901	−0.1985	−0.0258	0.0565	1.0000
Socialist legal origin	−0.3321	−0.2927	−0.3236	−0.3240	0.5475[a]	−0.4572[a]	−0.4169[a]
German legal origin	0.2101	0.2008	0.2023	0.1281	−0.1920	0.2444	−0.2141
Scandinavian legal origin	0.3391	0.3274	0.3378	0.2522	−0.2978	0.3109	−0.1727
English legal origin	0.2259	0.1998	0.1462	0.2412	−0.2324	0.0778	−0.4874[a]
Ln GDP/POP$_{1999}$	0.6900[a]	0.6703[a]	0.7483[a]	0.6123[a]	−0.6389[a]	0.7519[a]	−0.0767[b]
Ln(Number of procedures)	−0.5518[a]	−0.5234[a]	−0.5848[a]	−0.4435[b]	0.4662[a]	−0.4412[a]	0.4863[a]
Ln(Time)	−0.5420[a]	−0.5204[a]	−0.5635[a]	−0.4360[b]	0.4770[a]	−0.4921[a]	0.3976[b]
Ln(Cost)	−0.5070[a]	−0.4937[a]	−0.5656[a]	−0.4177[b]	0.4075[b]	−0.4588[a]	0.3472
Ln(Cost + time)	−0.5700[a]	−0.5478[a]	−0.6267[a]	−0.4745[a]	0.4713[a]	−0.5085[a]	0.3870[b]

a. Significant at 1 percent; b. significant at 5 percent; c. significant at 10 percent.

comes from a different source. Similarly, blocks of variables tend to be correlated with each other. In particular, democracy tends to be positively associated with competitive and limited executive and legislative branches. Legal origin, in contrast, is insignificantly correlated with other political variables (the exception is Socialist legal origin which has obvious correlations with democracy and limited government).[13] Income levels are positively as-

13. Consistent with this finding, La Porta et al. [2001] find that common law legal origin is associated with English constitutional guarantees of freedom, such

TABLE VI
(CONTINUED)

Socialist LO	German LO	Scandinavian LO	English LO	Ln GDP/ POP$_{1999}$	Ln (Number of procedures)	Ln (Time)	Ln (Cost)	Ln (Cost + time)
1.0000								
−0.1479	1.0000							
−0.1192	−0.0612	1.0000						
−0.3365	−0.1729	−0.0139	1.0000					
−0.1995	0.3409	0.3133	−0.0742	1.0000				
0.1538[b]	0.0030[b]	−0.3413[b]	−0.5069[a]	−0.4745[a]	1.0000			
0.1869	−0.0640	−0.2914	−0.4291[b]	−0.5014[a]	0.8263[a]	1.0000		
0.0319	−0.0727	−0.3007	−0.2172	−0.5953[a]	0.6354[a]	0.6147[a]	1.0000	
0.0851	−0.0933	−0.2786	−0.3094	−0.6244[a]	0.7434[a]	0.7793[a]	0.9605	1.0000

sociated with democracy as well as with competitive and limited executive and legislative branches, but not with the legal origin. The fact that countries with severe market failures have more abusive governments by itself limits the normative usefulness of the Pigouvian model.

In Table VII we present the results of regressing the number

---

as the independence of the judiciary and the accountability of the government to the law. These constitutional guarantees of freedom are strongly associated with economic freedoms, but less so with political freedoms.

TABLE VII
EVIDENCE ON REGULATION AND POLITICAL ATTRIBUTES

The table presents the results of running regressions for the log of the number of procedures as the dependent variable. We run seven regressions using various political indicators described in Table II and (log) GDP per capita. Robust standard errors are shown in parentheses below the coefficients.

Dependent variable	(1)	(2)	(3)	(4)	(5)	(6)	(7)
Executive de facto independence	-0.1249[a] (0.0322)						
Constraints on executive power		-0.1048[a] (0.0352)					
Effectiveness of legislature			-0.3301[a] (0.0778)				
Competition nominating				-0.2763[b] (0.0999)			
Autocracy					0.0545[b] (0.0178)		
Political rights						-0.3470 (0.2185)	
French legal origin							0.7245[a] (0.0916)
Socialist legal origin							0.4904[a] (0.1071)
German legal origin							0.7276[a] (0.1363)
Scandinavian legal origin							-0.0085 (0.1733)
Ln GDP/POP$_{1999}$	-0.0491 (0.0331)	-0.0634[c] (0.0352)	-0.0087 (0.0401)	-0.0902[b] (0.0358)	-0.0867[a] (0.0321)	-0.0939[b] (0.0386)	-0.1434[a] (0.0270)
Constant	3.1782[a] (0.2334)	3.2040[a] (0.2408)	2.8709[a] (0.2586)	3.3540[a] (0.2641)	2.7457[a] (0.2888)	3.1850[a] (0.2599)	2.9492[a] (0.1955)
R^2	0.3178	0.2872	0.3424	0.2475	0.2640	0.2350	0.6256
N	84	84	73	73	84	84	85

a. Significant at 1 percent; b. significant at 5 percent; c. significant at 10 percent.

of procedures on a constant and each of the political variables taken one at a time and the log of per capita income. In interpreting these regressions, we take the broad political measures of limited and representative government as being exogenous to entry regulation. It is possible, of course, that both the political and the regulatory variables are simultaneously determined by some deeper historical factors. Even so, it is interesting to know what the correlation is. Does the history that produces good government also produce many or few regulations of entry? The control for the level of development is crucial (and in fact our results without this control are significantly stronger). Market failures are likely to be both more pervasive and severe in poor countries than in rich ones. Moreover, our measures of good government are uniformly higher in richer countries. Without income controls, our political variables may just proxy for income levels. Imagine, for example, that the consumers in poor countries are exposed to a larger risk from bad firms entering their markets and selling goods of inferior quality. The Pigouvian planner would then need more tools to screen entrants in the poorer countries.

Holding per capita income constant, countries with more limited and representative governments have statistically significantly fewer procedures for entry regulation using five out of six measures of better government.[14] These results show that countries with more limited governments, governments more open to competition, and greater political rights have lighter regulation of entry even holding per capita income constant. Figure IV plots the number of procedures against the autocracy score and shows that regulation is increasing in autocracy. Regulation is heavy in autocratic countries such as Vietnam and Mozambique and light in democratic countries such as Australia, Canada, New Zealand, and the United States.

The log of per capita GDP tends to enter these regressions significantly. The interpretation of this result is clouded both because there are problems of multicollinearity with the political variables and because the direction of causation is unclear. In the public choice theory, burdensome regulation reflects transfers

---

14. Results are significant in all six regressions when we use time rather than number of procedures as the dependent variable. In contrast, results are insignificant in three regressions (competition in the legislature's nominating process, autocracy, and political rights) when using cost as the dependent variable.

34   *QUARTERLY JOURNAL OF ECONOMICS*

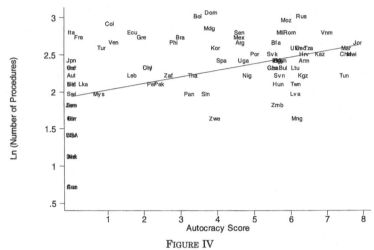

FIGURE IV
Autocracy and Number of Procedures
The scatter plot shows the values of the (log) number of procedures against the
autocracy score (higher values for more autocratic systems) for the 84 countries in
our sample with nonmissing data for the autocracy score.

from entrepreneurs or consumers, which are likely to be distortionary and, hence, associated with lower levels of income. Countries may be poor because regulation is hostile to new business
formation.

Holding per capita income constant, countries of French,
German, and Socialist legal origin have more regulations than
English legal origin countries, while countries of Scandinavian
legal origin have about the same. The result that civil law countries (with the exception of those in Scandinavia) regulate entry
more heavily supports the view that the legal origin proxies for
the state's proclivity to intervene in economic life [La Porta et al.
1999]. However, note that in itself this evidence does not discriminate among the alternative theories in the same way as the
evidence on democracy does: French origin countries might
merely be more prepared to deal with market failures than common law countries.

These results are broadly consistent with the public choice
theory that sees regulation as a mechanism to create rents for
politicians and the firms they support. The public choice theory
predicts that such rent extraction should be moderated by better
government to the extent that outcomes in such regimes come

closer to representing the preferences of the public. In contrast, these results are more difficult to reconcile with public interest unless one identifies it with political systems of countries such as Bolivia, Mozambique, or Vietnam, where corruption is widespread, governments are unlimited, and property rights insecure. Of course, it is possible that autocratic countries would perform even worse in the absence of heavy regulation because market failures are larger and alternative mechanisms of social control are inferior. Such a possibility strikes us as remote, especially since we hold the level of development constant.

VI. Conclusion

An analysis of the regulation of entry in 85 countries shows that, even aside from the costs associated with corruption and bureaucratic delay, business entry is extremely expensive, especially in the countries outside the top quartile of the income distribution. We find that heavier regulation of entry is generally associated with greater corruption and a larger unofficial economy, but not with better quality of private or public goods. We also find that the countries with less limited, less democratic, and more interventionist governments regulate entry more heavily, even controlling for the level of economic development.

This evidence is difficult to reconcile with public interest theories of regulation but supports the public choice approach, especially the tollbooth theory that emphasizes rent extraction by politicians [McChesney 1987; Shleifer and Vishny 1993]. Entry is regulated more heavily by less democratic governments, and such regulation does not yield visible social benefits. The principal beneficiaries appear to be the politicians and bureaucrats themselves.

WORLD BANK
DEPARTMENT OF ECONOMICS, HARVARD UNIVERSITY
SCHOOL OF MANAGEMENT, YALE UNIVERSITY
DEPARTMENT OF ECONOMICS, HARVARD UNIVERSITY

REFERENCES

Acemoglu, Daron, and Thierry Verdier, "The Choice between Market Failures and Corruption," *American Economic Review*, XC (2000), 194–211.
Banerjee, Abhijit, "A Theory of Misgovernance," *Quarterly Journal of Economics*, CXII (1997), 1289–1332.

36   *QUARTERLY JOURNAL OF ECONOMICS*

Central Intelligence Agency, *CIA World Factbook* (2001), published online. http://www.cia.gov/cia/publications/factbook/

Chidzero, Anne-Marie, "Senegal," in *The Informal Sector and Microfinance Institutions in West Africa,* Leila Webster and Peter Fidler, eds. (Washington, DC: The World Bank, 1996).

De Long J. Bradford, and Andrei Shleifer, "Princes and Merchants: European City Growth before the Industrial Revolution," *Journal of Law and Economics,* XXXVI (1993), 671–702.

Djankov, Simeon, Rafael La Porta, Florencio Lopez-de-Silanes, and Andrei Shleifer, "The Regulation of Labor," Harvard University manuscript in preparation, 2001a.

Djankov, Simeon, Rafael La Porta, Florencio Lopez-de-Silanes, and Andrei Shleifer, "Courts: The Lex Mundi Project," Harvard University, 2001b.

Djankov, Simeon, Caralee McLiesh, Tatiana Nenova, and Andrei Shleifer, "Who Owns the Media?" NBER Working Paper No. 8288, 2001.

De Soto, Hernando, *The Other Path* (New York, NY: Harper and Row, 1990).

Freedom House, *Freedom of the World* (New York, NY: Freedom House, 2001).

Friedman, Eric, Simon Johnson, Daniel Kaufmann, and Pablo Zoido-Lobaton, "Dodging the Grabbing Hand: The Determinants of Unofficial Activity in 69 Countries," *Journal of Public Economics,* LXXVI (2000), 459–494.

Henisz, Witold Jerzy, "The Institutional Environment for Economic Growth," *Economics and Politics,* XII (2000), 1–31.

Institute for International Management Development, *World Competitiveness Report* (Lausanne, Switzerland: IMD, 2001).

Jaggers, Keith, and Monty G. Marshall, "Polity IV Project," Center for International Development and Conflict Management, University of Maryland, 2000.

Johnson, Simon, Daniel Kaufmann, and Andrei Shleifer, "The Unofficial Economy in Transition," *Brookings Papers on Economic Activity,* 2 (1997), 159–239.

Kasnakoglu, Zehra, and Münür Yayla, "Unrecorded Economy in Turkey: A Monetary Approach" (1999), in *Informal Sector in Turkey, Volume I,* Tuncer Bulutay, ed. (Ankara, Turkey: SIS, forthcoming).

La Porta, Rafael, Florencio Lopez-de-Silanes, Andrei Shleifer, and Robert W. Vishny, "Law and Finance," *Journal of Political Economy,* CVI (1998), 1113–1155.

La Porta Rafael, Florencio Lopez-de-Silanes, Andrei Shleifer, and Robert W. Vishny, "The Quality of Government," *Journal of Law, Economics, and Organization,* XV (1999), 222–279.

La Porta, Rafael, Florencio Lopez-de-Silanes, Cristian Pop-Eleches, and Andrei Shleifer, "Guarantees of Freedom," manuscript, Harvard University, 2001.

McChesney, Fred S., "Rent Extraction and Rent Creation in the Economic Theory of Regulation," *Journal of Legal Studies,* XVI (1987), 101–118.

Olson, Mancur, "Autocracy, Democracy, and Prosperity," in Richard Zeckhauser, ed., *Strategy of Choice* (Cambridge, MA: MIT Press, 1991).

Peltzman, Sam, "Toward a More General Theory of Regulation," *Journal of Law and Economics,* XIX (1976), 211–240.

Pigou, Arthur C., *The Economics of Welfare,* 4th ed. (London: Macmillan and Co., 1938).

Reynolds, Thomas H., and Arturo A. Flores, *Foreign Law: Current Sources of Codes and Basic Legislation in Jurisdictions of the World* (Littleton, CO: F. B. Rothman, 1989).

Sananikone, Ousa, "Burkina Faso," in *The Informal Sector and Microfinance Institutions in West Africa,* Leila Webster and Peter Fidler, eds. (Washington, DC: The World Bank, 1996.)

Schneider, Friedrich, "The Value Added of Underground Activities: Size and Measurement of Shadow Economies and Shadow Economy Labor Force All over the World," mimeo, 2000.

Schneider, Friedrich, and Dominik H. Enste, "Shadow Economies: Size, Causes, and Consequences," *Journal of Economic Literature,* XXXVIII (2000), 77–114.

Shleifer, Andrei, and Robert W. Vishny, "Corruption," *Quarterly Journal of Economics,* CVIII (1993), 599–617.

THE REGULATION OF ENTRY 37

Shleifer, Andrei, and Robert W. Vishny, *The Grabbing Hand: Government Pathologies and their Cures* (Cambridge, MA: Harvard University Press, 1998).

SRI International, *International Practices and Experiences in Business Startup Procedures* (Arlington, VA: SRI, 1999).

Stigler, George J., "The Theory of Economic Regulation," *Bell Journal of Economics and Management Science,* II (1971), 3–21.

Tullock, Gordon, "The Welfare Cost of Tariffs, Monopoly, and Theft," *Western Economic Journal,* V (1967), 224–232.

Turnham, David, Bernard Salome, and Antoine Schwartz, *The Informal Sector Revisited* (Paris, OECD, 1990).

World Bank, "Administrative Barriers to Investment in Africa: The Red Tape Analysis," FIAS, Washington, DC, 1999.

——, *World Development Indicators* (Washington, DC: The World Bank, 2001).

World Economic Forum, *The Global Competitiveness Report 2001,* Klaus Schwab et al., eds. (New York, NY: Oxford University Press, 2001).

World Health Organization, *Causes of Death and Life, Birth Statistics* (Geneva, Switzerland: World Health Organization, 1998).

[13]

ELSEVIER

Available online at www.sciencedirect.com

ScienceDirect

Journal of Financial Economics 82 (2006) 591–629

JOURNAL OF
Financial
ECONOMICS

www.elsevier.com/locate/jfec

Entry regulation as a barrier to entrepreneurship [☆]

Leora Klapper[a], Luc Laeven[a,b], Raghuram Rajan[c,d,e,*]

[a]World Bank, 1818 H Street, NW, Washington, DC 20433, USA
[b]Centre for Economic Policy Research, 90-98 Goswell Road, London EC1 V 7RR, UK
[c]International Monetary Fund, 700 19th Street, NW, Washington, DC 20431, USA
[d]University of Chicago Graduate School of Business, 5807 South Woodlawn Avenue, Chicago, IL 60637, USA
[e]National Bureau of Economic Research, 1050 Massachusetts Avenue, Cambridge, MA 02138, USA

Received 22 November 2004; received in revised form 30 August 2005; accepted 9 September 2005
Available online 27 June 2006

Abstract

Using a comprehensive database of European firms, we study the effect of market entry regulations on the creation of new limited-liability firms, the average size of entrants, and the growth of incumbent firms. We find that costly regulations hamper the creation of new firms, especially in industries that should naturally have high entry. These regulations also force new entrants to be

[☆]We thank William Schwert, an anonymous referee, Allen Berger, Arnoud Boot, Nicola Cetorelli, Stijn Claessens, Mihir Desai, Simeon Djankov, Alexander Dyck, Saul Estrin, Raymond Fisman, Nicola Gennaioli, Paul Gompers, Luigi Guiso, Stephen Haber, Robert Hauswald, Thomas Hellman, Simon Johnson, Steven Kaplan, Naomi Lamoreaux, Joshua Lerner, Inessa Love, Vojislav Maksimovic, Atif Mian, Enrico Perotti, Michel Robe, Roberta Romano, Jean-Laurent Rosenthal, Jan Svejnar, Scott Stern, Gregory Udell, Christopher Woodruff, and seminar participants at the Fifth International Conference on Financial Market Development in Emerging and Transition Economies in Hyderabad, American University, University of Amsterdam, University of Maryland, the NBER Corporate Finance Program Meeting at the University of Chicago, the SME Conference at the World Bank, the Entrepreneurship Conference at Harvard Business School, the AEA meetings in Philadelphia, and the World Bank/NYU Workshop on Entry, Entrepreneurship, and Financial Development for valuable comments; Ying Lin and Victor Sulla for outstanding research assistance; Sebastian Roels at Bureau Van Dijk for help with the Amadeus data; and Brian Williams and Ryan Paul at Dun & Bradstreet for help with the Dun & Bradstreet data. Rajan thanks the National Science Foundation, the Center for the Study of the State and the Economy at the Graduate School of Business, University of Chicago for research support during part of this study. We also thank the World Bank for financial support. An earlier version of this paper circulated under the title "Business Environment and Firm Entry: Evidence from International Data." This paper's findings, interpretations, and conclusions are entirely those of the authors and do not necessarily represent the views of the World Bank, the IMF, their Executive Directors, or the countries they represent.

*Corresponding author. Fax: +1 202 623 7271.

E-mail address: rrajan@imf.org (R. Rajan).

larger and cause incumbent firms in naturally high-entry industries to grow more slowly. Our results hold even when we correct for the availability of financing, the degree of protection of intellectual property, and labor regulations.

JEL classification: G18; G38; L51; M13

Keywords: Entrepreneurship; Business incorporation; Regulatory barriers; Economic growth

1. Introduction

Entrepreneurship is a critical part of the process of creative destruction that Joseph Schumpeter (1911) argued is so important for the continued dynamism of the modern economy. That it helps economic growth has been documented in previous work (e.g., Hause and Du Rietz, 1984; Black and Strahan, 2002). Yet a number of countries put in place regulations that make it more difficult to start a new firm. Our focus in this paper is on the cost of meeting the regulatory requirements for setting up a limited liability company (we will use "entry costs" or "entry regulation" interchangeably since our measure proxies for both). We study the effect of such entry regulations on (i) the creation of new firms, (ii) the average size of firms that finally are able to incorporate, and (iii) the dynamism of incumbent firms.

We start by investigating the cross-country picture of new firm incorporation. We use a comprehensive, recently released database of corporations across a number of developed and transition countries in Europe to assess this picture. Some facts are striking. For instance, one might believe that Italy, with its myriad small corporations, should have tremendous incorporation of new firms (we use "incorporation of new firms" and "entry" interchangeably). Actually, the share of new corporations in Italy (the fraction of corporations that are one or two years old) is only 3.8% compared to 13.5% on average for France, Germany, and the United Kingdom.

What might account for these differences? One potential explanation is the cost of meeting the regulatory requirements for setting up a limited liability company. Why might such regulations exist? The early debate on incorporation emphasized the risk that crooks might register new companies with little capital and dupe unsuspecting investors or consumers. For instance, *The Times* of London thundered against the principle of free incorporation through limited liability in 1824:

> Nothing can be so unjust as for a few persons abounding in wealth to offer a portion of their excess for the information of a company, to play with that excess for the information of a company—to lend the importance of their whole name and credit to the society, and then should the funds prove insufficient to answer all demands, to retire into the security of their unhazarded fortune, and leave the bait to be devoured by the poor deceived fish (Halpern et al., 1980, p. 117).

Thus one motivation for requiring a firm to go through a detailed (and hence costly) bureaucratic process to register as a limited liability company is to screen out potential frauds and cheats. But there could be other motivations. For example, to the extent that information is generated during the process, it could help the tax authorities improve

L. Klapper et al. / Journal of Financial Economics 82 (2006) 591–629   593

collections, or it could help improve the accuracy of various censuses and hence the public decision-making process.

More recently, however, there is a growing view that costly regulations impede the setting up of businesses and stand in the way of economic growth (see De Soto, 1990; Djankov et al., 2002; World Bank, 2004). Do higher regulatory costs really have adverse effects? While Djankov et al. (2002) find that countries with higher entry costs have more corruption and larger unofficial economies—suggesting that the motivation for these regulations is not entirely benign—they do not measure the direct impact or entry costs, which is our focus.

First, we study whether entry costs affect the extent of incorporation, a necessary first step in determining whether these regulations have any effect. We focus on cross-industry, cross-country interaction effects. That is, we ask whether the fraction of new corporations is lower in an industry with a higher "natural" propensity for entry when the country has higher costs of complying with bureaucratic requirements for incorporation. The methodology, following Rajan and Zingales (1998), enables us to finesse a number of problems associated with the more traditional cross-country regressions—such as the problem that a healthy economy scores well on a number of cross-country variables, which makes it hard to estimate the direct effect of each variable in a cross-country regression (and equally hard to correct for all possible country variables that might matter). By focusing on interactions, we can absorb country-level variables and instead examine the differential effects of country-level variables across industries that might be most responsive to them. The downside of this methodology, of course, is that while it can tell us whether entry regulation works in predicted economic ways, it cannot tell us the overall magnitude of the effect, only the relative magnitude on "naturally high-entry" industries. But since our primary interest is in examining whether bureaucratic regulations affect entrepreneurship, this is not a major concern.

We find that the rate of new corporation creation in "naturally high-entry" industries is relatively lower in countries with higher entry costs, suggesting that these costs matter. Interestingly, they matter most in richer countries, or countries that are not corrupt, where the regulations on the books are more likely to be enforced. Our findings suggest an explanation for the low level of incorporation in Italy: the average direct cost associated with fulfilling the bureaucratic regulations for registering a new corporation in Italy is 20% of per capita GNP compared to 10% of per capita GNP on average for other G-7 European countries.

Second, we study the effect of bureaucratic entry regulations on the average size of entrant firms. Given that the high entry costs are largely fixed, they should be reflected in an increased average size of entrants into high-entry industries in countries with high costs. We indeed find this to be the case. The average value added of new firms in high-entry industries is disproportionately higher in countries that have higher entry costs. This means that not only do such regulations discourage small firms from setting up, they also force others to grow without the protection of limited liability until they reach a scale that makes the cost of incorporation affordable.

If entry regulations indiscriminately screen out small young firms, which are the source of Schumpeterian waves of creative destruction, then constraints on their emergence should have a chilling effect on incumbents and mute the disciplinary effects of competition, with older firms more likely to be lazy and less capable of enhancing productivity. If, by contrast, entry regulations are effective at screening, older firms that have come through the screening process could be better firms and more able to increase productivity. We therefore ask whether entry regulations affect the productivity growth of older incumbent firms. We find that the growth in value added per employee for firms older than two years is relatively lower in naturally high-entry industries when the industry is in a country with higher bureaucratic barriers to entry, consistent with the hypothesis that entry regulations indiscriminately screen out small young firms and inhibit the disciplinary effects of competition.

One might also expect the effects of the absence of competition to become more pronounced over time, with older incumbents in protected industries becoming far more reliant on the rents from incumbency than on efficiency gains. This is in fact the case. Value added per employee for older incumbents grows relatively more slowly in naturally high-entry industries in countries with costly bureaucratic barriers, although this effect is absent for young incumbents. Thus, costly entry regulations are a form of protection that has the most deleterious effect on the performance of seasoned incumbents.

In this regard, the comparison between high-entry-regulation Italy and the low-entry-regulation United Kingdom is particularly telling. Across all industries, firms start out larger when young in Italy, but grow more slowly so that firms in the United Kingdom are about twice as large by age ten (Fig. 1). This suggests that Italy has small firms not because there is too much entry but because there is too little!

Finally, to check whether entry regulations proxy for other aspects of the business environment that are likely to have an impact on entry, such as financial development, labor regulation, and protection of intellectual property, we include these environmental variables interacted with the characteristics of the industry they are most likely to influence. We find that these aspects of the business environment do matter, but primarily for the rate of incorporation, and not for the size of entrants or the productivity growth of incumbents. It is particularly noteworthy that the effect of entry regulations persists despite the inclusion of these other interactions.

In a related paper, Desai et al. (2003) use a cross-country approach and also find that entry regulations have a negative impact on firm entry. The cross-country approach has a number of limitations. In particular, variations in coverage in the database across

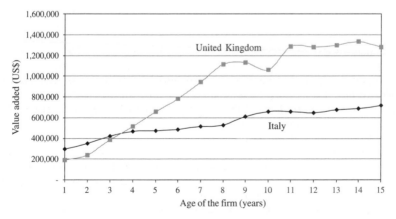

Fig. 1. Firm size and age.

L. Klapper et al. / Journal of Financial Economics 82 (2006) 591–629 595

countries could affect findings, a criticism that is less applicable to a within-country, cross-industry approach. Nevertheless, their findings are complementary to ours. Another related cross-country study is by Scarpetta et al. (2002), who use firm-level survey data from OECD countries to analyze firm entry and exit. They find that higher product market and labor regulations are negatively correlated with the entry of small and medium-sized firms SMEs) in OECD countries. Bertrand and Kramarz (2002) examine the expansion decisions of French retailers following new zoning regulations introduced in France and find a strong relation between increases in entry deterrence (such as rejection of expansion or entry decisions) and decreases in employment growth.

There is a substantial literature on entry into an industry (possibly by a firm from another industry) as distinguished from firm creation or entrepreneurship. It is the latter sense in which we use the term "entry." It would take us too much out of our way to describe the literature on industry entry, so we refer the reader to Gilbert (1989) for a comprehensive survey. Note that there are technological determinants of entry into an industry such as minimum scale, etc., that also affect firm creation. We assume these determinants carry over countries and are absorbed by industry indicators. Our focus is on environmental determinants of firm creation.

The paper proceeds as follows. In Section 2 we describe the data and in Section 3 we present the empirical methodology. We present the empirical results in Section 4. Section 5 concludes.

2. Data

2.1. Amadeus database

Central to our analysis is the firm-level Amadeus database. Amadeus is a commercial database provided by Bureau van Dijk. It contains financial information on over five million private and publicly owned firms across 34 Western and Eastern European countries. The database includes up to ten years of information per company, although coverage varies by country. Amadeus is especially useful because it covers a large fraction of new and SME companies across all industries. The Amadeus database is created by collecting standardized data received from 50 vendors across Europe. The local source for these data is generally the office of the Registrar of Companies.

The Amadeus database includes firm-level accounting data in standardized financial format for 22 balance sheet items, 22 income statement items, and 21 financial ratios. The accounts are transformed into a universal format to enhance comparison across countries, though coverage of these items varies across countries. We use period average exchange rates from the International Monetary Fund's International Financial Statistics to convert all accounting data into U.S. dollars.

In addition to financial information, Amadeus also provides other firm-level information. We use information on the year of incorporation to calculate the age of the firm. Amadeus also assigns companies a three-digit NACE code—the European standard of industry classification—which we use to classify firms and construct industry dummy variables. The NACE codes follow the NACE Revision 1 classification. In our analysis, we use NACE codes at a two-digit level so that we have a sufficient number of firms per industry.

2.2. Sample selection

We use the 2001 edition of Amadeus and limit our sample to the years 1998 and 1999.[1] There are two reasons to limit our analysis. First, there is the potential problem of survivorship: as companies exit or stop reporting their financial statements, Amadeus puts a "not available/missing" for four years following the last included filing. Firms are not removed from the database unless there is no reporting for at least five years (i.e., 1997 or earlier). So the data for firms from 1997 as reported in the 2001 database will not include firms that exited in 1997 or before. To avoid this potential survivorship bias, we restrict our attention to 1998 and 1999. A second reason is that efforts were made in 1998 to expand the coverage for Central and Eastern European countries allowing us to include more countries, but making the prior data less comparable. For example, the coverage of Central and Eastern European firms increased by 16% from 1997 to 1998, but less than 5%, on average, for the following two years.

As shown in Table 1, Column (i), we start with a sample in Amadeus of about 3.5 million annual observations over the years 1998–1999. We then impose a number of restrictions on the data. First, we require reporting firms to have some basic accounting information in their accounts over the years (i.e., data on total assets, sales, profit before tax, or employment). The reason for dropping those that do not report is that there could be country differences in the criteria for including firms with no information on their accounts. In addition, this criterion excludes any "phantom" firms established for tax or other purposes.

Next we delete from our sample firms that report only consolidated statements, to avoid double-counting firms and subsidiaries or operations abroad. For most firms in Amadeus, unconsolidated statements are reported and consolidated statements are provided when available. We also exclude certain industries. First, we drop several primary industries where the activity is country-specific (e.g., not all countries have uranium mines). These industries include agriculture (NACE code 1), forestry (NACE code 2), fishing (NACE code 5), and mining (NACE codes 10-14). We also exclude utilities (NACE codes 40-41), which tend to be regulated and largely state-owned industries in Europe. We drop the recycling industry (NACE code 37), which is difficult to match with a comparable SIC code(s). We also drop the financial services industries (NACE codes 65 and 66) because financial ratios for financial companies are not comparable to those of nonfinancial companies. In addition, financial institutions tend to be subject to specific entry restrictions (e.g., initial capital requirements) that do not apply to nonfinancial firms. (Barth et al. (2004) discuss financial sector regulations across countries). Finally, we drop the government/public sector, education (mainly public sector in Europe), the health and social sector, activities of organizations, private households, extra-territorial organizations, and firms that cannot be classified (NACE codes 75, 80, 85, 91, 92, 95, and 99).[2] We also exclude, by country, any industries with less than three firms (although we check whether such exclusion affects our results qualitatively). We are left with 47 NACE industries, which is the maximum number of observations per country.

---

[1] Due to lags in data collection, the coverage for the year 2000 is incomplete.

[2] All results are robust to the inclusion of excluded industries.

L. Klapper et al. / Journal of Financial Economics 82 (2006) 591–629   597

Table 1
Number of firms, corporations and employment, by country and year

Country	(i) Total Firms		(ii) Total Corporations		(iii) Total Employment	
	1998	1999	1998	1999	1998	1999
Austria	25,243	27,170	18,224	19,684	737,114	717,498
Belgium	229,171	244,361	215,709	230,352	1,459,269	1,501,236
Bulgaria	28,272	38,840	17,004	21,167	1,113,907	1,116,755
Czech Republic	7,153	7,613	7,153	7,613	1,424,975	1,472,515
Denmark	72,989	82,639	68,906	77,720	902,078	961,128
Estonia	10,438	27,407	10,243	26,737	269,042	321,308
Finland	47,646	57,781	46,286	55,765	789,208	867,984
France	652,376	676,781	584,274	604,155	7,640,624	7,724,623
Germany	468,865	519,759	334,305	372,167	10,266,932	10,005,253
Greece	17,617	18,604	17,297	18,280	708,412	710,973
Hungary	29,397	17,404	25,731	15,794	854,131	751,858
Ireland	15,184	10,587	13,835	9,759	104,543	78,324
Italy	117,670	126,514	111,736	120,393	4,598,602	4,808,664
Latvia	2,433	2,681	2,244	2,482	226,195	232,865
Lithuania	1,123	1,247	1,113	1,228	180,049	144,779
Netherlands	145,634	153,430	145,454	153,276	587,366	581,869
Norway	104,836	115,804	104,836	115,804	991,191	1,059,226
Poland	10,605	10,309	8,668	8,451	2,667,816	2,423,589
Portugal	21,351	23,798	20,734	23,096	396,088	195,393
Romania	302,705	318,020	287,657	303,374	4,027,310	3,506,044
Spain	166,688	180,621	164,879	178,662	4,849,609	4,894,020
Sweden	193,333	204,936	193,333	204,936	1,931,973	2,022,113
UK	506,610	863,498	491,891	833,033	10,712,104	10,545,236
Total	3,218,450	3,770,760	2,896,065	3,408,713	58,289,265	57,511,010

This table summarizes (i) the total number of firms, (ii) the total number of corporations (plc and ltd, or their equivalents) and (iii) employment from the Amadeus database. We exclude about 25,000 firms with no financial data (i.e., inactive firms). The total employment figures exclude firms with missing employment in all years. We use current employment figures to replace lagged employment figures if previous year(s) employment are missing and extrapolate forward employment figures if current year(s) employment is missing.

Finally, we exclude all legal forms other than the equivalent of public and private limited liability corporations.[3] In particular, we exclude proprietorships and partnerships. Two arguments prompt this. First, a big and common carrot behind registration as a corporation is limited liability, which allows entrepreneurs and investors to take risks. By contrast, the benefits of registration as other forms can vary considerably across countries, which will make the analysis harder to interpret. Second, the coverage of proprietorships and other unincorporated firms in Amadeus is poor and uneven: in most European countries, only limited liability companies are required to file statements. However, most European countries require all limited liability corporations to file financial statements,

---

[3]We include Plc and Ltd in the UK, AG and GmbH in Germany, and SA and SARL in France and exclude the GmbH & Co KG, which is a hybrid legal form (a combination of a partnership and a private limited company) used in Austria and Germany. The results do not alter when we include the latter.

598   *L. Klapper et al. / Journal of Financial Economics 82 (2006) 591–629*

which makes the coverage for corporations extensive and the best available. We use the information on legal form in Amadeus—which is country-specific—to identify public and private limited companies.

In Appendix A, we summarize the cross-country differences in the collection of company accounts in Amadeus. We exclude from our sample several European countries where the coverage is incomplete or the data quality is poor. First, we exclude Switzerland, since small firms are not required to file. Second, we exclude the countries of the former Republic of Yugoslavia (Bosnia-Herzegovina, Croatia, former Yugoslav Republic of Macedonia, and Federal Republic of Yugoslavia), which were at war during our sample period and where data coverage is limited. Third, we exclude Slovakia, Slovenia, Russia, and the Ukraine, which have only a very small number of total filings (i.e., less than 1,000 firms annually). These restrictions exclude 342,216 firms over the two years (9.8% of total firms).

As shown in Table 1, Column (ii), after applying these exclusion criteria, we have a smaller, comprehensive sample of incorporated firms in a large number of European countries, which enhances comparability across countries. These restrictions exclude 342,216 firms over two years (9.8% of total firms). Our sample now has over three million annual firms and 57 million employees.

We are not done yet. We have national statistics from Eurostat (European Commission, 2003) on numbers of, and employment in, firms of different sizes. In Table 2, we compare the ratio of firms and employment in Amadeus and in published national statistics in Eurostat (European Commission, 2003). Data, by firm size, are unavailable for non-EU countries. Columns (i) and (ii) show the coverage in Amadeus of large firms (the ratio of firms and employment at firms with more than 250 employees in Amadeus versus that in national statistics) and Columns (iii) and (iv) show the coverage of small firms (the ratio of firms and employment at firms with 10–50 employees in Amadeus versus that in national statistics). Column (v) shows the absolute value of the difference between the ratio of employment in small firms to the ratio of employment in large firms in Amadeus less the ratio of employment at small and large firms in national statistics. This ratio is used to test whether our Amadeus sample is biased towards larger firms. The discrepancy between Amadeus and national figures can also be explained by: (1) the lack of employment data for a significant number of firms in Amadeus, and (2) the fact that for the purpose of cross-country comparisons, our Amadeus dataset excludes proprietorships and partnerships.

We exclude a country from our dataset if two conditions are met: (1) the ratio of employment in firms with more than 250 employees in Amadeus to that in national statistics (Column (ii)) is less than 50%, and (2) the absolute difference between the ratio of the number of firms with 10–50 employees in Amadeus versus that in national statistics and the ratio of total employment at firms with 10–50 employees in Amadeus versus that in national statistics (Column (iv)) is more than 25%. Four countries do not meet the criteria: Iceland, Ireland, Luxembourg, and Portugal. Since these cutoffs could be considered somewhat arbitrary, we also test whether the qualitative results hold if we do not apply these criteria.

We believe that our inclusion criteria create the most comparable sample of firms across countries, but we should be cautious about deriving strong conclusions from direct cross-country comparisons. However, even if we have not eliminated all biases between countries, our basic test examines within-country differences across countries, and will not be affected unless there are systematic biases in reporting industries within a country.

L. Klapper et al. / Journal of Financial Economics 82 (2006) 591–629   599

Table 2
Comparison with National Statistics

Country	(i)	(ii)	(iii)	(iv)	(v)
	Coverage of large firms by number of		Coverage of small firms by number of		Relative coverage of small firms (%)
	Firms (%)	Employees (%)	Firms (%)	Employees (%)	
Austria	44.4	38.7	54.6	65.2	10.6
Belgium	70.0	57.4	65.9	50.6	15.3
Denmark	100.0	77.2	63.3	73.1	9.8
Finland	125.0	90.2	39.0	42.4	3.4
France	65.2	54.2	66.8	57.8	9.0
Germany	34.3	39.0	47.4	49.5	2.1
Greece	200.0	84.4	58.0	97.7	39.7
Iceland	30.0	39.3	6.2	37.9	31.7
Ireland	33.3	14.8	23.1	67.9	44.8
Italy	57.9	78.5	45.3	100.0	54.7
Luxembourg	40.0	38.3	2.9	82.2	79.3
Netherlands	14.3	11.9	31.5	46.4	14.9
Portugal	33.3	20.5	12.8	117.5	104.7
Spain	83.3	98.6	53.2	99.0	45.8
Sweden	114.3	105.6	43.7	47.8	4.1
UK	85.1	79.4	8.6	31.0	22.4

This table compares the number of corporations in Amadeus in 1999 with the total number of firms according to 1996 data from *Enterprises in Europe*: 6th report (European Commission, 2003). The Amadeus ratios are calculated using our extrapolated employment data. The national statistics (Eurostat) refer to all enterprises, including proprietorships. Enterprises with zero employees are excluded from both samples. *Enterprises in Europe* does not cover Eastern European countries, Norway, and Switzerland. In Column (i), we report the ratio of the number of firms with more than 250 employees in Amadeus to the number of firms with more than 250 employees in national statistics. In Column (ii), we report the ratio of total employment at firms with more than 250 employees in Amadeus to total employment at firms with more than 250 employees in national statistics. In Column (iii), we report the ratio of the number of firms with 10–50 employees in Amadeus to the number of firms with 10–50 employees in national statistics. In Column (iv), we report the ratio of total employment at firms with 10–50 employees in Amadeus to total employment at firms with 10–50 employees in national statistics. Column (v) indicates whether there is a bias in the relative coverage of large (versus small) firms in Amadeus and is equal to the absolute value of the difference between the ratio of employment in firms with 10–50 employees to employment in firms with more than 250 employees in Amadeus and the ratio of employment in firms with 10–50 employees to employment in firms with more than 250 employees in national statistics. All data are shown as percentages. Due to data unavailability, large firms in Iceland refer to firms with more than 100 (rather than 250) employees.

Our final sample includes 3,371,073 firms in 21 countries: Austria, Belgium, Bulgaria, the Czech Republic, Denmark, Estonia, Finland, France, Germany, Greece, Hungary, Italy, Latvia, Lithuania, the Netherlands, Norway, Poland, Romania, Spain, Sweden, and the United Kingdom.

2.3. Industry-level entry variables

We measure entry as the fraction of new firms to the total number of firms in an industry, where a new firm is defined as a firm that is one or two years old. We calculate entry at the two-digit NACE industry level averaged over the years 1998 and 1999. We refer to this variable as Entry. For a complete list of variable names and definitions, see Appendix B. Our empirical results are qualitatively robust to defining new firms as age equal to one or to using entry rates calculated for one year (1998 or 1999) only.

We require firms to survive at least one year and exclude firms in year 0. We exclude firms less than one year old to avoid frivolous filings and because of the difference in initial filing requirements across countries. In particular, in some countries firms in their first year do not have to file accounting information until after the end of their first year of operation, while in others they have up to one year to file. We check that the results are not qualitatively affected by including firms under one year old as new firms. The median share of firms of age zero over the period 1998–1999 is 2.5%.

Table 3
Entry rates and main explanatory variables by country, average 1998–1999

Country	(i) % of new firms (1 and 2 years old)	(ii) Number of entry procedures	(iii) Entry cost (% of per capita GNP)
Austria	13.00	9	27.28
Belgium	11.58	8	9.98
Bulgaria	8.60	10	14.41
Czech Republic	11.55	10	8.22
Denmark	13.66	3	10.00
Estonia	20.41	n.a.	n.a.
Finland	11.13	5	1.16
France	14.68	15	14.30
Germany	12.34	10	15.69
Greece	15.44	15	58.60
Hungary	17.38	8	85.87
Italy	3.46	16	20.02
Latvia	18.16	7	42.34
Lithuania	19.23	10	5.46
Netherlands	8.48	8	18.41
Norway	16.87	4	4.72
Poland	12.04	11	25.46
Romania	17.97	16	15.31
Spain	11.41	11	17.30
Sweden	7.90	6	2.56
UK	15.01	5	1.43
Averages			
Western Europe	11.92	8.85	15.50
Transition countries	15.67	10.29	28.15
All countries	13.35	9.35	19.93

Column (i) shows entry rates of new firms in Amadeus, averaged by country for the period 1998–1999. We exclude the agricultural, mining, utility, finance, and public sectors. We exclude country–industry observations based on fewer than three firm observations. New firms are defined as corporations one and two years old. Columns (ii–iii) show the number of entry procedures and entry costs as a percentage of per capita GNP, respectively (Djankov et al., 2002). All data are shown as percentages.

L. Klapper et al. / Journal of Financial Economics 82 (2006) 591–629   601

In Table 3, we describe the country averages of the entry variables that we use in our analysis. We calculate entry and new firm employment rates for all firms. As shown in Column (i), the average entry rate across industries and countries is about 13.3%. Since we define new firms as firms that are one or two years old, this is calculated over two years, on average, and corresponds to an average annual entry rate of about 6.6% (or 4.6% when excluding small firms). The entry rate varies from a high of 19.2% in Lithuania to a low of 3.5% in Italy. Overall, we find an average of about 15.7% of new firms in Eastern European countries, as compared to 11.9% for Western European countries. This difference reflects the recent emergence of a large number of private firms in the transition economies.

Djankov et al. (2002) have data on the procedures that are officially required for an entrepreneur to obtain all necessary permits, and to notify and file with all requisite authorities, in order to legally operate a business. These data refer to 1999 and are shown in Column (ii). These procedures include (i) obtaining all the necessary permits and licenses, and (ii) completing all the required inscriptions, verifications, and notifications to enable the company to start operation. To make the procedures and companies comparable across countries, the survey assumes that the intent is to open a limited liability company and that the founders complete all procedures themselves (without intermediaries). This means the entry barriers are likely to be more onerous for small firms where this latter assumption is likely to be true. We report in Table 3, Column (iii), the direct costs of setting up a new business expressed as a percentage of per capita GNP in U.S. dollars. The cost of entry varies from a high of 86% of GNP per capita in Hungary to a low of 1% of GNP per capita in Finland and the U.K.

In Table 4, Column (i), we present entry rates for a selection of industries based on (groupings of) two-digit NACE codes. The highest entry rates are in communications (telephone, wireless, etc.), computer services, and services, with the lowest entry into chemical manufacturing, construction, and transportation. The industries with high entry rates are generally those related to the high-tech sector, which experienced global growth over the late 1990s. Industries with lower entry rates are those that similarly faced a global decline in the late 1990s (construction) as well as traditionally more concentrated industries (such as chemicals).

As a comparison, we calculate one-year entry rates in the United States from the Dun & Bradstreet (D&B) database of over seven million U.S. corporations over the period 1998–1999. We refer to this variable as $Entry_{US}$. In Table 4, Column (iii), we present U.S. entry rates ($Entry_{US}$) for the same NACE codes. Complete two-digit NACE U.S. entry and exit rates are shown in Appendix C. We use the International Concordance between the U.S. 1987 SIC and the NACE Revision 1 industrial classifications to match the four-digit level SIC codes used by D&B with the two-digit level NACE codes used in Amadeus. As in Europe, we find similar high entry rates in the computer and communications industries in the United States and low entry rates in industries such as manufacturing of basic metals and machinery, suggesting common investment opportunity shocks in these industries. One way of conceptualizing our methodology (though not the only way) is that it essentially examines how different countries respond to these shocks.

In Table 5, we examine the size (measured by number of employees in Amadeus) distribution of entering firms, averaged over 1998 and 1999. An important caveat is that these data are less comprehensive since employment (which we need to classify firms) is missing for about 38% of observations in our sample. The data confirm that most of the

Table 4
Entry rates across Europe and the United States by two-digit NACE code

Industry	NACE code	(i) Europe Age 1 & 2	(ii) Europe Age 1	(iii) U.S. Age 1
Manufacturing	15–36	11.07	6.00	6.31
Food products and beverages	15	9.78	4.63	5.24
Tobacco products	16	16.12	15.23	7.45
Textiles	17	9.37	4.82	6.92
Wearing apparel; dressing and dyeing of fur	18	9.56	4.83	6.44
Luggage, handbags, saddlery and footwear	19	8.48	6.12	9.06
Wood and of products of wood and cork, except furniture	20	11.09	5.62	5.98
Pulp, paper and paper products	21	9.32	5.74	5.26
Publishing, printing and reproduction of recorded media	22	11.15	5.71	5.49
Coke, refined petroleum products and nuclear fuel	23	10.78	7.11	5.80
Chemicals, and chemical products	24	9.53	4.64	6.08
Rubber and plastic products	25	11.15	5.17	4.46
Other non-metallic mineral products	26	9.33	4.90	5.79
Basic metals	27	12.54	7.33	4.90
Fabricated metal products, except machinery and equipment	28	11.58	5.99	5.71
Machinery and equipment not elsewhere classified	29	10.46	4.86	4.30
Office machinery and computers	30	15.53	9.33	8.67
Electrical machinery and apparatus not elsewhere classified	31	11.06	5.82	5.92
Radio, television and communication equipment and apparatus	32	14.35	7.14	8.45
Medical, precision and optical instruments, watches and clocks	33	9.97	5.62	5.72
Motor vehicles, trailers and semi-trailers	34	10.78	5.47	5.20
Other transport equipment	35	12.90	6.94	7.96
Furniture; manufacturing not elsewhere classified	36	11.73	5.90	7.92
Construction	45	13.56	6.51	8.14
Trade	50–52	14.27	6.92	5.86
Sale, maintenance and repair of motor vehicles and motorcycles	50	13.15	6.21	5.05
Wholesale trade and commission trade, except of motor vehicles	51	14.65	7.00	5.35
Retail trade, except of motor vehicles and motorcycles	52	15.01	7.55	7.19
Hotels and Restaurants	55	14.73	7.42	5.95
Transportation	60–63	13.90	7.58	6.74
Land transport; transport via pipelines	60	15.56	7.82	8.41
Water transport	61	11.67	7.12	5.61
Air transport	62	13.53	8.62	6.19
Supporting and auxiliary transport activities, and travel agencies	63	14.20	6.95	6.77
Post and telecommunications	64	26.71	14.00	10.09
Services	70–74, 93	18.01	9.77	7.51
Real estate activities	70	15.76	8.20	5.33
Leasing of equipment and machinery	71	17.66	9.18	6.34
Computer services	72	22.19	12.49	10.73
Research and development	73	16.76	10.29	6.53
Other business activities	74	16.98	8.76	6.46
Other services activities	93	16.76	10.29	6.53
Total	15–93	13.27	7.09	6.65

This table shows entry rates of new firms across Europe and the U.S. by two-digit NACE industry codes. Column (i) shows European data from Amadeus, averaged across countries, and averaged for the years 1998–1999. Column (ii) defines new firms as corporations one year old, to compare to the U.S. data. In Column (iii), data on U.S. entry rates are from Dun & Bradstreet, averaged for the years 1998–99, and new firms are defined as corporations of age 1. Data are shown as percentages. We exclude the agricultural, mining, utility, finance, and public sectors (NACE codes 5–7, 10–14, 50–51, 65–67, 85, and 91–92). We also exclude country-industry observations based on less than three firm observations. "Total" is the average of all non-excluded two-digit NACE codes.

L. Klapper et al. / Journal of Financial Economics 82 (2006) 591–629   603

Table 5
Size distribution of new firms in Europe, by country and firm size, average of 1998 and 1999

	(i)	(ii)	(iii)	(iv)
	Percentage of new corporations with employment:			
Country	<10	10–50	50–250	> 250
Austria	61.32	29.89	7.04	1.76
Belgium	91.18	7.44	1.17	0.20
Bulgaria	54.51	24.10	16.64	4.75
Czech Republic	28.18	34.83	29.39	7.60
Denmark	82.57	15.42	1.74	0.27
Estonia	77.39	19.36	2.72	0.53
Finland	87.37	9.70	2.30	0.63
France	90.91	8.00	0.93	0.16
Germany	80.50	16.05	2.71	0.74
Greece	54.54	40.42	4.49	0.54
Hungary	43.03	38.90	14.83	3.24
Ireland	7.89	34.54	52.30	0.00
Italy	66.18	23.21	8.35	2.25
Latvia	50.02	31.37	14.80	3.81
Lithuania	36.38	47.04	12.79	3.78
Netherlands	57.67	23.15	16.33	2.85
Norway	86.42	11.68	1.55	0.36
Poland	19.50	28.42	41.87	10.20
Portugal	50.87	28.35	16.50	4.28
Romania	92.07	6.02	1.44	0.46
Spain	68.06	27.54	3.82	0.58
Sweden	91.32	7.54	0.98	0.17
United Kingdom	70.14	17.18	9.83	2.85
Averages				
Western Europe	69.80	20.01	8.67	1.18
Transition countries	50.14	28.76	16.81	4.30
All countries	62.96	23.05	11.50	2.26

This table shows the size distribution of new firms in Amadeus by country, averaged over the period 1998–99. New firms are defined as corporations that are one or two years old. Columns indicate percentages of total new corporations in a particular size category.

entry occurs in small firms. Interestingly, we find a greater fraction of new, larger firms in the Eastern European transition countries. This might suggest that new, private firms are emerging across all size groups, rather than only among small firms. It could also reflect a number of larger, state-owned firms that continue to be privatized and reincorporated following the transition. An exception to the transition countries is Romania, which includes over 200,000 firms with less than 10 employees. On average, about 63% of new firms have fewer than ten employees, 23% have 10–50 employees, 12% have 50–250 employees, and 2% have more than 250 employees. Since new firms in this largest category are likely to be existing firms that reincorporate following a merger or acquisition, we check that our qualitative results hold when we exclude new firms with more than 250 employees.

604   *L. Klapper et al. / Journal of Financial Economics 82 (2006) 591–629*

3. Methodology

We explore the differential effects of certain country characteristics on entry across industries with different natural demands for that characteristic. In other words, we are interested in the interaction between country and industry-specific variables. We use industry indicators to control for level differences across industries and country indicators to control for level differences across countries. The model is as follows:

$$Entry_{j,k} = Constant + \Phi_1 \cdot Industry\ dummies_j$$
$$+ \Phi_2 \cdot Country\ dummies_k$$
$$+ \phi_3 \cdot Industry\ share_{j,k}$$
$$+ \phi_4 \cdot (Industry\ characteristic_j \cdot Country\ characteristic_k)$$
$$+ e_{j,k}, \tag{1}$$

where a subscript j indicates industry j, a subscript k indicates country k, and uppercase coefficients indicate vectors. The dependent variable is the ratio of new firms to total firms of industry j in country k. The industry indicators correct for industry-specific effects. Similarly, the country indicators correct for country-specific variables.[4] The industry j share of total sales in country k captures an industry-specific convergence effect: we correct for the possibility that sectors that are large relative to the rest of the economy experience lower entry rates. We get similar results when we use value added rather than sales as a measure of relative industry size, but prefer to use sales as a measure of size because value added figures are missing for several industries in a number of countries. Finally, $\varepsilon_{j,k}$ is an error term with the usual distributional assumptions. The focus is on the interaction term and its coefficient ϕ_4.

The critical aspect, of course, is the country characteristic and the industry characteristic. The first country characteristic we focus on is the cost of fulfilling the bureaucratic requirements to register a company. Costly entry regulations will make it more difficult for new firms to enter. Djankov et al. (2002) calculate the direct costs associated with starting up a business as a percentage of per capita GNP in 1999. Following their work, we term the log of this variable EntCost. We use the log of the entry cost variable (which takes values of between zero and one because it is expressed in fractions of per capita GNP) so that in absolute terms higher costs are associated with lower values.

We would expect industries that naturally have low entry barriers to be most affected by regulations on entry. We therefore need to know what entry would look like if there were few artificial or infrastructural barriers to entry—not just bureaucratic barriers but also other potential barriers like rigid labor regulation or poor access to financing. Under the assumption that these barriers are low in the United States (for instance, entry costs in the U.S. are 0.5% of per capita GNP compared to an average of 20% of per capita GNP in our sample of European countries), we would expect the rate of entry in an industry in the United States to be a good proxy for the "natural" propensity for entry in that industry – reflecting technological barriers in that industry like economies of scale or incumbent

---

[4]One of the omitted variables that could explain cross-country variation in incorporation rates is differences in the tax regimes and tax treatments of corporations. In many countries, limited companies are set up for tax purposes rather than entrepreneurial activities. If this taxation difference varies across countries, this would create a hard to quantify bias. The country indicators, however, control for such differences across countries.

L. Klapper et al. / Journal of Financial Economics 82 (2006) 591–629   605

organizational efficiencies obtained from experience. Of course, there is a degree of heroism in assuming that entry in the United States does not suffer from artificial barriers (or even in assuming that there is a clear distinction between natural and artificial barriers). Nevertheless, all that is important for us is that the rank ordering of entry in the United States correspond to the rank ordering of natural barriers across industries, and that this rank ordering carry over to other countries. We do, however, check the robustness of the results to measures based on entry in other regions.

As a measure of industry share, we use the Amadeus database to construct the ratio of the industry's sales to total sales of firms in the country. We refer to this variable as Industry Share. We use the average of this variable for the years 1998–1999. We calculate this country-industry level variable for two-digit NACE industries using data in Amadeus. These industry shares of total sales are expected to capture a potential convergence effect.

In the basic regression then, EntCost is our country characteristic and Entry$_{US}$ is the industry characteristic indicating whether the industry has "naturally high entry." If, as hypothesized, bureaucratic entry requirements do have an effect, they should particularly impede entry in industries that are naturally prone to entry (or seen another way, entry into an industry that is a natural monopoly should be little affected by the existence of bureaucratic entry barriers). We thus expect coefficient ϕ_4 to be negative.

4. Results

4.1. Entry barriers and permutations

We report summary statistics for the country and industry level variables in Table 6. In Table 7, Column (i), we present the basic regression, estimated using a Tobit regression with censoring at zero and one. The coefficient of the interaction term is negative and significant at the 1% level. Since we use the log of entry cost, which takes values between zero and one, lower entry costs result in a more negative value for our entry cost variable. Together with the negative coefficient on the interaction term, this means that relative entry into industries with naturally high entry is disproportionately higher in countries with low regulatory barriers to entry.

Since this is a difference-in-difference estimate, it is worth pointing out what the coefficient means. Take an industry like retail trade (NACE code 52) that is at the 75th percentile of Entry$_{US}$ and an industry like manufacturing of pulp, paper, and paper products (NACE code 21) that is at the 25th percentile of Entry$_{US}$. The coefficient estimate suggests that the difference in entry rates between retail and pulp in the Czech Republic (which is at the 25th percentile in terms of EntCost with entry costs equal to 8% of per capita GNP) is 0.5 percentage points higher than the difference in entry rates between the same industries in Italy (which is at the 75th percentile in terms of EntCost with entry costs equal to 20% of per capita GNP). In other words, moving from Italy to the Czech Republic benefits the high entry retail sector relatively more. As a comparison, the mean difference in entry rates between the retail and pulp industries across countries is 5%. This suggests that the effect of regulatory entry barriers accounts for about 10% of the mean difference.

Since this basic result is critical to any further analysis, we attempt to rule out other explanations of this result by conducting a variety of robustness checks. In Column (ii) we use as an alternative measure of entry regulation the logarithm of the number of

Table 6
Summary statistics of country-level variables

Panel A: Summary statistics of country-level variables

Variable	(i) Number of countries	(ii) Mean	(iii) Median	(iv) Std. dev.	(v) Min	(vi) Max
Entry costs (EntCost)	20	0.20	0.15	0.21	0.01	0.86
Entry procedures (EntProc)	20	9.35	9.50	3.90	3.00	16.00
Bankrupty costs (bankcost)	20	0.13	0.08	0.11	0.01	0.38
Private credit (Priv)	21	0.58	0.58	0.38	0.10	1.20
Employment laws (EmpLaw)	20	1.55	1.68	0.36	0.80	2.18
Property rights (Prop)	21	4.14	4.00	0.85	2.00	5.00
Tax disadvantage (Tax)	21	−0.11	−0.10	0.09	−0.28	0.00

Panel B: Summary statistics of U.S. and Amadeus industry-level variables, by industry

Industry	(i) Sector code	(ii) NACE Industry Code	(iii) Entry rate (Entry$_{US}$)	(iv) Exit rate (Exit$_{US}$)	(v) Total Assets (Scale)	(vi) Total Revenues (Size)	(vii) External Finance (ExtFin)	(viii) Labor Intensity (LabInt)	(ix) R&D (R&D)
Manufacturing	1	15–36	6.31	21.71	318.44	385.41	26.60	23.94	3.15
Manufacture of chemicals		24	6.08	22.43	31.04	17.22	79.05	11.12	12.68
Manufacture of office machinery and computers		30	8.67	34.23	34.65	40.23	50.15	54.31	10.35
Manufacture of radio, television, and Communication equipment		32	8.45	27.43	42.95	51.69	32.76	19.61	10.62
Construction	2	45	8.14	19.89	97.24	127.54	46.98	22.27	0.50
Trade	3	50–52	5.86	20.30	104.70	209.29	54.79	43.56	0.00
Hotels and restaurants	4	55	5.95	15.88	52.82	62.65	42.51	95.70	0.00
Transportation	5	60–63	6.74	24.63	218.34	204.39	13.01	20.13	7.50
Communications	6	64	10.09	31.36	270.85	108.67	85.58	9.63	2.23
Services	7	70–74, 93	7.51	20.30	47.76	46.17	96.87	28.68	10.21
Computer services		72	10.73	25.61	17.85	20.95	123.86	22.81	17.57
Average	1–7	15–93	6.65	21.74	234.23	276.32	41.00	2.80	4.12
Median			6.14	20.66	94.36	126.06	28.05	1.96	1.31
Standard deviation			1.59	4.76	643.11	733.22	50.20	2.16	7.52

Panel A shows summary statistics of country-level variables. In the regressions, we use the logarithm of the entry costs, entry procedures, and bankruptcy costs as reported in Panel A. Panel B shows summary statistics of U.S. industry-level characteristics. Averages are reported across sector groups based on two-digit NACE industry codes. Entry rates, exit rates, external financial dependence, labor intensity, and R&D intensity are reported in percentages. See Appendix C for complete two-digit NACE U.S. entry and exit rates. We exclude the agricultural, mining, utility, finance, and public sectors and two-digit industries with fewer than 3 observations. See Appendix B for complete variable definitions and sources.

procedures required to set up a business from Djankov et al. (2002). The maximum value of number of entry procedures in the sample is 16, for Italy and Romania. We indeed find higher entry rates into industries with high entry in the U.S. in countries with fewer entry procedures. The coefficient estimate suggests that the difference in entry rates between retail and pulp in Sweden (which is at the 25th percentile in terms of the number of entry procedures) is 0.8 percentage points higher than the difference in entry rates between the same industries in Spain (which is at the 75th percentile in terms of the number of entry

Table 7
Determinants of entry rates

	(i)	(ii)	(iii)	(iv)	(v)
	Fraction of new firms				
	Entry costs	Entry procedures	EntCost & time	Excl. transition	EuroStat data
Industry Share	−0.092	−0.093	−0.095	0.157	
	(0.108)	(0.109)	(0.108)	(0.123)	
Entry$_{US}$ * EntCost	−0.175***			−0.110***	−0.198***
	(0.047)			(0.041)	(0.043)
Entry$_{US}$ * EntProc		−0.656***			
		(0.177)			
Entry$_{US}$ * EntCost&Time			−0.211***		
			(0.055)		
Observations	708	708	708	484	259

The reported estimates are from Tobit regressions. The dependent variable in columns (I–iv) is the ratio of new firms to total firms, averaged over the period 1998–1999, by two-digit NACE industry code and country (Amadeus). Industry Share is the industry share in sales (Amadeus). Entry$_{US}$ is the ratio of new firms to total firms in the U.S., by two-digit NACE industry code (Dun & Bradstreet). In Column (iv), we exclude transition countries. The dependent variable in Column (v) is the ratio of new firms to total firms for the year 1999 by Eurostat industry code and country, calculated using data from Eurostat. All regressions include a constant, country dummies and two-digit industry dummies, not shown. White (1980) standard errors are reported in parentheses. *** denotes significance at 1%. See Appendix B for complete variable definitions and sources.

procedures). In Column (iii) we include the monetized value of the entrepreneur's time to set up a business in the cost of entry and find similar results.

Next, we estimate using different samples. In Column (iv), we exclude transition countries. Privatization has resulted in the emergence of a large number of private firms in these economies, and we want to make sure our results are not driven by this. Our results are robust to the exclusion of these countries. Our results are also robust to adding back those countries that fail to meet our inclusion criteria (i.e., Iceland, Ireland, Luxembourg, and Portugal), and to dropping one country at a time (not reported in tables).

We also analyze "official" data from Eurostat, which is calculated by the European Union (EU) using confidential census data for a sample of nine EU countries, by "EU-industries," which are broader than two-digit NACE codes. We do not have data from this sample for non-EU transition countries or for certain industries. For example, whereas we have about 600 observations by country and two-digit NACE industry codes using the Amadeus database, Eurostat only includes about 250 observations. Eurostat provides entry rates, calculated as the one-year change in the number of firms, and exit rates, calculated as the number of firms exiting the industry, excluding mergers and acquisitions. Entry rates across countries and industries using the Amadeus database and Eurostat data are significantly correlated at about 67%. As shown in Column (v), our main regression results are robust to the substitution of entry rates from Eurostat. This suggests that our calculations using the Amadeus data are in line with official figures.

4.2. Robustness to outliers

Our estimation strategy can be thought of as a difference-in-difference estimation, where we divide the countries into two groups: high entry regulation (HR) and low entry regulation (LR) groups, and the industries into high entry (HE) and low entry (LE) groups. If we abstract away from any control variables, our estimate is: [HE(HR) – LE(HR)] – [HE(LR) – LE(LR)]. This estimate captures the average effect only. For robustness, we employ a similar non-parametric difference-in-difference estimation strategy to investigate whether the effect is generally present in all countries and industries.[5] We report the results of this procedure but do not include a separate table.

We first divide the countries into HR and LR, and then rank the industries from the lowest natural entry to the highest. Next, we pick the lowest natural entry industry (LWE) as our reference industry, and repeat the difference-in-difference estimation above for each remaining industry *J*, i.e., we compute: [*J*(HR) – LWE(HR)] – [(*J*(LR) – LWE(LR)], for each industry *J*. The effect is strongest for the computer and related activities (NACE 72) and post and telecommunications (NACE 64) industries. We also find that the effect tends to be larger for industries with higher natural entry.

Next, we repeat the exercise for countries, i.e., we divide industries into low entry (LE) and high entry (HE), and order countries from lowest to highest entry regulation. Again, we find that the average effect is consistent with our main results. The effect is strongest for Norway and the United Kingdom. What is reassuring is that no single industry or country appears to be driving the results. In particular, the results in Table 7 are also robust to (i) the exclusion of Italy, a developed country with relatively high entry barriers, and (ii) the exclusion of the following information technology-intensive industries: manufacture of communication equipment (NACE 32) and computer and related activities (NACE 72).

4.3. Alternative measures

In Table 8 we examine alternatives to U.S. entry rates as measures of the natural propensity to enter. Prior literature (Dunne et al., 1988) finds that exit rates and entry rates are strongly correlated—the more there is creation through young firms, the more destruction there also is. In Column (i) we calculate $Exit_{US}$, which is the share of firms that exit in the U.S. D&B data measured by the number of firms that exit in year *t* (because of closure or acquisition) as a percentage of all firms in year *t*-1. This measure is averaged for the industry over the period 1998–1999. $Exit_{US}$ should serve as a proxy for "natural entry" and when we replace $Entry_{US}$ with it in the regression, the interaction has the expected negative sign and is significant (this also suggests that our industry characteristics are not just picking up growth opportunities in the industry but some measure of the industry's natural dynamism).

One might think it obvious that bureaucratic costs would deter entry. What about other costs that weigh on entrants? For example, we expect that firms are more likely to enter and receive start-up financing if bankruptcy proceedings are less costly in the case of default. As a measure of bankruptcy costs, we use the actual cost of bankruptcy proceedings as the percentage of the estate that is consumed in bankruptcy proceedings

---

[5]We thank Atif Mian for this suggestion.

L. Klapper et al. / Journal of Financial Economics 82 (2006) 591–629   609

Table 8
Alternative proxies for natural propensity to enter

	(i)	(ii)	(iii)	(iv)	(v)	(vi)	(vii)	(viii)	(ix)
	Exit	Bankruptcy	Taxes	SME	Scale	Size		UK	Europe
Industry Share	−0.081	−0.083	−0.108	−0.083	−0.087	−0.088	−0.074	−0.143	−0.105
	(0.109)	(0.108)	(0.109)	(0.109)	(0.109)	(0.109)	(0.109)	(0.111)	(0.107)
Exit * EntCost	−0.032**								
	(0.015)								
Entry$_{US}$ * BankCost		−3.491***							
		(0.863)							
Entry$_{US}$ * EntCost			−0.207***						
			(0.050)						
Entry$_{US}$ * Tax			−2.429**						
			(1.228)						
SME * EntCost				−0.007*					
				(0.004)					
Scale * EntCost					0.002***				
					(0.001)				
Size * EntCost						0.002***			
						(0.001)			
Entry$_{US, 1990–2000}$ * EntCost							−0.142**		
							(0.064)		
Entry$_{UK}$ * EntCost								−0.095***	
								(0.022)	
Entry$_{Europe}$ * EntCost									−0.094***
									(0.015)
Observations	708	708	708	708	708	708	708	670	708

The reported estimates are from Tobit regressions. The dependent variable is the ratio of new firms to total firms, averaged over the period 1998–1999, by two-digit NACE industry and country (Amadeus). Industry Share is the industry share in sales (Amadeus). Exit is exit rates of U.S. firms, averaged over the period 1998–1999, by NACE industry (Dun & Bradstreet). EntCost is country-level entry cost (Djankov et al., 2002). Entry$_{US}$ is the ratio of new firms to total firms in the U.S., by NACE industry (Dun & Bradstreet) BankCost is the country-level bankruptcy cost (Djankov et al., 2003). Tax is the difference between the top corporate income and personal income tax rates in the country (PricewaterhouseCoopers). SME is the percentage of U.S. firms with fewer than 250 employees, averaged over the period 1998–1999, by NACE industry (D & B). Scale is the median assets of U.S. firms, averaged over the period 1998–1999, by NACE industry (Compustat). Size is the median sales of U.S. firms, averaged over the period 1998–1999, by NACE industry (Compustat). Entry$_{US, 1990–2000}$ is the entry rate of U.S. firms, averaged over the period 1990–2000, by NACE industry (D & B). Entry$_{UK}$ is the entry rate of U.K. firms, averaged over the period 1998–1999, by NACE industry (Amadeus). Entry$_{Europe}$ is the entry rate of firms in Europe, averaged over the period 1998–1999, by NACE industry (Amadeus). All regressions include a constant, and country and industry dummies, not shown. See Appendix B for complete variable definitions and sources. White (1980) standard errors are reported in parentheses. *, **, and *** denote significant at 10%, 5%, and 1%, respectively.

(Djankov et al., 2003). We find that entry is higher in high-entry industries in countries with lower cost of bankruptcy (Column (ii) in Table 8).

Another form of entry barrier is the differential income taxes for corporations compared to individuals, which can cause a tax penalty and make incorporation unattractive. In Column (iii) we include the interaction between Entry$_{US}$ and Tax Disadvantage, which is defined as the difference between the top corporate income tax and the top personal income tax rates in the country (obtained from PricewaterhouseCoopers

Worldwide Taxes 1999–2000).[6] We find that entry is significantly higher in high-entry industries in countries where tax rates on corporate income are much lower than those on personal income.

In Column (iv) we use the D& B data to calculate SME, which is the ratio of the number of Small and Medium Enterprises (SMEs), defined as businesses with less than 250 employees, to the total number of firms. Since new firms are generally also small, we expect greater entry into industries with larger shares of smaller firms. Indeed, we find a significantly negative coefficient, suggesting that higher entry costs discourage entry into industries with larger shares of SMEs. In Columns (v–vi), we use firm size as the industry characteristic. We use Compustat data of U.S. listed firms to calculate SCALE as the log of median assets of firms in an industry and SIZE as the log of median total sales. Assets and sales take values less than one (they are divided by 10 billion US dollars) so that the log is a negative number, and more negative values denote industries with firms of smaller size. Since entry costs are more negative when low, the positive coefficient estimate indicates that smaller scale/average size industries have relatively more entry in low entry cost countries.

Next, we examine the persistence of U.S. entry rates. Dunne and Roberts (1991) and Cable and Schwalbach (1991) study U.S. and international data, respectively, and find that the relation between industry characteristics and industry turnover patterns is stable over time. These results suggest stability of industry structures over time and countries. However, for robustness we compute the average of annual D & B entry rates of U.S. corporations from 1990–2000 (Entry$_{US, 1990–2000}$). The raw correlation between U.S. entry rates in 1998–1999 – the variable in the baseline regression—and U.S. entry rates over the 1990s is 0.32 and significant at the 5% level. When we replace the Entry$_{US}$ variables with Entry$_{US, 1990–2000}$, we find that the coefficient on the interaction term remains highly significant and of similar magnitude (Column (vii) in Table 8).

Finally, it could be that our results are driven by the peculiarities of industry structure in the U.S. Our method should work so long as we measure entry rates in a country where barriers to entry are thought to be small. In Column (viii), we use entry rates calculated for firms in the United Kingdom (Entry$_{UK}$). There are important differences between the United Kingdom and the U.S. For instance, the United Kingdom's bankruptcy system is more creditor-friendly and the composition of its industries is different. Nevertheless, the correlation between entry rates in the U.S. and in the United Kingdom is 0.60 and significant at the 1% level. The regression results (excluding industries of the United Kingdom) show that the coefficient on the interaction term remains highly significant. Column (ix) shows that our results are also robust to using entry rates calculated using firms across all European countries in our sample (Entry$_{Europe}$). The correlation between entry rates in the U.S. and the average entry rate across Europe is 0.60 and significant at the 1% level.

4.4. Causality

We have not fully addressed the issue of causality. We know the findings do not arise because there are fewer high natural entry industries in countries with high bureaucratic entry barriers—this is the virtue of correcting for industry effects. But there could be omitted variables that jointly drive the propensity to enter and the degree of bureaucratic

---

[6]Our measure of tax disadvantage differs from the measure used in Gordon and MacKie-Mason (1997) which takes taxation of corporate dividends into account.

entry barriers. One way to test the direction of causality is to use instruments. It has been generally found that the origin of a country's legal system seems to be strongly associated with the regulatory system in place today (see, for example, La Porta et al., 1999). While there has been some debate about the precise mechanism by which this association exists, a country's legal origin offers a proxy for predetermined components of regulation. When we instrument entry regulation with legal origin, we find that the coefficient estimate for the interaction term is highly significant, the same sign and approximately the same magnitude as shown earlier in Table 7 (Column (i) in Table 9). The legal origin variables explain 59% of the variation in the entry cost variable. Entry costs tend to be lowest in countries with Anglo-Saxon and Scandinavian legal origin and highest in countries with French legal origin.

The instrumental variable approach might still not fully address the causality problem: it could be that countries with large "high natural entry" industries have a strong entrepreneurial culture and select low entry regulation. (If legal origin also drives entrepreneurial culture, the instrument could be pre-determined, but might not satisfy the exclusion restriction—it might be correlated with other omitted variables that determine entry.) A crude way to correct for this is to include the interaction between $Entry_{US}$ and the aggregate rate of entry in the country (the fraction of new firms to total firms). If the aggregate rate of entry proxies for entrepreneurial culture, and so do entry costs, the inclusion of this new interaction variable should reduce the magnitude of the estimated coefficient on the basic interaction significantly. It does not (see Table 9, Column (ii)).

Another approach is to check whether the result holds when we restrict the sample to industries that are relatively small. These industries are unlikely to be responsible for the entry barriers since they have limited political clout. For each country, industries are defined to be small if their Industry Share is in the country's bottom textile in Industry Share. When we restrict our sample to small industries, we still find a strongly significant interaction coefficient of approximately the same magnitude as shown earlier in Table 7 (Column (iii) in Table 9). This suggests that industries that are unlikely to be responsible for the entry regulations are equally affected by it.

While entry regulation is not strongly correlated with economic development (as measured by per capita GDP) in our sample, we also confirm that our results are robust to the inclusion of the interaction of $Entry_{US}$ and the logarithm of per capita GDP (Column (iv) in Table 9). We have also checked whether the results are robust to controlling for growth opportunities. Following Fisman and Love (2003b), we use industry-level U.S. sales growth over the period 1990–2000 as proxy for industry growth opportunities. Our entry interaction variable still enters significantly at the 1% level when we add the interaction between U.S. sales growth and entry costs (not shown). We get similar results when we calculate average U.S. sales growth for the period 1980–1990.

Another concern is that countries with more untrustworthy populations erect higher bureaucratic barriers so as to screen would-be entrepreneurs more carefully. If this were true, bureaucratic barriers might affect entry, and might cause incumbents to become fat and lazy, but this is necessary because the alternative of unrestricted entry by charlatans would be much worse. One way to address this concern is to check whether the underlying population results in differential selection. More developed countries have better-developed information systems, better product inspections and quality control, better contract and law enforcement, and consequently, an entrepreneurial population less inclined to misbehavior. (The underlying population in wealthier countries might also be

L. Klapper et al. / Journal of Financial Economics 82 (2006) 591–629

Table 9
Causality and selection issues

	(i)	(ii)	(iii)	(iv)	(v)	(vi)	(vii)
	IV:Legal origin	Country-average entry	Small industries	Development	GDP	Corruption	Informal sector
Industry Share	-0.092 (0.090)	-0.089 (0.108)	-3.704* (2.085)	-0.128 (0.107)	-0.110 (0.108)	-0.117 (0.108)	-0.143 (0.108)
$Entry_{US}$ * EntCost	-0.175*** (0.055)	-0.164*** (0.048)	-0.191** (0.093)	-0.186*** (0.046)			-0.173*** (0.046)
$Entry_{US}$ * Country-average Entry		2.730 (2.672)					
$Entry_{US}$ * GDP per capita				0.419*** (0.092)			
Low GDP per capita * $Entry_{US}$ * EntCost					0.087 (0.127)		
High GDP per capita * $Entry_{US}$ * EntCost					-0.170*** (0.047)		
High Corruption * $Entry_{US}$ * EntCost						0.186 (0.128)	
Low Corruption * $Entry_{US}$ * EntCost						-0.168*** (0.047)	
$Entry_{US}$ * Informal							-0.057*** (0.013)
Observations	708	708	214	708	708	708	708

This table shows an instrumental variable regression with robust errors (Column (i)) and Tobit regressions with censoring at 0 and 1 (Columns (ii–viii)). The dependent variable is the ratio of new firms to total firms, averaged over the period 1998–1999, by two-digit NACE industry code and country. In column (i), we use the legal origin variable in La Porta et al. (1998) as instrument for entry regulations. The standard errors are corrected for clustering at the country level. Column (ii) includes an interaction of industry-level U.S. entry and the average entry rate for the country as a whole. Column (iii) shows Tobit regressions with the sample restricted to industries that are in the country's bottom tertile in industry share. Column (iv) includes an interaction of industry-level entry and the logarithm of per capita GDP in the country. Columns (v–vi) show Tobit results when we estimate different slopes for the interaction variables for whether the industry is in a country below or above the sample median per capita income (low GDP per capita and high GDP per capita), or above or below the sample median level of corruption (high corruption and low corruption). Column (vii) includes an interaction of industry-level entry and the share of the informal economy in the country (Informal) from Schneider (2002). All regressions include a constant and country and industry dummies, not shown. See Appendix B for complete variable definitions and sources. White (1980) standard errors are reported in parentheses. *, **, and *** denote significant at 10%, 5%, and 1%, respectively.

L. Klapper et al. / Journal of Financial Economics 82 (2006) 591–629   613

socialized to be more honest (less adverse selection) but for our purposes it is only necessary that the richer infrastructure gives them more incentive to behave, so there is less need for screening.) If bureaucratic rules are meant to screen entry efficiently, we should expect them to be particularly effective in low-income countries relative to high-income countries. In Column (v) of Table 9 we estimate different slopes for the interaction variable for whether the industry is in a country that is above or below the sample median per capita income. If, in fact, entry regulations screen more effectively in low-income countries where there is less alternative infrastructure to assure compliance, we should find the coefficient estimate for the interaction in below-sample-median income countries to be significantly more negative. It is not.[7] Similarly, we find that entry barriers work most effectively in preventing entry in low-corruption countries rather than in high-corruption countries (Column (vi) in Table 9), suggesting that they do not help select more carefully amongst an untrustworthy population.

Taken together, these results suggest that the regulation of entry seems to have causal effects, more so in wealthy countries or countries that are not corrupt than in poor or corrupt countries. Thus, it is unlikely that these regulations are particularly effective in screening populations in countries where other formal screening mechanisms do not exist or where the population is more likely to be untrustworthy.

Finally, we are concerned that there could be a high degree of underreporting of new firms, since we measure entry only into the formal sector. In countries where for tax avoidance and other reasons it is attractive to remain informal, we expect to see less entry into the formal sector and fewer firms choosing the legal form of a limited liability company. The correlation between our measure of the informal sector (Informal) calculated as the size of the informal economy as a percentage of official GNI averaged over the period 1999–2000 and the cost of entry regulations (EntCost) is 0.37 although not statistically significant at the 10 percent level. In column (vii), we include an interaction of $Entry_{US}$ and a measure of the share of the informal economy (Informal).

The coefficient estimate for the interaction between $Entry_{US}$ and Informal is negative and statistically significant, suggesting that underreporting of new firms is more likely in high-entry industries in countries with an inhospitable business environment. However, our main interaction variable between $Entry_{US}$ and EntCost remains highly significant and virtually unchanged in magnitude, suggesting that bureaucratic regulations have an independent effect over and above the effects of the inhospitable environment. This is not particularly surprising in light of our finding that bureaucratic regulations have the most impact in developed and less corrupt countries, which are unlikely to have an inhospitable business environment.

4.5. The consequences of preventing free entry

Entry regulations, at least in the way we measure them, could be thought of as a fixed cost. They should be reflected in an increased average size of entrants into high-entry industries in countries with high entry costs. In Table 10, Panel A, Column (i), the dependent variable is the average size of entrants (measured as the logarithm of average

---

[7]When allowing for different slopes for transition versus non-transition countries, we find a stronger effect for non-transition countries, i.e., for countries where we expect a stronger legal system etc. (not shown).

value added in millions of Euros in industry i in country j over the period 1998–1999, where value added is computed as earnings before interest, taxes, depreciation, and amortization, plus labor costs). The explanatory variables are the standard ones. We find that the average size of entering firms is indeed significantly higher in high-entry industries in countries with high entry costs. A one standard deviation increase in entry costs raises the average size of entrants by 0.78 million euros in an industry that is one standard deviation higher in natural entry rate, a substantial magnitude when compared to the median size of entrants across industries of 0.87 million euros.

While some of the lower entry we have found earlier could simply be because a number of small firms will be discouraged from setting up, others might have to grow without the protection of limited liability until they reach the scale to afford the cost of incorporation. In either case, entry costs could have a dampening effect on innovation and risk-taking.

An immediate question is whether entry regulation affects the ability or incentive of incumbents to enhance productivity. If entry regulations only serve to protect incumbents and prevent the disciplinary effects of competition, incumbent firms are less likely to be able, or forced, to enhance productivity. If, by contrast, regulations are effective at screening, incumbent firms that have come through the screening process could be better firms, more able to enhance productivity.

In Table 10, Panel A, Columns (ii–viii), we examine the effect of entry regulation on the relative performance of incumbent or established firms, defined as all firms more than two years old. We use the growth in value added per employee as a measure of firm performance. To reduce the influence of outliers, the dependent variable in the regressions in this table is censored.

In Panel A, Columns (ii–v), we present Tobit estimations where the dependent variable is the real growth in value added per employee over the period 1998–1999 averaged over all incumbent firms in the industry in a country. In Column (ii), the negative significant coefficient on the interaction variable indicates that incumbent firms in naturally high-entry industries have relatively less growth in value added when they are in a country with high entry regulations. We verify that this result is not simply because incumbents in countries with high entry costs are larger—the result survives when we include the average value added for incumbents in the industry in that country (not reported in the table).

Again, it is worth pointing out what the coefficient means by comparing the retail trade industry, which is at the 75th percentile of $Entry_{US}$, and the pulp and paper manufacturing industry, which is at the 25th percentile of $Entry_{US}$. The coefficient estimate suggests that the difference in real growth rates of value added per worker between retail and pulp in the Czech Republic (which is at the 25th percentile in terms of EntCost) is 0.7 percentage points higher than the difference in real growth rates between the same industries in Italy (which is at the 75th percentile in terms of EntCost). In other words, moving from Italy to the Czech Republic benefits the growth rate of the high-entry retail sector relatively more. Since the average real growth rate in value added per worker is 1%, this is a sizeable magnitude.

We also include other measures of firm entry. Column (iii) shows that our results are robust to the substitution of entry rates with the percentage of SMEs, defined as firms with less than 250 employees. The estimates in Columns (iv–v) indicate that incumbent firms in industries with smaller scale tend to increase productivity more slowly in countries with high regulatory entry barriers. Next, we test the direction of causality using legal origin as

Table 10
The consequences of preventing free entry

Panel A: Size of entrants and performance of incumbent firms

	(i) Size of entrants	(ii) Growth	(iii) SME	(iv) Scale	(v) Size	(vi) Legal origin	(vii) GDP	(viii) Corruption
Industry Share	2.334	−0.050	−0.030	−0.048	−0.040	−0.178	−0.038	0.012
	(3.890)	(0.530)	(0.529)	(0.530)	(0.530)	(0.378)	(0.531)	(0.530)
Entry$_{US}$ * EntCost	9.936***	−0.426**				−0.211*	−0.431**	
	(1.861)	(0.202)				(0.113)	(0.203)	
SME * EntCost			−0.039**					
			(0.015)					
Scale * EntCost				0.006**				
				(0.003)				
Size * EntCost					0.007**			
					(0.003)			
Low GDP per capita * Entry$_{US}$ * EntCost							−0.607	
							(0.607)	
High GDP per capita * Entry$_{US}$ * EntCost								
High Corruption * Entry$_{US}$ * EntCost								−0.456**
								(0.202)
Low Corruption * Entry$_{US}$ * EntCost								−1.394***
								(0.614)
Observations	484	572	572	572	572	572	572	572

Table 10 (continued)

Panel B: Performance of Young and Old Incumbent Firms

	(i)	(ii)
	Age 3–5	Age > 5
Entry$_{US}$ * EntCost	−0.038 (0.281)	−0.396** (0.199)
Wald test of equality of slope coefficients (p-value)	0.300	
Likelihood ratio test of equality of all regression coefficients (p-value)	0.001***	
Observations	472	615

Column (i) of Panel A reports OLS estimates. The dependent variable is the logarithm of the average value added (in millions of Euros) of entrants for each industry and country, averaged over the years 1998–1999. Entrants are defined as firms that are one or two years old. Columns (ii) to (v) of Panel A show Tobit regressions with alternative proxies for the propensity to enter. Column (vi) shows an instrumental variable regression. We use legal origin of the country as instrument for entry cost. Columns (vii–viii) show Tobit results when we estimate different slopes for the interaction variables for whether the industry is in a country below or above the sample median of per capita income, or above or below the sample median of corruption. The dependent variable in Columns (ii–viii) is the industry-level real growth in value added per employee of incumbent firms, defined as firms with age > 2. Panel B reports results from Tobit estimations. The dependent variable is the industry-level real growth in value added per employee of incumbent firms calculated for two age groups: age 3–5 and age > 5. Growth rates are averages for the period 1998–1999, by two-digit NACE industry and country, and excluding observations based on fewer than three firms. Growth observations are censored at −50% and +100%. Industry Share is the industry share in sales. Entry$_{US}$ is the ratio of new firms to total firms in the United States. EntCost is country-level entry costs. SME is the percentage of U.S. firms with fewer than 250 employees. Scale is the median assets of U.S. firms in an industry. Size is the median sales of U.S. firms in an industry. Entry$_{US}$, SME, Scale, and Size are averages for the period 1998–1999 and calculated at the two-digit NACE industry level. See Appendix B for complete variable definitions and sources. All regressions include a constant, country dummies, and two-digit industry dummies, not shown. White (1980) standard errors are reported in parentheses. In Panel B we report the p-value of a Wald test for whether the coefficients of the interaction term are equal across the two regressions and the p-value of a likelihood ratio test of equality of all regression coefficients across the two regressions. *, **, and *** denote significant at 10%, 5%, and 1%, respectively.

L. Klapper et al. / Journal of Financial Economics 82 (2006) 591–629   617

an instrument for entry regulation. Column (vi) shows that the results are robust to using instrumental variables, although the magnitude of the coefficient estimate for the interaction term is somewhat reduced. Finally, in Columns (vii) and (viii), we verify that the adverse effect on productivity growth is more pronounced in high GDP and low corruption countries, consistent with our earlier finding that these are the countries where entry barriers have an impact.

If the lower regulatory barriers indeed allow for more disciplining of entry, older incumbents should be particularly affected since they have survived much harsher competition. The effects should be far less pronounced for young incumbent firms because competition has not had time to work its selection effects. Put another way, older incumbents in protected industries should have become far more reliant on the rents from incumbency than on efficiency gains.

We split each industry in each country into incumbent young firms (firms between three and five years of age) and incumbent old firms (firms over five years of age) and compute value-added growth rates for each age segment. We then estimate the regression in Table 10, Panel A, Column (ii) for each segment. The regression estimates are in Table 10, Panel B. They suggest that the adverse interaction effects on growth are present primarily for the older firms, and a likelihood ratio test confirms the difference in coefficients across the two samples.

In sum, value added per worker grows relatively more slowly for older incumbents in naturally high-entry industries in countries with high bureaucratic barriers but not for young incumbents. This is consistent with older firms, who have had to survive greater competition in countries with low entry barriers, becoming relatively more efficient.

This has effects on overall growth rates. As a suggestive comparison, Fig. 1 plots average value added for firms in different age groups for two countries, high-barrier Italy and the low-barrier United Kingdom. Across all industries, firms start out larger when young in Italy, but grow more slowly so that firms in the United Kingdom are about twice as large by age ten.

Taken together, these results suggest that entry regulations adversely affect the growth of those industries that might be presumed to benefit most by the added selectivity that such regulation might bring. This strongly suggests that there are costs to such regulations that should be taken into account in evaluating any potential benefits.

4.6. Other regulations and the business environment

Thus far, the focus has been on entry regulations and their effect on firm entry, size, and growth. But there are other regulations and aspects of the business environment that might affect entry and firm growth, such as financial development, labor regulation, and protection of intellectual property. We want to make sure that the effect we have focused on thus far is not driven by these other aspects of the business environment. To the extent that onerous entry regulations go together with lower financial development, more stringent employee protection, and lower property rights protection, they could all capture similar aspects of an unfavorable business environment. We therefore consider the effects of the availability of financing, labor regulations, and the protection of intellectual property on firm entry and growth.

We focus on these three dimensions of the business environment because they have been found to explain variation in firm entry, size, and growth in previous literature. Black and

Strahan (2002) find that financial development following bank deregulation fostered firm entry in the United States. Di Patti and Dell'Ariccia (2004) find that entry is higher in informationally opaque industries in Italian regions that have a more concentrated banking sector. Fisman and Love (2003a) focus on access to trade credit rather than bank credit and find that industries with higher dependence on trade credit financing exhibit higher growth rates in countries with relatively weak financial institutions.

Stricter labor regulations, such as the ability to hire and fire workers, have also been found to correlate with firm entry. Scarpetta et al. (2002) use firm-level survey data from OECD countries and find that firm entry is lower in countries with stricter labor regulations.

There is also work related to the importance of property rights for firm size and firm growth. Kumar et al. (2002) find that the average size of firms in human capital and in R&D intensive industries is larger in countries that protect property rights and patents. Using survey data from five transition countries on the reinvestment of profits by entrepreneurs, Johnson et al. (2002) find lower investment by entrepreneurs in countries with weak property rights. Claessens and Laeven (2003) find that growth of industries that rely on intangible assets is disproportionately lower in countries with weak intellectual property rights. Except for the work by Scarpetta et al. (2002), none of these other papers also examine entry regulations.

We find that these aspects of the business environment have a significant impact, but primarily on the rate of incorporation and not on the productivity growth of incumbents. Importantly, when we control for these other aspects of the business environment, entry regulations remain an important determinant of new firm entry and the growth of incumbent firms.

4.6.1. Access to finance

First, we consider access to finance as an alternative determinant of firm entry and growth. Liquidity constraints can hinder people from starting businesses (see, e.g., Evans and Jovanovic, 1989). This suggests that entry rates should be lower in countries with less developed financial systems.[8] In fact, Rajan and Zingales (2003) suggest that the absence of regulations protecting investors could be a very effective barrier to new firm creation.

We use ExtFin, a measure of dependence on external finance (the industry-level median of the ratio of capital expenditures minus cash flow over capital expenditures – see Rajan and Zingales (1998) for details) as the industry characteristic. We also calculate an industry-level measure of reliance on supplier trade financing as the average ratio of accounts payable to total assets across all firms in the industry. Both measures are calculated for the period 1990–1999 for all U.S. listed firms in Compustat.

We also use alternative measures of access to financing. As a measure of banking development, we include the ratio of domestic credit to the private sector to GDP from the International Monetary Fund's International Financial Statistics. As a proxy for capital market development, we use the ratio of stock market capitalization to GDP from the World Bank Development Indicators. To measure country-level provisioning of supplier

---

[8]Rajan and Zingales (1998) find that there are more new establishments in industrial sectors with greater external financing needs in more developed financial systems. This is not exactly the same as our findings, since new establishments need not be new entry but could simply be new plants set up by existing firms.

L. Klapper et al. / Journal of Financial Economics 82 (2006) 591–629   619

trade credit, we use firm-level financial data in Amadeus to calculate the unweighted ratio of the sum of total accounts receivables to total assets for all firms.

In Table 11A, Column (i), we find as predicted that entry is higher in more financially dependent industries in countries that have higher financial development. We find similar results when substituting the stock market capitalization variable for the private credit variable. These results suggest that new firm creation depends on access to start-up capital.

Next, we use industry-level trade credit dependence. Industries with higher dependence on trade credit financing exhibit higher entry rates in countries with greater availability of trade credit (not shown). We find that supplier financing matters even after controlling for the effect of financial development and entry costs (not shown). In sum, these results suggest that the availability of both private (bank) credit and trade credit aids entry in financially dependent industries.

4.6.2. Labor regulation

We next turn to labor market regulation, specifically laws that prevent a firm from firing employees. This could cut both ways. One could argue that strict labor regulations protect

Table 11A
Other Regulations and the business environment

	(i)	(ii)	(iii)	(iv)	(v)	(vi)
	Entry rates				Size of entrants	Growth of incumbents
	Finance	Labor	Innovation	Horse race	Horse race	Horse race
Industry Share	−0.118	−0.108	−0.135	−0.157	2.690	−0.029
	(0.108)	(0.108)	(0.108)	(0.108)	(3.891)	(0.534)
Entry$_{US}$ * EntCost	−0.155***	−0.195***	−0.166***	−0.177***	9.506***	−0.420**
	(0.047)	(0.048)	(0.047)	(0.048)	(1.862)	(0.210)
ExtFin$_{US}$ * Priv	0.034***			0.016	0.344	0.005
	(0.010)			(0.012)	(0.619)	(0.052)
LabInt$_{US}$ * EmplLaw		−2.580**		−2.447**	−25.704	2.451
		(1.014)		(1.007)	(27.180)	(4.432)
R&D$_{US}$ * Prop			0.117***	0.093***	−2.330	0.045
			(0.030)	(0.034)	(1.881)	(0.148)
Observations	708	708	679	679	468	548

This table shows Tobit regressions with censoring at zero and one (Columns (i–iv and vi) and an OLS regression (Column (v)). The dependent variable in regressions (i–iv) is the ratio of new firms (defined as age 1–2) to total firms, averaged over the period 1998–1999, by two-digit NACE industry code and country. The dependent variable in regression (v) is the logarithm of the average value added (in millions of Euros) of entrants, defined as firms with age 1–2, for each industry and country. The dependent variable in regression (vi) is the industry-level real growth in value added per employee for firms with age42. Industry Share is the industry share in sales. Entry$_{US}$ * EntCost is the interaction of industry-level new entry ratios and country-level entry costs. ExtFin$_{US}$ * Priv is the interaction of industry-level external financial dependence for the period 1990–1999 (from Compustat) and country-level private credit-to-GDP. LabInt$_{US}$ * EmplLaw is the interaction of industry-level labor intensity and country-level employment laws index. R&D$_{US}$ * Prop is the interaction of industry-level R&D intensity and country-level Property rights. See Appendix B for complete variable definitions and sources. All regressions include a constant, country dummies, and industry dummies, not shown. White (1980) standard errors are reported in parentheses. *, **, and *** denote significant at 10%, 5%, and 1%, respectively.

employees and give them the confidence to join small, untested firms (much the way that good corporate governance offers investors confidence), thus reducing start up-costs. Regulations could also hamper the growth of large incumbent firms, whose adherence to regulations is more easily monitored, thus creating the space for new firms to enter. However, one could argue for the opposite effect of labor regulations on entry: the cost of compliance with regulations has fixed components that make them particularly costly for small businesses to meet, and could inhibit entry. Small firms might not be able to afford to keep their employees through downturns, and thus might underhire in the face of strict labor regulations.

We use the employment laws index of worker protection developed by Botero et al. (2004), which indicates the strictness of labor regulations in the country in 1997. This index was constructed by examining detailed provisions in the labor laws regarding alternative employment contracts, conditions of employment, and job security. The index takes values between zero and three, with higher values implying that regulation is more protective of a worker. We refer to this index as EmpLaw.

Following our methodology, we need to find an industry characteristic that would make an industry most susceptible to labor regulation. We would expect labor regulations to impinge the most on industries that are the most labor intensive. We calculate labor intensity, LabInt, from U.S. data as the industry median over all Compustat firms in that industry of the number of employees divided by the amount of fixed assets (in millions of dollars), and is calculated over all firm-years over the period 1998–1999. A higher score indicates higher labor intensity. We have explored the use of other measures of labor intensity such as employees over total assets and get similar results. In Table 11A, Column (ii), we find that labor regulations have a dampening effect on entry in labor-intensive industries.

4.6.3. Regulations protecting property

Now consider regulations protecting intellectual property. Strong patent protection could dissuade entry because it protects incumbents and forces new entrants to carve a wide path around existing intellectual property. On the other hand, new entrants do not have the organizational structure, finance, or intellectual capital to create a significant first-mover advantage and thus dissuade potential imitators. As a result, they might have a greater incentive to do research if they know their research will be protected legally.

Following the now familiar method, our country-level variable is Property Rights, which is an index of the protection of property in a country from the Economic Freedom Index constructed by the Heritage Foundation. This variable is estimated for the year 1997 and has been used previously by Claessens and Laeven (2003).

The industry variable measured from U.S. data, R&D, is a measure of dependence on research and development and equals the industry-level median of the ratio of research and development expenses to sales for Compustat firms in the same industry over the period 1990–1999. The numerator and denominator are summed over all years for each firm before dividing.

In Table 11A, Column (iii), the interaction variable is positive and significant, suggesting that there is more entry in R&D intensive industries in countries that protect property better. This echoes the findings of Claessens and Laeven (2003). We find similar results when using a more specific index of intellectual property rights from the World Economic Forum (2002) (not shown).

Table 11B
Correlations between regulatory variables

	EntCost	Priv	EmplLaw	Prop
EntCost	1.00			
Priv	−0.38	1.00		
	(0.10)			
EmplLaw	0.37	−0.44	1.00	
	(0.11)	(0.05)		
Prop	−0.29	0.70	−0.44	1.00
	(0.22)	(0.00)	(0.05)	

This table shows the correlations between the different country-level regulatory variables considered in the regressions reported in Table 11A. EntCost is country-level costs associated with entry regulation. Priv is the country-level ratio of private credit to GDP. EmplLaw is a country-level index of employment regulations. Prop is a country-level measure of protection of property rights. See Appendix B for complete variable definitions and sources. *P*-values are reported between brackets.

4.6.4. Business environment

Do higher entry costs reflect a generally hostile business environment? Because the correlations in Table 11B suggest that higher entry costs accompany lower private credit to GDP, more stringent employee protection, and lower property rights protection, these could all be aspects of an unfavorable business environment (or, put another way, good institutions tend to go together). But only the correlation with private credit is significant at the 10% level, suggesting there is some variation.

When we estimate a regression with all the interactions included in Table 11A, Column (iv), we find that all variables retain their predicted effect and statistical significance except the financial development interaction (not surprising since private credit is more strongly statistically correlated with entry costs and the other regulatory variables considered). The coefficient estimate of the entry costs interaction remains statistically significant and of similar magnitude in Table 11 A Column (iv) as in the baseline regression in Table 7, Column (i).

4.6.5. Performance of incumbents and other regulations

Do these other impediments to entry affect the average size of entrants? While low credit, high labor regulation, or low protection of property rights could particularly affect young firms, they are not just an up-front fixed cost that can be overcome by reaching the right size. For example, profitable firms can overcome constraints on external credit, firms that utilize labor very effectively can overcome high labor regulatory costs, and low protection of property rights can be overcome by being more secretive or more efficient at commercialization than the competition. Indeed, when we regress the average value added by entrants (our measure of size) against the various interactions, only the entry cost interaction is significant (Table 11A, Column (v)). This suggests that the other constraints on entry must be overcome by factors other than sheer size.

If the other constraints have to be overcome by being more efficient, then one might expect ambiguous effects of a hostile business environment (apart from entry costs) on the productivity growth of incumbents. On the one hand, the absence of the disciplinary effect of competition from new young entrants gives incumbents less incentive to be efficient. On the other hand, the hostile environment forces them to be more efficient in order to survive (and to have entered in the first place).

If we estimate the regression with the real growth in value added per employee of incumbent firms as a dependent variable, and include all the interactions in Table 11A, Column (vi), we find that none of the interaction terms with the other regulatory variables enters significantly. Importantly, the entry regulation interaction continues to enter negatively and is statistically significant and with a similar order of magnitude as the regressions reported in Table 10. In sum, there could well be offsetting effects of other constraints to entry as hypothesized above; or, put another way, firms need not be particularly clever or efficient to pay high bureaucratic costs of entry, they only need to be large enough to afford it.

5. Conclusion

This paper uses cross-country data to identify the impact of the business environment on entrepreneurship. We use the Amadeus database, which includes financial data on over three million firms in Western and Eastern Europe. These data improve upon previously used datasets in that they include (1) a large number of private, unlisted, and publicly traded corporations and (2) all sectors (i.e., not limited to manufacturing). This database offers a unique opportunity for us to construct entry rates across sectors and test the effect of diverse industry- and country-level characteristics on new firm creation.

To summarize our results, we find that entry regulations hamper entry, especially in industries that naturally should have high entry. Entrants are larger—suggesting that small firms are dissuaded from entering or have to grow without the protection of limited liability until they can afford the costs of incorporation. Also, the value added per employee in naturally "high-entry" industries grows more slowly in countries with high entry barriers. The effect is primarily seen in older firms, suggesting that entry barriers mute the disciplining effect of competition. Taken together, our findings suggest that entry regulations have significant adverse effects. Since we have not measured the value of all potential benefits, we cannot make a categorical statement about the net welfare effects of these regulations.

However, the effect of these entry regulations is seen primarily in developed countries or countries where there is little corruption. To the extent that the benefits of screening are small, and other benefits—such as the provision of greater information to the authorities—can be captured even with reduced costs (for example, by automating the process), a reduction in the cost of complying with regulations governing incorporation will have the most pronounced effect in developed countries such as those in Continental Europe, where existing entry regulations are most effectively enforced.

In developing countries or countries where corruption is a serious problem, entry regulations are unlikely to help screen out cheats. To the extent that such regulations increase the cost of entry (if nothing else, through the additional bribes that have to be paid), without any benefits in screening or information gathering, there could be merit to reducing the regulatory requirements substantially.

The broader point made is that entry regulation has costs over and above the direct costs of compliance and enforcement. While there could indeed be deeper politico-economic interests underpinning such regulation that negate any attempt at deregulation, authorities should weigh these "excess costs" of entry regulation carefully in deciding policy.

Appendix A

Details about collection of company accounts in Amadeus are given in Table 12.

Table 12

Country	Which companies have to file accounts?	Are all public and private limited companies required to file accounts?	Maximum period a company can take to file accounts after its year end	Maximum period between filing of accounts and records appearing in database
Austria	Public limited companies (AG) and private limited companies (GmbH).	Yes	12 months	3 months
Belgium	All public limited companies (SA/NV) companies, private limited companies (SPRL/BV/BVBA), partnerships, cooperatives, and European Economic Interest Groupings.	Yes	7 months	3 months
Bulgaria	Joint Stock companies (EAD).	No, only public limited companies.	n.a.	n.a.
Czech Republic	Joint stock companies, limited liability companies and cooperatives. Limited liability companies and cooperatives only if they meet at least one of the following two conditions in the previous year: equity > CZK 20 million and turnover > CZK 40 million.	No, only if they meet certain size criteria.	6 months	4–5 weeks
Denmark	Public limited companies (A/S), private limited companies (ApS), limited partnerships by shares (P/S), and some limited and general partnerships.	Yes	5–6 months	Less than 20 days
Estonia	Public limited companies, private limited companies, and cooperatives.	Yes	6 months	12 months
Finland	All joint-stock companies and all cooperatives that meet two of the following three conditions: turnover > FIM 20 million, total assets > FIM 10 million, number of employees > 50.	No, only if they meet certain size criteria.	8 months	n.a.
France	Public limited companies (SA), private limited companies (SARL), limited partnerships (SCS), general partnerships (SNC), and sole proprietorships with limited liability (EURL).	Yes	4–6 months	4 months
Germany	Public limited companies (AG), private limited companies (GmbH), and cooperatives (eG).	Yes	12 months	4–6 weeks
Greece	Public and private limited companies (SA).	Yes	6 months	20–40 days
Hungary	All companies, except proprietorships.	Yes	5 months	n.a.
Iceland	All public limited companies (HF), private limited companies (EHF), general cooperatives (SVF), and some partnerships and agricultural cooperatives.	Yes	8 months	6 weeks
Ireland	Public limited companies (plc) and private limited companies (ltd).	Yes	46 days	n.a.

Table 12 (*continued*)

Country	Which companies have to file accounts?	Are all public and private limited companies required to file accounts?	Maximum period a company can take to file accounts after its year end	Maximum period between filing of accounts and records appearing in database
Italy	Public limited companies (S.p.A.) and private limited companies (S.r.l.).	Yes	6 months	5 months
Latvia	All companies, except sole proprietorships and farms with annual turnover < LVL 45,000.	Yes	4–10 months	9 months
Lithuania	All companies.	Yes	5 months	n.a.
Luxembourg	Public limited companies (S.A.), private limited companies (S.A.R.L.) and cooperatives (S.C.).	Yes	6 months	2 months
Netherlands	Public limited companies (NV) and private limited companies (BV).	Yes	15 months	
Norway	All limited liability companies. Unlimited liability entities only if turnover > NOK 2 million.	Yes	6 months	2 months
Poland	All joint stock companies, limited liability companies, and partnerships that meet the following criteria: employees > 50, total assets > Euro 1 million, and net profits > Euro 3 million.	No, only if they meet certain size criteria.	9 months	n.a.
Portugal	All joint-stock companies and private limited companies.	Yes	6 months	2 months
Romania	Joint stock companies, limited liability companies, and partnerships limited by shares.	Yes	2.5 months	4 months
Slovak Republic	Joint stock companies (a.s.), limited liability companies (s.r.o.), and cooperatives if they meet two of three conditions: Assets > SKK 20 mln, turnover > SKK 40 mln, and number of employees > 20.	No, only if they meet certain size criteria.	12 months	4–5 weeks
Slovenia	All companies.	Yes	3 months	2–4 months
Spain	All public limited companies (S.A.), private limited companies (S.L.) and limited partnerships.	Yes	7 months	n.a.
Sweden	All public and private limited companies (AB).	Yes	6 months	n.a.
Switzerland	There are no legal requirements to file accounts. Listed public limited corporations (AG/SA) must file accounts to the stock exchange and publish audited statements in the official gazette.	No	n.a.	3 months
United Kingdom	Public limited companies (plc) and private limited companies (ltd).	Yes	7–10 months	10 weeks

Source: Amadeus, Bureau Van Dijk, Dun & Bradstreet Country Report Guides, and Primark Capital Markets Guide 1999. Note: Data excludes proprietorships in all countries.

L. Klapper et al. / Journal of Financial Economics 82 (2006) 591–629   625

Appendix B

Definition of Variables are given in Table 13.

Table 13

Variable	Description
Amadeus industry-level variables	
Entry	Share of new firms in the total number of firms. New firms are firms that are one or two years old. Average for the years 1998–1999. We calculate this country-industry level variable for two-digit NACE industries. Source: Amadeus.
Industry share	Ratio of the industry's sales to total sales. Average for the years 1998–1999. We calculate this country-industry level variable for two-digit NACE industries. Source: Amadeus.
Growth in value added per employee	Growth in value added per employee over the period 1998–99 averaged over all incumbent firms in the industry in a country. Incumbent firms are defined as firms that are more than two years old. Value added is computed as earnings before interest, taxes, depreciation and amortization, plus labor costs. We calculate this country-industry level variable for two-digit NACE industries. Source: Amadeus.
Size of entrants	Logarithm of average value added (in millions of Euros) of entrants, defined as firms that are one or two years old, over the period 1998–99. We calculate this country-industry level variable for two-digit NACE industries. Source: Amadeus.
Eurostat industry-level variables	
Eurostat entry	Entry rate for the year 1999 by Eurostat industry (based on two-digit NACE industries). Source: Eurostat.
Eurostat exit	Exit rate for the year 1999 by Eurostat industry (based on two-digit NACE industries). Source: Eurostat.
U.S. Benchmark variables	
Entry U.S. ($Entry_{US}$)	Entry rates for U.S. corporations. Calculated for two-digit NACE industries (original data on a four-digit SIC level). Average for the years 1998–1999. Source: Dun & Bradstreet.
Exit U.S. ($Exit_{US}$)	Exit rates for U.S. corporations. Calculated for two-digit NACE industries (original data on a four-digit SIC level). Average for the years 1998–1999. Source: Dun & Bradstreet.
Entry U.S. 1990s ($Entry_{US,\ 1990-2000}$)	Entry rates for U.S. corporations. Calculated for two-digit NACE industries (original data on a four-digit SIC level). Average for the years 1990–2000. Source: Dun & Bradstreet.
Entry U.K. ($Entry_{UK}$)	Entry rates for U.K. corporations. Calculated for two-digit NACE industries. Average for the years 1998–1999. Source: Amadeus.
Entry Europe ($Entry_{Europe}$)	Entry rates averaged across all corporations in the sampled European countries. Calculated for two-digit NACE industries. Average for the years 1998–1999. Source: Amadeus.
Total assets (Scale)	Industry-level median of total assets. We compute this measure for all U.S. firms for the year 1995. Calculated for two-digit NACE industries (original data on a four-digit SIC level). Source: Compustat.
Total revenues (Size)	Industry-level median of total revenues. We compute this measure for all U.S. firms for the year 1995. Calculated for two-digit NACE

Table 13 (*continued*)

Variable	Description
	industries (original data on a four-digit SIC level). Source: Compustat.
External financial dependence (ExtFin)	Industry-level median of the ratio of capital expenditures minus cash flow over capital expenditures. The numerator and denominator are summed over all years for each firm before dividing. Cash flow is defined as the sum of funds from operations, decreases in inventories, decreases in receivables, and increases in payables. Capital expenditures include net acquisitions of fixed assets. This definition follows Rajan and Zingales (1998). We compute this measure for all U.S. firms for the period 1990–1999. Calculated for two-digit NACE industries (original data on a four-digit SIC level). Source: Compustat.
R & D intensity (R&D)	Measure of dependence on research and development, equal to the industry-level median of the ratio of research and development expenses to sales. The numerator and denominator are summed over all years for each firm before dividing. We compute this measure for all U.S. firms for the period 1990–99. Calculated for two-digit NACE industries (original data on a four-digit SIC level). Source: Compustat.
Labor intensity (LabInt)	Measure of labor intensity, equal to the amount of employees per value added, industry medians of ratios over all firm-years in the relevant time period. We compute this measure for all U.S. firms for the period 1990–99. A higher score indicates higher labor intensity. Calculated for two-digit NACE industries (original data on a four-digit SIC level). Source: Compustat.
Country-Level Variables	
Entry cost (EntCost)	Cost of business registration, expressed as a percentage of per capita GNP. Data for the year 1999. Source: Djankov et al. (2002).
Entry cost and time (EntTime)	Cost of business registration, including the monetized value of the entrepreneur's time. Source: Djankov et al. (2002).
Entry procedures (EntProc)	Number of procedures to register a business. Data for the year 1999. Source: Djankov et al. (2002).
Bankruptcy cost (BankCost)	Actual cost of bankruptcy proceedings as a percentage of the estate. Data for the year 2003. Source: Djankov et al. (2003).
Informal sector (Informal)	Share of the informal economy, calculated as the size of the informal economy as a percentage of official GNI. Average over the period 1999–2000. Source: Schneider (2002).
Tax disadvantage (Tax)	Tax disadvantage is the difference between the top corporate income tax and the top personal income tax rates in the country (PricewaterhouseCoopers Worldwide Taxes 1999–2000).
Private credit to GDP (Priv)	Ratio of domestic credit to the private sector scaled by GDP, average over the period 1995–99. Source: International Monetary Fund's International Financial Statistics (IMF-IFS).
Stock market capitalization (MCap)	Ratio of stock market capitalization to GDP, average over the period 1995–99. Source: World Bank World Development Indicators (WDI).
Employment laws (EmpLaw)	Index of labor regulations from Botero et al. (2004). Ranges from zero to three. A higher score indicates that regulation is more protective of a worker. Data refer to 1997.
Property rights (Prop)	Index of property rights for the year 1997. Source: Index of Economic Freedom, Heritage Foundation. Ranges from one to five with higher score indicating greater protection of property rights (we reversed the original scale).

L. Klapper et al. / Journal of Financial Economics 82 (2006) 591–629   627

Appendix C

U.S. entry and exit rates, by two-digit NACE Revision 1 or two-digit 1987 U.S. SIC code are given in Table 14.

Table 14

NACE	Industry	Entry	Exit	SIC	Industry	Entry	Exit
10	Coal mining	3.05	4.08	10	Metal mining	3.42	2.72
11	Oil and gas extraction	4.45	1.35	12	Coal mining	3.05	4.08
13	Mining of metal ores	3.41	2.86	13	Oil and gas extraction	4.32	1.33
14	Other mining and quarrying	3.73	1.39	14	Nonmetallic minerals, except fuels	3.73	1.39
15	Food products and beverages	5.24	1.91	15	General building contractors	9.27	4.58
16	Tobacco products	7.45	1.40	16	Heavy construction contractors	4.98	2.00
17	Textiles	6.92	2.46	17	Special trade contractors	7.81	4.10
18	Wearing apparel; fur	6.44	3.03	20	Food and kindred products	5.24	1.91
19	Luggage, handbags, footwear	9.06	2.51	21	Tobacco manufactures	7.45	1.40
20	Wood, except furniture	5.98	3.29	22	Textile mill products	6.14	2.65
21	Pulp and paper	5.26	1.87	23	Apparel and other textile products	7.02	2.68
22	Publishing; printing	5.49	2.14	24	Lumber and wood products	6.39	3.17
23	Coke and petroleum products	5.80	0.81	25	Furniture and fixtures	5.03	2.59
24	Chemicals	6.08	1.45	26	Paper and allied products	5.26	1.87
25	Rubber and plastic products	4.46	1.79	27	Printing and publishing	5.49	2.14
26	Non-metallic mineral products	5.79	1.74	28	Chemicals and allied products	6.02	1.44
27	Basic metals	4.90	2.13	29	Petroleum and coal products	4.89	0.95
28	Fabricated metal products	5.71	1.98	30	Rubber and plastics	4.29	1.52
29	Machinery and equipment n.e.c.	4.30	1.74	31	Leather and leather products	9.00	2.37
30	Office machinery and computers	8.67	2.20	32	Stone, clay, and glass products	5.93	1.79
31	Electrical machinery	5.92	1.52	33	Primary metal industries	4.90	2.13
32	Communication equipment	8.45	2.27	34	Fabricated metal products	4.31	1.83
33	Instruments, watches and clocks	5.72	1.45	35	Machinery and equipment	4.52	1.75
34	Motor vehicles and trailers	5.20	2.42	36	Electrical and electronic equipment	7.07	1.89
35	Other transport equipment	7.96	2.18	37	Transportation equipment	6.77	2.27
36	Furniture; manufacturing n.e.c.	7.92	2.33	38	Instruments and related products	6.02	1.05
40	Electricity, gas, hot water	5.56	0.88	39	Miscellaneous manufacturing	8.62	2.25
41	Distribution of water	1.74	0.28	40	Railroads and rail transportation	4.87	2.48
45	Construction	8.14	4.14	41	Local passenger transit	5.90	3.98
50	Sale and repair of motor vehicles	5.05	2.74	42	Motor freight transportation	8.45	7.33
51	Wholesale trade	5.35	1.54	44	Water transportation	4.22	1.56
52	Retail trade	7.19	2.81	45	Transportation by air	4.65	1.55
55	Hotels and restaurants	5.95	2.54	46	Pipelines, except natural gas	2.22	0.44
60	Land transport	8.41	7.68	47	Transportation services	8.24	2.14
61	Water transport	5.61	1.95	48	Communications	8.80	1.77
62	Air transport	6.19	1.75	49	Electric, gas, and sanitary services	4.68	1.51
63	Supporting transport activities	6.77	1.67	50	Wholesale trade–durable goods	4.94	1.50
64	Post and telecommunications	10.09	2.14	51	Wholesale trade–nondurable goods	5.68	1.68
70	Real estate activities	5.33	1.56	52	Building materials	4.93	1.81
71	Renting of machinery, equipment	6.34	1.93	53	General merchandise stores	6.44	2.21
72	Computer and related activities	10.73	1.91	54	Food stores	5.72	2.28
73	Research and development	6.53	0.93	55	Automotive dealers; gas stations	4.68	2.02
74	Other business activities	9.65	4.60	56	Apparel and accessory stores	8.61	2.42
85	Health and social work	2.83	1.51	57	Furniture stores	7.56	2.61
90	Sewage; disposal; sanitation	5.43	2.22	58	Eating and drinking places	6.29	2.77
92	Recreation, culture and sports	6.46	2.35	59	Miscellaneous retail	7.55	2.97
93	Other services activities	6.46	3.67	65	Real estate	5.22	1.52

Table 14 (*continued*)

NACE	Industry	Entry	Exit	SIC	Industry	Entry	Exit
				70	Hotels and other lodging places	3.83	1.13
				72	Personal services	6.56	3.73
				73	Business services	11.49	5.68
				75	Automotive repair and services	5.47	3.31
				76	Miscellaneous repair services	8.09	4.14
				78	Motion pictures	9.58	3.47
				79	Amusement and recreation	6.20	2.43
				80	Health services	2.19	1.04
				83	Social services	4.52	2.70

Sample of all U.S. corporations from Dun & Bradstreet. Averages for the years 1998–1999. *Entry* is the percentage of new corporations (firms that are one year old). *Exit* is the percentage of firms that exited following formal bankruptcy proceedings.

References

Barth, J.R., Caprio Jr., G., Levine, R., 2004. Bank supervision and regulation: what works best? Journal of Financial Intermediation 13, 205–248.

Bertrand, M., Kramarz, F., 2002. Does entry regulation hinder job creation? Evidence from the French retail industry. Quarterly Journal of Economics 117, 1369–1413.

Black, S.E., Strahan, P.E., 2002. Entrepreneurship and bank credit availability. Journal of Finance 57, 2807–2833.

Botero, J., Djankov, S., La Porta, R., Lopez-de-Silanes, F., Shleifer, A., 2004. The regulation of labor. Quarterly Journal of Economics 119, 1339–1382.

Cable, J., Schwalbach, J., 1991. International comparisons of entry and exit: entry and market contestability. In: Geroski, P.A., Schwalbach, J. (Eds.), Entry and Market Contestability: An International Comparison. Blackwell Publishers, London, pp. 257–281.

Claessens, S., Laeven, L., 2003. Financial development, property rights, and growth. Journal of Finance 58, 2401–2436.

Desai, M., Gompers, P., Lerner, J., 2003. Institutions, capital constraints and entrepreneurial firm dynamics: evidence from Europe. Unpublished working paper. National Bureau of Economic Research.

De Soto, H., 1990. The Other Path. Harper and Row, New York.

Di Patti, E.B., Dell'Ariccia, G., 2004. Bank competition and firm creation. Journal of Money, Credit, and Banking 36, 225–252.

Djankov, S., La Porta, R., Lopez-de-Silanes, F., Shleifer, A., 2002. The regulation of entry. Quarterly Journal of Economics 117, 1–35.

Djankov, S., Hart, O., Nenova, T., Shleifer, A., 2003. Efficiency in bankruptcy. Unpublished working paper. Harvard University, Department of Economics.

Dunne, T., Roberts, M.J., 1991. Variation in producer turnover across US manufacturing industries. In: Geroski, P.A., Schwalbach, J. (Eds.), Entry and Market Contestability: An International Comparison. Blackwell Publishers, London, pp. 187–203.

Dunne, T., Roberts, M.J., Samuelson, L., 1988. Patterns of firm entry and exit in U. S. manufacturing industries. RAND Journal of Economics 19, 495–515.

European Commission, 2003. Enterprises in Europe, Sixth Report. Eurostat, Office for Official Publications of the European Communities, Luxembourg.

Evans, D.S., Jovanovic, B., 1989. An estimated model of entrepreneurial choice under liquidity constraints. Journal of Political Economy 97, 808–827.

Fisman, R., Love, I., 2003a. Trade credit, financial intermediary development and industry growth. Journal of Finance 58, 353–374.

Fisman, R., Love, I., 2003b. Financial dependence and growth revisited. Unpublished Working Paper, National Bureau of Economic Research.

Gilbert, R.J., 1989. Mobility barriers and the value of incumbency. In: Schmalensee, R.L., Willig, R.D. (Eds.), Handbook of Industrial Organization, vol. 1. Elsevier, Amsterdam, pp. 720–781.

Halpern, P., Trebilcock, M., Turnbull, S., 1980. An economic analysis of limited liability in corporate law. University of Toronto Law Review 30, 117–150.

Hause, J.C., du Rietz, G., 1984. Entry, industry growth, and the microdynamics of industry supply. Journal of Political Economy 92, 733–757.

Johnson, S., McMillan, J., Woodruff, C., 2002. Property rights and finance. American Economic Review 92, 1335–1356.

Kumar, K., Rajan, R., Zingales, L., 2002. What determines firm size? Unpublished working paper, University of Chicago.

La Porta, R., Lopez-de-Silanes, F., Shleifer, A., Vishny, R.W., 1999. The quality of government. Journal of Law, Economics, and Organization 15, 222–279.

Rajan, R., Zingales, L., 1998. Financial dependence and growth. American Economic Review 88, 559–586.

Rajan, R., Zingales, L., 2003. The great reversal: the politics of financial development in the 20th century. Journal of Financial Economics 69, 5–50.

Scarpetta, S., Hemmings, P., Tressel, T., Woo, J., 2002. The role of policy and institutions for productivity and firm dynamics: evidence from micro and industry data. Unpublished Working Paper, OECD.

Schneider, F., 2002. Size and measurement of the informal economy in 110 countries around the world. Unpublished Working Paper, World Bank.

Schumpeter, J.A., 1911. Theorie Der Wirtschaftlichen Entwicklung. Duncker & Humblot, Leipzig.

World Bank, 2004. Doing Business 2004: Understanding Regulation. World Bank and Oxford University Press, Washington DC.

Further reading

Gordon, R., MacKie-Mason, J.K., 1997. How much do taxes discourage incorporation? Journal of Finance 52, 477–505.

[14]

THE JOURNAL OF FINANCE • VOL. LX, NO. 1 • FEBRUARY 2005

Financial and Legal Constraints to Growth: Does Firm Size Matter?

THORSTEN BECK, ASLI DEMIRGÜÇ-KUNT,
and VOJISLAV MAKSIMOVIC*

ABSTRACT

Using a unique firm-level survey database covering 54 countries, we investigate the effect of financial, legal, and corruption problems on firms' growth rates. Whether these factors constrain growth depends on firm size. It is consistently the smallest firms that are most constrained. Financial and institutional development weakens the constraining effects of financial, legal, and corruption obstacles and it is again the small firms that benefit the most. There is only a weak relation between firms' perception of the quality of the courts in their country and firm growth. We also provide evidence that the corruption of bank officials constrains firm growth.

CORPORATE FINANCE THEORY SUGGESTS that market imperfections, such as those caused by underdeveloped financial and legal systems, constrain firms' ability to fund investment projects. Using firm-level data, Demirgüç-Kunt and Maksimovic (1998) show that firms in countries with developed financial institutions and efficient legal systems obtain more external financing than firms in countries with less-developed institutions. Although these findings show a strong effect of financial institutions and the legal system on firm growth, their conclusions are based on a sample of the largest firms in each of the economies they study. Their study relies on inferring firms' demand for external financing from a financial model of the firm.

In this paper, we use a size-stratified survey of over 4,000 firms in 54 countries to assess (1) whether financial, legal, and corruption obstacles affect firms' growth; (2) whether this effect varies across firms of different sizes; (3) whether small, medium-sized, and large firms are constrained differently in countries with different levels of financial and institutional development; (4) the specific characteristics of the legal system that facilitate firm growth; and (5) the importance of corruption in financial intermediaries to firm growth.

*Beck and Demirgüç-Kunt are at the World Bank. Maksimovic is at the Robert H. Smith School of Business at the University of Maryland. This paper's findings, interpretations, and conclusions are entirely those of the authors and do not necessarily represent the views of the World Bank, its executive directors, or the countries they represent. We would like to thank Jerry Caprio, George Clarke, Simeon Djankov, Jack Glen, Richard Green, the editor, Luc Laeven, Florencio Lopez-de-Silanez, Inessa Love, Maria Soledad Martinez Peria, Raghuram Rajan, and seminar participants at the World Bank, American University, Case Western Reserve, Georgetown University, Oxford University, the University of Minnesota and Yale University, and an anonymous referee for helpful comments.

138   *The Journal of Finance*

There is considerable evidence that firm size is related to a firm's productivity, survival, and profitability. As a result, understanding how financial, legal, and corruption obstacles affect firms of different sizes has policy implications. Significant resources are channeled into the promotion of small and medium-sized enterprises (SMEs). The World Bank alone has approved more than $10 billion in SME support programs in the past 5 years, $1.5 billion of it in the last year alone (World Bank Group Review of Small Business Activities (2002)).

A priori, it is not clear whether weak financial and legal institutions create greater obstacles to the growth of large or small firms. Large firms internalize many of the capital allocation functions carried out by financial markets and financial intermediaries. Thus, the development of financial markets and institutions should disproportionately benefit small firms. On the other hand, large firms are most likely to tax the resources of an underdeveloped financial or legal system, since they are more likely than small firms to depend on long-term financing and on larger loans. It is possible that financial development can disproportionately reduce the effect of institutional obstacles on the largest firms.

Our paper provides evidence relevant to reforming legal systems in developing countries. Although recent studies in international corporate finance predict a positive relation between the quality of the legal system and access to external financing, we actually know very little about how firms' perceptions conform to the conventional notions of what makes a legal system efficient (such as the impartiality of courts and whether court decisions are enforced). Moreover, we do not know whether these conventional notions help predict the effect of the legal system on firm growth. In this paper, we address both of these issues.

Our paper also provides evidence about the potential costs of monitoring by financial intermediaries. Several influential theoretical models and public policy prescriptions rely on monitoring by financial intermediaries to reduce misallocation of investment in economies with underdeveloped financial markets. Although the reduction of agency costs caused by firms' insiders is a major motivation for this monitoring, the models on which the policies are based typically do not consider the possibility of agency costs within banks. We examine evidence indicating that corrupt officials in financial intermediaries retard the efficient allocation of capital to smaller firms by relating firms' reports of bank corruption to the firms' growth rates.

Our paper builds on earlier studies, starting with La Porta et al. (1998), who argue that differences in legal and financial systems can explain much of the variation across countries in firms' financial policies and performance. Recent empirical evidence supports the view that the development of a country's financial system affects firm growth and financing. In addition to Demirgüç-Kunt and Maksimovic's (1998) firm-level results, Rajan and Zingales (1998a) show that industries that are dependent on external finance grow faster in countries with better developed financial systems.[1] Wurgler (2000) shows that

---

[1] In addition, Carlin and Mayer (2003) also argue that there exists a relation between a country's financial system and the characteristics of industries that prosper in the country. Demirgüç-Kunt

the rate at which resources are allocated to productive industries depends on the development of the financial system. Love (2003) shows that the sensitivity of investment to cash flow depends negatively on financial development. [2]

The richness of the survey's database allows us to go beyond earlier papers that infer the presence of institutional failures from past growth performance.[3] The firms that were surveyed reported whether specific features of the financial and legal systems in their countries and the corruption they faced were obstacles to their growth. Thus, we are able to analyze how firms in different financial and legal systems perceive obstacles to growth, and whether in fact there is a relation between these perceptions and firm growth. Our paper differs from earlier work in that we also examine the effect of corruption on firm growth.[4]

Second, the literature has less to say about how the state of a country's financial and legal institutions affects firms of different sizes.[5] We know that in developing economies, there are advantages in belonging to a business group (see Khanna and Palepu's (2000) study of India and Rajan and Zingales' (1998b) review of evidence on Asian capitalism). This finding contrasts with the prevailing view in the United States that the ability to escape market monitoring by recourse to internal capital markets makes large diversified firms inefficient (Scharfstein and Stein (2000), Rajan, Servaes, and Zingales (2000)).[6] However, studies of business groups in the emerging economies are limited to firms that choose to belong to such groups, and the extent to which these results generalize to other firms and to other institutional settings is unclear. Cross-country studies of financing choices have found different financing patterns for small and large firms, in the use of long-term financing and trade credit (Demirgüç-Kunt and Maksimovic (1999, 2001)). However, these studies rely on commercial databases of listed firms, so that even the "small" firms are relatively large.

The paper is organized as follows. Section I presents the data and summary statistics. Section II presents our main results. Section III presents conclusions and policy implications.

---

and Maksimovic (1999) show that the origin and efficiency of a legal system facilitates firms' access to external finance, particularly long-term finance. At the country level, King and Levine (1993), Levine and Zervos (1998), and Beck, Levine, and Loayza (2000) show that financial development promotes growth and that differences in legal origins explain differences in financial development.

[2] Rajan and Zingales (1998a) use the external financing by U.S. firms as a benchmark, under the assumption that firms in the same industries in other countries depend on similar amounts of external financing. Demirgüç-Kunt and Maksimovic (1998) rely on a financial planning model to identify firms that have access to long-term external financing.

[3] Exceptions are Schiffer and Weder (2001) who investigate different obstacles using WBES data and Clarke, Cull, and Peria (2003) who assess the impact of foreign bank entry on these obstacles.

[4] Empirical evidence based on cross-country comparisons does suggest that corruption has a major adverse effect on private investment and economic growth (Mauro (1996)). We look at whether corruption also has a significant impact in constraining firm growth.

[5] Except to study determinants of firm size by looking at the largest firms around the world (see Beck, Demirgüç-Kunt, and Maksimovic (2001b)).

[6] For evidence that large diversified firms in the U.S. economy do allocate resources efficiently, see Maksimovic and Phillips (2002).

I. Data and Summary Statistics

Our data set consists of firm survey responses from over 4,000 firms in 54 countries.[7] The main purpose of the survey is to identify obstacles to firm performance and growth around the world. Thus, the survey includes many questions on the nature of financing and legal obstacles to growth, as well as questions on corruption issues. General information on firms is more limited, but the survey includes data on numbers of employees, sales, industry, growth, and number of competitors. The survey also gives information on ownership, whether the firm is an exporter, and if it has been receiving subsidies from national or local authorities.

In addition to the detail on the obstacles, one of the greatest values of this survey is its wide coverage of SMEs. The survey covers three groups of firms. It defines small firms as those with 5–50 employees. Medium-sized firms are those that employ 51–500 employees, and large firms are those that employ more than 500 employees. Forty percent of our observations are from small firms, another 40% are from medium firms, and the remaining 20% are from large firms. Table AI in the Appendix reports the number of firms for each country in the sample. For each of the countries, we also use data on GDP per capita, GDP in U.S. dollars, growth rate of GDP, and inflation. We also use information on financial system development, legal development, and corruption. Country-level variables are 1995–1999 averages. To compile these averages, we follow Beck, Demirgüç-Kunt, and Levine (2000).

In Table I we summarize relevant facts about the level of economic development, firm growth, and firm-level obstacles in the sample countries. We provide details on our sources in Table AII in the Appendix. The countries in the sample show considerable variation in per-capita income. They range from Haiti, with an average GDP per capita of $369, to the United States and Germany, with per-capita incomes of around $30,000. We also provide the average annual growth rate of per-capita GDP as a control variable. If investment opportunities in an economy are correlated, there should be a relation between the growth rate of individual firms and the growth rate of the economy. The average inflation rate also provides an important control, since it is an indicator of whether local currency provides a stable measure of value in contracts between firms. The countries also vary significantly in their rates of inflation, from a low of 0% in Sweden and Argentina to 86% in Bulgaria.

In Table I, the column titled Firm Growth reports firm growth rates, which are sales growth rates for individual firms averaged over all sampled firms in each country. Firm growth rates also show a wide dispersion, from negative rates of −19% for Armenia and Azerbaijan to a positive 34% for Poland.

Table I also shows firm-level financing, legal, and corruption obstacles reported by firms averaged over all firms in each country. The World Business Environment Survey (WBES) asked enterprise managers to rate the extent to

---

[7] The WBES covers 80 economies. However, the sample is reduced because most firm-level or country-level variables are missing for 26 countries.

Table I

Economic Indicators and Obstacles to Firm Growth

GDP per capita is real GDP per capita in U.S. dollars. Inflation is the log difference of the consumer price index. Growth is the growth rate of GDP in current U.S. dollars. All country variables are 1995–1999 averages. Firm Growth is the percentage change in firm sales over the past 3 years (1996–1999). Financing, Legal, and Corruption are summary obstacles as indicated in the firm questionnaire. They take values between 1 and 4, with higher values indicating greater obstacles. We average firm variables over all firms in each country. Detailed variable definitions and sources are given in Table AII in the Appendix.

	GDP per Capita	Inflation	Growth	Firm Growth	Financing Obstacle	Legal Obstacle	Corruption Obstacle
Albania	806.78	0.15	0.03	0.25	3.04	2.76	3.40
Argentina	8000.15	0.00	0.02	0.10	3.03	2.27	2.59
Armenia	844.11	0.10	0.04	−0.19	2.48	1.51	1.99
Azerbaijan	407.75	0.03	0.05	−0.19	3.17	2.60	3.02
Belarus	2234.91	0.71	0.07	0.09	3.31	1.55	1.88
Belize	2737.70	0.01	0.00	0.13	3.14	1.54	2.00
Bolivia	938.55	0.06	0.01	0.07	3.00	2.81	3.53
Brazil	4491.67	0.07	0.00	0.04	2.67	2.58	2.49
Bulgaria	1414.61	0.86	−0.02	0.15	3.18	2.27	2.64
Canada	20548.97	0.01	0.02	0.17	2.11	1.46	1.40
Chile	5002.70	0.05	0.03	0.08	2.39	1.97	1.85
China	676.76	0.02	0.07	0.05	3.35	1.51	1.96
Colombia	2381.19	0.16	−0.01	0.04	2.71	2.41	2.87
Costa Rica	3692.47	0.12	0.04	0.25	2.63	2.24	2.59
Croatia	3845.27	0.05	0.05	0.09	3.32	2.69	2.56
Czech Republic	5158.04	0.07	0.00	0.10	3.17	2.18	2.07
Dominican Republic	1712.31	0.06	0.06	0.24	2.59	2.41	2.90
Ecuador	1538.48	0.30	−0.02	−0.03	3.34	3.09	3.52
El Salvador	1705.79	0.04	0.01	−0.01	2.98	2.37	2.80
Estonia	3663.49	0.10	0.05	0.61	2.44	1.70	1.92
France	27719.92	0.01	0.02	0.21	2.75	1.81	1.63
Germany	30794.03	0.01	0.01	0.10	2.60	2.14	1.86
Guatemala	1503.25	0.08	0.01	0.14	3.06	2.58	2.68
Haiti	368.73	0.14	0.00	−0.05	3.39	2.27	3.02
Honduras	707.52	0.16	0.00	0.13	2.93	2.40	2.93
Hungary	4705.65	0.15	0.04	0.29	2.61	1.30	1.94
Indonesia	1045.04	0.20	−0.02	−0.06	2.82	2.26	2.67
Italy	19645.96	0.02	0.01	0.16	1.98	2.27	1.90
Kazakhstan	1315.10	0.16	0.02	0.08	3.28	2.13	2.74
Kyrgizstan	800.34	0.22	0.04	−0.02	3.48	2.20	3.23
Lithuania	1907.93	0.09	0.03	0.08	3.00	2.24	2.44
Malaysia	4536.23	0.03	0.01	0.01	2.67	1.66	2.09
Mexico	3394.75	0.20	0.04	0.26	3.51	2.94	3.57
Moldova	667.74	0.18	−0.03	−0.14	3.39	2.47	2.90
Nicaragua	434.69	0.11	0.03	0.19	3.22	2.46	2.88
Pakistan	505.59	0.08	0.00	0.08	3.31	2.55	3.53
Panama	3123.95	0.01	0.02	0.07	2.13	2.36	2.74
Peru	2334.94	0.07	0.01	−0.01	3.10	2.55	2.85
Philippines	1125.81	0.08	0.01	0.07	2.69	2.24	3.13

(continued)

The Journal of Finance

Table I—*Continued*

	GDP per Capita	Inflation	Growth	Firm Growth	Financing Obstacle	Legal Obstacle	Corruption Obstacle
Poland	3216.04	0.13	0.05	0.34	2.48	2.32	2.28
Portugal	11582.33	0.03	0.03	0.12	1.82	1.86	1.77
Romania	1372.02	0.53	−0.02	0.07	3.28	2.60	2.88
Russia	2223.57	0.35	0.00	0.28	3.21	2.18	2.62
Singapore	24948.09	0.01	0.02	0.11	1.96	1.33	1.29
Slovakia	3805.41	0.07	0.04	0.11	3.38	2.08	2.44
Slovenia	10232.73	0.08	0.04	0.29	2.30	2.29	1.64
Spain	15858.03	0.02	0.03	0.26	2.22	1.97	2.08
Sweden	28258.28	0.00	0.02	0.23	1.85	1.49	1.19
Trinidad & Tobago	4526.28	0.04	0.04	0.20	2.93	1.44	1.66
Turkey	2993.89	0.58	0.01	0.10	3.11	2.28	2.86
Ukraine	866.52	0.26	−0.03	0.03	3.46	2.18	2.54
United Kingdom	20186.56	0.03	0.02	0.31	2.21	1.51	1.24
United States	29250.32	0.02	0.03	0.14	2.39	1.79	1.86
Uruguay	6113.60	0.15	0.02	0.03	2.70	1.87	1.84
Venezuela	3482.51	0.40	−0.02	−0.02	2.57	2.65	2.98

which financing, legal, and corruption problems presented obstacles to the operation and growth of their businesses. A rating of 1 denotes no obstacle; 2, a minor obstacle; 3, a moderate obstacle; and 4, a major obstacle. These ratings provide a summary measure of the extent to which financing, legal systems, and corruption create obstacles to growth, and we refer to them below as "summary" obstacles.

Table I shows that in the large majority of countries, firms report that the financing obstacle is the most important summary obstacle to growth.[8] Also, in general, the reported obstacles tend to be lower in developed countries such as the United Kingdom and the United States compared to those in developing countries.

Table II contains the sample statistics of our variables. In addition to the financial, legal, and corruption summary obstacles described above, and in order to understand the nature of these obstacles to growth better, the survey asked firms more specific questions. We also investigate responses to these questions.

Table II reports unaudited self-reports by firms. In self-reporting it is possible that unsuccessful firms may blame institutional obstacles for their poor performance. This possibility must be balanced by the likelihood that alternative data sources used in cross-country firm-level research, such as accounting data, are also subject to distortion. With accounting data, the auditing process provides a measure of quality control. However, the quality of the audit may vary systematically across countries and firm size.[9] Moreover, the incentives

---

[8] This is consistent with other studies that use the WBES (see Schiffer and Weder (2001)).

[9] Financial data used in previous studies are also subject to potential biases because country institutional factors can affect the properties of accounting data (see Ball, Kothari, and Robin (2000) and Hung (2001)).

Table II

Summary Statistics and Correlations

Panel A presents summary statistics and Panel B presents correlations. *N* refers to firm-level observations for 54 countries. Firm Growth is given by the percentage change in firm sales. Government and Foreign are dummy variables that take the value of 1 if the firm has government or foreign ownership and 0 if not. Exporter is a dummy variable that indicates if the firm is an exporting firm. Subsidized is also a dummy variable that indicates if the firm receives subsidies from the national or local authorities. Manufacturing and Services are industry dummies. No. of Competitors is the logarithm of the number of competitors the firm has. Size is a variable that takes the value of 1 if firm is small, 2 if it is medium-sized, and 3 if it is large. Small firms employ 5–50 employees, medium-size firms employ 51–500 employees, and large firms employ more than 500 employees. Inflation is the log difference of the consumer price index. GDP per capita is real GDP per capita in U.S. dollars, GDP is the logarithm of GDP in millions of U.S. dollars. Growth is the growth rate of GDP. All country variables are 1995–1999 averages. The different financing, legal, and corruption issues are survey responses as specified in the firm questionnaire. Higher numbers indicate greater obstacles, with the exception of "Firms must make 'additional payments' to get things done" and "Firms know the amount of 'additional payments' in advance." Detailed variable definitions and sources are given in Table AII in the Appendix.

Panel A: Summary Statistics

	N	Mean	SD	Min	Max
Firm Growth	4,255	0.13	0.59	−1	2
Government	4,255	0.13	0.34	0	1
Foreign	4,255	0.17	0.37	0	1
Exporter	4,255	0.35	0.48	0	1
Subsidized	4,255	0.10	0.35	0	1
Manufacturing	4,255	0.37	0.48	0	1
Services	4,255	0.47	0.50	0	1
No. of competitors	4,255	0.80	0.33	0	1.39
Size	4,254	1.78	0.72	1	3
Inflation	54	17.41	19.30	0.11	86.05
GDP per capita	54	560	772	369	30,794
GDP (million $)	54	24.72	1.96	20.30	29.74
Growth	54	0.02	0.03	−0.03	0.07
Financing	4,213	2.87	1.13	1	4
Legal	3,976	2.17	1.05	1	4
Corruption	4,000	2.43	1.17	1	4

(continued)

Entrepreneurship in Developing Countries

Table II—*Continued*

Panel A: Summary Statistics

	N	Mean	SD	Min	Max
Collateral requirements	3,954	2.54	1.17	1	4
Bank paperwork/bureaucracy	4,078	2.54	1.10	1	4
High interest rates	4,112	3.24	1.03	1	4
Need special connections with banks	3,958	2.19	1.09	1	4
Banks lack money to lend	3,861	2.10	1.22	1	4
Access to foreign banks	3,489	1.99	1.17	1	4
Access to nonbank equity	3,470	2.06	1.16	1	4
Access to export finance	3,017	1.99	1.19	1	4
Access to financing for leasing equipment	3,532	2.02	1.14	1	4
Inadequate credit/financial information on customers	3,712	2.21	1.13	1	4
Access to long-term loans	3,937	2.63	1.27	1	4
Availability of information on laws and regulations	4,211	2.92	1.42	1	6
Interpretation of laws and regulations are consistent	4,225	3.42	1.37	1	6
Overall quality and efficiency of courts	3,521	3.73	1.31	1	6
Courts are fair and impartial	3,933	3.75	1.39	1	6
Courts are quick	3,991	4.77	1.22	1	6
Courts are affordable	3,910	3.92	1.45	1	6
Courts are consistent	3,918	4.04	1.36	1	6
Court decisions are enforced	3,905	3.67	1.48	1	6
Confidence in legal system to enforce contract & prop. rights	4,206	3.35	1.38	1	6
Confidence in legal system – 3 years ago	3,935	3.46	1.40	1	6
Corruption of bank officials	3,574	1.72	1.05	1	4
Firms have to make "additional payments" to get things done	3,924	4.36	1.62	1	6
Firms know the amount of "additional payments" in advance	2,310	3.38	1.59	1	6
If "additional payments" are made, services are delivered	2,269	3.01	1.53	1	6
It is possible to find honest agents to replace corrupt ones	3,602	3.58	1.75	1	6
Proportion of revenues paid as bribes	2,831	2.35	1.47	1	7
Prop. of contract value that must be paid for govt. contracts	1,733	2.51	1.73	1	6
Mgmt's time (%) spent with officials to understand laws & regs	3,990	2.24	1.39	1	6

Panel B: Correlation Matrix of Variables

	Firm Growth	Govt	Foreign	Exporter	Subsidized	Manuf.	Services	No. of Comp.	Size	Inflation	GDP/Capita	GDP($)	Growth	Financing	Legal
Govt.	-0.0245*														
Foreign	0.0390***	-0.0258*													
Exporter	0.0844***	0.1001***	0.2368***												
Subsidized	-0.0049	0.1472***	0.0006	0.081***											
Manuf.	-0.0180	0.0855***	0.1165***	0.3448***	0.0219										
Services	0.0210	-0.0846***	-0.0312*	-0.2465***	-0.0759***	-0.7302***									
No. of Co.	0.0148	-0.0057	-0.1788***	-0.1211***	-0.0285*	-0.117***	0.0334**								
Size	0.0224	-0.0245*	0.0390***	0.0844***	0.0049	-0.0180	0.0210	0.0148							
Inflation	0.0010	0.1335***	-0.1231***	-0.1024***	0.0675***	0.0280*	-0.1262***	0.2640***	0.0010						
GDP/Cap	0.0489***	-0.0808***	0.1262***	0.1223***	0.0625***	-0.0460***	0.0739***	-0.2228***	0.0489***	-0.3655***					
GDP($)	0.0551***	-0.0960***	0.0799***	0.0058	0.0404***	-0.0391***	0.0559***	-0.1178***	0.0551***	-0.0789***	0.5666***				
Growth	0.0751***	0.0673***	0.0237	0.1275***	0.0231	0.0000	0.021	0.0281*	0.0751***	-0.3608***	0.1308***	-0.1007***			
Fin. Obst.	-0.0821***	0.0723***	-0.1732***	-0.052***	-0.0303*	0.0426***	-0.1317***	0.1039***	-0.0821***	0.1784***	-0.2518***	-0.1114***	-0.1226***		
Leg Obst.	-0.0676***	-0.0084	-0.0158	-0.0095	-0.0759***	0.0198	-0.0378*	0.0167	-0.0676***	0.0531***	-0.1737***	-0.0682***	-0.1411***	0.1901***	
Corruption	-0.0695***	-0.0713***	-0.0733***	-0.1025***		-0.001	-0.0338*	0.0479***	-0.0695***	0.1314***	-0.3322***	-0.1635***	-0.1815***	0.2809***	0.5754***

*, **, *** indicate significance levels of 10%, 5%, and 1%, respectively.

146   *The Journal of Finance*

to distort data are likely to be much higher in financial statements than in survey responses, since financial statements affect operational and financing decisions.

Although the possibility of data bias due to unaudited self-reporting can never be totally eliminated, we believe that it is unlikely to be a significant source of bias in this study. The stated purpose of the WBES survey is to evaluate the business environment, not firm performance. Firms were asked few specific questions about their performance and such questions were asked only at the end of the interview. This sequencing reduces the respondents' need to justify their own performance when answering the earlier questions about the business environment. Respondents were asked about a large range of business conditions and government policies. Thus, to the extent that firms need to shift blame for poor performance to outside forces, an unsuccessful firm that is not financially constrained is likely to find other, more immediate excuses for its internal failures.

To assess the importance of financing obstacles, the firms were asked to rate, again on a scale of 1–4, how problematic specific financing issues are for the operation and growth of their business. These are (1) collateral requirements of banks and financial institutions; (2) bank paperwork and bureaucracy; (3) high interest rates; (4) need for special connections with banks and financial institutions; (5) banks lacking money to lend; (6) access to foreign banks; (7) access to nonbank equity; (8) access to export finance; (9) access to financing for leasing equipment; (10) inadequate credit and financial information on customers; and (11) access to long-term loans.

Among the specific financial obstacles to growth, high interest rates stand out with a value of 3.24, which should be a constraint for all firms in all countries. Access to long-term loans, and bank collateral and paperwork requirements, also appear to be among the greater of the reported obstacles to growth.

The survey also included specific questions on the legal system. Businesses were asked if (1) information on laws and regulations was available; (2) if the interpretation of laws and regulations was consistent; and (3) if they were confident that the legal system upheld their contract and property rights in business disputes 3 years ago, and continues to do so now. These answers were rated between 1, fully agree, to 6, fully disagree.

The survey also asked businesses to evaluate whether their country's courts are (1) fair and impartial, (2) quick, (3) affordable, (4) consistent, and (5) enforced decisions. These are rated thus: 1 equals always, 2 equals usually, 3 equals frequently, 4 equals sometimes, 5 equals seldom, and 6 equals never. Finally, businesses were asked to rate the overall quality and efficiency of courts between 1, very good, to 6, very bad.

Looking at these legal obstacles to growth, speed of courts, which has a value of 4.77, seems to be one of the important perceived obstacles. Other important obstacles include the consistency and affordability of the courts. Below we examine whether in fact growth is related to the firms' perceptions of these obstacles.

The final set of questions we investigate relate to the level of corruption that firms must deal with. The questions are (1) whether corruption of bank

Financial and Legal Constraints to Growth 147

officials creates a problem (rated from 1 to 4 as described above); (2) if firms have to make "additional payments" to get things done; (3) if firms generally know what the amount of these "additional payments" are; (4) if services are delivered when the "additional payments" are made as required; and (5) if it is possible to find honest agents to circumvent corrupt ones without recourse to unofficial payments. Other questions include (6) the proportion of revenues paid as bribes (increasing in payment ranked from 1 to 7);[10] (7) the proportion of contract value that must be paid as "unofficial payments" to secure government contracts (increasing in payment ranked from 1 to 6);[11] and (8) the proportion of management's time in dealing with government officials about the application and interpretation of laws and regulations (increasing in time from 1 to 6). Unless specified, answers are ranked from 1 (always) to 6 (never).

Of the specific corruption obstacles reported, the need to make additional payments is the highest at 4.36. The second highest rated obstacle is firms' inability to have recourse to honest officials at 3.58.

One potential problem with using survey data is that enterprise managers may identify several operational problems, only some of which are constraining, while others can be circumvented. For this reason, we examine the extent to which the reported obstacles affect the growth rates of firms. To do this, we obtain benchmark growth rates by controlling for firm and country characteristics. We then assess whether the level of a reported obstacle affects growth relative to this benchmark. However, note that since many firms in our sample are not publicly traded, we do not have firm-level measures of investment opportunities, such as Tobin's Q. We use indicators of firm ownership, industry, market structure, and size as firm-level controls. Since the sample includes firms from manufacturing, services, construction, agriculture, and other industries, we control for industry effects by including industry dummy variables.

We also include dummy variables that identify firms as government-owned or foreign-controlled. Government-owned firms might grow at different rates because their objectives or their exposure to obstacles might differ from those of other firms. For example, they can have advantages in dealing with the regulatory system, and they could be less subject to crime or corruption by financial intermediaries and more exposed to political influences. The growth rate of foreign institutions can also be different because foreign entities might find it more difficult to deal with local judiciary or corruption. However, foreign institutions might be less affected by financing obstacles, since they could have easier access to the international financial system.

The growth rate of firms can also depend on the market structure in which they operate. Therefore, we also include dummy variables to capture whether the firm is an exporting firm, whether it receives subsidies from local and national governments, and the number of competitors it faces in its market.

[10] On the scale 1 equals 0%, 2 equals less than 1%, 3 equals 1–1.9%, 4 equals 2–9.99%, 5 equals 10–12%, 6 equals 13–25%, and 7 equals more than 25%.

[11] On the scale, 1 equals 0%, 2 equals less than 5%, 3 equals 6–10%, 4 equals 11–15%, 5 equals 16–20%, 6 equals more than 20%.

148   *The Journal of Finance*

Firm size can be a very important factor in how firm growth is constrained by different factors. Small firms are likely to face tougher obstacles in obtaining finance, accessing legal systems, or dealing with corruption (see, e.g., Schiffer and Weder (2001)). Here, size is a dummy variable that takes the value of 1 for small firms, 2 for medium firms, and 3 for large firms.

Panel B of Table II shows the correlation matrix for the variables in our study. Foreign firms and exporters have higher growth rates. Government-owned firms have significantly lower rates of growth. Also, firms in richer, larger, and faster-growing countries have significantly higher growth rates. As expected, higher financing, legal, and corruption obstacles correlate with lower firm growth rates.

Correlations also show that government-owned firms are subject to higher financing obstacles, but are subject to lower corruption. On the other hand, foreign-controlled firms and exporters face lower financing and corruption obstacles. Financing obstacles seem to be higher for manufacturing firms. Firms in service industries are less affected by all obstacles. To the extent that firms have a greater number of competitors, they seem to face greater financing obstacles and corruption.

All obstacles are significantly lower in richer, larger, and faster-growing countries, but are significantly higher in countries with higher inflation. Firms are also significantly larger in richer, larger, and faster-growing countries. Firm size itself is not correlated with firm growth. However, size is likely to have an indirect effect on firm growth because larger firms face significantly lower financing, legal, and corruption obstacles. All three obstacles are highly correlated with each other. Thus, firms that suffer from one are also likely to suffer from others.

We compute but do not report here the correlations of specific obstacles with summary financing, legal, and corruption obstacles, respectively. Overall, specific obstacles are highly correlated with the summary obstacles and with each other. The correlation between the summary corruption obstacle and the corruption of bank officials is significant and particularly high at 43%.

We next explore the relation between the financing, legal, and corruption obstacles and firm size, controlling for country-level institutional development. To capture institutional development, we use independently computed country-level measures of the size of the financial sector, development of the legal sector, and the level of corruption. Earlier work has shown that the level of financial development affects firm growth (see Demirgüç-Kunt and Maksimovic (1998)). As a measure of financial development, we use *Priv*, which is given by the ratio of domestic banking credit to the private sector divided by GDP. The index *Laworder* serves as our proxy for legal development and is an index of the efficiency of the legal system. It is rated between 1 and 6, with higher values indicating better legal development. Corruption is captured by *Corrupt*. This measure is an indicator of the existence of corruption, rated between 1 and 6, with higher values indicating less corruption.

In Table III, we regress the firm-level survey responses on size dummies and the country-level variables. The three size dummy variables are small, medium,

Financial and Legal Constraints to Growth   149

Table III
Firm-Level Obstacles and Institutional Development

The regression estimated is

$$\text{Firm Level Obstacle} = \alpha + \beta_1\,Priv * Small + \beta_2\,Priv * Medium + \beta_3\,Priv * Large$$
$$+ \beta_4\,Laworder * Small + \beta_5\,Laworder * Medium + \beta_6\,Laworder * Large$$
$$+ \beta_7\,Corrupt * Small + \beta_8\,Corrupt * Medium + \beta_9\,Corrupt * Large$$
$$+ \beta_{10}\,Small + \beta_{11}\,Medium + \varepsilon.$$

Firm-Level Obstacles—Financing, Legal, or Corruption—are summary obstacles as indicated in the firm questionnaire. They take values of 1–4, where 1 indicates no obstacle and 4 indicates a major obstacle. *Priv* is domestic bank credit to the private sector divided by GDP. *Laworder* is a national indicator (values between 1 and 6) that takes higher values for legal systems that are more developed. *Corrupt* is a corruption indicator (values between 1 and 6) at the national level that takes higher values in countries where corruption is lower. *Small*, *Medium*, and *Large* are dummy variables that take the value 1 if a firm is small (or medium or large) and 0 otherwise. Small firms employ 5–50 employees, medium-size firms employ 51–500 employees, and large firms employ more than 500 employees. These size dummies are interacted with *Priv*, *Laworder*, and *Corrupt*. We estimate all regressions using country random effects. At the foot of the table we report whether the coefficients are significantly different for large and small firms. We obtain firm-level variables from the WBES. Detailed variable definitions and sources are given in Table AII in the Appendix.

	Financing Obstacle		Legal Obstacle		Corruption Obstacle	
Priv	−0.531***		−0.316*		−0.461**	
	(0.190)		(0.194)		(0.235)	
Priv * Small		−0.167		−0.262		−0.624**
		(0.208)		(0.206)		(0.249)
Priv * Medium		−0.746***		−0.369*		−0.451*
		(0.205)		(0.203)		(0.247)
Priv * Large		−0.864***		−0.340		−0.191
		(0.242)		(0.233)		(0.276)
Laworder	−0.032		−0.137***		−0.245***	
	(0.053)		(0.054)		(0.065)	
Laworder * Small		−0.048		−0.146***		−0.225***
		(0.059)		(0.059)		(0.071)
Laworder * Medium		−0.036		−0.127**		−0.257***
		(0.056)		(0.056)		(0.068)
Laworder * Large		0.008		−0.135**		−0.250***
		(0.063)		(0.062)		(0.074)
Corrupt	−0.160***		−0.059		−0.129**	
	(0.052)		(0.053)		(0.065)	
Corrupt * Small		−0.135***		−0.053		−0.082
		(0.057)		(0.057)		(0.069)
Corrupt * Medium		−0.153***		−0.045		−0.143**
		(0.056)		(0.055)		(0.067)
Corrupt * Large		−0.221***		−0.097*		−0.172**
		(0.063)		(0.061)		(0.074)
Small	0.294***	−0.004	−0.036	−0.163	0.240***	−0.034
	(0.052)	(0.202)	(0.048)	(0.187)	(0.051)	(0.198)
Medium	0.229***	0.134	0.015	−0.184	0.147***	0.172
	(0.050)	(0.187)	(0.046)	(0.171)	(0.049)	(0.183)

(continued)

Table III—*Continued*

	Financing Obstacle		Legal Obstacle		Corruption Obstacle	
R^2-within	0.01	0.02	0.00	0.00	0.01	0.01
R^2-between	0.44	0.45	0.37	0.37	0.55	0.54
R^2-overall	0.08	0.08	0.06	0.06	0.13	0.13
Priv(large − small)		−0.700***		−0.080		0.438**
Laworder(large − small)		0.055		0.014		−0.024
Corrupt(large − small)		−0.085*		−0.046		−0.091*
No of firms	3,549	3,549	3,400	3,400	3,406	3,406
No of countries	49	49	49	49	49	49

*, **, *** indicate significance levels of 10%, 5%, and 1%, respectively.

and large. These variables take the value of 1 if the firm is small or medium or large, respectively, and 0 otherwise. We also report specifications in which we interact country-level variables with firm size.

Table III indicates that on average, the firms' perception of the financing and corruption obstacles they face relates to firm size, with smaller firms reporting significantly higher obstacles than large firms. In contrast, smaller firms report lower legal obstacles than do larger firms, but these differences are not significant.

Table III also shows that in countries with more developed financial systems and with less country-level corruption, firms report lower financing obstacles. These effects are more significant and the coefficients are greater in absolute value for the largest firms, particularly for financial development. The indicator of the quality of the legal system does not appear to explain the magnitude of the firm-level financing obstacles. The firm-level legal obstacles are significant and negatively related to the quality of the country's legal system. The corruption obstacles reported by firms in our sample are higher in countries with less-developed financial and legal systems and in countries that are rated as more corrupt. Lack of corruption at the country level is associated with a significant reduction in the level of corruption obstacles reported by larger firms. In contrast, financial development is significantly correlated with lower corruption obstacles reported by the smaller firms.

Table III shows that even after we control for the quality of a country's institutions, firm size is an important determinant of the level of financial and corruption obstacles. However, to determine if firm size really has an impact, we need to investigate both the level of the reported obstacles and how firm growth is affected by these obstacles.

II. Firm Growth and Reported Obstacles

The regressions reported in Table III indicate that firm size and a country's institutional development predict the obstacles that firms report. However, it

Financial and Legal Constraints to Growth   151

does not follow that they also predict the effect of these obstacles on firm growth. A firm's report that an existing economy-wide institutional obstacle constrains its growth might be accurate, but may not take into account the possibility that the obstacle may also benefit it by affecting its rivals. Obstacles might affect large and small firms differently. Table II also indicates that there is a high degree of correlation between variables of interest and other firm- and country-level controls that affect growth. Thus, we clarify the relation between firm-level characteristics and firm growth using multivariate regression.

We regress firms' growth rates on the obstacles they report. We initially introduce financial, legal, and corruption summary obstacles one at a time, and finally all together. In subsequent regressions, we substitute specific obstacles for these summary obstacles and introduce interaction terms. All regressions are estimated using firm-level data across 54 countries and country random effects. The regressions are estimated with controls for country and firm-specific variables discussed in Section II. The country controls are GDP per capita, GDP, country growth, and the inflation rate. Firm-specific controls are the logarithm of the number of competitors the firm has, and indicator variables for ownership of the firm (separate indicators for government- and foreign-owned firms), industry classification (separate indicators for manufacturing and service industries), and indicators for whether the firm is an exporter and whether it receives government subsidies. Specifically, the regression equations we estimate take the form

$$Firm\ Growth = \alpha + \beta_1\ Government + \beta_2\ Foreign + \beta_3\ Exporter$$

$$+ \beta_4\ Subsidized + \beta_5\ No.\ of\ Competitors$$

$$+ \beta_6\ Manufacturing + \beta_7\ Services + \beta_8\ Inflation$$

$$+ \beta_9\ GDP\ per\ capita + \beta_{10}\ GDP$$

$$+ \beta_{11}\ Growth + \beta_{12}\ Obstacle + \varepsilon. \tag{1}$$

To test the hypothesis that an obstacle is related to firm growth, we test whether its coefficient β_{12} is significantly different from zero. We also obtain an estimate of the economic impact of the obstacle at the sample mean by multiplying its coefficient β_{12} by the sample mean of the obstacle. This impact variable measures the total effect of the obstacle on growth, taking into account both the level of the mean reported obstacle and the estimated relation between the reported obstacle and observed growth.

Table IV shows how firm growth is related to the financing, legal, and corruption obstacles reported by firms. When entered individually, all reported obstacles have a negative and significant effect on firm growth, as expected. The impact of the obstacles on firm growth evaluated at the sample mean is negative, and in all cases, substantial.

Column 4 shows that financing and legal obstacles are both significant and negative, but corruption loses its significance in the presence of these two variables. This suggests that the impact of corruption on firm growth is captured

Table IV
Firm Growth: The Impact of Obstacles

The regression estimated is

$$Firm\ Growth = \alpha + \beta_1\ Government + \beta_2\ Foreign + \beta_3\ Exporter + \beta_4\ Subsidized$$
$$+ \beta_5\ No.\ of\ Competitors + \beta_6\ Manufacturing + \beta_7\ Services + \beta_8\ Inflation$$
$$+ \beta_9\ GDP\ per\ capita + \beta_{10}\ GDP + \beta_{11}\ Growth + \beta_{12}\ Financing$$
$$+ \beta_{13}\ Legal + \beta_{14}\ Corruption + \varepsilon.$$

Firm Growth is the percentage change in firm sales over the past 3 years. *Government* and *Foreign* are dummy variables that take the value of 1 if the firm has government or foreign ownership and 0 if not. *Exporter* is a dummy variable that indicates if the firm is an exporting firm. *Subsidized* is also a dummy variable that indicates if the firm receives subsidies from the national or local authorities. *No. of Competitors* is the logarithm of the firm's number of competitors. *Manufacturing* and *Services* are industry dummies. *Inflation* is the log difference of the consumer price index. *GDP per capita* is real GDP per capita in U.S. dollars. *GDP* is the logarithm of GDP in millions of U.S. dollars. *Growth* is the growth rate of GDP. Financing, Legal, and Corruption are summary obstacles as indicated in the firm questionnaire. They take values between 1 and 4, where 1 indicates no obstacle and 4 indicates major obstacle. We estimate all regressions using country random effects. We obtain firm-level variables from the WBES. Detailed variable definitions and sources are given in Table AII in the Appendix.

	(1)	(2)	(3)	(4)
Government	−0.070***	−0.083***	−0.074***	−0.070**
	(0.028)	(0.029)	(0.029)	(0.030)
Foreign	0.034	0.045*	0.045*	0.037
	(0.025)	(0.025)	(0.026)	(0.026)
Exporter	0.103***	0.104***	0.107***	0.105***
	(0.021)	(0.022)	(0.022)	(0.022)
Subsidized	0.001	0.002	0.007	0.007
	(0.026)	(0.027)	(0.027)	(0.027)
No. of competitors	−0.011	−0.016	−0.001	−0.005
	(0.031)	(0.032)	(0.032)	(0.033)
Manufacturing	−0.032	−0.023	−0.032	−0.035
	(0.028)	(0.029)	(0.030)	(0.030)
Services	0.027	0.052*	0.037	0.036
	(0.027)	(0.028)	(0.028)	(0.028)
Inflation	0.002**	0.002*	0.002	0.002
	(0.001)	(0.001)	(0.001)	(0.001)
GDP per capita	0.002	0.001	0.001	0.000
	(0.003)	(0.003)	(0.003)	(0.003)
GDP ($)	0.007	0.012	0.010	0.013
	(0.011)	(0.011)	(0.011)	(0.012)
Growth	0.021***	0.021***	0.020***	0.019***
	(0.007)	(0.007)	(0.008)	(0.008)
Obstacles				
Financing	−0.031***			−0.023***
	(0.009)			(0.009)
Legal		−0.029***		−0.023**
		(0.009)		(0.011)

(continued)

Financial and Legal Constraints to Growth 153

Table IV—*Continued*

	(1)	(2)	(3)	(4)
Corruption			−0.021***	−0.007
			(0.009)	(0.011)
Impact on growth evaluated at sample mean	−0.087***	−0.063***	−0.052***	−0.134***
R^2-with.	0.01	0.01	0.01	0.02
R^2-between	0.28	0.27	0.25	0.26
R^2-overall	0.02	0.03	0.02	0.03
No. of firms	4,204	3,968	3,991	3,800
No. of countries	54	54	54	54

*, **, *** indicate significance levels of 10, 5, and 1%, respectively.

by the financial and legal obstacles. This is reasonable because corruption in the legal and financial systems can be expected to degrade firms' performance.

When we look at the control variables, we see that the growth rates of government-owned firms are lower, and the growth rates of exporters are higher. Foreign firms also appear to grow faster, although this result is only significant at 10% in two specifications. We do not observe significant differences in the growth rates of firms in different industries. The coefficient of inflation is significant and positive in two of the four specifications. A significant inflation effect most likely reflects the fact that firm sales growth is given in nominal terms. The GDP growth rate and firm growth are significant and positively correlated, indicating that firms grow faster in an economy with greater growth opportunities. Most of the explanatory power of the model comes from between-country differences as indicated by the between-R^2 values of 25–28%.

In Table V, we look at how specific financial, legal, and corruption obstacles affect firm growth. We enter each of the specific obstacles in turn into equation (1). Although our regressions include the control variables, for the sake of brevity we do not report these coefficients.

Panel A shows that collateral requirements, bank paperwork and bureaucracy, high interest rates, the need to have special connections with banks, lack of money in the banking system, and access to financing for leasing equipment all have significant constraining effects on firm growth.

We note that although firms in the WBES survey rate the lack of access to long-term loans as an important obstacle, it is not significantly correlated with firm growth, suggesting that firms might be able to substitute short-term financing that is rolled over at regular intervals for long-term loans. Also, because we expect interest rates to constrain all firms, it is reassuring to see that those firms that perceive high interest rates as an important obstacle actually grow more slowly. We also note that some of these factors are likely to be correlated with lack of development of the financial system. Other potential constraints, such as access to foreign banks, access to nonbank equity, access

Table V
Firm Growth: The Impact of Obstacles

The regression estimated is

$$\text{Firm Growth} = \alpha + \beta_1\, \text{Government} + \beta_2\, \text{Foreign} + \beta_3\, \text{Exporter} + \beta_4\, \text{Subsidized} + \beta_5\, \text{No. of Competitors} + \beta_6\, \text{Manufacturing} + \beta_7\, \text{Services} + \beta_8\, \text{Inflation}$$
$$+ \beta_9\, \text{GDP per capita} + \beta_{10}\, \text{GDP} + \beta_{11}\, \text{Growth} + \beta_{12}\, \text{Obstacle} + \varepsilon.$$

Firm Growth is the percentage change in firm sales over the past 3 years. *Government* and *Foreign* are dummy variables that take the value of 1 if the firm has government or foreign ownership and 0 if not. *Exporter* is a dummy variable that indicates if the firm is an exporting firm. *Subsidized* is also a dummy variable that indicates if the firm receives subsidies from the national or local authorities. *No. of Competitors* is the logarithm of the firm's number of competitors. *Manufacturing* and *Services* are industry dummies. *Inflation* is the log difference of the consumer price index. *GPP per capita* is real GDP per capita in U.S. dollars. *GDP* is the logarithm of GDP in millions of U.S. dollars. *Growth* is the growth rate of GDP. Obstacles are financing obstacles in Panel A, legal obstacles in Panel B, and corruption obstacles in Panel C. Financing obstacles range between 1 and 4. Legal obstacles range between 1 and 6 (1 and 4 in the case of the summary obstacle). The range of the corruption indicators is indicated in parentheses after the variable name, with the first number indicating the least constraint. Unless otherwise noted, obstacles take higher values for higher obstacles and they are entered one at a time. We estimate all regressions using country random effects. We obtain firm-level variables from the WBES. Detailed variable definitions and sources are given in Table AII in the Appendix.

Panel A: Financing Obstacles

	Financing Obstacle	Collateral Requirements	Bank Paperwork/ Bureaucracy	High Interest Rates	Need Special Connections with Banks	Banks Lack Money to Lend	Access to Foreign Banks	Access to Nonbank Equity	Access to Export Finance	Access to Financing for Leasing Equipment	Inadequate Credit/ Financial Information on Customers	Access to Long-Term Loans
	-0.031***	-0.027***	-0.028***	-0.032***	-0.023***	-0.029***	-0.009	0.007	-0.009	-0.022**	0.001	-0.010
	(0.009)	(0.008)	(0.008)	(0.010)	(0.009)	(0.008)	(0.008)	(0.009)	(0.009)	(0.009)	(0.008)	(0.008)
R^2-with.	0.01	0.01	0.01	0.01	0.01	0.01	0.01	0.01	0.01	0.01	0.01	0.01
R^2-between	0.28	0.25	0.26	0.26	0.26	0.26	0.24	0.25	0.29	0.26	0.27	0.25
R^2-all	0.02	0.02	0.02	0.02	0.02	0.02	0.02	0.02	0.02	0.02	0.02	0.02
Impact	-0.087***	-0.070***	-0.070***	-0.104***	-0.051***	-0.062***	-0.002	0.001	-0.018	-0.045***	0.001	-0.027
N (firms)	4,204	3,945	4,069	4,103	3,949	3,853	3,482	3,464	3,007	3,524	3,703	3,928
N(country)	54	54	54	54	54	54	54	54	54	54	54	54

Panel B: Legal Obstacles

	Legal Constraint	Availability of Info. on Laws and Regulations	Interpretation of Laws and Regulations Is Consistent	Overall Quality and Efficiency of Courts	Courts Are Fair and Impartial	Courts Are Quick	Courts Are Affordable	Courts Are Consistent	Court Decisions Are Enforced	Confidence in Legal System to Enforce Contract and Property Rights	Confidence in Legal System— 3 Years Ago
	-0.029***	0.002	-0.003	-0.003	-0.004	0.005	-0.009	0.002	0.011	-0.005	0.004
	(0.009)	(0.006)	(0.007)	(0.008)	(0.007)	(0.008)	(0.007)	(0.007)	(0.007)	(0.007)	(0.007)
R^2-with.	0.01	0.01	0.01	0.01	0.01	0.01	0.01	0.01	0.01	0.01	0.01
R^2-between	0.27	0.27	0.26	0.27	0.27	0.28	0.30	0.27	0.31	0.28	0.32
R^2-all	0.03	0.02	0.02	0.02	0.02	0.02	0.02	0.02	0.03	0.02	0.02
Impact	-0.063***	0.006	-0.011	-0.014	-0.013	0.026	-0.035	0.007	0.039	-0.015	0.014
N (firms)	3,968	4,202	4,216	3,513	3,924	3,982	3,901	3,909	3,896	4,197	3,926
N(country)	54	54	54	54	54	54	54	54	54	54	54

Panel C: Corruption Obstacles

	Corruption Obstacle (1-4)	Corruption of Bank Officials (1-4)	Firms Have to Make "Additional Payments" to Get Things Done (6-1)	Firms Know in Advance the Amount of "Additional Payments" (6-1)	If "Additional Payments" Are Made, Services Are Delivered as Agreed (1-6)	If One Agent Asks for Payments It Is Possible to Find Others to Get the Correct Treatment without Payment (1-6)	Proportion of Revenues Paid as Bribes— Annual Figure for Each Firm (1-7)	Proportion of Contract Value That Must be Paid as "Payment" to Do Business with the Government (1-6)	Percentage of Senior Management's Time Spent with Government Officials to Understand Laws and Regulations (1-6)
	-0.021***	-0.017*	-0.003	-0.002	-0.012	-0.002	-0.037***	0.004	-0.012*
	(0.009)	(0.010)	(0.006)	(0.008)	(0.009)	(0.006)	(0.008)	(0.007)	(0.007)
R^2-with.	0.01	0.01	0.01	0.01	0.02	0.01	0.03	0.02	0.01
R^2-between	0.25	0.26	0.28	0.19	0.20	0.28	0.16	0.21	0.24
R^2-all	0.02	0.02	0.02	0.02	0.02	0.02	0.03	0.04	0.02
Impact	-0.052***	-0.030*	-0.014	-0.007	0.035	-0.006	0.087***	0.011	-0.027*
N (firms)	3,991	3,566	3,916	2,306	2,266	3,595	2,824	1,734	3,981
N(country)	54	54	54	53	53	53	53	52	54

*, **, *** indicate significance levels of 10%, 5%, and 1%, respectively.

to export finance, or inadequate information on customers are not significantly correlated with firm growth. Tests of the economic impact of the obstacles at the sample means indicate that the estimated coefficients, when significant, are sufficiently large to impact growth rates materially.

Panel B shows a significant and negative relation between the summary legal obstacle and firm growth. None of the specific legal obstacles has a significant coefficient. It appears that firms are able to work around these specific legal obstacles, although they find them annoying. Nevertheless, regressing the summary legal obstacle on the quality of the courts (i.e., their fairness, honesty, quickness, affordability, consistency, enforcement capacity, and confidence in the legal system), we find that these factors can explain 46% of the cross-country variation in the legal obstacle.[12] To further examine the importance of the specific legal obstacles taken together, we compute the predicted summary legal obstacle from this regression and introduce it as an independent variable in the firm growth equation in place of the actual summary legal obstacle. The coefficient of the predicted summary legal obstacle is positive yet insignificant, suggesting that the specific obstacles are at most weakly related to firm growth. This is also true if we run the regressions only for the sample of small firms. If we split the sample based on legal origin, the explanatory power of the specific descriptors is not significantly different in the common law countries compared to the civil law countries.[13]

Thus, although specific obstacles relate to the summary obstacle, they play a minor role in affecting growth. This finding suggests that the usual intuitive descriptors of how a good legal system operates predict survey responses well, but do not capture the effect of the legal system on firm growth.

Panel C of Table V shows that in addition to the summary corruption obstacle, the proportion of revenues paid as bribes has a negative and highly significant coefficient, indicating that it is a good indicator of corruption. Corruption of bank officials and the percentage of senior management's time spent with government officials also reduce firm growth significantly, but only at the 10% level. Again, the need to make payments or the absence of recourse to honest officials are not significant in regressions, despite their high levels as obstacles.

To investigate the relation between growth and reported obstacles for different-size firms, we next introduce firm size as an explanatory variable and interact the size dummies with individual obstacles. This specification posits that a firm might be affected by an obstacle, such as corruption, at three different levels: (1) at the country level, in that the general level of corruption may affect all the firms in the country; (2) at the "firm category" level, in that some firms (in our case different sized firms) might be affected differently; and (3) at the firm-specific level, in that firms have idiosyncratic exposures to corruption, depending on their business or financing needs. The equations are also estimated using random effects. Thus, the influence of the general

---

[12] If we use firm-level data and include random country effects, the between-R^2 is 41%.

[13] We are only able to do this using firm-level observations, since there are not enough degrees of freedom at the country level.

level of corruption in each country on firm growth is captured by the country random effects. The size variable picks up any systematic effects of exposure to corruption by firms of different sizes. The effect of firm-specific exposure to corruption is picked up by interacting the obstacles reported by each firm with a size dummy.

More generally, for each reported obstacle of interest, we regress firm growth on the control variables, firm size, the reported obstacle, and the interaction of the reported obstacle with three size dummies. These three variables, *Small*, *Medium*, and *Large*, take on the value 1 when the firm is small, medium-sized, and large, respectively, and 0 otherwise. The coefficients of interactions of the size dummies with an obstacle may differ because the impact of an obstacle can depend on firm size.

We also compute an economic impact variable for each firm size by multiplying the coefficients of the interacted variables by the mean level of reported obstacle for the subsample of firms of the corresponding firm size. To determine whether an obstacle affects the growth of large and small firms differently, we report and test the significance of the difference in the economic impacts of the obstacle for large and small firms. Thus, our reported impact variable, *Impact*(*L* − *S*), measures the difference between the total effect of the obstacle on large and small firms at their respective population means.

Our impact measure, *Impact*(*L* − *S*), also controls to a certain extent for a potential bias that could arise if some firms misestimate the effect of the obstacles on their growth, and if this misestimate is related to firm size. For example, if small firms systematically do not appreciate the real cost of the reported obstacles, they may, on average, underreport (relative to large firms) the magnitude of the obstacle. In that case, small firms might report, on average, λ times the true obstacle, where $\lambda < 1$. This in turn would bias upward the estimate of the interaction between *Small* and *Obstacle*. However, since the impact measure is defined as the difference of the products of the estimated coefficients and sample means of reported obstacles for large and small firms, it would therefore also not be affected by such scaling.[14]

In Table VI, we investigate whether financial, legal, and corruption obstacles affect firms differently based on their size. Panel A shows that financial obstacles affect firms differently, based on their size. The column titled 'Financial Obstacle' shows that the financing obstacle constrains the smallest firms the most and the largest ones the least. Multiplying the coefficients with the mean level of the summary financial obstacle for each respective subsample shows that the hypothesis that the economic impact of financing obstacles is the same for large and small firms can be rejected at the 10% level.

These differences become even clearer when we look at specific financing obstacles: The largest firms are barely affected. The only obstacle that affects these firms is that caused by high interest rates, which is different from 0 at

---

[14] As shown in the tables below, for almost all the regressions reported below, the conclusions we draw by testing for the differences of the economic impact variables match those drawn by simply testing for the differences in the coefficients.

Table VI

Firm Growth and Individual Obstacles: Large Compared to Small Firms

The regression estimated is

$$Firm\ Growth = \alpha + \beta_1\ Government + \beta_2\ Foreign + \beta_3 Exporter + \beta_4\ Subsidized + \beta_5\ No.\ of\ Competitors + \beta_6\ Manufacturing + \beta_7\ Services + \beta_8\ Inflation$$
$$+ \beta_9\ GDP\ per\ capita + \beta_{10}\ GDP + \beta_{11}\ Growth + \beta_{12}\ LSize + \beta_{13}\ Obstacle * Small + \beta_{14}\ Obstacle * Medium + \beta_{15}\ Obstacle * Large + \varepsilon.$$

Firm Growth is the percentage change in firm sales over the past 3 years. *Government* and *Foreign* are dummy variables that take the value of 1 if the firm has government or foreign ownership and 0 if not. *Subsidized* is also a dummy variable that indicates if the firm receives subsidies from the national or local authorities. *No. of Competitors* is the logarithm of the number of the firm's competitors. *Manufacturing* and *Services* are industry dummies. *Inflation* is the log difference of the consumer price index. *GDP per capita* is real GDP per capita in U.S. dollars. *GDP* is the logarithm of GDP in millions of U.S. dollars. *Growth* is given by the growth rate of GDP. *LSize* is given by logarithm of firm sales. Obstacles are financing obstacles in Panel A, legal obstacles in Panel B, and corruption obstacles in Panel C. Financing obstacles range between 1 and 4. Legal obstacles range between 1 and 6 (1 and 4 in the case of the summary obstacle). The range of the corruption indicators is indicated in parentheses after the variable name, with the first number indicating the least constraint. Unless otherwise noted, obstacles take higher values for higher obstacles and they are entered one at a time. Obstacles are multiplied by a vector of size dummy variables, Small, Medium, and Large. They take the value of 1 if a firm is small (or medium or large) and zero otherwise. Small firms employ 5–50 employees, medium-size firms employ 51–500 employees, and large firms employ more than 500 employees. For brevity only these coefficients ($\beta_{13} - \beta_{15}$) are reported below. *Impact (L − S)* gives the coefficient for large firms multiplied by the mean value of the obstacle for large firms minus the coefficient for small firms multiplied by the mean value of the obstacle for small firms. Its significance is based on a Chi-square test of these differences. We estimate all regressions using country random effects. Detailed variable definitions and sources are given in Table AII in the Appendix.

Panel A: Financing Obstacles

	Financing Obstacle	Collateral Requirements	Bank Paperwork/ Bureaucracy	High Interest Rates	Need Special Connections with Banks	Banks Lack Money to Lend	Access to Foreign Banks	Access to Nonbank Equity	Access to Export Finance	Access to Financing for Leasing Equipment	Inadequate Credit/ Financial Information on Customers	Access to Long-Term Loans
Large	−0.023**	−0.019	−0.012	−0.024**	−0.007	−0.020	−0.002	−0.004	0.005	−0.006	0.012	0.000
	(0.012)	(0.012)	(0.012)	(0.012)	(0.013)	(0.013)	(0.013)	(0.014)	(0.014)	(0.014)	(0.013)	(0.011)
Medium	−0.031***	−0.025***	−0.027***	−0.031***	−0.021**	−0.029***	0.000	0.002	−0.006	−0.023**	−0.001	−0.012
	(0.009)	(0.009)	(0.009)	(0.010)	(0.010)	(0.009)	(0.010)	(0.010)	(0.010)	(0.010)	(0.010)	(0.009)
Small	−0.034***	−0.031***	−0.031***	−0.037***	−0.028***	−0.034***	−0.002	0.000	−0.019*	−0.027***	−0.001	−0.012
	(0.009)	(0.009)	(0.009)	(0.010)	(0.010)	(0.010)	(0.010)	(0.011)	(0.011)	(0.011)	(0.010)	(0.009)
R^2-with.	0.01	0.01	0.01	0.01	0.01	0.01	0.01	0.01	0.01	0.01	0.01	0.01
R^2-between	0.29	0.25	0.26	0.27	0.27	0.28	0.26	0.28	0.30	0.30	0.28	0.27
R^2-all	0.03	0.03	0.03	0.03	0.02	0.03	0.02	0.02	0.03	0.03	0.02	0.02
Impact (L − S)	0.040*	0.038	0.050**	0.043*	0.051**	0.032	0.002	−0.007	0.047*	0.050***	0.028	0.033
N (firms)	4,182	3,926	4,048	4,083	3,928	3,832	3,463	3,444	2,990	3,504	3,682	3,907
N (country)	54	54	54	54	54	54	54	54	54	54	54	54

Financial and Legal Constraints to Growth 159

Panel B: Legal Obstacles

	Legal Obstacle	Availability of Info. on Laws and Regulations	Interpretation of Laws and Regulations Is Consistent	Overall Quality and Efficiency of Courts	Courts Are Fair and Impartial	Courts Are Quick	Courts Are Affordable	Courts Are Consistent	Court Decisions Are Enforced	Confidence in Legal System to Enforce Contract and Property Rights	Confidence in Legal System—3 Years Ago
Large	−0.013	0.016	0.006	0.012	0.011	0.013	−0.003	0.014	0.024***	0.010	0.017*
	(0.013)	(0.010)	(0.009)	(0.010)	(0.010)	(0.009)	(0.009)	(0.009)	(0.009)	(0.010)	(0.009)
Medium	−0.026***	0.002	−0.005	−0.002	−0.001	0.006	−0.007	0.003	0.010	−0.003	0.006
	(0.010)	(0.007)	(0.007)	(0.008)	(0.008)	(0.008)	(0.007)	(0.007)	(0.007)	(0.008)	(0.008)
Small	−0.040***	−0.002	−0.005	−0.091	−0.010	0.002	−0.013*	−0.004	0.007	−0.010	−0.003
	(0.011)	(0.007)	(0.008)	(0.008)	(0.008)	(0.008)	(0.007)	(0.008)	(0.007)	(0.008)	(0.008)
R^2-with.	0.02	0.01	0.01	0.01	0.01	0.01	0.01	0.01	0.01	0.01	0.01
R^2-between	0.26	0.28	0.27	0.26	0.27	0.29	0.30	0.27	0.31	0.28	0.32
R^2-all	0.03	0.02	0.02	0.02	0.02	0.02	0.02	0.02	0.03	0.02	0.03
Impact (L – S)	0.057**	0.049**	0.038	0.095***	0.078***	0.059**	0.041	0.073***	0.061**	0.063**	0.065**
N (firms)	3,946	4,180	4,295	3,496	3,902	3,960	3,880	3,888	3,874	4,175	3,905
N (country)	54	54	54	54	54	54	54	54	54	54	54

(continued)

Table VI—*Continued*

Panel C: Corruption Obstacles

	Corruption Obstacle (1-4)	Corruption of Bank Officials (1-4)	Firms Have to Make "Additional Payments" to Get Things Done (6-1)	Firms Know in Advance the Amount of "Additional Payments" (6-1)	If "Additional Payments" Are Made, Services Are Delivered as Agreed (1-6)	If One Agent Asks for Payments It Is Possible to Find Others to Get the Correct Treatment without Payment (1-6)	Proportion of Revenues Paid as Bribes—Annual Figure for Each Firm (1-7)	Proportion of Contract Value That Must Be Paid as "Payment" to Do Business with the Government (1-6)	Percentage of Senior Management's Time Spent with Government Officials to Understand Laws and Regulations (1-6)
Large	-0.007	-0.007	0.017	0.018	0.004	0.011	-0.013	0.020	-0.003
	(0.012)	(0.016)	(0.011)	(0.014)	(0.014)	(0.009)	(0.015)	(0.014)	(0.011)
Medium	-0.017*	-0.012	-0.001	-0.002	-0.005	-0.001	-0.033***	0.006	-0.014*
	(0.010)	(0.012)	(0.007)	(0.009)	(0.011)	(0.007)	(0.010)	(0.009)	(0.008)
Small	-0.030***	-0.024**	-0.011	-0.009	-0.018*	-0.009	-0.053***	-0.001	-0.017*
	(0.010)	(0.011)	(0.007)	(0.009)	(0.011)	(0.007)	(0.009)	(0.009)	(0.009)
R^2-with.	0.01	0.01	0.01	0.02	0.02	0.01	0.03	0.02	0.01
R^2-between	0.25	0.28	0.28	0.20	0.21	0.29	0.23	0.21	0.26
R^2-all	0.03	0.03	0.03	0.03	0.03	0.03	0.04	0.05	0.02
Impact (L – S)	0.060**	0.034	0.128***	0.084**	0.067*	0.052***	0.117***	0.047	0.029
N (firms)	3,969	3,545	3,896	2,293	2,255	3,581	2,805	1,712	3,963
N (country)	54	54	53	53	53	53	53	52	54

*, **, *** indicate significance levels of 10%, 5%, and 1%, respectively.

Financial and Legal Constraints to Growth   161

the 5% significance level. Largest firms are completely unaffected by collateral requirements, bank bureaucracies, the need for special connections (probably because they already have them), banks' lack of money, or any of the access issues. In contrast, medium-sized firms, and particularly small firms, are significantly and negatively affected by collateral requirements, bank paperwork and bureaucracy, high interest rates, the need for special connections with banks, banks' lack of money to lend, and access to financing for leasing equipment. The smallest firms are also negatively affected by obstacles to gaining access to export finance. The tests for the difference in the economic impact of specific financing obstacles on the largest and smallest firms confirm significant differences for most of the obstacles that significantly affect the growth of small firms. These results provide evidence that financial obstacles have a much greater impact on the operation and growth of small firms than on that of large firms.[15]

Panel B of Table VI shows that the summary legal obstacle leaves large firm growth unaffected, but has a significant, negative impact on the growth rates of medium-sized and especially small firms. The effect on the growth rate of large firms is insignificant, despite the fact that large firms report a higher level of the legal obstacle (Table III).

To evaluate the economic impact of each obstacle for each subsample of firms by size, we multiply the estimated coefficient by the mean reported level of the obstacle. At the subsample means, the predicted effect of the summary legal obstacle on annual firm growth is 2.8% for large firms, whereas it is 5.7% for medium firms and 8.5% for small firms. The difference between the predicted effects on large and small firms is statistically significant.[16] These results indicate that large firms are able to adjust to the inefficiencies of the legal system. However, the same does not seem to be the case for small and medium enterprises, which end up paying for the legal systems' shortcomings in terms of slower growth. Even looking at specific obstacles, which do not capture relevant differences as well as the summary obstacles, there is an indication that large firms may be using legal inefficiencies to their advantage because poor enforcement of court decisions appears to contribute to large firm growth rates. However, looking at the other specific obstacles, we do not see such an effect. For small firms, the affordability of the court system emerges as an obstacle, although the coefficient is significant only at 10%. The coefficients of the other more specific legal obstacles are not significantly different from 0. When we investigate whether this finding might be explained by the nonlinear coding of the responses to the questions on specific features of the legal system by rescaling the responses, the results are unchanged.

---

[15] Firm size itself never has a significant coefficient in the regressions, consistent with simple correlations reported in Table II.

[16] It is interesting to note that the estimates of the difference in the economic impact of specific legal obstacles on large and small firms are generally statistically significant, even in cases where the coefficients of the specific obstacle are not statistically different from zero. That can occur if the coefficients for large and small firms are of different sign or if the subsample means of the obstacle for large and small firms differs sufficiently.

Panel C shows that again, it is the small and medium-sized firms that are negatively affected by corruption. The mean effects on firm growth are 1.6%, 4.1%, and 7.5% for large, medium-sized, and small firms, respectively. The difference between the economic impact of corruption for large and small firms at the subsample mean is statistically significant at the 5% level. None of the corruption obstacles is significant for large firms. The corruption obstacle is negative but significant at 10% for medium-sized firms and negative and highly significant for small firms.

When we look at specific obstacles, we again see that it is the small and medium enterprises that are affected by bribes. Both coefficients are highly significant, although the impact on small firm growth is larger in magnitude. The percentage of a senior manager's time spent with officials to understand regulations reduces the growth rates of both small and medium-sized enterprises, but only at a 10% level of significance. In addition, small firms are significantly and negatively affected by variables that capture the corruption of bank officials and uncertainty that services will be delivered even after bribes are paid. We do not find a significant relation between firms' growth rates and the need to make bribe payments or the absence of recourse to honest officials, despite these variables' high reported ratings as obstacles. The tests of economic impact at the subsample means support the hypothesis that there is a more adverse effect of corruption on small firms than on large firms.

Next, we address the issue of whether obstacles affect firms similarly in all countries, or if their impact depends on the country's level of financial and legal development and corruption. To examine this issue, we focus on our three summary obstacles and introduce into our regressions a term for the interaction of the summary obstacle with a variable proxying for institutional development. The institutional variable is *Priv* when financial obstacles are being analyzed, *Laworder* when the legal obstacle is entered, and *Corrupt* when the corruption obstacle is entered. The coefficient of the interaction term measures whether the financial development of the economy has an effect on the relation between reported financial obstacles and firm growth. Thus, our specification is

$$\begin{aligned} Firm\ Growth = {} & \alpha + \beta_1\ Government + \beta_2\ Foreign + \beta_3\ Exporter \\ & + \beta_4\ Subsidized + \beta_5\ No.\ of\ Competitors \\ & + \beta_6\ Manufacturing + \beta_7\ Services + \beta_8\ Inflation \\ & + \beta_9\ GDP\ per\ capita + \beta_{10}\ GDP + \beta_{11}\ Growth \\ & + \beta_{12}\ Institution + \beta_{13}\ Obstacle \\ & + \beta_{14}\ Obstacle * Institution + \varepsilon. \end{aligned} \tag{2}$$

Table VII presents estimates of equation (2) for the summary financing, legal, and corruption obstacles. The results indicate that firms in financially and legally developed countries with lower levels of corruption are less affected by firm-level obstacles. In all three cases, the coefficient of the obstacle remains negative and significant, and the coefficient of the obstacle interacted

Financial and Legal Constraints to Growth 163

Table VII
Firm Growth and Obstacles: Impact of Institutional Development

The regression estimated is

$$\text{Firm Growth} = \alpha + \beta_1 \text{Government} + \beta_2 \text{Foreign} + \beta_3 \text{Exporter} + \beta_4 \text{Subsidized}$$

$$+ \beta_5 \text{No. of Competitors} + \beta_6 \text{Manufacturing} + \beta_7 \text{Services} + \beta_8 \text{Inflation}$$

$$+ \beta_9 \text{GDP per capita} + \beta_{10} \text{GDP} + \beta_{11} \text{Growth} + \beta_{12} \text{Institution}$$

$$+ \beta_{13} \text{Obstacle} + \beta_{14} \text{Obstacle} * \text{Institution} + \varepsilon.$$

Firm Growth is the percentage change in firm sales over the past 3 years. *Government* and *Foreign* are dummy variables that take the value of 1 if the firm has government or foreign ownership and 0 if not. *Exporter* is a dummy variable that indicates if the firm is an exporting firm. *Subsidized* is also a dummy variable that indicates if the firm receives subsidies from the national or local authorities. *No. of Competitors* is the logarithm of the number of the firm's competitors. *Manufacturing* and *Services* are industry dummies. *Inflation* is the log difference of the consumer price index. *GDP per capita* is real GDP per capita in U.S. dollars. *GDP* is the logarithm of GDP in millions of U.S. dollars. *Growth* is given by the growth rate of GDP. Obstacle is either Financing Legal or Corruption obstacle. The institutional variable is *Priv* when Financial constraint is entered, *Laworder* when Legal obstacle is entered, and *Corrupt* when Corruption obstacle is entered. *Priv* is domestic bank credit to the private sector divided by GDP. *Laworder* is a national indicator (values 1–6) that takes higher values for legal systems that are more developed. *Corrupt* (values 1–4) is a corruption indicator at the national level that takes higher values in countries where corruption is lower. Obstacles range between 1 and 4 and take higher values for greater obstacles. They are also interacted with the respective institutional variables. For brevity only these coefficients are reported below. Impact on growth is evaluated at the mean and is given by the product of the interaction term, the sample mean of the respective obstacle and the mean level of the institutional variable. We estimate all regressions using country random effects. Detailed variable definitions and sources are given in Table AII in the Appendix.

	Financing Obstacle	Legal Obstacle	Corruption Obstacle
Fin obstacle	−0.043***		
	(0.013)		
Fin. Obs. × Priv	0.045*		
	(0.029)		
Legal obstacle		−0.085**	
		(0.027)	
Legal Obs. × Laworder		0.014*	
		(0.009)	
Corruption obstacle			−0.084***
			(0.026)
Corruption Obs. × Corrupt			0.020***
			(0.008)
R^2-with.	0.01	0.01	0.01
R^2-between	0.17	0.26	0.36
R^2-all	0.02	0.02	0.03
Impact	0.039*	0.123*	0.155***
No. of firms	3,596	3,923	3,939
No. of countries	50	53	53

*, **, *** indicate significance levels of 10%, 5%, and 1%, respectively.

with the relevant development variable is positive and significantly different from zero.[17] Evaluating the coefficients at different levels of institutional development shows that in developed countries with *Priv* levels of 95% or higher, *Laworder* values of 6 and *Corrupt* values of 4 or higher, the impact of financial, legal, or corruption obstacles on firm growth is not significantly different from 0. In unreported regressions, we estimate equation (2) with each specific obstacle in turn. In separate regressions, we find positive and significant coefficients for the interaction between the level of development and the lack of money in the banking system, a consistent interpretation of laws, the amount of bribes to be paid, and the fraction of the contract value that must be paid to a government to secure the contract. These results also support the hypothesis that in countries where there is less corruption and better-developed financial and legal systems, firm growth is less constrained by the factors we examine.

We next investigate whether the effect of financial and institutional development on growth varies with firm size. For each summary obstacle, we augment our regression equations by interacting the summary obstacle with a measure of institutional development and with the firm-size dummies, *Small, Medium,* and *Large.* This gives us three triple interaction coefficients corresponding to the three triple interactions, *Obstacle ∗ Small ∗ Institution, Obstacle ∗ Medium ∗ Institution,* and *Obstacle ∗ Large ∗ Institution.*

Significance tests of the coefficient of the triple interactions show whether a marginal change in institutional development affects the relation between the summary obstacles and growth for small, medium, and large firms, respectively. We also test whether the marginal effect of a change in the country's financial system affects the sensitivity of the firm's growth to the financing obstacle equally for large and small firms. This difference in impact, *Impact(L − S),* is computed as the coefficient of the triple interaction term for large firms evaluated at the mean level of *Obstacle* for the subsample of large firms minus the coefficient of the triple interaction term for small firms evaluated at the mean level of *Obstacle* for small firms.

Taking into account firm sizes reinforces the results reported in Table VII. Table VIII shows that the relation between financing, legal, and corruption obstacles and the growth of firms of different sizes depends on the institutional setting.

The first column of Table VIII shows that small firms are again the most severely affected by financing obstacles. However, the interaction term of the financing obstacle with *Priv* and the small firm dummy variable has a positive sign and is significant, suggesting that a marginal development in a country's financial system relaxes the financial constraints on small firms.

In column 2 of the table, we see that marginal improvements in legal efficiency translate into a relaxing of legal constraints for small and medium-sized

---

[17] The variables *Priv* and *Laworder* are not significant when entered together with financing and legal obstacles. On the other hand, corruption enters positively and significantly in some specifications, even when entered together with firm-level corruption obstacles. This result indicates that lack of corruption is associated with higher firm growth.

Table VIII

Firm Growth and the Impact of Obstacles: Firm Size and National Differences

The regression estimated is

$$Firm\ Growth = \alpha + \beta_1\ Government + \beta_2\ Foreign + \beta_3\ Exporter + \beta_4\ Subsidized + \beta_5\ No.\ of\ Comp.$$

$$+ \beta_6\ Manuf. + \beta_7\ Services + \beta_8\ Inflation + \beta_9\ Gdp\ per\ capita + \beta_{10}\ GDP + \beta_{11}\ Growth$$

$$+ \beta_{12}\ Institution * Small + \beta_{13}\ Institution * Medium + \beta_{14}\ Institution * Large$$

$$+ \beta_{15}\ LSize + \beta_{16}\ Obstacle * Small + \beta_{17}\ Obstacle * Medium + \beta_{18}\ Obstacle * Large$$

$$+ \beta_{19}\ Obstacle * Small * Institution + \beta_{20}\ Obstacle * Medium * Institution$$

$$+ \beta_{21}\ Obstacle * Large * Institution + \varepsilon.$$

Firm Growth is the percentage change in firm sales over the past 3 years. *Government* and *Foreign* are dummy variables that take the value 1 if the firm has government or foreign ownership and 0 if not. *Exporter* is a dummy variable that indicates if the firm is an exporting firm. *Subsidized* is also a dummy variable that indicates if the firm receives subsidies from the national or local authorities. *No. of Competitors* is the logarithm of the number of the firm's competitors. *Manufacturing* and *Services* are industry dummies. *LSize* is given by logarithm of firm sales. *Inflation* is the log difference of the consumer price index. *GDP per capita* is real GDP per capita in U.S. dollars. *GDP* is the logarithm of GDP in millions of U.S. dollars. *Growth* is the growth rate of GDP. Institution is either *Priv, Laworder,* or *Corrupt. Priv* is domestic bank credit to the private sector divided by GDP. *Laworder* is a national indicator (values between 1 and 6) that takes higher values for legal systems that are more developed. *Corrupt* is a corruption indicator (values between 1 and 6) at the national level that takes higher values in countries where corruption is lower. *Obstacle* is either Financing, Legal, or Corruption. These are summary firm-level obstacles as indicated in the firm questionnaire. They take values between 1 and 4, where 1 indicates no obstacle and 4 indicates a major obstacle. *Small, Medium,* and *Large* are dummy variables. They take the value 1 if a firm is small (or medium or large) and 0 otherwise. Small firms employ 5–50 employees, medium size firms employ 51–500 employees, and large firms employ more than 500 employees. Financing obstacles are interacted with *Priv*, legal obstacles are interacted with *Laworder*, and corruption obstacles are interacted with *Corrupt*. These are also interacted with size dummies. Only these interaction terms are reported for brevity. Impact (L − S) is β_{21} evaluated at mean level of the institutional variable and mean obstacle for large firms minus β_{19} evaluated at mean level of the institutional variable and mean obstacle for small firms. Its significance is based on a Chi-square test of these differences. We estimate all regressions using country random effects. We obtain firm-level variables from the WBES. Detailed variable definitions and sources are given in Table AII in the Appendix.

	(1)	(2)	(3)
Financing Obstacle			
Large	−0.023		
	(0.016)		
Medium	−0.031**		
	(0.014)		
Small	−0.058***		
	(0.014)		
Large × Priv	−0.039		
	(0.051)		
Medium × Priv	0.021		
	(0.038)		
Small × Priv	0.097***		
	(0.039)		

(continued)

Table VIII—Continued

	(1)	(2)	(3)
Legal Obstacle			
Large		−0.060	
		(0.046)	
Medium		−0.092**	
		(0.040)	
Small		−0.104***	
		(0.044)	
Large × Laworder		0.009	
		(0.013)	
Medium × Laworder		0.018*	
		(0.010)	
Small × Laworder		0.015*	
		(0.010)	
Corruption Obstacle			
Large			−0.020
			(0.037)
Medium			−0.067**
			(0.028)
Small			−0.117***
			(0.029)
Large × Corrupt			0.002
			(0.013)
Medium × Corrupt			0.018**
			(0.009)
Small × Corrupt			0.026***
			(0.009)
R^2-within	0.02	0.02	0.02
R^2-between	0.34	0.26	0.43
R^2-overall	0.04	0.03	0.04
Impact(L − S)	−0.126***	−0.040	−0.197***
No. of firms	3,579	3,906	3,922
No. of countries	50	53	53

*, **, *** indicate significance levels of 10%, 5%, and 1%, respectively.

firms (albeit significant at the 10% level). The corruption results reported in column 3 indicate that as countries manage to reduce corruption, the constraining effect of corruption on the growth of small and medium-sized firms diminishes. The differential effect of the interaction of *Priv* and of the level of corruption on the growth of large and of small firms is statistically significant, indicating a material difference in the economic impact of these variables on the growth of large and small firms.

To address two possible sources of bias, we perform robustness checks of our specifications. Our estimates will be biased if firms that are not growing because of internal problems systematically shift blame to the legal and financial institutions and report high obstacles. This type of reverse causality problem,

Table IX
Sensitivity Test: IV Estimation and Using Real Firm Growth

The IV regression estimated is

$$Firm\ Growth = \alpha + \beta_1 Government + \beta_2 Foreign + \beta_3 Exporter + \beta_4 Subsidized$$

$$+ \beta_5\ No.\ of\ Competitors + \beta_6 Manufacturing + \beta_7 Services + \beta_8 Inflation$$

$$+ \beta_9\ GDP\ per\ capita + \beta_{10}\ GDP + \beta_{11}\ Growth + \beta_{12}\ Financing$$

$$+ \beta_{13}\ Legal + b_{14}\ Corruption + \varepsilon.$$

Firm Growth is the percentage change in firm sales over the past 3 years. *Government* and *Foreign* are dummy variables that take the value of one if the firm has government or foreign ownership and zero if not. *Exporter* is a dummy variable that indicates if the firm is an exporting firm. *Subsidized* is also a dummy variable that indicates if the firm receives subsidies from the national or local authorities. *No. of Competitors* is the logarithm of the number of the firm's competitors. *Manufacturing* and *Services* are industry dummies. *Inflation* is the log difference of the consumer price index. *GDP per capita* is real GDP per capita values in U.S. dollars. GDP is the logarithm of GDP in millions of U.S. dollars. *Growth* is the growth rate of GDP. Financing, Legal, and Corruption are summary obstacles as indicated in the firm questionnaire. They take values between 1 and 4, where 1 indicates no obstacle and 4 indicates a major obstacle. In Panel A, we estimate all regressions using instrumental variables, where the firm-level obstacles are instrumented by country-level institutional variables (*Priv, Laworder,* and *Corrupt*). In Panel B, obstacles are interacted with size dummies—small, medium, and large—and are instrumented by the three country-level institutional variables interacted by the three size dummies. In this specification we also control for *Size* in the regression. In Panel C, instead of interacting the obstacles with the three size dummies, we interact them with firm size. In Panel D, the dependent variable, *Firm Growth*, is replaced by real firm growth constructed using GDP deflator. Inflation is dropped from the specification. In Panel E, firm growth and obstacles are averaged for different size groups in each country. The averaged firm growth is regressed on averaged obstacles and all macro variables plus an interaction term of the averaged obstacle with a dummy variable that takes the value 1 if the firm is a small or medium firm and 0 otherwise. Each panel also reports Impact—the relevant coefficient evaluated at the mean level of the obstacle, or Impact (L − S), the differential impact on large versus small firms evaluated at the mean level of the obstacle for large and small firms. For brevity we report only the coefficients of the obstacles. Robust standard errors are reported in parentheses. We obtain firm-level variables from the WBES. Detailed variable definitions and sources are given in the Table AII in the Appendix.

	(1)	(2)	(3)
	Panel A		
Financing	−0.575***		
	(0.125)		
Legal		−0.029***	
		(0.009)	
Corruption			−0.021***
			(0.009)
Impact	−1.637***	−0.063***	−0.051***
No. of firms	3539	3390	3396

(continued)

Table IX—*Continued*

	(1)	(2)	(3)
Panel B			
Financing * large	−0.341***		
	(0.111)		
Financing * medium	−0.448***		
	(0.111)		
Financing * small	−0.790***		
	(0.186)		
Legal * large		0.073	
		(0.065)	
Legal * medium		0.023	
		(0.081)	
Legal * small		−0.104	
		(0.076)	
Corruption * large			−0.156**
			(0.081)
Corruption * medium			−0.207***
			(0.087)
Corruption * small			−0.272***
			(0.084)
Impact (L − S)	1.431***	0.382***	0.314***
No. of firms	3538	3389	3395
Panel C			
Financing	−0.046***		
	(0.013)		
Financing * size	0.002*		
	(0.001)		
Legal		−0.049***	
		(0.013)	
Legal * size		0.003**	
		(0.001)	
Corruption			−0.036***
			(0.012)
Corruption * size			0.002*
			(0.001)
R^2-within	0.01	0.01	0.01
R^2-between	0.31	0.28	0.27
R^2-overall	0.03	0.03	0.03
Impact (at mean size)	−0.032***	−0.029***	−0.021***
No. of firms	4,183	3,947	3,970

(continued)

if it exists, is likely to be most severe in the case of the summary obstacles.[18] To examine this possibility, we reestimate the specifications in Table IV by using *Priv, Laworder,* and *Corrupt* as the instrumental variables. The coefficients of

---

[18] We are grateful to the referee for pointing this out.

Financial and Legal Constraints to Growth　　　169

Table IX—*Continued*

	(1)	(2)	(3)
		Panel D	
Financing	−0.030***		
	(0.009)		
Legal		−0.030***	
		(0.009)	
Corruption			−0.021***
			(0.009)
R^2-within	0.01	0.01	0.01
R^2-between	0.28	0.28	0.27
R^2-overall	0.15	0.16	0.14
Impact	−0.085***	−0.065***	−0.051***
No. of firms	4204	3968	3991
No. of countries	54	54	54
		Panel E	
Financing	0.015		
	(0.0364)		
Financing * SME	−0.021**		
	(0.011)		
Legal		0.043	
		(0.038)	
Legal * SME		−0.027**	
		(0.014)	
Corruption			−0.003
			(0.032)
Corruption * SME			−0.024**
			(0.012)
R^2	0.12	0.12	0.12
Impact (L − SME)	0.060***	0.059***	0.058***
No. of observations	162	162	162
No. of countries	54	54	54

*, **, *** indicate significance levels of 10%, 5%, and 1%, respectively.

interest are reported in Panel A of Table IX. The coefficients show that the same variables remain significant at roughly comparable levels of significance.

In Panel B, we estimate the size splits for the three summary indicators using *Priv*, *Laworder*, and *Corrupt* interacted with the three size dummies as instrumental variables. Although the results for financing and corruption obstacles do not change significantly, those for the legal obstacle lose significance.

In Panel C, rather than looking at the differences between the three size groups, we interact the obstacles by firm size given by the logarithm of firm sales. Even when we use this continuous definition of firm size, we see that larger firms are less affected by the three obstacles.

Panel D shows the relation between the obstacles and firms' real growth. In this specification, we drop the rate of inflation variable from the right-hand side. Inspection of Panel D shows that adjusting the dependent variable for inflation does not alter the results.

In Panel E, we examine the robustness of our findings when we average the variables by country for different firm sizes. This procedure provides an alternative and more stringent test of the relation between firm growth and obstacles because it ignores the firm-level heterogeneity across firms in the same country belonging to the same size classification. Because this aggregation procedure reduces the degrees of freedom, in Panel D, we also reduce the number of independent variables and focus on the differences between SMEs and large firms. The results reported in Panel E are consistent with the firm-level results reported in earlier tables. There exist significant differences in the impact of financial, legal, and corruption obstacles on SMEs and large firms.

III. Conclusions

In this paper, we investigate whether the financial, legal, and corruption obstacles that firms report actually affect their growth rates. By making use of a unique survey database, we investigate a rich set of obstacles reported by firms and directly test whether any of these reported obstacles are significantly correlated with firm growth rates. The database also allows us to focus on differences in firm size, since it has good coverage of small and medium-sized enterprises in 54 countries. We investigate if the extent to which the firms are constrained by different obstacles depends on the level of development of the financial and legal systems. We are particularly interested in investigating the previously unexamined national level of corruption and its impact on firm growth.

Our results indicate that the extent to which financial and legal underdevelopment and corruption constrain a firm's growth depends very much on a firm's size. We show that it is the smallest firms that are consistently the most adversely affected by all obstacles.

Taking into account national differences between financial and legal development and corruption, we see that firms that operate in underdeveloped systems with higher levels of corruption are affected by all obstacles to a greater extent than firms operating in countries with less corruption. We also see that a marginal development in the financial and legal system and a reduction in corruption helps relax the constraints for the small and medium-sized firms, which are the most constrained.

All three obstacles—financial, legal, and corruption—do affect firm growth rates adversely. But not all specific obstacles are equally important, and the ones that affect firm growth are not necessarily the ones rated highest by the firms themselves. When we look at individual financing obstacles, we see that difficulties in dealing with banks, such as bank paperwork and bureaucracies, and the need to have special connections with banks, do constrain firm growth. Collateral requirements and certain access issues—such as financing for leasing equipment—also turn out to be significantly constraining. Macroeconomic issues captured by high interest rates and lack of money in the banking system also significantly reduce firm growth rates. Further, these effects remain

Financial and Legal Constraints to Growth   171

significant even after we control for the level of financial development. We are interested to find that another obstacle that is rated very highly by firms, access to long-term loans, does not affect their growth rates significantly. Perhaps, firms find it possible to substitute short-term funding for long-term loans.

Legal and corruption obstacles, particularly the amount of bribes paid, the percentage of senior management's time spent with regulators, and corruption of bank officials, also represent significant constraints on firm growth. However, other obstacles, such as the speed with which the courts work, or the need to make additional payments, both of which are rated very highly by firms as important obstacles, do not affect firm growth significantly. These results suggest that the surveys elicit all kinds of complaints that may appear equally important. However, our methodology allows us to distinguish between obstacles that are merely annoying from those that truly constrain firm performance.

There are two particularly interesting findings. First, corruption of bank officials does indeed affect firm growth, particularly for small firms. This finding provides evidence for the existence of institutional failure, which must be taken into account when modeling the monitoring role of financial institutions in overcoming market failures due to informational asymmetries. Second, while the intuitive descriptors of an efficient legal system are related to the summary obstacle, they are not related to firm growth. This finding suggests that the mechanism by which the legal system affects firm performance is not yet well understood.

There are several policy implications in our results. Development institutions devote a large amount of their resources to SMEs because they believe the development of the SME sector is crucial for economic growth and poverty alleviation and that small entrepreneurs face greater constraints. While this paper does not address the issue of SME impact on economic development, it does provide evidence confirming that indeed, small and medium-sized firms face greater financial, legal, and corruption obstacles compared to large firms, and that the constraining impact of obstacles on firm growth is inversely related to firm size. Our paper also shows that it is the small firms that stand to benefit the most from improvements in financial development and a reduction in corruption.

Appendix

Table AI
Number of Firms in Each Country

	Number of Firms
Albania	85
Argentina	76
Armenia	90
Azerbaijan	66
Belarus	95

(continued)

Table AI—*Continued*

	Number of Firms
Belize	14
Bolivia	61
Brazil	132
Bulgaria	100
Canada	73
Chile	67
China	69
Colombia	77
Costa Rica	49
Croatia	91
Czech Republic	78
Dominican Republic	73
Ecuador	46
El Salvador	48
Estonia	103
France	55
Germany	59
Guatemala	52
Haiti	42
Honduras	46
Hungary	91
Indonesia	67
Italy	54
Kazakhstan	85
Kyrgizstan	62
Lithuania	66
Malaysia	33
Mexico	35
Moldova	78
Nicaragua	51
Pakistan	55
Panama	47
Peru	65
Philippines	84
Poland	169
Portugal	49
Romania	95
Russia	372
Singapore	72
Slovakia	86
Slovenia	101
Spain	64
Sweden	68
Trinidad & Tobago	59
Turkey	112
Ukraine	165
United Kingdom	53
United States	61
Uruguay	55
Venezuela	54

The data source is WBES.

Financial and Legal Constraints to Growth   173

Table AII
Variables and Sources

Variable	Definition	Original Source
GDP	GDP in current U.S. dollars, average 1995–1999	WDI
GDP per capita	Real per capita GDP, average 1995–1999	WDI
Growth	Growth rate of GDP, average 1995–1999	WDI
Inflation rate	Log difference of Consumer Price Index	IFS, line 64
Priv	$\{(0.5) * [F(t)/P\_e(t) + F(t-1)/P\_e(t-1)] / [GDP(t)/ P\_a(t)]\}$, where F is credit by deposit money banks to the private sector (lines 22d), GDP is line 99b, P_e is end-of period CPI (line 64) and P_a is the average CPI for the year.	IFS
Laworder	Measure of the law and order tradition of a country. It is an average over 1995–1997. It ranges from 6, strong law and order tradition, to 1, weak law and order tradition.	ICRG
Corrupt	Measure of corruption in government. It ranges from 1 to 6 and is an average over 1995–1997. Lower scores indicate that "high government officials are likely to demand special payments" and "illegal payments are generally expected throughout lower levels of government" in the form of "bribes connected with import and export licenses, exchange controls, tax assessment, policy protection, or loans."	ICRG
Firm growth	Estimate of the firm's sales growth over the past 3 years.	WBES
Government	Dummy variable that takes on the value 1 if any government agency or state body has a financial stake in the ownership of the firm, 0 otherwise.	WBES
Foreign	Dummy variable that takes on the value 1 if any foreign company or individual has a financial stake in the ownership of the firm, 0 otherwise.	WBES
Exporter	Dummy variable that takes on the value 1 if firm exports, 0 otherwise.	WBES
Subsidized	Dummy variable that takes on value 1 if firm receives subsidies (including tolerance of tax arrears) from local or national government.	WBES
Manufacturing	Dummy variable that takes on the value 1 if firm is in the manufacturing industry, 0 otherwise.	WBES
Services	Dummy variable that takes on the value 1 if firm is in the service industry, 0 otherwise.	WBES
No. of competitors	Regarding your firm's major product line, how many competitors do you face in your market?	WBES
Firm size dummies	A firm is defined as small if it has between 5 and 50 employees, medium-sized if it has between 51 and 500 employees, and large if it has more than 500 employees.	WBES
Size	Logarithm of firm sales	WBES
Financing obstacle	How problematic is financing for the operation and growth of your business: no obstacle (1), a minor obstacle (2), a moderate obstacle (3), or a major obstacle (4)?	WBES

(continued)

174　　　　　　　　　　*The Journal of Finance*

Table AII—*Continued*

Variable	Definition	Original Source
Legal obstacle	How problematic is functioning of the judiciary for the operation and growth of your business: no obstacle (1), a minor obstacle (2), a moderate obstacle (3), or a major obstacle (4)?	WBES
Corruption obstacle	How problematic is corruption for the operation and growth of your business: no obstacle (1), a minor obstacle (2), a moderate obstacle (3), or a major obstacle (4)?	WBES
Collateral requirements	Are collateral requirements of banks/financial institutions no obstacle (1), a minor obstacle (2), a moderate obstacle (3), or a major obstacle (4)?	WBES
Bank paperwork/ bureaucracy	Is bank paperwork/bureaucracy no obstacle (1), a minor obstacle (2), a moderate obstacle (3), or a major obstacle (4)?	WBES
High interest rates	Are high interest rates no obstacle (1), a minor obstacle (2), a moderate obstacle (3), or a major obstacle (4)?	WBES
Need special connections with banks	Is the need of special connections with banks/financial institutions no obstacle (1), a minor obstacle (2), a moderate obstacle (3), or a major obstacle (4)?	WBES
Banks lack money to lend	Is banks' lack of money to lend no obstacle (1), a minor obstacle (2), a moderate obstacle (3), or a major obstacle (4)?	WBES
Access to foreign banks	Is the access to foreign banks no obstacle (1), a minor obstacle (2), a moderate obstacle (3), or a major obstacle (4)?	WBES
Access to nonbank equity	Is the access to nonbank equity/investors/partners no obstacle (1), a minor obstacle (2), a moderate obstacle (3), or a major obstacle (4)?	WBES
Access to export finance	Is the access to specialized export finance no obstacle (1), a minor obstacle (2), a moderate obstacle (3), or a major obstacle (4)?	WBES
Access to financing for leasing equipment	Is the access to lease finance for equipment no obstacle (1), a minor obstacle (2), a moderate obstacle (3), or a major obstacle (4)?	WBES
Inadequate credit/financial information on customers	Is inadequate credit/financial information on customers no obstacle (1), a minor obstacle (2), a moderate obstacle (3), or a major obstacle (4)?	WBES
Access to long-term loans	Is the access to long-term finance no obstacle (1), a minor obstacle (2), a moderate obstacle, (3) or a major obstacle (4)?	WBES
Availability of information on laws and regulations	In general, information on the laws and regulations affecting my firm is easy to obtain: (1) fully agree, (2) agree in most cases, (3) tend to agree, (4) tend to disagree, (5) disagree in most cases, (6) fully disagree.	WBES
Interpretation of laws and regulations are consistent	In general, interpretation of regulations affecting my firm is consistent and predictable: (1) fully agree, (2) agree in most cases, (3) tend to agree, (4) tend to disagree, (5) disagree in most cases, (6) fully disagree.	WBES

(*continued*)

Financial and Legal Constraints to Growth   **175**

Table AII—*Continued*

Variable	Definition	Original Source
Overall quality and efficiency of courts	Overall quality and efficiency of the judiciary/courts: (1) very good, (2) good, (3) slightly good, (4) slightly bad, (5) bad, (6) very bad.	WBES
Courts are fair and impartial	In resolving business disputes, do you believe your country's courts to be fair and impartial: (1) always, (2) usually, (3) frequently, (4) sometimes, (5) seldom, (6) never.	WBES
Courts are quick	In resolving business disputes, do you believe your country's courts to be quick: (1) always, (2) usually, (3) frequently, (4) sometimes, (5) seldom, (6) never.	WBES
Courts are affordable	In resolving business disputes, do you believe your country's courts to be affordable: (1) always, (2) usually, (3) frequently, (4) sometimes, (5) seldom, (6) never.	WBES
Courts are consistent	In resolving business disputes, do you believe your country's courts to be consistent: (1) always, (2) usually, (3) frequently, (4) sometimes, (5) seldom, (6) never.	WBES
Court decisions are enforced	In resolving business disputes, do you believe your country's courts to enforce decisions: (1) always, (2) usually, (3) frequently, (4) sometimes, (5) seldom, (6) never.	WBES
Confidence in legal system to enforce contract and property rights	I am confident that the legal system will uphold my contract and property rights in business disputes: (1) fully agree, (2) agree in most cases, (3) tend to agree, (4) tend to disagree, (5) disagree in most cases, (6) fully disagree.	WBES
Confidence in legal system— 3 years ago	I am confident that the legal system will uphold my contract and property rights in business disputes: 3 years ago: (1) fully agree, (2) agree in most cases, (3) tend to agree, (4) tend to disagree, (5) disagree in most cases, (6) fully disagree.	WBES
Corruption of bank officials	Is the corruption of bank officials: no obstacle (1), a minor obstacle (2), a moderate obstacle (3), or a major obstacle (4)?	WBES
Firms have to make "additional payments" in advance	It is common for firms in my line of business to have to pay some irregular "additional payments" to get things done: (1) always, (2) mostly, (3) frequently, (4) sometimes, (5) seldom, (6) never.	WBES
Firms know the amount of "additional payments" in advance	Firms in my line of business usually know in advance about how much this "additional payment" is: (1) always, (2) mostly, (3) frequently, (4) sometimes, (5) seldom, (6) never.	WBES
If "additional payments" are made, services are delivered	If a firm pays the required "additional payments," the service is usually also delivered as agreed: (1) always, (2) mostly, (3) frequently, (4) sometimes, (5) seldom, (6) never.	WBES

(*continued*)

176   *The Journal of Finance*

Table AII—*Continued*

Variable	Definition	Original Source
It is possible to find honest agents to replace corrupt ones	If a government agent acts against the rules, I can usually go to another official or to his superior and get the correct treatment without recourse to unofficial payments: (1) always, (2) mostly, (3) frequently, (4) sometimes, (5) seldom, (6) never.	WBES
Proportion of revenues paid as bribes	On average, what percentage of revenues do firms like yours typically pay per year in unofficial payments to public officials: (1) 0%, (1) less than 1%, (3) 1–1.99%, (4) 2–9.99%, (5) 10–12%, (6) 13–25%, (7) over 25%.	WBES
Proportion of contract value that must be paid for government contracts	When firms in your industry do business with the government, how much of the contract value must they offer in additional or unofficial payments to secure the contract: (1) 0%, (1) up to 5%, (3) 6–10%, (4) 11–15%, (5) 16–20%, (6) over 20%.	WBES
Management's time (%) spent with officials to understand laws and regulations	What percentage of senior management's time per year is spent in dealing with government officials about the application and interpretation of laws and regulations?	WBES

Sources of data: WDI = World Development Indicators; IFS = International Financial Statistics; ICRG = International Country Risk Guide; WBES = World Business Environment Survey.

REFERENCES

Ball, Ray, S. P. Kothari, and Ashok Robin, 2000, The effect of international institutional factors on properties of accounting earnings, *Journal of Accounting and Economics* 29, 1–51.
Beck, Thorsten, Asli Demirgüç-Kunt, and Ross Levine, 2000, A new database on the structure and development of the financial sector, *World Bank Economic Review* 14, 597–605.
Beck, Thorsten, Asli Demirgüç-Kunt, and Vojislav Maksimovic, 2001a, Financing patterns and constraints: The role of institutions, mimeo, World Bank.
Beck, Thorsten, Asli Demirgüç-Kunt, and Vojislav Maksimovic, 2001b, Financial and legal institutions and firm size, mimeo, World Bank.
Beck, Thorsten, Ross Levine, and Norman Loayza, 2000, Finance and the sources of growth, *Journal of Financial Economics* 58, 261–300.
Carlin, Wendy, and Colin Mayer, 2003, Finance, investment, and growth, *Journal of Financial Economics* 69, 191–226.
Clarke, George, Robert Cull, and Maria Soledad Martinez Peria, 2001, Does foreign bank penetration reduce access to credit in developing countries? Evidence from asking borrowers, mimeo, World Bank.
Demirgüç-Kunt, Asli, and Vojislav Maksimovic, 1998, Law, finance, and firm growth, *Journal of Finance* 53, 2107–2137.
Demirgüç-Kunt, Asli, and Vojislav Maksimovic, 1999, Institutions, financial markets and firm debt maturity, *Journal of Financial Economics* 54, 295–336.
Demirgüç-Kunt, Asli, and Vojislav Maksimovic, 2001, Firms as financial intermediaries: Evidence from trade credit data, World Bank Working paper.
Hung, Mingyi, 2001, Accounting standards and value relevance of financial statements: An international analysis, *Journal of Accounting and Economics* 30, 401–420.

Khanna, Tarun, and Krishna Palepu, 2000, Is group affiliation profitable in emerging markets? An analysis of diversified Indian business groups, *Journal of Finance* 55, 867–891.

King, Robert G., and Ross Levine, 1993, Finance and growth: Schumpeter might be right, *Quarterly Journal of Economics* 108, 717–738.

La Porta, Rafael, Florencio Lopez-de-Silanes, Andrei Shleifer, and Robert W. Vishny, 1998, Law and finance, *Journal of Political Economy* 106, 1113–1155.

Levine, Ross, and Sara Zervos, 1998, Stock markets, banks, and economic growth, *American Economic Review* 88, 537–558.

Love, Inessa, 2001, Financial development and financing constraints: International evidence from the structural investment model, World Bank Working paper No. 2694.

Maksimovic, Vojislav, and Gordon Phillips, 2002, Do conglomerate firms allocate resources inefficiently? Evidence from plant-level data, *Journal of Finance* 57, 721–767

Mauro, Paolo, 1996, The effects of corruption on growth, investment and government expenditure, IMF Working paper 96/98.

Rajan, Raghuram G., Henri Servaes, and Luigi Zingales, 2000, The cost of diversity: The diversification discount and inefficient investment, *Journal of Finance* 55, 35–80.

Rajan, Raghuram G., and Luigi Zingales, 1998a, Financial dependence and growth, *American Economic Review* 88, 559–587.

Rajan, Raghuram G., and Luigi Zingales, 1998b, Which capitalism? Lessons from the East Asian crisis, *Journal of Applied Corporate Finance* 11, 40–48.

Scharfstein, David S., and Jeremy C. Stein, 2000, The dark side of internal capital markets: Divisional rent-seeking and inefficient investment, *Journal of Finance* 55, 2537–2564.

Schiffer, Mirjam, and Beatrice Weder, 2001, Firm size and the business environment: Worldwide survey results, IFC Discussion Paper number 43.

World Bank, 2002, SME. World Bank Froup Review of Small Business Activities. Washington, DC: World Bank.

Wurgler, Jeffrey, 2000, Financial markets and the allocation of capital, *Journal of Financial Economics* 58, 187–214.

[15]

ELSEVIER

Journal of Development Economics
Vol. 68 (2002) 117–135

JOURNAL OF
Development
ECONOMICS

www.elsevier.com/locate/econbase

Growth of firms in developing countries, evidence from Côte d'Ivoire

Leo Sleuwaegen [a,b,*], Micheline Goedhuys [a]

[a]*Catholic University of Leuven, B-3000 Leuven, Belgium*
[b]*Erasmus University Rotterdam, Netherlands*

Received 30 November 1997; accepted 30 June 2001

Abstract

The paper presents evidence in support of a particular growth process of firms that is consistent with a missing middle in the size distribution of manufacturing firms in African countries. Firm growth is explained by size and age effects as a result of efficiency exploiting through scale enlargements and learning, but is strongly moderated by reputation effects and formal legitimation which facilitate access to output markets and resources. Complementing the model with data on growth obstacles as perceived by the owners of firms, medium sized firms are found to be strongly hurt by insufficient access to infrastructure and financial services. © 2002 Elsevier Science B.V. All rights reserved.

JEL classification: D92; L11; O17; O55
Keywords: Size distribution; Firm size; Firm growth; Learning; Legitimation

1. Introduction

In many African countries, even in countries with a comparatively large manufacturing sector, the size structure of firms is highly dualistic, with a small number of large firms producing the largest share of output and a very large number of small firms operating on the fringes of the economy. Micro-enterprises and small firms have insufficiently evolved into more productive formal activity firms, and they seldomly

---

* Corresponding author. Faculty of Economic and Applied Economic Science, Catholic University of Leuven, Naamsestraat 69, B-3000 Leuven, Belgium. Tel.: +32-16-32-69-13; fax: +32-16-32-67-32.
E-mail address: Leo.Sleuwaegen@econ.kuleuven.ac.be (L. Sleuwaegen).

118   L. Sleuwaegen, M. Goedhuys / Journal of Development Economics 68 (2002) 117–135

graduate into larger-scale operations, thereby sustaining the 'missing middle' in the size distribution of firms (Biggs and Oppenheim, 1986). For Côte d'Ivoire, it was estimated that 74% of employment in manufacturing takes place in firms with less than 10 employees, 4% in firms employing between 10 and 99 employees, while large firms account for 22% of employment in manufacturing.[1] This bi-modal distribution also appears in many other African countries, as illustrated in Tybout (2000).

This paper addresses the issue of the 'missing middle' by focusing on the industrial structure and growth of manufacturing firms in Côte d'Ivoire. As in many African countries, Côte d'Ivoire's size distribution of firms was largely shaped in its early post-independence period, when the development of a solid and modern industrial base was expected to come from large-scale investments by the state and foreign investors. In the last decade, the focus of attention shifted towards the mass of small-scale enterprises at the other edge of the size distribution. After more than a decade of structural adjustment, intending to remove barriers to the development of these smaller firms, the industrial structure is still bimodal.[2]

Existing theories on firm growth fail to explain firm dynamics that underlie the observed industrial structure in developing countries. They do not sufficiently take into account the institutional features of poorly developed markets and the high transaction costs involved in doing business and in securing the necessary inputs. The purpose of this paper is to explicitly consider these institutional elements in testing an empirical model of firm growth using data of manufacturing firms in Côte d'Ivoire. To further test the validity of the analysis, the results of the empirical model are contrasted with survey data on actual growth barriers as they are perceived by owners and managers of the firms.

The paper is organised as follows. Section 2 reviews the existing literature on firm size and growth and examines how institutional factors affect the growth process of firms in developing countries. After presenting the data in Section 3, an empirical model is proposed in Section 4 and tested against data on manufacturing firms in Côte d'Ivoire. Corroborating insights on the obstacles to firm development are derived from analysing the owners' and managers' perception in Section 5. Section 6 concludes.

2. Models of firm growth

Research on the size distributions of firms and the underlying firm dynamics commonly starts from Gibrat's (1931) law of proportionate effect (LPE). According to this law, firms grow each year following a random drawing from a distribution of growth rates. Stochastic

---

[1] Estimates are on the basis of data of the Ministry of Employment and Service, the ILO 1992 yearbook and the 1993 Census of the 'National Institute of Statistics' (INS).

[2] Data from the 1993 Census, the most complete list of formally registered firms, show that there is indeed a relative overrepresentation of firms in the largest and in the smallest size categories. Coverage of the manufacturing sector is extensive but not complete, especially for the smaller firm categories. A Shapiro–Wilk test on employment data rejected at the 5% confidence level the null-hypothesis that the size of firms is log-normally distributed. Taking into account that smaller firms are less completely represented, it can be assumed that the actual bimodal shape is even more pronounced.

L. Sleuwaegen, M. Goedhuys / Journal of Development Economics 68 (2002) 117–135   119

growth models including a whole generation of growth models based on weaker assumptions of the LPE generate skewed distributions (log-normal, Pareto, Yule) which fit the observed size distributions of firms in Western economies strikingly well (Ijiri and Simon, 1964).

In spite of the apparent power of Gibrat's law, an increasing number of empirical studies find evidence that goes against it. Most studies find a significant negative relationship between firm growth and firm size (Mansfield, 1962; Evans, 1987a; Kumar, 1985; Dunne and Hughes, 1994; McPherson, 1996; Das, 1995; for developing countries) and between firm growth and firm age (Evans, 1987a; Dunne and Hughes, 1994).

The negative age-growth and size-growth relationship is consistent with models of learning, which argue that the size distribution of firms is determined by the underlying distribution of managerial abilities within the population (Lucas, 1978). Jovanovic (1982) claims that, once firms are established in the industry, they learn about their efficiency. The process of competition forces the least efficient firms to exit and allows more efficient managers to learn about their efficiency and to adjust their scale of operations accordingly. Hence, young and small firms, which are in the initial process of uncovering their own efficiency level, grow faster and their growth rates are more volatile. According to Pakes and Ericson (1990), managers not only uncover their (fixed) level of efficiency through learning, they are also able to increase this level of efficiency in an active learning process through human capital formation.

However, the observed growth determinants do not explain the emergence of the dual market structure that is observed in many LDCs. If smaller firms are found to grow significantly faster than larger firms, a bimodal shape disappears automatically as successful small firms move up to the middle of the size distribution. Models of learning assume that competition among firms in an industry selects the more efficient firms into the industry, forcing inefficient firms to exit. In many LDCs, however, competition fails to operate as a selection mechanism, because of high sunk entry costs and a too low number of market participants. High transaction costs hamper the well functioning of markets (Tybout, 2000). Nugent and Nabli (1989, 1992) and Nugent (1996) argue that due to the existence of transaction and information costs in input markets, mainly credit and equity markets, the actual size distribution of firms can deviate from the 'natural' distribution which would emerge from exogenous factors like technology, market size, transport costs. In a similar vein, Tybout (2000) comments on several intertwining factors that may render the growth process of firms different from the one observed for industrialised countries, and account for the bimodal size distribution typical for many African countries. Among these factors, the lacking of a supportive institutional system for small and mid sized firms and the bias against small firms in industrial promotion policies and regulations show up as crucial elements.

An interesting parallel to these phenomena is found in the 'Organisational Ecology' theories focusing on the emergence of new industries, where it is argued that selection of organisations depends also on the degree of legitimation organisations enjoy within their environment. Legitimation refers to the social acceptance of an organisational form (Hannan et al., 1990; Hannan and Carroll, 1992). Lacking clear signals from market forces, reputation and legitimacy become important growth driving factors as they reduce transaction and information costs involved in dealing with a firm.

120   *L. Sleuwaegen, M. Goedhuys / Journal of Development Economics 68 (2002) 117–135*

Reputation and legitimacy are acquired through formal registration of a firm and its initial size. Registered firms enjoy the benefits of access to the legal system, to the formal banking sector and publicly administered employee benefits, instruments that are found to foster growth (Levensohn and Maloney 1997). Registration provides firms with an institutional standing in the eyes of law-enforcing agencies, consumers, suppliers, police and other key actors and facilitate contractual relationships with clients and suppliers and third parties. Formal firms are not only better positioned in output markets; they can also gain better access to scarce resources. In developing economies where both product and input markets are characterised by severe imperfections, firms compete heavily for inputs. Restricted access to a wide range of resources is typically experienced by managers and owners of firms as an important growth constraining factor. The lack of credit, management and skilled labour, the lack of access to industrial sites with suitable infrastructure facilities, regulatory constraints, the various kinds of taxes, price regimes, the lack of materials and spare parts are frequently mentioned to be among the growth hampering factors (see Section 5). Therefore, while formal registration may be a systematic choice for the more efficient and larger firms, the formal status may in itself act as a signalling mechanism, granting legitimacy and opening up additional growth opportunities.

With these processes at work, the growth of small firms will be lower than observed for industrialised countries and few small firms will make the transition into mid-range size classes where they are most vulnerable to the regulatory system. Firms that start large, on the other hand, will benefit from the system and, in spite that they may quickly attain the minimal efficient scale of operations, continue to grow at a rate that is higher than the one observed for industrialised countries. Levensohn and Maloney (1997) found indeed that payoffs of formality increase with the scale of operations. Due to the tax burden, higher labour costs and difficult licensing policy, small firms remain informal and avoid taxes and regulation, while large firms are influential enough to obtain special treatment (Gauthier and Gersovitz, 1997; Rauch, 1991). Moreover, if entry costs are high, especially entry into the formal sector, there is no guarantee that efficiency would converge to the best level, but substantial efficiency variation across firms may persist over time. This may further reinforce the skewed distribution in the formal sector with the most efficient firms growing faster and obtaining market shares that rise with the level of entry costs (Hopenhayn, 1992).

Following the foregoing arguments, we specify and test a model that hypothesises that the growth of firms in Côte d'Ivoire manufacturing follows a learning process that is strongly moderated by the particular environmental and institutional context of a developing country. More in particular, we hypothesise that, in the absence of well functioning markets, initial firm size and formal registration together with persisting efficiency differences strongly affect the firms' growth performance. As demand density and the availability of resources vary strongly with location, ownership and sector of activity in developing countries, these structural features are hypothesised to exert a further impact on the growth opportunities of firms (Tybout, 2000). Under the hypothesised growth process, few small firms will grow into a large size class and a bimodal firm size distribution in manufacturing will emerge.

L. Sleuwaegen, M. Goedhuys / Journal of Development Economics 68 (2002) 117–135   121

The proposed hypotheses will be tested against data on a heterogeneous group of firms, composed of firms of different startup size, age, formal status, technology and based in different regions of the country. The results of the empirical model are further interpreted against survey evidence on the managers' perception of growth obstacles, covering the same group of firms.

3. Data

The empirical analysis uses a unique data set covering the growth of a representative sample of Ivorian manufacturing firms. The data are obtained from a survey conducted in 1995 and 1996 in the framework of the World Bank project RPED (Regional Program on Enterprise Development in Africa). The data set includes 185 manufacturing firms for which historical data on sales, employment and other structural variables are available. The firms are active in one of the four main industrial sectors: agro-industries, textiles, wood working and metal working. Both formally registered and informal firms are included.

In line with other studies (McPherson and Liedholm, 1996; Mead and Morrisson, 1996), firms are defined as 'formal' if they are registered, fulfil all tax obligations and respect labour and other regulations. Following this definition, the formal firms were selected from the 1993 Census of the 'National Institute of Statistics' (INS) a census compiled from data of the 'Banque de Données Financières' (BDF) and the corporate tax authorities (DGI). It reports data of 4464 modern firms, i.e. firms with normal or simplified accounting records. These firms respect all fiscal obligations, including VAT, company taxes and business license taxes at local and national level. They have full access to all business support services organised by state agencies.

Table 1
Composition of the sample and size of the firms in terms of employment in 1995

	Number of firms	Average size	Standard deviation
All firms	185	144.4	433.3
By startup year			
1918–1969	35	327.4	341.3
1970–1979	45	265.7	784.8
1980–1986	48	47.1	74.2
1987–1995	57	18.3	21.9
By sector			
Agro-industries	48	227.6	705.4
Textiles	45	153.0	424.3
Wood working	46	130.9	226.1
Metal working	46	62.8	79.1
By formal status			
Formal	125	210.4	514.7
Semi-formal	22	12.2	18.7
Informal	38	3.8	4.6

The group of informal firms on the other hand pays at most local business license tax (*patente*). None of the informal firms have access to official business support services and training programs. A third and relatively small group of firms defines itself as semi-formal. The firms do not keep full records but nevertheless pay some taxes on turnover.

Foreign participation in industry is very important in Côte d'Ivoire as a result of former open-door policies that were aimed at stimulating foreign investment and attracting labour. Over the period 1980–1991, foreign ownership accounted for an average of 78% of total equity of private firms reporting to the BDF (World Bank, 1994). Extensive foreign ownership also characterises the sample firms. Most industrial activity is located in the industrial core region of Abidjan. A majority of the sample firms is also located there. Both managerially run and entrepreneurial[3] firms are included in the sample (Table 1).

4. Empirical model

Following previous work (Evans, 1987a), the basic empirical model follows a general growth function *g* in size and age:

$$G = \frac{S_{t'}}{S_t} = g(S_t, A_t) \tag{1}$$

where $S_{t'}$ and S_t are the size of a firm in period t' and in period t, respectively, and A_t is the age of the firm in period t. In accordance with the arguments proposed in Section 2, this functional relationship is further moderated through a set of institutional and firm specific variables X which interact with the basic function in the following way:

$$G = g(S_t, A_t) e^{bx} \tag{2}$$

Approximating the growth function *g* through a second order logarithmic expansion of a generalised function relating growth to size and age, the estimating equation corresponds to the following form:

$$\frac{\log(S_{t'}) - \log(S_t)}{d} = a_0 + a_1 \log(S_t) + a_2 \left[\log(S_t)\right]^2 + a_3 \log(A_t)$$

$$+ a_4 \left[\log(A_t)\right]^2 + a_5 \log(S_t) \times \log(A_t) + \sum_{i=1}^{n} b_i X_i \tag{3}$$

where *d* stands for the number of years over which growth is measured and *a* and *b* are coefficient vectors. The dependent variable in Eq. (3) corresponds to an average annual growth rate.

---

[3] A firm is defined as 'entrepreneurial' if the firm is owned by one or several individuals, who at the same time manage and control the firm.

The partial derivatives $g_s=(\mathrm{d}\ln G/\mathrm{d}\ln S)$ and $g_a=(\mathrm{d}\ln G/\mathrm{d}\ln A)$ allow to test for alternative theories of firm growth (Evans, 1987a,b). Gibrat's law implies that the partial derivative g_s equals zero. Alternatively, learning models of firm growth and efficient scale arguments imply $g_s<0$ and $g_a<0$.

4.1. Variables

The dependent variable is the average annual growth rate of employment and, alternatively, sales calculated over the entire period of a firm's existence from startup to 1994. The analysis is also performed analysing growth over a homogenous shorter period, from 1989 until 1994.

Following the proposed estimating equation, the set of explanatory variables includes initial firm size (SIZE) and firm age (AGE) as basic determinants of firm growth. Size is measured alternatively as deflated sales and employment, at startup or in the beginning of the period under consideration.

As moderating factors, and in contrast to some of the earlier work on industrialised countries, we do not assume that firms automatically converge to the same efficiency level, but, in the absence of strong market selection, efficiency differences may persist for a significant time period. The variable INEFF, measuring firm inefficiency, is to assess to what extent less efficient firm grow more slowly over time. This measure is derived from the estimation of a stochastic frontier production function at the sector level[4] (Goedhuys, 1999). The variable measures the distance of an individual firm's output level from its best practice output level. Average technical efficiency of our sample of firms is 0.47, indicating that on average only 47% of the output that would be attained under efficient production is actually produced. A negative effect of the variable INEFF on growth is expected.

In addition to age and size, a firm's reputation and legitimacy in the industry is explicitly accounted for by the variable FORMAL. The variable takes the value one for formally registered firms, and takes the value zero for informal and semi-formal firms.

Other moderators of the growth relationship include the sector to which the firm belongs and its location. Three binary variables account for possible different growth performance in the textiles, woodworking and metalworking industries (TEXTILES, WOOD, METAL), the reference sector being agro-industries. From interviews, it is clear that owners and managers consider the geographical location as important for the availability of resources. The availability of industrial sites, infrastructure, and access to raw materials and skilled labour were mentioned as the main location determinants by 80% of the firms. Only 8% of all firms choose their location with the intention to be close to clients or competitors. The largest market and the largest supply of resources is in Abidjan. Firms located in Abidjan are also more likely to engage in networking and subcontracting, thereby exploiting additional growth opportunities. A binary variable

---

[4] The estimated stochastic frontier production function takes the form $y_i=f(x_i,b)\exp(v_i-u_i)$ as introduced first by Aigner et al. (1977) and Meeusen and Van Den Broeck (1977). The value of the variable INEFF used in the analysis here corresponds to the value of u_i, the estimated inefficiency term of the individual firm i.

124   *L. Sleuwaegen, M. Goedhuys / Journal of Development Economics 68 (2002) 117–135*

(NABIDJAN) is included to capture the effect of being located outside the industrial core region of Abidjan.

In addition to the sectoral and locational impact, a firm specific measure of capital and related services is included to capture the extent to which firms need and have access to a wide range of resources, including capital and basic services (CAPITAL INTENSITY). Firms that are to some extent deprived from these inputs are expected to grow less. Capital intensity is measured as the share of the cost of electricity, water, fuel and telephone in total sales. In the sales growth regression, the cost of electricity, water, fuel and telephone per employee is used as an alternative to minimise spurious correlation.

Capital and technology sourcing from abroad is taken into account by making a distinction following the origin of capital: non-Ivorian African, European or Asian direct investment (AFRICAN, EUROPEAN, ASIAN). Foreign firms in Côte d'Ivoire are indeed found to import significantly more than their domestic counterparts (Harrison, 1996).

4.2. Estimation and results

To account for endogeneity of the variable FORMAL, the model is estimated with a two-stage least-squares procedure as proposed by Barnow et al. (1981). In doing so, we explicitly take into account sectoral variations and find support that firms run by professional managers as well as the more efficient, larger and older firms choose to be formally registered (consistent with the theoretical model of Rauch, 1991). The results of the probit equation explaining the probability that a firm is formally registered, are presented in Table 2.

Table 3 shows the estimated coefficients and standard errors for the growth regressions. The first two columns present the results for employment growth over the two different

Table 2
Results of the probit estimation that a firm is formally registered

	Coefficients	Standard errors
AGE	0.858**	0.381
SIZE	1.105***	0.324
TEXTILES	− 1.158*	0.662
WOOD	0.227	0.686
METAL	2.924**	1.250
INEFF	− 1.310**	0.568
ENTRFIRM	− 1.309*	0.752
HIGHEDUC	1.066	0.819
Constant	− 1.058	1.106
McFadden's R^2	0.742	
No. of observations	129	

ENTRFIRM equals one if the firm is an entrepreneurial firm, i.e. is owned by one or more individuals who at the same time manage the firm; HIGHEDUC equals one if the entrepreneur has received higher formal education of academic or equivalent level. Other explanatory variables as defined in the text.

   * Significant at the 0.10% level.
   ** Significant at the 0.05% level.
   *** Significant at the 0.01% level.

L. Sleuwaegen, M. Goedhuys / Journal of Development Economics 68 (2002) 117–135　　　125

Table 3
Regression results for employment and sales growth over the period startup-1994 and 1989–1994

	Employment growth		Sales growth	
	Startup-1994	1989–1994	Startup-1994	1989–1994
AGE	− 0.157***	− 0.146***	− 0.116*	− 0.116**
	(0.050)	(0.050)	(0.062)	(0.049)
SIZE	− 0.199*	− 0.185**	− 0.226***	− 0.233***
	(0.107)	(0.073)	(0.057)	(0.053)
SIZE^2	0.006	0.007	0.004	0.009**
	(0.006)	(0.006)	(0.004)	(0.004)
AGE*SIZE	0.041**	0.031***	0.038***	0.027***
	(0.019)	(0.010)	(0.012)	(0.010)
CAPITAL	0.183*	0.185**	0.020**	0.020**
INTENSITY	(0.108)	(0.081)	(0.009)	(0.009)
FORMAL	0.258	0.300**	0.534*	0.659***
	(0.220)	(0.123)	(0.276)	(0.229)
NABIDJAN	− 0.075	− 0.101**	− 0.218***	− 0.182***
	(0.065)	(0.046)	(0.075)	(0.064)
INEFF	− 0.002	− 0.006	− 0.008	− 0.010*
	(0.002)	(0.004)	(0.005)	(0.006)
AFRICAN	0.078	0.136*	0.022	0.051
	(0.067)	(0.082)	(0.084)	(0.089)
EUROPEAN	0.036	0.038	− 0.072	− 0.013
	(0.064)	(0.046)	(0.072)	(0.063)
ASIAN	− 0.063	− 0.049	− 0.060	− 0.019
	(0.071)	(0.050)	(0.102)	(0.079)
TEXTILES	0.133*	0.086	− 0.028	− 0.031
	(0.069)	(0.056)	(0.076)	(0.063)
WOOD	0.049	0.045	0.105*	0.101*
	(0.047)	(0.046)	(0.060)	(0.057)
METAL	0.076*	0.066*	0.056	− 0.017
	(0.040)	(0.035)	(0.077)	(0.054)
Constant	0.374***	0.329***	0.182	0.070
	(0.131)	(0.122)	(0.129)	(0.112)
N	107	129	66	107
R-Adj.	0.372	0.397	0.448	0.357

Standard errors (in parentheses) are estimated using White's consistent estimator (White, 1980).
　*　Significant at the 0.10% level.
　**　Significant at the 0.05% level.
　***　Significant at the 0.01% level.

periods, startup-1994 and 1989–1994. The last two columns present the sales growth regressions. In estimating the age effect, the restriction of fixing the coefficient of squared age to zero could not be rejected in any of the estimated equations. Hence, the restricted model is presented here.

Learning effects seem to be at work as suggested by Jovanovic's learning models. Younger firms seem to grow faster than older ones, as indicated by the negative and significant coefficient of the variable AGE. Learning is apparently a strong factor driving growth in a firm's initial years of operation. Evaluated at the sample means, the partial derivative of employment growth with respect to log (age) equals -0.06 from startup until 1994 and -0.04 over the period 1989–1994.

The negative relationship between growth and age does not hold for firms that start at a large scale. These findings suggest that startup size has an important effect on the subsequent growth performance of firms. Firms starting at a larger size, i.e. about 45 employees or more, tend to regress less fast in growth rate as they grow older. This means that firms that start small tend to grow fast in the initial years but the growth rate flattens out rapidly. Larger entrants on the contrary enjoy a better reputation from the start and face growth opportunities that improve over time despite that they quickly attain an efficient scale of operations, an effect that dampens their need to grow.

The relationship between initial size and employment growth is indeed significantly negative, implying that smaller firms grow faster than larger ones. The results are robust and hold over the different periods and samples of firms for which growth is measured.[5] They are consistent with studies conducted in other countries. The partial derivatives of the growth rate with respect to log size evaluated at the sample mean are negative. They equal -0.08 for the growth regression from startup until 1994 and -0.06 for growth over the period 1989–1994. The elasticity of end-of-period size with respect to beginning-of-period size is 0.73 for the period 1989–1994. The results go against Gibrat's law of random growth behaviour.[6]

Only surviving firms are included in the data set, which may imply a certain bias in the results. As failure is more common among smaller firms, the selection bias could affect the estimated firm size–growth relationship. McPherson (1996) analyses the possible selection bias resulting from the exclusion of exiting firms on the size–growth relationship in five southern African countries and finds this bias to be insignificant. In a similar way, Evans (1987a,b), Doms et al. (1995) and Audretsch (1995) find a significant relationship between firm growth and size, controlling for exit of firms. Relative to our particular sample, some of the possible selection bias could be mildered by restricting the analysis to the largest firms in the sample. Controlling for age, Fig. 1 plots the differential between actual firm size in 1994 and hypothetical size in 1994 for growth independent of size, against start size. It shows that firms that started at a smaller scale have actually grown into a larger than their hypothetical size while the opposite holds for firms that started at a larger scale. This implies that the actual growth rate of firms starting small is relatively larger and corroborates the estimated negative size–growth relationship.

The results of the growth equations also show that efficiency differences across firms are related to growth differences. Firms with higher levels of efficiency tend to grow faster as indicated by the coefficient of INEFF. This finding is in line with models of learning which predict that, through a process of competition firms adjust their size and grow into the size that is associated to their true efficiency level. But this finding also supports the

---

[5] Historical sales and employment data were not consistently available for all firms. In order to use the maximum information available from the data set, the size of the sample may therefore differ across estimating models. Running the different models on different subsamples and on the reduced sample of firms for which all information about employment and sales growth was consistently available, did not produce any different results.

[6] The elasticity of end-of-period size with respect to beginning-of-period size is $E_S = 1 + dg_s$, while the elasticity of end-of-period size with respect to age is $E_A = dg_a$.

L. Sleuwaegen, M. Goedhuys / Journal of Development Economics 68 (2002) 117–135   127

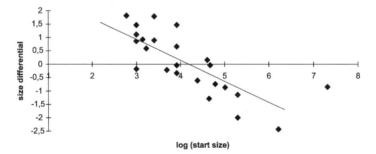

Fig. 1. Size differentials for the largest firms in the sample. Note: size differential = (actual firm size in 1994) − (estimated firm size in 1994 under the hypothesis of growth independent of start size, controlling for age). To estimate the hypothetical size, firms are regrouped into age cohorts. For each age cohort, the average compound growth rate is calculated. The hypothetical size in 1994 is estimated by applying this growth rate to the respective firm's initial size over the period of existence.

hypothesis that substantial efficiency variation in growth performance goes together with the existence of strong entry barriers.

In line with our main hypothesis, transactional advantages operate favourably for the growth of formally registered firms, as indicated by the coefficient of the instrumented variable FORMAL. This implies that, controlling for efficiency, size and age of firms, the formal status has an additional effect on the growth of the firm. The formal character of a firm increases its estimated annual growth rate over the entire period since startup by 0.26. For the period 1989–1994, the formal status increases the expected annual growth rate with 0.30.

Corroborating these findings, capital intensive firms, i.e. firms with more intensive use of electricity, fuel, water and telephone, grow significantly faster. This supports the hypothesis that access to a wider range of resources works positively on firm growth. Although small labour intensive firms realise strong growth rates in the beginning stages of their growth path, this growth moderates very rapidly towards a lower or zero level as these firms reach the size where economies of scale are fully exploited. Firms that are able to apply a more capital intensive technology and use related services more intensively can reap additional scale economies and grow larger.

Geographical location also has an impact on firm growth. The better supplied Abidjan region seems more conductive to firm development than other regions in the country. External scale economies and urbanisation economies that reduce competition for resources seem to account for these differences in growth performances. The presumed effects of foreign ownership, offering firms the opportunity of sourcing abroad, are not significant.

The estimation of the sales growth equation produces comparable results. The negative age-growth and size-growth relationship seems robust. Evaluated at the sample means, the partial derivatives of growth with respect to size and age equal − 0.11 and 0.05, respectively, for the entire period since startup and − 0.07 and 0.03 for the 5-year growth period. The interaction term between size and age is again positive and significant, and implies that the size at which the age effect turns positive is nearly half the average initial size at which growth is measured.[7] Firms located in Abidjan, that are formal and are capital intensive again seem to grow significantly faster. Sectoral effects also do not produce clear variations in the growth performance of firms.

4.3. Comparison with other studies

The results from other studies of firm growth in developing countries, though taking a different perspective, are consistent with our results (e.g. Mc Pherson, 1996; Goedhuys and Sleuwaegen, 1999, for various other African countries), or shed additional light on certain aspects our findings. Analysing firm growth in an infant industry in India, Das (1995) found a positive age–growth relationship, which he interpreted to imply that for infant industries reputation building over time and learning is decisive for entrepreneurial success. Since the Indian economy is also characterised by a 'missing middle', the author grants support for our hypothesis that reputation effects may be a critical explanation for the bifurcation of the size distribution of firms in emerging economies. Evidence that micro-enterprises and small firms are in a disadvantaged position in gaining access to inputs, is provided by Mead and Liedholm (1998) for several African and Caribbean countries and by McCormick et al. (1997) for Nairobi's small and medium sized garment producers. The latter study also stresses the need to include social variables in the formal analysis of firm growth. For Indonesia, the liberalisation of markets, including primarily capital markets, appears to have made the transition towards a larger size a more continuous process (Aswicahyono et al., 1996).[8]

Equally interesting is to compare our results with those obtained for industrialised countries. While formal status should not be a real issue, Storey (1994) nonetheless reports that the legal status of the firm and the form of incorporation exert an important impact on the financing and growth of firms in the UK.

In reviewing the empirical studies on firm growth in industrialised countries, Sutton (1997, p. 46) reports that for any given size of firm, 'the proportional rate of growth is smaller according as the firm is older, but its probability of survival is greater'. As to size effects, across a broad spectrum of analyses (Hall, 1987; Dunne et al., 1988, 1989; Audretsch, 1995; Wagner, 1992; Cabral, 1995; Mata et al., 1995), the observed growth rates tend also to be negatively related to initial size, but weakens or disappears for larger firms, suggesting that Gibrat's law would hold if firms can start or attain the minimum efficient scale of output (Geroski, 1995; Hart and Oulton, 1996a,b).

To further illustrate the difference in growth regime of firms in a developed country versus the one observed for firms in a developing country such as Côte d'Ivoire, one particular source of data on entry and growth of German firms allows us to make a relevant and direct comparison with our results. The data set of ZEW-Foundation Panel West of

---

[7] Sales approximating 27 millions F.CFA. and 76 millions F.CFA. at start and in 1989, respectively.

[8] Introduction of market forces through liberalisation has enhanced a steady growth of medium sized firms (100–499 employees), mainly at the expense of larger units (500 or more employees). Smaller firms (20–99 employees) have revealed a great deal of dynamism over the period 1975–1991.

L. Sleuwaegen, M. Goedhuys / Journal of Development Economics 68 (2002) 117–135   129

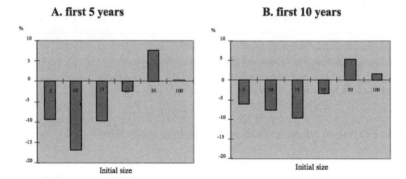

Fig. 2. Growth differential following initial size (average growth of Ivorian firms minus average growth of German firms).

German firms, based on CREDITRFORM data, contains extensive information on new startups in manufacturing between 1989 and 1997.[9] A comparison of both data sets reveals a strong difference between Côte d'Ivoire and Germany in growth performance according to initial size and the chances of smallest firms to grow into a large size.

In particular, the data reveal that for firms with over 100 employees at the end of the period, 28% started as a micro-enterprise (1–4 employees) and 32% as a small firm (5–49 employees). This contrasts strongly with the data for Côte d'Ivoire where very few of the firms with more than 100 employees started at a size below 15 employees.

Moreover, the German firms' transition into a larger size takes place in a relatively short period of existence, as firms in the German panel are a maximum of 10 years old. In Côte d'Ivoire, on the contrary, the large firms are all relatively old firms; the average age is 29 years, with none of the firms younger than 5 years old and only one firm of less than 10 years of age.

The importance of a large initial size for the growth of firms in Côte d'Ivoire shows up most clearly in Fig. 2.

Fig. 2A shows the difference in average growth rates between Ivorian and German firms for the first 5 years, respectively, 10 years, for firms with an initial size of 5, 10, 15, 25, 50 and 100 employees.[10] Smaller firms grow relatively faster in Germany than in Côte d'Ivoire. Interestingly, the opposite is observed for firms of 50 employees and more. This

---

[9] Georg Licht and Dirk Engel of the Centre for European Economic Research kindly provided this information.

[10] For Côte d'Ivoire, growth is based on 1989–1994 employment growth rates, conform to the model presented in Secton 2. The German growth rates are taken from Harhoff et al. (1998) and are derived from a model with exactly the same structure as presented in this paper. The growth rates cover manufacturing firms for the same period and are based on the CREDITREFORM data set. CREDITREFORM is the largest German credit rating agency with a comprehensive database of German firms. Almost all firms, which are registered in the trade register, enter CREDITREFORM's database.

implies that, in comparison to German firms, smaller firms grow slowly into a larger size while larger firms grow relatively faster, a finding that is consistent with the missing middle in the firm size distribution.

In order to relate our findings to the hypothesised growth barriers, the following section relates the growth obstacles, as perceived by the owners and managers of the firms, to the underlying characteristics of the firms.

5. Obstacles to growth: the owners' and managers' perceptions

In the RPED survey, the interviewed person, the manager or owner of the firm was presented a list of 17 factors and was asked to report whether these factors are an obstacle to the growth of the firm. The answers to the questions are the respondents' subjective and personal view and are a reflection of the growth constraints experienced in more recent years. Table 4 shows the list of growth hampering factors and their associated severity according to the percentage of respondents that see it as an obstacle. The ranking differs strikingly from similar survey results for industrialised countries. For instance, in the study by Kamshad and Hay (1995), which is most comparable to our analysis, intensity of competition is ranked by far the most important constraint to the growth of small and medium sized firms in the UK. Financial constraints and resource availability appear as much less important growth hampering factors, while infrastructure and the provision of utilities do not appear at all. The list of growth barriers for Ivorian firms illustrates the distorting role of government intervention and the strong competition for resources in developing countries,[11] a process in which small and medium sized firms find themselves in a disadvantaged position compared to larger firms (see also Fafchamp, 1994).

The growth analysis pointed to differences in growth as being explained by a firm's initial size and their formal status and implied a serious slow down in growth for firms in the medium size range. To analyse to what extent the respondent's perceived growth obstacles align with this growth process, the more severe growth barriers are regrouped into four different types of obstacles: (a) *regulatory barriers* including taxes, corruption practices or problems related to obtaining investment benefits, (b) *market constraints* arising from insufficient demand or competition of imports, (c) *infrastructure* including a lack of business support services and the deficient provision and pricing of public utilities, and (d) *financial constraints* including primarily the availability of credit.

Table 5 shows the proportion of owners and managers which report that the growth of their firm suffers from fore-mentioned types of obstacles for firms that are classified

---

[11] Evidence that capital constraints, deficient infrastructure and regulatory problems with the obtention of licences and permits are common in third world countries is abundantly available. Rondinelli and Kasarda (1992) describe these problems for small enterprises in Indonesia, Kenya, the Philippines, Colombia, Peru and other countries. From the RPED survey conducted in Burundi, Tanzania, Kenya, Cameroun, Ghana, Zambia and Zimbabwe it is clear that a lack of credit is the most frequently mentioned growth barrier, generally followed by deficient infrastructure and business support services and insufficient demand.

L. Sleuwaegen, M. Goedhuys / Journal of Development Economics 68 (2002) 117–135   131

Table 4
Obstacles to growth, the perception of the owners or managers

Obstacle	No obstacle	Obstacle	Severe obstacle
(1) Taxes	58	45	26
(2) Lack of credit	59	26	34
(3) Lack of demand	69	33	27
(4) Lack of business support services	72	35	22
(5) Corruption	85	18	26
(6) Price public services	88	33	8
(7) Problems obtaining investment benefits	93	19	17
(8) Competition of illegal imports	96	16	17
(9) Lack of infrastructure	104	18	7
(10) Regulations on activities	107	14	8
(11) Labour regulations	107	19	3
(12) Competition of legal imports	113	9	7
(13) Problems obtaining licenses	119	6	4
(14) Price controls	121	6	2
(15) Regulation on location	122	5	2
(16) Regulation on equity capital	125	2	2
(17) Foreign exchange controls	128	1	0
Number of observations : 129			

Numbers of respondents, out of a total of 129, reporting (. . .) as no obstacle, obstacle or severe obstacle.

according to their size in 1994, measured by employment.[12] A χ^2-test formally tests whether the incidence of reporting the respective growth obstacle is related to the size of the firm.

The results strongly support the hypothesis that firm growth obstacles vary systematically with the size of the firm, with small and medium sized firms appearing as most constrained (χ^2-test rejects independence from size at 1% significance level for all barriers). Large firms, exceeding 250 employees, and micro-enterprises (1–4 employees) less frequently report to have experienced growth constraining factors.

For firms of over 250 employees, a lack of credit appears to be least constraining. This stresses the strong position of large firms in financial markets and is in line with the arguments developed above, that reputation effects operate favourably for larger firms. A similar pattern can be observed for infrastructure,[13] in line with the argument that large firms often develop their own substitute services when public infrastructure proves unsatisfactory, or they may enjoy a priority status with government officials regarding the provision and distribution of support services and utilities (Tybout, 2000). Regulation in general is strongly hampering the growth of small and medium sized firms. Market constraints show up as less severe for micro and small firms which are most often focusing on serving niches in the local market.

---

[12] The sample therefore corresponds to the sample used for the employment growth equation from 1989 until 1994, being the largest sample for which data are available.

[13] These results are in line with the findings of McCormick et al. (1997) that it is especially the growing small firms in the garment sector in Kenya that face difficulties in raising additional funds and finding suitable secure premises to expand further.

Table 5
Proportion of firms reporting the respective growth obstacle, by size class in 1989

Employment	1–4 employees	5–99 employees	100–249 employees	250+ employees	Value
Financial constraints	35 (35)	66 (86)	71	29	15.158
Market conditions	35 (35)	59 (100)	82	67	10.637
Infrastructure	35 (35)	66 (71)	71	33	13.287
Regulation	42 (45)	75 (43)	71	62	9.356

In parentheses, the proportion of informal firms reporting to perceive the respective factor as a growth constraint.

To assess whether there are marked differences between formal and informal firms, within the micro and small size classes, the proportion of informal firms reporting the respective obstacle is given in parentheses in Table 5. The proportion of informal small firms is significantly higher for market conditions and lower for regulation (χ^2 significant at the 5% level). Also in line with expectations, financial constraints form more an obstacle for informal firms, once they attain a larger size.

In summary, the results with respect to the perceived obstacles to growth illustrate the vulnerable position of mid-sized firms and provides corroborating evidence for the theoretical framework and empirical growth model presented in the previous sections. The size dependence of the constraining factors fits well with the asymmetric growth process observed for manufacturing firms in Côte d'Ivoire.

6. Summary and conclusions

This paper presents empirical support for the proposition that the bimodal size structure of manufacturing firms observed in Côte d'Ivoire, as well as in many other African countries, is consistent with a complex growth process of firms competing for resources. Within the growth process, legitimation and reputation effects interact with dynamic learning of firms in imperfect input and output markets.

The empirical model revealed a negative relationship between a firm's growth, its age and its size, consistent with efficiency maximisation through learning. However, in comparison to the growth process of firms in Western economies, small firms grow relatively slower and larger firms grow relatively faster in Côte d'Ivoire. Moreover, very few small firms grow to a large scale, whereas formally registered firms that start at a large scale appear to benefit from a different regime with a relatively stronger growth performance as they grow older, suggesting other mechanisms are at work. In line with the arguments developed in this paper, the difference in growth regimes is consistent with the process of reputation and legitimation as mechanisms to compete for resources. Within such a competitive process, scarce resources needed to expand activities are not solely allocated to the most efficient firms, but also to those—large—firms that enjoy recognition and legitimacy in the industry. Reputation effects are found important in the African context where transaction and information costs are very high and where markets are poorly developed with little transparency as to firms' activities, performance and strengths.

The results from a survey on growth obstacles perceived by managers and firm owners support the above assertions and corroborate the findings of the empirical growth model. Firms experience restrained access to inputs as a major growth barrier, thereby revealing a fierce process of competition for resources. The most severely input constrained group of firms are the small and medium sized firms whose growth process tends to be crowded out by larger established competitors.

From a policy perspective, the results call for policies and aid measures that are less biased against medium sized firms. Our findings stress the need to develop efficient institutions that improve the functioning of input and output markets supporting the growth of all firms in developing countries.

Acknowledgements

We would like to thank one anonymous referee and the participants of the conference 'The Impact of Technological Change on Industry and Firm Performance' held in August, 1997 in Rotterdam and in particular we are grateful to David Audretsch, Martin Carree and Steven Klepper. Financial support from the Belgian Fund for Scientific Research (FWO-G.0196.96 N) is gratefully acknowledged.

References

Aigner, D., Lovell, C., Schmidt, P., 1977. Formulation and estimation of stochastic frontier production models'. Journal of Econometrics 6, 21–37.

Aswicahyono, H., Bird, K., Hill, H., 1996. What happens to industrial structure when countries liberalise? Indonesia since the Mid-1980s. The Journal of Development Studies 32, 340–363.

Audretsch, 1995. Innovation, growth and survival. International Journal of Industrial Organisation 13, 441–457.

Barnow, B., Cain, G., Goldberger, A., 1981. Issues in the Analysis of Selection Bias. Department of Economics, University of Wisconsin.

Biggs, T.S., Oppenheim, J., 1986. What drives the size distribution of firms in developing countries? Employment and enterprise policy analysis discussion paper no. 6 (HIID, Cambridge, MA).

Cabral, L., 1995. Sunk costs, firm size and firm growth. Journal of Industrial Economics 43, 161–172.

Das, S., 1995. Size, age and firm growth in an infant industry: the computer hardware industry in India. International Journal of Industrial Organisation 13, 111–126.

Doms, M., Dunne, T., Roberts, M., 1995. The role of technology use in the survival and growth of manufacturing plants. International Journal of Industrial Organisation 13, 523–542.

Dunne, P., Hughes, A., 1994. Age, size, growth and survival: UK companies in the 1980s. The Journal of Industrial Economics 42, 115–140.

Dunne, T., Roberts, M., Samuelson, L., 1988. Patterns of firm entry and exit in U.S. manufacturing industries. RAND Journal of Economics 19, 495–515.

Dunne, T., Roberts, M., Samuelson, L., 1989. The growth and failure of US manufacturing plants. Quarterly Journal of Economics 104, 671–698.

Evans, D.E., 1987a. The relationship between firm growth, size and age: estimates for 100 manufacturing industries. The Journal of Industrial Economics 35, 567–582.

Evans, D.E., 1987b. Tests of alternative theories of firm growth. Journal of Political Economy 95, 657–674.

Fafchamp, M., 1994. Industrial structure and micro-enterprises in Africa. The Journal of Developing Areas 29, 1–30.

Gauthier, B., Gersovitz, M., 1997. Revenue erosion through tax exemption and evasion in poor countries. Journal of Public Economy 64, 404–424.

Geroski, P.A., 1995. What do we know about entry? International Journal of Industrial Organization 13, 421–440.

Gibrat, R., 1931. Les inégalités économiques. Sirey, Paris.

Goedhuys, M., 1999. Industrial organisation in developing countries, evidence from Côte d'Ivoire', PhD dissertation, Katholieke Universiteit Leuven.

Goedhuys, M., Sleuwaegen, L., 1999. Barriers to growth of firms in developing countries: evidence from Burundi. In: Audretsch, D.B., Thurik, R. (Eds.), Innovation, Industry Evolution and Employment. Cambridge Univ. Press, Cambridge, UK, pp. 297–314.

Hall, B., 1987. The relationship between firm size and firm growth in the US manufacturing sector. Journal of Industrial Economics 36, 583–606.

Hannan, M.T., Carroll, G.R., 1992. Dynamics of organizational populations; Density, Legitimation and Competition. Oxford Univ. Press, New York.

Hannan, M.T., Ranger-Moore, J., Banaszak-Holl, J., 1990. Competition and the evolution of organizational size distributions. In: Singh, J. (Ed.), Organisational Evolution: New Directions. Sage, Newbury Park, CA, pp. 246–268.

Harhoff, D., Stahl, K., Woywode, M., 1998. Legal form, growth and exit of West German firms—empirical results for manufacturing, construction, trade and service industries. Journal of Industrial Economics 46, 453–488.

Harrison, A., 1996. Determinants and effects of foreign direct investment. In: Roberts, M.J., Tybout, J.R. (Eds.) 1996, Industrial Evolution in Developing Countries, Micro Patterns of Turnover, Productivity and Market Structure. Oxford Univ. Press, New York, US, pp. 163–186.

Hart, P.E., Oulton, N., 1996a. Growth and size of firms. Economic Journal 106, 1242–1252.

Hart, P.E., Oulton, N., 1996b. Job creation and variation in corporate growth. London National Institute of Economic and Social Research. Discussion paper, 95.

Hopenhayn, H., 1992. Entry, exit and firm dynamics in long run equilibrium. Econometrica 60, 1127–1150.

Ijiri, Y., Simon, H.A., 1964. Business firm growth and size. The American Economic Review 54, 77–89.

Jovanovic, B., 1982. Selection and the evolution of industry. Econometrica 50, 649–670.

Kamshad, K., Hay, M., 1995. Barriers to growth in SMEs: an econometric analysis, London Business School, working paper series, number 158.

Kumar, M.S., 1985. Growth, acquisition activity and firm size: evidence from the United Kingdom. The Journal of Industrial Economics 33, 327–338.

Levensohn, A., Maloney, W., 1997. The Informal Sector, Firm Dynamics and Institutional Participation. University of Illinois, Mimeo.

Lucas, R.E., 1978. On the size distribution of business firms. The Bell Journal of Economics 9, 508–523.

Mansfield, E., 1962. Entry, Gibrat's Law, innovation and the growth of firms. The American Economic Review 52, 1023–1051.

Mata, J., Portugal, P., Guimares, P., 1995. The survival of new plants: start-up conditions and post-entry evolution. International Journal of Industrial Organization 13, 459–482.

McCormick, D., Kinyanjui, M., Ongile, G., 1997. Growth and barriers to growth among Nairobi's small and medium sized garment producers. World Development 25, 1095–1110.

McPherson, M.A., 1996. Growth of micro and small enterprises in southern Africa. Journal of Development Economics 48, 253–277.

McPherson, M.A., Liedholm, C., 1996. Determinants of small and micro enterprise registration: results from surveys in Niger and Swaziland. World Development 24, 481–487.

Mead, D., Liedholm, C., 1998. The dynamics of micro and small enterprises in developing countries. World Development 26, 61–74.

Mead, D.C., Morrisson, C., 1996. The informal sector elephant. World Development 24, 1611–1619.

Meeusen, W., Van Den Broeck, J., 1977. Efficiency estimation from Cobb–Douglas production functions with composed error. International Economic Review 18, 435–444.

Nugent, J.B., 1996. What explains the trend reversal in the size distribution of Korean manufacturing establishments? Journal of Development Economics 48, 225–251.

Nugent, J.B., Nabli, M.K., 1989. An institutional analysis of the size distribution of manufacturing establishments: an international cross-section study, CES International Economics Research Paper no. 62.

Nugent, J.B., Nabli, M.K., 1992. Development of financial markets and the size distribution of manufacturing establishments: international comparisons. World Development 20, 1489–1499.

Pakes, A., Ericson, R., 1990. Empirical implications of alternative models of firm dynamics, Columbia University Working Paper.

Rauch, J.E., 1991. Modelling the informal sector formally. Journal of Development Economics 35, 33–47.

Rondinelli, D., Kasarda, J., 1992. Foreign trade potential, small enterprise development and job creation in developing countries. Small Business Economics 4, 253–265.

Storey, D., 1994. The role of legal status in influencing bank financing and new firm growth. Applied Economics 26, 129–136.

Sutton, J., 1997. Gibrat's legacy. Journal of Economic Literature 35, 40–59.

Tybout, J.R., 2000. Manufacturing firms in developing countries: how well do they do and why. Journal of Economic Literature 38, 11–44.

Wagner, J., 1992. Firm size, firm growth and persistence of change: testing Gibrat's Law with establishment data from Lower Saxony, 1978–1989. Small Business Economics 4, 125–131.

White, H., 1980. A heteroskedasticity-consistent covariance matrix estimator and a direct test for heteroskedasticity. Econometica 48, 817–832.

World Bank, 1994. Republic of Côte d'Ivoire Private Sector Assessment, Report no 12885-IVC, the World Bank, Washington, DC, 96 pp.

[16]

THE QUALITY OF THE LEGAL SYSTEM, FIRM OWNERSHIP, AND FIRM SIZE

Luc Laeven and Christopher Woodruff*

Abstract—We show that firm size is increasing with the quality of the legal system in Mexico. A 1-standard-deviation improvement in the quality of the legal system is associated with a 0.15–0.30 standard deviation increase in firm size. We also show that the legal system affects firm size by reducing the idiosyncratic risk faced by firm owners. The legal system has a smaller impact on partnerships and corporations than on proprietorships, where risk is concentrated in a single owner. All of the findings are robust to instrumenting for legal quality using historical conditions. By focusing on firms in a single country, the data draw attention to the importance of informal institutions.

I. Introduction

THAT institutions affect economic outcomes is now well established. In a seminal paper, Acemoglu, Johnson, and Robinson [henceforth, AJR] (2001) show that property rights institutions affect GDP per capita in a causal fashion. There is also evidence suggesting specific channels through which institutions affect economic outcomes. Acemoglu et al. (2003) show a causal channel between historical determinants of institutional quality and macroeconomic volatility, and Besley (1995) and Johnson, McMillan, and Woodruff (2002a) provide evidence on the relationship between institutions and the willingness of entrepreneurs to invest in their enterprises.

In this paper, we explore in more detail the link between the institutional environment and investment by entrepreneurs. We develop a framework in which the institutional environment affects the level of idiosyncratic risk faced by an entrepreneur investing an increasing share of his assets in a single firm. Entrepreneurs can mitigate the effect of idiosyncratic risk by diversifying ownership, that is, by incorporating and taking on equity partners. In the absence of diversified ownership, we show that lower-quality institutions limit the size of an entrepreneur's firm. The framework predicts that institutional quality will have a more limited impact where ownership is diversified.

Received for publication June 17, 2004. Revision accepted for publication July 25, 2006.

* Laeven is at the International Monetary Fund and CEPR, and Woodruff is at the Graduate School of International Relations and Pacific Studies, University of California San Diego.

The authors thank Daron Acemoglu (the editor), two anonymous referees, Franklin Allen, Thorsten Beck, Luis Cabral, Stijn Claessens, Simon Johnson, Ross Levine, Inessa Love, John McMillan, Bernard Yeung, and seminar participants at the 2004 annual meetings of the American Economic Association, Carnegie Mellon University, CEPR Gerzensee, New York University, University of Pittsburgh, Centro de Investigación y Docencia Económicas (CIDE), and the University of Southern California for helpful comments, Gerardo Leyva and Benito Arciniega at Instituto Nacional de Estadística Geografía e Informática (INEGI) for providing the data from the Mexican economic census, and Guillermo Noguera and Augusto Nieto for research assistance. The paper was largely written while the first author was at the World Bank. This paper's findings, interpretations, and conclusions are entirely those of the authors and do not represent the views of the International Monetary Fund, its executive directors, or the countries they represent.

We take this framework to data from a census of firms in Mexico. The census data allow us to distinguish between proprietorships and firms that are incorporated.[1] We find that firms located in Mexican states with weak legal environments are smaller than those located in states with better legal environments. Moreover, consistent with the model, we find that the effect of the legal system is larger for those industries in which proprietorships make up a larger percentage of firms. Our data suggest that reduction of idiosyncratic risk is one important channel through which the quality of the institutional environment affects the investment decisions of entrepreneurs.

Does the quality of the legal system affect the efficiency of the economy through the firm size channel we identify in this paper? According to the theoretical framework developed here, the answer is yes. We present results from a translog production function that provide empirical support for an efficiency effect as well. Where a better legal system reduces idiosyncratic risk, capital is allocated more efficiently among entrepreneurs.

We deal with the endogeneity of institutions in what is now a standard manner, using instruments for institutional quality. In particular, we use differences in historical circumstances, as suggested by AJR (2001) and Engerman and Sokoloff (2002). We show that the efficiency of the legal system varies across states in Mexico in a systematic way with historical circumstances. In particular, the quality of legal institutions is lower where the indigenous population was more prevalent one hundred years ago. Consistent with the work of Engerman and Sokoloff (2002), legal-system quality is also lower in states with higher levels of activity in production of agricultural crops with high economies of scale.

Recent work on "unbundling" institutions suggests several important ways of thinking about the institutional environment that are applicable to our paper (see Acemoglu & Johnson, 2005; and Acemoglu, 2005). First, we use contemporary measures of institutional quality that are related to the narrow institutions of financial contracting. However, the quality of narrow institutions is likely to be highly correlated with broader institutional quality. The instruments we use to overcome endogeneity problems are similar to those used by AJR (2001) and Engerman and Sokoloff (2002) to describe the formation of broad institutions. We do not have instruments that allow us to unbundle broad and narrow institutions. Hence, while we describe

[1] A sole proprietorship is an unincorporated business that is owned by one individual, with no distinction between the liabilities of the firm and the personal liabilities of the owner. It is the simplest form of business organization.

The Review of Economics and Statistics, November 2007, 89(4): 601–614

narrow institutions related to financial contracting, many of our results might also be interpreted as representing the effects of the broader institutional environment on outcomes. We return to this issue in the concluding section of the paper.

We believe our paper contributes to unbundling of institutions in a different dimension. Economic outcomes are affected by both formal and informal institutions. Formal institutions include the laws that govern economic relationships and the formal structure by which those relationships are governed—whether courts operate by civil or common law, for example. Informal institutions are well-established but unwritten norms that govern the functioning of bureaucracies, legislatures, and judiciaries. Informal institutions affect how formal laws are applied and enforced. Though formal institutions are sometimes measured directly (for example, Djankov et al., 2003; and Persson & Tabellini, 2003), informal institutions are inherently more difficult to identify. Measures of informal institutions generally must be based on impressionistic measures of institutions that conflate the formal and informal. In practice, most commonly used measures of institutions reflect a mixture of the formal and the informal.

We suggest that one method of isolating the impact of informal institutions is to examine environments in which formal institutions do not vary but informal institutions do. By using data from a single country where economic relations are governed largely by national laws, we are able to isolate differences in the quality of informal institutions. In this regard, Mexico is a particularly interesting example. Between 1929 and 1989, a single party controlled the presidency, the legislature, and every governorship and state legislature in the country. At least until 1989, then, the formal institutions governing the country and each of its federal entities were essentially the same. Since 1989, formal institutions have begun to change in modest ways,[2] but formal institutions were still very homogeneous in 1998, when the data we use were gathered. In spite of the presence of very similar formal institutions, however, the institutional environment varies markedly across states within Mexico.

Methodologically, our work is related to Kumar, Rajan, and Zingales [henceforth, KRZ] (2002), who examine the determinants of firm size across thirteen European countries. They find that more efficient legal systems are associated with larger firm sizes across countries in Western Europe, an effect especially pronounced in industries characterized by low levels of capital intensity. They posit that the reason for this is that all legal systems in Europe are of high enough quality to protect investment in physical capital. Variation among the European countries, therefore, shows up in the more challenging area of intangible assets

such as intellectual property. Our paper complements KRZ (2002) in that the legal environment in Mexico varies from bad to less bad, while the legal environment in Western Europe varies from good to very good.[3] Hence, protection of more basic contracts is less certain in Mexico.

The paper is organized as follows: section II presents a simple model of the link between firm size, ownership, and the quality of the legal system, and derives testable implications of the model. Section III describes the data. Section IV presents the regression results, and section V provides concluding remarks.

II. Investment, Firm Size, and Legal Institutions

We develop a simple analytical framework based on Lucas's (1978) model determining the distribution of firm size. Our intention is not to break new theoretical ground but rather to focus ideas. We make an explicit consideration of the quality of the legal system. An increase in the quality of the legal system reduces the risk faced by entrepreneurs and lowers their required rate of return to capital. We focus on the effect of idiosyncratic risk faced by the entrepreneurs who invest an increasing share of their wealth in an enterprise. The inclusion of idiosyncratic risk generates a set of predictions about the relative impact of improvements in the legal system on proprietorships and corporations. A critical distinction between proprietorships and corporations is that in the latter, owners are able to both limit and diversify their risk through equity sharing arrangements, albeit at the cost of creating agency problems that may subject outside investors to stealing by insiders.[4] Among the firms in our data, corporations and limited partnerships represent the primary vehicle for diversifying risk. Generally, the literature equates equity investments with stock markets. However, our data are dominated by firms that are far too small to issue publicly traded equity securities.[5]

We begin by establishing a benchmark distribution of firm size in an economy with fully diversified ownership. We then consider an economy of owner-managed proprietorships in which a single owner bears all of the risk and creditors of the business can make claims on the owner's nonbusiness assets. We show that an improvement in the quality of the legal system that reduces idiosyncratic risk allows an expansion of investment by higher-ability entrepreneurs. In a perfect legal system, the distribution among proprietorships will approach that of the benchmark case of

---

[2] To give a couple of examples, 23 of Mexico's 32 federal entities have passed freedom of information acts since 2000, and 15 have independent tribunals to govern the careers of judges, including appointments and promotions.

[3] The rule of law as measured by the Political Risk Services group and averaged over the period 1990–1999 is 9.72 for the sample of eleven European countries in KRZ (2002), but only 4.73 for Mexico (with higher scores denoting better rule of law). Even the lowest score across countries in Europe, 7.82 for Greece, is well above the score for Mexico.

[4] There is a large literature on the agency problems in corporations and partnerships (for example, Alchian & Demsetz, 1972; Holmstrom, 1982; and Fama & Jensen, 1983).

[5] Moreover, because bank loans in Mexico are generally more than fully collateralized with real estate (see Gelos & Werner, 2002; and La Porta, Lopez-de-Silanes, & Zamarripo, 2003), debt does not alleviate idiosyncratic risk.

the incorporated economy. The framework suggests that in an economy with a mixture of corporations and proprietorships, the relationship between firm size and the quality of the legal environment will be strongest in sectors where there is a larger proportion of proprietorships.

Consider an economy composed of corporations only. Each agent can become an entrepreneur and produce output Y using capital K and labor L according to $Y = \Omega \theta K^\alpha L^{(\beta-\alpha)}$, where $\alpha < \beta < 1$.[6] The parameter Ω indicates the quality of the legal system, with $\Omega \in [0, 1]$; θ is a measure of the entrepreneurial talent of the agent, with $\theta \in [0, 1]$ and talent increasing in θ. Every entrepreneur faces decreasing returns to scale,[7] but higher-ability entrepreneurs produce higher levels of output both on average and at the margin.

An entrepreneur with a given talent level produces more output where the legal system is more efficient. For example, the legal system may affect the production function of a firm through the demand for products. Better legal systems may increase the demand for a given firm's output by increasing the number of available trading partners (Johnson et al., 2002b).

Each agent weighs the profit from being an entrepreneur against the endogenously determined wage rate. Given that all firms are corporations whose owners are fully diversified, we assume that all face the same interest rate, r, and pay the same wage rate, w. Each potential entrepreneur then chooses K and L according to

$$w = (\beta - \alpha)\theta \Omega K^\alpha L^{(\beta-\alpha-1)}, \tag{1}$$

and

$$r = \alpha \theta \Omega K^{\alpha-1} L^{(\beta-\alpha)}. \tag{2}$$

Denote the levels of labor and capital that satisfy equations (1) and (2) as $L^*(\theta)$ and $K^*(\theta)$. Then the profit for an agent from self-employment is $Y(K^*(\theta), L^*(\theta)) - wL^*(\theta) - rK^*(\theta)$. This implies that entrepreneurs with higher θ will run larger firms. Lucas (1978) shows that an equilibrium exists in which agents with the highest levels of entrepreneurial ability become entrepreneurs and the remaining agents become wage workers. In this equilibrium, the distribution of firm size depends on the distribution of entrepreneurial talent and the economy's capital-to-labor ratio.

Proposition 1: Firm size increases with the quality of the legal system, even when ownership is fully diversified.

The proof of proposition 1 is straightforward. An improvement in the legal system causes an increase in the demand for labor and capital from all entrepreneurs. This

puts upward pressure on wage and rental rates, inducing entrepreneurs with low ability to leave self-employment for wage work. As a result, average firm size increases.

We now examine the equilibrium distribution of firm size in an economy where all firms are proprietorships, each of which is owned by a single agent. Investment comes from the personal wealth of the owner, invested directly or used as collateral for loans. We assume all loans are fully collateralized, consistent with bank lending markets in Mexico (La Porta et al., 2003). This is an important assumption because full collateralization implies that debt does not reduce the risk to the owner. An individual's risk can be diversified only by making equity investments in other firms, assumed away in the proprietorship economy. The owner faces unlimited liability for losses incurred operating the business. The production function and the distribution of entrepreneurial talent are as before. All agents earn the same rate of return on capital invested without risk outside the business. However, the risk premium required for capital invested in the business, denoted as ρ, is increasing in the level of investment for all levels of capital investment, $\rho \geq 1$ and $\rho_K > 0$. A better legal system provides a more certain operating environment and allows firms to protect profits from bureaucrats with kleptocratic tendencies.[8] Hence, idiosyncratic risk is a decreasing function of the quality of legal enforcement. The legal system now not only enters the production function directly, but also impacts investments by reducing the idiosyncratic risks faced by this entrepreneur. We assume that all agents have similar aversion to idiosyncratic risk, and that the distribution of wealth and entrepreneurial ability are uncorrelated.

Proposition 2: The positive impact of the quality of the legal system on firm size is greater for proprietorships, where idiosyncratic risk plays a larger role, than for corporations.

Again, the proof is straightforward. As before, maximizing agents choose labor according to equation (1), but the cost of capital now includes a return to idiosyncratic risk, so optimal investment is now

$$r = \frac{\alpha \theta \Omega K^{\alpha-1} L^{(\beta-\alpha)}}{\rho(K, \Omega)}. \tag{3}$$

The effect of idiosyncratic risk on the distribution of firm sizes can be seen by comparing the impact of an increase in θ on the level of capital (and labor) demanded by a single firm in equations (2) and (3). For equation (2), $\partial^2 Y/\partial K \partial \theta$ is $\alpha \Omega K^{\alpha-1} L^{(\beta-\alpha)}$; for equation (3), the same cross partial adjusted for idiosyncratic risk is $\dfrac{\alpha \Omega K^{\alpha-1} L^{(\beta-\alpha)}}{\rho(K, \Omega)}$. Since K is

---

[6] Kihlstrom and Laffont (1979) develop a similar model in which it is the degree of risk aversion rather than entrepreneurial talent that determines whether individuals become entrepreneurs or workers.

[7] Alternatively, we could write the production function as $Y = \Omega K^{(\alpha\theta)} L^{(1-\alpha)\theta}$, in which the scale factor is a function of entrepreneurial ability. This produces identical predictions with additional complexity.

[8] There is ample evidence that an improvement in the legal protection of property positively affects investment. See, among others, Besley (1995), Johnson et al. (2002a), Claessens and Laeven (2003), and Banerjee and Iyer (2005).

increasing in θ, the latter is smaller, indicating that a change in entrepreneurial ability is associated with a smaller increase in capital employed. Hence, an increase in entrepreneurial ability is associated with a smaller increase in the size of the firm when idiosyncratic risk is incorporated.

The consideration of idiosyncratic risk reduces the average firm size through an indirect route as well. The reduction in investment by the most able entrepreneurs will result in lower market wage rates. This will induce additional entry into self-employment. The new entrants will have lower entrepreneurial ability than the marginal entrant in the economy without idiosyncratic risk, and hence will employ less capital and labor than the previous marginal entrant. An improvement in the legal system also reduces idiosyncratic risk where the latter is not eliminated through dispersed ownership. This results in an additional increase in firm size wherever proprietorships are important.

The quality of the legal system may also affect the distribution of legal forms. However:

Proposition 3: The effect of the quality of the legal system on the ratio of proprietorships to corporations is theoretically ambiguous.

The proof is straightforward. An improvement in the legal system reduces the cost of moving to the corporate form of organization by reducing the cost of finding outside partners. It also directly increases the benefits of incorporation by increasing the demand for the firm's goods. However, since an improvement in the legal system also reduces idiosyncratic risk among proprietors, it reduces the benefits of incorporation and increases the size of existing proprietorships. If the latter effect outweighs the former, an improvement in the quality of the legal system could result in an increase in proprietorships relative to corporations.

We provide empirical evidence in support of propositions 1 to 3 in section IV.

III. Data

Our data on firm investment and employment come from the Mexican economic census of 1998 carried out by Instituto Nacional de Estadística Geografía e Informática (INEGI). The data are given in reference to December 31, 1998. The economic census covers the manufacturing, commerce, services, and construction sectors. Data are gathered for every location of each firm in Mexico, but INEGI does not make the firm-level data available. Instead, the data were provided to us at the two-digit industry level, by state and by employment size. There are as many as twelve size bins in each state/industry.[9]

The data have two important limitations. First, the bins are derived from plant-level data. Both our framework and most of the theories explaining firm size distributions refer to enterprise-level data rather than plant data. We have no way to aggregate the data at the enterprise level. Instead, INEGI provided us data by industry/state bin for the sample of domestically owned firms that operate from a single location within Mexico. For most of the analysis, we limit the sample to these firms for whom the data represent both the plant and enterprise level. Foreign-owned firms are excluded because they are quite likely to have operations outside of Mexico, and they may have access to courts in other countries that operate in a different institutional environment. Even if we could aggregate the data to the firm level, it is not clear what measure of institutional quality would be appropriate for a firm operating in multiple states. Firms with multiple plants located in different states are likely to use courts in different states depending on where disputes arise.[10] We will show, however, that the results we report below are robust to including the foreign-owned and multiplant firms.

The second issue is that the data are organized according to the number of workers, while the theoretical framework is based on the level of capital stock. This should not be a major concern because there is a strong correlation between labor and capital in the data.[11] The median level of invested capital increases monotonically with the bin size measured by employment.

In our standard regression specification, we exclude several industries that are dominated by government-owned firms: oil and gas extraction, coal mining, water and electricity, and education and medical services. We also exclude the fishing industry, both because the industry remains dominated by cooperatives established with significant government assistance and because the regional location of fishing is determined by geography. Finally, the census data do not include firms involved in agricultural production, though agricultural processing firms are included. There are 32 states and 24 two-digit sectors, resulting in 768 potential state/sector data points. Since some states have no employment in some sectors, we have about 700 observations for most of the regressions.

We begin by benchmarking the Mexican data to data on firm-size distribution from the 1997 U.S economic census. Average firm size in Mexico is much smaller than in the United States. While more than 96% of firms in Mexico employ 10 employees or fewer, only about 78% in the United States do so. As a percentage of the total firms, the number of large firms with more than 500 employees is about eight times larger in the United States than in Mexico.

---

[9] These are 0–2 workers, 3–5 workers, 6–10 workers, 11–15 workers, 16–20 workers, 21–30 workers, 31–50 workers, 51–100 workers, 101–250 workers, 251–500 workers, 501–1,000 workers, and 1,001 or more workers. So, for example, an observation is the number of firms employing 6–10 workers in the textile industry located in the state of Jalisco.

[10] The single-plant firms in our data are generally forced to use the courts in the state where the firm is located.
[11] The correlation between number of workers and fixed assets at the bin level is 0.48 and statistically significant at the 1% level. The data show that invested capital is strictly increasing in the number of workers.

THE QUALITY OF THE LEGAL SYSTEM, FIRM OWNERSHIP, AND FIRM SIZE   605

TABLE 1.—FIRM SIZE, QUALITY OF LEGAL SYSTEM, INDIGENOUS POPULATION, AND CROPS BY STATE

State	Average Firm Size	Weighted Average Size	Typical Firm Size	Share of Small Firms	Judicial Efficiency	Judicial Factor	Private Credit	Indigenous	Crops
Aguascalientes	4.12	142.04	2.03	0.56	4.59	2.88	0.13	0.00	0
Baja California	5.44	279.33	2.92	0.52	3.14	0.74	0.10	0.02	1
Baja California Sur	4.24	68.87	2.14	0.64	2.53	−0.62	0.05	0.02	1
Campeche	3.56	210.16	2.06	0.65	3.21	0.17	0.03	0.42	0
Chiapas	2.38	97.67	1.29	0.79	2.97	−0.24	0.06	0.36	2
Chihuahua	4.19	189.12	2.05	0.59	2.71	−0.43	0.08	0.07	1
Coahuila	4.64	192.82	2.92	0.51	3.40	1.03	0.09	0.00	1
Colima	3.40	74.34	1.31	0.71	3.14	0.08	0.07	0.00	2
Distrito Federal	5.34	578.83	3.31	0.48	2.53	0.15	0.67	0.02	0
Durango	3.81	171.11	2.04	0.57	3.34	0.85	0.06	0.01	1
Guanajuato	3.67	150.14	2.04	0.61	3.03	0.07	0.10	0.01	1
Guerrero	2.63	112.09	1.28	0.74	1.69	−1.80	0.03	0.25	4
Hidalgo	3.00	120.39	1.28	0.64	2.11	−0.15	0.04	0.29	2
Jalisco	3.98	227.97	2.04	0.61	2.39	0.40	0.15	0.00	3
México	3.19	202.60	2.04	0.60	3.20	1.02	0.07	0.13	1
Michoacán	2.67	84.57	1.28	0.77	1.94	−1.34	0.07	0.05	3
Morelos	2.73	63.96	1.29	0.72	3.27	0.64	0.07	0.17	2
Nayarit	2.81	185.78	1.28	0.73	2.49	−1.14	0.04	0.03	4
Nuevo León	5.55	296.17	3.24	0.48	3.00	0.47	0.26	0.00	2
Oaxaca	2.19	79.16	1.28	0.81	2.64	0.15	0.02	0.52	3
Puebla	2.90	106.70	1.28	0.66	2.54	0.37	0.10	0.32	3
Querétaro	4.40	177.03	2.91	0.51	3.24	0.07	0.08	0.10	0
Quintana Roo	4.45	108.86	2.05	0.59	2.46	−1.02	0.10	0.69	0
San Luis Potosí	3.30	138.52	2.06	0.63	2.84	−0.15	0.08	0.06	2
Sinaloa	3.80	147.40	2.06	0.64	2.67	−0.19	0.19	0.03	2
Sonora	3.93	189.57	2.04	0.62	3.06	0.52	0.18	0.12	2
Tabasco	3.62	248.38	2.05	0.61	3.11	0.89	0.09	0.09	3
Tamaulipas	3.82	210.08	2.04	0.59	3.01	1.38	0.06	0.00	2
Tlaxcala	2.61	57.56	1.27	0.68	2.19	−0.88	0.04	0.16	0
Veracruz	2.83	253.56	1.28	0.71	2.20	−1.49	0.06	0.20	4
Yucatán	3.46	272.85	2.05	0.62	2.03	−1.77	0.12	0.69	0
Zacatecas	2.42	65.03	1.28	0.79	2.26	−1.50	0.04	0.00	1
Total	3.60	172.79	1.93	0.64	2.78	−0.02	0.10	0.15	2

Average size is the unweighted average firm size in terms of workers. Weighted average size is the employee-weighted average of average firm size in each of the bins. Typical firm size is the logarithm of the average firm size in the bin where the median worker is located. Share of small firms is the share of employment in firms with 0–20 employees. Judicial efficiency is based on 1998 survey data from ITAM/GMA and is measured as the average of seven individual indicators. Judicial efficiency factor is the first principal component of the seven judicial efficiency indicators. Private credit is private credit to GDP in 2000. Indigenous is the share of the indigenous population in 1900. Crops is the number of cultivated crops with large economies of scale (sugar, coffee, rice, and cotton) in 1939, from the 1940 census. All firm size figures exclude firms with multiple establishments and firms with foreign ownership. Data on firm size distribution, private credit, indigenous population, and crops are from INEGI. More detailed definitions of the alternative size variables can be found in the main text.

The numbers confirm Tybout's (2000) observation that employment in developing countries (such as Mexico) is disproportionately concentrated in very small firms.

Comparing the distribution of employment by legal form of organization in Mexico and the United States, we find that in Mexico a much larger share of employment is concentrated in single proprietorships (38% versus 6% in the United States). Because the majority of proprietorships are smaller firms, this is consistent with the previous finding.

Table 1 shows Mexican state-level data for several different measures of firm size, all of which are highly correlated. The firm-size measures are based on data for single-location, domestically owned firms only.[12] The first column shows the simple average firm size, calculated as the sum of employees and contract employees[13] divided by the number of units reported in the census. For Mexico as a whole, there is an average of 13.6 employees per unit reporting in the census. The simple average number of employees per firm can be misleading because the average may be brought down by a large number of very small firms.[14] We thus consider several alternative firm-size measures. We will find that our basic results are robust to any of these definitions.

Davis and Henrekson (1997) and KRZ (2002) suggest an alternative calculation of firm size that weights each bin by the number of employees in that bin. This employee-weighted firm size is given by

$$\sum_{bin=1}^{n} \left(\frac{N_{bin}^{emp}}{N_{sec}^{emp}} \right) \times \left(\frac{N_{bin}^{emp}}{N_{bin}^{estab}} \right),$$

---

[12] The share of multiplant or foreign-owned firms in total employment ranges from as low as 11% in Nuevo Leon to as high as 52% in Chihuahua. On average, about 24% of employees are employed by multiplant firms with foreign ownership. These employees are concentrated in the large firms.

[13] In order to avoid labor laws requiring firms to share profits with employees, firms sometimes establish independent entities that exist only to hire workers for the firm. These workers are reported as contract employees.

[14] For example, the average size of firms in an industry in which a single firm hires 10,000 employees and nine firms hire one employee each is roughly 1,000. If the same industry instead had 99 firms hiring one employee each, the average firm size would be roughly 100. But in the sense of most theories of firm size, these two industries are not as different as is indicated by the difference in simple average firm size.

where N_{bin}^{emp} is the total number of employees reported in the given bin, N_{sec}^{emp} is the total number of employees in the sector, and N_{bin}^{estab} is the number of establishments in the bin. This alternative measure of average firm size places more weight on larger firms, and hence dampens the impact of a large number of very small firms. The second column of table 1 shows the employee-weighted average firm size. Indeed, this produces a significantly larger average firm size. For Mexico as a whole, the average firm size is now just over 1,100 employees.[15] Finally, the third column of table 1 shows the percentage of employment found in firms with fewer than 20 workers. Across states within Mexico, there is considerable variation in firm size by any of these three measures. For example, the employee weighted average firm size ranges from 275 in the state of Zacatecas to more than 5,000 in the Federal District.

The second major component of our data is the quality of legal institutions. These come from a survey conducted in 1998 under the direction of the Center for the Study of Law at the Instituto Tecnológico Autónomo de México (ITAM/GMA 1999).[16] The ITAM project focused on collection of bank debt through local courts in each of Mexico's 32 federal entities. Bank debt was chosen as the focus of the ITAM/GMA study because banks are centralized but must collect debts in the location of the debtor; that is, they must operate in the courts of each state. From our perspective, the focus of the study on the legal enforcement of financial contracts is fortunate because it fits closely with our model. The data gathered come from interviews with a total of 519 lawyers working for banks directly and as outside counsel (ITAM/GMA, 1999, p. 32).

The relevant commercial laws are national in scope, with only minor variation across states. McNeece and Poelstra (2003), for example, note that "Mexican civil codes [vary] from state to state, though most are based on the Federal Civil Code" (p. 5). The more important variation across states comes from the effect that state laws and state legal enforcement have on the application of law by courts and the ability of claimants to enforce verdicts. State laws vary, for example, on the ease with which collateral can be claimed by a victor in a court decision. We construct a measure of the efficiency of legal enforcement in each state by taking an average of the responses to seven different questions. Each of these questions reflects the judgment of lawyers in the survey, and each is scaled from 1 (worst) to 5 (best). The questions relate to the following: (i) the quality of judges (mean value 3.76); (ii) the impartiality of judges

(1.94),[17] (iii) the adequacy of judicial resources (1.88); (iv) the efficiency of enforcement of rulings (2.71); (v) the efficiency of the judicial administration more generally (2.69); (vi) the cost, ease of use, and completeness of property registries (3.33); and (viii) the adequacy of local legislation related to contract enforcement (3.14). The index is shown in the fifth column of table 1, and a graphical presentation of the index across Mexican states is shown in figure 1.

The data point to rather substantial differences in state-level judicial efficiency (varying from a score of 1.69 to 4.59 on a scale from 1 to 5), suggesting that despite the same legal origin and formal laws in each state, stark differences exist in the practice and enforcement of the law across states.[18] While there is some pattern of legal institutions improving as we move north in Mexico, figure 1 makes clear that geography alone does not explain the variation in judicial effectiveness. We return to this issue later when we address concerns with endogeneity between judicial effectiveness and firm size.[19] The fifth column of table 1 shows the first principal component from a factor analysis of the seven measures of judicial efficiency.

The other columns of table 1 show our indicator of financial development by state and our two historical instruments. Financial market development is a more concrete output measure that is determined in part by the ability to write and enforce financial contracts. We use it as a robustness check for the legal quality results. Financial market development is proxied by the ratio of private credit to GDP. These data are the best available measure of access to finance.[20] However, these data have two limitations. First, a

---

[15] Both the simple average firm size and the weighted average firm size in Mexico are close to the average in the median European country reported by KRZ (2002).

[16] The survey was conducted again in 2001 (Sarre and López Ugalde, 2002). Using the average of the two surveys rather than just the 1998 survey produces somewhat stronger results in most of the regressions that we report in the next section.

---

[17] Since the survey was administered to lawyers who generally work for banks, it could be that a high rating on "impartiality" actually reflects a bias in favor of the banks. Given Levine's (1998) finding that rules favoring creditors are associated with higher levels of financial development, we do not see this as a great concern.

[18] Figure 1 shows that judicial efficiency tends to be higher in the northern and central states of Mexico, as well as in some of the southern states. The states in the western and eastern parts of Mexico tend to score low on the judicial effectiveness scale. Aguascalientes has the highest score (4.59) and Guerrero, the lowest (1.69).

[19] Other researchers have noted variation in both the organization and effectiveness of courts across states in Mexico. Cantú and Caballero (2002) show that courts in Mexico differ organizationally in several regards. Negrón Ruiz (2003) discusses the establishment of state judicial councils, which reinforce the independence of the judiciary, in 15 of Mexico's 32 federal entities (see Fix-Fierro, 2003, for a discussion of the importance of the judicial councils). At the state level, many of these characteristics are correlated with the measure of effectiveness we use here. For example, courts in states that provide more information about court cases are more efficient, as are courts in states in which selection and promotion of judges is carried out in a more autonomous fashion.

[20] We cannot use a more direct measure of firm debt finance because the 1998 census shows only data on the total interest expense of firms; there are no data on total debt. Interest payments are an imperfect measure of access to finance, and may be jointly determined with the measures of firm size which are our primary focus. Furthermore, interest rates paid by firms are likely to vary across states, industries, and firms of different sizes.

THE QUALITY OF THE LEGAL SYSTEM, FIRM OWNERSHIP, AND FIRM SIZE   607

FIGURE 1.—JUDICIAL EFFICIENT BY MEXICAN STATE

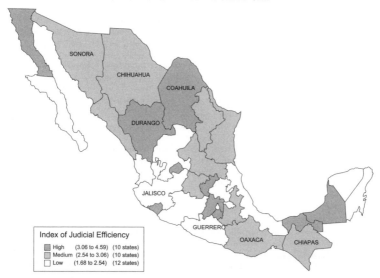

Index of Judicial Efficiency

■ High   (3.06 to 4.59) (10 states)
▨ Medium (2.54 to 3.06) (10 states)
□ Low   (1.68 to 2.54) (12 states)

substantial part of bank lending taking place outside Mexico City is attributed to the Federal District, due to internal reporting procedures at Mexican banks. As a result, credit figures from banks overstate bank activity in the Federal District and understate bank activity in other states. We therefore check that the regression results where we include private credit to GDP are robust to excluding the observations from the Federal District. Second, as mentioned before, previous research has shown that financial market development itself is a function of the efficiency of the legal system (Levine, 1998).

Neither judicial efficiency nor financial market development can be considered exogenous to economic outcomes such as investment and firm size. We address the endogeneity issue by using instruments. The cross-country literature suggests two instruments that are relevant in the Mexican context. Following AJR (2002) and Acemoglu and Johnson (2005), we use historical data on the share of indigenous-speaking people in a given state in 1900. Where the share of indigenous population was higher, European settlers were more likely to develop institutions designed to exploit local labor. In the context of Mexico, the *encomienda* system imported by the Spanish treated indigenous labor as a resource to be used by the immigrant Europeans (Gibson, 1966). Hence, the presence of a larger share of indigenous people might be expected to be associated with a worse institutional environment. The 1900 data are the earliest measure of indigenous population available to us at the state level.[21]

Engerman and Sokoloff (2002) suggest a related instrument. They note that some agricultural crops have higher production economies of scale than others. In particular, they identify sugar, coffee, rice, and cotton as crops with large economies of scale. Where production of these crops is prevalent, the distribution of land and income is likely to be more unequal. Engerman and Sokoloff show that this inequality is reflected in political institutions (for example, the universality of the right to vote in elections). Using data from the 1940 census of agriculture (the first with detailed state-level production data), we identify the number of these four crops produced in each of Mexico's 32 federal entities. This second instrument picks up geographic and climatological differences that may be reflected in regional differences in the quality of institutions. The correlation between the two instruments is quite low (0.05), and when used together the two instruments pass standard overidentification tests. As we discuss below, both explain a significant share of the state-level variation in institutional quality.

---

[21] The states of Quintana Roo and Baja California Sur were created after 1900, carved out of Yucatán and Baja California, respectively. For these states, we use data from the 1930 census, the first census after they became states.

TABLE 2.—LEGAL FORMS OF ORGANIZATION BY SECTOR IN MEXICO

Sector	Sector Code	Incorporation Intensity
Mining of metals	23	0.60
Mining of nonmetals	29	0.19
Food, beverages, and tobacco	31	0.04
Textiles and leather	32	0.11
Lumber products	33	0.05
Paper products and printing	34	0.20
Chemicals, pharmaceuticals, and plastics	35	0.49
Ceramics, glass, and clay	36	0.04
Basic metals	37	0.78
Metal products and equipment	38	0.13
Other manufacturing	39	0.08
Construction	50	0.76
Wholesale	61	0.27
Retail	62	0.03
Transport	71	0.12
Communications	72	0.19
Real estate	82	0.29
Leasing	83	0.09
Restaurants and hotels	93	0.04
Recreation	94	0.08
Professional services	95	0.09
Repair and maintenance	96	0.03
Other services	97	0.40
Total		0.20

This table shows the importance of legal persons with limited liability versus physical persons with unlimited liability by industrial sector for Mexico. Incorporation intensity is the share of legal persons with limited liability in the total number of firms. The category of legal persons with limited liability includes *sociedades anonimas* (SAs) and *sociedades de responsabilidad limitada* (SRLs). The total number of firms includes individual proprietorships. We exclude other types of legal forms from these total figures.

To explore the differential effect of the quality of the legal system on firms with differences in the degree of idiosyncratic risk, we construct a variable measuring the number of firms with limited liability and multiple owners as a percentage of all firms in a particular industry. We will refer to this variable as the incorporation-intensity measure. The category of firms with limited liability includes *sociedades anonimas* (SAs) and *sociedades de responsabilidad limitada* (SRLs). For simplicity, we refer to these as the corporate legal form, though they include limited partnerships as well. The total number of firms includes these as well as individual proprietorships. We exclude other types of legal forms from these total figures. We also report the share of employment in firms with limited liability and multiple owners.

Table 2 shows the incorporation intensity by industry. A lower number indicates that proprietorships are a more typical legal form of organization in the given industry. The corporate form tends to be more common in the mining and manufacturing industries, while businesses with unlimited liability are common in the services and retail sectors.

Our regressions also control for the effect of market size, measured as the log of population in the state. In robustness checks, we include measures of GDP per capita and education levels in the states. These are not included in the base regressions, because they are themselves endogenous to institutional quality. The data on these variables are from INEGI.

The three firm-size measures are highly correlated and most of the correlations between firm size and judicial efficiency or financial market development are significant as well. The exception is that weighted average firm size is not correlated with judicial efficiency. Judicial efficiency is also not significantly correlated with financial market development. The direction of causation of correlations between judicial effectiveness and economic performance is, of course, not clear. This is an issue we will address in the empirical work below.

IV. Empirical Results

Across industries, the variation in the size of firms is consistent with well-established patterns (see the discussion in KRZ, 2002). Average firm size is positively associated with capital intensity (measured as fixed assets per worker) and with wage levels. We are more interested in regional variation in the size of firms, and we will use information on how institutional variables differ among states to investigate this.

The model predicts that state-level variation in legal efficiency has a positive impact on average firm size (proposition 1). We test this prediction by aggregating all firm-size classes at the sectoral level in each state, and by running regressions using the log of the employee-weighted firm size at the state/industry level as the dependent variable. The regression model is as follows:

$$Size_{ij} = \alpha_i + \beta B_j + \gamma \Gamma_{ij} + \varepsilon_{ij},$$

where $Size_{ij}$ is a measure of average firm size of industry i in state j, α_i is an industry fixed effect, B_j is a vector of state-level variables, Γ_{ij} is a vector of variables that vary by industry and state, and ε_{ij} is the error term. As state-level variables we include a measure of market size and a measure of legal institutions. All regressions include sector-level fixed effects. The regressions, reported in table 3, have 699 observations across 32 states and 24 industries. Not all industries are represented in each state. Although the regressions are based on state-/industry-level data, the institutional variables vary only at the state level.

The first column of table 3 reports an OLS regression for the above model, using the log of weighted average firm size as the dependent variable, and with errors corrected for clustering at the state level.[22] Market size as measured by the log of population has a very strong and positive effect on firm size. A 1-standard-deviation increase in log population (0.8) is associated with a 0.27-standard-deviation increase in the weighted average size of firms. A 1-standard-deviation increase in judicial effectiveness (0.56) increases the weighted firm size by one-sixth of a standard deviation.

[22] Random-effects regressions with random effects at the state level produce very similar results.

THE QUALITY OF THE LEGAL SYSTEM, FIRM OWNERSHIP, AND FIRM SIZE 609

TABLE 3.—CROSS-STATE DETERMINANTS OF FIRM SIZE DISTRIBUTION

	(1)	(2)	(3)	(4)
	OLS	IV	IV	IV
Market size	0.501*** (0.091)	0.591*** (0.140)	0.591*** (0.140)	0.595*** (0.134)
Judicial efficiency	0.420*** (0.097)	0.981* (0.506)	1.137*** (0.419)	0.757** (0.301)
R-squared	0.51	0.47	0.45	0.51
States	32	32	32	32
Observations	699	699	699	699
First Stage: Judicial Efficiency				
Market size		−0.115 (0.127)	−0.042 (0.113)	0.013 (0.186)
Indigenous population		−0.150** (0.070)	−0.145** (0.069)	−0.169** (0.079)
Crops			−0.149* (0.077)	−0.185* (0.100)
Geographical controls	No	No	No	Yes
Hansen overidentification test (p-value)			0.63	0.63
F-test of identifying instruments		0.03	0.03	0.03
Partial R-squared		0.15	0.25	−0.22
R-squared		0.17	0.27	0.29
Observations		32	32	32

The dependent variable is the logarithm of the weighted average firm size. All regressions are at the state/industry level. Columns 2 to 4 report instrumental variable (IV) regressions. As instruments we use the log of the share of the indigenous population in 1900 and the number of cultivated crops with large economies of scale (sugar, coffee, rice, and cotton) in 1939. In column 4 we add variables measuring state-level average rainfall and temperature, both measured over the 1925–34 period, and the percentage of land that is tropical (as opposed to temperate or arid). We report the first stage for the IV regressions in the lower part of the table. We exclude the electricity, water, oil and gas extraction, coal mining, fishing, and medical and educational services industries and observations based on fewer than three firms. Regressions include the logarithm of total population in a state as a measure of the size of the market. Judicial efficiency is based on survey data from ITAM/GMA at year-end 1998 and is measured as the average of seven individual indicators (on a scale from 0 5): perceived quality of judges; perceived impartiality of judges; adequacy of resources for materials; efficiency in the enforcement of resolutions; efficiency of public ministry of justice; efficiency of public registry of real estate property; and adequacy of local legislation for the enforcement of contracts. A higher score indicates more efficiency. Industry fixed effects are included, but not reported. Standard errors are reported in parentheses and are corrected for potential dependence of observations within states (clusters). We also report the p-value of an F-test of the identifying instruments, the partial R-squared of the identifying instruments, and the p-value of the Hansen overidentification test of all instruments. *, **, *** denotes significance at 10%, 5%, and 1%, respectively.

We get similar results when not controlling for market size, although the statistical significance of judicial efficiency is somewhat reduced.

Column 2 of table 3 repeats the regression, instrumenting for judicial efficiency with the share of indigenous population in 1900. The first-stage regression is reported at the bottom of the table. The instrument is significant and explains 15% of the variation in the judicial efficiency measure. Instrumented judicial efficiency remains highly statistically significant. The measured coefficient is about two times larger than the OLS estimate.

Column 3 of table 3 repeats the regression using two instruments for judicial efficiency: the share of indigenous population in 1900 and the production of crops that have large economies of scale in 1939. The instruments are both significant and explain 25% of the variation in the judicial efficiency measure. The instruments pass a standard test of overidentification, indicated by the Hansen statistic. Instrumented judicial efficiency remains highly statistically significant.

The overidentification test provides some confirmation of the validity of the instruments. Nevertheless, some concern with exclusion restrictions remains. In particular, the prevalence of crops with large economies of scale may be the result of geographical and climatological factors that affect both crop choice and economies of scale in production more generally. We do find that geographical variables are associated with the prevalence of large-scale-economy crops. Average rainfall and temperature, both measured from 1925 to 1934, and the proportion of land area classified as tropical are all significantly associated with the prevalence of large-

scale-economy crops.[23] Together, they explain about a quarter of the cross-state variance in both crops with large economies of scale and historical indigenous population. In column 4 of table 3 we report the first-and second-stage regressions with these variables added as additional regressors in the IV regression. None of the geographical controls are significant in either the first or the second stage. The instruments remain significant in the first-stage regression, and instrumented judicial efficiency remains significant almost at the 1% level in the second stage, with a coefficient smaller than the IV regression without geographical controls.

One might also be concerned that historical and current indigenous population shares are correlated, and that current indigenous share is related to firm size directly. The former is the case. The correlation between indigenous share in 1900 and indigenous share in 2000 is 0.90. However, when we include indigenous share in 2000 as an additional regressor, judicial efficiency remains significant at the 10% level. Moreover, if we use only crops with large economies of scale as an instrument, and include either historical or current indigenous share as a regressor, neither measure of indigenous share is associated with firm size, and judicial efficiency (instrumented only with large-scale-economy crops) is significant at the 5% level. Given the compelling arguments for a connection between indigenous population and institutional development made by AJR (2001) and Acemoglu and Johnson (2005), and the lack of evidence that

[23] The source of the geographical data is INEGI.

TABLE 4.—ALTERNATIVE SIZE MEASURES, ALTERNATIVE INSTITUTIONAL MEASURES, AND ALTERNATIVE SAMPLES

	(1) Average Firm Size	(2) Typical Firm Size	(3) Share of Small Firms	(4) Invested Capital	(5) Judicial Factor	(6) Private Credit	(7) GDP and Education	(8) All Firms	(9) All Sectors	(10) All Bins
Market size	0.216**	0.388**	−0.066**	0.992***	0.396***	0.126	0.519***	0.621***	0.545***	0.585***
	(0.100)	(0.172)	(0.028)	(0.206)	(0.125)	(0.114)	(0.064)	(0.147)	(0.138)	(0.142)
Judicial efficiency	0.746**	1.345**	−0.227***	1.604**			0.514**	1.060**	1.039***	1.158***
	(0.302)	(0.535)	(0.082)	(0.658)			(0.209)	(0.419)	(0.390)	(0.416)
Judicial factor					0.619***					
					(0.235)					
Private credit						5.967**				
						(2.923)				
Per capita income							0.236			
							(0.265)			
Schooling							2.043*			
							(1.094)			
Hansen test (p-value)	0.67	0.56	0.59	0.23	0.36	0.71	0.42	0.30	0.20	0.27
R-squared	0.64	0.45	0.52	0.33	0.46	0.45	0.55	0.44	0.49	0.44
States	32	32	32	32	32	32	32	32	32	32
Observations	699	699	699	699	699	699	699	699	799	706

This table reports instrumental variables (IV) regressions. The dependent variable is the logarithm of the weighted average firm size, unless otherwise noted. As instruments for judicial efficiency we use the log of the share of the indigenous population in 1900 and the number of cultivated crops with large economies of scale (sugar, coffee, rice, and cotton) in 1939. We exclude the electricity, water, oil and gas extraction, coal mining, fishing, and medical and educational services industries. We exclude observations based on fewer than three firms. Industry fixed effects are included in the regressions, but not reported. The dependent variable in regression (1) is the logarithm of unweighted average firm size in terms of workers. The dependent variable in regression (2) is the logarithm of the average firm size in the bin where the median worker is located, referred to as the "typical" firm size. The dependent variable in regression (3) is the share of workers in firms with fewer than 20 employees. The dependent variable in regression (4) is average firm size weighted by the level of invested capital stock. In regression (5) we use the first principal component of the seven judicial efficiency questions as an alternative measure of judicial efficiency. In regression (6) we use state-level private credit to GDP rather than judicial efficiency. Data on private credit are from INEGI. In regression (7) we control for state-level log per capita income and education. Schooling is the share of population in each state aged fifteen years and over with at least nine years of schooling education in 1990. The dependent variable in regression (8) is the average firm size for all firms (including foreign-owned and multiplant firms). In regression (9) we include all industries (including government sectors). In regression (10) we include observations based on fewer than three firms. Market size is the logarithm of state population. Standard errors are corrected for potential dependence of observations within states (clusters). We also report the p-value of an F-test of the identifying instruments and the p-value of the Hansen overidentification test of all instruments. *, **, *** denotes significance at 10%, 5%, and 1%, respectively.

indigenous share and firm size are directly related, we use both instruments in the remaining regressions. The robustness of the results to various instrumenting strategies and controls is, however, reassuring.

Table 4 presents results from alternative measures of firm size, alternative measures of institutions, and several alternative samples. All regressions are estimated using an IV approach with the share of indigenous population in 1900 and the production of crops with large economies of scale in 1939 as instruments for judicial efficiency.[24] Looking at the alternative definitions of firm size first, the results are very similar if we use the simple unweighted average firm size (column 1). We also obtain similar (somewhat stronger) results when we define the state/industry firm size as being the size bin that includes the median worker. We refer to this as the "typical" firm size (column 2). We find similarly significant results if we regress the share of workers in the state/sector working in firms with fewer than 20 workers (column 3). Note that the coefficient on judicial efficiency is negative in this case, indicating that better legal systems are associated with a smaller percentage of the workers being employed in small firms. Indeed, the results are robust to using a cutoff of 10, 50, 100, or 250 workers instead of 20 workers to define small firms. In column 4, we use the log of weighted average firm size in terms of invested capital levels rather than employees as the dependent variable, and again find similar results.

Columns 5 and 6 repeat the regression in column 3 of table 3, using alternative measures of institutional quality. In column 5, we use the first principal component of the seven judicial efficiency questions as an alternative measure of institutions. The standard deviation of the factor is about 80% larger than the standard deviation of the straight average, so the results are quite similar, both in magnitude and significance. In column 6, we replace judicial efficiency with a standard measure of financial market development, the ratio of private credit to GDP. The financial development measure is based on more concrete data than our survey-based measure of judicial efficiency, and thus may be a more palatable indication of financial contracting for those concerned with subjective measures. We want to stress, however, that the financial development measure is based on debt, while the financial contracts most relevant in our model are ownership contracts. The results are similar, consistent with the notion that financial market development itself is a function of the efficiency of the legal system. The ratio of private credit to GDP has a standard deviation of about 10%, suggesting that a 1-standard-deviation increase in credit is associated with an increase of about 0.36 of a standard deviation in firm size. This is comparable to the level effect of judicial efficiency in the IV regressions.[25,26]

Column 7 adds the level of per capita income in the state and the percentage of the population aged fifteen and older with at least nine years of schooling. These are excluded from the base regressions because they are likely to be

[24] We obtain similar results in all regressions when using OLS with clustering at the state level instead.

[25] We obtain very similar results when using the number of bank branches per capita in the state as measure of financial development. We obtain data on bank branches per capita in 2000 from INEGI.

[26] The IV regressions in columns 5 and 6 pass the standard identification tests, such as the F-test of identifying instruments and the Hansen overidentifying test.

TABLE 5.—FIRM SIZE DISTRIBUTION, QUALITY OF THE LEGAL SYSTEM, AND NATURAL PROPENSITY TO INCORPORATE

	(1)	(2)	(3)	(4)	(5)	(6)	(7)
	OLS with Clustering	OLS with State Fixed Effects	IV with State Fixed Effects	OLS with Clustering	OLS with State Fixed Effects	IV with State Fixed Effects	IV: Organizational Form
				Controlling for Other Channels			
Market size	0.501***			0.502***			0.024
	(0.091)			(0.091)			(0.023)
Judicial efficiency	0.572***			1.346*			0.126**
	(0.127)			(0.707)			(0.060)
Judicial efficiency × Incorporation intensity	−0.798**	−0.863***	−1.713***	−0.759**	−0.810***	−1.631**	
	(0.299)	(0.312)	(0.632)	(0.284)	(0.291)	(0.656)	
Judicial efficiency × Vertical integration				−0.172	−0.145	−0.812	
				(0.456)	(0.471)	(0.806)	
Judicial efficiency × Capital intensity				−0.059	−0.068	−0.174	
				(0.059)	(0.062)	(0.174)	
F-test of overidentifying restrictions			0.00			0.00	0.03
Hansen overidentification test (p-value)			0.44			0.80	0.72
R-squared	0.52	0.60	0.59	0.52	0.60	0.59	0.66
States	32	32	32	32	32	32	32
Observations	699	699	699	699	699	699	667

The dependent variable in regressions (1) to (6) is the weighted average firm size. The dependent variable in regression (7) is the ratio of corporations to proprietorships at the industry/state level. Incorporation intensity is the ratio of corporations to proprietorships at the industry level. Vertical integration is the ratio of value added to sales at the industry level. Capital intensity is the ratio of fixed assets plus inventories to employment at the industry level. Incorporation intensity, vertical integration, and capital intensity are calculated based on data from the 1998 Mexican economic census. Columns 1 and 4 report OLS regressions with clustering at the state level. Columns 2 and 5 report OLS regressions with state fixed effects. Columns 3 and 6 report instrumental variables (IV) regressions with state fixed effects, and column 7 reports an IV regression without state fixed effects. As instruments for judicial efficiency (or finance), we use the log of the share of the indigenous population in 1900 and the number of cultivated crops with large economies of scale (sugar, coffee, rice, and cotton) in 1939. We drop the construction sector in the regression reported in column 7 because of missing data on organizational form at the industry/state level. All regressions exclude the electricity, water, oil and gas extraction, coal mining, fishing, and medical and educational services industries. We further exclude observations based on fewer than three firms. Industry fixed effects are included in all regressions and state fixed effects in regression (2), (3), (5), and (6), but these are not reported. Judicial efficiency is based on survey data from ITAM/GMA and is measured as the average of seven individual indicators. Standard errors are reported in parentheses and corrected for potential dependence of observations within states (clusters). We also report the p-value of an F-test of the identifying instruments and the p-value of the Hansen overidentification test of all instruments. *, **, *** denotes significance at 10%, 5%, and 1%, respectively.

endogenous to the quality of the legal system (and institutions more broadly). We do not have separate instruments for them. Their coefficients should be interpreted with some caution as a result. For our purposes, a key point worth noting is that when they are included, the measure of judicial efficiency remains significant. The coefficient on judicial efficiency is reduced in magnitude by nearly 50%, however.

The results are also robust to including foreign and multiplant firms in the sample (column 8), to including the sectors dominated by the government, such as electricity and mining (column 9),[27] and to including sectors with bins containing fewer than three firms (column 10).[28] Thus, the results are robust to various measures of firm size and institutions, and to various ways of defining the sample. Both the results in this table and those in table 3 are robust to the exclusion of one industry or state at a time. Hence, no industry or state appears to be driving the results.

A. *Legal Quality and Corporate Form*

A key prediction of the model is that the legal system will have a larger impact on the size of proprietorships than on

[27] If we run the regression in column 10 only for the government sectors, then the coefficient on judicial efficiency is smaller in magnitude, as expected, and no longer statistically significant; the number of observations in this case is reduced to only 100.

[28] In many of these sectors, we had to estimate the number of firms from the total number of employees, and hence we chose not to include them in our base regressions. Also, these regressions are less subject to outliers in state/sector firm-size estimates.

the size of corporations (proposition 2). To test this differential effect, we add to the regressions a variable measuring the percentage of firms in the industry that are corporations and the interaction of this term with the measure of the quality of the legal system. The structure of the regression model is now

$$Size_{ij} = \alpha_i + \beta B_j + \gamma \Gamma_{ij} + \xi L_i \Omega_j + \varepsilon_{ij},$$

where L_i is the incorporation intensity in industry i and Ω_j is the quality of the legal system in state j. The other variables are as before. Again, all regressions include sector-level fixed effects.

Table 5 reports OLS and IV regressions of the extended model. We include industry fixed effects in all regressions and state fixed effects in the regressions reported in columns 2 and 3. The OLS regression reported in column 1 does not include state fixed effects but instead controls for market size and judicial efficiency directly. We find that the interaction term is negative and significant. This indicates that the efficiency of the legal system has less effect in sectors with greater incorporation intensity. In other words, changes in the quality of the legal system impact sectors where proprietorships predominate (such as services) more than sectors where corporations predominate (such as manufacturing of basic metals). Indeed, the negative coefficient on the interaction term is larger in magnitude than the original positive coefficient on judicial efficiency. However, the standard deviation on incorporation intensity is only 0.20, so the combined level and interaction effect is positive.[29]

How much does the impact of incorporation intensity vary with the quality of the legal system? A specific example may help clarify what the coefficient on the interaction term means. Take an industry such as "repair and maintenance" that is at the 25th percentile of our measure of incorporation intensity (in other words, relatively many proprietorships) and an industry such as "wholesale trade" that is at the 75th percentile of incorporation intensity. The coefficient estimate in column 3 of table 5 suggests that the difference in average firm size between "repair and maintenance" and "wholesale trade" in Jalisco (that is at the 25th percentile of judicial efficiency) is 0.14 higher than the difference in average firm size between the same industries in Baja California (that is at the 75th percentile of judicial efficiency). In other words, moving from Jalisco to Baja California benefits the sector where proprietorships predominate relatively more. As a comparison, the mean difference in average firm size between the "wholesale" and "repair and maintenance" sectors across states is 0.83. This suggests that the effect of judicial efficiency accounts for about 17% of the mean difference. This is an economically significant effect.

Next, we consider several alternative channels through which judicial efficiency may affect firm size. First, the effect could depend on the degree of vertical integration of the firm. We would expect the effect of judicial efficiency on firm size to be more pronounced for nonvertically integrated firms because a nonvertically integrated firm relies more on the judicial system to enforce contracts with suppliers and customers (Johnson et al., 2002b). A highly vertically integrated firm does not rely on the judicial system as much since all activities are internalized. As a measure of vertical integration at the sector level we use the ratio of total value added to total sales in the sector, where a value of 1 means that firms in the sector are highly vertically integrated and a value of 0 means that firms are not vertically integrated.[30]

Judicial efficiency could also affect firm size differently depending on the capital intensity of the sector, as in KRZ (2002). They find that the effect of judicial efficiency on firm size is more pronounced for firms in sectors with low levels of capital intensity. As a measure of capital intensity at the sector level, we use the ratio of total fixed assets plus inventories to total employment in the sector. An additional reason for controlling for capital intensity is that corporations tend to be more capital intensive and so our measure

of incorporation intensity might be picking up the effects of capital intensity rather than the effect of diversified ownership.

The regressions reported in columns 4 to 6 of table 5 repeat those reported in columns 1 to 3 but also consider the differential effect of vertical integration and capital intensity on firm size by including interaction terms between judicial efficiency and vertical integration and between judicial efficiency and capital intensity.[31] Consistent with our prior regressions, we find a negative coefficient on the interaction term between judicial efficiency and vertical integration, although the effect is not statistically significant. We also find a negative coefficient on the interaction term between judicial efficiency and capital intensity, consistent with the findings of KRZ (2002), although again the effect is statistically insignificant. Importantly, our main result is unaffected. Incorporation intensity remains an important channel through with judicial efficiency affects firm size, even after controlling for the degree of vertical integration and capital intensity.

Finally, we consider the effect of judicial efficiency on the relative share of corporations among all firms. As we discussed above, the theoretical prediction on the sign of judicial efficiency is ambiguous (proposition 3). The results shown in column 7 of table 5 indicate that firms in states with higher-quality judicial systems are more likely to be incorporated. Since the regression includes sector fixed effects, this should be interpreted as a within-sector effect. This is consistent with better financial contracting environments making the identification of equity partners easier, and with the judicial system making it easier to expand customer bases.

B. Efficiency Effects

The theoretical framework implies that increased firm size is associated with increased efficiency in the economy. Where idiosyncratic risk is reduced, capital is allocated more efficiently among entrepreneurs. Thus, theoretically at least, improvements in the quality of the legal system improve the efficiency of the economy. The implication of the theory is that these consequences should show up as increasing returns to scale. The existing literature examining returns to scale among firms in developing countries suggests that returns to scale are modest if present at all (Tybout, 2000). However, most of this literature is limited to an examination of the manufacturing sector. One exception is the paper by Pagano and Schivardi (2003), which finds that productivity growth is increasing in firm size across industries in Europe. Like us, they use data from both

---

[29] We find qualitatively similar results when we define incorporation intensity in terms of employment rather than number of firms. This is hardly surprising given that the correlation between these two measures at the sectoral level is 0.94. We also find similar results when using the alternative measures of average firm size considered in table 4.

[30] When we use the distinction between manufacturing, which is interfirm-contracting intensive, and retail/service sectors as an alternative measure of interfirm contracting instead of vertical integration we obtain similar results.

[31] The correlation between incorporation intensity and vertical integration is −0.26 (significant at 1%), and the correlation between incorporation intensity and capital intensity is +0.33 (significant at 1%), hence, incorporation intensity captures sector-specific differences that are to a large extent distinct from those captured by vertical integration or capital intensity.

THE QUALITY OF THE LEGAL SYSTEM, FIRM OWNERSHIP, AND FIRM SIZE 613

TABLE 6.—QUALITY OF THE LEGAL SYSTEM AND FIRM PRODUCTIVITY

	(1) OLS	(2) IV
Judicial efficiency	0.118**	0.352**
	(0.047)	(0.155)
ln(Capital)	0.464*	0.405*
	(0.232)	(0.218)
ln(Labor)	0.404*	0.473**
	(0.218)	(0.201)
ln(Materials)	−0.040*	−0.044**
	(0.023)	(0.022)
ln(Capital) × ln(Labor)	0.064	0.049
	(0.046)	(0.042)
ln(Capital) × ln(Materials)	0.014***	0.015***
	(0.004)	(0.004)
ln(Labor) × ln(Materials)	−0.028***	−0.030***
	(0.004)	(0.004)
ln(Capital)^2	−0.024	−0.018
	(0.022)	(0.020)
ln(Labor)^2	−0.030	−0.020
	(0.027)	(0.024)
ln(Materials)^2	0.009***	0.009***
	(0.001)	(0.001)
F-test of overidentifying restrictions		0.03
Hansen overidentification test (*p*-value)		0.25
R-squared	0.95	0.94
States	32	32
Observations	699	699

Dependent variable is the logarithm of sales (output) at the industry/state level. We estimate the following translog production function: $\ln(Y) = \ln(K) + \ln(L) + \ln(M) + \ln(K) \times \ln(L) + \ln(K) \times \ln(M) + \ln(L) \times \ln(M) + \ln(K)^2 + \ln(L)^2 + \ln(M)^2 + \varepsilon$, where Y is output as measured by gross production, K is capital as measured by fixed assets, L is labor as measured by number of employees, and M is materials as measured by raw materials and intermediate goods. Column 1 reports an OLS regression and column 2 reports an instrumental variables (IV) regression. As instruments for judicial efficiency (or finance), we use the log of the share of the indigenous population in 1900 and the number of cultivated crops with large economies of scale (sugar, coffee, rice, and cotton) in 1939. We further exclude the electricity, water, oil and gas extraction, coal mining, fishing, and medical and educational services industries. We exclude observations based on fewer than three firms. Standard errors are reported in parentheses and corrected for potential dependence of observations within states (clusters). We also report the *p*-value of an *F*-test of the identifying instruments and the *p*-Value of the Hansen overidentification test of all instruments. *, **, *** denotes significance at 10%, 5%, and 1%, respectively.

manufacturing and service sectors, where the presence of proprietorships is greater.

We provide some additional evidence of efficiency effects by running regressions for a basic translog production function and including judicial efficiency on the right-hand side. Table 6 reports the results of this exercise. After controlling for capital, labor, and material inputs, we find that the output of firms (as measured by the log of sales) increases with the quality of the legal system. We estimate the production function using both OLS and IV. The coefficient on our standard measure of judicial efficiency when estimating using OLS is 0.12 (column 1), indicating that a 1-standard-deviation increase in the quality of the legal system is associated with an increase in sales of about 0.03 standard deviations. The increase is substantially larger in the IV estimation (column 2)—almost 0.10 standard deviations. Overall, these results suggest that improvements in the quality of the legal system are associated with improvements in the efficiency of the economy.

V. Conclusions

We draw three broad conclusions from the model and the data. First, the data show the importance of informal insti-

tutions in determining outcomes. The formal laws governing both economic transactions and broader relationships between individuals and the state (or elites) are very similar across states in Mexico. The perceived efficiency of the legal system varies. The variation is consistent with historical factors previously identified in cross-country research as affecting the quality of institutions. The variation in the quality of the legal system is reflected in a variation in the size of firms.

Second, the results provide support for the idea that one of the ways an improved legal system affects economic outcomes is by diminishing idiosyncratic risk. Empirically, this support comes primarily from the interaction between legal quality and incorporation intensity. The coefficient on this interaction indicates that legal systems have a larger effect on firm size in industries dominated by proprietorships than in industries where corporations are more prevalent. Idiosyncratic risk is reduced away when liability is limited and ownership is dispersed—that is, when firms are organized as corporations.

We interpret our collective results as indicating that contracting institutions are important in the efficiency of the economy. This conclusion differs to some extent from that of Acemoglu and Johnson (2005) who find that broader property rights measures affect economic outcomes but narrower contracting institutions have no effect. However, the difference between our results and theirs may not be so great. That is, it may still be the case that contracting institutions are of second-order importance to broader property rights institutions. None of our regressions controls for broader property rights institutions, which are likely to be highly correlated with our measures of narrow contracting institutions. But even if we interpret judicial efficiency as proxying for broader measures of institutions in the initial regressions (reported in tables 3 and 4), then the results in table 5 suggest that individuals are able to contract around these difficulties. That is, where they are able to incorporate and diversify ownership, the effect of weaker institutions is markedly diminished. Thus, we believe that, taken as a whole, our results show that narrow contracting institutions matter.

REFERENCES

Acemoglu, D., "Constitutions, Politics and Economics: A Review Essay on Persson and Tabellini's *The Economic Effects of Constitutions,*" *Journal of Economic Literature* 43 (2005), 1025–1048.
Acemoglu, D., and S. Johnson, "Unbundling Institutions," *Journal of Political Economics* 113 (2005), 949–995.
Acemoglu, D., S. Johnson, and J. Robinson, "The Colonial Origins of Comparative Development: An Empirical Investigation," *American Economic Review* 91 (2001), 1369–1401.
—— "Reversal of Fortune: Geography and Institutions in the Making of the Modern World Income Distribution," *Quarterly Journal of Economics* 117 (2002), 1231–1294.
—— "Institutions as the Fundamental Cause of Long-Run Growth," *Handbook of Economic Growth* (2005), 385–472.
Acemoglu, D., S. Johnson, J. Robinson, and Y. Thaicharoen, "Institutional Causes, Macroeconomic Symptoms: Volatility, Crises and Growth," *Journal of Monetary Economics* 50 (2003), 49–123.

Alchian, A. A., and H. Demsetz, "Production, Information Costs, and Economic Organization," *American Economic Review* 62 (1972), 777–795.

Banerjee, A., and L. Iyer, "History, Institutions and Economic Performance: The Legacy of Colonial Land Tenure Systems in India," *American Economic Review* 95 (2005), 1190–1213.

Besley, T., "Property Rights and Investment Incentives: Theory and Evidence from Ghana," *Journal of Political Economy* 103 (1995), 903–937.

Cabral, L. M. B., and J. Mata, "On the Evolution of the Firm Size Distribution: Facts and Theory," *American Economic Review* 93 (2003), 1075–1090.

Cantú, H. A., and J. A. Caballero, "La Reforma Judicial en las Entidades Federativas," in Serna and Caballero (Eds.), *Estado de Derecho en Transicion Juridica* (Mexico City: UNAM Instituto de Investigaciones Juridicas, 2002).

Claessens, S., and L. Laeven, "Financial Development, Property Rights, and Growth," *Journal of Finance* 58 (2003), 2401–2436.

Cohen, W. M., and S. Klepper, "Firm Size and the Nature of Innovation within Industries: The Case of Process and Product R&D," this REVIEW 78:2 (1996), 232–243.

Davis, S. J., and M. Henrekson, "Explaining National Differences in the Size and Industry Distribution of Employment," University of Chicago Mimeograph (1997).

Djankov, S., R. La Porta, F. Lopez-de-Silanes, and A. Shleifer, "Courts," *Quarterly Journal of Economics* 118 (2003), 453–517.

Engerman, S. L., and K. Sokoloff, "Factor Developments, Inequality, and Paths of Development among New World Economies." NBER working paper no. 9259 (2002).

Fama, E. F., and M. C. Jensen, "Separation of Ownership and Control," *Journal of Law and Economics* 26 (1983), 301–325.

Fix-Fierro, H., "Judicial Reform in Mexico," in Jensen and Heller (Eds.), *Beyond Common Knowledge: Empirical Approaches to the Rule of Law* (Stanford, CA: Stanford University Press, 2003).

Gelos, G. R., and A. M. Werner, "Financial Liberalization, Credit Constraints, and Collateral: Investment in the Mexican Manufacturing Sector," *Journal of Development Economics* 67 (2002), 1–27.

Gibson, C., *Spain in America* (New York: Harper Colophon Books, 1966).

Holmstrom, B., "Moral Hazard in Teams," *Bell Journal of Economics* 13 (1982), 324–340.

Instituto Tecnológico Autónomo de México and Gaxiola Moraila y Asociados, S.C. (ITAM/GMA), "La Administración de Justicia de las Entidades Mexicanas a Partir del Caso de la Cartera Bancaria," Mexico City (1999).

Johnson, S., J. McMillan, and C. Woodruff, "Property Rights and Finance," *American Economic Review* 92 (2002a), 1335–1356.

——— "Courts and Relational Contracts," *Journal of Law, Economics and Organization* 18 (2002b), 221–277.

Kihlstrom, R. E., and J.-J. Laffont, "A General Equilibrium Entrepreneurial Theory of Risk-Taking Based on Risk-Aversion," *Journal of Political Economy* 87 (1979), 719–748.

Kumar, K., R. Rajan, and L. Zingales, "What Determines Firm Size?" University of Chicago GSB Working paper (2002).

La Porta, R., F. Lopez-de-Silanes, and G. Zamarripa, "Related Lending," *Quarterly Journal of Economics* 118 (2003), 231–268.

Levine, Ross. "The Legal Environment, Banks, and Long-Run Economic Growth," *Journal of Money, Credit, and Banking* 30:3 (1998), 596–613.

Lucas, R. E., "On the Size Distribution of Firms," *Bell Journal of Economics* 9 (1978), 508–523.

McMillan, J., and C. Woodruff, "The Central Role of Entrepreneurs in Transition Economies," *Journal of Economic Perspectives* 16 (2002), 153–170.

McNeece, J. B., and M. T. Poelstra, "Secured Transactions under Mexican Law," Luce, Forward, Hamilton, and Scripps, LLP, Working paper (2003).

Negrón Ruiz, A. Pérez, "El Consejo de la Judicatura Estatal: Refuerzo de la Independencia del Poder Judicial en el Estado de Michoacán," Revista Juridica, Universidad Latina de América (2003).

Pagano, P., and F. Schivardi, "Firm Size Distribution and Growth," *Scandinavian Journal of Economics* 105 (2003), 255–274.

Persson, T., and G. Tabellini, *The Economic Effects of Constitutions: What Do the Data Say?* (Cambridge: MIT Press, 2003).

Sarre, M., and A. López Ugalde, *Administración de Justicia en México. Indicadores en materia mercantil e hipotecaria* (Mexico: ITAM-Gaxiola Moralia, 2002).

Tybout, J. R., "Manufacturing Firms in Developing Countries: How Well Do They Do, and Why?" *Journal of Economic Literature* 38 (2000), 11–44.

[17]

The Central Role of Entrepreneurs in Transition Economies

John McMillan and Christopher Woodruff

A ll sorts of small enterprises boomed in the countryside, as if a strange army appeared suddenly from nowhere," remarked Deng Xiaoping, reflecting in 1987 on the first eight years of China's economic reforms (Zhao, 1996, p. 106). These startup firms drove China's reform momentum; they were arguably the single main source of China's growth. But their rapid emergence, Deng said, "was not something I had thought about. Nor had the other comrades. This surprised us." The reformers had not foreseen the key to their own reforms. The other ex-communist economies had similar experiences. As in China, new firms were drivers of reform. They strengthened the budding market economy by creating jobs, supplying consumer goods, mobilizing savings and ending the state firms' monopoly. As in China, also, the reformers usually did not anticipate the force of entry.

Of the two routes to a private sector—privatizing the existing firms and creating new ones—the policy debates focused almost exclusively on the former. Little attention was given to what reform policies would foster entry. Dusan Triska, for example, the architect of Czechoslovakia's privatization program, said privatization "is not just one of the many items on the economic program. It is the transformation itself" (Nellis, 2001, p. 32). It is not surprising that those who had spent their lives under central planning did not foresee the impact of entrepreneurship, but few analysts from the West predicted it either.

The reason for underestimating entrepreneurship, perhaps, was a sense that setting up a business, risky anywhere, is especially risky in an economy undergoing

■ *John McMillan is Professor of Economics, Graduate School of Business, Stanford University, Stanford, California. Christopher Woodruff is Assistant Professor of Economics, Graduate School of International Relations and Pacific Studies, University of California at San Diego, La Jolla, California. Their e-mail addresses are ⟨mcmillan_john@gsb.stanford.edu⟩ and ⟨cwoodruff@ucsd.edu⟩.*

deep reform. With prices volatile as a result of the reforms, it is unclear which lines of business are going to be the most profitable. State firms, fearing competition, harass the new firms, and corrupt bureaucrats extort bribes. Without the normal market-supporting institutions, the new firms usually cannot rely on the courts to enforce their contracts; bank loans are unobtainable for most; and there is little legal or regulatory provision for shareholding.

These handicaps notwithstanding, large parts of the new market economy arose spontaneously, through the initiatives of entrepreneurs. They succeeded by self-help: they built for themselves substitutes for the missing institutions. Reputational incentives substituted for court enforcement of contracts. Trade credit (loans from firm to firm along the supply chain) substituted for bank credit. Reinvestment of profits substituted for outside equity.

In this paper, we summarize entrepreneurial patterns in the transition economies, particularly Russia, China, Poland and Vietnam.[1] Markets developed spontaneously in every transition country, but they were built at varying speeds. Some governments impeded the entrepreneurs' self-help by creating conditions that made it hard for informal contracting to work; others created an environment that was conducive to self-help. The spontaneous emergence of markets, furthermore, has its limits. As firms' activities became more complex, they came to need formal institutions. Some governments fostered entrepreneurship by building market-supporting infrastructure; others did not (Frye and Shleifer, 1997). We will argue that the success or failure of a transition economy can be traced in large part to the performance of its entrepreneurs.

The Environment for Entrepreneurship

All the transition economies, from the former Soviet Union and central and eastern Europe to China and Vietnam, were similar in one important respect: their planned economies had been dominated by large firms, producing few consumer goods. Small and medium-sized firms were almost nonexistent, although they are a large part of every market economy. Trade and services were also a much smaller part of the transition economies than is typical for a market economy. As reform led to greater flexibility in prices, wages and production decisions, the imbalances inherited from the planned economy created enormous profit opportunities for entrepreneurs. Entrepreneurs responded by starting enterprises at a rapid—though varying—rate in each of the transition countries.

Some governments actively made it hard for entrepreneurs to operate. Expropriation of profits through official corruption was the most conspicuous of such actions. Managers of startup manufacturing firms were asked in a survey whether "extralegal" payments were needed in order to receive government services or a

---

[1] Our focus will be on the state's role in encouraging startup firms, not on efforts to create a market sector by revamping the old state firms; on that issue, see Djankov and Murrell (2002), Megginson and Netter (2001) and Nellis (2001).

business license (Johnson, McMillan and Woodruff, 2002b). More than 90 percent of Russian managers said they were, compared with about 20 percent of Polish managers. Corruption deters investment. Those firms in the sample that were the most concerned about corruption invested nearly 40 percent less than those least concerned. The mafia is a further deterrent to entrepreneurship. Asked whether payments to private agencies were necessary for "protection" of their activities, more than 90 percent of Russian managers and 8 percent of Polish managers said they were.

Managers were asked in the same survey whether they would invest $100 today if they expected to receive $200 in two years (an implied annual rate of return of 40 percent). The responses to this question give an indication of both the opportunity cost of money and the security of property. A striking 99 percent of the Russian managers said they would not, compared with 22 percent of the Polish managers.

Illegitimate takings aside, official policies often make it expensive to set up firms. Entrepreneurs must apply for business licenses to establish that their company's name is unique and provide proof of their startup capital; then they must file with the tax and labor authorities. In Russia, setting up a new business takes an entrepreneur over two months and costs 38 percent of per capita GDP in official fees (Djankov et al., 2002). In Poland, it takes nearly a month and costs 28 percent of per capita GDP. In Vietnam, it takes nearly six months and costs a striking 150 percent of per capita GDP.

The government's decisions on privatizing state firms may also have affected the environment for new firms. Mass privatization could add to the general uncertainty, thus deterring entry. Across Russia's regions, more new firms have been formed where there was less privatization of small state enterprises, though more entry has occurred where there was more privatization of large-scale state enterprises (Berkowitz and Holland, 2001). The continued presence of state enterprises also raised barriers to entry. They absorbed scarce capital and received regulatory favors (as did the privatized firms). Anecdotes abound of state firms stifling new entrants to prevent them from becoming competitors.

Not only did governments impede entrepreneurship, formal institutions to underpin entrepreneurial activity developed only slowly. In Vietnam in the mid-1990s, for example, after a decade of reform, the market institutions were still inadequate. Banks almost exclusively served state-owned firms. There were no credit-reporting bureaus. Courts able to enforce contracts between private firms were just being created. Among manufacturers we surveyed between 1995 and 1997, less than 10 percent said that courts or the government could enforce a contract with a buyer or seller, and just 10 percent said that they had received credit from banks when they started their business (McMillan and Woodruff, 1999b). In another survey carried out in 1997, 74 percent of private firms reported having no debts to banks, and such debts represented only 20 percent of the capital among the 24 percent of the firms that did have them (Ronnås, 1998).

Profits and Entry

Four transition countries, Poland, Russia, China and Vietnam, span the range of entrepreneurship patterns. Poland was among the most successful in fostering new private firms. Russia was among the least successful, though entry occurred even there. China took a distinctive path with entry of competitive enterprises run by local governments. Vietnam offers an example of robust growth of private firms even with an almost total absence of formal institutions to facilitate business.

A telling measure of the success of a transition economy's reforms is the time path of entrants' profits. Figure 1 shows the path of profits in the five years following the start of transition in China (1979–1984) and in Poland and Russia (1990–1995). In China, at the start of the reform era in 1979, the average profits of nonstate firms were 28 percent of invested capital. This is very high in comparison to earnings in a mature market economy: small businesses in the United States typically earn returns between 9 percent and 15 percent of assets.[2] As China's transition proceeded, the new firms' profits declined steadily through the first decade of reform, falling to 15 percent of invested capital in 1984 and leveling out at 6 percent in 1991 (Naughton, 1995, p. 150).

In Poland, profit rates of manufacturing firms in their first year of operation fell from an average of 25 percent of invested capital for firms formed in 1990 to 6 percent for firms formed in 1995. In Russia, also, profits earned by entrants were high at the start of the reforms: firms established in 1990 earned an average profit of 17 percent on invested capital in their first year of operation. By contrast with China and Poland, however, profits did not decline over time: first-year profits for firms established in 1995, at 16 percent, were almost as high as those for the firms established in 1990 (Johnson, McMillan and Woodruff, 2002b).[3]

The high profits earned in all three countries early in the transition are easily explained. The starting point was a heavily distorted economy with unfilled market niches. Firms that were able to overcome the impediments to doing business and produce and sell goods and services were very profitable. In Poland and China, as market-supporting institutions developed, the impediments declined and so rents

---

[2] The U.S. data are from the National Survey of Small Business Finances (Federal Reserve Board of Governors, 1994). The NSSBF sampled 273 manufacturing firms with between 10 and 250 employees. The return on invested capital averages 15 percent. However, in the surveys of firms in the five eastern European countries, profits as a percentage of assets were obtained in categories, with the lowest category being "negative" and the highest category being "41 percent or greater." When these categories are used with the U.S. data, the average return on invested capital is 9 percent rather than 15 percent. It is likely, then, that the data from Poland and Russia discussed in this section understate somewhat the return to capital.

[3] A word of caution about comparing the profit data from China on the one hand and Russia and Poland on the other: The Polish and Russian data are from surveys of about 300 manufacturers in each country in 1997 (Johnson, McMillan and Woodruff, 2002b). Firms were asked about profits in their first year of operation. Figure 1 shows the average profit rate of firms beginning operation in each year. As such, they are subject to possible recall and selection bias. The China data were gathered contemporaneously from firms operating at the time.

The Central Role of Entrepreneurs in Transition Economies   157

Figure 1
Time Path of Profits

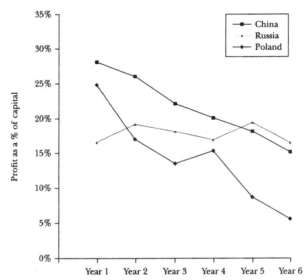

Notes: The horizontal axis shows the number of years into reform. For China, year 1 means 1979 and year 6 means 1984. For Poland and Russia, year 1 means 1990 and year 6 means 1995.
Sources: China: Naughton (1996, p. 150). Poland and Russia: Johnson, McMillan and Woodruff (2002b).

fell. Russia's stalled transition shows up in the absence of any decline in profit levels.

Data on the rate of entry of new firms are consistent with the profit paths shown in Figure 1. Entry occurred rapidly in China. Most of the new entrants there were not private firms, but rural enterprises run by local governments, called township and village enterprises. The share of China's industrial output accounted for by rural enterprises increased from 9 percent in 1978 to 30 percent in 1991 (Naughton, 1995, p. 164). Since none of the increase in output of rural firms in China came from privatized state firms, all of it is attributable to newly formed firms. The entry of these new enterprises was driven by the extraordinarily high rates of profit available early in the reforms. The competition engendered by rapid entry was the primary cause of the fall in profits.

Entry in Poland was also rapid. Industrial employment in Poland's private sector firms increased from 15 percent in 1991 to 37 percent in 1994, according to Konings, Lehmann and Schaffer (1996), using data collected by the Polish Central Statistical Office. The 21-percentage-point increase was apparently largely the result of new entrants, since privatized firms represented only 6 percent of industrial employment in 1994. At least one-sixth of industrial employment in Poland in 1994, then, was in de novo firms ("de novo" meaning started from scratch rather than being spun off from state-owned firms). The level of self-employment in Poland increased from 6 percent of the labor force in 1988 to 12 percent in 1993 (according to Earle and Sakova, 1999, using labor market surveys).[4] Although most of the firm-level studies in transition countries focus on manufacturing, entry may have been even more important in the service sector, given the underdevelopment of the service sector in the centrally planned economies. In Poland, the service sector grew from 40 percent of nonagricultural GDP in 1989 to 66 percent of GDP in 1997.

Russia, by contrast, saw less rapid entry. A 1995 study found that just 6 percent of manufacturing employment was in de novo firms (Richter and Shaffer, 1996). Self-employment in Russia in the early years of the transition increased only from 2 percent of the labor force in 1988 to 3 percent in 1993 (Earle and Sakova, 1999). Confirmation of the slowness of entry comes from data collected by Djankov and Nenova (2001) on employment in manufacturing firms with fewer than 50 employees in 1997. Since small firms were uncommon in the planned economy, small size is a rough proxy for de novo startups. They find that small firms represented 24 percent of manufacturing employment in Poland, but only 10 percent in Russia, and that the employment share of small firms in the Russian service sector more than doubled from 13 percent in 1989 to 30 percent in 1997.[5] All data on increasing shares in Russia need to be interpreted in the context of a shrinking economy. For example, Russia also saw services increase from 40 percent of the nonagricultural economy in 1989 to 62 percent in 1997. The share of services increased in spite of the fact that output of services actually declined by 1 percent per year during the 1990s; manufacturing declined much more rapidly.

The speed of entry in China, Poland and Russia was consistent with the time path of profits shown in Figure 1. Robust entry in China and Poland brought plummeting profits. In Russia, entry was slower, and profits remained high.

In Vietnam, also, the available data indicate that entry of private firms was robust (though we are unaware of any profit data there). Vietnam is an intriguing example, for it is an extreme case in its lack of formal market-supporting institutions. Yet Vietnam's private sector boomed. The number of registered private firms grew by 40 percent per year between 1993 and 1997. Private sector employment grew from 3.8 million to 10.2 million between 1988 and 1992, while employment in state firms fell from 4.1 million to 3.0 million and in cooperatives fell from 20.7 million to 18.6 million. In the following three years, from 1992 to 1995, private

[4] The labor survey data indicate that the majority of the self-employed work for their own account. These workers may represent not robust entry, but desperation in the face of unemployment (Earle and Sakova, 2000). Nevertheless, in 1993, over 4 percent of Poland's workforce were self-employed people who also hired others, a level much higher than in the other transition countries examined by Earle and Sakova.

[5] Djankov and Nenova (2001) data also show that employment in small firms grew rapidly in Poland during the 1990s, from an average of 8 percent in 1990–1992 to 23 percent in 1996–1998. (Comparable data for Russia are not available.) For Russia, small manufacturing firms are defined as those with fewer than 100 employees, rather than 50, as in Poland, hence the difference between Poland and Russia is understated. The service sector data for Russia and Poland are from the World Development Indicators database.

sector employment grew by more than 2.4 million, during which time state sector employment remained constant.[6] Substantially all of this private sector growth came from new entry or expansion of household enterprises, mostly retail and repair shops or small manufacturing enterprises. Vietnam has had no formal program of privatization. Though there were some ad hoc spin-offs from state-owned firms, these represent a minority of the private firms. For example, only 6 percent of firms we surveyed in 1995 said that more than half of their equipment came from state-owned firms (McMillan and Woodruff, 1999b).

Entry was robust, then, in Poland, Vietnam and, in its own way, in China, while it was comparatively weak in Russia. Other transition countries saw entry to varying degrees. Ukraine and the rest of the former Soviet Union were like Russia, for example, whereas Slovakia was more like Poland. Profits were high early in the transition because the inefficiencies of the planned economy left unsatisfied demands and unfilled market niches. Where reform was successful, it brought competitive markets, eroding profits. Where it was less successful, the entrants' profits remained high.

Entrepreneurs' Strategies

In the early years of economic transition, the absence of credit markets, courts and other market institutions created substantial impediments to entry. Potential entrants had to find money with which to purchase equipment and inputs. They had to identify reliable suppliers and customers when most firms were new and little information was available. The unusually high profit rates early in the transition provided a strong incentive for entrepreneurs. But what substituted for the missing formal institutions?

How did the entrepreneurs succeed in overcoming the lack of market-supporting institutions? Ongoing relationships among firms substituted for the missing institutions. Firms relied on the logic of the incentives to cooperate that arise in playing a repeated game. Where courts and laws are unreliable for settling disputes, firms trust their customers to pay their bills and their suppliers to deliver quality goods out of the prospect of future business. Interviews with Vietnamese managers, for example, indicate that they think quite consciously in terms of building relationships with specific customers and suppliers (McMillan and Woodruff, 1999a).[7]

Early in the process of transition, repeated game incentives work especially

---

[6] Registration data are from McKenzie (2000); employment data from Wolff (1999, p. 63). Joint ventures between state firms and foreign investors are included in the state sector. Beginning in 1993, statistics for collectives and private firms were combined. The increase of 2.4 million jobs is for private firms and collectives combined; however, it is reasonable to presume that collectives continued to decline (their output shrank from 2.7 percent of GDP in 1992 to 0.8 percent in 1998), meaning the employment increase is attributable to private firms.

[7] On the interaction between formal and informal contracting mechanisms, see Baker, Gibbons and Murphy (1994).

well. When it is hard to locate alternative trading partners, because firms are scarce or market information is inadequate or transport costs are high, firms make efforts to maintain their existing relationships. They recognize that they are to some extent locked in with their trading partners, which provides an incentive to behave cooperatively (Kranton, 1996; Ramey and Watson, 2001). The evidence we present in this section suggests that self-enforcing contracts are all that is needed to support a lot of entrepreneurship, especially at the start of the reforms.

Evidence from Vietnam is especially pertinent here, since formal institutions were almost nonexistent for some years after its transition began. Consider access to capital. Even in developed market economies, a major source of capital for small- and medium-sized firms is trade credit from suppliers. The lack of formal financial markets meant that credit from suppliers was even more important to private sector firms in transition countries. In 53 percent of the relationships between the manufactures we surveyed and their customers, some portion of the bill was paid on credit. That suppliers were willing to offer credit in the absence of formal enforcement of contracts is noteworthy. What gave the suppliers confidence that they would be paid? The willingness to sell goods on credit depended upon repeated interactions, according to the managers we surveyed (McMillan and Woodruff, 1999a). Trading relationships most often began with cash transactions, as the partners "tested" each other. Firms got contractual assurance by dealing with firms they knew through having dealt with them before.

Informally enforced trade rests on the shadow of the future. A firm lives up to its agreements because it wants to go on doing business with this trading partner. For the future to weigh heavily enough to induce cooperative behavior, the discounted value of the future profit stream must outweigh whatever immediate profits could be squeezed from the deal. Some of the conditions in the transition economies actually worked against cooperation. The scarcity of credit meant the opportunity cost of capital was high. With high discount rates, firms have an incentive to take current profits rather than wait for future profits. Moreover, as we saw, profits tended to decline over time. To the extent that this was predictable, the gains from forward-looking behavior were lowered. That firms were nevertheless able to operate mutually beneficial relationships is striking.

Other circumstances of the transition aided informal contracting. Cooperation is easier to sustain when severing the relationship results in higher costs. Early in the transition, trading partners were most often located in the same city or even the same neighborhood. There were usually few firms nearby producing any given product. When a supplier severed a relationship with a customer, the customer had to incur a high cost of searching for another trading partner. As a result, trading partners tended to be locked in with each other, inducing them to try to sustain their existing relationships (Kranton, 1996; Ramey and Watson, 2001).

Cooperation is more easily sustained, also, if punishment for malfeasance comes not only from the trading partner who has been cheated but also from other firms in the community. We found that gossip was important in Vietnam's manufacturing community. Firms gathered information about potential or existing trading partners from other firms. Sometimes this information gathering was organized. Trade associations helped firms to work productively with each other, by spreading information about who had breached contracts and coordinating the sanctioning of them. This meant that reneging brought more severe consequences than merely losing the business of the offended party and thus increased the likelihood of cooperation (McMillan and Woodruff, 2000; Recanatini and Ryterman, 2000).

The self-help mechanisms evolved over time to support more complex transactions. Early in the transition, firms sold mostly to customers located in the same city or limited sales to customers about whom they had prior information from family members, friends or other firms with whom they did business. They were likely to inspect a customer's factory or store before selling to it. These are ways to reduce the risk of dealing with new trading partners, though they involve costs of exclusion or of time spent investigating trading partners. Relationships with firms located in distant cities are harder to manage than local sales, but limiting the circle of trading partners means passing up some opportunities for growth. Sales to customers located in other cities, and to customers about whom the manufacturer had no prior information, became more common as the transition progressed.

Table 1 illustrates these changes using data from surveys in three transition countries, Vietnam, Poland and Russia. The surveys asked firms about the characteristics of their oldest and newest customer relationships. The table splits relationships into those that began earlier and later in the transition. Relationships labeled "old" are those begun in the first six years of reform, before 1993 in Vietnam and before 1995 in Poland and Russia, while those labeled "new" were formed between 1994 and 1997 in Vietnam and between mid-1995 and 1997 in Poland and Russia. All of the variables shown on Table 1 are measured at the start of the relationship and, as such, are indicators of the formation of new relationships rather than the development of the specific bilateral relationships.

These data show statistically significant increases in transactions with customers from other cities, with customers about whom nothing was known at the start of the relationship, and in relationships that were initiated without the seller having visited the buyer's factory or store. In Poland, for example, 35 percent of the customer relationships started by surveyed firms between 1989 and mid-1995 involved customers from a different city, compared with 45 percent of relationships started in 1995 or after. About 39 percent of the newer customers in Poland were anonymous when the trading relationship began, compared with 27 percent of the older customers. Trading started in 38 percent of the new Polish relationships without the seller visiting the buyer's facility, compared with 29 percent of the older relationships.

The patterns in the other countries are similar, both for Vietnam and Russia, as shown in the table, and for Slovakia, Romania and Ukraine, which are not shown. Further evidence on the increase over time in the sophistication of dealings comes from Bulgaria, where quality incentives developed. Suppliers became increasingly willing to guarantee quality and to replace substandard goods based on their trading relationships (Koford and Miller, 1998).

These data suggest that the problems of governing more complex relationships

Table 1
Development of Relationships with Trading Partners

	Vietnam Relationships		Poland Relationships		Russia Relationships	
	Old	*New*	*Old*	*New*	*Old*	*New*
Located in a different city	28.8%	38.9%	35.0%	45.0%	14.5%	31.8%
		(2.27)		(2.40)		(3.44)
Previously unknown	57.6%	65.5%	27.0%	38.9%	n.a.	n.a.
		(1.74)		(2.94)		
Did not visit before first transaction	36.6%	50.5%	28.8%	37.5%	35.3%	30.8%
		(3.00)		(2.16)		(0.70)
Number of firms	191	281	226	342	344	66

Notes: Old relationships are those initiated prior to 1993 in Vietnam and prior to 1995 in Poland and Russia. In parentheses: *t*-values for differences between old and new relationships. The data on "previously unknown" for Vietnam and Poland are not directly comparable because of differences in the survey instrument. Entries marked "n.a." are not available in the survey used in the given country.
Sources: Johnson, McMillan and Woodruff (2000); McMillan and Woodruff (1999b).

can be overcome not only where courts work relatively well, as in Poland, but even where courts do not function at all, as in Vietnam. Receiving no help from the state, entrepreneurs made do for themselves, by relying on the incentives that arise in ongoing relationships. Repeated games substituted for the courts; trade credit and profit reinvestment substituted for financial markets. The mechanism of self-help supported increasingly sophisticated transactions—at least in the early years of transition.

State Support for Entrepreneurship

Self-help in creating market institutions is not a permanent solution for entrepreneurs. It faces a number of natural limits.

First, the development of the market as the transition proceeds lowers the costs of searching out new trading partners, which weakens a firm's threat to cut off dealings if a trading partner reneges on a deal. The cost of breaking a relationship falls. Firms then become less willing to cooperate with each other, and the need for workable laws of contract and courts able to enforce them becomes more pressing.

Second, repeated games entail personalized interfirm relationships. When firms are small, they need only deal with customers and suppliers with whom they have a particular connection: those located nearby, or managed by a friend or relative, or coming via personal recommendations. Firms were able to some extent to overcome these limitations, as noted above: even in Vietnam, they were able to trade at a distance. Such informal mechanisms are limited, however. To grow beyond a certain size, firms need to manage arms-length anonymous dealings: for example, to begin trading with firms in distant cities rather than just with geographically nearby firms. Anonymous trades need a greater extent of formal contractual assurance.

Third, as products become more complex, there is an increased need to order them, and to commit to buy them, in advance of production. Without the courts, suppliers may be unwilling to switch to producing complex goods and services.

Fourth, although firms can for a while grow incrementally by investing their retained earnings, they reach a point where, to take advantage of economies of scale, they must make big discrete jumps in their investments. Having a long-delayed return, such investments are unlikely to be made on the basis of ongoing relationships. Sunk costs tempt someone to renege: a purchaser after the costs are sunk may renegotiate the buying price, or the government after the costs are sunk may impose a specific tax. Large-scale investments require legal protection.

Finally, as profits decline through the process of economic transition, while investments often become larger and longer term, firms can rely less on retained earnings to grow and increasingly need access to external finance.

A role for the government, even early in the transition, is to set a stable platform for entrepreneurs' self-help. Macroeconomic instability, common at the beginning of a reform program, can undermine informal cooperation. Consider a trading relationship in which the seller allows the buyer to pay with a 30-day delay. In stable times, the ability to delay payment has a predictable value to the buyer and cost to the seller. The value of continuing the relationship is also predictable. The level of credit offered can be set in such a way that repayment is in the seller's interest. But now suppose that, after the goods are delivered by the seller, there is some unforeseen shock that increases the value to the buyer of not making the required payment and affects only the trading partners' current payoffs, not the stream of future gains from the relationship (such as a sharp decrease in bank credit or a rapid decline in the buyer's demand). If the shock makes the gains from reneging large enough, the buyer will not pay.[8]

Risks were inherent in any trading relationship in all of the transition countries, but the policies of some governments magnified them. Unstable macroeconomic conditions made it harder to predict the behavior of trading partners. High and variable rates of inflation and economic growth led to fluctuations in a trading partner's gain from breaking the cooperative relationship. Macroeconomic stability was conducive to the development of informal trading relationships. On this score, countries like Slovakia, where inflation peaked in 1991 at 35 percent, and Poland, where inflation peaked in 1990 at 75 percent, fared well. Russia and Ukraine, where price stability was longer in coming, fared worse. Of course, the lack of entry in Russia and Ukraine may have contributed to macroeconomic instability as well as the other way around. We know of no data that would allow us to separate the

---

[8] The situation we have in mind is similar to the Rotemberg and Saloner's (1986) model of price wars during economic booms. In their model, collusion is most likely to break down in a boom when the demand for the product is high, because that is when an individual seller's gain from undercutting the group-maximizing price is highest. Hence, collusion is harder to sustain in industries with more variable demand.

directions of causation. But given the importance of informal trading arrangements early in the transition, theory suggests that, by making relationships harder to establish, macroeconomic instability created a barrier to entry.

While contracting is mainly supported by informal relationships among firms, the courts also foster it. The courts in the transition economies are still inadequate; it takes a long time to build a well-functioning legal system. The evidence shows, however, that even these highly imperfect courts facilitate doing business. Managers of startup firms were asked in a 1997 survey whether they could appeal to the courts to enforce a contract with a trading partner. In Poland, 73 percent said they could, and in Russia, 56 percent said they could. Belief in the courts affects behavior. Those who say the courts are effective offer more trade credit and are more willing to take on new trading partners (Johnson, McMillan and Woodruff, 2002a; see also Frye and Shleifer, 1997; Hendley, Murrell and Ryterman, 1999). By making it easier for new firms to enter, workable courts improve on relational contracting and boost overall productivity. Even weak courts can be useful.

The absence of well-functioning credit markets matters less early in transition than later. In place of external funds, firms reinvest from their own profits. The high profits mean that entrepreneurs have the resources they need for expansion, without needing to borrow. Retained earnings has been the biggest single source of investible funds for startup firms in transition economies. In addition, where interfirm relationships are working well, firms receive trade credit from their suppliers. Trade credit was almost nonexistent among Russian firms as of 1997, but in Poland it was as large a source of firms' capital as bank loans (Johnson, McMillan and Woodruff, 2002b). As entry occurs and profit rates are driven downward, however, credit markets become more important. In Vietnam, there is some evidence that credit markets were beginning to reach new private firms: 24 percent of firms in a 1997 survey reported having bank credit, up from 8 percent in 1991 (Hemlin, Ramamurthy and Ronnås, 1998).

An alternative source of capital is equity markets. State support is needed for an equity market to develop. In Poland, a regulatory agency that intervened to protect minority shareholders from expropriation by insiders allowed the stock market to develop rapidly (Glaeser, Johnson and Shleifer, 2001). New issues were offered regularly. In the Czech Republic, by contrast, the absence of regulatory oversight meant people were, rightly, reluctant to invest in firms because they feared the managers would misuse their money, and so the stock market stayed inactive. Why is regulation needed for equity markets? Informal creation of share ownership is difficult. Fixed costs of issuing shares to a large group of investors prevent a slow buildup of the relationship, with investors testing entrepreneurs as trading partners in Vietnam reported doing. Because outside shareholders lack information on the firm's internal affairs, managers can easily expropriate the returns owed to the shareholders (Johnson and Shleifer, 2001). Prospective shareholders need legal and regulatory protection before they are willing to hand their money over to firms.

Entrepreneurs running de novo startups in Poland reported that an average of 25 percent of their equity capital was owned by private firms or people other than the top manager's family. This is a somewhat higher level of outside ownership than other countries for which such data are available: Vietnam, at 19 percent, Slovakia, 19 percent, and Romania, 14 percent (Johnson, McMillan and Woodruff, 2000; McMillan and Woodruff, 1999b). The lesson, once again, is that informal mechanisms work only up to a point. Investors are willing to entrust their money to managers they have some reason to believe in, perhaps because of ties of family or ethnicity or because the manager comes recommended by a trusted third party. Large firms with diversified shareholding cannot develop by such informal mechanisms, but some degree of outside ownership can.

Evidence that self-help mechanisms in financial markets have limits comes from Earle and Sakova's (2000) study of entrepreneurship in Poland, Russia and four other eastern European countries. Employers, as compared to wage workers, are more likely to have received property during posttransition restitution and to have had higher earnings in 1988. Also, the parents of those who became employers were more likely to have owned a business prior to communism and more likely to have had a university degree than are the parents of wage workers. These findings suggest that access to capital was a binding constraint on entry, one not entirely overcome by informal credit.

China did things differently with its new firms. Entry occurred in the non-standard form of the township and village enterprises (Che and Qian, 1998; Whiting, 1996). These firms were publicly owned, by communities of a few thousand people. They were managed by village government, and the profits were shared between villagers and local government by explicit rules. Around 60 percent of profits were reinvested, and the remainder was paid as bonuses to workers or used for local public goods such as education, roads and irrigation. Managerial discipline in the township and village enterprises came from the fact that these enterprises had no access to government subsidies to cover any losses and faced intensely competitive product markets.

The township and village enterprises received some benefits from having the village government as a partner. Access to state banks and to rationed inputs was eased. Public ownership helped remedy the lack of laws protecting against arbitrary expropriation by the state, as well as helping with contract enforcement. Moreover, China's local governments, arguably, did not sabotage their township and village enterprises by overtaxing them because they could see that if they did, the firms would fail and their own revenue source would be lost.

The township and village enterprise organizational form was a transitional device. After a decade and a half of growth, they began to be privatized. By the late 1990s, more than half of them were partially or fully privately owned (Li and Rozelle, 2000). By the turn of the century, the township and village enterprises were well on their way to becoming conventional firms.

Entrepreneurs require more from the state, in the medium and long run, than the absence of interference. If firms are to be able to grow to yield economies of scale, they need laws of contract so they can take on anonymous dealings and financial regulation so they can get bank loans and outside shareholding.

Welfare Effects of Entrepreneurship

The creation of jobs has been arguably the most important welfare benefit of the new entrants. Given the distortions and inefficiencies in the communist planned economy, the old firms had to shed jobs during the transition, and new entrants were needed to take up the slack. New firms have usually been the fastest-growing segment in transition economies. In Poland and in Russia, de novo manufacturing firms grew faster, invested at a higher rate and generated faster employment growth than did privatized firms (Belka et al., 1995; Richter and Schaffer, 1996; Johnson, McMillan and Woodruff, 2000). In Vietnam, the private sector created (in net terms) some 10 million jobs in the seven years from the start of reforms, while the state-owned and collective firms shed workers.

This pattern is repeated in most of the transition economies for which data exist. In Estonia, small privately owned firms—mostly startups—created almost all of the new jobs between 1989 and 1994 (Haltiwanger and Vodopivec, 2000). In Romania, 86 percent of de novo manufacturing firms created jobs between 1994 and 1996, while only 13 percent of privatized firms did so. In Slovakia, 79 percent of de novo firms grew, against 52 percent of privatized firms (Johnson, McMillan and Woodruff, 2000). De novo firms in Bulgaria, Hungary and Romania between 1990 and 1996 grew more quickly than did privatized or state-owned firms (Bilsen and Konings, 1998). Though de novo firms represented less than 3 percent of employment in the samples in Bulgaria and Romania, they created more than half of the new jobs. In a sample of firms from 25 transition countries, Carlin et al. (2001) find that sales and employment grow faster in de novo firms than in privatized or state firms; they also find that productivity gains are smaller, probably reflecting that new firms start at a higher level of efficiency than the state firms and thus have less room for productivity growth.

The key difference does not seem to be between state-owned and private firms, but rather that de novo firms outgrew all other firms. Many studies find little difference between the performance of state-owned firms and privatized firms. The finding that de novo firms perform better than privatized and state-owned firms is not quite universal, however. The Johnson, McMillan and Woodruff (2000) data show essentially no difference in the growth rates of startups and privatized firms in Russia and Ukraine. Lizal and Svejnar (2001) find that the rates of investment of private firms in the Czech Republic were somewhat lower on average than those of state-owned firms in the 1992–1998 time period and that small firms in the Czech Republic were credit constrained while large firms were not (which may explain in part their first finding). Taken as a whole, then, the evidence indicates that de novo firms were more dynamic than privatized state firms, except perhaps where the latter had favored access to capital.

Entrepreneurial firms provide other benefits. Small new firms are dynamic. They learn and change rapidly, and thus they provide a large number of independent experiments on how to do business. One measure of this dynamism is their job churning. In a study of Estonia, Haltiwanger and Vodopivec (2000) separate the net change in employment into the creation of new jobs by expanding firms and the destruction of existing jobs by shrinking firms. For state-owned firms, in the first half of the 1990s, job creation was small and job destruction among these enterprises was large. In the private sector, there was a lot of job creation. Yet, surprisingly, the private sector also had higher rates of job destruction than the state enterprise sector. These data indicate more flux in the private sector, with some firms expanding rapidly and others contracting. The simultaneous high rates of job creation and job destruction were especially pronounced among the smallest firms, those with fewer than 20 workers. This could be attributable to learning by the small firms, which is especially important in the transition setting, where costs and demands are subject to far wider uncertainty than in a stable economy.

New firms also provide competitive discipline for the pre-existing firms. State-owned and privatized firms in eastern Europe and the former Soviet Union are significantly more likely to have undergone restructuring if they faced competition (Carlin et al., 2001; Djankov and Murrell, 2002). In China through the 1980s, while the township and village enterprises burgeoned, the state firms' markup of price over marginal cost fell by 15 percent; the increased competitiveness of the output market was associated with an increased total factor productivity for the state firms (Li, 1997).

There is some evidence, also, that a transition economy's overall performance is correlated with entry. Comparing economic growth rates of the different regions of Russia, Berkowitz and DeJong (2001) find that the faster-growing regions have more entry of new firms.

Implications for Policy

In the early 1990s, a common view among those advising the reforming countries was that the overriding objective was to get the government out of the economy. Once the prohibitions on market activity were abolished, the argument went, the private sector would quickly take over. Later, in light of the grim performance of Russia and the rest of the former Soviet Union, this simple view was supplanted by a recognition that reforming an economy is exceedingly hard. Success requires a complex package of microeconomic reform, macroeconomic stability and institution building.

Our analysis speaks to both views. On the one hand, it says there is something in the leave-it-to-the-market view. Profit-driven entrepreneurs can do a remarkable amount, even to the extent of creating temporary replacements for the key social institutions of property rights and contract.

On the other hand, our analysis says getting the government out achieves its aim only in a narrow set of circumstances. The self-help substitutes for market-supporting institutions work well only for firms that are small. Larger firms, dealing with many suppliers and customers and trading at a distance, cannot rely solely on personalized relationships to undergird their transactions. Formal institutions are needed, therefore, both by privatized firms and, after a while, by startup firms if they are to grow to an efficient scale. Moreover, government policy does matter even at the level of the small startups, for the business environment must be reasonably stable and predictable if the shadow of the future is to give firms reason to be able to trust each other. If you keep your word only because of the prospect of future gains, you are more likely to renege when the business environment is very noisy. Corrupt bureaucrats and politicians, by extorting bribes, discourage entrepreneurs from investing (Johnson, McMillan and Woodruff, 2002b). High and volatile inflation could undermine firms' attempts at self-help contracting. Mass privatization, by adding to the uncertainty about which lines of business are going to be profitable, might disrupt the nascent interfirm relationships.

The same ambivalence between the force of informal mechanisms and their limits, by the way, is seen in many developing countries. In Africa and Latin America, firms lacking access to the courts engage in a remarkable range of productive activity (de Soto, 1989; Fafchamps, 2001; Woodruff, 1998). The lack of market-supporting institutions, however, makes it hard or impossible for these firms to grow into sophisticated corporations.

The economic transition has been far more painful in some ex-communist countries than in others. Relative success came in those countries where new market activities were quickly established. Ironically, and contrary to the leave-it-to-the-market view, markets arose faster where the government did not completely withdraw, but rather set a stable platform. New firms entered and grew more slowly in Russia, where the government abruptly ceased controlling prices and rapidly privatized the state firms, than in China, where the government mostly continued doing what it had been doing before. [9]

Conclusion

The importance of entrepreneurs in the transition economies is a reminder that the task of economic transition is not just a matter of government officials enacting certain policies or setting certain rules of operation for the new economy. Entrepreneurs acted as reformers, too. Indeed, much of the task of devising the new ways of doing business in transition economies has been taken on by entrepreneurs.

"By pursuing his own interest," Adam Smith (1776 [1976], volume 1, pp. 477–78) famously wrote of the merchant, "he frequently promotes that of society more effectually than when he really intends to promote it." The entrepreneurs in the transition countries exemplify Smith's dictum. By creating jobs, supplying consumer goods, constraining the market power of the state firms and building reform momentum, they have produced real welfare gains.

■ *We thank David Ahn, Simon Board, Simeon Djankov, Brad De Long, John Earle, Alan Krueger, Barry Naughton, Timothy Taylor and Michael Waldman for helpful comments. McMillan thanks the Stanford Graduate School of Business for research support.*

---

[9] On the parallel roles of bottom-up and top-down forces in developing market rules and procedures, see McMillan (2002).

References

Baker, George, Robert Gibbons and Kevin J. Murphy. 1994. "Subjective Performance Measures in Optimal Incentive Contracts." *Quarterly Journal of Economics.* 109:4, pp. 1125–156.

Belka, Marek et al. 1995. "Enterprise Adjustment in Poland: Evidence from a Survey of 200 Private, Privatized, and State-Owned Firms." Centre for Economic Performance Discussion Paper No. 233, April.

Berkowitz, Daniel and David DeJong. 2001. "Entrepreneurship and Post-Socialist Growth." William Davidson Institute Working Paper No. 406.

Berkowitz, Daniel and Jonathan Holland. 2001. "Does Privatization Enhance or Deter Small Enterprise Formation?" *Economics Letters.* 74:1, pp. 53–60.

Bilsen, Valentijn and Jozef Konings. 1998. "Job Creation, Job Destruction and Growth of Newly Established, Privatized and State-Owned Enterprises in Transition Economies: Survey Evidence from Bulgaria, Hungary and Romania." *Journal of Comparative Economics.* 26:3, pp. 429–45.

Brown, David and John Earle. 2001. "Privatization, Competition, and Reform Strategies: Theory and Evidence from Russian Enterprise Panel Data." SITE Working Paper No. 159, Stockholm School of Economics.

Carlin, Wendy et al. 2001. "Competition and Enterprise Performance in Transition Economies: Evidence from a Cross-Country Survey." CEPR Discussion Paper No. 2840.

Che, Jiahua and Yingyi Qian. 1998. "Institutional Environment, Community Government, and Corporate Governance: Understanding China's Township Village Enterprises." *Journal of Law, Economics, and Organization.* 14:1, pp.1–23.

de Soto, Hernando. 1989. *The Other Path.* New York: Harper and Row.

Djankov, Simeon and Peter Murrell. 2002. "Enterprise Restructuring in Transition: A Quantitative Survey." *Journal of Economic Literature.* 40:3, pp. 739–92.

Djankov, Simeon and Tatiana Nenova. 2001. "Constraints to Entrepreneurship in Kazakhstan." World Bank, March.

Djankov, Simeon et al. 2002. "The Regulation of Entry." *Quarterly Journal of Economics.* 117:1, pp. 1–37.

Earle, John and Zuzana Sakova. 1999. "Entrepreneurship from Scratch: Lessons on the Entry Decision into Self-Employment from Transition Economies." IZA Discussion Paper No. 79.

Earle, John and Zuzana Sakova. 2000. "Business Start-ups or Disguised Unemployment? Evidence on the Character of Self-Employment from Transition Countries." *Labour Economics.* 7:5, pp. 575–601.

Fafchamps, Marcel. 2001. "Networks, Communities and Markets in Sub-Saharan Africa: Implications for Firm Growth and Investment." *Journal of African Economies.* 10:0, pp. 109–42.

Federal Reserve Board of Governors. 1994. *National Survey of Small Business Finance.* Washington, D.C.: Board of Governor of the Federal Reserve and U.S. Small Business Administration.

Frye, Timothy and Andrei Shleifer. 1997. "The Invisible Hand and the Grabbing Hand." *American Economic Review.* Papers and Proceedings, 87:2, pp. 354–58.

Glaeser, Edward, Simon Johnson and Andrei Shleifer. 2001. "Coase versus the Coaseans." *Quarterly Journal of Economics.* 114:3, pp. 853–900.

Haltiwanger, John and Milan Vodopivec. 2000. "Gross Worker and Job Flows in a Transition Economy: An Analysis of Estonia." Mimeo, University of Maryland, November.

Hemlin, Maud, Bhargavi Ramamurthy and Per Ronnås. 1998. "The Anatomy and Dynamics of Small Scale Private Manufacturing in Vietnam." Mimeo, Stockholm School of Economics.

Hendley, Kathryn, Peter Murrell and Randi Ryterman. 1999. "Law, Relationships, and Private Enforcement: Transactional Strategies of Russian Enterprises." Mimeo, University of Wisconsin, January.

Johnson, Simon and Andrei Shleifer. 2001. "Privatization and Corporate Governance." Mimeo, MIT.

Johnson, Simon, John McMillan and Christopher Woodruff. 2000. "Entrepreneurs and the Ordering of Institutional Reform: Poland, Slovakia, Romania, Russia and Ukraine Compared." *Economics of Transition.* 8:1, pp. 1–36.

Johnson, Simon, John McMillan and Christopher Woodruff. 2002a. "Courts and Relational Contracts." *Journal of Law, Economics, and Organization.* 18:1, pp. 221–77.

Johnson, Simon, John McMillan and Christopher Woodruff. 2002b. "Property Rights and Finance." *American Economic Review.* Forthcoming.

Koford, Kenneth and Jeffrey B. Miller. 1998. "Contractual Enforcement in an Economy in Transition." Mimeo, Department of Economics, University of Delaware.

Konings, Jozef, Hartmut Lehmann and Mark E. Schaffer. 1996. "Job Creation and Job Destruction in a Transition Economy: Ownership, Firm Size and Gross Job Flows in Polish Manufacturing." *Labour Economics.* 3:2, pp. 299–317.

Kranton, Rachel E. 1996. "Reciprocal Exchange: A Self-Sustaining System." *American Economic Review.* 86:4, pp. 830–51.

Le, Wei. 1997. "The Impact of Economic Reform on the Performance of Chinese State Enterprises, 1980–1989." *Journal of Political Economy.* 105:5, pp. 1080–106.

Li, Hongbin and Scott Rozelle. 2000. "Saving or Stripping Rural Industry: An Analysis of Privatization and Efficiency in China." *Agricultural Economics.* 23:3, pp. 241–52.

Lizal, Lubomir and Jan Svejnar. 2001. "Investment, Credit Rationing, and the Soft Budget Constraint: Evidence from the Czech Republic." *Review of Economics and Statistics.* 83:1, pp. 92–99.

McKenzie, John. 2000. "Creating a Market in Management Training for Vietnam's Private Firms." International Labour Organization Working Paper.

McMillan, John. 2002. *Reinventing the Bazaar: A Natural History of Markets.* New York: Norton.

McMillan, John and Christopher Woodruff. 1999a. "Dispute Prevention Without Courts in Vietnam." *Journal of Law, Economics, and Organization.* 15:3, pp. 637–58.

McMillan, John and Christopher Woodruff. 1999b. "Interfirm Relationships and Informal Credit in Vietnam." *Quarterly Journal of Economics.* 114:4, pp. 1285–320.

McMillan, John and Christopher Woodruff. 2000. "Private Order under Dysfunctional Public Order." *Michigan Law Review.* 98:8, pp. 2421–458.

Megginson, William L. and Jeffry M. Netter. 2001. "From State to Market: A Survey of Empirical Studies on Privatization." *Journal of Economic Literature.* 39:2, pp. 321–89.

Naughton, Barry. 1995. *Growing Out of the Plan.* New York: Cambridge University Press.

Nellis, John. 2001. "The World Bank, Privatization, and Enterprise Reform in Transition Economies: A Retrospective Analysis." Mimeo, Operations Evaluation Department, World Bank.

Ramey, Garey and Joel Watson. 2001. "Bilateral Trade and Opportunism in a Matching Market." *Contributions to Theoretical Economics.* 1:1, ⟨http//www.bepress.com/bejte/contributions/vol1/iss1/art3/⟩.

Recanatini, Francesca and Randi Ryterman. 2000. "Disorganization or Self-Organization?" Mimeo, World Bank.

Richter, Andrea and Mark Schaffer. 1996. "The Performance of *De Novo* Private Firms in Russian Manufacturing," in *Enterprise Restructuring and Economic Policy in Russia.* Commander, Fan and Schaffer, eds. Washington, D.C.: World Bank, pp. 253–74.

Ronnås, Per. 1998. "The Transformation of the Private Manufacturing Sector in Vietnam in the 1990s." Stockholm School of Economics Working Paper No. 241.

Rotemberg, Julio and Garth Saloner. 1986. "A Supergame-Theoretic Model of Price Wars during Booms." *American Economic Review.* 76:3, pp. 390–407.

Smith, Adam. 1976 [1776]. *An Enquiry into the Nature and Causes of the Wealth of Nations.* Chicago: University of Chicago Press.

Whiting, Susan H. 1996. "Contract Incentives and Market Discipline in China's Rural Industrial Sector," in *Reforming Asian Socialism.* J. McMillan and B. Naughton, eds. Ann Arbor: University of Michigan Press, pp. 63–110.

Wolff, Peter. 1999. *Vietnam: The Incomplete Transformation.* London: Frank Cass Press.

Woodruff, Christopher. 1998. "Contract Enforcement and Trade Liberalization in Mexico's Footwear Industry." *World Development.* 26:6, pp. 979–91.

Zhou, Kate Xiao. 1996. *How the Farmers Changed China.* Boulder: Westview Press.

[18]

Available online at www.sciencedirect.com

SCIENCE DIRECT®

ELSEVIER

Journal of Comparative Economics 34 (2006) 338–356

Journal of
COMPARATIVE
ECONOMICS

www.elsevier.com/locate/jce

Entrepreneurship and the evolution of income distributions in Poland and Russia

Daniel Berkowitz [a], John E. Jackson [b,*]

[a] *University of Pittsburgh, WWPH 4711, Pittsburgh, PA 15260, USA*
[b] *Department of Political Science, University of Michigan, 7766 Haven Hall, Ann Arbor, MI 48109, USA*

Received 14 December 2004; revised 14 December 2005

Available online 10 March 2006

Berkowitz, Daniel, and Jackson, John E.—Entrepreneurship and the evolution of income distributions in Poland and Russia

Differences in the evolution of Polish and Russian income distributions in the post-socialist era can be attributed to different rates of entry of new enterprises. Using regional differences during early privatization as instruments to estimate the impact of this entry, we find that a one-standard-deviation increase in the share of the workforce in new or small enterprises increases the share of income earned by the lowest forty percent of the population by 1.4% and by 1.25% in Polish and Russian regions, respectively. Poland's greater success in de novo firm entry contributes to its more equitable income distribution during the transition. *Journal of Comparative Economics* **34** (2) (2006) 338–356. University of Pittsburgh, WWPH 4711, Pittsburgh, PA 15260, USA; Department of Political Science, University of Michigan, 7766 Haven Hall, Ann Arbor, MI 48109, USA.
© 2006 Association for Comparative Economic Studies. Published by Elsevier Inc. All rights reserved.

JEL classification: D3; O87; P2

Keywords: De novo firms; Spin-offs; Early privatization; Exclusion restrictions; Income distribution

1. Entrepreneurship and the evolution of income distributions in Poland and Russia

Income inequality increased in the transitional economies in Central and Eastern Europe and the former Soviet Union (CIS) according to UNICEF (2001) and World Bank (2000). The more

---

* Corresponding author.
E-mail address: jjacksn@umich.edu (J.E. Jackson).

0147-5967/$ – see front matter © 2006 Association for Comparative Economic Studies. Published by Elsevier Inc. All rights reserved.
doi:10.1016/j.jce.2006.02.003

D. Berkowitz, J.E. Jackson / Journal of Comparative Economics 34 (2006) 338–356   339

successful transitional economies in Central and Eastern Europe experienced relatively modest increases in inequality of about 0.05 in their Gini coefficients from 1987–1989 to 1997–1999 with coefficients still at or below the OECD average of 0.31 by the end of the 1990s. In contrast, the CIS countries, which are regarded as having less successful transitions, had average increases in their Gini coefficients of 0.17 during the same period so that, with the exception of Belarus, all of these countries have Gini coefficients well above the OECD average. These observations raise the intriguing issue of whether the relatively rapid and successful creation of a capitalist market economy has a salutary impact on income distribution. In this paper, we investigate the increased inequality by examining the relationship between the rates of creation and growth of new and small private enterprises and the changes in the income share of the bottom two quintiles within regions in Poland and Russia.

Russia and Poland illustrate two quite different transition experiences. Poland's real GDP increased annually beginning with the third year of the transition and exceeded its pre-transition level by the sixth year. According to UNICEF data, the Gini coefficient measuring income inequality increased from 0.28 to 0.33 between 1987–1989 and 1997–1999 in Poland.[1] However, Russia experienced a major contraction from 1991 to 1998 and, by 2003, real GDP was still below the pre-transition level despite significant growth after 1998. Accompanying this fall in income is a considerable increase in inequality. According to the UNICEF data, the Gini coefficient for income increased from 0.27 to 0.47 between 1987–1989 and 1997–1999 in Russia.[2] We use these contrasting experiences to test propositions about how entry and growth of new small firms is related to changes in the distribution of income. In the next section, we present arguments for why increased small enterprise growth flattens the income distribution and benefits those in the lower quintiles. Section 3 describes the regional variations in income distributions and the size of the small enterprise sector in Poland and Russia. In the following section, we discuss our estimation methods, which recognize the endogeneity of new firm creation and growth, and present the statistical results. In the concluding section, we draw on our comparison of the Polish and Russian experiences to suggest why Poland did not have the large increase in income inequality that occurred in Russia.

2. New firm entry and changes in income distribution

The entry of small enterprises consists of the creation of de novo firms, spin-offs from state enterprises, and small scale privatization of state firms. In all three situations, we expect higher rates of small enterprise creation to promote a more equitable income distribution. First, new small enterprises were the sole source of job creation in many transitional economies and offset layoffs resulting from the introduction of hard budget constraints, privatization, and restructuring of state-owned firms. Bilsen and Konings (1998) provide evidence from Romania, Bulgaria and Hungary; while Jackson et al. (2005) demonstrate this for Poland and Jurjada and Terrell (2001) provide evidence from the Czech Republic and Estonia. The wages earned in these jobs increase incomes at the lower end of the income distribution because they are greater than unemployment benefits.

Second, based on the Schumpeterian notion of creative destruction, new small enterprises will exhibit higher productivity than the firms that they are replacing. Using a detailed sample of 24

---

[1] Keane and Prassad (2002) provide an overview of the dynamics of the income distribution in Poland during the 1990s.

[2] Luttmer (2002) provides a comparison of the income distributions in Poland and Russia.

340   *D. Berkowitz, J.E. Jackson / Journal of Comparative Economics 34 (2006) 338–356*

countries, Bartelsman et al. (2004) document that, in the post-socialist transition economies, new firms are primarily small and the firms that they are replacing are large state enterprises. These authors show that productivity gains from entry and exit are highest in transition economies. Klapper et al. (2004) corroborate this finding. Comparing new and old manufacturing firms in Slovenia, De Loecker and Konings (2006) find that the net entry of de novo private firms is an important determinant of the growth in total factor productivity. Using longitudinal data on cohorts of new and old enterprises in Poland, Jackson et al. (2005) find that both survival and growth are strongly related to average sales per worker within new firms indicating that the most productive firms are employing a larger share of the workforce. These authors also show that wage growth among surviving firms in a cohort is strongly related to sales per worker and to sales growth. Moreover, their analysis indicates that wage growth is tied more closely to productivity growth in the surviving small enterprises than in state-owned and former-state-owned firms. In the short run, regional incomes depend on factors other than the number and growth of new firms, e.g., unemployment.[3] However, in the longer run, the equilibrium wage in a competitive labor market will reflect this higher level of productivity in the surviving new firms.

Finally, a high rate of entry and survival of new firms increases the competitiveness of product and labor markets so that monopoly rents are eliminated over time, as McMillan (1995) discusses. Johnson et al. (2002) argue that, during the first years of transition, small de novo and spin-off firms in Poland and Russia entered sectors that had been dominated by large state enterprises under socialism, such as consumer goods, light manufacturing, trade and services. The inefficiencies of the state enterprises created considerable profit opportunities for initial entrants in these sectors. Over time, the continued entry of firms reduced profits. Johnson et al. (2002) show that rents decreased as competition increased in Poland starting in 1995. However, McMillan and Woodruff (2002) argues that the slow development of supporting institutions and lower rates of firm entry led to the persistence of high profits in Russia.[4] Frye and Shleifer (1997) present evidence that, by 1996, small firms in Warsaw were operating in a more competitive market than their counterparts in Moscow. Thus, the small enterprise sector provides employment through job creation and also boosts productivity. If the entry of small enterprises is accompanied by the reduction of monopoly rents because of increased competition and if distortionary regulations are removed gradually, we expect payments to labor to reflect more accurately the marginal productivity of labor over time so that the entry of small enterprises leads to higher wages. These arguments predict a positive association between the rate of new and small firm creation and the equality of the income distribution in transitional economies. The remaining sections test this prediction by relating changes in the income share of the lowest two quintiles to the size and growth of the de novo firm sector in regions in Poland and in Russia.

3. Income distribution and new firm creation in Poland and Russia

Our estimates of regional income distributions and of the size of the small enterprise sector in Poland come from specialized data collections. The Polish Central Statistical Office does not

---

[3] Jackson (2003) and Tichit (2006) discuss the relationship between wages and unemployment in transition economies.

[4] An additional explanation given for the elimination of monopoly rents in Poland and their persistence in Russia is that Poland became more open to foreign trade. However, from EBRD (2003, pp. 178 and 186), we calculate the share of trade in GDP during years seven through ten of transition, i.e., 1996 to 1999 in Poland and 1998 to 2001 in Russia, to be 42.2% in Poland and 54.0% in Russia. Furthermore, the share of trade with non-transition countries during these years is 35.2% in Poland, which is less than the comparable share of 37.4% in Russia.

D. Berkowitz, J.E. Jackson / Journal of Comparative Economics 34 (2006) 338–356   341

disseminate publicly data on the regional distribution of income. The Institute for Social Studies at the University of Warsaw has conducted the Polish General Polish Social Survey (PGSS) since 1992, as discussed by Cichomski and Morawski (2002). This survey contains a nationally representative random sample of about 1600 households in 1992, 1993, and 1994 and about 2300 households in 1997 and 1999.[5] One of the questions asks for total monthly family income. The 1992, 1993, and 1994 samples are pooled and family incomes in 1993 and 1994 are adjusted to 1992 price levels using the consumer price index. These data constitute the 1993 sample. Similarly the 1997 and 1999 surveys are pooled and 1999 incomes are adjusted to 1997 levels. These data make up the 1998 sample. Each sample is disaggregated by region, i.e., voivodship, of which there are forty-nine.

Measures of income distribution, or inequality, are computed for each region based on the respondents residing in that region. These measures are the income shares of the lowest and the lowest two quintiles in both 1993 and 1998 and the changes in these shares between 1993 and 1998. Table 1 provides descriptive statistics for the means and ranges of these measures among voivodships with the Warsaw region omitted. The average income share of both the first and second quintile is essentially equal in 1993 and 1998 at about 22%. The average share for the first quintile is also comparable across the periods at about 8%. The standard deviation of regional shares of the first two quintiles increased between 1993 and 1998 while the range decreased by 2.5%. For the first quintile, both the standard deviation and the range of income shares increased between 1993 and 1998. The stability of mean income shares between 1993 and 1998 disguises substantial variation in changes in the shares. The range of these changes is large, from −9.8% to +12.2%, with a standard deviation of 4.3% for the first and second quintiles combined. These statistics indicate considerable regional variations in the change in shares; our interest is to investigate whether these changes are related to the size and growth of the small enterprise sector.

Table 1
Descriptive measures of income distributions and survey sample sizes for Poland

Variable	1993 Shares	1998 Shares	ΔShares
1st Quintile income shares			
Regional mean	7.9%	8.1%	0.1%
Regional median	7.9%	7.8%	0.1%
Regional st. deviation	1.1%	1.5%	1.7%
Regional minimum	5.3%	5.9%	−3.6%
Regional maximum	10.34%	14.7%	4.7%
1st and 2nd Quintile income shares			
Regional mean	21.7%	21.9%	0.2%
Regional median	21.4%	21.8%	0.3%
Regional st. deviation	2.6%	3.0%	4.3%
Regional minimum	15.7%	17.1%	−9.9%
Regional maximum	28.8%	27.8%	12.2%
Sample sizes			
National	4569	4151	
Regional mean	95.2	86.5	
Regional median	81	73.5	
Regional minimum	22	21	
Regional maximum	542	428	

Note: the Warsaw region is omitted from all statistics.

---

[5] A study was made in 1995 but we do not include it in our analysis.

The lower half of Table 1 shows the regional sample sizes on which these distributional statistics are calculated. Two important considerations must be given to the evaluation of these statistics. First, their accuracy relative to the population values in the regions is a function of sample size. In our statistical analysis, we weight by these sample sizes to adjust for sampling errors. The alternative strategy of combining regions with smaller sample sizes presents two problems. It reduces the degrees of freedom in our analysis relating changes in regional income shares to the de novo sector. In addition, regions with small samples are not contiguous so that any aggregation is arbitrary. For these reasons, we keep the regions intact and weight by sample size. Second, the PGSS study is a representative sample for the nation but not for each voivodship. Hence, our measure of a region's income distribution may be calculated from a non-representative subset of a region's population.

Given the available data, we have no option but to use these regional income distributions despite this potentially serious problem. To discern its likely severity, we compare the sample sizes in each voivodship with the corresponding populations and conjecture that the greater is the proportional difference the less likely is the voivodship to be represented adequately in the PGSS sample. The simple correlation of the sample size and population variables is 0.93. The ratio of the regional sample size to the voivodship population divided by ten is 1.19 with a standard deviation of 0.37; the log of this ratio has a mean of 0.13 and a standard deviation of 0.32. We correlated this ratio and its log with a series of variables characterizing each voivodship, e.g., population, average salary, and the rates of creation of both de novo firms and jobs. None of the individual correlations is close to being statistically significant with the lowest p-level at 0.25. The multiple regression in which all the variables are included has an adjusted R-squared of -0.13 and an F-statistic of 0.51 with eleven and thirty-six degrees of freedom, which implies a p-level of 0.88. Based on these comparisons, we conclude that the regional sample sizes and populations are highly correlated and we find no systematic variation in the deviations from this ratio. Thus, with corrections for sampling error, we expect to obtain good estimates of the relationship between small enterprise creation and income inequality and to have reliable estimates of their uncertainty.

Measuring the size and growth of the small enterprise sector in transitional economies is a daunting task. However, we have access to a dataset developed by the Economics and Statistics Research Office of the Polish Central Statistical Office (GUS) that enables us to focus on small de novo firms and spin-offs as opposed to small privatized firms in Poland. The GUS created longitudinal data tracking individual firms from annual reports filed by individual enterprises that measure the entry, survival, and growth of new firms for the period 1990 through 1997, as Jackson et al. (1999, 2005) describe. The filings are linked to follow the survival and employment growth of small firms that existed in 1990 and the entry, survival, and growth of new firms that entered after 1990. From these data, we calculate the number of firms in each region in 1997 that were small in 1990 or had entered since then along with their total employment. These numbers for employment and firms are denominated by the size of the workforce and by population, respectively. Hence, we take the density of these firms per capita, their employment share in 1997, and the change in their employment share from 1993 to 1997 as measures for the size of the small enterprise sector in each region. Table 2 reports the summary statistics for these variables.

One limitation of these data is that the GUS did not require firms with five or fewer employees to report. Consequently, the very smallest sector is omitted. Another agency collects data on firm registrations by region but their data for firms with five or fewer employees overstate considerably the number of de novo firms. Hence, these data are not reliable and we do not use them in this

D. Berkowitz, J.E. Jackson / Journal of Comparative Economics 34 (2006) 338–356   343

Table 2
Description of Poland's de novo economy

Variable	1990[a]	1993	1997
Firms/thousand population			
Mean	0.32		1.92
Median	0.30		1.69
St. deviation	0.13		0.79
Minimum	0.13		0.79
Maximum	0.73		4.42
New employment/workforce			
Mean	0.01	0.05	0.11
Median	0.01	0.04	0.10
St. Deviation	0.01	0.02	0.05
Minimum	0.00	0.02	0.04
Maximum	0.04	0.10	0.23
ΔNew employment/workforce, 1993–1997			
Mean			0.07
Median			0.06
St. deviation			0.03
Minimum			0.02
Maximum			0.15

Notes. Entries for 1990 refer to firms with six to one hundred employees.

[a] Warsaw region omitted.

study.[6] Jackson et al. (2005) compare the GUS and registry data for firms of all sizes and find no evidence of systematic regional differences or biases between the two data sources. These authors conclude that the GUS data provide more reliable estimates of local de novo firms and spin-off activity because they track both growth and exit. Hence, we use these data despite the omission of very small firms. The GUS data have several advantages over the usual data that measure the size of the small and medium enterprise (SME) sector or that track the registration of new firms. First, in the conventional data on SMEs, the most successful new firms will no longer by classified as SMEs as they grow over time. Hence, the more successful is a region in promoting entry and growth of a small enterprise sector, the more likely is the SME data to understate its size and importance. Second, most data on the size of the private sector do not separate de novo and spin-off firms from privatized firms. The latter may have a quite different impact on promoting the competition and growth needed for a healthy market economy than the former group. In summary, we conclude that the GUS data are the best available information on the size and growth of small de novo and spin-off firms in Poland so that we use them to measure the number and employment of the most successful of these firms on a regional basis.

The Warsaw region is dropped from the Polish sample because it is an outlier whose inclusion would influence the results unduly. As the capital city, Warsaw has a very high proportion of government employees, whose wages are not determined by market forces but are more reflective of political interests. Warsaw also had a large de novo private sector by 1997 and received the dominant share of foreign investment, which accounted for about half of all employment in new

---

[6] Some registrations are for tax purposes solely and the agency responsible for these data does not record exits. Both of these considerations lead to overstatements of the size of this sector. Including these data for firms with five or fewer employees with our data on those with over five employees would imply more job creation than job loss during the transition, which is inconsistent with the ten percent unemployment rate in 1997.

foreign owned firms. Hence, Warsaw has the largest proportion of workforce in de novo private domestic and foreign firms of any region. Nonetheless, Table 2 indicates the substantial variation in the size of the de novo sector across regions.

For Russia, we use published regional data supplied by the official Russian statistical agency in Goskomstat Rossii (1996, 2001, 2002) to characterize the income distribution and small enterprise formation. These data contain representative regional surveys of household income, regional registries of small enterprises, and data on the number of employees and sales in these new enterprises. The regional income distribution is reported in 1995, 2000 and 2001 and the methodology does not change over time. Russia contains 89 regions; the 1995 national survey covers 75 of the regions and the 2001 survey covers 77 of them. We match data from the national sample with our regional data set, which includes early privatization data and other regional covariates, and obtain a sub-sample of 66 regions in 1995 and 2001. The cities of Moscow and St. Petersburg are excluded.

Table 3 reports the share of income held by the bottom 20-percent and the bottom 40-percent of the regional income distribution in 1995 and 2001 and illustrates several patterns. First, income distribution within Russian regions becomes slightly more inequitable during this time period measured by either the national mean or the regional mean. Households in the bottom 40-percent of the income distribution lose, on average, one percentage point of their share of overall income; households in the bottom 20-percent lose about a half percentage point. Hence, the changes in the Russian income distribution from 1995 to 2001 are considerably different from the relatively stable income distribution in Poland from 1993 to 1998 reported in Table 1.

Second, comparing Tables 1 and 3, we see that the income distribution exhibits less variation over time in Russia than in Poland. The standard deviation in regional income shares in Russia decreases from 2.7% in 1995 to 1.7% in 2001, whereas in Poland it increases from 2.6% in 1993 to 3.0% in 1998. The changes in income shares within regions are also more stable in Russia between 1995 and 2001 than in Poland between 1993 and 1998. For the lowest two quintiles, the

Table 3
Descriptive measures of income distributions and survey sample sizes for Russia

Variable	1995 Shares	2001 Shares	ΔShares
1st Quintile income shares			
National mean (full sample)	7.6%	7.1%	
Regional mean (analyzed sub-sample)	7.7%	7.2%	−0.5%
Regional median	8.0%	7.3%	−0.7%
Regional st. deviation	1.3%	0.9%	1.2%
Regional minimum	4.7%	4.7%	−3.3%
Regional maximum	10.1%	8.5%	2.5%
1st and 2nd Quintile income shares			
National (full sample)	20.0%	19.0%	
Regional mean (analyzed sub-sample)	20.1%	19.1%	−1.0%
Regional median	20.9%	19.4%	−1.4%
Regional st. deviation	2.7%	1.7%	2.5%
Regional minimum	13.9%	13.9%	−6.5%
Regional maximum	24.8%	21.8%	5.2%
Sample sizes (number of regions)			
National (full sample)	75	77	
Regional (analyzed sample)	66	66	
Actual number of regions	89	89	

Note: the cities of Moscow and St. Petersburg are omitted from all statistics.

D. Berkowitz, J.E. Jackson / Journal of Comparative Economics 34 (2006) 338–356   345

standard deviation of the change in income shares is smaller in Russia than in Poland at 2.5% and 4.3%, respectively, and the range of the changes is smaller in Russia than in Poland, i.e., −6.5% to 5.2% compared to −9.9% to 12.2%. Nevertheless, we have sufficient variation in the change in Russian regional income shares to estimate the relationship between income shares and the size and growth of the small enterprise sector.

We use small enterprise employment as a share of the regional workforce and the registry of small enterprises per 1000 people as measures of small enterprise development. Legally registered small enterprises include spin-offs from state enterprise and start-ups as well as privatized small state enterprises. Thus, we can not separate small de novo and spin-off firms from small privatized firms in Russia as we did in Poland. Before 1996, small enterprises were defined by employment ceilings in that, over the course of a year, a small enterprise could hire no more than 200 workers on average and employment ceilings varied across branches, e.g., 100 in scientific services and 15 in retail trade. However, starting in 1996, small enterprises have been defined by both ownership structure and employment in Russia. Regarding ownership, no matter how small an enterprise may be, it is not legally defined as a small enterprise if it has an outside owner, e.g., a large company, a charitable organization, or a social or religious organization, that owns at least 25% of the initial enterprise capital. In addition, employment ceilings have changed and become smaller; for example, the highest ceiling is 100 applying to industry, construction and transport while the ceiling for retail trade has been increased to 30 employees on average per year. Because the definition of a Russian and Polish small enterprise is different, our data cannot be used to compare the penetration of small enterprise in these two countries.

Table 4 reports data on the evolution of small enterprises in Russia for pairs of years in which the definitions are comparable and for which data are available. Remarkably, the number of small enterprises per capita and the share of the labor force employed in small enterprises decreases over time. Employment shares increase in only one region in our sub-sample, namely, Nizhni Novgorod. The cities of Moscow and St. Petersburg are outliers because the increase in the labor force employed in small enterprises in these cities is three to four standard deviations above the

Table 4
Description of Russia's small enterprises

Variable	1996	2001
Firms/population (1000)		
Mean	3.84	2.34
Median	3.76	2.18
St. deviation	1.41	1.02
Minimum	1.71	1.09
Maximum	9.40	5.98
Small employment/workforce	1995	2001
Mean	0.13	0.07
Median	0.13	0.07
St. deviation	0.02	0.03
Minimum	0.08	0.02
Maximum	0.20	0.14
Δ *Employment share, 1995–2001*		
Mean		−0.06
Median		−0.06
St. deviation		0.03
Minimum		−0.15
Maximum		0.01

346   *D. Berkowitz, J.E. Jackson / Journal of Comparative Economics 34 (2006) 338–356*

median region in our sub-sample and one to two standard deviations above Nizhny Novgorod. Moscow is 4.6, 2.6, and 4.8 standard deviations above the mean and St. Petersburg is 4.5, 3.5, and 5.2 standard deviations above the mean for the 2001 small enterprise employment share, the 1995 to 2001 change in small enterprise employment share, and in 2001 enterprises per capita. Moreover, the extent of foreign activity in Moscow and St. Petersburg sets these two regions apart from the rest of Russia. In 2001, they attracted 48% of foreign investment. Moscow and St. Petersburg have the highest and second highest proportions of the regional workforce employed in foreign joint enterprises that are also small enterprises. Hence, we exclude these two cities from our analysis. However, even if we were to include Moscow and St. Petersburg in the sample, small enterprise development would remain much more dynamic over time in Poland than in Russia.

4. The empirical results

In this section, we present the empirical analysis of the influence of small enterprise development on income distribution in Poland 1998 and Russia 2001. We begin with the following equation:

$$\Delta DIST_t = \alpha + \beta SMENT + \gamma X + \delta DIST_{t-1} + \varepsilon_t, \tag{1}$$

where $\Delta DIST_t$, $DIST_{t-1}$, $SMENT$, and X denote respectively the change in income distribution measured as the share of income going to the bottom 40-percent of the distribution in a region between periods t and $t - 1$, the income distribution in period $t - 1$, small enterprise development, and a vector of regional covariates. In this vector, we include log population to capture the extent of the market and education because both of these variables are important determinants of income distribution and small enterprise development. The primary measure for small enterprise development, denoted $SMENT$, is the employment share of the sector in 1997 in Poland and in 2001 in Russia. This variable is also measured by the number of de novo private firms per thousand people and by the change in the de novo firm share of private employment from 1993 to 1997 for Poland and from 1995 to 2001 for Russia.

Estimating Eq. (1) is complicated by the possibility of reverse causality. Using formal models, Gabszewicz and Thisse (1980) and Shaked and Sutton (1982) show that the entry of new firms in markets characterized by monopolistic competition is related to the distribution of income. Empirical studies argue that more equitable income distributions are associated with higher rates of economic growth. Aghion et al. (1999) provide a summary of this research and Forbes (2000) gives a contrary view. Keane and Prassad (2002) report a strong negative correlation between GDP growth and inequality for fourteen transition countries during the first eight years of the transition. If GDP growth is related to the growth of de novo firms as we hypothesize, our measures of small enterprise development will be endogenous.

To address this potential endogeneity problem, we use early privatization and initial conditions as instruments that should provide consistent estimates for the relationship between new enterprise development and changes in income equality. Because of differences in data availability and in their approaches to reforms, the precise variables differ in each country. For Russia, the two instruments are large and small scale privatizations in 1993, defined as the number of privatized firms in each category per 1000 of the population, as reported in Goskomstat Rossii

(1994).[7] In Poland, data for only large scale privatization, defined as the proportion of the 1993 workforce employed in firms privatized to that time, are available. Additional relevant initial condition variables are the proportion of the 1990 non-farm workforce employed in state-owned enterprises and the proportion of the workforce employed in private enterprises with fewer than one hundred employees.[8]

The first requirement for our instruments is that they be related to the size of the de novo enterprise sector. McMillan (1995) argues that early privatization leads to the emergence of a regulatory environment that enhances the entry and development of small enterprises. If properly implemented, privatization weakens the political connections of the controllers of formerly state owned enterprises. Hence, both national and local governments would have no incentive to use tax and regulatory policy to protect state-owned enterprises against entry by small enterprises. Furthermore, governments can expand their tax base and enhance the standard of living by developing a pro-small-business regulatory environment. Alternatively, if privatization fails to eliminate these political connections, the old situation in which governments have an incentive to protect the large enterprises remains. Berkowitz and Holland (2001) find strong positive relationships between new firm registrations and federal and regional privatization in Russia, but small negative relationships for local privatization. Hence, we conclude that the greater is the degree of capture of government agencies by the privatized firms and the smaller is the separation of these firms from the government, the weaker will be the relationship between privatization and new firm entry.

Poland and Russia have quite different privatization experiences. Poland proceeded very slowly with large scale privatization while Russia privatized very rapidly. Alexeev (1999), Berkowitz and Li (2000), Black et al. (2000), Frye and Shleifer (1997), Hellman (1998) and Shleifer and Vishny (1993) argue that early Russian privatization led to a corrupt regulatory environment that persisted through at least the mid-1990s, while early Polish privatization had the opposite effect. Johnson et al. (2002), Hellman et al. (2003) and Karatnycky et al. (2001) and Transparency International (1996) document far less corruption in Poland than in Russia, while Hellman et al. (2003) reports relatively less governmental capture in Poland. We expect these differences to produce a stronger association between large scale privatization and new firm growth in Poland than in Russia.

Initial conditions are important to the development of the Polish de novo private sector. Poland had a nascent small private sector and a varied mix of state-owned, collective, and large domestic and foreign enterprises at the beginning of the transition, the concentration of which varied substantially by region. Given the importance of agglomeration, learning, and political effects, the presence of a significant number of small private enterprises at the beginning of the transition gives a region a substantial advantage in expanding its de novo sector as the transition proceeds. Moreover, we expect the presence of state-owned enterprises at the beginning of the transition to depress the entrepreneurial process and, as a result, decrease the growth and ultimately the size of the de novo sector. These enterprises pay higher wages, raising labor costs and reducing labor supply for new enterprises. Even within the less-corrupt Polish environment, large firms are able to exert undue influence on institutions ranging from financial organizations to governments

---

[7] Regional privatization combined voucher and cash privatization of large and medium-sized companies. To avoid potential problems associated with over-identification, we do not include early regional privatization in Russia.

[8] For the equation with new firms per thousand of the population as the measure for *SMENT*, the variables representing initial conditions are the proportion of the 1990 non-farm workforce employed in state-owned enterprises and the number of small firms per one thousand people in 1990.

and obtain preferential treatment and various subsidies, which create an unfavorable climate for enterprise creation. Finally, empirical evidence from the US and Poland in Jackson and Rodkey (1994) and Jackson and Marcinkowski (1999) indicates that both individuals residing in regions dominated by large organizations, independent of the size of their own employer, and employees in large organizations express less support for entrepreneurs and are less likely to say they would undertake entrepreneurial activity. Considering these three factors, we expect to find a negative relationship between a region's density of state-owned enterprises and the development of its de novo sector in Poland. However, these initial conditions are relatively unimportant in explaining the development of the de novo sector in Russia due to the lack of a small private sector and the fact that virtually all employment was in state-owned firms at the beginning of the transition.

A second requirement for our instruments is that they are not related systematically to the change in the income share of the bottom two quintiles after controlling for new firm entry, lagged income shares, education and population. In other words, the effect of an instrument on income shares is only through its relationship to new firm creation and growth. To validate empirically this identifying assumption, we take a two-step approach. First, we control for the influence of the initial income distribution in the estimating equation. Initial conditions and early privatization are determined prior to our measure of initial income shares so that, if these variables affect inequality directly, their strongest effects should be on this variable and not on the subsequent change in income. Second, we validate our exclusion restrictions by employing over-identification tests based on Hansen (1982) and Baum et al. (2003). These tests examine whether the identifying variables are correlated individually or jointly to the changes in the income distribution conditional on firm entry and the other covariates in Eq. (1). If we cannot reject the null hypothesis of no correlation, we find statistical corroboration for the validity of this requirement.[9]

Based on these propositions the first stage regression used to identify the impact of *SMENT* on $\Delta DIST$ is:

$$SMENT = \alpha_1 + \beta_1 PRIV + \beta_2 COND_0 + \gamma_1 X + \varepsilon_1, \tag{2}$$

where *PRIV* denotes privatization during 1990 to 1993 for Poland and small and large privatization in 1993 for Russia and $COND_0$, which applies only to Poland, is the 1990 employment in small private and in state-owned firms.[10] Therefore, we use the variables in *PRIV* and in $COND_0$ as over-identifying restrictions in estimating Eq. (1) for either Poland or Russia.[11]

Table 5 contains the empirical results of estimating Eqs. (1) and (2) for Poland.[12] In panel A, we report 2SLS estimates of Eq. (1) and, in panel B, we provide test statistics to check for

---

[9] As in all conventional statistical tests, a failure to reject the null hypothesis does not mean we can accept it. However, the higher is the probability of getting our statistical results by chance under the null, the more likely the null is to be correct.

[10] Privatized employment in 1993 and state-owned employment in 1990 are measured by the non-farm workforce because we are using these variables to measure the concentration of industrial and commercial activity in these firms. For the small private and de novo sectors, we are seeking variables to assess the level of participation of the entire workforce in these enterprises.

[11] Hahn and Hausman (2002) and Chao and Swannson (2006) show that over-identification can create bias when two stage least squares (2SLS) is used. Simulation results in Chao and Swannson show that one way to offset this bias is to use limited information maximum likelihood estimation (LIML). Because the difference between our 2SLS and LIML estimates are negligible, we report only the 2SLS results but the LIML results are available upon request.

[12] We also estimated the equations with Warsaw included. In each first-stage estimation, the dfits statistic for Warsaw is about six times larger than both the next largest value and the conventional threshold for concluding that the observation may be problematic. Hence, we report the results with Warsaw excluded.

D. Berkowitz, J.E. Jackson / Journal of Comparative Economics 34 (2006) 338–356   349

Table 5
Income distribution and small enterprises in Poland

Measure of small enterprise development	Employment share of workforce, 1997	New enterprises per capita, 1997	Δ Employment share, 1993–1997
A. Second stage 2SLS estimates dependent variable is share of income going to bottom 40-percent			
Small enterprise development, (instrumented)	30.6^* (10.7) QS: 1.44	2.00^* (0.79) QS: 1.58	57.3^* (24.6) QS: 1.72
Log population, 1998	-1.01^* (0.45)	-1.14^* (0.54)	-1.32^* (0.58)
Education, 1998	-1.35^{**} (0.77)	-1.46^{**} (0.85)	-1.36^{**} (0.80)
Income share, 1993	-1.50^* (0.22)	-1.50^* (0.21)	-1.50^* (0.23)
Centered R^2	0.64	0.64	0.63
B. Over-identification tests for 2SLS estimates: t-statistics			
Employment in private firms in 1990 per 1000 workforce (*p*-value)	-0.62 (0.54)		-0.09 (0.93)
1990 private employment per 1000 population (*p*-value)		-0.42 (0.68)	
Employment in state-owned firms, 1990 (*p*-value)	0.01 (0.99)	0.09 (0.93)	0.34 (0.74)
Employment in firms privatized 1990–1993 per 1000 workforce (*p*-value)	0.76 (0.45)	0.50 (0.62)	0.49 (0.63)
J-test for joint exclusion of privatization variables (*p*-value)	0.54 (0.76)	0.25 (0.88)	0.19 (0.91)
C. OLS estimates of the second stage			
Small enterprise development, 1998	22.2^* (8.70) QS: 1.25	1.27^* (0.42) QS: 2.15	34.6^* (13.1) QS: 1.3
Log population, 1998	-0.72 (0.49)	-0.71 (0.43)	-0.78 (0.49)
Education	-1.17 (0.71)	-1.18 (0.72)	-1.09 (0.69)
Share, 1993	-1.51^* (0.22)	-1.51^* (0.21)	-1.51^* (0.22)
Centered R^2	0.65	0.65	0.65
D. First stage reduced form OLS regression (dependent variables is small enterprise development, 2001)			
Privatization variables (excluded instruments)			
Employment in private firms in 1990 per 1000 workforce	3.64^* (0.92)		1.56^* (0.73)
Per 1000 population		2.76^* (0.69)	

(*continued on next page*)

350   *D. Berkowitz, J.E. Jackson / Journal of Comparative Economics 34 (2006) 338–356*

Table 5 (*continued*)

Measure of small enterprise development	Employment share of workforce, 1997	New enterprises per capita, 1997	Δ Employment share, 1993–1997
Employment in state-owned firms, 1990	-0.16^*	-2.98^*	-0.14^*
	(0.08)	(1.39)	(0.06)
Employment in firms privatized 1990–1993 per 1000 workforce	0.51^*	10.76^{**}	0.38^{**}
	(0.21)	(5.80)	(0.19)
Log population, 1998	0.05^*	0.91^*	0.04^*
	(0.01)	(0.22)	(0.01)
Education, 1998	0.01	0.14	0.00
	(0.01)	(0.17)	(0.01)
Income share, 1993	-0.001	-0.02	-0.001
	(0.002)	(0.03)	(0.002)
F-statistic for excluded instruments	13.1	7.51	5.15
p-value of F-statistic	0.000	0.000	0.004
Partial R^2 of excluded instruments	0.52	0.44	0.35

Notes. (1) The standard errors of the point estimates are reported in parentheses. (2) The standard errors in the second stage have a small sample correction; first and second stage standard errors are corrected for heteroskedasticity. (3) QS denotes quantitative significance, which is the impact of a one-standard-deviation difference in small enterprise development, using the actual sample, on income distribution. (4) Small private firms in 1990 have fewer than 100 employees.

[*] Significance at the 5% level.

[**] Idem, 10%.

the validity of our instruments. Panel C contains corresponding Ordinary Least Squares (OLS) estimates and panel D presents the first stage estimates of the influence of early privatization and initial conditions on small enterprises.

Small enterprise development in 1997 in Poland, whether measured by employment share, enterprises per capita, or change in employment share, has the expected positive impact on the change in income distribution between 1993 and 1998 and is always significant at the 5 percent level. To gauge the quantitative significance (QS) of small enterprises, we compute the impact of a one-standard-deviation increase in small enterprise development on income distribution. These values for all three measures are about one half of a standard deviation of income going to the bottom 40-percent in 1998, which is 3% in our sample. Panel B provides two sets of tests to check the validity of excluding early privatization from the 2SLS estimates in Eq. (1). First, we provide t-statistics and associated p-values to test the null hypothesis that each instrument can be excluded separately from the second stage. For example, the t-statistic for employment in private firms in 1990 divided by the workforce reported in the first regression column tests the null hypothesis that this variable's coefficient is not statistically different from zero if only it is included in the second stage while using the identifying restriction that the other instruments are excluded. In the nine cells for the three regression columns, the lowest p-value associated with these t-statistics is 0.45 indicating that the null hypothesis for an individual test can be rejected. Second, we report the J-statistic to test the null hypothesis that the three privatization instruments are not jointly correlated with the error term in the second stage estimates, as suggested by Hansen (1982) or Baum et al. (2003). All the p-values are above 0.75 indicating that the null hypothesis cannot be rejected for the joint tests. Hence, we conclude that the variables characterizing early privatization and initial conditions are valid instruments.

D. Berkowitz, J.E. Jackson / Journal of Comparative Economics 34 (2006) 338–356   351

Panel C reports OLS point estimates of the impact of small enterprises on income distribution. In all three cases, the 2SLS points estimate are higher suggesting that the 2SLS procedure has corrected for some simultaneity bias. Panel D reports the first-stage OLS estimates of the impact of early privatization and employment in state-owned enterprises on small enterprise development. In each case, early privatizations have strong positive and statistically significant coefficients and the concentration of state-owned enterprises has a significant negative impact on subsequent small enterprise development. The F-statistic to test for excluded instruments indicates that the early privatization measures and the initial concentration of state enterprise cannot be jointly excluded from the first stage. The partial R^2 measures the share of the variance explained by these instruments and corroborates the considerable strength of these instruments.

Table 6 is arranged similarly to present the results for Russia.[13] Panel A shows that all three variables measuring small enterprise employment have a positive and statistically significant impact on income distribution in 2001. The quantitative significances of all three variables are substantial compared to the 2.2 percent standard deviation in regional income distribution. As in Poland, the entry of new firms and the consequent employment created is strongly and positively related to the increases in income share of the lower two quintiles. The t-test statistics and J-test statistics in panel B provide validation for using early large and small privatization as instruments. The OLS estimates of the impact of these variables on income distribution in Panel C are positive and substantially lower than the corresponding 2SLS estimates. Panel D indicates that early privatization is always positively associated with subsequent small enterprise devel-

Table 6
Income distribution and small enterprises in Russia

Measure of small enterprise development	Employment share of workforce, 2001	New enterprises per capita, 2001	Δ Employment share, 1995–2001
A. Second stage 2SLS estimates			
Small enterprise development	38.9*	1.46*	76.5**
(instrumented)	(10.5)	(0.59)	(38.4)
	QS: 0.98	QS: 1.49	QS: 2.30
Log population, 2001	−0.82*	−0.85*	−2.29*
	(0.26)	(0.39)	(0.76)
Education, 1994	−0.19*	−0.47*	−0.16
	(0.09)	(0.20)	(0.16)
Income share, 1995	−0.79*	−0.80*	−0.98*
	(0.08)	(0.10)	(0.17)
Centered R^2	0.64	0.44	0.16
B. Over-identification tests for 2SLS estimates: t-statistics			
Large privatization, 1993	0.08	0.60	0.90
(p-value)	(0.94)	(0.55)	(0.37)
Small privatization, 1993	−0.08	−0.48	−0.41
(p-value)	(0.94)	(0.63)	(0.68)
J-test for joint exclusion of privatization	0.01	0.35	0.64
variables (p-value)	(0.94)	(0.55)	(0.42)

(continued on next page)

[13] Although we exclude Moscow and St. Petersburg because of their potential to exert undue influence, our results are robust to their inclusion if we use small enterprise shares to measure new enterprises. However, the results are somewhat noisier if we use the small enterprises per capita or the change in employment shares with these cities included. A table similar to Table 6 with Moscow and St. Petersburg included is available upon request from the authors.

D. Berkowitz, J.E. Jackson / Journal of Comparative Economics 34 (2006) 338–356

Table 6 (*continued*)

Measure of small enterprise development	Employment share of workforce, 2001	New enterprises per capita, 2001	Δ Employment share, 1995–2001
C. OLS estimates of the second stage			
Small enterprise development, 2001	21.5*	0.20	7.94
	(6.67)	(0.26)	(7.29)
	QS: 0.54	QS: 0.20	QS: 0.24
Log population, 2001	−0.70*	−0.60*	−0.74**
	(0.27)	(0.30)	(0.37)
Education, 1994	−0.13	−0.10	−0.06
	(0.08)	(0.09)	(0.08)
Income share, 1995	−0.76*	−0.73*	−0.75*
	(0.08)	(0.08)	(0.08)
Centered R^2	0.66	0.63	0.63
D. First stage reduced form OLS regression (dependent variable is small enterprise development)			
Privatization variables (excluded instruments):			
Large privatization, 1993	0.22*	3.61	0.05
(firms per 1000 population)	(0.07)	(2.24)	(0.08)
Small privatization, 1993	0.09*	2.88*	0.06*
(firms per 1000 population)	(0.02)	(1.31)	(0.03)
Log population, 2001	0.009*	0.29**	0.024*
	(0.003)	(0.16)	(0.00)
Education, 1994	0.003*	0.27*	0.001
	(0.001)	(0.06)	(0.001)
Income share, 1995	0.003*	0.09*	0.004*
	(0.001)	(0.03)	(0.001)
F-statistic for excluded instruments	28.8	4.86	3.11
p-value of F-statistic	0.000	0.011	0.052
Partial R^2 of excluded instruments	0.40	0.22	0.09

Notes. (1) The standard errors of the point estimates are reported in parentheses. (2) The standard errors in the second stage include a small sample correction; first and second stage standard errors are corrected for heteroskedasticity. (3) QS denotes quantitative significance, which is the impact of a one-standard-deviation difference in small enterprise development, using the actual sample, on income distribution.

* Significance at the 5% level.

** Idem, 10%.

opment. The early small privatization measures are statistically significant in all 3 models and the early large scale privatization variable is significant in one model. The F-test for excluded instruments and the partial R^2 values show that these instruments are strongest in the equation for employment share in 2001 and weaker for the other two measures.

In Table 7, we compute the indirect quantitative significance of early privatization on income distribution in a two-step approach. First, we multiply a one-standard-deviation change in one of the early privatization measures by its impact on small enterprise formation and obtain the quantitative significance of a particular form of early privatization on small enterprises. Second, we take this statistic and multiply it by that impact of small enterprises on the subsequent income distribution. Regardless of whether we use employment, the number of small firms, or the change in employment as the measure of early small enterprise development in Poland, early privatiza-

D. Berkowitz, J.E. Jackson / Journal of Comparative Economics 34 (2006) 338–356   353

Table 7
Indirect quantitative significance of early privatization on income distribution

A. Poland

Measure of small enterprise development	Employment share of workforce, 1997	New enterprises per capita, 1997	Δ Employment share, 1993–1997
Early privatization			
Employment in private firms in 1990	0.686		0.549
Private firms in 1990		0.718	
Employment in firms privatized 1990–1993	0.335	0.467	0.465
State-owned employment 1990	−0.431	−0.513	−0.707

B. Russia

Measure of small enterprise development	Employment share of workforce, 2001	New enterprises per capita, 2001	Δ Employment share, 1995–2001
Early privatization:			
Large privatization, 1993	0.31	0.19	0.15
Small privatization, 1993	0.41	0.48	0.50

Note. Indirect quantitative significance is computed as a one-standard-deviation increase in the early privatization variable times the impact of that early privatization variable on small enterprise formation times the impact of the small enterprise variable on income distribution.

tion is associated with a 0.6 to 0.7 percentage point increase in the income shares of the bottom 40-percent of the distribution. Privatizations from 1990 to 1993 are associated with only about a 0.3 to 0.5 percentage point increase in shares while increases in the employment in state-owned enterprises in 1990 are associated with a 0.4 to 0.7 percentage point decrease in these income shares. In Russia, a one-standard-deviation change in small and large privatization is associated with about a 0.45 and 0.20 percent increase in the income shares of the lowest two quintiles.

Hence, evidence from both countries indicates that early small privatization is relatively more important than privatization and initial employment in state-owned firms for income distribution. Moreover, as the table indicates, the impact of early privatization on income distribution is much stronger in Poland than in Russia. Therefore, we conclude that early privatization through its impact on small enterprise development has been a more powerful force for promoting an equitable income distribution in Poland than in Russia.

5. Conclusion

In our empirical work, we find a strong positive relationship between the size and the growth of the de novo sector and the income share of the bottom two quintiles of the distribution in both Poland and Russia. The average impact of a one-standard-deviation increase in any measure of new enterprise activity on the income share of this group is approximately 1.6%. Finding consistent evidence for these two countries having two quite different transition experiences lends credibility to the proposition that new firm creation leads to a more equitable distribution of income in post-socialist countries. In addition, Berkowitz and DeJong (2005) find that a one–standard-deviation increase in the size of the small firm sector is associated with a one and a half percent increase in annual income growth from 1993 to 2000 in Russia. In a similar analysis for Poland, we find that each measure of de novo firm activity used in this paper is significantly related to income growth with a one-standard-deviation increase associated with a one percent higher annual income growth rate.[14] Taken together, these results indicate that new firm creation is associated with both larger income and a larger portion of income distributed to the lower quintiles, making the members of this group better off in both absolute and relative terms. These results also suggest that a positive association between per capita income and income distribution is due in part to small enterprise activity. In addition, according to United Nations (2005), overall growth in Russia since 2001 is associated with some improvement in the income distribution. Investigating these interesting issues requires additional data and sophisticated systems tests so that we leave it to future research.

Our empirical work allows us to make inferences about the strikingly different changes in the income distributions in Poland and Russia during the first decade of their respective transitions. A critical aspect of the differences in the experiences of the two countries is the rate and character of new private firm creation. Kornai (2000) considers Poland's transition to be based on a high level of organic de novo firm creation and of spin-offs from old state firms in contrast with Russia where the emphasis was on privatization with much lower rates of de novo creation and of spin-offs. Our Polish and Russian data are not comparable because the former measures new firm creation and their employment growth while the latter measures the size of the small enterprise sector, although most of this activity is likely to be new firms. However, the evidence presented in this paper demonstrates strong growth of the de novo sector in Poland by 1997. Employment in these firms more than doubled between 1993 and 1997 and the most successful regions exhibit very dynamic de novo sectors. In contrast, the small enterprise sector in Russia actually decreased between 1995 and 2001. Hence, our data indicate that the small private enterprise sector is a much more dynamic part of the Polish transition relative to Russia, as Kornai contends. Our empirical results show that these new firms are also crucial to promoting aggregate economy growth, to creating an economic middle class, and to maintaining a relatively equitable income distribution. Hence, we conclude that the different experiences with the creation of new small firms are a major reason why the income distributions in Poland and Russia diverged so dramatically during the 1990s.

Acknowledgments

We thank Erik Berglof and Ariel Pakes for suggesting this topic. We also thank Yuri Andrienko for help with the Russian data and Jacek Klich, Krystyna Poznańska and Józef Chmiel for help with the Polish economic data. We are grateful to the Institute for Social Studies at the University of Warsaw for sharing the PGSS data. We also thank John Bonin, the Editor, and an anonymous referee for useful comments.

References

Aghion, Philippe, Caroli, Eva, Garcia-Peñalosa, Cecilia, 1999. Inequality and economic growth: The perspective of the new growth theories. Journal of Economic Literature 37 (4), 1615–1660.
Alexeev, Michael, 1999. The effect of privatization on wealth distribution in Russia. Economics of Transition 7 (2), 449–465.
Bartelsman, Eric J., Haltiwanger, John, Scarpetta, Stefano, 2004. Microeconomic evidence of creative destruction in industrial and developing countries. Discussion paper 114/3. Tinbergen Institute.
Baum, Christopher F., Schaffer, Mark E., Stillman, Steven, 2003. Instrumental variables and GMM: Estimation and testing. The Stata Journal 3 (1), 1–31.

---

[14] A table of the statistical results is available upon request from the authors.

Berkowitz, Daniel, DeJong, David N., 2005. Entrepreneurship and post-socialist growth. Oxford Bulletin of Economics and Statistics 67 (1), 25–46.

Berkowitz, Daniel, Holland, Jonathan, 2001. Does privatization enhance or deter small enterprise formation? Economics Letters 74, 53–60.

Berkowitz, Daniel, Li, Wei, 2000. Tax rights in transition economies: A tragedy of the commons? Journal of Public Economics 76, 369–397.

Bilsen, Valentijn, Konings, Jozef, 1998. Job creation job destruction and employment growth in newly established firms in transition countries: Survey evidence from Romania, Bulgaria and Hungary. Journal of Comparative Economics 26 (3), 429–445.

Black, B., Kraakman, R., Tarassova, A., 2000. Russian privatization and corporate governance: What went wrong? Stanford Law Review 52, 1731–1810.

Chao, John, Swanson, Norman, 2006. Alternative approximations of the bias and MSE of the IV estimator under weak identification with an application to bias correction. Journal of Econometrics. In press.

Cichomski, Bogdan, Morawski, Pawel, 2002. Polish General Social Surveys: Machine readable data file 1992–1999. Institute for Social Studies, University of Warsaw, Warsaw, Poland.

De Loecker, Jan, Konings, Jozef, 2006. Creative destruction and productivity growth: Evidence from Slovenia. European Journal of Political Economy. In press.

European Bank for Reconstruction and Development. Transition report 2003: Integration and regional cooperation. EBRD, London.

Forbes, Kristin, 2000. A reassessment of the relationship between inequality and growth. American Economic Review. 90 (4), 869–887.

Frye, Timothy, Shleifer, Andrei, 1997. The invisible hand and the grabbing hand. American Economic Review 87, 354–358.

Gabszewicz, J., Thisse, Jaskold J.-F., 1980. Entry (and exit) in a differential industry. Journal of Economic Theory 22, 327–338.

Goskomstat Rossii, 1994. Rossiskiy Statisticheskiy Yezhegodnik. Goskomstat Rossii, Moskva.

Goskomstat Rossii, 1996. Rossiskiy Statisticheskiy Yezhegodnik. Goskomstat Rossii, Moskva.

Goskomstat Rossii, 2001. Regiony Rossii. Goskomstat Rossii, Moskva.

Goskomstat Rossii, 2002. Regiony Rossii. Goskomstat Rossii, Moskva.

Hahn, Jinyong, Hausman, Jerry, 2002. Notes on bias in estimators for simultaneous equation models. Economics Letters 75, 237–241.

Hansen, Lars Peter, 1982. Large sample properties of generalized method of moment estimators. Econometrica 50, 1029–1054.

Hellman, Joel S., 1998. Winners take all: The politics of partial reforms in post-Communist transitions. World Politics 50 (2), 203–234.

Hellman, Joel S., Jones, Geraint, Kaufman, Daniel, 2003. Seize the state, seize the day: State capture, corruption and influence in transition economies. Journal of Comparative Economics 31 (4), 751–773.

Jackson, John E., 2003. A computational political economy model of transition. In: Fidrmuc, Jan, Campos, Nauro (Eds.), Political Economy of Transition and Development: Institutions, Politics, and Policies. Kluwer Academic, Boston/Dordrecht/London, pp. 117–137.

Jackson, John E., Marcinkowski, Aleksander S., 1999. The entrepreneurial attitudes of Poles. In: Hauser, Ewa, Wasilewski, Jacek (Eds.), Lessons in Democracy. Univ. of Rochester Press/Jagiellonian Univ. Press, Rochester, NY/Kraków, Poland, pp. 171–200.

Jackson, John E., Rodkey, Gretchen R., 1994. The attitudinal climate for entrepreneurial activity. Public Opinion Quarterly 58 (3), 358–380.

Jackson, John E., Klich, Jacek, Poznańska, Krystyna, 1999. Firm creation and economic transitions. Journal of Business Venturing 14 (5/6), 427–450.

Jackson, John E., Klich, Jacek, Poznańska, Krystyna, 2005. The Political Economy of Poland's Transition: New Firms and Reform Governments. Cambridge Univ. Press, Cambridge, England/New York, NY.

Johnson, Simon, McMillan, John, Woodruff, Christopher, 2002. Property rights, finance and entrepreneurship. American Economic Review 92, 1335–1356.

Jurjada, Štepán, Terrell, Katherine, 2001. What drives the speed of job reallocation during episodes of massive adjustment? Working paper #601. Institute for the Study of Labor (IZA), Bonn, Germany.

Karatnycky, Adrian, Motyl, Alexander, Schnetzer, Amanda, 2001. Nations in Transit. Freedom House, New York, NY.

Keane, Michael, Prassad, Enwar, 2002. Inequality, transfers and growth: New evidence from economic transition in Poland. Review of Economics and Statistics 84 (2), 324–341.

Klapper, Leora, Laeven, Luc, Rajan, Raghuram, 2004. Business environment and firm entry: Evidence from international data. Working paper 10380. NBER.

Kornai, János, 2000. Ten years after 'The Road to a Free Economy': The author's self-evaluation. Paper prepared for the Annual Bank Conference on Development Economics. World Bank, Washington, DC.

Luttmer, Erzo F.P., 2002. Measuring economic mobility and inequality: Disentangling real events from noisy data. Available at http://www.nber.org/~luttmer/mobility.pdf. Harris School of Public Policy Studies, University of Chicago, Chicago, IL.

McMillan, John, 1995. Markets in transition. Chapter 6. In: Kreps, David M., Wallis, K.F. (Eds.), Advances in Economics and Econometrics. Cambridge Univ. Press, Cambridge.

McMillan, John, Woodruff, Christopher, 2002. The central role of entrepreneurs in transition economies. Journal of Economic Perspectives 16, 153–170.

Shaked, Avner, Sutton, John, 1982. Relaxing price competition through product differentiation. Review of Economic Studies 49 (1), 3–13.

Shleifer, Andrei, Vishny, Robert, 1993. Corruption. Quarterly Journal of Economics 58 (3), 599–617.

Tichit, Ariane, 2006. The optimal speed of transition revisited. European Journal of Political Economy. In press.

Transparency International, 1996. TI Corruption Perception Index 1996. Available at http://www.transparency.org/cpi/1996/cpi1996.pdf. Berlin.

UNICEF. 2001. A Decade of Transition. Regional Monitoring Project No. 8. UNICEF Innocenti Research Centre. Florence, Italy.

United Nations, 2005. Human Development Report 2005. United Nations Development Program, New York.

World Bank, 2000. Making Transition Work for Everyone: Poverty and Inequality in Europe and Central Asia. World Bank, Washington, DC.

[19]

Property Rights and Finance

By Simon Johnson, John McMillan, and Christopher Woodruff*

Which is the tighter constraint on private sector investment: weak property rights or limited access to external finance? From a survey of new firms in post-communist countries, we find that weak property rights discourage firms from reinvesting their profits, even when bank loans are available. Where property rights are relatively strong, firms reinvest their profits; where they are relatively weak, entrepreneurs do not want to invest from retained earnings. (JEL D23, P23)

Property rights are fundamental: entrepreneurs will not invest if they expect to be unable to keep the fruits of their investment. Country-level studies consistently show that less secure property rights are correlated with lower aggregate investment and slower economic growth (Stephen Knack and Philip Keefer, 1995; Paolo Mauro, 1995; Jakob Svensson, 1998; Daron Acemoglu et al., 2001). The microeconomic evidence is more limited, but Timothy Besley (1995), for example, finds in Ghana a significant link between property rights and investment.

Secure property rights may be necessary for entrepreneurial investment, but are they sufficient? External finance could also matter for investment and growth, for if bank credit is not available it may be hard for entrepreneurs to take advantage of new opportunities. There is evidence that a well-functioning financial system contributes to investment and growth (Ross

Levine, 1997; Raghuram Rajan and Luigi Zingales, 1998). Is external finance, in addition to secure property rights, necessary for entrepreneurs to invest, or is property-rights security all that is needed? Broad cross-country studies cannot answer this question because effective protection for property rights is positively correlated with the use of external finance. For example, Rafael La Porta et al. (1997, 1998, 2000) show more external finance is available when there is a stronger legal system in general and more effective protection of investors in particular, while Asli Demirgüç-Kunt and Vojislav Maksimovic (1998) find that firms invest more from external funds in countries with secure property rights.

Recent experience in Eastern Europe and the former Soviet Union offers an experiment that can help disentangle the effects of property rights and external finance. Although all these former communist countries have relatively weak institutional environments, there is considerable variation in the extent to which property rights are protected. For example, Timothy Frye and Shleifer (1997) and Shleifer (1997) provide evidence that the Russian government acts like a "grabbing hand," discouraging entrepreneurs from investing, while the Polish government does not. In general, property rights have proven more secure in Poland than in other parts of Eastern Europe and the former Soviet Union. Within countries, also, there is variation in both the perceived security of property rights and in the access to bank credit. Given these countries' banking systems, small firms are able to borrow only if they can provide adequate collateral. Owning collateral is therefore a good proxy for at least having the possibility to

* Johnson: Sloan School of Management, MIT, 50 Memorial Drive, Cambridge, MA 02142 (e-mail: sjohnson@mit.edu); McMillan: Graduate School of Business, Stanford University, 518 Memorial Way, Stanford, CA 94305 (e-mail: mcmillan_john@gsb.stanford.edu); Woodruff: Graduate School of International Relations and Pacific Studies, University of California-San Diego, La Jolla, CA 92093 (e-mail: cwoodruff@ucsd.edu). We thank Timothy Besley, Bengt Holmström, Takeo Hoshi, James Rauch, Andrei Shleifer, and two anonymous referees for comments, Todd Mitton for help with the Worldscope data, Mark Schankerman for help in facilitating the surveys, and the European Bank for Reconstruction and Development for funding the surveys in Poland, Slovakia, and Romania, and the National Council for Soviet and East European Research for funding the surveys in Russia and Ukraine. For support, Johnson thanks the MIT Entrepreneurship Center and McMillan thanks the Stanford Graduate School of Business.

borrow. Firm-level evidence from these post-communist countries therefore allows us to determine whether secure property rights are (a) necessary, (b) sufficient, or (c) necessary and sufficient for investment by entrepreneurs.

Our data come from a 1997 survey of recently formed and relatively small manufacturing firms in five transition countries: Poland, Romania, Slovakia, Ukraine, and Russia. The perceived security of property rights and the use of bank credit vary considerably both across and within these countries. As an outcome variable, we focus on the amount entrepreneurs choose to reinvest out of their profits. This provides a robust measure of investment, as our survey work indicates, that is comparable across firms.

Our approach has two parts, both of which are designed to be straightforward to implement in countries where standard financial information is hard to obtain. First, we explain the data we were able to obtain, putting particular emphasis on what our investigation shows is a reasonable way to ask questions about sensitive financial information and property-rights issues (Section I).[1] Second, we test whether secure property rights are sufficient for investment by entrepreneurs (Sections II and III).

The entrepreneurs in our sample reinvest less of their retained earnings when they perceive their property rights to be insecure, irrespective of whether they own the collateral that is generally needed to obtain credit. This effect is large. Those entrepreneurs in our sample with the least secure property rights invest nearly 40 percent less of their profits than those with the most secure property rights (specifically, entrepreneurs with the least secure perceived property rights reinvest 32 percent of their profits, while those with the most secure reinvest 56 percent). Secure property rights are necessary for the entrepreneurs in our sample to take full advantage of opportunities to invest. Moreover, we find that the absence of bank finance does not prevent the entrepreneurs in our sample from investing. Controlling for property rights, there is no evidence that access to bank

credit leads to more investment for these firms. Secure property rights are therefore also sufficient for investment. In fact, the firms in our sample with weak perceived property rights and high levels of unreinvested profits do not want to borrow.

Part of the explanation for these results is that, for the firms in our sample, retained earnings have consistently been large, and therefore have been a source of potential investment funds. Many of these new firms are extremely profitable because the relatively hostile business environment creates barriers to entry and because the partially reformed economy offers entrepreneurs lucrative unfilled niches.[2] High profits mean that entrepreneurs have the resources they need for expansion, without needing to borrow. The issue is not whether entrepreneurs have enough resources, but rather whether they want to invest their retained earnings or instead consume these earnings, perhaps outside the country.

At the low level of institutional development of the countries in our sample, secure property rights are both necessary and sufficient to induce investment by entrepreneurs. The availability of bank loans surely matters for growth, but perhaps only once property rights are perceived to be secure. If property rights are insecure, it is immaterial whether or not finance is available. Our findings thus add empirical detail to the view that certain market-supporting institutions will work only after other institutions have been built (McMillan, 1997; Shleifer and Vishny, 1998).

Because our survey covers only firms already in existence, we cannot infer anything about the relative importance of property rights and finance for potential entrepreneurs who are considering entry. We focus instead on entrepreneurs who are already in business with small-scale operations. Our question is: under what conditions

---

[1] For more detail on the survey see Appendices A, B, and C, which are on the *American Economic Review* web site: ⟨www.aeaweb.org/aer⟩. The questionnaire and the complete raw data are available at ⟨http://www-irps.ucsd.edu/faculty/cwoodruff/data.htm⟩.

[2] High profits to new entrants appear to have been common in the early stages of reform in the formerly planned economies. China's newly entering rural firms had an average rate of profit on capital of 40 percent in 1978, the first year of reform; in subsequent years this profit rate fell as China's marketization proceeded (Barry Naughton, 1995, p. 150). Anecdotal evidence that early entrants in Poland earned high profits is given in Johnson and Gary W. Loveman (1995).

will these entrepreneurs reinvest their profits to make their businesses grow?

I. The Data

A. *The Sample*

We surveyed private manufacturing firms in May and June of 1997 in Russia and Ukraine and from September to December of 1997 in Poland, Slovakia, and Romania.[3] The survey was designed to find similar relatively small firms in comparable cities in all five countries.

We chose the countries explicitly to look for variation in institutional conditions. The previously available cross-country evidence, for example from European Bank for Reconstruction and Development (EBRD, 1996) and Shleifer (1997), suggested that property rights were less secure in countries further to the East. We intentionally surveyed only firms that were going concerns, in order to focus on investment decisions by firms that had managed to enter an industry and survive. Other researchers have found that weak property rights increase barriers to entry (Simeon Djankov et al., 2002). Daniel Berkowitz and David N. DeJong (2002) find variation across Russian regions in the rate of formation of new firms is associated with the degree of local political support for reform. This paper looks instead at the effects of weak property rights on entrepreneurial investment conditional on entry having occurred.

The sample includes about 300 manufacturing firms with between seven and 270 employees in each country; the total sample size for most variables is about 1,400 observations. Some of the firms were started from scratch and others were spun off from state enterprises, which probably reflects characteristics of the population of firms. In our sample for Poland, Romania, and Slovakia, start-ups far outnumber spin-offs; in Russia and especially Ukraine, spin-offs predominate. We control for these characteristics of the firms in our regression analysis.

B. *The Questions*

The survey design incorporated both experience of previous surveys on these topics and the results of pilot studies we carried out in each country. The pilots tested precisely how people understood various questions and established the best ways to ask about sensitive information. For the purposes of this paper, the most important issue was how to ask about profits and their reinvestment.

We expected respondents would be reluctant to answer questions about the specific nominal amounts of profits and investments, and we found this to be the case. However, they were more willing to answer questions posed in terms of ratios. We also found that respondents found it much easier to answer questions that posed this ratio in terms of a closed-end question listing various ranges from which they could choose. For example, our key question was: "How much did you reinvest out of profits during 1996?" We offered respondents six choices: 0 percent, 1–10 percent, 11–25 percent, 26–49 percent, 50–75 percent, or more than 75 percent. Both the use of ratios and the closed categories represent compromises. We obtain much higher response rates: in the case of reinvestment rates, the response rate exceeded 94 percent.[4] But we have only categorical rather than continuous data. As a result, our regressions will be ordered probits.

Previous research indicated that for particularly sensitive issues, for example relating to bribes and other issues linked to security rights, the response rate was higher when we posed the questions in terms of asking about "firms in your industry" rather than the entrepreneur's own firm.[5] Our assumption, based on other

---

[3] We chose these three countries on the basis of country-level measures that indicated substantial variation in institutional environment. The survey is described in more detail in Appendix A, and Appendix C summarizes our key questions about finance, profits, investment, and property rights. (These Appendices are available at ⟨www.aeaweb.org/aer⟩.)

[4] For questions where the range of potential responses ranged too widely to use categories, we did ask for specific nominal amounts. In these cases—for example, when we asked firms how much capital they invested in the firm at start-up—response rates were much lower.

[5] This way of asking about sensitive issues, such as property rights and underground economic activity, was developed by Daniel Kaufmann in his earlier empirical work; see, for example, Joel Hellman et al. (2000). The

TABLE 1—PERCEIVED SECURITY OF PROPERTY RIGHTS

Survey result	All countries	Poland	Slovakia	Romania	Russia	Ukraine
1) Percentage of respondents who say firms make extralegal payments for government services	37.3 (1,117)	20.1 (298)	38.2 (306)	20.0 (315)	91.2 (114)	86.9 (84)
2) Percentage of respondents who say firms make extralegal payments for licenses	37.9 (1,128)	19.3 (300)	42.2 (303)	17.0 (317)	91.7 (120)	87.5 (88)
3) Percentage of respondents who say firms make payments for protection	24.4 (1,163)	7.9 (302)	14.9 (308)	0.6 (320)	92.9 (126)	88.8 (107)
4) Percentage of respondents who say firms make unofficial payments for ongoing registration	14.0 (805)	0.4 (234)	3.0 (236)	19.1 (267)	80.0 (55)	76.9 (13)
5) Percentage of respondents who say firms make unofficial payments for fire/sanitary inspection	19.2 (881)	2.8 (254)	12.1 (248)	21.8 (289)	67.9 (56)	91.2 (34)
6) Percentage of respondents who say firms make unofficial payments for tax inspection	12.9 (843)	0.8 (247)	2.5 (242)	17.3 (289)	75.6 (45)	85.0 (20)
7) Tax payments to government as a percentage of sales for firms in industry	18.9 (1,130)	15.5 (277)	16.4 (278)	17.2 (321)	26.9 (119)	28.0 (135)
8) Percentage of respondents who say courts cannot be used to enforce contracts	31.6 (1,470)	27.1 (303)	32.1 (308)	13.1 (321)	44.2 (269)	45.4 (269)
Number of entrepreneurs surveyed	1,471	303	308	321	269	270

Note: The number of observations is given in parentheses below each response level.

experience, is that answers to this question reflect the entrepreneur's own experience. At least one respondent confirmed this, telling our survey firm that he knew the questions were designed to "disguise the fact that [the survey] was after information about his own firm." He responded to the questions anyway.

C. *Measuring Property Rights*

The entrepreneur's beliefs about the security of his or her property rights are indicated by responses to several survey questions. We asked entrepreneurs first whether firms in their industry make "extralegal payments" for government services, and second whether firms in their industry make "extralegal payments" for licenses. More than 90 percent of the Russian entrepreneurs and almost 90 percent of Ukrainian entrepreneurs answered affirmatively to these questions (see the first two rows of Table 1).

results seem consistent with available cross-country evidence and across surveys.

Only one in five entrepreneurs in Poland and Romania said firms make extralegal payments for services or licenses. The response rates for these questions are well above 98 percent in the three Eastern European countries, but are 40 percent or less in Russia and Ukraine. One reasonable interpretation of a refusal to answer the question, in this context, is that the entrepreneur makes these payments and—for obvious reasons—does not want to discuss them.

We also asked whether firms make payments for "protection" of their activities, finding a similar pattern of responses across the countries (in the third row of Table 1). We chose not to ask directly about whether firms made payments to organized crime, because we expected that most entrepreneurs would not admit this. However, the indirect question probably picks up whether a firm believes it is likely to be subject to extortion by some form of mafia—although we would caution that anecdotal evidence suggests this sort of organized crime often operates with the tacit protection of some local government officials.

For further measures of property-rights security, we asked entrepreneurs whether they make "unofficial" payments for specific services: payments for renewing their business registration, and payments to fire, sanitary, and tax inspectors (see the fourth, fifth, and sixth rows of Table 1). Though the response rates to these questions are lower, the pattern is the same. A majority of entrepreneurs in Russia and Ukraine say such payments are common, while a minority of entrepreneurs in the other three countries say the same. We use these detailed corruption measures to check the robustness of results from our basic regression.

Official payments to government are also higher in Russia and Ukraine, where tax payments are more than one quarter of sales, compared to about a sixth of sales in Eastern Europe (see the seventh row of Table 1).[6] We control for tax payments as a percent of sales to see whether this is a direct disincentive to invest. We do find some evidence that investment rates are negatively impacted by higher tax rates, though in contrast to other results, the tax rate findings are not robust.

Using courts to enforce contracts with trading partners is a logically distinct activity from protecting property rights. Nevertheless the effects on investment are similar. Inadequate contractual enforcement could put firms' profits at risk and make them reluctant to invest. Asked whether courts could be used to enforce an agreement with a customer or supplier, most firms in all of the countries said they could. Affirmative answers to this question ranged from 87 percent in Romania to 56 percent in Ukraine (see the last row of responses in Table 1).

Overall, Table 1 shows that the five countries fall into two distinct groups—the three East European countries have relatively more secure

property rights than do the two former Soviet Union countries. Courts are less reliable in resolving commercial disputes in Russia and Ukraine, and interactions with the government are also more costly in these countries. This is consistent with the existing evidence that the regulatory environment in Eastern Europe is less hostile to business activity than in the former Soviet Union (see, for example, Frye and Shleifer, 1997).

Entrepreneurs' perceptions of the security of property rights may vary within a country for three reasons. First, different firms may face different realities. Interaction with the government may be more frequent in some industries than in others. Activities may vary in the ease with which they can be hidden from government bureaucrats. And some entrepreneurs may have connections that allow them to avoid extortion. In our data, for example, entrepreneurs who previously worked as high-level entrepreneurs in state-owned enterprises are less likely to say bribes are paid. Second, entrepreneurs may differ in their perceptions. This is especially likely in an economy undergoing deep reform, where institutions and circumstances change quickly. We find, for instance, that older entrepreneurs are less likely to say bribes are paid. Third, the responses may reflect some other characteristic of the firm or the entrepreneur. In our regressions we control for as many characteristics as possible, but some unobserved attributes may matter for investment.

D. *An Index of the Insecurity of Property Rights*

Table 2 shows the correlations among our property-rights measures for individual firms in all five countries. Not surprisingly, most are highly correlated. Extralegal payments for services and extralegal payments for licenses have a correlation coefficient of 0.66, while the correlation between payments for "protection" and either of these measures is larger than 0.50.

For our regression analysis, we combine the three main property-rights questions—extralegal payments for licenses, extralegal payments for services, and paying for protection—into an additive index of property-rights insecurity for

---

[6] We asked entrepreneurs to report taxes as a percent of total sales. Firms in Eastern Europe and the former Soviet Union routinely underreport sales to avoid taxes and extortion (Johnson et al., 1997). In separate questions, entrepreneurs indicated that the percentage of sales hidden by firms in their industry is about 41 percent in Ukraine, 29 percent in Russia, and around 6 percent in the other three countries. It may be that some entrepreneurs reported taxes and profits as a percent of official sales rather than total sales. If so, then the tax burden and profit rates will be overstated, especially for Russia and Ukraine. But this should not affect our analysis of reinvestment rates.

TABLE 2—CORRELATIONS AMONG VARIOUS INDICATORS FOR THE SECURITY OF PROPERTY RIGHTS

Indicator	Payments for services	Payments for licenses	Payments for protection	Index of property rights
Firms make extralegal payments for licenses	0.66 (1,105, <0.01)			
Firms make payments for protection	0.52 (1,109, <0.01)	0.54 (1,122, <0.01)		
Index of property rights insecurity	0.87 (1,099, <0.01)	0.87 (1,099, <0.01)	0.79 (1,099, <0.01)	
Courts cannot enforce contracts	0.1 (1,117, <0.01)	0.11 (1,117, <0.01)	0.22 (1,163, <0.01)	0.15 (1,099, <0.01)
Tax payments as a percentage of sales for firms in industry	0.24 (996, <0.01)	0.24 (1,007, <0.01)	0.31 (1,042, <0.01)	0.29 (981, <0.01)
Firms make unofficial payments for ongoing registration	0.29 (775, <0.01)	0.27 (783, <0.01)	0.36 (789, <0.01)	0.38 (769, <0.01)
Firms make unofficial payments for fire/sanitary inspection	0.33 (840, <0.01)	0.32 (843, <0.01)	0.29 (857, <0.01)	0.39 (830, <0.01)
Firms make unofficial payments for tax inspection	0.36 (816, <0.01)	0.34 (818, <0.01)	0.32 (828, <0.01)	0.43 (806, <0.01)
Firm had loan before 1996	0.15 (1,072, <0.01)	0.16 (1,082, <0.01)	0.26 (1,115, <0.01)	0.20 (1,055, <0.01)
Firm has collateral	−0.05 (997, 0.13)	−0.03 (1,006, 0.28)	−0.03 (1,040, 0.28)	−0.05 (980, 0.09)

Notes: Correlations are for all five countries combined. The number of observations and significance level are in parentheses.

(*continued overleaf*)

each firm. The property-rights index we construct ranges from 0 to 3, with 3 indicating that the entrepreneurs said all three payments were common, 2 indicating an affirmative response to two of the payments, 1 indicating an affirmative response to one of the payments, and 0 indicating an affirmative response to none. A higher value of this index therefore represents less secure property rights.

An alternative index for property rights insecurity would equal one if firms make any one of the three types of payments and zero otherwise. Either of these indexes can be justified theoretically.

The additive index is appropriate if responding affirmatively to more than one question indicates a greater level of insecurity than responding affirmatively to only one question. The either/or index is appropriate if one bribe-taker has the same effect as multiple bribe-takers. According to the model of Shleifer and Vishny (1993), if two or more corrupt bureaucrats coordinate so as to maximize their total bribes, they will extract the same total amount

as a monopoly extortionist. If they compete with each other, however, their total bribes will, by prisoners'-dilemma logic, exceed the bribe-maximizing amount. The data show the effects of corruption are additive, as discussed below (Section III), suggesting the rate of total bribes might exceed what even the bribe-takers would want.

A belief that courts are not effective in enforcing contracts is positively correlated with the corruption measures, but the correlation is smaller. The correlation between courts and the index for insecurity of property rights is 0.15. While this correlation may seem low, it probably reflects the fact that believing the courts can enforce private contracts is quite different from trusting the government not to expropriate your property. With regard to courts, the issue is presumably whether judges are incompetent or corruptible. With regard to security of property rights, the issue is to what extent members of the executive feel constrained to act responsibly and within the law. Even in environments where the executive is quite predatory

TABLE 2—*Continued.*

Courts enforce	Taxes as a percentage of sales	Bribes registration	Bribes fire/sanitary	Bribes taxes	Loan before 1996
0.11 (1,130, <0.01)					
0.06 (805, 0.09)	0.19 (756, <0.01)				
0.03 (881, 0.40)	0.17 (820, <0.01)	0.49 (757, <0.01)			
0.01 (843, 0.74)	0.16 (789, <0.01)	0.47 (734, <0.01)	0.63 (811, <0.01)		
0.06 (1,302, 0.02)	0.15 (1,094, <0.01)	0.16 (739, <0.01)	0.16 (863, 0.01)	0.08 (828, 0.02)	
−0.05 (1,217, 0.08)	−0.04 (1,018, 0.25)	0.08 (739, 0.03)	0.03 (805, 0.37)	0.04 (769, 0.29)	0.30 (1,189, <0.01)

(Russia, for example), we see considerable willingness on the part of entrepreneurs to rely on courts for the enforcement of contracts with other entrepreneurs.

In the main regressions, we use the effectiveness of courts alongside the index of property rights. We also run regressions using the components of the index separately. Finally, an alternative index of property rights that we use in the regressions, ranging from 0 to 4, adds to the first index the measure of the ineffectiveness of courts (that is, we add one if the entrepreneur thinks the courts cannot be used to enforce contracts and zero otherwise).

E. *Reinvestment of Profits*

Initial entrants in transition economies often earn large profits, which decline over time as new firms enter (McMillan, 1997). Our data are consistent with this at the country level. Table 3 (second line) shows the firms' average profit after taxes as a percent of sales in 1996. Re-

ported after-tax profits are much higher in Russia (21 percent) and Ukraine (18 percent), where there has been the least progress with economic reform, than in Poland (10 percent), where the transition has progressed much further. Romania is in between (13 percent). Slovakia appears to be the outlier in this pattern, with profit rates much lower than in any of the other countries (6 percent).[7] Entrepreneurs were also asked to estimate profit rates after taxes in their industry, as a percent of sales. As we would expect, the estimates of industry profits and the firm's own profit rates are highly correlated ($p = 0.41$). At the country level, these estimates, also shown in Table 3 (third line),

---

[7] Responses to questions about the entrepreneur's own profits were provided in categories. Appendix B (at ⟨www.aeaweb.org/aer⟩) explains how the numbers in Table 3 were calculated from these responses. The profit data are also compared in Appendix B to data from the National Survey of Small Business Finance, conducted in 1993 in the United States among similarly sized firms (Federal Reserve Board of Governors, 1994).

TABLE 3—USE OF INTERNAL FINANCE

Measure	Poland	Slovakia	Romania	Russia	Ukraine
Number of firms	303	308	321	269	270
1996 profit after taxes, percentage of annual sales	9.9	5.7	12.9	20.6	18.0
Estimated industry profit rate after taxes	11.1	10.0	13.4	17.6	14.3
Profit reinvestment, percentage of profits after taxes	52.6	42.3	52.8	38.8	29.6
Unreinvested profit, percentage of annual sales	4.8	3.6	5.7	11.7	12.3
Profit after taxes in first year of operation, for firms started in:					
1989–1991	9.9	2.4	8.3	4.3	7.6
1992–1993	4.2	−0.2	7.8	4.5	6.6
1994–1996	2.1	−1.1	6.7	3.9	7.4
Start-ups:					
Number of firms	237	238	281	128	82
1996 profit after taxes, percentage of annual sales	10.5	6.0	13.4	20.8	19.0
Estimated industry profit rate after taxes	11.3	9.8	13.8	18.3	14.9
Profit reinvestment, percentage of profits after taxes	53.6	44.8	54.2	37.5	29.4
Unreinvested profit, percentage of annual sales	4.8	3.7	5.8	12.2	12.9
Spin-offs:					
Number of firms	66	70	40	123	183
1996 profit after taxes, percentage of annual sales	7.7	4.6	9.6	20.3	17.7
Estimated industry profit rate after taxes	10.1	10.6	10.5	17.1	14.0
Profit reinvestment, percentage of profits after taxes	49.0	33.7	42.5	39.4	29.6
Unreinvested profit, percentage of annual sales	5.0	3.5	5.0	11.2	12.1

Notes: Profit reinvestment as a percentage of profits excludes firms with zero or negative profits. In order to make the data more comparable to the external finance data shown in Table 4, we assume that firms with negative or zero profits reinvest zero percent of sales and have unreinvested profits of zero percent of sales. Profit reinvestment as a percentage of annual sales is calculated by multiplying profits as a percentage of sales by profit reinvestment as a percentage of profits. Unreinvested profits as a percentage of sales is calculated as profits as a percentage of sales times one minus profit reinvestment as a percentage of profits. See Appendix B at ⟨www.aeaweb.org/aer⟩ for more details on the calculations.

indicate a similar pattern, but with less variation across countries.[8]

These profit rates are high relative to the available data for large firms in these countries. The best data are for Poland. According to the most recent data in Worldscope, average profit/

[8] Throughout, we use the reported rate of profit as a proxy for the firm's cash flow available for reinvestment. In reality, profits and cash flow may diverge for a number of reasons, in particular depreciation. However, information on depreciation recorded by the firms is not available from the survey.

sales for Polish firms from all industries is about 5 percent.[9] However, this average hides considerable disparity. In particular, large firms operating in sectors with substantial barriers to entry, for example due to regulations, had profits as a percent of sales that were comparable to the small firms in our sample.

These data are consistent with the idea that the insecurity of property rights may deter entry into the small-firm sector (Djankov et al., 2002). In addition, these partially reformed post-communist economies offer entrepreneurs lucrative unfilled niches. There is also presumably a survivorship bias for small firms. We are measuring only the firms that have not gone out of business (although arguably this should overstate the importance of external finance and understate the importance of expropriation risk). Large firms may not show such a bias because, in these countries, the government may provide implicit subsidies that prevent them from going out of business.

Entrepreneurs also reported profits as a percentage of sales during their firm's first full year of operation. We show in Table 3 (see the sixth, seventh, and eighth lines) the average first-year profit rates by country and by year in which the firms began operation. In Poland, firms started between 1989 and 1991, just after the reforms, reported earning an average of 9.9 percent of sales during their first year of operation. First-year profits were markedly lower—4.2 percent of sales— for firms started in 1992 or 1993, and lower still for the most recent group of entrants (2.1 percent of sales for firms entering between 1994 and 1996). These data are consistent with our expectation that entry leads to lower profit rates.

A downward trend over time in profit rates for entrants in their first year of business is also evident in Slovakia and Romania, though the rate of fall is not as steep as in Poland. There is even less difference across time in the profit rates of start-up firms in either Russia or Ukraine. Firms entering between 1989 and 1991 had average first-year profit rates of 4.3 percent and 7.6 percent of sales in Russia and Ukraine,

respectively. Those entering five years later had average profit rates of 3.9 percent and 7.4 percent of sales, respectively.[10]

We also asked what fraction of 1996 profits after taxes were reinvested in the firm. Polish and Romanian firms reinvested the highest fraction, slightly more than 50 percent on average (fourth line of Table 3). Reinvestment rates average about 40 percent in Slovakia and Russia, and 30 percent in Ukraine.[11] We also compute the profits entrepreneurs choose not to reinvest in their businesses (fifth line of Table 3). Unreinvested profits as a percentage of sales are highest in Russia and Ukraine, where they exceed 10 percent of sales, and lower in Romania (5.9 percent of sales), Poland (5.2 percent), and Slovakia (5.1 percent). In Russia and Ukraine, where property rights are the least secure, entrepreneurs are on average the most reluctant to reinvest their profits.

Table 3 also divides these data into start-ups and spin-offs. Start-ups are more profitable than spin-offs in all five countries, though the difference is much greater in Poland and Romania than in the other three countries. Start-ups reinvest a greater proportion of their profits than spin-offs in Poland, Slovakia, and Romania.

F. *External Finance*

The survey contains three indications of having received bank credit. First, we asked firms what their sources of start-up capital were. A minority of firms, ranging from 6.6 percent of Polish firms to 27 percent of Slovakian firms, obtained part of their start-up capital from bank loans (see the second line of Table 4). Second, we asked whether they obtained a loan at some point in the past. Over 90 percent of Russian firms and 79 percent of Ukrainian firms say they have received loans at some time (third line of Table 4). Only half of Slovakian and Romanian firms have had a loan at

---

[9] Worldscope also has data for Russia and Slovakia, although this is available for fewer firms. The average profit–sales ratio in Russia for 1999 is 7.11 percent, although firms with substantial market power show higher profit rates. Almost all the Slovak firms show losses.

[10] *T*-tests comparing the profit rate in the early period (1990–1992) with the profit rate in the last period (1994–1996) indicate that the drop in first-year profit rates is significant at the 1-percent level in Poland ($t = 3.38$) and in Slovakia ($t = 2.96$), but not in Romania ($t = 0.99$), Russia ($t = 0.30$), or Ukraine ($t = 0.61$).

[11] See Appendix B at ⟨www.aeaweb.org/aer⟩ for the details of these calculations as well as some caveats to their interpretation.

TABLE 4—SOURCES OF EXTERNAL FINANCE

Measure	Poland	Slovakia	Romania	Russia	Ukraine
Number of firms	303	308	321	269	270
Percentage of firms with bank loans at start-up	6.6	27.0	9.7	15.2	12.2
Percentage of firms with bank loans ever	70.0	51.0	49.8	92.4	79.0
Percentage of firms with bank loans in 1996	48.8	27.6	24.1	17.0	13.8
Percentage of firms with collateral at the time of interview	95.7	80.8	94.4	87.2	75.5
Average 1996 loan, percentage of annual sales					
All firms (no loan = 0 percent)	2.3	2.5	1.7	2.3	0.8
Firms with loans	4.8	10.6	7.3	24.7	13.4
Accounts payable, percentage of annual sales					
All firms	2.7	3.4	NA	0.1	0.7
Firms with 1996 loans	2.5	4.2	NA	0.04	0.3
Start-ups:					
Number of firms	237	238	281	128	82
Percentage of firms with bank loans:					
ever	72.2	42.4	46.6	95.4	81.9
in 1996	50.6	22.7	20.8	12.0	11.1
Average 1996 loan, percentage of annual sales (no loan = 0 percent)	2.5	2.0	1.7	1.7	1.3
Accounts payable, percentage of annual sales	2.5	3.2	NA	0.1	0.9
Spin-offs:					
Number of firms	66	70	40	123	183
Percentage of firms with bank loans:					
ever	62.1	80.0	72.5	89.4	78.5
in 1996	42.4	44.3	47.5	21.5	14.6
Average 1996 loan, percentage of annual sales (no loan = 0 percent)	1.5	4.4	2.2	2.8	0.6
Accounts payable, percentage of annual sales	3.2	4.0	NA	0.1	0.7

Note: For details of variable definitions, see Section II of the text.

some point in the life of the enterprise. Third, we asked whether they obtained loans from banks in 1996, the year before the survey. The greatest percentage of current borrowers was in Poland, where just under half (49 percent) of firms said they had loans in 1996. About a quarter of firms in Slovakia and Romania said they had loans in 1996, with lower percentages in Russia (17 percent) and Ukraine (14 percent).[12]

[12] There are no reliable comparable data on credit to the private sector across transition countries, but the ratio of broad money to GDP provides a rough indicator. In 1996,

Although fewer firms in Russia and Ukraine received loans than in the other three countries, the average loan size was larger there. Loans average less than 5 percent of a borrower's

broad money was 37.5 percent of GDP in Poland, 28.9 percent in Romania, 13.1 percent in Russia, 71 percent in Slovakia, and 11.16 percent in Ukraine (EBRD, 1997). The real money supply in Russia and Ukraine fell dramatically between 1991 and 1996, which partially accounts for credit becoming harder to get in these two countries (EBRD, 1997). Of course, our sample has quite different characteristics from the large state or privatized firms that receive (or do not receive) most of the credit in these transition economies.

annual sales in Poland, more than 10 percent of annual sales in Slovakia and Ukraine, and almost 25 percent of annual sales in Russia. As a result, the variation across countries in the total funds provided by banks is small. Including firms who do not receive loans, Slovakian firms received the most credit in 1996, amounting to 2.5 percent of annual sales. In Poland and Russia, finance provided by banks represents 2.3 percent of annual sales, in Romania 1.7 percent, and in Ukraine 0.8 percent.

Even though Polish firms are much more likely to have obtained a loan in 1996 than firms in the other four countries, the Polish credit markets are underdeveloped by western standards. In the United States, small and medium-sized firms are surveyed periodically by the Federal Reserve Board of Governors (FRBG). Among the 344 firms in the 1993 National Survey of Small Business Finances (NSSBF) that are manufacturers with between ten and 270 employees, 84 percent reported having a loan at the time of the survey. This level is substantially higher than the 49 percent rate in Poland. Moreover, loan amounts were 16 percent of sales among the group of small U.S. manufacturers, several times the levels in any of the countries we surveyed.[13]

Compared to a developed capital market, loans in our five countries are also much more likely to require collateral. While 20 percent of bank loans obtained by U.S. firms were without collateral, less than 2 percent of the firms in our sample obtaining loans did so without collateral. A lack of collateral, however, is not the main reason for less borrowing in our sample than in the United States. More than 75 percent of firms in each of the countries—and more than 90 percent of firms in Poland and Romania—say they were able to offer collateral to banks. At least in the minds of entrepreneurs, a lack of collateral does not appear to be a major constraint on borrowing.[14]

An alternative source of external funds is credit received from other firms. We measure trade credit by the level of accounts payable reported by firms (the eighth and ninth rows of Table 4). Trade credit is almost nonexistent in Russia (0.1 percent of annual sales) and is low in Ukraine (0.7 percent), but is an important source of capital in Poland (2.7 percent) and Slovakia (3.4 percent). Credit received from suppliers is comparable in size to credit received from banks in Poland, Slovakia, and Ukraine. Reliable data for this question are not available for Romania.[15] (For more on trade credit, see Johnson et al., 2002, where we use trade credit as a measure of a firm's trust in its trading partner.)

Profit reinvestment is a larger source of investment capital than either bank funds or trade credit in all five countries, as is seen by comparing Tables 3 and 4 (except that trade credit is bigger than profit reinvestment in Slovakia). In Poland, firms internally generate funds for investment averaging 9.9 percent of sales (Table 3, second line). Bank loans average 2.3 percent of sales for the whole sample and 4.8 percent of sales for firms receiving loans in Poland (Table 4, sixth and seventh lines). In contrast, we estimate that firms in Russia and Ukraine have unreinvested profits averaging 12 percent of sales (Table 3, fifth line). This suggests the Russian and Ukrainian firms could have used their unreinvested profits in productive projects (earning high rates of return), but for some reason they chose not to. The potential for using retained earnings as a source of capital is seen from the fact that, in all five countries, the capital available from unreinvested profits exceeds the capital provided by banks (compare the fifth row in Table 3 with the sixth row in Table 4).

Table 2 shows correlations between the various measures of property rights on the one hand and variables indicating access to credit on

---

[13] When lines of credit are excluded, loans were 5.8 percent of sales among the small manufacturers in the NSSBF survey. Both of these averages assign a value of zero to firms without loans. (See Appendix B, at ⟨www.aeaweb.org/aer⟩, for more discussion of the NSSBF data.)

[14] While the response rate to the collateral question was more than 99 percent in Romania, it was only 76 percent in Ukraine and 61 percent in Russia. If nonrespondents are less

likely to have collateral, then the numbers in Table 2 may overstate the availability of collateral in Russia and Ukraine. Still, as a lower bound (taking all nonrespondents as having no collateral), the survey indicates that more than half of firms in Russia (53 percent) and Ukraine (57 percent) are able to offer collateral.

[15] Apparently respondents misunderstood what we were asking. This question may not have been translated properly.

the other. We would be concerned if access to capital is strongly correlated with security of property rights, because that would make it difficult to disentangle access to credit from security of property. We measure the ability to access credit in 1996 with two variables—an indication that the firm received a bank loan at some point before 1996, and an indication that the firm has collateral that can be used to obtain a loan. The correlations indicate that firms with less secure property rights are more likely to have had a loan before 1996. Firms with less secure property rights are less likely to have collateral to offer banks, but the correlation is small and is significant only for the index of insecurity and for a lack of confidence in courts. Hence, we are not concerned that our measures of insecure property rights are proxying for a lack of access to credit.[16]

G. Assessment

The cross-country evidence suggests that property rights are an important determinant of investment by entrepreneurs. In Poland, where property rights are relatively secure, we find high rates of reinvestment. In contrast, in Russia and Ukraine, where property rights are weak, we find that the level of unreinvested profits is high; entrepreneurs there have the ability to do much more investment than they actually do. The next question is whether these results hold in the firm-level data when we control for characteristics of the firm and entrepreneur.

II. A Framework for Investment Decisions

This section lays out a simple framework that explains and defends the assumptions needed for our regression analysis. A firm's desired investment level is a function of both industry and firm-specific factors. Firms in growing in-

---

[16] The correlations between property rights and access to credit are driven primarily by differences across countries. When Poland, Slovakia, and Romania are separated from Russia and Ukraine, insecure property rights are positively correlated with a lack of collateral. However, the correlations are low, all below 0.11, and there is no correlation between security of property rights and having had a loan before 1996. In Russian and Ukraine, firms with less secure property rights are more likely to have collateral to offer and to have had a loan before 1996.

dustries are faced with more investment opportunities than are firms in declining industries. Production in a capital-intensive industry also necessitates higher investment levels. More able entrepreneurs will find investments more profitable in any industry. All of these factors affect the profitability of potential investments.

Investment demand also depends on the ability of entrepreneurs to retain any profits they make. Entrepreneurs may be unwilling to invest when returns are insecure. The effect of entrepreneurs' perceptions of property rights on investment decisions is the main issue we want to explore. Suppose that the firm makes its investment and borrowing decisions simultaneously, and extortion, if it occurs, comes after any profits are realized, so that firm's demand for investable funds is given by

$$(1) \qquad I^d = I(\pi, s, r^I, r^L)$$

where π represents expected (pre-extortion) profits, s represents the amount of those profits that will be extracted by corrupt bureaucrats or criminals, r^I represents the interest rate the entrepreneur can earn by investing the firm's profits outside the firm and r^L the interest rate the entrepreneur pays on borrowed money. Investable funds may be obtained either internally from retained earnings or externally through credit markets. Thus:

$$(2) \qquad I^d = R + L^d$$

where R represents reinvested earnings and L^d is the firm's demand for loans.

The usual assumption is that the value to the firm of internal funds, r^I, is less than the cost to the firm of external funds, r^L. The wedge between the two interest rates arises because entrepreneurs have better information about their prospects than outside lenders or investors. Lenders demand a premium to offset their informational disadvantage. The difference between r^I and r^L creates a pecking order in which internal funds are exhausted first before external funds are obtained (Stewart C. Myers and Nicholas S. Majluf, 1984; Lakshmi Shyam-Sunder and Myers, 1999). This idea was developed from the experience of firms in the United States. The wedge between the value of internal funds and the cost of external funds is likely to be larger in transition countries than in developed market economies because information sources are missing and investment uncertainties are much greater in transition countries. Information asymmetries are therefore likely to be more severe.

Firms in transition economies have another reason to prefer internal financing in addition to borrower/lender information asymmetries. External financing makes it hard for firms to hide their activities from tax collectors or the mafia. The effective cost of external finance in Russia is increased, according to Anna Meyendorff (1998), by the fact that firms that apply for a bank loan are more likely to have to pay their taxes. According to Richard Lotspeich (1996), firms are reluctant to disclose information to banks for fear it will be leaked to the mafia. Given these conditions, the assumption that the value of internal funds is less than the cost of external funds is a reasonable one to make in examining the investment decisions of firms.

The difference in cost of internal and external funds leads to a discontinuity between the investment of internal funds and the decision to seek external funds. Investment projects must have an expected return (after extortion and adjusted for risk) comparable to r^I to be profitable when financed by internal funds, but a return comparable to r^L to be profitable when financed by external funds. As a result, a firm's decision to invest internally generated funds is made independently of a decision to seek external finance. This allows us to estimate econometrically an equation for reinvestment of profits independent of the demand for external finance.

We represent the pecking-order hypothesis by supposing that firm i has a maximum amount of money that it is willing to reinvest out of its current profits, E_i; this might be the total current profit, or it might be strictly less than that. We assume E_i depends on entrepreneur-specific characteristics. Then the pecking-order hypothesis implies:

$$(3) \qquad I^d = R \qquad \text{if } I^d \leq E_i$$
$$I^d = E_i + L^d \qquad \text{if } I^d > E_i.$$

This gives us the main equation we will esti-

mate, relating the firm's willingness to reinvest its profits to its expected profits and the security of its property rights:

$$(4) \qquad R = I(\pi, s, r^I) \qquad \text{if } I^d \leq E_i$$
$$R = E_i \qquad \text{if } I^d > E_i.$$

In our data, we will use explicit measures of π and s. Differences in r^I across firms in the sample will be subsumed in country/industry control variables.

If the assumption that investment of internally generated funds is independent of access to external funds were invalid, then investment of internal and external funds would need to be examined simultaneously. There are (at least) three reasons that investment of internal funds might depend on access to external funds. First, r^L may not be higher than r^I if loans are subsidized by the government. This does not appear to be the case in our data. Subsidies were most important in loans to state-owned firms. There are no state-owned firms in our sample. Only in Romania do we find that interest rates paid by firms spun off from state-owned enterprises are lower than those paid by de novo start-ups. In the remaining countries, there are no significant differences in loan rates between the two groups of firms. Moreover, across the sample, loans given by state banks have higher interest rates than loans given by private banks. In Poland and Slovakia, where loans are equally divided between state and private banks, interest rates are nearly the same, with rates from state banks very slightly higher than rates from private banks.

Second, entrepreneurs for whom property rights are insecure may prefer to invest bank funds in their businesses and to divert internally generated funds to more secure accounts. This implies that firms receiving loans should invest, on average, a lower proportion of their own profits than firms without loans. The data suggest this is not the case. Among the most profitable firms (those with profits 10 percent or more of sales) who are investing less than half of their profits, loans are infrequent. Only 64 of 476 (13 percent) of these firms received loans in 1996. On the other hand, 104 of the 259 (40 percent) firms investing more than 75 percent of

TABLE 5—REINVESTMENT RATES, FIRMS WITH AND WITHOUT LOANS

Reinvestment rate[a]	Percentage of firms	
	Firms with loans in 1996	Firms without loans in 1996
0–25 percent	26.0	33.0
26–49 percent	21.0	31.5
50–75 percent	21.3	18.2
76–100 percent	31.7	17.4

[a] Percentage of after-tax profits.

their profits received loans.[17] The survey does not indicate whether a loan received in 1996 represented new capital, or a rollover of a loan from previous years. But we would expect that firms investing most of their profits are both more likely to roll over existing loans and more likely to take out new loans. In either case, firms that are investing aggressively will be more likely to have a loan in 1996, as the data suggest.

Finally, investment may be lumpy, with the minimal investment larger than retained earnings can accommodate. Given the level of technology used by small-scale manufacturers in these countries, however, it seems unlikely that investments are lumpy. Moreover, Table 5 shows that 35 percent of firms without loans in 1996 reinvested half or more of their profits, indicating that the lack of external finance does not preclude internally funded investment. (By comparison, 53 percent of firms with loans in 1996 invested half or more of their profits.) Further evidence on this is discussed in Section III, where we use a firm's ability to offer collateral and loans prior to 1996 as a measure of access to loans in the 1996 reinvestment equation. If investments are lumpy then reinvestment should be positively associated with collateral; we find no significant interaction.

Thus, examining reinvestment of profits in-

dependent of access to external finance appears to be reasonable for our data. In the next section, we examine the determinants of the firm's decision to reinvest from its profits [equation (4)]. The main hypothesis is that firms reinvest less if they perceive their property rights to be more insecure.

III. Determinants of Profit Reinvestment

Security of property rights is positively correlated with profit reinvestment rates at the country level, as we saw in Section I. Reinvestment rates are highest in Poland and Romania, where extralegal payments and payments for protection are lowest and the reliability of the courts is highest. Reinvestment rates are lowest in Ukraine and Russia, where extralegal payments are highest and courts less effective. Reinvestment rates are affected, however, by factors other than property rights.

A. *Basic Specification*

In this subsection, we estimate the reinvestment-demand equation (4), with the percentage of its profits a firm reinvests as the dependent variable and our property-rights indices as independent variables. Our data on reinvestment rates are categorical rather than continuous, and hence we use ordered probit regressions (although we have checked the robustness of our results using alternative specifications). We control for factors affecting investment demand other than property rights: the industry profit rate (as a proxy for expected investment opportunities more generally),[18] the age of the firm, access to external finance (represented by whether the firm had collateralizable assets), entrepreneur characteristics, and other industry effects.

---

[17] Because of the categorical responses, we cannot determine how many firms obtained new loans and invested more than 100 percent of their profits, though it is likely that some did. Just over a fifth of the firms reported investing more than 75 percent of profits, the highest reinvestment category. In Poland, 35 percent of firms reported investing at least 75 percent of profits.

[18] We do not use the firm's own profit rate due to concern about reverse causation: higher investment levels might lead to higher rates of profits. Given our belief that the manager's estimate of industry conditions is based on his own experience, use of industry profits does not completely eliminate endogeneity concerns. However, none of the results we report are altered if we use the firm's profit rate during its first year of operation, or exclude all measures of profits.

TABLE 6—ORDERED PROBITS FOR REINVESTMENT RATE IN 1996

Variable	(1)	(2)	(3)	(4)	(5)	(6)	(7)	(8)	(9)
Index for perceived insecurity of property rights	−0.17 (5.51)	−0.12 (3.39)	−0.12 (1.97)	−0.18 (2.83)	−0.0003 (0.01)		−0.18 (2.87)		−0.17 (2.88)
Dummy for believing courts ineffective		−0.18 (2.01)	−0.18 (1.85)	−0.15 (1.31)	−0.11 (0.47)		−0.16 (1.32)	−0.45 (1.95)	−0.23 (1.85)
Index for perceived insecurity of property rights including courts (four-element index)						−0.17 (2.93)			
Estimated industry profit rate		0.005 (1.13)	0.004 (0.91)	0.01 (1.80)	−0.02 (0.97)	0.01 (1.81)	0.01 (1.86)	−0.07 (1.55)	0.01 (1.90)
Log of firm age		−0.25 (3.34)	−0.30 (3.73)	−0.25 (2.35)	−0.77 (3.51)	−0.25 (2.36)	−0.25 (2.40)	−0.35 (1.22)	−0.33 (2.69)
Dummy for being a start-up		0.30 (2.80)	0.35 (2.73)					−0.04 (0.15)	
Tax payments as a percentage of sales		−0.01 (1.69)	−0.01 (1.68)	−0.004 (0.92)	−0.02 (1.50)	−0.004 (0.93)	−0.003 (0.86)		−0.002 (0.43)
Dummy for collateral to offer bank									−0.11 (0.64)
Dummy for obtaining loan prior to 1996									0.14 (1.57)
Industry controls	no	yes	yes	yes	yes	yes	yes	yes	yes
Country controls	no	no	yes	yes	yes	yes	yes	yes	yes
Manager characteristics included in regression	no	no	yes	yes	yes	yes	yes	yes	yes
Number of observations:	815	815	815	619	196	619	574	116	559
Chi-square:	30.3	236.2	570.4	722.9	28.3	314.6	549.2	98.8	263.6
Probability:	<0.001	<0.001	<0.001	<0.001	0.005	<0.001	<0.001	<0.001	<0.001

Notes: Regressions are ordered probits. The dependent variable is the firm's profit reinvestment rate, divided into categories, with a higher value indicating more investment as a percentage of profits (see Appendix B at ⟨www.aeaweb.org/aer⟩ for details). Numbers in parentheses are *t*-statistics based on robust standard errors. Country and industry controls are interacted when both are included. Manager controls are manager's age and education level, an indicator that the manager was previously a high-level manager in a state-owned enterprise and an indicator that the manager has previous experience in the private sector. Columns (1)–(6) present results for all five countries from regressions including:
   1) all firms, without country and industry controls;
   2) all firms, without country controls;
   3) all firms, with country controls;
   4) start-ups only;
   5) spin-offs only;
   6) the four-element alternative index of security of property rights.
Column (7) presents results from regressions including only start-ups in Poland, Slovakia, and Romania. Column (8) presents results using all firms in Russia and Ukraine only. Finally, column (9) gives results for start-ups with loan variables, using data from all five countries. (See text for additional details.)

Table 6 presents the results of these regressions. There are six categories of responses to the reinvestment question, increasing in the rate of reinvestment. A positive coefficient indicates that an increase in the level of the independent variable increases the chance that a firm is in a higher reinvestment category.[19] We exclude

from the regression sample firms that had zero or negative profits in 1996, since we are unable to measure their reinvestment rate. We also exclude firms not operating at the start of the

---

similar to those reported. We prefer the ordered probit because it does not require the assumption that investment rates are exactly at the midpoint of the categories specified in the survey. (See Appendix B at ⟨www.aeaweb.org/aer⟩ for the details on the six categories of responses to the reinvestment question.)

[19] We have run all of the regressions using ordinary least squares, using the midpoint of the reinvestment categories, with robust standard errors. The results are qualitatively

year in 1996. Both start-ups and spin-offs are included in the initial regressions (first and second columns). Recall that the questions on which the key independent variables are based refer to payments made by firms in the respondent's industry. To be conservative, we therefore report *t*-values based on standard errors adjusted for clustering for 44 industry/country groups. Adjusting for clustering has only a small effect on the standard errors in these regressions and does not affect the significance level for any of our results.

The first column of Table 6 includes only the index that represents the insecurity of property rights. Greater insecurity is associated with lower levels of profit reinvestment, and this effect is highly significant. The second column adds the variable that indicates the entrepreneur thinks courts are ineffective. Ineffective courts are associated with lower levels of investment as well, an effect significant at the 0.05 level. Additional variables added in the second column control for the entrepreneur's estimate of the industry profit rate[20] and tax rate, the log age of the firm in years, a dummy variable indicating that the firm is a start-up and nine industry dummy variables. Older firms invest a lower proportion and start-ups a higher proportion of their profits. Higher tax rates are associated with lower investment rates, though the effect is significant at only the 0.10 level. The regression also controls for the age of the firm and whether the firm is a start-up.

Our index for the insecurity of property rights is additive. An alternative index would take a value of one if firms make any one of the three types of payments, and a value of zero otherwise. Both indices have theoretical merit, but the additive index explains the data better. The either/or index is significant ($\beta = -0.27$, $t = 3.48$), but has a lower *t*-value and results in a lower χ^2 (60.8 vs. 65.4 with the additive index).

The additive index can be used to create four dummy variables, the first representing an index value of zero, the second representing an index value of one, and so on. When dummies representing index values of three, two, and one are used in place of the index (with the value zero being the base group), the coefficients are -0.35, -0.26, and -0.14, respectively. These results suggest that the effects of corruption are additive, perhaps because multiple affirmative responses indicate stronger convictions on the part of the entrepreneur. Alternatively, the better performance of the additive index may indicate that those extracting payments do not coordinate their activities, consistent with the model of Shleifer and Vishny (1993).

The first two regressions do not control for country effects. Since much of the variance in security of property rights is across countries rather than within country, this measures the full effect of property rights. However, there may be other factors that vary across countries and affect the demand for investment. If so, then these other country-level effects will be correlated with our measures of property rights. The regressions in columns (3)–(9) control for differences in each industry in each country using 39 industry/country dummy variables. We include interacted controls because the factors affecting investment demand in the food industry in Poland, for example, may differ from factors affecting investment demand in the food industry in Russia. Neither the index of property rights nor the reliability of the courts is much affected by the inclusion of the industry/country dummies, though the index is now significant only at the 0.05 level.[21]

B. *Alternative Specifications*

The regressions in columns (3)–(9) also include a set of four variables measuring entrepreneur characteristics. These variables measure the age, years of schooling, and prior work experience of the entrepreneur. The two work experience variables indicate whether the entre-

---

[20] We use the entrepreneur's estimate of industry profits rather than the firm's own profits because we believe the former are more likely to represent the expected profits from new investments. Additionally, own profits may be determined in part by reinvestment, creating endogeneity problems. Nevertheless, when we rerun all of the regressions in Table 6 with own profits replacing industry profits, we find that own profits are significant everywhere that industry profits are significant. The property-rights index and courts results are not affected.

[21] Because response rates were lower in Russia and Ukraine, only 14 percent of the observations in the regressions are firms in those countries. This may explain why the country controls have only a small impact on the property-rights variables.

preneur previously was a high-level manager in a state-owned enterprise and whether the entrepreneur had prior experience in the private sector. The coefficients of these controls for entrepreneur characteristics (not shown on Table 6) indicate that investment rates are higher for younger entrepreneurs ($\beta = -0.01$, $t = 2.77$ in the third-column specification) and for entrepreneurs who were previously high-level managers at state-owned enterprises ($\beta = 0.24$, $t = 2.98$ in the third-column specification). Education and private sector experience have no significant effect.

We split the sample, in the fourth and fifth columns, into firms that are start-ups and those that were spun off from a state enterprise. For start-ups, the coefficients are similar to those obtained for the whole sample, though the measure of courts is not significant at the 0.10 level. The industry tax rate is not significant in either subsample. However, the entrepreneur's estimated profit rate for the industry is significant at the 0.10 level among start-ups. Among spinoffs, no variable measuring property rights has any effect on investment. The industry profit rate has the wrong sign and is insignificant. There are significant differences between the behavior of spin-offs and start-ups, with the regressions doing a better job explaining the behavior of start-ups. Given that most of the spin-offs underwent downsizing after being privatized, other factors may play an important role in determining reinvestment rates for these firms. For the regressions in the sixth, seventh, and ninth columns we limit the sample to start-up firms.

The regression in the sixth column uses an alternative index of security of property rights. This alternative index ranges from zero to four—it adds one to the original index if the entrepreneur thinks courts are ineffective for enforcing contracts. As with the original index, a higher value represents less secure property rights. The four-element index has the expected negative sign, and is significant at the 0.01 level.

Last, we divide the sample by region, first considering investment among start-ups in Poland, Slovakia, and Romania (the seventh column), and then considering all firms in Russia and Ukraine (the eighth column). (The number of start-ups with nonmissing responses in Russia and Ukraine is too small for us to use only start-ups in this regression.) The two property-

rights measures both have the expected sign in the three Eastern European countries. The index is significant at the 0.01 level; the significance of the effectiveness of courts falls below the 0.10 level. In Russia and Ukraine, the effectiveness of courts is significant. The index of property rights is not included in this regression because there is not enough variation in the index in the Russia/Ukraine sample to make the results meaningful. (Only three of 116 firms in the sample answer "no" to any of the three questions in the index!)

The ordered probit coefficients represent changes in the probabilities of being in each category of investment. Hence, giving an economic interpretation of their magnitude is difficult. To gain a better picture of the effect of property rights on investment, we calculate the probability of being in each investment category conditional on different values of the property-rights index. We use the regression reported in the sixth column of Table 6, using the four-element security index. The results are shown in Table 7. The bottom row of the table shows the weighted average reinvestment rate for each value of the index, using the midpoint of each reinvestment category. Firms with the most secure property rights (those with an index value of zero) have an average predicted reinvestment rate of 55.1 percent; those with the least secure property rights have an average predicted reinvestment rate of 33.5 percent. The most insecure firms' investment is therefore 39 percent lower than the investment of the most secure firms.

In sum, the index of property rights has a significant effect on firms' investment rates, especially among de novo start-ups. We find only weak evidence that tax rates affect investment demand. The lack of robustness in the tax effects may reflect a lack of variance in taxes across firms, since statutory tax rates vary only across countries. Alternatively, perhaps it is the clandestine and unpredictable nature of the unofficial payments, rather than just the fact that some profits will be taken, that discourages firms from investing.

C. Access to Credit

Our framework assumes that the decision to invest internally generated funds is independent

TABLE 7—PREDICTED PROFIT REINVESTMENT RATE FROM THE ORDERED PROBIT RESULTS
IN TABLE 6, COLUMN (6)

Profit reinvestment rate (percent)	All firms	4	3	2	1	0
	Percentage of firms in investment category					
		Insecurity of property-rights index[a]				
0	3.3	9.2	6.5	4.4	3.2	1.9
1–10	13.7	25.0	21.0	16.6	13.6	10.4
11–25	10.9	14.9	14.0	12.4	11.1	9.5
26–49	20.2	21.3	21.8	21.3	20.6	19.2
50–75	21.0	16.1	18.4	20.3	21.4	22.0
76–100	30.8	13.5	18.3	25.0	30.2	36.9
Weighted investment rate:	49.9	33.5	39.0	45.3	49.8	55.1

Notes: We calculate the probability of being in each investment category conditional on different values of the property-rights index. We use the regression reported in column (6) of Table 6, utilizing the four-element security index (i.e., including belief in the effectiveness of the courts). The last row of Table 7 shows the weighted average reinvestment rate for each value of the index, using the midpoint of each reinvestment category.

[a] Scale for insecurity of property-rights index ranges from 0 (most secure) to 4 (least secure).

of access to external funds. It is possible, however, for internal and external funds to complement one another. If investment projects are lumpy, then firms may need outside finance in order to undertake investment projects at all. In this case, those not receiving loans would not invest internal funds either. We cannot include a direct measure of whether the firm has a loan because the latent variable—investment demand—determines (at least in part) both reinvestment of profits and demand for loans. Instead, we test for the importance of loans by including variables that are correlated with access to finance but that we expect are uncorrelated, or only weakly correlated, with investment demand.[22] We include two variables, one indicating that the firm has collateralizable assets, and the other indicating the firm received a loan prior to 1996. Both of these variables are strongly correlated with receiving a loan in 1996. Collateral is necessary for access to loans. Only six of 310 firms reporting loans in 1996 said they did not provide collateral. Loans obtained prior

to 1996 provide an additional indication of creditworthiness. In most cases (69 percent) where firms had loans prior to 1996 and in 1996 as well, the firm obtained both loans from the same bank. Given that our sample is limited to firms with positive profits in 1996, we believe these two variables are good indications of access to credit.[23] Neither has a significant effect on the rate of reinvestment (ninth column of Table 6). The inclusion of the instruments for bank finance has little impact on the magnitude or significance of the coefficient on the index of property-rights insecurity. The variable measuring the reliability of courts is now significant at the 0.10 level.

In unreported regressions available from the authors, we pursued an alternative test for an interaction between security of property rights and use of external credit. We included the index of insecurity as an independent variable in a regression with the receipt of a loan in 1996 as the dependent variable. We found that the index of insecurity has no effect on the likelihood a firm obtained a loan in 1996. This provides additional evidence that less secure property rights did not encourage entrepreneurs to invest

[22] Because investment opportunities may be correlated across time within a firm, we had some concern that either of these variables might be partially endogenous to current reinvestment rates. Their insignificance in the reinvestment equation suggests that endogeneity of our measures through temporal correlation of investment rates is not a serious problem.

[23] Our results are consistent with those found by Andrzej Bratkowski et al. (2000), who find for a sample of new firms in the Czech Republic, Hungary, and Poland that loans are significantly associated with collateral and past loans.

TABLE 8—ORDERED PROBITS FOR REINVESTMENT RATE IN 1996:
ALL FIVE COUNTRIES, START-UPS ONLY

Dummy variables	(1)	(2)	(3)	(4)	(5)	(6)
Firms make extralegal payments for services	−0.42 (4.33)					
Firms make extralegal payments for licenses		−0.11 (0.84)				
Firms make payments for protection			−0.34 (1.60)			
Firms make unofficial payments—ongoing registration				−0.40 (3.04)		
Firms make unofficial payments—fire and sanitary inspections					−0.31 (2.45)	
Firms make unofficial payments—tax inspection						−0.27 (1.76)
Courts cannot be used to enforce contracts	−0.16 (1.39)	−0.14 (1.20)	−0.13 (1.13)	−0.21 (1.65)	−0.14 (1.21)	−0.20 (1.63)
Controls included	industry/ country	industry/ country	industry/ country	industry/ country	industry/ country	industry/ country
Manager characteristics	yes	yes	yes	yes	yes	yes
Number of observations:	619	619	619	499	538	529
Chi-square:	428.4	339.8	235.2	512.3	470.2	169.1
Probability:	<0.001	<0.001	<0.001	<0.001	<0.001	<0.001

Notes: All regressions are ordered probits. The dependent variable is the level of investment, divided into categories, with a higher value indicating more investment as a percentage of profits (see Appendix B at ⟨www.aeaweb.org/aer⟩ for details). All regressions also include the entrepreneur's estimate of the industry profit rate and the age of the firm. Numbers in parentheses are *t*-statistics based on robust standard errors.

from bank funds rather than from their own profits. In the regressions, both the availability of collateral and receipt of loans prior to 1996 had large and significant effects on the likelihood a firm received credit in 1996, suggesting that banks' willingness to lend is an important determinant of credit availability. The level of unreinvested profits also has a large and significant effect on the likelihood a firm received credit. The last result suggests an indirect link between property rights and credit: firms perceiving property rights as insecure invest less, and so demand less credit. Low levels of observed credit may result from a lack of demand as well as a lack of supply.

D. Further Robustness Checks

Table 8 reports regressions that use the components of the index one at a time. We use the sample of start-ups in these regressions. Among

the elements of the index, extralegal payments for government services clearly have the most significant effect (the first column). Payments for protection fall just below the 0.10 level of significance, and payments for licenses is insignificant as well (the third and second columns, respectively).

The fourth, fifth, and sixth columns of Table 8 replace the components of our index with the responses to questions about bribes paid for specific services. All three types of bribes—payments for ongoing registration, payments for fire/sanitary inspection, and payments for tax inspection—are negatively and significantly associated with reinvestment levels. The sample size in these regressions varies and is smaller than the other regressions because the response rate for these questions is generally lower. The variable representing trust in the courts has the correct sign in all of the regressions reported on Table 8, though it is insignificant in all but one of the specifications (see the last row of coefficients in each column).

Our findings are also robust to alternative ways of defining the dependent variable. Ordinary least-squares regressions using the midpoint of the investment categories (i.e., five for the 1–10 percent category, eighteen for the 11–25 percent category, and so on) produces very similar results. Probits for over/under 75 percent reinvestment or over/under 50 percent reinvestment also produce similar findings.

E. *Caveats to Our Interpretation*

In the regressions, we treat property rights as exogenous to the investment decisions of our firms. There are at least two reasons why this may not be a valid assumption. First, higher investment rates may lead to more secure property rights, as in the model of Besley (1995). While it is plausible that very large firms in post-communist transition countries may endogenously create property rights by becoming "too big to fail," we do not view this as likely for our firms, given their relatively small size.

Of more concern is the possibility that higher reinvestment rates and more secure property rights may both reflect the optimism of the responding managers. Managers may also attempt to justify an unwillingness to invest by saying that property rights are insecure. In either of these cases, endogeneity of property-rights security arises from our inability adequately to control for manager characteristics. We lack direct measures of a manager's attitudes, but managers who say property rights are less secure also say their own profits and their industry's profits are higher. Insecurity is also significantly correlated with characteristics of the manager that we can measure. For example, older managers and managers who formerly worked as a high-level manager of a state-owned enterprise say property rights are more secure. These correlations suggest there is an important exogenous component of our insecurity index. Nevertheless, the estimated impacts of insecurity on investment may be overstated if unmeasured manager characteristics are important.

Alternatively, our regression coefficients may understate the effects of property-rights insecurity. Since we surveyed existing firms, our sample omits both failed firms and potential firms

that were deterred from entering. Both failure and the decision not to enter presumably reflect the insecurity of property rights. Additionally, because our regressions look at the determinants of firms' marginal investment decisions in their current lines of activity, we cannot pick up possible intersectoral distortions. For example, certain industries might be especially susceptible to extortion; the insecurity of property rights might cause entrepreneurs to shun those industries. If capital is more susceptible to extortion than labor, weak property rights may also cause production to be inefficiently labor intensive. We have no way of determining the net effect of the biases of opposite directions.

In summary: Weak perceived property rights have a consistently negative effect on reinvestment in our regressions. The index of property rights is significant in all subsamples apart from spin-offs. The measure of trust in courts has a less robust effect on reinvestment, but is significant for the full sample. The availability of collateral is not correlated with the reinvestment of profits.

IV. Conclusion

Firms' investment is affected by the perceived security of property rights, as shown by both our cross-country data and firm-level regressions. Reinvestment rates are lowest in Russia and Ukraine, where bribes for government services and licenses are common, firms make payments for protection, and the courts are least effective, and highest in Poland and Romania, where property rights are the most secure. Within countries, also, there is also significant variation, as our firm-level regressions indicate. The entrepreneurs who perceive their property rights to be the least secure reinvest 32 percent of their profits, while those with the most secure property reinvest 56 percent. Insecurity of property rights, all else equal, reduces a firm's investment by over a third.

Most of the firms say they were able to offer collateral to banks (more than three-quarters of the firms in each of the countries). Lack of collateral, therefore, does not appear to have been a binding constraint on firms' investment. There are two reasons why, until now, external credit has not been essential for private-sector development. First, insecure property rights mean firms have limited incentive to invest and therefore little demand for external finance (especially in Russia and Ukraine). Second, the high profits of early entrants in all these transition economies meant that firms that wished to invest were able to do so. The potential for using retained earnings as a source of investment is seen from the fact that, in all five countries, unreinvested profits exceed the funds provided by banks. Our evidence indicates, then, that secure property rights have been both necessary and sufficient for investment.

Although the firms have had little demand for external finance at the time of our survey, they will begin to need access to credit as these economies develop their market-supporting institutions. This is because legal and bureaucratic reforms increase the demand for investable funds by solidifying property rights;[24] and because profits will be driven down to normal levels as transaction costs fall and market competition increases, so investment from internal funds will not be sustainable.

REFERENCES

Acemoglu, Daron; Johnson, Simon and Robinson, James. "The Colonial Origins of Comparative Development: An Empirical Investigation." *American Economic Review*, December 2001, *91*(5), pp. 1369–401.

Berkowitz, Daniel and DeJong, David N. "Policy Reform and Growth in Post-Soviet Russia." *European Economic Review*, 2002 (forthcoming).

Besley, Timothy. "Property Rights and Investment Incentives: Theory and Evidence from Ghana." *Journal of Political Economy*, October 1995, *103*(5), pp. 903–37.

Bratkowski, Andrzej; Grosfeld, Irena and Rostowski, Jacek. "Investment and Finance in De Novo Private Firms: Empirical Results from the Czech Republic, Hungary, and Poland." *Economics of Transition*, March 2000, *8*(1), pp. 101–16.

[24] Low reinvestment may be the result of a high required rate of return, rather than a high probability of expropriation, because imperfect financial markets mean entrepreneurs bear a large amount of idiosyncratic risk. Improved capital markets would then facilitate investment because they would increase diversification possibilities and reduce idiosyncratic risk.

Demirgüç-Kunt, Asli and Maksimovic, Vojislav. "Law, Finance, and Firm Growth." *Journal of Finance*, December 1998, *53*(6), pp. 2107–37.

Djankov, Simeon; La Porta, Rafael; Lopez-de-Silanes, Florencio and Shleifer, Andrei. "The Regulation of Entry." *Quarterly Journal of Economics*, February 2002, *117*(1), pp. 1–37.

European Bank for Reconstruction and Development. *Transition report*. London: EBRD, 1996.

Federal Reserve Board of Governors. *National survey of small business finance*. Washington, DC: Federal Reserve Board, 1994.

Frye, Timothy and Shleifer, Andrei. "The Invisible Hand and the Grabbing Hand." *American Economic Review*, May 1997 (*Papers and Proceedings*), *87*(2), pp. 354–58.

Hellman, Joel; Jones, Geraint; Kaufmann, Daniel and Schankerman, Mark. "Measuring Governance and State Capture: The Role of Bureaucrats and Firms in Shaping the Business Environment." Workshop on the Institutional Foundation of a Market Economy, Berlin, February 2000.

Johnson, Simon; Kaufmann, Daniel and Shleifer, Andrei. "The Unofficial Economy in Transition." *Brookings Papers on Economic Activity*, Fall 1997, (2), pp. 159–221.

Johnson, Simon and Loveman, Gary W. *Starting over in Eastern Europe*. Boston, MA: Harvard Business School Press, 1995.

Johnson, Simon; McMillan, John and Woodruff, Christopher. "Entrepreneurs and the Ordering of Institutional Reform: Poland, Slovakia, Romania, Russia and Ukraine Compared." *Economics of Transition*, March 2000, *8*(1), pp. 1–36.

_____. "Courts and Relational Contracts." *Journal of Law, Economics, and Organization*, Spring 2002, *18*(1), pp. 221–77.

Knack, Stephen and Keefer, Philip. "Institutions and Economic Performance: Cross-Country Tests Using Alternative Institutional Measures." *Economics and Politics*, November 1995, *7*(3), pp. 207–28.

La Porta, Rafael; Lopez-de-Silanes, Florencio; Shleifer, Andrei and Vishny, Robert. "Legal Determinants of External Finance." *Journal of Finance*, July 1997, *52*(3), pp. 1131–50.

_____. "Law and Finance." *Journal of Political Economy*, December 1998, *106*(6), pp. 1113–55.

_____. "Investor Protection and Corporate Governance." *Journal of Financial Economics*, October–November 2000, *58*(1–2), pp. 3–28.

Levine, Ross. "Financial Development and Economic Growth: Views and Agenda." *Journal of Economic Literature*, June 1997, *35*(2), pp. 688–726.

Lotspeich, Richard. "An Economic Analysis of Extortion in Russia." Unpublished manuscript, Indiana State University, 1996.

Mauro, Paolo. "Corruption and Growth." *Quarterly Journal of Economics*, August 1995, *110*(3), pp. 681–712.

McMillan, John. "Markets in Transition," in David M. Kreps and Kenneth F. Wallis, eds., *Advances in economics and econometrics: Theory and applications*. Cambridge: Cambridge University Press, 1997, pp. 210–39.

Meyendorff, Anna. "Tax Avoidance and the Allocation of Credit." Unpublished manuscript, William Davidson Institute, University of Michigan, May 1998.

Myers, Stewart C. and Majluf, Nicholas S. "Corporate Financing and Investment Decisions When Firms Have Information that Investors Do Not Have." *Journal of Financial Economics*, June 1984, *13*(2), pp. 187–221.

Naughton, Barry. *Growing out of the plan.* New York: Cambridge University Press, 1995.

Rajan, Raghuram and Zingales, Luigi. "Financial Dependence and Growth." *American Economic Review*, June 1998, *88*(3), pp. 559–86.

Shleifer, Andrei. "Government in Transition." *European Economic Review*, April 1997, *41*(3–5), pp. 385–410.

Shleifer, Andrei and Vishny, Robert W. "Corruption." *Quarterly Journal of Economics*, August 1993, *108*(3), pp. 599–617.

_____. *The grabbing hand: Government pathologies and their cures.* Cambridge, MA: Harvard University Press, 1998.

Shyam-Sunder, Lakshmi and Myers, Stewart C. "Testing Static Tradeoff Against Pecking Order Models of Capital Structure." *Journal of Financial Economics*, February 1999, *52*(1), pp. 219–44.

Svensson, Jakob. "Investment, Property Rights and Political Instability: Theory and Evidence." *European Economic Review*, July 1998, *42*(7), pp. 1317–41.

[20]

Available online at www.sciencedirect.com

SCIENCE ⊘ DIRECT°

ELSEVIER

Journal of Financial Economics 77 (2005) 117–146

JOURNAL OF
Financial
ECONOMICS

www.elsevier.com/locate/econbase

Institutions, ownership, and finance: the determinants of profit reinvestment among Chinese firms ☆

Robert Cull[a],*, Lixin Colin Xu[b,c]

[a]*Development Research Group, The World Bank, 1818 H Street, NW, Mail Code MC3-300, Washington, DC 20433, USA*
[b]*Development Research Group, World Bank, Washington, DC 20433, USA*
[c]*Guanghua School of Management, Peking University, Beijing 100871, PR China*

Received 26 July 2003; received in revised form 24 March 2004; accepted 24 May 2004
Available online 3 March 2005

Abstract

Johnson et al. (2002. American Economic Review 92 (5), 1335–1356) examine the relative importance of property rights and external finance in several Eastern European countries. They find property rights to be overwhelmingly important, while external finance explains little of firm reinvestment. McMillan and Woodruff (2002. Journal of Economic Perspectives 16 (3), 153–170) further conjecture that as transition moves along, market-supporting (financial) institutions should become more important. This paper reexamines those issues in the context of China in 2002, when the transition had moved far. We also find that secure property rights are a significant predictor of firm reinvestment. However, in line with McMillan and Woodruff, we find that access to external finance in the form of bank loans is also associated with more reinvestment. Following Acemoglu and Johnson (2003. Unbundling institutions. Unpublished working paper 9934, National Bureau of Economic Research,

---

☆ We thank George Clarke, David Dollar, David Scott, and Shuilin Wang for useful comments, and Mani Jandu for excellent assistance in copy editing. The survey was funded by the Department for International Development of the United Kingdom and the Multi-Donor Funded Knowledge for Change Program, to which we are grateful. The findings, interpretations, and conclusions expressed in this paper are entirely ours. They do not necessarily represent the views of the World Bank, its executive directors, or the countries they represent. We alone bear responsibility for any mistakes and inaccuracies.

*Corresponding author.

E-mail address: rcull@worldbank.org (R. Cull).

118   R. Cull, L.C. Xu / Journal of Financial Economics 77 (2005) 117–146

Cambridge, MA), we separate our proxies for the security of property rights into two groups: those measuring the risk of expropriation by the government and those measuring the ease and reliability of contract enforcement. Whereas those authors' cross-country results suggest that risk of expropriation is the more severe impediment to economic development, ours indicate that both expropriation risk and contract enforcement play a role in Chinese firms' reinvestment decisions. We also find that another aspect of property rights, the extent of private ownership, is associated with greater reinvestment. At China's current stage of development, expropriation risk, contract enforcement, access to finance, and ownership structure all appear to matter for reinvestment decisions. Some evidence also exists that access to finance and government expropriation affect small firms more than large ones.

JEL classification: D23; G31; P2; L2

Keywords: China; Property rights; Banking; Investment

1. Introduction

In recent years, two strands of research on growth and development have evolved more or less independent of one another. The first finds that secure property rights are an important precondition for growth, especially for countries in transition from a planned to a market economy. In particular, a series of cross-country studies find that less secure property rights are associated with lower investment and slower growth (Knack and Keefer, 1995; Mauro, 1995; Svensson, 1998; Acemoglu et al., 2001; Claessens and Laeven, 2003). The second finds that financial sector development is a robust determinant of growth (Levine, 1997; Rajan and Zingales, 1998; Levine et al., 2000). While these two sets of findings need not be contradictory, knowing which factor has greater influence on growth could be important for policy makers with limited time and resources. However, Johnson, McMillan, and Woodruff (JMW, 2002) point out that it is hard to separate the effects of property rights from external financing with country-level data because external financing is strongly influenced by the security of property rights (La Porta et al., 1997, 1998, 2000; Demirguc-Kunt and Maksimovic, 1998).

Following this line of thought, JMW (2002) use micro data to highlight that secure property rights could be central to the earliest stages of development of a market economy. (Few micro-studies link investment behavior with property rights, with notable exceptions in Besley, 1995; Jacoby et al., 2002.) For a sample of firms from Poland, Romania, Russia, Slovakia, and Ukraine, JMW find that entrepreneurs choose to reinvest a higher share of their profits when property rights are perceived to be more secure. Proxies for access to external finance are not significantly associated with reinvestment rates, from which they conclude that, at least until now, insecure property rights have been a more serious impediment to investment and firm growth than a lack of finance in a number of transition countries.

Though intriguing, the JMW results on the importance of property rights should be viewed in context. The transition countries of Europe and the former Soviet

R. Cull, L.C. Xu / Journal of Financial Economics 77 (2005) 117–146   119

Union underwent rapid transformations from planned to developed economies. Under this big bang approach to economic development, the security of newly established rights to property would be uncertain in a rapidly changing environment, and thus likely an important determinant of whether firms grew. Moreover, financial institutions in these countries were notoriously poor intermediaries and were undergoing their own chaotic transformations.[1] Finally, firms in the JMW sample tend to have high profit margins, which likely makes them less reliant on external finance for investment. These conditions made it likely that the security of property rights would be a more important determinant of firm growth than access to external finance.

By contrast, Demirguc-Kunt and Maksimovic (DKM, 1998) find that access to external finance contributed to the sales growth of firms in 20 industrialized and ten developing countries, none of which was in transition from a planned to a market economy. In addition, reliance on long-term finance was greater in countries with efficient legal systems, an active stock market, and a large banking sector, none of which was characteristic of the economies in transition. The DKM results, viewed in combination with those of JMW, suggest that economies in the early stages of transition might be the rare current example in which the security of property rights matters much more for growth than access to external finance.

Although it might be tempting to generalize the JMW results to all transitional countries, there are important unsettled issues to consider. By construction, the JMW sample is composed of firms with substantial retained earnings, many in industries largely protected from competition. Firms in competitive industries with less retained earnings likely are in greater need of external finance, which might make the JMW results less applicable to transitional countries facing a great deal of competition (such as China).

The JMW results are put in perspective in a recent survey on entrepreneurs and transition by McMillan and Woodruff (2002). They suggest that the overwhelming importance of property rights relative to external financing might not hold as transition progresses. In particular, the need for market-supporting institutions increases when competition forces down profit margins and when relational contracting gives way to formal contracting, often because products and transactions become more complex such that ex ante contracting is needed to coordinate buyers and sellers. While the conjecture sounds plausible, no formal econometric evidence is offered to indicate that as market transition moves along, the relative importance of market-supporting institutions increases. In this paper, we offer such evidence using the most populous transitional country, China, as the backdrop.

---

[1] On the difficulties of bank privatization in the Czech Republic, Hungary, and Poland, see Bonin and Wachtel (2000). In the Czech case, the state banks had long-standing creditor relationships with many of the large state-owned enterprises privatized through vouchers. Because those firms represented a large share of their portfolios, bank managers had strong incentives to prop up troubled firms through further lending and rollovers to avoid revealing their own insolvency (Hrncir, 1993; Capek, 1994; Brom and Orenstein, 1994; Desai, 1996). Cull et al. (2002) confirm that privatized firms with close links to the Czech banking system performed worse than all others.

120   *R. Cull, L.C. Xu / Journal of Financial Economics 77 (2005) 117–146*

We add to the JMW results in a number of ways. First, we offer evidence from China, a country whose transition to a market economy has been more gradual than those in Europe and the former Soviet Union. Lacking a big bang, uncertainties regarding the security of property rights could be less severe, and China thus offers a potentially interesting contrast to most other transitional economies. The time period we cover is 2000–2002, during which China had made progress in its transition and likely satisfied the conditions for the increasing importance of market-supporting institutions (such as competition and more arm's-length relationships between buyers and sellers). Second, we have detailed data on the ownership structure of our firms, in particular the extent to which they are privately owned. We thus are able to distinguish two different aspects of property rights: perceptions about how secure those rights are (which is the focus of JMW) and ownership structure. We test explicitly whether investment behavior is different for firms with a higher share of private ownership. Third, our sample is composed of less profitable firms, on average, than those studied by JMW, at least in part because the level of protection from competition enjoyed by Chinese firms is lower than that enjoyed by firms in some transition economies in the 1990s. This feature helps us assess whether the JMW results (i.e., that access to external finance does not affect reinvestment) are largely attributable to a sample of relatively profitable firms that had little need for external finance.

Following Acemoglu and Johnson (2003), we separate our proxies for the security of property rights into two groups: those measuring the risk of expropriation by the government and those measuring the ease and reliability of contract enforcement. In a cross-country analysis, those authors find that the risk of expropriation is the more severe impediment to economic development, and they speculate that individuals can alter the terms of formal and informal contracts to avoid the adverse effects of contracting institutions but are unable to do so against the risk of expropriation. By contrast, we find that both expropriation risk and contract enforcement play a role in Chinese firms' reinvestment decisions. At this stage of the transition, individuals could still be learning how to tailor their contracting to offset weak supporting institutions.

We confirm many of the JMW results regarding the importance of secure property rights for reinvestment decisions. Given where China is in terms of economic growth and financial development, the continued importance of secure property rights for investment might come as a surprise to some. Table 1 offers a comparison between China and the countries in the JMW sample in terms of standard indicators of the security of property rights and financial development. The general impression is that China is in the middle of the pack in terms of property rights, trailing both Poland and Slovakia. However, regarding financial development, China is well ahead of the JMW countries. It might come as less surprise, therefore, that in line with the McMillan and Woodruff conjecture, access to external finance is a significant predictor of firm reinvestment in China.

One should not take the figures for China's financial development at face value. Under corporatization, which had affected most Chinese firms by the turn of the 21st century and thus explains the relatively high ratio of private credit to gross domestic

Table 1
Financial development and property rights in China and JMW countries

Country	Financial development indicators (2001)			Property rights indicators (1997)	
	LL/GDP (%)	BANK/GDP (%)	PRIV/GDP (%)	Rule of law	Corruption
China	150.1	129.2	119.7	-0.27^a	-0.38^a
Poland	42.5	34.5	27.6	0.51	0.44
Romania	19.6	11.7	6.3	-0.26	-0.28
Russia	n.a.	n.a.	n.a.	-0.79	-0.69
Slovakia	65.8	63.7	27.3	0.12	0.16
Ukraine	14.4	9.7^b	7.3^b	-0.70	-0.79

n.a. is not available.
LL/GDP is the ratio of liquid liabilities to gross domestic product (GDP). BANK/GDP is the ratio of deposit money banks' assets to GDP. PRIV/GDP is the ratio of private credit extended by deposit money banks to GDP. The source of all the indicators of financial development is the electronic version of the International Monetary Fund's *International Financial Statistics*. Those indicators are available via the internet in the World Bank financial structure database, http://www.worldbank.org/research/projects/finstructure/database.htm. Indicators of the security of property rights are taken from Kaufman et al. (2003). Their indicators are normally distributed, with a mean of zero and a standard deviation of one. The larger the value, the better the country. Their index for rule of law is composed of several indicators that measure the extent to which agents have confidence in and abide by the rules of society. These include perceptions of the incidence of crime, the effectiveness and predictability of the judiciary, and the enforceability of contracts. Corruption measures the extent to which corruption is controlled based on perceptions from survey respondents.
[a] Average data 2000–2002.
[b] 1999 data.

product (GDP) in Table 1, the performance of many majority-state-owned firms was converging to that of private firms. (See Zhu (1999), Lin and Zhu (2001) and Xu et al. (2005) for analysis of the effects of the recent corporatization and associated reforms.) However, state-owned enterprises (SOEs) continue to receive a disproportionately large share of the credit extended by the main (and largely state-owned) banks in China, and recent empirical research shows that state banks have grown increasingly inefficient in allocating credit as they have been increasingly forced to bail out poorly performing state-owned enterprises (Lardy, 1998; Cull and Xu, 2000, 2003). These bailouts come in the form of stability loans to keep SOEs afloat, as many or most of them maintain excessive employment.[2] We therefore view loans extended by state-owned banks to state enterprises as having a strong bailout component instead of as true external finance awarded on the basis of creditworthiness. For private firms, which are the focus of this analysis, these agency problems should be much less severe. Both the banks and their ultimate owner, the government, have an incentive to lend any excess funds to the best private borrowers.

---

[2] Bai et al. (2000) suggest that SOEs typically face multiple tasks. Bai and Xu (2002) present evidence consistent with the notion that the chief executive officer of a SOE likely faces multiple tasks. Shleifer and Vishny (1994) also emphasize that employment maintenance tends to be an important objective of SOEs.

122   *R. Cull, L.C. Xu / Journal of Financial Economics 77 (2005) 117–146*

Section 2 discusses relevant theoretical issues and lays out the JMW framework for investment decisions. Section 3 describes our data set. Section 4 formalizes our testable hypotheses, while Sections 5 and 6 contain the empirical results. Section 7 concludes.

2. Framework for investment decisions

JMW offer a framework for evaluating the effects of insecure property rights on investment decisions, based on the financial pecking order described in Myers and Majluf (1984). With minor modifications for the Chinese case, we rely on the same framework to illustrate our central hypotheses and defend the assumptions implicit in the regressions that follow.

The firm's demand for investable funds is given by

$$I^d = I(p, s, r^I, r^E), \tag{1}$$

where p is the firm's profits, s is the amount of those profits taken by corrupt officials or criminals, r^I is the interest rate that the firm owner could earn by investing profits outside the firm, and r^E is the interest rate the owner must pay for external loans.

Funds for investment are generated internally or borrowed externally, and therefore

$$I^d = R + L^E, \tag{2}$$

where R is reinvested earnings and L^E is the firm's demand for external loans. Under the pecking-order hypothesis, the cost of internal funds r^I is assumed to be less than the cost of external funds r^E. This is because the borrower has better information about the quality of its investment opportunities than does the lender. The lender, therefore, requires compensation in the form of a higher interest rate. Because external funds are more costly, firm owners first exhaust internal funds to support investment before turning to credit markets, and thus a pecking order exists between the two sources of finance.

JMW assume that firm i is willing to reinvest a maximum amount E_i of its current profits $(E_i \leqslant p)$. The wedge between the value of internal funds and the cost of external funds implies that

$$I^d = R \quad \text{if} \quad I^d \leqslant E_i$$

and

$$I^d = E_i + L^E \quad \text{if} \quad I^d > E_i. \tag{3}$$

The assumptions underlying (3) give rise to the equation estimated by JMW:

$$R = I(p, s, r^I) \quad \text{if} \quad I^d \leqslant E_i$$

and

$$R = E_i \quad \text{if} \quad I^d > E_i. \tag{4}$$

R. Cull, L.C. Xu / Journal of Financial Economics 77 (2005) 117–146   123

Their data provide explicit proxies for p and s. Country and industry control variables capture differences across firms in r^I. We follow the same strategy, except that we also include some firm-level proxies for r^I. The key insight is that the firm's decision to invest internally generated funds is made independently of its decision to borrow external funds. This allows JMW to estimate an equation for profit reinvestment independent of the demand for external finance.

As JMW note, there are at least three reasons that the investment of internal funds might depend on access to external funds. First, the pecking-order hypothesis might not hold if the government subsidizes loans so that $r^E < r^I$. Although JMW offer evidence that this is relevant only for loans to state enterprises in their sample, the same might not hold for China, where state banks continue to dominate the financial system and interest rates remain highly regulated.

Second, insecure property rights might compel owners to invest bank funds in their firms and divert internal profits to more secure investment opportunities. In this way, we would expect a negative relation between access to loans and reinvestment rates. While we find this somewhat unlikely given China's reasonably high scores on indicators of the security of property rights (see Table 1), our regressions will offer a test of whether it might be true.

Third, investment could be lumpy, in the sense that the scale of efficient investment is larger than retained earnings can support. Thus, firms need both internal and external funds to undertake investment, which implies a positive association between reinvestment rates and access to finance. For their sample, JMW point out that 35% of the firms without access to loans reinvested half or more of their profits, which suggests that lack of external finance did not impede internally financed investment. However, JMW deliberately sampled small firms, ranging in employees from seven to 270. The average firm in our sample has 133 employees, and more than 10 percent employ at least a thousand. Therefore, lumpy investment could lead to a positive relation between reinvestment and access to loans in our case.

3. Data

Our data come from a survey of firms for the period between 2000 and 2002, conducted in early 2003 by the World Bank (jointly with the Enterprise Survey Organization of China) on the investment climate in China. The survey enables us to study variation in firm-level financing decisions across a number of industries.

Firms were drawn from 18 cities that were selected to achieve balanced representation across five regions: (1) Northeast: Benxi, Changchun, Dalian, and Haerbin; (2) Coastal: Hangzhou, Jiangmen, Shenzhen, and Wenzhou; (3) Central: Changsha, Nanchang, Wuhan, and Zhenzhou; (4) Southwest: Chongqing, Guiyang, Kunming, and Nanning; (5) Northwest: Langzhou and Xi'an. The total sample is composed of 2,400 firms, 100 or 150 from each city (Fig. 1).

The questionnaire has two parts. Part one, based on interviews with the manager of a firm, contains questions on general information about the firm and the manager, innovation, market environment, relationships with clients and suppliers, location of

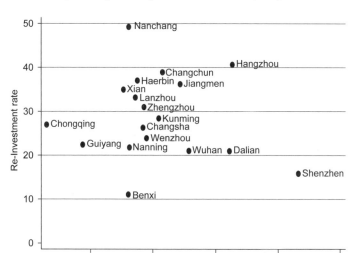

Fig. 1. Reinvestment rate and income level for the 18 cities.

manufacturing plant, relations with government, and international trade. Part two is based on interviews with the firm's accountant and personnel manager, who provided quantitative information on production, costs, employee training, schooling, and wages. While most of the qualitative questions pertained only to the year 2002, many quantitative questions also requested information for 2000–2002. Therefore, in the regressions the qualitative variables are time-invariant, while quantitative ones vary over 2000–2002.

Firms were sampled randomly subject to a few constraints. First, the survey sampled only the following industries: for manufacturing, apparel and leather goods, electronic equipment, electronic components, consumer products, and vehicles and vehicle parts; for services, accounting and related services, advertising and marketing, business logistics services, communication services, and information technology services.[3] Second, the size restriction of firms as measured by number of employees was prespecified.[4] Once these constraints were roughly satisfied, the surveyors randomly drew the required number of firms from an electronic list of firms in that city.

The data contain both private firms and state-owned enterprises. For comparability to JMW, we restrict our analysis to that of private firms, defined as those with private ownership of more than 50%. Besides the comparability reason, our

---

[3] In certain cities, a few additional industries were included because of the inability to sample a sufficient number of firms.

[4] For manufacturing (service) firms, the minimum number of employees is 20 (15). When there were not sufficient firms from a particular sector in a city, the size constraint was loosened.

R. Cull, L.C. Xu / Journal of Financial Economics 77 (2005) 117–146   125

narrower focus is also shaped by our concerns that the behavior of state and private firms differs greatly. For instance, access to bank loans by state enterprises could be much more reflective of a soft budget constraint than loans for private firms (Cull and Xu, 2000, 2003). Government officials could harass state enterprises in a different manner and amount relative to private firms, and the impact could differ.

For our purposes, the key survey questions deal with firm managers' perceptions about the security of property rights. Following Acemoglu and Johnson (2003), we separate the property rights variables into two groups: those that measure the risk of government expropriation and those that measure the ease and reliability of contract enforcement. We also designed our property rights questions to mimic those used by JMW. See the appendix for a comparison.

The first expropriation variable measures the extent to which the government acts as a helping instead of a grabbing hand. It is the manager's response to: "Among the government officials that your firm regularly interacts with, what is the share (0–100) of that interaction that is oriented toward helping rather than hindering firms?" The mean response is 35, with a standard deviation of 31. Therefore, substantial disagreement exists about the general tendency for government officials to help firms. The second expropriation variable is the manager's estimate of informal payments to government regulators divided by total sales. Most responses tended toward zero so that the mean is only 0.2%, but the standard deviation is 1.6 percentage points. To the extent that it measures the likelihood and severity of government expropriation and can thus be viewed as an additional tax (Bardhan, 1997), this variable should be negatively associated with profit reinvestment.

Three variables measure the ease and reliability of contract enforcement. The first is the manager's response to: "On a scale of 0–100%, what is the likelihood that the legal system will uphold your contract and property rights in business disputes?" Responses range from zero to 100, with a mean of 62, and a standard deviation of 39. A second variable is a dummy equal to one if a firm has signed a formal contract with a client. Because a firm would sign a contract only if it expected that it had some chance of being protected in case of dispute, we expect those that do so to have greater faith in the contract enforcement system. However, because 91% of firms report some formal contracting (see Table 2), this variable might not explain substantial variation in reinvestment rates. The third contract enforcement variable measures owners' perceptions of the ability of courts to resolve payment disputes. It is the actual percentage of disputes over payment that were resolved by court action (as reported by the manager). Its average value is 7%, with a standard deviation of 23%. As with the other two proxies for contract enforcement, we hypothesize that higher values are a reflection of greater faith in the enforcement of contracts and thus should be positively associated with reinvestment.

One might expect little variation in survey responses in a relatively authoritarian country such as China. However, the means and standard deviations reported in Table 2 indicate a large variation in the responses regarding property rights. Moreover, the sample statistics mask substantial variation across cities (see Table 3). In cities such as Changsha, Chongqing, Hangzhou, and Jiangmen, respondents indicate that roughly half of government officials' contact with firms was a help, not

Table 2
Summary statistics of main variables

Only firms with positive profits enter the reinvestment regressions and summary statistics. Firm-level observations are calculated by averaging each firm's responses from 2000 to 2002. Reinvestment is the firm manager's assessment of the percentage of profits that were reinvested in the firm in the last year. Percent private ownership is the percentage of total shares held by private interests. Dummy: access to bank loan equals one if the firm has at least one loan from a bank. Share of input purchased via trade credit is the percentage reported by the manager. Collateral as percent value of loan is the manager's assessment of the collateral required on a typical loan, expressed as a percentage of the loan's face value. Percent total sales spent on informal payments to government officials is also reported by the manager. Percent disputes resolved via court is the manager's assessment of the share of the firm's business disputes that are resolved in the courts. Dummy: sign formal contract equals one if the firm has signed at least one formal contract with a client. Likelihood of upholding contract is the manager's response to: "On a scale of 0–100, what is the likelihood that the legal system will uphold your contracts and property rights in business disputes?" Government officials help instead of hinder firms is the manager's response to: "Among government officials that your firm regularly interacts with, what share of their contact is oriented toward helping rather than hindering firms?" Profit/sales is the ratio of current profits to current sales. Chief executive officer (CEO) schooling is the years of formal education for the current CEO. CEO tenure is the years that the current CEO has held that post in this firm. Dummy: deputy CEO equals one if the current CEO was the deputy CEO at that firm prior to becoming CEO. Dummy: government official equals one if the current CEO was a government official just prior to becoming CEO at that firm. Percent growth in employment is relative to employment one year prior. It is calculated from the yearly employment figures. Total factor productivity is calculated by estimating a fixed-effects output production function (that is regressing the constant value of output onto the constant value of capital stock, of material inputs, and labor), allowing for industry-specific coefficients for each variable including the constant. The residual including the fixed effect is the total factor productivity.

Variable	Number of firms	Mean	Standard deviation	Minimum	Maximum
Reinvestment	705	0.27	0.37	0.00	1.00
Percent private ownership	760	0.96	0.12	0.50	1.00
log(city population)	727	6.38	0.55	5.05	8.04
log(GDP per capita), in 2000 yuan	727	9.48	0.37	8.55	10.74
log(number of employees)	760	4.32	1.30	0.00	9.37
log(firm age)	760	1.82	0.76	0.00	3.96
Dummy: access to bank loan	760	0.28	0.35	0.00	1.00
Share of input purchased via trade credit	710	0.09	0.20	0.00	1.00
Collateral as percent value of loan	758	0.25	0.44	0.00	3.00
Percent total sales spent on informal payments to government officials	760	0.002	0.02	0.00	0.49
Percent disputes resolved via court	743	0.07	0.23	0.00	1.00
Dummy: sign formal contract	754	0.91	0.29	0.00	1.00
Likelihood of upholding contract	671	0.62	0.39	0.00	1.00
Government officials help instead of hinder firms	731	0.35	0.31	0.00	1.00
CEO schooling	758	14.35	2.75	0.00	18.00
CEO tenure	760	6.56	4.22	0.50	29.00
Dummy: deputy CEO before becoming CEO	755	0.36	0.48	0.00	1.00
Dummy: was a government official before becoming CEO	755	0.06	0.24	0.00	1.00
Total factor productivity	648	0.14	1.57	−3.18	4.73
Percent employment growth	725	0.16	0.30	−0.46	2.56
Profit/sales	759	0.07	0.11	0.00	1.53

R. Cull, L.C. Xu / Journal of Financial Economics 77 (2005) 117–146   127

Table 3
Property rights protection and contract enforcement across 18 cities

City	Risk of expropriation by government		Ease and reliability of contract enforcement		
	To what extent do government officials that you regularly have contact with help rather than hinder firms? (scaled 0–1)	Share of total sales spent on informal payments to government officials	What percentage of your business disputes have been resolved by court action?	Percent of firms that have signed at least one formal contract with a client	On a scale of 0–1, what is the likelihood that the legal system would uphold your contracts and property rights in business disputes?
Northeast					
Benxi	0.289	0.0002	0.069	0.706	0.679
Changchun	0.449	0.0001	0.036	0.967	0.691
Dalian	0.283	0.0001	0.001	0.939	0.554
Haerbin	0.398	0.0042	0.124	0.951	0.577
Coastal					
Hangzhou	0.574	0.0001	0.208	0.944	0.743
Jiangmen	0.449	0.0002	0.093	1.000	0.531
Shenzhen	0.346	0.0098	0.190	0.861	0.661
Wenzhou	0.202	0.0001	0.045	0.897	0.402
Central					
Changsha	0.455	0.0007	0.039	0.917	0.620
Nanchang	0.415	0.0004	0.097	0.985	0.815
Wuhan	0.343	0.0001	0.021	1.000	0.605
Zhengzhou	0.435	0.0001	0.049	0.731	0.825
Northwest					
Lanzhou	0.246	0.0002	0.051	0.884	0.511
Xian	0.212	0.0138	0.014	0.950	0.428
Southwest					
Chongqing	0.453	0.0043	0.123	0.917	0.883
Guiyang	0.222	0.0004	0.030	0.927	0.408
Kunming	0.325	0.0001	0.054	0.791	0.702
Nanning	0.279	0.0000	0.139	0.949	0.558

a hindrance, while for cities such as Guiyang, Wenzhou, and Xian, that figure was only about 20%. The percentage of sales used for informal payments to government officials shows similar variation, with respondents from cities such as Changsha, Dalian, Hangzhou, Jiangmen, Kunming, Nanning, Wenzhou, Wuhan, and Zhengzhou reporting almost no such payments, while those from Shenzhen and Xian reported that such payments composed roughly 1% of sales.

Substantial variation across cities also exists regarding the ease and reliability of contract enforcement. Managers of private firms from Hangzhou, for instance,

128   *R. Cull, L.C. Xu / Journal of Financial Economics 77 (2005) 117–146*

resolve 21% of their disputes via the court system, yet the percentage is only 0.1% for Dalian. The likelihood of upholding contract and property rights also varies across cities. Chongqing leads with an average response of 88%, which is more than twice the figure for the last-place city on this dimension, Wenzhou. Finally, the share of firms that have signed at least one formal contract with a client is 100% for Jiangmen and Wuhan, which is 40% higher than Benxi at 71%.

One might be concerned that the variation in survey responses is not an indication of true underlying variation in the security of property rights, but merely that survey respondents' perceptions differ. We argue that the responses reflect differences in the security of property rights for three reasons. First, the institutions associated with contract enforcement, in particular the legal system, vary in their effectiveness across regions in a country as vast as China. Second, a firm's relations with the state likely depend upon its size, the political importance of its sector, and, for firms with a high share of state ownership, the level of government responsible for its oversight. These differences are especially likely to affect the level of informal payments required by regulators. Third, respondents' knowledge about the security of property rights is dictated by the nature of their business, which varies across sectors. Those that engage in long-term contracts are likely keenly aware of the security of those agreements.

Firms also vary in their responses to financial questions (Table 2). With respect to external finance, 28% of our private firms have access to bank loans. In addition, the typical firm purchases 9% of its inputs with trade credit, although the standard deviation of that average is 20%, with some firms financing all input purchases in this manner. Firms also vary in the amount of collateral they are required to provide to secure loans. The average private firm posts 25 cents of collateral per dollar borrowed, but the standard deviation is 44 cents.

Table 4 indicates that access to finance also differs greatly across cities. For example, almost 58% of private firms in Wenzhou have access to loans, which is more than nine times higher than firms in Benxi. The difference in access to trade credit is also striking. Firms in Hangzhou buy 19% of their inputs via trade credit, seven times more than firms in Changsha. On average, firms in Chongqing provide 39 cents in collateral for every dollar that they borrow, while in Lanzhou they provide only five. In short, our sample contains rich variation in both perceptions about the security of property rights and access to finance, and that variation appears to have a strong city-specific component to it.

Our sample has at least two other notable features. First, the average ratio of profits to sales for our private firms is 7.5%, which is lower than the averages for the private firms in most of the JMW sample: 21% for firms in Russia, 18% in Ukraine, 13% in Romania, 10% in Poland, and 6% in Slovakia. This feature of our sample is relevant because, lacking internal funds, firms in more competitive industries might have greater need of external funds to finance investment.

Second, the correlations between our property rights variables and financial variables tend to be low (Table 5). As JMW note, high correlations could be a sign that measures of insecure property rights are proxying for a lack of access to finance. The correlations between access to bank loans (the key financial variable in our

R. Cull, L.C. Xu / Journal of Financial Economics 77 (2005) 117–146   129

Table 4
Access to finance across 18 cities

Share of firms with access to loans is the city-level average of a dummy variable that equals one if the firm has at least one loan from a bank. Share of input purchased via trade credit is the percentage reported by the manager. Collateral as percent value of loan amount is the manager's assessment of the collateral required on a typical loan, expressed as a percentage of the loan's face value.

City	Share of firms with access to loans	Share of input purchased via trade credit	Collateral as percent value of loan
Northeast			
Benxi	0.057	0.045	0.168
Changchun	0.172	0.146	0.275
Dalian	0.143	0.109	0.289
Haerbin	0.157	0.039	0.244
Coastal			
Hangzhou	0.486	0.188	0.376
Jiangmen	0.325	0.131	0.081
Shenzhen	0.139	0.088	0.158
Wenzhou	0.580	0.069	0.265
Central			
Changsha	0.364	0.026	0.240
Nanchang	0.323	0.042	0.369
Wuhan	0.152	0.030	0.250
Zhengzhou	0.203	0.108	0.194
Northwest			
Lanzhou	0.136	0.094	0.048
Xian	0.339	0.134	0.326
Southwest			
Chongqing	0.348	0.179	0.388
Guiyang	0.450	0.033	0.320
Kunming	0.338	0.032	0.391
Nanning	0.124	0.120	0.223

analysis) and the expropriation risk variables are insignificant. The correlation between the access to bank finance and the two contracting variables (the percentage of disputes resolved via courts and the dummy for the existence of a formal contract with a client) are either insignificant or significant but small in magnitude. The pattern of correlations is similar to that found in the JMW sample. This suggests that the property rights and financial variables capture different sources of variation, and thus including both in profit reinvestment regressions is reasonable.

4. Hypotheses

We test whether access to external finance or property rights better explains firms' investment decisions. We control also for firm characteristics, ownership structure,

130 R. Cull, L.C. Xu / Journal of Financial Economics 77 (2005) 117–146

Table 5
The correlation coefficients for key variables

Percent disputes resolved via court is the manager's assessment of the share of the firm's business disputes that are resolved in the courts. Dummy: sign formal contract equals one if the firm has signed at least one formal contract with a client. Likelihood of upholding contract is the manager's response to: "On a scale of 0–100, what is the likelihood that the legal system will uphold your contracts and property rights in business disputes?" Government officials help instead of hinder firms is the manager's response to: "Among government officials that your firm regularly interacts with, what share of their contact is oriented toward helping rather than hindering firms?" Percent total sales spent on informal payments to government officials is reported by the manager. Dummy: access to bank loan equals one if the firm has at least one loan from a bank. Share of input purchased via trade credit is the percentage reported by the manager. Collateral as percent value of loan is the manager's assessment of the collateral required on a typical loan, expressed as a percentage of the loan's face value.

Variable	Percent disputes resolved via the court	Dummy: sign formal contract	Likelihood of upholding contract	Government officials help firms	Percent sales on informal payments to government officials	Dummy: access to bank loans	Percent inputs purchased via trade credit
Contract enforcement							
Dummy: sign formal contract							
Correlation coefficient	0.026						
p-value for the null that the correlation is zero	0.486						
Number of observations	737						
Likelihood of upholding contract							
Correlation coefficient	0.039	0.025					
p-value for the null that the correlation is zero	0.314	0.517					
Number of observations	659	665					
Risk of expropriation							
Government officials help rather than hinder firms							

(continued overleaf)

	(1)	(2)	(3)	(4)	(5)	(6)	(7)
Correlation coefficient	−0.049	0.041	0.320				
p-value for the null that the correlation is zero	0.190	0.266	0.000				
Number of observations	716	725	662				
Percent total sales spent on informal payments to government officials							
Correlation coefficient	0.012	0.022	0.032	0.049			
p-value for the null that the correlation is zero	0.737	0.532	0.408	0.182			
Number of observations	743	743	671	731			
Financial							
Dummy: access to bank loan							
Correlation coefficient	0.092	0.048	−0.051	0.025	0.044		
p-value for the null that the correlation is zero	0.011	0.186	0.184	0.499	0.230		
Number of observations	743	754	671	731	760		
Share of input purchased via trade credit							
Correlation coefficient	0.019	−0.009	0.015	0.034	−0.016	0.068	
p-value for the null that the correlation is zero	0.616	0.798	0.698	0.364	0.662	0.067	
Number of observations	695	706	637	686	710	710	
Collateral as percent value of loan							
Correlation coefficient	0.069	0.018	0.071	0.067	−0.008	0.388	0.022
p-value for the null that the correlation is zero	0.056	0.619	0.065	0.068	0.821	0.000	0.546
Number of observations	742	752	669	729	758	758	709

132   *R. Cull, L.C. Xu / Journal of Financial Economics 77 (2005) 117–146*

and industry affiliation using the following reduced form equation

$$REINVESTMENT_{it} = \alpha + \beta'_1 \, FIRM_{it} + \beta'_2 \, CITY_{it} + \beta_3 \, PRIVATE_i$$
$$+ \beta'_4 \, EXPROPRIATION_i + \beta'_5 \, CONTRACT_i$$
$$+ \beta_6 \, BANK_{it-1} + \beta'_7 \, FINANCIAL_i + \varepsilon_{it}. \qquad (5)$$

For firm i in year t, *REINVESTMENT* is its profit reinvestment rate as reported by the firm manager. *FIRM* is a vector of control variables, composed of the log of the number of employees and the log of firm age. Large firms, those with more employees, are likely to have different investment needs than smaller ones, and size therefore should be controlled for. Older firms are likely to require less investment, because any investments to exploit scale economies were likely to have occurred in the past, and upgrading their dated technology is more difficult and thus less likely. Additional control variables are subsumed within *CITY*, a vector that includes the log of the level of city GDP per capita (measured in 2000 yuan) and the log of city population.

The variables of interest are those related to property rights and access to finance. Our variables capture two separate aspects of property rights. The first, expropriation risk (denoted by the vector *EXPROPRIATION*), is captured by the two variables described in Section 3, informal payments to government officials as a share of total sales and the manager's assessment of whether government officials tend to be a help or a hindrance in their regular interactions with firms. In the profit reinvestment regressions, we expect the share of informal payments to have a negative sign, while the manager's assessment of government officials' helpfulness should have a positive one.

Our proxies for contract enforcement are the three variables described in previous Section 3 (denoted *CONTRACT*): the firm manager's belief that the legal system will uphold his property rights in a dispute (scaled from 0 to 100), the percentage of commercial disputes the firm resolves via the courts, and a dummy variable indicating whether the firm has signed at least one formal contract with a client. For the reasons laid out in Section 2, we expect that reinvestment is positively associated with the contract enforcement variables.

We also argue that ownership structure is itself a measure of the security of property rights. Direct state ownership is often associated with the pursuit of political objectives at the expense of other stakeholders in the firm. The control rights of the manager and other owners are often weakened to achieve social objectives or to provide private benefits to politicians and bureaucrats. (See Shleifer (1998) and Megginson and Netter (2001) for excellent summaries of theories and evidence on the impact of ownership structure on performance.) A higher share of private ownership implies that the owner or manager of a firm can have greater confidence in being shielded from government interference, and therefore a higher expected return on investment. We thus expect a positive relationship between private ownership and reinvestment rates. In Eq. (5), the percentage of private ownership is denoted as *PRIVATE*.

We include separate variables for access to bank loans and additional aspects of access to external finance. The key variable is *BANK*, a dummy equal to one if the

R. Cull, L.C. Xu / Journal of Financial Economics 77 (2005) 117–146   133

firm has access to loans from domestic banks, which are almost all state-owned in China. (See Lardy (1998) and Cull and Xu (2000, 2003) for a breakdown of the assets of the Chinese banking sector by type of ownership.) If investment is lumpy as described in Section 2 or the pecking order hypothesis regarding the relative price of internal and external funds does not hold, access to bank loans could be positively associated with reinvestment. If neither of those hypotheses is true, we expect *BANK* to be insignificant. Because current access to bank loans and reinvestment could both be determined by investment demand, we follow JMW and control for past access to bank loans, in particular whether the firm had access to bank loans in the previous three years.

FINANCE is a vector containing two variables, one that measures access to alternative sources of external finance, another measuring the terms on which bank loans are secured by the firm. The first is the percentage of inputs bought with trade credit. Some observers of the Chinese economy suggest that trade credit is an indirect means of channeling bank loans to profitable firms. State-owned enterprises obtain loans from state banks, then relend them to their trading partners that lack access to funds. If the relending hypothesis is correct, the trade credit variable provides an indication of trading partners' willingness to supply funds to the firm. As with *BANK*, the sign on trade credit depends on whether that source of funds is a substitute or a complement for internal funds.

As an indication of banks' willingness to lend to a firm, we include the manager's estimate of the collateral required on a typical loan, expressed as a percentage of its face value. Higher collateral requirements indicate that banks are less willing to supply funds, thus making it more difficult to finance investment through bank loans. Because this could necessitate greater reliance on internal funds to finance investment, we expect that the collateral variable could be positively associated with the rate of profit reinvestment. Ideally we would like to include financial variables in our reinvestment regressions that are correlated with access to external funds but that are uncorrelated, or weakly correlated, with investment demand. Because the trade credit and the collateral variables capture the willingness to supply funds to the firm, these seem like good candidates. The bank loan dummy variable is more susceptible to criticism on these grounds, but we offer a series of robustness checks to address this potential problem.

We also experimented with variables such as the percentage of loans in foreign currency, a dummy variable indicating whether the firm has an overdraft facility (which can serve as a sort of line of credit), and the number of banks that have extended loans to the firm. None of these was significant in the reinvestment regressions, and thus we drop them from the results that follow.

5. Base results

Table 6 presents the basic results. Again, the sample for the reinvestment equations includes only those private firms with positive profits. Because we have multiple observations from each firm, our panel regressions on the left hand side of

Table 6 allow for clustering at the firm level to obtain correct standard errors. On the right-hand side of Table 6, we offer collapsed cross-sectional regressions in which a firm's average value for each variable enters the regression. Thus, there is one observation per firm in the cross-sectional regressions. The shortcoming of using the collapsed version is that we sacrifice some time-variant information.

Although the correlations in Table 5 indicate that mulitcollinearity between the property rights and financial variables is not a major problem, we present regressions in which each group of variables enters separately to demonstrate that our main results are robust to alternative specifications.[5] Because the share of private ownership is conventionally controlled for in these types of regressions and is less subject to multicollinearity problems, it is included in all specifications. However, our main results hold whether or not that variable is included.

Our results for property rights and profit reinvestment corroborate those in JMW. Given China's stage of development, this might come as a surprise to some. It also suggests that China's development pattern is not inherently different from other transition economies, at least not in every respect. As in JMW, the variables related to contract enforcement are typically of the hypothesized signs and often significantly associated with reinvestment. The proxy for reliance on courts is positive and significant. A one standard deviation increase on that measure (0.24) is associated with a 4 percentage point increase in the rate of profit reinvestment. This is large considering that the average reinvestment rate is 27%.

The effects of signing a formal contract with a client appear to be even larger. Those firms that did so had reinvestment rates 8–13 percentage points higher than those that did not. The significance of that result is slightly stronger in the clustered regressions than in the cross-sectional regressions. Finally, owners who express greater faith that their rights would be protected by the legal system also reinvest more than others, although the coefficient is small and insignificant.

The variables related to risk of government expropriation are also of the hypothesized signs, although the manager's assessment of the helpfulness of government officials is significant while the share of sales devoted to informal payments is not. A one standard deviation increase in government helpfulness (31 percentage points) is associated with a 3 percentage point increase in the rate of profit reinvestment. Although the payments variable is insignificant in the base results, it achieves significance in some of the robustness checks that follow. However, its magnitude is relatively small. A one standard deviation on that measure implies an increase in reinvestment of less than half a percentage point. In short, proxies for both the risk of expropriation and the ease and reliability of contract

---

[5]We also ran regressions that we do not report in which the property rights variables enter the regression one at a time. Qualitative results are similar to those in Table 6, except that the manager's perception of whether contracts and property rights would be upheld is significant.

R. Cull, L.C. Xu / Journal of Financial Economics 77 (2005) 117–146   135

enforcement are significant predictors of reinvestment rates, and some appear to be economically important.

Ownership structure also appears to have a strong effect on profit reinvestment. The share of private ownership, which we argue is a fundamental reflection of the security of property rights, is positive and significant, and its magnitude indicates that it is economically important. A one standard deviation increase in private ownership (0.12) for private firms is associated with an increase in the reinvestment rate by 2.4–3.6 percentage points, depending on the specification. Clearly the implied magnitude would be much larger if we use the standard deviation of the sample of both private and state firms.

Unlike JMW, we find that access to bank loans is positively and often significantly associated with the rate of profit reinvestment in both the clustered and cross-sectional regressions. Those firms with a loan had reinvestment rates 4–10 percentage points higher than those that did not. The result is consistent with the conjecture that as transition progresses and competition increases, the complexity of transactions also increases. Supporting institutions, including financial ones, become increasingly important for firm growth. Interpreting the bank loan coefficient and assessing its validity are one focus of our robustness checks. This result appears to undercut the pecking-order hypothesis described in Section 2, either because the price of internal funds is not lower than that of external funds or perhaps because investment is lumpy and requires both internal and external funds to be undertaken. The collateral variable is positive and generally significant, suggesting that firms that are required to post more collateral are more reliant on internal funds for investment. The trade credit variable is also positive, but generally statistically insignificant. The positive sign for trade credit indicates perhaps that type of finance is a complement to internal funds, but the large standard error warns against a strong conclusion. None of the city-level or firm-level controls is significant across multiple specifications. Most are never significant. However, some weak indications are that the reinvestment rate is higher in larger and younger firms.

6. Robustness checks

To test the robustness of our base results, we re-run our regressions on sub-samples of our firms based on size. We also perform median regressions to confront outliers, control for characteristics of CEOs in our base regressions, and offer additional tests of whether bank loans are being directed to better performing firms.

6.1. JMW equivalent sample

Although our results are substantially similar to those for the transition economies studied by JMW, some differences exist, and these might be attributable to the nature of our respective samples. Our sample contains firms that are notably larger

Table 6
Determinants of reinvestment

Standard errors are in parentheses. *, **, and *** represent statistical significance at the 10%, 5% and 1% percent level respectively. All models estimated via ordinary least squares. Standard errors in full sample models (1–5) allow for clustering at the firm level. Collapsed sample models (6–10) allow one observation per firm. For a firm with multiple observations, its average value for each variable enters the regressions. Percent private ownership is the percentage of total shares held by private interests. Dummy: access to bank loan equals one if the firm has at least one loan from a bank. Share of input purchased via trade credit is the percentage reported by the manager. Collateral as percent value of loan is the manager's assessment of the collateral required on a typical loan, expressed as a percentage of the loan's face value. Percent total sales spent on informal payments to government officials is also reported by the manager. Government officials help instead of hinder firms is the manager's response to: "Among government officials that your firm regularly interacts with, what share of their contact is oriented toward helping rather than hindering firms?" Percent disputes resolved via court is the manager's assessment of the share of the firm's business disputes that are resolved in the courts. Dummy: sign formal contract equals one if the firm has signed at least one formal contract with a client. Likelihood of upholding contract is the manager's response to: "On a scale of 0–100, what is the likelihood that the legal system will uphold your contracts and property rights in business disputes?" GDP is gross domestic product.

Variables	Full sample: standard errors clustered at firm level					Collapsed sample: one observation per firm				
	(1)	(2)	(3)	(4)	(5)	(6)	(7)	(8)	(9)	(10)
Percent private ownership	0.238 (0.112)**	0.185 (0.114)	0.291 (0.122)**	0.272 (0.123)**	0.300 (0.122)**	0.283 (0.120)**	0.214 (0.123)*	0.311 (0.133)**	0.294 (0.138)**	0.319 (0.139)**
Financial										
Dummy: access to bank loan	0.039 (0.024)		0.046 (0.026)*		0.047 (0.027)*	0.046 (0.043)		0.083 (0.049)*		0.099 (0.051)*
Share inputs purchased via trade credit	0.111 (0.077)		0.051 (0.086)		0.077 (0.089)	0.122 (0.073)*		0.036 (0.081)		0.083 (0.084)
Collateral as percent value of loan	0.092 (0.034)***		0.074 (0.036)**		0.081 (0.038)**	0.100 (0.034)***		0.054 (0.037)		0.065 (0.039)*
Property rights government expropriation										
Percent sales spent on informal payments		-0.142 (0.503)		-0.095 (0.402)	-0.086 (0.431)		-0.242 (0.657)		-0.087 (0.660)	-0.093 (0.673)

(continued overleaf)

R. Cull, L.C. Xu / Journal of Financial Economics 77 (2005) 117–146   137

	(1)	(2)	(3)	(4)	(5)	(6)	(7)	(8)	(9)	(10)
Government officials help instead of hinder firms	0.106 (0.052)**			0.095 (0.056)*	0.110 (0.058)*	0.116 (0.050)**			0.113 (0.054)**	0.126 (0.055)**
Contract enforcement										
Percent disputes resolved via courts		0.171 (0.073)**		0.156 (0.078)**	0.159 (0.082)*		0.152 (0.065)**		0.142 (0.078)*	0.144 (0.079)*
Dummy: sign formal contract		0.102 (0.044)**		0.121 (0.050)**	0.126 (0.050)**		0.079 (0.052)		0.097 (0.057)*	0.099 (0.058)
Likelihood of upholding contract		0.014 (0.040)		0.022 (0.044)	0.022 (0.045)		0.017 (0.039)		0.019 (0.043)	0.024 (0.044)
Other controls										
log(city population)			0.004 (0.034)	0.018 (0.034)	-0.002 (0.036)			0.015 (0.035)	0.026 (0.035)	0.004 (0.036)
log(gdp per capita), in 2000 yuan			0.009 (0.047)	0.014 (0.048)	0.015 (0.050)			0.014 (0.047)	0.021 (0.051)	0.021 (0.052)
log(number of employees)			0.026 (0.014)*	0.020 (0.014)	0.008 (0.015)			0.022 (0.015)	0.020 (0.015)	0.004 (0.016)
log(firm age)			-0.041 (0.023)*	-0.031 (0.024)	-0.029 (0.024)			-0.036 (0.023)	-0.029 (0.023)	-0.024 (0.024)
Number of observations	2,072	1,913	1,493	1,359	1,312	660	608	590	537	514
R^2	0.03	0.03	0.05	0.08	0.09	0.03	0.03	0.06	0.08	0.10

than those sampled by JMW, and somewhat less profitable. In columns 1 and 2 of Table 7, we present results for Chinese firms with 270 or fewer employees, which was the maximum value in the JMW sample. This reduces the number of active observations by about one-fifth, but the results are similar to the base results. There are two exceptions.

First, the informal payments variable is now significant in the clustered regressions, although it continues to be insignificant in the cross-sectional regression. The magnitudes across the two specifications are similar, implying a decrease in the reinvestment rate by roughly 1 percentage point with a one standard deviation increase in informal payment. Second, access to bank loans is now no longer statistically significant. This is especially interesting because the result is the same as in the JMW paper. Thus part of the reason for our earlier discovery of a significant effect of the banking variable could be attributable to the differences in samples with JMW.

6.2. Outliers

The summary statistics in Table 2 make clear that extreme observations are possible for a number of our variables. To test whether those observations are driving our results, we run median regressions, which tends to decrease the influence of extreme observations relative to ordinary least squares. Our results (columns 3 and 4) become somewhat stronger, with the same qualitative conclusions. The finance variables, for instance, are all significant now. These results suggest that outliers have a dampening effect on our base results.

6.3. Firm size: split-sample tests

To test whether the relations between property rights, access to finance, and investment are different for firms of different sizes, we split the sample in half based on the number of employees (columns 5–8, Table 7). Small firms, those below the sample median in employees, appear to be more fearful of expropriation than large firms. Unlike in the base results, the informal payments variable is significant at the 1% level in the clustered regression (column 7). For small firms, the government helpfulness measure increases in significance to the 5% level in the cross-sectional regression. By contrast, neither of the expropriation proxies is significant for large firms in either the clustered or the cross-sectional regression.

Regarding contract enforcement, the percentage of disputes resolved via courts is positive and significant for large firms in the pooled regressions, but not small ones. This suggests, perhaps, that firms need to be of a certain size to make use of the formal judicial system. The dummy for a formal contract is significant only for small firms. This could be because nearly all large firms have signed at least one contract, and thus that variable cannot explain variation in their reinvestment rates. Moreover, access to bank loans is significant only for small firms. This could be because large firms have access to alternative sources of finance and are therefore less

R. Cull, L.C. Xu / Journal of Financial Economics 77 (2005) 117–146   139

reliant on bank loans. Both types of firms might face lumpy investment opportunities, but only the small ones are absolutely dependent on some bank finance to undertake projects. Finally, the collateral variable is significant only for small firms. This is another indication that small firms are more subject to financial constraints. Taken together, these results suggest that the profit reinvestment decisions of small firms are more sensitive to potential expropriation and access to external funds than those of larger firms.

6.4. CEO characteristics

JMW offer robustness checks that control for entrepreneur characteristics, to confront the possibility that higher reinvestment rates and more secure property rights both reflect the optimism of the responding manager. We do the same using four variables that summarize the experience of each firm's chief executive officer (CEO): his years of schooling, tenure with the firm as CEO, and dummies to indicate whether he was the firm's deputy CEO prior to becoming CEO and whether he was a government official prior to becoming CEO. None of those variables is significant when added to our base specification. The qualitative results for the property rights variables and access to bank loans are the same as in the base results (see columns 9 and 10, Table 7).

6.5. Determinants of access to loans

We find that access to bank loans by private firms was positively and significantly related to reinvestment rates and suggest that this finding is consistent with the notion that improvement in market-supporting (financial) institutions might be important as transition drags along. Yet the conclusion rests on an important premise: The Chinese banking sector has to perform reasonably well for private firms before the importance of the financial sector can be highlighted as a market-supporting institution.

We now provide evidence that the Chinese banking sector is working reasonably well for the private firms. Table 8 offers models of the determinants of access to bank loans. In column 1, we include three measures of firm performance (total factor productivity; employment growth; and profitability, i.e., the ratio of profit to sales) and the control variables from the reinvestment specifications. All three measures of firm performance are positively associated with access to bank loans and the productivity and employment variables are significant at the 10% and 1% level, respectively. Thus the Chinese banks tend to allocate funds to firms with better performance.

This is not to say that all lending by China's state banks to private firms is based solely on economic criteria. When we regress access to bank loans on the property rights variables (column 2), both informal payments and government helpfulness are positive and significant, suggesting perhaps that firms with close relationships with the government also are more likely to receive loans from state

140   R. Cull, L.C. Xu / Journal of Financial Economics 77 (2005) 117–146

Table 7
Determinants of reinvestment, robustness checks

Standard errors are in parentheses. *, **, and *** represent statistical significance at the 10%, 5% and 1% level, respectively. All models estimated via ordinary least squares, except for models 3 and 4, which are estimated via median regressions. Standard errors in clustered models (1, 3, 5, 7, 9) allow for clustering at the firm level. Collapsed sample models (2, 4, 6, 8, 10) allow one observation per firm. For a firm with multiple observations, its average value for each variable enters the regressions. Control variables include log(city population), log(gdp per capita), log(number of employees), and log(firm age). GDP is gross domestic product. Percent private ownership is the percentage of total shares held by private interests. Dummy: access to bank loan equals one if the firm has at least one loan from a bank. Share of input purchased via trade credit is the percentage value of loan. Collateral as percent value of loan is the manager's assessment of the collateral required on a typical loan, expressed as a percentage of the loan's face value. Percent total sales spent on informal payments to government officials is also reported by the manager. Government officials help instead of hinder firms is the manager's response to: "Among government officials that your firm regularly interacts with, what share of their contact is oriented toward helping rather than hindering firms?" Percent disputes resolved via court is the manager's assessment of the share of the firm's business disputes that are resolved in the courts. Dummy: sign formal contract equals one if the firm has signed at least one formal contract with a client. Likelihood of upholding contract is the manager's response to: "On a scale of 0–100, what is the likelihood that the legal system will uphold your contracts and property rights in business disputes?" In models 9 and 10, four variables are included to describe chief executive officer (CEO) characteristics: CEO schooling, CEO tenure, a deputy CEO dummy variable, and a former government official dummy variable. CEO schooling is the years of formal education for the current CEO. CEO tenure is the years that the current CEO has held that post in this firm. Dummy: deputy CEO equals one if the current CEO was the deputy CEO at that firm prior to becoming CEO. Dummy: government official equals one if the current CEO was a government official just prior to becoming CEO at that firm. JMW is Johnson et al. (2002).

Variable	JMW sample		Median regressions		Large firms		Small firms		Include CEO characteristics	
	Clustered	Collapsed	Clustered	Collapsed	Clustered	Collapsed	Clustered	Collapsed	Clustered	Collapsed
	(1)	(2)	(3)	(4)	(5)	(6)	(7)	(8)	(9)	(10)
Percent private ownership	0.432	0.467	0.184	0.207	0.280	0.364	0.415	0.303	0.243	0.278
	(0.145)***	(0.190)**	(0.031)***	(0.100)**	(0.146)*	(0.167)**	(0.195)**	(0.304)	(0.126)*	(0.143)*
Financial										
Dummy: access to bank loan	0.028	0.094	0.036	0.075	0.034	0.024	0.050	0.148	0.048	0.104
	(0.033)	(0.057)	(0.008)***	(0.036)**	(0.034)	(0.071)	(0.043)	(0.078)*	(0.027)*	(0.051)**
Share inputs purchased via trade credit	0.051	0.051	0.114	0.106	0.006	0.093	0.226	0.111	0.080	0.086
	(0.113)	(0.104)	(0.019)***	(0.058)*	(0.099)	(0.105)	(0.164)	(0.151)	(0.089)	(0.084)

(continued overleaf)

R. Cull, L.C. Xu / Journal of Financial Economics 77 (2005) 117–146   141

	(1)	(2)	(3)	(4)	(5)	(6)	(7)	(8)	(9)	(10)
Collateral as percent value of loan	0.121 (0.042)***	0.091 (0.045)**	0.146 (0.009)***	0.105 (0.028)***	0.040 (0.047)	0.034 (0.049)	0.121 (0.063)*	0.133 (0.073)*	0.080 (0.038)**	0.064 (0.039)
Property rights										
Government expropriation										
Percent sales spent on informal payments to govt. officials	−0.424 (0.135)***	−0.450 (0.722)	−0.155 (0.119)	−0.202 (0.229)	3.018 (1.830)	2.958 (1.921)	−0.541 (0.155)***	−0.585 (0.732)	−0.096 (0.409)	−0.137 (0.674)
Government officials help instead of hinder firms	0.101 (0.066)	0.126 (0.062)**	0.165 (0.012)***	0.142 (0.040)***	0.087 (0.075)	0.089 (0.079)	0.146 (0.087)*	0.179 (0.082)**	0.131 (0.058)**	0.148 (0.056)***
Ease of contract enforcement										
Percent disputes resolved via courts	0.227 (0.121)*	0.194 (0.101)*	0.255 (0.018)***	0.218 (0.056)***	0.166 (0.098)*	0.130 (0.093)	0.093 (0.152)	0.170 (0.173)	0.158 (0.081)*	0.144 (0.079)*
Dummy: sign formal contract	0.165 (0.057)***	0.136 (0.064)**	0.055 (0.013)***	0.032 (0.041)	0.115 (0.086)	0.121 (0.099)	0.161 (0.059)***	0.116 (0.076)	0.112 (0.051)**	0.090 (0.058)
Likelihood of upholding contract	0.038 (0.050)	0.042 (0.049)	0.014 (0.010)	0.025 (0.031)	0.030 (0.063)	0.050 (0.066)	0.010 (0.063)	0.005 (0.062)	0.014 (0.045)	0.019 (0.044)
Control variables included?	Yes	Yes	Yes	Yes	Yes	Yes	Yes	Yes	Yes	Yes
CEO characteristics included?	No	No	No	No	No	No	No	No	Yes	Yes
Number of observations	1020	414	1312	514	656	262	656	252	1297	509
R^2	0.11	0.12	0.11		0.12	0.12	0.14	0.15	0.11	0.11

Table 8

Determinants of access to bank loans

Standard errors are in parentheses. *, **, and *** represent statistical significance at the 10%, 5% and 1% level, respectively. All models estimated via ordinary least squares. The dependent variable is the three-year average of the dummy variable that is equal to one if the firm has at least one loan from a bank in the previous three years. Percent growth in employment is relative to the employment one year prior. It is calculated from the yearly employment figures. Total factor productivity is calculated by estimating a fixed-effect output production function (that is, regressing the constant value of output onto the constant value of capital stock, of material inputs, and labor), allowing for industry-specific coefficients for each variable including the constant. The residual including the fixed effect is the total factor productivity. Profit/sales is the ratio of profits over sales. Percent total sales spent on informal payments to government officials are reported by the manager. Government officials help instead of hinder firms is the manager's response to: "Among government officials that your firm regularly interacts with, what share of their contact is oriented toward helping rather than hindering firms?" Percent disputes resolved via court is the manager's assessment of the share of the firm's business disputes that are resolved in the courts. Dummy: sign formal contract equals one if the firm has signed at least one formal contract with a client. Likelihood of upholding contract is the manager's response to: "On a scale of 0–100, what is the likelihood that the legal system will uphold your contracts and property rights in business disputes?" GDP is gross domestic product.

Variable	(1)	(2)	(3)
Performance			
Total factor productivity	0.028		0.037
	$(0.014)^*$		$(0.015)^{**}$
Percent growth in employment	0.161		0.159
	$(0.062)^{***}$		$(0.065)^{**}$
Profits/sales	0.043		0.067
	(0.185)		(0.196)
Control			
log(city population)	−0.099	−0.046	−0.056
	$(0.042)^{**}$	(0.044)	(0.045)
log(gdp per capita), in 2000 yuan	−0.154	−0.079	−0.084
	$(0.057)^{***}$	(0.063)	(0.064)
log(number of employees)	0.108	0.119	0.108
	$(0.017)^{***}$	$(0.018)^{***}$	$(0.019)^{***}$
log(firm age)	−0.022	−0.044	−0.030
	(0.027)	(0.028)	(0.029)
Property rights			
Government expropriation			
Percent sales spent on informal payments		1.124	1.170
to government officials		$(0.294)^{***}$	$(0.237)^{***}$
Government officials help instead of		0.109	0.116
hinder firms		$(0.065)^*$	$(0.066)^*$
Ease of contract enforcement			
Percent disputes resolved via courts		−0.054	−0.066
		(0.092)	(0.093)
Dummy: sign formal contract		0.104	0.073
		(0.068)	(0.069)
Likelihood of upholding contract		−0.196	−0.193
		$(0.052)^{***}$	$(0.054)^{***}$
Number of observations	646	566	547
R^2	0.16	0.17	0.19

R. Cull, L.C. Xu / Journal of Financial Economics 77 (2005) 117–146   143

banks.[6] However, the firm performance variables remain significant when property rights variables are included in the specification (column 3). Because the property rights variables are already included in the reinvestment specifications, the bank loans variable could be capturing lending based on legitimate economic criteria.

7. Conclusions

Our evidence from Chinese firms confirms that secure property rights are a key determinant of profit reinvestment, thus complementing results from European transition countries. Our results further indicate that both the risk of government expropriation and the ease and reliability of contract enforcement affect firms' profit reinvestment decisions. This stands in contrast to cross-country results indicating that risk of expropriation is the more important of these two aspects of property rights in explaining growth. Our speculation is that our regressions are highlighting Chinese firms' adaptation to an imperfect and evolving system of contract enforcement. The cross-country evidence likely summarizes periods long enough to have permitted economic actors to create contracts that compensate for weaknesses in institutions.

In contrast to evidence from other transition countries, profit reinvestment by the firms in our sample is positively associated with access to bank loans. This could be because investment is lumpy in the sense that both internal and external funds are required to undertake investment projects, and because the price of external funds does not always exceed that of internal funds given China's extensive regulation of interest rates. More generally, the result is consistent with the conjecture that, as transition progresses and competition increases, the complexity of transactions also increases. Supporting institutions, including financial ones, become increasingly important for firm growth. Although Chinese banks are rife with incentive problems, especially in their lending to state-owned enterprises, robustness checks indicate that the better performing private firms are more likely to receive loans. This suggests that the loans are supporting valid investment. In addition, access to bank loans appears to affect the reinvestment patterns of small firms more than it does large ones, as do fears of government expropriation. This could be because larger, better established firms have access to more sources of external funds and are better able to protect themselves from expropriation.

Finally, we also find that the share of private ownership has a positive effect on profit reinvestment rates. At this stage of China's transition, expropriation risk, contract enforcement, access to finance, and ownership structure all appear to matter for the investment decisions of firms.

---

[6]Another hypothesis offered by JMW is that less secure property rights encourage entrepreneurs to invest more from bank funds instead of their own profits. They reject that hypothesis because they find no significant link between their index of the insecurity of property rights and the use of bank loans. In our case, the positive sign on the government helpfulness variable would seem to invalidate the hypothesis.

Appendix

Comparison between Johnson, McMillan, Woodruff (JMW, 2002) and Chinese survey questions

	JMW transition countries	China
Expropriation by government	1. Do firms in your industry make extralegal payments for government services? 2. Do firms in your industry make extralegal payments for licenses? 3. Do firms in your industry make payments for protection? 4. Do firms in your industry make unofficial payments for ongoing registration? 5. Do firms in your industry make unofficial payments for fire/sanitary inspection? 6. Do firms in your industry make unofficial payments for tax inspection?	1. What percentage of total sales is spent on informal payments to government officials in any of the following agencies: tax, labor and social security, fire and construction safety, health and infectious disease control, police station, environmental agency, and the standards bureau? 2. Among government officials that your firm regularly interacts with, what share of their contact is oriented toward helping rather than hindering firms?
Contract enforcement	1. Can firms in your industry use courts to enforce an agreement with a customer or supplier?	1. On a scale of 0–100, what is the likelihood that the legal system will uphold your contracts and property rights in business disputes? 2. Has your firm signed at least one formal contract with a client? 3. What is the actual percentage of business disputes that were resolved by court action?

References

Acemoglu, D., Johnson, S., 2003. Unbundling institutions. Unpublished working paper 9934, National Bureau of Economic Research, Cambridge, MA.

Acemoglu, D., Johnson, S., Robinson, J., 2001. The colonial origins of comparative development: an empirical investigation. American Economic Review 91 (5), 1369–1401.

Bai, C.-E., Xu, L.C., 2002. The system of incentives for CEOs with multitasks: theory and evidence from Chinese state-owned enterprises. Mimeo, World Bank, Washington, DC.

Bai, C.-E., Li, D.D., Tao, Z., Wang, Y., 2000. A multi-task theory of the state-enterprise reforms. Journal of Comparative Economics 28 (4), 716–738.

Bardhan, P., 1997. Corruption and development: a review of the issues. Journal of Economic Literature 35 (3), 1320–1346.

Besley, T., 1995. Property rights and investment incentives: theory and evidence from Ghana. Journal of Political Economy 103 (5), 903–937.

Bonin, J., Wachtel, P., 2000. Lessons from bank privatization in Central Europe. In: Rosenblum, H. (Ed.), Bank Privatization: Conference Proceedings of a Policy Research Workshop Held at the World Bank, March 15–16, 1999. Federal Reserve of Dallas, Dallas, TX, pp. 35–51.

Brom, K., Orenstein, M., 1994. The privatized sector in the Czech Republic: government and bank control in a transitional economy. Europe-Asia Studies 46 (6), 893–928.

Capek, A., 1994. The bad debts problem in the Czech economy. Moct-Most 4 (3), 59–70.

Claessens, S., Laeven, L., 2003. Financial development, property rights, and growth. Journal of Finance 58 (6), 2401–2436.

Cull, R., Xu, L.C., 2000. Bureaucrats, state banks, and the efficiency of credit allocation: the experience of Chinese state-owned enterprises. Journal of Comparative Economics 28 (1), 1–31.

Cull, R., Xu, L.C., 2003. Who gets credit? The behavior of bureaucrats and state banks in allocating credit to Chinese state-owned enterprises. Journal of Development Economics 71 (2), 533–559.

Cull, R., Matesova, J., Shirley, M., 2002. Ownership and the temptation to loot: evidence from privatized firms in the Czech Republic. Journal of Comparative Economics 30 (1), 1–24.

Demirguc-Kunt, A., Maksimovic, V., 1998. Law, finance, and firm growth. Journal of Finance 53 (6), 2107–2137.

Desai, R.M., 1996. Reformed banks and corporate governance in the Czech Republic, 1991–1996. Post Soviet Geography and Economics 37 (8), 463–494.

Hrncir, M., 1993. Financial intermediation in former Czechoslavakia: lessons and progress evaluation. Economic Systems 17 (4), 301–327.

Jacoby, H., Li, G., Rozelle, S., 2002. Hazards of expropriation: tenure insecurity and investment in rural China. American Economic Review 92 (5), 1420–1447.

Johnson, S., McMillan, J., Woodruff, C., 2002. Property rights and finance. American Economic Review 92 (5), 1335–1356.

Kaufman, D., Kraay, A., Mastruzzi, M., 2003. Governance matters III: governance indicators for 1996–2002. Policy Research Working Paper 2196, World Bank, Washington, DC.

Knack, S., Keefer, P., 1995. Institutions and economic performance: cross-country test using alternative institutional measures. Economics and Politics 7 (3), 207–228.

La Porta, R., Lopez-de-Silanes, F., Shleifer, A., Vishny, R., 1997. Legal determinants of external finance. Journal of Finance 52 (3), 1131–1150.

La Porta, R., Lopez-de-Silanes, F., Shleifer, A., Vishny, R., 1998. Law and finance. Journal of Political Economy 106 (6), 1113–1155.

La Porta, R., Lopez-de-Silanes, F., Shleifer, A., Vishny, R., 2000. Investor protection and corporate governance. Journal of Financial Economics 58 (1–2), 3–28.

Lardy, N.R., 1998. China's Unfinished Economic Reform. Brookings Institution Press, Washington, DC.

Levine, R., 1997. Financial development and economic growth: views and agenda. Journal of Economic Literature 35 (2), 688–726.

Levine, R., Loayza, N., Beck, T., 2000. Financial intermediation and growth: causality and causes. Journal of Monetary Economics 46 (1), 31–77.

Lin, Y., Zhu, T., 2001. Ownership restructuring in Chinese state industry: an analysis of evidence on initial organizational changes. China Quarterly 166, 305–341.

Mauro, P., 1995. Corruption and growth. Quarterly Journal of Economics 110 (3), 681–712.

McMillan, J., Woodruff, C., 2002. The central role of entrepreneurs in transitional economies. Journal of Economic Perspectives 16 (3), 153–170.

Megginson, W.L., Netter, J.M., 2001. From state to market: a survey of empirical studies on privatization. Journal of Economic Literature 39 (2), 321–389.

Myers, S.C., Majluf, N.S., 1984. Corporate financing and investment decisions when firms have information that investors do not have. Journal of Financial Economics 13 (2), 187–221.

Rajan, R., Zingales, L., 1998. Financial dependence and growth. American Economic Review 88 (3), 559–586.

Shleifer, A., 1998. State versus private ownership. Journal of Economic Perspectives 12 (4), 133–150.

Shleifer, A., Vishny, R.W., 1994. Politicians and firms. Quarterly Journal of Economics 109 (4), 995–1025.

Svensson, J., 1998. Investment, property rights, and political instability: theory and evidence. European Economic Review 42 (7), 1317–1341.

Xu, L.C., Zhu, T., Lin, Y.-M., 2005. Politician control, agency problems, and firm performance: evidence from a national survey of ownership restructuring in China. Economics of Transition 13 (1), 1–24.

Zhu, T., 1999. China's corporatization drive: an evaluation and policy implications. Contemporary Economic Policy 17 (4), 530–539.

Part IV
Who are the Entrepreneurs?

[21]

ENTREPRENEURSHIP IN CHINA AND RUSSIA COMPARED

Simeon Djankov
World Bank

Yingyi Qian
University of California Berkeley

Gérard Roland
University of California Berkeley

Ekaterina Zhuravskaya
CEFIR

Abstract
We compare results from a pilot study on entrepreneurship in China and Russia. Compared to non-entrepreneurs, Russian and Chinese entrepreneurs have more entrepreneurs in their family and among childhood friends, value work more relative to leisure and have higher wealth ambitions. Russian entrepreneurs have a better educational background and their parents were more likely to have been members of the Communist Party but Chinese entrepreneurs are more risk-taking and greedy and have more entrepreneurs among their childhood friends. (JEL: M13, 012, P12)

1. Introduction

The recent development and transition literatures have emphasized the importance of a strong and healthy small and medium enterprise sector for economic growth and development. Endogenous growth theory (Aghion and Howitt 1997) has emphasized the Schumpeterian approach to growth which advances that entrepreneurial dynamism is fundamental for innovation and growth.

We have launched a research project trying to better understand the determinants of entrepreneurship using surveys of individuals that are being conducted in five large developing and transition countries: Russia, Brazil, China, India, and Nigeria. The samples include both entrepreneurs and non-entrepreneurs in order to understand how these groups differ in terms of three broad sets of variables put forward in social sciences as factors that potentially affect entrepreneurship: (1) individual characteristics such as skills, education, and intellectual and personality traits; (2) sociological variables such as family background, social origins, social networks, values, and beliefs; and (3) perceptions of the institutional,

Acknowledgments: We thank Irina Levina and Xiaolu Wang for excellent research assistance, and the International Finance Corporation for financial support.

E-mail addresses: Djankov: sdjankov@worldbank.org; Qian: yqian@econ.Berkeley.edu; Roland: groland@econ.berkeley.edu; Zhuravskaya: EZhuravskaya@cefir.ru

social, and economic environment that businesses face. Whereas recent economic research has very much emphasized the role of credit institutions (Banerjee and Newman 1993) or of institutions securing property rights (Johnson, McMillan, and Woodruff 2002; Besley 1995; Che and Qian 1998; Djankov, Glaeser, and Schleifer 2002; Frye and Zhuravskaya 2000; Roland and Verdier 2003), we want to take a more comprehensive approach and try to disentangle the role these factors play in promoting entrepreneurship across a variety of settings.

This paper reports and compares some findings from a pilot survey conducted in Russia in 2003–2004 and in China in 2004–2005.

2. The Data

In both Russia and China, we surveyed individuals in seven large cities in four different regions. To capture some of the regional heterogeneity in these countries, the regions were selected to maximize the cross-regions variation in the business climate. In Russia, the survey was done in Moscow; in Nizhny Novgorod and Dzershinsk in the Nizhegorodskaya Oblast; in Perm and Chaykovsky in the Permskaya Oblast; and in Rostov on the Don and Taganrog in the Rostovskaya Oblast. In China, the survey was conducted in Beijing; in Wuhan and Huangshi in Hubei Province; in Guangzhou and Zhongshan in Guangdong Province; and in Xi'An and Baoji in Shaanxi Province.

In each country, we first surveyed a random sample of about 400 entrepreneurs—100 in Moscow and Beijing metropolitan areas and 50 in each of the other six cities. These surveys were conducted in the fall of 2003 in Russia and in the fall of 2004 in China. We define *entrepreneur* as an owner-manager of a business with five or more employees because we wanted to make sure that individuals who we call entrepreneurs in our sample are more than just self-employed. After completion of the surveys of entrepreneurs in the respective countries, we conducted a survey of about 550 non-entrepreneurs in the same cities using a similar instrument.[1] We defined *non-entrepreneurs* as individuals who are not working for their own business. Non-entrepreneur surveys took place during the spring of 2004 and 2005 in Russia and China, respectively. In both countries 80% of respondents in the non-entrepreneur sample were chosen randomly conditional on matching the age, gender, and educational attainment of entrepreneurs from the respective entrepreneur surveys and 20% were chosen at random. Finally, in each country a short survey was run among a random sample of 1,200 individuals (with the same breakdown across cities) asking nine questions about their

---

1. For hundred entrepreneurs and 550 non-entrepreneurs was the target sample size given to the survey firms in both countries. In reality, these firms interviewed a slightly larger number of individuals to make sure that in the end we had the targeted number of valid questionnaires. The actual number of observations in the empirical analysis depends on the response rates for each particular question.

personal characteristics, including a question about whether or not they are an entrepreneur or self-employed to get data on prevalence of entrepreneurship across cities. In all of the empirical analysis, the observations are weighted with weights equal to the inverse of the probability for a particular respondent (entrepreneur or non-entrepreneur) to get into our sample. The weights reflect differences in entrepreneurship, age, gender, and education across cities in the population, as well as the city size.

3. Comparing Entrepreneurs to Non-entrepreneurs in China and Russia

In this section, we summarize differences in individual characteristics, social environment, values, beliefs, and perceptions of institutional environment for entrepreneurs and non-entrepreneurs in both countries. We report means for entrepreneurs and non-entrepreneurs in both countries on various questions from the survey. In order to have comparability, the means are conditional on gender, age, and education (with a quadratic term) of respondents and on city dummies. The standard errors and p-values for the differences in means between entrepreneurs and non-entrepreneurs are adjusted to allow for clustering of the error terms at the level of cities (Table 1).

First, we summarize differences in individual characteristics of entrepreneurs and non-entrepreneurs. Entrepreneurs on average are more mobile across jobs and geographically. In Russia, entrepreneurs have lived in significantly more localities than non-entrepreneurs and have had a significantly higher number of distinct professional activities. Although these differences have the same sign in China, they are statistically insignificant. In China, however, entrepreneurs worked in a significantly higher number of industries compared to non-entrepreneurs. This is in line with recent findings of Lazear (2002) who surveyed the population of former Stanford MBA students and found that those with a higher number of jobs and shorter job tenures before business school were most likely to become entrepreneurs afterwards.

In line with a common perception that entrepreneurship is associated with risk-taking, entrepreneurs report significantly lower risk aversion than non-entrepreneurs. When asked whether respondents were willing to accept one of two risk-neutral gambles—(1) win $10 with probability 1/2 and lose $10 with probability 1/2 or (2) win $20 with probability 1/2 and lose $20 with proba-bility 1/2—77% of entrepreneurs in Russia and 90% of entrepreneurs in China responded "yes" (compared to 67% and 57% of non-entrepreneurs in Russia and China, respectively).

Entrepreneurs report higher levels of satisfaction with life compared to non-entrepreneurs. First, in Russia, a significantly higher share of entrepreneurs (92%) answered "yes" to the question whether they are happy compared to 73% of non-entrepreneurs. In China, this difference has the same sign but is

TABLE 1. Entrepreneurs in Russia and China (comparison of means).

	Russia			China		
	Entrepreneurs	Non-entrepreneurs	p-value for test of difference in means	Entrepreneurs	Non-entrepreneurs	p-value for test of difference in means
Individual characteristics						
Number of localities lived	2.42	2.18	0.01 ***	1.85	1.55	0.15
Number of distinct professional activities	2.76	2.54	0.06 *	2.40	2.13	0.24
Number of industries respondent worked in				1.85	1.58	0.00 ***
Accept a risk neutral gamble, %	77	67	0.00 ***	90	57	0.01 ***
Very happy or quite happy in life, %	92	73	0.00 ***	92	91	0.76
Very successful or quite successful in life, %	74	37	0.00 ***	64	43	0.01 ***
Good health, self described, %	12	07	0.00 ***	51	37	0.09 *
Got ill last week, %	25	30	0.02 **	04	08	0.00 ***
Height, cm	172.58	172.38	0.43	169.04	168.22	0.02 **
Married, %	74	60	0.00 ***	84	80	0.53
Number of children	1.34	1.31	0.22	1.19	99	0.00 ***
Religious believer, %	68	78	0.00 ***	12	08	0.09 *
Cognitive text score	3.32	3.15	0.15	3.92	3.80	0.62
Top 10% in secondary school (self reported), %	44	34	0.00 ***	37	38	0.82
Top 10% in high school, college or university (self reported), %	41	38	0.13	36	38	0.10
Speak foreign language, %	38	58	0.01 **	35	49	0.22
Motivation, greed						
Retire if won 100 times GDP per capita, %	08	27	0.00 ***	05	24	0.02 **
Retire if won 500 times GDP per capita, %	18	29	0.00 ***	14	37	0.00 ***

(Continued)

TABLE 1. CONTINUED

	Russia			China		
	Entrepreneurs	Non-entrepreneurs	p-value for test of difference in means	Entrepreneurs	Non-entrepreneurs	p-value for test of difference in means
Retire if won 5000 times GDP per capita, %	.	.	.	31	44	0.05 *
Not retire if won a large sum: I like what I do, %	82	69	0.00 ***	74	75	0.93
Not retire if won a large sum: I want more money, %	50	28	0.00 ***	70	43	0.01 ***
Not retire if won a large sum: my work serves useful social purpose, %	70	37	0.00 ***	18	81	0.00 ***
Sociological characteristics						
Father has secondary special or higher education, %	73	48	0.00 ***	29	27	0.57
Mother has secondary special or higher education, %	73	48	0.00 ***	14	18	0.46
Father was a boss or director, %	19	12	0.00 ***	30	13	0.02 **
Mother was a boss or director, %	08	00	0.00 ***	06	03	0.10
Father was a worker or employee without special education, %	43	44	0.43	56	72	0.01 **
Mother was a worker or employee without special education, %	30	53	0.00 ***	70	71	0.86
Father was a member of the communist party, %	48	37	0.00 ***	40	31	0.42
Mother was a member of the communist party, %	19	12	0.01 ***	10	15	0.01 ***
Members of the family were running business, %	57	34	0.00 ***	49	24	0.00 ***

Djankov et al.   Entrepreneurship in China and Russia   357

Had childhood friends who became entrepreneurs, %	59	37	0.00	***	45	28	0.01	**
Had adolescent friends who became entrepreneurs, %	67	48	0.00	***	60	24	0.00	***
Values								
Friends are very important, %	43	53	0.01	***	60	66	0.16	*
Relations with parents are very important, %	84	92	0.00	***	86	88	0.10	
Financial well-being is very important, %	53	58	0.02	**	73	62	0.08	*
Leisure time is very important, %	23	26	0.02	**	19	20	0.85	
Health is very important, %	75	80	0.00	***	93	88	0.20	
Service to others is very important, %	21	29	0.00	***	19	19	0.92	
Political freedom is very important, %	62	74	0.03	**	73	28	0.00	***
Power is very important, %	10	07	0.00	***	32	26	0.01	**
Work is very important, %	75	53	0.00	***	80	63	0.00	***
Intellectual achievement is very important, %	43	49	0.00	***	24	33	0.02	**
Values of legal social norms								
Not paying a fare can be justified to some degree, %	77	76	0.68		08	05	0.48	
Shirking at work can be justified to some degree, %	54	58	0.27		23	07	0.00	***
Accepting a bribe can be justified to some degree, %	32	18	0.00	***	19	06	0.00	***

(Continued)

TABLE 1. CONTINUED

	Russia			China		
	Entrepreneurs	Non-entrepreneurs	p-value for test of difference in means	Entrepreneurs	Non-entrepreneurs	p-value for test of difference in means
Trust						
Most people can be trusted, %	16	22	0.05 **	56	54	0.79
Have a lot of trust in family members, %	90	86	0.00 ***	96	92	0.48
Have a lot of trust in friends, %	49	48	0.17	58	58	0.98
Have a lot of trust in colleagues, %	26	20	0.02 **	38	33	0.46
Have a lot of trust or some trust in businessmen, %	61	66	0.06 *	71	46	0.02 **
Have a lot of trust or some trust in subordinates, %	79	82	0.06 *	95	83	0.02 **
Have a lot of trust or some trust in other people from town, %	54	85	0.00 ***	42	50	0.29
Have a lot of trust or some trust in foreigners, %	44	70	0.00 ***	29	38	0.39
Have a lot of trust or some trust in local government officials, %	40	40	1.00	69	59	0.07 *
Have a lot of trust or some trust in regional government officials, %	39	42	0.38	68	64	0.43
Have a lot of trust or some trust in central government officials, %	40	41	0.76	75	75	0.99
Individual perceptions of institutions						
People in your town are favorable toward entrepreneurs, %	67	65	0.36	68	60	0.33
Local government is favorable toward entrepreneurs, %	49	53	0.26	82	70	0.00 ***

(continued overleaf)

Regional government is favorable toward entrepreneurs, %	51	0.01 ***	78	76	0.74
Central government is favorable towards entrepreneurs, %	57	0.08 *	81	90	0.10 *
Private entrepreneurs pay bribes to avoid regulations, %	72	0.00 ***	50	54	0.57
Private entrepreneurs pay bribes to change rules, %	56	0.00 ***	40	50	0.39
Businessmen are subject to theft of property, %	88	0.18	70	98	0.08 *
Would go to court against a business relation if cheated, %	66	0.01 **	90	88	0.48
Would go to court against a government official if abused, %	62	0.00 ***	80	73	0.00 ***
It is relatively easy to find money to start a business in town, %	21	0.02 **	38	26	0.28

Note: The reported differences in means are conditional on city-level variation, age, gender, education, and education squared. Standard errors (and *p*-values) are adjusted to allow clusters of error term at the level of cities.
*Significant at 10% level; **Significant at 5% level; ***Significant at 1% level.

insignificant. Second, entrepreneurs report to be in significantly better health than non-entrepreneurs in both countries. Finally, entrepreneurs are taller than non-entrepreneurs. The difference in height is statistically significant only in China. In addition, entrepreneurs marry more often and have more children. The difference in percent married is significant in Russia and insignificant in China; while the difference in the number of children is significant in China only.

There are important differences between the two countries in religiosity and school achievement of entrepreneurs compared to non-entrepreneurs. Russian entrepreneurs tend to be less religious but Chinese entrepreneurs are more religious. However, religiosity is very low in China (12% among entrepreneurs) and relatively high in Russia (68%).

Russian entrepreneurs report to have been higher achievers in school, but this is not the case for China. Entrepreneurs tend to speak fewer foreign languages, an interesting fact. They scored higher than non-entrepreneurs on a test of cognitive ability, focusing on short-term recall (a digit-span test, available from the authors upon request) but the difference is not significant.

Another important difference that emerges relates to leisure-work choices of entrepreneurs and non-entrepreneurs. Respondents were asked whether they would retire if they received a windfall income of 100 or 500 times (5,000 times also in China) the annual GDP per capita of the country. Entrepreneurs were much less likely to respond positively than non-entrepreneurs. In both countries, a very strong reason for not retiring was the desire to earn more money. In Russia, job satisfaction and a feeling of being socially useful also played a significant role but not in China, where one finds the opposite.

Now let us focus on social environment. Compared to non-entrepreneurs, a larger share of parents of Russian entrepreneurs (73% vs. 48%) achieved higher or special education. There are no differences in parents' education in China. Nevertheless, fathers of entrepreneurs in both countries were more likely to have been bosses or directors (19% vs. 12% in Russia and 30% vs. 13% in China). In Russia, both parents of entrepreneurs were more likely to have been members of the Communist Party, but not in China. Not only is there no significant difference for fathers in China but mothers of entrepreneurs were less often members of the Communist Party (10% compared to 15% for non-entrepreneurs).

A very large difference that emerges in both countries is the proportion of entrepreneurs in one's family and among one's friends. Entrepreneurs in both countries are much more likely to have entrepreneurs in their family (57% in Russia and 49% in China, compared to respectively 34% and 24% among non-entrepreneurs). Respondents were asked to name five friends from their childhood and adolescence and then to report how many of these five have become entrepreneurs. The difference in response for entrepreneurs and non-entrepreneurs is striking. In China, for example, 60% of entrepreneurs had adolescent friends who became entrepreneurs compared to 24% among non-entrepreneurs.

We also asked questions about values and beliefs. Although there are statistically significant differences between entrepreneurs and non-entrepreneurs, the magnitude of the differences is not very large except for a few cases. A major difference is the value attached to work: 75% of Russian and 80% of Chinese entrepreneurs consider work to be very important in their life compared to 53% and 63% for non-entrepreneurs in Russia and China. This is consistent with the labor–leisure preferences reported above. Note that Chinese entrepreneurs value political freedom very strongly compared to non-entrepreneurs (73% vs. 28%) whereas Russian entrepreneurs value political freedom significantly less than non-entrepreneurs (62% vs. 74%) even though they value it highly. Entrepreneurs seem to value relations with parents significantly less than non-entrepreneurs in both countries. Asked about social norms, entrepreneurs in both countries consider that bribes are more acceptable. This probably reflects their greater experience in the business environment rather than intrinsic values. Chinese entrepreneurs consider that shirking at work can be justified. We asked many questions about trust, but no strong pattern emerged. Russian entrepreneurs are considerably less trustful of foreigners and of people out of town whereas there is no significant difference in China. It is worth noting that Russians (both entrepreneurs and non-entrepreneurs) trust the government at all levels substantially less than Chinese (for example, 37% of respondents had at least some trust in the central government in Russia compared to 77% in China).

Finally, we compare individual perceptions of entrepreneurs and non-entrepreneurs about the institutional environment controlling for the average differences across cities. Chinese entrepreneurs find that local government is more favorable to entrepreneurs (82% positive answers vs. 70% for non-entrepreneurs). In Russia, entrepreneurs find that local government is less favorable (only 49% of positive answers) even though the difference is not significant. In general, the perception of different levels of government regarding their attitude to entrepreneurs is more negative among Russian entrepreneurs compared to non-entrepreneurs. In China, it is only more negative with respect to the central government and even there the percentage of positive answers is higher than in Russia. Entrepreneurs in China also feel more secure with respect to theft of property. Russian entrepreneurs tend to distrust the courts more than non-entrepreneurs. In China, it is the opposite. When asked if they would go to court if abused by a government official, roughly 72% say yes in both countries. However, only 62% of Russian entrepreneurs respond positively whereas 80% of Chinese entrepreneurs do.

To summarize the main results of this section, entrepreneurs in both countries are risk-taking and have more entrepreneurs in their families and among their childhood and adolescence friends. Entrepreneurs value work very highly and are greedy. Russian entrepreneurs tend to come from a higher educational background but have a more negative perception of the institutional environment in which they operate compared to Chinese entrepreneurs. The latter tend to have a positive view of local governments' attitude towards entrepreneurs.

4. Results of Multivariate Probit Regressions

In this section, we report results of multivariate analysis. We explain variation in individual decisions to become an entrepreneur in probit regressions with independent variables that can plausibly be considered exogenous to this decision. The main objective of these regressions is to see which variables are robustly associated to entrepreneurship and also to compare the differences between Russia only and China only.

The results are reported in Table 2. Column 1 in Table 2 reports pooled results, columns 2 and 3 report separate results for Russia only and China only, and columns 4 and 5 present a regression where all dependent variables include interactions with China dummy. The fourth column should thus be read as result for Russia[2] and the coefficients in the fifth column represent the difference in China relative to Russia. As above, all regressions include city-fixed effects and controls for gender, age, and a quadratic function of education. Standard errors are adjusted for clusters in error terms at the city level.

The pooled results in Table 2 show that entrepreneurship is positively associated with the father having been a member of the Communist Party, the mother having been a boss or a director, having family and friends being entrepreneurs (social network), greed (not willing to retire to earn more money), and a positive perception of the attitude of the local population toward entrepreneurs. However, when looking at the country regressions, one sees that only the social network variables and greed are robustly significant in both countries. Note from columns 2 and 3 that height has a negative coefficient in Russia and a positive one in China. Columns 2 and 4 show that, for Russia, having had a father in the Communist Party and a mother director has positive correlation with entrepreneurship as well as for reporting to have been among the top 10% in school and also a positive perception of the population's attitude toward entrepreneurs. Column 5 shows the significant differences between entrepreneurship in China and Russia. Chinese entrepreneurs are more greedy and risk-taking (the Russia coefficient is negative but this is not the case in other specifications), are more likely to have entrepreneurs among their former school friends and were less good in school.

In terms of the importance of the different effects, because the reported coefficients are marginal effects, looking at column 1, the two most-important effects are greed and having friends entrepreneurs. A one standard deviation increase in greed, increases the probability of being an entrepreneurs by about 9% while a

---

2. The results of column 2 and 4 are identical when the data are not weighted but they are slightly different because the weights are different in a regression including one versus countries.

TABLE 2. Entrepreneurship in Russia and China. Probit regressions. Marginal effects reported.

	Pooled	Russia only	China only	Russia and China compared	
				Russia	Difference in China relative to Russia
Father with secondary or higher education	0.003 [0.021]	-0.014 [0.012]	0.004 [0.007]	-0.008 [0.007]	0.018 [0.019]
Father was a member of the communist party	0.073 [0.036]**	0.108 [0.023]***	0.011 [0.023]	0.066 [0.015]***	-0.034 [0.036]
Mother was a boss or director	0.271 [0.116]**	0.371 [0.136]***	0.066 [0.047]	0.283 [0.124]**	-0.054 [0.030]*
Mother with secondary or higher education	-0.034 [0.023]	-0.013 [0.009]	-0.016 [0.008]*	-0.008 [0.005]	-0.031 [0.022]
Family members entrepreneurs	0.039 [0.006]***	0.05 [0.003]***	0.012 [0.007]*	0.03 [0.003]***	-0.001 [0.009]
Friends entrepreneurs (from the last place of study)	0.06 [0.010]***	0.075 [0.009]***	0.032 [0.011]***	0.045 [0.006]***	0.029 [0.012]**
Cognitive test score	0.007 [0.007]	-0.006 [0.007]	0.003 [0.005]	-0.004 [0.004]	0.011 [0.013]
Height	0 [0.002]	-0.005 [0.001]***	0.001 [0.000]***	-0.003 [0.001]***	0.006 [0.001]***
Risk-loving	0.061 [0.053]	-0.033 [0.009]***	0.08 [0.006]***	-0.019 [0.006]***	0.327 [0.069]***
Top 10% in secondary school (self reported)	0.021 [0.026]	0.087 [0.011]***	-0.009 [0.010]	0.053 [0.008]***	-0.059 [0.016]***
Greed	0.186 [0.073]**	0.097 [0.019]***	0.155 [0.015]***	0.059 [0.012]***	0.246 [0.060]***
City population perceived favorable towards entrepreneurs	0.043 [0.020]**	0.035 [0.017]**	0.011 [0.011]	0.021 [0.010]**	0.006 [0.025]
Government perceived favorable towards entrepreneurs	-0.002 [0.008]	0.006 [0.006]	-0.001 [0.006]	0.003 [0.004]	-0.005 [0.013]
Observations	1530	726	804	1530	

Note: Robust standard errors corrected for clusters of error term at city level in brackets. Also control for gender, age, education, and education squared.
*Significant at 10% level; **Significant at 5% level; ***Significant at 1%level.

TABLE 3. Institutions and plans to expand sales and employment. Entrepreneur sample.

	Planned sales growth	Planned employment growth	Planned sales growth	Planned employment growth
Average city-level corruption	−1.702 [0.608]**	−1.503 [0.751]*		
Average city-level efficiency of courts			1.215 [0.418]**	1.047 [0.591]
Country	0.364 [0.091]***	0.026 [0.268]	0.294 [0.136]*	−0.035 [0.326]
Observations	362	342	362	342

Notes: Robust standard errors corrected for clusters of error term at city level in brackets. Also control for gender, age, education, and education squared.

*Significant at 10% level; **Significant at 5% level; ***Significant at 1% level. All regressions include industry dummies and all the regressors as in the first column of Table 2.

one standard deviation increase in the "friends entrepreneurs" variable increases this probability by 7.2%.

As with most cross-section OLS regressions, we cannot rule out the possibility that an omitted variable simultaneously influenced entrepreneurship decisions of our respondents and of their families and friends. Thus, at this stage, we cannot establish a causal link between social networks and entrepreneurship; but we hope to address the question of causality in the subsequent stages of this project.

So far we have held the variation in city-level institutional environment constant by including city dummies. To evaluate the effect of city-level institutional environment, we regress a dummy (Table 3) that equals one if entrepreneur plans to expand sales or employment on the average city-level measures of corruption and efficiency of courts (as reported in Table 1). These regressions include controls (not shown) for industry dummies and all individual characteristics as reported in Table 2. As above, error terms are clustered at the city-level. As one can see, these institutional variables are significant and have the expected sign. Note also the country effect showing the stronger economic dynamism in China.

5. Conclusions

Russian and Chinese entrepreneurs have common characteristics relative to non-entrepreneurs controlling for age, gender, and education. They are more risk-taking, place a higher value on work relative to leisure, are greedy and are much more likely to have entrepreneurs in their family as well as among childhood and adolescence friends. There are also differences however, Russian entrepreneurs have a better educational background which is not the case for Chinese entrepreneurs and are more risk-taking and greedy and are even more likely than in Russia to have had school friends who became entrepreneurs. In future work, we want to understand better in particular the role of social networks and the channels through which they operate for entrepreneurs.

References

Aghion, Philippe, and Peter Howitt (1997). *Endogenous Growth Theory*. MIT Press.

Banerjee, Abhijit, and Andrew Newman (1993). "Occupational Choice and the Process of Development." *Journal of Political Economy*, 101(2), 1276–1298.

Besley, Tim (1995). "Property Rights and Investment Incentives: Theory and Evidence from Ghana." *Journal of Political Economy*, 103, 903–937.

Che, Jiahua, and Yingyi Qian (1998). "Insecure Property Rights and Government Ownership of Firms." *Quarterly Journal of Economics*, 113, 467–496.

Djankov, Simeon, Ed Glaeser, and Andrei Shleifer (2002). "The Regulation of Entry." *Quarterly Journal of Economics*, 1117(1), 1–37.

Frye, Timothy, and Ekaterina Zhuravskaya (2000). "Rackets, Regulation and the Rule of Law." *Journal of Law, Economics, and Organization*, 16, 478–502.

Johnson, Simon, John McMillan, and Chris Woodruff (2002). "Property Rights and Finance." *American Economic Review*, 92, 1335–1356.

Lazear, Edward (2002). "Entrepreneurship." NBER Working Paper No. w9109.

Roland, Gérard, and Thierry Verdier (2003). "Law Enforcement and Transition." *European Economic Review*, 47, 669–685.

[22]

Advances in Economic Analysis & Policy

| Volume 3, Issue 1 | 2003 | Article 4 |

Ethnic Ties and the Provision of Credit: Relationship-Level Evidence from African Firms

Raymond J. Fisman[*]

*Columbia University GSB, rf250@columbia.edu

Ethnic Ties and the Provision of Credit: Relationship-Level Evidence from African Firms*

Raymond J. Fisman

Abstract

This paper studies the effect of ethnic ties on trade credit provision. Previous work in Africa has found that entrepreneurs of Asian and European descent are more likely to obtain credit from their suppliers. However, since these analyses use firm-level data, one cannot distinguish the effect of community ties from that of unobserved firm quality that is correlated with the owner's ethnic background. Using data on specific supplier relationships of African firms, this paper more directly examines the effect of ethnic ties on trade credit provision. Results from random and fixed-effects models indicate that firms are twice as likely to obtain credit from suppliers from within the owners' ethnic communities as from outsiders, suggestive of a very strong effect of communal ties. However, these ties accounts for only a small proportion (15 percent) of the overall preferential credit access enjoyed by entrepreneurs of non-African descent.

KEYWORDS: Trade Credit, Ethnicity

*Associate Professor, Columbia University GSB, Uris 823, 3022 Broadway, New York, NY 10027, Phone: 212-854-9157, Fax: 212-854-9895

Erratum

In Table 4, the headings for column 6 and 7 are reversed. The correct heading for column 6 is "BACKGROUND VALUE=1." The correct heading for column 7 is "BACKGROUND VALUE=0." These are typographical errors and none of the results or conclusions of the paper are affected.

Trade credit is an important form of financing for businesses in a broad range of industries and economies. Even in the United States, with its extremely well-developed financial markets, trade credit is the largest single source of short-term financing (Petersen and Rajan, 1997). In less-developed countries, where formal lenders are scarce at best, trade credit plays an even more significant role in funding firms' activities. Hence, understanding the determinants of credit access is potentially important for both the theory and practice of development. This paper considers the role of ethnic ties in promoting credit provision, by examining the determinants of credit access of firms in four African countries. In particular, I examine whether entrepreneurs of Asian and European descent are more likely to receive credit from suppliers of the same origin, relative to suppliers from different backgrounds.

There are numerous reasons that credit provision might be higher within such communities. Since entrepreneurs from these communities often have higher levels of wealth and human capital, they may be more likely to receive trade credit from any of their suppliers; I will refer to this as the *background* effect. Alternatively, preferential credit access may come *only* from members of their own community; I refer to this as the *ties* effect, which may operate through a number of channels. These may broadly be divided into two classes: Network-based explanations and discrimination-based explanations.

The most prominent network-based theory is laid out by Granovetter (1985), in his description of the ' embeddedness' of business relations in a social context. He argues that when transactions take place within a tight-knit community there is less scope for opportunistic behavior, since such actions will result in social sanction and exclusion from the communal business network. Trust, thus engendered, allows for mutually beneficial cooperation between commercial enterprises in situations where there exists the potential for opportunistic behavior that might otherwise have precluded such cooperation. This explanation is closely related to several theoretical and historical studies in economics. In particular, it is similar to the notion of communal enforcement formalized by Kandori (1996), and also closely parallels the arguments spelled out by Greif (1993) in his analysis of Maghribi trading networks. A closely related network-based theory holds that communal ties may be a useful means of channeling information about credit-worthiness. This is the story emphasized by Fafchamps and Minten (2002). A further distinction is necessary within the realm of network-based explanations. As embodied in the economic models described above, networks may operate through a decentralized set of dyadic ties that collectively diffuse information about 'bad' behaviors. Alternatively, communities may have a leader, or centralized authority, that acts to sanction violators. Guinnane (2001) discusses the church as an example of such a coordinating body in nineteenth century Germany.

Another set of explanations for preferential credit access is based on discrimination against trading partners of different backgrounds. For example, Platteau (2000) argues that firms may exhibit 'preferential honesty,' whereby they are less likely to renege on within-community contracts. If this is the case, it will be perfectly rational for suppliers to avoid providing trade credit to firms outside of their communities. More generally, there exists a large body of literature on the effect of race and discrimination in many types of markets (see, for example, Loury, 1998, Donohue, 1998).

Differentiating among these explanations of the role of communal ties is beyond the scope of this paper. Rather, my goal is to measure the extent that ethnic ties, as distinct from ethnic *backgrounds*, are responsible for the preferential credit access enjoyed by some groups. To be more precise, as mentioned above, some groups may have preferential access because they

Advances in Economic Analysis & Policy , Vol. 3 [2003], Iss. 1, Art. 4

are more likely to receive credit from suppliers from within their own community (the effect of ethnic ties), or they may be more likely to receive credit from *all* suppliers because members of the group present a better credit risk for reasons that are not readily observable to the econometrician (the effect of ethnic backgrounds). While previous work has had difficulty distinguishing between these effects since analyses were done at the firm level, the relationship-level data in this study will allow for a cleaner distinction between the impact of background versus ties.

Earlier work in this area by Fafchamps (1997, 2000) found that members of Asian and European minority groups in Zimbabwe are more likely to have access to trade credit than their counterparts of African descent. This test does not isolate the effect of communal ties, however. Most importantly, problems of omitted variable bias, as suggested above, are severe. Ethnicity is often highly correlated with measures of owner 'quality' such as education and experience, and with measures of firm 'quality' such as size and profitability. If great disparities exist across groups in observable measures of firm quality, it seems very likely that there are also substantial differences in *unobserved* firm quality (for example, due to the transmission of information and skills). Thus, Fafchamps cannot effectively distinguish the effect of communal ties from the effect of similar backgrounds of community members.

To overcome these difficulties, we require data on the relationships of a firm with each of its suppliers, which allows for a comparison of credit access across different types of relationships, holding firm characteristics constant. In this paper, I am able to follow this methodology by taking advantage of a particularly rich data set, collected by the Research Program on Enterprise Development at the World Bank, to more convincingly examine the role of communal ties in promoting cooperation across firms. Through surveys, relationship-level information was collected on the suppliers of firms in several African countries. These data include information on whether each of the firm's main suppliers comes from the firm owner's ethnic group.[1] This allows for the *direct* measurement of the effect of communal ties (i.e., same ethnic community), as distinct from ethnic background (i.e., Asian, European, or African). Using a random-effects specification, I find that a firm is far more likely to obtain goods on credit from a supplier that is a part of the same ethnic community. Furthermore, since the data contain multiple observations per firm, it is possible to use a fixed-effects model to more rigorously control for differences in quality across firms. Using this more restrictive approach, I find that there remains a statistically significant and large effect from ethnic ties. For an average firm, the results imply that an Asian or European owned firm is more than twice as likely to obtain credit from a supplier whose owner is of the same origin as from an 'outside' supplier.

With these data, I am further able to assess the extent to which ethnic ties account for the preferential credit access enjoyed by Asian and European firms. In contrast to previous studies, I find that these ties account for only a small proportion (15 percent) of the difference in credit access between African and non-African firms, essentially because the number of within-community transactions is relatively small.

The rest of this paper is organized as follows: Section 1 describes the empirical approach. Section 2 gives a description of the data used in the paper. The empirical results are presented in section 3, including a decomposition of the difference in credit access for African versus non-

---

[1] The survey allows for some flexibility in the definition of ethnicity, to include consideration of ethnic divisions among those of African descent. I will focus primarily on the three main ethnic divisions in these African business communities: European, Asian, and African (see the data section below for further details). See, for example, Forster et al (2000) for a general discussion of ethnicity in Africa.

African owned firms; finally, a discussion of the results and some conclusions are given in section 4.

1. Empirical Approach

The standard estimations examining the effect of ethnicity (or other personal characteristics) on credit access use some variant on the following (see Munnell, et al, 1996; Blanchflower et al., 1998; Fafchamps, 2000):

$$P(CREDIT_i = 1) = \alpha + \beta_1*BACKGROUND_i + \beta_2*X_i + \beta_3*CW_i + \varepsilon_i \qquad (1)$$

where $CREDIT_i$ is an indicator variable for credit access for firm i, CW_i represents measures of credit worthiness, X_i is a vector of other firm characteristics, and $BACKGROUND_i$ is the ethnicity of the firm's owner. Within this framework, evidence of differential credit access would be indicated by a significant coefficient on $BACKGROUND$. However, the different interpretations assigned to β_1 by the papers listed above highlight the difficulties in using firm-level data to study credit access. In particular, the effect of ethnicity could derive from ethnic ties or differential firm quality that is correlated with $BACKGROUND$.

A more complete model of credit access would take into account unobserved 'quality' differences across firms, the characteristics of the firm's supplier, and also the nature of the relationship between the two firms. Thus, what we wish to estimate is:

$$P(CREDIT_i = 1) = \alpha + \beta_1*BACKGROUND_i + \beta_2*X_i + \beta_3*CW_i + UQ_i$$
$$+ \beta_4*R_{si} + \beta_5*SC_{si} + \beta_6*TIES_{si} + \varepsilon_{si} \qquad (2)$$

where UQ_i represents unobserved quality of the firm, SC_{si} are the characteristics of supplier s, and R are the characteristics of the relationship between the two firms (e.g., length of relationship). $TIES_{si}$, the specific supplier characteristic that is the focus of this paper, denotes whether the supplier is of the same ethnic background as the firm. If unobserved quality is treated as a fixed effect (α_i), the coefficients on the firm-level characteristics cannot be identified, and the model is reduced to:

$$P(CREDIT_i = 1) = \alpha_i + \beta_4*R_{si} + \beta_5*SC_{si} + \beta_6*TIES_{si} + \varepsilon_{si} \qquad (3)$$

Now, the characteristics of the firm are held constant, and the coefficient on $TIES$ reflects solely the differential credit access that the firm receives from suppliers of its own ethnicity.

Unfortunately, fixed effects are extremely restrictive in the context of the binary choice model that I will use to estimate (3), since within-firm variation is required in the dependent variable. I will therefore also consider a model that treats unobserved quality as a random variable, estimating (2) as a random effects model.

II. Data

The data used in this paper come from surveys administered by the Regional Program on Enterprise Development (RPED) at the World Bank during 1992-95, to five former British

Advances in Economic Analysis & Policy , Vol. 3 [2003], Iss. 1, Art. 4

colonies in Sub-Saharan Africa: Ghana, Kenya, Tanzania, Zambia, and Zimbabwe.[2] Three rounds of the survey were conducted in each country; where possible, the same firms were visited in each round. The survey instrument covered a wide variety of topics including: Basic statistics on the firms' operations; the history of the firms and their owners; use of technology; competition and competitors (only in the later rounds); labor; financing and contractual relations; conflict resolution; regulation; infrastructure; and use of business support services.

While the use of survey data raises concerns of data quality, I believe that they are minimal with regard to the analyses in this paper. Most importantly, errors generally arise from misreporting or mismeasurement of accounting data, such as sales, capital, and expenses. All critical regressions below do not require these data as controls, because of the fixed effects specifications. In fact, almost all of the results are derived using only very simple, survey-based variables that are relatively straightforward for the survey respondents to estimate. Deliberate misreporting, while also often a concern, is unlikely to be driving the reported results. First, the survey was carried out by an independent organization (as opposed to the government) so there was less incentive for managers to mislead or withhold information. Furthermore, it is unclear why misreporting would be systematically correlated with any of the variables that I use.[3]

The data are drawn primarily from the Finance section of the first round of the survey, which included information on the firm's relationships with up to three of its primary suppliers. Of crucial interest for this paper is the form of payment that was required by the supplier. Three options were available in the survey: Credit, cash, and advance payment. Virtually all relationships were characterized by credit or cash transactions. Responses were used to construct the dummy variable *CREDIT* that takes on a value of one if purchases with a particular supplier were largely credit based. This will be the dependent variable in most of what follows.

I also require information on the ethnicity of the firm's supplier. This is given by the variable *TIES*, which takes on a value of one if the owner of both the firm and its supplier were members of the same ethnic community. It is inferred from responses to the following survey question, with reference to each primary supplier: "Is the person you deal with a member of the same tribe or ethnic group?" The phrasing of this question allowed each owner to make his own judgment about whether he considered his supplier to be a part of his ethnic community. Given the manner in which communal ties are posited to operate, this is an appropriate way of defining connections. This is important, since the three main ethnic groupings that I consider in this paper – European, Asian, and African descent – are by no means homogeneous. For example, the Jewish community in Zimbabwe is of European descent, but considers itself to be very distinct from that country's British colonizers. Similarly, the Chinese and East Indian communities in Africa have relatively little interaction, though they would both be identified as Asian in the survey.

There are several relationship-level characteristics that likely affect credit access, and may be correlated with supplier ethnicity, and hence should be included as controls. Length of relationship with the supplier is particularly important: If the development of trust (required for credit provision) is a gradual process, length of relationship will be an important determinant of credit provision. Thus, if ethnically tied supplier relationships tend to be longer in duration, this could create omitted variable problems (in fact, ethnic ties and length of relationship are only

---

[2] While I have access to these five databases, Ghana is omitted from the analyses, because its survey did not collect data on ethnicity.

[3] The one exception is the reporting of credit transactions in Tanzania, for religious reasons. I will discuss this issue further below.

very weakly correlated). I include as a control *LENGTH*, the reported length of the relationship with a given supplier, in years.

Frequency of interaction may also be an important predictor of credit access: Frequent transactions will put a supplier in a better position to retaliate quickly for non-payment, suggesting a positive relationship between credit provision and frequency of purchase. From a demand perspective, however, there will be less need for credit between parties that transact frequently, which argues for a negative relationship. Also, frequent interaction may be a signal of cash flow problems that would be positively correlated with credit risk. Overall, the predicted effect is ambiguous. I define *FREQUENCY* as the frequency with which purchases were made from a given supplier. These values range from daily (*FREQUENCY* =6) to yearly (*FREQUENCY*=0). Firms were given the option of responding that the frequency of interaction was "Occasional" – I omit observations where this ambiguous response was given.

Finally, I include a variable *COMPETITION*, which proxies for the degree of product market competition for the supplied good. This has been shown to be important determinant of credit access in other work (Fisman and Raturi, 2003), since supplier credit can be used to establish market power in otherwise competitive markets. It is defined as a dummy variable that takes on a value of one if there is more than one supplier available to provide the materials purchased.

For the random-effects specifications, I also include firm-level controls. In these regressions, I will be able to look at the effect of the ethnic background of the firm's owner (as distinct from the effect of ethnic ties), which I will denote by *BACKGROUND*, a dummy variable taking on a value of 1 if the firm's owner is of Asian or European descent.

In terms of other controls, the primary concern in firm-level regressions is controlling for firm quality and reputation, which is surely correlated with credit access. The proxies for reputation/quality that I use closely parallel those utilized by Fafchamps (2000):

- *SIZE* - Following on previous work using the RPED data, I use total employment (given by (full-time workers) + 0.5*(part-time workers)) as a measure of firm size. The reason for using employment is that number of workers is much less likely to be mismeasured or misreporting than sales or assets.
- *AGE* – firm's age.
- *GENDER* – dummy variable equal to one if the firm's owner is female.
- *SUBSIDIARY* – a dummy variable denoting whether the firm is a subsidiary of a conglomerate.

Industry and country dummies are also included where appropriate. The sectors covered by the survey include: Food Processing; Textiles and Clothing; Wood and Furniture; and Metal Products.

All variable definitions are summarized in the Data Appendix.

The original sample included 860 firms, with 1938 relationships. Observations were dropped that did not include information on the basic variables, including length of relationship (227) [4], possible ethnic ties to supplier (228), whether the supplier provided goods on credit (4), and whether the supplier was a monopolist (2). This yielded a sample of 614 firms with 1478 relationships. For the random effects model, firm size is also required as a basic control; this variable was missing for 11 firms, reducing the sample to 603 firms/1451 relationships. For the

---

[4] Deletions were done sequentially; number of dropped variables in parentheses.

Advances in Economic Analysis & Policy , Vol. 3 [2003], Iss. 1, Art. 4

fixed effects specification, as mentioned above, we require within-firm variation in *CREDIT*; this drastically reduces the sample size to 88 firms/242 relationships.

Basic summary statistics for the firms are listed in Table 1, both for the full sample, and for the sample divided by ethnicity and by country. Several patterns are worth noting: most importantly, the difference in credit access between African and non-African firms is very large.

Table 1 - Summary Statistics: Mean Values for Primary Variables

	Full Sample	*BACKGROUND*=1	*BACKGROUND*=0	Kenya	Tanzania	Zambia	Zimbabwe
Firm-Level Variables							
BACKGROUND	0.42	1	0	0.51	0.24	0.4	0.56
ASIAN	0.29	0.7	0	0.5	0.24	0.27	0.11
EURO	0.13	0.3	0	0.01	0	0.13	0.45
log(*SIZE*)	2.97	3.85	2.34	2.54	2.57	2.99	4.11
SUBSIDIARY	0.017	0.012	0.02	0	0.019	0.006	0.053
AGE	16.9	22.6	12.9	16.6	13.9	16.1	22.9
GENDER	0.1	0.037	0.15	0.093	0.06	0.11	0.19
Obs.	603	253	350	163	160	166	114
Relationship-Level Variables							
CREDIT	0.25	0.44	0.10	0.33	0.05	0.13	0.59
TIES	0.08	0.12	0.05	0.14	0.05	0.04	0.11
log(*LENGTH*)	9.97	13.06	7.47	8.18	8.28	8.81	15.71
COMPETITION	0.83	0.79	0.87	0.88	0.85	0.78	0.83
FREQUENCY	2.35	2.54	2.16	1.87	2.62	2.49	2.44
Obs.	1478	660	818	338	385	447	308

For variable definitions, please see the data appendix

However, there are also clearly vast differences across the two groups on observable characteristics that might account for this differential.

Another important statistic to note is that the proportion of Asian/European firms' suppliers that are members of the same ethnic group (i.e., *TIES* = 1) is only about 12 percent, which suggests that such ties are unlikely to be responsible for the bulk of the differential in credit access. This number may seem low, given the high percentage of *BACKGROUND*=1 firms in the overall population. For example, in Kenya, 50 percent of the firms in the sample are Asian-owned; hence, random matching would lead to E[*TIES*]= 0.25 ((0.5)^2), almost as high as the actual mean value of *TIES* among Asian firms in Kenya. The primary explanation for this apparent discrepancy is straightforward: the Asian and European populations within each of the countries in the sample are divided into distinct sub-populations (see discussion above). If the European and Asian communities in each country were divided into just two (equally sized) groups each, random matching would lead to a mean value of *TIES* that is approximately half of its actual value, which is consistent with at least some vertical clustering of firms by ethnicity. Furthermore, some transactions in the data may be arm's length-type purchases in an anonymous market. Ethnicity (and hence ethnic ties) would be irrelevant for these transactions, and these

Fisman: Ethnic Ties and the Provision of Credit

would therefore be listed as being associated with suppliers outside of the firm's ethnic community.

The other relevant summary statistic is the extremely low rate of credit provision among Tanzanian firms. This is entirely a result of low reported credit provision by Asian firms: for non-Asians, the rate of credit access is comparable to that of other countries in the sample. One possible explanation is that the Asian (Arab) community in Tanzania is Moslem, and quite devout. Hence, because of the strict prohibition against lending in Islam, Asian owners would be unlikely to be involved in credit transactions (or may simply be reluctant to admit to allowing such transactions – if enumerators had asked about 'payment facilities' rather than credit, different results may have been obtained). Note that this is likely to bias the results against finding any effect of ethnic ties: owners may be *less* likely to obtain credit from other Asian firms, because of these restrictions. In fact, in the subsample of Asian firms in Tanzania, among the within-community transactions firms never report that supplier credit was granted (0 out of 7 transactions). Finally, to get a sense of the effect of ethnic ties in the raw data, Table 2 shows the average rate of credit access, disaggregated by *TIES*, and by country, both for the full sample and also for firms with *BACKGROUND* = 1. With the exception of Tanzania (see the above caveat), it is readily apparent that Asian/European firms are more likely to obtain goods on credit from suppliers within their ethnic communities. Note, however, that the extent of this effect varies across countries. This will make it important to consider the effect of *TIES* by country, which I do below. Furthermore, given the systematic differences across firms that appear in the summary statistics, the multivariate analyses below should be more informative with respect to the true nature of the effect of ethnic ties.

Table 2: Average Rates of Credit Access, by Ethnicity of Supplier

	Full Sample		*BACKGROUND*=1 Firms	
	TIES=0	*TIES*=1	*TIES*=0	*TIES*=1
Kenya	0.27	0.66	0.42	0.70
Tanzania	0.05	0.14	0.11	0.00
Zambia	0.13	0.21	0.21	0.44
Zimbabwe	0.59	0.64	0.75	0.90
All Countries	0.23	0.49	0.41	0.66

TIES is a dummy variable that takes on a value of one if the firm reported that the owner of its supplier and the firm's owner were of the same ethnicity. *BACKGROUND* is dummy variable that takes on a value of one if the firm's owner is of Asian or European descent.

III. Econometric Results
Before estimating the model from Section I, it is useful to look at analyses similar to the firm-level regressions that previous papers have reported. I use the basic specification from Fafchamps (2000):

$$P_i = \alpha + \beta_1 * BACKGROUND_i + \beta_2 * \log(SIZE_i) + \beta_3 * X_i + INDUSTRY_I + COUNTRY_C + \varepsilon_i \quad (4)$$

where P_i is the proportion of suppliers that provide the firm with goods on credit; X_i is a vector of additional controls; $INDUSTRY_I$ and $COUNTRY_C$ are industry and country fixed-effects

Advances in Economic Analysis & Policy , Vol. 3 [2003], Iss. 1, Art. 4

respectively, and ε_i is the error term. Table 3 reports the results. Consistent with previous work, the coefficient on *BACKGROUND* is very large and significant, i.e., Asian/European firms receive much more trade credit. To get a sense of how much of this effect comes from intra-community transactions, columns (6)-(10) report the results of the same regression, with *TIES*=1 relationships dropped from the sample. The coefficient on *BACKGROUND* is reduced by about 20 percent, suggesting that at least some of the preferential access to credit from suppliers enjoyed by Asian/European firms may be derived from within-community relationships. However, the *BACKGROUND* coefficient remains very large and statistically significant; since all within-community transactions have been omitted from the sample, the coefficient on *BACKGROUND* now reflects the effect of ethnic background, rather than ethnic ties. This strongly suggests that previous studies may have significantly overestimated the presence of ethnic ties. To more carefully examine the possibility of a direct effect of ethnic ties, I now turn to the full models of credit provision outlined above in (2) and (3).

Fisman: Ethnic Ties and the Provision of Credit

Table 3 - Firm-Level Regressions on the Determinants of Credit Access

	(1)	(2)	(3)	(4)	(5)	(6)	(7)	(8)	(9)	(10)
log(*SIZE*)	0.063	0.062	0.061	0.060	0.055	0.064	0.064	0.062	0.061	0.054
	(0.011)	(0.011)	(0.012)	(0.014)	(0.015)	(0.011)	(0.011)	(0.012)	(0.014)	(0.015)
BACKGROUND	0.129	0.126	0.122	0.126	0.128	0.100	0.097	0.094	0.097	0.097
	(0.035)	(0.035)	(0.035)	(0.039)	(0.039)	(0.036)	(0.036)	(0.037)	(0.040)	(0.040)
SUBSID		0.248	0.245	-0.008	-0.005		0.257	0.255	0.002	0.007
		(0.094)	(0.094)	(0.067)	(0.065)		(0.095)	(0.095)	(0.062)	(0.061)
log(*AGE*)			0.010	0.006	0.007			0.008	0.006	0.007
			(0.017)	(0.018)	(0.018)			(0.017)	(0.017)	(0.017)
GENDER				0.134	0.147				0.149	0.164
				(0.043)	(0.042)				(0.042)	(0.041)
EDU					0.010					0.014
					(0.017)					(0.017)
Wood	0.120	0.125	0.124	0.159	0.159	0.099	0.105	0.104	0.145	0.145
	(0.039)	(0.039)	(0.039)	(0.042)	(0.042)	(0.041)	(0.041)	(0.041)	(0.044)	(0.044)
Food	0.015	0.017	0.016	0.040	0.040	0.016	0.019	0.018	0.043	0.043
	(0.040)	(0.040)	(0.040)	(0.043)	(0.043)	(0.041)	(0.040)	(0.040)	(0.043)	(0.043)
Textiles	0.041	0.039	0.038	0.065	0.058	0.050	0.048	0.047	0.075	0.067
	(0.041)	(0.040)	(0.040)	(0.044)	(0.043)	(0.042)	(0.041)	(0.041)	(0.045)	(0.044)
Tanzania	-0.252	-0.255	-0.254	-0.249	-0.242	-0.224	-0.228	-0.227	-0.223	-0.214
	(0.037)	(0.037)	(0.037)	(0.038)	(0.040)	(0.037)	(0.037)	(0.037)	(0.038)	(0.039)
Zambia	-0.220	-0.222	-0.221	-0.214	-0.214	-0.183	-0.185	-0.185	-0.178	-0.177
	(0.038)	(0.038)	(0.038)	(0.039)	(0.039)	(0.040)	(0.039)	(0.039)	(0.040)	(0.040)
Zimbabwe	0.133	0.120	0.121	0.109	0.120	0.173	0.159	0.159	0.142	0.155
	(0.053)	(0.054)	(0.054)	(0.056)	(0.057)	(0.056)	(0.057)	(0.057)	(0.060)	(0.062)
Const	0.065	0.066	0.048	-0.088	-0.120	0.033	0.035	0.020	-0.131	-0.176
	(0.048)	(0.048)	(0.054)	(0.060)	(0.077)	(0.050)	(0.049)	(0.056)	(0.060)	(0.076)
TIES=1 Firms excluded	No	No	No	No	No	Yes	Yes	Yes	Yes	Yes
Obs	603	603	603	534	533	578	578	578	515	514
R2	0.38	0.38	0.38	0.35	0.35	0.35	0.36	0.36	0.313	0.31

Standard Errors in parentheses. Dependent Variable in all regressions is *CREDIT,* a dummy variable that takes on a value of one if the primary method of payment to the supplier was through trade credit. For additional variable definitions, please see the data appendix.

Advances in Economic Analysis & Policy , Vol. 3 [2003], Iss. 1, Art. 4

For ease of interpretation, linear regression models with heteroskedasticity-corrected errors are often used in estimating binary choice models. However, given some of the complications associated with short-panel fixed effect models, this simplified approach could lead to biased coefficients in the context of this paper.[5] In the analyses that follow, I will utilize two different models: random effects logit, and conditional fixed effects logit (as developed by Chamberlain, 1980). As already mentioned above, the sample size will be considerably smaller for the fixed effect specifications.

I begin with the random effects model:

$$P(CREDIT_{si} = 1) = \Lambda(\beta_1 * LENGTH_{si} + \beta_2 * COMPETITION_{si} + \beta_3 * FREQUENCY_{si} +$$

$$\beta_4 * TIES_{si} + \beta_5 * \log(SIZE_i) + \beta_6 * AGE_i + \beta_7 * BACKGROUND_i + \textbf{INDUSTRY}_I +$$

$$\textbf{COUNTRY}_C + \eta_i + \varepsilon_{si})$$

where i is a firm index and s is a relationship index; **INDUSTRY**$_I$ is a vector of industry dummies and **COUNTRY**$_C$ is a vector of country dummies; $\Lambda(.)$ is the logistic function; η_i is a firm-specific random effect, and ε_{si} is the error term.

The results are listed in Table 4. The coefficients are, for the most part, consistent with earlier work in this area: Firm size, a proxy for a company's reliability and reputation, is large and statistically significantly different from zero. *AGE* is relatively small in size and significance, which is somewhat surprising – the age of an establishment should be a reasonable proxy for its reliability in repaying its debts.

Among the relationship specific variables: the coefficient on *LENGTH* is positive, and generally significant, consistent with the idea that there is a gradual build-up of trust that precedes the provision of credit. In the regressions that include *FREQUENCY*, its coefficient is not significant, which may be because of the counteracting effects described in the Data section.[6] The coefficient on *COMPETITION*, is positive, and generally significant.

The coefficient of primary interest in this paper, *TIES*, is statistically significantly different from zero at the one percent level, indicating the possible importance of the role of ethnic ties. Note, however, that the coefficient on *BACKGROUND* is also highly significant and very large, indicating that unobserved firm quality of Asian/European firms induces all suppliers, regardless of ethnicity, to provide more credit to Asian and European firms.

---

[5] In reality, using linear probability models in the analyses yields qualitatively identical results, which are available from the author.
[6] Consistent with the story, when the average of *FREQUENCY* is included as a regressor, its coefficient is positive and the coefficient on *FREQUENCY* becomes negative and significant.

Fisman: Ethnic Ties and the Provision of Credit

Table 4 - Random Effects Regressions on the Determinants of Supplier Credit Access

	(1)	(2)	(3)	(4)	Tanzania Excluded (5)	BACKGROUND VALUE =0 (6)	=1 (7)	(8)
BACKGROUND	1.575	1.745	1.706	1.504	1.597			1.439
	(0.443)	(0.475)	(0.470)	(0.536)	(0.454)			(0.459)
log(SIZE)	0.775	0.776	0.672	0.567	0.786	0.148	1.419	0.788
	(0.149)	(0.152)	(0.153)	(0.205)	(0.154)	(0.172)	(0.298)	(0.152)
TIES	1.823	1.808	1.622	1.601	1.664	2.060	0.923	0.813
	(0.504)	(0.515)	(0.504)	(0.515)	(0.516)	(0.662)	(0.834)	(0.842)
LENGTH	0.020	0.025	0.030	0.021	0.026	0.018	0.028	0.020
	(0.016)	(0.017)	(0.018)	(0.023)	(0.017)	(0.019)	(0.033)	(0.016)
BACKGROUND* TIES								1.541
								(1.061)
COMP		0.908	0.968	1.024				
		(0.387)	(0.396)	(0.458)				
FREQ			-0.083	-0.077				
			(0.099)	(0.113)				
SUBSID				-1.410				
				(2.467)				
log(AGE)				0.339				
				(0.325)				
GENDER				2.163				
				(0.818)				
EDU				0.157				
				(0.269)				
Country Dummies	Yes	Yes	Yes	Yes	Yes	Yes	Yes	Yes
Sector Dummies	Yes	Yes	Yes	Yes	Yes	Yes	Yes	Yes
Obs	1451	1451	1205	1047	1069	651	800	1451

Standard Errors in parentheses. Dependent Variable in all regressions is *CREDIT*, a dummy variable that takes on a value of one if the primary method of payment to the supplier was through trade credit. For additional variable definitions, please see the data appendix.

Advances in Economic Analysis & Policy , Vol. 3 [2003], Iss. 1, Art. 4

In looking at the summary statistics, it is apparent that some entrepreneurs of African descent report transactions with *TIES* = *1*, reflecting within-community transactions among this group.   The relative dominance of businesses owned by those of European and Asian background in the countries in the sample may weaken the potential use of ethnic ties in promoting cooperation among entrepreneurs of African descent, which would attenuate the average effect of *TIES*.   To examine this possibility, I include an interaction term *BACKGROUND*TIES* in an additional specification in column (8). Alternatively, the model may be run with the sample split into *BACKGROUND*=1 and *BACKGROUND*=0 firms. These results are reported in columns (6) and (7), and are consistent with the previously described hypothesis: the coefficient on *TIES* is large and significant for Asian/European firms, but not for the subsample of African-owned firms. Similarly, in the full sample regression, the coefficient on the interaction term *BACKGROUND*TIES* is positive, though not significant at conventional levels. When we restrict the sample to non-Tanzanian firms, all point estimates increase in magnitude (see column (5)).   Finally, the basic regressions were run for each country individually, limiting the sample to *BACKGROUND* = 1 firms. This could not be done for Tanzania, because of the empty cell of *TIES* = 1 and *CREDIT* = 1 firms. For all other countries, the coefficient on *TIES* was positive and significant, taking on values of 1.8,1.5, and 5.7 in Kenya, Zambia, and Zimbabwe respectively.[7]

While I have tried to control for unobserved quality that might be correlated with the relationship-specific regressors, omitted variable bias is always a potential problem with random effects models. All of the preceding regressions were thus repeated using Chamberlain's (1980) conditional fixed-effects model. Because the maximum likelihood estimation in this case is conditional on the total number of suppliers from which a firm receives goods on credit, all observations for which there is no within firm variation in *CREDIT* will drop out of the maximum likelihood expression, reducing the sample size to 88 firms with 248 relationships. The fixed-effects specification is as follows:

$$P(CREDIT_{si} = 1) = \Lambda(\beta_1 * LENGTH_{si}, + \beta_2 * TIES_{si} + \alpha_i)$$

The results are listed in Table 5; the magnitudes of coefficients are marginally smaller than those obtained with the random effects model. When all firms from all countries are included, the coefficient on *TIES* is not statistically significantly different from zero at conventional levels. This is, however, driven entirely by within-community transactions among *BACKGROUND*=0 firms: when the sample is split by *BACKGROUND*, the coefficient on *TIES* is significant in the *BACKGROUND*=1 subsample, and actually negative in the *BACKGROUND*=0 subsample (though not significant). The coefficient on *TIES* remains marginally smaller than the coefficient reported in the random effects model. However, this is driven by the difference in sample rather than the actual specification. When the random effects specification was repeated with the 88 firms with variation in *CREDIT*, the coefficients on the relationship-specific variables were virtually identical to those obtained in the fixed effects specification.

---

[7] This actually results in a much smaller effect of ethnic ties on the rate of credit access for firms in Zimbabwe (see below). One possible explanation is that the better court system and presence of a credit reference agency reduces the importance of communal networks.

Entrepreneurship in Developing Countries

Fisman: Ethnic Ties and the Provision of Credit

Table 5 – Fixed Effects Regressions of Determinants of Credit Access

	Full Sample	BACKGROUND=1	BACKGROUND=0	Full Sample	Tanzania Excluded
TIES	0.961	1.693	-0.958	-1.094	-1.100
	(0.621)	(0.806)	(1.254)	(1.240)	(1.240)
LENGTH	0.026	0.016	0.076	0.025	0.023
	(0.020)	(0.021)	(0.054)	(0.020)	(0.020)
BACKGROUND* TIES				2.796	2.800
				(1.479)	(1.479)
Obs	248	162	86	248	224

Standard Errors in parentheses. Dependent Variable in all regressions is *CREDIT,* a dummy variable that takes on a value of one if the primary method of payment to the supplier was through trade credit. For additional variable definitions, please see the data appendix.

Interpreting the magnitude of the effect implied by the coefficient on *TIES* is not straightforward, since it is a function of firm characteristics. In particular, since the country dummies' coefficients are all highly significant, the size of the effect will be country-dependent. Estimating the effect for an average firm implicitly takes a weighted average across countries.[8] Using this approach, the probability of receiving credit for an Asian/European firm increases by more than 100 percent, going from 0.29 to approximately 0.75, in moving from a relationship with a supplier outside the owner's ethnic community to a within-community relationship. This effect is slightly increased by the exclusion of Tanzania from the sample. Looking at each country separately, the changes in probability associated with going from a within-community transaction to an outside-community transaction are listed in Table 6. Note that, because of the shape of the logistic function, these values are particularly sensitive to the choice of firm characteristics for Zimbabwe, where the rate of credit access is very high.

Table 6
Probability of Obtaining Credit for BACKGROUND=1
Firms, from Logit Regression Results

	TIES=0	TIES=1
Full Sample	0.29	0.75
Kenya	0.27	0.73
Zambia	0.11	0.35
Zimbabwe	0.95	1.00

---

[8] This is not truly a weighted average, because of the non-linear nature of the logistic function.

Advances in Economic Analysis & Policy , Vol. 3 [2003], Iss. 1, Art. 4

The other sense in which the importance of ethnic ties in promoting credit provision may be assessed is the extent to which this accounts for the total difference in credit access enjoyed by non-African firms. While the effect of *TIES* is large, there are few enough *TIES* = 1 relationships that ethnic ties seem to account for only a small percentage of the higher level of credit access of non-African firms. To be more precise: the difference in the probability of obtaining credit for *BACKGROUND*=1 vs. *BACKGROUND*=0 firms is 0.34 (0.44-0.10). Given that the probability of obtaining credit is 45 percentage points higher in a relationship involving ethnic ties, and that 12 percent of relationships involve ethnic ties, this suggests that only about 15 percent (0.45*0.12/0.34) of the total difference in credit access may be attributed to the effect of ethnic ties. The rest may be attributed to differences in observable characteristics, such as firm size, and also unobservables, as reflected by the extremely large coefficient on *BACKGROUND*.[9]

Robustness Checks
Interpreting the coefficient on *TIES* as the effect of ethnic ties is potentially complicated by the possibility that the ethnicity of a supplier proxies for supplier quality in the provision of credit. While the fixed effects model above would absorb any such omitted variable bias across firms, it does not deal with within-firm unobserved supplier differences. Note, however, that theory would perhaps argue that this biases the reported coefficients *towards* zero. The reason is that, all else equal, the owner of a given firm may prefer to transact with suppliers of his own ethnicity. Therefore, an outsider will face a higher hurdle in attracting an 'ethnic' firm as a customer. Thus, conditional on having chosen to transact with an 'outside' firm, we might expect this outside firm to be of particularly 'high-quality'. We may observe some very tentative evidence of this: within-community (*TIES* = 1) transactions are, on average, less than half as large as those involving suppliers outside the owner's ethnic group.[10] To the extent that transaction size is correlated with firm size,[11] and that firm size is further correlated with a firm's ability to provide credit,[12] this suggests that suppliers outside of owners' communities may indeed be better credit providers in general. Hence, this casual evidence points to a downward bias on the reported coefficients on *TIES*.

Endogeneity of controls is also a concern. For example, suppose that a firm approaches two suppliers to obtain credit. Further imagine that one supplier, A, grants credit while the other, B, does not. In this case, we may expect the firm to continue buying from A, while buying only occasionally, if at all, from B. In this case, length of relation and frequency of purchases are caused by credit, instead of the opposite. Controlling for length of relationship and frequency of

---

[9] Perhaps a more natural way to think about this is as a decomposition of the various components of credit access, using the method pioneered by Oaxaca (1973). However, Belman and Hayward (1990) have noted some of the complications in trying to apply this method to non-linear models. Depending on the specification that is used, this method provides a fairly wide range of decompositions. However, the fundamental finding, i.e., that most of the preferential credit access of ethnic firms does not come from within-community relationships, is broadly found to be true when this type of decomposition is implemented.

[10] The number of firms for which we have observations on transactions size is very small (n=395), which is why this variable is not used as a control.

[11] This relationship is very strong among firms in the RPED sample: average transaction size with clients is highly correlated with firm size (ρ=0.55).

[12] In a regression looking at credit provision, I found that by far the strongest predictor of whether a firm provides its customers with goods on credit is firm size. Unfortunately, data on ethnicity of customers was not collected, so I cannot use these data to examine the primary hypothesis of this paper.

purchase may thus bias the coefficient of the *TIES* variable because these variables capture part of the effect of *TIES* on credit. We explore this possibility by dropping these controls from the regressions. This results in a very small reduction in the coefficient on *TIES* (about 5 percent), but does not fundamentally impact the previously reported results.

Finally, the deletion of observations in order to include the controls may raise concerns of selection bias. However, when both the random- and fixed-effects regressions were repeated with the original (unabridged) sample, the resultant coefficients changed only slightly.

IV. Discussion and Conclusions

In this paper, I have shown that firms are far more likely to be provided with trade credit by suppliers that are members of their ethnic communities: the results imply that a firm with average characteristics is more than twice as likely to obtaining credit from a within-community supplier as from an 'outside' supplier. The other main finding of this paper is that most of the preferential trade credit access enjoyed by Asian and European firms in Africa is *not* attributable to communal ties.

Overall, however, these results hint at the potentially large role that ethnic ties play in governing economics transactions. Therefore, developing a better understanding the channels through which these communal ties impact firm behavior – discrimination versus networks; decentralized versus centralized enforcement – is an important next step in this research agenda.

Advances in Economic Analysis & Policy , Vol. 3 [2003], Iss. 1, Art. 4

Data Appendix

Relationship Variables

CREDIT – dummy variable denoting whether purchases with a particular supplier were largely credit based.

TIES – dummy variable that takes on a value of one if the firm reported that the owner of its supplier and the firm's owner were of the same ethnicity.

COMPETITION – dummy variable denoting whether there is more than one supplier available to provide the materials purchased.

LENGTH – the reported length of the relationship with a given supplier, in years.

FREQUENCY – the frequency with which purchases were made from a given supplier. These values range from daily (FREQUENCY =6) to yearly (FREQUENCY=0).

Firm Variables

BACKGROUND – dummy variable that takes on a value of one if the firm's owner is of Asian or European descent

SIZE - total firm employment, given by (full-time workers) + 0.5*(part-time workers).

OVERDRAFT – dummy variable denoting whether the firm has access to overdraft facilities.

AGE – firm's age.

ASIAN – dummy variable that takes on a value of one if the firm's owner is of Asian descent.

EURO – dummy variable that takes on a value of one if the firm's owner is of European descent.

GENDER – dummy variable equal to one if the firm's owner is female.

SUBSIDIARY – dummy variable denoting whether the firm is a subsidiary of a conglomerate.

References

Arrow, Kenneth J. "Models of Job Discrimination." *Racial Discrimination in Economic Life*, Anthony H. Pascal (ed.). Lexington, Mass.: Heath, 1972.

Arutyunyan, Yuri. "Armenians in Moscow." *Immigration and Entrepreneurship: Culture, Capital, and Ethnic Network*, Ivan Light, Parminder Bhachu (eds.), London: Transaction, 1993.

Becker, Gary S. *The Economics of Discrimination.* Chicago: The University Of Chicago Press, 1971.

Belman, Dale and John S. Hayward. "Application of the 'Oaxaca Decomposition' to Probit Estimates: The Case of Unions and Fringe Benefit Provision." *Economics Letters*, 32 (1), January 1990, pp. 101-4.

Blanchflower, David G., Philip B. Levine, David J. Zimmerman. "Discrimination in the Small Business Credit Market." *National Bureau of Economic Research Working Paper* 6840, December, 1998.

Borjas, George J. "Ethnicity, Neighborhoods, and Human Capital Externalities." *American Economic Review*, 85 (3), June 1995, pp. 365-90.

Chamberlain, Gary. "Analysis of Covariance with Qualitative Data." *Review of Economic Studies*, 47, 1980, pp. 225-238.

Chamberlain, Gary. "Panel Data." *Handbook of Econometrics, Volume II*, Zvi Griliches and Michael D. Intriligator (eds.). New York: North-Holland, 1984.

Donohue, John. "Discrimination in Employment." *The New Palgrave Dictionary of Economics and the Law*, Peter Newman (ed.). London: MacMillan, 1998.

Fafchamps, Marcel. "Trade Credit in Zimbabwean Manufacturing," *World Development*, 25(3): 795-815, April 1997.

Fafchamps, Marcel. "Ethnicity and Credit in African Manufacturing." *Journal of Development Economics*, 61:205-235, 2000.

Fafchamps, Marcel and Bart Minten. "Returns to Social Network Capital Among Traders", *Oxford Economic Papers*, 54: 173-206, April 2002.

Fisman, Raymond J. and Mayank Raturi. "Does Competition Encourage Cooperation? Evidence on the Effect of Competition on Trade Credit Provision." *Review of Economics and Statistics,* forthcoming, 2003.

Forster, Peter, Michael Hitchcock, and Francis Lyimo, *Race and ethnicity in East Africa.* London: MacMillan, 2000.

Advances in Economic Analysis & Policy , Vol. 3 [2003], Iss. 1, Art. 4

Granovetter, Mark, ''Economic Action and Social Structure: The Problem of Embeddedness,'' *American Journal of Sociology*, 91(3): 481-510, 1985.

Greene, William H. *Econometric Analysis*, 4th edition, Prentice-Hall: New Jersey, 2000.

Greif, Avner. "Contract Enforceability and Economic Institutions in Early Trade: the Maghribi Traders' Coalition." *American Economic Review*; 83(3), June 1993, pp. 525-48.

Guinnane, Timothy. "Cooperatives as Information Machines: German Rural Credit Cooperatives, 1883-1914." *Journal of Economic History*, 61(2): 366-389, 2001.

Kandori,-Michihiro. "Social Norms and Community Enforcement." *Review of Economic Studies*, 59(1), January 1992, pp. 63-80.

Landa, Janet T. "Trust, Social Capital, and Gift Giving: Chinese Middleman-Entrepreneurship." *International Sociological Association* paper, 1998.

Loury, Glenn. ""Discrimination in the Post-Civil Rights Era: Beyond Market Interactions," *Journal of Economic Perspectives*, 12 (2), Spring 1998, pp. 117-126.

Munnell, A.G., M.B Tootell, L.E. Browne and J. McEneaney. "Mortgage lending in Boston: interpreting HMDA data." *American Economic Review*, 86(1), March 1996, pp. 25-53.

Oaxaca, Ronald. "Male-Female Wage Differentials in Urban Labor Markets." *International Economic Review*, 14(3), October 1973, pp. 693-709.

Platteau, Jean-Philippe, *Institutions, social norms, and economic development*, Reading, U.K.: Harwood Academic, 2000.

Rogers, Alisdair and Stephen Vertovec. *The Urban Context: Ethnicity, Social Networks, and Situational Analysis*, Berg: Oxford, 1995.

Yambert, Karl A. "Alien Traders and the Ruling Elites: The Overseas Chinese in Southeast Asia and the Indians in East Africa." *Ethnic Groups*, 3(3), pp. 173-198.

Zhou, Yu. "Inter-Firm Linkages, Ethnic Networks, and Territorial Agglomeration: Chinese Computer Firms in Los Angeles." *Papers in Regional Science*, 75(3), July 1996, pp. 265-91.

[23]

THE JOURNAL OF FINANCE • VOL. LVIII, NO. 5 • OCTOBER 2003

Family Firms

MIKE BURKART, FAUSTO PANUNZI, and ANDREI SHLEIFER*

ABSTRACT

We present a model of succession in a firm owned and managed by its founder. The founder decides between hiring a professional manager or leaving management to his heir, as well as on what fraction of the company to float on the stock exchange. We assume that a professional is a better manager than the heir, and describe how the founder's decision is shaped by the legal environment. This theory of separation of ownership from management includes the Anglo-Saxon and the Continental European patterns of corporate governance as special cases, and generates additional empirical predictions consistent with cross-country evidence.

MOST FIRMS IN THE WORLD are controlled by their founders, or by the founders' families and heirs. Such family ownership is nearly universal among privately held firms, but is also dominant among publicly traded firms. In Western Europe, South and East Asia, the Middle East, Latin America, and Africa, the vast majority of publicly traded firms are family controlled (La Porta, Lopez-de-Silanes, and Shleifer (1999), Claessens, Djankov, and Lang (2000), European Corporate Governance Network (2001), Faccio and Lang (2002)). But even in the United States and the United Kingdom, some of the largest publicly traded firms, such as Wal-Mart Stores and Ford Motor, are controlled by families.

A crucial issue in the discussion of family firms from the perspective of corporate governance and finance is succession. For nearly every entrepreneurial firm that does not fail, there comes a moment when the founder no longer wishes to manage it. This can happen from the very beginning, when founders seek professional managers to run their firms, as is the case in high technology start-ups in the United States. Alternatively, a founder can retire or cut his work load later in

*Burkart is from the Stockholm School of Economics, Panunzi is from Università di Bologna, and Shleifer is from Harvard University. We are grateful to Mara Faccio, Julian Franks, Rob Gertner, Denis Gromb, Simon Johnson, Rafael La Porta, Enrico Perotti, Jeremy Stein, Daniel Wolfenzon, the editor, an anonymous referee, and seminar participants at Bologna, INSEAD, London Business School, the NBER Corporate Finance Conference (Chicago), Padua, Salerno, Stockholm School of Economics, Venice, and Zurich for helpful comments and discussions. Financial support from Università Bocconi (Ricerca di Base), from the Bank of Sweden Tercentenary Foundation, and from the Gildor Foundation is gratefully acknowledged. Robin Greenwood provided excellent research assistance. This paper is produced as part of a CEPR project on Understanding Financial Architecture: Legal Framework, Political Environment, and Economic Efficiency, funded by the European Commission under the Human Potential—Research Training Network program (Contract No. HPRN-CT-2000-00064).

life, and appoint either an heir or a professional as a successor. When control is turned over to a professional, ownership and management become separated.

The patterns of separation of ownership and management vary across countries. In the United States, founders often hire professional managers early on. By the time a founder retires, his family retains only marginal ownership. In such Berle and Means (1932) corporations, professional managers exercise nearly full control. In Western Europe, significant ownership typically stays with the family after the founder retires. His children either hire a manager, as in BMW or Fiat, or run the firm themselves, as in Peugeot. In emerging markets, both management and ownership tend to stay with the family when the founder retires. Occasionally in both developed and emerging markets, a manager marries into the family, as happened at Bombardier in Canada, Matshushita in Japan, and Worldwide Shipping in Hong Kong.

There are three broad theories of the benefits to a family of preserving control.[1] According to the first, there is a significant "amenity potential" of family control. The term "amenity potential," suggested by Demsetz and Lehn (1985), refers to nonpecuniary private benefits of control, meaning utility to the founder that does not come at the expense of profits. A founder may derive pleasure from having his child run the company that bears the family name. Alternatively, in some industries, such as sports or the media, a family can participate in or even influence exciting social, political, and cultural events through ownership of firms. This reason for family control suggests that there will be a distribution of ownership patterns within a country, with companies delivering a large amenity potential of control staying in family hands. Indeed, in their study of initial public offerings of German companies, Ehrhardt and Nowak (2001) find that families nearly universally retain control, with "amenity potential" being the crucial reason.

If the amenity potential is large, we expect families to try to maintain control as long as they can. Only if a firm desperately needs capital and cannot raise it without a control change, or if the founder dies and significant inheritance taxes are due, will control be sold off. Some recent research indeed points to the importance of these considerations. In a cross section of 20 countries, Wells (1998) finds a higher incidence of widely held, as opposed to family-controlled, firms in countries with higher inheritance taxes. Bhattacharya and Ravikumar (2001, 2002) present theoretical models linking the persistence of family control to imperfect capital markets. In our model, we recognize the role of the amenity potential in keeping some firms under family control. But we use a framework that simultaneously explains capital market underdevelopment and the prevalence of family ownership based on institutional characteristics of a country.

A second reason for the preservation of family control is that the name itself may be a carrier of a reputation, in both economic and political markets. Families

---

[1] A related literature describes *how* control is maintained by a dominant shareholder, which may or may not be a family. This literature focuses on pyramids, multiple classes of stock with different voting rights, voting trusts, and so forth (see, e.g., Grossman and Hart (1988), Prowse (1995), Zingales (1994), and Nenova (2003)).

may stand for quality (as advertisements often argue) or for political connections (Faccio (2002)). Italy's Agnellis have stayed close to the government, sometimes having family members in the cabinet, and always securing public transfers to Fiat. Such "reputational benefits" would be diluted if control is surrendered to an outsider. This theory suggests, counterfactually, that ceteris paribus family-controlled firms would be more valuable than firms controlled by professionals. Although it deserves a closer analysis, the connection between family control and politics is not considered in this paper.

We focus on a third theory of family ownership, namely the possibility of expropriation of outside investors that comes with control. Unlike the amenity potential, such private benefits of control, as described by Jensen and Meckling (1976), do come at the expense of profits accruing to the outside investors. In our theory, the principal benefit of hiring a professional is that he is likely to be a better manager. The principal cost is that now the professional manager, rather than the founder, controls the company and so can expropriate investors. We argue that a crucial factor shaping the attractiveness of delegated management is the degree of legal protection of outside shareholders from expropriation (or tunneling) by the insiders. Earlier research shows that such protection varies sharply across countries, and that this variation predicts the differences in financial development and ownership structures (La Porta et al. (1997, 1998, 2000a, 2000b), Johnson et al. (2000)). In this paper, we examine the costs and benefits of delegating management from this perspective. This allows us, in particular, to examine the costs and benefits of keeping the succession of management inside the family.

We present a model of a founder looking for a manager to succeed him. We assume that there is no superior manager available with sufficient resources to buy the firm outright. When such a manager (or a company) is available, the firm is simply sold to them—as often happens. Absent an outright buyer, the founder chooses among three options. He can sell out completely in the stock market and create a widely held firm run by a professional manager. He can hire a professional manager but stay on as a large shareholder to monitor him. He can also keep the firm inside the family by either staying on as a less than ideal manager or by passing management to a family member, who is generally not as talented as a professional. The founder maximizes his welfare, equal to the sum of the value of the retained block, the revenues from selling shares to investors, and the amenity potential obtained only if the family keeps control.

We study the trade-off between superior management by the professional outsider and his discretion to expropriate shareholders. If the founder stays on as a large shareholder and monitors, he can control expropriation to some extent. In our framework, both the law and the monitoring reduce managerial expropriation. We show that when the family's amenity potential from managing the firm is very large, ownership and management are never separated. In contrast, management and ownership are always separated when the discrepancy between the managerial abilities of the professional and the founder (or heir) is very large and the amenity potential is small. Except for these extremes, the decision to keep control in the family depends on the quality of legal protection.

2170   *The Journal of Finance*

When legal protection of outside investors is very good, there is no need for monitoring in equilibrium, and the best arrangement is a widely held professionally managed firm. When legal protection of outside investors is moderate, the benefits of professional managers are still high enough for the entrepreneur to surrender control, but it pays for him or his family to stay on as large shareholders and monitor the manager. Finally, with sufficiently weak shareholder protection, the founder's ability to control expropriation is too limited, and management stays with his family even when someone else can run the firm better. In general, this analysis leads to a prediction of a negative relationship between investor protection and ownership concentration, consistent with a range of empirical evidence.

We consider two versions of the model, one in which the founder—when he detects expropriation—forces the manager to stop it and pay dividends, and another in which he and the manager just share the spoils. In the first version, as in Shleifer and Vishny (1986), the founder provides a public good to the minority shareholders by monitoring the manager. In the second version, monitoring is no longer a public good, the benefits of which are shared by all shareholders. In fact, the only effect of monitoring is to raise the founder's share of the loot. The basic results we describe hold in both specifications, but the second version also yields the empirically accurate prediction of a positive premium paid for a controlling block of shares.

At a theoretical level, the model combines in one unified framework the twin conflicts essential to understanding corporate governance: that between the manager and the outside shareholders, and that between the large shareholder and the minority shareholders. By doing so, the model sheds light on the different prevalent patterns of ownership and management among countries. It shows, for example, why Anglo-Saxon patterns of corporate governance, with widely held firms and traditional conflicts between professional managers and dispersed shareholders (Berle and Means (1932)), are likely to be a feature of countries with very good legal protection of minority shareholders. It explains why "family" firms, in which the founder's family is a significant shareholder or even the manager over several generations, are such an enduring phenomenon in countries with less effective legal protection of shareholders (La Porta et al. (1999), Claessens et al. (2000)). Indeed, it explains how, in such countries, the twin conflicts coexist between the manager and the large shareholder, and between the two of them combined and the minority shareholders. The model is moreover consistent with the evidence that family management is generally inferior to professional management (Morck, Strangeland, and Yueng (2000), Perez-Gonzales (2001)).[2] The basic trade-off between the benefits of delegated management and the costs of giving up control—especially when legal protection is poor—appears consistent with a great deal of data.

---

[2] For a sample of S&P 500 firms, Anderson and Reeb (2003) present evidence that Tobin's Qs are actually higher for family than for nonfamily businesses. They also find that performance measures deteriorate at high levels of family ownership, consistent with the view that entrenched family control is associated with inferior performance even in the United States.

Our paper joins a growing theoretical literature on corporate governance in the regimes of poor investor protection. Bebchuk (1999) shows that poor legal protection renders dispersed ownership structure unstable, because it allows extraction of significant private benefits. Himmelberg, Hubbard, and Love (2001) and La Porta et al. (2002) study theoretically and empirically the determination of ownership structure when firms raise funds to finance investment. Burkart and Panunzi (2001) and Shleifer and Wolfenzon (2002) analyze the impact of legal shareholder protection on the optimal ownership structure. Shleifer and Wolfenzon consider owner–managers and examine the relationship between legal protection and inside equity. Burkart and Panunzi assume that the professional manager and the large shareholder are distinct parties and analyze the relationship between the law and outside ownership concentration. By making the separation of ownership and management a choice variable, the present model extends and generalizes these two papers.

The paper is organized as follows. Section I outlines the model. Section II examines the founder's decision to hire a professional manager and to float shares when he cannot share private benefits. Section III analyzes the case with collusion between founder and professional manager and derives implications for share value, block premium, and agency costs of separating ownership and management. Section IV concludes. Mathematical proofs are in the Appendix.

I. The Model

Figure 1 presents the model's timeline. We consider a firm initially fully owned by its founder. At date 0, the founder decides whether to appoint a professional manager to run the firm or keep management in the family. Simultaneously, he decides what fraction $1 - \alpha$ of the shares to sell to dispersed shareholders. The family keeps the remaining fraction α. All shareholders are risk neutral. If management stays in the family, there is no separation of ownership and management. If the founder appoints a professional manager, ownership and management are separated. In this case, the founder may also offer a wage and the professional manager accepts or rejects the offer to run the company at date 1.

At date 3, the firm generates revenues that depend on the identity of the manager. If control remains inside the family, total revenues generated are v_F. In addition, the amenity potential B accrues to the founder. While B may differ across founders and industries, it does not reduce revenues v_F. If a professional manager runs the firm, total revenues are v_M. The professional manager may enjoy some

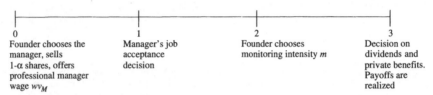

0	1	2	3
Founder chooses the manager, sells 1-α shares, offers professional manager wage wv_M	Manager's job acceptance decision	Founder chooses monitoring intensity m	Decision on dividends and private benefits. Payoffs are realized

Figure 1. The timing of the model.

amenity potential from running the firm. He also has an outside option. To economize on notation, let c denote the professional manager's utility when pursuing his outside option net of the foregone amenity potential. For simplicity, the outside option of the founder or the family is normalized to zero.

ASSUMPTION 1: $v_M - c > v_F$.

There are two interpretations of the model. Under the first, the choice is between the founder himself, who is becoming outdated or reluctant to manage, and a professional outsider. Under the second, the founder definitely retires from management, and chooses as his successor either a professional manager or his heir. In both interpretations, retaining management inside the family reduces the profitability of the firm relative to hiring a professional.

Assumption 1 is consistent with a recent study by Morck et al. (2000) of corporate control of Canadian firms. They find that heir-controlled firms have lower returns on sales and assets than comparable firms. Furthermore, firms with founder control have earnings that are lower than those of widely held firms but higher than those in heir-controlled firms. Perez-Gonzales (2001) provides evidence on firm performance following inherited control by studying 162 family transitions in the United States. In 38 percent of these cases, family members inherit the CEO position. These family CEOs are promoted to the post an average of nine years earlier than professional managers and are detrimental to firm performance—the return on assets falls by 16 percent within two years of transition and by 25 percent compared with unrelated CEOs.

In this model, if the founder is the best manager himself, there is no reason for him ever to sell equity. He stays on as the manager, keeps 100 percent of the firm, and there are no agency problems or conflicts. This assumption distinguishes the model from the papers of La Porta et al. (2002), Shleifer and Wolfenzon (2002), and Himmelberg et al. (2001), where equity is raised to finance investment projects, and therefore the size of the firm is endogenous.

The problems arise when the founder is no longer the best manager. He must then choose between hiring a more qualified outsider to manage and staying on (or equivalently naming a mediocre son as a successor). We assume that the competent professional outsider has neither the resources nor the external funds to just buy the firm himself. As we show below, the outsider's inability to raise external funds is consistent with the assumptions of the model, since to buy the firm, he has to pay for the private benefits accruing to the founder, which he cannot pledge to investors. Unless the superior manager is himself wealthy, he has to work for the family. Hiring a professional separates ownership from management.

At date 2, shareholders can monitor the professional manager and thereby deprive him of at least some private benefits. The monitoring technology is discussed below.

At date 3, the revenues can either be paid out to all shareholders proportionally to their ownership stakes or diverted to generate private benefits Φ. In countries with weakest shareholder protection, such private benefits take the form of outright theft. More commonly, they take the form of transactions with related parties, expropriation of corporate opportunities, transfer pricing, excessive salaries and perquisites, and so on (see Johnson et al. (2000)).

Whoever manages the firm chooses the level of expropriation, subject to being monitored and partially impeded by the law. The noncontractible expropriation decision is modeled as the choice of $\phi \in [0,1]$, such that security benefits (dividends) are $(1 - \phi)v_i$, and private benefits are $\Phi = \phi v_i$, $i = M, F$. Expropriation of shareholders is limited by the law. To model legal shareholder protection, we assume that the law sets an upper bound $\bar{\phi} \in [0, 1]$ on the fraction of revenues that can be (at no cost) diverted by the party in control.[3] Stronger legal protection corresponds to lower values of $\bar{\phi}$.

The law is not the only determinant of the fraction of resources diverted for private benefits. The other is monitoring, which occurs when a professional manager is hired. Although in principle all shareholders can monitor the manager, the free-rider problem prevents small shareholders from choosing to incur the cost. In equilibrium, only the large shareholder monitors to reduce the fraction of resources appropriated by the manager.[4] Recall that the legal upper bound on private benefits of control is $\bar{\phi}v_M$. Following Pagano and Röell (1998), we assume that the large shareholder can at a cost $k(m^2/2)$ reduce private benefit extraction by mv_M, where $m \in [0,1]$ and $k > 0$.

The private benefits Φ differ from the amenity potential B in two respects: They come at the expense of security benefits and their size depends on the legal shareholder protection and (in the absence of collusion) on the monitoring intensity.

Private monitoring and the law are alternative mechanisms for reducing expropriation of shareholders. In our model, when k is strictly positive, monitoring is costly to the founder whereas reliance on the law is free. Some legal protection, such as disclosure mandated by law, is indeed enforced by the authorities and is truly free to the founder though not to the society. Other kinds of legal protection require an investment in resources by the founder, such as litigation. What we require is not that the law be literally free to the founder, but that reducing managerial extraction by a given amount through a combination of stricter rules and less monitoring be cheaper for the founder and the shareholders than achieving the same protection through a combination of weaker laws (higher $\bar{\phi}$) and more monitoring (higher m).

Alternatively, one can think of legal protection as reducing the cost of monitoring. Our framework can accommodate this interpretation. The cost parameter k would then be a measure of shareholder protection: The law protects shareholders by increasing the effectiveness of monitoring.[5] Under this formulation,

---

[3] The amount $\bar{\phi}v_i$ is the legal upper bound that can be extracted as private benefits of control, irrespective of the form in which those benefits are enjoyed. In particular, wages in excess of market value are already incorporated in $\bar{\phi}v_i$.

[4] We assume that there is no reason for the founder to sell his shares to another large shareholder who would monitor, since, if anything, the founder has a comparative advantage at monitoring because of his knowledge. In addition, the founder may want to retain his stake because of some residual amenity potential.

[5] Modeling the differences in legal shareholder protection by varying the efficiency of the monitoring technology or by changing the upper bound on diversion is equivalent when the

private monitoring and the law are complements rather than substitutes. The crucial feature of our model is that better legal protection mitigates the agency problem between the management and the shareholders either by directly reducing the scope of expropriation or by making the founder's intervention more effective.

We assume that corporate and other law governing investor protection matters, and that firms cannot opt into more protective legal regimes via a contract, such as cross-listing or a better corporate charter. This assumption is consistent with the evidence that legal rules governing investor protection in different countries have significant consequences for financial development (La Porta et al. (1997, 1998, 2000b)). This assumption is also consistent with recent theory and evidence pointing to the limited usefulness of such contractual solutions (Siegel (2002), Nenova (2003)). If a founder could opt into a more protective legal regime before selling any shares, he would do so, since in equilibrium he bears the monitoring cost of reducing managerial expropriation.

If a professional manager is hired, the question arises whether a monitoring founder can enjoy a part of the private benefits. We consider both the cases of collusion and no collusion between the professional manager and the founder. Excluding the founder from the spoils of extraction is tantamount to assuming that his interests and those of the small shareholders are perfectly congruent. This case is most appropriate when the legal duties of the large shareholder, perhaps as a board member, bar him from complicity with the manager in expropriating shareholders. In contrast, when the founder and the professional manager can share the private benefits, they may collude at the expense of minority shareholders. This assumption might be more suitable for weaker legal regimes. The second assumption complicates the model, in that rent-seeking monitoring, intended to capture some of the private benefits rather than serve all shareholders, becomes attractive. We solve the model under the first assumption in the next section, and under the second in Section III.

II. Owner-Manager or Professional Manager

We analyze the founder's decision whether to hire a professional manager in steps. We begin by considering the founder's maximization problem for the cases of nonseparation and separation of ownership and management. In each case, we solve the model by backward induction, going from the date 3 expropriation decision, to the founder's date 2 monitoring intensity, to the manager's date 1 job acceptance choice. We then can determine the optimal number of shares that the founder retains in cases of separation and nonseparation. Having done that, we can compare the founder's welfare in different legal environments, that is, different values of $\bar{\phi}$. This enables us to infer under what circumstances the founder chooses to separate ownership from management.

founder and the small shareholders have congruent interests. With collusion between the founder and the professional manager (Section III), this equivalence breaks down because monitoring protects the founder but not the shareholders from managerial expropriation.

A. No Separation of Ownership and Management

Due to the simplicity of the model, the case of no separation does not yield precise predictions, notably for the ownership structure. At date 3, the founder decides how to allocate the revenues. While the law does not influence the amenity potential B, it constrains the founder to divert no more than $\bar{\phi}v$ of the revenues as private benefits Φ. Unless he owns all the shares, in which case he is indifferent between any $\phi \in [0, \bar{\phi}]$, he extracts the legal upper bound $\bar{\phi}$. Absent a professional manager, there is neither date 2 monitoring nor a date 1 job acceptance decision. Hence, we move directly to the founder's date 0 decision as to which fraction of shares to sell to outside investors. The founder maximizes his welfare $V^{NS} = \alpha(1 - \bar{\phi})v_F + \bar{\phi}v_F + (1 - \alpha)(1 - \bar{\phi})v_F + B$.   The first term, $\alpha(1 - \bar{\phi})v_F + \bar{\phi}v_F$, is the value of his date 3 block; the second term, $(1 - \alpha)(1 - \bar{\phi})v_F$, is the proceeds from selling $1 - \alpha$ shares at date 0; the final term is the amenity potential. Since diversion is efficient and since the founder is by assumption neither financially constrained nor risk averse, the optimal ownership structure is indeterminate when ownership and management are separated.

LEMMA 1: *For any* $\bar{\phi} \in [0, 1]$, $V^{NS}(\alpha*) = v_F + B$ *and* $\alpha* \in [0, 1]$.

The founder's welfare is equal to $v_F + B$—total revenues under his management plus the amenity potential of managing the company. Even though private benefit extraction decreases with the quality of the law, the founder's welfare is independent of the legal environment. Since the extraction of private benefits is efficient, each diverted dollar reduces the security benefits by a dollar. Diversion reduces the price at which the founder can sell shares to investors, but increases the value of his block by an identical amount. The sum of security and private benefits (including both the amenity potential B and private benefits Φ) is constant.

B. Separation of Ownership and Management

What happens when ownership and management are separated? The founder gives up the amenity potential B and also transfers to the professional manager the opportunity to divert corporate revenues as private benefits rather than pay them out as dividends to the shareholders. While the law constrains diversion, the founder can further limit private benefit extraction through monitoring. Monitoring may also induce opportunistic behavior by the founder even when he does not share in the private benefits. Once the professional manager has signed on to run the firm and revenues are realized, the founder has an incentive to reduce the professional manager's private benefits by monitoring more. Anticipating high levels of monitoring, the professional manager may reject the offer to run the firm. That is, the founder may overmonitor in the sense that the ex post optimal monitoring level exceeds the ex ante optimal amount (Pagano and Röell (1998)). To induce the manager to agree to run the firm, the founder has to commit himself not to monitor excessively. He can do so by dispersing some of the shares to small investors because the actual monitoring intensity is determined by the size of the founder's equity stake (Burkart, Gromb, and Panunzi (1997)). In addition (or instead), the founder may offer the professional manager monetary incentives to convince him to run the firm.

We solve the game by backward induction, beginning with the date 3 resource allocation decision. Total revenues under the professional manager are v_M. The law stipulates that $(1 - \bar{\phi})v_M$ must be paid out either to shareholders as dividends or to the professional manager as salary. What fraction of the remaining $\bar{\phi}v_M$ is actually diverted depends on monitoring. The founder who monitors with intensity m can control the use of an additional fraction m (or at most $\bar{\phi}$) of v_M. Being excluded from sharing private benefits, the founder forces the professional manager to pay out all of them as dividends. The professional manager then has discretion over $\max\{0, (\bar{\phi} - m)v_M\}$ in resources. He strictly prefers to extract them as private benefits, unless he is the sole shareholder.

Since private benefit extraction is efficient, there are no gains to shareholders from using monetary incentives to resolve the conflict over resource allocation. To induce the manager to abstain from extracting an additional dollar, shareholders have to offer him this dollar as a transfer. Monetary incentives (henceforth called the wage) can, however, play a role in inducing the manager to accept the job of running the firm. Let wv_M denote the wage paid to the professional manager when he accepts the job offer from the founder.[6]

At date 2, the founder chooses the monitoring intensity. For a given block α and for a given wage rate w, the founder maximizes $\alpha(1 - w - \bar{\phi} + m)v_M - k(m^2/2)$.[7] He receives a fraction α of the security benefits net of the wage bill less his monitoring costs. Since the law already shields $(1 - \bar{\phi})v_M$ of the revenues from private benefit extraction, the founder never monitors more than $\bar{\phi}$. Hence, $m = \min\{\bar{\phi}, \alpha(v_M/k)\}$ and weakly increases with the block size.

At date 1, the manager agrees to run the firm if the sum of the wage and the private benefits exceeds his outside utility c.[8] The condition $(w + \bar{\phi} - m)v_M \geq c$ can be rewritten as

$$m \leq \bar{m} = w + \bar{\phi} - \frac{c}{v_M}. \tag{1}$$

High levels of monitoring and strict legal rules reduce the professional manager's private benefits and may thus discourage him from running the firm. Offering him a higher wage can sway him to accept the job. Higher ownership concentration and better legal protection make it more difficult to satisfy the professional manager's participation constraint, whereas higher wages make it easier. This is the basic trade-off when ownership and management are separated.

At date 0, the founder chooses the ownership structure and the wage to maximize his welfare $V^s = [1 - w - \bar{\phi} + m]v_M - k(m^2/2)$ subject to the manager's participation constraint.

If the founder were to choose an ownership structure such that $\bar{\phi} < \alpha(v_M/k)$, the professional manager would be left with zero private benefits. Consequently,

---

[6] The subsequent analysis implicitly assumes that $\bar{\phi} + w < 1$, which holds in equilibrium.

[7] The range $m \in [0,1]$ implies that $k \geq v_M$.

[8] An alternative interpretation of the model is one where the manager has to exert an effort to generate revenues v_M and where c is the disutility of the effort.

the founder would have to offer a wage $w = c$ to induce the professional manager to accept the job. Leaving some private benefits to the professional manager in exchange for a lower wage saves on monitoring costs. Hence, the founder always chooses an ownership structure such that $\bar{\phi} > \alpha(v_M/k)$ and $m = \alpha(v_M/k)$.

Inserting the monitoring level $m = \alpha(v_M/k)$ into the founder's welfare yields $V^S = \left[1 - w - \bar{\phi} + (\alpha v_M/k)\right]v_M - \left[(\alpha v_M)^2/2k\right]$ with $dV^S/d\alpha = (1 - \alpha)v_M^2/k \geq 0$ and $dV^S/dw = -v_M < 0$. The founder's welfare increases with ownership concentration and decreases with the wage, provided that the professional manager's participation constraint is satisfied.

A binding participation constraint is obviously in the interest of the founder as any managerial rent comes at his expense. Sometimes, however, the founder cannot avoid leaving some rents to the professional manager. More precisely, there are parameter values for which the participation constraint $(w + \bar{\phi} - m)v_M \geq c$ does not bind despite a fully concentrated ownership structure and a zero wage. This occurs when $\bar{\phi} > v_M/k + c/v_M$. We want to allow for the possibility of legal regimes in which the professional manager can extract a rent.

ASSUMPTION 2: $\dfrac{v_M}{k} + \dfrac{c}{v_M} < 1$.

Since $\bar{\phi} \leq 1$, Assumption 2 is a necessary condition for $\bar{\phi} > v_M/k + c/v_M$ to hold.

LEMMA 2:

(i) *For* $\bar{\phi} \leq c/v_M$, $\alpha^* = 0$, $w^* = c/v_M - \bar{\phi}$, $m^* = 0$, *and* $V^S(\alpha^*, w^*, \bar{\phi}) = v_M - c$.

(ii) *For*

$$\frac{c}{v_M} < \bar{\phi} \leq \frac{c}{v_M} + \frac{v_M}{k}, \qquad \alpha^* = \frac{k}{v_M}\left(\bar{\phi} - \frac{c}{v_M}\right), \qquad w^* = 0, \qquad m^* = \bar{\phi} - \frac{c}{v_M},$$

$$V^S(\alpha^*, w^*, \bar{\phi}) = v_M - c - \frac{k}{2}\left(\bar{\phi} - \frac{c}{v_M}\right)^2.$$

(iii) *For*

$$\bar{\phi} > \frac{c}{v_M} + \frac{v_M}{k}, \qquad \alpha^* = 1, \qquad w^* = 0, \qquad m^* = \frac{v_M}{k},$$

$$and \quad V^S(\alpha^*, w^*, \bar{\phi}) = v_M(1 - \bar{\phi}) + \frac{v_M^2}{2k}$$

When legal protection is strong (case (i)), then even in the absence of monitoring, private benefits are insufficient to induce the professional manager to run the firm. Ownership is then completely dispersed and the professional manager is offered a wage equal to the difference between his outside utility and the private benefits. The founder's welfare $V^S(\alpha^*, w^*, \bar{\phi})$ is at its highest possible level under separation $(v_M - c)$ and does not depend on legal rules.

When legal protection is moderate (case (ii)), expected private benefits exceed the outside utility c. As a result, the founder has to monitor the professional manager to limit the size of his rent. Setting the wage equal to zero minimizes the monitoring intensity that keeps the professional manager's participation constraint binding. Since monitoring is costly, this dominates all other combinations of positive wage and monitoring level that also leave no rent to the professional manager. A positive wage and concentrated ownership do not coexist in equilibrium. Due to the monitoring costs, the founder's welfare $V^S(\alpha*, w*, \bar{\phi})$ is below its highest possible level. Moreover, $V^S(\alpha*, w*, \bar{\phi})$ decreases in both $\bar{\phi}$ and k: Less legal protection entails a higher optimal level of monitoring, and a higher k makes monitoring more expensive.

When legal protection is poor (case (iii)), the founder cannot avoid leaving a rent to the professional manager. Offering a zero wage and retaining all shares to implement a monitoring level $m = v_M/k$ is all that the founder can do. The resulting rent to the professional manager is equal to $R = [\bar{\phi} - (v_M/k)] v_M - c$. The founder's welfare $V^S(\alpha*, w*, \bar{\phi})$ is equal to the highest possible level $(v_M - c)$ less monitoring costs and managerial rent. As in the range with moderate legal protection, $V^S(\alpha*, w*, \bar{\phi})$ decreases in both $\bar{\phi}$ and k.[9]

We now turn to the final step of determining the conditions under which the founder chooses to hire a professional manager. The answer follows from comparing the founder's welfare under no separation V^{NS} (Lemma 1) to that under separation V^S (Lemma 2). The next propositions describe the overall equilibrium outcomes.

PROPOSITION 1. *(i) If $v_F + B \geq v_M - c$, ownership and management are never separated. (ii) If $v_M^2/2k \geq v_F + B$, ownership and management are always separated.*

When the family's amenity potential B exceeds the professional manager's superior ability net of his outside option ($B \geq v_M - c - v_F$), separation of ownership and management is never optimal, irrespective of the quality of legal protection. A necessary condition for separation is that $B < v_M - c - v_F$. At the other extreme, if the discrepancy between the managerial abilities of the professional and the founder (or his heir) is very large, keeping management in the family is always a bad choice. The founder or the family retains an ownership stake of a size depending on the quality of the legal protection as described in Lemma 2, but gives up control. The condition $v_M^2/2k \geq v_F + B$ is intuitive if we consider the founder's welfare under separation at its minimum when the law provides no protection ($\bar{\phi} = 1$). In this case, all dividend payments are exclusively due to monitoring, a fully concentrated ownership structure is optimal, and $V^S = v_M^2/2k$, which is still better than keeping control in the family.

Proposition 1 sheds light on some of the reasons for observing a variation in ownership structures *within* a country, so the legal protection of investors is held

---

[9] The conclusions of Lemma 2 also obtain if we use the efficiency of monitoring (cost parameter k) rather than the upper bound on diversion as the measure of legal shareholder protection, with one difference. Since the founder and the small shareholders have congruent interests, legal protection and monitoring are substitutes when $\bar{\phi}$ is the measure of legal protection, but are complements when k is the measure of legal protection.

roughly constant. Even with very strong protection of investors, a founder might want to keep control in the family if the amenity potential is very large or if the heir is relatively competent. Consistent with this prediction, Demsetz and Lehn (1985) document the pervasiveness of family control in the media and professional sports companies in the United States. Conversely, even with very weak investor protection, family control is likely to be surrendered when the heir is at a particularly strong disadvantage in management. Thus, in Western Europe, one often sees professionally managed firms in relatively "technical" areas, such as utilities and telecommunications.

Consider now the parameter range of "moderate" amenity potential and relative competency of the heir: $v_M^2/2k < v_F + B < v_M - c$. In this range, the law shapes the attractiveness of hiring a professional manager. Denote by $\bar{\phi}* \in (c/v_M, 1)$ the unique value of $\bar{\phi}$ such that $V^S(\alpha*, w*, \bar{\phi}) = V^{NS}$. This value exists because $v_M^2/2k < v_F + B$.

PROPOSITION 2. *If* $v_M^2/2k < v_F + B < v_M - c$ *there are three regimes:*

   (i)   *When legal shareholder protection is strong* ($\bar{\phi} \leq c/v_M$), *ownership and management are separated, and ownership is fully dispersed.*
   (ii) *When legal protection is moderate* ($\bar{\phi} \in (c/v_M, \bar{\phi}*]$), *ownership and management are separated, and the founder retains a block.*
   (iii) *When legal protection is poor* ($\bar{\phi} > \bar{\phi}*$), *there is no separation of ownership and management.*

When legal rules are very protective, that is, with $\bar{\phi} \leq c/v_M$, the separation of ownership and management allows the founder to capitalize on the superior ability of the professional manager and only give up the amenity potential B. Strong legal protection also solves at no cost to the founder the agency conflict over the allocation of revenues. More precisely, the law restricts private benefit extraction below the professional manager's outside utility. Letting this manager divert corporate resources is part of his compensation package, which needs to be supplemented by a wage. In this case, selling all the equity and hiring a professional manager is the optimal choice for the founder.

In this model, a legal system with strong protection of outside shareholders is socially desirable. The best manager is hired to run the firm, and no resources are wasted on monitoring. This conclusion is driven by the assumption that law enforcement is free—at least from the viewpoint of the founder. If better legal protection imposes higher enforcement costs on the society, we would have to compare these costs with the social costs of private monitoring.[10]

Once investor protection falls below the threshold c/v_M, the separation of ownership and management involves a trade-off. On the one hand, the firm is run by a more qualified manager. On the other hand, the founder has to incur monitoring

---

[10] The private and social calculations are further complicated when there are private costs of compliance with legal rules. For example, the costs of complying with better accounting and disclosure standards might be higher.

costs (and possibly leave a rent to the professional manager) as well as give up the amenity potential B.

When ownership and management are separated, the founder's welfare V^S decreases with $\bar{\phi}$, because weaker legal protection entails higher monitoring costs and (possibly) an increasing managerial rent. In contrast, when ownership and management are not separated, the founder's welfare is $v_F + B$ and independent of the quality of legal protection. Hence, there exists a unique threshold value $\bar{\phi}^*$ below which the cost of separating ownership and management (monitoring costs, managerial rent, and B) is less than the gain in managerial efficiency $(v_M - c - v_F)$. In this case, the founder or family simply retains an ownership stake whose size depends on legal protection (Lemma 2). Conversely, for $\phi > \bar{\phi}^*$, the forgone efficiency loss associated with keeping control in the family is smaller than the agency costs of separating ownership and management. This holds when the sum of B and revenues under family control exceeds the net dividends under separation.

Propositions 1 and 2 can be described in a simple diagram, which shows the gains and costs of appointing a professional manager as a function of the degree of legal protection $\bar{\phi}$ (Figure 2). The gain is independent of $\bar{\phi}$ and is reflected by the horizontal line $v_M - c - v_F$. The cost includes the monitoring cost, managerial rent, and the forgone amenity potential B. As Proposition 1 and Figure 2 show, B could be very high, in which case there is no separation regardless of the legal regime, or very low, in which case there is separation for any legal regime. In the intermediate range, it follows from Lemma 2 that below $\bar{\phi} \leq c/v_M$ the cost is constant and equal to B; in the range $c/v_M < \bar{\phi} \leq c/v_M + v_M/k$ the cost increases at an increasing rate; and above $\bar{\phi} > c/v_M + v_M/k$ the cost increases linearly in $\bar{\phi}$. The parameter restrictions $v_M^2/2k < v_F + B < v_M - c$ ensure that the two lines cross at $c/v_M < \bar{\phi}^* < 1$, that is, we are in the parameter range where Proposition 2 applies.

The model has a clear implication for how the law shapes ownership structure.

PROPOSITION 3. *When ownership and management are separated and $\alpha^* \in (0,1)$, more concentrated ownership structures go together with weaker legal protection, that is, $d\alpha/d\bar{\phi} \geq 0$.*

The founder's objective when ownership and management are separated is to pay the professional manager no more than his outside utility. Both legal protection and monitoring restrict the manager's extraction of private benefits. Since the law does this at no cost, the founder resorts to monitoring only to the extent that the law leaves the manager a payoff in excess of his outside utility. To keep the manager's participation constraint binding, the founder has to monitor more as legal protection deteriorates. Thus, for $\bar{\phi} \in (c/v_M, c/v_M + v_M/k]$, legal protection and ownership concentration are inversely related when ownership and management are separated.[11]

---

[11] The (inverse) relationship between ownership concentration and legal protection depends crucially on the absence of wealth constraints for the founder and the assumed monitoring

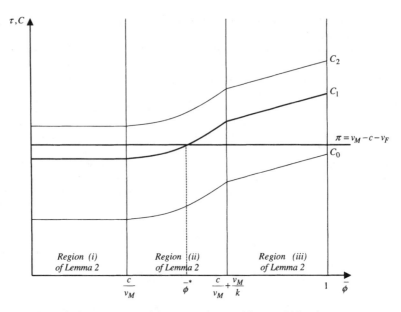

C = monitoring cost + managerial rent + amenity potential = cost of delegation

$\pi = v_M - c - v_F$ = benefit of delegation

C_1 obtains for $\dfrac{v_M^2}{2k} < v_F + B < v_M - c$ $\Big\}$ Law Matters: Proposition 2

C_0 obtains for $\dfrac{v_M^2}{2k} > v_F + B$ Law does not matter: delegation

C_2 obtains for $v_F + B > v_M - c$ Law does not matter: family management $\Big\}$ Proposition 1

Figure 2. Illustration of Lemma 2, Proposition 1, and Proposition 2.

Propositions 2 and 3 make strong empirical predictions, namely that family ownership should be common around the world, and relatively more common in countries with poor investor protection. Recent empirical work is consistent with these predictions. Family control is the dominant form of corporate ownership around the world. Looking at the 20 largest firms in 27 wealthy economies, La Porta et al. (1999) find that families or individuals control 30 percent in number and 25 percent in value of the top 20 firms in each country. These numbers are higher for smaller firms. Family transitions are a frequent and important occurrence: Only about one-third of family-controlled firms are run by their founders;

technology. In particular, the positive relationship between optimal monitoring intensity and ownership concentration relies on the assumption that the incentive to monitor depends on the ownership stake but is independent of legal protection. In contrast, when legal protection has a direct impact on the (marginal) return from monitoring, changes in investor protection have an ambiguous effect on ownership concentration (Burkart and Panunzi (2001)).

the rest are run by descendants or by families that came to own them later. In addition, La Porta et al. show that widely held firms are more common in countries with good shareholder protection: 34 percent versus 16 percent in the countries with a low level of protection. Moreover, ownership patterns tend to be relatively stable. In short, when expropriation is a concern, firms remain family controlled.

Claessens et al. (2000) find that, with the exception of Japan, more than 50 percent of all publicly traded firms in nine East Asian countries are controlled by families and that the top 15 families control significant shares of country wealth.[12] East Asian countries outside Japan are indeed known for particularly poor protection of outside investors. Faccio and Lang (2002) find higher incidence of family firms in countries with inferior shareholder protection in a large sample of West European corporations. The European Corporate Governance Network (2001) documents the prevalence of concentrated corporate ownership in OECD countries.

Propositions 1 and 2 together predict both the general tendencies in ownership patterns across countries and the existence of possibly large variation within each country. In our model, the sources of within-country variation are the amenity potential of control and the differences in skill between heirs and professionals. Of course, there are other potential sources of within-country variation. If firms require outside finance for expansion, or to pay inheritance taxes, ownership is likely to become dispersed. Such dispersion is.compatible with the preservation of family control if shares with inferior voting rights are sold in the market. This external finance effect is likely to reinforce our finding: Since valuations in countries with weaker investor protection are lower, using markets to raise funds is less attractive, raising the attractiveness of family control (Shleifer and Wolfenzon (2002)). Another force toward ownership dispersion—diversification—is also less powerful in markets with lower valuations.

Propositions 1 and 2 analyze the institutional conditions under which professional managers are hired. Alternatively, one can consider the managerial efficiency gain necessary to have separation of ownership and management in a regime with weak legal protection.

COROLLARY 1: *The separation of ownership and management requires higher managerial skills in regimes with poorer legal shareholder protection.*

The founder's welfare under separation V^S increases with both the professional manager's ability (higher $v_M - c$ values) and the quality of the law (lower $\bar{\phi}$ values). In contrast, the founder's welfare under no separation V^{NS} is independent of $\bar{\phi}$. Ceteris paribus, the switch from keeping family control to hiring a professional manager requires a more able professional manager when legal protection is less effective: Such legal regimes are associated with higher agency costs of

---

[12] In Taiwan, the top 15 families control 20.1 percent of listed corporate assets; in Hong Kong, Indonesia, Korea, Malaysia, the Philippines, Singapore, and Thailand, the top 15 families control more than 25 percent of listed corporate assets.

separation of ownership and management. To make hiring a professional manager nonetheless worthwhile, the efficiency gain must be larger.

This section has analyzed how legal rules affect the trade-off between the benefits and costs of separating ownership and management. The model makes accurate predictions about the patterns of such separation in different countries. Some implications of our basic model do, however, clash with the empirical evidence. In particular, the model implies that the founder's block trades at a discount when ownership and management are separated. There is some evidence of negative block premia, but they are the exception rather than the rule. In a study of 63 large block sales in the United States that are not necessarily made by founders, Barclay and Holderness (1989) report that about 20 percent were priced at a discount from the postannouncement exchange price. On average, however, block premia are both positive and higher in countries with weaker protection of outside shareholders (Zingales (1994), Dyck and Zingales (2003), Nenova (2003)). The reason for the negative block premia in our model is that all shareholders benefit in proportion to their stakes from monitoring, but only the founder bears the cost. The negative block premium follows from the assumption that the founder cannot extract any private benefits, thereby ensuring that monitoring is a public good. In the next section, we allow the founder to benefit privately from his monitoring activity.

A final theoretical point concerns our assumption that ownership structure remains stable once the manager has agreed to run the company. If the founder had the opportunity and incentive to retrade ex post, he may want to increase his stake and extract a higher fraction of private benefits from the manager. This, in turn, would affect the decision of the manager to accept the offer to run the company. For the model in this section, we can prove that, so long as trade in not anonymous, the purchase of an additional fraction of shares is not profitable for the founder. Because shareholders free ride on the entire value improvement implied by the founder's final holding,[13] the founder does not make a profit on the additional shares acquired in the retrading stage. Moreover, the increase in the monitoring costs due to the larger final holding exceeds the increase in the value of the shares owned initially by the founder. Matters are more complicated when trade is anonymous (DeMarzo and Urosevic (2000)), or when the founder shares some of the private benefits of control with the manager, as happens in the next section. In these instances, we need to make the assumption that there is no retrading, or alternatively that the manager's wage can be conditioned on the founder's final equity stake.

III. Transferable Private Benefits of Control

In Section II, the founder cannot by assumption extract any private benefits Φ unless he manages the firm himself. The founder's interest and that of the minority shareholders are perfectly congruent when a professional manager runs the

---

[13] A proof of a similar result is contained in Burkart et al. (1997) and Pagano and Röell (1998).

firm. In this section, we consider the other extreme, where the private benefits are perfectly transferable, thereby aligning the founder's interest in expropriation with that of the professional manager. For example, the founder and the manager can jointly create a private company that does business with the public firm, and divert cash flows to their private company through related transactions at nonmarket prices, such as asset sales, transfer pricing, or loan guarantees.

The possibility of sharing the spoils with the professional provides a new rationale for monitoring, namely to secure for the founder a larger share of the private benefits. Monitoring becomes a rent-seeking activity. Below we repeat the analytical steps of the previous section for this case of transferable private benefits, and establish that the existence of the three patterns of separation of ownership and management holds as before. We then explore the implications of the model for the relationship between legal protection, share value, block premium, and the agency costs of separating ownership and management. Transferable private benefits only matter in the presence of a professional manager, leaving unchanged the founder's welfare in the case of no separation (Lemma 1). We therefore move directly to the case of separation of ownership and management.

At date 3, the law imposes that $(1 - \bar{\phi})v_M$ be paid out either as dividends to all shareholders or as the wage to the professional manager. The founder and the professional manager bargain over how to share the remaining $\bar{\phi}v_M$. For simplicity, we assume Nash bargaining with equal bargaining power. That is, both the founder and the manager receive their outside options plus half the surplus. The payoff that each party obtains if bargaining were to break down, that is, the outside option, depends on monitoring. If the founder monitors with intensity m, his outside option is $\alpha m v_M$, which corresponds to his share of security benefits salvaged from managerial expropriation. Due to the constraint $m \leq \bar{\phi}$, the outside option is equal to $\min\{\alpha m v_M, \alpha \bar{\phi} v_M\}$. The outside option of the professional manager is the fraction of revenues that he does not have to pay out to shareholders. For the same reason, $(m \leq \bar{\phi})$, this is equal to $\max\{0, (\bar{\phi} - m)v_M\}$. The surplus to be shared in the bargaining between the founder and the manager is the difference between $\bar{\phi}v_M$ and the sum of the two outside options, and is equal to $\min\{(1 - \alpha)m v_M, (1 - \alpha)\bar{\phi} v_M\}$. Under the assumption of equal bargaining power, the founder receives in the bargaining a payment equal his outside option plus half the surplus, or $\min\{[(1 + \alpha)/2]\bar{\phi} v_M, m[(1 + \alpha)/2]v_M\}$, and the manager likewise gets $\max\{\bar{\phi}[(-1 - \alpha)/2]v_M, (\bar{\phi} - m[(1 + \alpha)/2])v_M\}$. Since these payoffs exceed their outside options, the founder and the manager always agree to set $\phi = \bar{\phi}$. They expropriate minority shareholders to the maximum, and share the spoils.[14]

---

[14] The question arises again whether there are any gains from using monetary incentives to induce the manager to abstain from extracting private benefits. At first glance, this seems possible, since the manager receives only half of the surplus. While the use of such a compensation scheme is in the minority shareholders' interest, the founder prefers ex post to extract private benefits. Since such extraction is efficient, the founder is ex ante indifferent. All that matters is to keep the manager's participation constraint binding, that is, to leave him no rents.

At date 2, the founder chooses the monitoring intensity to maximize $\{\alpha(1 - w - \bar{\phi}) + [(1+\alpha)/2]m\}v_M - k(m^2/2)$. Since the law already protects $(1 - \bar{\phi})v_M$ of the revenues from extraction, there is no gain from monitoring more than $\bar{\phi}$. The founder therefore chooses $m = \min\{\bar{\phi}, [(1+\alpha)/2k]v_M\}$. If $\bar{\phi} < (1+\alpha)v_M/2k$ holds, monitoring does not depend on the block size and is purely driven by the prospect of extracting a part of the private benefits. Otherwise $(\bar{\phi} \geq (1+\alpha)v_M/2k)$, monitoring is a function of both private benefits and the ownership stake.

Indeed, decomposing the first-order condition into $\alpha(v_M/k) + [(1-\alpha)/2](v_M/k)$ reveals the two motives for monitoring. The first term reflects monitoring in the absence of collusion aimed at preventing managerial expropriation of the founder's stake α. The second term captures the additional monitoring that the founder undertakes to appropriate some of the private benefits. While monitoring increases as before with the block size α, the second term implies that monitoring is positive even when the founder retains no shares, that is, $m(0) > 0$. This implies that the founder cannot withdraw from the firm. To remove this purely mechanical feature of the model, we impose the following assumption.

ASSUMPTION 3: *If the founder retains less than $\underline{\alpha} > 0$, he abstains from monitoring.*

Assumption 3 simply means that, to monitor effectively, the founder must have some power over the manager, and for that he needs a minimum ownership stake. This stake may enable him to sit on the board, to have enough shares to convene an extraordinary shareholder meeting, to have standing in litigation, or to exercise power in other ways. When the stake of the founder is below the threshold $\underline{\alpha}$, he has no power vis-à-vis the manager. Put differently, owning a stake below $\underline{\alpha}$ and dispersing the shares among small investors enables the founder to commit not to interfere through monitoring in the running of the firm.[15]

When $\alpha \geq \underline{\alpha}$, the founder monitors in part to avoid expropriation by the professional manager, but he does so only to help himself. Indeed, from the minority shareholders' perspective, monitoring is a pure rent-seeking activity. The founder and the professional manager agree to set $\phi = \bar{\phi}$ irrespective of the monitoring intensity m.[16] This result illustrates an important difference between legal shareholder protection and monitoring: While the law protects all the shareholders, monitoring in this model is a form of self-protection by the founder, which has either positive or negative externalities for other investors.

At date 1, the professional manager agrees to run the firm if $(w + \bar{\phi} - m(1+\alpha)/2)v_M \geq c$. The condition that the wage and the manager's share of the

---

[15] In the absence of collusion, fully dispersed ownership $(\alpha = 0)$ ensures no monitoring $(m(0) = 0)$. Introducing a threshold $\underline{\alpha}$ in Section II would have complicated the analysis without adding any insight.

[16] If one introduces a dead-weight loss associated with private benefit extraction, monitoring also benefits minority shareholders because the founder internalizes part of the inefficiency and hence reduces the level of diversion (Burkart and Panunzi (2001)).

private benefits exceed the outside utility can be rewritten as

$$m \leq \bar{m} \equiv \min \left\{ \bar{\phi}, \frac{(\bar{\phi} + w)v_M - c}{\frac{1+\alpha}{2} v_M} \right\}. \tag{2}$$

The maximum level of monitoring compatible with the professional manager's participation constraint weakly decreases with the founder's stake. A larger block increases the founder's outside option in the bargaining, thereby reducing the share of private benefits that the professional manager obtains. Nonetheless, as $(1 + \alpha)/2 \leq 1$ the threshold $\bar{m}$ is higher for a given wage w and legal protection $\bar{\phi}$ when the founder and professional manager collude than in the absence of collusion. Withholding $(1 - \alpha)mv_M$ from the minority shareholders makes it more likely that the professional manager's participation constraint is satisfied.

At date 0, the founder chooses ownership α and wage w to maximize his welfare

$$V^S = (1 - \bar{\phi} - w)v_M + \frac{1 + \alpha}{2} m v_M - k \frac{m^2}{2} \tag{3}$$

The founder's welfare is composed of three terms: The first, $(1 - \bar{\phi} - w)v_M$, is the dividends accruing to all shareholders if there were no monitoring (again, the founder obtains this amount as the value of the block and as the proceeds from selling shares at date 0); the second, $[(1 + \alpha)/2]mv_M$, is the share of private benefits that the founder extracts due to monitoring in the bargaining with the manager; the third, $km^2/2$, is the monitoring cost.

ASSUMPTION 4: $\underline{\alpha} \leq (2kc/v_M^2) - 1$.

Assumption 4 is purely technical, made to restrict the number of cases. The threshold $\underline{\alpha} > 0$ (Assumption 3)[17] and Assumption 4 imply that the equilibrium monitoring intensity m^* is either zero or given by the first order condition $m = (1 + \alpha^*)v_M/2k$.[18] In the absence of Assumption 4, monitoring intensity for small $\bar{\phi}$ values would be determined by the legal threshold ($m^* = \bar{\phi}$), leaving the ownership structure indeterminate in that range of $\bar{\phi}$ values. Nonetheless, all our results on founder welfare, share value, and separation of ownership and management are robust with respect to relaxing Assumptions 3 and 4.

LEMMA 3:

(i) For $\bar{\phi} \leq c/v_M$, $\alpha < \underline{\alpha}$, $w^* = (c/v_M) - \bar{\phi}$, $m^* = 0$, and $V^S(\alpha^*, w^*, \bar{\phi}) = v_M - c$.

---

[17] As $\underline{\alpha} > 0$, Assumption 4 implies that $v_M/2k \leq c/v_M$.
[18] Rearranging Assumption 4 to $(1 + \underline{\alpha})v_M/2k \leq c/v_M$ shows that for all $\bar{\phi} \leq c/v_M$ the first order condition and not the constraint $m \leq \bar{\phi}$ determines the monitoring intensity. Since monitoring is zero in equilibrium for $\bar{\phi} \leq c/v_M$, the constraint $m \leq \bar{\phi}$ never binds in equilibrium.

(ii) *For*

$$\frac{c}{v_M} < \bar{\phi} \leq \frac{c}{v_M} + \frac{(1+\alpha)^2}{8k} v_M, \quad \alpha < \underline{\alpha}, \quad w* = 0, \quad m* = 0, \quad and$$

$$V^S = (1 - \bar{\phi}) v_M.$$

(iii) *For*

$$\frac{c}{v_M} + \frac{(1+\alpha)^2}{8k} v_M < \bar{\phi} \leq \frac{c}{v_M} + \frac{(1+\alpha)^2}{4k} v_M, \quad \alpha* = \underline{\alpha},$$

$$w* = \frac{c}{v_M} - \bar{\phi} + \frac{(1+\alpha)^2}{4k} v_M,$$

$$m* = \frac{1+\alpha}{2k} v_M, \quad and \quad V^S = v_M - c - \frac{(1+\alpha)^2}{8k} (v_M)^2.$$

(iv) *For*

$$\frac{c}{v_M} + \frac{(1+\alpha)^2}{4k} v_M < \bar{\phi} \leq \frac{c}{v_M} + \frac{v_M}{k}, \quad \alpha* = \frac{2}{v_M}\sqrt{k(\bar{\phi}v_M - c)} - 1, \quad w* = 0,$$

$$m* = \sqrt{\frac{\bar{\phi}v_M - c}{k}}, \quad and \quad V^S(\alpha*, w*, \bar{\phi}) = v_M - c - \frac{\bar{\phi}v_M - c}{2}.$$

(v) *For*

$$\bar{\phi} > \frac{c}{v_M} + \frac{v_M}{k}, \quad \alpha* = 1, \quad w* = 0, \quad m* = \frac{v_M}{k}, \quad and$$

$$V^S(\alpha*, w*, \bar{\phi}) = v_M(1 - \bar{\phi}) + \frac{v_M^2}{2k}.$$

LEMMA 3—illustrated in Figure 3—replicates Lemma 2 with an added twist due to collusion and a discontinuity in the feasible monitoring level.[19] In particular, region (i) coincides with region (i) in Lemma 2 and region (v) coincides with region (iii) of Lemma 2. The differences between transferable and nontransferable

---

[19] There is another difference between Lemma 2 and 3. When legal protection is measured by the upper bound on diversion, the founder's welfare under separation V^S decreases with $\bar{\phi}$ both in the case of transferable and in the case of nontransferable private benefits. When legal protection is measured by monitoring efficiency, V^S does not always decrease with k in the case of transferable private benefits (region (iii) of Lemma 3). Since monitoring in this setting is also a rent-seeking activity, lower k values lead to more monitoring in equilibrium—a cost ultimately paid by the founder.

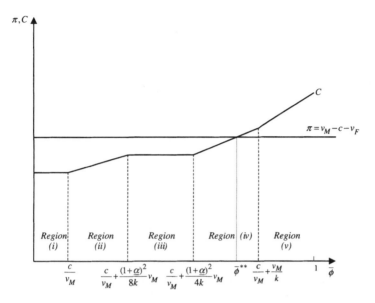

C= monitoring cost + managerial rent + amenity potential = cost of delegation.
$B = v_M - c - v_F$ = benefit of delegation.

In *region (i)*, ownership is dispersed $\alpha^* < \underline{\alpha}$, wage rate is $w^* = c/v_M - \underline{\phi}$ and managerial rent is $R = 0$.

In *region (ii)*, $\alpha^* < \underline{\alpha}$, $w^* = 0$ but $R = \underline{\phi} v_M - c > 0$ (due to undermonitoring).

In *region (iii)*, $\alpha^* = \underline{\alpha}$, $w^* = c/v_M - \underline{\phi} + (1+\underline{\alpha})^2 v_M / 4k > 0$ but $R = 0$ (due to overmonitoring)

In *region (iv)*, $\alpha^* = (2/v_M)\sqrt{k(\bar{\phi} - c/v_M)} - 1 \in (\underline{\alpha}, 1)$, $w^* = 0$ and $R = 0$.

In *region(v)*, $\alpha^* = 1$, $w^* = 0$ and $R = \bar{\phi} v_M - c > 0$.

Figure 3. Illustration of Lemma 3.

private benefits appear in the intermediate range of legal protection.[20] In region
(iv), weak legal protection permits private benefits to an extent that sharing
them between the founder and the professional manager is compatible with the
participation constraint and a zero wage. Indeed, to avoid leaving a rent to the
manager, the founder has to retain $\alpha > \underline{\alpha}$ and monitor accordingly. In contrast, in
regions (ii) and (iii), where the law is more protective, a zero wage, sharing
of private benefits, and satisfying the professional manager's participation
constraint are not compatible with each other. Because of the discontinuity in

---

[20] Irrespective of Assumptions 3 and 4, the equilibrium outcome with collusion is more complicated than Lemma 2. In the absence of Assumptions 3 and 4, the complication is due to the
fact that monitoring may be determined by the law ($m* = \bar{\phi}$) rather than by the first order
condition.

monitoring, the founder faces a trade-off between under- and overmonitoring. More precisely, the founder has the option to either not monitor or to monitor at least $m = (1 + \underline{\alpha})v_M/2k$. While abstaining from monitoring concedes a rent to the professional manager, monitoring with intensity $m = (1 + \underline{\alpha})v_M/2k$ requires a positive wage to satisfy the participation constraint. In region (ii), the sum of the wage and the monitoring cost when $m = (1 + \underline{\alpha})v_M/2k$ exceeds the rent that the professional manager can extract. Hence, it is optimal to fully disperse ownership and to leave the manager with a rent of $R = \bar{\phi}v_M - c$. The reverse holds in region (iii): Overmonitoring and compensating the professional manager with a wage to satisfy the participation constraint is less costly to the founder. Consequently, the optimal ownership concentration jumps to $\alpha* = \underline{\alpha}$.

Another implication of Lemma 3 is that the founder cannot gain from selling the entire company to a penniless professional manager who would raise funds in the capital market. From the discussion of the no separation case, it follows that the professional manager could raise at most $(1 - \bar{\phi})v_M$ in the market. Moreover, he will never pay more than $v_M - c$. Simple inspection shows that the founder's welfare V^S is always at least as large as the minimum of $(1 - \bar{\phi})v_M$ and $v_M - c$. Hence selling the entire company to a penniless manager is weakly dominated by selling some stock in the market and hiring a professional manager.

The feature of Lemma 3 that is both crucial for the subsequent results and robust to relaxing Assumptions 3 and 4 is that the agency cost of separation of ownership and management rises as investor protections become weaker. When $\bar{\phi}$ increases, the professional manager can appropriate a larger fraction of the revenues. This in turn implies either more monitoring or a larger rent. Since the founder ultimately bears the agency cost, his welfare weakly decreases with $\bar{\phi}$.

The final step in analyzing the founder's decision to hire a professional manager and to float part of the equity is the comparison of Lemma 1 with Lemma 3. Since Lemmas 2 and 3 coincide for $\bar{\phi} \leq c/v_M$ and $\bar{\phi} > c/v_M + v_M/k$, Proposition 1 continues to hold. When the amenity potential is very high ($B > v_M - c - v_F$), it is never optimal for the founder to separate ownership and management. As before, a necessary condition to have separation is $B \leq v_M - c - v_F$. Also, if the discrepancy between the competence of the professional manager and that of the founder is very large ($v_M^2/2k \geq v_F + B$), separation is always superior.

In the remaining case ($v_M^2/2k < v_F + B < v_M - c$), the decision to separate or not depends on legal protection. When legal protection is good ($\bar{\phi} \leq c/v_M$), ownership and management are separated, and ownership is fully dispersed. When legal protection is less strong ($\bar{\phi} > c/v_M$), the founder's welfare V^S under separation and collusion (weakly) decreases with $\bar{\phi}$. Hence, Proposition 2 also continues to hold: There exists a unique threshold $\bar{\phi}** \in (c/v_M, 1]$ above which the sum of agency cost and forgone amenity potential B exceeds the loss in managerial efficiency, and keeping management in the family is optimal. The threshold $\bar{\phi}**$ again denotes the $\bar{\phi}$ value where $V^S(\alpha*, w*, \bar{\phi}) = V^{NS}$. As we show below, $\bar{\phi}**$ is smaller than the threshold $\bar{\phi}*$ derived in the previous section. The only qualitative difference from the case with nontransferable private benefits is that separation and concentrated ownership may or may not be an equilibrium outcome. That is, the threshold value $\bar{\phi}**$ at which the founder switches to no separation may entail either a concentrated or a dispersed ownership structure under separation: Both $\alpha*(\bar{\phi}**) > \underline{\alpha}$ and $\alpha*(\bar{\phi}**) = 0$ are possible.

From the founder's perspective, legal protection and monitoring are substitutes: Both restrict the professional manager's ability to extract private benefits. While monitoring is costly, better legal protection comes at no cost to the founder. This has two implications. First, as legal protection improves, the level of monitoring falls, which in turn entails a less concentrated ownership structure. Proposition 3 thus also holds with transferable private benefits: Legal protection and ownership concentration are inversely related under separation of ownership and management. Second, weaker legal protection raises the agency cost of separation. Hence, hiring a professional manager in regimes with weaker legal rules requires higher managerial skills (Corollary 1).

The quality of the law also affects share value, defined as the total amount of dividends paid out to all shareholders at the final date.

PROPOSITION 4. *Share value increases as legal shareholder protection improves.*

From the minority shareholders' perspective, monitoring is not a substitute for legal protection when private benefits are transferable. Ex post, both the founder and the manager prefer to extract private benefits. As a rent-seeking activity, monitoring merely determines how the two split these private benefits. In contrast, the law prescribes that no less than $(1 - \bar{\phi})v_M$ is used for dividends and wage payments. Hence, the expected share value is equal to $S = (1 - \phi - w)v_M$. For $\bar{\phi} \leq c/v_M$, better legal protection unambiguously increases share value because the reduction in private benefits exceeds the wage increase.[21] Nonetheless, the minority shareholders are indifferent to the quality of the legal rules because they always get what they pay for. Because the minority shareholders anticipate at date 0 that the founder and the manager will divert the fraction $\bar{\phi}$ of revenues, the founder's proceeds from selling $(1 - \alpha)$ shares are equal to $(1 - \alpha)S$.

Proposition 4 also holds when the founder or his family keeps control over the firm. Since the founder sets $\phi = \bar{\phi}$ at date 3 (unless $\alpha = 1$), better laws boost share value because a larger fraction of the proceeds has to be paid out as dividends.

La Porta et al. (2002) examine the valuation of companies (relative to their assets) in different countries, with different levels of shareholder protection. They find that companies in countries with above the world median measures of shareholder protection have Tobin's Qs about 20 percent higher than do comparable companies in countries with below world median shareholder protection. The positive association between investor protection and the valuation of corporate assets survives a variety of controls for industry, ownership structure, and growth opportunities. Claessens et al. (2002) find similar evidence of higher valuation of companies in more protective legal regimes using data from East Asia.

---

[21] In contrast, variations in k have no impact on share value because a more efficient monitoring technology does not benefit the minority shareholders when the founder and the manager collude. This independence suggests that modeling legal (minority) shareholder protection in terms of efficient monitoring technology may not be appropriate.

The positive relationship between share value and legal protection also has implications for the value of the controlling block.

COROLLARY 2: *Total block premium $V^S - S$ increases as legal shareholder protection falls.*

When $\alpha* \in (\underline{\alpha}, 1)$, the founder responds to lower investor protection by monitoring more. Hence, his welfare is reduced by these extra monitoring costs (and possibly by the rent paid to the manager). In contrast, monitoring has no positive impact on share value, and the law is the only safeguard of dividends. As a result, changes in the quality of the law have a larger impact on share value than on the founder's welfare. Corollary 2 also holds when management and ownership are not separated. Since the founder does not monitor in this case, his welfare is independent of the law, while share value decreases with the quality of the law.

A number of recent empirical studies examine the valuation of block premia in different jurisdictions. For example, Zingales (1994) presents evidence of a very significant premium on the high voting rights shares trading on the Milan stock exchange. Nenova (2003) explicitly compares the value of a corporate voting right across legal jurisdictions in a sample of 661 dual-class firms from 18 countries. She presents striking evidence that control is more highly valued in countries with inferior protection of minority shareholders, consistent with Corollary 2. Using a different methodology for computing block premia, Dyck and Zingales (2003) extend and confirm Nenova's findings.

In contrast to minority shareholders whose wealth is independent of the law, the founder's welfare V^S increases with the quality of the law when ownership and management are separated. The possibility of colluding with the manager also affects the founder's welfare.

PROPOSITION 5: *Collusion between the founder and the manager increases the agency costs of separating ownership and management.*

In equilibrium, the agency cost of separating ownership from management is the sum of the monitoring cost and the managerial rent. Compared to the case with nontransferable private benefits, the equilibrium level of monitoring is higher when private benefits are transferable. This is so for two reasons. First, the rent-seeking motive induces the founder to monitor more for a given α and $\bar{\phi}$. Higher levels of monitoring allow the founder to appropriate a larger share of the private benefits. From an ex ante perspective, however, the founder bears the cost of such wasteful monitoring himself. Second, the professional manager receives a larger payoff for a given monitoring intensity m. Rather than increasing the dividends for all shareholders by mv_M, the founder and the professional manager withhold the minority shareholders' share $(1 - \alpha)mv_M$ and split it among themselves. Consequently, collusion requires higher monitoring levels in order to avoid leaving a rent to the professional manager. When private benefits are transferable, the impossibility of fine-tuning monitoring (undermonitoring) also allows the manager to obtain a positive rent in the range $\bar{\phi} \in [c/v_M, c/v_M + (1 + \underline{\alpha})^2 v_M/8k]$. The rent in very poor legal regimes ($\bar{\phi} > c/v_M + v_M/k$) is identical with nontransferable and transferable private benefits, as the two cases coincide once ownership is fully concentrated ($\alpha = 1$).

The present model formalizes legal shareholder protection as a limit on the share of corporate resources that the party in control can divert as private benefits. The law can protect shareholders in other ways as well. One possibility suggested by Proposition 5 is that legal rules can hinder or prevent collusion between the founder and the manager. Examples of such legal rules are equal treatment provisions and fiduciary duties. In fact, Proposition 5 provides a rationale for such rules. They reduce the agency costs of separation of ownership from management, thereby increasing the founder's welfare.[22]

Collusion influences the founder's welfare when ownership and management are separated as well as his decision whether to hire a professional manager.

COROLLARY 3: *Collusion between the founder and the manager is detrimental to the hiring of a professional manager, that is $\bar{\phi}^{**} \leq \bar{\phi}^{*}$.*

When ownership and control are separated, the founder's welfare is lower with transferable than with nontransferable private benefits. In contrast, collusion has no impact on his welfare when control is kept in the family. Hiring a professional manager is therefore comparatively less attractive when private benefits are transferable.

IV. Conclusion: The Separation of Ownership from Management

It is often claimed that there are two paradigms of corporate governance: the Anglo-Saxon paradigm centered on the conflict between the shareholders and the manager, and the rest of the world's paradigm where the conflict is between large and small shareholders. We show that the two paradigms are special cases of a single model of managerial succession, in which the founder must simultaneously decide whether to hire an outside professional manager (as opposed to keeping management in the family) and how much of the shares to float. We argue that this decision is to some extent shaped by the degree of legal protection of minority shareholders, and derive implications for optimal succession and ownership structures from this premise.

We show that in the regimes with the strongest legal protection of minority shareholders, the optimal solution for the founder is to hire the best professional manager and sell off the entire firm in the stock market—unless his amenity potential of keeping control in the family is huge. This gives rise to the Anglo-Saxon model, in which the law is the principal constraint on managerial discretion and the agency conflict is between the manager and small minority shareholders. With intermediate protection of minority shareholders, the founder still hires a professional manager, but the law is not strong enough to control managerial

---

[22] In contrast, minority shareholder wealth is affected neither by the quality of the law nor by collusion. When purchasing shares at date 0, they pay no more than the date 3 share value.

discretion, and the founder or his children must stay on as large shareholders to monitor the manager. This gives rise to the twin problems of a conflict between the manager and the controlling shareholders, but also between the two of them and minority outside investors. When the protection of minority shareholders is the weakest, the agency problems are too severe to allow for separation of ownership and management. The founding family must stay on and run the firm; they can only afford to cede control to a professional manager if they make him a member of the family. The separation of ownership and management is thus an indication of a superior corporate governance environment. The lack of such separation, and the prevalence of family firms, is evidence of financial underdevelopment.

Our analysis raises the question of why entrepreneurs do not lobby the government for better investor protection. In the model, if a country improves investor protection ex ante, before the entrepreneur has sold off any shares in the market, he would be strictly better off. On the other hand, for a founder who has already sold a substantial fraction of his company, an improvement in investor protection entails a reduction of the private benefits of control, while the gains in the valuation of publicly traded shares accrue not to him but to the public shareholders. Many of these founders are therefore worse off from the improvement in the corporate governance environment, and indeed, in developing countries the established families generally oppose such reforms (La Porta et al. (2000b)). The new entrepreneurs, as well as firms with significant needs for outside financing, would benefit from legal reform, but their voices are rarely as influential as those of publicly traded family firms in the political debate.

Appendix

Proof of Lemma 2: For $\bar{\phi} > (c/v_M) + (v_M/k)$, the professional manager's participation constraint $(w + \bar{\phi} - \alpha v_M/k)v_M \geq c$ is slack for any admissible pair (α, w). Since $dV^S/d\alpha > 0$ and $dV^S/dw < 0$, $\alpha^* = 1$ and $w^* = 0$ is the solution. Thus, for $\bar{\phi} > (c/v_M) + (v_M/k)$, $m(\alpha = 1) = v_M/k$, $V^S(\alpha^*, w^*, \bar{\phi}) = (1 - \bar{\phi})v_M + (v_M^2/2k)$, and the professional manager receives a rent $R = [\bar{\phi} - (v_M/k)]v_M - c$ (part iii).

For $\bar{\phi} \leq (c/v_M) + (v_M/k)$ the professional manager's participation constraint binds. Rearranging this binding constraint to $\alpha = [w + \bar{\phi} - (c/v_M)](k/v_M)$ and substituting α into the objective function yields

$$V^S = v_M - c - \frac{k}{2}\left(w + \bar{\phi} - \frac{c}{v_M}\right)^2,$$

which decreases with w. Consequently, the founder sets w at the lowest value compatible with $w \geq 0$ and $\alpha \geq 0$. Hence, $w = \max\{0, (c/v_M) - \bar{\phi}\}$, and there are two cases: For

$$\bar{\phi} \leq c/v_M, \quad \alpha^* = 0, \quad w^* = (c/v_M) - \bar{\phi},$$

$$m^* = 0, \quad \text{and} \quad V^S(\alpha^*, w^*, \bar{\phi}) = v_M - c \qquad \text{(part i)}.$$

For

$$\frac{c}{v_M} + \frac{v_M}{k} \geq \bar{\phi} > \frac{c}{v_M}, \quad \alpha* = k\left(\frac{\bar{\phi}}{v_M} - \frac{c}{(v_M)^2}\right), \quad w* = 0, \quad m* = \bar{\phi} - \frac{c}{v_M}, \quad \text{and}$$

$$V^S(\alpha*, w*, \bar{\phi}) = v_M - c - \frac{k}{2}\left(\bar{\phi} - \frac{c}{v_M}\right)^2 \quad \text{(part ii)}. \quad \text{Q.E.D.}$$

Proof of Proposition 1: By Lemma 1, $V^{NS} = v_F + B$, and by Lemma 2, $V^S \leq v_M - c$. Thus, if $B > v_M - c - v_F$, $V^{NS} > V^S$ for $\bar{\phi} \in [0, 1]$. Since V^S decreases with $\bar{\phi}$, V^S reaches its minimum, $v_M^2/2k$, at $\bar{\phi} = 1$. Therefore, if $v_F + B < v_M^2/2k$, then $V^S > V^{NS}$ for $\bar{\phi} \in [0, 1]$. Q.E.D.

Proof of Proposition 2: For $\bar{\phi} \leq c/v_M$, $V^S = v_M - c$ and $V^{NS} = v_F + B$. If $B < v_M - c - v_F$, then separation and fully dispersed ownership are optimal. For

$$\frac{c}{v_M} + \frac{v_M}{k} \geq \bar{\phi} > \frac{c}{v_M}, \quad V^S(\alpha*, w*, \bar{\phi}) = v_M - c - \frac{k}{2}\left(\bar{\phi} - \frac{c}{v_M}\right)^2,$$

and

$$dV^S/d\bar{\phi} = -k(\bar{\phi} - c/v_M) < 0,$$

while for

$$\bar{\phi} > \frac{c}{v_M} + \frac{v_M}{k},$$

$V^S(\alpha*, w*, \bar{\phi}) = (1 - \bar{\phi})v_M + (v_M^2/2k)$ and $dV^S/d\bar{\phi} = -v_M < 0$. Moreover, the two expressions for V^S coincide when $\bar{\phi} = (c/v_M) + (v_M/k)$. Hence, V^S decreases with $\bar{\phi}$ and is continuous in $\bar{\phi}$ for $\bar{\phi} > c/v_M$. Since V^{NS} is independent of $\bar{\phi}$ (Lemma 1), there exists a unique $\bar{\phi}* \in (c/v_M, 1)$ where $V^{NS} = V^S$ provided that $V^{NS} > V^S(\bar{\phi} = 1)$, that is, $v_F + B > v_M^2/2k$. Hence, separation dominates no separation for $\bar{\phi} \leq \bar{\phi}*$, and the reverse holds for $\bar{\phi} > \bar{\phi}*$. Q.E.D.

Proof of Corollary 1: As V^{NS} is independent of $\bar{\phi}$, it suffices to show that $dV^S/dv_M > 0$ and $dV^S/d\bar{\phi} < 0$ for $\bar{\phi} > c/v_M$. Since the latter is proved above, we only need to show that $dV^S/dv_M > 0$. In region (iii) $dV^S/dv_M = (1 - \bar{\phi}) + v_M/k > 0$, and in region (ii)

$$dV^S/dv_M = 1 - k(\bar{\phi} - \frac{c}{v_M})\frac{c}{(v_M)^2} \geq 1 - k\left[\frac{c}{v_M} + \frac{v_M}{k} - \frac{c}{v_M}\right]\frac{c}{v_M^2} = 1 - \frac{c}{v_M} > 0$$

as $\bar{\phi} \leq \frac{c}{v_M} + \frac{v_M}{k}$.

Q.E.D.

Proof of Lemma 3: For $\bar{\phi} > (c/v_M) + (v_M/k)$, the monitoring intensity is given by

$$m = \frac{1+\alpha}{2k}v_M \leq \frac{v_M}{k} < \bar{\phi},$$

and the professional manager's participation constraint

$$(w + \bar{\phi} - \frac{1+\alpha}{2}m)v_M \geq c$$

is slack for any admissible pair (α, w). Hence, as in Lemma 2, $\alpha^* = 1$, $w^* = 0$, $m^* = v_M/k$, and $V^S(\alpha^*, w^*, \bar{\phi}) = (1 - \bar{\phi})v_M + (v_M^2/2k)$ (part v).

Consider now the range $\bar{\phi} \leq (c/v_M) + (v_M/k)$. Suppose that the monitoring intensity is given by the FOC $m = [(1+\alpha)/2k]v_M$. That is, abstract from the discontinuity in monitoring and from the possibility that $[(1+\alpha)/2k]v_M > \bar{\phi}$. Then the participation constraint must be binding. Rearranging the constraint to $w = (c/v_M) - \bar{\phi} + \{[m(1+\alpha)]/2\}$ and substituting w in the founder's objective function yields $V^S = v_M - c - k(m^2/2)$ which decreases with m. Thus, the founder chooses the lowest monitoring intensity compatible with $m \geq 0$ and $w \geq 0$. For $\bar{\phi} \leq c/v_M$, $m = 0$, that is, $\alpha < \underline{\alpha}$, and $w = (c/v_M) - \bar{\phi}$. Otherwise, $w = 0$ is optimal. Substituting the FOC $m = [(1+\alpha)/2k]v_M$ into the professional manager's participant constraint yields the corresponding optimal ownership concentration $\alpha = (2/v_M)\sqrt{k(\bar{\phi}v_M - c)} - 1$ and monitoring intensity $m = \sqrt{(\bar{\phi}v_M - c)/k}$.

This is the solution to the founder's maximization problem only if it satisfies the conditions that the monitoring intensity is both given by the FOC, that is, $m^* \leq \bar{\phi}$, and feasible, that is,

$$m^* \notin \left(0, \frac{1+\alpha}{2k}v_M\right).$$

Zero monitoring trivially satisfies both conditions and $\alpha^* < \underline{\alpha}$ and $w^* = (c/v_M) - \bar{\phi}$ is indeed the solution for $\bar{\phi} \leq c/v_M$. The founder's welfare is $V^S(\alpha^*, w^*, \bar{\phi}) = v_M - c$ (part i).

For

$$\frac{c}{v_M} < \bar{\phi} \leq \frac{c}{v_M} + \frac{v_M}{k},$$

the first condition $(m^* \leq \bar{\phi})$ is equivalent to $\sqrt{(\bar{\phi}v_M - c)/k} \leq \bar{\phi}$, which is always satisfied because of Assumption 4. Given $m = \sqrt{(\bar{\phi}v_M - c)/k}$, the second condition $(m^* \geq [(1+\underline{\alpha})/2k]v_M)$ is equivalent to

$$\bar{\phi} \geq \frac{c}{v_M} + \frac{(1+\underline{\alpha})^2}{4k}v_M.$$

Therefore, $w* = 0$, $\alpha* = (2/v_M)\sqrt{k(\bar{\phi}v_M - c)} - 1$, and $m* = \sqrt{(\bar{\phi}v_M - c)/k}$ is the solution only for

$$\frac{c}{v_M} + \frac{(1+\alpha)^2}{4k}v_M < \bar{\phi} \leq \frac{c}{v_M} + \frac{v_M}{k}.$$

The founder's resulting welfare is

$$V^S(\alpha*, w*, \bar{\phi}) = v_M - c - \frac{\bar{\phi}v_M - c}{2} \qquad \text{(part iv).}$$

For

$$\frac{c}{v_M} < \bar{\phi} \leq \frac{c}{v_M} + \frac{(1+\alpha)^2}{4k}v_M,$$

the only two possible optimal levels of monitoring are $m = 0$ and $m = [(1+\alpha)/2k]v_M$. If $m = 0$ (that is, $\alpha < \underline{\alpha}$), $w = 0$ and $V^S = (1 - \bar{\phi})v_M$. If $m = [(1+\alpha)/2k]v_M$ (i.e., $\alpha = \underline{\alpha}$), the participation constraint implies

$$w = \frac{c}{v_M} - \bar{\phi} + \frac{(1+\alpha)^2}{4k}v_M,$$

and $V^S = v_M - c - [(1+\alpha)/8k]v_M^2$. Simple calculations show that $v_M - c - \left[(1+\alpha)^2/8k\right]v_M^2 > (1 - \bar{\phi})v_M$ holds for

$$\bar{\phi} > \frac{c}{v_M} + \frac{(1+\alpha)^2}{8k}v_M.$$

Thus, for

$$\frac{c}{v_M} < \bar{\phi} \leq \frac{c}{v_M} + \frac{(1+\alpha)^2}{8k}v_M,$$

$\alpha* < \underline{\alpha}$, $w* = 0$, $m* = 0$, and $V^S(\alpha*, w*, \bar{\phi}) = (1 - \bar{\phi})v_M$ (part ii), while for

$$\frac{c}{v_M} + \frac{(1+\alpha)^2}{8k}v_M < \bar{\phi} \leq \frac{c}{v_M} + \frac{(1+\alpha)^2}{4k}v_M, \quad \alpha* = \underline{\alpha}, \quad w* = \frac{c}{v_M} - \bar{\phi} + \frac{(1+\alpha)^2}{4k}v_M,$$

$$m* = \frac{1+\alpha}{2k}v_M, \quad \text{and} \quad V^S(\alpha*, w*, \bar{\phi}) = v_M - c - \frac{(1+\alpha)^2}{8k}v_M^2. \qquad \text{(part iii).}$$

Q.E.D.

Proof of Proposition 4: We need to show that over the five regions of Lemma 3 share value $S = (1 - \bar{\phi} - w*)v_M$ (weakly) decreases with $\bar{\phi}$. To this end, we substitute the optimal wage $w*$ from Lemma 3 into $S = (1 - \bar{\phi} - w*)v_M$. To establish that share value does not increase from one region to the next, we also explicitly derive (when necessary) the share value at the lower and/or upper bound of the regions.

In region (i) $w* = c/v_M - \bar{\phi}$ making the share value constant and equal to $S = v_M - c$.

In region (ii) $w* = 0$ and $S = (1 - \bar{\phi})v_M$, which decreases with $\bar{\phi}$. At the lower bound of region (ii) $(\bar{\phi} = c/v_M)$ share value is equal to $S = v_M - c$, and at the upper bound

$$\left(\bar{\phi} = \frac{c}{v_M} + \frac{(1+\alpha)^2}{8k} v_M \right), \quad S = v_M - c - \frac{(1+\alpha)^2}{8k} v_M^2.$$

In region (iii),

$$w* = \frac{c}{v_M} - \bar{\phi} + \frac{(1+\alpha)^2}{4k} v_M$$

making the share value constant and equal to

$$S = v_M - c - \frac{(1+\alpha)^2}{4k} v_M^2.$$

At the transition from region (ii) to region (iii)

$$\left(\bar{\phi} = \frac{c}{v_M} + \frac{(1+\alpha)^2}{8k} v_M \right)$$

the share value is discontinuous jumping from

$$v_M - c - \frac{(1+\alpha)^2}{8k} v_M^2 \quad \text{to} \quad v_M - c - \frac{(1+\alpha)^2}{4k} v_M^2.$$

In regions (iv) and (v), $w* = 0$ and $S = (1 - \bar{\phi})v_M$, which decreases with $\bar{\phi}$. At the lower bound of region (iv)

$$\left(\bar{\phi} = \frac{c}{v_M} + \frac{(1+\alpha)^2}{4k} v_M \right),$$

share value is equal to

$$S = v_M - c - \frac{(1+\alpha)^2}{4k} v_M^2$$

and decreases thereafter at a constant rate v_M. Q.E.D.

Proof of Corollary 2: The block premium is meaningful only in the range where $1 > \alpha* > 0$, that is, in regions (iii) and (iv) of Lemma 3. In region (iii), $\alpha* = \underline{\alpha}$ and

$$V^S(\alpha*, w*, \bar{\phi}) - S = \frac{(1+\alpha)^2}{8k} v_M^2,$$

which is independent of $\bar{\phi}$. In region (iv),

$$\alpha* = \frac{2}{v_M} \sqrt{k(\bar{\phi} v_M - c)} - 1 \quad \text{and} \quad V^S(\alpha*, w*, \bar{\phi}) - S = \frac{\bar{\phi} v_M - c}{2}$$

which increases with $\bar{\phi}$ and is equal to

$$V^S(\alpha^*, w^*, \bar{\phi}) - S = \frac{(1+\alpha)^2}{8k} v_M^2$$

at the lower bound

$$\left(\bar{\phi} = \frac{c}{v_M} + \frac{(1+\alpha)^2}{4k} v_M\right).$$

Q.E.D.

Proof of Proposition 5: Denote by $V^{S_{NC}}$ the founder's welfare in the absence of collusion (Lemma 2) and by V^{S_C} his welfare with collusion (Lemma 3). As the subsequent comparison shows, $V^{S_{NC}} \geq V^{S_C}$ in the interval

$$\frac{c}{v_M} < \bar{\phi} \leq \frac{c}{v_M} + \frac{v_M}{k},$$

while $V^{S_{NC}}$ and V^{S_C} coincide for $\bar{\phi} \leq c/v_M$ and for $\bar{\phi} > (c/v_M) + (v_M/k)$, that is, in regions (i) and (v) of Lemma 3.

For

$$\frac{c}{v_M} < \bar{\phi} \leq \frac{c}{v_M} + \frac{(1+\alpha)^2 v_M}{8k},$$

$V^{S_{NC}} \geq V^{S_C}$ is equivalent to

$$c + \frac{k}{2}\left(\bar{\phi} - \frac{c}{v_M}\right)^2 \leq \bar{\phi} v_M.$$

Rearranging this inequality, we obtain

$$\frac{k}{2v_M}\left(\bar{\phi} - \frac{c}{v_M}\right)^2 \leq \left(\bar{\phi} - \frac{c}{v_M}\right),$$

which can be rewritten as

$$\bar{\phi} \leq \frac{c}{v_M} + 2\frac{v_M}{k}.$$

This condition is always satisfied for

$$\bar{\phi} \leq \frac{c}{v_M} + \frac{(1+\alpha)^2 v_M}{8k}.$$

For

$$\frac{c}{v_M} + \frac{(1+\alpha)^2 v_M}{8k} < \bar{\phi} \leq \frac{c}{v_M} + \frac{(1+\alpha)^2 v_M}{4k},$$

$V^{S_{NC}} \geq V^{S_c}$ is equivalent to

$$\frac{k}{2}\left(\bar{\phi} - \frac{c}{v_M}\right)^2 \leq \frac{(1+\alpha)^2}{8k} v_M^2.$$

Since the LHS increases with $\bar{\phi}$, it is sufficient to check that the inequality is satisfied at the upper bound of the interval. Substituting

$$\bar{\phi} = \frac{c}{v_M} + \frac{(1+\alpha)^2 v_M}{4k}$$

into the inequality and rearranging yields $(1+\alpha)/2 \leq 1$ which always holds.
  For

$$\frac{c}{v_M} + \frac{(1+\alpha)^2 v_M}{4k} < \bar{\phi} \leq \frac{c}{v_M} + \frac{v_M}{k},$$

$V^{S_{NC}} \geq V^{S_c}$ is equivalent to

$$\frac{k}{2}\left(\bar{\phi} - \frac{c}{v_M}\right)^2 \leq \frac{\bar{\phi} v_M - c}{2}.$$

Rearranging this inequality, we obtain

$$k\left(\bar{\phi} - \frac{c}{v_M}\right)^2 \leq v_M\left(\bar{\phi} - \frac{c}{v_M}\right),$$

which can be rewritten as

$$\bar{\phi} - \frac{c}{v_M} \leq \frac{v_M}{k}.$$

This condition is always satisfied for $\bar{\phi} \leq \frac{c}{v_M} + \frac{v_M}{k}$. Q.E.D.

REFERENCES

Anderson, Ronald, and David Reeb, 2003, Founding family ownership and firm performance: Evidence from the S&P 500, *Journal of Finance* 58, 1301–1328.

Barclay, Michael, and Clifford Holderness, 1989, Private benefits from control of public corporations, *Journal of Financial Economics* 25, 371–395.

Bebchuk, Lucien, 1999, A rent extraction theory of corporate ownership and control, NBER Working Paper 7203.

Berle, Adolph, and Gardiner Means, 1932, *The Modern Corporation and Private Property* (Macmillan, New York).

Bhattacharya, Utpal, and B. Ravikumar, 2001, Capital markets and the evolution of family businesses, *Journal of Business* 74, 187–220.

Bhattacharya, Utpal, and B. Ravikumar, 2002, From cronies to professionals: The evolution of family firms, Mimeo, University of Indiana.

Burkart, Mike, Denis Gromb, and Fausto Panunzi, 1997, Large shareholders, monitoring, and the value of the firm, *Quarterly Journal of Economics* 112, 693–728.

Burkart, Mike, and Fausto Panunzi, 2001, Agency conflicts, ownership concentration and legal shareholder protection, Financial Markets Group (LSE) Discussion Paper 378.

Claessens, Stijn, Simeon Djankov, Joseph Fan, and Larry Lang, 2002, Disentangling the incentive and entrenchment effects of large shareholdings, *Journal of Finance* 57, 2379–2408.

2200   *The Journal of Finance*

Claessens, Stijn, Simeon Djankov, and Larry Lang, 2000, The separation of ownership and control in East Asian corporations, *Journal of Financial Economics* 58, 81–112.

DeMarzo, Peter, and Branko Urosevic, 2000, Optimal trading by a large shareholder, Mimeo, Stanford Graduate School of Business.

Demsetz, Harold, and Kenneth Lehn, 1985, The structure of corporate ownership: Causes and consequences, *Journal of Political Economy* 93, 1155–1177.

Dyck, Alexander, and Luigi Zingales, 2003, Private benefits of control: An international comparison, *Journal of Finance*, forthcoming.

Ehrhardt, Olaf, and Eric Nowak, 2001, Private benefits and minority shareholder expropriation— Empirical evidence from IPOs of German family owned firms, CFS Working Paper 2001/10.

European Corporate Governance Network (ECGN), 2001 Fabricio Barca, Marco Becht, eds. *The Control of Corporate Europe* (Oxford University Press, Oxford).

Faccio, Mara, 2002, Politically-connected firms: Can they squeeze the State? Mimeo, University of Notre Dame.

Faccio, Mara, and Larry Lang, 2002, The ultimate ownership of Western European corporations, *Journal of Financial Economics* 65, 365–395.

Grossman, Sanford, and Oliver Hart, 1988, One share–one vote and the market for corporate control, *Journal of Financial Economics* 20, 175–202.

Himmelberg, Charles, Glenn Hubbard, and Inessa Love, 2001, Investor protection, ownership, and capital allocation, Mimeo, Columbia University.

Jensen, Michael, and William Meckling, 1976, Theory of the firm: Managerial behavior, agency costs and capital structure, *Journal of Financial Economics* 3, 305–360.

Johnson, Simon, Rafael La Porta, Florencio Lopez-de-Silanes, and Andrei Shleifer, 2000, Tunneling, *American Economic Review Papers and Proceedings* 90, 22–27.

La Porta, Rafael, Florencio Lopez-de-Silanes, and Andrei Shleifer, 1999, Corporate ownership around the world, *Journal of Finance* 54, 471–517.

La Porta, Rafael, Florencio Lopez-de-Silanes, Andrei Shleifer, and Robert Vishny, 1997, Legal determinants of external finance, *Journal of Finance* 52, 1131–1150.

La Porta, Rafael, Florencio Lopez-de-Silanes, Andrei Shleifer, and Robert Vishny, 1998, Law and finance, *Journal of Political Economy* 106, 1113–1155.

La Porta, Rafael, Florencio Lopez-de-Silanes, Andrei Shleifer, and Robert Vishny, 2000a, Agency problems and dividend policies around the world, *Journal of Finance* 55, 1–33.

La Porta, Rafael, Florencio Lopez-de-Silanes, Andrei Shleifer, and Robert Vishny, 2000b, Investor protection and corporate governance, *Journal of Financial Economics* 58, 3–27.

La Porta, Rafael, Florencio Lopez-de-Silanes, Andrei Shleifer, and Robert Vishny, 2002, Investor protection and corporate valuation, *Journal of Finance* 57, 1147–1170.

Morck, Randall, David Stangeland, and Bernard Yeung, 2000, Inherited wealth, corporate control, and economic growth?, in Morck Randall, ed. *Concentrated Corporate Ownership* (NBER Conference Volume, University of Chicago Press, Chicago, IL).

Nenova, Tatiana, 2003, The value of corporate voting rights and control: A cross-country analysis, *Journal of Financial Economics* 68, 325–352.

Pagano, Marco, and Ailsa Röell, 1998, The choice of stock ownership structure: Agency costs, monitoring and the decision to go public, *Quarterly Journal of Economics* 113, 187–225.

Perez-Gonzales, Francisco, 2001, Does Inherited Control Hurt Firms' Performance? Ph.D. dissertation, Harvard University.

Prowse, Steven, 1995, Corporate governance in an international perspective: A survey of corporate control mechanisms among large firms in the US, UK, Japan and Germany, *Financial Markets, Institutions and Instruments* 4, 1–63.

Shleifer, Andrei, and Robert Vishny, 1986, Large shareholders and corporate control, *Journal of Political Economy* 94, 461–488.

Shleifer, Andrei, and Daniel Wolfenzon, 2002, Investor protection and equity markets, *Journal of Financial Economics* 66, 3–27.

Siegel, Jordan, 2002, Can foreign firms bond themselves effectively by submitting to U.S. law? Mimeo, MIT.

Wells, Philippe, 1998, *Essays in International Entrepreneurial Finance*, Ph.D. dissertation, Harvard University.

Zingales, Luigi, 1994, The value of a voting right: A study of the Milan stock exchange, *Review of Financial Studies* 7, 125–148.

[24]

Available online at www.sciencedirect.com

ScienceDirect

Journal of Financial Economics 88 (2008) 466–498

ELSEVIER

JOURNAL OF
Financial
ECONOMICS

www.elsevier.com/locate/jfec

Mixing family with business: A study of Thai business groups and the families behind them ☆

Marianne Bertrand[a], Simon Johnson[b,*],
Krislert Samphantharak[c], Antoinette Schoar[b]

[a]*Graduate School of Business, University of Chicago, Chicago, IL 60637, USA*
[b]*Sloan School of Management, Massachusetts Institute of Technology, Cambridge, MA 02142, USA*
[c]*School of International Relations and Pacific Studies, University of California at San Diego, La Jolla, CA 92093, USA*

Received 13 April 2007; received in revised form 26 December 2007; accepted 7 April 2008
Available online 21 May 2008

Abstract

How does the structure of the families behind business groups affect the group's organization, governance, and performance? We construct a unique dataset of family trees and business groups for 93 of the largest business families in Thailand. We find a strong positive association between family size and family involvement in the ownership and control of the family businesses. The founders' sons play a central role in both ownership and board membership, especially when the founder of the group is dead. Greater involvement by sons is also associated with lower firm-level performance, especially when the founder is dead. One hypothesis that emerges from our analysis is that part of the decay of family-run groups over time is due to the dilution of ownership and control across a set of equally powerful descendants of the founder, which creates a "race to the bottom" in tunneling resources out of the group firms.
© 2008 Elsevier B.V. All rights reserved.

JEL classification: D13; G30; J12; Z19

Keywords: Corporate governance; Excess control; Groups; Families

1. Introduction

Family firms have attracted a lot of interest over the last few years. Recent research shows that the U.S. model of dispersed ownership, with strong separation of ownership and control, is unusual. Instead, most firms around the world are likely to be part of a group of companies, linked together through common

---

☆ We thank Thorsten Beck, Utpal Bhattacharya, Alexander Dyck, Francisco Pérez-González, Randall Morck, Andrei Shleifer, and seminar participants at Emory University, INSEAD, the Mitsui Life Symposium on Global Financial Markets (University of Michigan), the IMF, the MIT Organization Lunch, the MIT Finance Lunch, Vanderbilt University, UCSD, UCLA, the NBER Conference in Corporate Finance, and the European Summer Symposium in financial markets at Gerzensee for many helpful comments. We particularly thank the organizers and participants at the Darden-World Bank emerging markets conference in May 2006.
*Corresponding author.
E-mail address: sjohnson@imf.org (S. Johnson).

0304-405X/$ - see front matter © 2008 Elsevier B.V. All rights reserved.
doi:10.1016/j.jfineco.2008.04.002

M. Bertrand et al. / Journal of Financial Economics 88 (2008) 466–498   467

ownership, with ultimate ownership and control often lying with a single family. La Porta, Lopez-de-Silanes, and Shleifer (1999) show that a large fraction of public and private firms around the world are family-controlled. Family-controlled firms often use pyramidal ownership structures to exert control over a large network of firms.[1] While family firms appear to be more prevalent in countries with weak minority shareholder protection, a number of recent studies show that family involvement is quite widespread, even in the U.S.[2]

The finance literature has generally treated the families behind business groups as monolithic entities. Most economic theories of family businesses focus on the role of families as second-best solutions to imperfections in the financial markets, the market for corporate control, or the market for managerial talent (see, e.g., Burkart, Panunzi, and Shleifer, 2003; Caselli and Gennaioli, 2005). These models generally assume that trust relationships between family members can serve to (partially) solve principal-agent problems between owners and outside managers, if monitoring of managers is difficult. However, these theories typically ignore the fact that families are composed of individual members who have their own personal objectives and claims over the family businesses. This divergence in objectives might even lead to an erosion of trust within families, especially once the founder has passed control to the next generation.

Our goal is to explore how these within-family dynamics affect the organization, governance, and performance of business groups. For this analysis, we created a new data set that contains detailed information on the family trees—starting with the founder and following until the current generation—and the exact network structure of over 90 of the largest family business groups in Thailand.[3] We have three main sets of findings. First, we document in detail how control, management, and ownership are allocated across different family members. The sons of the founder are central in ownership and control for these groups and substantially increase their ownership once the founder is gone. In groups where the founder has a relatively greater number of sons, the sons hold a significantly larger fraction of the ownership and control rights of the group firms. In fact, we find that sons "crowd out" the ownership and control rights of other family members.

Second, we show that families where the founder has a relatively greater number of sons are associated with lower firm-level performance. Family structure appears to be a major determinant of firm-level performance. This effect is especially pronounced when the founder is dead. In contrast, the correlation between firm performance and the number of daughters or number of other family members is much smaller and in most cases insignificant.

Third, we identify a possible governance channel for these performance results. Families that have relatively more sons tend to show a larger discrepancy between control and ownership rights (excess control), which is usually associated with poor governance and incentives for tunneling. The same increase in excess control cannot be found in families that have relatively more daughters or other family members. Moreover, sons show higher levels of excess control once the founder is gone. A parallel relation can be found for the organizational structure of the groups. Once the founder is gone, larger families are associated with larger groups (more firms in the group) and groups that are more pyramidal in structure. Finally, we find that, controlling for family ownership, excess control by the founder's sons is associated with lower firm-level performance, again especially when the founder is dead. The same effect of excess control is not found for other family members. This suggests that a family member's ability to extract resources from a group firm depends on that family member's position within the family hierarchy and not just whether he or she has a position on the firm board.

One interpretation that emerges from our analysis is that the decay of family-run groups over time might in part reflect infighting for group resources as control becomes more diluted among rival family members, and in particular among the sons of the founder. If powerful insiders compete against each other, this could lead to "a race to the bottom" where one brother tries to tunnel resources out of the firm before another brother does.

---

[1] Anderson and Reeb (2003) find that founding families are present in one third of S&P 500 firms and hold on average about 18% of the equity in these firms. See also Claessens, Djankov, and Lang (2000) for a study of family involvement in East Asian countries, and the work of the European Corporate Governance Network reported in Gugler (2001) for a similar study for European countries.

[2] See also Bhattacharya and Ravikumar (2003) and Pérez-González (2006).

[3] Our data sources do not allow us to determine which family members have died (we are able to do this for founders only after substantial additional work for each). For this reason, measures of family size, number of sons, etc. are measured from the start of the family business, unless otherwise noted.

These rivalries across family members seem to become more pronounced when the founder of the family group has more sons and when the founder himself is gone.

However, we should stress that our analysis does not allow us to rule out additional explanations for the negative relation between family size (and especially number of sons) and firm performance. A greater number of sons could lead to worse management decisions within the group if these family insiders crowd out potentially more able professional managers. In addition, the average quality of a son could be lower as the number of sons increases, because of the limited parental resources that have to be shared across a larger set of children. The founder might feel compelled to let his sons manage the group firms irrespective of their ability because of personal preferences or cultural inheritance norms (see Bertrand and Schoar, 2006).

There are a number of reasons why we focus our analysis on Thailand. First, Thailand is one of the few countries where detailed family structure data can be constructed with reasonable accuracy. For the major family groups now in existence, we are able to identify the founder who created the family business and the lineage of his children and future generations, in some cases for up to five generations. Second, there is a great deal of publicly available data for both publicly traded and privately held Thai family firms, which enables us to explore the role of private firms in more detail than is possible in many countries. Given the structure of business groups, this is an important improvement over previous studies that focus only on the public firms within family groups. These data were collected for 1996, i.e., a year before the financial crisis. For each business group, we construct organizational charts that describe the network structure of the groups as of 1996.

Our paper builds on several recent studies that document that family firms have lower stock market valuations and lower rates of return on average than non-family firms, although none of these studies have data on the private firms within the family business groups (see, e.g., Claessens, Djankov, Fan, and Lang, 2002; Cronqvist and Nilsson, 2003). More recently, Pérez-González (2006) and Villalonga and Amit (2006) show for U.S. firms that this negative performance effect is in large part related to the passing of active management and control from the founder to the descendants. Bennedson, Nielsen, Pérez-González, and Wolfenzon (2007) show a similar result for the case of small private firms in Denmark and are able to use gender composition as an instrument for the availability of male heirs. Our data allow us to go a step further and investigate the family dynamics and changes in governance structure associated with larger families and founder succession in business groups. But not all papers conclude that family firms perform worse on average. For example, Anderson and Reeb (2003) find higher performance for family firms in the U.S., while Khanna and Palepu (2000) show that business groups in India (which are for the most part family-controlled) on average perform better than stand-alone firms in matched industries. Morck, Stangeland, and Yeung (2000) offer an explanation for the positive outcomes of family firms in some countries. If the government plays a central role in the economy, family connections can provide access to limited resources that in turn can lead to an even greater concentration of political influence in the hands of a few families. Marman (2002) provides a similar description of the emergence of family firms in South Korea and Israel.

Our results are also related to the sociology literature on family groups that tends to focus more on detailed descriptions of within-family dynamics. For example, a number of sociological studies, relying for the most part on case studies, interviews or anecdotal evidence, have stressed the importance of cultural factors in explaining the emergence of family firms. Redding (1990), Jones and Rose (1993) and Whyte (1996) explore this argument in the context of Chinese families. These papers suggest that family traditions and inheritance rules might be central to the evolution of family businesses. They also highlight the possibility of conflicts within business families and how those might alter the direction and growth of the businesses.

The rest of this paper is organized as follows. In Section 2 we provide some brief background information on Thai business history, including the evolution of family businesses. Section 3 explains how our data were collected on the families and their groups of firms. Section 4 discusses the descriptive statistics. Section 5 establishes that greater family involvement, particularly by sons of the founder, is associated with worse performance. Section 6 presents our main findings and Section 7 concludes.

2. Brief historical background

The Thai economy was integrated into the world economy in 1855 when the Bowring Treaty was signed between Britain and Siam. This treaty ended the Siamese King's monopoly power over international trade and

M. Bertrand et al. / Journal of Financial Economics 88 (2008) 466–498   469

lowered the tariff on exports and imports. In the wake of this increased openness, European businesses entered Thailand, mainly through trading houses and banks and in the forestry, mining, and engineering sectors. Over the same period, the number of Chinese immigrants increased. Almost 3 million Chinese immigrants arrived in Thailand between 1882 and 1931. By the end of the 1920s, almost 12% of the total population of Thailand was of Chinese origin (Limlingan, 1986). Most of these immigrants were poor and worked as laborers in the growing export industries such as rice milling. But a number of these immigrants became entrepreneurs in various industries such as agriculture, trade, and mining, and started to expand their business extensively. The origin of some of the best-known business families can be traced back to this period (Suehiro, 1997).

The revolution of 1932 marked the end of the absolute monarchy in Thailand and led to an expansion of many family business groups that are important to this date. After the Second World War, Thailand entered a long period of successive military dictatorships that lasted until the 1970s. During this period, the government and military leaders became involved in business through shareholdings or board participation in both state-owned enterprises and private companies. These connections allowed such companies to grow rapidly. The First National Economic Development Plan was introduced in 1961, marking the beginning of the industrialization of the country. The manufacturing sector started to expand rapidly but was concentrated around a few family business groups that had connections with the banking sector and the government. The financial liberalization of the late 1980s and early 1990s created investment opportunities in real estate, telecommunications, and tourism and gave rise to new business groups that grew rapidly and eventually became as important as the old groups in shaping the modern Thai corporate sector.

3. Data

The data for this project were collected from a number of different sources. In the following we will give an overview of the data collection process. The Appendix explains precisely how we obtained our sample of firms, including how we ascertained that a family controls a particular firm.

3.1. Firms

Each registered firm in Thailand has to submit annual financial statements, audited by an authorized auditor, to the Ministry of Commerce. Registered firms include registered partnerships, privately held limited companies, and publicly traded companies. The financial statements of the largest 2,000 firms are published every year in a book series called *Thailand Company Information* (TCI). The criteria that TCI uses for including firms are (1) annual revenues of at least 200 million baht (approximately 8 million U.S. dollars, using 1996 exchange rates), (2) listed on the Stock Exchange of Thailand, or (3) one of the leading companies in its industry. We collect this information for the cross section of all firms in 1996, since we want to capture the groups' structures and organization before the Asian financial crisis. In total, our sample contains 2,153 firms in 1996, which includes all publicly traded firms and the largest privately held firms in Thailand.

The TCI database contains financial, ownership, and board composition information at the firm level. For all firms, the financial information includes total assets, total liabilities, total revenues, and net profits. The database also reports ownership data, the names of and the percentage of company shares held by each shareholder, and the names of directors on the firm's board. For publicly traded firms, specific board positions held by a particular person are also reported. The database provides information on industry classification similar to one-digit and two-digit SIC codes, as well as the founding year for each firm. We supplement these data with follow-up requests made to the Department of Business Development in the case of missing information. (The Department of Business Development was previously known as the Department of Commercial Registration until the government reorganization that became effective in October 2002.) We had to hand-collect the data for our business groups, since TCI only publishes these data in book format (rather than electronically).

For publicly listed firms, we can obtain additional information from the Stock Exchange of Thailand's *Listed Company Info.* These data are available in electronic format and distinguish between consolidated and unconsolidated financial statements. We use unconsolidated financial statements in our analysis when looking at the outcomes of subsidiary firms within a business group.

470   *M. Bertrand et al. / Journal of Financial Economics 88 (2008) 466–498*

3.2. Families

To construct family trees for the family business groups in our sample, we rely on a number of sources. We start with a publication by the Brooker Group (2003) entitled *Thai Business Groups: A Unique Guide to Who Owns What*, which covers the 150 leading business groups in Thailand and the history of each of these groups from the time the first business was founded. We then construct family trees for these business groups: for each of the groups, we identify the founder and trace all of his direct descendants to the youngest generation that is active in business. We exclude family members who are younger than 15 years in 1996. We can infer this from the person's title, since in Thailand people drop their junior title when they turn 15.

Since the Brooker book does not provide full coverage of all family members, we gather more detailed descriptions from alternative sources. First, we collect family tree information from the funeral books published and distributed for the group founders or other family members. It is customary in Thailand when a public person dies that the descendants compile a funeral book that contains information about the person's life and his or her family relationships. These funeral books are available at the National Library in Bangkok. Second, we compile data from various biographical accounts written on Thai families. For example, Sapphaibul (2001a, b) provides detailed information on 55 of the most famous business families. We supplement this information with articles, obituaries, wedding announcements, and anniversary announcements of these businesses families in various local magazines and newspapers. A complete list of the biography and funeral books as well as the articles is in the Appendix. Finally, we conduct informal interviews with family members of a few business families to verify the accuracy of our data.

The descriptive data are then systematically coded in the form of family trees. We include in our family trees all of the family members we identify, whether or not they are involved in the family business. The founder generation is coded as generation one, his children are generation two, and so on. For each family member, we collect information on his or her specific position in the family tree (defined as the relationship to the founder), gender, birth order (defined as the rank order of children within a specific marriage), and biological versus adopted status. We also code information on education, working experience, and involvement in the family business, but these data are less complete. We identify whether the founder is still alive in 1996 and whether an heir has taken over. (Note that we cannot systematically track whether a given family member is still alive for most of the other family members.) Finally, we collect information on the name of the spouse(s) for each family member. This information is especially interesting for the founder, since several founders have multiple wives and also children from multiple wives. We do not, however, count spouses as part of the family when we construct measures of family size. We carefully keep track of changes in last names, especially for married female family members and their descendants.

Since we have to rely on secondary sources to construct the family trees, there is some concern that there is a bias towards coverage of family members who are involved in business, while family members who are more private will not be mentioned in these sources. We limit our sample to 93 families for which we can cross-check our information using several different sources. But even for these families, there is still some concern that our information is not complete. With regard to the coverage of female family members, the proportion of females including all generations and adopted children is 38%, whereas the proportion of females in the family trees excluding the first generation (the founders) and excluding adopted children is 42%, suggesting some data inconsistencies.

Fig. 1 displays a sample family tree. The Bhirom Bhakdi family owns and manages a beer business in Thailand under the brand "Singha." Boonrawd Satrabutr started the family business in 1932. Boonrawd is coded as the first generation in our data. He adopted Wit, a nephew, as his son. He and his wife later had two other sons, Prachuab and Chamnong Wit, Prachuab, and Chamnong are considered as the family's second generation. There are 11 family members in the third generation: five males and six females, the sons and daughters of Wit, Prachuab, and Chamnong.

Each individual in the family tree then has to be matched to the ownership and board composition data collected at the firm level, allowing us to determine whether a specific family member is involved in the family business, in what capacity (through ownership and/or control), and in which firms. There are two major data challenges in this matching exercise. First, there are typically many different English spellings for a given Thai name, forcing us to do most of this matching by hand. Second, special care has to be taken in matching female

M. Bertrand et al. / Journal of Financial Economics 88 (2008) 466–498   471

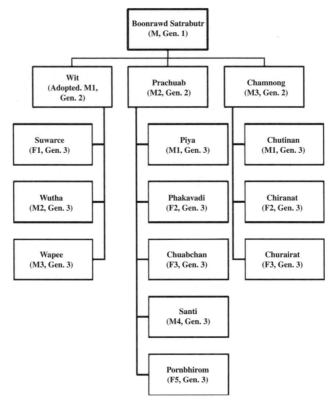

Fig. 1. Bhirom Bhakdi Family.

family members to the ownership and board information as they may have dropped their maiden name after getting married. To alleviate any bias that might result from the change in last name we also match all the daughters of a given family by first name only. This creates a unique match in all but one case, since in Thai culture it is very uncommon that two children within a family are given the same first name. Overall, we identify the firms that belong to each of our 93 business families. The criterion is that the family as a whole has the highest percentage of ultimate ownership in that company. Ultimate ownership is defined as the cash-flow rights derived from holding shares in the firm directly or indirectly through pyramids or cross-shareholdings. Taken as a whole, the 93 families in our dataset control more than 40% of all the assets in our 1996 sample of Thai firms.

4. Descriptive statistics

Table 1 provides an overview of the 93 business families in our sample. While the average family has 12.9 members, there is wide variation in family size: the largest family has as much as 122 members and the smallest has one. Note that we use here all family members in the family tree (but not children under age 15 at the time of our study—it is impossible to ascertain exactly how many of them are present in most families), regardless of whether we have evidence that they are involved in the business, since we would create endogeneity bias in

472 *M. Bertrand et al. / Journal of Financial Economics 88 (2008) 466–498*

Table 1

Summary statistics: family characteristics

The unit of observation is a family. All the data are approximately as of 1996. Family size is the total number of direct descendants of the founder of each business group, including the founder himself. Specifically, family size does not include spouses, founder's siblings, and descendants of founder's siblings. Number of generations is defined as the number of generations of the family from the founder (generation 1) to the latest generation that is active in family business. Number of male family members is the total of number of direct descendants of the founder, including the founder himself. Number of female family members is the total number of direct descendants of the founder. Number of sons (daughters) is the total number of founder's sons (daughters) from all wives. Multiple wives is a dummy variable with the value of one if the founder had more than one wife, and zero otherwise. Founder dead is a dummy variable with the value of one if the founder was dead by 1996 and zero otherwise. The number of observations in full sample is 93 families, except for multiple wives, where the number of observations is 72.

Variable	Mean	Std. Dev.	Min	Max
Family size	12.94	17.51	1	122
Number of generations	2.47	0.72	1	5
Number of male family members	9.06	10.28	1	69
Number of female family members	5.88	8.08	0	51
Number of sons	3.26	2.57	0	14
Number of daughters	2.40	2.30	0	12
Multiple wives	0.24	0.43	0	1
Founder dead	0.48	0.50	0	1

the family size variable otherwise. Due to data limitations, family size does not include spouses or the founder's siblings (and their descendants). In-laws are also excluded. We are not confident in our ability to collect high-quality data on these relatives across all families.

There are two main sources of variation in family size: the number of children each couple has, and the number of generations that have passed since the founder started the business. On average, each family group has been around for 2.5 generations, with a minimum of one generation (three families), and a maximum of five generations (only one family).[4] The vast majority of the families in our data span two or three generations. The average number of male direct descendants of the founder is 9.1 and the average number of female direct descendants of the founder is 5.9. The number of sons is 3.3 and the number of daughters is 2.4. These calculations include the founder's children from all wives. For 72 out of the 93 families, we have been able to ascertain if the founder had more than one wife.[5] This was the case in 17% of the 72 families. Finally, we document that the founder is dead in 45 of the families in our sample.

Table 2 reports characteristics of the firms that these families own and operate. Every family in our sample controls at least one firm; 16 out of 93 families control only one firm (for which we have data), while the remaining families control groups of firms. (By our criterion of assigning a firm to the family with highest ownership, no firms in our sample are owned by, controlled by, or involve more than one family.) The average family in our sample controls 6.56 distinct companies in 1996. There is wide variation among families, with the biggest family group owning 58 firms. Since this family presents a large outlier in our group size distribution, we rerun all our results without this family; the results are robust to this omission. The average return on assets of the groups, calculated as net profits in 1996 divided by 1996 year-end total book assets, is only 3%, while leverage is over 70%, measured as total liabilities divided by book value of total assets (again for 1996). The low average ROA and high leverage reflect the timing of the data, which was at the onset of the Asian financial crisis. On average, the groups in our sample own 1.9 public firms and 4.7 private firms. To provide a better picture of the structure of the groups in our sample, we calculate the "depth" of the groups measured as the largest number of vertical ownership links between firms within a group. We set the depth of firms at the top of the group structure as zero. For example, if firm A owns B and firm B owns C, we calculate the depth of

---

[4]Eight families in our sample are four or more generations old. However, several second-generation family members are still alive in these families. In fact, in four out of these eight families, we identify second-generation members with ownership and/or board positions in 1996. We replicate the main parts of our analysis by dropping those four families that are four or more generations old and for which we do not see second-generation family members with ownership and/or board positions. The main regression results do not change.

[5]In some instances the founder has more than one wife at the same time, while in other cases the wives are consecutive. We do not differentiate between these two kinds of multiple wife situations in our analysis.

M. Bertrand et al. / Journal of Financial Economics 88 (2008) 466–498

Table 2

Summary statistics: firm characteristics

Panel A: The unit of observation is a firm. All data are as of 1996. Return on assets is the net profit divided by the total assets at the end of the year. Leverage is group total liabilities divided by group total assets. Residual return on assets is the residual from the OLS regression of return on assets on one-digit SIC fixed effects and the natural logarithm of firm total assets across all firms in the full sample, including firms not belonging to the 93 families. Firm age is as of 1996.

Panel B: The unit of observation is a family business group. All data are as of 1996. Number of firms is the number of public and private firms in our sample that belonged to families. Log of total assets is the natural logarithm of group total assets in thousands of baht at the end of the year. Return on assets is the net profit divided by the total assets at the end of the year. Leverage is group total liabilities divided by group total assets. Group age is defined as the age of the oldest firm for each group in our sample. Group depth is defined as the maximum depth of the deepest firm in the group, where maximum depth is the longest chain that vertically traces the firm to the family's ultimate ownership. Number of firms owning a particular firm is the largest number of group firms with ownership in a particular firm in the same group. Number of firms owned by a particular firm is the largest number of group firms that are owned by a particular firm in the same group. The total number of groups in the full sample is 93. When computing group structure variables, two groups are dropped out due to their complicated structure of cyclical cross-shareholdings.

Variable	Number of firms	Mean	Std. Dev.	Min	Max
Panel A: Firm level					
Return on assets	586	0.03	0.07	−0.11	0.21
Residual return on assets	586	0.10	7.25	−19.86	19.71
Leverage	586	0.71	0.25	0.21	1.10
Firm age	586	18.06	13.57	0	114
Panel B: Group level					
Number of firms	93	6.56	9.21	1	58
Number of public firms	93	1.90	2.58	0	19
Number of private firms	93	4.66	7.81	0	53
Log of total assets	93	16.43	1.77	12.54	21.22
Returns on assets	93	0.03	0.04	−0.11	0.21
Leverage	93	0.69	0.18	0.29	1.10
Group age	93	32.10	16.98	7	114
Group depth	91	1.64	1.55	0	7
Number of firms owning a particular firm	91	1.57	1.67	0	7
Number of firms owned by a particular firm	91	2.33	3.94	0	23

the group as two. Table 2 shows that the average depth of the groups in our sample is 1.64, where the flattest groups have a depth of zero (i.e., they are not pyramidal at all) and the deepest group has seven levels, i.e., seven layers below the firm at the top of the group. We also calculate two more statistics on the complexity of the upstream and downstream ownership holdings within the groups. "Number of firms owning a particular firm" calculates the largest number of upstream ties of an individual firm in the groups, while "number of firms owned by a particular firm" describes the same for downstream ties. The values for these are 1.57 and 2.33, respectively.

Panel A of Table 3 reports the ownership structure of the firms across different family members and Panel B shows the board involvement of the family members. The average family ownership stake is 45.2% for the firms in our sample, and on average 6.23 family members have ownership stakes in at least one firm within the family group. The sons of the founder on average hold 12.6% of the outstanding equity in the group firms while the daughters hold only 5.5%. About 1.4 sons on average have ownership in at least one of the group firms but only 0.8 of the daughters do. Overall, the proportion of family ownership held by the sons is 28% while the daughters own only 10% of the equity that is in the hand of family members.

Panel B shows that the numbers are even more skewed for the distribution of board positions that provide control rights over the firm. On average there are 1.24 family members with board positions. About 51% of sons hold at least one board position. The fraction of family board positions held by the sons is 40%. In contrast, the fraction family ownership held by daughters of the founder is 8% and only 10% of daughters hold board positions.

474 *M. Bertrand et al. / Journal of Financial Economics 88 (2008) 466–498*

Table 3

Summary statistics of family involvements

The unit of observation is a family business group. For each observation, the variables are computed as the arithmetic average across firms in the group. The data are as of 1996. The number of observations in the full sample is 93 groups (families) except for those for fraction of family board positions because some families do not hold any board positions in some family-owned firms.

Family ownership is the total percentage of ultimate ownership directly or indirectly held by family members in a particular firm. Number of family members with ownership is the number of family members that directly or indirectly own a particular firm. Sons' (daughters's) ownership is the total percentage of ultimate ownership directly or indirectly held by all founder's sons (daughters). Number of sons (daughters) with ownership is the number of founder's sons (daughters) that directly or indirectly own a particular firm. Fraction of family ownership held by sons (daughters) is computed as sons' (daughters') ownership divided by family ownership. Fraction of family ownership held by others is the fraction of family ownership not held by the founder's sons or daughters.

Number of family member with board positions is the number of family member with board positions in at least one of the group firms. Number of sons (daughters) with board position is the number of the founder's sons (daughters) with board positions in at least one of the group firms. Fraction of board positions held by sons (daughters) is computed as the number of founder's sons (daughters) on the board divided by the number of all family members on board for a particular firm. Fraction of board positions held by others is computed as the number of family board positions not held by founder's sons or daughters divided by the number of board positions held by any family members for a particular firm.

Variable	Number of families	Mean	Std. Dev.	Min	Max
Panel A: Involvement in ownership					
Family ownership (%)	93	45.17	25.37	3.64	100.00
Number of family members with ownership	93	6.23	4.82	1	36.57
Sons' ownership (%)	93	12.61	15.52	0	63.08
Daughters' ownership (%)	93	5.49	10.14	0	45.50
Number of sons with ownership	93	1.39	1.38	0	6
Number of daughters with ownership	93	0.81	1.11	0	5
Fraction of family ownership held by sons	93	0.28	0.28	0	1
Fraction of family ownership held by daughters	93	0.10	0.16	0	1
Fraction of family ownership held by others	93	0.62	0.33	0	1
Panel B: Involvement in board positions					
Number of family members with board positions	93	1.24	0.87	0	5
Number of sons with board positions	93	0.51	0.65	0	4
Number of daughters with board positions	93	0.10	0.25	0	1
Fraction of family board positions held by sons	85	0.40	0.39	0	1
Fraction of family board positions held by daughters	85	0.08	0.22	0	1
Fraction of family board positions held by others	85	0.52	0.41	0	1

5. Family structure and family involvement in the business

As a first step toward understanding the role of individual family members in the performance and governance of group firms, we analyze the ownership and control positions of the different family members. We focus on two types of involvement: board membership and share ownership. We analyze how family involvement in the business (board membership and ownership) varies with the size and composition of the family. The idea behind this analysis is to understand whether greater "availability" of family members is associated with more family members taking part in business. A possible alternative would be to select the same number of family members to run the firms, after choosing from a larger talent pool.

5.1. Ownership structure

In Table 4, we first compute for each family the number of family members who hold some ownership in at least one of the group firms. In Column 1 we regress the number of family members who have some ownership in one of the group firms on the size of the family measured as the number of family members across all generations. These regressions are estimated at the firm level, but standard errors are clustered at the family (i.e., group) level to account for the fact that the decisions to involve family members could be made at the central group level and not at the level of the individual firm. We also include dummy variables for the number of generations since the group was founded and a control for the age of the business group, measured as the

M. Bertrand et al. / Journal of Financial Economics 88 (2008) 466–498   475

Table 4

Family involvement in business ownership for 93 families

The unit of observation is a firm ($n = 521$). Number of family members with ownership is the number of family members that directly or indirectly own a particular firm. Fraction of family ownership held by sons (daughters) is computed as sons' (daughters') ownership divided by family ownership. Fraction of family ownership held by others is the fraction of family ownership not held by the founder or his sons or daughters. Family size is the total number of direct descendants of the founder of each business group, including the founder himself. Founder dead is a dummy variable with the value of one if the founder was dead by 1996 and zero otherwise. Number of sons (daughters) is the total number of founder's sons (daughters) from all wives. Number of others is family size minus the number of sons and daughters. Firm age is as of 1996. All regressions are estimated using OLS and controlled for number of generations fixed effects. Standard errors are clustered at family-group level. Robust standard errors are in parentheses. * Represents coefficients significant at 10%; ** significant at 5%; and *** significant at 1%.

| | Number of family members with ownership | | Fraction of family ownership (× 100) held by | | | | | | |
| | | | Sons | | | Daughters | | | Others |
	(1)	(2)	(3)	(4)	(5)	(6)	(7)	(8)	(9)
Family size	0.241	0.243			−0.371			0.020	
	(0.086)***	(0.087)***			(0.196)*			(0.085)	
Founder dead? (Yes = 1)		−0.605		20.372	20.499		−0.043	−0.454	−20.359
		(1.285)		(8.437)**	(8.182)**		(8.241)	(8.514)	(10.652)*
Number of sons			2.651	2.140	3.542			0.268	−3.751
			(1.390)*	(1.398)	(1.437)**			(0.857)	(1.407)***
Number of daughters						0.369	0.370	0.174	1.066
						(0.629)	(0.601)	(0.793)	(1.617)
Number of others									0.291
									(0.231)
Firm age	0.034	0.036	0.044	−0.006	−0.003	0.133	0.133	0.134	−0.119
	(0.024)	(0.025)	(0.107)	(0.098)	(0.096)	(0.067)*	(0.066)**	(0.067)**	(0.119)
Constant	1.498	1.787	20.258	11.388	13.191	4.091	4.111	3.438	82.220
	(1.704)	(1.597)	(8.626)**	(7.423)	(7.543)*	(2.978)	(5.826)	(6.070)	(9.506)***
R-squared	0.55	0.55	0.39	0.42	0.43	0.08	0.08	0.08	0.41

year in which the oldest firm in the group was established. All results are robust to running median regressions or dropping the largest families from the sample.

If the involvement of family members is not sensitive to the "supply" of members, we should not see a relation. However, we find a strong positive correlation between the size of the family and the number of family members who are involved in business. The estimated coefficient of 0.241 means that for every four additional family members, one additional person will have ownership. In Column 2 we show that even when we include a dummy variable for whether the founder is dead we find no change in the coefficient on family size; the coefficient on the dummy is negative but not significant. This suggests that even if the founder is dead there is no significant difference in the overall holdings of the family members.

But these effects mask stark differences in the roles of different relatives of the founder, which we explore in the remaining columns of Table 4. We break down ownership by the fraction of family ownership held by sons of the founder, daughters of the founder, and other family members (excluding the founder). In Columns 3–5 we look at the ownership of sons as a function of the number of sons. Column 3 shows that the fraction of sons' ownership increases sharply with the number of sons. Indeed, the estimated coefficient is 2.651 which is economically quite large. An extra son in the family is roughly equivalent to 3% more of the group ownership in the hands of the sons. This suggests that the fraction of the group ownership held by the sons is closely tied to the number of sons in the family. Interestingly, in Column 4 when we include a dummy for whether the founder is dead, we find a very large positive and significant coefficient. The effect is equivalent to a 20% larger ownership stake by the sons in firms when the founder has died, suggesting that most of the founder's shares go to the sons after his death. In Column 5 we also include a control for family size. The coefficient on family size is negative but barely significant so that other family members have a minor crowd-out effect on the sons.

When we repeat the same analysis for the daughters in Columns 6–8, we find no significant relation between the number of daughters and their fraction of ownership in the group firms. Moreover, the holdings of daughters are not higher in families where the founder dead. We find similar results when looking at "other" family members (apart from the children of the founder) in Column 9. There is no significant relation between the share of family ownership held by other family members and the number of other family members. However, there is a strong negative relation between the number of sons in the family and the ownership for other family members. There is no such negative result for the number of daughters. Thus, sons crowd out other family member but not their sisters. However, the sisters do not seem to have much of the ownership to start with.

The results in Table 4 suggest that the number of family members with ownership stakes in the business increases with the number of "available" people in the family. However, this result is entirely driven by the sons of the founders. If the founder has more sons, they increase their ownership stake at the expense of other family members. Once the founder has passed away, the ownership stakes of the sons increase, while the stakes of other family members, including daughters of the founder, do not.

5.2. Board positions

Table 5 repeats the regressions from Table 4 but the dependent variable is the number of board positions held by various family members. Parallel to the family ownership, we find that involvement of family members on the boards of firms increases with the size of the family (Column 1), and there is no significant change in the overall number of board positions when the founder is dead (Column 2). As before, we find a very strong relation between the number of sons of the founder and the fraction of board positions held by the sons

Table 5

Family involvement in board positions for 93 families

The unit of observation is a firm. Number of family member with board positions is the number of family member with board position in a given firm. Fraction of board positions held by sons (daughters) is computed as the number of founder's sons (daughters) on board divided by the number of all family members on board for a particular firm. Fraction of board positions held by others is computed as the number of family board positions not held by the founder nor his sons or daughters, divided by the number of board positions held by any family members for a particular firm. Family size is the total number of direct descendants of the founder of each business group, including the founder himself. Founder dead is a dummy variable with the value of one if the founder was dead by 1996 and zero otherwise. Number of sons (daughters) is the total number of founder's sons (daughters) from all wives. Number of others is family size minus number of sons and daughters. Firm age is as of 1996. All regressions are estimated using OLS and controlled for number of generations fixed effects. Standard errors are clustered at family-group level. Robust standard errors are in parentheses. * Represents coefficients significant at 10%; ** significant at 5%; and *** significant at 1%.

| | Number of family members with board positions | | Fraction of family's board positions (× 100) held by: | | | | | | |
| | | | Sons | | | Daughters | | | Others |
	(1)	(2)	(3)	(4)	(5)	(6)	(7)	(8)	(9)
Family size	0.013	0.014			−0.746			−0.145	
	(0.003)***	(0.003)***			(0.242)***			(0.077)*	
Founder dead? (Yes = 1)		−0.174		3.474	4.778		2.026	2.655	−6.636
		(0.237)		(9.438)	(8.698)		(6.045)	(5.947)	(10.384)
Number of sons			3.821	3.753	6.551				−7.011
			(1.278)***	(1.303)***	(1.494)***				(1.287)***
Number of daughters						1.026	1.003	1.521	1.993
						(0.359)***	(0.369)***	(0.511)***	(1.245)
Number of others									0.702
									(0.255)***
Firm age	0.020	0.020	0.062	0.058	0.049	0.038	0.036	0.036	−0.064
	(0.004)***	(0.004)***	(0.114)	(0.113)	(0.123)	(0.064)	(0.059)	(0.059)	(0.118)
Constant	0.424	0.507	24.394	22.634	26.607	1.545	0.415	1.713	71.414
	(0.155)***	(0.231)**	(6.646)***	(8.163)***	(7.516)***	(1.980)	(4.603)	(4.632)	(8.977)***
Observations	580	580	323	323	323	323	323	323	323
R-squared	0.08	0.08	0.20	0.21	0.24	0.06	0.06	0.07	0.29

M. Bertrand et al. / Journal of Financial Economics 88 (2008) 466–498   477

(Column 3). But in contrast to the effect of founder death on ownership, the fraction of board positions held by the sons is not significantly higher when the founder is dead (Column 4), suggesting that the sons assume board positions before the founder is dead, but ownership only passes on afterwards. In Column 5 we see that the number of other family members has a negative and significant (albeit small) relation with the fraction of board positions held by the sons.

In Columns 6–8 we see that the fraction of board position held by daughters is positively related to their number in the family, but the relation is much weaker than for the sons. In Column 7 we show that the fraction of daughters' board positions is not higher in families where the founder is dead. And in larger families, other family members reduce the share of board seats for daughters (Column 8). In Column 9 we find a significant and positive relation between the fraction of board seats held by other family members and the number of "others" in the family. Again, this is in contrast to the ownership results where a larger number of other family members does not result in a higher fraction of ownership. The coefficient on the number of sons is negative, indicating that sons crowd out board positions of other family members.

One concern about seeing effects from founder's sons and not from the daughters is that our data on daughters might be less complete than for sons. However, given that the daughters included in our sample are more likely to be the ones with ownership and position, the regression coefficients for daughters should be positively biased, if anything. This is contrary to our results.

6. Real effects of family structure on the businesses they run

We now turn to the question of whether the differences in the size and composition of families are associated with differences in group performance. Several hypotheses have been put forward as to why we might expect lower performance for groups run by larger families. If family managers are less skilled than outside managers, greater involvement of family members will negatively affect performance. Larger family involvement might also lead to more infighting over resources and segregation of business lines across family members. It is also possible that business families are faced with a quantity/quality tradeoff: as the number of family members increases, the amount of resources that can be devoted to each family member declines, leading to lower average managerial quality. Under these views, a larger family would have worse performance at the group and firm level.

On the other hand, one might conjecture that the market for corporate control and top executive talent is thin in Thailand. A larger family offers a deeper talent pool of potential managers to draw from. Moreover, if governance of professional (outside) managers is difficult to establish, relying on trust relationships along kinship lines might be preferable since it could serve as a substitute for direct monitoring. These theories would imply that larger families would be positively related to group performance.

6.1. Family structure and firm performance

In Table 6 we study the relation between firm performance and the structure of the families behind the firms. Panel A presents regressions for all firms in the group and separately breaks out groups where the founder dead or alive. Panel B examines private and public firms. The unit of observation is a group firm (i.e., a firm that belongs to a family group). The dependent variable is residual return on assets, computed as the residual from a regression of firm-level ROA (1996 net profits divided by 1996 year-end total assets) on one-digit industry codes and a control for the measure of the log of total firm assets. The estimation of residual ROA includes all firms in our dataset, not just the group firms. Therefore, residual ROA measures the performance of the firms net of industry and firm size effects.

All regressions in Table 6 also include a dummy variable for the number of generations since the group was started and a control for the age of the firm. Standard errors are clustered at the family-group level. In Column 1, we regress residual ROA on the size of the family, measured as the number of people in the family tree. The coefficient on family size is negative and not significant. However, when we include a measure for the number of sons in Column 2, the coefficient on the number of sons is negative and highly significant. The estimated coefficient is −0.34. This means that a one-standard-deviation increase in the number of sons leads to a 1% decrease in the residual ROA of the family firms. This effect is quite large since all industry variation has

Table 6

Firm performance and family structure

The unit of observation is a firm. Residual return on assets is the residual from the OLS regression of return on assets on one-digit SIC fixed effects and natural logarithm of firm's total assets across all firms in the full sample, including firms not belonging to the 93 families. Number of sons (daughters) is the total number of founder's sons (daughters) from all wives. Sons from different wives is a dummy variable with value of one if there are founder's sons from different founder's wives, and zero otherwise. Firm age is as of 1996. All regressions are estimated using OLS and controlled for number of generations fixed effect. Contants are included but not reported here. Standard errors are clustered at the family-group level. Robust standard errors are in parentheses. * Represents coefficients significant at 10%; ** significant at 5%; and *** significant at 1%.

	Dependent variable: Residual ROA ($\times$ 100)							
	All Firms				Founder Dead		Founder alive	
	(1)	(2)	(3)	(4)	(5)	(6)	(7)	(8)
Family size	−0.043	0.000	0.014	0.016	0.023	0.017	−0.530	−0.136
	(0.032)	(0.025)	(0.023)	(0.023)	(0.022)	(0.021)	(0.425)	(0.791)
Number of sons		−0.340	−0.473	−0.284	−0.483	−0.334	0.348	0.117
		(0.156)**	(0.132)***	(0.160)*	(0.114)***	(0.151)**	(0.797)	(0.948)
Sons from different wives			−0.386		−0.402		4.649	
			(0.802)		(0.681)		(2.828)	
Number of daughters				−0.216		−0.145		−0.291
				(0.108)**		(0.085)*		(0.821)
Firm age	0.026	0.024	0.036	0.022	0.049	0.048	0.001	−0.052
	(0.020)	(0.020)	(0.020)*	(0.020)	(0.021)**	(0.021)**	(0.063)	(0.060)
Observations	586	586	507	586	309	337	198	249
R-squared	0.03	0.04	0.05	0.04	0.08	0.07	0.04	0.02
Number of families	93	93	93	93	37	45	33	48

	Public		Private	
	(9)	(10)	(11)	(12)
Family size	0.068	0.068	−0.025	−0.023
	(0.021)***	(0.023)***	(0.035)	(0.037)
Number of sons	−0.393	−0.279	−0.427	−0.231
	(0.166)**	(0.225)	(0.180)**	(0.195)
Sons from different wives	−1.711		0.376	
	(1.303)		(1.138)	
Number of dauthers		−0.129		−0.191
		(0.200)		(0.150)
Firm age	0.022	0.013	0.032	0.019
	(0.029)	(0.031)	(0.031)	(0.028)
Observations	151	169	356	417
R-squared	0.05	0.04	0.06	0.05
Number of families	52	62	55	75

already been taken out. The coefficient on the family size measure becomes insignificant and very close to zero. In Column 3, we add a dummy for the presence of sons from different wives (of the founder). The coefficient on the multiple wives dummy is negative but not significant. In Column 4 we add the number of daughters of the founder, and find a negative effect that is similar in magnitude to the effect of sons. The presence of an additional daughter of the founder reduces ROA by 0.216.

When we separate out firms where the founder is still alive versus those where the founder is dead (Columns 5–8), we find a dramatic asymmetry in the results. In firms where the founder is dead (Columns 5 and 6), we see a significant and robust negative relation between performance and the number of sons, and a somewhat smaller negative relation for the number of daughters. In contrast, for firms in groups where the

M. Bertrand et al. / Journal of Financial Economics 88 (2008) 466–498   479

founder is still active (Columns 7 and 8) we find a positive but not significant relation between firm performance and the number of sons. These results indicate that the negative relation between firm performance and the number of sons (and to a lesser degree the number of daughters) is only present in families where the founder has passed away. While the founder is still alive, the composition of the family does not appear to affect firm performance. These findings are consistent with previous studies such as Pérez-González (2006) and Villalonga and Amit (2006), who also find that the performance of family firms is particularly poor once the founder is gone.

In Panel B of Table 6 we separate family firms into those that are publicly traded and those that are private. When we compare the results for private and public firms in Panel B we find that the negative relation between the number of sons and firm performance is approximately of the same magnitude in both types of firms. There is no evidence of a significant negative effect of daughters when we divide up the firms in this fashion.

These results are interesting along a number of dimensions. They suggest that the lower performance of family firms is not uniformly due to a greater involvement of all family members if the family is larger. Instead, our results suggest that the sons of the founder play a particular role, since the poor performance of family firms is mainly associated the number of founders' sons in the family. The results are not consistent with the hypothesis that trust relationships among family members (in particular the sons) and the ability to draw from a deeper talent pool in larger families provide a source of comparative advantage to these families. These findings are instead more supportive of theories that suggest efficiency losses through greater involvement of sons. As we discussed before, an alternative explanation for this finding could be that family firms forgo the opportunity of hiring outsiders whose managerial skills might be superior to those of family members; such a difference in managerial quality between family members and outsiders might be especially acute in larger families because of the quantity-quality tradeoff in raising children. We unfortunately do not have data on the talent or educational background of sons, which could help us test this alternative story more directly. However, we do not think that this hypothesis is very plausible since these are some of the richest families in Thailand where the quality-quantity tradeoff would not be binding. Moreover, the results in the following section suggest that changes in governance structure do play an important role in the performance of group firms.

6.2. Governance and family structure

A number of papers have documented that pyramidal group structures allow the expropriation of minority shareholders by the shareholders of higher-up group firms through tunneling resources out of these firms (see, e.g., Bertrand, Mehta, and Mullainathan, 2002; Claessens, Djankov, and Lang, 2000). A similar logic can apply between family members or, in our context, even between sons of the founder. One plausible explanation for the lower performance of family groups with more sons is that the dilution of ownership among equally powerful sons increases the amount of tunneling from lower-down group firms. If the sons of the founder do not trust each other to use their control rights in the interest of the firm, there can be a "race to the bottom" where one brother tries to tunnel resources out of group firms before another brother can do so.

To investigate whether the performance results can be explained by a deterioration in the governance structure of family groups with more sons, we first analyze whether families with more sons display a greater discrepancy between cash flow and control rights, which provides incentives for tunneling. We construct several measures of the discrepancy between control and ownership for each of the firms in the groups covered in our sample. We follow the standard measures of excess control defined as the gap between total family ownership and total family control as calculated in La Porta, Lopez-de-Silanes, and Shleifer (1999), and Claessens, Djankov, and Lang (2000). However, our data also allow us to also compute similar measures of excess control for each individual family member's ownership and control rights within each of the group firms. Given the central role played by sons, it is of interest to contrast excess control by sons with excess control by other family members.

In Table 7 we analyze whether groups become more pyramidal (i.e., larger excess control structures) if there are more family members (and sons in particular), especially once the founder is gone. While certainly not a proof of tunneling, such evidence would be consistent with greater *incentives* to tunnel. In Panel A of Table 7 we first regress the existence of family excess control (i.e., a dummy for whether total family control is larger

480 M. Bertrand et al. / Journal of Financial Economics 88 (2008) 466–498

Table 7
Excess control and family structure

The unit of observation is a firm. "Family Control > Family Ownership" is a dummy variable with the value of one if the family has voting rights more than its cash flow rights. "Number of Sons with Control > Ownership" is the number of founder's sons whose voting rights exceed their cash flow rights. Difference in sons' control and ownership is the average difference between voting rights and control rights across founder's sons. Number of sons (daughters) is the total number of founder's sons (daughters) from all wives. All regressions are estimated using OLS and controlled for number of generations fixed effects. Constants are included but not reported here. Standard errors are in parentheses.
* Represents coefficients significant at 10%; ** significant at 5%; and *** significant at 1%.

Panel A: Dependent variable = Family control > Family ownership? (Yes = 1)

	All firms		Founder dead		Founder alive		Public		Private	
	(1)	(2)	(3)	(4)	(5)	(6)	(7)	(8)	(9)	(10)
Number of sons	0.013	0.012	0.021	0.027	-0.057	-0.057	0.026	0.025	0.010	0.006
	(0.007)*	(0.008)	(0.007)***	(0.009)***	(0.018)***	(0.018)***	(0.013)*	(0.015)*	(0.008)	(0.010)
Number of daughters		0.003		-0.010		0.003		0.002		0.006
		(0.008)		(0.009)		(0.017)		(0.015)		(0.010)
Observations	586	586	337	337	249	249	169	169	417	417
R-squared	0.02	0.02	0.04	0.04	0.11	0.11	0.10	0.10	0.02	0.03
Number of families	93	93	45	45	48	48	62	62	75	75

Panel B: Dependent variable = Number of sons with control > Ownership

	All firms		Founder dead		Founder alive		Public		Private	
	(11)	(12)	(13)	(14)	(15)	(16)	(17)	(18)	(19)	(20)
Number of sons	0.264	0.326	0.259	0.342	0.126	0.147	0.398	0.458	0.223	0.264
	(0.025)***	(0.030)***	(0.033)***	(0.040)***	(0.040)***	(0.039)***	(0.046)***	(0.051)***	(0.030)***	(0.035)***
Number of daughters		-0.116		-0.143		-0.135		-0.133		-0.074
		(0.029)***		(0.040)***		(0.037)***		(0.052)**		(0.035)**
Observations	586	586	337	337	249	249	169	169	417	417
R-squared	0.31	0.33	0.28	0.31	0.05	0.10	0.51	0.53	0.26	0.27
Number of families	93	93	45	45	48	48	62	62	75	75

Panel C: Dependent variable = Difference in sons' control and Ownership

	All firms		Founder dead		Founder alive		Public		Private	
	(21)	(22)	(23)	(24)	(25)	(26)	(27)	(28)	(29)	(30)
Number of sons	0.501	0.895	0.348	0.834	0.764	0.865	0.981	1.306	0.347	0.711
	(0.119)***	(0.137)***	(0.159)**	(0.191)***	(0.168)***	(0.164)***	(0.210)***	(0.230)***	(0.143)**	(0.169)***
Number of daughters		-0.741		-0.836		-0.649		-0.727		-0.655
		(0.135)***		(0.190)***		(0.156)***		(0.232)***		(0.169)***
Observations	586	586	337	337	249	249	169	169	417	417
R-squared	0.12	0.16	0.09	0.14	0.09	0.15	0.27	0.31	0.09	0.12
Number of families	93	93	45	45	48	48	62	62	75	75

M. Bertrand et al. / Journal of Financial Economics 88 (2008) 466–498   481

than total family ownership) on the number of sons, controlling for the number of generations the group has been in existence. As before, this family excess control variable includes the holdings of all family members. We find a positive but only marginally significant relation. In Column 2, we include the number of daughters in the regression and find no significant relation between family excess control and the number of daughters. However, we find a very different picture if we separate the groups where the founder is dead versus those where he is still alive. For groups where the founder is dead we find a strong positive relation between the measure of family excess control and the number of sons in the firms (Column 3). We do not find this relation for the number of daughters (Column 4). However, for groups where the founder is still present, this relation is negative and significant (Column 5). Again, we do not find this result for the number of daughters (Column 6).

We replicate these results for the private and public firms within the groups in Columns 7–10. The sensitivity of family excess control to the number of sons is larger and more significant in public firms. This indicates that a greater number of sons is associated with especially high tunneling incentives in publicly traded firms, especially when the founder is gone. Of course, because we do not directly measure tunneling, there are other possible interpretations for this finding. For example, it could also reflect a desire by founders to have each son manage a (more prestigious) publicly traded firm, leading to an increase in the number of publicly traded firms in the lower levels of the pyramidal structure.

In Panel B of Table 7 we focus on excess control in the hands of sons relative to the rest of the family. The dependent variable is a simple count of the number of sons with excess control. This measure of excess control allows us to understand whether sons in particular see an increase in excess control once the founder is dead. We find that families with more sons also have a larger number of sons with excess control (Column1). However, when we include the number of daughters as an explanatory variable (Column 2) we find a significant negative coefficient. This suggests that in families with more daughters, daughters crowd out some of the excess control from the sons. However, the number of sons that have excess control is much larger for families where the founder is dead (Columns 3–6). In fact, the coefficient on the number of sons is about twice as large when the founder is gone (Column 14) versus when he is still alive (Column 16). And again, we find that the results are stronger for public firms than for private firms (Columns 17–20).

We replicate the results using a measure of the average difference between control and ownership among sons at a given firm (Panel C, Columns 21–30). We find that a greater number of sons is associated with a higher average difference between control and ownership for sons. The relation is stronger when the founder is dead and in the subset of publicly traded firms.

Overall, these results further suggest that the presence of more sons leads to a governance structure that is more pyramidal, which means that the gap between control and ownership rights becomes more skewed in the hands of the sons. This allows for more "expropriation positions" for sons once the founder is gone. Moreover, if the trust relationship among the sons is not strong, there are increased incentives for tunneling by the sons as they race to secure their part of the profits before one of the other brothers can tunnel it out.

We should note that it is theoretically possible that an increase in the number of controlling shareholders might *improve* corporate governance. For example, Gomes and Novaes (2006) suggest that under certain conditions it is optimal for founders to share control with multiple outside shareholders to increase the value of the firm, instead of just selling ownership stakes to outside shareholders. Their model assumes that under shared control each of the large shareholders has *veto power* over decisions that would reduce the value of their individual ownership stakes. This can enhance the overall value of the firm if private benefits are distributed unequally among controlling shareholders and if projects with low public benefits but high private benefits can thus be blocked. Thus, the critical difference between these results and our interpretation relies on the assumption that even controlling shareholders *cannot exercise effective veto power* if each controlling shareholder can tunnel resources from the firm unilaterally. In other words, the hypothesis we propose in the current paper relies on the idea that controlling shareholders cannot block each other's transgressions and thus engage in a race to the bottom. These types of misbehaviors become more pronounced when there are more sons involved as large shareholders. While we admittedly cannot prove this assumption, we think it is a reasonable description of emerging markets where enforcement is weak. In contrast, the board negotiation process described in Gomes and Novaes (2006) might be more representative of shareholder behavior in more developed capital markets.

In regressions not reported here, we also directly analyze how the depth of business groups relates to family size. This analysis very much parallels the analysis in Table 7. We defined depth as the maximum number of layers within a group separating a group firm from the firm(s) at the top of that group. This variable ranges from 0 to 6, with a mean of about 2. Not surprisingly, we find that larger families are associated with deeper groups. In families where the founder is dead, we see a strong positive relation between the number of sons and group depth. But there is a negative and barely significant relation when the founder is still around. In other words, consistent with the results in Table 7, larger families are associated with deeper and more pyramidal group structures once the founder is dead.

6.3. Group size and diversification and family structure

The above analysis suggests that the organizational and control structure of groups is importantly related to the size and composition of the families behind them, especially once the founder is dead. We now discuss the possible relation between family structure and other group characteristics. Specifically, we analyze whether the number of firms in a group and its level of industry concentration change when there are more sons in the group or when the founder is dead. In Table 8, we regress these different group characteristics on our family structure variables. The regressions in this table are performed at the family level. All regressions in this table include a control for the age of the group.

The first dependent variable we consider is the number of firms in the group (as of 1996). Column 1 of Table 8 documents a positive and statistically significant correlation across families between the number of firms in the group and the number of sons in the family but not a significant relation with the total number of family members. In Column 2 we focus only on families where the founder is dead and find that this positive relation between the number of group firms and the number of sons is entirely driven by the those families where the founder is dead. Interestingly, neither family size nor the number of sons is correlated with group size in families where the founder is still alive (Column 3). In Columns 4–6, we repeat the previous regression but use

Table 8
Group size, industry concentration, organization structure, and family size

The unit of observation is a family business group. Number of firms is the number of public and private firms in our sample that belonged to a given family. Total assets is group's total assets in millions of baht. Industry concentration is computed as the squareroot of the summation of the squares of the fraction of group assets in each industry to total group assets in all industries. Specifically, the concentration index equals one if the group is concentrated in only one industry. Industries are classified approximately at the two-digit SIC. Family size is the total number of direct descendants of the founder of each business group, including the founder himself. Number of sons is the number of founder's sons. Group age is defined as the age of the oldest firm for each group in our sample. All regressions are estimated using OLS. Standard errors are in parentheses. * Represents coefficients significant at 10%; ** significant at 5%; and *** significant at 1%. The total number of groups in the full sample is 91 (two groups are eliminated due to their complicated structure of cyclical cross-shareholdings).

	Number of firms			Total assets (millions Baht)			Industry concentration (2-digit SIC)		
	All firms	Founder dead	Founder alive	All firms	Founder dead	Founder alive	All firms	Founder dead	Founder alive
	(1)	(2)	(3)	(4)	(5)	(6)	(7)	(8)	(9)
Family size	0.079	0.056	0.007	2.469	2.212	−1.989	−0.001	0.000	−0.002
	(0.050)	(0.068)	(0.194)	(1.324)*	(1.995)	(3.325)	(0.002)	(0.002)	(0.014)
Number of sons	0.548	1.336	−0.408	2.403	7.475	3.216	−0.002	−0.031	0.040
	(0.314)*	(0.523)**	(0.414)	(8.369)	(15.443)	(7.094)	(0.012)	(0.015)**	(0.030)
Group age	0.096	0.086	0.084	2.113	2.279	1.150	−0.004	−0.004	−0.004
	(0.047)**	(0.073)	(0.047)*	(1.266)*	(2.144)	(0.806)	(0.002)**	(0.002)*	(0.003)
Constant	0.121	−1.610	3.212	−45.623	−59.297	2.291	0.849	0.929	0.747
	(1.717)	(3.194)	(1.440)**	(45.748)	(94.322)	(24.672)	(0.065)***	(0.093)***	(0.104)***
Number of observations	91	44	47	91	44	47	91	44	47
R-squared	0.20	0.27	0.12	0.13	0.12	0.05	0.08	0.20	0.13

Entrepreneurship in Developing Countries

total assets as a dependent variable. We find that larger families are associated with larger total group assets; however, the effect is economically much smaller. Moreover, we do not find any relation with the number of sons in the group. These combined results suggest that the average size of the firms within a group declines with the number of male family members. In other words, the assets of the group tend to be divided into more separate firms with a larger number of sons in the family once the founder is gone.

In Columns 7–9, we use the Herfindahl concentration index (at the Thai equivalent of the two-digit SIC level) as a dependent variable. We find that the industry concentration of a group declines when there are more sons in the family but only when the founder is gone. This result can be seen as a corollary to the previous result for the number of firms in a group, since a group can become more diversified when there are more firms within the group.

6.4. Firm performance and excess control

In a final step, we want to investigate whether there is a direct relation between the performance of group firms and the level of excess control by family members. If the poor performance of family firms after the founder's departure is in part explained by deteriorating governance due to the many sons who are vying for the group's assets, we would expect to find a direct relation between excess control and firm performance. Of course, we need to be careful not to make any inference about the direction of causality from this analysis, since we have already seen that both performance and governance are related to family structure.

To investigate this question, in Panel A of Table 9 we first regress firm-level (residual) ROA on total family ownership in the firm and on a dummy variable for excess family control (i.e., total family control is larger than total family ownership). For the precise construction of the measure please see the Appendix. If there is excess control at the individual level, there is excess control at the family level. We use a control for the year the firm was established in all the regressions. Moreover, we include family fixed effects in all regressions to control for fixed differences in the use of control between families. Across all groups, in Column 1, we find a strong robust negative correlation between total family ownership and firm performance. This is in line with our prior findings in Table 7 that groups with larger families perform worse. Higher excess control for the family overall is negatively correlated with residual ROA in the full sample, but the effect is not significant. There is a significant negative relation between family ownership and residual ROA once the founder is dead (Column 3), but no such relationship when the founder is still alive (Column 5). The coefficient on excess family control is negative (but insignificant) when the founder is dead but positive when he is still alive.

We now break out total family control and ownership into individual-specific measures of excess control. Specifically, we contrast excess control in the hands of sons with excess control in the hands of other family members. In Column 2 we find a strong negative correlation between residual ROA and the measure of excess control of the sons, but no effect for other family members. We then divide families into those where the founder is dead (Column 4 of Panel A) versus those where the founder is still involved (Column 6 of Panel A). We find a large and significant negative correlation between residual ROA and the measure of excess control of the sons when the founder is gone but no effect on the other family members. In contrast, for those groups where the founder is still involved there is no significant relation between residual ROA and excess control of the sons. We find parallel results when we use the *number* of sons with excess control but the coefficient estimates (not reported) are not significant at traditional levels.

One possible interpretation for the asymmetry we observe between sons and other family members is that it reflects differences in ownership stakes. It might be that the gap between control and ownership of any shareholder (not only sons) reduces profitability but only when the degree of control is sufficiently large for this shareholder to be relevant. We check this possibility (results not reported) by creating a dummy variable that equals one when sons' ownership is more than 25% (zero otherwise) and another dummy variable that equals one when other family members' ownership is more than 25% (zero otherwise). We then interact these dummy variables with sons' excess control and others' excess control, respectively. The results confirm that even when others own more than 25%, their excess control does not affect profitability. On the contrary, sons' excess control matters both when their ownership is less than 25% and when their ownership is more than 25%. Hence, it appears that sons' excess control differentially impacts profitability relative to other family members' excess control, even when these other family members are relevant shareholders. We do find,

Table 9
Firm performance, family ownership, and excess control
The unit of observation is a firm. Residual return on assets is the residual from the OLS regression of return on assets on one-digit SIC fixed effects and the natural logarithm of firm total assets across all firms in the full sample, including firms not belonging to the 93 families. Family ownership is the total percentage of ultimate ownership directly or indirectly held by family members in a particular firm. "Family ownership" is a dummy variable with the value of one if the family has voting rights that exceed its cash flow rights. Difference in sons' control and ownership is the average difference between voting rights and control rights across founder's sons. Difference in others' control and ownership is the average difference between voting rights and control rights across family members other than founder's sons. All regressions are estimated using OLS and controlled for family fixed effects. Constants are included but not reported here. Standard errors are clustered at the family-group level. Robust standard errors are in parentheses. * Represents coefficients significant at 10%; ** significant at 5%; and *** significant at 1%.

Dependent variable: residual ROA ($\times$ 100)	All firms		Founder dead		Founder alive	
	(1)	(2)	(3)	(4)	(5)	(6)
Family ownership	−0.036	−0.036	−0.050	−0.045	−0.011	−0.020
	(0.016)**	(0.015)**	(0.018)***	(0.018)**	(0.030)	(0.026)
Family control > Family ownership? (Yes = 1)	−1.059		−2.308		1.134	
	(1.148)		(1.496)		(1.533)	
Difference in sons' control and ownership		−0.168		−0.167		−0.344
		(0.049)***		(0.052)***		(0.265)
Difference in others' control and ownership		0.023		0.026		0.035
		(0.051)		(0.096)		(0.073)
Observations	586	586	337	337	249	249
R-squared	0.26	0.27	0.20	0.21	0.36	0.36
Number of families	93	93	45	45	48	48

Dependent variable: residual ROA ($\times$ 100)	Public		Private	
	(7)	(8)	(9)	(10)
Family ownership	−0.044	−0.028	−0.029	−0.030
	(0.051)	(0.045)	(0.020)	(0.018)*
Family control > Family ownership ? (Yes = 1)	−1.245		−1.091	
	(2.772)		(1.497)	
Difference in sons' control and ownership		0.203		−0.202
		(0.078)**		(0.060)***
Difference in others' control and ownership		−0.255		0.047
		(0.142)*		(0.055)
Observations	169	169	417	417
R-squared	0.51	0.53	0.26	0.28
Number of families	62	62	75	75

however, that the negative effect of sons' excess control on performance is stronger when their ownership is higher.

These results are striking. They indicate that excess control in the hands of sons is strongly negatively associated with firm performance, but excess control in the hands of other family members does not have the same effect. This might suggest that potential governance abuses within a family are not merely a function of the excess control rights a family member holds, but it is also determined by the person's position within the family. A son of the founder might have greater freedom than other family members to use excess control rights to his benefit. This might provide insight into the internal dynamics of the family and could suggest that there is a layer of governance or power structure within the family itself that affects the way family members can exercise their ownership and control rights within family firms.

Finally, in Panel B of Table 9 we run the same set of regressions but for public and private firms. We find that the negative relation between performance and excess control by sons is entirely driven by private firms (contrast Column 11 with Column 13). For public firms the relation between firm performance and excess

M. Bertrand et al. / Journal of Financial Economics 88 (2008) 466–498   485

control by sons is actually positive and significant. If the public firms within a family group are important for the image of the family or even as a way for the sons to maintain liquidity of their ownership stakes, then the observed positive relation for public firms could be suggestive of the propping of public firms where sons hold excess control. Overall, these findings reinforce a governance interpretation for our findings, as we expect tunneling to be more prominent in opaque private firms and propping in more visible public firms.[6]

Our findings suggest that not all family members have the power or inclination to take advantage of their excess control position at group firms. Only excess control in the hands of sons appears to significantly hurt performance, and predominantly at private firms. In addition, the contrast between groups where the founder is no longer present and those where the founder is still alive suggests that the founder has a disciplining effect on his sons' behavior. The fact that performance is negatively related to the number of sons with excess control suggests that the amount of distortion might be driven by competition between the sons over a given company's resources.

7. Conclusion

Families run a large fraction of firms around the world. Families themselves, however, are not monolithic entities but are composed of individual members who can have different stakes and objectives in family businesses. We take a first step in going beyond the case-study evidence to ask whether constraints imposed by family structure affect the corporate structure and performance of family-run firms.

We show that the larger is the family, in particular the more sons the founder has, the more positions within family firms are held by family members instead of outside managers and board members. The number of sons of the founder is pivotal. Groups that are run by larger families (especially more sons) tend to have lower performance. These effects are especially pronounced in groups where the founder is no longer active and ultimate control has passed on to an heir.

We also analyze how the pyramidal ownership structure of group firms affects the performance of the firms. Firms where many sons of the founder indirectly own a fraction of the ownership show lower performance. This finding is consistent with the hypothesis that having several sons with excess control can lead to a "race to the bottom", where each son is trying to tunnel resources out of the company before his brothers do the same.

Overall, our findings provide novel evidence that wider family involvement in business groups alters business decisions and the performance of family-run firms. One hypothesis that emerges from our analysis is that the decay of family-run groups over time is due in part to increased incentives on the part of family members to tunnel resources out of the firm as control becomes more diluted among different family members. A slightly different interpretation is that outright infighting for group resources leads to inefficient decision making. Conflicts between different parts of the family might lead to distortions in the governance structure and internal operations of these groups. These conflicts seem to be especially important once the founder has died or retired.

A deeper question in this context is why families do not separate control rights (i.e., management) more effectively from the ownership structure of the firm by placing management control in the hand of professionals while retaining ownership control within the family. Such arrangements are widely used in many European countries where family firms are still prevalent. This would allow family members to fight over the cash flow streams without distorting the efficiency of the business decisions within the firms. We conjecture that a potential answer to this question lies in the limited enforcement of contracts and governance in a country like Thailand. It could be that cash flow rights de facto can only be guaranteed in conjunction with control rights. Therefore, family members have to stay directly involved in the operations of the business if they want to protect their cash flow rights. Our analysis suggests that individual family members might have to be concerned not only about expropriation by outsiders but also expropriation by other (more powerful)

---

[6]At first glance, one could view these findings as inconsistent with the findings in Table 7, where we find a stronger relationship between excess control and number of sons in public firms than private firms. However, it is important to stress again that the analysis in Table 7 only captures tunneling incentives, and not tunneling opportunities or actual tunneling. A given level of incentives for tunneling in public firms might not translate in as much opportunities for tunneling in these firms given the stronger external monitoring public firms are subject to.

family members. For example, the fact that weaker family members, such as daughters of the founder, are less likely to hold board positions in firms where sons of the founder are also on board is quite suggestive in this regard. Similarly, our findings that larger families and greater family involvement are associated with a breakdown of group assets into a larger set of (smaller) firms could also indicate that access to cash flow for a given family member requires control rights for that family member.

Appendix A

A.1. Firm data

Our firm-level data are from Thailand. Each registered firm in Thailand has to submit annual financial statements, audited by an authorized auditor, to the Ministry of Commerce. Registered firms include registered partnerships, privately held limited companies, and publicly traded companies. The database is physically assembled and maintained by the Ministry's Department of Business Development.[7] We access this database in several ways.

(1) *Direct request made to the Department of Business Development*: The Department makes the database available to general public upon request. The database contains all the information each firm submits to the Ministry. For each firm, the information include the registration number, registration date, address, name of the firm, notes on change of status or change of names, types of business, the report of the shareholder meetings, financial statements, list of shareholders (names, nationality, profession, number of shares, date of acquire or purchase), and list of the directors. The coverage is all registered firms in Thailand for all available years. The data is not digitalized and must be requested on firm-by-firm basis based only on the registration number. The request must be made in person. Fees are charged based on the number of firms, the number of years, and the type of requested data.

(2) *Thailand Company Information (TCI)*: The Department of Business Development gives a right to Advanced Research Group Co., Ltd. to publish the financial statements of approximately the top 2,000 registered firms in a series of books called *Thailand Company Information* (TCI). The books have been released annually since 1987. The TCI database contains financial, ownership, and board composition information at the firm level. For all firms, the financial information includes total assets, total liabilities, total revenues, and net profits. Ownership data report the names of the shareholders and the percentage of company shares directly held by each shareholder. The database includes information of the names of directors on the firm's board. For publicly traded firms, specific positions on the board held by a particular person are also reported. The database provides information on industry classification similar to one-digit and two-digit SIC codes, and the founding year for each firm. All data in TCI are translated into English.

(3) *Business Online (BOL)*: The Department of Business Development also cooperates with Business Online Public Co., Ltd. to digitalize the basic information of over 600,000 registered companies in Thailand. The information includes the company's name, registration number, address, financial statement, list of shareholders, and directors. As BOL was established in 1996, the database contains only information in recent years. (At the time of working on our project, the BOL financial data went back to 1993 while the shareholder and director information went back only to 1997.) The data are available for purchase in digital format. The price is based on the number of firms, the number of years, and type of the data. Most of the data are in English, except for shareholder and director information, which is mostly in Thai.

(4) *Listed Company Info (SET)*: In addition to submitting an annual report to the Ministry of Commerce, all the listed firms must submit the same report and additional data to the Stock Exchange of Thailand (SET). The data that SET makes available to the investors and general public include the company profile, quarterly consolidated and unconsolidated financial statements, daily trading information, and announcement and news. The data are digital and come in a series of CD-ROMs. Recently, the Stock Exchange of Thailand changed the format of the data from CD-ROM to online access. Unfortunately, the online access contains only the data for the past five years. All the data are in English.

---

[7]The Department of Business Development was previously known as the Department of Commercial Registration until the government reorganization that became effective in October 2002.

M. Bertrand et al. / Journal of Financial Economics 88 (2008) 466–498   487

We construct our dataset from several sources listed above. We start by taking the list of firms directly from *Thailand Company Information* 1997–1998, which publishes the financial data for the end of 1996. The criteria that TCI use in selecting the firms to be included are that the firm must either (1) have annual revenues of at least 200 million Baht (approximately eight million U.S. dollars), (2) be listed on the Stock Exchange of Thailand, or (3) be one of the leading companies in its industry. In total, there are 2,153 firms included in TCI's 1996 list. All of these firms form our sample for 1996. Our 1996 sample therefore includes all publicly traded firms and the largest privately held firms in Thailand. For all firms, we get the general firm's profiles (registration number, name, type of business, and founding year) from the TCI 1997–1998 books.

The 1996 information on shareholders, board of directors, and financial statements come from two sources. For non-listed firms, we rely on the TCI books for all of these data as it was the only source available except by direct request to the Department of Business Development. However, for listed firms, we get the data from SET's *Listed Company Info* CD-ROMs because the data are digitalized and distinguish between consolidated and unconsolidated financial statements. We use unconsolidated financial statements in our analysis.

A.2. Family data

Our objective is to construct family trees for the family groups in our sample that are as accurate and comprehensive as possible. For that purpose we rely on a number of sources. We start with information from a publication by the Brooker Group entitled *Thai Business Groups: A Unique Guide to Who Owns What*. This book identifies the 150 leading business groups in Thailand and covers the history of each of these groups since the time the first business was founded until today. The next step is constructing family trees of these business families listed in the Brooker book. Specifically, for each of the family business groups, we identify its founder and try to trace all of his direct descendants to the youngest active generation. To make the definition of family size consistent across families, we do not count the founder's siblings and their descendants as a part of the family when we compute family size because this set of information is incomplete for many families. However, the information is useful when we analyze the involvement of family members in the family business so we still collect the information on the founder's siblings and their descendants whenever possible. We also ignore family members who are younger than 15 in the late 1990s by including in our family tree only individuals with Mr., Mrs., Miss, Lady (Thanpuying and Khunying), Dr., or military titles.[8]

Although the Brooker book helps us identify the prominent business families and construct some family trees, it does not provide systematic information on the full family trees of all the families. We therefore gather more detailed descriptions of the business families from several alternative sources. The most useful source is from various biography books written on several Thai millionaires. For example, Sapphaibul (2001a, b) provides impressive information on 55 of the most famous business families. In addition, it is customary in Thailand when a public person dies that the descendants compile a funeral book that contains information about the person's life and his or her family relationships. When available, we also collect the family tree information from the funeral books published and distributed for the group founders or other family members. Next, we supplement the information with articles from various local magazines and newspapers. These articles are usually either a story about a famous family or an interview with a group founder or his descendants. The full list of the biography and funeral books as well as articles is at the end of this Appendix. We also collect a number of small news clips from social columns in several daily newspapers. Most of these news clips are obituaries or announcements of engagements, weddings, divorces, deaths, funeral arrangements, and anniversary celebrations. Finally, we conduct informal interviews with family members of a few business families to verify the accuracy of our data.

With the descriptive information we gather from these sources, we code the information systematically. We include in our family trees all of the family members we identify, whether or not they are involved in the family business. The founder generation is coded as generation one, his children are generation two, and so on. For each family member, we collect information on their specific position in the family tree (defined as the relationship to the founder), gender, birth order (defined as the rank order of children within a specific marriage), and biological versus adopted status. With less coverage and accuracy, we also code the

---

[8]In Thailand, a person drops his or her junior title and starts using Mr. or Miss when he or she turns 15.

488   *M. Bertrand et al. / Journal of Financial Economics 88 (2008) 466–498*

information on individual education, work experience, and involvement in family business. We also rely on these sources to identify which specific family members, if any, are designated as "heirs" of the family business. Note that we cannot systematically track whether a given family member in our family tree is still alive or not. However, we do know for all families whether the founder is still alive or not as of 1996.

Finally, for each family member, we collect information on the name of the spouse(s) whenever possible. This information will be especially interesting for the founders, since several of them have multiple wives and also children from multiple wives. We do not, however, count spouses as part of the family when we construct measures of family size. We carefully keep track of changes in last names, especially for married female family members and their descendants. We also gather information on relationships across families through marriages.

As a whole, we construct family trees for 93 business families. Ninety of them are among the Brooker's list; three of them are additional. By alphabetical order, the families included in our data are Asadathorn, Asavabhokin, Assakul, Bencharongkul, Bhirom Bhakdi, Bodiratnangkura, Boondicharern, Boonnamsap, Boonsoong, Bulakul, Bulsook, Chaiyawan, Chansiri, Chansrichwala, Charnvirakul, Chearavanont, Chirathivat, Chokwatana, Chotitawan, Darakananda, Dumnernchanvanit, Hetrakul, Horrungruang, Jantaranukul, Jungrungruangkit, Kanathanavanich, Karnasuta, Karnchanachari, Karnchanapas, Kiangsiri, Kitiparaporn, Krisdathanont, Kunanantakul, Kuvanant, Lailert/YipInTsoi/Chutrakul, Lamsam, Laohathai, Lee-Issaranukul, Leelaprachakul, Leelasithorn, Leenutaphong, Leeswadtrakul, Leophairatana, Lertsumitr-kul, Mahadumrongkul, Mahagitsiri, Maleenont, Nakornsri, Narongdej, Nithivasin, Osathanugrah, Phaoenchoke, Phatraprasit, Phenjati, Phodhivorakhun, Phongsathorn, Phornprapha, Piyaoui, Poolvoralaks, Prasarttong-Osot, Raiva/Sila-on, Ratanarak, Sermsirimongkol, Shinawatra, Sirivadhanabhakdi, Sophonpa-nich, Srifuengfung, Sriorathaikul, Srivikorn, Sukosol, Supsakorn, Suriyasat, Tangkaravakoon, Tangmati-tham, Tantipipatpong, Tantipong-anant, Techaruvichit, Tejapaibul, Tejavibul, Tuchinda, Uahwatanasakul, Umpujh, Vacharaphol, Vanich, Vilailuck, Viraporn, Viriyabhan, Viriyaprapaikit, Vongvanij, Wanglee, Wattanavekin, Wongkusolkit, and Yoovidhaya. The main characteristics of each family are shown in Table A1.

A.3. Matching family data with firm data

The next task is putting the firm data and the family data together. First, we match the names listed as shareholders and directors to the names listed in our constructed family trees. It is very common that a Thai name is translated into different versions of English spelling so we pay careful attention when we match the names.

Next, we identify firms that belong to each of our 93 business families. The criterion is that the family as a whole has the highest percentage of ultimate ownership in that company. Ultimate ownership is defined as the cash-flow rights derived from holding shares in the firm directly or indirectly through pyramids or cross-shareholdings. The main characteristics of each family business group are shown in Table A2.

Note that we are very careful in matching female family members by looking at both their current last name and their maiden name. Specifically, to alleviate the concern that we overlook a female family member because she changes her last name after marriage, we match the female names in two steps:

First step: Starting with the family trees, we match the records where *both* the first name *and* the last name are perfectly identical (after correcting for various ways of spelling the same Thai names in English). Out of 4,408 records of ownership, 3,269 individual names and last names (74.16%) were matched in this first stage. Note that we considered both the original last name of the individual and the last name of her husband. Out of 232 daughters in our family trees, 102 have the husband's last name. Obviously, we may miss some of the last names, but it is also likely that some of the daughters without the husband's last name were indeed not married, and when they got married the last name in the firm database at the Ministry of Commerce might not be updated. We address this concern in the second step.

Second step: For each of the names in the family tree that are not matched in the first step, we check whether it could have been due to the change in last name. Specifically, we perform a match between family tree and firm records just based on *first* names. We can confidently apply this strategy since it is extremely rare in the Thai culture to give the same first name to more than one person within the same family. This is done for each

Entrepreneurship in Developing Countries

M. Bertrand et al. / Journal of Financial Economics 88 (2008) 466–498

Table A1

Family characteristics

The unit of observation is a family. Families are ranked by number of generations, family size, and number of sons, respectively. The data are approximately as of 1996. Family size is the total number of direct descendants of the founder of each business group, including the founder himself. Family size does not include spouses, the founder's siblings and descendants of the founder's siblings. Number of generations is defined as the number of generations of the family from the founder (generation 1) to the latest generation that is active in family business. Number of sons (daughters) is the total number of founder's sons (daughters) from all wives. Multiple wives is a dummy variable with the value of one if the founder had more than one wife, and zero otherwise. Founder dead is a dummy variable with the value of one if the founder was dead by 1996 and zero otherwise.

Family	Number of generations	Family size	Number of		Multiple wives?	Founder dead?	Family	Number of generations	Family size	Number of		Multiple wives?	Founder dead?
			Sons	Daughters						Sons	Daughters		
1	5	122	3	2	1	1	48	2	7	4	2	0	1
2	4	99	6	6	1	1	49	2	7	4	2	n.a.	1
3	4	34	6	1	1	1	50	2	7	4	2	0	0
4	4	33	5	2	0	1	51	2	7	2	4	0	0
5	4	27	4	2	0	1	52	2	7	2	4	0	1
6	4	25	1	2	0	1	53	2	6	5	0	n.a.	0
7	4	21	5	5	0	1	54	2	6	4	1	0	0
8	4	20	3	0	1	1	55	2	6	3	2	0	0
9	3	59	14	12	1	1	56	2	6	3	2	0	1
10	3	38	8	2	0	1	57	2	6	3	2	0	0
11	3	34	8	4	1	1	58	2	6	3	2	0	0
12	3	29	5	4	0	1	59	2	6	2	3	0	0
13	3	25	5	3	1	1	60	2	6	2	3	0	0
14	3	23	10	0	n.a.	0	61	2	6	1	4	0	0
15	3	21	8	8	0	1	62	2	6	0	5	0	0
16	3	19	4	8	1	1	63	2	5	4	0	n.a.	0
17	3	17	7	4	1	1	64	2	5	4	0	n.a.	0
18	3	16	6	1	0	0	65	2	5	3	1	0	0
19	3	16	2	1	0	1	66	2	5	3	1	0	1
20	3	15	6	6	n.a.	1	67	2	5	3	1	0	1
21	3	15	6	5	0	0	68	2	5	3	0	0	1
22	3	15	3	0	0	1	69	2	5	2	2	n.a.	0
23	3	14	2	3	0	0	70	2	5	2	2	0	0
24	3	13	2	2	0	1	71	2	5	1	3	0	0
25	3	12	5	4	1	1	72	2	5	1	3	n.a.	0
26	3	12	2	2	0	1	73	2	5	1	3	0	0
27	3	12	1	6	0	1	74	2	4	3	0	n.a.	0
28	3	11	4	0	n.a.	1	75	2	4	3	0	0	0
29	3	11	3	1	0	1	76	2	4	2	1	0	0
30	3	11	2	4	0	1	77	2	4	2	1	1	0
31	3	11	1	0	0	1	78	2	4	1	2	0	0
32	3	11	0	2	0	1	79	2	4	1	2	0	1
33	3	10	4	3	0	0	80	2	4	1	2	0	0
34	3	8	2	4	n.a.	0	81	2	4	1	2	0	1
35	3	7	3	2	0	1	82	2	4	1	2	0	0
36	3	6	3	0	n.a.	1	83	2	4	0	2	0	0
37	3	5	1	0	n.a.	1	84	2	3	2	0	n.a.	0
38	2	20	8	10	0	0	85	2	3	1	1	0	0
39	2	16	9	5	0	0	86	2	3	1	1	0	1
40	2	13	10	2	1	1	87	2	2	1	0	n.a.	0
41	2	12	4	7	1	0	88	2	2	1	0	0	0
42	2	11	4	1	1	0	89	2	1	0	0	n.a.	1
43	2	11	4	3	0	0	90	2	1	0	0	n.a.	1
44	2	10	4	2	1	0	91	2	1	0	0	n.a.	0
45	2	9	4	4	1	1	92	1	1	0	0	n.a.	0
46	2	8	4	3	n.a.	0	93	1	1	0	0	n.a.	0
47	2	8	2	5	1	0							

490 M. Bertrand et al. / Journal of Financial Economics 88 (2008) 466–498

Table A2
Group characteristics

The unit of observation is a family business group. All data are as of 1996. Family numbers correspond to those assigned in Table A1. Number of firms is the number of public and private firms in our sample that belonged to families. Log of total assets is the natural logarithm of group total assets in thousand baht at the end of the year. Return on assets is net profit divided by total assets at the end of the year. Leverage is group total liabilities divided by group total assets. Group age is defined as the age of the oldest firm for each group in our sample. Group depth is defined as the maximum depth of the deepest firm in the group, where firm's maximum depth is the longest chain that vertically traces the firm to the family's ultimate ownership. Number of firms owning a particular firm is the largest number of group firms that own a particular firm in the same group. Number of firms owned by a particular firm is the largest number of group firms that are owned by a particular firm in the same group.

Family	Number of firms — All	Public	Private	Log total assets	ROA (×100)	Leverage	Group age	Group depth	Number of firms — Owning	Owned
1	8	4	4	18.25	1.03	0.90	63	4	3	3
2	14	7	7	20.34	2.00	0.89	64	4	4	7
3	18	7	11	21.22	1.43	0.74	52	5	6	11
4	25	1	24	18.23	7.34	0.65	44	3	3	11
5	22	6	16	17.90	3.79	0.65	114	3	2	8
6	2	1	1	15.42	2.69	0.57	66	0	0	0
7	4	1	3	17.76	-0.01	0.92	49	3	1	1
8	5	0	5	17.12	9.10	0.65	63	1	3	3
9	31	6	25	18.43	1.56	0.69	39	4	2	6
10	35	19	16	17.90	3.75	0.52	44	7	5	23
11	4	0	4	16.21	-0.71	0.96	31	2	6	2
12	1	1	0	15.11	8.54	0.53	27	0	0	0
13	9	1	8	16.48	2.11	0.68	38	3	4	4
14	1	0	1	15.63	0.10	1.05	46	1	0	0
15	4	0	4	15.02	0.44	0.93	54	1	0	0
16	46	7	39	19.19	0.78	0.60	29	5	7	21
17	11	1	10	17.90	5.71	0.73	29	4	2	6
18	8	0	8	16.34	0.83	0.90	20	1	1	1
19	4	0	4	17.16	0.97	0.83	29	2	1	1
20	4	0	4	15.73	7.74	0.54	33	1	1	1
21	2	2	0	18.16	1.38	0.57	28	1	0	0
22	3	3	0	17.05	-1.27	0.75	8	0	0	0
23	7	1	6	17.46	3.95	0.61	41	5	2	3
24	3	2	1	15.51	6.33	0.59	26	1	1	0
25	2	2	0	15.46	-4.25	0.72	16	1	1	1
26	4	1	3	16.13	5.87	0.60	32	3	2	2
27	2	0	2	15.72	9.28	0.39	35	2	1	1
28	8	0	8	16.22	5.77	0.67	24	2	2	2
29	2	2	0	16.50	3.44	0.68	23	0	0	3
30	2	2	0	13.53	0.58	0.69	48	2	1	0
31	1	1	0	12.92	4.45	0.40	18	0	0	1
32	4	0	4	15.85	-3.51	1.00	22	1	1	0
33	7	1	6	16.16	20.86	0.30	29	1	3	3

Family	Number of firms — All	Public	Private	Log total assets	ROA (×100)	Leverage	Group age	Group depth	Number of firms — Owning	Owned
48	8	4	4	19.05	2.99	0.71	67	3	3	3
49	2	0	2	14.44	10.62	0.68	7	2	1	0
50	5	0	5	18.60	-0.27	0.33	55	2	3	3
51	1	0	1	14.74	4.88	1.10	18	0	0	0
52	9	4	5	19.95	1.73	0.89	51	6	7	6
53	1	0	1	15.68	-0.13	0.87	28	0	0	0
54	13	6	7	16.87	4.71	0.41	27	3	4	12
55	10	1	9	19.75	-0.32	0.29	27	4	4	6
56	1	1	0	14.50	-1.37	0.66	27	0	0	0
57	2	1	1	15.11	12.03	0.49	23	1	1	1
58	4	3	1	16.56	4.63	0.55	11	2	1	3
59	3	2	1	14.41	4.54	0.58	26	0	0	0
60	58	5	53	20.28	1.14	0.91	62	4	2	2
61	7	2	5	16.55	7.33	0.64	31	2	1	2
62	6	2	4	16.13	2.42	0.62	26	2	5	5
63	1	1	0	15.70	1.13	0.79	23	1	2	2
64	3	0	3	13.70	-0.25	0.89	27	1	1	0
65	6	5	1	17.88	3.60	0.61	31	1	1	0
66	6	2	4	18.30	5.80	0.58	16	4	3	3
67	2	0	2	14.59	-0.05	0.74	30	1	1	1
68	3	1	2	14.27	8.15	0.53	8	1	1	0
69	7	0	7	15.70	-1.07	0.78	33	1	1	1
70	2	1	1	15.25	0.40	0.46	32	2	2	0
71	1	0	1	13.58	1.09	0.69	27	0	0	0
72	13	3	10	17.99	-1.68	0.81	33	2	2	4
73	1	1	0	15.27	3.30	0.49	25	0	0	0
74	4	2	2	15.34	11.84	0.51	15	1	1	1
75	2	0	2	14.31	6.41	0.59	17	1	1	0
76	4	4	0	16.38	0.48	0.62	34	1	1	3
77	2	0	2	15.39	-1.62	0.87	19	1	1	6
78	3	1	2	16.60	8.20	0.72	13	0	0	0
79	2	2	0	15.15	-5.22	0.48	23	0	0	0
80	5	4	1	16.86	2.69	0.40	26	1	4	1

(continued overleaf)

34	3	2	1	16.75	-11.11	0.90	24	3	2	2
35	17	3	14	17.48	1.66	0.59	43	4	4	1
36	3	1	2	16.17	7.69	0.58	44	0	0	0
37	4	0	4	17.12	4.84	0.56	34	1	1	1
38	3	2	1	17.25	0.48	0.80	37	0	1	0
39	1	0	1	13.52	0.89	0.96	7	2	0	2
40	4	2	2	18.70	1.31	0.91	57	0	4	0
41	2	0	2	14.92	0.01	0.83	18	2	0	2
42	4	2	2	16.12	4.74	0.58	17	2	1	1
43	2	0	2	15.81	5.87	0.69	32	1	2	0
44	1	0	1	13.47	0.51	0.47	10	0	0	0
45	2	0	2	15.69	0.73	0.43	21	1	1	0
46	3	0	3	17.47	-0.16	0.97	54	0	4	2
47	1	0	1	15.66	0.60	0.95	16	0	0	0

81	1	0	1	13.22	0.63	0.77	17	0	0	0
82	8	4	4	17.84	11.99	0.43	13	2	1	4
83	2	0	2	15.73	2.38	0.72	22	1	1	1
84	4	2	2	17.48	0.88	0.91	24	1	1	3
85	16	4	12	17.47	1.03	0.73	35	3	3	8
86	1	1	0	18.60	0.91	0.90	47	0	0	0
87	4	4	0	16.69	-1.35	0.69	43	1	1	2
88	3	3	0	17.76	0.07	0.82	26	2	2	1
89	5	1	4	17.39	0.25	0.90	47	0	0	0
90	1	0	1	13.69	1.71	0.69	23	2	2	3
91	7	3	4	17.32	4.80	0.60	23	2	2	1
92	7	2	5	16.81	0.55	0.83	38	0	0	0
93	1	1	0	12.54	-11.20	1.10	11	0	0	0

of the families. There is only one case where we find the same first name in the family tree and firm records, but different last names. For this particular one case, we do not consider this person as a family member.

Given that we only identify one case in step 2, we are quite confident that our name matching covers most of the family members listed in our family trees and there is no systematic bias between male and female family members in the matching process.

A.4. References for family information

A.4.1. Books
In English
Brooker Group, The. Thai Business Groups 2001: A Unique Guide to Who Owns What, 4th edition. Bangkok, 2001.
Brooker Group, The. Thai Business Groups: A Unique Guide to Who Owns What, 5th edition. Bangkok, 2003.
Suehiro, A. Capital Accumulation in Thailand: 1855–1985. Chiangmai, Thailand: Silk Worm Books, 1996.
In Thai
Chantimathorn, Sathien. *Chin Sophonpanich: The King of Finance.* Bangkok: Matichon Publishing, 1988.
Jaiyen, Boonchai. Lives of Thai Millionaires: Their Family and Their Business. Bangkok, undated.
Jaiyen, Boonchai. Heirs of Thai Millionaires: Their Family and Their Business. Bangkok, undated.
Jaiyen, Boonchai. *The Riches Man in Thailand: Charoen Sirivadhanabhakdi.* Bangkok: Dokya Group Publishing, 2003.
Kongnirandornsuk, Supranee. Studying Crisis for New Opportunities, Manager Classic No.1, Bangkok: Se-Education, 2002.
Limthongkul, Sonti. *Mafia (Chao Por)*, Manager Classic No.5, Bangkok: Se-Education, 2002.
Limthongkul, Sonti. *New Comer*, Manager Classic No.3, Bangkok: Se-Education, 2002.
Maneenoi, Chupong. *Lives of 25 Millionaires (Set 2).* Bangkok: Finance and Banking Publishing, 1986.
Sabphaibul, Athiwat. *The Great Four Warriors.* Bangkok: Vanasarn Publishing, 2003.
Sabphaibul, Thanawat. *25 Business Millionaires.* Bangkok: Pim Kam Publisher, 2003.
Sabphaibul, Thanawat. *Life of the Lamsam Millionaire*, 2nd edition. Bangkok: Bangkok Biz News Publisher, 2000.
Sabphaibul, Thanawat. *The Legend of 55 Business Families: Book 1.* Bangkok: Nation Publishing, 2001.
Sabphaibul, Thanawat. *The Legend of 55 Business Families: Book 2.* Bangkok: Nation Publishing, 2001.
Saengthongkam, Wirat, and Kongnirandornsuk, Supranee, eds. *The Player*, Manager Classic No.7, Bangkok: Se-Education, 2002.
Saengthongkam, Wirat; Thangsriwong, Pandop; and Damrongsunthornchai, Somsak. *70-Year Chirathivat: Central*, Manager Classic No.7, Bangkok: Se-Education, 2002.
Yipphan. *Yesterday Millionaires: The Merchants.* Bangkok: Nation Publishing, 2003.
Yipphan. *Yesterday Millionaires: The Bankers.* Bangkok: Nation Publishing, 2003.
Young Blood, Business Interest, Special Issue, 1993.

A.4.2. Funeral Books (All are in Thai)
Attaphorn Leenutphong, 2001.
Bancha Lamsam, August 1992.
Boonkrong Bulakul, February 1980.
Nongyao Kanchanacharee, November 1996.
Samrit Chirathivat, November, 1992.
Shin Sophonpanich, April 1987.
Thanpuying Niramol Suriyasat, 2003.
Tiam Chokwatana, August 1991.
Tan Sew Ting Wanglee, November 1985.

M. Bertrand et al. / Journal of Financial Economics 88 (2008) 466–498   493

A.4.3. Magazine and Newspaper Articles (All are in Thai)

"108 Years of British Dispensary (L.P.)," *Manager Magazine*, June 2000.

"24 Key Men of Laemthong Bank," *Who's Who in Business & Finance*, February 1996, pp. 32–48.

"6 Heirs of Maleenont Family," *Manager Magazine*, June 1999.

"After Tiam: Profits Rather Than Growth," *Manager Magazine*, September 1991, pp. 192–200.

"Anan Asavabhokin and 'Land And House'," *Who's Who in Business & Finance*, May 1995, pp. 14–41.

"Angubokul Family," *Praew*, July 2004, pp. 160–162.

"Anuphong Asavabhokin: Waiting to Prove Himself," *Manager Magazine*, May 2003.

"Apirak Vanich: Following Akapoj," *Manager Magazine*, July 1992, pp. 80–81.

"Asavabhokin Family: The Owner of Land & House," *Boss Magazine*, July 1998, pp. 78–81.

"Assakul Family: The Owner of Ocean Insurance," *Boss Magazine*, Special Edition 1996, pp. 182–185.

"Assakul: Quiet and Deep Business," *Businessman Magazine*, undated, pp. 87–94.

"Attaporn Leenutphong: The Legend of Yontrakit," *Manager Magazine*, March 2001.

"Banthoon Lamsam—Somkid Jatusripitak," *Manager Magazine*, September 2003.

"Before Nailing the Coffin of Chanut Piyaoui," *Manager Magazine*, undated, pp. 146–155.

"Bencharongkul Family: The Owner of UCOM Group," *Boss Magazine*, Special Edition 1996, pp. 106–109.

"Bhirom Bhakdi and the Legend of Thai Beer," *Businessman Magazine*, undated, pp. 20–30.

"Bhirom Bhakdi Family: The Owner of Singha Beer," *Boss Magazine*, August 1997, pp. 174–177.

"Boonnam Boonnamsap: A Chinese in Japanese Body," *Manager Magazine*, December 1990, pp. 103–127.

"Boonrawd Diversifying to Yacht Market," *Who's Who in Business & Finance*, October 1996, pp. 50–81.

"Boonsithi Chokwatana 'Saha Group Will Be Ten Times Bigger'," *Who's Who in Business & Finance*, March 1996, pp. 14–26.

"Bulakul Family, Part 1," *Praew*, No.1, April 2005, pp. 366–368.

"Bulakul Family, Part 2," *Praew*, No.2, April 2005, pp. 376–378.

"Bulakul Family: The Owner of Maboonkrong Building," *Boss Magazine*, Special Edition 1996, pp. 174–177.

"Bulsook Family: The Owner of Thai Pepsi," *Boss Magazine*, Special Edition 1996, pp. 158–161.

"Central Group: The Change of Generations," *Manager Magazine*, April 2003.

"Central to the 3rd Generation: Maybe Not Chirathivat's? *Manager Magazine*, October 1986.

"Chai Chaiyawan: The 2nd Generation of the Family," *Who's Who in Business & Finance Magazine*, January 1996, pp. 23–28.

"Chai Sophonpanich 'I Cannot Retire'," *Manager Magazine*, June 2003.

"Chaiyudh Srivikorn: Heir of the Family," *Who's Who in Business & Finance*, February 1995, pp. 64–67.

"Chanut Piyaoui," *Manager Magazine*, February 2000.

"Chanut Piyaoui: Dividing the Wealth," *Manager Magazine*, February 2001.

"Chansrichawala Family: The Owner of Siam Vidhaya Group," *Boss Magazine*, Special Edition 1996, pp. 122–125.

"Charoen Sirivadhanabhakdi: Transferring the Army to His Children," *Manager Magazine*, March 2003, pp. 34–54.

"Chatikavanich Family: The Owner of Loxley," *Boss Magazine*, July 1997, pp. 190–193.

"Charn Issara: Ready to Retire?" *Manager Magazine*, 1988, pp. 6–33.

"Chearavanont Family: The Owner of CP Group," *Boss Magazine*, Special Edition 1996, pp. 54–57.

"Cherdchu Sophonpanich: Who Is He?" *Manager Magazine*, October 2003.

"Chirathivat Family: King of Thai Department Stores, Part 1," *Praew*, No.1, March 2005, pp. 326–328.

"Chirathivat Family: King of Thai Department Stores, Part 2," *Praew*, No.2, March 2005, pp. 350–352.

"Chirathivat Family: The Owner of Central Department Store," *Boss Magazine*, October 1997, pp. 168–171.

"Chirathivat: Family Council," *Manager Magazine*, October 2000.

"Chokwatana Conquering Consumer Product Empire," *Businessman Magazine*, undated, pp. 62–73.

"Chokwattana Family: King of Thai Customer Products, Part 1," *Praew*, No.1, September 2004, pp. 384-386.

"Chokwattana Family: King of Thai Customer Products, Part 2," *Praew*, No.2, September 2004, pp. 272–274.

"Chokwatana Family: The Owner of Sahapattanaphibul," *Boss Magazine*, Special Edition 1996, pp. 102–105.

"Chokwattana's Third Generation: Thammarat Chokwattana and Theerada Amphanwong," *Manager Magazine*, March 2003.

"Cholvicharn Family: The Owner of Union Bank," *Boss Magazine*, Special Edition 1996, pp. 74–77.

"Chuan Tangmatitham: Grow and Split," *Businessman Magazine*, undated, pp. 137–140.

"Critical Period of Samart Group," *Manager Magazine*, February 1992, pp. 150–162.

"Darakananda Family: The Owner of Saha-Union," *Boss Magazine*, Special Edition 1996, pp. 210–213.

"Doctor Boon Vanasin," *Who's Who in Business & Finance Magazine*, January 1990, pp. 125–129.

"Dr.Chaiyudh Kanasutra," *Manager Magazine*, undated, pp. 25–47.

"Exclusive Chatree Sphonpanich," *Who's Who in Business & Finance*, December 1994, pp. 14–26.

"Heir of Chatree," *Who's Who in Business & Finance*, December 1994, pp. 36–37.

"Hetrakul Family: The Owner of Daily News," *Boss Magazine*, Special Edition 1996, pp. 110–113.

"Issara Family: The Owner of Charn Issara Tower," *Boss Magazine*, Special Edition 1996, pp. 126–129.

"Jakkapak Family: The Owner of Finance One," *Boss Magazine*, Special Edition 1996, pp. 130–133.

"Kamron Tejapaibul and Mahanakorn Bank,"undated, pp. 35–38.

"Kanasutra Family: The Owner of Ital-Thai Group," *Boss Magazine*, April 1996, pp. 86–89.

"Kanasutra General Assembly: Exciting till the End," *Manager Magazine*, January 1987, pp. 76–87.

"Karnchanachari Family: The Owner of Seaw-National," *Boss Magazine*, Special Edition 1996, pp. 190–193.

"Karnchanapas Family: The Owner of Muangthong Thani," *Boss Magazine*, Special Edition 1996, pp. 66–69.

"Karnchanapas Family: The Road to Real-Estate Tycoon, Part 1," *Praew*, No.2, November 2004.

"Karnchanapas Family: The Road to Real-Estate Tycoon, Part 2," *Praew*, No.1, December 2004, pp. 422–424.

"Karnchanapas Family: The Road to Real-Estate Tycoon, Part 3," *Praew*, No.2, December 2004, pp. 328–330.

"Keeree Kanchanapas," *Manager Magazine*, April 2003.

"Keeree Karnchanapas: The Great Dragon," *Manager Magazine*, April 1991, pp. 138–152.

"Khunying Sasima Srivikorn," *Manager Magazine*, October/November 1987, pp. 146–155.

"Kiet Srifuengfung," *Manager Magazine*, October/November 1987, pp. 117–129.

"Krisdathanont Family: The Owner of Krisda Mahanakorn," *Boss Magazine*, Special Edition 1996, pp. 206–209.

"Lamsam: The Great Family," *Businessman Magazine*, undated, pp. 36–47.

"Land And House: How Long It Will Last?" *Manager Magazine*, September 1993, pp. 102–122.

"Leenutaphong Family: From Scraps to Automobile Empire," *Praew*, No.1, October 2004, pp. 402–404.

"Leenutphong Family: The Owner of Yontrakit," *Boss Magazine*, Special Edition 1996, pp. 170–173.

"Leeswadtrakul Family: The Owner of Anoma Hotel," *Boss Magazine*, Special Edition 1996, pp. 194–197.

"Lenso: To the Telecommunication Business," *Manager Magazine*, April 1994, pp. 110–118.

"Luanchai Vongvanich's Vision," *Who's Who in Business & Finance*, February 1996, pp. 22–30.

"M. Thai Group," *Who's Who in Business & Finance*, January 1995, pp. 55–58.

"Maboonkrong: A Memorial for Sirichai Bulakul," undated, pp. 82–96.

"Mahadamrongkul Family: The Owner of Nakornluang Thai Bank," *Boss Magazine*, Special Edition 1996, pp. 30–33.

"Mahadamrongkul: Setting Time, Finding Future," *Manager Magazine*, December 1993, pp. 144–156.

"Maleenont Family: The Founder of Channel 3," *Boss Magazine*, Special Edition 1996, pp. 125–128.

"Mazda Took over Sukosol," Manager Magazine, May 1999.

"Narin Naruela and Tower Records," *Who's Who in Business & Finance*, January 1997, pp. 51–55.

"New Blood," *Manager Magazine*, May 2003.

"Osathanugrah Family: The Owner of Osotspa," *Boss Magazine*, Special Edition 1996, pp. 50–53.

"Osotspa 2000," *Who's Who in Business & Finance*, April 1995, pp. 15–43.
"Osotspa: Osathanugrah's Monopoly," *Manager Magazine*, undated, pp. 89–99.
"Pathra Sila-on: The Oldest Sister of S&P," *Manager Magazine*, September 2001.
"Phenjati Family: The Owner of Phenjati Tower," *Boss Magazine*, Special Edition 1996, pp. 198–201.
"Phornprapa Family: The Owner of Siam Motor," *Boss Magazine*, November 1997, pp. 176–179.
"Phornprapa: Toward Thai Automobile Empire," *Businessman Magazine*, undated, pp. 74–85.
"Piyaoui Family: The Owner of Disit Thani Hotel," *Boss Magazine*, Special Edition 1996, pp. 178–181.
"Pong Sarasin on the Political Road," *Manager Magazine*, December 1990, pp. 169–170.
"Poolvoralaks Family: King of Thai Movie Theaters, Part 1," *Praew*, No.1, January 2005, pp. 298–300.
"Poolvoralaks Family: King of Thai Movie Theaters, Part 2," *Praew*, No.2, January 2005, pp. 294–296.
"Poolvoraluks Family: The Owner of RGV Theaters," *Boss Magazine*, Special Edition 1996, pp. 142–145.
"Pornsanong Tuchinda: The Last Heir of Thai Dhanu Bank?" *Manager Magazine*, November 1999.
"Prachai Leophairatana: Local Hero," *Manager Magazine*, May 2000.
"Prapa Viriyaprapaikit: Difficult to Read," *Manager Magazine*, undated, pp. 156–159.
"Sahakol Air: Will Prasert Prasarttong-Osot Fail?" *Manager Magazine*, January 1987, pp. 88–95.
"Sarasin Family: The Owner of Thai Coca-Cola," *Boss Magazine*, Special Edition 1996, pp. 86–89.
"Sasima Srivikorn: Reaching to the Star," *Manager Magazine*, March 1999.
"Sawas Horrungruang: Dead Man Walking," *Manager Magazine*, January 2003.
"Shinnawatra Family: The Owner of Shin Group," *Boss Magazine*, August 1998, pp. 98–101.
"Siam Motor: How Pornthip-Kasem Keep It?" *Manager Magazine*, undated, pp. 38–84.
"Siam Motor: The End of Thavorn or Phornprapa?" *Manager Magazine*, November 1986, pp. 61–97.
"Singha Beer: Reorganization," *Manager Magazine*, August 2003.
"Sirivadhanabhakdi Family: The Owner of Mekong Brandy," *Boss Magazine*, Special Edition 1996, pp. 46–49.
"Sophonpanich: From Bank to Business," *Businessman Magazine*, undated, pp. 22–34.
"Sophonpanich: Managing the Business Bequest," *Manager Magazine*, undated, pp. 39–64.
"Srifuengfung Family: The Owner of Thai-Asahi Glass," *Boss Magazine*, December 1997, pp. 170–173.
"Srifuengfung Is Thai-Asahi Glass," *Businessman Magazine*, undated, pp. 106–113.
"Srivikorn Family: From Landlord to Tycoon," *Praew*, June 2004, pp. 110–112.
"Srivikorn Family: The Owner of President Hotel," *Boss Magazine*, Special Edition 1996, pp. 134–137.
"Subaru Music Award," *Businessman Magazine*, undated, pp. 51–55.
"Sunrise at Channel 3: The Golden Era of Maleenont's Second Generation," *Manager Magazine*, June 1999.
"Supachai Chearavanont: Crisis Coming with Opportunities," *Manager Magazine*, September 1999.
"Supachai Umpujh: From Stock-Checking Boy to Owner of the Mall Group," *Manager Magazine*, August 1987, pp. 115–124.
"Supaluck Umpujh," *Manager Magazine*, April 2003.
"Surang Dumnernchanvanit (1932–2002)," *Manager Magazine*, February 2003.
"Surangrat Chirathivat: Central Iron Lady," *Manager Magazine*, October 1990, pp. 8–9.
"Suriyon Raiva: The First Tycoon," *Manager Magazine*, October/November 1987.
"Suthichart Chirathivat: The Leader of Generation 3," *Manager Magazine*, March 2003.
"Suvit Wanglee on His Heir," *Who's Who in Business & Finance*, January 1995, pp. 35–54.
"Suvit Wanglee: The Gentleman of Nakornthon Bank," *Businessman Magazine*, undated, pp. 24–29.
"Syberia: Internet Café," *Who's Who in Business & Finance*, January 1997, pp. 29–32.
"Tangkaravakoon Family, Part 1," *Praew*, No.2, October 2004, pp. 370–372.
"Tangkaravakoon Family, Part 2," *Praew*, No.1, November 2004, pp. 376–378.
"Tangmatitham Family: The Owner of Mankong Kehakarn," *Boss Magazine*, Special Edition 1996, pp. 186–189.
"Tejapaibul Family: The Legend, Part 1," *Praew*, No.1, February 2005, pp. 318–320.
"Tejapaibul Family: The Legend, Part 2," *Praew*, No.2, February 2005, pp. 302–304.
"Tejapaibul Family: The Owner of Srinakorn Bank," *Boss Magazine*, Special Edition 1996, pp. 62–65.
"Tejapaibul: The Greatness of Udane," *Businessman Magazine*, undated, pp. 48–56.

"Thai Banks before the Fall (1962–1997)," *Manager Magazine*, February 2000.
"Thai Dhanu Bank and Its Challenge," *Who's Who in Business & Finance*, March 1996, pp. 27–47.
"Thai-Asahi Glass," *Businessman Magazine*, undated, pp. 47–51.
"The 60 Hotels in the Hand of an Iron Lady, Khunying Chanut Piyaoui," *Who's Who in Business & Finance*, July 1995, pp. 16–35.
"The Doctor Who Cure Wongkusolkit," *Manager Magazine*, February 1991, pp. 42–44.
"The End of Euchukiet-Pathraprasit Legend of Bank of Asia 1998," *Manager Magazine*, August 1998.
"The End of Srinakorn Bank: Not Surprising," *Manager Magazine*, June 2003.
"The Fighting of the Machine Mogul," *Manager Magazine*, December 1990, pp. 128–151.
"The Future of British Dispensary in the Hands of Anurut and Luenchai Vongvanich," *Who's Who in Business & Finance*, February 1996, pp. 15–21.
"The Greatness of Soon Hua Seng," *Manager Magazine*, pp. 140–159.
"The Heavy Loads on Srivikorn Family," *Manager Magazine*, March 1999.
"The Last Paper of Dr. Chaiyud Kanasutra," *Manager Magazine*, February 1999.
"The Latest Situation of Wanglee Family," *Manager Magazine*, August 1999.
"The Man Behind...," *Manager Magazine*, July 2003.
"The Man in front of Bancha Lamsam," *Manager Magazine*, February 1992.
"The New Leader of Central," *Manager Magazine*, May 1992.
"The Thai Rungrueng Empire," *Manager Magazine*, December 1987, pp. 113–132.
"Theerada Amphanwong (Chokwattana)," *Manager Magazine*, May 1999.
"Theeraphong Chansiri: The man behind TUF," *Manager Magazine*, October 1998.
"Time to Prove: Suthipong Chirathivat," *Manager Magazine*, June 1998.
"To the Future with Petrochemicals," *Manager Magazine*, May 2000.
"Tracking Sophonpanich's Wealth Abroad," *Who's Who in Business & Finance*, December 1994, pp. 31–35.
"Trouble on Central-Chirathivat," *Manager Magazine*, February 2003.
"Tuchinda Family: The Owner of Thai Dhanu Bank," *Boss Magazine*, Special Edition 1996, pp. 150–153.
"Two Roles, Two Leaders in Sahaphat," *Manager Magazine*, May 1999.
"Umpujh Family: The Owner of The Mall," *Boss Magazine*, Special Edition 1996, pp. 138–141.
"Unveiling 7,000 Million Empire of Prapad Phodhivorakhun," April 1996, pp. 14–32.
"Unveiling the Heirs of Business Empires," *Thairath*, July 28, 2004.
"Unveiling the Management Team of Nakornthon Bank," *Who's Who in Business & Finance*, December 1995, pp. 28–38.
"Unveiling the Management Team of Union Bank of Bangkok," *Who's Who in Business & Finance*, July 1995, pp. 36–64.
"Vacharaphol Family: The Owner of Thairath Newspaper," *Boss Magazine*, Special Edition 1996, pp. 82–85.
"Vanasin Family: The Owner of Thonburi Hospital," *Boss Magazine*, Special Edition 1996, pp. 202–205.
"Vanich Family," *Manager Magazine*, December 1999.
"Vanich-Chai Chaiyawan and the Future of Thai Insurance," *Who's Who in Business & Finance*, January 1996, pp. 15–22.
"Vichai Poolvoralaks: High-Tech Movie Theaters?" *Manager Magazine*, January 1998.
"Viriyaprapaikit Family: The Owner of Sahaviriya Group," *Boss Magazine*, September 1997, pp. 168–171.
"Viriyaprapaikit: Growth fromVision," *Businessman Magazine*, undated, pp. 114–118.
"Vongvanich Family: The Owner of British Dispensary," *Boss Magazine*, March 1997, pp. 183–186.
"Wanglee Family: The Owner of Nakornthon Bank," *Boss Magazine*, August 1998, pp. 84–87.
"Wanglee: Slow but Sure," *Businessman Magazine*, undated, pp. 57–61.
"Wanglee's Family Saga," undated, pp. 104–122.
"Wattanavekin Family: The Owner of Kiatnakin Finance," *Boss Magazine*, Special Edition 1996, pp. 166–169.
"Wisut Poolvoralaks: A Man Who Makes Thais Love Thai Movies," *Manager Magazine*, January 2000.
"Yoovidhaya Family: The Owner of Red Bulls," *Boss Magazine*, Special Edition 1996, pp. 70–73.

M. Bertrand et al. / Journal of Financial Economics 88 (2008) 466–498   497

A.5. Construction of excess control measures

Individual ownership is calculated by summing a given family member's direct and indirect ownership over a given firm. Direct ownership is simply the percentage of shares that a given family member owns. When there is a chain shareholding along the pyramid, we also compute the indirect ownership along the chain by calculating the product of shares held by a given individual along the chain. The calculation is more complicated if there is more than one chain for each firm.

In such cases, the total indirect ownership is the sum of the ownership over all chains that can be traced back to the given family member. For example, Firm X is 30% owned by Mr. A and 70% owned by firm Y. Firm Y is 40% owned by Mr. A. We say that Mr. A directly owns 30% of firm X. He also indirectly owns 40%*70% = 28% of firm X through firm Y along the pyramid chain. His ownership in firm X is therefore 30 + 28 = 58%.

Control is based on the voting rights of a given family member. Due to a one-share-one-vote rule, direct control rights are simply the shares that the family member holds. However, in case of a chain shareholding, control over the voting rights of a firm is the weakest link, i.e., the smallest share along each chain. Total indirect control is defined as the sum of the control over all chains. Finally, ultimate control is the sum of direct and indirect control for each family member. Using the previous scenario, Mr. A directly controls 30% of the voting rights of firm X. He also indirectly controls min {40%, 70%} = 40% over firm X. His control in firm X is therefore 30 + 40 = 70%. Using this approach, we can define a measure of excess control (i.e., extent of control greater than or in excess of ownership stake) at the individual level. In the example above, Mr. A has excess control over firm X (by 12%).

References

Anderson, R., Reeb, D., 2003. Founding-family ownership and firm performance: evidence from the S&P 500. Journal of Finance 63, 1301–1328.
Bennedson, M., Nielsen, K., Pérez-González, F., Wolfenzon, D., 2007. Inside the family firm: the role of families in succession decisions and performance. Quarterly Journal of Economics 122, 647–691.
Bertrand, M., Schoar, A., 2006. The role of family in family firms. Journal of Economic Perspectives 20, 73–96.
Bertrand, M., Mehta, P., Mullainathan, M., 2002. Ferreting out tunneling: an application to Indian business groups. Quarterly Journal of Economics 117, 121–148.
Bhattacharya, U., Ravikumar, B., 2003. Capital markets and the evolution of family businesses. Journal of Business 74, 187–220.
Brooker Group, 2003. Thai Business Groups: A Unique Guide to Who Owns What.
Burkart, M., Panunzi, F., Shleifer, A., 2003. Family firms. Journal of Finance 58, 2167–2202.
Caselli, F., Gennaioli, M., 2005. Dynastic management. Unpublished working paper, London School of Economics (earlier version was NBER Working Paper No 9442).
Claessens, S., Djankov, S., Lang, L., 2000. The separation of ownership and control in East Asian Corporation. Journal of Financial Economics 58, 81–112.
Claessens, S., Djankov, S., Fan, J., Lang, L., 2002. Disentangling the incentive and entrenchment effects of large shareholders. Journal of Finance 62, 2741–2771.
Cronqvist, H., Nilsson, M., 2003. Agency costs of controlling minority shareholders. Journal of Financial and Quantitative Analysis 38, 695–719.
Gomes, A., Novaes, W., 2006. Sharing of control versus monitoring as corporate governance mechanisms. Unpublished working paper.
Gugler, K., 2001. Corporate Governance and Economic Performance, European Corporate Governance Network. Oxford University Press, Oxford.
Jones, G., Rose, M., 1993. Family capitalism. Business History 35, 1–16.
Khanna, T., Palepu, K., 2000. Is group affiliation profitable in emerging markets? An analysis of diversified Indian business groups. Journal of Finance 55, 867–891.
La Porta, R., Lopez-de-Silanes, F., Shleifer, A., 1999. Corporate ownership around the world. Journal of Finance 54, 471–518.
Limlingan, V.S., 1986. The Overseas Chinese in ASEAN: Business Strategies and Management Practices. Vita Development Corp., Manila.
Marman, D., 2002. The emergence of business groups: Israel and South Korea compared. Organization Studies 23, 737–758.
Morck, R., Stangeland, D., Yeung, B., 2000. Inherited wealth, corporate control, and economic growth: the Canadian disease, in concentrated corporate ownership. In: Morck, R. (Ed.), NBER Conference Volume. University of Chicago Press.
Pérez-González, F., 2006. Inherited control and firm performance. American Economic Review 96, 1559–1588.
Redding, S.G., 1990. The Spirit of Chinese Capitalism. W. de Gruyter, New York.

Sapphaibul, T., 2001a. The Legend of 55 Business Families: Book 1. Nation Publishing, Bangkok.
Sapphaibul, T., 2001b. The Legend of 55 Business Families: Book 2. Nation Publishing, Bangkok.
Suehiro, A., 1997. Capital Accumulation in Thailand 1855–1985. Silkworm Books, Chiang Mai, Thailand.
Villalonga, B., Amit, R., 2006. How do family ownership, management, and control affect firm value? Journal of Financial Economics 80, 385–417.

Part V
Entrepreneurs, Politicians
and Rent-Seeking

[25]

Entrepreneurship: Productive, Unproductive, and Destructive

William J. Baumol

New York University and Princeton University

The basic hypothesis is that, while the total supply of entrepreneurs varies among societies, the productive contribution of the society's entrepreneurial activities varies much more because of their allocation between productive activities such as innovation and largely unproductive activities such as rent seeking or organized crime. This allocation is heavily influenced by the relative payoffs society offers to such activities. This implies that policy can influence the allocation of entrepreneurship more effectively than it can influence its supply. Historical evidence from ancient Rome, early China, and the Middle Ages and Renaissance in Europe is used to investigate the hypotheses.

> It is often assumed that an economy of private enterprise has an automatic bias towards innovation, but this is not so. It has a bias only towards profit. [HOBSBAWM 1969, p. 40]

When conjectures are offered to explain historic slowdowns or great leaps in economic growth, there is the group of usual suspects that is

I am very grateful for the generous support of the research underlying this paper from the Division of Information Science and Technology of the National Science Foundation, the Price Institute for Entrepreneurial Studies, the Center for Entrepreneurial Studies of the Graduate School of Business Administration, New York University, and the C. V. Starr Center for Applied Economics. I am also very much indebted to Vacharee Devakula for her assistance in the research. I owe much to Joel Mokyr, Stefano Fenoaltea, Lawrence Stone, Constance Berman, and Claudia Goldin for help with the substance of the paper and to William Jordan and Theodore Rabb for guidance on references.

[*Journal of Political Economy*, 1990, vol. 98, no. 5, pt. 1]

regularly rounded up—prominent among them, the entrepreneur. Where growth has slowed, it is implied that a decline in entrepreneurship was partly to blame (perhaps because the culture's "need for achievement" has atrophied). At another time and place, it is said, the flowering of entrepreneurship accounts for unprecedented expansion.

This paper proposes a rather different set of hypotheses, holding that entrepreneurs are always with us and always play *some* substantial role. But there are a variety of roles among which the entrepreneur's efforts can be reallocated, and some of those roles do not follow the constructive and innovative script that is conventionally attributed to that person. Indeed, at times the entrepreneur may even lead a parasitical existence that is actually damaging to the economy. How the entrepreneur acts at a given time and place depends heavily on the rules of the game—the reward structure in the economy—that happen to prevail. Thus the central hypothesis here is that it is the set of rules and not the supply of entrepreneurs *or the nature of their objectives* that undergoes significant changes from one period to another and helps to dictate the ultimate effect on the economy via the *allocation* of entrepreneurial resources. Changes in the rules and other attendant circumstances can, of course, modify the composition of the class of entrepreneurs and can also alter its size. Without denying this or claiming that it has no significance, in this paper I shall seek to focus attention on the allocation of the changing class of entrepreneurs rather than its magnitude and makeup. (For an excellent analysis of the basic hypothesis, independently derived, see Murphy, Shleifer, and Vishny [1990].)

The basic proposition, if sustained by the evidence, has an important implication for growth policy. The notion that our productivity problems reside in "the spirit of entrepreneurship" that waxes and wanes for unexplained reasons is a counsel of despair, for it gives no guidance on how to reawaken that spirit once it has lagged. If that is the task assigned to policymakers, they are destitute: they have no means of knowing how to carry it out. But if what is required is the adjustment of rules of the game to induce a more felicitous allocation of entrepreneurial resources, then the policymaker's task is less formidable, and it is certainly not hopeless. The prevailing rules that affect the allocation of entrepreneurial activity can be observed, described, and, with luck, modified and improved, as will be illustrated here.

Here, extensive historical illustrations will be cited to impart plausibility to the contentions that have just been described. Then a short discussion of some current issues involving the allocation of entrepreneurship between productive and unproductive activities will be offered. Finally, I shall consider very briefly the means that can be used to change the rules of the game, and to do so in a manner that stimulates the productive contribution of the entrepreneur.

I.   On the Historical Character of the Evidence

Given the inescapable problems for empirical as well as theoretical study of entrepreneurship, what sort of evidence can one hope to provide? Since the rules of the game usually change very slowly, a case study approach to investigation of my hypotheses drives me unavoidably to examples spanning considerable periods of history and encompassing widely different cultures and geographic locations. Here I shall proceed on the basis of historical illustrations encompassing all the main economic periods and places (ancient Rome, medieval China, Dark Age Europe, the Later Middle Ages, etc.) that the economic historians almost universally single out for the light they shed on the process of innovation and its diffusion. These will be used to show that the relative rewards to different types of entrepreneurial activity have in fact varied dramatically from one time and place to another and that this seems to have had profound effects on patterns of entrepreneurial behavior. Finally, evidence will be offered *suggesting* that such reallocations can have a considerable influence on the prosperity and growth of an economy, though other variables undoubtedly also play substantial roles.

None of this can, of course, be considered conclusive. Yet, it is surely a standard tenet of scientific method that tentative confirmation of a hypothesis is provided by observation of phenomena that the hypothesis helps to explain and that could not easily be accounted for if that hypothesis were invalid. It is on this sort of reasoning that I hope to rest my case. Historians have long been puzzled, for example, by the failure of the society of ancient Rome to disseminate and put into widespread practical use some of the sophisticated technological developments that we know to have been in its possession, while in the "High Middle Ages," a period in which progress and change were hardly popular notions, inventions that languished in Rome seem to have spread like wildfire. It will be argued that the hypothesis about the allocability of entrepreneurial effort between productive and unproductive activity helps considerably to account for this phenomenon, though it certainly will *not* be claimed that this is all there was to the matter.

Before I get to the substance of the discussion, it is important to emphasize that nothing that follows in this article makes any pretense of constituting a contribution to economic history. Certainly it is not intended here to try to explain any particular historical event. Moreover, the analysis relies entirely on secondary sources, and all the historical developments described are well known to historians, as the citations will indicate. Whatever the contribution that may be offered by the following pages, then, it is confined to enhanced understanding and extension of the (nonmathematical) theory of entrepreneurship in general, and not to an improved analysis of the historical events that are cited.

II. The Schumpeterian Model Extended: Allocation of Entrepreneurship

The analysis of this paper rests on what seems to be the one theoretical model that effectively encompasses the role of the entrepreneur and that really "works," in the sense that it constitutes the basis for a number of substantive inferences.[1] This is, of course, the well-known Schumpeterian analysis, whose main shortcoming, for our purposes, is the paucity of insights on policy that emerge from it. It will be suggested here that only a minor extension of that model to encompass the *allocation* of entrepreneurship is required to enhance its power substantially in this direction.

Schumpeter tells us that innovations (he calls them "the carrying out of new combinations") take various forms besides mere improvements in technology:

> This concept covers the following five cases: (1) the introduction of a new good—that is one with which consumers are not yet familiar—or of a new quality of a good. (2) The introduction of a new method of production, that is one not yet tested by experience in the branch of manufacture concerned, which need by no means be founded upon a discovery scientifically new, and can also exist in a new way of handling a commodity commercially. (3) The opening of a new market, that is a market into which the particular branch of manufacture of the country in question has not previously entered, whether or not this market has existed before. (4) The conquest of a new source of supply of raw materials or half-manufactured goods, again irrespective of whether this source already exists or whether it has first to be

---

[1] There has, however, recently been an outburst of illuminating writings on the theory of the innovation process, analyzing it in such terms as *races* for patents in which the winner takes everything, with no consolation prize for a close second, or treating the process, alternatively, as a "waiting game," in which the patient second entrant may outperform and even survive the first one in the innovative arena, who incurs the bulk of the risk. For an overview of these discussions as well as some substantial added insights, see Dasgupta (1988).

created. (5) The carrying out of the new organization of any industry, like the creation of a monopoly position (for example through trustification) or the breaking up of a monopoly position. [(1912) 1934, p. 66]

The obvious fact that entrepreneurs undertake such a variety of tasks all at once suggests that theory can usefully undertake to consider what determines the *allocation* of entrepreneurial inputs among those tasks. Just as the literature traditionally studies the allocation of other inputs, for example, capital resources, among the various industries that compete for them, it seems natural to ask what influences the flow of entrepreneurial talent among the various activities in Schumpeter's list.

Presumably the reason no such line of inquiry was pursued by Schumpeter or his successors is that any analysis of the allocation of entrepreneurial resources among the five items in the preceding list (with the exception of the last—the creation or destruction of a monopoly) does not promise to yield any profound conclusions. There is no obvious reason to make much of a shift of entrepreneurial activity away from, say, improvement in the production process and toward the introduction of new products. The general implications, if any, for the public welfare, for productivity growth, and for other related matters are hardly obvious.

To derive more substantive results from an analysis of the allocation of entrepreneurial resources, it is necessary to expand Schumpeter's list, whose main deficiency seems to be that it does not go far enough. For example, it does not explicitly encompass innovative acts of technology transfer that take advantage of opportunities to introduce already-available technology (usually with some modification to adapt it to local conditions) to geographic locales whose suitability for the purpose had previously gone unrecognized or at least unused.

Most important for the discussion here, Schumpeter's list of entrepreneurial activities can usefully be expanded to include such items as innovations in rent-seeking procedures, for example, discovery of a previously unused legal gambit that is effective in diverting rents to those who are first in exploiting it. It may seem strange at first blush to propose inclusion of activities of such questionable value to society (I shall call them acts of "unproductive entrepreneurship") in the list of Schumpeterian innovations (though the creation of a monopoly, which Schumpeter does include as an innovation, is surely as questionable), but, as will soon be seen, this is a crucial step for the analysis that follows. If entrepreneurs are defined, simply, to be persons who are ingenious and creative in finding ways that add to their own wealth, power, and prestige, then it is to be expected that not all of them will be overly concerned with whether an activity that achieves these goals adds much or little to the social product or, for that matter, even whether it is an actual impediment to production (this notion goes back, at least, to Veblen [1904]). Suppose that it turns out, in addition, that at any time and place the magnitude of the benefit the economy derives from its entrepreneurial talents depends *substantially,* among other variables, on the allocation of this resource between productive and unproductive entrepreneurial activities of the sorts just described. Then the reasons for including acts of the latter type in the list of entrepreneurial activities become clear.

Here no exhaustive analysis of the process of allocation of entrepreneurial activity among the set of available options will be attempted. Rather, it will be argued only that at least *one* of the prime determinants of entrepreneurial behavior at any particular time and place is the prevailing rules of the game that govern the payoff of one entrepreneurial activity relative to another. If the rules are such as to impede the earning of much wealth via activity A, or are such as to impose social disgrace on those who engage in it, then, other things being equal, entrepreneurs' efforts will tend to be channeled to other activities, call them B. But if B contributes less to production or welfare than A, the consequences for society may be considerable.[2]

As a last preliminary note, it should be emphasized that the set of active entrepreneurs may be subject to change. Thus if the rules of the game begin to favor B over A, it may not be just the same individuals who switch their activities from entrepreneurship of type A to that of type B. Rather, some persons with talents suited for A may simply drop out of the picture, and individuals with abilities adapted to B may for the first time become.entrepreneurs. Thus the allocation of entrepreneurs among activities is perhaps best described in the way Joan Robinson (following Shove's suggestion) analyzed the allocation of heterogeneous land resources (1933, chap. 8): as the solution of a jigsaw puzzle in which the pieces are each fitted into the places selected for them by the concatenation of pertinent circumstances.

III.   Entrepreneurship, Productive and Unproductive: The Rules Do Change

Let us now turn to the central hypothesis of this paper: that the exercise of entrepreneurship can sometimes be unproductive or even

---

[2] There is a substantial literature, following the work of Jacob Schmookler, providing strong empirical evidence for the proposition that even the allocation of inventive effort, i.e., the directions pursued by inventive activities, is itself heavily influenced by relative payoff prospects. However, it is now agreed that some of these authors go too far when they appear to imply that almost nothing but the demand for the product of invention influences to any great extent which inventions will occur. For a good summary and references, see Abramovitz (1989, p. 33).

destructive, and that whether it takes one of these directions or one that is more benign depends heavily on the structure of payoffs in the economy—the rules of the game. The rather dramatic illustrations provided by world history seem to confirm quite emphatically the following proposition.

PROPOSITION 1. The rules of the game that determine the relative payoffs to different entrepreneurial activities *do* change dramatically from one time and place to another.

These examples also suggest strongly (but hardly "prove") the following proposition.

PROPOSITION 2. Entrepreneurial behavior changes direction from one economy to another in a manner that corresponds to the variations in the rules of the game.

A. *Ancient Rome*

The avenues open to those Romans who sought power, prestige, and wealth are instructive. First, it may be noted that they had no reservations about the desirability of wealth or about its pursuit (e.g., Finley 1985, pp. 53–57). *As long as it did not involve participation in industry or commerce,* there was nothing degrading about the wealth acquisition process. Persons of honorable status had three primary and acceptable sources of income: landholding (not infrequently as absentee landlords), "usury," and what may be described as "political payments":

> The opportunity for "political moneymaking" can hardly be over-estimated. Money poured in from booty, indemnities, provincial taxes, loans and miscellaneous extractions in quantities without precedent in Graeco-Roman history, and at an accelerating rate. The public treasury benefited, but probably more remained in private hands, among the nobles in the first instance; then, in appropriately decreasing proportions, among the *equites,* the soldiers and even the plebs of the city of Rome. . . . Nevertheless, the whole phenomenon is misunderstood when it is classified under the headings of "corruption" and "malpractice", as historians still persist in doing. Cicero was an honest governor of Cilicia in 51 and 50 B.C., so that at the end of his term he had earned only the legitimate profits of office. They amounted to 2,200,000 sesterces, more than treble the figure of 600,000 he himself once mentioned (*Stoic Paradoxes* 49) to illustrate an annual income that could permit a life of luxury. We are faced with something structural in the society. [Finley 1985, p. 55]

Who, then, operated commerce and industry? According to Veyne (1961), it was an occupation heavily undertaken by freedmen—former slaves who, incidentally, bore a social stigma for life. Indeed, according to this writer, slavery may have represented the one avenue for advancement for someone from the lower classes. A clever (and handsome) member of the lower orders might deliberately arrange to be sold into slavery to a wealthy and powerful master.[3] Then, with luck, skill, and drive, he would grow close to his owner, perhaps managing his financial affairs (and sometimes engaging in some homosexual activity with him). The master then gained cachet, after a suitable period, by granting freedom to the slave, setting him up with a fortune of his own. The freedmen, apparently not atypically, invested their financial stakes in commerce, hoping to multiply them sufficiently to enable them to retire in style to the countryside, thereafter investing primarily in land and loans in imitation of the upper classes.

Finally, regarding the Romans' attitude to the promotion of technology and productivity, Finley makes much of the "clear, almost total, divorce between science and practice" (1965, p. 32). He goes on to cite Vitruvius's monumental work on architecture and technology, in whose 10 books he finds only a single and trivial reference to means of saving effort and increasing productivity. Finley then reports the following story:

> There is a story, repeated by a number of Roman writers, that a man—characteristically unnamed—invented unbreakable glass and demonstrated it to Tiberius in anticipation of a great reward. The emperor asked the inventor whether anyone shared his secret and was assured that there was no one else; whereupon his head was promptly removed, lest, said Tiberius, gold be reduced to the value of mud. I have no opinion about the truth of this story, and it is only a story. But is it not interesting that neither the elder Pliny nor Petronius nor the historian Dio Cassius was troubled by the point that the inventor turned to the emperor for a reward, instead of turning to an investor for capital with which to put his invention into production?[4] . . . We must

---

[3] Stefano Fenoaltea comments that he knows no documented cases in which this occurred and that it was undoubtedly more common to seek advancement through adoption into an upper-class family.

[4] To be fair to Finley, note that he concludes that it is *not* really interesting. North and Thomas (1973, p. 3) make a similar point about Harrison's invention of the ship's chronometer in the eighteenth century (as an instrument indispensable for the determination of longitude). They point out that the incentive for this invention was a large governmental prize rather than the prospect of commercial profit, presumably because of the absence of effective patent protection.

> remind ourselves time and again that the European experi-
> ence since the late Middle Ages in technology, in the econ-
> omy, and in the value systems that accompanied them, was
> unique in human history until the recent export trend com-
> menced. Technical progress, economic growth, productivity,
> even efficiency have not been significant goals since the be-
> ginning of time. So long as an acceptable life-style could be
> maintained, however that was defined, other values held the
> stage. [1985, p. 147]

The bottom line, for our purposes, is that the Roman reward system, although it offered wealth to those who engaged in commerce
and industry, offset this gain through the attendant loss in prestige.
Economic effort "was neither the way to wealth nor its purpose. Cato's
gods showed him a number of ways to get more; but they were all
political and parasitical, the ways of conquest and booty and usury;
labour was not one of them, not even the labour of the entrepreneur"
(Finley 1965, p. 39).

B. *Medieval China*

In China, as in many kingdoms of Europe before the guarantees of
the Magna Carta and the revival of towns and their acquisition of
privileges, the monarch commonly claimed possession of all property
in his territories. As a result, particularly in China, when the sovereign was in financial straits, confiscation of the property of wealthy
subjects was entirely in order. It has been claimed that this led those
who had resources to avoid investing them in any sort of visible capital
stocks, and that this, in turn, was a substantial impediment to economic expansion (see Balazs 1964, p. 53; Landes 1969, pp. 46–47;
Rosenberg and Birdzell 1986, pp. 119–20; Jones 1987, chap. 5).

In addition, imperial China reserved its most substantial rewards in
wealth and prestige for those who climbed the ladder of imperial
examinations, which were heavily devoted to subjects such as Confu-
cian philosophy and calligraphy. Successful candidates were often
awarded high rank in the bureaucracy, high social standing denied to
anyone engaged in commerce or industry, even to those who gained
great wealth in the process (and who often used their resources to
prepare their descendants to contend via the examinations for a position in the scholar bureaucracy). In other words, the rules of the game
seem to have been heavily biased against the acquisition of wealth *and
position* through Schumpeterian behavior. The avenue to success lay
elsewhere.

Because of the difficulty of the examinations, the mandarins
(scholar-officials) rarely succeeded in keeping such positions in their

own families for more than two or three generations (see Marsh 1961, p. 159; Ho 1962, chap. 4 and appendix). The scholar families devoted enormous effort and considerable resources to preparing their children through years of laborious study for the imperial examinations, which, during the Sung dynasty, were held every 3 years, and only several hundred persons in all of China succeeded in passing them each time (E. A. Kracke, Jr. in Liu and Golas [1969, p. 14]). Yet, regularly, some persons not from mandarin families also attained success through this avenue (see, e.g., Marsh [1961] and Ho [1962] for evidence on social mobility in imperial China).

Wealth was in prospect for those who passed the examination and who were subsequently appointed to government positions. But the sources of their earnings had something in common with those of the Romans:

> Corruption, which is widespread in all impoverished and backward countries (or, more exactly, throughout the pre-industrial world), was endemic in a country where the servants of the state often had nothing to live on but their very meager salaries. The required attitude of obedience to superiors made it impossible for officials to demand higher salaries, and in the absence of any control over their activities from below it was inevitable that they should purloin from society what the state failed to provide. According to the usual pattern, a Chinese official entered upon his duties only after spending long years in study and passing many examinations; he then established relations with protectors, incurred debts to get himself appointed, and then proceeded to extract the amount he had spent on preparing himself for his career from the people he administered—and extracted both principal and interest. The degree of his rapacity would be dictated not only by the length of time he had had to wait for his appointment and the number of relations he had to support and of kin to satisfy or repay, but also by the precariousness of his position. [Balazs 1964, p. 10]

Enterprise, on the other hand, was not only frowned on, but may have been subjected to impediments deliberately imposed by the officials, at least after the fourteenth century A.D.; and some historians claim that it was true much earlier. Balazs tells us of

> the state's tendency to clamp down immediately on any form of private enterprise (and this in the long run kills not only initiative but even the slightest attempts at innovation), or, if it did not succeed in putting a stop to it in time, to take over

and nationalize it. Did it not frequently happen during the course of Chinese history that the scholar-officials, although hostile to all inventions, nevertheless gathered in the fruits of other people's ingenuity? I need mention only three examples of inventions that met this fate: paper, invented by a eunuch; printing, used by the Buddhists as a medium for religious propaganda; and the bill of exchange, an expedient of private businessmen. [P. 18]

As a result of recurrent intervention by the state to curtail the liberty and take over any accumulated advantages the merchant class had managed to gain for itself, "the merchant's ambition turned to becoming a scholar-official and investing his profits in land" (p. 32).

C. The Earlier Middle Ages

Before the rise of the cities and before monarchs were able to subdue the bellicose activities of the nobility, wealth and power were pursued primarily through military activity. Since land and castles were the medieval forms of wealth most highly valued and most avidly sought after, it seems reasonable to interpret the warring of the barons in good part as the pursuit of an economic objective. For example, during the reign of William the Conqueror (see, e.g., Douglas 1964), there were frequent attempts by the barons in Normandy and neighboring portions of France to take over each other's lands and castles. A prime incentive for William's supporters in his conquest of England was their obvious aspiration for lands.[5] More than that, violent means also served to provide more liquid forms of income (captured treasure), which the nobility used to support both private consumption and investment in military plant and equipment, where such items could not easily be produced on their own lands and therefore had to be purchased from others. In England, with its institution of primogeniture (the exclusive right of the eldest son to inherit his father's estate), younger sons who chose not to enter the clergy often had no socially acceptable choice other than warfare as a means to make their fortunes, and in some cases they succeeded spectacularly. Thus note the case of William Marshal, fourth son of a minor noble, who rose

---

[5] The conquest has at least two noteworthy entrepreneurial sides. First, it involved an innovation, the use of the stirrup by the Normans at Hastings that enabled William's warriors to use the same spear to impale a series of victims with the force of the horse's charge, rather than just tossing the spear at the enemy, much as an infantryman could. Second, the invasion was an impressive act of organization, with William having to convince his untrustworthy allies that they had more to gain by joining him in England than by staying behind to profit from his absence by trying to grab away his lands as they had tried to do many times before.

through his military accomplishments to be one of the most powerful and trusted officials under Henry II and Richard I, and became one of the wealthiest men in England (see Painter 1933).

Of course, the medieval nobles were not purely economic men. Many of the turbulent barons undoubtedly enjoyed fighting for its own sake, and success in combat was an important avenue to prestige in their society. But no modern capitalist is a purely economic man either. What I am saying here is that warfare, which was of course pursued for a variety of reasons, was *also* undertaken as a primary source of economic gain. This is clearly all the more true of the mercenary armies that were the scourge of fourteenth-century France and Italy.

Such violent economic activity, moreover, inspired frequent and profound innovation. The introduction of the stirrup was a requisite for effective cavalry tactics. Castle building evolved from wooden to stone structures and from rectangular to round towers (which could not be made to collapse by undermining their corners). Armor and weaponry became much more sophisticated with the introduction of the crossbow, the longbow, and, ultimately, artillery based on gunpowder. Military tactics and strategy also grew in sophistication. These innovations can be interpreted as contributions of military entrepreneurs undertaken at least partly in pursuit of private economic gains.

This type of entrepreneurial undertaking obviously differs vastly from the introduction of a cost-saving industrial process or a valuable new consumer product. An individual who pursues wealth through the forcible appropriation of the possessions of others surely does not add to the national product. Its net effect may be not merely a transfer but a net reduction in social income and wealth.[6]

---

[6] In saying all this, I must not be interpreted as taking the conventional view that warfare is an unmitigated source of impoverishment of any economy that unquestionably never contributes to its prosperity. Careful recent studies have indicated that matters are more complicated (see, e.g., Milward 1970; Olson 1982). Certainly the unprecedented prosperity enjoyed afterward by the countries on the losing side of the Second World War suggests that warfare need not always preclude economic expansion, and it is easy to provide earlier examples. The three great economic leaders of the Western world preceding the United States—Italy in the thirteenth–sixteenth centuries, the Dutch Republic in the seventeenth and eighteenth, and Great Britain in the eighteenth and nineteenth—each attained the height of their prosperity after periods of enormously costly and sometimes destructive warfare. Nevertheless, the wealth gained by a medieval baron from the adoption of a novel bellicose technique can hardly have contributed to economic growth in the way that resulted from adoption of a new steelmaking process in the nineteenth century or the introduction of a product such as the motor vehicle in the twentieth.

D. The Later Middle Ages

By the end of the eleventh century the rules of the game had changed from those of the Dark Ages. The revival of the towns was well under way. They had acquired a number of privileges, among them protection from arbitrary taxation and confiscation and the creation of a labor force by granting freedom to runaway serfs after a relatively brief residence (a year and a day) in the towns. The free-enterprise turbulence of the barons had at least been impeded by the church's pacification efforts: the peace and the (later) truce of God in France, Spain, and elsewhere; similar changes were taking place in England (see, e.g., Cowdrey [1970]; but Jones [1987, p. 94] suggests that some free-enterprise military activity by the barons continued in England through the reigns of the earlier Tudors in the sixteenth century). All this subsequently "gave way to more developed efforts to enforce peace by the more organized governments of the twelfth century" (Brooke 1964, p. 350; also p. 127). A number of activities that were neither agricultural nor military began to yield handsome returns. For example, the small group of architect-engineers who were in charge of the building of cathedrals, palaces, bridges, and fortresses could live in great luxury in the service of their kings.

But, apparently, a far more common source of earnings was the water-driven mills that were strikingly common in France and southern England by the eleventh century, a technological innovation about which more will be said presently. An incentive for such technical advances may have been the monopoly they conferred on their owners rather than any resulting improvement in efficiency. Such monopoly rights were alike sought and enforced by private parties (Bloch 1935, pp. 554–57; Brooke 1964, p. 84) and by religious organizations (see below).

The economic role of the monks in this is somewhat puzzling—the least clear-cut part of our story.[7] The Cistercian abbeys are generally assigned a critical role in the promotion of such technological advances. In some cases they simply took over mills that had been constructed by others (Berman 1986, p. 89). But the Cistercians improved them, built many others, and vastly expanded their use; at

---

[7] Bloch (1935) notes that the monasteries had both the capital and the large number of consumers of flour necessary to make the mills profitable. In addition, they were less likely than lay communities to undergo military siege, which, Bloch notes, was (besides drought and freezing of the waterways) one of the main impediments to adoption of the water mill, since blocking of the waterway that drove the mill could threaten the besieged population with starvation (pp. 550–53).

least some writers (e.g., Gimpel 1976, pp. 3–6) seem to suggest that the Cistercians were the spearhead of technological advance.

Historians tell us that they have no ready explanation for the entrepreneurial propensities of this monastic order. (See, e.g., Brooke [1964, p. 69] and also a personal communication to me from Constance Berman. Ovitt [1987, esp. pp. 142–47] suggests that this may all have been part of the twelfth-century monastic drive to reduce or eliminate manual labor in order to maximize the time available for the less onerous religious labors—a conclusion with which Bloch [1935, p. 553] concurs.) But the evidence suggests strongly that avid entrepreneurs they were. They accumulated vast tracts of land; the sizes of their domesticated animal flocks were enormous by the standards of the time; their investment rates were remarkable; they sought to exercise monopoly power, being known, after the erection of a water mill, to seek legal intervention to prevent nearby residents from continuing to use their animal-powered facilities (Gimpel 1976, pp. 15–16); they were fierce in their rivalrous behavior and drive for expansion, in the process not sparing other religious bodies—not even other Cistercian houses. There is a "record of pastoral expansionism and monopolies over access established by the wealthiest Cistercian houses . . . at the expense of smaller abbeys and convents . . . effectively pushing out all other religious houses as competitors" (Berman 1986, p. 112).

As with early capitalists, the asceticism of the monks, by keeping down the proportion of the monastery's output that was consumed, helped to provide the resources for levels of investment extraordinary for the period (pp. 40, 83). The rules of the game appear to have offered substantial economic rewards to exercise of Cistercian entrepreneurship. The order obtained relatively few large gifts, but instead frequently received support from the laity and from the church establishment in the form of exemptions from road and river tolls and from payment of the tithe. This obviously increased the *marginal* yield of investment, innovation, and expenditure of effort, and the evidence suggests the diligence of the order in pursuing the resulting opportunities. Their mills, their extensive lands, and their large flocks are reported to have brought scale economies and extraordinary financial returns (chap. 4). Puritanical, at least in earlier years, in their self-proclaimed adherence to simplicity in personal lifestyle while engaged in dedicated pursuit of wealth, they may perhaps represent an early manifestation of elements of "the Protestant ethic." But whatever their motive, the reported Cistercian record of promotion of technological progress is in diametric contrast to that of the Roman empire.

E. Fourteenth Century

The fourteenth century brought with it a considerable increase in military activity, notably the Hundred Years' War between France and England. Payoffs, surely, must have tilted to favor more than before inventions designed for military purposes. Cannons appeared as siege devices and armor was made heavier. More imaginative war devices were proposed: a windmill-propelled war wagon, a multibarreled machine gun, and a diving suit to permit underwater attacks on ships. A pervasive business enterprise of this unhappy century of war was the company of mercenary troops—the *condottiere*—who roamed Europe, supported the side that could offer the most attractive terms, and in lulls between fighting, when unemployment threatened, wandered about thinking up military enterprises of their own, at the expense of the general public (Gimpel 1976, chap. 9; see also McNeill 1969, pp. 33–39). Clearly, the rules of the game—the system of entrepreneurial rewards—had changed, to the disadvantage of productive entrepreneurship.

F. Early Rent Seeking

Unproductive entrepreneurship can also take less violent forms, usually involving various types of rent seeking, the type of (possibly) unproductive entrepreneurship that seems most relevant today. Enterprising use of the legal system for rent-seeking purposes has a long history. There are, for example, records of the use of litigation in the twelfth century in which the proprietor of a water-driven mill sought and won a prohibition of use in the vicinity of mills driven by animal or human power (Gimpel 1976, pp. 25–26). In another case, the operators of two dams, one upstream of the other, sued one another repeatedly at least from the second half of the thirteenth century until the beginning of the fifteenth, when the downstream dam finally succeeded in driving the other out of business as the latter ran out of money to pay the court fees (pp. 17–20).

In the upper strata of society, rent seeking also gradually replaced military activity as a prime source of wealth and power. This transition can perhaps be ascribed to the triumph of the monarchies and the consequent imposition of law and order. Rent-seeking entrepreneurship then took a variety of forms, notably the quest for grants of land and patents of monopoly from the monarch. Such activities can, of course, sometimes prove to contribute to production, as when the recipient of land given by the monarch uses it more efficiently than the previous owner did. But there seems to have been nothing in the structure of the land-granting process that ensured even a tendency toward transfer to more productive proprietors, nor was the individual who sought such grants likely to use as an argument in favor of his suit the claim that he was likely to be the more productive user (in terms of, say, the expected net value of its agricultural output).

Military forms of entrepreneurship may have experienced a renaissance in England in the seventeenth century with the revolt against Charles I. How that may have changed the structure of rewards to entrepreneurial activity is suggested by Hobsbawm (1969), who claims that at the end of the seventeenth century the most affluent merchants earned perhaps three times as much as the richest "master manufacturers."[8] But, he reports, the wealthiest noble families probably had incomes more than 10 times as large as those of the rich merchants. The point in this is that those noble families, according to Hobsbawm, were no holdovers from an ancient feudal aristocracy; they were, rather, the heirs of the Roundheads (the supporters of the parliamentary, or puritan, party) in the then-recent Civil War (pp. 30–32). On this view, once again, military activity would seem to have become the entrepreneur's most promising recourse.

But other historians take a rather different view of the matter. Studies reported in Thirsk (1954) indicate that ultimately there was little redistribution of property as the result of the Civil War and the restoration. Rather it is noted that in this period the "patrician élites depended for their political power and economic prosperity on royal charters and monopolies rather than on talent and entrepreneurial initiative" (Stone 1985, p. 45). In this interpretation of the matter, it was rent seeking, not military activity, that remained the prime source of wealth under the restoration.

By the time the eighteenth-century industrial revolution ("the" industrial revolution) arrived, matters had changed once again. According to Ashton (1948, pp. 9–10), grants of monopoly were in good part "swept away" by the Monopolies Act of 1624, and, we are told by Adam Smith (1776), by the end of the eighteenth century they were rarer in England than in any other country. Though industrial activity continued to be considered somewhat degrading in places in which industry flourished, notably in England during the industrial revolution there was probably a difference in degree. Thus Lefebvre (1947, p. 14) reports that "at its upper level the [French] nobility . . . were envious of the English lords who enriched themselves in bourgeois

---

[8] The evidence indicates that the wealth of affluent families in Great Britain continues to be derived preponderantly from commerce rather than from industry. This contrasts with the record for the United States, where the reverse appears to be true (see Rubinstein 1980, pp. 22–23, 59–60).

ways," while in France "the noble 'derogated' or fell into the common mass if [like Mirabeau] he followed a business or profession" (p. 11). (See, however, Schama [1989], who tells us that "even a cursory examination of the eighteenth-century French economy . . . reveals the nobility deeply involved in finance, business and industry—certainly as much as their British counterparts. . . . In 1765 a royal edict officially removed the last formal obstacles to their participation in trade and industry" [p. 118].) In England, primogeniture, by forcing younger sons of noble families to resort to commerce and industry, apparently was imparting respectability to these activities to a degree that, while rather limited, may have rarely been paralleled before.

The central point of all the preceding discussion seems clear—perhaps, in retrospect, self-evident. If entrepreneurship is the imaginative pursuit of position, with limited concern about the means used to achieve the purpose, then we can expect changes in the structure of rewards to modify the nature of the entrepreneur's activities, sometimes drastically. The rules of the game can then be a critical influence helping to determine whether entrepreneurship will be allocated predominantly to activities that are productive or unproductive and even destructive.

IV. Does the Allocation between Productive and Unproductive Entrepreneurship Matter Much?

We come now to the third proposition of this article.

PROPOSITION 3. The allocation of entrepreneurship between productive and unproductive activities, though by no means the only pertinent influence, can have a profound effect on the innovativeness of the economy and the degree of dissemination of its technological discoveries.

It is hard to believe that a system of payoffs that moves entrepreneurship in unproductive directions is not a substantial impediment to industrial innovation and growth in productivity. Still, history permits no test of this proposition through a set of anything resembling controlled experiments, since other influences *did*, undoubtedly, also play important roles, as the proposition recognizes. One can only note what appears to be a remarkable correlation between the degree to which an economy rewarded productive entrepreneurship and the vigor shown in that economy's innovation record.

Historians tell us of several industrial "near revolutions" that occurred before *the* industrial revolution of the eighteenth century that are highly suggestive for our purposes (Braudel [1986, 3:542–56]; for a more skeptical view, see Coleman [1956]). We are told that two of the incipient revolutions never went anywhere, while two of them were rather successful in their fashion. I shall report conclusions of some leading historians on these episodes, but it should be recognized by the reader that many of the views summarized here have been disputed in the historical literature, at least to some degree.

A. Rome and Hellenistic Egypt

My earlier discussion cited ancient Rome and its empire as a case in which the rules did not favor productive entrepreneurship. Let us compare this with the evidence on the vigor of innovative activity in that society. The museum at Alexandria was the center of technological innovation in the Roman empire. By the first century B.C., that city knew of virtually every form of machine gearing that is used today, including a working steam engine. But these seem to have been used only to make what amounted to elaborate toys. The steam engine was used only to open and close the doors of a temple.

The Romans also had the water mill. This may well have been the most critical pre-eighteenth-century industrial invention because (outside the use of sails in transportation by water) it provided the first significant source of power other than human and animal labor: "it was able to produce an amount of concentrated energy beyond any other resource of antiquity" (Forbes 1955, 2:90). As steam did in more recent centuries, it offered the prospect of providing the basis for a leap in productivity in the Roman economy, as apparently it actually did during the eleventh, twelfth, and thirteenth centuries in Europe. Yet Finley (1965, pp. 35–36), citing White (1962), reports that "though it was invented in the first century B.C., is was not until the third century A.D. that we find evidence of much use, and not until the fifth and sixth of general use. It is also a fact that we have no evidence at all of its application to other industries [i.e., other than grinding of grain] until the very end of the fourth century, and then no more than one solitary and possibly suspect reference . . . to a marble-slicing machine near Trier."

Unfortunately, evidence of Roman technical stagnation is only spotty, and, further, some historians suggest that the historical reports give inadequate weight to the Roman preoccupation with agricultural improvement relative to improvement in commerce or manufacture. Still, the following quotation seems to summarize the weight of opinion: "Historians have long been puzzled as to why the landlords of the Middle Ages proved so much more enterprising than the landlords of the Roman Empire, although the latter, by and large, were much better educated, had much better opportunities for making technical and scientific discoveries if they had wished to do so"

(Brooke 1964, p. 88). It seems at least plausible that some part of the explanation is to be found in the ancient world's rules of the game, which encouraged the pursuit of wealth but severely discouraged its pursuit through the exercise of productive entrepreneurship.[9]

B. Medieval China

The spate of inventions that occurred in ancient China (before it was conquered by the barbarian Yuan dynasty in 1280) constituted one of the earliest potential revolutions in industry. Among the many Chinese technological contributions, one can list paper, (perhaps) the compass, waterwheels, sophisticated water clocks, and, of course, gunpowder. Yet despite the apparent prosperity of the Sung period (960–1270) (see, e.g., Liu and Golas 1969), at least some historians suggest that none of this spate of inventions led to a flowering of *industry*[10] as distinguished from commerce and some degree of general prosperity. And in China too, as we have seen, the rules did not favor productive entrepreneurship. Balazs (1964, p. 53) concludes that

> what was chiefly lacking in China for the further development of capitalism was not mechanical skill or scientific aptitude, nor a sufficient accumulation of wealth, but scope for individual enterprise. There was no individual freedom and no security for private enterprise, no legal foundation for rights other than those of the state, no alternative investment other than landed property, no guarantee against being penalized by arbitrary exactions from officials or against intervention by the state. But perhaps the supreme inhibiting

[9] It has been suggested by historians (see, e.g., Bloch 1935, p. 547) that an abundance of slaves played a key role in Roman failure to use the water mill widely. However, this must imply that the Romans were not efficient wealth seekers. As the cliometric literature has made clear, the cost of maintaining a slave is not low and certainly is not zero, and slaves are apt not to be efficient and dedicated workers. Thus if it had been efficient to replace human or animal power by the inanimate power of the waterways, failure to do so would have cut into the wealth of the slaveholder, in effect saddling him with the feeding of unproductive persons or keeping the slaves who turned the mills from other, more lucrative, occupations. Perhaps Roman landowners *were* fairly unsophisticated in the management of their estates, as Finley (1985, pp. 108–16) suggests, and, if so, there may be some substance to the hypothesis that slavery goes far to account for the failure of water mills to spread in the Roman economy.

[10] Also, as in Rome, none of this was associated with the emergence of a systematic body of science involving coherent theoretical structure and the systematic testing of hypotheses on the basis of experiment or empirical observation. Here, too, the thirteenth-century work of Bishop Grosseteste, William of Henley, and Roger Bacon was an early step toward that unique historical phenomenon—the emergence of a systematic body of science in the West in, say, the sixteenth century (see Needham 1956).

factor was the overwhelming prestige of the state bureaucracy, which maimed from the start any attempt of the
bourgeoisie to be different, to become aware of themselves
as a class and fight for an autonomous position in society.
Free enterprise, ready and proud to take risks, is therefore
quite exceptional and abnormal in Chinese economic history.

C. Slow Growth in the "Dark Ages"

An era noted for its slow growth occurred between the death of
Charlemagne (814) and the end of the tenth century. Even this period
was not without its economic advances, which developed slowly, including the beginnings of the agricultural improvements that attended the introduction of the horseshoe, harness, and stirrup, the
heavy plow, and the substitution of horsepower for oxen, which may
have played a role in enabling peasants to move to more populous
villages further from their fields (see White 1962, p. 39 ff.). But, still,
it was probably a period of significantly slower growth than the industrial revolution of the eleventh–thirteenth centuries (Gimpel 1976),
about which more will be said presently. We have already seen that
this was a period in which military violence was a prime outlet for
entrepreneurial activity. While this can hardly pretend to be *the* explanation of the relative stagnation of the era, it is hard to believe that it
was totally unimportant.

D. The "High Middle Ages"

A good deal has already been said about the successful industrial
revolution (and the accompanying commercial revolution sparked by
inventions such as double-entry bookkeeping and bills of exchange
[de Roover 1953]) of the late Middle Ages, whose two-century duration makes it as long-lived as our own (see Carus-Wilson 1941; White
1962; Gimpel 1976).
   Perhaps the hallmark of this industrial revolution was that remarkable source of productive power, the water mills, that covered the
countryside in the south of England and crowded the banks of the
Seine in Paris (see, e.g., Gimpel 1976, pp. 3–6; Berman 1986, pp. 81–
89). The mills were not only simple grain-grinding devices but accom-
plished an astonishing variety of tasks and involved an impressive
variety of mechanical devices and sophisticated gear arrangements.
They crushed olives, ground mash for beer production, crushed cloth
for papermaking, sawed lumber, hammered metal and woolens (as
part of the "fulling" process—the cleansing, scouring, and pressing of

woven woolen goods to make them stronger and to bring the threads closer together), milled coins, polished armor, and operated the bellows of blast furnaces. Their mechanisms entailed many forms of ingenuity. Gears were used to translate the vertical circular motion of the efficient form of the waterwheel into the horizontal circular motion of the millstone. The cam (a piece attached, say, to the axle of the waterwheel, protruding from the axle at right angles to its axis of rotation) served to lift a hammer and to drop it repeatedly and automatically (it was apparently known in antiquity, but may not have been used with waterwheels). A crank handle extending from the end of the axle transformed the circular motion of the wheel into the back and forth (reciprocating) motion required for sawing or the operation of bellows. The most sophisticated product of all this mechanical skill and knowledge was the mechanical clock, which appeared toward the end of the thirteenth century. As White (1962, p. 129) sums up the matter, "the four centuries following Leonardo, that is, until electrical energy demanded a supplementary set of devices, were less technologically engaged in discovering basic principles than in elaborating and refining those established during the four centuries before Leonardo."[11]

In a period in which agriculture probably occupied some 90 percent of the population, the expansion of industry in the twelfth and thirteenth centuries could not by itself have created a major upheaval in living standards.[12] Moreover, it has been deduced from what little we know of European gross domestic product per capita at the beginning of the eighteenth century that its average growth in the preceding six or seven centuries must have been very modest, since if the poverty of that later time had represented substantial growth from

[11] As was already noted, science and scientific method also began to make an appearance with contributions such as those of Bishop Grosseteste and Roger Bacon. Walter of Henley championed controlled experiments and observation over recourse to the opinions of ancient authorities and made a clear distinction between economic and engineering efficiency in discussing the advisability of substituting horses for oxen. Bacon displayed remarkable foresight when he wrote, circa 1260, that "machines may be made by which the largest ships, with only one man steering them, will be moved faster than if they were filled with rowers; wagons may be built which will move with incredible speed and without the aid of beasts; flying machines can be constructed in which a man . . . may beat the air with wings like a bird . . . machines will make it possible to go to the bottom of seas and rivers" (as quoted in White [1962, p. 134]).

[12] But then, much the same was true of the first half century of "our" industrial revolution, which, until the coming of the railways, was centered on the production of cotton that perhaps constituted only some 7–8 percent of national output (Hobsbawm 1969, p. 68). Initially, the eighteenth-century industrial revolution was a very minor affair, at least in terms of investment levels and contributions to output and to growth in productivity (perhaps 0.3 percent per year) (see Landes 1969, pp. 64–65; Feinstein 1978, pp. 40–41; Williamson 1984).

eleventh-century living standards, much of the earlier population would surely have been condemned to starvation.

Still, the industrial activity of the twelfth and thirteenth centuries was very substantial. By the beginning of the fourteenth century, according to Gimpel (1976), 68 mills were in operation on less than one mile of the banks of the Seine in Paris, and these were supplemented by floating mills anchored to the Grand Pont. The activity in metallurgy was also considerable—sufficient to denude much of Europe of its forests and to produce a rise in the price of wood that forced recourse to coal (Nef [1934]; other historians assert that this did not occur to any substantial degree until the fifteenth or sixteenth century, with some question even about those dates; see, e.g., Coleman [1975, pp. 42–43]). In sum, the industrial revolution of the twelfth and thirteenth centuries was a surprisingly robust affair, and it is surely plausible that improved rewards to industrial activity had something to do with its vigor.

E. The Fourteenth-Century Retreat

The end of all this period of buoyant activity in the fourteenth century (see the classic revisionist piece by Lopez [1969] as well as Gimpel [1976, chap. 9]) has a variety of explanations, many of them having no connection with entrepreneurship. For one thing, it has been deduced by study of the glaciers that average temperatures dropped, possibly reducing the yield of crops (though recent studies indicate that the historical relation between climatic changes and crop yields is at best ambiguous) and creating other hardships. The plague returned and decimated much of the population. In addition to these disasters of nature, there were at least two pertinent developments of human origin. First, the church clamped down on new ideas and other manifestations of freedom. Roger Bacon himself was put under constraint.[13] The period during which new ways of thinking brought rewards and status was apparently ended. Second, the fourteenth century included the first half of the devastating Hundred Years' War. It is implausible that the associated renewal of rewards to military enterprise played no part in the economic slowdown.

F. Remark on "Our" Industrial Revolution

It need hardly be added, in conclusion, that *the* industrial revolution that began in the eighteenth century and continues today has brought

---

[13] The restraints imposed by the church had another curious effect: they apparently made bathing unfashionable for centuries. Before then, bathhouses had been popular as centers for social and, perhaps, sexual activity; but by requiring separation of the sexes and otherwise limiting the pleasures of cleanliness, the church undermined the inducements for such sanitary activities (see Gimpel 1976, pp. 87–92).

to the industrialist and the businessperson generally a degree of wealth and a respect probably unprecedented in human history. The fact that this period yielded an explosion of output at least equally unprecedented is undoubtedly attributable to a myriad of causes that can probably never be discovered fully and whose roles can never be disentangled. Yet the continued association of output growth with high financial and respectability rewards to productive entrepreneurship is surely suggestive, even if it can hardly be taken to be conclusive evidence for proposition 3, which asserts that the allocation of entrepreneurship *does* really matter for the vigor and innovativeness of an economy.

V. On Unproductive Avenues for Today's Entrepreneur: A Delicate Balance

Today, unproductive entrepreneurship takes many forms. Rent seeking, often via activities such as litigation and takeovers, and tax evasion and avoidance efforts seem now to constitute the prime threat to productive entrepreneurship. The spectacular fortunes amassed by the "arbitrageurs" revealed by the scandals of the mid-1980s were *sometimes*, surely, the reward of unproductive, occasionally illegal but entrepreneurial acts. Corporate executives devote much of their time and energy to legal suit and countersuit, and litigation is used to blunt or prevent excessive vigor in competition by rivals. Huge awards by the courts, sometimes amounting to billions of dollars, can bring prosperity to the victor and threaten the loser with insolvency. When this happens, it must become tempting for the entrepreneur to select his closest advisers from the lawyers rather than the engineers. It induces the entrepreneur to spend literally hundreds of millions of dollars for a single legal battle. It tempts that entrepreneur to be the first to sue others before those others can sue him. (For an illuminating quantification of some of the social costs of one widely publicized legal battle between two firms, see Summers and Cutler [1988].)

Similarly, taxes can serve to redirect entrepreneurial effort. As Lindbeck (1987, p. 15) has observed, "the problem with high-tax societies is not that it is impossible to become rich there, but that it is difficult to do so by way of productive effort in the ordinary production system." He cites as examples of the resulting reallocation of entrepreneurship " 'smart' speculative financial transactions without much (if any) contribution to the productive capacity of the economy" (p. 15) as well as "illegal 'business areas' such as drug dealing" (p. 25).

In citing such activities, I do not mean to imply either that rent-seeking activity has been expanding in recent decades or that takeover bids or private antitrust suits are always or even preponderantly unproductive. Rather, I am only suggesting where current rent-seeking activities are likely to be found, that is, where policy designers should look if they intend to divert entrepreneurial talents into more productive channels.

The main point here is to note that threats of takeovers are sometimes used as a means to extract "greenmail" and that recourse to the courts as a means to seek to preserve rents through legally imposed impediments to competition does indeed occur, and to suggest that it is no rare phenomenon. This does, then, become an attraction for entrepreneurial talent whose efforts are thereby channeled into unproductive directions. Yet, to the extent that takeovers discipline inefficient managements and that antitrust intervention sometimes is legitimate and sometimes contributes to productivity, it would seem that it will not be easy to change the rules in a way that discourages allocation of entrepreneurial effort into such activities, without at the same time undermining the legitimate role of these institutions. Some promising proposals have been offered, but this is not a suitable place for their systematic examination. However, a few examples will be reported in the following section.

VI. Changes in the Rules and Changes in Entrepreneurial Goals

A central point in this discussion is the contention that if reallocation of entrepreneurial effort is adopted as an objective of society, it is far more easily achieved through changes in the rules that determine relative rewards than via modification of the goals of the entrepreneurs and prospective entrepreneurs themselves. I have even gone so far as to use the same terms to characterize those goals in the very different eras and cultures referred to in the discussion. But it would be ridiculous to imply that the attitudes of a wealth-seeking senator in Rome, a Sung dynasty mandarin, and an American industrialist of the late nineteenth century were all virtually identical. Still, the evidence suggests that they had more in common than might have been expected by the casual observer. However, even if it were to transpire that they really diverged very substantially, that would be of little use to the designer of policy who does not have centuries at his or her disposal and who is notoriously ineffective in engendering profound changes in cultural influences or in the structure of preferences. It is for this reason that I have chosen to take entrepreneurial goals as given and to emphasize modification in the structure of the rewards to different activities as the more promising line of investigation.

This suggests that it is necessary to consider the process by which those rules are modified in practice, but I believe that answers to even this more restricted question are largely beyond the powers of the historians, the sociologists, and the anthropologists into whose domains it falls. One need only review the disputatious literature on the influences that led to the revival of trade toward the end of the early Middle Ages to see how far we still are from anything resembling firm answers. Exogenous influences such as foreign invasions or unexpected climatic changes can clearly play a part, as can developments within the economy. But the more interesting observation for our purposes is the fact that it is easy to think of measures that *can* change these rules quickly and profoundly.[14]

For example, the restrictions on royal grants of monopolies imposed by Parliament in the Statute of Monopolies are said to have reduced substantially the opportunities for rent seeking in seventeenth- and eighteenth-century England and may have moved reluctant entrepreneurs to redirect their efforts toward agricultural improvement and industry. Even if it did not succeed to any substantial extent in reallocation of the efforts of an unchanged body of entrepreneurs from one of those types of activity to the other, if it increased failure rates among the rent seekers while not impeding others who happened to prefer productive pursuits, the result might have been the same. Similarly, tax rules can be used to rechannel entrepreneurial effort. It has, for instance, been proposed that takeover activity would be reoriented substantially in directions that contribute to productivity rather than impeding it by a "revenue-neutral" modification in capital gains taxes that increases rates sharply on assets held for short periods and decreases them considerably for assets held, say, for 2 years or more. A change in the rules that requires a plaintiff firm in a private antitrust suit to bear both parties' legal costs if the defendants are found not to be guilty (as is done in other countries) promises to reduce the frequency with which such lawsuits are used in an attempt to hamper effective competition.

As has already been said, this is hardly the place for an extensive discussion of the design of rational policy in the arena under consideration. The objective of the preceding brief discussion, rather, has been to suggest that there are identifiable means by which the rules of the game can be changed effectively and to illustrate these means concretely, though hardly attempting to offer any generalizations about their character. Certainly, the few illustrations that have just been offered should serve to confirm that there exist (in principle)

---

[14] Of course, that still leaves open the critical metaquestion, How does one go about changing the society's value system so that it will *want* to change the rules? But that is not the issue with which I am grappling here, since I see no basis on which the economist can argue that society *ought* to change its values. Rather, I am positing a society whose values lead it to favor productivity growth and am examining which instruments promise to be most effective in helping it to pursue this goal.

testable means that promise to induce entrepreneurs to shift their attentions in productive directions, *without any major change in their ultimate goals*. The testability of such hypotheses indicates that the discussion is no tissue of tautologies, and the absence of references to the allocability of entrepreneurship turned up in extensive search of the literature on the entrepreneur suggests that it was not entirely self-evident.

VII. Concluding Comment

There is obviously a good deal more to be said about the subject; however, enough material has been presented to indicate that a minor expansion of Schumpeter's theoretical model to encompass the determinants of the *allocation* of entrepreneurship among its competing uses can enrich the model considerably and that the hypotheses that have been associated with the model's extension here are not without substance, even if none of the material approaches anything that constitutes a formal test of a hypothesis, much less a rigorous "proof." It is also easy to confirm that each of the hypotheses that have been discussed clearly yields some policy implications.

Thus clear guidance for policy is provided by the main hypothesis (propositions 1–3) that the rules of the game that specify the relative payoffs to different entrepreneurial activities play a key role in determining whether entrepreneurship will be allocated in productive or unproductive directions and that this can significantly affect the vigor of the economy's productivity growth. After all, the prevailing laws and legal procedures of an economy are prime determinants of the profitability of activities such as rent seeking via the litigative process. Steps such as deregulation of the airlines or more rational antitrust rules can do a good deal here.

A last example can, perhaps, nail down the point. The fact that Japan has far fewer lawyers relative to population and far fewer lawsuits on economic issues is often cited as a distinct advantage to the Japanese economy, since it reduces at least in part the quantity of resources devoted to rent seeking. The difference is often ascribed to national character that is said to have a cultural aversion to litigiousness. This may all be very true. But closer inspection reveals that there are also other influences. While in the United States legal institutions such as trebled damages provide a rich incentive for one firm to sue another on the claim that the latter violated the antitrust laws, in Japan the arrangements are very different. In that country any firm undertaking to sue another on antitrust grounds must first apply for permission from the Japan Fair Trade Commission. But such permission is rarely given, and, once denied, there is no legal avenue for appeal.

The overall moral, then, is that we do not have to wait patiently for slow cultural change in order to find measures to redirect the flow of entrepreneurial activity toward more productive goals. As in the illustration of the Japanese just cited, it may be possible to change the rules in ways that help to offset undesired institutional influences or that supplement other influences that are taken to work in beneficial directions.

References

Abramovitz, Moses. *Thinking about Growth, and Other Essays of Economic Growth and Welfare.* New York: Cambridge Univ. Press, 1989.

Ashton, Thomas S. *The Industrial Revolution, 1760–1830.* London: Oxford Univ. Press, 1948.

Balazs, Etienne. *Chinese Civilization and Bureaucracy: Variations on a Theme.* New Haven, Conn.: Yale Univ. Press, 1964.

Berman, Constance H. "Medieval Agriculture, the Southern French Countryside, and the Early Cistercians: A Study of Forty-three Monasteries." *Trans. American Philosophical Soc.* 76, pt. 5 (1986).

Bloch, Marc. "Avènement et conquêtes du moulin a eau." *Annales d'Histoire Économique et Sociale* 7 (November 1935): 538–63.

Braudel, Fernand. *Civilization and Capitalism, 15th–18th Century.* Vols. 2, 3. New York: Harper and Row, 1986.

Brooke, Christopher N. L. *Europe in the Central Middle Ages, 962–1154.* London: Longman, 1964.

Carus-Wilson, Eleanora M. "An Industrial Revolution of the Thirteenth Century." *Econ. Hist. Rev.* 11, no. 1 (1941): 39–60.

Coleman, Donald C. "Industrial Growth and Industrial Revolutions." *Economica* 23 (February 1956): 1–22.

———. *Industry in Tudor and Stuart England.* London: Macmillan (for Econ. Hist. Soc.), 1975.

Cowdrey, H. E. J. "The Peace and the Truce of God in the Eleventh Century." *Past and Present,* no. 46 (February 1970), pp. 42–67.

Dasgupta, Partha. "Patents, Priority and Imitation or, the Economics of Races and Waiting Games." *Econ. J.* 98 (March 1988): 66–80.

de Roover, Raymond. "The Commercial Revolution of the 13th Century." In *Enterprise and Secular Change: Readings in Economic History,* edited by Frederic C. Lane and Jelle C. Riemersma. London: Allen and Unwin, 1953.

Douglas, David C. *William the Conqueror: The Norman Impact upon England.* Berkeley: Univ. California Press, 1964.

Feinstein, C. H. "Capital Formation in Great Britain." In *The Cambridge Economic History of Europe,* vol. 8, pt. 1, edited by Peter Mathias and M. M. Postan. Cambridge: Cambridge Univ. Press, 1978.

Finley, Moses I. "Technical Innovation and Economic Progress in the Ancient World." *Econ. Hist. Rev.* 18 (August 1965): 29–45.

———. *The Ancient Economy.* 2d ed. London: Hogarth, 1985.

Forbes, Robert J. *Studies in Ancient Technology.* Leiden: Brill, 1955.

Gimpel, Jean. *The Medieval Machine: The Industrial Revolution of the Middle Ages.* New York: Holt, Reinhart and Winston, 1976.

Ho, Ping-Ti. *The Ladder of Success in Imperial China, 1368–1911.* New York: Columbia Univ. Press, 1962.

Hobsbawm, Eric J. *Industry and Empire from 1750 to the Present Day.* Harmondsworth: Penguin, 1969.

Jones, Eric L. *The European Miracle: Environments, Economies, and Geopolitics in the History of Europe and Asia.* Cambridge: Cambridge Univ. Press, 1987.

Landes, David S. *The Unbound Prometheus: Technological Change and Industrial Development in Western Europe from 1750 to the Present.* New York: Cambridge Univ. Press, 1969.

Lefebvre, Georges. *The Coming of the French Revolution, 1789.* Princeton, N.J.: Princeton Univ. Press, 1947.

Lindbeck, Assar. "The Advanced Welfare State." Manuscript. Stockholm: Univ. Stockholm, 1987.

Liu, James T. C., and Golas, Peter J., eds. *Change in Sung China: Innovation or Renovation?* Lexington, Mass.: Heath, 1969.

Lopez, Robert S. "Hard Times and Investment in Culture." In *The Renaissance: A Symposium.* New York: Oxford Univ. Press (for Metropolitan Museum of Art), 1969.

McNeill, William H. *History of Western Civilization.* Rev. ed. Chicago: Univ. Chicago Press, 1969.

Marsh, Robert M. *The Mandarins: The Circulation of Elites in China, 1600–1900.* Glencoe, Ill.: Free Press, 1961.

Milward, Alan S. *The Economic Effects of the Two World Wars on Britain.* London: Macmillan (for Econ. Hist. Soc.), 1970.

Murphy, Kevin M.; Shleifer, Andrei; and Vishny, Robert. "The Allocation of Talent: Implications for Growth." Manuscript. Chicago: Univ. Chicago, 1990.

Needham, Joseph. "Mathematics and Science in China and the West." *Science and Society* 20 (Fall 1956): 320–43.

Nef, John U. "The Progress of Technology and the Growth of Large-Scale Industry in Great Britain, 1540–1640." *Econ. Hist. Rev.* 5 (October 1934): 3–24.

North, Douglass C., and Thomas, Robert Paul. *The Rise of the Western World: A New Economic History.* Cambridge: Cambridge Univ. Press, 1973.

Olson, Mancur. *The Rise and Decline of Nations: Economic Growth, Stagflation, and Social Rigidities.* New Haven, Conn.: Yale Univ. Press, 1982.

Ovitt, George, Jr. *The Restoration of Perfection: Labor and Technology in Medieval Culture.* New Brunswick, N.J.: Rutgers Univ. Press, 1987.

Painter, Sidney. *William Marshal: Knight-Errant, Baron, and Regent of England.* Baltimore: Johns Hopkins Press, 1933.

Robinson, Joan. *The Economics of Imperfect Competition.* London: Macmillan, 1933.

Rosenberg, Nathan, and Birdzell, L. E., Jr. *How the West Grew Rich: The Economic Transformation of the Industrial World.* New York: Basic Books, 1986.

Rubinstein, W. D., ed. *Wealth and the Wealthy in the Modern World.* London: Croom Helm, 1980.

Schama, Simon. *Citizens: A Chronicle of the French Revolution.* New York: Knopf, 1989.

Schumpeter, Joseph A. *The Theory of Economic Development.* Leipzig: Duncker and Humblot, 1912. English ed. Cambridge, Mass.: Harvard Univ. Press, 1934.

Smith, Adam. *An Inquiry into the Nature and Causes of the Wealth of Nations.* 1776. Reprint. New York: Random House (Modern Library), 1937.

Stone, Lawrence. "The Bourgeois Revolution of Seventeenth-Century England Revisited." *Past and Present,* no. 109 (November 1985), pp. 44–54.

Summers, Lawrence, and Cutler, David. "Texaco and Pennzoil Both Lost Big." *New York Times* (February 14, 1988).

Thirsk, Joan. "The Restoration Land Settlement." *J. Modern Hist.* 26 (December 1954): 315–28.

Veblen, Thorstein. *The Theory of Business Enterprise.* New York: Scribner, 1904.

Veyne, Paul. "Vie de trimalcion." *Annales: Économies, Societés, Civilisations* 16 (March/April 1961): 213–47.

White, Lynn T., Jr. *Medieval Technology and Social Change.* Oxford: Clarendon, 1962.

Williamson, Jeffrey G. "Why Was British Growth So Slow during the Industrial Revolution?" *J. Econ. Hist.* 44 (September 1984): 687–712.

[26]

THE ALLOCATION OF TALENT:
IMPLICATIONS FOR GROWTH*

KEVIN M. MURPHY
ANDREI SHLEIFER
ROBERT W. VISHNY

A country's most talented people typically organize production by others, so they can spread their ability advantage over a larger scale. When they start firms, they innovate and foster growth, but when they become rent seekers, they only redistribute wealth and reduce growth. Occupational choice depends on returns to ability and to scale in each sector, on market size, and on compensation contracts. In most countries, rent seeking rewards talent more than entrepreneurship does, leading to stagnation. Our evidence shows that countries with a higher proportion of engineering college majors grow faster; whereas countries with a higher proportion of law concentrators grow more slowly.

INTRODUCTION

When they are free to do so, people choose occupations that offer them the highest returns on their abilities. The ablest people then choose occupations that exhibit increasing returns to ability, since increasing returns allow "superstars" to earn extraordinary returns on their talent [Rosen, 1981]. In these occupations, being slightly more talented enables a person to win a tournament, to capture a prize, to be promoted, or otherwise to gain a lot by being slightly better than the next person. For example, since everyone wants to listen to the best singer, she can earn a lot more than a marginally inferior singer, especially with records and tapes. In occupations with increasing returns to ability, absolute advantage is the critical determinant of pay.

Some people have strong comparative advantage from natural talent for particular activities, such as singing, painting, or playing basketball. These people can earn vastly more by practicing these occupations than any others. But other people do not have such great specialized abilities, but at the same time possess great intelligence, energy, or other generally valuable traits. Such people

*We are grateful to Robert Barro, William Baumol, Olivier Blanchard, Avinash Dixit, Steve Kaplan, Anne Krueger, Paul Romer, Lawrence Summers, and Robert Waldmann for helpful comments. We also appreciate the support from the National Science Foundation and the Sloan and Bradley Foundations.

can become one of the best in many occupations, unlike the best singer or basketball player. They can become entrepreneurs, government officials, lawyers, speculators, clerics, etc. All these occupations exhibit increasing returns to ability, in that having marginally greater talent leads to a significantly higher payoff. The ablest people then choose occupations when returns to being a superstar are the highest. In this paper we discuss what determines their choices, and then argue theoretically and empirically that the allocation of talent has significant effects on the growth rate of an economy.

What determines the attractiveness of an occupation to talent? First, the size of the market is crucial: being a superstar in a large market pays more than being a superstar in a small market and so will draw general talent. A person of great general athletic ability, for example, would rather be the tenth best tennis player than the first best volleyball player, since far fewer people would pay to watch him play volleyball. Second, attractive activities have weak diminishing returns to scale. A superstar would want to spread her ability advantage over as large a share of the market as possible, but is limited by constraints on her time, physical ability, and more generally the size of the firm she can run. A surgeon can operate, at most, sixteen hours a day, unless of course she can teach others to use the procedure and reap a return on their time. In contrast, an inventor who can embody her idea in a product overcomes the constraints on her physical time, but is still limited by the size of the firm she can run. Because of stronger diminishing returns to scale, even the most successful doctors do not make as much money as successful entrepreneurs. The faster returns to scale in an activity diminish, the less attractive it is to a person of high ability.

Finally, the compensation contract—how much of the rents on their talent the superstars can capture—determines the sector's attractiveness to talent. For example, if returns to innovation are not protected by patents and cannot be captured by an entrepreneur, entrepreneurship becomes less attractive. When individual output is difficult to measure or is not sufficiently rewarded when measured, talented people are underpaid. Teamwork without attribution is unattractive to superstars, as is horizontal equity. The more of the rents on her talent a superstar can keep, the more likely she is to join a sector.

In different countries and time periods, talented people chose occupations in which it was the most attractive to be a superstar.

THE ALLOCATION OF TALENT   505

When markets in a country are large and when people can easily organize firms and keep their profits, many talented people become entrepreneurs. Examples of such countries might be Great Britain during the Industrial Revolution, the United States in the late nineteenth and early twentieth centuries, and some East Asian countries today. In many other countries talented people do not become entrepreneurs, but join the government bureaucracy, army, organized religion, and other rent-seeking [Tullock, 1967; Krueger, 1974] activities because these sectors offer the highest prizes. In Mandarin China, Medieval Europe, and many African countries in this century, government service, with the attendant ability to solicit bribes and dispose of tax revenue for the benefit of one's family and friends, was the principal career for the ablest people in the society [Baumol, 1990]. In Latin America and parts of Africa today as well as in many other countries through history, the most talented people often joined the army as a way to access the resources from their own countries (as well as from foreign conquests). In eighteenth century France, the best and the brightest also became rent seekers. The great chemist Lavoisier's main occupation was tax collecting, and Talleyrand was a bishop with a large tax income despite his prodigious entrepreneurial skills shown when he escaped to the United States after the French revolution. These examples show that in fact talent is often general rather than occupation-specific, and therefore its allocation is governed not just by comparative advantage but also by returns to absolute advantage in different sectors.

Which activities the most talented people choose can have significant effects on the allocation of resources. When talented people become entrepreneurs, they improve the technology in the line of business they pursue, and as a result, productivity and income grow. In contrast, when they become rent seekers, most of their private returns come from redistribution of wealth from others and not from wealth creation. As a result, talented people do not improve technological opportunities, and the economy stagnates. Landes [1969] believes that the differential allocation of talent is one of the reasons why England had the Industrial Revolution in the eighteenth century but France did not. In more recent times the allocation of talent to the rent-seeking sectors might be the reason for stagnation in much of Africa and Latin America, for slow growth in the United States, and for success of newly industrializing countries where these sectors are smaller.

The allocation of talent to rent seeking is damaging for several reasons. First, as the rent-seeking sectors expand, they absorb labor and other resources and so reduce income. The enormous size of government bureaucracies in some LDCs illustrates this effect. Second, the tax imposed by the rent-seeking sector on the productive sector reduces incentives to produce, and therefore also reduces income. A striking example of this is the difficulty of starting a firm in today's Peru described in De Soto's [1989] *The Other Path*. Finally, if the most talented people become rent seekers, the ability of entrepreneurs is lower, and therefore the rate of technological progress and of growth is likely to be lower. The flow of some of the most talented people in the United States today into law and financial services might then be one of the sources of our low productivity growth. When rent-seeking sectors offer the ablest people higher returns than productive sectors offer, income and growth can be much lower than possible.

The sharp distinction we draw between productive and rent-seeking activities is exaggerated. Pure entrepreneurial activities raise current income because resources are used more efficiently, contribute to growth because technology is improved, and take profits away from competitors. Or take the case of traders in financial markets. Trading probably raises efficiency since it brings security prices closer to their fundamental values. It might even indirectly contribute to growth if more efficient financial markets reduce the cost of capital. But the main gains from trading come from the transfer of wealth to the smart traders from the less astute who trade with them out of institutional needs or outright stupidity. Even though efficiency improves, transfers are the main source of returns in trading. The same is true for some kinds of law, such as divorce and contract law, the army and the police in some countries, and to some extent organized religion. Although few activities are pure rent seeking or pure efficiency-improving, the general point remains: talent goes into activities with the highest private returns, which need not have the highest social returns.

Olson [1982] also addresses the relationship between rent seeking and growth. His idea is that "cumulative distortions" due to rent seeking reduce growth. Olson does not deal with the allocation of talent. Magee, Brock, and Young [1989] discuss rent seeking in great detail and present a model of the allocation of labor between rent seeking and production. Like us, they present some evidence that lawyers have a detrimental effect on growth, using different data. They do not focus on the allocation of talent. Baumol [1990] makes the same basic point as we do that entrepreneurship can be "productive" or "unproductive," and the allocation of people between the two activities depends on the relative returns and provides many interesting historical examples. The ideas in our paper were developed independently. In particular, Baumol does not discuss the role of increasing returns to ability in explaining why rent seeking and productive entrepreneurship are in fact competing for the very same people, who are the ablest in the society.

Section I of the paper presents a one-sector model of entrepreneurship and growth and discusses the increasing returns to ability that draw the ablest people into entrepreneurship. We abstract from alternative uses of high ability to stress the importance for growth of allocating talent into the entrepreneurial activities. Section II then considers the allocation of talent between two sectors with increasing returns to ability. It also explains why talented people may be drawn into sectors that experience an improvement in technology or an increase in demand, making growth in these sectors self-sustaining. Section III introduces pure rent seeking as an alternative activity with increasing returns to ability and shows when the ablest people switch to rent seeking. We also discuss the implications of rent seeking for growth. Section IV presents some evidence on the effect of lawyers and engineers on growth. Section V concludes.

I. Entrepreneurship and Growth: A One-Sector Model

This section presents a model of entrepreneurship and growth. The model is based on Lucas [1978] and has been previously used by Kuhn [1988]. In the model high-ability people become entrepreneurs and hire low-ability people in their firms. When they do, they improve the current productive techniques. As the improvement of the technique is imitated, everyone's productivity rises, and income grows. In the model we set up, the rate of technological progress and of income growth is determined by the ability of the ablest person engaged in entrepreneurship. The model thus illustrates the importance for growth of allocating the ablest people to the productive sector of the economy.

We assume that there is a distribution of abilities in the population, with the support of $[1,a]$ and the density function $f(A)$. We measure a person's ability by how much he can improve the technology he operates. Ability in our model is unidimensional: we do not address the allocation of people to jobs because of particular aptitude in those jobs. Each person is alive for one period, and the distribution of abilities is the same each period.

We assume that there is only one good in the economy, which is produced by many firms. Each firm is organized by an entrepreneur. If a firm is organized by an entrepreneur with ability A, its profits are given by

$$(1) \qquad y = s \cdot A \cdot F(H) - w \cdot H,$$

where s is the common state of technology, F is the constant over time production function, H is the aggregate human capital (ability) of all the workers employed by this entrepreneur, w is the workers' wage, and the price of the good is normalized to be 1. We can think of $s \cdot A$ as the productivity parameter of the firm, where s is the public level of technology and A is the entrepreneur's contribution. The entrepreneur takes the current state of technology s and the wage w as given. F is a standard concave production function.

The profit function (1) builds in our key assumptions. The abler entrepreneurs can earn more than proportionately to their ability higher profits from operating the same technology as the less able entrepreneurs. This is because their output and therefore revenues rise with their ability but their costs do not. There is, therefore, an increasing return to ability. This assumption makes it more attractive for the ablest people to become entrepreneurs, for two reasons. First, they can earn more than proportionately higher profits for a fixed size of the firm H. Second, the abler expand the size of the firm so that they can spread their ability advantage over a larger scale. The concavity of the production function F determines how strongly the returns diminish with scale, and so measures how much one can benefit from high ability.

The first-order condition with respect to H is given by

$$(2) \qquad s \cdot A \cdot F'(H) = w,$$

so the abler people, obviously, run larger firms. In the extreme case of constant returns to scale, the ablest entrepreneur captures the whole market. In the case of diminishing returns, his ability to expand is limited, but he still runs a larger firm.

Each person in the model lives for one period. He decides whether to become an entrepreneur or a worker. If he becomes an entrepreneur, he picks the size of his firm $H(A)$ according to (2) and then earns a profit as in (1). If he becomes a worker, he earns

THE ALLOCATION OF TALENT   509

$w \cdot A$. We have the increasing return to ability in entrepreneurship since someone with double the ability earns double the income as a worker, but more than double the income as an entrepreneur for a fixed firm size. In fact, what matters here is that returns to ability in entrepreneurship *relative* to other work be increasing.

A person becomes an entrepreneur when

$$(3) \qquad s \cdot A \cdot F(H(A)) - w \cdot H(A) > w \cdot A,$$

and a worker otherwise. The abler people become entrepreneurs in equilibrium, and the less able ones become workers. There is a cutoff ability A^* such that those with higher ability become entrepreneurs and those with lower ability become workers.

The demand for workers by entrepreneurs must equal the supply of workers:

$$(4) \qquad \int_1^{A^*} Af(A)dA = \int_{A^*}^a H(A) f(A)dA.$$

Equation (4) describes how the real wage adjusts. If there are too many workers and too few entrepreneurs, there is excess supply of labor, and so the best workers want to switch to entrepreneurship. Conversely, if there are too few workers, the wage is high, and the marginal entrepreneurs would rather become workers.

To specify the growth model, we need to describe the evolution of technology s. We assume that the state of technology today is the state last period times the ability of the ablest entrepreneur last period:

(5) $s(t) = s(t - 1) \cdot$ (maximum ability of an entrepreneur at $t - 1$).

This assumption says that last period's best practice becomes common knowledge this period and is therefore accessible to any entrepreneur, who can then improve on it. The constantly improving technology generates permanent growth in our model. In addition, the assumption that the entrepreneur does not capture the future returns from his innovation builds in the standard externality, as in Arrow [1962]. As in Arrow, this assumption generates inefficiency in some versions of the model.

The model we present does not distinguish between innovation and running firms. In fact, they are distinct activities and in principle can be done by different people. In this case, how the returns from innovation and managing are divided can influence the willingness of people to become innovators. This is one of the examples of how contracting can influence the allocation of talent. Historical experience, especially from the British Industrial Revolution, shows that the two functions (innovation and management) have very often been combined in the same person, suggesting that the problem of splitting the rewards is substantial enough to overcome the forces of comparative advantage.

This model is essentially static, since agents take the state of technology as given. The equilibrium is easy to describe. Each period all agents with ability above A^* become entrepreneurs, and those below A^* become workers. The profit function and the income of workers are homogenous in s and w, which means that A^* is constant over time. The same part of the distribution becomes entrepreneurs each period. Technology, wages, profits, and income per capita all grow at the constant rate $a - 1$ given by the ability of the best entrepreneur. This person determines the rate of growth of this economy.

The allocation of resources in this economy is first-best efficient. This means both that the growth rate is efficient, and that the cutoff ability level A^* between entrepreneurs and workers is efficient. The latter result obtains because both the social and the private product of the least able entrepreneur is exactly equal to his wage as a worker. The efficiency of the growth rate is very special: it is a consequence of having only one sector and not having any effort supply decisions by entrepreneurs that might be distorted. At the same time the flavor of the result that more talented people are allocated to entrepreneurial activities with beneficial consequences for growth is going to be preserved in more general specifications.

This simple model illustrates several general principles. First, the ablest people in the society enter occupations where they can take advantage of increasing returns to ability. In this model there is only one such activity—entrepreneurship—and so the question of *which* sector with increasing returns to ability to enter does not arise. When the ablest people become entrepreneurs, they organize production and improve the available techniques. Second, the growth rate of the economy is determined by the ability of the entrepreneurs. It is therefore essential for growth that the ablest people turn to entrepreneurship. Next, we examine the implications of introducing an alternative sector that competes for the talents of the entrepreneurs.

II. A Two-Sector Model

In this section we discuss the allocation of talent between sectors. The determinant of attractiveness of a sector that we model formally is the extent of diminishing returns to scale. Nonetheless, in interpreting the results, it is important to remember that market size and contracts also affect the allocation of talent.

Suppose that there are two sectors rather than one. Each sector has its own concave production function, but they are identical in all the other respects. Suppose also that preferences are Cobb-Douglas, so that the same fixed share of income is spent on a given good each period. Denote the share of income spent on good 1 by b. For this model we can prove the following:

PROPOSITION. If the production function for good 1 is more elastic than that for good 2, then each period the ablest people down to some constant over time threshold ability level A_1 become entrepreneurs in sector 1, the next range of ability down to a constant over time A_2 become entrepreneurs in sector 2, and the least able people become workers.

The ablest people are all drawn into the sector with less diminishing returns (higher elasticity of output with respect to labor), because they run larger firms there and so can spread their ability advantage over a larger scale. The quasi rents accruing to talent are higher in that sector. Productivity in each sector grows at the rate given by the ability of the ablest entrepreneur in that sector, which of course is higher in sector 1. The real wage grows at the rate $g = a^b \cdot A_1^{1-b}$, which is the weighted average of productivity growth rates in the two sectors. At the same time the price of good 1 falls over time relative to that of good 2, since technological progress is faster in sector 1. The fall in the relative price of good 1 exactly offsets the increase in the relative productivity, so that in equilibrium revenues and profits in each sector grow at the same rate g as do the wages. Because revenues, profits, and wages all grow at the rate g, the cutoff ability levels A_1 and A_2 between sectors remain constant over time.

There is a stark inefficiency in this model. At the social optimum the ablest person becomes an entrepreneur in one sector, and the second ablest person in the other sector. That way both sectors' productivity grows at the maximum possible rate. In equilibrium, however, the second ablest person would rather be in

512   *QUARTERLY JOURNAL OF ECONOMICS*

the sector with less rapidly diminishing returns, since the first one captures only a small part of that sector, and there is still more money for the ablest person to make in this than in the other sector. Each person is quasi-rent seeking, and quasi rents on ability are higher in sector 1. As a result, all the ablest people become entrepreneurs in sector 1, where the externality from all of them other than the ablest is zero. In contrast, the person generating the externality in sector 2 is much less able, and as a result that sector's productivity grows at a much lower rate. The pursuit of quasi rents by the able people unbalances growth of the two sectors, with the result that one grows inefficiently slowly.

This inefficiency is much more general than our model, in which only the ablest person determines the rate of technological progress, would suggest. Obviously, the result that people of comparable ability bunch into the same sector does not depend on the form of externality. So unless such bunching generates the maximum externality, there will be an inefficiency. We see no reason why bunching of people of comparable ability into the same sector is optimal, so many types of externality generate an inefficiency. For example, if the externality depends on the *average* or *total* ability of entrepreneurs in a given sector, it may still be efficient to have very similar distributions of abilities in the two sectors. One can argue perhaps that there is an agglomeration economy of people with comparable abilities working in the same sector, and that the pace of innovation depends on that. In this case, one would want many innovators of comparable ability working together. But again, there is no reason to think that the number of people needed to take advantage of the agglomeration economy is as large as this model would put into the same sector, or that the agglomeration economy is the highest in the sector where the most talented people go. The equilibrium we have is inefficient, except by coincidence. Of course, the inefficiency is smaller when individuals have comparative advantage at working in particular sectors or when there are increasing returns to agglomeration of talent.

The ablest people tend to flow into a sector where they can spread their ability advantage over the largest scale. In the model this means that they run the largest firms in the economy, a prediction that seems patently false. We have assumed in this model that the compensation arrangements enable the ablest people to collect full quasi rents from their talents (though none of the future rents because of perfect imitation). If this is not the case in some sectors, the ablest people would move into sectors where they *collect* the most even if firms are smaller. The reasons that people cannot collect full quasi rents have to do with imperfect contracting and problems of allocating output to individuals. The allocation is then determined by the compensation contract, and not just by technology.

In fact, differences in contracts between industries are probably as important or more important than physical diminishing returns to scale. In industries where it is easy to identify and reward talent, it might be possible to pay the able people the true quasi rents on their ability and so to attract them. This is probably true in industries at the early stages of their development, where able people can start and run firms rather than work as part of a team. Perhaps the reason the auto industry attracted enormous talent when it started but attracts much less talent now is that talent was easier to identify and reward then. Starting one's own company is obviously the most direct way to capitalize on one's talent without sharing the quasi rents. Talent will then flow into industries where it is easy to start a firm, which would be newer and less capital-intensive industries. Also, talent will flow into sectors with less joint production, so it is easier to assign credit and reward contributions. Finally, the most talented people will not go into activities where horizontal equity and other ethical considerations prevent them from capturing the quasi rents on their ability. Meritocracy is an obvious attractor of talent.

We emphasize that what matters for the allocation of talent is the relative rewards in different sectors. If all sectors tax quasi rents to ability equally, then obviously the compensation contract will not make any of them more attractive. This logic also suggests that there are two ways for a particular sector to be attractive to the high-ability people. The first is for this sector to have attractive compensation contracts; the second is for the other sectors to have unattractive contracts. For example, the reason that more talented people might become investors in Japanese manufacturing might not be that they are particularly well rewarded there, but rather that compensation in law or government is even less attractive. Alternative opportunities are thus a key determinant of the allocation of talent.

The Cobb-Douglas assumption on preferences gives the result that the allocation of talent across sectors is constant over time. If we relaxed this assumption, the allocation of talent would change over time, and the analysis would become more complicated. The

Cobb-Douglas assumption also has the unfortunate implication that the *level* of technology in a sector does not affect who goes into it. There is thus no sense in which the most talented people are attracted to "hot" sectors that experience a technology shock or a price rise (although of course the sector to which the best people go grows faster). To analyze how the allocation of talent might change in response to such shocks, in order to explain, for example, the U. S. experience in the 1970s and 1980s, we need to depart from the simple framework. Below we consider one plausible framework and look at the static allocation problem rather than a growth model.

Consider a one-period model with two sectors with prices p_1 and $p_2 < p_1$ and identical production functions. In our current model this could not be an equilibrium since all entrepreneurs would rather be in sector 1 than in sector 2. But suppose that there are only a fixed number of firms, n_1 in sector 1 and n_2 in sector 2, and there is no free entry. Then entrepreneurs bid for the opportunity to run the firms, and the owners of these firms earn quasi rents on their fixed factor. The equilibrium is easy to describe. The ablest n_1 people go into sector 1, the next n_2 go into sector 2, and the rest become workers. Let the ability of the least able entrepreneur in sector 1 be A_1 and that of the least able entrepreneur in sector 2 be A_2. The entrepreneur with ability A_2 earns $w \cdot A_2$, and the rest of his profits go to the fixed factor in sector 2. Similarly, the least able entrepreneur in sector 1 earns what the ablest entrepreneur in sector 2 does, and the rest of his profits go to the fixed factor in sector 1.

In this equilibrium the abler people enter the hotter sector with the higher price, and free entry does not make them indifferent between sectors. The reason that the abler people end up in the hotter sector is that they bid more for the fixed factors because it is worth more to them to gain access to these factors. The fixed factors get the rents of the least able people gaining access to them, just as in Ricardo, and the abler people earn quasi rents on their ability as well.

We describe this extension for two reasons. First, it explains why the implausible feature of our basic model, namely that the level of technology does not affect the allocation of talent, is not really a problem. More importantly, this extension helps explain some episodes of why changes in particular sectors can attract a different type of talent into that sector. Suppose that there is a technological improvement in some sector, say financial services, and so the output per unit of ability in that sector rises sharply.

Suppose also that demand is elastic and that the number of firms in that sector is fixed in the short run. In this case, we might see that the ability of people moving into this sector rises, since they are able to profit the most working in a scarce number of firms. By doing so, they would pay the most to the owners of those firms for the privilege of working there. Without free entry we would see that some of the benefits of the productivity increase would go to the firm owners, and some to the new employees who can produce the most.

When the ability of the most talented employees joining a sector rises, so does technological progress in that sector. This illustrates an important positive feedback in this model: when a sector with elastic demand experiences a positive technology shock, it attracts better talent, and so technology improves further. Such continuation of the original innovation or other rent-creating shock through attraction of talent describes growth of many industries [Porter, 1990]. This model might explain, for example, the enormous technological progress in the U. S. financial services in the 1980s, after deregulation.

III. Rent Seeking and Growth

In this section we introduce rent seeking into the one-sector growth model. We have described rent seeking in detail in the introduction; here we simply take it to be a tax on the profits of the productive sector. Specifically, we assume that when an entrepreneur earns a profit y, $T \cdot y$ is taken away by rent seekers through bribes, taxes, fees, and other costs of doing business in a rent-seeking society. We assume that T is exogenous. One might argue in contrast that the amount of rent seeking is a function of the level of development, so that T is a function of the level of income or the stability of government [Olson, 1982]. For simplicity, we assume that there is no productive component to rent seeking; it is therefore not a completely accurate description of financial services, law, or organized religion. We assume that rent seekers tax profits rather than all income, including wages, to simplify the analysis. This assumption leads to a distortion of allocation of people between entrepreneurship and work, but to no distortion in the size of the firm once a person becomes an entrepreneur. Of course, some taxes, such as the famous growth tax in India which imposes a penalty on revenue increases beyond a certain rate,

516   *QUARTERLY JOURNAL OF ECONOMICS*

distort the size of the firm as well [Little, Mazumdar, and Page, 1987].

The rent-seeking technology is also subject to increasing returns to ability and diminishing returns to scale. We assume that the rents collected by a person with ability A are given by

(6)
$$R = \frac{A \cdot G(H) \cdot T \cdot Y}{\int\limits_{\text{rent seekers}} AG(H)f(A)\,dA} - w \cdot H,$$

where H is the total human capital or ability of others that this rent seeker employs, Y is the aggregate profits of the entrepreneurs, and $G(H)$ is the concave production function in the rent-seeking sector. In this specification the *share* of total gross rents $T \cdot Y$ collected by the rent seeker of ability A is proportional to $A \cdot G(H)$. Total gross rents collected by the rent seekers thus automatically add up to the total revenues lost by the entrepreneurs. We assume for simplicity that there is no technological progress in rent seeking. This assumption allows us to keep the model homogeneous in the state of technology s. The rent-seeking technology, like the productive technology, allows abler people to earn higher profits at a fixed size H as well as to expand H to maximize profits. In this respect, rent seeking is similar to entrepreneurship.

Each person now has three choices: entrepreneurship, work, and rent seeking, and he picks the most attractive option. If it is one of the former two, he also sets the size of the firm. In equilibrium the wage adjusts until the combined demand for workers by the productive and the rent-seeking sector is equal to the supply of workers:

(7) $\int\limits_{\text{rent seekers}} H(A)f(A)\,dA + \int\limits_{\text{entrepreneurs}} H(A)f(A)\,dA = \int\limits_{\text{workers}} Af(A)\,dA.$

We consider two cases. In the first the production function (F) for output is more elastic with respect to H than the production function (G) for rent seeking; in the second it is the other way around. The results are similar to those of the two-sector model. In the first case the ablest people go into the productive sector where firms are the largest, the next group goes into rent seeking, and the least able become workers. The cutoff ability levels are constant because the model is homogeneous in the level of technology s and so the allocation decision is the same each period. In this case the level of technology s, productivity, wages, profits, and aggregate returns to rent seekers all grow at the rate a—the ability of the ablest person in the economy. The growth rate is optimal since this person is an entrepreneur. However, the level of income is lower than it would be without rent seeking. First, some workers are allocated to the rent-seeking rather than productive sector, and as a result output is forgone. Put differently, demand for workers in the rent-seeking sector drives up wages and so reduces equilibrium employment in the productive sector. Second, the less able entrepreneurs become rent seekers, and so do not organize production. Although this does not lead to the reduction in the growth rate, it leads to a once-and-for-all reduction in the level of income.

The situation is worse when the production function for rent seeking is more elastic and so the ablest people become rent seekers since firms (correcting for compensation contracts) are the largest in that sector. The next group becomes entrepreneurs, and the least able are workers. Now output grows at a lower rate than a, since the ablest entrepreneur is no longer the ablest person available. We now have three distortions from rent seeking. It absorbs labor; it distorts the choice of least able entrepreneurs who now become workers; and finally, it turns the ablest people, who are pivotal for growth, into rent seekers. The model thus captures the crucial point that rent seeking can reduce growth (and not just the level of income) because it attracts potential innovators and entrepreneurs. As the ability of the ablest person who becomes an entrepreneur falls, so does the growth rate.

This model makes several interesting predictions. First, suppose that the tax rate T on entrepreneurial profits falls. This fall can correspond to the improvement in the property rights as suggested by North and Thomas [1973], and also to a reduction in corruption or in taxes. The first direct effect of this fall is to reduce the size of the rent-seeking sector. Workers move out of this sector and into production. Also, in the case where the ablest people are entrepreneurs, the ablest rent seekers move out and become entrepreneurs since incentives for this activity have improved. Although the growth rate in this case remains at a, the level of income jumps as resources move from rent seeking into entrepreneurship and production.

The case where the ablest persons were rent seekers is different. As the tax rate T falls, the least able rent seekers become entrepreneurs, and so the ability of the best entrepreneur rises. As a result, not only does the level of income jump, but the growth rate increases also as the person determining the growth rate of technology is now more talented. This result demonstrates perhaps the most important cost of a large rent-seeking sector (high T). By drawing people out of entrepreneurship and into rent seeking, it reduces the growth rate of the economy permanently. The result also demonstrates how a one-time reduction in the extent of rent seeking can permanently raise the growth rate of the economy. Barro [1991] finds that countries with smaller government consumption relative to GDP grow faster, which is what our theory would predict if government consumption was a measure of the tax rate T.

In this model, changes in the tax rate T do not affect whether the ablest person is an entrepreneur or a rent seeker. The reason is that the ablest person has the strongest comparative advantage at being in the sector that he is in, and so is the last to switch. For example, as T rises, there is more entry into the rent-seeking sector, but the entry is by people who have the least attachment to other sectors. This entry drives down the returns without affecting the allocation of inframarginal people. Where the ablest person goes is determined in the model only by the relative elasticity of the two production functions, or how fast the diminishing returns set in the two activities. Since the career choice of the ablest people determines the growth rate, how fast returns to scale diminish in entrepreneurship and in rent seeking is one of the key determinants of growth.

More generally, the allocation of talent between entrepreneurship and rent seeking is determined by market size and by the nature of contracts as well as by firm size (diminishing returns to scale) in the two types of activities. The puzzle that must be addressed is why, in most countries and times, talented individuals choose rent-seeking activities, and the entrepreneurial choice is a fairly rare exception. Rent seeking seems to have an inherent advantage as a career choice. Table I summarizes some characteristics of countries and markets that influence the allocation of talent; in the following we try to discuss why the choice is so often rent seeking.

Rent-seeking activities are attractive when the potential amounts to be taken are large. When the "official" rent-seeking sectors such as the government, religion, or the army are big and powerful, the resources (and power) that a talented person gets by joining them and succeeding are large. As a result, these sectors attract talent. In such countries the official institutions have

TABLE I
FACTORS FAVORING RENT SEEKING AND ENTREPRENEURSHIP

	Factors making rent seeking an attractive choice	Factors making entrepreneurship an attractive choice
Market size	Large resources go to "official" rent-seeking sectors, such as the government, army, or religion. Poorly defined property rights make wealth accessible to "unofficial" rent seekers. Large wealth that is up for grabs, especially relative to smaller goods markets.	Large markets for goods. Good communications and transportation that facilitate trade.
Firm size	Substantial authority and discretion of rent seekers (such as government officials, army, etc.) enable them to collect large sums unhindered by law or custom.	Easy entry and expansion, few diminishing returns in operations, access to capital markets.
Contracts	Ability to keep a large portion of collected rents. In firms, observability of output that yields appropriate rewards.	Clear property rights, patent protection. No expropriation of rents by rent seekers. Ability to start firms to collect quasi rents on talent.

well-defined property rights over private wealth. Because the "official" rent-seeking institutions are and have been extremely powerful in most countries, this type of rent seeking often attracts talent.

Countries with poorly defined property rights also attract talent into rent seeking, since success at redefining these property rights brings high rewards. Rent seeking pays because a lot of wealth is up for grabs. In these cases, rent seeking is "unofficial" and takes the form of bribery, theft, or litigation. In the United States today, lobbying to influence the Congress and litigation are examples of this activity, which is so attractive because the redistributed wealth is enormous. In many countries such "unofficial" rent seekers are official agents of the government, who use their official positions to collect unofficial rents. Customs officials in Equatorial Guinea take a cut of meat and liquor imports allegedly to "inspect" them. Like the "official" rent seeking, "unofficial" rent seeking outcompetes entrepreneurship for talent when wealth available for taking is larger.

Importantly, rent seeking unlike entrepreneurship usually deals with capital and other forms of wealth, which rent seekers fight over. Entrepreneurship typically allows the innovator to capture a portion of a market for some period of time, which is in most cases much less lucrative than getting one's hands on a piece of the country's wealth. Moreover, a country with large wealth but slow growth is especially attractive for rent seeking. The reason is that new goods often have more than unitary income elasticity of demand, and therefore future growth is essential for the profitability of innovation. Slow growth then reduces the attractiveness of innovation and entrepreneurship. This logic suggests that the productivity growth slowdown can be self-sustaining: as talent leaves entrepreneurship and growth slows, the returns to entrepreneurship fall farther relative to those to rent seeking. We thus expect rent seeking to prosper in countries with substantial wealth and slow growth, such as the United States and Argentina today.

Feasible firm size, broadly interpreted, also often benefits rent seeking at the expense of entrepreneurship. When rent seekers such as government officials or the military have substantial authority and discretion, they can expand their operations and collect larger sums unhindered by law or custom. In this respect, poorly defined property rights are responsible not just for large potential markets for rent seeking, but also for the ability of rent seekers to run larger "firms."

In entrepreneurship physical diminishing returns to scale are only one limitation on firm size. In many less developed countries legal restrictions on entry and on expansion, such as industrial capacity licensing, are a government-imposed limitation on firm size that makes entrepreneurship less attractive. Access to credit is also a crucial determinant of feasible firm size, and therefore of the attractiveness of entrepreneurship. Because rent seekers themselves often limit the ability of entrepreneurial firms to expand to maximize their own income, high returns to rent seeking often go with low returns to entrepreneurship. Entry and capacity restrictions, for example, invite bribes. In contrast, in countries where firms can easily organize and expand with few constraints from the state and from the capital markets, entrepreneurship will be attractive to the most talented relative to rent seeking. When rent seekers tax entrepreneurs by limiting firm expansion, the ablest entrepreneurs suffer, and the best potential entrepreneurs become rent seekers.

Perhaps the single most important determinant of the allocation of talent is the compensation contract. The ability of rent seekers to keep a large portion of the rents on their talents, whether legally or illicitly, raises the attractiveness of rent seeking. In many countries official positions come with a territory of being able to collect bribes. People pay hundreds of thousands of dollars for positions with the power to allocate supposedly free water to farmers in India, since these jobs give them monopoly rights to charge for water. Tax farmers throughout history bid fortunes for positions. Illegal rent seeking is the most attractive when it is protected by the state. What distinguishes these rent-seeking activities is that, at the margin, rent seekers can keep all or most of the return from their ability.

In market rather than official rent seeking, such as some forms of law and speculation, the output of rent seeking is often easily observable, and therefore can be rewarded. This might not be true in entrepreneurial jobs where the inventor cannot start his own firm but must work as part of a team in a large firm. In mature manufacturing industries in the United States, for example, it is extremely hard to identify individual contributions and to reward them accordingly even if they are identified. The difficulty of observing output might drive the potential entrepreneurs out of such industries and into rent seeking. The observability of output and the possibility of rewarding talent is probably the most important reason why so many talented people go into rent seeking in the United States today.

To summarize, talent in the rent-seeking sectors in many countries benefits from property rights that enable rent seekers to claim a substantial part of the productive output through official and unofficial expropriation. As talent joins the rent-seeking sectors, it expands and improves them. The higher taxes on productive activities reduce the returns to entrepreneurship, and drive even more talent into rent seeking. Large rent-seeking institutions and weak rent-protecting institutions draw talent out of entrepreneurship. One benefit of the shrinking rent-seeking institutions, such as the decline of central government, is that talent moves into productive activities. As the *New York Times* described Hungary's move to capitalism, "Government now has to compete with business for talented workers."

In some countries entrepreneurs have managed at least in part to avoid the tax from rent seekers by becoming rent seekers themselves. In these countries it is common for government officials to own businesses run either by themselves or by their relatives, and to protect these businesses from competition or from bribes by virtue of their government positions. Misallocation of talent nonetheless persists, since a large portion of these people's time is spent in rent-seeking activities designed to foster their own businesses at the expense of those of the competitors.

Our model has one additional interesting implication. Suppose that the most lucrative sector for the most talented is rent seeking and that there is a dominant group in the population that has access to that sector. Suppose that this group now excludes some ethnic or racial minority from access to the rent-seeking sector, such as the army or the government. In this case, the ablest people from the excluded group must go into other sectors, one of which might very well be entrepreneurship. If the exclusion is effective, and if the overall distribution of abilities is the same for each group, this means that the ability of the ablest entrepreneurs rises. The growth rate of the economy then also rises as a result of this exclusion. Moreover, exclusion of others benefits the dominant group, both because it leaves them a greater share of the rent-seeking pie, and because the size of that pie rises as the quality of entrepreneurship improves. Competition for the rent-seeking positions may in part explain why Jews have been excluded from many rent-seeking occupations in Europe, the Chinese in Malaysia, and the Indians and Lebanese in Africa. Faster growth can be one of the few inadvertent benefits of discrimination in rent seeking. Of course, discrimination against minorities in entrepreneurship hurts both them and the majority.

IV. Some Evidence

A major implication of our paper is that the allocation of talented people to entrepreneurship is good for growth, and their allocation to rent seeking is bad for growth. Unfortunately, it is hard to directly measure the allocation of talent to these two types of activities. Barro [1991] provides some evidence that high government consumption and a high number of coups, both of which might measure the extent of rent seeking, have a negative effect on growth, but this finding is too indirect. An alternative approach is to associate individual occupations with entrepreneurship and rent seeking. Magee, Brock, and Young [1989] have in fact found data on the number of lawyers in 35 countries, and found that countries with more lawyers grow more slowly. We have not found data on the numbers of people in different occupations in different countries, but instead used data on college enrollments in different fields for a large cross section of countries collected by UNESCO. We use the data on college enrollment in law as a measure of a talent allocated to rent seeking, and on college enrollment in engineering as a measure of talent allocated to entrepreneurship. Although lawyers do different things in different countries, and undergraduate enrollments might not be a good proxy for the extent of each activity, these are the best measures of rent seeking and entrepreneurship we could find.

We use Barro's [1991] data set that augments the Summers and Heston [1988] data base. In fact, we frame our analysis as an extension of Barro's regressions. The variables we use for each country are the growth rate of real GDP per capita between 1970 and 1985, real GDP per capita in 1960, average from 1970 to 1985 of the ratio of real government consumption (exclusive of defense and education) to real GDP, primary school enrollment rate in 1960, average from 1970 to 1985 of the ratio of real private investment to real GDP, and the number of revolutions and coups. Although these are not all of Barro's variables, they are the most important ones, and include measures of general investment in human capital (primary education), in physical capital (private investment), and of government consumption.

We add to Barro's list the ratio of college enrollments in law to total college enrollments in 1970, and the same ratio for engineering. The reason that we choose total enrollments rather than population or population of a given age as a denominator is that we are interested in the allocation of the ablest people between fields. Fractions of college enrollment in law and engineering in fact measure the incentives to be in these fields as opposed to being in college more generally. Looking at the ratios to population would tell us less about the allocation of the ablest people and more about incentives to go to college. The intersection of the sample of countries for which data on college enrollments by field are available for 1970 with Barro's 98-country sample for which data on investment and government consumption are available yields 91 observations.

We run the regressions first for all 91 countries in the sample, and then for the 55 countries that have more than 10,000 college students. The idea of looking at countries with more than 10,000 students is to reduce the problem of college attendance abroad. We found this approach preferable to running population-weighted regressions since some large population countries have a significant commitment to education abroad. In addition, the subsample with large college enrollments gets rid of some smaller countries that probably have less reliable data, and might be preferred for this reason as well. Table II presents the summary statistics for the engineering and law variables in the total and the restricted sample.

Table III presents the basic results of the regression of 1970 to 1985 growth rate on law and engineering enrollments, controlling only for the 1960 GDP. In the regression for all countries, we find a positive and significant effect of engineers on growth, and a negative and basically insignificant ($t = 1.2$) effect of lawyers on growth. The signs of the coefficients are consistent with the theory that rent seeking reduces growth, while entrepreneurship and innovation raise it. If an extra 10 percent of enrollment was in engineering, which corresponds roughly to doubling average engineering enrollments, the growth rate would rise 0.5 percent per year. If an extra 10 percent were in law, which also roughly corresponds to doubling enrollments, growth would fall 0.3 percent per year. If we look at countries with large student populations, the effect of engineers more than doubles and becomes more significant. The negative effect of lawyers also doubles, but remains insignificant. The R^2 of the second regression is a lot higher as well.

Of course, we cannot interpret these relationships as struc-

TABLE II
SUMMARY STATISTICS FOR ENGINEERING AND LAW MAJOR AS PERCENTAGE OF
COLLEGE STUDENTS

	Full sample		Countries with 10,000 or more students	
	Engineering	Law	Engineering	Law
Mean	10.39	8.89	12.03	7.25
Median	9.08	5.52	10.25	5.61
25th percentile	3.83	2.65	7.26	3.10
75th percentile	14.31	11.20	15.92	10.05

TABLE III
REGRESSIONS OF GROWTH OF REAL GDP PER CAPITA BETWEEN 1970 AND 1985 ON
PROPORTIONS OF MAJORS IN ENGINEERING AND LAW (IN 1970)

Model	All countries (1)	> 10,000 students (2)
Constant	0.013	0.015
	(0.005)	(0.004)
Engineering	0.054	0.125
	(0.027)	(0.037)
Law	−0.031	−0.065
	(0.025)	(0.049)
GDP 1960	0.000	−0.002
	(0.001)	(0.001)
N	91	55
R^2	0.09	0.23

tural, since law and engineering enrollments might be correlated with other sources of growth. Accordingly, we next consider the Barro regression augmented by our law and engineering variables, and then decompose the reduced-form effects on law and engineering on growth into direct effects and indirect effects operating through correlation with other variables.

Table IV presents the results of the augmented Barro regression for the whole and the large college population samples. In both regressions investment in physical and in human capital increase growth, while government consumption and revolutions reduce growth. There is also some evidence of convergence as in Barro, although it is not clear that it makes sense to define convergence holding investment constant. The direct effects of lawyers and engineers are very insignificant in the whole sample, with the sign on engineers switching to negative. In contrast, the direct effect of engineering in the reduced sample is still positive and almost significant, although it falls to under half of the total effect in Table III. More surprisingly, the direct effect of lawyers is negative and significant in the reduced sample, and its absolute value is higher than in the whole sample. Based on this sample, Table IV confirms the direct negative relationship between rent seeking and growth, and the direct positive relationship between entrepreneurship and growth.

The positive direct effect of engineers, and the negative direct effect of lawyers, are consistent with our theory, which says that the rate of technological progress is determined by the allocation of talent. If engineering is an attractive major, the quality of talent in

526   *QUARTERLY JOURNAL OF ECONOMICS*

TABLE IV
DETERMINANTS OF GROWTH RATE OF REAL GDP PER CAPITA BETWEEN 1970
AND 1985

Model	(1)	(2)
Constant	0.018	0.020
	(0.010)	(0.011)
Investment	0.086	0.085
	(0.032)	(0.039)
Primary school enrollment	0.022	0.012
	(0.009)	(0.011)
Government consumption	−0.145	−0.064
	(0.040)	(0.053)
Revolutions and coups	−0.028	−0.035
	(0.009)	(0.009)
GDP 1960	−0.007	−0.006
	(0.001)	(0.001)
Engineering	−0.010	0.054
	(0.023)	(0.034)
Law	−0.024	−0.078
	(0.020)	(0.040)
N	91	55
R^2	0.47	0.56
Sample	All	≥ 10,000 students

engineering is higher, therefore entrepreneurs are of higher quality, the rate of technological progress is greater, and the growth rate of GDP per capita is higher. This argument of course assumes a positive correlation between the fraction of college majors in engineering and the rate of technological progress that they will generate and does not deal with the abilities of engineers. Similarly, if law is an attractive major, the quality of rent seekers is higher, and hence, indirectly, the quality of entrepreneurs is lower, and technological progress and income growth are smaller. Of course, there may be other mechanisms that explain these direct effects, and our theory also predicts that there may be indirect effects of the allocation of talent on growth. For example, less rent seeking and more technological progress are likely to raise physical investment.

To decompose the total effect of lawyers and engineers on growth from Table III into the direct and indirect effects, Table V presents the estimates from auxiliary regressions of Table IV independent variables (investment, primary education, government consumption, and revolutions) on lawyers and engineers. In all these regressions, we control for 1960 real GDP. High engineering enrollments predict high investment in pure and physical capital, low government consumption, and low revolutions and coups. This suggests that some of the effect of engineers on growth comes from the fact that countries with many engineering majors also do many other things that are good for growth, such as educate the young and accumulate capital. They also avoid things that are bad for growth, such as government consumption and revolutions. Our engineering variable might be a proxy for good incentives and the efficiency of allocation on a variety of margins.

In contrast to the finding for engineers, the correlations between Table IV independent variables and law enrollments are weak and insignificant. To our surprise, lawyers do not have a significant negative effect on investment, which they would if rent seekers specialized in redistribution of physical capital. The results suggest that most of the effect of lawyers on growth is direct.

TABLE V
REGRESSIONS OF TABLE II INDEPENDENT VARIABLES ON PROPORTIONS OF MAJORS
IN ENGINEERING AND LAW

A. Estimated auxiliary regressions for engineering		
Model	(1)	(2)
Investment	0.243	0.432
	(0.081)	(0.119)
Primary schooling	0.904	1.02
	(0.271)	(0.408)
Government consumption	−0.142	−0.181
	(0.056)	(0.078)
Revolutions and coups	−0.090	−0.300
	(0.265)	(0.445)
N	91	55
Sample	All	≥ 10,000 students
B. Estimated auxiliary regressions for law		
Model	(1)	(2)
Investment	−0.093	0.055
	(0.076)	(0.160)
Primary schooling	−0.093	0.576
	(0.254)	(0.548)
Government consumption	0.006	−0.089
	(0.053)	(0.105)
Revolutions and coups	−0.121	0.141
	(0.248)	(0.597)
N	91	55
Sample	All	≥ 10,000 students

528   *QUARTERLY JOURNAL OF ECONOMICS*

Table VI decomposes the total effect into the direct and the indirect effects. For engineers the direct effect on growth is trivial for the whole sample, but about half of the total for the reduced sample. As we mentioned, this direct effect is consistent with the view that allocating good people to entrepreneurial activities is good for growth. In both samples the indirect effects are large because engineering enrollments are strongly positively correlated with investment in physical and human capital, which are positively correlated with growth, and negatively correlated with government consumption, which is negatively correlated with growth. This result suggests that in countries that invest and have a good labor force attract their able people into engineering as well, and that as a result of this allocation of resources they grow. They do all the right things at the same time. They also avoid high government consumption, which discourages engineering majors, as well as reduces growth. Avoiding revolutions does not discourage engineering concentrators, and so there is no indirect effect there. Our results suggest, not surprisingly, that people choose the engineering major when other conditions in the economy make investment in industry-related human capital attractive.

The indirect effects of law enrollments on growth are all

TABLE VI
DECOMPOSITION OF THE EFFECT OF ENGINEERING AND LAW MAJORS ON GROWTH
INTO DIRECT AND INDIRECT EFFECTS

A. Estimated effects for engineering		
Model	(1)	(2)
Investment	0.021	0.037
Primary schooling	0.020	0.012
Government consumption	0.021	0.012
Revolutions and coups	0.002	0.003
Direct	−0.010	0.054
Total	0.054	0.125
B. Estimated effects for law		
Model	(1)	(2)
Investment	−0.008	0.005
Primary schooling	−0.002	0.007
Government consumption	−0.001	0.006
Revolutions and coups	0.004	−0.005
Direct	−0.024	−0.078
Total	−0.031	−0.065

trivial. By far the main effect is direct, which in the reduced sample is even larger in magnitude than the total effect. This evidence from the reduced sample might mean that the most important effect of lawyers on growth is the opportunity cost of not having talented people as innovators. The small indirect effect suggests that lawyers reduce growth creating activities but not through reducing the incentives to invest.

In summary, the sample with large college enrollments reveals a large direct and large indirect positive effect of engineers on growth, and a large direct negative effect of lawyers on growth. One, but not the only one, interpretation of these findings is that the allocation of talent is important for growth. The allocation of talent into engineering seems to occur in countries that also invest in human and physical capital, suggesting that some countries just do things right.

V. CONCLUSION

Among the many explanations of the recent U. S. productivity growth slowdown, two deal with human capital. The first is that the quality of the U. S. human capital stock is not growing as fast as it used to, or perhaps is even deteriorating. The poor quality of schools, the declining test scores, and even the declining relative wages of high school graduates [Murphy and Welch, 1988] suggest that this might be a problem. The second explanation is that human capital is allocated improperly for growth, and in particular the ablest young people become rent seekers rather than producers. The fact that many of the most talented young people become lawyers and security traders is cited as evidence for this explanation.

In this paper we have presented some theoretical reasons why the second concern might in fact be important, and some empirical evidence that suggests that this concern might be real. Lawyers are indeed bad, and engineers good, for growth. This suggests that private incentives governing the allocation of talent across occupations might not coincide with social incentives. Some professions are socially more useful than others, even if they are not as well compensated. The findings on engineers also suggest that countries that have many engineering majors also invest in human and physical capital. We do not know what is the exogenous cause of these relationships. However, it is quite possible that policies that raise investment or improve the quality of human capital will

530   *QUARTERLY JOURNAL OF ECONOMICS*

indirectly make engineering a more attractive career, and in this way increase growth.

UNIVERSITY OF CHICAGO
HARVARD UNIVERSITY
UNIVERSITY OF CHICAGO

REFERENCES

Arrow, Kenneth J., "The Economic Implications of Learning by Doing," *Review of Economic Studies*, XXIX (1962), 155–73.
Barro, Robert J., "Economic Growth in a Cross-Section of Countries," *Quarterly Journal of Economics*, CVI (1991), 407–43.
Baumol, William J., "Entrepreneurship: Productive, Unproductive, and Destructive," *Journal of Political Economy*, XCVIII (1990), 893–921.
De Soto, Hernando, *The Other Path* (New York: Harper and Row, 1989).
Krueger, Anne, "The Political Economy of the Rent-Seeking Society," *American Economic Review*, LXIV (1974), 291–303.
Kuhn, Peter, "Unions in a General Equilibrium Model of Firm Formation," *Journal of Labor Economics*, VI (1988), 62–82.
Landes, David, *The Unbound Prometheus* (New York: Cambridge University Press, 1969).
Little, Ian M. D., Dipak Mazumdar, and John M. Page Jr., *Small Manufacturing Enterprises: A Comparative Analysis of India and Other Economies* (New York: Oxford University Press for the World Bank, 1987).
Lucas, Robert E., Jr., "On the Size Distribution of Business Firms," *Rand Journal of Economics*, IX (1978), 508–23.
Magee, Stephen P., William A. Brock, and Leslie Young, *Black Hole Tariffs and the Endogenous Policy Theory* (Cambridge: Cambridge University Press, 1989).
Murphy, Kevin M., and Finis Welch, "The Structure of Wages," mimeo, 1988.
North, Douglass C., and Robert Paul Thomas, *The Rise of the Western World: A New Economic History* (Cambridge: Cambridge University Press, 1973).
Olson, Mancur, *The Rise and Decline of Nations* (New Haven: Yale University Press, 1982).
Porter, Michael E., *The Competitive Advantage of Nations* (New York: Free Press, 1990).
Rosen, Sherwin, "The Economics of Superstars," *American Economic Review*, LXXI (1981), 845–58.
Summers, Robert, and A. Heston, "A New Set of International Comparisons for Real Product and Price Levels: Estimates for 130 Countries," *Review of Income and Wealth*, XXXIV (March 1988), 1–25.
Tullock, Gordon, "The Welfare Cost of Tariffs, Monopoly and Theft," *Western Economic Journal*, V (1967), 224–32.

[27]

Politically Connected Firms

By Mara Faccio*

The incentive for corporations to become politically connected has been recognized among economists for many years and has probably been recognized by citizens of affected countries for many more. As economists have noted, the source of such value can take various forms, including preferential treatment by government-owned enterprises (such as banks or raw material producers), lighter taxation, preferential treatment in competition for government contracts, relaxed regulatory oversight of the company in question, or stiffer regulatory oversight of its rivals, and many other forms.[1] However, as emphasized by Andrei Shleifer and Robert W. Vishny (1994), politicians themselves will extract at least some of the rents generated by connections, and corporate value will be enhanced only when the marginal benefits of the connections outweigh their marginal costs.

In this paper, I provide a comprehensive look at corporate political connections around the globe. I address two main questions: What common characteristics do countries with widespread political connections share? And, do connections add to company value?

To answer these questions, I assemble a database that includes 20,202 publicly traded firms in 47 countries. A company is identified as being connected with a politician if at least one of its large shareholders (anyone controlling at least 10 percent of voting shares) or one of its top officers (CEO, president, vice-president, chairman, or secretary) is a member of parliament, a minister, or is closely related to a top politician or party. I define close relationships in Section I. I do not include contributions to political campaigns or direct (undisclosed) payments to politicians in my analysis, but the connections I document are likely to be more durable than one-time campaign contributions or cash payments.

I find corporate political connections to be relatively widespread; they exist in 35 of the 47 countries in my sample. Generally speaking, connections are less common in the presence of more stringent regulation of political conflicts of interest. On the other hand, connections are particularly common in countries that are perceived as being highly corrupt, in countries that impose restrictions on foreign investments by their citizens, and in more transparent systems. Perhaps this last effect is simply due to greater access to information in such economies. The number of identifiable cases within any individual country is not necessarily large. A strict application of my criteria yields a subsample of connected firms of less than 3 percent (541) of the total sample. As might be expected, connections are more widespread among larger firms: connected firms represent 7.72 percent of the world's stock market capitalization. In some countries, political connections are quite common. In Russia, for example, connected firms represent 86.75 percent of the market capitalization. I caution the reader that my findings are descriptive in nature and do not imply any causality. The cross-country approach taken in this study differs from previous work, where the

* Vanderbilt University, Owen Graduate School of Management, 401 21st Avenue South, Nashville, TN 37203 (e-mail: mara.faccio@owen.vanderbilt.edu). I thank Massimo Belcredi, Bernardo Bortolotti, Lorenzo Caprio, Tom Cosimano, Serdar Dinç, Simeon Djankov, Ray Fisman, Mariassunta Giannetti, Richard Green, Tom Gresik, E. Han Kim, Meziane Lasfer, Paolo Mauro, Todd Mitton, Randall Morck, David Parsley, Susan Rose-Ackerman, Andrei Shleifer, David Stolin, and especially three anonymous referees, Richard Rogerson (the editor), John McConnell, Paul Schultz, and Ron Masulis for their helpful comments, and Patricia Peat and Suzanne Bellezza for editorial help. I am deeply indebted to the parliaments, governments, and stock exchange regulators that replied to my questionnaire on conflicts of interest. I also benefited from comments from workshop participants at Indiana University, Stockholm School of Economics, Università Cattolica (Milan), Università di Lugano, University of Michigan, University of Notre Dame, Syracuse University, Vanderbilt University Law School, the IMF, the 2003 AFA meeting in Washington, D.C., and the 2002 METU International Conference in Economics in Ankara. I also wish to thank Larry Lang for sharing data on group affiliation in Asia.

[1] Evidence of preferential treatment by government-controlled banks is provided by Michael Backman (1999) and I. Serdar Dinç (2005). Evidence of tax discounts is documented by Hernando De Soto (1989). The regulatory benefits enjoyed by politically connected firms are discussed by George J. Stigler (1971) and De Soto (1989).

focus has been on specific countries and specific types of connections that make cross-country comparison impossible.[2]

To examine the second question, whether connections add to company value, I perform an event study around the time of the announcements that officers or large shareholders are entering politics, or that politicians are joining boards. I find a significant increase in corporate value, but only when those involved in business enter politics. Furthermore, the stock price impact of a new connection is larger whenever a businessperson is elected as prime minister, rather than as a member of the parliament, and whenever a large shareholder, rather than an officer, enters politics. These results complement the work of Fisman (2001), who concludes that in Indonesia a considerable percentage of well-connected firms' value comes from political connections. In particular, he compares returns across firms with differing degrees of political exposure at the time of rumors of Indonesian President Suharto's worsening health. Around that time, stock prices of firms closely connected with Suharto dropped more than the prices of less well-connected firms, and the stock price reactions were more severe when the news was more negative.

I. Incidence of Political Connections

A. *Definition of Connections*

I say a company is connected with a politician if one of the company's large shareholders

[2] In the United States, researchers have examined the role of connections created by contributions to electoral campaigns (e.g., Brian E. Roberts, 1990; Randall S. Kroszner and Thomas Stratmann, 1998; James Ang and Carol Marie Boyer, 2000). Anup Agrawal and Charles R. Knoeber (2001) focus on the political experience of outside directors. Non-U.S. studies generally look at connections generated by means other than campaign contributions. In a study of Canadian firms, Randall K. Morck et al. (2000) discuss the political influence of dominant business families. Raymond Fisman (2001) examines established friendships with top politicians in Indonesia. Simon Johnson and Todd Mitton (2003) analyze political connections in Malaysia and label connected firms as those whose officers or large shareholders are affiliated with top government officials. A few other studies rely on specific cases of corruption (e.g., Joel S. Hellman et al., 2003; Jakob Svensson, 2003). Pranab Bardhan (1997) and Susan Rose-Ackerman (1999) offer excellent analyses of the literature on corruption.

or top officers is: (a) a member of parliament (MP), (b) a minister or the head of state, or (c) closely related to a top official.

Connections with Members of Parliament.— Firms may be connected through an MP in two ways. First, at least one of their top officers may sit in the national parliament as of 2001.[3] As in Stijn Claessens et al. (2000) and Faccio and Larry H. P. Lang (2002), top officers are defined as a company's CEO, president, vice-president, chairman, or secretary. For example, Lord Browne of Maddingley, a member of the British House of Lords, is the CEO of British Petroleum. BP is therefore classified as connected with a member of parliament through an officer.

Second, companies are classified as connected when at least one large shareholder is a member of parliament. Large shareholders are defined as anyone directly or indirectly controlling at least 10 percent of shareholder votes. A good example of this is one of the most influential families in Italy, the Agnelli family. Giovanni Agnelli had a life term as senator. Through a complex ownership structure, the Agnelli family controls *directly* or *indirectly* more than 10 percent of the votes in 18 Italian listed firms. Those firms are all classified as connected with a member of parliament. A firm is not classified as connected if a family member of an MP is a large shareholder or a top officer of a firm. Thus, although Giovanni Agnelli's brother Umberto is a top officer of IFIL, this company is not considered to be connected through an officer (but it is included in the sample because of Giovanni Agnelli's ownership).

Connections with a Minister or Head of State.—There are three types of connections with a minister or head of state: as officer; as large shareholder; or through a relative. A relative may be a spouse, child, sibling, or parent. Ian MacFarlane, Australian Minister for Small Business, for example, is chairman of two Australian listed firms: Central Pacific Minerals and Southern Pacific Petroleum. These firms are therefore classified as connected with a minister (through an officer). Italy's Prime Minister Sil-

[3] For most countries, politicians are identified as of the first half of 2001 (data are generally not available before that date). For Colombia, Luxembourg, Sri Lanka, Taiwan, and Zimbabwe, politicians are identified as of June 2003.

vio Berlusconi is a large shareholder of four Italian listed firms: Arnoldo Mondadori Editore, Mediaset, Mediolanum, and Standa. All these companies are defined as politically connected with a minister (through a large shareholder). Finally, Malaysian Prime Minister Mohamad Mahathir's son, Mirzan, and Silvio Berlusconi's daughter, Marina, are either large shareholders or top officers of several listed corporations. All of these connections are included.

Companies Closely Related to a Top Official.— Close relationships are a bit more ambiguous. Since they lack the definitional objectivity of the first two connection types, I place them in a separate category. Connections of this type occur when a person who was a head of state or prime minister between 1997 and 2001 (or one of their relatives) was also a top executive or a large shareholder of the company during 1997 or 2001 (except for the cases that fall into the paragraph directly above); when a government minister or a member of parliament as of 2001 was a top executive or large shareholder of the company during 1997; when a large shareholder or a top officer is a friend of a minister or MP;[4] when a large shareholder or a top officer is a politician in another country; or when a large shareholder or a top officer is known to be associated with a political party. Well-known relationships with political parties are illustrated by members of the UMNO party in Malaysia (see Edmund Terence Gomez and K. S. Jomo, 1997; Johnson and Mitton, 2003). Notice that, in my definition, I include only those cases where the firm's officer or large shareholder served as a minister as of 1997 or after, since connections with politicians who served farther back in time are less likely to have a major impact on firm activities.

The necessity of relying on publicly available sources for information on close relationships, such as friendship or well-known cases of relationships with political parties, produces an incomplete picture. For example, no political connections are identified in Argentina. To re-

duce any potential bias, these less objective connections are treated as a separate group in the country-level analysis, and separate regression estimates are made using two different dependent variables; *% of firms connected to a minister or MP* (which includes only connections with MPs, ministers, or heads of state) and *% of firms connected with a minister or MP, or a close relationship.* The first set of regressions relies only on objective connections and will thus provide objective results. As I will show, the results are qualitatively the same when the less objective relationships are included.

B. Data and Descriptive Statistics

I start with the countries for which the Worldscope database provides coverage. For each country, I gather names of members of parliament and government (as of 2001) using the *Chiefs of State* directory and the official Web site of each country's government and parliament. Overall, data sources allow me to identify politicians in 47 countries. Former heads of state or prime ministers are identified for all countries using sources listed in Appendix A, panel G.[5] Names of politicians are cross-checked with names of the top officers of 20,202 listed companies covered in Worldscope.[6] Worldscope generally includes only a company's CEO, president, vice-president, chairman, or secretary, and in some instances another officer, all of whom are identified by family name and initials. Names that match members of parliaments or governments are cross-checked using the Extel database, company Web sites, and extensive searches on Lexis-Nexis. Whenever I cannot find the *full* names of officers, I elimi-

---

[4] Cases of friendship represent just a few of the connections overall, as most of them are not reported in *Forbes.* For example, President George W. Bush and Vice-President Dick Cheney are friends of many chief executives, particularly in the energy sector, but I do not find this cited in *Forbes,* so it is not included in my connection variables.

[5] The Appendix is available from the author.
[6] Worldscope provides full coverage of developed markets. Coverage is limited for Argentina, Chile, Colombia, the Czech Republic, Hungary, India, Israel, New Zealand, Peru, Poland, Russia, Sri Lanka, Taiwan, Turkey, Venezuela, and Zimbabwe. For these markets, companies need to satisfy at least one of the following conditions in order to be included in Worldscope: (a) five or more broker estimates; (b) market capitalization equal to or greater than $100 million; (c) inclusion in the FTSE All-World, IFC Investible, Dow Jones Global, MSCI World, MSCI EMF, SSBMI, or S&P Global indexes; (d) listing of an ADR on the NYSE, ASE, Nasdaq, or OTC trading of a sponsored ADR; (e) inclusion in the EASDAQ or EURO.NM; (f) listing on the NYSE, ASE, or Nasdaq.

nate the observation. Much of the time, connections based on initials alone are misleading; think how many Kims and Parks there are in Korea. I prefer to understate rather than to considerably overstate connections. To avoid understating family affiliations in Asia, where family names may not be the same, I integrate country-specific family affiliation data taken from sources listed in Appendix A, panel F. If not covered in those sources, connections are excluded when the family name does not coincide. So, for example, Canadian Prime Minister Jean Chrétien is the father-in-law of Paul Desmarais, an important Canadian tycoon. This case does not show up in my data, because the two do not share the same family name.

The names of large shareholders come from a number of sources published by each country's stock exchange or supervisory authority. I also rely on Claessens et al. (2000) for shareholders in East Asian countries, and on Faccio et al. (2001) and Faccio and Lang (2002) for shareholders in West European countries. These authors have collected data from the various publications of the stock exchanges and supervisory authorities.[7] When ownership data cannot be found in those sources, the data are collected from Worldscope and Extel.

Further information on political connections comes from Agrawal and Knoeber (2001) for the U.S.; Backman (1999) for Asia; Gomez and Jomo (1997) and Johnson and Mitton (2003) for Malaysia; Fisman (2001) for Indonesia;[8] and the Stationery Office (2001) for the United Kingdom. *The Economist, Forbes,* and *Fortune* provide information on well-known cases of friendships between top politicians and entrepreneurs. State-owned firms are not included in my sample of political connections unless a member of parliament or of government sits on the board or is a large shareholder.

---

[7] Most of these data on board membership and share ownership are for the 1996–1999 period. Extel is used to update them.

[8] Fisman (2001) identifies connections based on the Suharto Dependency Index, developed by the Castle Group, a leading economic consultant in Indonesia. The index ranges from one (least dependent) to five (most dependent). In my definition of connections, I include only groups rated five.

Overall, I find 607 connections involving 541 firms. Table 1 shows that 59.5 percent of connections involve top officers, while 40.5 percent of cases involve large shareholders. In 15.5 percent of cases, the connection is with the country's leader or a minister; in 59.6 percent of cases the connection is with a member of parliament. Finally, in 24.9 percent of cases, mostly concentrated in Malaysia and Indonesia, the connection consists of a close relationship with a politician.

Table 2 shows that connected firms represent 2.68 percent of all listed corporations and 7.72 percent of the world's market capitalization. When I focus on the largest 50 firms in each market, I find that 6.92 percent of them have political connections. Thus, larger firms exhibit connections more often, consistent with evidence provided in Agrawal and Knoeber (2001) and Johnson and Mitton (2003). Some countries exhibit only a few cases of connections or no connections at all (12 of 47 countries). On the other hand, in Indonesia, Italy, Malaysia, Russia, and Thailand, over 10 percent of listed corporations are politically connected. In Ireland, Malaysia, Russia, Thailand, and the United Kingdom, connected corporations account for more than 20 percent of the market capitalization. In Russia, connected firms actually represent 86.75 percent of the market capitalization, and in the United Kingdom they represent 39.02 percent.

A few caveats are in order. First, the count of connections is far from comprehensive. For many countries, data on ownership are lacking, and families may control firms through nominee accounts or shell entities. Disclosure regulations also differ significantly across countries. To limit the impact of these factors, I investigate only large shareholders, i.e., those who control at least 10 percent of votes—a level of control that forces disclosure almost everywhere. Second, in some countries, connections with local officials may be more important than connections with central government officeholders. There is no comprehensive and accurate information on identifies of those local government officials. Finally, there are many ways to create a political connection. I focus on a direct measure of connections that is observable for all countries. Other instruments, such as campaign contributions, are not observable for most countries.

TABLE 1—CLASSIFICATION OF CONNECTIONS BY TYPE

	Connections through large shareholder	Connections through top officer	Total	(%)
Connections with MPs	45	317	362	59.6
Connections with ministers	64	30	94	15.5
Closely related firms	137	14	151	24.9
Of which:				
Cases of friendship	*10*	*1*	*11*	*1.8*
Former heads of state or prime ministers	*12*	*5*	*17*	*2.8*
Current politicians who have left the firm				
after 1997	*0*	*2*	*2*	*0.3*
Foreign politicians	*2*	*6*	*8*	*1.3*
Political parties	*113*	*0*	*113*	*18.6*
Total	246	361	607	
(%)	40.5	59.5		

Notes: Connections with MPs include firms whose large shareholder or top officer of the company sits in a national parliament. *Connections with ministers* include firms with a shareholder controlling at least 10 percent of the voting stock or a top officer who holds a government office, is king or president of the country. *Closely related firms* are those with a shareholder controlling at least 10 percent of the voting stock or a top officer who has a close relationship with at least one top politician. Close relationships include: (a) friends, (b) former heads of state or prime ministers (and their relatives), (c) current politicians who have left the firm after 1997, (d) foreign politicians, and (e) well-known cases of relationships with political parties. *Connections through large shareholder* include those cases in which a shareholder controlling at least 10 percent of the firm's voting stock sits in a national parliament, holds office in the government, is the head of state, or is closely related to a top politician or political party. *Connections through top officer* include those cases in which a company's top officer sits in a national parliament, holds office in the government, is the head of state, or is closely related to a top politician or political party.

II. Where Are Political Connections More Common?

To examine the incidence of connections in different countries, I identify a number of variables that are potentially associated with connectedness.

A. Variable Definitions

Connections.—I use two variables to measure the incidence of political connections at the country level. The first variable, *% of firms connected with a minister or MP,* is the number of firms connected with a minister or MP, excluding cases of close relationships, divided by the total number of firms listed in a country. This ratio ranges from a minimum of 0 percent for the countries listed above as having no connections to a maximum of 12 percent in Russia. This index relies only on connections that can be objectively established. The second variable, *% of firms connected with a minister or MP, or a close relationship,* is the number of all connected firms, including cases of close relationships, divided by the total number of firms listed in a country. This ratio ranges from a minimum

of 0 percent in Argentina, Brazil, the Czech Republic, New Zealand, Norway, Peru, Poland, South Africa, Venezuela, and Zimbabwe to a maximum of 22.08 percent in Indonesia. This index includes less objective connections, as discussed earlier. Since ratios of connected firms are by construction constrained to be tween 0 and 100 percent, the regression analysis in Section IIB uses a two-boundary Tobit model (see Takeshi Amemiya, 1984, for a discussion).

Regulatory Environment.—A regulatory score is constructed based on regulations that prohibit or set limits on the business activities of public officials. The results are shown in Table 3. I start by looking at each country's constitutional law, and then I look at the rules of procedure for each chamber of the parliament. Third, I consult the regulations included in the Inter-Parliamentary Union's Web site (http://www.ipu.org/parline-e/parlinesearch.asp), under the field "code (rules) of conduct." Fourth, I conduct Internet searches using combinations of the following keywords: *country name* + "incompatibilities" + "member* parliament." For ministers, I use the keywords: *country name* + "conflict* of interest*" + "minister*" as well as *country name* + "code

TABLE 2—COUNTRY DISTRIBUTION OF FIRMS WITH POLITICAL CONNECTIONS

	No. of firms with available data	No. of firms connected with a minister or MP	% of firms connected with a minister or MP	No. of firms connected through close relationships	% of firms connected with a minister or MP, or a close relationship	% of top 50 firms connected with a minister or MP, or a close relationship	Connected firms as % of market capitalization
Argentina	38	0	0.00	0	0.00	0.00	0.00
Australia	287	2	0.70	0	0.70	0.00	0.32
Austria	110	1	0.91	0	0.91	2.00	0.25
Belgium	157	6	3.82	0	3.82	8.00	18.77
Brazil	167	0	0.00	0	0.00	0.00	0.00
Canada	534	7	1.31	0	1.31	2.00	2.53
Chile	89	2	2.25	0	2.25	4.00	1.43
Colombia	32	0	0.00	0	0.00	0.00	0.00
Czech Rep.	63	0	0.00	0	0.00	0.00	0.00
Denmark	228	7	3.07	0	3.07	6.00	2.52
Finland	132	2	1.52	0	1.52	0.00	0.14
France	914	16	1.75	4	2.19	10.00	8.03
Germany	840	11	1.31	2	1.55	2.00	1.20
Greece	153	1	0.65	0	0.65	0.00	0.09
Hong Kong	405	3	0.74	5	1.98	6.00	2.33
Hungary	27	1	3.70	0	3.70	3.85	2.81
India	323	9	2.79	0	2.79	2.00	1.83
Indonesia	154	12	7.79	22	22.08	24.00	12.76
Ireland	82	2	2.44	0	2.44	4.00	22.83
Israel	55	2	3.64	0	3.64	4.26	8.13
Italy	233	24	10.30	0	10.30	16.00	11.27
Japan	2,395	31	1.29	1	1.34	2.00	1.34
Luxembourg	23	1	4.35	0	4.35	4.55	10.48
Malaysia	445	23	5.17	65	19.78	44.00	28.24
Mexico	94	6	6.38	2	8.51	12.00	8.14
Netherlands	238	1	0.42	0	0.42	0.00	0.01
New Zealand	50	0	0.00	0	0.00	0.00	0.00
Norway	206	0	0.00	0	0.00	0.00	0.00
Peru	37	0	0.00	0	0.00	0.00	0.00
Philippines	114	1	0.88	4	4.39	8.00	16.16
Poland	57	0	0.00	0	0.00	0.00	0.00
Portugal	101	3	2.97	0	2.97	4.00	2.00
Russia	25	3	12.00	2	20.00	36.36	86.75
Singapore	229	18	7.86	0	7.86	4.00	2.59
South Africa	212	0	0.00	0	0.00	0.00	0.00
South Korea	313	7	2.24	1	2.56	4.00	8.95
Spain	200	3	1.50	0	1.50	0.00	0.82
Sri Lanka	18	0	0.00	0	0.00	0.00	0.00
Sweden	280	3	1.07	0	1.07	4.00	1.02
Switzerland	243	6	2.47	0	2.47	4.00	0.69
Taiwan	237	2	0.84	6	3.38	10.00	12.74
Thailand	279	23	8.24	19	15.05	34.00	41.62
Turkey	84	1	1.19	0	1.19	0.00	0.14
UK	2,149	154	7.17	0	7.17	46.00	39.02
US	7,124	6	0.08	8	0.20	6.00	4.94
Venezuela	18	0	0.00	0	0.00	0.00	0.00
Zimbabwe	8	0	0.00	0	0.00	0.00	0.00
All countries	20,202	400	1.98	141	2.68	6.92	7.72

	Total number of connections	Of which:			
		Ownership		Directorship	
		N	%	N	%
Argentina	0	.	.	.	.
Australia	2	0	0.0	2	100.0
Austria	1	0	0.0	1	100.0
Belgium	6	0	0.0	6	100.0
Brazil	0	.	.	.	.
Canada	7	0	0.0	7	100.0
Chile	2	0	0.0	2	100.0
Colombia	0	.	.	.	.
Czech Rep.	0	.	.	.	.

(continued overleaf)

TABLE 2—*Continued.*

		Of which:			
		Ownership		Directorship	
	Total number of connections	N	%	N	%
Denmark	7	0	0.0	7	100.0
Finland	2	0	0.0	2	100.0
France	22	10	45.5	12	54.5
Germany	16	5	31.3	11	68.8
Greece	1	0	0.0	1	100.0
Hong Kong	8	5	62.5	3	37.5
Hungary	1	0	0.0	1	100.0
India	10	2	20.0	8	80.0
Indonesia	34	34	100.0	0	0.0
Ireland	3	0	0.0	3	100.0
Israel	2	0	0.0	2	100.0
Italy	29	21	72.4	8	27.6
Japan	35	4	11.4	31	88.6
Luxembourg	1	0	0.0	1	100.0
Malaysia	94	87	92.6	7	7.4
Mexico	8	2	25.0	6	75.0
Netherlands	1	0	0.0	1	100.0
New Zealand	0	.	.	.	.
Norway	0	.	.	.	.
Peru	0	.	.	.	.
Philippines	6	5	83.3	1	16.7
Poland	0	.	.	.	.
Portugal	3	1	33.3	2	66.7
Russia	7	2	28.6	5	71.4
Singapore	19	10	52.6	9	47.4
South Africa	0	.	.	.	.
South Korea	8	1	12.5	7	87.5
Spain	3	1	33.3	2	66.7
Sri Lanka	0	.	.	.	.
Sweden	3	0	0.0	3	100.0
Switzerland	7	0	0.0	7	100.0
Taiwan	9	6	66.7	3	33.3
Thailand	46	37	80.4	9	19.6
Turkey	1	0	0.0	1	100.0
UK	189	13	6.9	176	93.1
US	14	0	0.0	14	100.0
Venezuela	0	.	.	.	.
Zimbabwe	0	.	.	.	.
All countries	607	246	40.5	361	59.5

Notes: No. of firms with available data is the number of firms included in Worldscope. *No. of firms connected with a minister or MP* is the number of firms with a shareholder controlling at least 10 percent of the voting stock or a top officer who is a member of parliament or government, excluding close relationships. *% of firms connected with a minister or MP* is the number of firms connected with a minister or MP as a proportion of the total number of firms in a given country. *No. of firms connected through close relationships* is the number of firms with a shareholder controlling at least 10 percent of the voting stock or a top officer who is a member of parliament or government, plus all identified cases of close relationships. *% of firms connected with a minister or MP, or a close relationship* is the number of all connected firms as proportion of the total number of firms in a particular country. *% of top 50 firms connected with a minister or MP, or a close relationship* is the number of connected firms as proportion of the largest 50 firms (based on end of 1997 market capitalization) in a particular country. For countries with fewer than 50 firms in the sample, this fraction is computed based on the available companies. *Total number of connections* is the overall number of connections identified in a given country. If two officers of the same company sit as ministers, the number of connections would be two, while the number of connected firms would be one. *Ownership* and *directorship* denote whether the company is connected through a large shareholder or through a top officer.

conduct" + "minister*." From the Web sites of each parliament and government, I gather contact information (generally e-mail addresses), which I use to send a questionnaire concerning the specific conflicts of interest described below. My questionnaire is sent to each chamber of the parliament and to at least three ministers, as well as to each country's securities regulatory authority. Information from these sources is used to construct six regulatory subscores (numbered 1–6 below), an aggregate regulatory score, and a disclosure score for each country. These scores are presented from left to right in Table 3. For the six regulatory subscores and for

TABLE 3—REGULATION INDEX

	Restrictions on ownership by MPs	Restr. on directorships by MPs	Restrictions on MPs in constitution	Restrictions on own. by ministers	Restrictions on directorships by ministers	Restrictions on ministers in constitution	Regulatory score	Mandatory disclosure of assets
Argentina	0	1^{CI}	0	0	1^{CI}	0	2	1
Australia	0	0	0	1^{CI}	1^{TOT}	0	2	1
Austria	1^A	1^A	0	0	0	0	2	1
Belgium	0	0^{GOV}	0	0	0	0	0	0
Brazil	1^{CI}	$1^{R,CI}$	1	0	1^{TOT}	0	4	1
Canada	0	0	0	$1^{CI,A}$	$1^{R,A}$	0	2	0
Chile	0	1^{TOT}	1	0	0	0	2	0
Colombia	0	1^{CI}	1	0	1^{CI}	1	4	0
Czech Rep.	0	0^{GOV}	0	0	0	0	0	1
Denmark	0	0	0	0	1^{TOT}	0	1	0
Finland	0	0	0	0	1^{CI}	0	1	0
France	0	$1^{GOV,CI}$	0	0	0	1	2	1
Germany	0	0	0	0	1^A	1	2	1
Greece	0	1^{CI}	1	0	1^{CI}	1	4	0
Hong Kong	0	0	0	0	1^A	0	1	1
Hungary	0	0	0	0	1^{CI}	0	1	1
India	0	0	0	0	0	0	0	0
Indonesia	0	0	0	0	0	0	0	0
Ireland	1^{CI}	$1^{R,CI}$	0	1^{CI}	$1^{R,CI}$	0	4	1
Israel	0	$1^{R,CI}$	1	0	$1^{R,CI}$	1	4	1
Italy	0	0^{GOV}	0	0	0	0	0	1
Japan	0	0	0	0	0	0	0	1
Luxembourg	0	0^{GOV}	0	0	0	0	0	0
Malaysia	0	0	0	0	0	0	0	0
Mexico	0	0	0	0	0	0	0	0
Netherlands	0	0	0	0^{GOV}	1^{TOT}	0	1	0
New Zealand	0	0	0	1^{CI}	1^{CI}	0	2	1
Norway	0	0	0	0	$1^{A,CI}$	0	1	0
Peru	1^{CI}	1^{CI}	1	1^{TOT}	1^{TOT}	1	6	0
Philippines	$1^{GOV,CI}$	$1^{GOV,CI}$	1	1^{CI}	$1^{GOV,CI}$	1	6	1
Poland	0^{GOV}	0^{GOV}	1	0	0	0	1	1
Portugal	1^{CI}	1^{TOT}	0	0	0	0	2	1
Russia	0	1^R	1	0	0	0	2	1
Singapore	0	0	0	1^{CI}	1^A	1	3	0
South Africa	0	0	0	1^{CI}	$1^{R,CI}$	1	3	1
South Korea	0	1^{TOT}	0	0	0	0	1	0
Spain	0	0	0	1^{TOT}	1^{TOT}	1	3	1
Sri Lanka	0	1	1	0	0	0	2	1
Sweden	0	0	0	0	1^{CI}	0	1	0
Switzerland	0	0^{GOV}	0	1	1	0	2	1
Taiwan	0	0^{GOV}	0	0	0	0	0	1
Thailand	0	0^{GOV}	0	1^{CI}	1^{TOT}	1	3	1
Turkey	0	1^{CI}	1	0	1^{CI}	1	4	1
UK	0	0	0	1^{CI}	1^{TOT}	0	2	1
US	1^{CI}	$1^{R,CI}$	0	$1^{CI,A}$	$1^{CI,A}$	0	4	1
Venezuela	0	0^{GOV}	0	0	0	0	0	1
Zimbabwe	0	0	0	0	1^R	1	2	0

[A] indicates a restriction that can be waived by obtaining a special *authorization*.

[CI] indicates a restriction applying to possible *conflicts of interest*, or where the firm obtains benefits from the government.

[GOV] indicates some minor restrictions applying to *government-controlled* firms.

[R] indicates major restrictions, although the politician may hold non-*remunerated* directorships.

[TOT] indicates that MPs/ministers are *totally* forbidden to hold directorships. Regulation variables are defined in Section II.

the disclosure score, a value of one is assigned if the country has at least one restriction in that category, and zero otherwise.

1. *Restrictions on ownership by members of parliament.* Restrictions include both those that completely forbid MPs to hold stock and those that allow MPs to hold stock in some instances. For example, the Brazilian *Código de Ética* forbids senators to own companies that would benefit from a contract with the government. Similarly, in Ireland, office holders are not allowed to have any financial interests that might conflict or be seen to conflict with their position.

2. *Restrictions on board membership by MPs.*
First, restrictions include those that completely
forbid MPs to sit on a board. This is the case in
Chile, Portugal, and South Korea. I also consider partial restrictions, which allow MPs to sit
on boards as long as the position (a) is not
remunerated; (b) does not represent a conflict of
interest; or (c) a waiver is granted. Partial restrictions apply in 13 countries. For example,
Rule XLVII of the U.S. House of Representatives stipulates that members shall not serve
with compensation as an officer or member of
the board of any association, corporation, or
other entity. The French regulation prohibits
MPs from sitting on the boards of companies
that derive advantage from the state or from a
public body. In Austria, the Incompatibility Act
requires MPs holding a leading position in a
joint-stock company to reveal their position to
the president of the Chamber. The Incompatibility Committee decides on the acceptability of
such a function.

3. *Whether major restrictions against board
membership or ownership of public companies
by members of the parliament are expressed in
the constitution.* Major restrictions include
those forbidding (to some extent) MPs to sit as
a company officer or to own a company, but
they do not include generic provisions on conflicts of interest (as in the Hungarian Constitution), or ways to determine incompatibilities
through law (as in the Portuguese Constitution).
Furthermore, restrictions need to apply to all
MPs, and not just to a few. I indicate, for
example, that the Malaysian Constitution does
not set major restrictions, since its provisions
pertain only to the president of the Senate and
the speaker of the House of Representatives.

4. *Restrictions on ownership by ministers,
following the restrictions as for MPs.* These
restrictions may come from any of the sources.
Restrictions on ownership by ministers are
identified in 14 countries.

5. *Restrictions on board membership by ministers.* In Australia, Brazil, Denmark, the Netherlands, Peru, Spain, Thailand, and the United
Kingdom, ministers may not sit on a board. In
some other countries, ministers are allowed to
sit on boards as long as the position (a) is not
remunerated; (b) does not represent a conflict of
interest (e.g., the company either has a contract
with the state or enjoys special privileges or
concessions, or receives a regular state subsidy

by virtue of a special law); or (c) a waiver is
granted.

6. *Major restrictions on board membership
or ownership by ministers expressed in the constitution.* Constitutional restrictions applying to
ministers are more common than restrictions
applying to MPs; they show up in 13 countries.

I add these six scores together to create an
aggregate score (*regulatory score*), which
ranges from 0 for Belgium, the Czech Republic,
India, Indonesia, Italy, Luxembourg, Malaysia,
Mexico, Taiwan, and Venezuela, to 6 for Peru
and the Philippines.[9]

In addition to this restrictions-based variable,
I include the dummy variable *mandatory disclosure of assets,* which takes the value of one if
government officials are required to disclose
personal assets, and zero otherwise. This variable is based on information from the Parline
database and from the questionnaires sent to
parliaments and governments.

I expect connections to be less common in
countries with more stringent regulations (e.g.,
more widespread and stronger restrictions). The
expected impact of disclosure rules is much less
clear. On the one hand, disclosure may discourage connections, as it increases the likelihood
that abuses are detected and punished. On the
other hand, disclosure makes it more likely that
connections are picked up in my sample. The
correlation coefficient for restrictions and incidence of connections, reported in Table
4, shows that, as expected, restrictions are associated with a lower proportion of connections.
Disclosure requirements are also associated
with fewer connections, at least in the univariate
analysis.

Corruption.—I employ three measures of
perceived corruption. My first proxy for corruption, *Kaufmann et al. corruption,* is defined as
the exercise of public power for private gains; it
includes various measures ranging from the frequency of "additional payments to get things
done" to the effects of corruption on the business environment. This variable comes from
Daniel Kaufmann et al. (1999a and 1999b). It is
an indicator variable that is based on a statistical
compilation of perceptions regarding the quality

---

[9] Details on each country's regulations are available
from the author.

TABLE 4—DETERMINANTS OF THE FREQUENCY OF CONNECTIONS (CORRELATION COEFFICIENTS)

	Kaufmann et al. corruption	German corruption	Corruption ICRG	Quality of legal environment	Cross-border restrictions	Democratic in all years since 1950
% of firms connected with a minister or MP	0.10	0.22	0.11	−0.06	0.25	0.00
% of firms connected with a minister or MP, or a close relationship	0.27	0.38	0.32	−0.23	0.41	−0.18
% of top 50 firms connected with a minister or MP, or a close relationship	0.14	0.22	0.12	−0.06	0.29	−0.05

	Press freedom index	Secondary school enrollment	Ln{GDP (per capita)}	Regulatory score	Mandatory disclosure of assets
% of firms connected with a minister or MP	0.28	0.04	−0.02	−0.22	−0.13
% of firms connected with a minister or MP, or a close relationship	0.42	−0.08	−0.23	−0.23	−0.09
% of top 50 firms connected with a minister or MP, or a close relationship	0.33	0.07	−0.10	−0.16	−0.01

Notes: % *of firms connected with a minister or MP* is the ratio of firms connected with a minister or MP as a proportion of the total number of firms in a given country. % *of firms connected with a minister or MP, or a close relationship* is the number of all connected firms as a proportion of the total number of firms in a particular country. % *of top 50 firms connected with a minister or MP, or a close relationship* is the number of connected firms as proportion of the largest 50 firms (based on end-of-1997 market capitalization) in a particular country. For countries with fewer than 50 firms in the sample, this fraction is computed based on the available companies. Kaufmann et al. (1999a, b) corruption is defined as the exercise of public power for private gains, and measures various aspects, ranging from the frequency of "additional payments to get things done" to the effects of corruption on the business environment. "The indicator reflects the statistical compilation of perceptions of the quality of governance of a large number of survey respondents in industrial and developing countries, as well as nongovernmental organizations, commercial risk rating agencies, and think tanks during 1997 and 1998." Originally scaled from about −2.5 to 2.5; rescaled from 0 to 10, with higher scores for higher corruption. Source: Kaufmann et al. (1999a, b), *http://www.worldbank.org/wbi/governance/datasets.html#dataset. German corruption* is the German exporters' corruption index developed by Neumann (1994). The index ranges from 0 to 5, with higher scores denoting higher levels of corruption. *Corruption ICRG* is the International Country Risk Guide's assessment of the corruption in government. Higher scores indicate "high government officials are likely to demand special payments" and "illegal payments are generally expected throughout lower levels of government" in the form of "bribes connected with import and export licenses, exchange controls, tax assessment, policy protection, or loans." Average of the months of April and October of the monthly index between 1982 and 1995. Scale from 0 to 10; the original scale is inverted so that lower scores correspond to lower levels of corruption (source: La Porta et al., 1998). *Quality of legal environment* is the average between *efficiency of the judicial system* and *rule of law. Efficiency of the judicial system* is an assessment of the "efficiency and integrity of the legal environment as it affects business, particularly foreign firms" produced by the country-risk rating agency Business International Corporation. It "may be taken to represent investors' assessments of conditions in the country in question." Average between 1980 and 1983. Scale from 0 to 10, with lower scores for lower efficiency levels (source: Mauro, 1995). *Rule of law* is an assessment of the law-and-order tradition in the country produced by the country-risk rating agency International Country Risk. Average of the months of April and October of the monthly index between 1982 and 1995. Scale from 0 to 10, with lower scores for lower efficiency levels (source: La Porta et al., 1998, and World Bank, *http://www.worldbank.org/wbi/governance/datasets.html#dataset*). *Cross-border restrictions* is a dummy variable that equals 1 if there is any restriction on the purchase of securities or outward direct investment in a specific country, and zero otherwise (source: IMF, "Exchange Arrangements and Exchange Restrictions"). *Democratic in all years since 1950* is dummy variable that equals 1 if (i) the executive is elected, (ii) the legislature (at least its lower house) is elected, (iii) more than one party contests elections, and (iv) during the last three elections of the executive there has been at least one turnover of power between parties (source: Treisman, 2000). *Press freedom index* measures the amount of freedom journalists and the media have in each country and the efforts made by governments to see that press freedom is respected. Reporters without Borders sent a questionnaire based on the main criteria for such freedom and asking for details of direct attacks on journalists (such as murders, imprisonment, physical assaults, and threats) and on the media (censorship, confiscation, searches, and pressure). It also asked about the degree of impunity enjoyed by those responsible for such violations. The index of press freedom is a portrait of the situation based on events between September 2001 and October 2002. Scale from 0 to 100, with lower scores for more freedom (source: Reporters without Borders, "Worldwide Press Freedom Index," *http://www.rsf.fr/ article.php3?id_article=4118*). The original index is not available for Luxembourg (replaced in the sample with the average between France and Belgium), New Zealand (replaced in the sample with Australia, and Singapore). *Secondary school enrollment* is the ratio of the number of children of official school age (as defined by the national education system) who are enrolled in school to the population of the corresponding official school age. Secondary education completes the provision of basic education that began at the primary level and aims at laying the foundations for lifelong learning and human development by offering more subject- or skill-oriented instruction using more specialized teachers. Average 1987–1999 (source: World Bank, *http://sima-ext.worldbank.org/query/*). *Ln{GDP (per capita)}* is the natural log of gross domestic product (in US$) on a purchasing-power-parity basis divided by population; computed for 1999 (source: World Bank, *http://sima-ext.worldbank.org/query/*). *Regulatory score* is formed by adding: (i) restrictions on ownership by MPs, (ii) restrictions on directorships by MPs, (iii) restrictions on ownership by ministers, (iv) restrictions on directorships by ministers, (v) restrictions on directorships by ministers, (vi) restrictions on ministers in constitution. The index ranges from 0 to 6 (source: Table 3). *Mandatory disclosure of assets* is a dummy variable that takes the value of 1 if government officials are required to declare personal assets and zero otherwise (source: Table 3).

of governance in industrial and developing countries, collected in a survey of a large number of respondents, as well as the opinion of nongovernmental organizations, commercial risk rating agencies, and think tanks (during 1997 and 1998). The second measure of corruption that I employ, *German corruption*, was developed in Peter Neumann (1994). This index is compiled from interviews with German exporters, and it indicates the proportion of transactions involving bribes. To put together this index, Neumann interviewed on average ten individuals per foreign importing country, with a guarantee of strict confidentiality. This proxy of corruption has been used by other researchers, such as Alberto Ades and Rafael Di Tella (1997) and Shang-Jin Wei (2000), and has the benefit of being relatively "objective," since bribing foreign government officials was not a crime in Germany when the survey was done.[10] The third measure of corruption in the table,

[10] I thank a referee for suggesting this proxy for corruption. I also thank Rafael Di Tella for providing me with a copy of Neumann's (1994) article.

corruption ICRG, is the International Country Risk Guide's assessment of corruption in governments. Ex ante, it is not clear whether corruption and connections should be complements or substitutes. The correlation coefficients in Table 4 show, however, that connections are positively related to corruption.

Quality of the Legal Environment.—Quality of legal environment is the average of efficiency of the *judicial system* and *rule of law.* The first is an assessment of the efficiency and integrity of the legal environment as it affects business, particularly foreign firms, produced by the country-risk rating agency, Business International Corporation. It may be taken to represent investors' assessments of conditions in the country in question. The index is scaled from 0 to 10; lower scores represent lower efficiency levels (see Paolo Mauro, 1995). The *rule of law* is an assessment of the law and order tradition in the country produced by the country-risk rating agency, International Country Risk. It also is scaled from 0 to 10, with lower scores for lower efficiency levels.[11] Ex ante, one would expect countries with better legal systems to display a lower incidence of connections. A good legal regime should exhibit more transparency of regulation, uniform application of the law, and rigorous enforcement of penalties associated with violations of the law. This hypothesis is supported by the negative correlations in Table 4.

Openness.—Cross-border restrictions are used as proxy for openness in the economy. They take the value of one if there is any restriction on the purchase of foreign securities or outward direct investment by citizens, and zero otherwise. Measures of this variable come from the International Monetary Fund's "Exchange Arrangements and Exchange Restrictions." Capital restrictions allow politicians to insulate the country from international capital flows, ensuring connected corporations' access to capital, both from domestic private investors and banks (Johnson and Mitton, 2003; Raghuram G.

Rajan and Luigi Zingales, 2003). Thus, I expect connections to be more prevalent in countries with capital restrictions. The relevant coefficients in Table 4 confirm that connections are more common in countries that restrict capital outflows.

Democracy, Freedom of Press, Education, and Economic Development.—As a proxy for democracy, I use *democratic in all years since 1950,* an indicator variable that takes the value of one if (a) the executive is elected; (b) the legislature (or at least its lower house) is elected; (c) more than one party contests elections; and (d) during the last three elections of the executive there has been at least one turnover of power between parties. This variable is taken from Daniel Treisman (2000). Democratic systems might serve to discourage connections, because political opponents have an incentive to discover and publicize abuses of office. Further, connections may be seen as less valuable if officials can be voted out.

The *press freedom index* measures the extent of freedom journalists and the media have in each country and of the efforts made by governments to see that press freedom is respected, as measured by Reporters without Borders. Increased freedom of press should discourage connections since it encourages the detection and punishment of abuses. As with any other transparency variable, however, we may uncover a positive association between the freedom of the press and connections if more transparent systems are, in general, better able to tolerate connections because a misuse would be more likely to be punished. Furthermore, a positive mechanical association would result if connections are easier to detect in more transparent economies.

A similar effect may show up for education-related variables. A proxy for education, *secondary school enrollment,* is the proportion of children of official secondary school age (as defined by the country) enrolled in school to the population of that age.

I also use the natural log of per capita GDP, *Ln{GDP (per capita)}*, as a proxy for economic development (see Mauro, 1995; Treisman, 2000). We may see fewer connections in more developed countries, as the benefits of being close to politicians may be smaller there. On the other hand, more developed countries may be more transparent, so that a higher proportion of

---

[11] I also use a number of proxies for the regulation of entry developed by Simeon Djankov et al. (2002), such as their "number of procedures," "time," and "cost" variables, but none of them is significant in explaining the incidence of connections.

connections that exist are included in the sample because they are easier to detect in more transparent economies.

B. *Regression Results*

Using regressions based on a two-boundary Tobit specification, I test the significance of the relations between the connections variables and the independent variables. All regressions include the natural log of per capita GDP as a control variable. I start by using the objective measure of connections, *% of firms connected with a minister or MP*, as dependent variable. In Table 5, models (1), (2), and (8) to (10) show that two of the three proxies for perceived corruption are positively and significantly associated with the connection index. This finding is intriguing and indicates three possible explanations. First, it may be that in some countries corruption is not helpful enough to obtain significant benefits, so businessmen need to become personally involved in politics in order to "squeeze the state." Alternatively, it may be the case that corruption emerges as a response to political connections if companies without political connections need to bribe politicians in order to obtain the minimum benefits necessary to ensure the survival of the firm. Third, it may be that my measure of connections is a proxy for corruption, which is observable at the firm level. Of course, these results need to be interpreted with the following caveat: my measure of political connections includes only cases that are readily observable, and overt connections might be more common in countries in which corruption is more widely accepted. Model (3) shows that connections are less common in countries with better legal environments. This result is statistically significant in regressions (9) and (10).

Model (4) shows that countries that restrict foreign financial investment by residents have a significantly higher incidence of political connections. Democratic governments are associated with a higher incidence of connections, but the relationship is not statistically significant (model 5). Similarly, less freedom of press is associated with a higher incidence of connections. Model (6) shows that better education is associated with more connections. This result may be due to the fact that democracies and systems with better education are in general

better able to tolerate connections because a misuse would be more likely to be punished. Finally, Model (7) indicates that restrictions on connections are, as one would expect, associated with fewer connections. The mandatory disclosure of assets is also associated with fewer connections.

Several of the explanatory variables are highly correlated with one another and it would be difficult to disentangle their individual effects. Thus, I further assess the validity of the results using a stepwise procedure, adding independent variables one at a time until the best regression model is obtained. Most of the results continue to hold for models (8) to (10). Corruption, for example, continues to be positively associated with connections for two of the three measures. Similarly, connections remain more common in countries that restrict foreign investment by residents. Connections are less common in the presence of more restrictive regulations. They remain more common in more transparent systems, such as democracies, and in countries with higher secondary school enrollment.

Models (11) to (13) show that these results are generally robust to changes in the incidence of connections variable; these models use *% of firms connected with a minister or MP, or a close relationship,* the less objective measure of connections. One difference between models (11) to (13) and models (8) to (10) is that when using the less objective measure of connections the relationship between connections and corruption is weakened. Additionally, although I find a positive association between the democratic structure of the country and the incidence of connections, this association is no longer significant at conventional levels.

The coverage of the Worldscope dataset is such that more firms are included for some countries than for others. A way to minimize Worldscope sampling issues is to focus on the largest firms in each country. I therefore use the variable *% of top 50 firms connected with a minister or MP, or a close relationship,* which is the incidence of connections among the largest 50 firms in each country. For countries with fewer than 50 firms in the sample, this fraction is computed based on the available companies. In models (14) to (16), countries that restrict foreign financial investment by residents continue to display a significantly higher incidence

TABLE 5—DETERMINANTS OF THE FREQUENCY OF CONNECTIONS: TWO-BOUNDARY TOBIT REGRESSION ESTIMATES

Indep. variables:	Dep. var.: % of firms connected with a minister or MP						
	(1)	(2)	(3)	(4)	(5)	(6)	(7)
Kaufmann et al. corruption	0.41						
	(0.53)						
German corruption		0.95					
		(0.11)					
Quality of legal environment			−0.31				
			(0.53)				
Cross-border restrictions				3.73			
				(0.02)			
Democratic in all years since 1950					1.14		
					(0.21)		
Press freedom index					0.14		
					(0.08)		
Secondary school enrollment						0.12	
						(0.19)	
Regulatory score							−0.49
							(0.16)
Mandatory disclosure of assets							−0.71
							(0.55)
Ln{GDP (per capita)}	1.34	2.00	1.24	2.09	1.58	−3.67	0.34
	(0.35)	(0.14)	(0.38)	(0.02)	(0.22)	(0.18)	(0.67)
Intercept	−12.25	−18.67	−7.66	−19.20	−15.56	28.09	0.00
	(0.42)	(0.17)	(0.48)	(0.03)	(0.23)	(0.19)	(1.00)
N obs.	47	45	42	46	46	43	47
R^2 adj. (%)	<0	0.27	<0	1.31	5.22	1.77	<0

Indep. variables	Dep. var.: % of firms connected with a minister or MP			Dep. var.: % of firms connected with a minister or MP, or a close relationship		
	(8)	(9)	(10)	(11)	(12)	(13)
Kaufmann et al. corruption	0.36			−0.23		
	(0.53)			(0.97)		
German corruption		1.00			1.20	
		(0.08)			(0.18)	
Corruption ICRG			1.50			2.20
			(0.00)			(0.01)
Cross-border restrictions	2.70	1.94	2.28	5.73	4.51	4.74
	(0.03)	(0.13)	(0.07)	(0.02)	(0.07)	(0.06)
Democratic in all years since 1950	1.63	1.88	2.35	0.88	1.71	2.42
	(0.16)	(0.07)	(0.00)	(0.66)	(0.39)	(0.19)
Secondary school enrollment	0.03	0.03	0.04	0.09	0.11	0.13
	(0.39)	(0.43)	(0.12)	(0.16)	(0.16)	(0.08)
Regulatory score	−0.58	−0.62	−0.73	−1.11	−1.08	−1.33
	(0.02)	(0.01)	(0.00)	(0.05)	(0.04)	(0.00)
Ln{GDP (per capita)}	0.66	1.31	2.74	−1.54	−0.72	1.93
	(0.57)	(0.38)	(0.02)	(0.56)	(0.82)	(0.50)
Intercept	−8.35	−14.74	−31.64	10.25	−1.24	−31.00
	(0.49)	(0.27)	(0.01)	(0.69)	(0.96)	(0.26)
N obs.	43	42	42	43	42	42
R^2 adj. (%)	10.40	24.81	32.12	16.40	23.67	29.13

TABLE 5—*Continued.*

Indep. variables	Dep. var.: % of top 50 firms connected with a minister or MP, or a close relationship			Dep. var.: % of firms connected with a minister or MP. Robustness test: Addition of regional dummies		
	(14)	(15)	(16)	(17)	(18)	(19)
Kaufmann et al. corruption	−0.71			0.13		
	(0.76)			(0.83)		
German corruption		0.76			0.70	
		(0.78)			(0.39)	
Corruption ICRG			3.97			1.32
			(0.03)			(0.01)
Cross-border restrictions	16.62	15.33	13.90	2.47	1.56	1.91
	(0.02)	(0.03)	(0.04)	(0.01)	(0.22)	(0.05)
Democratic in all years since 1950	4.36	5.54	7.60	0.84	1.28	1.58
	(0.44)	(0.31)	(0.17)	(0.51)	(0.32)	(0.06)
Secondary school enrollment	0.25	0.29	0.33	−0.03	−0.03	−0.01
	(0.14)	(0.17)	(0.09)	(0.26)	(0.43)	(0.76)
Regulatory score	−2.24	−2.10	−2.54	−0.45	−0.52	−0.62
	(0.07)	(0.07)	(0.02)	(0.02)	(0.03)	(0.00)
Ln{GDP (per capita)}	−1.74	−0.99	4.99	0.80	1.56	2.65
	(0.77)	(0.90)	(0.45)	(0.53)	(0.43)	(0.05)
Europe				−3.24	−11.42	−25.15
				(0.81)	(0.53)	(0.08)
North America				−3.68	−11.52	−26.20
				(0.79)	(0.53)	(0.07)
South America				−7.97	−15.69	−29.97
				(0.58)	(0.41)	(0.03)
Asia				−3.28	−10.88	−25.87
				(0.81)	(0.54)	(0.07)
Austral. & New Zealand				−6.14	−14.05	−28.08
				(0.64)	(0.44)	(0.05)
Africa				−27.03	−32.91	−44.76
				(0.05)	(0.05)	(0.00)
Intercept	−1.13	−15.42	−83.76			
	(0.98)	(0.82)	(0.19)			
N obs.	43	42	42	43	42	42
R^2 adj. (%)	<0	<0	<0	41.27	47.56	54.60

Notes: All variables are defined in Table 4. The *p*-values, reported in parentheses below the coefficients, are computed using Huber/White correction for heteroskedasticity (see White, 1980).

of connections. Similarly, restrictions on political connections are associated with a significantly lower proportion of connections. Finally, although the ICRG measure of perceived corruption is positively and significantly associated with the incidence of connections, the associations with the German corruption index and the Kaufmann et al. proxy are not significant.

To check the robustness of my results, I exclude countries with limited data coverage in Worldscope (see footnote 6). All variables maintain the signs displayed in models (8) to (10), although only corruption and the regulatory score remain significant at conventional levels. As a second check, to verify that the results are not driven by a regional factor, I add regional dummies to the regressions (models (17) to (19)). In all regressions, the regulation variable remains significantly associated with the incidence of connections. Moreover, in at least some of the regressions, the coefficients on the cross-border restrictions indicator, democracy, and on the ICRG's measure of corruption remain significantly associated with the incidence of connections.

III. The Value of Connections

To see whether connections add value, I run an event study around announcements of (a) officers or large shareholders entering politics and (b) politicians joining boards. If connections add value, announcements should be associated with a positive cumulative abnormal return (CAR).

Several factors limit the sample size. First, the dates of appointments *and* elections must be identifiable. I am able to identify the election dates in 572 cases. All international data sources covered in Lexis-Nexis, Reuters, *The Financial Times,* and *The Economist* allow identification of the dates of board appointments or of acquisition of ownership for only 328 cases. The lack of data forces exclusion of many interesting connections, such as those involving several companies related to Suharto (who came to power in 1967), the King of Thailand, Mahathir, several Russian politicians, and anyone who came to power before press releases are available. Second, it must be possible to verify whether a particular politician was an officer before the election or appointment to office, as well as whether someone later appointed an officer was already a politician at that time. Application of this requirement reduces the sample to 296 observations. Third, stock price series must be available from Datastream or Bloomberg LP, which reduces the sample to 245 observations.

There will be a stock price reaction to an election only if the outcome is a surprise. In a number of cases, the outcome of an election was easy to call in advance. To deal with anticipation, I conduct keyword searches in *Factiva* using the terms "surprise*," "unexpect*," or "unpredict*," and include only those elections reported as being surprising. I consider all appointments of politicians to corporate boards as surprises, unless the press mentions the name of the politician as a potential candidate in advance. I follow a similar procedure for appointments to political positions. I am left with a final sample of 157 announcements, of which 48 are appointments of politicians to a board and 109 are "elections." While appointments are generally not clustered on a particular day, some of the connections created by elections are clustered. Overall, the 109 elections and appointments are spread over 48 different days or countries. Since in the presence of clustering, observations may not be independent, the standard errors reported in Table 6 and in footnotes 12 and 13 are corrected using the procedure described in Jeffry Wooldridge (2002, pp. 405–10).

I use the Stephen J. Brown and Jerold B. Warner (1985) standard event study methodology to calculate the market-adjusted CARs for the five-day period around the announcement dates (days -2 to $+2$). The event date is defined as the election date for officers and large shareholders entering politics, and as the day of appointment to the board for politician appointment. The results for the whole sample, reported in Table 6, panel A, indicate that the announcement of a new connection results in an abnormal return of 1.43 percent (p-value $= 0.09$). In panel B, an event study centered on elections reveals an average excess return of 2.29 percent (p-value $= 0.05$) whenever a businessperson enters politics, which suggests that, for this subsample, benefits outweigh the costs of connections. For the 48 announcements of appointments of a politician to a board, I find that companies experience an insignificant average CAR of -0.53 percent (p-value $= 0.27$). This suggests that, for this subsample of announcements, the benefits of connections do not exceed the costs.[12]

Furthermore, for the elections subsample, I find that connections with more powerful politicians and with businesspeople with more vested interests in the company result in larger announcement returns: for example, a connection through a large shareholder results in a five-day CAR of 4.47 percent, while a connection through an officer results in a CAR of only 1.94 percent (see panel C). Similarly, while a connection through a member of the parliament results in a value increase of "only" 1.28 percent, a connection with a minister or a close relationship results in an average value increase of 12.31 percent (panel D). Finally, panel E shows that connections create more value in

---

[12] It would be rational for controlling shareholders to charge the costs of connections to firms in which she is diluting her ownership stake through some control-enhancing devices (see, for example, Marianne Bertrand et al., 2002). I test for this possibility by comparing the announcement returns, around appointments of politicians to boards, of companies controlled through a pyramid to those of companies directly controlled by their largest shareholder. In support of the expropriation hypothesis, I find an average announcement return of -2.05 percent (p-value $= 0.06$) for companies controlled through a pyramid and of 0.03 percent (p-value $= 0.97$) for companies directly controlled by their largest shareholder. The difference between the two is statistically significant with a p-value of 0.06.

TABLE 6—THE VALUE OF CONNECTIONS

	N. Obs.	Average CAR (%)	(p-value)
Panel A: Overall results			
Full sample	157	1.43	(0.09)
Panel B: Results by the way the connection is established			
Appointments of politicians on corporate boards	48	−0.53	(0.27)
Company large shareholders and officers entering politics	109	2.29	(0.05)
Panel C: Officers versus large shareholders entering politics			
Large shareholders entering politics	15	4.47	(0.02)
Officers entering politics	94	1.94	(0.15)
Panel D: Officers and large shareholders taking on higher versus lower political office			
Appointment or election as a minister (either directly or through a close relationship)	10	12.31	(0.32)
Appointment or election as an MP	99	1.28	(0.02)
Panel E: Results by level of corruption (Kaufmann et al. corruption measure)			
Countries with corruption ≥ sample median	58	4.32	(0.08)
Countries with corruption < sample median	51	−0.02	(0.97)

Notes: Abnormal (%) returns are computed using a standard market-adjusted approach. The event window goes from day -2 to day $+2$. The event date is defined as the election date (or date of appointment of the politician, if different) in the case of officers/large shareholders elected as politicians, and as the date the appointment was announced, in the case of appointment of politicians to the board. Datastream's index for the connected company's home country is used as the measure of market returns. Panels C through E focus on the subsample of 109 elections (of large shareholders and/or officers to political office). Standard errors are corrected for clustering in the election dates.

countries with high corruption (i.e., those with a Kaufmann et al. corruption index greater than or equal to the sample median) than in countries with low corruption; the average CARs for these two subsamples are of 4.32 percent and -0.02 percent, respectively.[13]

[13] Because Rita Ramalho (2003) documents a long-term drift in performance in the year following the collapse of connections (with Brazilian President Collor de Mello), I test whether my sample firms exhibit abnormal performance in the year following the establishment of a connection. For this purpose, I measure one-year buy-and-hold returns (Brad Barber and John Lyon, 1997), starting on the second day after the announcement of the establishment of a connection (e.g., the last day of my event study window) and ending 262 trading days (approximately one year) after the establishment of the connection. To measure abnormal buy and hold returns, I assume that the expected return for company j is equal to its home country's stock market index return. Data are available to compute the abnormal return for 149 out of the 157 firms included in Table 6. For this sample, the average abnormal one-year return is 4.85 percent, with a p-value of 0.17. Thus, my results do not support Ramalho's findings.

IV. Conclusion

In this paper, I build a completely new measure of political connections for over 20,000 listed companies from 47 countries. I define a company as politically connected if one of its large shareholders or top officers is a member of parliament, a minister, or is closely related to a top politician or party. Overall, 541 firms are politically connected, representing almost 8 percent of the world's market capitalization. I find that political relationships are not equally common across countries. Connections are particularly common in countries with higher levels of corruption, countries imposing restrictions on foreign investments by their residents, and countries with more transparent systems. Connections are less common in countries with regulations that set more rigorous limits on political conflicts of interest.

I also find that different relationships between business people and politicians have different value. No significant price effect is detected for appointments of politicians to corporate boards. This result is consistent with the hypothesis that politicians extract rents from companies they manage (De Soto, 1989; Shleifer and Vishny, 1994), and that in equilibrium the costs of connections may offset their benefits. Stock prices increase significantly, however, when a businessperson enters politics, suggesting that rent seeking is, as one might expect, much less of a problem in this case. Additionally, firm value increases more when a businessperson is elected prime minister, rather than as a member of the parliament. Because the number of prime minister positions is quite limited, only a few businesspeople can succeed in becoming prime minister.

REFERENCES

Ades, Alberto and Di Tella, Rafael. "National Champions and Corruption: Some Unpleasant Interventionist Arithmetic." *Economic Journal*, 1997, *107*(443), pp. 1023–42.

Agrawal, Anup and Knoeber, Charles R. "Do Some Outside Directors Play a Political Role?" *Journal of Law and Economics*, 2001, *44*(1), pp. 179–98.

Amemiya, Takeshi. "Tobit Models: A Survey." *Journal of Econometrics*, 1984, *24*(1–2), pp. 3–61.

Ang, James and Boyer, Carol M. "Finance and Politics: Special Interest Group Influence during the Nationalization and Privatization of Conrail." Clarkson University, Economics and Financial Studies Working Papers: No. A-4, 2000.

Backman, Michael. *Asian eclipse: Exploring the dark side of business in Asia*. Singapore: John Wiley and Sons, 1999.

Barber, Brad M. and Lyon, John D. "Detecting Long-Run Abnormal Stock Returns: The Empirical Power and Specification of Test Statistics." *Journal of Financial Economics*, 1997, *43*(3), pp. 341–72.

Bardhan, Pranab. "Corruption and Development: A Review of Issues." *Journal of Economic Literature*, 1997, *35*(3), pp. 1320–46.

Bertrand, Marianne; Mehta, Paras and Mullainathan, Sendhil. "Ferreting Out Tunneling: An Application to Indian Business Groups." *Quarterly Journal of Economics*, 2002, *117*(1), pp. 121–48.

Brown, Stephen J. and Warner, Jerold B. "Using Daily Stock Returns: The Case of Event Studies." *Journal of Financial Economics*, 1985, *14*(1), pp. 3–31.

Claessens, Stijn; Djankov, Simeon and Lang, Larry H. P. "The Separation of Ownership and Control in East Asian Corporations." *Journal of Financial Economics*, 2000, *58*(1–2), pp. 81–112.

De Soto, Hernando. *The other path: The invisible revolution in the Third Worlds*. New York: Harper and Row Publishers, 1989.

Dinç, I. Serdar. "Politicians and Banks: Political Influences on Government-Owned Banks in Emerging Countries." *Journal of Financial Economics*, 2005, *77*(2), pp. 453–79.

Djankov, Simeon; La Porta, Rafael; Lopez-de-Silanes, Florencio and Shleifer, Andrei. "The Regulation of Entry." *Quarterly Journal of Economics*, 2002, *117*(1), pp. 1–37.

Faccio, Mara and Lang, Larry H. P. "The Ultimate Ownership of Western European Corporations." *Journal of Financial Economics*, 2002, *65*(3), pp. 365–95.

Faccio, Mara; Lang, Larry H. P. and Young, Leslie. "Dividends and Expropriation." *American Economic Review*, 2001, *91*(1), pp. 54–78.

Fisman, Raymond. "Estimating the Value of Political Connections." *American Economic Review*, 2001, *91*(4), pp. 1095–1102.

Gomez, Edmund T. and Jomo, K. S. *Malaysia's political economy: Politics, patronage and profits*. Cambridge: Cambridge University Press, 1997.

Hellman, Joel S.; Jones, Geraint and Kaufmann, Daniel. "Seize the State, Seize the Day: State Capture and Influence in Transition Economies." *Journal of Comparative Economics*, 2003, *31*(4), pp. 751–73.

Johnson, Simon and Mitton, Todd. "Cronyism and Capital Controls: Evidence from Malaysia." *Journal of Financial Economics*, 2003, *67*(2), pp. 351–82.

Kaufmann, Daniel; Kraay, Aart and Zoido-Lobatón, Pablo. "Governance Matters." World Bank Policy Research Paper No. 2196, 1999a.

Kaufmann, Daniel; Kraay, Aart and Zoido-Lobatón, Pablo. "Aggregating Governance Indicators." World Bank Policy Research Paper No. 2195, 1999b.

Kroszner, Randall S. and Stratmann, Thomas. "Interest-Group Competition and the Organization of Congress: Theory and Evidence from Financial Services' Political Action Committees." *American Economic Review,* 1998, *88*(5), pp. 1163–87.

La Porta, Rafael; Lopez-de Silanes, Florencio; Shleifer, Andrei and Vishny, Robert W. "Law and Finance." *Journal of Political Economy,* 1998, *106*(6), pp. 1113–55.

La Porta, Rafael; Lopez-de-Silanes, Florencio; Shleifer, Andrei and Vishney, Robert W. "The Quality of Government." *Journal of Law, Economics, and Organization,* 1999, *15*(1), pp. 222–79.

Mauro, Paolo. "Corruption and Growth." *Quarterly Journal of Economics,* 1995, *110*(3), pp. 681–712.

Morck, Randall K.; Stangeland, David A. and Yeung, Bernard. "Inherited Wealth, Corporate Control, and Economic Growth: The Canadian Disease?" in Randall K. Morck, ed., *Concentrated corporate ownership.* Chicago: University of Chicago Press, 2000, pp. 319–69.

Neumann, Peter. "Böse: Fast alle bestechen (Flaunting the Rules: Almost Everyone)." *Impulse,* 1994, *4,* pp. 12–16.

Rajan, Raghuram G. and Zingales, Luigi. "The Great Reversals: The Politics of Financial Development in the Twentieth Century." *Journal of Financial Economics,* 2003, *69*(1), pp. 5–50.

Ramalho, Rita. "The Effects of Anti-Corruption Campaign: Evidence from the 1992 Presidential Impeachment in Brazil." Unpublished Paper, 2003.

Roberts, Brian E. "A Dead Senator Tells No Lies: Seniority and the Distribution of Federal Benefits." *American Journal of Political Science,* 1990, *34*(1), pp. 31–58.

Rose-Ackerman, Susan. *Corruption and government: Causes, consequences, and reform.* Cambridge: Cambridge University Press, 1999.

Shleifer, Andrei and Vishny, Robert W. "Corruption." *Quarterly Journal of Economics,* 1993, *108*(3), pp. 599–617.

Shleifer, Andrei and Vishny, Robert W. "Politicians and Firms." *Quarterly Journal of Economics,* 1994, *109*(4), pp. 995–1025.

Stigler, George J. "The Theory of Economic Regulation." *Bell Journal of Economics and Management Science,* 1971, *2*(1), pp. 3–21.

Svensson, Jakob. "Who Must Pay Bribes and How Much? Evidence from a Cross Section of Firms." *Quarterly Journal of Economics,* 2003, *118*(1), pp. 207–30.

Treisman, Daniel. "The Causes of Corruption: A Cross-National Study." *Journal of Public Economics,* 2000, *76*(3), pp. 399–457.

Wei, Shang-Jin. "Local Corruption and Global Capital Flows." *Brookings Papers on Economic Activity,* 2000, *0*(2), pp. 303–46.

White, Halbert. "A Heteroskedasticity-Consistent Covariance Matrix Estimator and a Direct Test for Heteroskedasticity." *Econometrica,* 1980, *48*(4), pp. 817–38.

Wooldridge, Jeffrey M. *Econometric analysis of cross section and panel data.* Cambridge, MA: MIT Press, 2002.

[28]

Estimating the Value of Political Connections

By Raymond Fisman*

As the Indonesian economy went into a downward spiral in the latter half of 1997, there was much speculation and debate as to the reasons behind the sudden decline. Most explanations gave at least some role to investor panic, which had led to a massive outflow of foreign capital. At the root of this hysteria, however, were concerns that the capital that had flowed into Indonesia and elsewhere in Southeast Asia had not been used for productive investments. Much of this discussion focused on the role of political connections in driving investment. The claim was that in Southeast Asia, political connectedness, rather than fundamentals such as productivity, was the primary determinant of profitability and that this had led to distorted investment decisions. Obviously, the degree to which this type of problem was truly responsible for the Asian collapse depends very much on the extent to which connectedness really was a primary determinant of firm value. In making the argument that this was in fact the case, anecdotes about the business dealings of President Suharto's children were often cited as evidence. Such stories suggest that the value of some firms may have been highly dependent on their political connections. However, investigations in this area have not progressed beyond the level of case study and anecdote. That is, there has been no attempt to estimate the degree to which firms rely on connections for their profitability.

There are numerous difficulties that would

affect any attempt to value political connections, which probably accounts for the paucity of work in this area. In countries where political decision-making is decentralized, simply defining political connectedness is an extremely complicated proposition. For example, in India, analyzing a firm's political associations would require information on its relationships with numerous government decision-making bodies as well as some way of aggregating these connections. Even with a specific measure in mind, collecting the appropriate data would be difficult because business–politics relations is often a taboo topic of conversation and because connections tend to shift considerably over time. Finally, assuming that an appropriate measure were found, it is not clear how one would estimate the *value* of these connections. Simple measures of profitability are unsuitable: in equilibrium, well-connected firms may not earn higher profits, even if they are earning tremendous political rents, because of the resources they may be required to devote to rent-seeking activities. Also, it is plausible that unobservables such as business acumen are correlated with the ability to establish political connections.

By looking at Indonesia, I am able to overcome these problems. Because of Indonesia's highly centralized and stable political structure (until the very end of Suharto's reign), it is possible to construct a credible index of political connectedness. Moreover, my "event study" approach described below allows for a relatively clean measure of the extent to which firms relied on these connections for their profitability.

To infer a measure of the value of connections, I take advantage of a string of rumors about former Indonesian President Suharto's health during his final years in office. I identify a number of episodes during which there were adverse rumors about the state of Suharto's health and compare the returns of firms with differing degrees of political exposure. First, I

* Graduate School of Business, 614 Uris Hall, Columbia University, 3022 Broadway, New York, NY 10027. I thank George Baker, Richard Caves, Gary Chamberlain, Rafael Di Tella, Tarun Khanna, Sendhil Mullainathan, Jan Rivkin, James Schorr, Dr. Sjahrir, Joseph Stern, Peter Timmer, Lou Wells, and seminar participants at Harvard University and the University of California at San Diego for many helpful comments on earlier versions of this paper; two anonymous referees provided thoughtful insights and suggestions. I am also very grateful to the many members of the Indonesian business community who were kind enough to meet with me during my visits to Jakarta. Any remaining errors are my own.

show that in every case the returns of shares of politically dependent firms were considerably lower than the returns of less-dependent firms. Furthermore, the magnitude of this differential effect is highly correlated with the net return on the Jakarta Stock Exchange Composite Index (JCI) over the corresponding episode, a relationship that derives from the fact that the return on the JCI is a measure of the severity of the rumor as perceived by investors. Motivated by these initial observations, I run a pooled regression using all of the events, allowing for an interaction between "political dependency" and "event severity." The coefficient on this interaction term is positive and statistically significant, implying that well-connected firms will suffer more, relative to less-connected firms, in reaction to a more serious rumor. My results suggest that a large percentage of a well-connected firm's value may be derived from political connections.

A few earlier papers dealt with related issues, beginning with Anne O. Krueger's (1974) pioneering work, which focused on rent-seeking behavior and efficiency losses resulting from restrictive trade policies. As Krueger herself concedes, however, the proxies she uses for the value of rents are very rough. Moreover, while her paper finds economic rents to be a substantial percentage of total GDP, it deals only with *aggregate* political rents and is therefore unable to say anything directly about the rents obtained by individual firms. A paper in the political science literature (Brian E. Roberts, 1990) looks more directly at the valuation of political connections. It examines the effect of Senator Henry Jackson's (unexpected) death on various constituent interests and on the constituent interests of his successor on the Senate Armed Services Committee. Robert's event study showed that share prices of companies with ties to Senator Jackson declined in reaction to news of his death whereas the prices of companies affiliated with his successor increased. Not surprisingly, the reported effects are quite small—the companies' ties to the two senators presumably reflected only a small fraction of the full value of their aggregate political connections. Thus, although Roberts' paper showed that connections matter, it did not address the larger question that I attempt to answer here: *How much* do connections matter?

The rest of the paper is structured as follows: Section I describes the data that were acquired

for this project. In Section II, I present the paper's basic econometric results and provide an interpretation of the implied effect. Section III looks at some issues of robustness. Finally, conclusions and the implications of the results are given in Section IV.

I. Data

Four separate types of data were acquired for this study: 1) stock market and accounting data for companies traded on the Jakarta Stock Exchange (JSX); 2) data on the group affiliations of all JSX firms; 3) a measure of the political dependence of a subset of these firms; and 4) a series of "events" related to the condition of Suharto's health.

A. *Accounting and Share Price Data*

The accounting data were taken from the *Financial Times'* Extel Financials Database (1997). I used data from 1995 because it is the most recent year with reasonably broad coverage. The accounting variables used include total assets (ASSETS), total debt (DEBT), taxes (TAX), net income (NI), and the international standard industrial classification (ISIC) code of the firm's industry.

For stock price data, I use the *Financial Times'* Extel Securities Database (1997). Unfortunately, there are a few gaps in its coverage of Indonesian firms; to fill in these holes, I used data from Investamatic Database (1998), a financial services data base that is commonly used by Southeast Asian securities firms.

B. *Group Affiliation*[1]

In Indonesia, group affiliations are not publicly reported; they must be inferred by looking at a firm's major shareholders and by examining

---

[1] Diversified business groups (called *grupos* in Latin America, *chaebol* in Korea, *business houses* in India, and *keiretsu* in Japan) are ubiquitous yet poorly understood organizational forms that dominate the private sectors of many countries. Such groups are comprised of a diverse set of businesses, often initiated by a single family (this is certainly the case in Indonesia), and bound together by equity cross-ownership and common board membership. See Yoshihara Kunio (1988) for a detailed description of groups in Southeast Asia.

the composition of its board and management. Several consulting firms in Jakarta collect and sell this information, which facilitates the collection of these data. My primary source is *Top Companies and Big Groups in Indonesia* (Kompass Indonesia, 1996), which lists the top 200 Indonesian groups along with their affiliated companies. This publication was last revised in 1996 and, as a result, is slightly outdated; for newer firms, the *Indonesian Capital Markets Directory 1997* (Jakarta Stock Exchange, 1997) was used to fill in the blanks. No mention of the Tahija Group was made in either of these primary sources. Firms affiliated with this group were identified by using a list of Tahija-affiliated companies given in a recent *AsiaMoney* article (Matthew Montagu-Pollock, 1995). Finally, all group membership classifications were confirmed by investment analysts in Jakarta in December 1997, which resulted in only slight revisions. There were virtually no changes in the group affiliations of publicly traded companies in the period under study, so there is no need to deal with shifts in ownership.

C. *Political Connectedness*

As a measure of political connections, I use the Suharto Dependency Index (1995) (referred to by the variable *POL* below) developed by the Castle Group, a leading economic consulting firm in Jakarta. Over the past few years, the group assisted over 150 multinationals with entry and market strategies for Indonesia. Its services include "partner searches" to help foreigners find appropriate local business partners and "customized profiles of Indonesian business groups." Among its more popular products is a *Roadmap of Indonesian Business Groups* (1998), which outlines the relationships among these groups along with information about their holdings and government connections.

The index itself was put together for a seminar given to members of the Jakarta business community in early 1996 and is based on the subjective assessments of a number of top consultants at the Castle Group (including the president, James W. Castle). It consists of a numerical rating of the degree to which each of the 25 largest industrial groups in Indonesia is dependent on political con-

nections for its profitability.[2] The ratings range from one (least dependent) to five (most dependent). Most of these groups have multiple companies listed on the JSX, yielding a total sample of 79 firms.[3] All of the companies affiliated with President Suharto's children (Bimantara and Citra Lamtoro Groups) received a score of five, as did those owned by longtime Suharto allies Bob Hasan (Nusamba Group), Liem Sioe Liong (Salim Group), and Prajogo Pangestu (Barito Pacific Group). At the other extreme, firms owned by the Bakrie brothers and Julius Tahija were given a score of one. For this paper, I subtracted one from the index to facilitate the interpretation of coefficients in regressions involving interaction terms.

Some basic summary statistics of firms, by degree of political dependence, are listed in Table 1. There do not appear to be any systematic differences in size or debt structure across firm type.

D. *Information on Suharto's Health*

During 1995–1997, the Indonesian financial markets were occasionally hit by rumors about Suharto's health. To determine the relevant events, the keywords SUHARTO, HEALTH and INDONESIA, and (STOCK or FINANCIAL) were used in a Lexis-Nexis literature search. This returned 484 stories, most of which referred to one or more of the six episodes outlined in the unpublished Appendix.[4] For nearly all of these episodes, it was possible to

---

[2] Definition from a conversation with James Castle, August 12, 1998.

[3] A number of publicly traded companies are associated with several groups, which raises the issue of how to classify companies with multiple affiliations. In my sample, there were 12 firms for which this problem arose. Of these, only three had multiple "top 25" groups as shareholders. For these three firms, I took a simple arithmetic average of the level of political dependency of the top 25 affiliated groups (in only one of these cases was there a difference of more than one among the rankings of the multiple owners). For the others, each firm was assigned the political dependency of the one top 25 group with which it was affiliated. Because I do not have any measure of dependency for smaller groups, this is my best guess of the firm's overall political dependency. All of the analyses below were repeated excluding firms with multiple affiliations; this affected the results only slightly.

[4] The few articles that did not refer to one of these events were unrelated to Suharto's personal health.

TABLE 1—SUMMARY STATISTICS BY DEGREE OF POLITICAL DEPENDENCE AS MEASURED
BY THE SUHARTO DEPENDENCY INDEX

POL	1	2	3	4	5	All firms	Observations
Observations	5	34	10	16	14	79	
	2,145.76	2,228.57	2,206.20	1,634.08	1,765.51	2,033.19	
Assets	(2,843.63)	(3,989.85)	(3,676.99)	(2,561.07)	(2,230.52)	(3,321.59)	76
	707.18	791.32	813.25	397.83	712.57	717.37	
Debt	(702.84)	(1,478.83)	(976.28)	(461.06)	(1,070.83)	(1,186.85)	70
Return on assets							
(net income)/	0.038	0.058	0.043	0.037	0.050	0.050	
(total assets)	(0.031)	(0.058)	(0.023)	(0.032)	(0.029)	(0.044)	76
Tax rate (taxes							
paid)/(pretax	0.23	0.24	0.16	0.22	0.15	0.21	
income)	(0.05)	(0.12)	(0.14)	(0.16)	(0.12)	(0.13)	74

Sources: All data are from the *Financial Times' Extel Database* (1997); Assets and Debt are expressed in millions of 1995 rupiah.

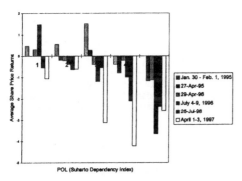

POL (Suharto Dependency Index)

FIGURE 1. EFFECT OF POLITICAL DEPENDENCE ON SHARE
PRICE RETURNS

ascertain the date when rumors first hit the Jakarta Exchange—there was generally a specific triggering *event*, which I take as the start of the episode. I assumed that each episode came to an end when it was (1) explicitly put to rest by the revelation of new information or (2) it was reported that analysts had factored the new information about Suharto's health into their pricing of securities.

II. Results

Figure 1 shows the share price returns for the six episodes, with the Suharto Dependency Index on the horizontal axis. The graph strongly suggests that politically dependent firms, on av-

erage, lost more value during these episodes than did less-dependent firms.

To get a sense of the magnitude of the effect of political dependence during each episode, I ran a set of regressions using the following specification:

$$(1) \qquad R_{ie} = \alpha + \rho \cdot POL_i + \varepsilon_{ie}$$

where R_{ie} is the return on the price of security i during episode e, POL_i is the firm's Suharto Dependency Number, and ε_{ie} is the error term.[5] The results of this set of regressions are listed in Table 2; consistent with the raw pattern illustrated in Figure 1, ρ is negative in every instance.

Now, in each episode, investors were reacting to a different piece of news, so we expect the coefficient on POL_i to differ across events. More precisely, a more severe threat to Suharto's health should intensify the effect of political dependence, hence the magnitude of ρ should be increasing with event severity. As a measure of the market's concerns regarding the threat to Suharto's health in each episode, I use

[5] All regressions reported in this paper use standard errors that correct for heteroskedasticity. I also ran regressions using an error structure that only allowed for the correlation of ε_{ei}s for each company, i.e., Cov(ε_{ei}, ε_{ej}) ≠ 0 if and only if $i = j$. The regressions were also run using an error structure that allowed for the correlation of ε_{ei}s within each group. These various approaches yielded very similar sets of standard errors.

TABLE 2—EFFECT OF POLITICAL CONNECTIONS ON CHANGES IN SHARE PRICE, SEPARATE ESTIMATION FOR EACH EVENT

	Jan. 30–Feb. 1, 1995	April 27, 1995	April 29, 1996	July 4–9, 1996	July 26, 1996	April 1–3, 1997
POL	−0.58* (0.34)	−0.31 (0.18)	−0.24* (0.15)	−0.95*** (0.27)	−0.57*** (0.22)	−0.90** (0.35)
Constant	1.29 (0.79)	0.21 (0.32)	0.12 (0.46)	0.83 (0.64)	−0.07 (0.41)	0.77 (0.97)
R^2	0.037	0.043	0.025	0.147	0.078	0.075
Observations	70	70	78	79	79	79

Note: Robust standard errors are in parentheses.
   * Significantly different from 0 at the 10-percent level.
   ** Significantly different from 0 at the 5-percent level.
   *** Significantly different from 0 at the 1-percent level.

the return on the Jakarta Stock Exchange Composite Index net of broader Southeast Asian effects[6] [referred to using $NR_e(JCI)$]. The preceding observations suggest that the coefficient on *POL* should be more negative if the threat to Suharto's health, as proxied by $NR_e(JCI)$, is greater.[7] This turns out to be the case: the correlation between ρ and $NR_e(JCI)$ is 0.98. This implies a specification where observations from all events are pooled together, with an interaction term, $NR_e(JCI) * POL_i$, added to allow the effect of political dependence to vary across events, depending on the event's severity. Thus, I use the following full-sample specification:

$$(2) \quad R(P_{ie}) = \alpha + \rho_1 \cdot POL_i$$

$$+ \rho_2 \cdot NR_e(JCI) + \rho_3$$

$$\cdot [NR_e(JCI) \cdot POL_i] + \varepsilon_{ie}.$$

TABLE 3—EFFECT OF POLITICAL CONNECTIONS ON CHANGES IN SHARE PRICE

	(1)	(2)
POL	−0.60** (0.11)	−0.19 (0.15)
NR(JCI)	0.25 (0.14)	−0.32 (0.28)
NR(JCI) · POL		0.28* (0.11)
Constant	0.88 (0.27)	0.06 (0.35)
R^2	0.066	0.078
Number of observations	455	455

Note: Robust standard errors are in parentheses.
   * Significantly different from 0 at the 5-percent level.
   ** Significantly different from 0 at the 1-percent level.

The results of this regression are listed in Table 3.[8]

If the severity of a rumor affects politically dependent firms more than less-dependent firms, then the coefficient on the interaction term $NR_e(JCI) \cdot POL_i$ should be positive. The estimated coefficient, ρ_3, is statistically significant at 5 percent and is equal to 0.28. Thus, if the overall market declined by 1 percent in reaction to news about Suharto's health, we might expect a firm with $POL = x$ to drop 0.28 percent more than a firm with $POL = x - 1$.

---

[6] To net out broader Southeast Asia effects, I ran the following "market model" for daily returns during 1994:

$$R_t(JCI) = \alpha + \sum_{m \in M} \beta_m \cdot R_t(m) + \varepsilon_t$$

where $R_t(JCI)$ is the return on the Jakarta Composite on day t, $R_t(m)$ is the return on market index m, and M is the set of ASEAN market indices (including Tokyo's Nikkei 225, Hong Kong's Hang Seng, Singapore's Straits Times, Bangkok's SET, Taiwan's Weighted, Philippines' Composite, Kuala Lumpur's Composite, and Seoul's Composite). This produced a set of coefficients reflecting the degree of correlation between the JCI and other market indices. For each episode e, the *net* return for the JCI is then given by

$$NR_e(JCI) = R_e(JCI) - [\hat{\alpha} + \sum_{m \in M} \beta_m \cdot R_e(m)].$$

[7] It may seem somewhat circular to use $NR_e(JCI)$ as a measure of the severity of the threat to Suharto's health when many of the firms in my sample are constituents of the JCI. Note, however, that $NR_e(JCI)$ is a difference, of which the coefficient on *POL* is a difference in differences. As Section III, subsection B, illustrates, these two variables need not be correlated.

[8] Regressions were also run using log(ASSETS), log(DEBT), and industry dummies as controls. These additions did not alter the size of significance of the interaction term.

One problem with the events described above is that they cannot be used to infer the full value of connections because the associated rumors only *increased* the probability that Suharto would leave office. To estimate the full value of connections would require an event involving Suharto's sudden and unexpected removal from office. (To the extent that connections were expected to continue to have some value even after Suharto, the shifts in share prices associated with such an event would understate the full value of connections.) However, no such event took place.[9]

In the absence of an actual sudden regime shift, we may be able to infer what the coefficient on *POL* would have been in such an event by using equation (2). During a visit to Jakarta in August 1997, I asked a number of investment bankers how much they thought the Jakarta Composite Index would have dropped if Suharto had died suddenly; 20 percent was the modal response to this question. If this value is taken as the best estimate of investor expectations, then (2) implies that the coefficient on *POL* would have been about 5.8 in the event of a sudden regime shift. This suggests that, in reaction to such an event, the returns for a firm with *POL* = 4 would have been about 23 percentage points lower than the returns for a firm with *POL* = 0. Thus, for plausible parameters, the results suggest that connections were very valuable for well-connected firms (though this calculation involves an inference that is quite far out of sample).

---

[9] Although Suharto was forced from office in May 1998, it is difficult to utilize this event for a number of reasons. Most importantly, there were many confounding events that took place simultaneously, including a drastic devaluation of the Indonesian rupiah, rioting and general political instability, and the implementation of an IMF rescue package. Moreover, by the end of 1997, shares on the Jakarta Stock Exchange were very thinly traded, making it relatively easy for prices to be manipulated. There are also serious difficulties in trying to define an appropriate event window: expectations of a regime shift had begun to form long before Suharto was replaced, so it is difficult to allow for a reasonably short event window. Finally, it is not even clear that Suharto's removal from power was actually accompanied by a regime change, given that he was succeeded by his longtime associate and apparent ally, B. J. Habibie.

Thus, although Suharto's children's companies declined quite drastically over the first few months of 1998, there is no systematic relationship between share price returns and political dependence, perhaps owing to the difficulties described above.

III. Robustness

A. *Thinly Traded Firms*

Whenever the market received adverse information regarding Suharto's health, it declined on average. However, if a company was not traded on that day, it would register no price change, even if it suffered a decline in its underlying value. There are two counteracting biases that may result, and the overall effect depends on their relative strengths. The intuition for a bias toward zero is that, among firms with zero trading volume, no "difference in difference" in returns between different types of firms will be recorded, even if there is such an effect on the underlying values of the securities. This could similarly bias the coefficient on $POL \cdot NR_e(JCI)$ toward zero. The direction of the second source of bias depends on whether connected or unconnected firms are more thinly traded. Suppose that unconnected firms are more likely to have zero trading volume. Then, what is being interpreted as the effect of connectedness may be a manifestation of the general market decline—a smaller decline in unconnected firms is observed simply because they are not being traded. This could also potentially bias the coefficient on the interaction term away from zero if an increase in the size of the rumor decreased the proportion of non-traded well-connected firms relative to non-traded unconnected companies. The data show that the opposite is true so, if anything, a bias toward zero may result.

To further examine the overall bias that these effects may have on the results, I revisited all of the basic models, limiting the sample to the set of firm–event observations where the firm had a positive trading volume during the relevant period. This affected the interaction term in Table 3 only slightly.

B. *Are Politically Dependent Firms More Sensitive to Bad News?*[10]

As noted previously, the JSX consistently declined whenever Suharto's health was

---

[10] This section essentially examines whether politically dependent firms have high betas.

brought into question. If politically dependent firms are more sensitive to bad news of any kind, then they will register larger losses on such days. This could be the source of the "difference in differences" that is being interpreted as the connectedness effect. To examine this possibility, I analyzed share price returns in reaction to other shocks that were more or less unrelated to the longevity of the Suharto regime. The beginning of the Southeast Asian financial crisis in 1997 provides a suitable example. The above analyses were repeated for trading days in the week following August 12, when the rupiah was floated by the Indonesian government. On these days, there was no relationship between share price returns and dependence. Similarly, there was no relationship between returns and political dependence on trading days following those days when the S&P 500 Index lost more than 2 percent.

C. Appropriateness of the Event Window

There may be some concern that trading on inside information prior to the onset of the rumors described in the unpublished Appendix could lead to price changes among well-connected firms earlier than my chosen starting day. When regressions were run using *total* returns over an event window expanded to include the two days (or one day) prior to the onset of the actual event, for all events except April 25–27, 1995, there was simply a minor attenuation of the results.

D. Monotonicity of POL

I have assumed throughout a linear specification for *POL*. It would be of concern if the relationship between *POL* and R_{ie} were not, at a minimum, monotonic. If this were not the case, it would bring into question the validity of the Castle Index and/or the appropriateness of my analyses. To examine this possibility, I ran the following, which allows *POL* to have a flexible functional form:

$$(3) \quad R_{ie} = \alpha + \sum_{p=2}^{5} \beta_p I_{POL \geq p} + \sum_{e=2}^{6} \gamma_e + \varepsilon_{ie}$$

where

$$I_{POL \geq p} = \begin{cases} 0 & \text{if} \quad POL < p \\ 1 & \text{if} \quad POL \geq p \end{cases}$$

and the γ_es provide event fixed effects.

The coefficients on the indicator variables were uniformly negative, ranging from -0.35 to -0.87. These results are consistent with the use of the Castle Index as a measure of political dependence.

We may go a little further by testing for the equality of the β_ps with the test statistic $F(3, 445) = 0.24$ (3 restrictions, 455 observations, and 10 variables). This implies that the hypothesis of equality of coefficients cannot be rejected at any significance level below 86 percent. Thus, the use of a linear specification on *POL* is also justified.

IV. Conclusion

This paper has concentrated on the valuation of rents for a relatively small subsample of Indonesian firms. However, the 25 groups associated with these firms account for a very large percentage of economic activity in Indonesia, with revenues of more than U.S. $60 billion in 1995 (as a frame of reference, Indonesia's GNP in 1995 was about U.S. $200 billion). Thus, for a very large part of the Indonesian economy, political connections apparently matter a lot.

Although the preceding analysis focused on Indonesia, there is reason to believe that the results apply to many other countries. For example, in Transparency International's frequently cited "Perceived Corruption Ranking (1998)," Indonesia ranks 45th out of the 54 countries surveyed. It was perceived as being less corrupt than, among others, India, Russia, Pakistan, China, Nigeria, and Bangladesh. To the extent that perceived corruption is a reasonable proxy for the prevalence of political rents, the results of this paper suggest that political connections may play an important role in many of the world's largest and most important economies.

REFERENCES

Corruption Perception Index. Berlin: *Transparency International*, 1998.

Extel Financials Database. London: *Financial Times,* 1997.

Extel Securities Database. London: *Financial Times,* 1997.

Investamatic Database. Singapore: *The Investamatic Group,* 1998.

Jakarta Stock Exchange. *Indonesian capital markets directory 1997.* Jakarta: Institute for Economic and Financial Research, 1997.

Kompass Indonesia. *Top companies and big groups in Indonesia.* Jakarta: Kompass Indonesia, 1996.

Krueger, Anne O. "The Political Economy of the Rent-Seeking Society." *American Economic Review,* June 1974, *64*(3), pp. 291–303.

Kunio, Yoshihara. *The rise of ersatz Capitalism in South-East Asia.* Singapore: Oxford University Press, 1988.

Montagu-Pollock, Matthew. "Who's Who in Indonesia." *AsiaMoney,* December 1995, *6*(10), pp. 89–93.

Roadmap of the Indonesian Ecomomy. Jakarta: *The Castle Group,* 1998.

Roberts, Brian E. "A Dead Senator Tells No Lies: Seniority and the Distribution of Federal Benefits." *American Journal of Political Science,* February 1990, *34*(1), pp. 31–58.

Suharto Dependency Index. Jakarta: *The Castle Group,* 1995.

[29]

ELSEVIER

Available online at www.sciencedirect.com

ScienceDirect

Journal of Financial Economics 88 (2008) 554–580

JOURNAL OF
Financial
ECONOMICS

www.elsevier.com/locate/jfec

Political connections and preferential access to finance: The role of campaign contributions [☆]

Stijn Claessens[a,b,c,*], Erik Feijen[d], Luc Laeven[a,c]

[a]*International Monetary Fund, 700 19th Street N.W., Washington, DC, 20431, USA*
[b]*University of Amsterdam, Roetersstraat 11, 1018 WB Amsterdam, The Netherlands*
[c]*CEPR, 90-98 Goswell Road, London, EC1V 7RR, UK*
[d]*World Bank, 1818 H Street N.W., Washington, DC, 20433, USA*

Received 17 May 2006; received in revised form 27 September 2006; accepted 18 November 2006
Available online 1 July 2007

Abstract

Using novel indicators of political connections constructed from campaign contribution data, we show that Brazilian firms that provided contributions to (elected) federal deputies experienced higher stock returns than firms that did not around the 1998 and 2002 elections. This suggests that contributions help shape policy on a firm-specific basis. Using a firm fixed effects framework to mitigate the risk that unobserved firm characteristics distort the results, we find that contributing firms substantially increased their bank financing relative to a control group after each election, indicating that access to bank finance is an important channel through which political connections operate. We estimate the economic costs of this rent seeking over the two election cycles to be at least 0.2% of gross domestic product per annum.
© 2007 Elsevier Ltd All rights reserved.

JEL classification: D7; G1; G2; G3; P48

Keywords: Campaign contributions; Elections; Corruption; Preferential lending

1. Introduction

This paper studies the political connections individual firms buy by contributing to campaigns of election candidates and the possible channels politicians use to repay these contributions. The paper addresses two fundamental political economy questions: Do higher campaign contributions imply more future firm-specific

---

[☆] We would like to thank an anonymous referee, Markus Brunnermeier, Aslı Demirgüç-Kunt, Mihir Desai, Joost Driessen, Raymond Fisman, Simon Johnson, Leora Klapper, Ross Levine, Christian Leuz, Florencio Lopez-de-Silanes, Enrico Perotti, Lev Ratnovski, Ernesto Revilla, David Samuels, Konstantinos Tzioumis, Paolo Volpin, seminar participants at the Darden conference on emerging markets, George Washington University, the Indian School of Business, the University of Amsterdam, Tilburg University, and the World Bank for detailed discussions or comments on earlier drafts, and David Samuels for sharing part of the data on campaign contributions. The findings, interpretations, and conclusions expressed in this paper are entirely ours. They do not represent the views of the International Monetary Fund, the World Bank, their executive directors, or the countries they represent.

*Corresponding author. International Monetary Fund, 700 19th Street N.W., Washington, DC, 20431, USA. Tel.: +202 623 7641.
E-mail address: sclaessens@imf.org (S. Claessens).

doi:10.1016/j.jfineco.2006.11.003

S. Claessens et al. / Journal of Financial Economics 88 (2008) 554–580 555

political favors? And, if so, what are these political favors? We find supporting empirical evidence for the hypothesis that campaign finance buys firm-specific political favors by exploiting a novel data set of firm- and candidate-level contribution data for the 1998 and 2002 Brazilian elections. Using a firm fixed effects framework to mitigate omitted variable problems, we find evidence that access to bank finance is one of these favors.

There are a number of reasons that Brazil is a good case to test the impact of political connections on stock prices and access to external banking finance. First, Brazil is known for odious relations between politicians and firms, as recent revelations have further confirmed. Second, and related, given Brazil's limited level of institutional development and significant distortions, the value of political connections is likely greater than in more developed countries. Much of this value could come from preferential access to finance as Brazil is among the countries with the highest interest rates and lowest degree of financial intermediation in the world. Moreover, the two largest commercial banks are government-owned and a large portion of external financing is extended by government-owned development banks, making financing more easily influenced by politicians. Third, Brazil is one of the few countries that register campaign contributions at the individual candidate level. Brazilian law also dictates individual registration and justification of campaign expenditures by each candidate. Although many contributions and expenditures remain unregistered, the law makes it more difficult for a politician to spend unofficial money on campaigning. And, although there could still be other ways to influence politicians, campaign contributions can be expected to be important means to do so. The detailed data enable us to construct new measures of political connections.

This paper contributes to the literature in the following ways. We make two methodological innovations. First, we improve upon the relatively crude measures of political connections often used in the non-US political connections literature. We are able to do so because we have detailed data on candidate-level campaign contributions. Our data have three advantages. (1) They are more objective compared with the data typically used in this literature to identify whether there exists a connection between politicians and firms. (2) They enable the intensity of a connection to be measured instead of simply having an indication of its presence. (3) They allow for an investigation into whether it matters for firm value and access to finance how contributions are distributed over different types of candidates. Second, we mitigate the omitted variable problem that plagues the literature on political connections by using a panel data framework with firm fixed effects to exploit the variation over time in our measures of political connections.

Supported by these methodological innovations, our research attests to the growing literature that in an environment with many distortions political connections can have a significant impact on firm value and access to bank finance. First, we find that the cross-sectional variation in stock market responses at the announcement of the election results can in part be explained by the campaign contributions of individual firms to federal deputies. After controlling for industry fixed effects, we still find a strong link between stock market reactions and contributions of individual firms, suggesting that contributions help shape policy on a firm-specific, not ideological, basis. Apparently, the stock market expected deputies to shape policy to benefit their campaign donors specifically. Second, we find that bank financing of firms that made more contributions to (elected) federal deputies increased more relative to other firms in the four years following each election, even after controlling for a host of firm characteristics and unobserved firm fixed effects.

Third, we show that it matters for firm value and access to finance how contributions are distributed across different types of candidates. We find that contributions to winning candidates have a consistently larger impact on firm value and access to finance. This result further alleviates concerns about the presence of a simultaneity bias and suggests there is a direct channel from contributions to political favors. If higher firm value and better access to finance would allow for larger contributions but contributions do not buy political favors, we should have found similar effects for contributions to winning and losing candidates. We also find that contributions to incumbent candidates and candidates affiliated to the president have a consistently larger impact on firm value and access to finance, suggesting that the strength of political connections depends on the characteristics of the candidate.

Taken together, our research shows that political connections matter through preferential access to finance. In theory, this could still be socially beneficial. In countries with weak financial and legal institutions, access to finance on arm's-length principles could be difficult, potentially making political connections a socially desirable alternative. However, our analysis shows that firms that make more contributions have significantly

556 *S. Claessens et al. / Journal of Financial Economics 88 (2008) 554–580*

lower returns on assets, despite having higher investment rates. We estimate the economic costs of capital misallocation associated with political connections to be at least 0.2% of gross domestic product (GDP) per annum.

Our paper contributes to two related strands of literature. First are studies of the relation between campaign contributions and policy outcomes (e.g., Snyder, 1990; Grossman and Helpman, 1996; Coate, 2004). This literature has found it difficult to disentangle the matching of ideological voting dispositions of politicians with preferences of firms from the incentives of politicians to provide contributors with specific favors. Combined with simultaneity bias (e.g., Durden and Silberman, 1976; Grenzke, 1989), this has made it hard to establish whether contributions have a substantial influence on political decision-making because politicians act according to their ideology (e.g., Chappell, 1982) or because contributions are used to forge cozy alliances between politicians and specific contributors (e.g., Stratmann, 1995; Kroszner and Stratmann, 1998). The literature has used event-study methodologies to try to overcome these problems but has found mixed results (e.g., Roberts 1990; Ansolabehere, Snyder, and Ueda, 2004; Jayachandran, 2004; Shon, 2006; Fisman, Fisman, Galef, and Khurana, 2006).

Second are studies of the influence of special interests on economic outcomes, without specific reference to campaign contributions. This literature finds that firms have strong incentives to forge alliances with politicians and that such connections affect economic outcomes, in part through affecting the general institutional environment (e.g., Krueger, 1974; Acemoglu, 2007; Morck, Wolfenzon, and Yeung, 2005). The channels for political influence are likely multiple. Rajan and Zingales (2003), for example, argue that incumbents have incentives to oppose financial development because it creates more competition. To maintain their rents, incumbents use political channels to retard financial development.

Some cross-country and country-specific evidence shows that political connections matter for firm value, including through preferential access to financing. Fisman (2001) finds that the market value of politically connected firms in Indonesia under President Suharto declined more when adverse rumors circulated about the health of the president. A number of other papers also take an event-study approach and find similar results for other countries (e.g., Johnson and Mitton, 2003; Ramalho, 2003; Ferguson and Voth, 2005; Faccio, 2006; Faccio and Parsley, 2006). For France, Bertrand, Kramarz, Schoar, and Thesmar (2004) show that favors between politicians and firms operate in both directions with firms reciprocating favors in the form of job creation.

Evidence also exists that political connections can provide preferential access to finance in emerging markets. Khwaja and Mian (2005) using loan-level data for Pakistan find that politically connected firms (firms with a director participating in an election) borrow twice as much and have 50% higher default rates than control firms, with connected firms obtaining exclusively loans from government-owned banks. Charumilind, Kali, and Wiwattanakantang (2006) find similar evidence for lending patterns in Thailand. Cole (2004) in the case of India and Dinc (2005) for a larger set of emerging countries also find that government-owned banks are often subject to capture by politicians.

The remainder of the paper is structured as follows. Section 2 describes the Brazilian political system and the context of the 1998 and 2002 elections. Section 3 lays out the methodology used. Section 4 describes the data. Section 5 provides a discussion of the results and the robustness checks. Section 6 concludes.

2. The Brazilian political system and the context of the 1998 and 2002 elections

In this section, we give a brief overview of the electoral system in Brazil and the institutional setup for campaign contributions. Brazil, like the United States, is a presidential and federal republic with a bicameral National Congress (Congresso Nacional) consisting of the Federal Senate, or Upper House (81 seats), and the Chamber of Deputies, or Lower House (513 seats).[1] Although the Brazilian executive has arguably more discretionary power than his US counterpart, the 1988 constitution empowered Congress to oppose the president and influence policy and legislation significantly. As in the US, the president and vice president are elected on the same ticket. However, in Brazil the president and the vice president are directly elected by a

[1] This section is largely based on information provided by the International Foundation for Election Systems (2005) and Instituto Universitário de Pesquisas do Rio de Janeiro (2005).

S. Claessens et al. / Journal of Financial Economics 88 (2008) 554–580 557

simple, popular majority vote for a four-year term, whereas in the US they are elected by a college of representatives who in turn are elected by popular majority vote from each state, with the number of representatives in proportion to the states' population. In terms of state elections, Brazil consists of 27 federal units, composed of 26 states and the Federal District, with each unit electing its own governor. The Senate includes three senators from each federal unit (compared with two in the US). They are elected by majority voting in staggered elections and serve eight-year terms. Members of the Chamber of Deputies are elected for a four-year term via a party-list, state-proportional system. Compared with the US, Brazil has a smaller Upper House (81 versus 100 seats in the US) and a larger Lower House (513 versus 435 seats in the US), and both senators and representatives in Brazil have longer terms in office (in the US they serve six and two years, respectively). Another large difference between the two countries is that the US has a two-party system, whereas Brazil has about 15 significant political parties. The most important parties are the Brazilian Social Democratic Party (PSDB), the Workers' Party (PT), the Liberal Front Party (PFL), and the Brazilian Democratic Movement Party (PMDB). Despite the large number of parties in Brazil, party discipline tends to be weak, resulting in individualized elections and few party votes.

Before 1993, businesses and individuals were prohibited from contributing to candidates directly. Triggered by campaign finance scandals, Congress passed a law (Law no. 8713) in 1993, which allowed contributions for all offices directly but required candidates to submit an overview of all their campaign contributions and sources, at the donor level, to electoral courts. Noncompliance can result in fines or removal of candidacy or appointment, and several state courts have imposed such penalties (e.g., Veja, 1998). Individuals can donate up to 10% and companies up to 2% of their gross annual income. Furthermore, campaign funding is individual-based and not channeled via the party to which the candidate is affiliated.

Because of weak party organization and limited party links, politicians cannot rely much on party branding and recognition to get elected. As a consequence, politicians take their own actions to get exposure to the public. To finance their campaign activities, candidates have strong demand for contributions. Individual firms in turn could be willing to make contributions because elected officials can provide political favors. Elected officials can presumably affect the distribution of export subsidies, bank recapitalization, financial sector regulations, the allocation of pork-barrel funds and other government contracts, and the provision of external financing from (state-owned) banks. While politicians have ex post incentives to renege on promises (because it is impossible to write and enforce a contract for political favors based on campaign finance), repeated interactions of businesses with individual politicians are common in Brazil. Although politicians switch positions often, with turnover of deputies in elections consistently over 60%, many politicians have long-lasting political careers in various representations. Typically, a politician spends a term in the chamber and continues in state or local levels of government (Samuels, 2001, 2002). This practice provides for a credible commitment mechanism.[2]

Because of a constitutional amendment, the 1998 election was the first in which the sitting president, Fernando Cardoso (PSDB), was allowed to run for reelection and he won the first round with 53.1% of votes. His close runner-up was Luiz Inácio (Lula) da Silva (PT) with 31.7% of votes. While the 1998 presidential election was not a big surprise, the election was close for many deputies and the announcement of election results resolved much uncertainty about the political future of individual deputies. In the 2002 election, six presidential candidates participated in the first round and results were less predictable. Because no single candidate obtained a majority of the votes, the two candidates with the most votes advanced to the second round. These candidates were Lula da Silva with 46.4% and Jose Serra (PSDB) with 23.2% of votes. Lula da Silva won the second round with 61.3% of votes.

The following positions were open during the two elections: president (1 position), governors (27 positions), senators (27 positions in 1998 and 54 positions in 2002), and federal deputies (513 positions). In our empirical analysis, we focus on the results for elections of federal deputies, but we also report results in which we control for contributions to candidates for all positions.

---

[2]Kroszner and Stratmann (1998) argue that, in the United States, to overcome this commitment problem, legislators have an incentive to create specialized standing committees that enable repeated interaction between special interests and committee members. Standing committees give rise to a reputational equilibrium in which special interests give high contributions to committee members who carry out favors for them.

3. Methodology

This section discusses the specific hypotheses we test, the construction of measures of the strength of political connections, and the econometric methodology we use to explain the cross-sectional variation in stock returns and the degree of access to finance.

If the market expects that contributions lead to benefits for individual firms because of future political favors, firm value, i.e., its stock price, should increase at the announcement of the candidate supported being elected. If the election leads to the appointment of candidates with a certain political ideology, then we would expect to find more general valuation changes for entire industries or even for the economy as a whole. Therefore, if individual firms have strong connections and experience significant positive stock returns around the election announcement relative to other firms in their industries, we can conclude that the market expects firm-specific political favors.

Regarding the channels through which political connections pay off, we focus on access to finance. Political favors can come in many forms, but given the many distortions in the Brazilian financial system, including subsidized credit and lending requirements, the large market share of state-owned banks in Brazil and the unattractive interest rate environment for borrowers, preferential access to finance is a likely candidate.[3] Specifically, we hypothesize that contributions gain a firm access to more bank loans, possibly at preferential terms. We therefore expect that the bank financing by firms with political connections increases more relative to a control group of firms in the four years following election.

Based on this discussion, we develop the following two main empirical hypotheses. The first hypothesis is that politically more active firms (i.e., those providing more campaign contributions) are more likely to receive future firm-specific political favors, which in turn means these firms' stock market value increases more following the announcement of the election result.

Value Hypothesis. *Using contributions to federal deputy candidates as a proxy for political connections, better connected firms have significantly higher stock market returns.*

The second main hypothesis is that firms with larger campaign contributors are more likely to receive preferential access to bank financing.

Access Hypothesis. *Using contributions to federal deputy candidates as a proxy for political connections, better connected firms have significantly greater increases in financing from banks in the four years following the election.*

We further develop two subhypotheses for our main hypotheses, based on which candidates receive contributions. First, we formulate the Winners Subhypothesis because elected deputies are expected to be better able to extend political favors.

Winners Subhypothesis. *Using contributions to winning federal deputy candidates as a proxy for political connections, better connected firms have significantly higher returns and greater access to finance.*

Because it is not a priori clear whether contributions to losing candidates destroy market value, we compare in our empirical work the effect of contributions to winning federal deputy candidates with both that of making no contributions and making contributions to losing federal deputy contributions. Similarly, we expect that contributions to deputy candidates who already served as a deputy (i.e., incumbent candidates) or who are related to the president are likely to have more impact than contributions in general. Therefore, we formulate the following Political Subhypothesis.

---

[3]According to La Porta, Lopez-de-Silanes, and Shleifer (2002), the share of the assets of the top ten banks in Brazil controlled by the government was 57% in 1995 (a bank is considered controlled by the government if its stake in the bank is larger than 20% and the state is the largest shareholder). Brazilian interest rate spreads are among the highest in the world, averaging around 58% in 1998 and 44% in 2002, with lending rates averaging around 86% in 1998 and 63% in 2002 (source: World Development Indicators database of the World Bank).

S. Claessens et al. / Journal of Financial Economics 88 (2008) 554–580   559

Political Subhypothesis. *Using contributions to federal deputy candidates who are incumbent deputies or who are affiliated to the president as a proxy for political connections, better connected firms have significantly higher returns and greater access to finance.*

The two subhypotheses help us to identify whether there is a causal link from connections to firm value and access to finance, thereby alleviating concerns about endogeneity. If political contributions translate into political favors and therefore matter for firm value and access to finance, we would expect that contributions to winners, incumbents, and presidential affiliates systematically have a greater impact than contributions in general. After all, contributions to losing deputies cannot be expected to lead to many gains from firm-specific political favors, and there was considerable uncertainty on who would win the elections. If firms give more contributions merely because they are more highly valued or have better access to finance (for reasons other than political connections), then the effect of contributions to winning deputies should not differ systematically from contributions to losing deputies. Similarly, if contributions matter irrespective of party affiliation, then it is less likely that contributions are made for political favors.

To test our hypotheses, we construct a novel data set of campaign contributions and collect financial data. As we argue, the aim of campaign finance is to acquire political influence. However, the functional form of how campaign contributions translate into political influence is nontrivial. Therefore, using contribution data, we construct three different, yet simple and intuitive, measures of how contributions could translate in terms of strength of political connections for donors.

Our first measure is simply the absolute amounts a firm donates altogether to candidates for the four different positions at stake in the 1998 election. Arguably, a donor benefits more if she contributed to winning, not losing, candidates. Hence, we also split each of the measures into the amount provided to winners and to losers.

Our second measure is based on the relative contributions among donors in which we consider competition between donors to gain political influence with a specific candidate. To build a connection with a candidate could require a larger contribution if this candidate already receives a large amount of contributions from other firms. As an alternative measure of the strength of a political connection, we therefore consider the firm's contribution as a fraction of total contributions received by the candidate. This measure gives equal weight to each candidate's share in total contributions.

Our third measure is based on the relative amounts among donors and candidates. In addition to acknowledging competition among donors, we consider heterogeneity of the political influence of candidates. That is, politicians differ in their ability to define, lobby, and decide over issues on the political agenda. Compared with entrants, for example, incumbents could be better able to exert political influence. As a consequence, some politicians attract more and some fewer contributions and we can think of the total contributions received by a candidate as proxy for its overall political influence. We thus construct a new measure defined as the firm's contribution for all candidates in a state as a ratio of all contributions by all firms to all candidates in a state.

For our dependent variables, we use abnormal rates of return and increased access to finance. For the rates of return, we use a standard event-study approach to construct cumulative abnormal returns (MacKinlay, 1997). This approach mitigates the simultanity problem that firm value and political connections could be correlated. We define the estimation window as the period (τ_0, τ_1) and the event window as (τ_1, τ_2). The event itself is at $\tau = 0$ when the election results became publicly known and where $\tau_0 < \tau_1 < 0 < \tau_2$. Next, we calculate daily stock returns for companies listed on the Brazilian stock market BOVESPA using $R_{i,t} = \ln(P_{i,t}/P_{i,t-1})$, where $P_{i,t}$ is the stock price index of company i at time t. To calculate the abnormal returns, we estimate a simple capital asset pricing model (CAPM) using the market return on the whole São Paolo stock market as measured by the BOVESPA index. We adopt this methodology to calculate cumulative abnormal returns for both elections in 1998 and 2002. The event dates are the days when the election results for federal deputies became known, October 9, 1998 and October 8, 2002, respectively (Reuters, 1998, 2002).

We estimate the following regression model for the cumulative abnormal returns:

$$y_{it} = \beta' x_{it-1} + \gamma z_{it} + \theta_t + \eta_j + \lambda_k + \varepsilon_{it}, \tag{1}$$

560								S. Claessens et al. / Journal of Financial Economics 88 (2008) 554–580

where y_{it} is the cumulative abnormal return (CAR) of firm i around the elections in year t; x_{it-1} is a vector of firm-level control variables averaged over the electoral cycle; z_{it} is a measure of campaign contributions made by firm i for the elections at the beginning of electoral cycle t; θ_t is an election year fixed effect; η_j is an industry fixed effect for industry j in which firm i operates; λ_k is a state fixed effect for state k in which the headquarters of firm i are located; and ε_{it} is the error term. Firm-level control variables are lagged to the previous electoral cycle. In the base regression, we estimate this model over the two election periods as pooled ordinary least squares (OLS) with clustering of standard errors at the firm level. In robustness checks, we also estimate the model using a balanced sample.

In addition, we analyze the impact of contributions on access to finance. As a proxy for access to finance, we use the growth in bank financing scaled by total assets of firm i over the four-year electoral cycle t, the period that the representatives were elected to office and able to extend political favors.[4] We call it l_{it}, growth in bank leverage, and define it as:

$$l_{it} = \frac{\text{Bank debt}_{t+1}}{\text{Total assets}_{t+1}} - \frac{\text{Bank debt}_t}{\text{Total assets}_t}. \tag{2}$$

Using this access to finance indicator, we estimate the following regression model:

$$l_{it} = \beta' x_{it-1} + \gamma z_{it} + \theta_t + \alpha_i + \varepsilon_{it}, \tag{3}$$

where x_{it-1} is a vector of firm-level control variables, lagged to the previous electoral cycle; z_{it} is a measure of campaign contributions made by firm i at the beginning of electoral cycle t; θ_t is an electoral cycle fixed effect; α_i is a firm fixed effect; and ε_{it} is the error term. We estimate the regression model over the two electoral cycles using pooled OLS with firm fixed effects and clustering of standard errors at the firm level. By including firm fixed effects, we mitigate an omitted variables problem. In robustness checks, we also estimate the model using a balanced sample.

The Value Hypothesis predicts that the coefficient γ for the campaign contribution measures to deputy candidates in Model 1 is positive and statistically and economically significant. The Access Hypothesis predicts that the coefficient γ for the amount of campaign contributions in Model 3 is positive and statistically and economically significant. According to the Winners Subhypothesis, this coefficient is positive and significant in both models for political connection measures for winning deputy candidates, and it is significantly larger than the coefficient for political connection measures for losing deputy candidates. The Political Subhypothesis predicts that the coefficient γ for the campaign contribution measures for incumbent candidates or candidates affiliated with the president in both models is positive and larger than that for nonincumbents and nonaffiliates, respectively. Although we already include firm fixed effects, changes over time in firm-level characteristics could affect the result. We therefore include several firm characteristics as control variables. Following the capital structure literature (e.g., Rajan and Zingales, 1995), we include the following control variables: log of total assets (proxy for firm size), ratio of fixed assets to total assets (proxy for asset tangibility), ratio of total liabilities to total assets (proxy for firm leverage), ratio of earnings before interest and taxes to total assets (proxy for operating profitability), and sales growth (proxy for growth opportunities). All firm-level control variables are four-year averages and lagged to the previous electoral cycle. We also consider separately the effect of contributions on bank debt of different maturity and on other types of debt financing.

4. Data

This section describes the sources of the firm-level campaign contributions, the stock market and financial data, and it provides some descriptive statistics.

---

[4]Deputies likely extend such political favors during their term in office following the elections because many deputies are not reelected. Deputy turnover is high at over 60% in both the 1998 and 2002 elections. Samuels (1998) reports that turnover has been similarly high in all democratic elections since 1945.

S. Claessens et al. / Journal of Financial Economics 88 (2008) 554–580   561

4.1. Data sources

The data for both the 1998 and 2002 elections are collected by the Brazilian national election court, the Tribunal Superior Eleitoral (TSE) (Tribunal Superior Eleitoral, 2005), and contains detailed information about donors and recipients. Each entry corresponds to a single contribution. For each documented candidate we know the name, the state, candidate number, party, and position (federal deputy, senator, governor, or president). Furthermore, we know the name of the donor, the size of its contribution, and the type (individual, corporate, political party, or unknown). Most contributions come from individuals and are relatively small. The database does not provide information on contributions of firms to political parties, which are thought to be small given the limited role of parties in Brazil. Data on whether deputy candidates lost or won were taken from the TSE. In each election, 513 deputy candidates were to be appointed. In compiling our campaign contributions data set, we had to correct some trivial differences in donor names.

In the construction of our political connection measures, we assume that if a listed firm does not appear in the official contribution data, the firm did not donate in any way to political candidates and hence becomes part of the control group. This should bias downward the coefficients on contributions in the regressions. We converted all data to 1998 Brazilian Real (BRL), which had an average exchange rate of $0.86 per BRL.

For the CAR tests, we use data on publicly traded firms taken from Thomson's Financial Datastream. For 159 actively traded listed firms in 1998 and 216 firms in 2002 we have data on campaign contributions, stock prices, and market capitalization. We use the sectoral classification as defined by Datastream: Basic Industries, Cyclical Consumer, Financials, General Industrials, Information Technology, Non-cyclical Consumer, Non-cyclical Services, Resources, and Utilities. To estimate state fixed effects, we collect from company websites the name of the state in which the company's headquarters is located.

To construct time-varying, firm-level controls we use accounting data from Economatica, a private financial information service, which covers Latin American countries. We collect data on total assets, fixed asset tangibility ratio, profitability ratio, financial leverage ratios, and other basic financial ratios.

4.2. Descriptive statistics

The contribution database organizes contributions by source: corporate, private, political party, or unknown. We focus on corporate contributions because they are most numerous and largest, and they relate closest to our hypotheses of political connections. Table 1 provides the definitions and the sources of the variables we use. Table 2 presents some descriptive statistics of corporate contributions. The descriptive

Table 1

Definition of variables

This table reports the variables used in our regression analyses and their description. Data sources: D = Datastream; T = Tribunal Superior Eleitoral (TSE); E = Economatica. Exchange rate in 1998: 1 Brazilian Real (BRL) ~0.86$.

Variable	Description	Source
CAR	Cumulative abnormal return (in percent); event window covers from 20 days before to 20 days after the election	D
Contributions to deputies	Total absolute amount the firm contributed to federal deputy candidates, in 100,000 of 1998 BRL	T
Contributions to winning deputies	Total absolute amount the firm contributed to federal deputy candidates who won the election	T
Contributions to losing deputies	Total absolute amount the firm contributed to federal deputy candidates who lost the election	T
Cumulative share in contributions to winning deputies	Firm's share in total contributions to winning federal deputy candidates	T
Cumulative share in contributions to losing deputies	Firm's share in total contributions to losing federal deputy candidates	T
Cumulative share in contributions to winning deputies in the state	Firm's contribution to winning candidates in a particular state as a fraction of total contributions received by winning candidates in that state, aggregated over all winning candidates and states	T

562   *S. Claessens et al. / Journal of Financial Economics 88 (2008) 554–580*

Table 1 (*continued*)

Variable	Description	Source
Cumulative share in contributions to losing deputies in the state	Firm's contribution to losing candidates in a particular state as a fraction of total contributions received by losing candidates in that state, aggregated over all losing candidates and states	T
Contributions to (non)incumbent deputies	Total amount the firm contributed to (non)incumbent federal deputy candidates	T
Contributions to deputies (non)affiliated to president coalition	Total amount the firm contributed to federal deputy candidates that are (not) affiliated to the coalition parties of the presidential candidate who won the elections (Fernando Cardoso in 1998 and Luiz Inácio (Lula) da Silva in 2002)	T
Contributions to candidates at other levels	Total amount the firm contributed to candidates at other levels of government (senator, governor, president)	T
Growth in bank leverage	The average growth in the ratio of bank debt to total assets during the four years following the election	E
Growth in short-term bank leverage	Average growth in the ratio of short-term bank debt to total assets during the four years following the election	E
Growth in long-term bank leverage	Average growth in the ratio of long-term bank debt to total assets during the four years following the election	E
Growth in other liabilities to total assets	Average growth in the ratio of liabilities other than bank debt to total assets during the four years following the election	E
Growth in debentures to total assets	Average growth in the ratio of debentures to total assets during the four years following the election	E
Growth in liabilities to total assets	Average growth in the ratio of liabilities to total assets during the four years following the election	E
Growth in interest expense to sales	Average growth in the ratio of interest expense to total sales during the four years following the election	E
Growth in fixed assets to total assets	Average growth in the ratio of fixed assets to total assets during the four years following the election	E
Growth in collateral to total assets	Average growth in the ratio of cash, receivables, inventories, and fixed assets to total assets during the four years following the election	E
CAPEX to total assets	Average ratio of capital expenditures to total assets during the four years following the election	E
Return on assets	Average ratio of pre-tax profits to total assets during the four years following the election	E
Log of total assets	Average of the logarithm of total assets during the four years following election (we use the one election period lag of this variable), in thousands of 1998 BRL	E
Fixed assets ratio	Average of the ratio of fixed assets to total assets during the four years following the election	E
Liabilities to total assets	Average of the ratio of total liabilities to total assets during the four years following the election	E
EBIT ratio	Average of the ratio of earnings before interest and taxes during the four years following the election	E
Sales growth	Average of real sales growth during the four years following the election	E
Bank debt to total assets	Average of the ratio of bank debt to total assets during the four years following the election	E
Initial Tobin's Q	Tobin's Q (ratio of market value of equity plus book value of total liabilities to book value of total assets) in the election year	E

statistics show that corporate campaign contribution activity was larger and more focused in 2002 than in 1998. Arguably, the reason is that the shape of the political landscape in 2002 was more uncertain because by law President Cardoso could not be reelected. In 1998, 889 federal deputy candidates received 5,580 corporate contributions for a total amount of 65,315,860 BRL, or an average per candidate of 73,471 BRL, while in 2002, 493 federal deputy candidates received 8,223 corporate contributions for a total amount of 108,572,813 BRL, or an average per candidate of 220,229 BRL. The average size of a corporate contribution was 11,705 BRL in 1998 and 13,204 BRL in 2002.

Contribution activity of listed firms did not increase as much. The 540 listed firms in our sample account for 15.9% in 1998 (10,372,432 BRL) and 12% in 2002 (13,000,882 BRL) of total corporate contributions to

S. Claessens et al. / Journal of Financial Economics 88 (2008) 554–580   563

Table 2
Descriptive statistics of campaign contributions to federal deputy candidates
This table reports summary statistics of campaign contributions for the whole universe of contributions and for the subsample of listed firms that officially contributed to candidates who ran for the position of federal deputy during the Brazilian elections of 1998 or 2002. Amounts are in 1998 Brazilian Real (1BRL ~0.86$).

Variable	1998	2002
Universe of corporate contributions		
Total amount of contributions (BRL)	65,315,860	108,572,813
Total number of contribution	5,580	8,223
Average size of a contribution	11,705	13,204
Number of candidates	889	493
Average sum of contributions per candidate (BRL)	73,471	220,229
Listed firms		
Total number of firms (including non-contributors)	540	540
Total amount of contributions (BRL)	10,372,432	13,000,882
	(15.9% of universe)	(12% of universe)
Number of contributions	423	664
Average size of contribution per firm (BRL)	24,521	19,580
Number of listed donor firms	60	72
Average number of contributions per firm	7.1	9.2
Average total of contributions per firm (BRL)	172,874	180,568
Average number of parties to which a firm contributed	2.6	3.5
Average number of contributions per party per firm	2.0	2.0
Listed firms with data on CAR in sample		
Number of firms	159	216
Number of donor firms	39	56
Average amount per firm (BRL)	238,980	213,020
Total contributions by firms (BRL)	9,320,211	11,929,130

federal deputies. Deputy candidates received campaign contributions from 60 listed firms in 1998 and from 72 listed firms in 2002. The average size of a corporate contribution for listed firms is significantly larger: 24,521 BRL in 1998 and 19,580 BRL in 2002. The total contribution per listed firm was 172,874 BRL in 1998 and 180,568 BRL in 2002. There is no evidence of party loyalty among listed firms. On average, listed firms spread their contributions over 2.6 parties in 1998 and over 3.5 parties in 2002, and they made 2.0 contributions on average to candidates belonging to the same party in each election. Taken together, we conclude that listed firms tried to hedge their bets in 2002 to deal with increased political uncertainty.

Although we have 540 listed firms in our sample for both 1998 and 2002, we have data on cumulative abnormal returns for only 159 firms in 1998 and 216 firms in 2002. Of those firms, 39 contributed in 1998 and 56 contributed in 2002. These firms represent almost all political activity of listed firms. They account for around 90% of contributions of listed firms in both elections.

Table A1 shows the number and average amount of contributions by political party. We find that the three main parties, PFL, PSDB, and PMDB, ranked highest as recipient in terms of number and size of contributions. The data also show that little party loyalty exists among contributors as firms donate to multiple and different parties in both election years. Again, the low loyalty between 1998 and 2002 is likely due to expectations that the political direction would change dramatically after the second and last term of President Cardoso.

Table 3 shows descriptive statistics for the dependent and independent variables used when pooled over 1998 and 2002. We have a total of 375 firm-year observations, of which 159 and 216 are for 1998 and 2002, respectively. Panel A starts with the statistics for the contributions. The table shows that winning deputy candidates received significantly larger contributions than losers did; the average contribution to a winner is 40,000 BRL and only 16,700 BRL to a loser. This difference is statistically significant at a 1% level, suggesting that on the whole campaign donors successfully targeted future winners. However, there was remaining uncertainty about future winners and losers, because many contributors gave to losers as well. This suggests

564   S. Claessens et al. / Journal of Financial Economics 88 (2008) 554–580

Table 3
Descriptive statistics of listed Brazilian firms that contributed to campaigns of federal deputy candidates

This table reports summary statistics of campaign contribution variables, dependent variables, and control variables for the sample of all listed Brazilian firms for which we have data. This includes both contributing and noncontributing firms. Reported numbers pertain to both the 1998 and 2002 election cycles. BRL = Brazilian Real; EBIT = earnings before interest and taxes.

Variable	Number of observations	Mean	Standard deviation	Minimum	Maximum
Panel A. Measures of political connections (1998 and 2002)					
Contributions to deputies (in 100,000 BRL)	375	0.567	2.014	0.000	15.200
Contributions to winning deputies (in 100,000 BRL)	375	0.400	1.496	0.000	13.000
Contributions to losing deputies (in 100,000 BRL)	375	0.167	0.617	0.000	5.236
Cumulative share in contributions to winning deputies	375	0.096	0.845	0.000	15.565
Cumulative share in contributions to losing deputies	375	0.055	0.461	0.000	8.170
Cumulative share in contributions to winning deputies in the state	375	0.008	0.064	0.000	1.062
Cumulative share in contributions to losing deputies in the state	375	0.004	0.060	0.000	1.155
Contributions to incumbent deputies (in 100,000 BRL)	375	0.335	1.290	0.000	10.400
Contributions to nonincumbent deputies (in 100,000 BRL)	375	0.232	0.827	0.000	6.956
Contributions to deputies affiliated to president coalition (in 100,000 BRL)	375	0.343	1.362	0.000	13.400
Contributions to deputies not affiliated to president coalition (in 100,000 BRL)	375	0.224	0.923	0.000	8.122
Contributions to candidates at other levels (in 100,000 BRL)	375	0.652	3.378	0.000	55.185
Panel B. Dependent variables (1998 and 2002)					
CAR (in percent)	375	−4.341	64.240	−982.353	110.474
Growth in bank leverage	168	−0.001	0.259	−0.701	1.594
Growth in short-term bank leverage	168	−0.023	0.311	−1.032	0.837
Growth in long-term bank leverage	168	0.020	0.406	−1.897	1.938
Growth in other liabilities to total assets	168	0.051	0.135	−0.346	0.498
Growth in liabilities to total assets	168	0.024	0.107	−0.271	0.446
Growth in interest expense to sales	158	−0.086	0.468	−2.106	1.550
Growth in fixed assets to total assets	168	−0.043	0.098	−0.533	0.271
Growth in collateral to total assets	164	−0.012	0.142	−0.972	1.053
CAPEX to total assets	160	0.052	0.040	0.000	0.212
Return on assets	168	0.029	0.093	−0.200	0.200
Initial Tobin's Q	166	0.628	0.272	0.100	2.035
Panel C. Control variables (1998 and 2002)					
Log of total assets (in BRL)	168	13.806	1.824	9.472	18.900
Fixed assets ratio	168	0.381	0.202	0.000	0.905
Liabilities to total assets	168	0.601	0.228	0.011	1.000
EBIT ratio	168	0.072	0.070	−0.100	0.200
Sales growth	165	0.018	0.168	−0.500	0.387
Bank debt to total assets	168	0.261	0.185	0.000	1.000
Short-term bank debt to total assets	168	0.139	0.153	0.000	1.000
Long-term bank debt to total assets	168	0.133	0.144	0.000	1.000

there was enough uncertainty to elicit a stock market response after the announcement of results if the market expected firm-specific political favors as a result of contributions. Furthermore, evidence shows some tenure and party affiliation effects because the average contribution to an incumbent candidate or a candidate affiliated with a coalition party of the president is significantly larger than the average contribution to nonincumbent or nonaffiliates, respectively (both differences are statistically significant at the 5% level). This suggests that contributors expected incumbents and presidential affiliates to be more effective in granting political favors or have a higher probability to be elected, or both.

In Panel B, we provide summary statistics for our main dependent variables, starting with the cumulative abnormal returns variable. For the main analysis, we choose the window for estimating the normal returns to be one hundred trading days and the event window for the CAR to be 41 trading days, i.e., $(\tau_0, \tau_1, \tau_2) = (-120, -20, 20)$. The average CAR was negative, −4.34%, but not statistically different from

S. Claessens et al. / Journal of Financial Economics 88 (2008) 554–580   565

zero. The second main dependent variable is the average growth in bank leverage over the election cycle. Growth in bank leverage was slightly negative on average for both cycles, but not statistically different from zero, and displayed a large dispersion, possibly because of variation in political connections. In terms of our other access to finance variables, we find that average growth varied. Short-term bank debt declined, long-term bank debt increased, other liabilities increased, total liabilities increased, and interest expense declined (with only the latter three representing statistically significant changes). In terms of the asset side of the balance sheet, there are no clear patterns. Fixed assets and assets that are easily collateralizable (such as cash, receivables, and inventories) declined as a share of firms' total assets, although the change is statistically significant only for fixed assets. At the same time, total capital expenditures as a ratio to total assets increased on average (statistically significant at 1%). The average return on assets was positive and significantly different from zero at the 1% level.

Panel C pertains to firm-level control variables, where we always use data lagged by one election cycle. Average log of total assets (reported in thousands of BRL) is about 13.8, indicating that the average firm has about 1 billion BRL in total assets. Earnings before interest and taxes (EBIT) ratio and sales growth are positive on average (although only EBIT growth is statistically significant) and firms are on average for 26% financed by banks (as indicated by the ratio of bank debt to total assets).

Table 4 shows simple correlations between the most important dependent and independent variables. Both cumulative abnormal returns and increases in financial leverage are positively correlated with campaign contributions to deputies, although the correlations are not statistically significant. Contributions to winners are highly correlated with contributions to losers (0.78 and significant at the 1% level), confirming that contributors could not perfectly distinguish future winners from losers.

5. Empirical results

In this section, we provide results of our empirical analyses whether the market expected firm-specific future political favors and whether contributions were associated with (preferential) future access to finance.

5.1. Campaign contributions and stock returns

Table 5 presents OLS regressions for the Value Hypothesis that the market expects political firm-specific future favors for firms that contributed to deputy candidates. The dependent variable is the CAR, expressed in percentage points, for each listed firm for which we have nonzero data on stock returns. Our pooled sample of both 1998 and 2002 data contains 375 observations that represent 238 firms. The advantage of the pooled approach is that we use all information available, although we do not estimate a firm fixed effect for firms for which we have information for only one election cycle. Hence, we prefer to use the unbalanced panel in the results that follow. Besides pooled regressions, however, we analyze a balanced panel of 274 observations for

Table 4
Correlations between dependent variables and contributions
   This table reports correlations between the main dependent variables, cumulative abnormal returns (CAR), and growth in bank leverage as well as several measures of political connections based on campaign contribution data. *P*-values are reported between brackets. Total number of observations is 375 for all pairwise correlations, except for correlations with growth in bank leverage, where the number of observations is 168. Data cover both the election cycles of 1998 and 2002.

Variable	CAR	Growth in bank leverage	Contributions to deputies	Contributions to winning deputies
Growth in bank leverage	−0.078			
	(0.336)			
Contributions to deputies	0.061	0.006		
	(0.241)	(0.934)		
Contributions to winning deputies	0.061	0.022	0.981	
	(0.241)	(0.778)	(0.000)	
Contributions to losing deputies	0.056	−0.017	0.885	0.779
	(0.279)	(0.825)	(0.000)	(0.000)

Table 5

Impact of contributions on cumulative abnormal returns

This table reports ordinary least squares (OLS) regressions of the form $y_{it} = \beta' x_{it-1} + \gamma z_{it} + \theta_t + \eta_j + \lambda_k + \varepsilon_{it}$, where y_{it} is the cumulative abnormal return of firm i around the elections in year t; x_{it-1} is a vector of firm-level control variables averaged over the electoral cycle; z_{it} is a measure of campaign contributions made by firm i for the elections at the beginning of electoral cycle t; θ_t is an election-year fixed effect; η_j is an industry fixed effect; λ_k is a state fixed effect; and ε_{it} is the error term. Firm-level control variables are lagged to the previous electoral cycle. The dependent variable is the cumulative abnormal return (in percent), calculated with an event window covering the 20 days before and 20 days after the election. We include data for the two election cycles (1998–2001 and 2002–2005) and estimate the model as pooled OLS with clustering of standard errors at the firm level. We exclude firms with no stock price variation over the event window. Contributions to (winning and losing) deputies is the total absolute amount firms contributed to all (winning and losing) federal deputy candidates. Regressions 7 and 8 include only observations for 1998 and 2002, respectively. Regression 9 includes observations for 1998 and the following firm-level control variables, calculated as averages over the previous election cycle: logarithm of total assets; ratio of fixed assets to total assets; ratio of total liabilities to total assets; ratio of earnings before interest and taxes (EBIT) to total assets; and real growth in sales. Industry, state, and time fixed effects are included in all regressions, but these are not reported. White (1980) heteroskedasticity-consistent standard errors corrected for clustering at the firm level are reported in parentheses. *, **, and *** indicate significance at 10%, 5%, and 1% level, respectively.

Variable	Cumulative abnormal returns								
	Basic (pooled) (1)	Winners (pooled) (2)	Winners and losers (pooled) (3)	Basic (balanced) (4)	Winners (balanced) (5)	Winners and losers (balanced) (6)	1998 (7)	2002 (8)	Firm controls (9)
Contributions to deputies	1.749***			1.797***			2.331***	0.988	7.451***
	(0.486)			(0.510)			(0.816)	(0.626)	(2.675)
Contributions to winning deputies		2.458***	2.849**		2.300***	1.883*			
		(0.654)	(1.166)		(0.654)	(1.095)			
Contributions to losing deputies			−1.243			1.526			
			(2.740)			(3.356)			
Log of total assets									−4.378
									(3.694)
Fixed assets to total assets									−45.665
									(32.149)
Liabilities to total assets									10.834
									(37.083)
EBIT to total assets									−91.500
									(127.994)
Sales growth									71.781
									(49.533)
Industry fixed effects?	Yes	Yes	Yes	Yes	Yes	Yes	Yes	Yes	Yes
State fixed effects?	Yes	Yes	Yes	Yes	Yes	Yes	Yes	Yes	Yes
Time fixed effects?	Yes	Yes	Yes	Yes	Yes	Yes	No	No	No
Number of observations	375	375	375	274	274	274	159	216	56
Number of firms	238	238	238	137	137	137	159	216	56
R-squared	0.06	0.06	0.06	0.11	0.11	0.11	0.15	0.08	0.46

137 firms. The drawback of using a balanced panel is that we lose many firms (101 firms out of 238 firms). As our main explanatory variable, we use the amount of contributions to all deputies. For all our CAR regressions, we report White (1980) heteroskedasticity-consistent standard errors corrected for clustering at the firm level. In addition, industry, state, and time fixed effects are included in each regression, but they are not reported.

Regression 1 confirms our Value Hypothesis by showing a positive coefficient of 1.749 for total contributions made by a firm (in 100,000 BRL). The effect is statistically significant at the 1% level and economically important. A one standard deviation increase in contributions implies an increase in the CAR of

S. Claessens et al. / Journal of Financial Economics 88 (2008) 554–580 567

3.5% (2.014∗1.749). This effect is substantial because the average CAR for the 1998 and 2002 elections pooled was −4.3%, with an average of −6.8% in 1998 and −2.6% in 2002. We find a significant positive industry effect for General Industrials and significant state effects for Rio Grande do Norte (positive) and Sergipe (negative). In addition, the dummy for the 2002 election cycle enters positively, but not significantly.

Regression 2 supports the Winner Subhypothesis by showing a coefficient of 2.458 for contributions to winners that is larger than the coefficient for total contributions in Regression 1, although the difference in the coefficients in not statistically significant. In Regression 3 we also control for contributions to losing deputies because it could be that stock prices react negatively to news that connected deputy candidates lost the election. While it is hard to disentangle the effect of contributions to winning deputies from that of losing deputies because the correlation between the two variables is high (0.78), we find that the effect of contributions to winning deputies is even larger once we control for contributions to losing deputies. This result implies that a one standard deviation increase in contributions to winners lead to an CAR increase of about 4.0% (1.496∗2.849). The coefficient for contributions to losing deputies enters negatively, though not statistically different from zero. Together, these results support the Winner Subhypothesis and confirm the importance of political connections. They also provide additional support that contributions buy firm-specific political favors, i.e., there exists a causal link from contributions to firm outcomes.

In Regressions 4–6, we use a balanced panel and replicate the results of Regressions 1–3. The coefficients in Regressions 4 and 5 are significant at the 1% level and not substantially affected by the reduction in sample size. The result in Regression 6 is also qualitatively similar to that in Regression 3, although the significance of the result is somewhat reduced.

Next, we investigate the effect of contributions in each election cycle separately by splitting the sample into the two election periods. Regressions 7 and 8 show that our main result is primarily driven by the 1998 election (coefficients are significant at the 1% level). For the 2002 election, contributions do not have a significant impact on CARs. This is not surprising, given that the political landscape was expected to change dramatically because Cardoso was not eligible for a third term. In addition, it became more likely that the left-wing presidential candidate Lula would represent a completely different ideology. Consequently, markets were not able to price the value of political connections as easily as in 1998. In Regression 9 for the 1998 election, we control for firm attributes used in the capital structure literature and for sales growth, our proxy for growth opportunities. This makes the main result less susceptible to the critique that the results are due to firms gaining value in anticipation of future investment opportunities. The main caveat of this robustness test is that our sample decreases significantly from 159 to 56 firms because of a lack of accounting information for many firms. Nevertheless, the regression shows that the effect of contributions is significant at the 1% level and more than three times as large when compared with the coefficient in Regression 1.

In Table 6, we subject our main result to a more detailed analysis by using alternative measures of political connections. First, we refine our contribution measures. In Regression 1, we take into account possible competition among donors for political influence. We create a new variable that sums the contributions that a firm gave to each winning candidate as a fraction of total contributions to that candidate to create a proxy for the strength of political connections. For example, if a firm provided 80% of all campaign funds to winning candidate A and 30% of winning candidate B, then this contribution variable takes a value of 1.1. We create a similar variable for contributions to losing candidates. When including these two alternative measures of contributions, we find a positive effect of contributions to winners on CARs, although the effect is not statistically significant.

In Regression 2, we further refine the analysis by taking into account the intrastate competition between donors to establish a political connection with a specific candidate. For each firm, we use the firm's contribution to each candidate in a particular state as a fraction of total contributions received by all candidates in that state, aggregated over all candidates and states, as an alternative measure of political connections. For example, if a firm provided 1,000 BRL of campaign funds to winning candidate A in state S1 and 2,000 BRL of winning candidate B in state S2, and total contributions in state S1 were 10,000 BRL and total contributions in state S2 were 20,000 BRL, then this contribution variable would take a value of 0.2. We create a similar variable for contributions to losing candidates in the state. We find that the coefficient for this alternative variable of contributions to winning deputies is positive and significant at the 1% level. These

Table 6

Impact of alternative measures of contributions on cumulative abnormal returns

This table reports pooled ordinary least squares (OLS) regressions of the form $y_{it} = \gamma z_{it} + \theta_t + \eta_j + \lambda_k + \varepsilon_{it}$, where y_{it} is the cumulative abnormal return of firm i around the elections in year t; z_{it} is a measure of campaign contributions made by firm i for the elections at the beginning of electoral cycle t; θ_t is an election-year fixed effect; η_j is an industry fixed effect; λ_k is a state fixed effect; and ε_{it} is the error term. Firm-level control variables are lagged to the previous electoral cycle. The dependent variable is the cumulative abnormal return (in percent). We include data for the two election cycles (1998–2001 and 2002–2005) and estimate the model as pooled OLS with clustering of standard errors at the firm level. Cumulative share in contributions to (winning and losing) deputies (in the state) is the firm's cumulative share in total contributions to (winning and losing) federal deputy candidates (in the state). Contributions to (non)incumbent deputies is the total amount the firm contributed to (non)incumbent federal deputy candidates. Contributions to deputies (not) affiliated to the coalition parties of the president is the total amount the firm contributed to federal deputy candidates who are (not) affiliated to the coalition parties of the presidential candidate who won the elections. Contributions to candidates at other levels is contributions to candidates at other levels of government (governor, senator, or president). Industry, state, and time fixed effects are included in all regressions, but these are not reported. White (1980) heteroskedasticity-consistent standard errors corrected for clustering at the firm level are reported in parentheses. ** and *** indicate significance at 5% and 1% level, respectively.

Variable	Cumulative abnormal returns				
	Share of deputy (1)	Share of deputy in state (2)	Incumbents (3)	Affiliation (4)	Other candidates (5)
Cumulative share in contributions to winning deputies	5.023 (3.210)				
Cumulative share in contributions to losing deputies	−7.509 (6.136)				
Cumulative share in contributions to winning deputies in the state		60.779*** (23.348)			
Cumulative share in contributions to losing deputies in the state		−49.405** (19.672)			
Contributions to incumbent deputies			2.765** (1.253)		
Contributions to nonincumbent deputies			0.063 (2.006)		
Contributions to deputies affiliated to president coalition				2.871*** (0.947)	
Contributions to deputies not affiliated to president coalition				−0.131 (1.278)	
Contributions to deputies					1.268** (0.622)
Contributions to candidates at other levels					0.428 (0.396)
Industry fixed effects?	Yes	Yes	Yes	Yes	Yes
State fixed effects?	Yes	Yes	Yes	Yes	Yes
Time fixed effects?	Yes	Yes	Yes	Yes	Yes
Number of observations	375	375	375	375	375
Number of firms	238	238	238	238	238
R-squared	0.06	0.06	0.06	0.06	0.06

results imply that not only absolute amounts matter for firm valuation, but that the distribution of contributions over candidates is important as well.

Next, we test the Political Subhypothesis, i.e., we assess whether the tenure of the deputy candidate and the affiliation to the coalition parties of the president matter for the relation between contributions and firm value. Therefore, in Regressions 3 and 4 we include separately contributions to (non) incumbent candidates and (non) affiliated candidates. First, in Regression 3 we find that the effect on the CARs of the contributions to incumbent deputies (i.e., candidates that were in power at the time of the election) is significant at the 5% level. The effect of contributions to nonincumbent deputies is insignificant. Taken together, these results suggest that incumbent deputies are expected to affect firm-specific favors more than nonincumbents do. Second, in Regression 4 we analyze the effect of deputy party affiliation. In doing so, we create a new variable,

S. Claessens et al. / Journal of Financial Economics 88 (2008) 554–580   569

contributions to deputies affiliated to the president. For 1998, we define this as those contributions that went to candidates of PSDB (the party of Cardoso), or parties that were part of the Cardoso coalition: PMDB, PSDB, PFL, and Brazilian Progressive Party (PPB). For 2002, we define this as those contributions that went to candidates of PT (the party of Lula) or parties who were part of the Lula coalition: Liberal Party (PL), Communist Party of Brazil (PCdoB), Party of National Mobilization (PMN), and Socialist People's Party (PPS). We find that contributions to deputies affiliated to the president translate into higher market valuation (significant at the 1% level) whereas contributions to unaffiliated deputies do not have a statistically significant effect. The coefficients of the incumbency and affiliation variables are larger than the coefficient of total contributions in the basic regression (2.77 and 2.87 compared with 1.75). These results suggest that a deputy was more likely expected to deliver favors when he was an incumbent or a member of a presidential coalition party. Similar to the logic already described, this shows that the distribution of contributions matters and strengthens our hypothesis that contributions cause firm-specific political favors and not that better performing firms are merely able to donate more.

One concern with our results could be that contributions to a deputy candidate proxy for connections with politicians at other levels of government. However, Regression 5 shows that the main result is unaffected when we control for contributions to candidates at other levels of government, i.e., president, governor, and senator. While the positive coefficient on contributions to candidates at other levels suggests that markets also expected political favors from them, this effect is not statistically significant. Hence, we conclude that contributions to individual deputy candidates pay off in terms of higher firm valuation surrounding the elections.

In Table 7, we subject our main result to several additional robustness checks. First, in Regression 1 we shorten the event window to avoid possible contamination of the CAR by other events after the elections. In

Table 7
Impact of contributions on cumulative abnormal returns, robustness
This table reports pooled ordinary least squares regressions of the form $y_{it} = \gamma z_{it} + \theta_t + \eta_j + \lambda_k + \varepsilon_{it}$, where y_{it} is the cumulative abnormal return of firm i around the elections in year t; z_{it} is a measure of campaign contributions made by firm i for the elections at the beginning of electoral cycle t; θ_t is an election-year fixed effect; η_j is an industry fixed effect; λ_k is a state fixed effect; and ε_{it} is the error term. Firm-level control variables are lagged to the previous electoral cycle. The dependent variable in Regression 1 is the cumulative abnormal return (in percent), calculated with an event window covering the 20 days before and five days after the election. The dependent variable in Regression 2 is the buy-and-hold return (in percent), calculated with an event window covering the 20 days before and 20 days after the election. The dependent variable in Regressions 3–5 is the cumulative abnormal return (in percent), calculated with an event window covering the 20 days before and 20 days after the election. In Regression 3, we exclude firms that operate in the financial services and utilities industries. In Regressions 4 and 5, we exclude firms that made no contributions to federal deputy candidates. Contributions to deputies is the total absolute amount the firm contributed to federal deputy candidates in one-hundred thousands of 1998 Brazilian Real at the beginning of the election cycle. Industry, state, and time fixed effects are included in all regressions, but these are not reported. White (1980) heteroskedasticity-consistent standard errors corrected for clustering at the firm level are reported in parentheses. * and ** indicate significance at 10% and 5% level, respectively.

Variable	Cumulative abnormal returns with shorter window	Buy-and-hold strategy	Cumulative abnormal returns		
			Excluding banks and utilities	Excluding firms that did not contribute	Excluding firms that did not contribute
	(1)	(2)	(3)	(4)	(5)
Contributions to deputies	0.825**	2.263*	1.404**	1.259*	
	(0.362)	(1.196)	(0.708)	(0.699)	
Contributions to winning deputies					1.663*
					(0.886)
Industry fixed effects?	Yes	Yes	Yes	Yes	Yes
State fixed effects?	Yes	Yes	Yes	Yes	Yes
Time fixed effects?	Yes	Yes	Yes	Yes	Yes
Number of observations	375	375	292	95	95
Number of firms	238	238	189	72	72
R-squared	0.06	0.05	0.08	0.26	0.26

doing so, we adjust the event window to 20 days before and five days after the announcement of the election results. We find that contributions still matter (significant at the 5% level), although the coefficient is of smaller magnitude, perhaps because the effects of political favors are assessed by the markets over a longer period. Second, in Regression 2 we use the buy-and-hold return (BHR) of the firm's stock as an alternative dependent variable. The main result is confirmed although the statistical significance is somewhat weaker (significant at the 10% level). The economic impact of the result is significant: A one standard deviation increase in contributions implies an increase in the BHR of 4.6% (2.014∗2.263). Third, in Regression 3 we drop banks and utilities because these firms are more regulated by the government and could potentially distort the main result. The results, however, again do not change qualitatively and remain significant at the 5% level. Fourth, in Regression 4 we re-run our main specification on the subsample of firms that contributed to deputies, excluding firms that do not contribute. Again, our results are significant (at the 10% level) and do not change qualitatively, although the sample is much reduced, to less than one hundred observations. Fifth, in Regression 5 we re-run Regression 2 of Table 5 when excluding firms that do not contribute and find similar results, offering additional support for the Winners Subhypothesis. Finally, in unreported regressions we find that results are robust to winsorizing cumulative abnormal returns at the 5% and 95% level.

5.2. Preferential access to finance as a political favor

In Section 5.1 we establish that campaign contributions are associated with higher stock returns around the time of election, suggesting that the market expected future, firm-specific political favors. In this subsection we investigate whether access to finance is such a favor.

As our basic test of the Access Hypothesis, we analyze whether the financial leverage over the election cycles of 1998 and 2002 (spanning the years 1998–2001 and 2002–2005, respectively) of firms that made higher contributions to (elected) federal deputies increased more during the four years following the election relative to a control group of listed firms that did not contribute to deputy candidates. Because our hypothesis is that firms benefit via preferential access to bank credit, we focus on financing that is provided by banks and use the growth in bank financing as a share of total assets (growth in bank leverage) over an election cycle as our dependent variable, as per the model specification in Eq. (2). In all leverage regressions, we drop financial companies such as banks and insurance companies because they are suppliers of finance. Because we do not have accounting data for some firms, the size of the pooled sample decreases to 168 observations that represent a balanced panel of 84 firms. In all our access to finance regressions, standard errors of coefficients are corrected for heteroskedasticity following White (1980) and for clustering at the firm level. In addition, firm and time fixed effects are included in each regression, but these are not reported. We use firm fixed effects to control for time-invariant, unobserved firm characteristics to mitigate the problem of omitted variables. In addition, the time fixed effect controls for election-specific influences.

Table 8 presents our main leverage regressions. Regression 1 confirms the Access Hypothesis: Campaign contributions positively affect a firm's access to finance, as measured by the growth rate in bank leverage, following an election. The coefficient on contributions is 0.047 and highly significant, at the 1% level. The result also has economic significance. A one standard deviation increase in contributions to deputies implies a 9.4% increase in bank leverage growth in the four-year period following an election (2.014∗0.047). Because average leverage growth was almost zero, this is a large effect, also relative to the individual election cycles (i.e., an average leverage growth of 6.4% over the first and -6.6% over the second election cycle).

Regression 2 confirms the Winner Subhypothesis: Political connections to winning deputies paid off more in terms of higher access to financing. The coefficient is significant at the 1% level and almost twice as large as in Regression 1, indicating that giving to winners matters more. The winners finding further mitigates concerns about simultaneity problems. Similarly as for the CAR regression, the fact that the coefficient for winners is greater than that for total contributions serves as a robustness check of our hypothesis that contributions imply political favors. A higher coefficient does not support the idea that some firms were just better able to give contributions and increase their access to finance, because it clearly mattered to whom the contributions were given. Correspondingly, the economic effect of giving to winners is substantial. A one standard deviation increase in contributions to winners translates into a 12.1% increase in bank leverage growth over the four-year period following an election (1.496∗0.081).

S. Claessens et al. / Journal of Financial Economics 88 (2008) 554–580 571

Table 8
Impact of contributions on growth in bank leverage

This table reports ordinary least squares regressions of the form $l_{it} = \beta' x_{it-1} + \gamma z_{it} + \theta_t + \alpha_i + \varepsilon_{it}$, where l_{it} is the growth in bank leverage of firm i over the electoral cycle t; x_{it-1} is a vector of firm-level control variables; z_{it} is a measure of campaign contributions made by firm i for the elections at the beginning of electoral cycle t; θ_t is an electoral cycle fixed effect; α_i is a firm fixed effect; and ε_{it} is the error term. The dependent variable is the growth in bank leverage (defined as the ratio of total bank debt to total assets) over the election cycle (either the period 1998–2001 or the period 2002–2005). Contributions to deputies is the total absolute amount in one-hundred thousands of 1998 Brazilian Real firms contributed to federal deputy candidates at the beginning of the election cycle. We include the following firm-level control variables, calculated as averages over the previous election cycle: log of total assets is the logarithm of total assets; fixed assets to total assets is the ratio of fixed assets to total assets; liabilities to total assets is the ratio of total liabilities to total assets; EBIT to total assets is the ratio of earnings before interest and taxes to total assets; and sales growth is real growth in sales. Firm-level control variables are lagged to the previous electoral cycle, except in Regression 7 in which we include contemporaneous values of the control variables. Firm fixed effects and election period fixed effects are included in the regressions, but these are not reported. White (1980) heteroskedasticity-consistent standard errors corrected for clustering at the firm level are reported in parentheses. *, **, and *** indicate significance at 10%, 5%, and 1% level, respectively.

Variable	Growth in bank leverage						
	Basic (pooled)	Winners (pooled)	Winners and losers (pooled)	Firm controls (pooled)	Firm controls (balanced)	Without liabilities to total assets (pooled)	Contemporaneous control variables (pooled)
	(1)	(2)	(3)	(4)	(5)	(6)	(7)
Contributions to deputies	0.047*** (0.015)			0.030** (0.014)	0.030** (0.014)	0.042* (0.022)	0.039** (0.017)
Contributions to winning deputies		0.081*** (0.028)	0.099 (0.073)				
Contributions to losing deputies			−0.033 (0.089)				
Log of total assets				−0.090 (0.056)	−0.090 (0.057)	−0.108 (0.077)	0.026 (0.088)
Fixed assets to total assets				0.310 (0.477)	0.310 (0.481)	0.381 (0.528)	0.398 (0.380)
Liabilities to total assets				−0.917*** (0.343)	−0.917** (0.345)		
EBIT to total assets				0.122 (0.616)	0.122 (0.621)	0.608 (0.776)	−1.234 (0.753)
Sales growth				0.125 (0.168)	0.125 (0.169)	0.050 (0.172)	0.170 (0.238)
Firm fixed effects?	Yes	Yes	Yes	Yes	Yes	Yes	Yes
Time fixed effects?	Yes	Yes	Yes	Yes	Yes	Yes	Yes
Number of observations	168	168	168	143	120	143	165
Number of firms	84	84	84	83	60	83	84
R-squared	0.04	0.04	0.04	0.08	0.08	0.06	0.02

When we further split contributions to winning deputies from contributions to losing deputies in Regression 3, we still find a positive coefficient for contributions to winning deputies although the effect is no longer statistically significant. It appears hard to disentangle the effect between winners and losers because the two variables are highly correlated at 0.78.

Our results could be influenced by time-varying firm characteristics. Therefore in Regression 4, we add one-election period lagged firm characteristics to control for any changes over the election cycle in size, asset tangibility, total leverage, profitability, and sales growth. Including past sales growth could be especially relevant because it controls for the possibility that leverage merely increases in anticipation of future investment opportunities, not as a result of political favors. Our main result is confirmed, as the coefficient for contributions has the same order of magnitude and is significant at the 5% level. We also find that firms substitute other liabilities for bank debt.

Regression 5 repeats Regression 4 for the balanced sample. Our results are almost identical. Regressions 1–3 are based on a pooled sample that is already balanced, so we do not repeat those regressions for a balanced sample. When we add firm control variables, we lose observations in the balanced panel because of missing data. Hence, we continue our analyses with the pooled approach, which includes more observations.

Regression 6 reports similar results when we do not include initial liabilities to total assets as a control variable, although the coefficient for contributions is slightly less significant with a *P*-value of 5.6%. Regression 7 shows that the results are robust to using contemporaneous control variables. Although contemporaneous variables could be contaminated by the effects of access to finance during the period studied, the advantage of using contemporaneous control variables is that we do not lose as many observations. We find that the coefficient for contributions is not affected.

Similar to the CAR regressions in Table 6, we subject our main result to further analyses by using alternative measures of political connections. Table 9 shows the results. First, we use the refined contribution

Table 9
Impact of alternative measures of contributions on growth in bank leverage

This table reports ordinary least squares regressions of the form: $l_{it} = \gamma z_{it} + \theta_t + \alpha_i + \varepsilon_{it}$, where l_{it} is the growth in bank leverage of firm i over the electoral cycle t; z_{it} is a measure of campaign contributions made by firm i for the elections at the beginning of electoral cycle t; θ_t is an electoral cycle fixed effect; α_i is a firm fixed effect; and ε_{it} is the error term. The dependent variable is the growth in bank leverage (defined as the ratio of total bank debt to total assets) over the election cycle (either the period 1998–2001 or the period 2002–2005). Cumulative share in contributions to (winning and losing) deputies (in the state) is the firm's share in total contributions to (winning and losing) federal deputies (in a particular state). Contributions to (non)incumbent deputies is the total absolute amount the firm contributed to (non)incumbent federal deputy candidates. Contributions to deputies (not) affiliated to president coalition is the total absolute amount the firm contributed to federal deputy candidates that are (not) affiliated to the coalition parties of the presidential candidate that won the elections (Fernando Cardoso in 1998 and Luiz Inácio (Lula) da Silva in 2002). Contributions to candidates at other levels is contributions to candidates at other levels of government (governor, senator, or president). Firm fixed effects and election period fixed effects are included in the regressions, but these are not reported. White (1980) heteroskedasticity-consistent standard errors corrected for clustering at the firm level are reported in parentheses. *, **, and *** indicate significance at 10%, 5%, and 1% level, respectively.

Variable	Growth in bank leverage				
	Share of deputy (1)	Share of deputy in state (2)	Incumbents (3)	Affiliation (4)	Other candidates (5)
Cumulative share in contributions to winning deputies	0.428*				
	(0.224)				
Cumulative share in contributions to losing deputies	−0.297				
	(0.180)				
Cumulative share in contributions to winning deputies in the state		5.119**			
		(2.298)			
Cumulative share in contributions to losing deputies in the state		−5.269			
		(4.347)			
Contributions to incumbent deputies			0.053***		
			(0.008)		
Contributions to nonincumbent deputies			0.037		
			(0.040)		
Contributions to deputies affiliated to president coalition				0.046**	
				(0.022)	
Contributions to deputies not affiliated to president coalition				0.048	
				(0.031)	
Contributions to deputies					0.059**
					(0.016)
Contributions to candidates at other levels					−0.008
					(0.009)
Firm fixed effects?	Yes	Yes	Yes	Yes	Yes
Time fixed effects?	Yes	Yes	Yes	Yes	Yes
Observations	168	168	168	168	168
Number of firms	84	84	84	84	84
R-squared	0.06	0.06	0.04	0.04	0.04

measures that take the distribution of contributions across candidates into account. Regression 1 shows the results when using contribution measures that correct for competition among firms in contributions to the same deputy, and Regression 2 shows the results when correcting for intrastate competition for contributions among candidates. In both cases, we make a distinction between contributions to winning and losing deputies, as before. We find that our main results are confirmed as the coefficients for the alternative contribution measures to winning deputies are positive and statistically significant.

Next, we assess the validity of the Political Subhypothesis, i.e., whether the tenure of the deputy candidate and the candidate's affiliation to the president matter for the relationship between contributions and access to finance. Regressions 3 and 4 report that contributions to incumbents and affiliation to the coalition parties of the president clearly matter for bank leverage growth, while contributions to non-incumbents and nonaffiliates have an insignificant effect. We conclude that incumbency and affiliation of deputies translate into improved access to finance. These results are in line with the results for the CARs in which we also find that incumbency and affiliation are important.

To make sure that contributions to deputies do not simply capture contributions to other candidates, we control in Regression 5 for contributions to candidates at other levels of government (including senator, governor, and president). Our results for contributions to deputies are not affected. The coefficient for contributions to candidates at other levels is not statistically different from zero, suggesting that the access to finance channel operates mostly at the deputy level.

Table 10 reports robustness checks similar to Table 7 regarding the impact of contributions on bank leverage growth. In Regression 1 we include the year before the election as an alternative base year to calculate the change in bank debt, to make sure that the result we find is not driven by changes in bank leverage during the election year. The coefficient is still significant and of the same order of magnitude as in earlier regressions. In Regression 2 we exclude utilities because they tend to be heavily regulated (we already exclude financial companies, which also tend to be regulated, from all leverage regressions) and find results that are virtually

Table 10

Impact of contributions on growth in bank leverage, robustness

This table reports ordinary least squares regressions of the form $l_{it} = \gamma z_{it} + \theta_t + \alpha_i + \varepsilon_{it}$, where l_{it} is the growth in bank leverage of firm i over the electoral cycle t; z_{it} is a measure of campaign contributions made by firm i for the elections at the beginning of electoral cycle t; θ_t is an electoral cycle fixed effect; α_t is a firm fixed effect; and ε_{it} is the error term. The dependent variable is the growth in bank leverage (defined as the ratio of total bank debt to total assets) over the election cycle. In Regression 1, the election cycles are defined as the periods 1997–2001 and 2001–2005 (i.e., we include the growth rate during the election year); in all other regressions, the election cycles are the periods 1998–2001 and 2002–2005. Contributions to deputies is the total absolute amount the firm contributed to federal deputy candidates in one-hundred thousands of 1998 Brazilian Real at the beginning of the election cycle. Contributions to all candidates is the total absolute amount the firm contributed to all types of election candidates (federal deputy, governor, senator, or president). In Regression 2, we exclude firms that operate in the utilities industries (firms that operate in the financial services industries are not included in any of the leverage growth regressions). In Regressions 3 and 4, we exclude firms that did not make contributions to federal deputies. Firm fixed effects and election period fixed effects are included in the regressions, but these are not reported. White (1980) heteroskedasticity-consistent standard errors corrected for clustering at the firm level are reported in parentheses. ** and *** indicate significance at 5% and 1% level, respectively.

Variable	Growth in bank leverage			
	Including election year to compute growth of bank leverage (1)	Excluding utilities (2)	Excluding firms that did not contribute to deputies (3)	Excluding firms that did not contribute to deputies (4)
Contributions to deputies	0.034** (0.016)	0.047*** (0.015)	0.046*** (0.007)	
Contributions to winning deputies				0.061*** (0.020)
Firm fixed effects?	Yes	Yes	Yes	Yes
Time fixed effects?	Yes	Yes	Yes	Yes
Observations	168	146	43	43
Number of firms	84	73	32	32
R-squared	0.03	0.04	0.02	0.04

574   S. Claessens et al. / Journal of Financial Economics 88 (2008) 554–580

identical to those reported in Regression 1 of Table 8. In Regression 3 we exclude firms that were not reported as contributors to deputies in our data. Again, our results are unaffected. The number of observations falls dramatically when considering only those firms that have contributed. Finally, in Regression 4 we consider contributions to winning deputies while excluding firms that did not contribute to deputies. We again confirm our earlier result.

Next, in Table 11, we investigate whether the influence of contributions can also be found for other forms of debt financing and for the price of bank financing. First, we check whether the results differ between short-term and long-term bank debt. Short-term bank debt represents that portion of bank debt payable within one year, including the current portion of long-term bank debt, while long-term bank debt represents all interest-bearing bank debt obligations, excluding amounts due within one year. Because much of long-term bank credit in Brazil is extended by state-owned banks, it could be that the political access to bank finance channel operates mostly through the extension of long-term bank credit. However, the effect could be more pronounced for short-term bank loans, because short-term debt contracts are more likely to be renegotiated than long-term debt contracts during the four-year election cycle. We find that both short-term and long-term bank debt increase following contributions to deputies (Regressions 1 and 2), suggesting that contributions buy improved access to bank finance irrespective of the maturity of the debt.

Second, to check for any effects on other forms of debt, we next use the growth in other liabilities (i.e., liabilities other than bank debt) relative to total assets as our dependent variable. Other liabilities include accounts payables, bonds, debentures, and arrears. If preferential access would come strictly from bank credit, we should not find a significant effect from contributions on these other forms of debt. Regression 3 shows that contributions do not have a significant effect on the growth of other liabilities, suggesting that political connections operate mostly through access to bank credit. Regression 4 shows that the effect of contributions on the growth of overall liabilities (i.e., the sum of bank debt and other liabilities) is still positive and statistically significant, indicating that while politically connected firms could substitute some liabilities for bank debt, their overall liabilities still increase relative to other firms.

Table 11
Impact of contributions on bank debt of different maturity, other types of debt, and interest expenses
This table reports ordinary least squares regressions of the form: $p_{it} = \gamma z_{it} + \theta_t + \alpha_i + \varepsilon_{it}$, where p_{it} is the dependent variable for firm i over the electoral cycle t; z_{it} is a measure of campaign contributions made by firm i for the elections at the beginning of electoral cycle t; θ_t is an electoral cycle fixed effect; α_i is a firm fixed effect; and ε_{it} is the error term. The dependent variable in Regression 1 is the growth in short-term bank leverage (defined as the ratio of short-term bank debt to total assets) over the election cycle. The dependent variable in Regression 2 is the growth in long-term bank leverage (defined as the ratio of long-term bank debt to total assets) over the election cycle. The dependent variable in Regression 3 is the growth in the ratio of liabilities other than bank debt to total assets over the election cycle. Other liabilities include accounts payables, bonds, debentures, and arrears. The dependent variable in Regression 4 is the growth in the ratio of total liabilities to total assets over the election cycle. The dependent variable in Regression 5 is the growth in the ratio of total interest expense on debt to total assets over the election cycle. Contributions to deputies is the total absolute amount the firm contributed to federal deputy candidates in one-hundred thousands of 1998 Brazilian Real at the beginning of the election cycle. Firm fixed effects and election period fixed effects are included in the regressions, but these are not reported. White (1980) heteroskedasticity-consistent standard errors corrected for clustering at the firm level are reported in parentheses. * and ** indicate significance at 10% and 5% level, respectively.

Variable	Growth in short-term bank leverage (1)	Growth in long-term bank leverage (2)	Growth in other liabilities to total assets (3)	Growth in total liabilities to total assets (4)	Growth in interest expense to total sales (5)
Contributions to deputies	0.050* (0.026)	0.033* (0.019)	−0.008 (0.005)	0.014** (0.007)	−0.007 (0.029)
Firm fixed effects?	Yes	Yes	Yes	Yes	Yes
Time fixed effects?	Yes	Yes	Yes	Yes	Yes
Observations	168	168	168	168	158
Number of firms	84	84	84	84	82
R-squared	0.03	0.01	0.01	0.05	0.14

S. Claessens et al. / Journal of Financial Economics 88 (2008) 554–580 575

Third, in addition to gaining access to an increased amount of debt financing, firms could also benefit from making contributions to politicians by gaining access to debt financing at preferential terms. Therefore we assess the impact of contributions on the cost of debt, as measured by the change in the ratio of interest expense on total interest-bearing debt obligations to total sales over the election cycle. Regression 5 finds a negative effect, suggesting that contributions lower the cost of all debt financing. The effect is, however, not statistically significant. We have data only on total interest expenses and not a breakdown of interest expenses by type of debt, including bank debt. We cannot therefore rule out that politicians could have some sway over the cost of bank financing as well.

The positive impact on access to bank financing we found in Table 11 could also be driven by an increase in assets that serve as collateral for attracting financing. The increase in assets in turn could be the result of politicians influencing government contracts, concessions, or other interventions that lead to preferential investment (opportunities) that in turn allow the firm to attract financing. We have no specific evidence whether increased access to financing arises through favors extended by politicians directly (via their connections with banks or other financial institutions) or indirectly because a political connection with a deputy increases the collateral or the franchise value of the firm via enhanced business opportunities. However, the data do not support the view that improved access to finance is the result of an increase in assets that can serve as collateral for debt finance. Regression 1 in Table 12 shows that contributions do not significantly impact the growth in fixed assets relative to growth in total assets. Regression 2 even reports that collateralizable assets as a share of total assets decrease in a statistically significant way over the election cycle the more firms contribute. These results also do not lend support for the notion that assets increase in response to improved investment opportunities.

Table 12

Impact of contributions on allocation and quality of investments

This table reports ordinary least squares regressions of the form $p_{it} = \gamma z_{it} + \theta_t + \alpha_i + \varepsilon_{it}$, where p_{it} is the dependent variable for firm i over the electoral cycle t, unless otherwise noted; z_{it} is a measure of campaign contributions; θ_t is an electoral cycle fixed effect; α_i is a firm fixed effect; and ε_{it} is the error term. The dependent variable in Regression 1 is the growth in fixed assets to total assets, averaged over the election cycle t. The dependent variable in Regression 2 is the growth in collateral to total assets (where collateralizable assets are defined as the sum of cash and cash-equivalent investments, accounts receivables, inventories, and fixed assets), averaged over the election cycle t. The dependent variable in Regression 3 is capital expenditure to total assets, averaged over the election cycle t. The dependent variable in Regression 4 is the ratio of pre-tax profits to total assets, averaged over the election cycle t. Contributions to deputies is the total absolute amount the firm contributed to federal deputy candidates in one-hundred thousands of 1998 Brazilian Real at the beginning of the election cycle. The dependent variable in Regressions 5 and 6 is the Tobin's Q of firm i at the beginning of the electoral cycle t. The dependent variable in Regression 7 is capital expenditure to total assets of firm i at the beginning of the electoral cycle t. In Regressions 1–5, z_{it} is the campaign contributions made by firm i for the elections at the beginning of electoral cycle t. In Regressions 6 and 7, z_{it} is a dummy variable indicating whether firm i has made any campaign contributions to federal deputy candidates for the elections at the beginning of electoral cycle t. Firm fixed effects and election-period fixed effects are included in the regressions, but these are not reported. White (1980) heteroskedasticity-consistent standard errors corrected for clustering at the firm level are reported in parentheses. * and *** indicate significance at 10% and 1% level, respectively.

Variable	Growth in fixed assets to total assets	Growth in collateral to total assets	Capital expenditure to total assets	Return on assets	Initial Tobin's Q	Initial Tobin's Q	Initial capital expenditure to total assets
	(1)	(2)	(3)	(4)	(5)	(6)	(7)
Contributions to deputies	−0.007	−0.009*	0.002	−0.014***	−0.040***		
	(0.010)	(0.005)	(0.002)	(0.003)	(0.012)		
Contributions (yes = 1; no = 0)						−0.070*	0.048*
						(0.037)	(0.027)
Firm fixed effects?	Yes	Yes	Yes	Yes	Yes	Yes	Yes
Time fixed effects?	Yes	Yes	Yes	Yes	Yes	Yes	Yes
Observations	168	164	160	168	166	166	141
Number of firms	84	84	84	84	84	84	78
R-squared	0.06	0.01	0.01	0.01	0.12	0.17	0.11

This raises the question: What do firms do with the increased financing? The increased access to bank financing could be used for an increase in investment or it could serve to finance lower operational cash flows. We find from Regression 3 that firms that make more political contributions invest at a somewhat higher rate as measured by the ratio of capital expenditures to total assets, although the coefficient is not significant. This suggests that the improved access to finance led to some degree to enhanced investment and was not simply used to cover operational losses or to tunnel firm resources away from investors.

Next, we analyze the allocational efficiency of the investment of contributing firms relative to other firms. From an overall resource allocation point of view, it is important to know whether contributions imply that more productive firms end up investing more as their financing constraint is released, or whether it is the less efficient firms that benefit from more external financing. Regression 4 shows that the relationship between firm performance, as measured by the change in the average pre-tax return on assets over the election cycle, and contributions is negative and statistically significant. In other words, the performance of firms during the post-election period is significantly lower, the more contributions they provide. Regression 5 repeats the analysis with the initial Tobin's Q at the beginning of the election cycle as the dependent variable and shows that firms' valuation before the election was significantly lower the more contributions they made. Together, these regression results suggest that contributing firms perform worse and that the additional investment generated by improved financing has not been efficient.

The results so far suggest that political favors do not mostly come in the form of increased business opportunities, as one would expect this to be reflected in higher profits and an increase in fixed and collateralizable assets over total assets, but rather that political favors come in the form of improved access to finance for often poorly performing firms. Further evidence of the possible links between contributions and preferential investment opportunities comes from the distribution of contributions across industries. If political favors come in the form of large contracts or concessions by the government, then one would expect highly regulated industries or industries dependent on government contracts to be the main contributors of campaign finance. However, the data are not consistent with this prediction either (Table A2 reports the share of firms in each three-digit industry that contributed to the campaigns of deputy candidates). While contributions are common in some highly regulated industries, such as the financial sector, in other highly regulated industries, such as the electricity and telecom sectors, there are no contributing firms. Also, while contributions appear to be common in industries such as basic industries (which includes the construction industry) and the oil and mining industries, in which government concessions are common, other industries in which government concessions are less common, such as the engineering and equipment manufacturing industries, also appear major campaign finance contributors. In other words, campaign contributions are not an industry-specific phenomenon that can be easily related to the occurrence of government regulation or contracts. Taken together, this suggests that the political economy channel of contributions goes predominantly directly through increased access to financing.

5.3. Economic costs of rents

While it is rather heroic to infer the cost to the economy at large of the rents extracted by contributing firms, let alone to assess the welfare implications of such rents, in this subsection we make an attempt to quantify the cost of the investment distortion that could arise by extending preferential bank credit to contributing firms. A welfare loss would arise if the rate of return on investment financed by this credit is lower than that on resources invested elsewhere. We estimate this investment distortion cost by comparing the return on investment generated by contributing firms with that of noncontributing firms. This is a lower bound measure as there are likely a variety of other costs associated with the investment distortion that we do not capture. Our intention is just to estimate those costs that can be inferred from our analysis.

Following Khwaja and Mian (2005), we use the differential in Tobin's Q to gauge the difference in investment returns. Regression 6 of Table 12 shows that the Tobin's Q of contributing firms at the time of the election is 0.07 lower than that of noncontributing firms (after taking out firm fixed and election year effects), suggesting that there is some misallocation of credit. This difference in Tobin's Q is substantial given that the average Tobin's Q in both election years is about 0.63 (see Table 3, Panel B). We next estimate the cost of the investment distortion by calculating how much additional return would have been generated if the bank

S. Claessens et al. / Journal of Financial Economics 88 (2008) 554–580   577

financing extended to contributing firms would have financed investments of noncontributing firms. This depends on how much investment was the result of the financing generated by the contributions. Regression 7 of Table 12 shows that the annual investment rate (as measured by the ratio of capital expenditure to total assets) at the time of the election is 0.048 higher for contributing firms (after taking out firm fixed and election year effects). If we next assume that a reallocation of resources would not affect the return on investment (Tobin's Q) of both contributing and noncontributing firms, we can get a welfare measure. This simple measure suggests that the investment distortion over the two election cycles is 0.34% ($= 0.048*0.07$) per annum of the average firm's total assets.

On average, the firms in our sample have about 1.0 billion 1998 BRL in total assets (Table 3 presents the summary statistics for the log of total assets). If we assume that the investment distortion is similar for all 540 listed firms, including those that are not included in our sample, then the gross cost of the investment distortion arising from contributions by listed firms is about 1.8 billion 1998 BRL ($= 540*1.0*0.0034$) per annum. Brazil's GDP in 1998 was 914 billion BRL, so this figure amounts to about 0.2% of GDP per annum. This is somewhat less than the 0.3–1.9% of GDP per annum cost of preferential access to financing computed for Pakistan by Khwaja and Mian (2005). We should keep in mind, though, that our estimate is a lower bound because it includes only the listed firms and therefore a subset of the firms in the country.[5] In any case, 0.2% of GDP per annum is a substantial welfare loss.

6. Conclusions

This paper addresses the question whether campaign contributions made by firms are associated with future firm-specific favors. We provide empirical support for the existence of such a link based on an analysis of the 1998 and 2002 elections in Brazil. We find robust evidence that higher campaign contributions to federal deputy candidates are associated with higher stock returns around the announcement of the election results. Contributing to deputy candidates that win the election has an even larger positive impact on stock returns.

Besides establishing a link between campaign finance and political favors at the firm level using candidate-level campaign data, we investigate the possible channel for political favors. We study the relationship between campaign contributions and future access to finance. Using a firm fixed effects framework to mitigate the problem of omitted variables, we find that the bank leverage of firms that made contributions to (elected) federal deputies increased substantially during the four years following the election. This suggests that contributing firms gained preferential access to finance from banks. Although we do not have direct evidence of preferential lending and associated benefits for contributing firms, it is reasonable to assume given the high interest rate environment in Brazil that the gross benefits of increased access to finance likely exceeded the cost paid by firms in the form of campaign contributions, the more so because contributions tend to be small compared with the size of contributing firms. In a crude way, we estimate the cost of the investment distortion associated with extending preferential bank credit to contributing firms to be at least 0.2% of GDP per annum.

While finance might not be the only channel through which firms benefit from political favors, our results support the notion that it is an important channel through which contributing firms benefit from political connections. More generally, our findings provide new evidence on the value of political connections in emerging markets. It corroborates other evidence that the rents from corruption are particularly large when there are government-imposed distortions, with negative welfare effects, and implies that the operation of corporations in such environments, including their financing and financial structure, depends on their relationships with politicians.

Appendix

Contributions by political partly and inversely are given in Tables A1 and A2.

---

[5]On average, the listed firms in our sample are responsible for about 14% of total corporate contributions made to federal deputies, so (by simple extrapolation) the cost could be as much as 1.4% of GDP per annum.

578 S. Claessens et al. / Journal of Financial Economics 88 (2008) 554–580

Table A1

Contributions by political party

This table lists the number of contributions of firms and the average amount of contributions by political party. Amounts are in 1998 Brazilian Real (1BRL ≈0.86$).

Political party	English name of political party	Listed firms in 1998 and 2002		Listed firms in 1998		Listed firms in 2002	
		Number of contributions	Average amount of contributions	Number of contributions	Average amount of contributions	Number of contributions	Average amount of contributions
PAN	Party of the Nation's Retirees	–	–	–	–	–	–
PCdoB	Communist Party of Brazil	4	8,305	3	12,566	5	4,043
PDT	Democratic Labor Party	33.5	9,871	13	7,037	54	12,704
PFL	Liberal Front Party	112.5	160.517	112	297,889	113	23,145
PGT	General Party of the Workers	0.5	2,244	–	–	1	4,488
PHS	Humanist Party of Solidarity	0.5	669	–	–	1	1,338
PL	Liberal Party	7	6,376	1	682	13	12,069
PMDB	Brazilian Democratic Movement Party	74.5	24,442	67	29,768	82	19,116
PPB	Brazilian Progressive Party	42	10,799	–	–	84	21,598
PMN	Party of National Mobilization	–	–	–	–	–	–
PP	Progressive Party	24.5	9,399	49	18,797	–	–
PPS	Socialist People's Party	19.5	16,801	4	13,750	35	19,851
PRTB	Brazilian Labor Renewal Party	3	12,657	–	–	6	25,314
PRONA	Party of the Reconstruction of the National Order	–	–	–	–	–	–
PRP	Progressive Republican Party	0.5	1,655	1	3,310	–	–
PSB	Brazilian Socialist Party	25	17,716	16	20,844	34	14,587
PSC	Christian Social Party	1.5	387	–	–	3	774
PSDB	Brazilian Social Democracy Party	129.5	24,444	123	25,610	136	23,278
PSDC	Christian Social Democratic Party	3	8,009	–	–	6	16,018
PST	Social Labor Party	0.5	3,674	–	–	1	7,348
PSL	Social Liberal Party	–	–	–	–	–	–
PSTU	United Socialist Workers' Party	–	–	–	–	–	–
PT	Workers' Party	31	17,384	16	14,715	46	20,053
PTdoB	Labor Party of Brazil	–	–	–	—	–	–
PTB	Brazilian Labor Party	27	13,578	18	11,861	36	15,295
PTN	National Labor Party	–	–	–	–	–	–
PV	Green Party	4	2.964	–	–	8	5,927
Total		543.5	14,723	423	15,727	664	13,719

Table A2

Contributions by industry

This table reports for each industry the total number of listed firms for which we have data on campaign contributions, the number of firms that contributed to the campaign finance of deputy candidates, the number of firms that did not contribute, and the share of firms that contributed. Data are for the years 1998 and 2002 for our sample of listed firms. Contributions are in 1998 Brazilian Real.

Industry	Number of firms	Contributors	Noncontributors	Contributors as share of total number of firms	Total contributions
1998					
Basic Industries (including Metals, Steel, Chemicals, Building Materials, Paper, Construction)	40	16	24	0.40	5,409,987
Cyclical Consumer Goods (including Textile, Leisure Goods, Leather, Clothing, Footwear)	21	6	15	0.29	399,802

S. Claessens et al. / Journal of Financial Economics 88 (2008) 554–580   579

Table A2 (*continued*)

Industry	Number of firms	Contributors	Noncontributors	Contributors as share of total number of firms	Total contributions
Cyclical Services (including Retail, Hotels, Entertainment, Publishing)	8	0	8	0.00	0
Financials (including Banks, Insurance)	14	4	10	0.29	2,314,500
General Industries (including Engineering, Electric Equipment, Diversified)	20	5	15	0.25	975,000
Information Technology (including Computer Hardware)	1	1	0	1.00	20,000
Investment Companies	12	2	10	0.17	21,000
Non-Cyclical Consumer Goods (including Food, Tobacco, Healthcare)	10	2	8	0.20	87,422
Non-Cyclical Services (including Telecom Fixed Line, Telecom Wireless)	5	0	5	0.00	0
Resources (including Oil, Gas, Mining)	6	3	3	0.50	92,500
Utilities (including Electricity, Water)	22	0	22	0.00	0
Total	159	39	120	0.25	9,320,211
2002					
Basic Industries (including Metals, Steel, Chemicals, Building Materials, Paper, Construction)	45	21	24	0.47	7,143,643
Cyclical Consumer Goods (including Textile, Leisure Goods, Leather, Clothing, Footwear)	30	7	23	0.23	303,500
Cyclical Services (including Retail, Hotels, Entertainment, Publishing)	7	0	7	0.00	0
Financials (including Banks, Insurance)	18	4	14	0.22	1,504,935
General Industries (including Engineering, Electric Equipment, Diversified)	30	13	17	0.43	1,838,486
Information Technology (including Computer Hardware)	1	1	0	1.00	76,810
Investment Companies	13	3	10	0.23	45,852
Non-Cyclical Consumer Goods (including Food, Tobacco, Healthcare)	14	5	9	0.36	861,598
Non-Cyclical Services (including Telecom Fixed Line, Telecom Wireless)	21	0	21	0.00	0
Resources (including Oil, Gas, Mining)	8	0	8	0.00	0
Utilities (including Electricity, Water)	29	2	27	0.07	154,309
Total	216	56	160	0.26	11,929,130

References

Acemoglu, D., 2007. The form of property rights: oligarchic vs. democratic societies. Mimeo. Journal of the European Economic Association, forthcoming.

Ansolabehere, S., Snyder, J., Ueda, M., 2004. Campaign finance regulations and the return on investment from campaign contributions. Mimeo. Massachusetts Institute of Technology, Cambridge, MA.

Bertrand, M., Kramarz, F., Schoar, A., Thesmar, D., 2004. Politically connected CEOs and corporate outcomes: evidence from France. Mimeo. University of Chicago, Chicago, IL.

Coate, S., 2004. Pareto-improving finance policy. American Economic Review 94, 628–655.

Chappell, H., 1982. Campaign contributions and congressional voting: a simultaneous Probit—Tobit model. Review of Economics and Statistics 64, 77–83.

Charumilind, C., Kali, R., Wiwattanakantang, Y., 2006. Connected lending: Thailand before the financial crisis. Journal of Business 79, 181–218.

Cole, S., 2004. Fixing market failures or fixing elections? Agricultural credit in India. Mimeo. Massachusetts Institute of Technology, Cambridge, MA.

Dinc, S., 2005. Politicians and banks: political influences on government-owned banks in emerging countries. Journal of Financial Economics 77, 453–479.

Durden, G., Silberman, J., 1976. Determining legislative preferences for the minimum wage: an economic approach. Journal of Political Economy 84, 317–329.

Faccio, M., 2006. Politically connected firms. American Economic Review 96, 369–386.

580   *S. Claessens et al. / Journal of Financial Economics 88 (2008) 554–580*

Faccio, M., Parsley, D., 2006. Sudden deaths: taking stock of political connections. Mimeo. Vanderbilt University, Nashville, TN.
Ferguson, T., Voth, H., 2005. Betting on Hitler: the value of political connections in Nazi Germany. Quarterly Journal of Economics, forthcoming.
Fisman, R., 2001. Estimating the value of political connections. American Economic Review 91, 1095–1102.
Fisman, D., Fisman, R., Galef, J., Khurana, R., 2006. Estimating the value of connections to Vice President Cheney. Mimeo. Columbia University, New York, NY.
Grenzke, J., 1989. PACs and the congressional supermarket: the currency is complex. American Journal of Political Science 33, 1–24.
Grossman, G., Helpman, E., 1996. Electoral competition and special interest politics. Review of Economic Studies 63, 265–286.
Instituto Universitário de Pesquisas do Rio de Janeiro, 2005. Dados eleitorais do Brasil. ⟨http://www.iuperj.br/⟩.
International Foundation for Election Systems, 2005. ⟨http://www.electionguide.org⟩.
Jayachandran, S., 2004. The Jeffords effect. Mimeo. University of California at Los Angeles, Los Angeles, CA.
Johnson, S., Mitton, T., 2003. Cronyism and capital controls: evidence from Malaysia. Journal of Financial Economics 67, 351–382.
Kroszner, R., Stratmann, T., 1998. Interest-group competition and the organization of Congress: theory and evidence from financial services' political action committees. American Economic Review 88, 1163–1187.
Krueger, A., 1974. The political economy of the rent-seeking society. American Economic Review 64, 291–303.
Khwaja, A., Mian, A., 2005. Do lenders favor politically connected firms? Rent provision in an emerging financial market. Quarterly Journal of Economics 120, 1371–1411.
La Porta, R., Lopez-de-Silanes, F., Shleifer, A., 2002. Government ownership of banks. Journal of Finance 57, 265–301.
MacKinlay, C., 1997. Event studies in economics and finance. Journal of Economic Literature 35, 13–39.
Morck, R., Wolfenzon, D., Yeung, B., 2005. Corporate governance, economic entrenchment, and growth. Journal of Economic Literature 43, 655–720.
Rajan, R., Zingales, L., 1995. What do we know about capital structure? Some evidence from international data. Journal of Finance 50, 1421–1460.
Rajan, R., Zingales, L., 2003. The great reversals: the politics of financial development in the 20th century. Journal of Financial Economics 69, 5–50.
Ramalho, R., 2003. The effects of an anti-corruption campaign: evidence from the 1992 presidential impeachment in Brazil. Mimeo. Massachusetts Institute of Technology, Cambridge, MA.
Reuters, 1998. Final results for Brazilian general election. October 9.
Reuters, 2002. Final results for Brazilian general election. October 8.
Roberts, B., 1990. A dead senator tells no lies: seniority and the distribution of federal benefits. American Journal of Political Science 34, 31–58.
Samuels, D., 1998. Careerism and its consequences: federalism, elections, and policy-making in Brazil. Ph.D. Dissertation. University of California at San Diego, San Diego, CA.
Samuels, D., 2001. Does money matter? Credible commitments and campaign finance in new democracies: theory and evidence from Brazil. Comparative Politics 34, 23–42.
Samuels, D., 2002. Pork barreling is not credit claiming or advertising: campaign finance and the sources of the personal vote in Brazil. Journal of Politics 64, 845–863.
Shon, J., 2006. Do stock return vary with campaign contributions? The Bush versus Gore 2000 presidential elections, Unpublished working paper. City University of New York, New York, NY.
Snyder, J., 1990. Campaign contributions as investments: the US House of Representatives, 1980–1986. Journal of Political Economy 98, 1195–1227.
Stratmann, T., 1995. Campaign contributions and congressional voting: does the timing of contributions matter? Review of Economics and Statistics 771, 127–136.
Tribunal Superior Eleitoral, 2005. ⟨http://www.tse.gov.br/⟩.
Veja, 1998. Castigo Rápido. August 12, 45.
White, H., 1980. A heteroskedasticity-consistent covariance matrix estimator and a direct test for heteroskedasticity. Econometrica 48, 817–838.

Name Index